The Official History of in England and Wales

Volume I of *The Official History of Criminal Justice in England and Wales* frames what was known about crime and criminal justice in the 1960s, before describing the liberalising legislation of the decade.

Commissioned by the Cabinet Office and using interviews, British Government records, and papers housed in private, and institutional collections, this is the first of a collaboratively written series of official histories that analyse the evolution of criminal justice between 1959 and 1997. It opens with an account of the inception of the series, before describing what was known about crime and criminal justice at the time. It then outlines the genesis of three key criminal justice Acts that not only redefined the relations between the State and citizen, but also shaped what some believed to be the spirit of the age: the abolition of capital punishment, and the reform of the laws on abortion, and homosexuality. The Acts were taken to be so contentious morally and politically that Governments of different stripes were hesitant about promoting them formally. The onus was instead passed to backbenchers, who were supported by interlocking groups of reformers, with a pooled knowledge about how to effectively organise a rhetoric that drew on the language of utilitarianism, and the clarity and authority of a Church of England. This came to play an increasingly consequential and largely unacknowledged part in resolving what were often confusing moral questions.

This book will be of much interest to students of criminology and British history, politics and law.

Paul Rock is an Emeritus Professor of Sociology at the London School of Economics. His published work has focused chiefly on the evolution of criminal justice policies in Canada and England and Wales, particularly for victims of crime, and on developments in criminological theory.

Whitehall Histories: Government Official History Series

ISSN: 1474–8398

The Government Official History series began in 1919 with wartime histories, and the peacetime series was inaugurated in 1966 by Harold Wilson. The aim of the series is to produce major histories in their own right, compiled by historians eminent in the field, who are afforded free access to all relevant material in the official archives. The Histories also provide a trusted secondary source for other historians and researchers while the official records are not in the public domain. The main criteria for selection of topics are that the histories should record important episodes or themes of British history while the official records can still be supplemented by the recollections of key players; and that they should be of general interest, and, preferably, involve the records of more than one government department.

The Rise and Fall of a National Strategy
The United Kingdom and the European
Community: Volume 1
Alan S. Milward

Secret Flotillas
Vol. I: Clandestine Sea Operations to Brittany,
1940–1944
Vol. II: Clandestine Sea Operations in the
Mediterranean, North Africa and the Adriatic,
1940–1944
Sir Brooks Richards

SOE in France
An Account of the Work of the British Special
Operations Executive in France 1940–1944
M. R. D. Foot

**The Official History of the Falklands
Campaign**
Vol. I: The Origins of the Falklands War
Vol. II: War and Diplomacy
Sir Lawrence Freedman

**The Official History of Britain and the
Channel Tunnel**
Terry Gourvish

Churchill's Mystery Man
Desmond Morton and the World of Intelligence
Gill Bennett

The Official History of Privatisation
Vol. I: The Formative Years 1970–1987
Vol. II: Popular Capitalism 1987–1997
David Parker

Secrecy and the Media
The Official History of the D-Notice System
Nicholas Wilkinson

The Official History of the Civil Service
Reforming the Civil Service, Vol. I: The Fulton
Years, 1966–1981
Rodney Lowe

**The Official History of North Sea Oil and
Gas**
Vol. I: The Growing Dominance of the State
Vol. II: Moderating the State's Role
Alex Kemp

**The Official History of Britain and the
European Community**
Vol. II: From Rejection to Referendum,
1963–1975
Vol. III: The Tiger Unleasged, 1975–1985
Stephen Wall

**The Official History of the Joint
Intelligence Committee**
Vol. I: From the Approach of the Second World
War to the Suez Crisis
Michael S. Goodman

**The Official History of the Cabinet
Secretaries**
Ian Beesley

**The Official History of the UK Strategic
Nuclear Deterrent**
Vol. I: From the V-Bomber Era to the Arrival of
Polaris, 1945–1964
Vol. II: The Labour Government and the Polaris
Programme, 1964–1970
Matthew Jones

**The Authorised History of British Defence
Economic Intelligence**
A Cold War in Whitehall, 1929–90
Peter Davies

**The Official History of Criminal Justice
in England and Wales**
Vol. I: The 'Liberal Hour'
Vol. II: Institution-Building
Paul Rock

For more information about this series, please visit:
https://www.routledge.com/Government-Official-History-Series/book-series/SE0789

The Official History of Criminal Justice in England and Wales

Volume I: The 'Liberal Hour'

Paul Rock

Routledge
Taylor & Francis Group

LONDON AND NEW YORK

First published 2019 by Routledge

2 Park Square, Milton Park, Abingdon, Oxon, OX14 4RN
605 Third Avenue, New York, NY 10017

Routledge is an imprint of the Taylor & Francis Group, an informa business

First issued in paperback 2020

British Library Cataloguing-in-Publication Data
A catalogue record for this book is available from the British Library

Library of Congress Cataloging-in-Publication Data
Names: Rock, Paul Elliott, author.
Title: The official history of criminal justice in England and Wales : volume one: the "Liberal hour" / Paul Rock.
Description: 1 Edition. | New York : Routledge, 2019– |
Series: Whitehall histories: government official history series |
Includes bibliographical references and index.
Identifiers: LCCN 2018043358 (print) | LCCN 2018061730 (ebook) |
ISBN 9780429892226 (Web PDF) | ISBN 9780429892219 (ePub) |
ISBN 9780429892202 (Mobi) | ISBN 9781138601673 (hardback) |
ISBN 9780429469923 (e-book)
Subjects: LCSH: Administration of justice--England--History. |
Administration of justice--Wales--History.
Classification: LCC HV9960.G7 (ebook) | LCC HV9960.G7 R635 2019
(print) | DDC 364.942--dc23
LC record available at https://lccn.loc.gov/2018043358

ISBN: 978-1-138-60167-3 (hbk)
ISBN: 978-0-367-73032-1 (pbk)

Typeset in Bembo by
Servis Filmsetting Ltd, Stockport, Cheshire

Contents

Lists of figures

Preface

This is the opening volume of a much lengthier, collaborative study that was commissioned in 2009 to cover critical episodes in the history of criminal justice between 1959 and 1997. The genesis, scope, development and workings of that project are discussed here, in the preface, and the larger context of crime and criminal justice in mid-century, the history's starting point, in Chapter 1. The remainder of the book examines an important body of reforms, lauded by some as the signal achievement of the time, the liberalising legislation that was passed under the Labour administrations of the 1960s. The abolition of capital punishment and the reform of the laws on abortion and private sexual relations between adult men were taken not only critically to redefine the relations between the state and its people but also somehow to mark the spirit of the age. They deserve a prominent place in any history of criminal justice.

Other volumes will follow to describe how a number of existing criminal justice institutions were reformed and others were created anew, amounting to the construction of a system of a sort that nationalised, rationalised, consolidated and 'disembedded' what had often been a hotchpotch of antique practices rooted in local traditions and loyalties. They will record how some changes could trace their bloodlines back to the great state-building project of the first decades of the nineteenth century, whilst others were driven more dramatically and precipitately by crises and scandals in the prisons, police and courts. Our hope is that the whole will chart, perhaps for the very first time, the emergence of several key components of the criminal justice system of England and Wales as they were arrayed at the end of the twentieth century.

Scope, sources and methods

The Government Official History programme was started in 1919 under the auspices of the Committee of Imperial Defence, the forerunner of the Cabinet Office, with the intention of 'compiling the naval and military history of the nation'. After 1945 its main task became the preparation and publication of the history of the Second World War, although its range became extended to include social policy (albeit in a wartime context).[1] And then, in 1966, Harold Wilson, in consultation with the Cabinet Secretary, decided to enlarge its scope to embrace what were called selected episodes of peacetime history so that 'important periods in our history [could] be recorded in comprehensive and authoritative narratives, written while the official records could still be supplemented by reference to the personal recollections of the public men who were involved',[2] and the expectation was that some four histories would be in preparation at any one time.[3] Its aim has more recently been described by the Histories, Openness and Records Unit of the Cabinet Office, the body responsible for the programme, as the production of 'authoritative accounts of major national events'[4] ... '[constituting] major histories in their own right, compiled by historians eminent in their field, who are afforded free access to all relevant material in the official archives ... [They] also provide a trusted secondary source for other historians and researchers while the official records are not in the public domain'. The latest examples included studies of the Joint Intelligence Committee,[5] the relations between Britain and the European Community,[6] North Sea oil and gas,[7] privatisation[8] and the civil service.[9]

The process of initiating a new official history was remarkably labyrinthine, reflecting the seriousness with which the exercise was viewed. Topics for the programme were selected by the Cabinet Committee on Official Histories on which all the major government departments were represented. Proposals then passed to a group of privy counsellors, one from each of the major political parties, and their approval conferred the authority for an historian to gain access to records of all the previous administrations, and the then 30-year rule was waived.[10]

Soundings having been taken, an invitation to submit applications was extended to two of us separately at the London School of Economics in early February 2008. Accompanying it was a prospectus detailing what a history of criminal justice might contain, and it began:

> The Official History would examine the significant changes in the Criminal Justice System over the last 40 years ... It would chart the position before, during and after our [*sic*] changes to the system. An appropriate starting point would probably be the Beeching Report, the abolition of the Assizes and the introduction of the single Crown Court in 1971. Ten years later a report issued by the Royal Commission on Criminal Procedure ... led directly to the establishment of the Crown Prosecution Service in 1986. ...

There then followed a list of some other recent developments that might warrant description: the emergence of trilateral arrangements between ministers for governing the criminal justice system; the creation of the Office for Criminal Justice Reform; the merger of the Court Service and Magistrates' Courts Committees to form Her Majesty's Courts Service; the bringing together of the Prison and Probation Services under the National Offender Management Programme; the formation of the Serious and Organised Crime Agency; the founding of the Ministry of Justice; relations with the criminal justice agencies and professions, and the like. Some of these, as we will explain, eventually fell outside the time period agreed for the History but it remained a very substantial brief.

All scholars are fond of imagining that theirs is a field of such breadth and complexity that it is difficult to master. Those of us who had been approached certainly believed that no one individual could cover the ground which was envisaged. So it was that we went to a third colleague and the three of us agreed to submit a joint proposal which would draw on our rather different areas of competence: David Downes with his broad interest in youth justice and penal politics; Tim Newburn with his interest in the development of policing, policy development, youth justice and the liberalisation of criminal justice; and me with my interest, *inter alia*, in the development of policies for victims of crime and the workings of the Crown Court. Over the years the three of us had collaborated in several ways on a number of studies, including successive editions of *Understanding Deviance*, a criminology text book; we had worked and taught together cordially in the same institution; and supposed (with good reason) that we could work together again on what could prove to be a very substantial undertaking, perhaps the largest single piece of research in any of our careers.

Our own answering submission accepted, built on and then went beyond the original brief, in particular, going beyond the institution-centred picture of criminal justice which it painted. After all, the academy is abuzz with conversations about crime, criminal justice and criminology and there can be no limit to the number of interesting questions which can be put. Intellectual ambition conceived a grand *tour d'horizon* that embraced not only the empirically driven themes listed by the Cabinet Office but also a plenitude of structural and conceptual developments in the regulation of crime and crime control. And it was that new, broader proposal which went to ministers and eventually won their endorsement, although the then Home Secretary, Jacquie Smith,[11] stipulated that the history could not extend beyond 1997, the date when the New Labour Government of Tony Blair had come to power. We ourselves accepted that the work should begin in the 1960s, but that was eventually modified more precisely to 1959, a year marked by the publication of the major White Paper, *Penal Practice in a Changing Society*.[12] The Prime Minister, Gordon Brown, finally announced the project in the House of Commons in February 2009[13] and we were formally awarded a five-year commission two months later.

We had been under ambitious. Many of the major events we describe had had a long gestation: thus the 1967 Sexual Offences Act had to be understood in large measure as a reaction to the so-called Labouchère amendment to the 1885 Criminal Law Amendment Act and its criminalisation of 'gross indecency'; the 1967 Abortion Act was the culmination of a long campaign to unravel the meaning of the word 'unlawful' in the 1861 Offences Against the Person Act; and the Murder (Abolition of Death Penalty) Act 1965 had its roots not only in the recommendations of the 1931 report of the Select

Committee on Capital Punishment but also in the anomalies and contradictions of the 1957 Homicide Act. The history of the police must return to the construction of its mandate in the face of the public disorder of the 1820s and 1830s. More generally, it would have been quite impossible to examine the reform of the penal system in the 1960s and beyond without reference to prison administration in earlier periods. No accounts could be reckoned adequate unless they returned to those earlier beginnings. Conversely, we recognised that to provide a detailed pre-history of all sectors of the criminal justice system would prove so substantial a task that we have limited that choice to subjects that could not be grasped without it.

Second, we had not perhaps fully enough anticipated what the unexpected might bring. The academic history of criminal justice in England and Wales is curiously patchy and underdeveloped and we knew there was abundant scope for fresh discovery. We were also long familiar with the way in which research has emergent properties, but the more we foraged, the more we hit upon new sources and informants – informants who were often extraordinarily generous – the more we discovered ourselves being propelled into important and hitherto unexplored regions. Many of those whom we met proved eager to talk about what had been some of the most absorbing episodes in their professional lives. They were frequently interesting and articulate people who devoted time to discussing events with us, sometimes with remarkable powers of recall; recommending others whom we might contact in a cascading process of 'snowballing'; and who lent or gave us their personal papers and memoirs. It could be a revelatory process, leading from time to time to our own petty versions of Cesare Lombroso's vision of a plain appearing under a flaming sky,[14] and our work changed course more than once.

We had been over ambitious, and that for a number of reasons, some of which again we perhaps should have anticipated. Before the appearance of what has been labelled the 'paperless office', Whitehall and the criminal justice agencies were awash with documents. Major policies could be supported by their own retinues of files, housed in The National Archives and in and around the archives of the different Departments and offices of State – the Cabinet Office, Home Office, Ministry of Justice, Treasury, Treasury Counsel, private, local and university archives and elsewhere. Professional organisations have their own records. There are ancillary sources – the scholarly articles, published secondary histories, biographies, autobiographies, newspaper and journal reports. Each episode of policymaking – such as a Royal Commission or a commission of inquiry – could produce hundreds of files and thousands of papers, all of which had to be read attentively, not only for the main thrust of their argument but also for the revealing chance observation or scribbled note – what the 1962 Guide for Public Record Officers called the 'unselfconscious minutes'.[15] More recent events could still be recalled in interview by those whom Harold Wilson had described as the public men (and presumably women) who were involved. All this will be perfectly familiar to any historian, but it did rather take us aback and we were chastened. Our task was proving to be quite gargantuan, especially if it was undertaken conscientiously enough to resemble what the Cabinet Office called an authoritative account of major national events, and it led rapidly and inexorably to the conclusion that it would be best to concentrate on a number of detailed case studies of especially significant episodes, including the hitherto unrecorded introduction of the single Crown Court in 1971 and the establishment of the Crown Prosecution Service in 1986 which the Cabinet Office had inserted at the very head of its inventory of topics. In making our choice, we were mindful that we had already covered a number of important episodes in some depth elsewhere – for example, the rebuilding of Holloway Prison in 1977, an event which marked a pivotal moment in the treatment of women prisoners;[16] the emergence of a greater responsiveness to the needs of prosecution witnesses in Crown Court proceedings;[17] the growth of policy transfers, particularly between the United States and England and Wales;[18] the emergence of private security as a complement to State policing;[19] early post-war forms of delinquency;[20] and the origins and development of services for victims of crime.[21] It seemed otiose to return to ground that had been described elsewhere.

If there was glut in some places, there was famine in others. A number of areas of history are now blank and irretrievable. Thousands of files have been discarded. No doubt many of those documents were ephemera, papers that had effectively been superseded, reviews of possible courses of action that had led nowhere, files of the kind that a government committee on legal records was to call 'valueless … uninformative and incomplete', … 'massive accumulations, forests of documents … . [in which there] may be hidden … a small quantity of useful information'.[22] Other documents may have been lost or never returned by officials. But over and over again, we stumbled upon voids in the historical evidence. Thus, although the papers of all Royal Commissions and many interdepartmental committees are meticulously preserved, the adjoining material that must once have documented the deliberations that initiated them, and the adjoining material that documented their consequences, may no longer remain.

Official records were to be the very foundation of our work and the practices that shaped their creation and retention became a matter of vital methodological and evidential importance to us. After all, what could be more germane to our project? They dictate almost all that can still be known about crime, lawmaking, law enforcement and policymaking in the period covered by this history. Those who compiled them were certainly heedful of the fact that they should leave a record of everything they deemed to be material to the development of policy. But the process was never simple.

It is worth reporting in some detail what former senior officials in the Home Office, then the leading Department of State in the field of criminal justice, said about the role of files in the latter half of the twentieth century. Officials identified themselves as participants in a great tradition that demanded proper service. One, Sir Quentin Thomas,[23] consulted several of his contemporaries before telling me that:

The Home Office we all joined (in the sixties or before), and to an extent Whitehall, had a present and a past and it assumed a future. There was in short a sense of continuity, infused by a sense of tradition. Although this could have been a strong inertial force it did not seem like that. Innovation was not inhibited and (as it seems to me at least) crime and its treatment was seen as intractable but not inevitable or impervious to intervention. Hence the minor institution of Noters, which you may have come across.[24] When a file settled a new point of policy or casework, it was, or should have been, marked "Noters to Note" so a central record was kept of these precedents. The cup would be passed on. This sense of continuity was probably more pronounced in the Home Office than elsewhere.[25]

There was in consequence a careful adherence to rule and convention. First, there were what might be called primary procedures. David Faulkner,[26] an official who had long been at the centre of things, said:

> There were some formal rules, supplemented by some notes on good practice. Every substantive paper had to be registered to a numbered file with a separate note of its dates and title so that it was easy to tell if a paper was missing. 'Spent drafts' were to be removed when they had served their purpose (unless they contained amendments made by a minister or very senior official); everything else had to be retained and removing papers or losing or destroying files were serious offences. 'Substantive papers' meant almost everything that was written down, apart from handwritten notes giving passing comments or advice to a member of staff, and certainly anything that was typed. There was discretion about how much to record from telephone calls or informal conversions, but good practice was to record anything that influenced what you did next (for example to show who you'd consulted and what they'd said), and private secretaries recorded everything that ministers heard or said while they were in the office. ... My impression was that the rules were followed conscientiously in my time.[27]

But a number of secondary rules were also in play. Sir Quentin stated:

> I guess any letter from or reply to a member of the public would be filed; as I suppose would other substantive contacts with people or bodies outside the department. So a note of a meeting held in, say, DHSS [the Department of Health and Social Security] ought to be on the file. But a note recording a telecon [teleconference] with DHSS setting up the meeting would be ephemeral. ... A note recording representations about a substantive issue from, say, the Magistrates Association should be filed.
>
> A file on a developing policy issue ought to show and track early papers, probably including early drafts of what became, say, a substantive submission to the Home Secretary perhaps proposing a demarche by writing

to ministerial colleagues. But in some cases a file would be "weeded" subsequently to remove early drafts which by then had been superseded. (Obviously the main concern was to advance business rather than to create a trail for history.) Probably a note recording an informal meeting within a division would not need to be filed; but if outsiders were present it probably would.[28]

It is clear that files were integral to the work of government, acting, in effect, as evidence of what had been done, as a *memoire* of why it had been done, and as a guide to future action, and they not only reported but also lent structure to the manner in which decisions were taken.[29] Bob Morris, who had joined the Home Office in 1961, rising to the rank of Assistant Undersecretary of State; Private Secretary to the Home Secretary, and later, the Head of the Crime Policy Planning Unit between 1979 and 1981, recollected:

> Meticulous record keeping was accepted as a necessary discipline. Staff were entirely aware that the Home Secretary exercised significant powers affecting the life of individuals, a consciousness reinforced particularly but by no means only because of the existence of capital punishment until 1965. Getting the facts right (often in murky situations) was of paramount importance. Sloppy record keeping could lead to indefensible decision-making. These disciplines were part of every officers' socialisation even where, as in immigration control until 1969, there was no system of administrative appeal. This was overwhelmingly because MPs could very speedily bring matters to the floor of the Commons and ministers would have to account for themselves – a situation that continued after immigration appeals were introduced and even when judicial review became more accessible to complainants from the 1980s.

Files were never treated as simple accumulations of paper. They were much more than that. It was important to attend to their *content*: they had to contain intelligible, interlinked, properly annotated and chronologically sequenced records serviceable for present and future use. The prime imperative was that anything that appreciably affected the course of policymaking had to be documented – John Croft, Head of the Home Office Research Unit between 1972 and 1983, recalled that he was 'rather insistent that everything went on record'. More specifically, *An Introduction to Files and Letter Writing in the Home Office*, produced in 1976 and in use during his time, contained models of the minutes sheets that all files must possess, and of the '"minute sheet language" which is standard to the Home Office'. Minutes were not to be addressed to any named person: they were supposed to 'present a complete "micro-story" of the subject'; they should 'present all the facts both for and against your case'; they should be bold, accurate and to the point.[30] It was important to attend to the *appearance* of files, and being 'good on paper', the art of writing in a pleasing, literate and succinct manner, was prized in the heyday of the civil service (although Sir Quentin remembered that it was a skill that could become rather too clever, too game-like – too much of an end in itself – on occasion). It was important to attend to their *handling*. It was almost as if they were ritual objects – and ritual too had its proper observances. Bob Morris said:

> Important minutiae all flowed from the overall mission. Thus there was procedural standardisation: papers had to be hole-punched two-thirds up the foolscap (later A 4) sheet; minutes were filed on the left and correspondence, notes and so on were filed on the right and their addition noted by date sequentially on the minute sheet. Other, lesser departments outside the HO, it was implied, followed a contemptible practice of hole-punching their papers at the top left hand corner of minute sheets and correspondence so that the holes were more vulnerable to being breached in use and papers lost or muddled as a result. In transit, files in the same series either general or personal were tied together by white tape. If files of different series travelled together, then they were bound in blue tape to signify their heterogeneity ... there was no red tape in the HO. ...[31]

Yet, for all their importance, in a paper world that existed before the widespread appearance of the office computer and the photocopier, before even the advent of the electric typewriter,[32] there were some very real logistical and technical limits on what could be done:

> Most operational discussions resulted in action rather than a note of the discussion itself. More significant meetings, especially with other government departments or outside bodies, were recorded, copied to files and circulated to all the parties. The shortage of typing resource – few officers even at Principal level had access to secretarial assistance – in effect rationed what was formally recorded. Reproduction of meeting notes relied on the Gestetner system of cutting specially prepared skins on typewriters from which the ribbons had been removed.[33] This system limited the number of legible copies that could be reproduced, and I was advised to make sure to retain the Gestetner skin under lock and key should additional copies ever be required. Having been told that some typing work was sent outside London for completion, I was still surprised on the first occasion when a slip falling out of some returned typing read 'Typed and checked in Carlisle'.[34]

Given their criticality, it became imperative to establish how many files had been retained and how many thrown away, largely as a result of the 1958 Public Records Act,[35] enacted at the very opening of our period and still in force whilst we worked.[36] A detailed history of the sequence of events that led up to, and succeeded, the passing of the Act appears in two papers in *Archives*,[37] the journal of the British Records Association. Here, I shall merely offer a truncated account of what came to pass.

The Act was a response to the report[38] of a committee appointed in 1952 to review the existing arrangements for record management under the chairmanship of Sir James Grigg, a former Secretary of State for War,[39] a man described by Edward Playfair, the Treasury official who nominated him, as 'bubbling over with mental energy and at the top of his form'.[40] The committee was the government's answer to what an official working in the Public Record Office, John Collingridge, called 'the very alarming state of affairs revealed by the information produced by Departments in response to a questionnaire sent out by an organisation and methods team of the Treasury in 1951'.[41] The Treasury was the Department of State officially responsible for the PRO. It provided its premises, and, through its minister, the Chancellor of the Exchequer, was accountable for its doings to Parliament. It was also the regulatory department within Whitehall where organisation and methods analysis was being developed with some gusto;[42] and it had come to conclude that at a time of harsh financial cuts that were falling especially heavily on the PRO,[43] 'a radical change might be required in present practice in order to ensure only documents worthy of permanent retention were passed to the Public Record Office, and to ensure that the problem of providing permanent storage space did not grow out of hand'.[44] The Act was to transfer the management of the public records to the Lord Chancellor, who, as head of the judiciary, was thought best equipped to assume responsibility for legal records;[45] and a newly created Keeper of the Public Records (appointed from 1 January 1959), assisted by an Advisory Council on Public Records, who would be required to sift through 'mountains of records',[46] and not only decide which were to be retained but also control what Theodore Plucknett, Professor of Legal History at the London School of Economics, and a former chairman of the Master of the Rolls Archives Committee, called the officials' 'dangerous power of destruction'.[47] Government papers were to be retained within their departments for five years, at which point a 'first review' took place to determine whether they were thought to have any present or future administrative value. Those that survived would then be reassessed by Departmental Records Officers after a further 25 years to decide whether they had lasting historical importance and, if so, whether they should be transferred to The National Archives. They were, as my articles in *Archives* suggested, governed by rules emanating from Theodore Schellenberg,[48] the former Director of Archival Management in the National Archives and Records Service in Washington, and they followed a Linnaean scheme which laid down that files could be assessed as having both a primary value to the organisation that created them and a secondary value to the historian that recorded not only how the organisation functioned formally but also the substantive decisions that it had taken. And the outcome was to be that something like 98% of official papers came to be discarded over the years in which we had an interest.[49]

It is almost certain that most of what was lost was indeed of little historical worth, but there *were* omissions which hampered our work. Indeed, the staff of The National Archives themselves confessed to us that they were occasionally bemused at how a number of important items had failed to pass review during that era.[50] There are, for example, no files on the decision taken in 1929 to appoint a Select Committee on capital punishment, and none on what government made of it; none on the decision to appoint the Wolfenden Committee that reported in 1957, and none on what government made of it; none on the Home Secretary's decision to accede to representations made in support of an important appeal against the conviction of three young men for the death of Maxwell Confait in 1972, none on the Royal Commission on Criminal Procedure that stemmed from the appeal, and none on the decision to establish the Crown Prosecution Service that flowed from the Royal Commission.

There was to be another source of disappointment. Scholars are wont to believe that theirs is a field of central importance not only to themselves but to the wider world. Pursuing the history of criminal justice soon cut us down to size. Criminal justice does not actually appear to loom very large in the world of politics and politicians: even the memoirs of former Home Secretaries can be quite unenlightening about decisions we deemed consequential. Politicians are taken up with far grander matters. We shall show, for instance, how the copious papers – published and unpublished – of that great liberal reformer, Roy Jenkins, have almost nothing to say about some of the matters that concerned us most: abortion law reform, homosexual law reform, the establishment of the Royal Commission on Criminal Procedure, and much else. Jenkins was evidently quite bored with the mundane work of the Home Office, being much more engaged with the literary and social world, the leadership of the Labour Party and Britain's entry to the European community. And, in contrast, other politicians were far too modest to leave any trace at all. Perhaps the reason was, as Bob Morris suggested, that criminal justice policy-making stretches over such long periods of time that politicians find it difficult to claim possession of what has been done: 'one of the characteristics of CJ policy development is often the sheer length of the process. This means that politicians – rarely in office for much more than two years at a stretch[51] – impact but fleetingly and, unless engaged in the legislative implementation, cannot 'own' or 'claim' the projects. Political careers much depend on claiming credit in some way but the opportunities to do so are often fortuitous'. Time and time again, we had thin pickings. What we had believed to be a rich field was all too often a desert.

It was not helpful, too, that many criminal justice agencies never replied to our requests for information: individual police services, including the Metropolitan Police, the Police Federation and the Police Superintendents Association, the Courts and Tribunal Service, and Bar Council were, for example, almost invariably deaf to our entreaties. There were palpable exceptions: the librarians of the Howard League, Liberty, Lambeth Palace, the Westminster Diocesan Archives, the Methodist International Centre, Lincoln's Inn, the Wellcome Trust, the Law Society and the British Medical Association were exemplary, and we are more than grateful to them. Yet it does remain the case that, although we were not without experience of hunting in archives (David Downes is a trained historian; Tim Newburn had worked extensively in and on government; and I had devoted much of my working life to observing the workings of the Home Office and scouring its files), we could not do much to rectify the fact that the history of criminal justice is pockmarked by vast tracts of *terra incognita*. We were obliged as a corollary to select and phrase our case histories pragmatically on the basis of what it was still possible to see and hear.

We had promised to write seamlessly and as one, producing a single, uniform narrative. But we soon realised that we were working on different substantive areas at different rates with different styles and different trajectories and sometimes in different places (I was ensconced in Philadelphia for significant periods during the first few years, for example). One is reminded of the question that Mike Phillipson once put to Ian Taylor, Paul Walton and Jock Young, the co-authors of *The New Criminology*,[52] in 1973. He asked, in effect, how it could be possible for three people to speak with one voice.[53] We discovered that we could not do so, determining at an early stage to assume direct personal responsibility for own individual contributions, ceasing to pretend that they were the joint work of several hands, but nevertheless passing drafts back and forth for comment, emendation, cross-reference and the enhancement of consistency and coherence. Quite routinely, drafts were also shown to the principals whom we had interviewed, that being a matter not only of good manners, good professional practice and an honouring of promises made but also of methodological prudence. After all, it is the principals' world we are attempting to describe; it is they who are expert about the details and circumstances of their actions; and the early drafts of a history can often get things wrong. It is easy enough to construct a plausible narrative, but plausibility is not validity, and a subject's endorsement is as good a test of phenomenological adequacy as any. Quite as routinely, and again following good scholarly practice, we showed early drafts to established academic authorities in a number of the areas we examined. We were, as a result, more than fortunate in gaining informed advice that led us away from error and into greater understanding, and we warmly acknowledge the assistance we received in the chapters that follow.

Work on the history proved to be a massive exercise that was made possible only because of the support and advice offered by a host of people to whom we owe a commensurately massive debt: Roger Smethurst, Teresa Stirling and Sally Falk of the Official Histories Team at the Cabinet Office; Richard Chown of the Ministry of Justice who shepherded these two volumes through to official clearance; Joyce Lorinstein, who was exemplary in her transcription of interviews; the admirable Nicky Tudor who copy-edited the typescripts; the ever-patient Beth Lund-Yates at Routledge; and the innumerable men and women whom we consulted, who lent or gave us their private papers and memoirs, who recommended others to whom we might turn, and who read and commented, often with great patience, on drafts as they emerged. We shall acknowledge them all in their turn as our narrative unfolds. Unless otherwise stated, it should be assumed that quotations attributed to them stemmed from interview. We have been given full access to official documents and are alone responsible for the statements made and the views expressed.

June 2018

Notes

1   See, for example, R. Titmuss (1950); *Problems of Social Policy*, HMSO, London.
2   HC Deb 9 March 1966 Vol. 725 cc561–3W.
3   *Manual of Records Administration* (1983); London: Public Record Office, 1.13.5.
4   http://webarchive.nationalarchives.gov.uk/20070701080507/cabinetoffice.gov.uk/about_the_cabinet_office/units.asp#horu
5   M. Goodman (2014); *The Official History of the Joint Intelligence Committee: Volume I: From the Approach of the Second World War to the Suez Crisis*, Routledge, London.
6   S. Wall (2014); *The Official History of Britain and the European Community, Vol. II: From Rejection to Referendum*, Routledge, London.
7   A. Kemp (2014); *The Official History of North Sea Oil and Gas, Vol. II: Moderating the State's Role, Routledge*, London.
8   D. Parker (2012); *The Official History of Privatisation, Vol. II, Popular Capitalism, 1987–97*, Routledge, London.
9   R. Lowe (2011); *The Official History of the British Civil Service, Reforming the Civil Service, Volume I: The Fulton Years, 1966–81*, Routledge, London.
10   The 30-year rule was to be revised and, in 2013, the government began transferring records to The National Archives when they were 20 years old.
11   Jacquie Smith obtained a BA from Oxford in PPE, became Labour Member of Parliament for Redditch in 1991, Minister for Schools in 2003, and Home Secretary in 2007.
12   *Penal Practice in a Changing Society*, Cmd 645, HMSO, London.
13   HC Deb, 27 February 2009, c38WS.
14   C. Lombroso (1911); introduction to G. Lombroso-Ferrero; *Criminal Man According to the Classification of Cesare Lombroso*, New York: G.P. Putnam's Sons, xii.
15   Foreword to *A Guide for Departmental Record Officers (Revised)* (1962); no provenance, Public Record Office, 1.
16   See P. Rock (1996); *Reconstructing a Women's Prison: The Holloway Redevelopment Project, 1968–88*, Oxford: Clarendon Press and David Downes' chapter ('The Pursuit of Innovation') in his forthcoming volume in this history.
17   See P. Rock (2001); *The Social World of an English Crown Court*, Oxford: Clarendon Press.
18   See T. Newburn and T. Jones (2007); *Policy Transfer and Criminal Justice: Exploring US Influence over British Crime Control Policy*, Maidenhead: Open University Press.
19   See T. Jones and T. Newburn (1998); *Private Security and Public Policing*, Oxford: Clarendon Press.
20   D. Downes (1966); *The Delinquent Solution: A Study in Subcultural Theory*, London: Routledge and Kegan Paul.
21   See P. Rock (1990); *Helping Victims of Crime: The Home Office and the Rise of Victim Support in England and Wales*, Clarendon Press; P. Rock (1998); *After Homicide: Practical and Political Responses to Bereavement*, Oxford: Clarendon Press; P. Rock (2004); *Constructing Victims' Rights: The Home Office, New Labour and Victims*, Oxford: Clarendon Press.
22   *Report of the Committee on Legal Records* (1966); Cmnd. 3084, London: HMSO, 2, 8.
23   Sir Quentin Thomas joined the Home Office in 1966, becoming the Private Secretary to the Permanent Secretary in 1970; a member of the Crime Policy Planning Unit 1974–1976; and the Under Secretary between 1988 and 1991; before leaving to join the Northern Ireland Office.
24   Bob Morris, another senior official, described 'Noters' thus: 'To facilitate the official

memory, the HO had set up a Noters team at the centre of the registration system. This team, never more I believe than two officers, maintained where recommended by divisional officers, central ledger notes of papers thought to be of special significance. This would have included all bill papers, cabinet papers and significant policy or personal case files. The system was instituted in the late nineteenth century and was an invaluable resource. Confronted when working on policing in 1971 with some ancient, decayed regulations made in February 1898 under an 1897 Act, I was able to identify and summon the original documents and understand the long-running saga behind them reaching back to the 1870s. ...' (email, 3 February 2016).

25 Email, 8 February 2016.

26 David Faulkner was born in 1934. He joined the Home Office as an Assistant Principal in 1959, worked in the Private Office (serving as Private Secretary to the Home Secretary between 1969 and 1970) and then in the Prison Department, the Establishment Department, and finally, as the Head of the Criminal and Research and Statistical Departments between 1982 and 1990.

27 Email, 1 February 2016.

28 Bob Morris, email, 3 February 2016.

29 See M. Power (1999); *The Audit Society: Rituals of Verification*, Oxford: Oxford University Press.

30 Taken from my *Helping Victims of Crime, op. cit.*, 27–8.

31 Email, 6 February 2016.

32 Bob Morris recalled that 'Computers had been around since the 1968 creation of the Joint Automatic Data Processing Unit which was shared with the Metropolitan police. The Police National Computer had been introduced with great success from the very early 1970s. Personal computers made the greater impact on working practices: the typing pools collapsed and the introduction of digital storage challenged the older forms of record keeping. Whereas managing a Northern Ireland Inquiry in 1971 (the Compton inquiry into allegations of brutality during the internment operation of 9 August 1971) had still relied on typewriters, word-processors and their greater productivity were becoming to be talked of if not generally accessible by the time of a UK prisons inquiry 1978–9. Work in Croydon 1986–91 was assisted by a Wang processor but without any fax or internet capability. Getting material to ministers in Whitehall still relied on messengers travelling to Whitehall by public transport. In the HO personal computers did not arrive on desks until into the 1990s. I recall conspiring with the Principal Establishment Officer: never mind the theory, just get the bloody things on desks. By the time I left we had email which I observed did something to democratise working practices and challenge former hierarchical working styles'.

33 David Gestetner invented a system of duplication by means of stencils which were eventually adapted for use in typewriters (see http://tottenham-summerhillroad.com/gestetner_duplicators_tottenham.htm)

34 Email, 6 February 2016.

35 The Public Records Act 1958, Chapter 51: An Act to make new provision with respect to public records and the Public Record Office, and for connected purposes.

36 See http://www.nationalarchives.gov.uk/documents/information-management/best-practice-guide-appraising-and-selecting.pdf which states that 'For over 50 years public records bodies have followed the system of appraisal established by the Grigg Report in 1954'.

37 P. Rock (2016); "The Dreadful Flood of Documents': The 1958 Public Record Act and its Aftermath. Part 1: The Genesis of the Act'. *Archives*, vol. LI, no. 132–3, 1–22; (2017); "The Dreadful Flood of Documents': The 1958 Public Record Act and its Aftermath. Part 2: After-effects'. *Archives*, Vol. LII, 26–50.

38 Committee on Departmental Records (1954); *Report*, Cmd. 9163, London: HMSO.

G. Martin, the Keeper of Public Record between 1982 and 1988, remarked in 1988 that the committee's recommendations 'have served the Office and its users ever since'. G. Martin (1988); 'The Public Records in 1988', in G. Martin and P. Spufford (eds.) *The Records of the Nation: The Public Record Office 1838–1988*, Woodbridge: The Boydell Press, 22.

39 Sir James Grigg, 1890–1964, was successively a civil servant, serving as Principal Private Secretary to a number of Chancellors of the Exchequer between 1921 and 1930; the Chairman of the Board of Inland Revenue in 1930; the Permanent Undersecretary of State for War, 1939–1942; and the Member of Parliament for East Cardiff between 1942 and 1945 (http://www.ukwhoswho.com/view/article/oupww/whowaswho/U52160/GRIGG_Rt_Hon._Sir_Percy_James?index=1&results=QuicksearchResults&query=0)

40 Edward Playfair to Sir Edward Bridges, 1 February 1952, Treasury file OM68/3/01.

41 J. Collingridge (1955–59); 'Implementing the Grigg Report', *Journal of the Society of Archivists*, 1, 179. The report revealed that the 53 departments consulted housed some 1,100,000 linear feet of records not still in current use but not yet old enough to be reviewed for destruction; and 300,000 linear feet of records awaiting possible destruction, of which it was estimated that 50,000 would be passed to the PRO for preservation. The Treasury inquiry into the PRO was only one of a number conducted at the time. Others included the Tate Gallery, the Wallace Collection, the National Maritime Museum and the British Museum.

42 The methodology had first been advocated in 1915 by the Royal Commission on the civil service, the MacDonnell Commission, Cd 7832, and it grew in and around Whitehall, but it appears only to have come properly into its own in the latter half of the 1940s. See C. Krishnamoorthy (1953); 'Organisation and Methods in the British Government', *The Indian Journal of Political Science*, Vol. 14, No. 2, 113–122 and I. Pitman (1948); 'Organisation and Methods: An Important Select Committee Report', *Public Administration*, Vol. 26, No. 1, 1–9. One source, *The Civil Service Yearbook*, was not published in the war years between 1941 and 1945, but it appears that an Organisation and Methods Division was established at some point in that time. In 1940 there was no reference to a Treasury Organisation and Methods Division, but by 1946, the Division was 69 strong. By 1951, the year of the inspection of the PRO, it was 119 strong. The Treasury Organisation and Methods Division issued its first *OandM Bulletin for the diffusion of news ideas and opinions among Organisation and Methods Officers in the Civil Service* in August 1945 with a circulation of some 480 as part of a pioneering attempt to feel 'their way through uncharted seas' (H. Wilson Smith (1945); Foreword, *OandM Bulletin*, Vol. 1, No. 1, 1. H. Wilson Smith was Treasury Under-Secretary). It also appears to have initiated a Treasury O and M Course at much the same time (see (1949); 'The Treasury Course – A Commentary', *OandM Bulletin*, Vol. 4, No. 1, 21).

43 A draft letter to the Master of the Rolls from Sir Edward Bridges of 1 February 1952 recited that 'as it happens, the cut hits the Public Record Office arithmetically almost harder than anyone else'. Treasury file OM68/3/01. The PRO Museum, founded in 1886, was to be closed that year at a saving of four posts and some £1,300 *per annum* (HC Deb 13 May 1952 Vol. 500 cc103–4W) Aneurin Bevan's comment was that 'It may be that we have to make economies in this or that direction, but the trouble is – as I have said on a number of occasions – that in the hierarchy of the Government machine the Treasury is now practically supreme. That may suit some people, but it has a most appalling consequence on public administration ...' (HC Deb 14 July 1952 Vol. 503 cc1808–90).

44 Indecipherable, note to Mr Simpson, the Director of Organisation and Methods at the Treasury, 29 November 1951, Examination of the Workings of Public Records Acts, Treasury file OM68/3/01.

45 Notes for Supplementaries, draft statement for the Prime Minister, 1 July 1955, PREM

11 911. The Master of the Rolls wrote to Sir James on 29 November 1955 to say that 'One reason which, I confess, much influenced me (and I think Bridges also) was the position of the Legal Records. It seemed to me that any difficulties of segregation would be best dealt with if the Lord Chancellor were Head of All Records. ...' PJGG10(2) Churchill Archives Centre, Cambridge. The decision had been taken against Sir James' advice. He told the Master of the Rolls 'As you know I was not consulted when the Treasury decided to make the Lord Chancellor the Minister responsible for departmental records and I do not agree with the decision'. Note to, 12 March 1957, PJGG10(2) Churchill Archives Centre, Cambridge.

46 See T. Plucknett (1959); 'The Public Records Act 1958', *The Modern Law Review*, Vol. 22, No. 2, 182.

47 *Ibid.*

48 Schellenberg is cited formally in The National Archives (2004); *Appraisal Policy: Background paper – The 'Grigg System' and Beyond*, Appraisal Project Board, 2.

49 In 2013, The National Archives released figures for the retention of files dated 1982 or before (https://www.gov.uk/government/publications/twenty-year-rule-on-public-records). It may be seen that at the beginning of this century beween 4% and 9% were transferred:

Progress of historic review programme, 2013 to 2014: files dated 1982 or earlier

	31 Mar 2014 – number of files	30 Jun 2014 – number of files	30 Sep 2014 – number of files
Total volume (brought forward)	10,481	7,773	7,565
Awaiting review	0	0	0
Selection review	0	0	0
Awaiting TNA sign-off of selection review	891 (8.5%)	903 (11%)	903 (12%)
Sensitivity review	24 (<1%)	24 <1%	4 (<1%)
Preparation for transfer	9,202 (88%)	6,198 (80%)	5,719 (76%)
Awaiting TNA sign-off for transfer	364 (3.5%)	648 (8%)	939 (12%)
Transferred	452	469	661

50 I have chosen to focus on the history of record management at TNA but it should be noted that other collections have also been depleted or scattered. For instance, the Home Office library, a once impressive collection of holdings of the annual statistics relating to crime and justice, publications of the Home Office Research Unit and relevant criminological studies from both the UK and overseas is now only a shadow of itself. We were told by the Head of the Home Office Knowledge and Information Management Unit that the creation of the Ministry of Justice in 2007 saw its criminal justice material being transferred to that Ministry's library. Two years later, and following what was called a restructure at the Home Office, it was decided to move to an electronic library service with a range of online material being made available to staff through their desktop computers. A small hard copy collection of departmental publications was also retained in the Information Services Centre at 2 Marsham Street. Other material, it was said, was transferred to the British Library, The National Archives and the Ministry of Justice.

51 There were to be 14 Home Secretaries between 1959 and 1997, one, Roy Jenkins, serving twice, and their average tenure of office was two and a half years.

52 I. Taylor, P. Walton and J. Young (1973); *The New Criminology*, London: Routledge and Kegan Paul.
53 M. Phillipson (1973); 'Critical Theorising and "The New Criminology"', in 'Review Symposium', *The British Journal of Criminology*, Vol. 13, No. 4, 399.

Bibliography

J. Collingridge (1955–59); 'Implementing the Grigg Report', *Journal of the Society of Archivists*, Vol. 1, 179–184

Committee on Legal Records (1966); *Report*, Cmnd. 3084, London: HMSO

D. Downes (1966); *The Delinquent Solution: A Study in Subcultural Theory*, London: Routledge and Kegan Paul

M. Goodman (2014); *The Official History of the Joint Intelligence Committee: Volume I: From the Approach of the Second World War to the Suez Crisis*, London: Routledge.

T. Jones and T. Newburn (1998); *Private Security and Public Policing*, Oxford: Clarendon Press

A.Kemp (2014); *The Official History of North Sea Oil and Gas, Vol. II: Moderating the State's Role*, London: Routledge

C. Krishnamoorthy (1953); 'Organisation and Methods in the British Government', *The Indian Journal of Political Science*, Vol. 14, No. 2, 113–122

C. Lombroso (1911); introduction to G. Lombroso-Ferrero; *Criminal Man According to the Classification of Cesare Lombroso*, New York: G.P. Putnam's Sons

R. Lowe (2011); *The Official History of the British Civil Service, Reforming the Civil Service, Volume I: The Fulton Years, 1966–81*, London: Routledge

G. Martin (1988); 'The Public Records in 1988', in G. Martin and P. Spufford (eds.) *The Records of the Nation: The Public Record Office 1838–1988*, Woodbridge: The Boydell Press, 43–48

T. Newburn and T. Jones (2007); *Policy Transfer and Criminal Justice: Exploring US Influence over British Crime Control Policy*, Maidenhead: Open University Press

D. Parker (2012); *The Official History of Privatisation, Vol. II, Popular Capitalism, 1987–97*, London: Routledge

M. Phillipson (1973); 'Critical Theorising and "The New Criminology"', in 'Review Symposium', *The British Journal of Criminology*, Vol. 13, No. 4, 398–400

I. Pitman (1948); 'Organisation and Methods: An Important Select Committee Report', *Public Administration*, Vol. 26, No. 1, 1–9

T. Plucknett (1959); 'The Public Records Act 1958', *The Modern Law Review*, Vol. 22, No. 2, 182–183

M. Power (1999); *The Audit Society: Rituals of Verification*, Oxford: Oxford University Press

Public Record Office (1962); *A Guide for Departmental Record Officers (Revised)*, London: Public Record Office

—(1983); *Manual of Records Administration*, London: Public Record Office

P. Rock (1990); *Helping Victims of Crime: The Home Office and the Rise of Victim Support in England and Wales*, Oxford: Clarendon Press

—(1996); *Reconstructing a Women's Prison: The Holloway Redevelopment Project, 1968–88*, Oxford: Clarendon Press

—(1998); *After Homicide: Practical and Political Responses to Bereavement*, Oxford: Clarendon Press

—(2001); *The Social World of an English Crown Court*, Oxford: Clarendon Press

—(2004); *Constructing Victims' Rights: The Home Office, New Labour and Victims*, Oxford: Clarendon Press

—(2016); "The Dreadful Flood of Documents': The 1958 Public Record Act and its Aftermath. Part 1: The Genesis of the Act'. *Archives*, Vol. LI, nos. 132–3, 1–22

—(2017); "The Dreadful Flood of Documents': The 1958 Public Record Act and its Aftermath. Part 2: After-effects'. *Archives*, Vol. LII, 26–50

I. Taylor, P. Walton and J. Young (1973); *The New Criminology*, London: Routledge and Kegan Paul

R. Titmuss (1950); *Problems of Social Policy*, London: HMSO

S. Wall (2014); *The Official History of Britain and the European Community, Vol. II: From Rejection to Referendum*, London: Routledge

1 Crime in the late 1950s and 1960s

A Preamble

Introduction

Let me set the scene for the chapters that are to come, laying out something of what was known about the state of crime in mid-century, roughly the starting point of this history. It was thought to be a troubled time, and a persistent growth in crime was taken to be a sign of the malaise. Driven numerically almost entirely by the growth of property crime rather than by personal violence, recorded crime had risen nearly continually throughout much of the twentieth century, and it had risen steeply[1] and for reasons that were obscure. It was eventually to reach a peak in about 1994, and it declined thereafter for a long while, again for reasons that were obscure. A few simple charts should make the point:[2]

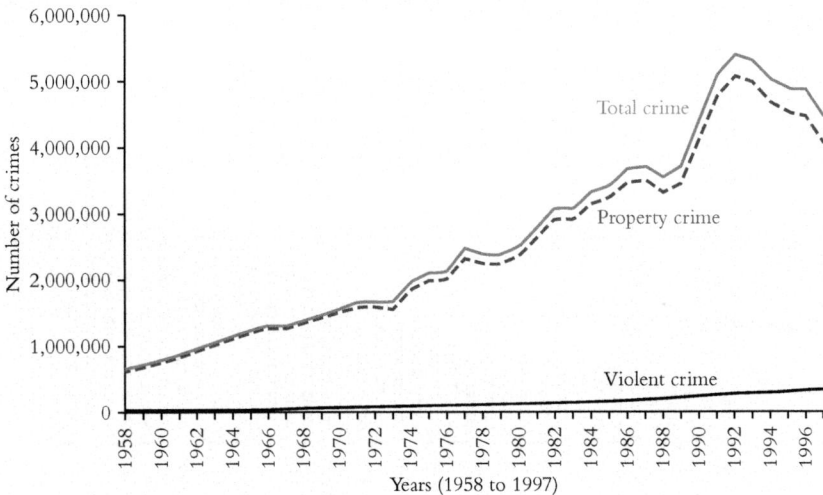

Figure 1.1[3] Recorded crime: property and violent crime

Property crime itself consisted almost entirely of breaking and entering and what were then called larceny offences, an omnibus term that covered the unlawful taking of the personal property of another:[4]

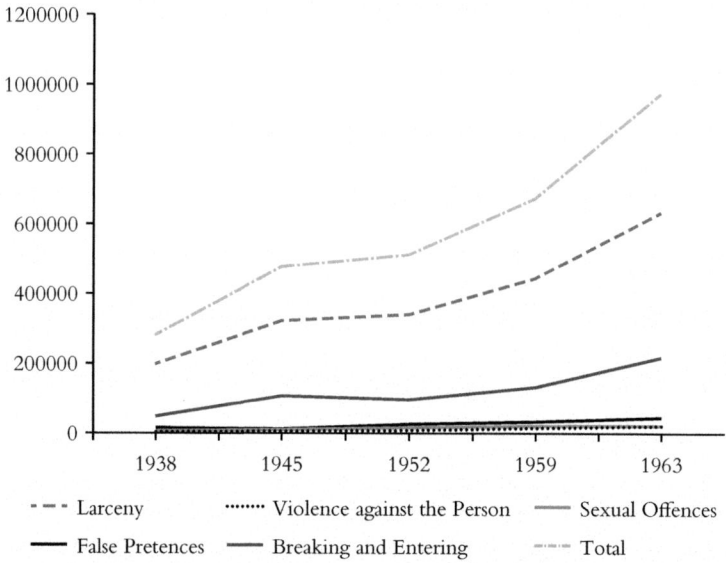

Figure 1.2[5] Recorded crime 1938–1963

Crime had risen absolutely. It had risen disproportionately when set against population increase:

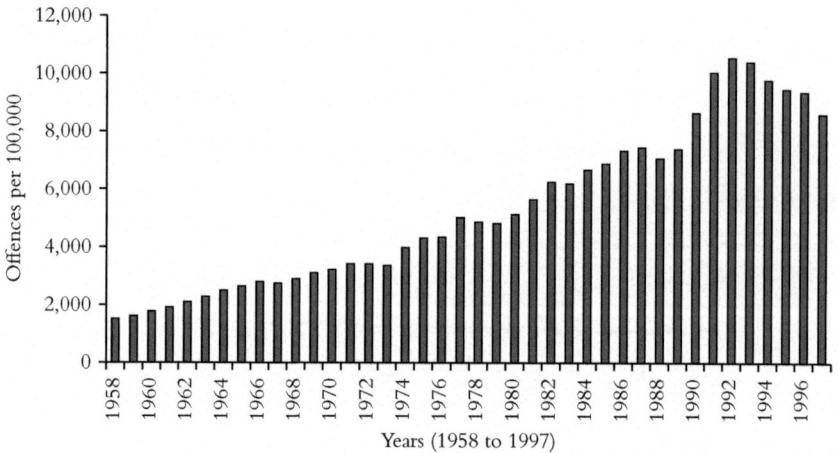

Figure 1.3[6] Notifiable offences recorded by the police per 100,000 population, England and Wales

It had risen in ragged fashion against general levels of unemployment:

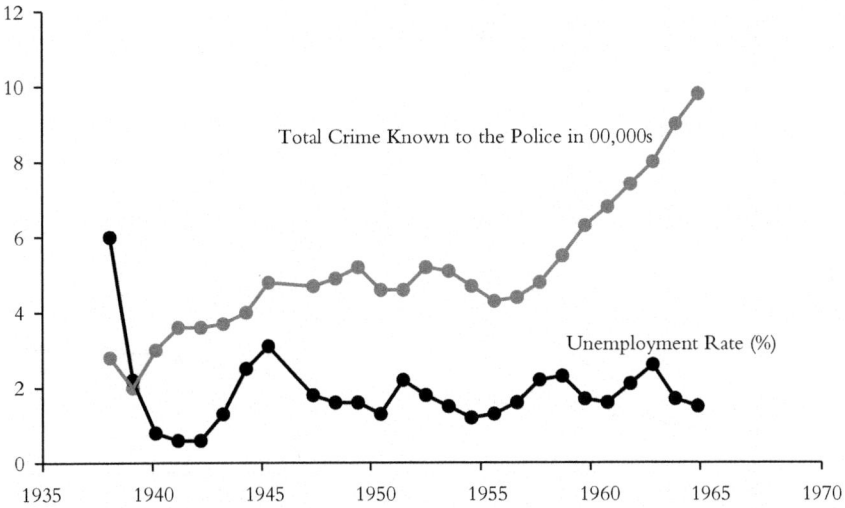

Figure 1.4[7] Crime and unemployment

It sometimes kept pace with the growth in the availability of particular targets:

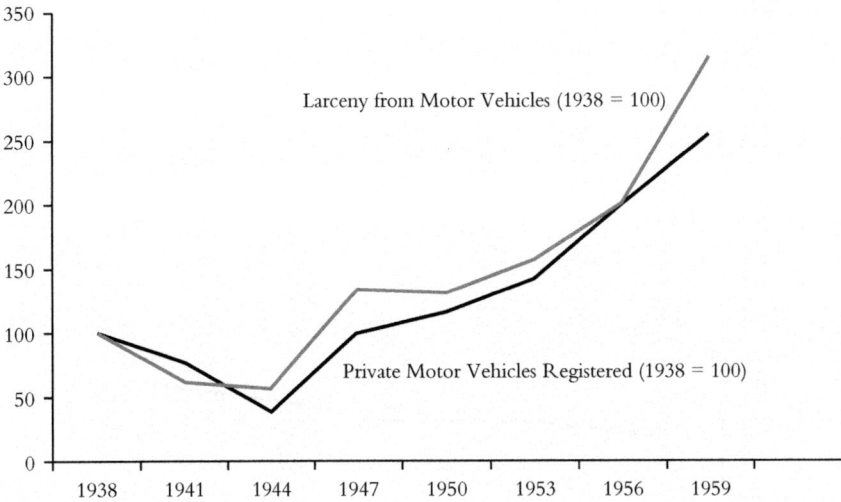

Figure 1.5[8] The number of private cars and larceny from motor vehicles 1938–1959

But it would just as often soar ahead again:

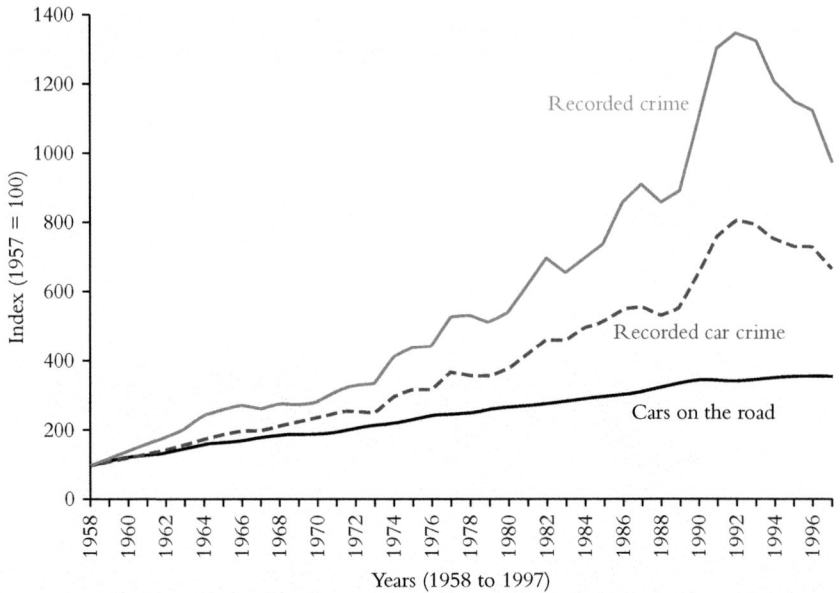

Figure 1.6[9] Recorded crime, recorded car crime and cars on the road

And it continuously outstripped not only the growth of personal wealth in England and Wales, crudely measured, but also the growth of expenditure on education:

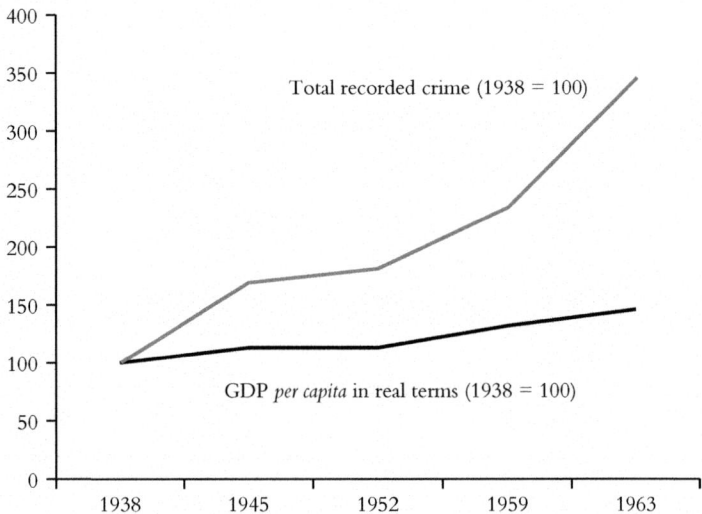

Figure 1.7[10] Crime and GDP *per capita* 1938–1965

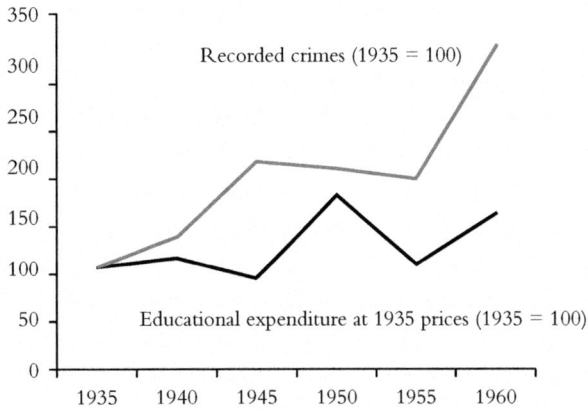

Figure 1.8[11] Educational expenditure and crime rates 1935–1960

The surge in offending had a momentum that appeared unstoppable, incomprehensible and deeply disquieting. Crime could inflict physical pain and material loss (and material loss may have significant symbolic and psychological repercussions[12]); it could generate fear, insecurity, anger and mistrust; its presence on any scale could challenge claims about the competence and authority of the state; and the *manner* in which the state responded in its work of prevention, detection, adjudication and punishment could raise difficult questions about justice, fairness and propriety.[13] Nicola Lacey observed that 'criminal justice policy and the institutions through which that policy is realised have a particular importance in establishing the legitimacy and credibility of governments ... the power to convict and punish represents the most vivid exercise of state force in relation to individual citizens'.[14] It is thus hardly remarkable that public attention had long focused on the official rates, and that policymakers, politicians and practitioners had had in their turn repeatedly to defend their management of the criminal justice system.

Although they might now appear modest enough, those rates were almost invariably regarded by people writing in the late 1950s and the 1960s as new;[15] disturbingly large; extraordinarily rapid in their growth;[16] largely inexplicable;[17] threatening,[18] and indicative of a major, somehow perverse transformation of the society of England and Wales. Their increase offended common-sense expectations about what should have been the proper links between national prosperity,[19] education,[20] employment,[21] want[22] and criminality.[23] Crime should have *declined*, not grown, after the Second World War. Leon Radzinowicz,[24] Wolfson Professor of Criminology at the University of Cambridge, and perhaps the foremost criminologist of his day, remarked in 1965:

> In England and Wales, ... the amount of indictable crime known to the police has more than trebled over the past twenty-five years in spite of the rise in the standard of living of all classes, of the improvement of housing, health and educational services and of protective legislation. The young

are richer than ever before and have a wider range of opportunities, but it is amongst them that the increase in the crime rate has been sharpest.[25]

And in like vein, Lord Pakenham,[26] later the Earl of Longford, the reforming Labour peer, writing in the 1950s, remarked how an article in *The Times*[27] had prompted him to form:

a very strong impression that crime had been increasing for twenty years, at a time when the Welfare State was being established, the condition of the poor much improved, and extreme want being abolished.[28]

He was later to be charged with chairing the Study Group on Crime Prevention and Penal Reform, an influential group that became known as the Longford Committee, which had been commissioned as part of the party's modernisation programme 'to advise the Labour Party on the recent increase in recorded crime, the present treatment of offenders, and the new measures, penal or social, required both to assist in the prevention of crime and to improve and modernise our penal practices'.[29] Its conclusions were to become available a few months before a new Labour administration came into office in October 1964, and we shall see that they were to anticipate and indeed influence a number of its decisions.

Changes in the figures appeared more dramatic and threatening still when, as was often the case,[30] what would now look like quite humble numerical increases were represented as percentages. In 1969, for example, the Secretary of State for the Home Department and the Secretary of State for Scotland reported in a memorandum that 'there was an increase in England and Wales in indictable offences of violence against the person of 33.3 per cent (from 17,601 to 23,470) between 1961 and 1964. ... For robbery, the corresponding increases were 30.5 per cent (2,349 in 1961 and 3,066 in 1964) ...'[31] So depicted, it seemed impossible to ignore or disparage what was in train. The University of Cambridge criminologist, Derek McClintock, opened his 1963 study of crimes of violence in London with the observation:

The increase during the last decade in the incidence of crimes against the person, especially those that are classified as of a violent nature, has led to a great uneasiness and even anxiety among a large proportion of the population, as well as among those concerned with the maintenance of law and order.[32]

Some Members of Parliament declared that matters were out of control,[33] and even that avowedly most liberal of Home Secretaries, Roy Jenkins,[34] was obliged to state in 1966:

One of the most menacing ... forces at the present time is the crime wave, which causes an immense amount of fear, suffering and economic loss. For the past 10 years at least crime has been growing at an alarming rate. This dangerous situation must be brought under control.[35]

Criminality was thought to be mushrooming especially amongst the young,[36] (one third of all those found guilty of indictable offences each year were under the age of 17, and one half under 21 in the early 1960s[37]), and it seemed that there was something peculiarly amiss with those who had been born in and around the wartime years,[38] the so-called affluent teenagers,[39] who should have had no pretext to offend. They were members of the markedly 'delinquent generations', represented by the Teddy Boys[40] and other young 'hooligans' whose early upbringing was supposed to have gone awry during the war,[41] and whose adolescence had been disorientated by the rapidity of the pace of social change that succeeded it.[42] R.A. Butler[43] commissioned a Conservative Party report on 'The Rising Tide; Youth in the 1960's' [*sic*] 'To consider the problems facing young people in their 'teens and in their early twenties ...', and the ensuing study stated that: 'It is certainly extremely disappointing that juvenile delinquency has not receded with the virtual banishment of really serious poverty. "The crime problem", as the Albemarle Report[44] observed, "is very much a youth problem"'.[45]

In 1965, another Conservative Party report reflected 'The nature of the problem which confronts us can be simply stated. We are experiencing a crime wave of substantial proportions ... [and there has been] a startling increase in the number of crimes committed by young people under the age of 21'.[46] Not only were the young offending in unusually heavy numbers, but the early onset of their offending was a worrying portent of future criminality. It was thought imperative to confront them at the very beginning of their delinquent careers lest matters became even worse. A draft White Paper on 'young people in trouble' written in the same month and same year as the Conservative Party Report on the 'rising tide' declared that:

> A recurrent theme has been the urgent need to concentrate resources on the prevention and treatment of juvenile delinquency. A high proportion of adult criminals have been juvenile delinquents, so that every advance in dealing with the young offender helps also to attack adult crime.[47]

Something appeared to be afoot, and it brought about what David Garland called 'a new experience of crime'. It was during this period that popular, political and expert responses to crime began to change. There was more property to steal, but crime was growing in volume even faster than the increase in the number of suitable targets, and it was being spread by an increasingly mobile population who could move about by motorcar to victimise households that, for demographic and economic reasons of divorce and work pattern,[48] were less and less securely protected. For the middle class, especially, crime was no longer quite so distinctively an infrequent event committed by small numbers of troubled, poor people who were socially and geographically distant. It was apparently ubiquitous, swelling, substantial and menacing. The changes:

> that gave rise to the high crime rates of the 1960s and subsequent dec-
> ades ... transformed the middle-class experience of crime. From being a
> problem that mostly affected the poor, crime (and particularly vandalism,
> theft, burglary and robbery) increasingly became a daily consideration for
> anyone who owned a car, used the subway, left their house unguarded
> during the day, or walked the city streets at night.[49]

The public response

Whatever stance they might privately have wished to take, and whatever policies they may have sought to promote,[50] Home Secretaries of both parties were
constrained throughout the period to convey publicly that they were aware
that crime was mounting dangerously, and that they were attempting tirelessly
to confront the problem. The Home Secretary between 1957 and 1962, R.A.
Butler, in particular, was assailed with unremitting complaints about the crime
wave from within the Conservative Party, and, above all, with almost unanimous protest from party associations about the dilution of punishments, the
abolition of corporal punishment and plans to abolish capital punishment. Lord
Windlesham, a former Home Office minister, recollected that R.A. Butler had
talked about 'the 'blood curdling demands' made annually at the Conservative
Party Conference for the restoration of corporal punishment which had 'quite
clouded his time as Chairman of the Party. ...'[51] And R.A. Butler himself
recalled that 'I [have] had to take an awful lot of opposition ... [including calls
for] birching and flogging ... which haunted me almost every week of my
time at the Home Office ...'[52] He had faced a brief but abortive attempt to stir
up a populist campaign against what was depicted by his critics as his craven
response to crisis.[53] In January 1960, he had had to write to Sir Eric Edwards,
deputy chairman of the party and the formal conduit for those protests and
recriminations: 'The Government is seriously concerned about the increase
in crime, especially amongst young people, and legislation is in preparation to
provide more effective means of combating it. The Government is certainly
not adopting a "soft" approach in this matter. ...'[54] And that became a formula
that he was obliged to deploy again and again in reply to remonstrations emanating from party members across the country.[55]

The state of knowledge

There were in public currency at least two dominant clusters of explanation to
make sense of, and manage, the rise in crime, although they differed principally
in nuance, language and mode of analysis rather than in substance. Both inevitably refracted the ethical, political, occupational and religious preoccupations
of the day. Tett may have claimed that 'The modern world is littered with

pockets of specialist knowledge, where technical experts work in mental and structural silos',[56] but her observation does not extend to knowledge about crime. The Prison Commissioner between 1922 and 1947, Alexander Paterson, observed that 'Everyone is interested in the criminal; everyone has views on the subject of crime'.[57] Crime impinges on everybody. Everybody can be, or can rehearse being, its victim, bystander, witness or perpetrator. Everybody is obliged continually to make personal, social and moral judgements about the risks, hazards and dilemmas it presents; everybody can, or thinks he or she can, understand crime and its causes;[58] and there seem in consequence to be no discernible 'mental and structural silos' inhibiting the construction and dissemination of arguments about its causes and remedies. If only for very practical reasons, everybody has to be an expert of a sort,[59] claiming an entitlement to comment, and the outcome has been the creation of a number of criminologies, some vernacular, some more academic, that have come from time to time to play a political role. An official who had joined the Home Office in the early 1960s observed in interview: 'the fate of the Home Secretary rather than the Transport Secretary for example, is that everybody knows what the solution is, you know. Everybody is his own Home Secretary'.

One cluster, more political and lay than scholarly, was a blend of common sense, moralistic theorising and popular psychology[60] that distilled a number of anxieties about the condition of England.[61] It touched on a collapse of discipline,[62] especially in the home,[63] 'mistakes in upbringing'[64] and the erosion of stable domestic life that had been precipitated by the dislocations of the Second World War, a growing involvement of women in the work force and the breakdown of the conventional nuclear family.[65] It was taken for granted that crime was in the main a breach of moral rules whose roots lay in moral failings and whose explanation must be pitched in moral terms.[66] It could take the form, at one pole, of the proclamation of simple imperatives,[67] and, at the other, of long, omnibus and somewhat vague lists that, tacitly invoking the principle that like causes like – that bad effects must have bad causes – pointed to the consequences of a decline in deference, defective socialisation, defective adherence to religious and ethical instruction, defective school discipline, defective informal and formal social control, and moral defects in the content of the evermore consequential and ubiquitous mass media,[68] and the supposed deleterious effects of 'horror comics', 'rock 'n' roll' and, indeed, much of American culture generally. R.A. Butler presaged his 1959 White Paper, *Penal Practice in a Changing Society*,[69] with the declaration that the report 'cannot be expected to deal with those deep-seated causes of crime which are reached not so much by legislation or administrative action, but by self-discipline, family responsibility and the influence and action of the Churches and other bodies which act as a leaven within the community'.[70]

Lord Longford, the politician and important Church layman, regarded by Cardinal Heenan,[71] the Archbishop of Westminster, as one of the premier Catholic peers, had also drafted his own very similar catalogue of probable causes of crime at very much the same time. They included 'The psychological and moral influence of [the offender's] family environment, operating especially, but not exclusively, during the first few years'; and 'The moral and psychological atmosphere of his time (including the attitude to the law) associated with, for example: great developments of opinion, including religious attitudes; far-reaching social changes such as the emergence of the Welfare State; the economic situation including any unemployment, short-ages, and so forth; catastrophes such as the war ...'[72] Merlyn Rees, a Member of Parliament who was himself to become a Home Secretary in 1976, said that delinquency 'raised issues of home and family, personality, school, work – or lack of it – and other factors'.[73] And Henry Brooke,[74] R.A. Butler's succes-sor as Conservative Home Secretary between 1962 and 1964, told the newly formed Advisory Committee on Juvenile Delinquency in February 1964 that there is one:

> purpose I want this committee to serve. Through it I want to see the accu-mulated knowledge and the resources of all Government Departments used on these problems of delinquency. I am sure you will agree that the home and the family and the personality, the school, work or the lack of it, housing conditions and other local facts, all have to be taken into account in striving to reduce delinquency.[75]

In their emphasis on the workings of informal social control, they were, of course, underscoring an important truth: most crime is affected only at the margins by the operation of the criminal justice system. Much crime is not reported; much reported crime is not recorded; and much recorded crime does not reach the courts or prisons. It is the impact of a medley of shaming, guilt, praise and recrimination, the bestowing and withdrawing of affection, practical surveillance, gossip, the management of stakes in conformity, target hardening, prudent conduct[76] and much else that principally counts. Formal social control touches most crime but little. Figure 1.9 makes the point.[77]

The other main cluster of explanations, more in vogue in the university, cor-rectional institution and clinic, was also a multi-factorial *potpourri*. The new and rather tentative academic study of crime was then what David Downes would have called a *rendezvous* enterprise: eclectic, multi-disciplinary, polycentric and more heavily disposed to the empirical than the theoretical, the concrete than the abstract. Consider the founding preoccupations of the discipline's principal vehicle in the United Kingdom, *The British Journal of Delinquency* – later *The British Journal of Criminology* – that had been launched in July 1950 with the revealing declaration that:

> Clinical contributions will of course receive special consideration, but it is hoped to publish articles, both theoretical and practical, from trained workers in the various departments of criminology; namely, medical psychology, psychiatry, psychoanalysis, organic medicine, educa-tional psychology, sociology, economics, anthropology, psycho-biology

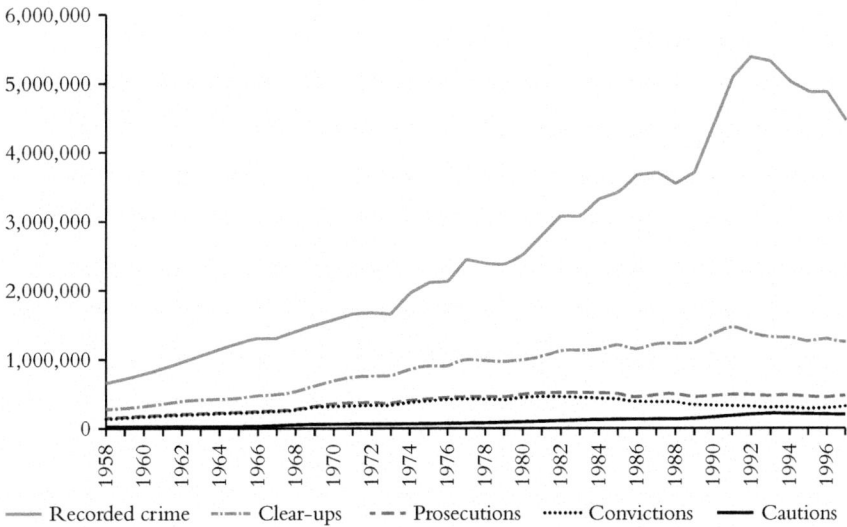

Figure 1.9[78] Recorded crime and clear-ups; indictable prosecutions, and the numbers convicted

- The number of prosecutions and the number of convictions for indictable offences have changed little over the period.
- There was an increase in the number of offenders who were not processed by the courts but instead received a formal caution from the police.

and statistics; also from social workers, probation officers, prison and other institutional personnel. ...'[79]

Crime, it was to be said repeatedly, could not be attributed to a single cause but to a multitude of antecedent conditions that included the psychological, economic and social circumstances of the offender. Each condition played its part and each demanded its own proper accounting and analysis.[80] The explanation of crime was so complex, remarked Howard Jones,[81] the author of an early British textbook, that 'some criminologists [have been led] to abandon the quest for systematic theories, and to lay emphasis instead upon causal *factors*. ...'[82] That was also the theme of *Comparative Criminology: A Textbook*, written by Hermann Mannheim,[83] formerly the Reader in Criminology at the London School of Economics, which surveyed the parts played in criminology by statistics; prediction studies; individual case studies and typological methods; action research; physical-anthropological-biological aspects; geography and physical health; the positivist school; heredity, twins and glands; psychoses, alcoholism and drug addiction; neuroses and psychopathy; mental deficiency; Freud, Jung and Adler; class and conflict; white-collar crime; ecological theory; culture conflict; racial and other minorities; the family and school; the crowd; organised crime; gangs; and age and sex.[84] And another textbook, *Crime and Punishment in Britain*, also published in 1965, and written by Nigel Walker, then the Reader in Criminology at the University of Oxford,[85] also followed an encyclopaedic course to review constitutional theories, theories of mental illness, psychoanalytic theories, theories centred on weakness of ego, weakness of super-ego, the affectionless character, broken homes; individualistic explanations couched in terms of 'inborn differences between delinquents and non-delinquents, whether congenital or hereditary', 'maladjustment resulting from faulty upbringing', and 'weak ethical learning as a normal result of working-class ways of child-rearing'; and 'environmental explanations' in terms of 'economic conditions', 'deteriorating urban areas' and 'sub-cultures with unofficial codes of conduct'. None of these modes of analysis necessarily contradicted or displaced the others, Walker observed, because 'hypotheses may avoid conflict if they are offered as explanations of different groups of observations'.[86]

Authors during that period quite legitimately tended to regard their works as pioneering and novel. Nigel Walker said simply 'My notes looked better when turned into a text-book: at that time there wasn't a British one'.[87] But they certainly did not write with confidence (Howard Jones reflected: 'Some may feel that the claim of criminology to be called a science is very much open to question; its methods, like those of other social sciences, are often highly subjective, and it has been able so far to establish no scientific laws that can claim general validity'[88]). They believed themselves to be members of a novel and marginal calling[89] (in 1966, Hermann Mannheim was obliged to say that 'in Great Britain at least, progress towards the formation of an independent profession of criminologists has been very erratic and generally unsatisfactory;'[90] and his colleague, Lord Chorley, a specialist in the law of banking and shipping, called criminology 'the Cinderella of the social sciences'[91]). And they were not wholly convinced of the utility of their discipline (Lord Longford recalled of one prominent academic that 'When Mrs Wootton[92] was asked what help the criminologists could give to the Home Secretary today about the causes of crime, she replied 'not very much'. ...'[93]).

The substance and form of the criminology of the late 1950s and the 1960s flowed in some significant part from those for whom crime was a practical preoccupation: the doctors, policy officials, psychiatrists, prison governors and others who treated, measured[94] and managed the criminal.[95] There were few others equipped to develop the craft. They were professionally positioned at close quarters to their subject (the *British Journal of Criminology* called them the 'forensic specialists whose work brings them into intimate contact with the problem of delinquency'[96]). It was they who, as a matter of course, supplied many of the data which were to become the materials, catalysts, objects, contexts and products of analysis.[97] Criminology was steeped in psychiatry, psychology and psychoanalysis. It was instrumental, emphasising its usefulness to reform, rehabilitation, correction and policy-making. It was intended to make 'criminal justice and penal institutions effective and decent'.[98] It was heavily quantitative. It was given to the construction of typologies of delinquents, delinquency, offenders, patients and modes of treatment. *The British*

Journal of Criminology talked affectionately in the mid-1960s of how 'modern criminological science pursues its ambitious psycho-social courses, and eager young researchers penetrate every nook and cranny of the field, bearing in their hands a variety of test schedules and questionnaires of the most recondite statistical particularity ...'[99]

Those 'test schedules and questionnaires of the most recondite statistical particularity' did indeed largely epitomise how many people of influence thought that research could and should proceed. Tom Lodge, an actuary by vocation,[100] who came to play a pivotal role in the 1950s and 1960s, first as the Home Office Statistical Adviser, and then as the co-founder and first Director of the new Home Office Research Unit, put it that criminological research objectives 'may be considered as falling into four categories:

1) To evolve and develop systems of observation, description and measurement;
2) To evolve, develop or modify relevant theory in the light of sound observation and measurement;
3) To provide assistance in management problems (operational research). This involves the study of case load size, types of institutions and like problems;
4) To assist in the development of training of treatment staff through the study of systems of communication'.[101]

His list of desiderata admittedly stemmed from within government (although it was not confined to government), but it would have been approved by many falling outside, and it made its mark on the external research that government chose to support.

I have remarked that, for all their protestations of scientificity and rigour, criminologists tended to betray a nervousness about their fledgling science.[102] Home Office officials were certainly not impressed by the quantity and quality of criminology practised in the universities at the end of the 1950s and the beginning of the 1960s. Sir Charles Cunningham,[103] the Permanent Undersecretary, was dismissive as he reminded Henry Brooke, the Home Secretary in 1963 that: 'In the 1959 White Paper we also included brief particulars of current research on crime for which the Home Office had no responsibility. This was the result of a circular to Vice-Chancellors. The harvest however was meagre and we would not propose to issue a similar circular on this occasion'.[104]

To be sure, there were the rudiments of organised research within the Home Office itself: it had 'funded some in-house research by its own prison staff early in the century and then had bought research through contracts in the 1930s'.[105] A co-ordinating body called the Research Committee on Delinquency (later the Home Office Research Committee) had been established in 1954. But what had been done was undeveloped and tentative. Matters eventually came to a head in 1957 with the appointment of a new and ambitious Home Secretary, R.A. Butler, who had written to his prime minister immediately on taking office to say that 'I shall be unable to fulfil my mission here unless I find it possible to press forward a comprehensive plan of penal reform. ... I must leave behind some permanent record of my period of office here or I shall feel not only that I have been disloyal to myself, but also that I have failed in my duty to you and the Government which you lead. ...'[106] And the immediate trigger for his desire to bolster scientific research on crime and the penal system, research that could act as a handmaiden to that grand political project, was, we are told, his reading of an article by C.H. Rolph,[107] published in *The New Statesman* on 2 February 1957, and written in the guise of an open letter addressed to him just nineteen days after his appointment as Secretary of State.

C.H. Rolph had opened with the assertion that 'Your new appointment brings you an opportunity that must be rare in the history of your office. It will not much longer suit the social conscience to shrug off the state of the prisons, even the existence of prisons, as "the black flower of civilised society"'.[108] And he then proceeded to catalogue at length the reforms a new Home Secretary might achieve (he said later that 'it touches on all the familiar problems, all of which could have been ... dredged up from long-forgotten government blue books'[109]). In a somewhat opaque passage, he talked of the need to dispel some of the ignorance that obscured officials' understanding of the impact of their actions, and, in particular, their ignorance about the effects of different types of imprisonment on different types of prisoner:

> We simply do not know, and no research will ever tell us, how many first offenders might, whether or not they have gone to prison or even been caught, have committed that one offence only throughout their lives. We do not know (because we do not adequately inquire) how many of them cannot at the moment respond to any kind of treatment. We know that there is in prison, at this moment, a group of people who will become recidivist *because they are there*. But, again, we do not know how many there are. ...
>
> Therefore, Mr. Home Secretary, I take leave to reproduce here an extract from Section 77 of the Criminal Justice Act, 1948:

> > (3) There shall be paid out of moneys provided by Parliament –
> > (f) towards the expenditure of any body of persons approved by the Secretary of State in the conduct of research into the causes of delinquency and the treatment of offenders, and matters connected therewith such sums as the Secretary of State may with approval of the Treasury direct, and subject to such conditions as he may with the like approval determine.[110] ...

> Would it be fair to say that this kind of financial provision is too readily relied upon as passing the buck to the Treasury? The buck resides at that address already: it is for other departments to get it into movement, bearing in mind that a provision like Section 77(3)(f) is an expression of the

will of parliament, upon which many high hopes were founded. In nine years, the grants thus made have totalled less than £100,000.[111]

The Home Secretary promptly set officials to enquire quite how much they had indeed spent on penological research since 1948, and the figure *they* unearthed was a mere £11,934.[112] It was a sum deemed quite inadequate, especially by a Home Secretary who wished to make his mark on crime and the management of the prison estate,[113] and it jolted the Home Office into taking a stand. It was an opportune moment. Tom Lodge was able to say:

> The two main handicaps to research hitherto have been shortage of money and shortage of competent research workers. A subsidiary restricting factor has been the lack of adequate data, and it is a point of some importance that the working out of methods of providing data for study can itself be regarded as research ...
>
> If it can be assumed that money will be available, we can consider how best to organise an expanded research programme. So far, a few small research studies have been carried out within the Home Office in the ordinary course of duty, and one larger study has been carried out by the Social Survey with the guidance of a committee of Home Office staff. But the usual method has been to invite some department of a University to undertake research with the help of a Home Office grant. This method has the advantage that the University contributes part of the cost and provides free, or almost free, the services of suitably qualified directing staff; another feature of this method is that the Home Office, while able to prevent the publication of anything too embarrassing, is not committed to agree with the conclusions of the research worker.
>
> A certain expansion of research by this method could, and should, be brought about, but there are two limitations on any large expansion. The first is the shortage of suitable University departments and the second is our inability to direct these departments to do what we want or to get it done in a reasonable time.
>
> The Universities to which so far we have given grants have been Oxford University (the Reader in Criminology), Cambridge University (Department of Criminal Science), London School of Economics (the Reader in Criminology), University College London (Department of Psychology). Undoubtedly there are a few other University Departments that would undertake research if we offered a grant, but most of the suitable ones are small and the scope for expansion in this way cannot be large. It can be admitted that our knowledge of this field is not complete, because it is not easy to go and investigate a University department when there is no prospect of offering them a grant. In the field of juvenile delinquency it should certainly be possible to arrange a moderate research programme through Universities, but it is doubtful whether there can be any great expansion in the field of adult criminology or penology.

... What is perhaps even more important, we have on only very few occasions been able to induce University departments to set about research with what we regard as sufficient attention to scientific rigour and the use of modern statistical techniques. One of the most important aspects of research on penology is the comparison (as measured by the proportion of reconvictions in any group) of the results of differing forms of treatment. This can be done only by extracting comparable groups for comparison.[114]

A week later, on 13 March 1957, the Home Secretary told the House of Commons:

Hon. Members may remember an interesting article by Mr. C. H. Rolph which appeared in the New Statesman, which has, I think, wisely and rightly stimulated a great deal of discussion. This article chided the Home Office for spending less than £100,000 on research in nine years. I should like to be quite frank ... and say that figures given recently in the House of Commons show that we have spent only about £12,000. This is the biggest initial shock which has come to me in examining this problem ... I acknowledge straight away that this is quite unsatisfactory.

Some useful work has, of course, been done ... But, in my opinion, much more work must be done, notably on imprisonment itself, which is the subject of this Supplementary Estimate. On this huge topic we must have more accurate information, and I propose to give first priority, therefore, to the best methods of expanding our research programme.[115]

Sir Frank Newsam,[116] the Permanent Undersecretary, a man on the brink of retirement, went to the Treasury the very next day with the proposal that the Home Office should have its own dedicated research unit to study the treatment of offenders. Criminological research should be put on a firmer institutional footing, and it would be research that could satisfy the state's need for highly focused and practical enquiry marked by rigour, statistics and policy relevance:

... [the] limitations are so serious that it is proposed that expansion of research should take place mainly by setting up an expanded Home Office research organisation. ... It is tentatively estimated that a useful research organisation could be set up in the Home Office by appointing two persons with some knowledge of statistics (possibly in conjunction with psychology or sociology) and four executive and clerical officers. It would be necessary to make some arrangements for the mechanical processing of data, but at first this could probably be done either by the Social Survey or by borrowing electronic computer time from some other Department. ...[117]

Sir Frank's immediate successor, Sir Charles Cunningham, appointed in September 1957, then 'lost no time in setting up for the first time a professional research unit, and encouraged the creation of the Cambridge Institute of Criminology'.[118] The Research Unit was established within the Home Office's Establishments and Organisation Division and Common Services in 1959–1960. Its programme of work was based at first on the 'medico-psychological model',[119] guided in large measure by that rather precise political mandate and the financial provisions of section 77 of the 1948 Criminal Justice Act. It was intended that there would be 'Studies of the results of treatment: Probation (already begun); Young prisoners; Adult prisoners; Borstal trainees (one study already done); Approved school trainees (one study already done)'.[120] And its first reports faithfully adopted as their series title the phrase 'the causes of delinquency and the treatment of offenders', although they sometimes strayed from those themes in practice. Study number 2[121] was *Time Spent Awaiting Trial* (1960) by Evelyn Gibson (in 'a purely factual way, this report describes the procedure for bringing to trial persons charged with criminal offences, examines the use of remands by magistrates' courts, and analyses the length of time spent awaiting trial and sentence … '); number 3 was *Delinquent Generations* by Leslie Wilkins (1960); number 4 was *Murder* by Evelyn Gibson and Stan Klein (1961), a study which was to have a political impact at a critical time; and number 5 was *Persistent Criminals* by W.H. 'Doc' Hammond and Evelyn Chayen (1963) ('on the criminal histories of all men who were liable to preventive detention in 1956'). Segments of crime and the criminal justice system of England and Wales were thereby being professionally mapped for the very first time.

Tom Lodge has been described by Chris Nuttall, a former colleague and eventual successor, as 'what you would expect from an actuary – correct, precise, and careful. … His interests were eclectic and he knew his way around the civil service – a very important skill for the head of a small but growing research institute which was seen as an irrelevance by many senior Home Office civil servants'.[122] By 1965, and under Lodge's direction, the new Unit was operating with ten staff:[123] two statisticians; three senior research officers; four research officers; and a senior executive officer.[124] Home Office grants for criminological research work in universities had increased to more than £50,000 a year,[125] equivalent to some £950,000 in 2018 prices.

The unit grew, and it grew in a relatively benign climate,[126] for some long while following the pattern set at its birth. It had been laid down from the outset the kinds of problem that should be studied, and those that should *not* be studied. It was to be 'pragmatic, interdisciplinary, correctional, reform-ist and positivist'.[127] It would focus on very specific questions of interest to the politician and the policymaker,[128] not on the larger matters which were less amenable to policy intervention, precise measurement, or, one may sup-pose, insulation from political, academic and social controversy.[129] Tom Lodge reported:

> The Home Office [followed] a course, to which it kept, more or less, for many years, involving:

    (i) an emphasis on the study of offenders and their treatment rather than the study in society of the social and socio-psychological origins of delinquency or the effect of different methods of law enforcement or delinquency prevention;

    (ii) the study of delinquents under the age of 21, with a preference for those between 17 and 21, rather than, say, research on the organisation of adult prisons.

Also, the link between research and statistics led to an emphasis on methodology and to a preoccupation, though ideas were still far from clear, with the logic of research design.[130]

By the end of the 1970s, John Croft, Tom Lodge's successor, whose tenure lasted from 1972 to 1983, could write about an establishment of fifty (an establishment that he considered needed no further expansion[131]) and a budget of £1,000,000 a year – equal to £4.4 million in 2018 – still devoted, quite inevitably and properly, to exploring in a determinedly objective manner, and emulating (where possible) the style of the natural sciences,[132] those problems of crime and criminal justice that interested government:

> [A research programme must be] designed for and applied to the requirements of those running the system … [its] objectives … must be dictated by practicalities and by the stance which government adopts in pursuing an active policy or reacting passively to events … a passive policy would confine research to recording the effects of, say, legislation with the limited aim of introducing modifications in legal and administrative procedures … an active policy, by contrast, would be prepared to encourage the exploration of policy options in more adventurous ways. …[133]

He later observed in interview that some subjects were actually more difficult to examine than others – for example, what was called 'social research' on the police was for a long while resisted by the Police Department, an examination of the differential arrest and imprisonment rates of ethnic minority suspects being especially contentious (ministers had said 'we can't possibly let that go forward … they were obviously very nervous'. They had not elaborated why they had jibbed in that fashion but their reluctance might have stemmed from an apprehension that project would frighten the Trades Union Congress). But there was never any censorship of even politically unpalatable findings when they *were* produced, 'We never held back anything' he said, although there could be what he called a judicious 'rewording' of sensitive passages from time to time.[134]

So criminologically substantial had the unit become that a former Head recalled 'We really dominated the scene, apart from Cambridge. There was something at LSE [the London School of Economics] of course, and there was something at Oxford. But there wasn't much else'.[135] Over the course of the first few years, there were to be in-house studies of 'criminal histories and the effectiveness of different treatments';[136] the 'criteria of successful treatment of offenders'; the classification of offenders (the 'object is to assist the selection of treatment for offenders by providing data on the varying responses to particular types of treatment of different classes of offenders'); approved schools ('the object is to investigate the effects of various kinds of training on different types of offender'); female offenders (including a 'study of the female offenders in the Metropolitan area, with special reference to the incidence of crime at different ages; this study also included a five year follow-up of those sentenced in 1957' and 'a study of women prisoners and borstal detainees discharged in 1953, with particular reference to the factors affecting reconviction'); and externally funded studies of restitution to victims of crime by Stephen Schafer; sentencing in magistrates courts by Roger Hood; and much else.[137]

As the unit grew, it became large enough and confident enough to acquire a distinctive culture, style and voice. It was no longer simply a handmaiden of the policy makers. Mike Hough who joined it in 1974 recalled:

> It carried out as much in-house research as it commissioned from universities, and it exercised considerable autonomy in setting its research programme. Links with policy divisions of the Home Office were distant, and we saw ourselves as producing 'big picture' research to provide a contextual understanding of crime problems, rather than acting under the direction of policy officials to address the questions that they wanted us to address. By current standards these officials were not 'hands-on' commissioners of research, but would engage with research (both positively and defensively) when it was presented to them. There was no direct political involvement (as I recall) in the publication process – although, then as now, senior officials took into account the likely reactions of their ministers. Publication in peer-reviewed academic journals, as well as in Home Office reports, was routine.[138]

How much impression the unit had on policy making is moot. It was not uniform. Neither was it consistent. It certainly influenced arguments about the deterrent impact of the death penalty – the next two chapters will make that plain. The British Crime Survey, launched in 1981, forced a major reappraisal of the structure, volume, trajectory and impact of crime in England and Wales. And its work on situational crime prevention, linked to Ron Clarke, Kevin Heal and Gloria Laycock; and on community initiatives, linked to Mary Tuck, galvanised policy at home and abroad.[139] The unit also made its mark on how officials began to construct argument. Bob Morris, who had joined the Home Office in 1961, becoming Assistant Private Secretary to the Home Secretary in 1964, remembered:

> It certainly made an impact on me and the way in which one did business and the way in which you expected to see evidence rather than just

argument. ... I mean business before the accessibility of certain kinds of social science research [was conducted] in terms of rhetorical argument, you know, and without appeals to evidence of a kind that had to be made and we didn't need to have policy descriptions. ... I think that's what it did, it seems to me.

But it was perhaps inevitable that the relations between the Home Office researcher, official and politician were always contingent. Mike Hough, a distinguished member of the unit, a co-author of the first British Crime Survey, claimed:

> In my own experience, there is a large element of luck and happenstance in determining when research achieves an impact, and when it sinks like a stone. Having something coherent to say is, of course, a precondition. To be able to say it with authority is also important. Timing is a critical factor; scale can be important; having non-academic allies – or, at least, sympathetic listeners – is critically important, whether these are politicians and their advisers, civil servants, non-government organisations, criminal justice agencies, non-departmental public bodies or journalists. What is undeniably the case – and what is very obvious to anyone who has engaged with policy for any length of time – is that criminologists are indeed minor players with small voices in the policy arena, and that their research will achieve little if they fail to foster, in some way or other, forms of reach into the political process.[140]

The other principal innovation, a new Institute of Criminology, was to be established at the University of Cambridge, outside the Home Office, and it effectively acted as the twin of the new Research Unit (Tom Lodge remarked that one should not ignore 'the close links between the Institute and the Research Unit and ... their common origin in the forces that for many years had been building up to make inevitable the development in Great Britain of scientific criminological research'[141]).

Alexander Paterson, the reforming Commissioner of Prisons, had floated the idea of a Chair of Criminology to be founded at the University of Oxford in 1932;[142] but it was to be the Howard League[143] and its sometime secretaries, Margery Fry[144] and Hugh Klare,[145] who had activated it by responding to a 1957 United Nations Educational, Scientific and Cultural Organisation review of the teaching of social sciences[146] that had disclosed the meagre provision of criminology in England.[147] The League, electing to promote the idea of an institute of criminology, and conceiving that it should be installed in the University of London, had written to R.A. Butler, and arranged a meeting with him in July of that year. But the University of London appeared disinclined to act as a host[148] whilst the University of Cambridge embraced the prospect, although it was difficult enough at first to secure money from the state (despite good will from the Home Secretary[149] and Permanent Undersecretary[150]), or from a university or private bodies such as the Nuffield Foundation.

Proposals for an Institute had been written into the 1959 White Paper, *Penal Practice in a Changing Society*,[151] with a statement in paragraphs 18 and 22 that:

> Research is not necessarily best conducted by official agencies. The outlook, training and environment of the academic worker give him advantages in some kinds of research over the staff of a Government Department. ... There is not at present any agency outside the Home Office which can keep [knowledge of crime and criminals] under constant and critical survey; which can keep track of what is being done; and which can serve as a focus of constructive thinking about delinquency in all its aspects. For this reason special importance attaches to the indication given by Cambridge University that it is prepared, if the necessary funds can be made available, to consider the establishment of an institute of criminology. ... [The new institute's] purposes would be various. It would teach criminology ... and it would undertake and encourage research on the highest academic standard. ... It would also, it may be hoped, be able from time to time to bring together groups of those concerned with the administration of justice and the treatment of offenders. By doing so, it would help to keep them abreast of current thought and the findings of research; and it would at the same time strengthen its own contacts with those doing the practical work of which it would study the results.

R.A. Butler eventually attracted the interest of the Wolfson Foundation,[152] itself newly formed, which donated £150,000 (or over £3,227,000 at 2017 prices), and Leon Radzinowicz of the Cambridge Department of Criminal Science was appointed the Institute's Director and first Professor. Ann Oakley remarked that 'as the country's first Professor of Criminology and Director of the first Institute of Criminology, in Cambridge, [he] had a direct interest in turning criminology into something that it clearly was not, namely a research-based science'.[153] He was a baronial academic figure – a 'continental Professor'[154] – a man not easily crossed, one with whom staff had clientilistic, 'bilateral relationships'.[155] Below him there were to be three Assistant Directors of Research and a number of research assistants, whose work was, and was expected to be, funded (but 'not dictated'[156]) by a Home Office over which he exerted some considerable influence.[157] In its opening decade, the government supported research on offenders as employees;[158] homosexuality;[159] crimes of violence in London;[160] robbery in London;[161] and the habitual prisoner.[162] Perhaps, John Croft conceded, the two institutions had been harnessed a 'bit too much', particularly over the issue of money and support for 'everything they did', but he had been obliged to accept it, and there was little that could be done.

The Institute also had something of a practical bent, Leon Radzinowicz having promised that it would:

> provide an environment in which systematically planned research on problems of limited scope would in time build up a body of objective

information and lead eventually to the solution of more fundamental issues. It would be concerned with such problems as trends in crime, the treatment of offenders, the medical and social aspects of criminal behaviour, the administration and enforcement of the criminal law and the reform both of the substantive criminal law and of criminal procedure.[163]

It would be interdisciplinary and international. It would play a wide role in the affairs of the nation. It would teach, conduct research and tender expert advice. It would forge connections with major institutions and powers in and around the criminal justice system, recruiting an 'Advisory Council ... [which] include[d] Lord Justice Devlin, the Bishop of London, the Baroness Wootton ... Professor Sir Aubrey Lewis, head of the Maudsley Institute, and Sir Charles Cunningham, Permanent Under-Secretary of State at the Home Office'.[164] And it would routinely bring those powers together in its National Conferences, organised from 1964 onwards.

Consider the composition of that very first National Conference on Research and Teaching in Criminology held in Cambridge. It would have been something of a microcosm of English and Welsh criminology proper. Of the 72 people attending, 42 or 58% were academics in post or in training; 20 being students and staff at the new Cambridge Institute of Criminology itself. The others were recruited largely from penal institutions and the Prison Staff College (six); the probation service (three); medical institutions (six); and the Home Office (nine, including three from the new Research Unit). Sessions were chaired by James Douglas of the Medical Research Council, and by Sir Charles Cunningham and Tom Lodge of the Home Office. Its themes were 'Ways of Classifying Offences for Criminological Research'; 'Interviewing in Criminological Surveys'; 'Family Patterns in Delinquency'; 'Prognosis in Young Criminals'; 'Research into Probation'; 'Research in Penal Institutions'; and 'Research in Criminology' (the former Home Office official, David Faulkner,[165] remarked in interview that there was 'never big money compared with medicine or other subjects but at least research [was] being taken seriously and research was one of the things that were prominent in the White Paper itself'.).

In may be seen that, in David Garland's phrase, criminology in England and Wales had begun life as an 'institutionally-based, administratively-oriented' discipline,[166] and that that orientation had been reinforced in the new organisations created to take it forward, organisations that Loader and Sparks would later say were peopled by 'associate members' of 'loosely affiliated liberal elites'.[167] It remained in that vein for some substantial time, but it had also started in the 1960s to betray the influence of a better-established and more substantial, robust, vigorous and avowedly sociological American criminology.[168] There were the first stirrings of what was to be called 'labelling theory',[169] the doctrine that informal and formal social control also makes it mark in constructing criminal and deviant behaviour.[170] There were the beginnings of talk about *anomie*,[171] relative deprivation, culture and subculture, and the impact of rising expectations in a society marked by structured social and economic inequalities (and Hermann Mannheim and Nigel Walker had themselves both touched on those themes in their textbooks). For some, *anomie* theory promised to resolve the seeming paradox posed by the presence of youthful crime in the midst of plenty by arguing that, in conditions of rapid social change and apparent prosperity, when controls were weakened and all were supposedly motivated to achieve material rewards in an unequal world, the young and relatively deprived, approaching the transition to work, might experience frustration and resort to illegitimate paths to success. Delinquency could then be understood as the fruit of what were called structured contradictions.[172] Barbara Wootton, a blower of 'a fresh and cold wind through the scene',[173] asserted that it was relative deprivation, not absolute poverty, that was the chief cause of crime, and it was the relative deprivation experienced by the young that deserved special attention:[174]

> For the young men and women of the working classes the outstanding effect of the social changes of the past twenty years has been to create tastes and expectations without the chance of satisfying them. A society in which everybody knows and keeps to his place can be less frustrating than one which pays lip service to social equality, but does not offer equality in opportunity, let alone in any fuller sense. To hear some people talk, you would think that the "welfare state" had opened up to all on equal terms the varied opportunities that normally await the child of the successful professional or business man: yet in actual fact social contrasts are only one degree less marked than they were.[175]

There were occasions when the two prime models of explanation, the one founded on common sense and the other on science, clashed. They clashed within the Home Office[176] and they clashed within Parliament. It was Barbara Wootton, again, who observed how she had long sought to:

> ... challenge ... 'the conventional wisdom' with demands for the factual and quantitative basis of generalisations about human affairs. Wide indeed is the gulf which separates the social scientists who are accustomed to make these demands from those who are content to rest upon 'informed opinion', not because (as may well be the case) relevant evidence is not available, but through sublime indifference to the obligation to look for it. ...[177]

Despite their commonalities, the relations between the two sets of ideas, of social science and informed lay opinion, were complex, fluid and sometimes confusing. They both stemmed from a common soil in the problems, preoccupations and typifications of everyday life.[178] They sometimes overlapped and sometimes diverged (people do, after all, inhabit multiple worlds and throughout this history it will be possible to see them moving back and forth for reasons that may have been instrumental or adventitious or a mark of the sheer pluralism and muddle of modern life). Explanations seeped from one area to the next, and one can read quite sophisticated adaptations of the new American sociology of crime and deviance in the documents of both major political parties, just as one can read in those documents not only very similar moral diagnoses of the state of the nation, but also, on occasion, both sets of accounts coexisting in the same place.[179]

There were, moreover, a number of moral and experiential claims that could never be openly made, and from time to time principals may have believed themselves constrained to speak the public language of science in the promotion of their more private convictions. They had, in effect, to practise doublespeak.

The 1950s and 1960s were riddled with taboos about what could and could not be said openly. For example, I shall show in another chapter how it was that very few in and around the campaign for homosexual law reform could acknowledge publicly being homosexual or claim to know homosexual men. None could proudly laud the gay life. Few homosexual men who testified before the Wolfenden Committee were prepared to shed their anonymity. The very name of the Secretary of the Homosexual Law Reform Society, Antony Grey, was a *nom de guerre*.[180]

That was in public. In *private*, matters could be otherwise. Roy Jenkins, later to become Home Secretary, a man who had himself almost certainly engaged in a homosexual affair,[181] remarked in 1959:

> What is particularly hypocritical about the Government's refusal to act on homosexual law reform is that none of its leading members (nor those of any other major institution in the national life) apply social disapproval to conduct, which, for public consumption, they insist on keeping subject to the full rigours of the criminal law.[182]

Differences or claims were not trumpeted. There was little public talk of extending greater inclusiveness to deviant populations.[183] That was to come later, if at all. Instead of boldly campaigning for rights, members of deviant groups and their champions argued instead in the name of ameliorating the miserable, clandestine and unenviable lot of unfortunates who were harried by the law, homosexual men and the women who had undergone illegal abortions, for instance. They spoke of civilised values and a greater tolerance of those who were persecuted.

If there were shifting boundaries between the formal and colloquial versions of reasoning about crime and justice, there were also the first stirrings of a schism *within* the coalition of practical and academic criminologists. For a period, and whilst the number of academic criminologists had been small, the two wings had had to collaborate together, sometimes uneasily, in meetings, seminars, editorial boards and conferences. But they started to draw apart towards the latter half of the 1960s as a new and distinct sociology of crime and deviance began to emerge, partly under the spell of its American sister discipline, partly under the impact of a new radicalism and its resuscitation of 'the tradition of grand sociology',[184] and partly in response to the growth of a critical mass of young Turks which coalesced as the universities expanded and junior staff were appointed *en masse*.[185] Hugh Klare, the chairman of the Howard League and sponsor of a pioneering 1966 first British Congress of Crime, was reported to have been disappointed at the outcome of his attempt to bring them together. The minutes of a meeting of the League's Executive Committee recorded that: 'There had been a language barrier between the academic criminologists and the practical people in the field. And a large congress always posed special problems of communication. ... Several members who had attended the Congress had felt that too much jargon had been used. ...'[186] Two years later, there was to be an even more consequential fissure within the body of criminology at the Third National Conference organised by the University of Cambridge. A group of renegades discovered that they had become numerous and confident enough to decamp to found a new and independent National Deviancy Symposium at the University of York 'in conscious opposition to Cambridge's National Conferences'.[187] They effected what David Downes called 'a deliberate break with what was seen as the stranglehold on the subject by the orthodox criminology of the South-East. The great appeal ... was to younger sociologists who saw in deviance an escape route from the positivist methods ... of much British sociology'.[188] A volume of papers delivered at that Symposium was prefaced by the comment that there were:

> feelings towards official criminology [which] ranged from distrust at its orientation towards administrative needs and impatience with its highly empirical, anti-theoretical bias, to simply a mild lack of interest in the sort of studies that were being conducted. ... So, as our own theory might put it – we found ourselves with a common identity problem ...[189]

A view from Cambridge was that that rupture was 'to some extent inevitable and to some extent misguided'[190] (Leon Radzinowicz described the new deviancy theorists as 'a group of naughty schoolboys playing a nasty game on their stern headmaster'[191]) and a view from the Home Office Research Unit[192] was that:

> the fact that the older established universities seemed to get the lion's share of the grants made them, and the Home Office, resented by less privileged institutions. This fuelled the criticisms of the Home Office and the Cambridge Institute of Criminology by the National Deviancy Symposium in the mid-1970s, a group of mostly left-wing sociologists. The criticisms were mostly brushed aside by the Home Office, but nevertheless were demoralising to the Unit's researchers, who were labelled as 'administrative criminologists',[193] supposedly undertaking plodding, atheoretical work serving the government.[194]

But scepticism was more endemic still. It spread beyond the schismatics and those whom they castigated to pervade the entire body of criminology. It was not as if *any* significant portion of the world of academics, practitioners, policy-makers and politicians took what Wootton had called the 'factual and quantitative basis of generalisations about human affairs' to be secure. Within government and the university there were widespread and grave uncertainties about what passed for assured scientific knowledge about crime and criminal justice.[195]

There were, above all, grave doubts about the meaning and reliability of the *statistics* of recorded crime[196] which underpinned reports about individual instances and classes of offending, on the one hand, and about crime waves,[197] on the other. Lord Longford observed quite typically at the end of the 1950s:

> My first conclusion must relate to the appalling incapacity of our criminal statistics to reveal the true state of crime in the country. ... the mournful truth must be told that among independent experts there is no kind of disposition to give them the same sort of credence as a practical index of crime that we give to those, for example, produced by the Treasury, Board of Trade, or other Government departments ...'[198]

And the Labour Party group which he came to chair, the Study Group on Crime Prevention and Penal Reform that produced the report, *Crime: A Challenge to Us All*,[199] frankly admitted in its preliminary working notes 'The impossibility of making an accurate assessment [of crime rates] on the basis of the criminal statistics as at present compiled. ...'[200] A year later, in 1965, a draft White Paper prepared by the Conservative government lamented that 'the criminal statistics as at present compiled do not enable us to measure and analyse [the actual volume of crime] as accurately as it is desirable we should be able to do. Our knowledge of the precise incidence and gravity of crime is incomplete'.[201]

The official statistics were those reported to or observed by the police and other agencies and then recorded and collated to form the published crime figures that were laid before the public, officials and politicians.[202] They were, Leon Radzinowicz said, 'the most difficult, and certainly one of the most imperfect, of all branches of statistics: difficult to compile, difficult to comprehend and difficult to interpret'.[203] They were acknowledged to be but the apex of a largely invisible pyramid of actions, interactions and decisions about which phenomena were to be observed, reported, notified, classified and eventually documented as criminal[204] (Leon Radzinowicz estimated that they amounted to no more than 15% of the whole,[205] and that was a figure that attained a robust facticity in later discussion). At the base of the pyramid there was supposed to be the so-called[206] 'dark figure' of crime,[207] the 'real' but largely inaccessible pool of offences which did not and perhaps could never come into view. In an illuminating passage, the Departmental Committee on Homosexual Offences and Prostitution was informed by its Secretary in 1956 that it was quite quixotic to attempt to assess the actual volume and distribution of homosexual acts in England and Wales because:

> With every step in the process of criminal administration, the recorded figures become less symptomatic of the actual crime position. Offences known to the police, offenders arrested, offenders charged, offenders tried, offenders convicted and offenders received into penal establishments are a regressive scale in the representation of the volume and forms of crime. ... To the extent that offences are not reported to the police – and it is obvious that many homosexual acts which are offences against the law as it now stands never come to light – the figures of indictable offences known to the police fail to represent the state of crime ...[208]

In somewhat tardy[209] recognition of those failings, Henry Brooke established the Departmental Committee on Criminal Statistics (the 'Perks Committee') under the chairmanship of Tom Lodge's fellow actuary, Wilfred Perks,[210] in June 1963. It was:

> to be a Committee to consider what changes, if any, are desirable in existing arrangements in England and Wales for the recording and reporting for statistical purposes of information about criminal offences and proceedings, and about non-criminal proceedings in magistrates' courts, and in the collection and presentation of statistics relating to these matters.

The Committee was told[211] about the work of the American criminologists Thorsten Sellin and Marvin Wolfgang[212] on public estimations of the seriousness of crime – and the construction of an index of crime seriousness came to preoccupy it for some time. It was asked sociological questions by my fellow official historian, David Downes: 'Will we learn something of the ways in which offences come to the attention of the police: by, for instance, citizen – reportage, victim – reportage, or police observation? What proportion of the different offence-types reach the attention of the police by which avenue'. It was told something of the phenomenology and epidemiology of crime waves by the sociologist, John Wakeford: 'the statistics had been influenced by changes in police procedure and in social attitudes and ... a small post-war increase in these offences had led to greater public interest, which in turn had led to a greater proportion of offences being reported'. It was advised about the importance of what was called victim-precipitation:[213] 'more detailed information ... should be gathered about the nature, gravity, circumstances and the place of commission of all crimes. For example, in respect of crimes against the person, there should be an indication regarding the severity of the injury and the relationship, if any, between victims and attackers'. Indeed, it was to be informed by the statistician-criminologist, Leslie Wilkins,[214] that 'more useful information for purpose of social action could be derived from data about victims and the nature of the event as suffered by the victim than from information regarding the concept of "crime",' because 'the main purpose of the administration and government in the field of crime is not to protect morals but to protect the victim'.[215]

The Committee reported four and a half years later, [216] noting the attrition of data about crime as they passed through successive stages of the reporting process and how vital they were to decisions covering 'the whole field of law enforcement' (paragraph 30). It agreed in paragraph 23 that 'the purpose of collecting and publishing criminal statistics is to provide society with information, both as a matter of public interest and as a basis for action'. It recommended a reclassification of offences and the furnishing of a new standard list of crimes; the provision of more copious information about victims, types of property stolen and the like; the publication of critical statistics at regular intervals; and the introduction of a standard computer-driven organisation of data gathering and presentation. It recommended the presentation of an annual abstract of 'standard list' main offences recorded and cleared up, shown in relation to the size of the population; and a list, broken down by age and gender, of persons found guilty and cautioned. But what it could not remedy was the progressive loss of information and the inadequacy of recorded figures as an index of the 'actual' volume of criminal activity. In paragraphs 27 and 28 it observed that 'one of the problems with which we were at once faced was that of offences that do not come to the knowledge of the police. ... We concluded that the study of such unreported offences must be left to research workers ...'[217] A very similar review concluded much later that 'The Perks Report was only the start of a process ...'[218]

There remained disquiet about the condition, funding and potential capacity of *criminology* itself in England and Wales. Despite its relative maturity (it had been established back in the 1930s and 1940s by a triumvirate of refugees from Europe – Max Grünhut[219] at the University of Oxford, Leon Radzinowicz at the University of Cambridge and Hermann Mannheim at the London School of Economics[220]); despite the foundation of the two research centres in London and Cambridge in the late 1950s; and despite the growth of research externally funded by the Home Office; criminology in England and Wales remained thin. It continued to occupy a tenuous position in the academy, lacking numbers, coherence and authority. Gordon Rose observed at the beginning of the 1960s that 'The criminologist is a humble man and only too well aware of his failings. He has achieved a mild degree of respectability too recently to be anything else'.[221] Certainly, when I was interviewed in 1966 by Professor Max Beloff of All Souls College, Oxford – Max Grünhut's old college – to meet the procedural requirement of being 'upgraded' from probationer B.Litt. status to that of D.Phil. student, I was required slowly to repeat and spell the word 'criminology' several times as if it were an alien, suspect and somewhat disagreeable neologism.

Academic criminology was often outgunned by practitioners employed outside the university (Nigel Walker commented at the time that 'English criminology was largely the work of psychoanalysts, psychiatrists and psychologists'[222]).

It certainly had not led to enlightenment. Roy Jenkins said in late 1966 that 'we are still shrouded in a considerable fog of ignorance;'[223] and, on another occasion in the same year, he remarked: 'I don't think any of us … can say why [there is a crime wave]. There are various theories, we do a lot of research, we try to improve our knowledge about it, but I think it would be a very arrogant man who said I know why people … do criminal acts'.[224] Criminology had failed to produce any solid causal explanation of patterns and movements of crime;[225] and perhaps its only achievement had been to debunk existing theories. In what Ann Oakley, her biographer, described as a 'blistering attack on the confusions of criminology and the arrogance of social workers',[226] Barbara Wootton said: 'Up till now the chief effect of precise investigation into questions of social pathology has been to undermine the credibility of virtually all the current myths'.[227] (Perhaps it should be noted that that criminological self-doubt has never deserted the discipline. Fifty years later precisely the same lament would be heard.[228] Lucia Zedner commented that 'Whatever the causes of its disgruntlement, there can be few disciplines whose leading protagonists are so ready to denounce their common project as a failure'.[229] The examined academic life is never perhaps worth living.).

In short, neither common-sense reasoning nor the infant science of criminology appeared to offer much of a clue about how to contend with the seemingly remorseless rise in crime. Effective levers of change seemed to lie beyond governments which were nevertheless continually beset by populist and political demands for effectual action, for more police officers and the restoration of harsh penalties.[230] Stevenson remarked that 'Both the Conservative Party and wider public opinion … grew increasingly difficult to handle as reported crime figures soared on the back of the maturing post-war baby boom'.[231] As early as 1961, and even at a time of the brave new world of *Penal Practice in a Changing Society* – where so much that was innovative and promising appeared to be in the offing – Sir Charles Cunningham, a man with 'surprisingly liberal views',[232] submitted a bleak note to the Home Secretary:

> … We have to recognise … that the increase in crime is leading many people to question whether our existing methods are sufficient. So far, this questioning, although understandable in itself, has not been accompanied by any constructive ideas. The main suggestions which have been made are, first, the re-introduction of <u>corporal punishment</u> as a judicial penalty; second, the restoration of the <u>death penalty</u> for all murder; and, thirdly, the establishment of a new type of <u>non-residential</u> training …
>
> (emphases in the original)[233]

The Home Office

There was a constellation of Offices and Departments of State administering the criminal justice system, including the Lord Chancellor's Office and the offices of the Director of Public Prosecutions and the attorney general, and they will make their appearance as this history develops. But the giant of them all in the 1960s was the Home Office.[234] It had its origin in 1782 when the Earl of Shelburne was appointed Secretary of State with responsibility for domestic and colonial affairs,[235] and it was required at first to perform the great assortment of work that its twin, the Foreign Office, did *not* do. Its position as a general *factotum* department thereafter remained intact. The Home Secretary had been 'left with responsibility for all domestic affairs which did not come under the purview of another minister. For this reason he has been described as being in the position of a "residuary legatee"'.[236] His core roles were the maintenance of the Queen's Peace and the exercise of the Royal Prerogative of Mercy,[237] but they were but part of a vast and unwieldy portfolio that came in time not only to include law and order (and its component institutions and responsibilities of criminal legislation, pardons, reprieves, prisons, police and magistrates' courts); the factory inspectorate; British Summer Time; the control of mentally disordered persons; patents of nobility for peers; broadcasting issues; the extradition of fugitive offenders and the provision of mutual assistance to other states in criminal matters; the fire and emergency services; 'equal opportunities for women'; civil defence;[238] film censorship; Church matters; the Anatomy Act and its inspectorate;[239] mines; theatre safety; naturalisation; burial grounds and cremations; liquor licensing; vivisection; dangerous drugs; elections; and race and community relations. It was no wonder that, as we shall see, Home Secretaries were frequently unable to attend, or attend fully, to all the matters that are threaded through this history of criminal justice.

The Home Office of the 1960s was a large, sprawling and complex institution whose character may best be captured by examining it at a single point in time. Midway through the decade, in 1965,[240] at a time when a number of important developments were in train, the Home Secretary was Sir Frank Soskice, a Queen's Counsel and Labour Member of Parliament for Newport, Monmouthshire.[241] He was supported by a Private Secretary, first G.J. Otton[242] and then R. Shuffrey,[243] young 'high-flyers' conceived to be destined for high office;[244] a Minister of State (Alice Bacon[245]); two Parliamentary Undersecretaries of State, Lord Stonham[246] (who spoke for the Department in the House of Lords) and T. George Thomas;[247] and the Permanent Undersecretary of State: Sir Charles Cunningham. Below them were two men holding the rank of Deputy Undersecretary of State, one of whom was the Chairman of the two-year-old Prison Board; and, lower still, a legal adviser and twelve Assistant Undersecretaries of State with responsibilities severally for the Children's Department; the Civil Defence Department, including the Civil Defence Staff College, and the eleven Regional Civil Defence Headquarters; the Fire Department with its Communications Branch, Explosives Branch, Fire Service Inspectorate and Fire Service College; the Criminal Department with its five Assistant Secretaries (including Brian Cubbon, who was later to become Permanent Undersecretary of State), five Principals, and two Assistant Principals (one of whom was John Chilcot who later became Deputy Undersecretary in charge of the Police Department); the Probation and After-Care Department with its one Assistant Undersecretary of State, two Assistant Secretaries and three Principals; the Establishment and Organisation Department and Common Services, including the Chief Architects Branch and Directorate of Works, the Public Relations Branch and the Statistics Department, the Research Unit with its eleven staff; the Finance Department; and the General Department with its responsibility for dangerous drugs, Inspectors under the Cruelty to Animals Act, 1876, and the Staff Management Scheme; the Immigration and Nationality Department; the Forensic Science Laboratories based in seven regions across the country; the Scientific Advisers' Branch; and the Women's Voluntary Service for Civil Defence.

There was the Police Department, with its responsibilities directly for the Inspectors of Constabulary, the Police Planning and Research Branch and the Police College; and, indirectly, through its role in part funding, inspecting and coordinating police forces, for serving police officers nationally. Police forces were being amalgamated throughout the decade,[248] sometimes with considerable local resistance, displayed, for instance, in prolonged campaigning to prevent the unions of the Luton and Bedfordshire constabularies and of the Norwich and Norfolk constabularies.[249] The numbers of officers were growing: in 1952, there had been an officer for every 611 members of the population of England and Wales; in 1957, one for every 598; and, in 1962, one for every 581.[250] By 1965, there were some 83,000 in England and Wales,[251] 27,000 male and 1,000 female officers serving in the Metropolis alone.[252]

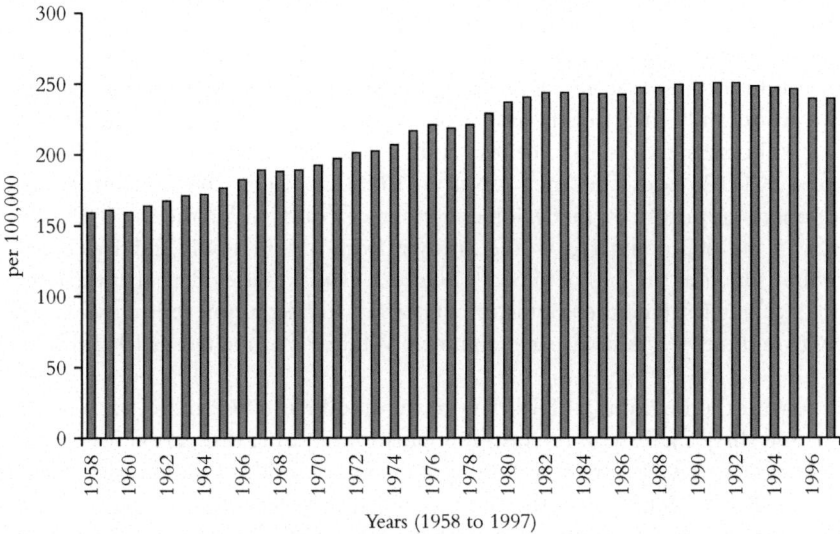

Figure 1.10[253] Number of police officers per 100,000 population

Yet police resources in the early 1960s were deemed to be in a parlous state: Ben Whitaker described how in 1964:

> The secretarial facilities for detectives can only be described as archaic: it is not uncommon for eleven sergeants and five inspectors to be waiting for the one ancient typewriter they have to share. There are only about 150 tape-recorders between all the Metropolitan police. ... The forensic laboratories are under such pressure that they are able to concentrate on only the most serious cases ...[254]

The answer was to be an accelerating 'modernisation' of the police, itself a part of the wider Labour enterprise of 'modernising' the nation.[255] Modernisation was to be achieved through more substantial recruitment,[256] and through training, reorganisation,[257] and amalgamations, coupled with a growing emphasis on enhancing conditions of work[258] and exploiting the promise of new technology (such as the new computers[259]), radio communication[260] and the use of motorcars. Roy Jenkins said in 1966 that:

> the equipment of the police [is important]. We are now making big strides in this direction, particularly with pocket radio sets, which will I believe greatly improve the effectiveness and morale of the individual policeman on the beat. A year ago the Metropolitan Police had only 25 such sets. Today they have 275. By the end of next year they should have a further 2500.[261]

There was the new Prison Board (until 1963, the semi-independent Prison Commission), administered by its Chairman, E. Gwynn, and, beneath him, the Director of Prison Medical Services, the Chief Psychologist, the Chaplain General of Prisons, the Catering Adviser, the Organiser of Physical Education and Industries and Stores, and the Governors, Deputy Governors Assistant Governors and officers of the numerous individual establishments: the 53 prisons, 20 borstals, two remand centres and 17 detention centres. The prison estate housed 20,123 convicted men (up from 19,833 in 1964) and 7,745 male civil prisoners, imprisoned chiefly for contempt of court under the 1869 Debtors Act;[262] and 603 convicted women (down from 635 in 1964) and 162 female civil prisoners at the end of 1965.[263] Figure 1.11 makes it evident that the estate was swelling fast (and the population of borstals and detention centres was swelling even faster[264]). A draft paragraph for a White Paper recited in 1963 that:

> From the beginning of 1959 until the middle of 1962 there was a steady and sharp increase in the prison population. During this period it was necessary to give priority in the use of resources, both of buildings and staff, to the development of the system for young offenders, and the establishments for adults became increasingly overcrowded and have suffered until recently from a serious shortage of staff. ...[265]

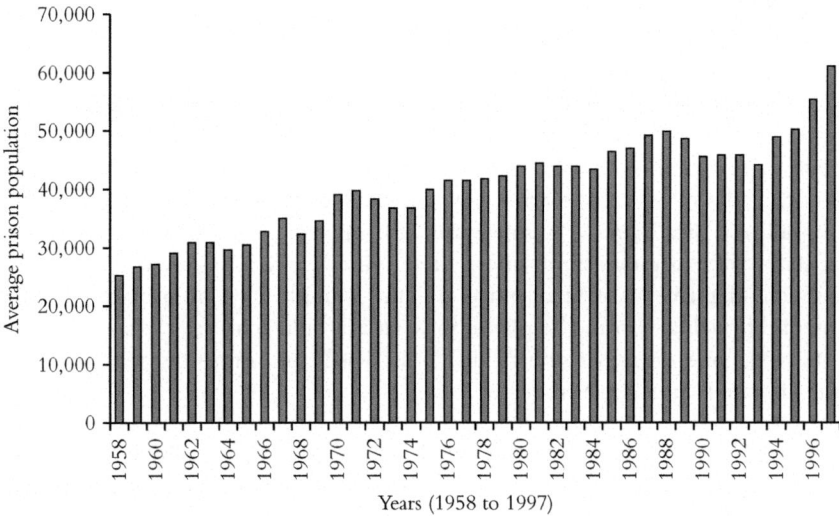

Figure 1.11[266] Average prison population

It was the pursuit of a reforming modernisation that again led prison admin-istrators to rely on the better-informed and managed classification, segregation, diagnosis, supervision and treatment of offenders, and of young offenders in particular. They too were turning to the new computers: information could be collected and collated mechanically in prisons to 'make it easier to trace relationships between offences, offenders and sentences'.[267] David Faulkner reflected in interview that there was a 'belief to begin with that our assessment and careful allocation to treatment programmes and ... remand centres like Risley and a psychiatric hospital like Grendon and the design of Holloway as a secure prison, would all have sort of instrumental effects in changing people, changing future conduct and reducing crime'.

And yet, overall, as R.A. Butler remarked in 1960, it is 'ironic that an over-due drive to modernise our penal methods and to introduce a more redemp-tive character into some of our penal treatment should coincide with a crime wave'.[268] At bottom, modernisation and all its accompaniments seemed to have had but a tangential bearing on the repression of crime and delinquency. The overriding problem, he said, was one of informal social control, and 'Improvement in moral standards is not an object that can, in my view, be attained by direct Government action; the problem is one for the community as a whole'.[269]

Those institutional trends in policing and penology did play one signal role. In what was something of a policy vacuum, where it was not entirely clear what it was that the state could and should do in the face of relentlessly and unaccountably rising numbers of offenders, defendants and prisoners (and of the 'delinquent generations' especially), and where the real motors of moral change were sensed to lie outside the state's grasp, they could at least be read as a visible proof of engagement. They were as much a part of a 'ritual of rationality',[270] a demonstration that something defensible was being done, as an obviously efficacious answer to the crime problem. The criminologist, Gordon Rose,[271] observed in 1964 that 'It can hardly [be] claim[ed] that much impact has been made upon the incidence of crime, but there has certainly been a great deal of activity. If crime could be reduced by ardent committee work ... the effect on the crime rate might have been larger'.[272] R.A. Butler himself told Sir Charles Cunningham, 'It is important in all these great offices of state to keep up an atmosphere of activity'.[273] Activity could reassure the public and convey a sense of purpose – and it might have an impact – but no unconditional faith could be placed in what it would achieve.[274] As one official reflected, 'one did what one could'.[275] In 1961, and in a note which I have already cited, Sir Charles reflected:

> If the conclusion is right that we should continue generally with our pre-sent policies ... we still have to face the public anxiety about the continu-ing increase in crime. There are some things we have been trying to do, and should continue to do:
>
> (a) We should press on with our efforts to make the police service as effective as possible, and to publicise developments (e.g. in train-ing) as widely as possible.
>
> (b) We should press on as hard as we can with our programme of development in all the services connected with the treatment of offenders, and again give as much publicity as we can to the progress that is being made.
>
> Plainly, however, nothing that has been done, or is in contemplation, seems likely to make a real impact on the extent of crime. That can presumably result only from a general change in the standard of conduct which is – super-imposed upon personal factors which cannot be easily influenced – largely responsible for the extent of criminal behaviour – particularly dishonesty. It is obviously not an easy matter to persuade the public that it is not enough to be indignant about the extent of crime – that there is an individual responsibility on the citizen to try to prevent it.[276]

And his colleague, Jean Nunn,[277] then head of the Home Office Children's Department, and another senior and experienced official, concurred:

> I found your note on crime, which you circulated with a covering note on 10 May, of great interest. I also found myself in very great agreement with it and indeed my own conclusions, which I had not put down in writing, were very much on the same lines. ... Although the public, or a large section of it, are convinced that some ready-made deterrent or punishment is at hand if only the Home Office would pluck up the

courage to use it, it does seem clear that we must now persuade people to think more in terms of crime prevention than punishment, treatment or even deterrence. I say this because, with the possible exception of police recruitment, I cannot convince myself that our other measures will in fact bring the problem under control and I fear that in two years, unless the delinquent generation theory works out even better, we shall be in even greater difficulties.[278]

Events

Future chapters in other volumes will dwell on the evolution of policing and prisons, but one matter should be flagged here. There is a tension at the heart of the criminal justice system. Police forces, courts and prisons not only work practically and symbolically to protect and reassure individuals. They control them. They do much of the 'dirty work' of society, the disagreeable but necessary tasks, often performed on behalf of those deemed to be the 'good people',[279] that touch on control, surveillance, coercion, restraint and confinement. Dirty work can be fraught, performed against the unwilling, resentful and defiant[280] who may resist what is done to them, and it is not uncommonly performed openly and before a critical public.

The Home Office combined masses of routine meetings, consultations, casework and the drafting of notes, proposals and memoranda, on the one hand, with the management of sudden crises and scandals flowing from its dirty work, on the other. Lord Windlesham remarked that 'The life of a Home Secretary has been depicted by several former holders of the office as being unduly susceptible to interruption by sudden and totally unexpected incidents which require all his attention'.[281] Politicians were at risk always of ambush by what Sir Brian Cubbon, a former Permanent Secretary, called 'events on the ground that can happen very quickly':[282] the shootings, riots, bombings, prison escapes, and alleged and proven miscarriages of justice which demand immediate action and an immediate response. 'Poor old Home Office,' [Sir Frank] Soskice had minuted on one file. 'We are not always wrong, but we always get the blame'.[283] One of his successors, James Callaghan, reported towards the end of the period covered by this chapter that he 'used to switch on the radio news at seven o'clock in the morning, mainly to find out what examples of alleged unfair treatment had cropped up during the night as a result of a Home Office decision'.[284] Another, Kenneth Clarke, recalled much later 'It's a department more likely to throw up problems and overnight crises than political rewards. It's partly a fire-fighting job ...'[285] And a later successor still, Kenneth Baker, said in interview that 'I found it a very defensive ministry. ... I think it was a sense of being overwhelmed by crises, the department is overwhelmed by crises. You've got to have a really clear, steady hand as Home Secretary not to be overwhelmed by it'. The epithet 'graveyard of political ambition' is as a result routinely applied to the department,[286] although, to be sure, it has as often been applied to other departments as well.

Crisis seemed to follow crisis in the 1960s. A Conservative party report observed that:

> Serious criminals are waging an ever more successful war upon society. Sometimes this takes a spectacular form amounting in effect to a military operation carefully planned against Society, like the mail train robbery. ...[287] Scarcely a week passes without some weekend coup in the form of a wage-snatch, a bank raid or a mail robbery. There are besides sporadic outbreaks of violence for its own sake, sometimes widely publicised, as were the exploits of Mods and Rockers at the seaside, but, more often mere hooliganism or individual knifings or shootings. ...[288]

There were the disturbances in seaside resorts[289] to which the report alluded (disturbances that were commemorated in Stan Cohen's *Folk Devils and Moral Panics*[290]); routine protests about executions that were pending or had been carried out, including agitation about the case of James Hanratty who was hanged in 1962,[291] and even more sustained and consequential agitation, lasting into the 1960s, about the mistrial and wrongful execution of Timothy Evans in 1950;[292] major, sometimes unruly, demonstrations about the nuclear bomb and American involvement in Vietnam;[293] cases of police incompetence in Cardiganshire and of corruption in Brighton, Worcester and Nottingham at the end of the 1950s that led to the institution of the Royal Commission on the Police in 1960;[294] the frauds committed by the Chief Constable of Southend in the 1960s,[295] the brutalities committed by the Sheffield police in 1963,[296] and the planting of evidence by Detective Sergeant Challenor at a demonstration against the Queen of Greece in July 1963[297] (which will also be discussed in a later chapter); and public and political[298] anxiety about the growing number of violent bank and mail[299] raids[300] and of crimes involving firearms[301] (anxiety that culminated in the Firearms Act 1965[302] and internal Home Office inquiries[303] and rumours about officers being armed[304]). Perhaps most dramatic of all was the shooting of three police officers in Shepherds Bush in August 1966, leading to the trial and conviction of Harry Roberts four months later.[305] There were escapes from prison,[306] including that of the 'great train robbers', Charles Wilson from Birmingham in August 1964[307] and Ronald Biggs and three others from Wandsworth in July 1965; of Frank Mitchell, the so-called 'mad axeman', from Dartmoor in December 1966;[308] and, most infamously, of the spy, George Blake,[309] in October 1966 from Wormwood Scrubs. Phillip Allen, Sir Charles Cunningham's successor, remembered:

> In October 1966 there blew up a sudden storm, something always likely to happen in the Home Office ... there came the news that the spy George Blake had escaped from Wormwood Scrubs prison. He was serving a sentence of forty-two years, the longest so far imposed by a British court, and had been responsible for the death of a number of British agents. The escape was serious news. Roy at once called a meeting at the Home Office

on Sunday morning, but it was pretty futile and Roy was not at all pleased by the contributions of the police and security representatives. Blake, as we now know, had gone to ground not all that far from the prison, but he was not traced. The publicity, naturally enough, was enormous.[310]

Prison escapes engendered worrying questions about security, the state's ability safely to confine dangerous offenders[311] and the sheer competence of politicians, policy-makers, prison administrators and officers.[312] They certainly raised embarrassing questions when it was being proposed that life imprisonment should replace capital punishment. They allowed Peter Rawlinson to remark in a debate on the abolition of the death penalty in 1965: 'Let no one forget that the people of this country are getting sick and tired of proposals to try to change criminals when they see daily their property and themselves being threatened and the State is unable even to keep in detention those criminals who have been sent to prison. I hope that a secure system of imprisonment will be created. I hope that it will be given absolute priority. I agree with some of my hon. Friends who wondered why this Bill was introduced if we were not able to provide a proper system for men who were sentenced to life imprisonment'.[313] Indeed, there were similar doubts within the Home Office itself. Some months later, James Callaghan, the Home Secretary at the end of the 1960s, was to be informed by an official that 'It seemed to us, on a review, that there were now a number of factors which made it no longer possible, even with vigilance, to have any certainty of keeping particularly dangerous men inside…'[314]

The crises collectively pointed to what Roy Jenkins called 'a pattern of wet impotence',[315] and it was impotence in the face of relentless media scrutiny. The Howard League described how the events were the subjects of 'avid, breathless and on occasions positively gleeful reporting …'[316] It is not therefore perhaps remarkable that the Home Office was ever thrown on the defensive, organised in large measure to protect its ministers from public and political embarrassment. It was precedent-driven, legalistic and, some would say, staid, formal and conventional. A number of its former senior officials believed it to be quite distinct, a place with its own special etiquette and customs, something of a 'distant planet as seen from the Cabinet Office'.[317] Lord Windlesham described it as 'conservative procedurally and cautious in outlook. … What is peculiar, even compared with other departments of government, is a special brand of stuffiness. There is a premium on thoroughness and accuracy'.[318] Papers, decisions and files would ascend stage by stage, carefully numbered and logged, through a well-defined hierarchy, accumulating commentary, chronology, narrative and context as they climbed up to the Permanent Undersecretary, the Private Office and thence to the Secretary of State himself.

The Department was organised in the ideal-typical manner once described by Max Weber:[319] stratified, with a clear division of labour and responsibility; and hierarchical, with intelligence and advice travelling upwards and instructions and commands downwards. So vertical was that system of communication that officials in contiguous departments might only very rarely encounter or know one another, having sometimes to be introduced on the occasions when they did meet. They might, moreover, acquire skills in one department that were not readily exportable to another:

> This results in transfer of the top civil servants between different divisions with little or nothing in common, and promotion may mean the loss to one division of an effective officer who will have little further use for his specialised experience, and his replacement by a newly promoted officer from another division with experience completely unrelated to his new responsibilities. ...[320]

I have described elsewhere the typical patterning of subterranean policymaking in the Home Office, the policymaking that is not always revealed in cabinet, ministerial and other official papers[321] where arguments had had time and grooming enough to become coherent, a history had been constructed and the immediate next steps seem transparent. Much mundane policy work was actually emergent, in that it had properties and meanings which form only as it unfolds; indeterminate, in that its future could not easily be foretold; environmentally constrained, in that it had to take account of, and not contradict too markedly, other policies already in place or in the making; contingent, in that it was likely to be affected by events that could arise unexpectedly; rhetorical, in that it was a matter chiefly of words and gestures politically deployed; opportunistic, in that it could seize upon other, sometimes unanticipated political developments; and a matter of *Realpolitik*, in that it had to defer, if only symbolically, to the powers of the criminal justice system, the judges, police, prison authorities and other departments of state, which could affect its future progress. In short, it could come to assume some odd guises which could not always be easily deciphered by the outsider or the historian long after the event.

Yet there was also a predictability of procedure which enabled policymakers routinely to get on with their work. Papers had to be framed in a set form using recognised arguments by approved officials; they had to move step by step and in the proper sequence before a fixed succession of committees, each committee making quite precise demands on what should be said; they had to observe the timetables and constraints set by planning, legislative, electoral and financial cycles; they had to go before other agencies and institutions for consultation and approval; and they had to make use of mandates, manifestos and policies already agreed. Those formal requirements were imprinted on the genetics of all policies, very similar arguments being rehearsed in proposal after proposal, and they tended to promote a stylisation, familiarity and entropy of style. And there was also a culture much remarked upon, the liberal culture of well-educated, professional men and women, trained in the humanities and classics, espousing, without overt political affiliation, an engrained respect for 'civilised' values and the promotion of what was called 'decency' in the treatment of suspects, defendants and prisoners. That may not have been quite how it was seen at the time by officials, and that is a matter to which I shall return in discussing the liberalising legislation of the 1960s. Bob Morris reflected in interview that:

> what you struggled for was some sort of rational principles to … explain and defend what was being done to people. And a strong feeling I remember amongst my colleagues which persisted throughout my time there was the feeling that imprisonment was such an incursion into people's lives that it should be used as sparingly as possible. … [But] one didn't notice [the larger picture]. One was too busy doing other things then. And these are retrospective glosses on events. The primary course they presented as individual problems and how to deal with capital punishment, how to deal with homosexual law reform, how to deal with abortion, weren't seen as part of some liberal process. They were seen as discrete problems which needed particular political solutions.

It should be noted, more or less in parenthesis, that, throughout much of the period, arguments finally submitted to the Home Secretary were heavily pruned, edited and refined to leave little trace of the indecisiveness and deliberations that had punctuated their upwards passage through the ranks.[322] Between 1957 and 1966, they would have been presented solely with the *chop* of the Permanent Undersecretary, Sir Charles Cunningham.[323] David Faulker said that 'no one else in the office had access to the Home Secretary effectively. So any submission to the Home Secretary went over Cunningham's initials'. And one Home Secretary, Roy Jenkins, himself remembered that:

> Everything came on one or two sheets of thick blue paper, boiled down to a few hundred words of lucid explanation, concluding with a clear recommendation, and boldly initialled 'C.C.C'. It was the most formidable display of intellectual energy and control over the Department, economical of the Secretary of State's time, provided that the recommendations were accepted and did not too frequently blow up in his face. But it was certainly not a system designed to allow the Home Secretary to weigh up different courses of action. No other course was outlined, there were no background documents from which an alternative could be devised, there was no indication whether or not there had been dissenting opinions as the file had made its way up through the various ranks of the hierarchy. All wrinkles had been smoothed away by the firm and skilled hands of the permanent secretary.[324]

With or without those wrinkles (and some would disagree with Faulkner's and Jenkins' accounts[325]), it was difficult enough for the Secretary of State to digest and analyse what came before him.[326] His duties were even wider, more taxing and more ill-assorted than those of the vast department he ran. He was not only responsible for the Home Office, but also for his constituents as a Member of Parliament: for speaking and voting in the House of Commons in the manner of any other Member; for attending the cabinet and its committees, sometimes deliberating on matters far removed from his own department's mandate; and for participating as a senior Officer of the Crown in the ceremonial life of the State.[327] Sir Frank Soskice's diary was littered with a rapid proliferation of engagements dwelling on very diverse matters. Take the entries for just five days, copied *verbatim* and quite at random from that specimen year of 1965:[328]

Feb 8
11.00   Subcommittee on redeployment of defence resources
11   Cabinet
11.30   Prime Minister Commonwealth immigration
…
4.30   Meeting on the police

Feb 9
10.30   Subcommittee on redeployment of defence resources
11.45   Memorial Service Lord Alexander[329]
2.15   Miss Bacon
3   Lord Boyd, CCC [Sir Charles Cunningham], GT
3.30   Three-line whip
5.30   Mr Walter Terry (Daily Mail)

Feb 10
Standing Committee C (Death Penalty Bill)
11.00   DOP (Arms for South Africa)

Feb 11 Thursday
10.30   Cabinet
…
3.30   Statement on firearms

Feb 12 Friday
10   HAC [Home Affairs Committee]
12.00   Thorpe Arch Prison
3.50   Grand Entrance B' Palace to meet HM on return from Sudan

His diary for the year opened on 4 January with a meeting with a deputation from the Advisory Committee on Juvenile Delinquency. The next day, he accompanied a constituency delegation to the Ministry of Labour. During the course of the month, he was to attend five full meetings of cabinet as well as meetings of its committees (the Ministerial Committee on Social Service, the Home Affairs Committee on the 8th and the Defence and Overseas Policy Committee to discuss Indonesia on 13 January and again on the 15th to discuss defence economics, the Polaris missile, and the Atlantic nuclear force). He attended the Memorial Service for Lord Monckton[330] on 14 January. As head of the Home Office, he attended the Department's tea party on 12 January ('all grades to be represented') and the Private Secretaries' party on the 15th. He met his Ministerial colleagues on 14 January to discuss the allocation of work and then saw them again at weekly intervals. He conducted another meeting with the Board of Deputies of British Jews to discuss racial incitement on the 14th, a subject of other meetings at other times in the month (the first Race Relations Bill was about to pass through the House of Commons, to be given the Royal Assent in November: it would outlaw discrimination on the 'grounds of colour, race, or ethnic or national origins' in public places[331]). He met a group from the British Council of Churches to discuss the implementation of the Wolfenden Report on the 17th. He met Sir Roger Hollis,[332] the Director of MI5,[333] on the 19th and 21st. He appeared before the Commonwealth Immigrants Committee on the 19th; and the Royal Commission on Penal Reform on the 12th and the 20th. He had meetings, formal and informal, with the judiciary on the 7th and the 17th; and with police officers on the 25th. He met the Parliamentary Commissioner on the 20th. He voted on a three-line whip on the 26th. He visited an approved school in Bristol on the 8th and MI5 headquarters on the 19th. There were internal departmental meetings on approved schools, immigration on the 25th, and the police on the 7th, 8th and 25th. And that was the business of one month alone.

During the remainder of the year, he attended investitures at Buckingham Palace, and was formally present when the Queen left the country on another State visit, and was present again on her return. He was present when she received an address from the Convocations of York and Canterbury. He visited his constituency in Wales on 12 occasions. He received 39 three-line whips to vote in divisions. He spoke four times in the House of Commons on the abolition of death penalty for murder; four times on the Firearms Bill; thrice on the Race Relations Bill; twice on the Criminal Evidence Bill; thrice in debates on passports, British nationality, Commonwealth immigrants and fugitive offenders; and once on animal experiments. He attended meetings of Standing Committee C on the Death Penalty Bill. He spoke with journalists and lobby correspondents. He visited prisons, approved schools, forensic science laboratories, police stations and fire stations. He was consulted about reprieves in capital cases (although he was adamant that no one should hang whilst he was in office) and about the release of prisoners on life sentences. And then he still had more work to do at the end of the day. Roy Jenkins remarked 'It was his habit … to proceed home each evening with ten or twelve brown pouches … stuffed with Home Office cases'.[334]

The politics of law and order

I opened this chapter quite carefully and deliberately by saying that crime in the late 1950s and 1960s appears significant when it is viewed through the special lens of a history of criminal justice. Most phenomena may be made to seem important if they are examined closely and attentively enough. At a greater distance, it is possible to construct the contrary argument that crime did *not* actually loom very large in the public politics of the time.[335] Many politicians, indeed, paid it no attention unless their ministerial duties obliged them to do so.[336] Bottoms and Stevenson remarked that:

> It is very important to emphasise ... that criminal justice policy was not, throughout this period, much of a party political issue. ... criminal justice policy-making ... was largely backstage policy-making – the work of Home Office civil servants, Royal Commissions, departmental committees; lobbying from relevant professional associations, penal reform bodies and trades unions, and so on.[337]

The political parties were largely exercised with other matters at the time. The archived files of the Conservative Party on juvenile delinquency and crime prevention were empty (although that may simply reflect poor record-keeping – reference has already been made to the party's 1965 inquiry into juvenile delinquency).[338] Meetings of its General Purposes Committee in the 1950s and 1960s[339] talked little about law and order, but at great length about communism in the trades unions, rates on property, local elections, home ownership, land nationalisation, Middle East policy, the 'colour bar', industrial relations, food hygiene, comprehensive schools, foodstuffs for livestock, drainage in rural areas, fuel costs, pensions, standards of roads in Wales, educational policy, the education of children of Her Majesty's Forces, the inspection and regulation of private schools, purchase tax on supplies to schools, and sundry other matters. Conservative Party Conference resolutions raised a great swathe of issues, including the problems of Berlin and Germany, local government in Greater London, education and the teaching of English, military pensions and officers' widows' pensions, inflatable life rafts, entry to the European Common Market, and local government elections, but little on law and order. The sole exception, which Bottoms and Stevenson also note, was their vociferous and frequent deploring of the abolition of capital and corporal punishment.[340]

Again, apart from the papers of the Study Group on Crime Prevention and Penal Reform – the Longford Committee – the Labour Party Archive in the People's History Museum, Manchester, contained nothing on crime and justice (although that may again reflect record-keeping practices as much as political preoccupations). No Labour Party conference resolutions were recorded as of 'Concern to the Home Policy Sub-Committee'.[341] During 1965–68, in what was to be an especially critical period for the politics of criminal justice, the Labour Party's *Annual Reports* made no reference to crime, criminal justice, capital punishment or the Sexual Offences Bill that was to decriminalise homosexual acts between consenting male adults in private, many of those matters having been entrusted to private member's bills. Alistair Service, the

Parliamentary lobbyist for the Abortion Law Reform Association in the latter half of the 1960s remembered that, with the exception of capital punishment, Harold Wilson did not busy himself with the other private member's bills that were in motion during his premiership: 'It was clear that we were not going to get strong positive support from the Government in the way that Harold Wilson had supported the ending of capital punishment. Wilson never mentioned any of the other social law reforms in his memoirs; quite extraordinarily he thought private member's bill reforms to be of no importance'.[342]

Election campaigns tend to flag what is considered salient, and crime and punishment played little part in them in the 1960s. Those matters were not the province of the public or the popular vote. They were the preserve of the legislator and expert, 'essentially technical issues, best governed by expert knowledge and empirical research',[343] although the experts, as I have said, had scant confidence in their abilities (they believed that although they might be able to manage affairs more efficiently than the laity, they had little certainty that crime rates themselves *could* be managed[344]). Manifestos made scant reference to law and order. Those of the Conservative Party would as a matter of course conclude with a short, neutral section on the area. The Labour Party initially neglected it altogether but then came in time to allude to it, using much the same language as the Conservatives. Thus the 1959 Labour manifesto contained no reference at all to crime or justice, but its Conservative Party counterpart contained a small, dispassionate passage towards the end:

> It will continue to be our policy to protect the citizens, irrespective of creed or colour, against lawlessness. We intend to review the system of criminal justice and to undertake penal reforms which will lead offenders to abandon a life of crime. A scheme for compensating the victims of violent crime for personal injuries will be considered.[345]

Five years later, the Labour Party manifesto again made no mention of crime and justice, but the Conservative Party programme talked briefly of strengthening the police and arresting the rise in crime committed by the young, using a language which Garland would describe as 'penal welfarism':[346]

> We shall continue to build up the strength of the police forces, and see that they are equipped with every modern scientific aid. ... We have asked it to give urgent priority to the growing problem of crime among the young. Meanwhile, we have increased the penalties for malicious damage and the compensation to those who suffer from this form of hooliganism. ...
>
> Much juvenile delinquency originates in broken or unhappy homes. We shall continue to support the work of marriage guidance. Local authorities will be encouraged, in co-operation with voluntary bodies, to develop their services of child care for young people deprived of normal home life and affection.

The 1966 Conservative Party manifesto contained a small section, 'To beat the Crime Wave', in which the battle language of a war against crime was newly invoked,[347] and it promised to:

> Place responsibility for law and order and for the war against crime on the Home Secretary and the Secretary of State for Scotland. Set up a central staff within the Home Office responsible for police strategy, intelligence and equipment. Accelerate the amalgamation of local police forces and establish a clear chain of command. Within a national force of this kind, local loyalties can and will be preserved. Ensure that the police have the organisation, manpower and equipment to do the job. Make offenders pay restitution for the injuries and damage they have done. Replace many short term sentences by substantial fines. Preserve the Juvenile Courts and expand the methods available for dealing with the problems of young people. Train those in prison to become useful members of the community.

On this occasion, for the first time, and at some length, there was also a reference to crime and law enforcement in the Labour Party manifesto, and its content was not dissimilar:

> *Law Enforcement*: For years Britain has been confronted by a rising crime rate, overcrowded prisons and many seriously undermanned police forces.
>
> *Strengthening the Police*.
>
> The slide in numbers has already been checked. Energetic action will now be taken to build up police strength in those areas confronted with a severe shortage. We shall ensure not only that police resources are used more efficiently, but that they receive the most modern scientific and technological equipment.
>
> There is also an urgent need for fewer – and larger – police forces. This cannot await the reports of the Royal Commission on Local Government. We shall, therefore, press ahead with a vigorous programme of amalgamations, to provide the police with the form of organisation best suited to the battle against crime.

Law and order were neglected elsewhere in campaigning[348] apart from the one exception of the election briefing materials distributed to party members by the Conservative Party in 1964, materials which contained but two short references, one to the 1959 Street Offences Act,[349] and the other to the death penalty, the latter being marked 'For Quakers – capital punishment – a matter of conscience'.[350]

The central forum of government policymaking, the cabinet, covered in its weekly meetings the entire span of foreign, colonial, economic and domestic problems, and it is patent that crime and justice, as a routine part of Bottoms' and Stevenson's 'backstage policy-making', necessarily played a modest role in its deliberations.[351] All proposals for White Papers and legislation[352] would appear in the government's name and, where schedules were constricted, they always demanded collective Ministerial scrutiny, approval and ranking. The question of granting extra parliamentary time to private member's bills could also come before cabinet, and the fate of such Bills could hinge on the government's blessing. David Steel's Abortion Law Reform Bill certainly needed extended time if it was to succeed, as did Sydney Silverman's Bill on the abolition of capital punishment, and we shall see that it was discussed in cabinet on a number of occasions throughout 1965.

There were set procedures. Thus, the preamble to a memorandum accompanying one Home Office draft White Paper recited 'I ask the agreement of my colleagues that I should present forthwith a White Paper setting in out in general terms my proposals ...' Arguments would be perused by the Home Affairs Committee[353] and by the Cabinet Secretary, who prepared a candid briefing for the prime minister-chairman, before they were submitted to the cabinet itself. In the specimen year of 1965, cabinet meetings were chiefly dominated by the economy and the balance of payments crisis; immigration; Southern Rhodesia; and iron and steel nationalisation, but there is also a record of copious discussion on the passage of Sydney Silverman's bill on capital punishment and on two Home Office draft White Papers. There was also consideration of the prospects of four criminal justice bills entering the legislative programme: in the event, they were to be graded 'Bills without Priority to be Considered for Second Reading Committee',[354] and only one was endorsed, emerging eventually as The Criminal Justice Act 1967 (c.80).[355]

There is a hint of the low importance believed to be attached to criminal justice matters, of the 'muteness of penal reform', or, perhaps, of the relative lack of political authority wielded by Sir Frank Soskice himself,[356] in a statement he offered to accompany his draft White Paper on the Adult Offender:

> I am anxious to publish these proposals very soon in the form of a White Paper because I think it would be most undesirable to have to remain, as it were, mute on the subject of penal reform for adult offenders until certainly next year and perhaps even the year after, if it is impossible to fit the Criminal Justice Bill into the programme...[357]

What many political commentators took to distinguish the politics of criminal justice in the 1960s was not conventional government legislation or penal reform at all but lawmaking initiated by private members. There was a wave of liberalising measures that had been presaged in Roy Jenkins' own dummy election manifesto, *The Labour Case*,[358] published in 1959. Tim Newburn observed of that time that '1960s Britain was characterised by a greater degree of freedom, the limited nature of which is guaranteed by law ... the major legislative changes of the period – the Obscene Publications Act, the Sexual

Offences Act, the Street Offences Act, the Abortion Act, the Theatres Act – are significant for their 'permissive' or 'liberalising' character'.[359]

Much of the remainder of this work will be a broad history of the central institutions of the criminal justice system, but those 'major legislative changes' warrant attention: the Murder (Abolition of Death Penalty) Act 1965 c.71; the Abortion Act 1967 c. 87; and the Sexual Offences Act 1967 c. 60 which decriminalised the commission of homosexual acts between adult men in private. They were all reforms introduced by private members, and they offer a glimpse of what Roy Jenkins described as 'the liberal hour',[360] a moment when some people believe that the *Zeitgeist* changed, when, in the words of Harold Wilson's biographer, Ben Pimlott, the Labour governments of the 1960s made Britain a more civilised place:

> The effect of this exceptional period of reform was to end a variety of judicial persecutions of private behaviour; quietly to consolidate a mood change in British society; and to provide a legal framework for more civilised social values. For hundreds of thousands, if not millions of people directly affected ... these were the important changes of the Wilson administration.[361]

It is on the ending of those judicial persecutions that the remainder of this book will now dwell.

Acknowledgements

I am grateful to Mike Hough and to John Croft, Director of the Home Office Research Unit, 1972–1983, for their comments on an earlier draft of this chapter.

Notes

1 Robert Reiner (2010); called the rise in recorded crime since the late 1950s 'spectacular'. 'Citizenship, Crime, Citizenship: Marshalling a Social Democratic Perspective', *New Criminal Law Review*, Vol. 13, No. 2, 253.

2 I am aware that any attempt to deploy statistics – especially longitudinal statistics of crime – to examine relations between offending rates and other indicators is fraught (see the discussion in R. Carr-Hill and N. Stern (1979); *Crime, the Police and Criminal Statistics: An Analysis of Official Statistics for England and Wales using Econometric Methods*, London: Academic Press; and in R. Hood *et al.*, 'Crime, Sentencing and Punishment in A. Halsey and J. Webb (eds.) (2000); *Twentieth Century British Social Trends*, London: Macmillan, 676–680). My sole intention is to underscore what informed observers at the time would have seen as the lack of what were commonly assumed to be clear connections between crime trends and other variables.

3 Taken from R. Taylor (1998); *Forty Years of Crime and Criminal Justice Statistics, 1958–1997*, London: RDS Home Office.

4 The term was replaced under The Theft Act 1968, Ch. 60.

5 Based on figures in H. Mannheim (1965); *Comparative Criminology: A Text Book*, London: Routledge and Kegan Paul, Vol. 1, 106.

6 Taken from R. Taylor (1998); *Forty Years of Crime and Criminal Justice Statistics, 1958–1997, op. cit.* 106, and http://socialdemocracy21stcentury.blogspot.co.uk/2013/04/uk-real-per-capita-gdp-19192001-where.html.

7 Based on figures in https://www.gov.uk/government/statistics/historical-crime-data and www.ons.gov.uk/ons/rel/lms/labour.../unemployment-since-1881.

8 Based on Figures in L. Wilkins (1959); *Social Deviance*, London: Tavistock, 55.

9 R. Taylor (1998); *Forty Years of Crime and Criminal Justice Statistics, 1958–1997, op. cit.*

10 Based on figures in H. Mannheim (1965); *Comparative Criminology: A Text Book, op. cit.*

11 Based on figures in https://www.gov.uk/government/statistics/historical-crime-data and http://www.ukpublicspending.co.uk/spending_chart_1926_1960UKm_15c1li111mcn_20t#

12 M. Maguire, and T. Bennett (1982); *Burglary in a dwelling: the offence, the offender and the victim*, London: Heinemann.

13 See T. Tyler (1990); *Why People Obey the Law*, London: Yale University Press

14 N. Lacey (2003); 'Principles, Politics, and Criminal Justice', in L. Zedner and A. Ashworth (eds.) *The Criminological Foundations of Penal Policy*, Oxford: Oxford University Press, 85.

15 Terence Morris (1989); claimed that 'The year 1960 is a key year: by showing an increase of approximately 70 per cent on the preceding five years ... it demonstrates that it was the late 1950s that saw the true beginnings of the modern crime problem'. *Crime and Criminal Justice since 1945*, Oxford: Basil Blackwell, 90.

16 Nigel Walker, then a Reader in Criminology at the University of Oxford, commented in 1965 that '... the increase over the last thirty years in indictable woundings recorded as 'known to the police' has been spectacular. Even when allowance is made for the increase in population, the *rate* appears almost eight times as high as it was before the war'. *Crime and Punishment in Britain*, Edinburgh: Edinburgh University Press, 19. And see F. McClintock and N. Avison (1968); *Crime in England and Wales*, London: Heinemann.

17 Bottoms and Stevenson (1968); reflected that 'many had expected a decrease in the figures with the return to post-war normality and the advent of the welfare state. ... But whatever the true explanation for the rise in crime, the crucially important point ... is that criminal justice policy-makers did not in any way expect increases of this magnitude – yet somehow, they had to cope with them'. A. Bottoms and S. Stevenson (1992); 'What Went Wrong?': Criminal Justice Policy in England and Wales, 1945–70', in D. Downes (ed.) *Unravelling Criminal Justice*, London: Macmillan, 5, 6.

18 See (2004); '"Gordon Riots" Fear As Crime Rate Keeps Rising', *The Times*, 30 May 1963.

19 Income and wealth were both becoming more equitably distributed at the time. See J. Hills (2004); *Inequality and the State*, Oxford: Oxford University Press, Ch. 2.

20 See B. Whitaker (1964); *The Police*, London: Eyre and Spottiswoode, 47.

21 Unemployment was low by historical standards. It was 1.5% in 1965, a rate that would be regarded by many economists as rather less than that necessary for the maintenance of a properly functioning labour market. There were areas of greater unemployment. In 1965, for instance, the rate was 0.9% in the South East and the Midlands, but 2.6% in the North East, North West and Wales. The working population was predominantly employed in manufacturing (at just under half the total), clerical work (11%), sales (10%) and the professions and management (11%). (All figures taken from S. Smith (1994); *Labour Economics*, 2nd edition, London: Routledge). Inflation rates fluctuated markedly, from 0.8% in 1960 to 4.4% in 1965 (A. Britton (2001); *Monetary Regimes of the Twentieth Century*, Cambridge: Cambridge University Press, 122).

22 The Chief Constable of Swansea was reported to have told his Watch Committee in 1957 that 'The pre-war theory that poverty and unemployment were major crime factors is no longer acceptable in these days of "overfull employment" when real poverty

is practically unknown'. In D. Jones (1990–91); "Where did it all go wrong?': Crime in Swansea, 1938–68', *Welsh History Review* Vol. 15, nos. 1–4, 264.

23 The White Paper, *Penal Practice in a Changing Society*, opened with the observation that: 'It is a disquieting feature of our society that, in the years since the war, rising standards in material prosperity, education and social welfare have brought no decrease in the high rate of crime reached during the war; on the contrary, crime has increased and is still increasing'. *Penal Practice in a Changing Society: Aspects of Future Development (England and Wales)* (February 1959); Cmnd. 645, London: HMSO.

24 Leon Radzinowicz, 1906–1999, studied at the Universities of Paris, Geneva, Rome and Cracow. His first post was at the Free University of Warsaw in 1932, he left for England in 1938 and was naturalised in 1947. He became a fellow of Trinity College, Cambridge, in 1948. He was a member of the Royal Commission on Capital Punishment (1949–1953), the Advisory Council on the Treatment of Offenders (1950–63) and the Advisory Council on the Penal System (1966–74). He was to be the founder and first director of the Cambridge Institute of Criminology and first Wolfson Professor of Criminology in 1959. (Based on Roger Hood's entry on Leon Radzinowicz in the Oxford Dictionary of National Biography (http://217.169.56.135/view/article/73693).)

25 *The Need for Criminology and a Proposal for an Institute of Criminology: Report by Professor Leon Radzinowicz Wolfson Professor of Criminology University of Cambridge presented to the Hon. Samuel I. Rosenman, President of the Association of the Bar of the City of New York, and approved by its Special Committee on the Administration of Criminal Justice under the Chairmanship of the Hon. Charles D. Breitel*, (1965); London: Heinemann, 29. And see Lord Windlesham (1993); *Responses to Crime*, Vol. 2, Clarendon Press, Oxford, 69.

26 Frank Pakenham, Lord Longford, 1905–2001, was a prominent Roman Catholic peer who held numerous political offices, including Chancellor of the Duchy of Lancaster (1947–48); Minister of Civil Aviation (1948–51); First Lord of the Admiralty (1951); Leader of the House of Lords (1964–68); and Lord Privy Seal (1964–65 and 1966–68).

27 'Growth of Serious Crime', *The Times*, 1st December 1952. In a lengthy article, one observation stood out: 'What is disturbing about the figures for crimes of both sex and violence is that, while there are fluctuations for larceny and the other offences, violence and sex, in particular, show an almost uninterrupted climb. The proportionate increase is high and many of the more blatantly violent offences show an alarming development in viciousness'.

28 Lord Packenham (1958); *Causes of Crime*, London: Weidenfeld and Nicolson, 17.

29 Report of the Labour Party Study Group on Crime Prevention and Penal Reform, RD773/May 1964, The Labour Party Archive in the People's History Museum, Manchester.

30 See, for example, reports in *The Times* during the period: on 4 December 1958 it was '31% Increase In Car Thefts'; on 22 July 1959 it was 'Brighton Crime Rise "Alarming"', on 20 September 1963 it was 'Police Severely Tested By 11% Rise In Crime'. ('Crime figures continue to be very bad and the Government are increasingly disturbed'); and so it went on.

31 *The Permanent Abolition of Capital Punishment for Murder*, Memorandum by the Secretary of State for the Home Department and the Secretary of State for Scotland, 6 May 1969. (To be sure, that portion of the memorandum sought to demonstrate that the rise in the number of homicides was small in contrast to the increases in offences of violence and robbery).

32 F. McClintock (1963); *Crimes of Violence: An Enquiry by the Cambridge Institute of Criminology into Crimes of Violence against the Person in London*, London: Macmillan, 1.

33 For example, Peter Thorneycroft, the Member for Monmouth, opened a debate on 2 February 1966 by moving, 'That this House notes with grave concern the mounting wave of crime together with the falling detection rate; [and] regrets that the

Government's actions and proposals in this sphere, particularly with regard to the police, appear inadequate to deal with this deteriorating situation. ... The background of the debate is a mounting crime wave. It is scarcely possible to pick up a newspaper without reading an account of some further breach of the criminal law – murder, robbery, violence, protection rackets, blackmail and every other kind of enormity. It is happening day by day and week by week ...'

34 Roy Jenkins, 1920–2003, was a Labour Member of Parliament from 1948, first for Southwark Central and then for Stechford in 1950. He became Economic Secretary to the Treasury, Minister for Aviation and then Home Secretary from 1964–1967 before becoming Chancellor of the Exchequer. One of his biographers, Anthony Howard, remarked that 'Jenkins's first spell as home secretary was undeniably the high point of his career until that date, and some might be tempted to say that nothing he did later (certainly not his second reluctant spell at the Home Office in 1974–6) surpassed it. He enjoyed regular debating triumphs in the House of Commons'. (*Oxford Dictionary of National Biography*, http://217.169.56.135/view/article/88739)

35 'The Criminal Justice Bill. Party Political Broadcast 1 December 1966', in R. Jenkins (1967); *Essays and Speeches*, London: Collins, 252.

36 A Conservative Party report remarked that there had been between 1938 and 1964 a 'startling increase in the number of crimes committed by young people under the age of 21. We have now reached a stage when half of those found·guilty of indictable crime come from this age-group'. (Conservative Party Archives at the Bodleian Library, Policy Group on Crime – Interim Report: Crime and Punishment, ACP (65) 12; PG/3/65/32, July 1965).

37 *The War Against Crime in England and Wales 1959–1964:* 20 March 1964 – revised draft of White Paper, 8.

38 The population of England and Wales amounted to 47,884,300 in 1965, of whom 3,741,000 (or some 8%) were aged 15–19. (*Registrar General's Statistical Review of England and Wales for the Year 1965, Part III. Commentary*, (1967); London: HMSO.

39 See, for example, M. Abrams (1961); *Teenage Consumer Spending in 1959*, London: London Exchange Press.

40 See S. Cohen and P. Rock (1970); 'The Teddy Boy', in V. Bogdanor and R. Skidelsky (eds.) *The Age of Affluence*, London: Macmillan.

41 See L. Wilkins (1960); *Delinquent Generations*, London: HMSO. The study opened on p. 1 with the statement: 'It has long been the opinion of many social workers and sociologists that evacuation and other disturbances of the lives of young children during the 1939–45 war would have a lasting effect upon the behaviour of these children. So far as is known this has not been confirmed statistically'. And it concluded on p. 9 by observing that children born during the war appear not to have been unduly affected but that 'the general theory that some birth years are associated with criminality is sustained by the current analysis. ... it seems that disturbances of social or family life had the most marked effect on subsequent criminality if they occurred when the children concerned were passing through their fifth year'. The report made quite a stir, attracting, for example, an editorial in *The Times*, 12 January 1961.

42 See G. Pearson (1983); *Hooligan: A History of Respectable Fears*, London: Macmillan, esp. Ch. 2.

43 R.A. Butler, 1902–1982, was the Conservative Member of Parliament for Saffron Walden from 1929 until 1965. He held a number of positions, including Chairman of the Conservative Research Department from 1945 to 1964; Chancellor of the Exchequer, 1951–1955; Lord Privy Seal and Leader of the House of Common in 1955; Home Secretary, 1957–1962; Deputy Prime Minister and First Secretary of State, 1962 to 1963; and Shadow Foreign Secretary 1964–1965

44 Ministry of Education (1960); *The Youth Service in England and Wales* ('The Albemarle Report'), London: HMSO. The report was prompted by what was held to be the

concatenation of a crisis in the youth services and an emerging problem of youth, and of youthful delinquency, in particular.

45 Conservative Party Archives at the Bodleian Library, ACP60/84, 31 July 1960.

46 Conservative Party Archives at the Bodleian Library, Policy Group on Crime; 'Interim Report – Crime and Punishment', ACP (65) 12, PG/3/65/32, 14 July 1965.

47 Cabinet Papers, CAB 128/3, 22 July 1965, para. 4.

48 See L. Cohen and M. Felson (1979); 'Social Change and Crime Rate Trends: A Routine Activity Approach', *American Sociological Review*, Vol. 44, No. 4, 588–608.

49 D. Garland (2000); 'The Culture of High Crime Societies', *British Journal of Criminology*, Vol. 40 No. 3, 359.

50 A group of former permanent undersecretaries and others, meeting at Birkbeck College on 2 July 2010 at a CCBH Witness Seminar on Home Office Organisation, concurred that, whilst their reputation as a 'Guardian-reading liberal *élite*' was misconceived ('we never knew the political views of any of our colleagues', said one), there was a pronounced gap between the high officials and the views of men and women on the street.

51 Lord Windlesham; *Responses to Crime, op. cit.*, 20.

52 'A Lifetime in the Jungle – Lord Butler in conversation with Robert McKenzie'. *The Listener*, Vol. 86, No. 2208, 22 July 1971, 110.

53 The fomenters of that campaign, the Anti-Violence League, claimed that they had reached the conclusion that 'the only effective means of forcing a change in the law is the formation of a nation-wide non-political and non-sectarian organisation, which will canalise the public demand and by sheer weight of numbers, influence and reverse the present disastrous policy of so-called "reform", which has resulted in a crime wave of violence and destruction hitherto unknown. No one – young and old alike – is safe to walk the streets, tend business, pay wages or even stay at home, without constant fear and apprehension'. Letter of 21 April 1961 in Labour Party Archives, People's History Museum. And see the report in *The Times*, 16 July 1961. The League's members included Sir Thomas Moore, M.P.; Sir Percy Sillitoe, the former Director General of MI5; and ex-Detective Superintendent Fabian of Scotland Yard.

54 Conservative Party Archives at the Bodleian Library, CC04/8/27, Letter of 11 January 1960.

55 He was subject to an incessant barrage. In 1960, for example, he was informed that the Northern Area Women's One-Day Conference had passed a resolution on 26 January that 'in view of the alarming increase in crimes of violence, this Conference strongly recommends to Her Majesty's Government that first priority should be given to: (a) Schemes for recruitment, and improved conditions in the Police Force and Prison Service; (b) Longer terms of imprisonment with the removal of amenities and no remission of sentence in these cases'. In the same year, he was informed that "That the Divisional Executive Committee of the Altrincham and Sale Division Conservative Association is seriously concerned with the continuing crimes of violence and urges the Government to re-introduce legislation to enable the Courts to sentence offenders to the birch as an effective punishment and deterrent." In June 1961, he was informed by the Chairman of the the North Fylde Conservative Association that members 'are very dissatisfied at the steps being taken to combat the rise in crime, and the Chairman was requested to write to the Home Secretary to inform him that the Association was of the opinion the reintroduction of birching would have a salutary effect'. And so it went on. His replies were invariant. He took crime seriously and had a variety of measures in place or in the offing to deal with the problems which it presented. He was to reflect 'My life history ha[s] been one of serving the Conservative Party and the Conservative Establishments

throughout the years. But I [have] had to take an awful lot of opposition, in which I stood out and in every case won. India [1935], education, Conservative reform … the birching and flogging at the Home Office, which haunted me almost every week of my time at the Home Office and on which I eventually won …' 'A Lifetime in the Jungle – Lord Butler in conversation with Robert McKenzie'. *The Listener, op. cit.*, 110.

56 G. Tett (2009); *Fool's Gold*, London: Abacus, xiv.

57 A. Paterson (1933); 'Should the Criminologist be Encouraged?', *Transactions of the Medico-Legal Society*, Vol. XXVI, 180.

58 Sir Brian Cubbon, the former Permanent Undersecretary, said at the Witness Seminar on Home Office Organisation of 2 July 2010, 'one thing is that you could go home and tell your wife about what you'd be doing and she'd understand you'.

59 Indeed, the former Home Secretary, Michael Howard, used almost precisely those words at the same Witness Seminar. 'Everyone's an expert', he said.

60 And most emphatically in the field of psycho-analysis. Williams, for instance, asserted that 'Early in life the absence of a good mother or mother substitute is of prime importance in the aetiology of delinquency. …' A.H. Williams (1965); 'The Treatment of Abnormal Murderers,' *Howard Journal of Penology and Crime Prevention*, Vol. 11, No. 4, 286–292.

61 See, for example, the report of a speech delivered by David Maxwell Fyfe, the Home Secretary, to a Conservative Political Centre meeting, in which he said the four main causes of crime were 'broken and unsatisfactory homes', a lack of parental control, the glorification of brutal violence and the decline of religion. (*The Observer*, 1 March 1953).

62 The *Report on the Work of the Prison Department for 1965* (1966) quoted approvingly the argument of the governor of a closed borstal that 'Traditional standards of morality, if ever implanted, had long since been abandoned by most of these youngsters, and 'the most difficult children of the State' nowadays show a lack of responsibility which is one of the most alarming features of late 20th century materialism'. Cmnd. 3088, London: HMSO, 19.

63 A Conservative Party working party listed the following inventory of causal factors: '(a) The Mother is of paramount importance. The link between mother and child very strong and fundamental. (b) Lack of security in the home can lead to delinquency. (c) Parents should be made to feel responsible for their children's behaviour. Odium is no longer attached to parents if the children go wrong. (d) The father as well as the mother should have responsibility for the discipline of his children. (e) Lack of discipline and lack of religious teaching in the home. The social outlook is different since the war and some children have little sense of purpose. (f) Parents are too frequently out leaving children alone. (g) Children are not taught enough in their homes to make their contribution to the world at large. (h) Broken homes are often a cause of delinquency'. Conservative Party Archives at the Bodleian Library: CCO4/8/155 Brief Notes on the preliminary findings of the Working Party on Parental Responsibility and Juvenile Delinquency at their first Meeting held on 10 December, 1959. A member of the group was reported to have said that 'children were not taught enough to make any contribution to the world at large or to feel citizens of the British Empire and she felt that mothers should be educated to bring up their children in this way … we must face the fact that the social outlook was not the same as before the war and that among those living on council estates there was very little sense of purpose for the lives of the children or of moral discipline or religion'. Report of the Meeting of the Working Party on Parental Responsibility and Juvenile Delinquency, 10 December 1959.

64 The phrase is used rather quizzically by N. Walker in *Crime and Punishment in Britain, op. cit.*, 69.

65 The number of dissolutions and annulments was again modest in retrospect, but it was growing, and its growth was regarded with some apprehension:

	1955	1960	1965
Number of Marriages:	357,918	343,614	371,127
Dissolutions and Annulments	28,314	28,542	42,981

(Registrar General's Statistical Review of England and Wales for the Year 1965, Part III. Commentary (1967); London: HMSO, 64, 65).

A report by a Conservative Party Women's National Advisory Committee Working Party on Parental Responsibility and Juvenile Delinquency commented that: 'There seems to be little doubt that many, though not all, cases of delinquency result from an unstable home life. Among those particularly liable to be affected are:-

Children of divorced or separated parents;
Adopted children;
The child whose mother goes out to work.

It would be both impossible and undesirable to dictate to a woman whether she should take on work outside her home or not, but we regard the present tendency for mothers to be away for long periods as harmful. Overtired mothers with frayed tempers have not enough time or energy left to give to the proper upbringing of their young. The child, who on return from school, faces an empty house, sometimes even a locked door, is more likely to get into mischief than one who finds Mother at home and ready with the tea – an unconscious symbol of security in the child's mind. ...' (Conservative Party Archives at the Bodleian Library, no date)

66 See T. Newburn; *Permission and Regulation* (1992); London: Routledge, 5. A Conservative Party report began trenchantly: 'Crime is a moral issue. It is concerned with the difference between right and wrong in an area which the State considers that difference to be of sufficient importance and relevance to interest itself in. No analysis of social or psychological causes of crime and no policy for dealing with it should be allowed to obscure this basic fact'. (Conservative Party Archives at the Bodleian Library, Policy Group on Crime – Interim Report: Crime and Punishment, ACP (65) 12; PG/3/65/32, July 1965). And for a discussion of the interplay between crime, socio-economic conditions and lay theorising in one locality, Swansea, see D. Jones (1990); "Where did it all go wrong?': Crime in Swansea, 1938–68', *Welsh History Review*, Vol. 15(1).

67 For example, the Roman Catholic Hierarchy issued a press statement on 21 October 1966 at a time when the law on abortion was under discussion: 'All direct destruction of life in the womb is immoral. No civil law can change the moral law which we are bound to obey. ... It is our duty to point out that certain clauses of the proposed Bill are contrary to the ethical code hitherto accepted not only by Catholics but by all who hold life sacred'.

68 The foreword to the Conservative Party report, *The Rising Tide*, observed in July 1960 that 'The authority of parents, teachers and employers is regarded differently than in the past. Mass media, especially T.V., now exert a stronger public influence; organised religion a weaker one than was once the case. ...' (Conservative Party Archives in the Bodeleian Library, ACP(60)78)

69 *Penal Practice in a Changing Society: Aspects of Future Development (England and Wales), op. cit.*

70 House of Commons debates, 2 February 1959.

71 John Heenan, Cardinal Archbishop of Westminister, 1905–1975, was ordained in 1930 and became an assistant priest in 1931. He was made superior of the Catholic

Missionary Society in 1947, Bishop of Leeds in 1951, Archbishop of Liverpool in 1957, and Archbishop of Westminster in 1963, becoming a cardinal in February 1965. (Based on Michael Gaine's entry in *The Oxford Dictionary of National Biography*, http://217.169.56.135/view/article/31215?docPos=2).

72 *Causes of Crime, op. cit.*, 39. He went on to say on p. 121 that 'there is no doubt that the psychological and moral influence of the family – especially as exercised during the first few years – has become far the most fashionable category among those who write and talk about the causes of crime. ...'

73 Quoted in HO291/117 7 Perks Committee Papers for Full Committee.

74 Henry Brooke, 1903–1984, was Conservative Member of Parliament for Lewisham West, 1938–1945; Member of Parliament for Hampstead, 1950–1966; Financial Secretary to the Treasury, 1954–1957; Minister of Housing and Local Government and Welsh Affairs, 1957–1961; Chief Secretary to the Treasury and Paymaster-General, 1961–1962; and Secretary of State for the Home Department, 1962–1964.

75 In a draft version of *The War Against Crime in England and Wales 1959–1964*, submitted to cabinet on 20 March 1964, C.P.(64) 80. A future Home Secretary, Merlyn Rees, alluded to the same bundle of factors in a debate in the House of Commons. Delinquency, he said, 'raised issues of home and family, personality, school, work – or lack of it – and other factors'. Cited in HO291/117 7 Perks Committee Papers for Full Committee.

76 Now described criminologically as 'responsibilisation'. See P. O'Malley (1992); 'Risk, Power and Crime-Prevention', *Economy and Society*, Vol. 21, No. 3.

77 http://rds.homeoffice.gov.uk/rds/pdfs/40years.pdf

78 Taken from R. Taylor (1998); *Forty Years of Crime and Criminal Justice Statistics, 1958–1997, op. cit.*

79 Editorial, *The British Journal of Delinquency* (1950); 1(1).

80 Mannheim remarked that 'in criminology there are no causes of crime which are both sufficient and necessary. There are only factors which may be 'necessary' to produce crime in conjunction with other factors. Neither crime in general nor any specific crime can ever be due to one single factor. ... This means a death blow to all one-factor theories of crime, such as Lombroso's, and leads straight to ... [the] theory of the multiplicity of factors'. *Comparative Criminology, op. cit.*, 8.

81 Howard Jones, 1918–2007, studied for a PhD under Hermann Mannheim at the LSE, became a lecturer in social studies and then senior lecturer in sociology at the University of Leicester 1953–65; was a Reader at Keele University 1965–69, where he introduced criminology; and then became a Professor at the University of Cardiff in 1969, where he was to be head of the then Department of Social Administration and School of Social Work until his retirement in 1984. (See M. Levi; Professor Howard Jones (1918–2007), http://www.cardiff.ac.uk/for/staff/obituaries/howardjones/professor-howard-jones.html).

82 H. Jones (1962); *Crime and the Penal System*, University Tutorial Press, London, second edition, 109 (emphasis in the original).

83 Mannheim was a German émigré of immense academic distinction who taught at the School between 1935 and 1955. On retirement, he began work on the two-volume *Comparative Criminology*. See Lord Chorley (1970); 'Hermann Mannheim: A Biographical Appreciation', *British Journal of Criminology*, Vol. 10, No. 4, 324–347.

84 *Comparative Criminology, op. cit.*

85 Nigel Walker was Reader in Criminology at the University of Oxford between 1961 and 1973, and the Wolfson Professor of Criminology at the University of Cambridge from 1973 to 1984.

86 *Crime and Punishment in Britain, op. cit.*, 105.

87 N. Walker (2003); *A Man Without Loyalties: A Penologist's Afterthoughts*, Chichester: Barry Rose, 100.

88 H. Jones; *Crime and the Penal System, op. cit.*, 1.
89 Criminology was not touched upon at all, for example, in J. Gould (ed.) (1965); *Penguin Survey of the Social Sciences 1965*, Harmondsworth: Penguin.
90 *Comparative Criminology: A Text Book, op. cit.*, 18.
91 'Hermann Mannheim: A Biographical Appreciation', *op. cit.*, 324.
92 Barbara Wootton, 1897–1988, was an influential criminologist-politician, who was appointed Professor at Bedford College of the University of London in 1948. She acted as the President of the British Sociological Association between 1959 and 1964. She served on four Royal Commissions, was created Baroness Wootton of Abinger in 1958, and was made a Companion of Honour in 1977.
93 *Causes of Crime, op. cit.*, 106.
94 Thus an editorial in *The Howard Journal of Penology and Crime Prevention* (1965); proclaimed that 'The public, prison staff and fellow prisoners all have a right to expect that every convicted murderer has a careful clinical examination, perhaps complemented by a battery of psychological tests, so that a proper diagnosis is established and a treatment plan worked out ...' Vol. 11, No. 4, 254–5.
95 See P. Rock (1994); introduction to *History of Criminology*, Aldershot: Dartmouth.
96 Editorial, *The British Journal of Delinquency* (1950); Vol. 1, No. 1.
97 Consider the contents of one specimen issue of the admittedly practitioner-leaning journal – the only criminological complement at the time to *The British Journal of Criminology* – *The Howard Journal of Penology and Criminology* (1966); Vol. XII, No. 1: H. Wilson; 'Pre-School Training of Culturally Deprived Children'; B. Biven and H. Holden; 'Informal Youth Work in a Cafe Setting'; G. Rose; 'Trends in the Use of Prediction'; H. Jones; 'Prison Officers as Therapists'; C. Smith; 'The Youth Service and Delinquency Prevention'; and D. Miller; 'Problems of Staff Training in a School for Delinquent Adolescent Boys'.
98 I. Loader (2006); 'Fall of the 'Platonic Guardians': Liberalism, Criminology and Political Responses to Crime in England and Wales', *British Journal of Criminology*, Vol. 46, No. 4, 567.
99 Editorial, *The British Journal of Criminology* (1965); Vol. 5 No. 2, 117.
100 See 'Seeking for Causes of Delinquency', *The Times*, 28 December 1961.
101 Tom Lodge, draft paragraph for *White Paper on Penal Practice*, 8 October 1963, CRI 61 15/1/5.
102 Such disparagement was diffuse and debilitating. Nigel Walker, also at the University of Oxford, was no less scathing about what was to become criminology's parent discipline of sociology: "Criminology [may have to be allotted] to the discipline of sociology – if discipline is not too strong a word'. *Crime and Punishment in Britain, op. cit.*, 19.
103 Charles Cunningham, 1906–1998, was appointed Secretary of the Scottish Department in 1948, and then became permanent Undersecretary of State at the Home Office between 1957 and 1966, when he was dismissed by the new Home Secretary, Roy Jenkins, in what Jenkins described as a 'shoot-out'. It was, Jenkins, said, 'at once the most difficult and most crucial encounter that I have ever had with any high-ranking civil servant. Over the subsequent decades, despite a strong natural tendency to question my own judgement in retrospect, although happily not to falter much at the time, I have never varied in my view that on this occasion I was right'. (R. Jenkins (1991); *A Life at the Centre*, London: Macmillan, 181.)
104 CRI61 15/1/5 Penal Reform Generally New White Paper on Penal Policy: CCC to S. of S. 19 July 1963. In the same file, it was made clear that those doubts about the universities, and the new universities in particular, were not easily dispelled. An official, later to become private secretary, Ralph Shuffrey, wrote to Leslie Wilkins in October 1963: 'It is not clear what can be said about the new Universities at this stage or why York in particular is mentioned; but you may possibly be able to think of something which should be said at this point. ...'

105 C. Nuttall (2003); 'The Home Office and Random Allocation Experiments', *Evaluation Review*, Vol. 27 No. 3, 268. He immediately added 'It had all been concerned with the effectiveness of penal treatments'.

106 PREM 11/4691.

107 C.H. Rolph was the *nom de plume* of Cecil Rolph Hewitt, who was born in London 1901; served in the City of London police between 1921–46; and then joined the editorial staff of the *New Statesman* between1947–70. He was to play a vigorous role in many of the campaigns centred on criminal justice reform in the 1960s, campaigns that will be covered elsewhere in this history. He said of his dual names, 'I never got it straight. I had manoeuvred my own identity into a hopeless muddle'. C.H. Rolph (1987); *Further Particulars*, Oxford: Oxford University Press, 127.

108 The allusion is to N. Hawthorne (1850); *The Scarlet Letter: A Romance*, Boston: Ticknor and Fields.

109 *Further Particulars, op. cit.*, 147.

110 He reproduced the section on funding in the 1948 Criminal Justice Act (Chapter 58 11 and 12 Geo 6). The matter had been raised in debate on the bill on 28 November 1947 by Major Vernon, the MP for Dulwich, who had said 'I have been utterly aston-ished that throughout this Debate no one has said one word about the provision of research into the early causes of crime and methods for dealing with those conditions. The hon. Member for Nelson and Colne (Mr. S. Silverman) pointed out that there were two ways of dealing with crime. He said that society may protect itself by terror, or society may protect itself by reforming the criminals. There is a third way in which society may protect itself, and that is by studying the causes responsible for a person first taking to criminal practices and the methods which may be adopted for dealing with those causes'. The matter was considered in Committee under Standing Order No. 69 on 14 April 1948 and the phrase cited by C.H. Rolph was introduced into the bill and approved in the House of Commons on the following day. The Home Secretary told the House a week later that 'I undertook, during Committee stage of the Criminal Justice Bill, to amend the Bill so as to take power to undertake research into the causes of delinquency and the treatment of offenders, and to make grants to approved bodies or persons engaged in such research. Amendments were made accordingly during Report stage and have been embodied in the Bill'. (Major Vernon, 1882–1975, was a Labour Member of Parliament between 1945–1951).

111 'Prisons and Prisoners', *New Statesman and Nation*, 2 February 1957, 136.

112 Brian Cubbon: Note on Mr Rolph's article in the New Statesman. ... 13 February 1957, HO291/504 Penal Reform General Suggestions for Inclusion in legislation: Home Office Legislation in the 1958/9 Session.

113 In an unpublished draft of a study of a history of criminal justice until 1970, lodged in the archives of the Institute of Criminology at the University of Cambridge, Simon Stevenson wrote 'One thing which seems clear is that the White Paper ... really took its origin not from external demand for action ... so much as from the deliberate min-isterial intention of encouraging debate. ... [although] Both the Conservative Party and wider public opinion now grew increasingly difficult to handle as reported crime figures soared on the back of the maturing post-war baby boom. ... Not least impor-tant of these features, this crime wave appeared to be accompanied by the emergence of a distinct teenage consumer–culture ...' 'The Butler Years', 1957–64, 134.

114 Letter to Miss Nunn, HO291/504 Penal Reform General Suggestions for Inclusion in Legislation: Home Office Legislation in the 1958/9 Session.

115 He later reflected how: 'in a Supply debate on the Supplementary Estimates for the Prison Commissioners I told the House that such was the paucity of information at my disposal that planning ahead was virtually impossible. I had ascertained that since 1948, when the Home Secretary was given power to spend money on research into criminological and penal matters, only £12,000 had been allocated – a hopelessly

inadequate sum. Although some useful work had begun in the Universities … this was only scratching the surface. A handful of research workers were attempting to under-take investigations into one of the most intractable problems on shoe-string budgets'. Lord Butler (1974); 'The Foundation of the Institute of Criminology in Cambridge', in R. Hood (ed.) *Crime, Criminology and Public Policy*, London: Heinemann, 1.

116 Frank Newsam, (1893–1964), was Permanent Secretary between 1948 and 30 September 1957.

117 HO291/504 Penal Reform General Suggestions for Inclusion in Legislation: Home Office Legislation in the 1958/9 Session.

118 The claim was made by Lord Allen of Abbeydale (formerly Sir Phillip Allen, himself a former permanent Undersecretary of State at the Home Office), in his entry on Sir Charles in the *Oxford Dictionary of National Biography*: http://217.169.56.135/view/article/70186?docPos=2.

119 See R. Clarke and D. Cornish (1983); *Crime Control in Britain: A Review of Policy Research*, Albany: State University of New York Press.

120 HO291/504 Penal Reform General Suggestions for Inclusion in legislation: Home Office Legislation in the 1958/9 Session Note from Tom Lodge.

121 Number 1, the report by L. Wilkins and H. Mannheim on *Prediction Methods in Relation to Borstal Training*, had been published in 1955 before the inception of the Research Unit.

122 C. Nuttall; 'The Home Office and Random Allocation Experiments', *op. cit.*, 269.

123 *The Times*, 28 December 1961.

124 *The British Imperial Calendar and Civil Service List 1965* (1965); London: HMSO.

125 *The War Against Crime in England and Wales 1959–1964:* 20 March 1964 draft of White Paper.

126 John Croft's comment was that 'politicians were at best tolerant of expenditure on criminological research, as was the Treasury' (letter, 30 March 2016). But there is some countervailing evidence. A 1965 Conservative Party report endorsed research fulsomely: 'It is essential that there should be a continuing and major programme of research into all aspects of crime – its causes, its prevention, its detection and its treatment. Research must be used not only to provide a body of reliable knowledge for the guidance of important decisions but also to evaluate different courses of action once they have been taken. Indeed, there is not a single aspect of the recom-mendations contained in this report, which should not be subject to research of some kind. This requirement contrasts sharply with the present under-use of research. Although appreciating a good start has been made in recent years under Conservative administration, the money and facilities available for research are still hopelessly inadequate. Research must be given considerably increased support if it is to play its proper part in the war against crime'. Policy Group on Crime – Interim Report: Crime and Punishment, ACP (65) 12; PG/3/65/32. Conservative Party Archives at the Bodleian Library. Very similarly, and at very much the same time, the Labour Party Study Group on Crime Prevention and Penal Reform reported under the sub-heading, 'More knowledge essential', that 'Problems as widespread and diverse as that of crime cannot be solved by a hit-or-miss policy, based on inadequate information, moral principles that may not be generally accepted, fallible human judgement and prejudice. Extensive research is essential, both into social problems generally and into the specific problem of crime and penal treatment'. Preliminary Outline for Report', RD727/March 1964, The Labour Party Archive in the People's History Museum, Manchester.

127 R. Clarke and D. Cornish (1983); *Crime Control in Britain: A Review of Policy Research, op. cit.*, 52.

128 Although John Croft observed that 'Up till the nineteen seventies the upper echelons of the Office were largely Oxbridge educated. … They were not particularly receptive

to research, although there were notable exceptions ...' (CCBH/LSE Ideas: The Home Office Research Unit, unpublished note, June 2010, 3).

129 Lucia Zedner commented that, as a statistician rather than a criminologist, Lodge's understanding of appropriate research was 'founded on assumptions about the hardness of hard data; the force of deductive reasoning; and the partiality of academic interpretation ...' 'Useful Knowledge? Debating the Role of Criminology in Post-war Britain', in L. Zedner and A. Ashworth (eds.) (2003); *The Criminological Foundations of Penal Policy: Essays in Honour of Roger Hood*, Oxford: Oxford University Press, 208.

130 T. Lodge (1974); 'The Founding of the Home Office Research Unit', in R. Hood (ed.) *Crime, Criminology and Public Policy, op. cit.*, 17–18.

131 He had deliberately curtailed the growth of the Unit so that it did not monopolise research at the expense of the universities (CCBH/LSE Ideas: The Home Office Research Unit, *op. cit.*): 'I didn't really believe in Government research' he said. 'There needed to be a small unit which would transfer research that ought to be done in the universities into policy if it was possible but I didn't believe that a large, in-house unit was the right thing'.

132 He wrote 'One of the problems of the social sciences is establishing the objective nature of the facts elucidated by research. Facts in the physical sciences, at least in modern times, are not susceptible to dispute on this score ... 'J. Croft (1980); *Research and Criminal Policy*, London: H.M.S.O., 4.

133 J. Croft (1978); *Research in Criminal Justice*, London: H.M.S.O., 4, 6.

134 For example, Simon Field's (1990) *Trends in Crime and Their Interpretation: A Study of Recorded Crime in Post-War England and Wales* (London: Home Office) could not talk about the relations between crime and unemployment at a difficult time in the political and economic fortunes of England and Wales.

135 In I. Loader; 'Fall of the 'Platonic Guardians', *op. cit.*, 566–7.

136 'The main aims are: (i) to study criminal careers and patterns of offending at all stages with special reference to predicting the continuance of criminality; (ii) if possible to establish norms (i.e. assessments of vulnerability to subsequent reconviction) of different offender groups; and (iii) to study methods of analysing biographical data'.

137 Extracted from *The War Against Crime in England and Wales 1959–1964:* 20 March 1964 – revised draft of White Paper; C.P.(64) 80.

138 M. Hough (2014); 'Confessions of a recovering 'administrative criminologist': Jock Young, quantitative research and policy research', *Crime Media Culture*, Vol. 10(3) 217.

139 It did indeed become a very major engine of intellectual innovation in criminology, particular with the introduction of the British Crime Survey in 1981. Ron Clarke identified 1981 as a turning point. It was then that 'HORU morphed into the Research and Planning Unit, or the RPU. ... The change of name signified its emphasised policy analysis role ...' He was able to say – quite rightly – that 'The Unit's outstanding achievement was its sustained production of an in-house programme of world class research. This covered the wide array of topics falling under the Home Office remit and resulted in many dozens, if not some hundreds of reports published in the Home Office's own research series or in professional and academic journals'. (R.V.G. Clarke; 'The Home Office Research Unit – an insider's view', paper delivered at CCBH/LSE IDEAS Witness Conference; The Home Office Research Unit, London School of Economics, 14 May 2010.) One of his colleagues, Mike Hough, reflected about that time that 'In the 1970s and early 80s we researchers had surprising autonomy, offering often unhelpful, or at least unwelcome commentary on policy – less to ministers, more to Mandarins'. ('Does Justice Policy Listen to Criminological Research?', School of Law, Birkbeck College, 8 March 2018, Slide 5.)

140 Review (2012) of I. Loader and R. Sparks, *Public Criminology?*, Routledge: London, 2010, *Criminology & Criminal Justice*, Vol.12(1), 105.

141 T. Lodge (1974); 'The Founding of the Home Office Research Unit', in R. Hood
    (ed.) *Crime, Criminology and Public Policy, op. cit.*, 11.
142 He said: 'I want a criminologist. ... I suggest ... that some public benefactor, realis-
    ing that a gap remains to be filled, should found a chair at Oxford University for a
    Professor of Criminology. ... I think there is a case for the man who will focus interest
    and direct study and research on this question of crime'. A. Paterson; 'Should the
    Criminologist be Encouraged?', *op. cit.*, 191, 200.
143 The Howard League for Penal Reform calls itself 'the oldest penal reform charity in
    the UK. It was established in 1866 and is named after John Howard, one of the first
    prison reformers'. (http://www.howardleague.org/who-we-are/) It was formed out
    of a merger between the Howard Association and the Penal Reform League in 1921,
    and its chief campaigns have been directed at children in prison, women prisoners,
    suicide and self-harm, community sentences, prison education, and young offenders
    (http://en.wikipedia.org/wiki/Howard_League_for_Penal_Reform). It convention-
    ally worked discreetly and moderately to become, as Mick Ryan argued, 'the pre-
    eminent group in the field of penal reform ... [i]n the immediate postwar period'.
    (M. Ryan (2003); *Penal Policy and Political Culture in England and Wales*, Winchester:
    Waterside Press, 19.
144 Margery Fry, 1874–1958, was a Quaker and a major political reformer, responsible for
    the institution of criminal injuries compensation and much else. She was the Honorary
    Secretary of the Penal Reform League from 1919–1926, a League which she amalga-
    mated with the Howard Association to form the Howard League for Penal Reform.
    She represented the League at the League of Nations, and succeeded in placing penal
    reform on its agenda.
145 Hugh Klare was Secretary of the Howard League for Penal Reform, 1949–1971.
146 *The University Teaching of Social Sciences, Criminology* (1957); Paris: UNESCO.
147 This account draws heavily on L. Radzinowicz (1988); *The Cambridge Institute of
    Criminology: Its Background and Scope*, London: H.M.S.O.
148 The history of the decision to site the new Institute was a subject of great acrimony in
    the criminological world. I could find no reference to it in the catalogues of archives
    held locally at the University of London and the London School of Economics and
    more widely elsewhere that might have held papers on the subject. Leon Radzinowicz's
    own account held that 'On the 7 March 1958, Mr Butler dispatched letters ... to the
    Vice-Chancellor of the University of London and to the Vice-Chancellor of the
    University of Cambridge. The gist of them was to ascertain whether either University
    was prepared to have an Institute of Criminology. ... The response from London was
    less than encouraging. To start with, the Vice-Chancellor did not answer, or even
    acknowledge the Home Secretary's letter until he was prompted by an enquiry from
    the Private Secretary as to whether the letter had been safely received. He then wrote
    (but only on 3 May) that it was still too early for him to give any firm statement. ...'
    (*The Cambridge Institute of Criminology, op. cit.*, 9). Terence Morris of the London School
    of Economics, and a former student of Mannheim, asserted that 'Mannheim, though
    he had a record of empirical and policy-oriented research, was not even consulted. At
    a private lunch given by the vice-chancellor, the principal, Douglas Logan, dismissed
    Mannheim's claims in a single sentence, but praised Radzinowicz, whom he knew
    well as a fellow Fellow of Trinity. The lunch was attended by the Undersecretary of
    State at the Home Office and the secretary of the royal commission on capital punish-
    ment, on which Radzinowicz had served. ... At the time, many in London, not least
    Mannheim, believed that the whole thing had been a stitch-up and the man with
    the needle was Logan. It will never be possible to know why the vice-chancellor
    did not acknowledge, let alone reply, to Butler's letter until prompted by the home
    secretary's private office. ... Mannheim wasted a disproportionate amount of energy
    in his retirement expressing his hatred of the "upstart Pole"; this degenerated into such

an obsession that any former pupil who visited Cambridge was re-categorised as an "unperson". ... In old age, Radzy was forgiving, even to Mannheim, in a generous tribute in the Dictionary of National Biography; Mannheim would never have done the same for him'. Obituary, Sir Leon Radzinowicz, *The Guardian*, Saturday 1 January 2000.

149 R.A. Butler informed the House of Commons on 31 July 1958: 'Discussions have been proceeding with university authorities and I am also consulting the University Grants Committee. I have now been informed by the Vice-Chancellor of Cambridge University that, provided the necessary funds can be made available, the university will be glad to consider the establishment of an institute of criminology, whose functions would include both teaching and research, as well as facilities for exchange of views and information with those concerned with the practical administration of the law. The nucleus of the institute would be the existing Department of Criminal Science, but it would be developed on a broader basis and steps would be taken to associate all interested Faculties with its management. I have told the Vice-Chancellor that I warmly welcome this proposal ...'

150 Commenting on the draft White Paper *Penal Practice in a Changing Society*, the Cabinet Secretary observed in a note to the prime minister, 'The proposals are bound to be expensive. ... All that the White Paper says on this subject ... is that "all this will cost a great deal of money ..." How much money? And how much time? And in what other respects may the Exchequer incur an additional liability – e.g. Cambridge would be prepared to establish an Institute of Criminology "if the necessary funds can be made available"? This would be a very valuable institution; but how much will it cost? And is there any suggestion that the Exchequer should contribute? (If a contribution were suggested, it might be a very good investment.)' Cabinet Secretary to PM 15 December 1958. PREM 11.

151 Cmd 645, February 1959.

152 The Foundation describes itself as a charity that 'was established in 1955. It aims to support excellence, generally through the funding of capital infrastructure in the fields of science and medicine, health, education and the arts & humanities. ... An important element of the Foundation's strategy is to seek collaboration with other expert bodies. Fruitful partnerships have included leading academic societies (notably the Royal Society and the British Academy), government departments, other grant-making trusts (such as the Wellcome Trust) and charities ranging from Help the Hospices to the Art Fund'. http://www.wolfson.org.uk/about-us/

153 A. Oakley; unpublished typescript of biography of Barbara Wootton, Ch. 14, 338, subsequently published in 2011 as *A Critical Woman: Barbara Wootton, Social Science and Public Policy in the Twentieth Century*, London: Bloomsbury Academic.

154 R. Hood (2002); 'Recollections of Sir Leon Radzinowicz', in A. Bottoms and M. Tonry (eds.) *Ideology, Crime and Criminal Justice: A Symposium in Honour of Sir Leon Radzinowicz*, Cullompton: Willan, xxi.

155 J. Martin; 'The Development of Criminology in Britain: 1948–1960', *op. cit.*, 173.

156 Roger Hood talked about 'a programme of research: for which permanent posts would need to be established to ensure academic freedom so that a research agenda could be negotiated with, and not dictated, by the Home Office or other funders'. He continued, 'For while he insisted on academic independence he was a pragmatist and knew that the most likely source of funds at that time would come from government and that access to individuals, public institutions, and the records of those caught up in the criminal justice system, could only be obtained if those in charge had confidence in the researchers and their academic integrity. That is why he did not seek to insulate the Institute from the Home Office and instead tried to make the Institute recipro-cally of value to the criminal justice system by including in his plans a short biennial course for senior criminal justice practitioners. This would inevitably lead to charges

in the early years of the Institute's existence of too close a collaboration, of official interference in academic freedom, and compliance of its staff with authority rather than being social critics of official policies. ...' R. Hood; 'Founder and Commander: Sir Leon Radzinowicz and the Launch of the Institute', presented at the Conference 'Challenging Crime' to celebrate 50 years of the Institute of Criminology, Cambridge, 24 September 2009, 6.

157   One former senior official told me that Sir Leon had been a 'very difficult man who had taken up a lot' of his time, a 'man of considerable power and personality', who had always gone 'direct to the top' of the Home Office, and had even been successful in securing the removal of one of the heads of the Research Unit.

158   J. Martin (1962); *Offenders as Employees: An Enquiry by the Cambridge Institute of Criminology*, London: Macmillan.

159   R. Hauser (1962); *The Homosexual Society*; London: Bodley Head.

160   F. McClintock (1963); *Crimes of Violence: An Enquiry by the Cambridge Institute of Criminology into Crimes of Violence against the Person in London*, Oxford: Oxford University Press.

161   F. McClintock and E. Gibson (1961); *Robbery in London: An Enquiry by the Cambridge Institute of Criminology*, London: Macmillan.

162   D. West; *The Habitual Prisoner: An Enquiry by the Cambridge Institute of Criminology*, London: Macmillan, 1963.

163   Quoted by R.A. Butler (1974) in 'The Foundation of the Institute of Criminology in Cambridge', in R. Hood (ed.) Crime, Criminology and Public Policy, *op. cit.*, 6.

164   *The Need for Criminology and a Proposal for an Institute of Criminology: Report* by Professor Leon Radzinowicz Wolfson Professor of Criminology University of Cambridge, *op. cit.*, 68–69. By the twenty-first century, the Advisory Council had been discontinued. Current staff at the Institute did not know quite when it was disestablished.

165   David Faulkner joined the Home Office in 1959 as an Assistant Principal; was Private Secretary to the Parliamentary Undersecretary of State between 1961 and 1963; was Private Secretary to the Home Secretary, 1969–70; Assistant Secretary, Prison Dept, 1970; Establishment Department, 1974; Police Department, 1976; Assistant Undersecretary of State, 1976; Undersecretary, Cabinet Office, 1978–80; Home Office; Assistant Undersecretary; of State; Director of Operational Policy, Prison Department, 1980–82; Deputy Undersecretary of State, 1982; Head of Criminal and Research and Statistical Departments, 1982–90; Principal Establishment Officer, 1990–92 (.http://www.ukwhoswho.com.gate2.library.lse.ac.uk/view/article/oupww/whoswho/U15527/FAULKNER_David_Ewart_Riley?index=1&results=QuicksearchResults&query=0)

166   'British Criminology before 1935', *British Journal of Criminology*, 28, 2, 7.

167   See I. Loader and R. Sparks; *Public Criminology?, op. cit.*

168   Hermann Mannheim talked of 'the dominant position held at present by American [sociological] criminology'. *Comparative Criminology, op. cit.*, x; and see J.P. Martin; 'The Development of Criminology in Britain: 1948–1960', *op. cit.*, 165–174. American criminology had diverse roots in penology, genetics, police management and studies of the the social organisation of crime, particularly at the University of Chicago in the 1920s and 1930s, and the University of Indiana in the 1940s and 1950s. One segment of criminology was to be institutionalised in the formation of the American Society of Criminology, whose birth has been traced to the meeting held in California in 1941 of a group of seven men teaching college courses in Police Science and Administration. Its first President was to be Orlando W. Wilson, Professor of Police Administration and Director of the Bureau of Criminology, University California, Berkeley (see A. Morris (1975); 'The American Society of Criminology: A History, 1941–1974'., *Criminology*, 123–167). Far more influential for the Young Turks in Britain were to

be the more avowedly sociological criminologists such as Edwin Lemert, David Matza and Howard Becker, and the journal and organisation with which *they* were associated: *Social Problems* and the Society for the Study of Social Problems ('the triple SP') that had been established in 1951.

169 Although they did not care for the term, labelling theory was to be linked with two American sociologists in particular. Edwin Lemert wrote about 'primary' and 'secondary' deviation, the one being 'mere' rule-breaking, the other the social behaviour that is shaped by reactions to the social response evoked by that rule-breaking (E. Lemert (1951); *Social Pathology*, New York: McGraw-Hill). Howard Becker wrote about how it was not deviance but the social organisation of the response to deviance which was primarily consequential in generating deviance and deviant roles (H. Becker (1963); *Outsiders*, New York: Free Press). The construction and application of deviant and criminal identities then became an object of inquiry in their own right. One of the first signs of the importation of labelling theory into England and Wales was the occasional publication in *The British Journal of Criminology* of papers by its American exponents. For example, in the midst of a number of highly positivistic articles on 'The Ganser Syndrome', 'The Incidence of a Criminal Record in 1,000 Consecutive 'Alcoholics'' and 'Views on 'Psychiatry and Approved Schools'' in the 1965 volume, there may be found Richard Quinney's 'Is Criminal Behaviour Deviant Behaviour?' (132–142). Quinney opened by asserting that 'The criminologist in his research usually proceeds on the premise that the criminal law embodies important social norms and that these norms are held by most persons in society. While these assumptions are rarely questioned in most studies of criminal behaviour, a few criminologists have nevertheless recognised that the relationship between the criminal law and social norms is problematic' (132). Labelling theory met with a cold reception at first. Barbara Wootton was scathing about it in her *Social Science and Social Pathology*, and Leon Radzinowicz took me aside to remark that it was a passing fad. It was to be the young Turks, Jock Young (1971); in *The Drugtakers*, London: MacGibbon and Kee, and Stan Cohen (1972); in *Folk Devils and Moral Panics*, London: MacGibbon and Kee, who were successfully to launch it in the United Kingdom.

170 Indications of what was beginning to emerge may be found in the proceedings of the 1971 British Sociological Association annual conference that were published as P. Rock and M. McIntosh (editors) (1974); *Deviance and Social Control*, London: Tavistock.

171 And, above all, the argument that was floated by Robert Merton (1938); in 'Social Structure and Anomie'. *American Sociological Review*, Vol. 3, No.5, 672–682 and then elaborated in his *Social Theory and Social Structure* (1957); Glencoe, Ill,: Free Press. Anomie theory was subsequently taken up and developed by the American criminologists, Richard Cloward and Lloyd Ohlin (1961); in *Delinquency and Opportunity*, London: Routledge and Kegan Paul.

172 Although David Downes (1966) was to question how marked the contradictions were in English society, and how, in a class-bound society, people did actually aspire uniformly to succeed in terms defined solely by monetary acquisition. See *The Delinquent Solution*, London: Routledge and Kegan Paul.

173 J. Martin (1988); 'The Development of Criminology in Britain 1948–60', *The British Journal of Criminology*, Vol. 28, No. 2, 172.

174 'Girls', she said, 'have the same parents as their brothers, and run the same risk of family breakdown. Yet at all ages males commit more than eight times as many crimes as females, and at the peak ages the rate is eleven times greater. … The simple truth is that far and away the most significant influences in the criminality of certain social groups are to be found in the conventions which govern masculine, and especially young masculine, behaviour'. B. Wootton (May 1959); *Contemporary Trends in Crime and its Treatment*, The Nineteenth Clarke Hall Lecture, The Rt Hon The Lord Pakenham in the Chair, 14–15.

175 *Ibid*, 10.
176 I shall show, for instance, how, in deliberations about abortion law reform, some ministers were wont to shift into taking strong moralising stances. Rather later, and more generally, it was to be the complaint of the staff of the Home Office Research Unit and outside researchers that their work was frequently disregarded by politicians (see T. Hope (2004); 'Pretend it Works: Evidence and Governance in the Evaluation of the Reducing Burglary Initiative', *Criminal Justice*, 4, 287–308). Home Office Research Unit staff would routinely take digests of information about victims and victimisation to the interdepartmental Victims Steering Group in the 1980s and 1990s, only, in their judgement, to be ignored (see P. Rock (2004); *Constructing Victims' Rights*, Oxford: Clarendon).
177 B. Wootton (1967); *In a World I Never Made: Autobiographical Reflections*, London: George Allen and Unwin, 214.
178 It could not be otherwise. Jack Douglas has made the claim that all social scientific reasoning is ultimately embedded in the common sense of everyday life. See his introduction to J. Douglas (ed.) (1971); *Understanding Everyday Life*, London: Routledge and Kegan Paul.
179 One interesting example is the interim report on crime and punishment produced by the Conservative Policy Group on Crime on 14 July 1965. It opened quite emphatically in paragraph 9 with the statement that 'Crime is a moral issue. It is concerned with the difference between right and wrong in an area which the State considers that difference to be of sufficient importance and relevance to interest itself in. No analysis of social or psychological causes of crime and no policy for dealing with it should be allowed to obscure this basic fact'. But it then proceeded in other paragraphs, and in paragraph 12 in particular, to rehearse a complex criminological argument based on anomie theory. A core statement reflects that 'The growing emphasis on equal opportunity for success, has created in our society for many people, higher aspirations than can be realised. "Getting on" is an accepted and approved goal for individuals, but the cost of this "achievement-orientation" is that individuals, in seeking to get on, reduce their loyalties to the groups and communities in which they have lived and make light of their commitments, in order to adjust to new relationships and to make new, materially advantageous, but more superficial, social contacts. As this occurs, an important support of the moral order – namely personal obligation – is lost. Equally, the emphasis on achievement creates for many a demand to get on by any means whatever and this in itself may well induce criminal response in order to command the goods, goals, and privileges which attainment of higher social status confers. Finally, this same disposition leads to a strong and widely diffused sense of discontent and frustration, for not all who are induced to want to get on will in fact succeed in doing so. For them the system may appear 'bogus', and they may feel more anger at this state of affairs than do men in a society where opportunities are fewer and the emphasis on achievement lower'. ACP (65) 12: PG/3/65/32 Conservative Party Archives at the Bodleian Library.
180 His obituary in *The Times* of 4 May 2010 said that '"Antony Grey" was a pseudonym that he assumed in 1962 when there were real dangers of police attention for any campaigner for gay rights. His actual name was Edgar Wright'.
181 See J. Campbell (2014); *A Well-Rounded Life*, London: Jonathan Cape, 33.
182 R. Jenkins (1959); *The Labour Case*, Mddx: A Penguin Special, 136.
183 And that is in some contrast to Dario Melossi's depiction of the period. D. Melossi (2008); *Controlling Crime, Controlling Society*, Cambridge: Polity Press, 6–7.
184 I. Taylor, P. Walton and J. Young (1973); *The New Criminology*, London: Routledge and Kegan Paul, 168.
185 There were 29 universities in England and Wales in 1950. Eight universities were founded in the 1950s; and fourteen in the 1960s. Undergraduate numbers doubled during the 1960s, and staff numbers followed in their train.

186 Minutes of the 844th meeting of the Executive Committee, 15 September 1966.
187 C. Walston (ed.) (2009); *Challenging Crime: A Portrait of the Cambridge Institute of Criminology*, London: Third Millennium Publishing, 22.
188 D. Downes (1988); 'The Sociology of Crime and Social Control in Britain, 1960–1987', *The British Journal of Criminology*, Vol. 28, No. 2, 177.
189 S. Cohen (1971); introduction to *Images of Deviance*, Harmondsworth: Penguin, 15.
190 L. Radzinowicz; *The Cambridge Institute of Criminology: Its Background and Scope, op. cit.*, 115. For a slightly fuller account, see S. Cohen (1981); 'Footprints in the Sand: A Further Report on Criminology and the Sociology of Deviance in Britain', in M. Fitzgerald, G. McLennan and J. Pawson (eds.) *Crime and Society: Readings in History and Theory*, London: Routledge.
191 L. Radzinowicz (1999); *Adventures in Criminology*, London: Routledge, 229.
192 Sir Brian Cubbon, a former Permanent Undersecretary, expressed his unhappiness about the response of academic criminologists to the accomplishments of the Home Office Research Unit at the Witness Seminar on Home Office Organisation of 2 July 2010.
193 Mike Hough wrote about how the new deviancy theorists had 'othered' him and his colleagues as 'administrative criminologists' leading to their stigmatisation in the eyes of the so-called radical criminologists. They 'acquired', he said, 'other connotations, most of them unflattering: unimaginative, atheoretical, politically suborned and corrupted by the pressures of grantsmanship'. He added 'We were reluctant civil servants, and viewed HORU as a body that was at one step removed from the Home Office. Taylor, Walton and Young's (1973) book The New Criminology was for most of us a seminal work. We admired the work of the National Deviancy Conference (NDC) criminologists, and adopted an ambiguous stance towards their criticisms'. ('Confessions of a recovering 'administrative criminologist', *op. cit.*, 216, 217). And see his description of the relations between the two wings of criminology as they revolved around their reception of the first British Crime Survey: Hough, M. (2018); 'The discovery of fear of crime in the UK,' in M. Lee and G. Mythen (eds.) *The Routledge International Handbook on Fear of Crime*, Milton Park: Routledge.
194 R. Clarke; 'The Home Office Research Unit – an insider's view', *op. cit.*
195 Indeed, by 1981, when the phrase 'nothing works' had come into currency, John Croft, the former head of the Home Office Research Unit, confessed that 'It is doubtful whether criminological research can solve problems. ... The positivist approach which informed much criminological research in the middle of this century was not of itself wrong, in the sense of being unscientific. Expectations were too high and the available techniques and skills were often applied to unsuitable issues. There was a mismatch between the expectations of those who commissioned research, the objectives of the investigations themselves, and the available technology. In these circumstances, it has been difficult to maintain the credibility of criminological research – at least, as an aid to policy formation – through almost three decades'. *Managing Criminological Research, op. cit.*, 3.
196 It was a widespread anxiety. For a review of the very comparable position in Scotland, see J. Shields and J. Duncan (1964); *The State of Crime in Scotland*, London: Tavistock.
197 Barbara Wootton remarked that 'The common practice of quoting records of indictable offences as indicative of trends in serious crime is far from satisfactory'. *Contemporary Trends in Crime and its Treatment*, The Nineteenth Clarke Hall Lecture, May 1959, 6. She said elsewhere 'that we should reject the official criminal statistics as evidence of criminal trends is hard doctrine, because it means that we must be content to confess ourselves quite ignorant as to whether our population is become more, or less, addicted to crime. Nevertheless, such ignorance has to be admitted'; *Social Science and Social Pathology*, London: George Allen & Unwin, 25.
198 *Causes of Crime, op. cit.*, 117.

199 *Crime: A Challenge to Us All*, Labour Party, London, 1964.

200 Study Group on Crime Prevention and Penal Reform: Preliminary Outline for Report, RD727/March 1964, The Labour Party Archive in the People's History Museum, Manchester.

201 *Developments in Penal Practice (England And Wales)*, draft, C.(65) 107.

202 For a statement of how the statistics were viewed from the Home Office Research Unit at the time, see the paper presented by Leslie Wilkins to the Royal Statistical Society Conference on Social Statistics, April 1962, and published as L. Wilkins (1963); 'The Measurement of Crime', *British Journal of Criminology*, Vol. 3, No. 4, 321–341.

203 'Problem of Counting Criminals', *The Times*, 12 August 1963.

204 Derek McClintock observed in his study of violence in London: 'it would appear that the discussions which take place are often based upon two important and unproved assumptions which, if acted upon, might result in the development of an erroneous penal policy. The first assumption is that all crimes of violence are automatically reported to the police and recorded by them and consequently any increase in the statistical trend in crimes of violence is taken to indicate that an *absolute* or *real* increase has occurred. The second assumption is that all, or at least the vast majority of, crimes of violence recorded by the police result in a detection and a conviction ... However, an examination of data collected in the course of the present enquiry showed that neither of these assumptions is in fact true. ...' *Crimes of Violence: An Enquiry by the Cambridge Institute of Criminology into Crimes of Violence against the Person in London*, *op. cit.*, 58.

205 See the remarks of Sir Peter Rawlinson in the House of Commons debate on crime of 2 February, 1966.

206 I use the word 'so-called' because the very idea of a pool of hidden but inherently unambiguous crimes is problematic. It is part of the work of victims, witnesses, police dispatchers, police officers, prosecutors, judges and juries to give definition to what are often, at least initially, shapeless and ill-resolved processes. See P. Waddington (1993); *Calling the Police: The Interpretation of, and Response to, Calls for Assistance from the Public*, Aldershot: Avebury.

207 See T. Sellin (1938); 'The Basis of a Crime Index', *Journal of Criminal Law and Criminology*, Vol. XXII, 333–356; and A. Biderman and A Reiss (1967); 'On Exploring the "Dark Figure" of Crime', *The Annals of the American Academy of Political and Social Science*, Vol. 374, No. 1, 1–15.

208 Note by the Secretary, Criminal Statistics, 25 July 1956, CHP/MISC/5.

209 See T. Lodge; 'The Founding of the Home Office Research Unit', *op. cit.*, 20.

210 Wilfred Perks, F.I.A., 1902–1970, was actuary of the Pearl Assurance Co., and was regarded by one of his colleagues as 'probably the best authority in the country on industrial life assurance' (F. M. Redington (1970); 'Memoirs', *Journal of the Institute of Actuaries*, 277).

211 HO291/117 7 Perks Committee Papers for Full Committee.

212 T. Sellin and M. Wolfgang (1964); *The Measurement of Delinquency*, New York: John Wiley.

213 See, for instance, H. von Hentig (1940); 'Remarks on the Interaction of Perpetrator and Victim', *Journal of Criminal Law and Criminology*, 31, 303–9.

214 Leslie Wilkins, 1915–2000, was elected a Fellow of the Royal Statistical Society and joined the Government Social Survey in 1946. In 1955, he was to publish with Hermann Mannheim an acclaimed study predicting borstal reconviction rates, the first of the Home Office research reports (L. Wilkins and H. Mannheim (1955); *Prediction Methods in Relation to Borstal Training*, HMSO: London). He left the Home Office nine years later after a *contretemps* following disclosure of his advice about the proper treatment of illegal drug abusers, joining the United Nations in Tokyo in 1966, being

appointed to a chair at the University of California at Berkeley in 1966, and then becoming dean of the school of criminal justice at the State University of New York, Albany, in 1969. (Based on the entry by Ken Pease in *The Oxford Dictionary of National Biography*, http://217.169.56.135/view/article/74314.)

215 Material in this paragraph has been based on HO 307/45 The Commission-Co-ordination with the Home Office – Statistics; Departmental Committee on Criminal Statistics: Summary of Evidence – Note by Secretaries.

216 Cmnd. 3448 (1967*)*.

217 Indeed, such a study was to be not at all practicable until much later when the introduction of complementary, contrasting surveys, based on a very different meth-odology, furnished some check against which the patterns, trends and constituents of recorded crime could be matched. The idea of adding more complexity to the analysis of crime data met some initial opposition from the Home Office and the Institute of Criminology (see M. de Castelbajac (2014); 'Brooding Over the Dark Figure of Crime', *British Journal of Criminology*, 54(5), 928–945. First there was to be the pioneering victimological work of Sparks, Genn and Dodd (R. Sparks, H. Genn and D. Dodd (1977); *Surveying Victims: A Study of the Measurement of Criminal Victimization, Perceptions of Crime, and Attitudes to Criminal Justice*, Chichester: Wiley) which surveyed three groups of Londoners in the early 1970s. They reported on p. 232 that 'When the project discussed in this book was first mooted, about six years ago, it was vehemently opposed by an eminent Polish criminologist who argued that the English criminal justice system had enough of a problem with its recorded crimes; it did not need to know – indeed it could not afford to find out – about crimes which were not recorded'. It was to be followed by the much larger Home Office *British Crime Survey* which was intended to 'improve the criminal justice data base', (See http://rds.homeoffice.gov.uk/rds/bcs1.html and http://rds.homeoffice.gov.uk/rds/pdfs07/bcs25.pdf) and which questioned a population of 11,000 people about their experience of victimisation in 1982, a survey which was to be repeated, elaborated and expanded at regular intervals thereafter, increasing to over 50,000 interviews from 2004–05. Then there was the Home Office *Offending, Crime and Justice Survey*, which questioned a population of 12,000 people about their offending in 2003, a survey which was repeated thereafter (see http://rds.homeoffice.gov.uk/rds/offending_survey.html).

Those two surveys were capable at last of producing estimates (albeit contrasting estimates) of the dark figure (I use the word 'estimate' because the original crime survey excluded some offences and some respondents – for example, the homeless and children under the age of 16). The first *Offending, Crime and Justice Survey* disclosed that 'it is clear that the C&JS gives a far higher estimate of the number of offenders than statistics from the criminal justice system. There were around 400,000 cautions or convictions in 2002 for the types of offence covered in the C&JS, compared with the 3.8 million estimate from the C&JS'. (T. Budd, C. Sharp and P. Mayhew (2005); *Offending in England and Wales: First results from the 2003 Crime and Justice Survey*, Home Office Research Study 275, London: Home Office Research, Development and Statistics Directorate, 21.) And the authors of the first British Crime Survey wrote:

'The summary report presented data about the extent of crime revealed by the survey, comparing, for those offence categories where it was possible, BCS esti-mates for 1981 with statistics recorded by the police. The survey indicated that there were around four times more offences of property loss and damage than in official statistics and around five times as many offences of violence'. (P. Mayhew and M. Hough (1983); 'The British Crime Survey', *The British Journal of Criminology*, Vol. 23, No. 4, 395).

218 *Review of Crime Statistics: A Discussion Document*, London: Home Office, July 2000, 7.

219 Max Grünhut, 1893–1964, was born in Germany and worked at the University of Bonn, where he taught and wrote about criminal jurisprudence until 1933, when he was dismissed from his post under the so-called 'Aryan clause' of German civil service law. He left Germany in early 1939 and was eventually admitted to All Souls College, becoming the first lecturer in criminology at Oxford in October 1947. He was to retire from his post in 1960. (Based on Roger Hood's entry in *The Oxford Dictionary of National Biography*, http://217.169.56.135/view/article/64539)

220 See R. Hood, 'Hermann Mannheim and Max Grünhut', *op. cit.*

221 G. Rose (1960); 'Criminology and Penology: Three Views', *The Howard Journal*, Vol. X, No. 3, 216.

222 *A Man Without Loyalties*, *op. cit.*, 97–98.

223 'Crime and Society', a speech to a regional conference of the Labour Party on 12 September 1966.

224 From transcript of *This Week*, Rediffusion Television, 17 February 1966.

225 Howard Jones remarked on the first page of his *Crime and the Penal System*, *op. cit.*, that 'it has been able so far to establish no scientific laws that can claim general validity'.

226 A. Oakley; unpublished typescript, Chapter 14, 326.

227 B. Wootton; *Social Science and Social Pathology*, *op. cit.*, 326. Offenders, she said, are likely to come from poor, large, discordant or broken criminal families; they are unlikely to be churchgoers; and they are prone to play truant from school. 'And beyond this we cannot go' (135).

228 See I. Loader and R. Sparks *Public Criminology?*, *op. cit*,

229 L. Zedner (2003); 'Useful Knowledge? Criminology in Post-war Britain', in L. Zedner and A. Ashworth (eds.) *The Criminological Foundations of Penal Policy*, *op. cit.*, 197–8.

230 Ian Loader claimed that 'the express and implied view [was] that untutored public sentiment towards crime is a dangerous thing – an object to be monitored and contained, steered down appropriate paths, taken on and argued with where necessary (most obviously, in this period, during the campaign to abolish capital punishment) but not to be followed, still less given governmental endorsement and expression'. 'Fall of the 'Platonic Guardians', *op. cit.*, 568.

231 S. Stevenson; 'The Butler Years', *op. cit.*, 135.

232 R. Jenkins; *A Life at the Centre*, *op. cit.*, 181.

233 Note by Sir Charles Cunningham for Discussion on Crime, The Rising Incidence of Crime, 10 May 1961, CRI60 431/5/92.

234 There were four political administrations in and about the 1960s: that of the Conservative prime minister, Harold Macmillan, from October 1959 to October 1964; those of the Labour prime minister, Harold Wilson, from October 1964 to March 1966, and again from March 1966 to June 1970; and that of Edward Heath, the Conservative prime minister, from 18 June 1970. Home Secretaries changed post largely in step with those changes in government: R.A. Butler from 14 January 1957 until 13 July 1962; Henry Brooke from 14 July 1962 until 16 October 1964; Sir Frank Soskice from 18 October 1964 until 23 December 1965; Roy Jenkins from 23 December 1965 until 30 November 1967; and James Callaghan from 30 November 1967 until 19 June 1970.

235 http://www.ndad.nationalarchives.gov.uk/AH/2/detail.html

236 J. Pellew (1982); *The Home Office*, London: Heinemann, 2.

237 See F. Newsam (1954); *The Home Office*, London: Allen and Unwin.

238 Civil defence was actually to play a major role in the work of the Home Office for some considerable time. See M. Smith (2010); 'Planning for the Last Time: Government Science, Civil Defence and the Public, 1945–68', PhD dissertation, University of Manchester.

239 The items that follow are based on Annex A of a paper presented by R.M. ['Bob'] Morris on 'The Home Office 1961–1997' at the CCBH Witness Seminar of 2 July 2010.

240 What follows is based upon *The British Imperial Calendar and Civil Service List 1965, op. cit.*

241 Sir Frank Soskice, 1902–1979, was called to the bar in 1926, becoming a Q.C. in 1945. He entered Parliament as Labour MP for East Birkenhead in 1945, and the prime minister, Clement Attlee, made him solicitor general that year. When the constituency of East Birkenhead was abolished in 1950, he became Member of Parliament for Sheffield Neepsend and, when that constituency too was abolished, he won a by-election at Newport, Monmouthshire, which he continued to represent until 1966. He was Home Secretary from October 1964-December 1965. (Based on the entry by Robert Pearce in *The Oxford Dictionary of National Biography*, http://217.169.56.135/view/article/31703)

242 G.J. Otton was to become deputy secretary at the Department of Health and Social Security in the 1970s.

243 Ralph Shuffrey graduated from Balliol College, Oxford, in 1947. He was to be awarded the CB and CVO, becoming a Home Office Deputy Undersecretary of State.

244 One illustrative case was that of Bob Morris who was an assistant private secretary to Frank Soskice at the age of 27, and whose Home Office career ended in 1997. His criminal justice relevant jobs were:

1962–3	C1 Division, Criminal Department
	General and prerogative casework including Prison Commission, life and capital cases.
1964–66	APS to Home Secretary
1971–73	F1 Division
	Financial and controls for Metropolitan Police, appointments of senior officers in E and W London. (Also Secretary to Compton Inquiry into complaints of Northern Ireland detainees following internment operation 9.8.71)
1973–6	Prison Dept
	Dept of Industries and Supply (industries and new prisons); P3 – adult sentenced male prisoners (Cat As, medical, force feeding etc.)
1976–8	Principal PS to Home Secretary
1978–9	Secretary to UK Prisons Inquiry (May Committee)
1979–81	Head Crime Police Planning Unit
1981–3	F2 Division – Reception of RCCP, police complaints, PACE No 1 Bill
1991–6	Criminal Justice and Constitutional Department – included Magistrates' courts, control of drugs, probation service

245 Alice Bacon, 1909–1993, became Labour MP for the north-east Leeds constituency in 1945; representing it until 1955 when constituency reorganisation led her to become MP for south-east Leeds until 1970. In 1957 she introduced an unsuccessful bill against capital punishment. She was to be Minister of State at the Home Office from 1964 to 1967 and then Minister of State for Education and Science from 1967 to 1970. (Based on C.M.P. Taylor's entry in *The Oxford Dictionary of National Biography*, http://217.169.56.135/view/article/51420).

246 Victor Collins, Lord Stonham, 1903–1971, was elected at the 1945 general election as the Labour Member of Parliament for Taunton, Somerset, a seat which he lost in 1950. He returned to parliament in a by-election in 1954, when he was elected as MP for Shoreditch and Finsbury. He was made a life peer in August 1958 as Baron Stonham. In Harold Wilson's Labour Government, 1964–1970, he served as a junior minister at the Home Office from 1964 to 1967, and as Minister of State in the Home Office until 1969. (Based on http://en.wikipedia.org/wiki/Victor_Collins,_Baron_Stonham)

247 George Thomas, 1909–1997, was first elected to Parliament as Labour MP for Cardiff Central in 1945. He became a junior minister first in the Home Office (1964–6) and

then in the Welsh Office; a Minister of State at the Commonwealth Office between 1967 and 1968; Secretary of State for Wales 1968–70; Deputy Speaker and, finally, Speaker of the House of Commons in February 1976. (Based on entry by Michael White in *The Oxford Dictionary of National Biography*, http://217.169.56.135/view/article/68815?docPos=3)

248 See, for example, C. Emsley (1991); *The English Police: A Political and Social History*, London: Longman.

249 See the article titled "No Retreat' from Police Mergers', *The Times*, 21 May 1966.

250 See B. Whitaker (1964); *The Police, op. cit.*, 55.

251 In 1965, the recorded strength of male police officers in England and Wales was 80,428 and of female officers, 2,868, up from 77,828 and 2,654 in 1964 (Central Statistical Office (1966); *Annual Abstract of Statistics No. 103 1966*, London: HMSO, 64).

252 *Report of the Commissioner of Police of the Metropolis for the year 1965*, London: HMSO, 1966.

253 http://rds.homeoffice.gov.uk/rds/pdfs/40years.pdf

254 B. Whitaker (1964); *The Police, op. cit.*, 54–55.

255 And, in that, it was on all fours with the wider conversation about 'modernisation' which was current in the 1960s. *Look Forward*, a pamphlet issued by the Labour Party in 1961, announced on p. 3 that 'The central feature of our postwar capitalist society is the scientific revolution. Both its pace and its extent are beyond the dream of previous generations. New discoveries and inventions now produce upheavals in five or ten years which previously took a century to complete'. And the 1964 Labour Party election manifesto opened with the statement: A New Britain – mobilising the resources of technology under a national plan; harnessing our national wealth in brains, our genius for scientific invention and medical discovery; reversing the decline of the thirteen wasted years; affording a new opportunity to equal, and if possible surpass, the roaring progress of other western powers …' And see http://www2.labour.org.uk/history_of_the_labour_party2.

256 1965, Alice Bacon claimed, 'was a record year for manpower since the end of the war' (House of Commons debate, 2 February 1966).

257 Roy Jenkins recalled that he had been engaged as Home Secretary with 'the preparation, presentation and defence of a major scheme of police reorganisation'. *A Life at the Centre, op. cit.*, 187.

258 R.A. Butler observed that 'the measure which I would put first in our fight against crime is the strengthening of the Police Force through the introduction of considerable improvements in their pay and conditions, and I hope that it will not be long before the effects of these reforms are seen'. Letter to C.J. Eastwood, 19 June 1961.

259 Lord Allen recollected that 'Roy [Jenkins], perhaps encouraged by his experiences at Bletchley Park, took a keen interest in the developments which were going on in the United States in the use of computers; and later set in train research projects which in due course led to the provision of the police national computer'. (P. Allen; 'A Young Home Secretary', *op. cit.*, 66). The first police computer to be used by the Metropolitan Police, an ICT 1301, was installed in the office of the Receiver for use on pay and crime statistics in 1963.

260 Lord Jellico thought it might be useful to introduce 'a short paragraph … on the initiative which the Home Office is taking regarding [police] equipment – standardisation, modern wireless, etc'. (White Paper on Developments in Penal Practice: Lord Jellico to S. of S., 26 September 1963, CRI61 15/1/5). Some two years later, Alice Bacon was able to inform the House of Commons on 2 February 1966 that 'Three years ago, expenditure on communications equipment, such as radios, was just over £500,000. By next year we shall spend nearly twice as much as that. In the same period, 10,000

more wireless sets will be in use and an additional £300,000 worth of equipment. At present 28 police forces have personal radios and in three months an extra 60 forces will get them'.

261 R. Jenkins; 'Crime and Society', in *Essays and Speeches*, London: Collins, 245.

262 See P. Rock (1973); *Making People Pay*, London: Routledge and Kegan Paul.

263 Figures are taken from *Report on the Work of the Prison Department 1965: Statistical Tables*, Cmnd. 3304, London: HMSO, 1966.

264 It was the special problem of the young offender that again received attention. The Department's report for the year 1965 noted that 'Amongst boys committed to borstals and detention centres the proportion of the criminally sophisticated, the feckless and inadequate and the mentally disturbed continue to increase. The record of further offences by boys released from these establishments suggests that from half to two-thirds of them are likely to be re-convicted within three years ...' The governor of a closed borstal was reported to have said that '1965 saw a crop of feckless and inadequate youths, most of whom had run the gamut of all the social agencies set up by the Criminal Justice Act 1948 to deal with the young offender. Traditional standards of morality, if ever implanted, had long since been abandoned by most of these youngsters, and 'the most difficult children of the State' nowadays show a lack of responsibility which is one of the most alarming features of late 20th century material-ism'. (*Report on the Work of the Prison Department 1965, op. cit.*, Chapter 1, para. 10, Chapter 4, para. 2).

265 Draft paragraph for *White Paper on Penal Practice*, October 1963, CRI 61 15/1/5; HO 291/516.

266 http://rds.homeoffice.gov.uk/rds/pdfs/40years.pdf

267 In correspondence touching on possible liaison between the aborted Royal Commission on the Penal System and the Home Office, it was remarked that 'Dr. Hammond [of the Research Unit] ... proposed a central record system covering an offender's ante-cedents, sentence and subsequent career. The records were to be maintained on a computer at Statistical Branch and compiled from particulars produced for courts by the police, probation officers and other agencies ... He envisaged that when a suf-ficient store of information had been built up, the computer would be able to produce lists of previous convictions and similar information very rapidly'. HO 307/45 The Commission-Co-ordination with the Home Office – Statistics – 5 July 1965.

268 Speech to New Bridge AGM, 22 February 1960 (CRI 15/1/81) And see A. Bottoms and S. Stevenson; 'What Went Wrong?': Criminal Justice Policy in England and Wales, 1945–70', *op. cit.*

269 Letter to Sir Eric Edwards, 12 January 1962, Conservative Party Archives at the Bodleian Library ACP (65) 12 PG/3/65/32.

270 See J. Meyer and W. Scott (1983); *Organizational environments: Ritual and rationality*, Beverley Hills: Sage.

271 Gordon Rose was Reader in Social Administration at the University of Manchester and the author of a number of works in criminology, including *The Struggle for Penal Reform: The Howard League and its Predecessors*, London: Stevens, 1961 and *Schools for Young Offenders*, London: Tavistock Publications,1967.

272 'Notes: The War Against Crime in England and Wales, 1959–1964', *British Journal of Criminology*, (1964); Vol. 4, No. 6, 606.

273 CRI2/7/36.

274 This pessimism looks like an early recognition of what Felson would later call the 'cops-and-courts fallacy', an acknowledgement that the criminal justice system alone could do little to shape the volume of crime. See M. Felson (2002); *Crime and Everyday Life*, London: Sage.

275 His larger observation was 'there are different ways of describing this, aren't there? On the one hand, you can say, this is activity rather than action you know. One the

other hand, you could say, you do what you can. And I can remember Soskice being very positive about re-equipping the police and equipping them with personal radios. I can remember very clearly. … I mean it was obvious [that there were] advantages of trying to improve the ability of the police to respond … you can't work five minutes in the Home Office and imagine you can change the world you know. And I wouldn't describe it as pessimism. I mean it's, it's realism about … what is happening. The greatest problems for Home Secretaries is how to represent some kind of intelligent community response to very complex social phenomena which are always changing and whose values and direction you cannot entirely grasp at the time you know. And you have to respond in ways which register politically and which are as positive as far as you can make it'.

276 Note by Sir Charles Cunningham for Discussion on Crime: The Rising Incidence of Crime, 10 May 1961, CRI 60 431/5/92.

277 Jean Nunn, 1916–1982, joined the Home Office in 1938, becoming Private Secretary to the Permanent Under-Secretary of State in 1941; acting principal in 1942; Principal Private Secretary to two Home Secretaries, James Chuter Ede and Sir David Maxwell-Fyfe; Assistant Under-Secretary of State in charge of the Children's Department in 1961, before leaving to join the Cabinet Office where she eventually became Deputy Secretary. (Based on Lord Allen of Abbeydale's entry in the *Oxford Dictionary of National Biography*, http://217.169.56.135/view/article/66883)

278 Jean Nunn to CCC, 18 May 1961, CRI60 431/5/92.

279 See E. Hughes (1962); 'Good People and Dirty Work', *Social Problems*, Vol. X (1), 3–11.

280 See L. Sherman (1993); 'Defiance, Deterrence, and Irrelevance: A Theory of the Criminal Sanction', *Journal of Research in Crime and Delinquency*, Vol. 30, no. 4, 445–473.

281 Lord Windlesham; *Responses to Crime*, Vol. 2, *op. cit.*, 11.

282 Said at the CCBH Witness Seminar on Home Office Organisation, *op. cit.*

283 In R. Jenkins; *A Life at the Centre, op. cit.*, 181.

284 J. Callaghan (1983); 'Cumber and Variableness', *The Home Office: Perspectives on Policy and Administration*, London: Royal Institute of Public Administration, 15.

285 'Getting to Know Kenneth Clarke' *Insight: The Staff Magazine for the Ministry of Justice*, June 2010, 6.

286 See, for example, 'Bubble Reputations at the Home Office', *The Times*, 6 December 1965; I. Hardman; 'Amber Rudd is reminded of the Home Office's reputation as a political graveyard', *The Spectator*, 25 April 2018 (https://blogs.spectator.co.uk/2018/04/amber-rudd-is-reminded-of-the-home-offices-reputation-as-a-political-graveyard/); R. Brazier (1997); *Ministers of the Crown*, Oxford: Clarendon; 169; B. Gibson (2007); *The New Home Office: An Introduction*, Winchester: Waterside Press, 144.

287 See Chapter 2 of Vol. 2.

288 Policy Group on Crime – Interim Report: Crime and Punishment, 14 July 1965, Conservative Party Archives at the Bodleian Library, ACP (65) 12, PG/3/65/32.

289 See, for example, the reports in *The Times* newspaper titled 'Police Pen Youths On Brighton Beach' (20 April 1965); 'Easter Incidents: Two Gaoled' (5 May 1965); '6 Months' Imprisonment for Seaside Assault: Incidents at Brighton and Great Yarmouth' (8 June 1965); and 'Greater Use of Weapons by Rowdies, Police Say' (9 June 1965).

290 S. Cohen (1972); *Folk Devils and Moral Panics: The Creation of the Mods and Rockers*, London: MacGibbon and Kee.

291 See *The Times*, 16 October 1961 and 8 March 1962. Although allegations about a miscarriage of justice were eventually allayed for some by the results of an inquiry conducted by Lewis Hawser, Q.C., and reported in *The Times* on 11 April 1975, the case continued to prompt many misgivings over a long period. See, for example, the letter by Terence Morris in *The Times* of 6 May 1982.

292 See L. Kennedy (1961); *10 Rillington Place*, London: Gollancz. Following a report by Mr. Justice Brabin, commissioned by the Home Office in 1965, Evans was awarded a free posthumous pardon (see the statement by Roy Jenkins in the House of Commons, 18 October 1966).

293 See the *Report of the Commissioner of Police of the Metropolis for the Year 1965, op. cit.*, and various newspaper reports, for example, in *The Times*, on 19 March 1968 ('Police bitter about Vietnam demonstration').

294 See *The Times* Tuesday, 5 January 1960. The Royal Commission reported in May 1962 as Cmnd. 1728.

295 See *The Times* report ('Southend Chief Constable Guilty: Two-Year Sentence on 17 Charges') of 23 November 1965.

296 See *The Times*, 18 November 1963.

297 See the obituary for Harold Challenor that appeared in *The Guardian* newspaper, 18 September 2008. The Challenor case is described in greater detail in Vol. 2.

298 Sir Frank Soskice had written to the Prime Minister on 8 January 1965, 'There is bound to be some demand, when Parliament meets, for an increase in the penalties for possessing a firearm without a certificate when this is required. ...'

299 There was to be a spate of reports in the newspapers in 1965 about raids on banks, shops and post offices. One such report in *The Times* on 13 December 1965 talked about 'The many highly lucrative robberies of jewellery and plate in recent weeks must leave the public convinced that organised crime is gaining the upper hand. ... Criminals are now raiding a society which has so far been used to defending itself only against crimes organised as erratically as may be expected from a class not hitherto noted for its intelligence. ... 'Another, two days later, again in *The Times*, reported how a 'Gang Get £41,065 In Wages Raid'. Terence Morris held that the building of motorways had considerably enhanced the mobility and brazenness of criminals: 'Birmingham gangs in high-speed cars were now able to make hit-and-run raids on London, and vice versa, he said. ...' (*The Times*, 24 November 1965).

300 Emmanuel Shinwell, M.P., had asked Henry Brooke in the House of Commons on 16 April 1964 about 'the exceptional number of raids accompanied by violence and the use of lethal weapons – including guns – and the danger to the public as well as to those concerned, who work in banks and other establishments ...'

301 In 1963, there had been 103 indictable offences in which firearms were used in the Metropolitan Police District. In 1964, there had been 172 such offences. Outside London, there had been 425 incidents in 1961 and 559 in 1964. (Statement by Sir Frank Soskice in the House of Commons, 2 March 1965).

302 The Firearms Act 1965, c. 44, instituted increased penalties for the use of firearms in the furtherance of crime; greater powers of search, forfeiture and arrest for the police who suspect the presence of firearms; greater powers of regulation of firearms dealers, and the like.

303 The Home Secretary asked for a 'background note on arming the police' in January 1963 (POL1091/1/23 Arming of Police General Note for S of S); a request repeated by the Permanent Undersecretary in 1966 (POL1091/1/23 Arming of Police General Minutes 17.8.1966). The advice typically tendered was that 'Firearms have been used by the police during the last 20 years on only a small number of occasions. There have been other occasions on which firearms have been used against the police, but not in any foreseeable circumstances which would justify any modification of the present practice. There has never been any strong agitation in favour of modification of the present policy. From time to time it has been suggested that it is out of date, and this suggestion has always been revived on the occasion of any outrage against the police, such as the recent shooting at Shepherd's Bush but there is no evidence of any strong feeling of this kind. The Police Federation have from time to time re-affirmed their opposition to the general arming of the police. It is conceivable that they may now

wish to review this policy, but there is at present no evidence of any likelihood of a change of mind. Subject to this there is certainly no backing amongst those with the most experience of practical policing for any suggestion that arming the police would assist them to check armed robberies. The fact that order can be preserved – save in the very last resort – without the use of armed police is one of the essential characteristics of the British system'. (3 POL1091/1/23 Arming of Police General – circular 19 May 1965) This seemed to be the line generally taken: a note of a meeting with members of the Police Federation on 23 August 1966, contained in the same file, stated that: 'In discussing the situation, the members of the Police Federation were entirely reasonable, and made it clear that they had no fixed ideas. Generally, they seemed disposed to accept the existing arrangements ... and they did not think it would be administratively feasible to carry arms in C.I.D. vehicles as a general practice...'

304 The inquiry was to become known to *The Daily Telegraph*, which reported on 29 August 1966 that: 'POLICE CHIEFS LIKELY TO BACK GUNS PLAN WEAPONS WANTED IN CARS. A suggestion that the driver of every police car should be armed is likely to be approved next weekend at a meeting of a special committee of chief constables. The general feeling is that the weapon issued should be some sort of small arm, probably a revolver or automatic pistol. ... The committee['s] six members are known to be against issuing arms to every policeman'. A Home Office official reported that 'Mr Burrows [Chief Constable of Oxford City Police and Assistant General Secretary of the Association of Chief Police Officers] ... had said ... when I read over extracts to him, that it was not accurate. Chief officers of police had no thought of carrying arms in every police car ...' (POL1091/1/23 Arming of Police General Minutes 30.8.1966)

305 See reports in *The Times*, 13 August, 15 September and 6 December 1966.

306 It was recorded that 'Escapes by prisoners, and precautions taken to prevent the escape of others, attracted public attention during the year. A series of searching enquiries took place, locally and centrally into problems of security in prisons. The number of prisoners who escaped from secure conditions was 71'. *Report on the Work of the Prison Department 1965, op. cit.,* 2.

307 The Secretary of State was informed that 'The problem of high security risk prisoners was brought home to us in 1964 when Wilson, the train robber, escaped from Birmingham prison with outside help. It seemed to us, on a review, that there were now a number of factors which made it no longer possible, even with vigilance, to have any certainty of keeping particularly dangerous men inside...' (12 ETG 173/10/1 Reports: Radzinowicz Report: Report of the Advisory Council on the Penal System on the Regime for Long-Term Prisoners in Conditions of Maximum Security: G.W. Penn to S. of S., 27 May 1968)

308 See the report in *The Times*, Tuesday, 13 December 1966 which talked about how he had been serving a life sentence imposed in October 1958 for robbery with violence. The police were quoted as saying 'He is a dangerous man who will stop at nothing. He is not to be trifled with'. There were later reports about stirrings within the House of Commons to demand Roy Jenkins' resignation over the matter (*The Times*, 16 December 1966).

309 George Blake, who had been working as a double agent for MI6 and the KGB, was convicted of spying and sentenced to 42 years' imprisonment in March 1962. It was the longest fixed-term sentence of imprisonment ever awarded in an English criminal court. See T. Morris (1989); *Crime and Criminal Justice since 1945*, Basil Blackwell, Oxford, 129.

310 P. Allen (2004); 'A Young Home Secretary' in A. Adonis and K. Thomas (eds.) *Roy Jenkins: A Retrospective*, Oxford: Oxford University Press, 69.

311 An internal Home Office report into the escape of Biggs concluded that: 'The concerted action of the prisoners on this exercise to aid the escape of their fellows, despite

the punishment which will follow, emphasises the difficulty of allowing men whose security is top security to associate without risk. … Until the Albany special prison is built … we shall have to recognise that prisoners whose security is as vital as is that of the Train Robbers will have to be severely deprived of normal prison conditions and that the area of the prison in which they are contained will have to be heavily guarded …' (HO 278/10 IPE 100/1/15:1)

312 The escape gave rise to major consternation and, first, the appointment of Lord Mountbatten to review prison security and then the reversal of his recommendations by a group chaired by Leon Radzinowicz. See *Report of the Inquiry into Prison Escapes and Security by Admiral of the Fleet, Lord Mountbatten of Burma*, Cmnd. 3175, London: HMSO, 1966 and *The Regime for Long-Term Prisoners in Conditions of Maximum Security*, Report of the Advisory Council on the Penal System, London: HMSO, 1968. The detailed history of those inquiries and their ramifications will be discussed in a separate volume.

313 HC Deb 13 July 1965 Vol. 716 cc358–465.

314 ETG 173/10/1 Reports Radzinowiciz Report: Report of the Advisory Council on the Penal System on the Regime for Long-Term Prisoners in Conditions of Maximum Security: G.W. Penn to S. of S., 27 May 1968.

315 R. Jenkins; *A Life at the Centre, op. cit.*, 201.

316 *Howard League Annual Report 1966–67*, London: Howard League, 1967, 1.

317 The phrase was Michael Moriarty's and had been spoken at the CCBH Witness Seminar on Home Office Organisation on 2 July 2010. Moriarty had been Deputy Undersecretary at the Home Office from 1984–1990.

318 Lord Windlesham; *Responses to Crime, op. cit.*, 12.

319 See M. Weber (rep. 1978); *Economy and Society*, Berkeley: University of California Press.

320 Labour Party Archives in the People's History Museum, Manchester: RD727/March 1964 Study Group on Crime Prevention and Penal Reform; Preliminary Outline for [Longford] Report.

321 P. Rock (2010); 'Comment on 'Public Criminologies'', *Criminology & Public Policy*, Vol. 9, No. 4, 751–768.

322 And those were the papers which were most difficult to find in the archives.

323 Lord Allen recollected that 'Roy, with his clear ideas of what he wanted to do, lost no time in putting the wheels in motion in his new Office, only for those early days to be overshadowed by rows with Sir Charles Cunningham, the Permanent Undersecretary of State … There were arguments about some staff appointments and changes of organisation, but the main struggle took place over the form of policy submissions. It was Cunningham's practice to limit what was put to the Home Secretary to a beautifully written memorandum of his own composition. There were no background documents, there was no indication whether there were any differences of opinion within the Department, no contemplation that the Home Secretary might want to weigh up other possible courses. Although Cunningham fought hard, rather surprisingly so, to keep this system in defiance of Roy's wishes, in the end he had to give way, as he was bound to. But it did not make for harmony … 'Phillip Allen; 'A Young Home Secretary', *op. cit.*, 62–63.

324 R. Jenkins; *A Life at the Centre, op. cit.*, 182.

325 An official who worked in the Home Secretary's private office at the time observed that 'I don't think that's a fair account. I mean Roy Jenkins dramatised … [his] confrontation with Charles Cunningham … the problem with dealing with Roy Jenkins, who was a very gifted person, was his extraordinary vanity. … I mean the vanity which always meant that he was the hero of his own anecdotes'.

326 One of his predecessors, J.R. Clynes, observed that 'I had to answer questions in the House on such subjects as drugs, Communism, juvenile employment, alien marriages, special schools, prison discipline, night clubs, the quality of beer, sweepstakes, police

prosecutions, street cries, policewomen, book censorship, factory hours, and a host of other matters – such a variety, in fact, that no one man could be an expert in them all'. J.R. Clynes (1937); *Memoirs 1924–1937*, London: Hutchinson and Co., 118.

327 It proved difficult to probe at all deeply into Sir Frank Soskice's work. There is no biography or autobiography. His family relate that he burnt most of his private papers and what remained was donated to the Parliamentary archives to form the Stow Hill papers. There was nothing in those archives that had anything of interest to say about the policy decisions and issues that arose during his period of office as Home Secretary. What was retained touched mainly on constituency business and his various honours and preferments, and it was singularly uninformative. A typical run consisted of:

STH/FS/2/2/5	Notification of appointment as Privy Councillor
STH/FS/2/2/6	Summons to a meeting of the Privy Council
STH/FS/2/2/7	Ceremony on taking the oath as Secretary of State, Home Department
STH/FS/2/2/8	Prime Minister's notification of intention to recommend conferment of a barony on Frank Soskice
STH/FS/2/2/9	Memorial to Earl Marshal requesting warrant assigning arms and crest
STH/FS/2/2/10	Notification of appointment as Lord Privy Seal
STH/FS/2/2/11	Invitation to a Buckingham Palace Party
STH/FS/2/2/12	Testimonial dinner to US Attorney General
STH/FS/2/2/13	Ceremonial when body of King George VI was brought to Westminster Hall
STH/FS/2/2/14	Presentation to Sir Winston Churchill
STH/FS/2/2/15	Memorial Service for Hugh Gaitskell
STH/FS/2/2/16	Privy Councillors' Dinner to celebrate 25th anniversary of marriage of Queen and Duke of Edinburgh

328 What follows is based on Sir Frank's official diary.

329 Lord Alexander, 1885–1965, was a former Minister of Defence and leader of the Labour group in the Lords.

330 Lord Monckton, 1891–1965, was a Conservative politician who had occupied a number of ministerial positions in the 1950s.

331 The Race Relations Act 1965, c. 73.

332 Sir Roger Hollis, 1905–1973, was the 6th Director General, 1956–1965.

333 MI5, the Security Service, has been established in 1909 as the Secret Service Bureau. During the 1960s, its principal preoccupation was with Soviet espionage (see https://www.mi5.gov.uk/output/1960-to-1989.html).

334 R. Jenkins; *A Life at the Centre, op. cit.*, 175.

335 See Lord Windlesham; *Responses to Crime, op. cit.*, 140.

336 For example, Anthony Benn (1996), that prolific chronicler and Labour politician, refers to it not at all in *The Benn Diaries*, London: Arrow; neither did the biography of the Labour prime minister, Harold Wilson: G. Eyre Noel (1964); *Harold Wilson and the 'new Britain': The Making of a Modern Prime Minister*, London: Campion Press.

337 A. Bottoms and S. Stevenson; 'What Went Wrong?', *op. cit.*, 6.

338 CC04/9/236 and CC04/9/131.

339 Conservative Party Archives in the Bodleian Library, CC04/6/45.

340 Typical of the period was a letter which Harold Macmillan, the Prime Minister, had to write to the Bristol Women's Conservative Association on 27 February 1957, weeks before the passing of the Homicide Act 1957 (Chapter 11 5 and 6 Eliz. 2: 'An Act to make for England and Wales (and for courts-martial wherever sitting) amendments of the law relating to homicide and the trial and punishment of murder, and for Scotland amendments of the law relating to the trial and punishment of murder

and attempts to murder'): 'I am, of course, well aware of the strongly held view of many supporters of our Party on the subject of capital punishment, It was because the Government believed that the country as a whole was not in favour of total abolition that the present Bill was introduced. Your members will be aware of the principle on which this Bill is based – the retention of capital punishment for the type of murder which strike [*sic*] particularly at the maintenance of public order – and also of the very special attention that was given in both Houses of Parliament to the question of murder by poisoning. ...' Conservative Party Archives in the Bodleian Library: ACP/58/60.

341 For example, the file RD529/Sept 1963/Home Policy Committee was void of matter on law and order.

342 In *Pioneers of Change: Interviews with people who made the 1967 Abortion Act possible*, http://www.bpas.org/js/filemanager/files/abortion_pioneers.pdf, 26.

343 D. Garland; 'The Culture of High Crime Societies', *op. cit.*, 352.

344 In a most significant remark, David Faulkner said in interview: 'I don't think I ever made a claim that the criminal justice system by itself can do something about crime. What I think I was sort of trying to do is to say that at least criminal justice should work in the sense that people get brought to trial in reasonable time, that if there are courses in prisons, they are actually provided and people actually go on them. And what is supposed to happen does happen and people know where they are and they're properly treated and people know where they stand and know what to expect. It was that sort of belief which of course goes with police response times and so on as well'.

345 See my account of the introduction of criminal injuries compensation in *Helping Victims of Crime*, Oxford: Clarendon, published in 1990.

346 See D. Garland (2001); *The Culture of Control*, Oxford: Clarendon. John Croft, too, would emphasise the importance of the post-war emergence of the welfare state and the social solidarity that had marked a beleaguered society in warfare in prompting a shift towards a new attitude to crime and criminal justice (and see G.D.H. Cole and R. Postgate (1971); *The Common People: 1746–1946*, London: Methuen.

347 The phrase echoed the title of a White Paper, *The War against Crime in England and Wales 1959–1964*, Cmnd. 2296, 1964. It was a novel phrasing that had prompted controversy in government. An official recalled it was 'the first use of this kind of combative language'. The Cabinet Secretary informed the prime minister when it was first submitted in draft form: 'The Cabinet considered the Home Secretary's previous paper rather briefly at the end of their meeting ... and, while it was agreed in principle that a Royal Commission should be appointed, the draft White Paper was not considered in detail. It was, however, suggested that the title – "The War Against Crime in England and Wales" – was not particularly appropriate. The Home Secretary [Henry Brooke] has suggested, but has not adopted, the alternative – "Society and the Criminal"'. The annex to Burke Trend's note repeated that 'The title – "The War Against Crime" – sounds over-dramatic and tends to set much of the contents in the wrong perspective'. CRI15/1/6 Penal Reform Generally White Paper on Penal Policy; Burke Trend to PM, 23 March 1964. (Burke Trend, 1914–1987, was Cabinet Secretary between 1963 and 1973).

348 *The Speakers' Handbook 1948–9 Supplement*, published by the Labour Party in 1949 and designed to enable 'socialists of all ages to draw their adversaries into detail', contained nothing on crime, criminal justice and law and order.

349 Street Offences Act 1959, CHAPTER 57 7 and 8 Eliz. 2: An Act to make, as respects England and Wales, further provision against loitering or soliciting in public places for the purpose of prostitution, and for the punishment of those guilty of certain offences in connection with refreshment houses and those who live on the earnings of or control prostitutes.

350 General Election Policy materials. App. C: Questions and Challenges to Labour Candidates. Conservative Party Archives in the Bodleian Library: C04/9/196. The advice given was that candidates 'will no doubt wish to answer this question in the light of their personal conviction as it is generally agreed that this is not a Party issue. Their attention is however drawn to the fact that the question does not relate solely to murder, it relates also to treason'.

351 It is noteworthy that a collection of short biographies of Lord Chancellors, including Lords Kilmuir, Dilhorne and Gardiner, politicians who were so prominent, say, in the debates about capital punishment, makes no mention at all of their involvement in the politics of criminal justice. It is as if such a politics was neither interesting nor memorable. See R. Heuston (1987); *Lives of the Lord Chancellors 1940–1970*, Oxford: Clarendon Press.

352 There were to be three criminal justice acts during the period: The Criminal Justice Act 1961 (9 & 10 Eliz.2 c.39); The Criminal Justice Administration Act 1962 (10 & 11 Eliz.2 c.15); and The Criminal Justice Act 1967 (c.80).

353 For example, Sir Frank Soskice attached a memorandum to a draft White Paper on 'Reforms Relating To Young People In Trouble' in which he noted that 'Following discussion on the Home Affairs Committee we have emphasised (in paragraph 1) the Government's intention to consult interested organisations and to seek their co-operation. The Committee also thought that since it may be some weeks before the White Paper is published, there would be merit in informing these organisations of what was proposed in advance of publication ...' C(65) 107 20 July 1965.

354 'The Queen's Speeches Committee ... consider it necessary to relegate to the reserve list Superannuation and Pirate Broadcasting; and to hold back Overseas Aid, Criminal Justice, Children and National Parks. This does not mean that it may not be possible to introduce one or more of these Bills late in the Session. It does mean that we should get on with other urgent Bills first and accept the risk that the four Bills in question may not be reached. If we cannot get Criminal Justice into the main programme I would hope that we should be able to take some parts of it in the form of separate Bills through the Second Reading Committee procedure. ...' Cabinet Legislative Programme, 1965–66, Memorandum by the Lord President of the Council, 18 October 1965, C(65) 133.

355 It was a typically omnibus Criminal Justice Act whose long title was: 'An Act to amend the law relating to the proceedings of criminal courts, including the law relating to evidence, and to the qualification of jurors, in such proceedings and to appeals in criminal cases; to reform existing methods and provide new methods of dealing with offenders; to make further provision for the treatment of offenders, the management of prisons and other institutions and the arrest of offenders unlawfully at large; to make further provision with respect to legal aid and advice in criminal proceedings; to amend the law relating to firearms and ammunition; to alter the penalties which may be imposed for certain offences; and for connected purposes'.

356 One of his officials observed: 'He was not regarded at all by his colleagues. I mean he was suffered by them, I think. ... Frank was not necessarily expected to be the Home Secretary. Not sure how far he expected to be the Home Secretary either but still, he was, he was just not up to it frankly'.

357 Cabinet: The Adult Offender: Draft White Paper; Memorandum by the Secretary of State for the Home Department, 30 November 1965, C(65)164.

358 R. Jenkins (1959); *The Labour Case, op. cit.*

359 T. Newburn; *Permission and Regulation, op. cit.*, 6.

360 R. Jenkins; *A Life at the Centre, op. cit.*, 210. He almost certainly borrowed the phrase from John Galbraith whose *The Liberal Hour* had been published by Hamish Hamilton in 1960.

361 B. Pimlott (1992); *Harold Wilson*, London: Harper Collins, 487.

Bibliography

M. Abrams (1961); *Teenage Consumer Spending in 1959*, London: London Exchange Press

P. Allen (2004); 'A Young Home Secretary', Ch. 6 in A. Adonis and K. Thomas (eds.) *Roy Jenkins: A Retrospective*, Oxford: Oxford University Press, 61–84

H. Becker (1963); *Outsiders*, New York: Free Press

A. Benn (1996); *The Benn Diaries*, London: Arrow

A. Biderman and A Reiss (1967); 'On Exploring the "Dark Figure" of Crime', *The Annals of the American Academy of Political and Social Science*, Vol. 374, No. 1, 1–15

A. Bottoms and S. Stevenson (1992); 'What Went Wrong?': Criminal Justice Policy in England and Wales, 1945–70', in D. Downes (ed.) *Unravelling Criminal Justice*, London: Macmillan, 1–45

R. Brazier (1997); *Ministers of the Crown*, Oxford: Clarendon

The British Imperial Calendar and Civil Service List 1965 (1965), London: HMSO

A. Britton (2001); *Monetary Regimes of the Twentieth Century*, Cambridge: Cambridge University Press

T. Budd, C. Sharp and P. Mayhew (2005); *Offending in England and Wales: First results from the 2003 Crime and Justice Survey*, Home Office Research Study 275, London: Home Office Research, Development and Statistics Directorate

J. Callaghan (1983); 'Cumber and Variableness', *The Home Office: Perspectives on Policy and Administration*, London: Royal Institute of Public Administration, 9–22

J. Campbell (2014); *A Well-Rounded Life*, London: Jonathan Cape

R. Carr-Hill and N. Stern (1979); *Crime, the Police and Criminal Statistics: An Analysis of Official Statistics for England and Wales using Econometric Methods*, London: Academic Press

M. de Castelbajac (2014); 'Brooding Over the Dark Figure of Crime', *British Journal of Criminology*, 54(5): 928–945

Central Statistical Office (1966); *Annual Abstract of Statistics No. 103 1966*, London: HMSO

Lord Chorley (1970); 'Hermann Mannheim: A Biographical Appreciation', *British Journal of Criminology*, Vol. 10, No. 4, 324–347

R. Clarke and D. Cornish (1983); *Crime Control in Britain: A Review of Policy Research*, Albany: State University of New York Press

R. Cloward and L. Ohlin (1961); *Delinquency and Opportunity*, London: Routledge and Kegan Paul

J.R. Clynes (1937); *Memoirs 1924–1937*, London: Hutchinson and Co.

L. Cohen and M. Felson (1979); 'Social Change and Crime Rate Trends: A Routine Activity Approach', *American Sociological Review*, Vol. 44, No. 4, 588–608

S. Cohen (1971); introduction to *Images of Deviance*, Harmondsworth: Penguin, 9–24

—(1972); *Folk Devils and Moral Panics*, London: MacGibbon and Kee

—(1998); 'Footprints in the Sand: A Further Report on Criminology and the Sociology of Deviance in Britain', in *Against Criminology*, London: Routledge, 67–94

—and P. Rock (1970); 'The Teddy Boy' in V. Bogdanor and R. Skidelsky (eds.) *The Age of Affluence*, London: Macmillan, 288–320

G.D.H Cole and R. Postgate (1971); *The Common People: 1746–1946*, London: Methuen

J. Croft (1980); *Research and Criminal Policy*, London: HMSO

J. Douglas (ed.) (1971); *Understanding Everyday Life*, London: Routledge and Kegan Paul

D. Downes (1966); *The Delinquent Solution*, London: Routledge and Kegan Paul

C. Emsley (1991); *The English Police: A Political and Social History*, London: Longman

M. Felson (2002); *Crime and Everyday Life*, London: Sage

S. Field (1990); *Trends in Crime and Their Interpretation: A Study of Recorded Crime in Post-War England and Wales*, London: Home Office

D. Garland (2000); 'The Culture of High Crime Societies', *British Journal of Criminology*, Vol. 40 No. 3, 347–375

—(2001); *The Culture of Control*, Oxford: Clarendon

B. Gibson (2007); *The New Home Office: An Introduction*, Winchester: Waterside Press

E. Gibson and S Klein (1969); *Murder, 1957 to 1968: a Home Office Statistical Division report on murder in England and Wales*, London: HMSO

J. Gould (ed.) (1965); *Penguin Survey of the Social Sciences 1965*, Harmondsworth: Penguin

R. Hauser (1962); *The Homosexual Society*; London: Bodley Head

N. Hawthorne (1850); *The Scarlet Letter: A Romance*, Boston: Ticknor and Fields

R. Heuston (1987); *Lives of the Lord Chancellors 1940–1970*, Oxford: Clarendon Press

J. Hills (2004); *Inequality and the State*, Oxford: Oxford University Press

Home Office (2000); *Review of Crime Statistics: A Discussion Document*, London: Home Office

R. Hood (ed.) (1974); *Crime, Criminology and Public Policy*, London: Heinemann

—(2002); 'Recollections of Sir Leon Radzinowicz', in A. Bottoms and M. Tonry (eds.) *Ideology, Crime and Criminal Justice: A Symposium in Honour of Sir Leon Radzinowicz*, Cullompton: Willan, xix–xxiii

—(2004); 'Hermann Mannheim and Max Grünhut: Criminological Pioneers in London and Oxford', *British Journal of Criminology*, Vol. 44, No. 4, 469–495

—*et al.*, (2000); 'Crime, Sentencing and Punishment in A. Halsey and J. Webb (eds.) *Twentieth Century British Social Trends*, London: Macmillan, 676–680

T. Hope (2004); 'Pretend it Works: Evidence and Governance in the Evaluation of the Reducing Burglary Initiative', *Criminal Justice*, 4, 287–308

M. Hough (2014); 'Confessions of a recovering 'administrative criminologist': Jock Young, quantitative research and policy research', *Crime Media, Culture*, Vol. 10(3), 215–226

—(2018); 'The discovery of fear of crime in the UK,' in M Lee and G. Mythen (eds.) *The Routledge International Handbook on Fear of Crime*, Milton Park: Routledge, 35–46

E. Hughes (1962); 'Good People and Dirty Work', *Social Problems*, Vol. X (1), 3–11

R. Jenkins (1959); *The Labour Case*, Mddx: A Penguin Special

—(1967); *Essays and Speeches*, London: Collins

—(1991); *A Life at the Centre*, London: Macmillan

D. Jones (1990–91); "Where did it all go wrong?': Crime in Swansea, 1938–68', *Welsh History Review* Vol. 15, nos. 1–4, 240–274

H. Jones (1962); *Crime and the Penal System*, University Tutorial Press, London

L. Kennedy (1961); *10 Rillington Place*, London: Gollancz

N. Lacey (2003); 'Principles, Politics, and Criminal Justice' in L. Zedner and A. Ashworth (eds.) *The Criminological Foundations of Penal Policy*, Oxford: Oxford University Press, 79–106

E. Lemert (1951); *Social Pathology*, New York: McGraw-Hill

I. Loader (2006); 'Fall of the 'Platonic Guardians': Liberalism, Criminology and Political Responses to Crime in England and Wales', *British Journal of Criminology*, Vol. 46, No. 4, 561–586

I. Loader and R. Sparks (2010); *Public Criminology?*, Routledge: London

Lord Longford (1958); *Causes of Crime* London: Weidenfeld and Nicolson

—(1964); *Crime: A Challenge to Us All*, Labour Party, London

M. Maguire, and T. Bennett (1982); *Burglary in a dwelling: the offence, the offender and the victim*, London: Heinemann

H. Mannheim (1965); *Comparative Criminology: A Text Book*, London: Routledge and Kegan Paul

J. Martin (1962); *Offenders as Employees: An Enquiry by the Cambridge Institute of Criminology*, London: Macmillan

—(1988); 'The Development of Criminology in Britain 1948–60', *The British Journal of Criminology*, Vol. 28, No. 2, 35–44

P. Mayhew and M. Hough (1983); 'The British Crime Survey', *The British Journal of Criminology*, Vol. 23, No. 4, 394–5

F. McClintock (1963); *Crimes of Violence: An Enquiry by the Cambridge Institute of Criminology into Crimes of Violence against the Person in London*, London: Macmillan

F. McClintock and E. Gibson (1961); *Robbery in London: An Enquiry by the Cambridge Institute of Criminology*, London: Macmillan

D. Melossi (2008); *Controlling Crime, Controlling Society*, Cambridge: Polity Press

R. Merton (1938); 'Social Structure and Anomie', *American Sociological Review*, Vol. 3, No. 5, 672–682

—(1957); *Social Theory and Social Structure*, Glencoe, Ill: Free Press

Ministry of Education (1960); *The Youth Service in England and Wales* ('The Albemarle Report'), London: HMSO

A. Morris (1975); 'The American Society of Criminology: A History, 1941–1974', *Criminology*, Vol.13(2), 123–167

T. Morris (1989); *Crime and Criminal Justice since 1945*, Oxford: Basil Blackwell

Lord Mountbatten (1966); *Report of the Inquiry into Prison Escapes and Security by Admiral of the Fleet, Lord Mountbatten of Burma*, Cmnd. 3175, London: HMSO

T. Newburn (1992); *Permission and Regulation* London: Routledge

G. Eyre Noel (1964); *Harold Wilson and the 'new Britain': The Making of a Modern Prime Minister*, London: Campion Press

C. Nuttall (2003); 'The Home Office and Random Allocation Experiments', *Evaluation Review*, Vol. 27 No. 3, 267–289

A. Oakley (2011); *A Critical Woman: Barbara Wootton, Social Science and Public Policy in the Twentieth Century*, London: Bloomsbury Academic

P. O'Malley (1992); 'Risk, Power and Crime-Prevention', *Economy and Society*, Vol. 21, No. 3, 252–275

A. Paterson (1933); 'Should the Criminologist be Encouraged?', *Transactions of the Medico-Legal Society*, Vol. XXVI, 180–200

J. Pellew (1982); *The Home Office*, London: Heinemann

Penal Practice in a Changing Society: Aspects of Future Development (England and Wales) (February 1959), Cmnd. 645, London: HMSO

B. Pimlott (1992); *Harold Wilson*, London: Harper Collins

Prison Department (1966); *Report on the Work of the Prison Department 1965: Statistical Tables*, Cmnd. 3304, London: HMSO

L. Radzinowicz (1965); *The Need for Criminology and a Proposal for an Institute of Criminology: Report by Professor Leon Radzinowicz Wolfson Professor of Criminology University of Cambridge presented to the Hon. Samuel I. Rosenman, President of the Association of the Bar of the City of New York, and approved by its Special Committee on the Administration of Criminal Justice under the Chairmanship of the Hon. Charles D. Breitel*, London: Heinemann

—(1968); *The Regime for Long-Term Prisoners in Conditions of Maximum Security*, Report of the Advisory Council on the Penal System, London: HMSO

—(1988); The Cambridge Institute of Criminology: its background and scope: a report, London: HMSO

—(1999); *Adventures in Criminology*, London: Routledge

F. M. Redington (1970); 'Wilfred Perks', *Journal of the Institute of Actuaries*, Vol. 96(2), 276–279

Registrar General's Statistical Review of England and Wales for the Year 1965, Part III. Commentary (1967), London: HMSO

R. Reiner (2010); 'Citizenship, Crime, Citizenship: Marshalling a Social Democratic Perspective', *New Criminal Law Review*, Vol. 13, No. 2, 241–261

Report of the Commissioner of Police of the Metropolis for the year 1965, London: HMSO, 1966

P. Rock (1973); *Making People Pay*, London: Routledge and Kegan Paul

—(1990); *Helping Victims of Crime*, Oxford: Clarendon

—(1994); introduction to *History of Criminology*, Aldershot: Dartmouth, xi–xix.

—(2004); *Constructing Victims' Rights*, Oxford: Clarendon

—(2010); 'Comment on 'Public Criminologies'', *Criminology & Public Policy*, Vol. 9, No. 4, 751–768

and M. McIntosh (editors) (1974); *Deviance and Social Control*, London: Tavistock

C.H. Rolph (1987); *Further Particulars*, Oxford: Oxford University Press

G. Rose (1960); 'Criminology and Penology: Three Views', *The Howard Journal*, Vol. X, No. 3, 212–216

—(1961); *The Struggle for Penal Reform: The Howard League and its Predecessors*, London: Stevens

—(1967); *Schools for Young Offenders*, London: Tavistock Publications

M. Ryan (2003); *Penal Policy and Political Culture in England and Wales*, Winchester: Waterside Press

L. Sherman (1993); 'Defiance, Deterrence, and Irrelevance: A Theory of the Criminal Sanction', *Journal of Research in Crime and Delinquency*, Vol. 30, no. 4, 445–473

T. Sellin (1938); 'The Basis of a Crime Index', *Journal of Criminal Law and Criminology*, Vol. XXII, 333–356

—and M. Wolfgang (1964); *The Measurement of Delinquency*, New York: John Wiley

J. Shields and J. Duncan (1964); *The State of Crime in Scotland*, London: Tavistock

M. Smith (2010); *Planning for the Last Time: Government Science, Civil Defence and the Public, 1945–68*, PhD dissertation, University of Manchester

S. Smith (1994); *Labour Economics*, 2nd edition, London: Routledge

R. Sparks, H. Genn and D. Dodd (1977); *Surveying Victims: A Study of the Measurement of Criminal Victimisation, Perceptions of Crime, and Attitudes to Criminal Justice*, Chichester: Wiley

I. Taylor, P. Walton and J. Young (1973); *The New Criminology*, London: Routledge and Kegan Paul

R. Taylor (1998); *Forty Years of Crime and Criminal Justice Statistics, 1958–1997*, London: RDS Home Office

G. Tett (2009); *Fool's Gold*, London: Abacus

T. Tyler (1990); *Why People Obey the Law*, London: Yale University Press

UNESCO (1957); *The University Teaching of Social Sciences, Criminology* Paris: UNESCO

N. Walker (1965); *Crime and Punishment in Britain*, Edinburgh: Edinburgh University Press.

—(2003); *A Man Without Loyalties: A Penologist's Afterthoughts*, Chichester: Barry Rose

C. Walston (ed.) (2009); *Challenging Crime: A Portrait of the Cambridge Institute of Criminology*, London: Third Millennium Publishing

M. Weber (rep. 1978); *Economy and Society*, Berkeley: University of California Press

D. West (1963); *The Habitual Prisoner: An Enquiry by the Cambridge Institute of Criminology*, London: Macmillan

B. Whitaker (1964); *The Police*, London: Eyre and Spottiswoode

L. Wilkins (1959); *Social Deviance*, London: Tavistock

—(1960); *Delinquent Generations*, London: HMSO

—(1963); 'The Measurement of Crime', *British Journal of Criminology*, Vol. 3, No. 4, 321–341

—and H. Mannheim (1955); *Prediction Methods in Relation to Borstal Training*, HMSO: London

A.H. Williams (1965); 'The Treatment of Abnormal Murderers,' *Howard Journal of Penology and Crime Prevention*, Vol. 11, No. 4, 286–292

Lord Windlesham (1993); *Responses to Crime*, Volume 2, Clarendon Press, Oxford

B. Wootton (1959); *Social Science and Social Pathology*, London: Allen & Unwin

—(1967); *In a World I Never Made: Autobiographical Reflections*, London: George Allen and Unwin

J. Young (1971); *The Drugtakers*, London: MacGibbon and Kee

L. Zedner (2003); 'Useful Knowledge? Criminology in Post-war Britain', in L. Zedner and A. Ashworth (eds.) *The Criminological Foundations of Penal Policy*, 197–236

2 The Liberal Hour I – Prologue
The Homicide Act 1957

Introduction

I shall begin this three-handed description of the liberal reforms of the 1960s by offering a broad outline of the rather detailed analysis that is to come in this and the next chapter. It will be my argument that, between the late 18th century and the mid-20th century, a stalemate existed in British politics over the abolition of capital punishment. Abolition was to come about as a faltering succession of seemingly small reforms which came progressively and incrementally to transform the mode of execution and pare down the numbers of offences and offenders eligible for the death penalty. The steps leading up to the unstable Homicide Act 1957 and its successor, the 1965 Murder (Abolition of Death Penalty) Act, took place in the central forum of a centralised state, in Parliament, and they were taken forward by legally trained backbenchers rather than by governments.[1] They were based on the broad political and moral issue of the very legitimacy of the death penalty and were fraught by 'Strong feelings [that lay] latent and from time to time [were] activated'.[2] The balance of opinion in government, the House of Commons and government committees of inquiry tended always to be finely divided (*The Times* reflected two years before the 1957 Act that 'For many years the principle of capital punishment has been neither decisively affirmed nor decisively rejected …'[3]) and, for the main part, the House of Lords and the Church of England had been adamantly hostile.

On the one hand, there were the arguments, much rehearsed, that abolition would be hazardous; the time was not ripe for a brash experiment; deterrence could not be proved not to work; killing was wrong and its heinousness had to be signified in the severity of the punishment that attended it; abolition would bring the law into disrepute; the criminal justice system had its full complement of safeguards against wrongful conviction; the pains of lifelong imprisonment were worse than those of execution;[4] and the public was unsympathetic to, and unready for, change. On the other hand, it was said, killing, even of murderers, was wrong; it could not be proved that deterrence worked;[5] states which had introduced abolition had not undergone any appreciable increase in homicide; the law was anomalous, unworkable and inconsistent; executions and the many reprieves which followed the passing of the death sentence brought the law into disrepute; irreversible miscarriages of justice could and did take place; no mitigation of the death penalty, other than its complete abolition, could succeed; and the role of the legislator was to lead public opinion, not to follow it.

At the heart of it all, it may be supposed, were clashing, deeply rooted, culturally framed[6] assessments of quite incommensurable and ambiguous risks and 'the two sides seldom [got] close enough together for the arguments of each to be convincingly cogent in terms of the other's honest assumptions'.[7] It was a problem that could not readily be resolved, and the same arguments were to be rehearsed interminably.[8] Sir Charles Cunningham, the Permanent Under-Secretary of State, who was at the epicentre of events for much of the 1960s, reflected:

> there is no doubt that the argument about the death penalty must be to a large extent a subjective one. Conclusions are likely to be based on personal judgements reached by reference more to ethical and psychological considerations than to objective or statistical analysis. There appears to be no conclusive evidence that the incidence of murder is materially influenced by the penalty attaching to the crime. ...[9]

The terms of the debate set in the early 19th century changed surprisingly little, but the stalemate was always potentially unsteady, and began to unravel around the mid-20th century, with the passage of the 1957 Act, which, following earlier legislation, further reduced the number of acts to which the death penalty could be applied, retaining it for what were supposed to be the most heinous examples of murder; and then the 1965 Act, which, for an experimental period of five years, effectively abolished capital punishment for all but a minute rump of offences.

Shifts in the composition and disposition of key figures in the armed forces, Church and House of Lords helped finally to tip the balance in favour of the abolitionists. But changes in the wider political arena were also crucial in explaining why abolitionists eventually attained supremacy. The emergence and eventual ascendance of the Labour Party was one critical factor. Another was that the House of Commons became more emboldened to challenge the House of Lords, for long a stronghold of retentionist sentiment. Moreover, the 'elite consensus' in Britain was far from automatic. It was manufactured by shrewd political entrepreneurs, most notably the diehard abolitionist Sydney Silverman, with the help of the Howard League for Penal Reform, established as a result of a merger in 1921, and the National Campaign for the Abolition of the Death Penalty, which was formed in 1925 and attracted a muster of distinguished intellectual and cultural supporters, most notably Lord Gardiner, who became its chairman. The content, continuity and consistency of the arguments and the manner in which they engendered an unstable compromise in the late 1950s need properly to be appreciated if the events of the 1960s are themselves to be understood.

Beginnings

Capital punishment is the most severe penalty available to the courts, and it conveys something of how judges, policy-makers and politicians view the standing of crime, criminals and criminal justice; make sense of their role and powers; and establish the mood, morals and mores of the nation. In an American context, David Garland said that 'death penalty practice has come to bear the distinctive hallmarks of ... political institutions and cultural conflicts',[10] and he further observed[11] that the ability of members of one group to impose the retention or abolition of the death sentence on members of another is redolent of what Joseph Gusfield once called 'status politics'.[12] Abolitionists and retentionists in England and Wales were two loosely configured social and political groupings, working in and through the state, that vied with one another over the centuries, and the Murder (Abolition of Death Penalty) Act, 1965, represented the culminating victory of one, 'a relatively narrow social group',[13] a liberal elite,[14] over the more popular and populist politics of others.[15] Indeed, Jeremy Horder would argue that, from the first, what he called a liberal-progressive elite composed of lawyers, legislators and others monopolised the work of reforming capital punishment to the effective exclusion of the citizenry as a whole.[16]

The history of abolition is worth telling because it attracted unusually strong passions, condensed unusually powerful symbolism (indeed, it is customary in any history of capital punishment to comment on the emotions it arouses[17]) and mobilised social and political forces in a manner foreign to much of the everyday history of criminal justice reform. The ending of executions in England and Wales was identified by some as the reckless experiment of a small coterie and by others as part of a civilising project. Roy Jenkins, the Labour Home Secretary, certainly thought it was timely. In 1959, and before he and his party regained office, he looked ahead and mused:

> The ghastly apparatus of the gallows continues to exist, and is used much more often than was thought likely when the Homicide Act [1957] was passing into law. Britain, despite our much-vaunted social and political maturity, still stands out as one of the few advanced countries which retains this presumptuously final penalty.[18]

It is with the groundwork of the besetting conflict over that presumptuously final penalty that this chapter will be concerned, a groundwork that culminated in the compromised Homicide Act of 1957, before I turn to abolition in the next. In what must be a reasonably brief description of political developments spanning some 150 years, it will necessarily skirt quite rapidly over a number of intricate and complicated themes. A repetitive, unstable pattern was to be in play over a very long period, a pattern which explains how it was that abolition came finally to pass into law, and my intention is to disclose a few of its broader contours.

Homicide rates were in long-term decline in Europe until the mid-1950s, when they began to climb to levels that nevertheless remained very low by historical standards.[19] According to Manuel Eisner, rates in England were always lower than in other, especially southern, European countries (Italy may have had a figure of 73 per 100,000 population in the fifteenth century, for example) but they did move in step with others across the continent. There were some 23 homicides for every 100,000 people in England in the thirteenth and the fourteenth centuries; seven in the sixteenth century; five in the seventeenth century; 1.5 in the eighteenth century; 1.3 at the end of the nineteenth century; and an average of 0.8 between 1900 and 1950.[20]

The 1950s then marked what the Dutch scholar, Pieter Spierenberg, called 'the trough of violence': 'In Europe west of the Iron Curtain, the 1950s were, on average, the least violent period in history. The decade had the lowest

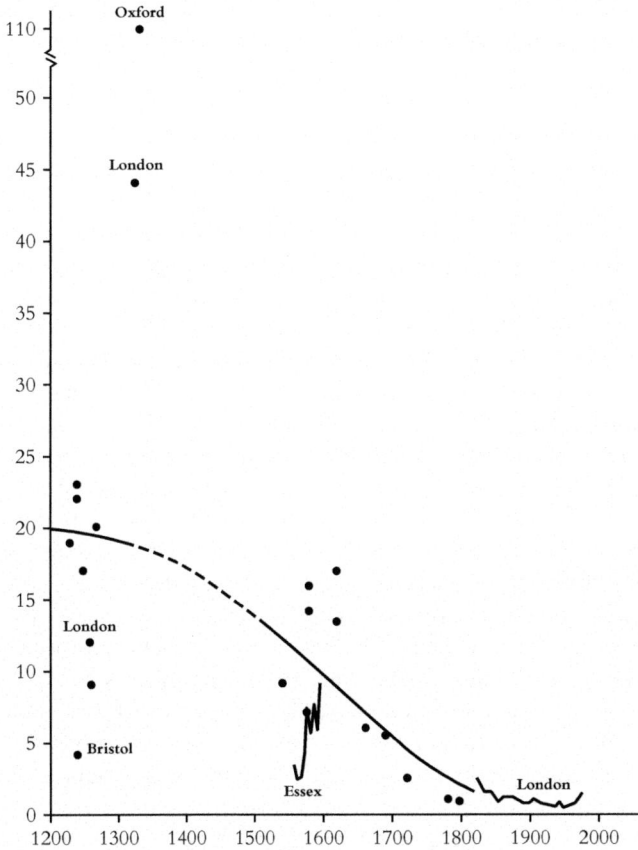

Figure 2.1 Homicides in England 1200–2000[21]

I am very grateful to Michael Tonry, the editor of *Crime and Justice*, for giving me permission to reproduce this image.

homicide rates ever. ...'[22] The prevailing scholarly explanation[23] for that continuous decrease has been grounded in Norbert Elias' notion of the 'civilising process',[24] the transformation of behaviour, emanating ultimately from the royal court as the centre of power, authority, delicacy and refinement, which gradually led to an erosion of the prickly culture of honour, a gentling of manners and the substitution of legal and other peaceful institutional procedures for the violent resolution of disputes by individuals intent on assault, feud or duel.[25] It was a decrease that was accelerated too by significant improvements in the medical response to serious injury, fewer and fewer people succumbing to their wounds as time went by.[26]

That decline in killing was mirrored in the decline in the number and ferocity of executions. Executions had once been the most public, brutal and theatrical of punishments in England and Wales, their ceremonial and cruel character having grown in tandem with the emergence of a centralised, weak state that sought in the sixteenth and seventeenth centuries to be seen to impress its will directly on the felon and on the audience that witnessed the death.[27] In 1930, a Select Committee of the House of Commons chose to call them an 'orgy of savage severity'.[28] Murder has always been described as an exceptional offence,[29] 'the most heinous of crimes', demanding a proportionate response from the state, and, in their turn, murder trials[30] and execution ritual for a long while took the guise of an elaborately engineered, conjoined and potent spectacle,[31] an artful piece of scene-setting,[32] that was part formal, part vernacular. The gallows or stake would be set up high in open view, perhaps on the roof of a gaol or on a scaffold or at the place where the offence had taken place. It could attract great crowds (at least 100,000, brought in by special 'cheap trains, all of which were densely packed',[33] were said to have witnessed the hanging of John Gleeson Wilson in Kirkdale in September 1849; tens of thousands attended the execution of the Mannings on the roof of Horsemonger Lane Gaol, the Surrey County Gaol, in Southwark three months later,[34] and of Catherine Wilson at Newgate Prison in October 1862.[35] And a hundred people were reported to have been rendered dead or insensible in the great press of the 40,000-strong crowd at the execution of John Holloway and John Haggerty in 1807[36]). At Newgate Prison there would be a Last Supper, a final 'solemn service of the condemned sermon ... preached in the chapel ... to repentant criminals who [were] about to expiate their crimes with their blood. ...'[37] The bell of the nearby St. Sepulchre-without-Newgate would toll before they left to make their way to the gallows.[38]

The day of execution itself might well be declared a public holiday, and people would arrive early and book rooms and vantage points from which to observe the hanging. In London until the end of the eighteenth century prisoners would go as if in procession to Tyburn, escorted by cavalry,[39] the wealthier arrayed in fine clothes (perhaps even decked out in wedding attire) and accompanied by professional mourners, receiving the ministrations of a clergyman exhorting repentance, offered nosegays, and stopping at intervals in seeming parody of the stages of the Cross (it has been said that much of the symbolism of capital punishment in Europe borrowed directly from a Christian iconography of martyrdom, suffering, death and repentance[40]). Executions were 'performative'.[41] There would be the ceremonial, often stylised and attentively reported[42] utterances of the dying man's or woman's last words, based on the right to confess on one's deathbed and prompted, not always successfully, in the hope that they would convey a model of penitence (McKenzie argued that it 'could all too easily shade into the forms and conventions of martyrological literature, with ordinary criminals borrowing the words and gestures of sixteenth- and seventeenth-century martyrs and political prisoners'[43]). There would be a hawking of souvenir ballads and purported confessions. Splinters from the gallows, pieces of the hangman's rope and halter, and executed people's possessions, blood and locks of hair were said to have magical properties in the cure, say, of ague and the toothache, just as relics of the true cross and martyred saints had miraculous powers. A touch of the dead man's or woman's hand was alleged to have curative properties.[44] Executioners like Jack Ketch and William Calcraft were part-heroic, part-demonic, public figures. As an additional penalty, the body of the hanged man or woman could be mutilated after death or go to the surgeons for dissection, and, being no longer whole, forfeit its prospects of resurrection and salvation.[45]

In all this, executions were far from being merely a practically simple or expedient method of carrying out a sentence. They took the form of an extravagantly didactic religious and secular rite (although their practical performance could actually be quite inept and shoddy,[46] their moral impact other than that intended, and the condemned could openly and defiantly contest their significance by, for example, mocking the ritual or protesting their innocence[47]). They were, at least in their design, 'grounded in cultural values and perceptions; ... they drew upon specific sensibilities and expressed particular emotions; they were sites of ritual performance and cultural production; and ... they produced diffuse cultural effects. ...'[48] And they did seem to have succeeded in stamping themselves deeply on the *conscience collective*, engendering strong popular sentiments of attachment and aversion to the very idea of capital punishment that persisted long after its public character had changed and its frequency had diminished. In 1922, the Howard League could still talk about the death penalty's 'immense dramatic hold upon the public mind'.[49] Perhaps that is part reason why executions were so difficult to bring to an end.[50]

'The rulers of eighteenth-century England cherished the death sentence', proclaimed Douglas Hay,[51] and there was certainly a great resort to the gallows as a penalty in law in the late eighteenth and early nineteenth centuries, the number of statutes prescribing the death sentence having risen from some 50 in 1688 to perhaps more than 200 in 1820,[52] all felonies except petty larceny and mayhem having become capital.[53] But convicted defendants could plead 'benefit of clergy' in its various forms until 1827 (benefit of clergy was a relic of the division of powers between the secular and ecclesiastical authorities – anyone who was literate enough to read the so-called 'hanging verse' was deemed for procedural purposes to be a cleric who was eligible for exemption from trial by a lay court[54]). Juries in the late eighteenth and early nineteenth centuries could at times refuse to convict, committing the 'pious perjury' of finding defendants guilty of non-capital offences rather than condemn a man or woman to death (Lord Suffield[55] told the House of Lords on 2 August 1833 that there had been what he claimed to be 555 perjured verdicts delivered at the Old Bailey in the previous 15 years[56]). Most of those condemned were eventually pardoned or had their sentences commuted, because, some say,[57] a conspicuous display of clemency shored up relations of authority, or, others have argued, because the threat of draconian sentences had to be deployed in a weakly policed state equipped with poor intelligence to cajole or bully those who had been apprehended into informing or turning evidence against otherwise inaccessible, untouchable or uncooperative suspects.[58] Until 1756, about two-thirds of those sentenced were actually hanged; between 1756 and 1772, the proportion shrank to one half; and between 1802 and 1808, it had declined to one eighth.[59]

The numbers of executions diminished, also, it has been claimed, as part of the civilising process[61] (although other explanations are on offer[62]) and hanging was eventually to become in effect a last resort.[63] What was 'really remarkable about the [eighteenth] century's penal policy is the almost constant search for viable secondary punishments', said James Sharpe,[64] and, after 1768, that major secondary punishment was transportation,[65] representing what was in effect exile in exchange for a commutation of the death sentence. Not only was there a steady decrease in the volume of executions but the overtly theatrical cruelty of the ceremony did not last.[66] Burning at the stake had once been the sentence for heresy and for treason committed by women[67] (and some 274 Protestants were burned in the reign of Mary Tudor alone[68]), but it was abolished in 1790 by the Treason Act (30 George III C. 48). Hanging, drawing and quartering had been the most severe punishment for men convicted of high treason, and many were killed in this fashion in the wake of the 1745 Jacobite rising – including 91 sentences passed by a Special Commission at Carlisle[69] – but there were only four more such sentences carried out thereafter in the 18th century, and that particular method of execution was to be abolished altogether by the Treason Act of 1814.[70] Exhibiting the bodies of the hanged in chains or gibbets was brought to an end in 1843.[71]

The progress to Tyburn was abandoned in 1784,[72] the sheriffs declaring that 'If we take a view of the supposed solemnity from the time at which the criminal leaves the prison to the last moment of his existence, it will be found

Period	Male	Female
1735–1799	6,069	375
1800–1899	3,365	172
1900–1964	748	15

Figure 2.2[60] Executions in England and Wales

to be a period full of the most shocking and disgraceful circumstances ... when they view the meanness of the apparatus, the dirty cart and ragged harness, surrounded by a sordid assemblage of the lowest among the vulgar, their sentiments are inclined more to ridicule than to pity'.[73] But if the Calvary had gone, the boisterousness and unseemliness of the crowds did not evaporate at the place of public execution itself,[74] and that was pretext enough to call for its end.[75] Charles Dickens had attended the Mannings' execution in 1849, and reported that:

> I was a witness of the execution at Horsemonger Lane this morning. I went there with the intention of observing the crowd gathered to behold it, and I had excellent opportunities of doing so, at intervals all through the night, and continuously from day-break until after the spectacle was over ... I believe that a sight so inconceivably awful as the wickedness and levity of the immense crowd collected at that execution this morning could be imagined by no man, and could be presented in no heathen land under the sun. The horrors of the gibbet and of the crime which brought the wretched murderers to it faded in my mind before the atrocious bearing, looks, and language of the assembled spectators. When I came upon the scene at midnight, the shrillness of the cries and howls that were raised from time to time, denoting that they came from a concourse of boys and girls already assembled in the best places, made my blood run cold. As the night went on, screeching, and laughing, and yelling in strong chorus of parodies on negro melodies, with substitutions of 'Mrs. Manning' for 'Susannah', and the like, were added to these. When the day dawned, thieves, low prostitutes, ruffians, and vagabonds of every kind, flocked on to the ground, with every variety of offensive and foul behaviour ...[76]

Public executions came to an end altogether nineteen years later under the Capital Punishment Amendment Act.[77] Thereafter, hanging took place behind walls, although it did not cease wholly to be a public event.

The continuous decline in the frequency, cruelty and visibility of capital punishment may be partially explained by the impact of a number of linked political and moral arguments that were urged persistently by those in and around Parliament until hanging's end in England and Wales.[78] One argument, lodged in the philosophy of an evolving liberal state, centred on the appropriateness, rationality, efficiency, expediency and fairness of methods of exercising state power.[79] It was to be but a strand of a catholic effort to reform the massively expanding and ever-more consequential systems of governance at the end of the eighteenth and beginning of the nineteenth centuries. And it took the form of an effort that brought about wholesale changes to the criminal law, the electoral franchise, policing, prisons, the slave trade and the ownership of slaves, the poor law, the supervision of factories and schools, and much else. Utilitarians, evangelicals nonconformists (and especially Quakers,[80] not the first abolitionists,[81] but certainly the founders of the first association for the abolition of the death penalty in 1783) and their Whig and Liberal confederates maintained that the overly generous use of the death penalty was wasteful, unchristian, oppressive, illogical and perverse in its consequences[82] (and, indeed, it is rather difficult at this point to resist a Whig interpretation of history). It was represented as part of the armoury of what was in effect an autocratic *ancien régime*. Instead of relying simply on tradition, usage, sentiments, or the religious precepts of the Old Testament, it was said, enlightened legislators should turn calmly to reason in organising the administrative machinery of the state. In the best of possible worlds, reason would transform penal justice into a coherent system that was clear, consistent and defensible. Problems should be split into their several parts, allowing rulers to ascertain, in the case of the criminal law, what should properly be subject to formal governance and what should not;[83] schematically codifying and reconciling the body of laws that were then drafted; enhancing the effectiveness and certainty of apprehension of malefactors;[84] devising proportionate measures of pain and repression which could conduce to the greatest good and inflict the least damage on society and perpetrator;[85] and justifying, in the process, the application, form, effectiveness and severity of every punishment. And, in all this, the power of the state should be curbed where possible. That Promethean utilitarian, Jeremy Bentham, said John Stuart Mill, 'found the philosophy of law a chaos, he left it a science: he found the practice of law an Augean stable, he turned the river into it which is mining and sweeping away mound after mound of its rubbish'.[86] 'The age of Law Reform and the age of Jeremy Bentham are one and the same', wrote Bentham's disciple, Lord Brougham.[87] Much later John Plamenatz would say that 'It was he who devised some of the best arguments in favour of many of the most important reforms undertaken in this country during the nineteenth century'.[88] Indeed, the voice of Bentham may be heard not only in the debates on capital punishment but also in almost everything else that is to come in this history of criminal justice.

Utility was represented by some as the unvarying test: 'While I dispute the pretensions of any theory which sets up an imaginary standard of justice not grounded on utility', further reflected John Stuart Mill, 'I account the justice which is grounded on utility to be the chief part, and incomparably the most sacred and binding part, of all morality'.[89] Reformers were not uniformly well disposed towards the abolition of capital punishment. Jeremy Bentham himself was a firm abolitionist, asking himself the question 'The punishment of death – shall it be abolished? I answer – *Yes*. Shall there be any exceptions to this rule? I answer, so far as regards *subsequential* offences, *No*. …'[90] John Stuart Mill was a retentionist: his case, purportedly founded on the felicific calculus, asserted that the death penalty was less oppressive than imprisonment for life.[91] But what was important in either case was the supposed ruthlessness of the application of reason and of the principle of utility. Hanging was said by those who were abolitionist to be inefficient, liable to give rise to ineradicable miscarriages of justice,[92] and overly and unreasonably harsh for its purpose. The case is well illustrated by an anecdote of the time. The sometime Solicitor General, Sir

Samuel Romilly,[93] a friend of William Wilberforce and of Jeremy Bentham, whose ideas he injected into the British political scene,[94] recalled an encounter he had had in June 1808 after he had moved a Bill to repeal the 1565 law (8 Eliz. I c. 4)[95] which had made picking pockets a capital offence:[96]

> It is but a few nights ago, that, while I was standing at the bar of the House of Commons, a young man … came up to me, and breathing in my face the nauseous fumes of his undigested debauch, stammered out, "I am against your Bill; I am for hanging all." I was confounded; and endeavouring to find out some excuse for him, I observed that I supposed he meant that the certainty of punishment affording the only prospect of suppressing crimes, the laws, whatever they were, ought to be executed. "No, no" he said, "it is not that. There is no good done by mercy. They only get worse; I would hang them all up at once."[97]

Romilly's own view, by contrast, was conveyed by the question:

> What better reason can be given for altering the law, than that it is not efficacious; and that, instead of its preventing crimes, crimes are multiplied under its operation? And if an alteration there must be, what can it be but to render the punishment less severe, but more certain in its operation?[98]

Those root arguments about reason, efficiency, proportionality and consistency were to be levelled until the last and they formed the first plank of a case formulated by a loose-coupled coalition against capital punishment. Hanging, it could be said, had been rendered increasingly unnecessary after 1829 by the introduction of police forces that replaced the need for often empty threats of draconian punishment by more effective and predictable state control. A second, nonconformist plank would invoke the clemency of the New Testament to say that the death penalty was immoral in its rejection of the sanctity of life, mercifulness and the possibility of personal redemption.[99] And a third, closely related plank, one that might be called humanitarian, pointed, as Norbert Elias had envisaged, at hanging as an instance of anachronistic, cruel and uncivilised punishment, a useless relic of a more barbarous, crude and irrational age which could no longer be stomached.[100] The 'enormously influential'[101] legal philosopher, Cesare Beccaria, a man whose ideas 'seeped into English thought [t]hrough Jeremy Bentham and Samuel Romilly',[102] said that the death penalty 'is not useful because of the example of savagery which it gives to men. If our passions or the necessity of war have taught us how to spill blood, laws, which exercise a moderating influence on human conduct, ought not to add to that cruel example. …'[103] John Stuart Mill talked of the origins of English law in a feudal system designed by 'a tribe of rude soldiers, holding a conquered people in subjection', and of how it had evolved slowly and fitfully through a 'struggle of centuries between the old barbarism and the new civilisation. …'[104] It was those contrasts between barbarism and civilisation, brutality and refinement, ignorance and enlightenment, reaction and reform, which had prompted him and others to deplore felons being executed in public, and to applaud the fact that in 1868 the 'laws by virtue of which rows of human beings might be seen suspended in front of Newgate ... have so greatly relaxed their most revolting and most impolitic ferocity. ...'[105] (Although as I have already remarked, executions did not cease altogether to be public. When the notorious, so-called Whitechapel Road murderer, the killer of Harriet Lane, Henry Wainwright, was executed at Newgate on 21 December 1875, for example, his hanging was witnessed by 'Mr. Alderman and Sheriff Knight, Mr. Sheriff Breffit, Mr. Under-Sheriff Baylis, Mr. Under-Sheriff Crawford, Mr. Sidney Smith, the Governor, and the Rev. Lloyd Jones, the Ordinary of Newgate ... [and] a limited number of strangers and representatives of the Press. ...'[106])

The campaign against capital punishment was thus from first to last rooted in a moral rhetoric[107] that employed the same words over and again for a hundred years or more to deplore killing[108] and maintain a belief in the idea of progress.[109] The death penalty 'is a survival from a ruder and a more barbarous time' said Ernest Thurtle,[110] the Member of Parliament for Shoreditch, when the campaign again came to a head in 1930.[111] Later still, Sydney Silverman, the Member of Parliament for Nelson and Colne, and prime mover behind the final abolition of capital punishment, argued in debate in the House of Commons on 14 April 1948:

> I would just summarise, very shortly, the qualities and aspects of this penalty which make it to all of us a revolting and barbaric thing. ... It is true that in the lifetime of most of us values of this kind have meant progressively less and less in the opinion of most communities. I suppose that after we have had two world wars with infinite loss of human life, after we have had the bombardment of cities and the wiping out of whole populations ... I suppose it may seem a very small matter whether half a dozen worthless human beings, who have themselves taken human life, should die or live.
>
> But, surely, it is the duty of all of us who value our civilisation not to depress still further those moral and spiritual values, but to seek to raise them, and to seek to raise them at precisely this moment when they are most in danger. If they are most in danger now, now is the time to restore the sense of the ultimate value of every human being, rather than to seek further to undermine that value. In the end these matters are decided not by the criminologists, nor by the politicians, nor by the philosophers. In the end they must be decided by moral standards. In the end the question we have to ask is this: Will what we are doing advance or repress the re-creation of the values of those standards in human minds?

'In 1956', we are told in an undated press release issued by the National Campaign for the Abolition of Capital Punishment, 'it was a predominantly

Conservative House of Commons which resolved, against the advice of the Government, "that the death penalty for murder no longer accords with the needs or the true interests of a civilised society"'. 'Hanging is an uncivilised form of punishment', a leaflet from the Campaign's Bristol branch claimed in 1964. And Kenneth Younger, a former Labour Cabinet minister, said in 1969:

> ... one does not need to be a starry-eyed liberal in order to assert that a society which no longer executes children for theft or hangs, draws and quarters its criminals in public is, to that extent, more civilised than one which did these things and thought them normal. ... The death penalty has long been in a category by itself in the British penal law, representing as it does the last remaining expression of an earlier philosophy under which punishment was physical, violent and irreversible.[112]

Those arguments were not unopposed. They were to meet with a continual counterpoint of resistance so effective that it took some one hundred and fifty years before an abolitionist majority could be secured in Parliament. Abolition, it was argued by the retentionists, would be foolhardy, putting the country at risk. It would be a 'most dangerous experiment' even for crimes other than murder and manslaughter, that was liable to give rise to a 'great evil'.[113] The populace might resort to lynch law if they were deprived of their executions,[114] lynching itself being defined as 'an outrage of individuals conspiring to supplant the law and act in defiance of the law'.[115] Prison and police officers would be defenceless. All nations had had capital punishment, it was an indispensable deterrent, popular opinion was generally supportive, and 'The fear of being hung not only prevented the criminal classes from committing murder, but it prevented murderers from seeking for accomplices'.[116]

The price of the liberty and freedom which freeborn Englishmen enjoyed, it could be claimed further, was the severity of punishments which were only very occasionally inflicted[117] (Koestler and Rolph put it that England had chosen executions when confronted with a choice between 'the cop and the hangman'[118]). If the laws were flouted, the only recourse could be to greater severity, not less.[119] If the laws were difficult to enforce, they should be made more severe.[120] If wise and experienced judges and politicians believed that hanging should be retained, it was impertinent, perhaps even rash, to challenge their judgement.[121] The English and Welsh trial system was so well designed that there were few, if any, instances of defendants improperly being convicted and punished.[122] Care and caution were exercised at every point[123] and the more egregious capital sentences were always amenable to the checks imposed by the exercise of the Royal Prerogative of Mercy (under the Regency, it was said, petitions 'forwarded to the fountain of mercy ... would always have due effect if a fair case were made out'[124]). It would come to be argued in time that the worst abuses of the death penalty had been removed, reserving capital punishment for only a small, core group of the most appalling offences and offenders. There it remained a deterrent[125] to which there was no viable alternative,[126] lengthy imprisonment being no more humane,[127] and proposals for abolition consequently being impracticable.[128]

It would be maintained over and over again that proposals for reform were premature. Public opinion was against them.[129] The electorate would not support them.[130] Parliament was not ready for them. It would never vote for them. The government had no plans to act upon them.[131] The government was not ready to reply to questions on them.[132] The government believed that they raised complex, perhaps insuperable, technical problems of drafting. There was no place for them in its busy legislative programme.

Early moves to abolition

The Attorney General, Sir Hartley Shawcross, reflected in 1948 on the progress of abolition that 'I suppose it is a characteristic of the development and reform of our criminal law down the centuries that we have proceeded on a rather empirical basis, following the maxim festina lente – hurry slowly – and, sometimes, perhaps, we have hurried very slowly indeed'.[133] And the probation officer and campaigner, Frank Dawtry,[134] echoed him when he claimed that:

> The campaign for abolition [was] a long one. The hope of any sudden and dramatic end to the use of capital punishment for murder, which sustained the abolitionists, was the sort of dream all idealists entertain in their hearts, though in their heads most of them know that ideals are usually achieved by stages. ... The death penalty in most abolitionist countries or states had gone by abrogation; first by diminution in its use, then a period of disuse, and then the legislation to confirm the situation.[135]

The progress of the campaign was to be marked by an almost interminable succession of committees, reports and minor reforms. So it was that a Select Committee in 1819 was appointed to examine the law on capital punishment for felonies,[136] and its report recommended in vain[137] the abolition of the death penalty for twenty seven offences.[138] It did not then realise its object, but the flow of private motions and public petitions for mitigation did not abate. In 1831, the Duke of Sussex informed the House of Lords that:

> 1,100 individuals, who were all liable to serve as Grand Jurors for the county of Middlesex ... [have urged] that their Lordships would take under their consideration the present state of the Criminal Law of this country, with a view to its revision and amendment; and to disconnect the punishment of death from crimes affecting merely the rights of property, but unaccompanied with violence and bloodshed. ... The petitioners stated, that their own private feelings of humanity had at various times caused a struggle within themselves, lest, by finding persons guilty, they should be accessory to a judicial murder; and that this feeling sometimes

induced Jurors and others to give what was vulgarly called a slip to the law, and that criminals, from this cause often escaped the hands of justice.[139]

In 1832, and partly as a result of the exertions of William Ewart, [140] the radical MP for the Dumfries District of Burghs, the death penalty was to be no longer imposed for shoplifting, sheep, cattle and horse stealing and for the theft of money or animals from a dwelling house.[141] In 1834, the City of London was obliged to discharge one of its two executioners for want of employment.[142] In 1836, the second report of a Royal Commission appointed by the Benthamite Lord Chancellor, Lord Brougham, to consolidate and encode the criminal law[143] observed that:

> We are induced to believe that the selection of a few culprits who alone are to suffer death out of a great number convicted for the same offence in point of law does not diminish but, on the contrary, tends to increase the number of offenders.[144]

No wholesale codification ensued but, in the following year, and by a majority of just one vote, William Ewart again succeeded in moving a Bill in the House of Commons 'for abolishing the punishment of death in certain cases,' thereby excluding 21 of the 37 offences then still attracting the death penalty.[145] By 1841, the death penalty had been removed for sacrilege, letter stealing, abortion, returning from transportation, forgery and coining, arson, burglary and theft from a dwelling house, and rape. In 1843, the M'Naghten Rule was introduced to offer the first formal legal definition of insanity that could be deployed by the defence at trial.[146] In 1847, following a petition from the magistrates of Kingston upon Hull, a Select Committee of the House of Lords produced two reports on the implementation of the criminal law, concentrating particularly on the treatment of juvenile offenders and transportation. Their second report concluded that there was no public mood for the abolition of capital punishment,[147] but that there was grave uncertainty about its deterrent effect, especially amongst those who were most familiar with prisoners. By 1861, the Criminal Law Consolidation Act had reduced the number of capital crimes to but four: murder, high treason, arson in a royal dockyard and piracy – in practical effect, therefore, murder. The absolutist state and its sanguinary punishments were evidently giving way to the bureaucratically administered, restrained and rational government of the middle and late nineteenth century; threats to the police; the gallows to the penitentiary; physical pain to moral discipline.[148]

As they gave way, so too the political, the raucous, the public and the spectacular in executions surrendered to the controlled, private and dully mechanical.[149] Petitions streamed out in support of the abolition of public executions.[150] In 1856, it was William Ewart again who moved the appointment of a 'Select Committee ... to inquire into the operation of the Law imposing the Punishment of Death',[151] and a House of Lords Select Committee did

indeed report unanimously in that year in favour of abolishing public executions,[152] but Sir George Grey, the Home Secretary, declared that the government had no intention of changing the position.[153] In February 1864, the
Member of Parliament for Oldham, Sir John Hibbert,[154] again turned to the
theme to talk about:

> the demoralising effect of public executions, and to move for papers on the
> subject. He felt that he need not apologise for calling the attention of the
> House to the subject after what he might designate as the disgusting display
> which took place in London the other morning, and which he thought a
> disgrace to the civilisation of the times in which they lived. He would not
> attempt to present to the House any overdrawn picture of the evils atten-
> dant on public executions, and he could not pass over without notice the
> very great alteration which had been made in the penal system during the
> last half century. They all knew the effect which civilisation had had on
> the penal code of this country, and were aware that while the former had
> advanced, so had the latter receded in its sanguinary character and savage-
> ness. The gibbet, the burnings, and the tortures of the old code had been
> progressively softened by the milder spirit of modern legislation. Referring
> to the early part of the present century, it would be found what the labours
> of a Romilly and a Macintosh[155] had done for their penal code. Although
> they had got rid of many of the barbarisms of former years, when women
> in cases of witchcraft were sentenced to be burnt, when persons refusing
> to answer were tortured, and when sentences for treason were of the
> same harsh character, there yet existed a relic of the same system, which
> he thought they ought also to endeavour to get rid of – these public
> executions.[156]

Four months later, William Ewart proposed:

> a Select Committee to inquire into the expediency of maintaining the
> punishment of death. It is now nearly a quarter of a century that the oppo-
> nents of capital punishment in this country have contended for its repeal.
> They hold it to be a great question of religion and civilisation. But, in a
> more practical point of view, and in one less connected with feeling and
> opinion, they support it, because they believe it would give certainty to
> justice and punishment to crime – and they base that belief on this maxim
> of the illustrious Beccaria: –"The certainty of even a moderate punish-
> ment will always make a greater impression than the fear of a more severe
> punishment, which is accompanied by the expectation of impunity." We
> apply this maxim to our present system, and we maintain that ours is not
> the more "moderate" system which "makes the greater impression," but
> that it is the "severer system which is accompanied by the expectation of
> impunity." Are we not justified in saying that great inconsistency, great
> uncertainty, prevail under our present system of capital punishment? Have

we not arrived, with regard to cases of murder, at a similar position to that which we held with regard to other crimes punished capitally many years ago?[157]

And his motion was passed and a Committee was appointed to inquire:

into the Provisions and Operation of the Laws now in force in the United Kingdom, under and by virtue of which the Punishment of Death may be inflicted upon persons convicted of certain crimes, and also into the manner in which Capital Sentences are carried into execution, and to report whether any, and if any what alteration is desirable in such Laws, or any of them, or in the manner in which such sentences are carried into execution.[158]

The Commissioners' final report was published on 8 January 1866. They recommended ending public executions but dissented amongst themselves by four to eight on whether there should be a total abolition of hanging.[159] They were as a result obliged to report that they had avoided 'the abstract question of the expediency of abolishing or maintaining Capital Punishment, on which subject there are differences of opinion', but they were 'all of opinion that certain alterations ought to be made in the existing law' (p. xlvii). The death penalty now remained in place in England and Wales solely for murder and treason, they said, and they saw no reason to alter that position, but murder punishable by death should be redefined and confined to 'all murders deliberately committed with express malice aforethought' and 'for all murders deliberately committed in, or with a view to, perpetration, or escape after the perpetration, or attempt at perpetration of any of the following felonies: murder, arson, rape, burglary, robbery or piracy' (p. l). Capital punishment should apply to cold-blooded, calculated killing, but not to other homicides committed recklessly or in anger: 'In all other cases of murder the punishment [should] be penal servitude for life, or for any period not less than seven years ...' (p. l, para. 3).

Their principal and more radical recommendation was not to be given effect. The Lord Chancellor[160] may have claimed that he 'thought the distinction raised by the clause a good one. He was of the opinion that there were crimes to which it was quite proper that the name of murder should continue to attach, whilst the capital punishment should be taken away. For instance, where a burglary was committed and resistance was made, and the burglars offered violence and killed a man, though without having had any intention to kill'. But others, anticipating the arguments that would continue all the way through to the Homicide Act 1957, professed doubts about whether the difference between the two categories of homicide was wide or clear enough. The Prime Minister, Earl Russell,[161] said that he did not 'think that the distinction between the two degrees of murder was drawn with sufficient distinction; and that as the clause now stood it might happen that crimes of one degree might be punished under the head of the other degree ... he remembered a case of a man being pushed by another into a river and drowned, which he thought under the wording of the clause would be murder of the second degree, though it appeared to him that if capital punishment was desirable it should apply to a case of that kind'. And the former Attorney General and Solicitor General, Lord Romilly,[162] said that 'He feared that if there were two classes of murder there would not be in the public mind the same degree of culpability attached to the crime as it was desirable should exist'. The then Lord Chief Justice recollected that he had: 'attended the meetings of the Committee, which sat eleven days; but at the end of that time it found that it could not agree upon a definition of the crime of murder – a result that was certainly very discouraging. His noble and learned Friend who succeeded to the Great Seal ... consulted the Judges on the general subject; but their opinions were by no means auspicious'.[163] On a vote taken on 31 May 1866, the House of Lords was evenly divided, and 'The Numbers being equal, it was (according to ancient Rule) Resolved in the Negative'. Although there had always been a distinction traced between murder and manslaughter,[164] that difficulty of successfully differentiating in fine detail between degrees of seriousness, between degrees of intent and, by extension, between capital and non-capital murder, repeatedly bedevilled that and all subsequent attempts to retain yet mitigate the death penalty in 1876, 1877, 1878,[165] 1882[166] and beyond into the twentieth century.

The Commission had also advocated separating infanticide as a crime from other forms of killing and that all executions should take place within prison grounds, out of the public eye. It was only the latter recommendation that was to be accepted immediately even though there were five dissentients in the Commission. The second reading of the Capital Punishment Amendment Bill was introduced on 7 May 1868 by the Tory Leader of the House of Lords, the Duke of Richmond,[167] who claimed that 'instead of public executions doing good or operating as a deterrent among criminals, the revolting scenes which, on many occasions, took place before the gallows, especially in the metropolis, did considerable harm, and ought to be prevented'. The Bill passed three weeks later, but it would be a further half century before infanticide was treated as manslaughter rather than murder and close to a century before murder was split into two categories – and then only as a compromise in an attempt to avoid total abolition.

In 1874, a Homicide Amendment Bill[168] which would have established the separate offences of infanticide, murder, manslaughter[169] and killing by negligence was scrutinised by a Select Committee of the House of Commons[170] and it was concluded warily on page *ix* of the subsequent report that the existing definition of murder 'which may be roughly stated as killing with malace [*sic*] aforethought, is far too narrow ... the attention of the Government and of the Parliament should be directed to the present disgraceful state of the definition of the law of Murder and Manslaughter ...' But the Select Committee further argued on page *iv* that it would be wrong to proceed in haste and that a very thorough process of examination and codification of the criminal law must take place before any attempt was made to construct separate classes of homicide:

> In the case of homicide, we have to deal not with technical terms, but with ordinary language, which is quite intelligible when used by a judge in directing a jury on a state of facts proved before them, but which when reduced to abstract propositions becomes obscure and ambiguous from the want of particulars to which the proposition applies, and from the want of a clear definition of the terms used. ... The Law of Homicide required very considerable alterations in substance before it is reduced to its simplest form, and made permanent in code. ... For these reasons, your Committee are of opinion that it is not desirable to proceed with the present Bill.

Thus it was that numerous, unremitting and usually unsuccessful attempts continued to be made by utilitarians, liberals, nonconformists and others to restrict or abolish the use of the death penalty, the baton being passed from Member of Parliament to Member of Parliament over the decades.[171] Their campaigning was fuelled from time to time by the dramatisation of incidents as they arose. One example was the execution of Edith Thompson in 1923 for the murder of her husband. Thompson had continually proclaimed her innocence; her guilt was taken by many to be uncertain; there was a sense that she was being punished as much for her adultery as for the murder; but she was nevertheless convicted and sentenced at the end of 1922; lost her appeal; was not reprieved by the Home Secretary and was taken to the gallows drugged and unconscious; a crowd having gathered to protest her hanging outside Holloway Prison on the day of her execution.[172] Her executioner killed himself two weeks later.[173] The whole episode amounted to another *cause célèbre* which reanimated the politics of abolition for a while.

Legislative encroachments continued to be made on the scope of the death penalty. There was the 1922 Infanticide Act[174] which effectively removed another capital crime from the statute book by reducing the offence to one of manslaughter (although no one had been executed for infanticide since 1899); the Children's Act of 1908[175] which ended the execution of children under 16, and the The Children and Young Persons Act of 1933[176] which raised the minimum age to 18.[177] (The Home Secretary who floated that change, William Joynson-Hicks, commented that that 'only gives legislative effect to what has been the practice for many years'.[178])

Two influential pressure groups were founded in the 1920s: the Howard League for Penal Reform in 1921 and the National Campaign for the Abolition of the Death Penalty, a body seeking 'to co-ordinate the efforts of all those working for the abolition of capital punishment',[179] in 1925. Although abolitionists were recruited from all political parties, there was a powerful addition to the abolitionist cause in the founding of the Labour Representation Conference in 1900 and its transformation seven years later into the Labour Party. I shall return to those organisations and their politics in the next chapter.

Courts Martial

Almost as important, and in the wake of the Great War, there was a closely coupled campaign[180] to moderate or eradicate the passing of death sentences by military courts.[181] Death sentences had been passed by the British Army on some 2,700 British soldiers in courts martial between 1914 and 1918 for such offences as sleeping on duty, cowardice, desertion, murder, mutiny and treason. Although over 90% of these sentences were later commuted to hard labour or penal servitude,[182] there were those who had been impelled by experience at first or second hand to hold that martial justice was overly draconian and procedurally unjust[183] with its very limited rights of representation and of appeal, especially from field courts.[184] The Independent Labour Party, for example, condemned 'the whole system of capital, corporal and field punishment, and ... call[ed] upon the Government to abolish capital punishment ...'[185]

In 1919, the Army Council was prompted to set up a Committee of Inquiry[186] that was to be chaired by Sir Charles Darling,[187] then a Judge of the King's Bench Division.[188] His ensuing report[189] opened with the observation that, as 'an inevitable result of the enormous expansion of the Army during the European War ...', there had been a great increase in the numbers of general courts martial, amounting to a figure of just under 35,000 in contrast to the 49 that had been conducted during the seven years before the war. It noted further that 'The difficulty of dealing with this sudden increase in the legal work of the Army was accentuated by the loss during the first few months of the war of so many of the regular officers who were familiar with military law' (para. 2), and by the difficulty of training newly recruited officers in law.

The majority report of the Committee was sanguine. Difficulties had in the main been overcome during the course of the conflict: 'having regard to all the circumstances, the work of courts martial during the war has been well done' (para. 3) although 'in certain points it is capable of improvement' (para. 4). Over one hundred observations and recommendations were circulated to Army Commands across the world[190] and then returned to the Army Council for approval.[191] The Commands endorsed what was proposed, and the proposals they approved were conservative. Change should be modest, and it would not touch on the death penalty. Two new committees[192] were to be formed to implement recommendations 6 to 8, relatively innocuous proposals which dealt with rectifying the disciplinary code's 'many minor defects of drafting and much repetition and overlapping, which render its study difficult even to lawyers' (6); the preparation of a handbook containing 'all those portions of the Army Act, Rules of Procedure and King's Regulations which relate to ... Courts-Martial' (7); and 'the more effective instruction of the proper tribunals for administering the law' (8). In the matter of sentencing, it was thought 'undesirable to set up any formal Court of Appeal from the decisions of Courts-Martial' (103); and, as to the 'right to petition for clemency, the decision [about sentences] ought to be left, as at present, to the military authorities, who alone are in a position to form a correct judgement as to what sentences the state of discipline in the Army ... requires' (105).[193] 'Nor', added the majority report, 'do we consider that any exception ought to be made in the case of death-sentences' (106). The one signal change wrought by the Committee was to be the reorganisation in 1923 of the Judge Advocate General's office so that separate departments came to deal with the office's prosecuting and judicial functions.[194]

Three members of the Committee, all Members of Parliament rather than currently serving officers, Major Christopher Lowther,[195] a former soldier and provost marshal;[196] Horatio Bottomley[197] and Stephen Walsh,[198] issued a separate, dissenting report urging a substantial reduction in the number of courts martial (para 4). They recommended the founding of a separate Court of Appeal for cases other than those involving death sentences (para. 8); and that 'no man on joining the army should forfeit the right of appeal for his life to a competent judicial tribunal' (para. 8).

In November 1919, the two reports were submitted jointly to Parliament, and that second, minority report became in effect the foundation of a platform for further sustained campaigning in Parliament. Members of Parliament, foremost amongst them Major Lowther, tried repeatedly and fruitlessly to introduce reforms each year as the annual Army and Air Force Bill was debated in the House of Commons.[199] The Bill renewed the powers of courts martial to impose more severe penalties more peremptorily than the civilian courts,[200] and, as a matter of routine, it would be the subject of largely barren attempts at curtailment.

So it was that, on 13 April 1920, Major Lowther sought to add a new clause to the Death Sentences (Appeal) Bill: 'In all cases of death sentences there should be a right of appeal to the Court of Criminal Appeal', which would have placed courts martial under the ultimate jurisdiction of the civilian courts. But he lost by 42 votes to 124. On 11 April 1921, he attempted to insert a version of the clause into the Army and Air Force (Annual) Bill, but again he failed by 63 votes to 161. On 1 March 1922, he endeavoured more boldly and comprehensively to bring in a bill 'to abolish in Great Britain the award of capital punishment for any crime or offence whatsoever'. 'I feel too deeply in this matter to indulge in any flowery language', he said, 'A Bill for the abolition of capital punishment is one which, if it does not induce the sympathy of the whole House, at any rate deserves serious reflection ... so long as I can, in my miserable small way, have the power to do so, I shall struggle on that account alone to have this horrible, this ghastly, responsibility which we all take upon ourselves removed, and which I consider is a blot upon any civilised nation'. But he was once more defeated, by 234 votes to 86. In March 1927, another ex-military Member of Parliament, Major Hills[201] sought to introduce major restrictions on the use of the death penalty in military courts,[202] and he too was defeated by 259 votes to 134. 'Year after year', observed a Member of Parliament, 'we have urged the abolition of the death penalty for [certain] offences, and we have had the same reply'.[203]

Yet the powers of courts martial did diminish over time. In 1925, there was a successful attack on the number of offences liable to the death penalty,[204] and in 1928, after another Committee, chaired by Captain King, had reported, the government abolished the death penalty for eight further offences,[205] leaving treachery, mutiny, cowardice and desertion as the only acts for which capital punishment remained the penalty.[206] Two years later, the Secretary of State for War, against the advice of his military advisers,[207] recommended the abolition of the death sentence for cowardice and offences allied to it.[208] What then remained at the outbreak of the Second World War were three capital military offences only.[209] Yet another Select Committee, the Oliver Committee, was eventually to be appointed in 1938 to inquire into the right of appeal which Christopher Lowther and his colleagues had urged,[210] but it was adjourned because of the war, and later reconvened as the Lewis Committee and its conclusions were accepted in 1950.[211]

Agitation and the rise of the Labour Party

Parallel campaigning continued to be directed at the imposition of the death penalty in civilian courts.[212] There was an unsuccessful bid in Parliament in 1923 to float the idea of a 'Royal Commission or other body' to investigate 'the whole question of capital punishment', but it was dismissed by the then Home Secretary, William Bridgeman.[213] In that same year, and just before it came to power, the Labour Party passed a resolution at its annual conference urging the party to secure 'the substitution of reformative treatment instead of the punitive treatment of criminals at present obtaining and the abolition of the death penalty'. The Party then formed minority administrations in 1924[214] and 1929–1935 and its rise to power raised hopes among abolitionists that its attitude would be significantly different from those of the other main parties (after all, a third of the new Labour Members of the 1924 Parliament were claimed by the Howard League to be abolitionist). Arthur Henderson,[215] the Home Secretary, was ready in 1924 to submit a memorandum on abolition to Cabinet but he was informed by the Prime Minister's Office that 'the Government cannot, within the first few months, commit themselves to every desire they have',[216] flagging a disinclination to act that was echoed in a statement made later by the Under-Secretary of State for the Home Department to the House of Commons.[217] Abolition was not at all pivotal to the government's aspirations and the first Labour Prime Minister, James Ramsay MacDonald,[218] was occupied with other matters.[219] In opposition, he had taken it to be his duty to 'position his turbulent and inexperienced party as the natural custodian of the liberal tradition through the ballot box. He had to show that it was now a potential party of government ...'[220] Elevated to power, 'Labour was to show it could rule responsibly'.[221] '[W]ork in the Home Office was not in the front line of Labour policy'[222] and abolition was a volatile, perhaps irresponsible issue.

The MacDonald Government voiced stock objections. The prospect of abolishing capital punishment always represented what Home Office officials would have called 'trouble', difficult to command unanimous government support,[223] difficult to steer through Parliament, and difficult to champion in the teeth of what looked like hostile public opinion (although there were no opinion polls in the 1920s). 'As a result,' Victor Bailey observed, 'two private member's bills failed to make progress, and [a] deputation of the Howard League, led by Labour stalwart George Lansbury, was fed [what was to become] the standard Home Office line: abolition had never commanded a majority in any Parliamentary division, there was little evidence of any public desire for abolition, and there was no feasible substitute for capital punishment'.[224]

There was thus in the 1920s a prolongation of a century's-old saga of unremitting campaigning, small gains and a lack of official enthusiasm for change. An abolitionist manifesto may have been widely distributed across Labour Party branches in 1927 (Tuttle suggested, 'from 1925 to [the 1960s], with the exception of the years during the Second World War, Great Britain was deluged with propaganda on behalf of the abolition of capital punishment'[225]). And there may have been recurrent attempts to introduce private member's bills,[226] chiefly by the Labour Member, Ernest Thurtle, and the Conservative MP, Vyvyan Adams,[227] a member of the Executive of the National Campaign for the Abolition of the Death Penalty, who was then the current baton-bearer, and a man who called capital punishment 'another kind of violent death, not accidental, but deliberate, cold-blooded, controllable and ceremonious'.[228] But government succeeded government without palpable change.

In 1925, another prime minister, Stanley Baldwin, followed James Ramsay MacDonald to evince no obvious interest in murder and capital punishment at a time when yet another attempt was being made by Ernest Thurtle to amend the Army and Air Force (Annual) Bill.[229] It is perhaps characteristic that, when asked by Major Hore-Belisha in the House of Commons 'Is the Prime Minister aware that there is a newspaper bill outside bearing the device "Murder, by Lord Birkenhead",[230] and may I ask what action he proposes to take in the matter?', he replied, 'I do not think that murder is a matter of public policy'.[231]

Yet there was to be one significant and perhaps surprising step taken against the wider pattern. In late 1929, William Brown[232] presented a new abolitionist Bill to Parliament[233] and, in the ensuing debate, reference was made by the seconder, Lieutenant-Commander Kenworthy,[234] himself a past unsuccessful mover of abolitionist legislation, to an amendment advocating a new inquiry into capital punishment[235] which had been drafted by Sir Herbert Samuel,[236] the former Liberal Home Secretary and current Foreign Secretary, but which had not been tabled.[237] J.R. Clynes, the Labour Home Secretary, was an avowed abolitionist (he confessed that 'I do not believe in this form of punishment ... Capital punishment seems to me more like an act of revenge than punishment for correction. I have carefully studied the figures on the matter, and I am convinced that hanging does not prevent murder or lessen crime statistics'[238]). But all his memoirs had to say of his part in the larger politics of hanging and the proposal to set up an inquiry was 'I was the only Home

Secretary who took a definite step towards the abolition of this form of punish-ment'.[239] He made no mention of Sir Herbert Samuel, James Barr, the Inquiry or its recommendations. There are no extant papers on the decision to appoint a Select Committee in the National Archives, or the archives of the Home Office and the Ministry of Justice, presumably an early victim of the policy of what Lord Hailsham had called the 'somewhat ruthless policy of shredding'. And the Cabinet discussion of the matter is not very revealing. It records that: 'The Cabinet agreed with the view of the Home Secretary that he should adopt a sympathetic attitude towards a Debate on this question and intimate that the Government would be glad to learn the views of the House of Commons. The Home Secretary should be authorised to announce, if neces-sary, that if the view of the House was clearly in favour of a change an Inquiry should be initiated'.[240] None of the secondary accounts of the history of the campaign, including Roy Calvert's own near-contemporary narrative, laid out in Chapter XI of his *Capital Punishment in the Twentieth Century*, explains the decision to accede to William Brown's request. Indeed, they rely simply and wholly on the Parliamentary record.

What John Clynes[241] said to the House was:

> We are wandering partly in the region of opinion and partly in the region of disputed fact. We cannot be sure of our ground. It is risky, and, I think, unhelpful to dogmatise too much on this question, but that does not mean that the facts should not be ascertained and that we should definitely defer action on this question when the facts have been ascertained. During the last 100 years this subject has been debated in the House of Commons on, I believe, 18 occasions, but on only one occasion was a majority recorded in favour of the introduction of a Bill, and then the majority was only one vote. How keen, then, has been the division of opinion! ... We cannot settle the matter altogether on statistics, but we must have statistics. ... A Committee would have to consider the facts presented by authority and brought forward through a channel that could be trusted. While on differ-ent sides of the House we have been in doubt on the question of figures and on points of argument, I think that the Government, whether Labour or otherwise, would be disposed to take some steps on whatever report a Select Committee might submit. My view is that in such a case a Bill would have to be introduced, but it could not be done upon a Motion so bare as the one now before the House. Any action must be taken on a Bill which either this Government or any other Government may be disposed to introduce.

Sir Herbert Samuel himself then moved that 'it is desirable that a Select Committee should be appointed to consider the question of capital punishment. ... The only question to which the House need seriously address itself in this – the whole matter resolves itself down to this – Does capital pun-ishment prevent murders, and, if it is abolished, are murders likely to increase?'

And, supported in part perhaps by those who would delay abolition, and in part by those who wished to promote it, it was resolved the next day 'That, in the opinion of this House, it is desirable that a Select Committee should be appointed to consider the question of Capital Punishment'. The Cabinet appeared favourably disposed.[242] On 7 November 1929, it was announced that 'arrangements are being made through the usual channels, and the customary notice will be given at an early date'. And the Committee began its business on 12 December 1929 with the task of exploring:

> the question of Capital Punishment in cases tried by civil courts in time of peace and to report whether another penalty, and, if so, of what nature, should be substituted for the sentence of death in such cases where that sentence is now prescribed by law.[243]

The Select Committee on Capital Punishment

The Committee was chaired by the Labour Member of Parliament for Motherwell, the Reverend James Barr,[244] and for an interim period, whilst Barr was incapacitated, by Sir John Power.[245] Its manner of proceeding was literary, exegetical, erudite and reflective. It noted the unwaveringly low numbers of people executed: 15 males killed in 1901, 22 in 1902, 24 in 1903, 16 in 1927, 13 in 1928 and seven in 1929, at an annual average rate of 14 over a 50-year period.

It recited the arguments of the retentionist and the abolitionist. On the one hand, it noted, there were appeals to natural justice; atonement; retribution; the State's right to self-defence; the deterrent potential of the death penalty; and, echoing John Stuart Mill (whom it quoted), capital punishment's greater humanity: 'a lifelong sentence is but to let men rot and decay, to doom them to an existence worse than death itself, and permanently to impair something more precious than the life of the physical body' (para. 60). The condemned man, it could be said, was worth little, and the Select Committee quoted its witness, Lord Darling, the former chairman of the 1919 Army Council Committee of Inquiry, and the man who did not think it right to review the power of courts martial to impose the death sentence: 'I think it is quite fair to take his life, and have done with it' (para. 61).

On the other hand, the Select Committee observed (showing the religious stamp of its Chairman), the abolitionist might say that 'every human life is of inestimable value, and ... life itself is the gift of the Creator which no man is empowered to take away' (para. 62). Respect for life is no less binding on the State than on the individual, and 'the more life is held sacred by the Government, the more likely it is to be preserved by the people. ...' (para. 63). The deterrent capacity of the death sentence was unproven, and, even if it were proven, the State should not take life. The death penalty unwarrantably precluded all hope of reformation (para. 65). It was irreparable. It had a deleterious and brutalising impact on prison officers, other prisoners and members of the public (para. 66) (and, in making those observations, it drew heavily on the testimony tendered by Margery Fry of the Howard League and by Roy Calvert of the National Campaign for the Abolition of the Death Penalty. Calvert, said Hugh Klare, was the first person to collect statistics on capital punishment – before him 'the arguments against the death penalty were moral and ethical'[246]).

The Committee moved on to 'deterrency' and observed how very many people were reprieved, how very few were hanged and how, in the past, the removal of the capital penalty from a range of crimes had actually been followed by a decline in offending. Any change in the law on death had always been fiercely contested, and the adverse consequences predicted by its antagonists had never materialised. Indeed, a reluctance to impose overly severe sanctions had had the perverse consequence of corrupting justice (para. 108). And the Committee recalled the numerous failed attempts that had been made over the decades to mitigate the law on homicide by grading offences.

The Committee's report was over 700 pages long. It devoted thirty pages to the experience of other countries, beginning with the dominions and colonies, moving on through South America to the USA (and it looked closely at figures state by state to note that identical trends in homicide rates could be observed in states that were abolitionist and those that were retentionist, those which had restored the death penalty and those which had not done so (paras. 331–2)). The abolitionist states, Maine and Minnesota, for example, were said to have some of the lowest murder rates. It received evidence about Europe, being briefed by the Home Office and by Roy Calvert. It held 27 sittings and heard 44 witnesses, including Margery Fry of the Howard League;[247] Lord Darling;[248] Roy Calvert; and Dr Maurice Hamblin Smith, a prison medical officer and the first man to teach criminology at an English university. (In his evidence of 2 July 1930, Hamblin Smith recommended a discontinuance 'with suitable safeguards of capital punishment': capital punishment, he said, did not allow for the treatment of the prisoner; it fomented unwholesome sympathy for the condemned; it encouraged imitative crimes; and it fed people's worst instincts, pandering to the emotion of revenge.) It heard William Temple,[249] the Archbishop of York, who said that vengeance was illegitimate in Christian theology and who declared himself an abolitionist. It quoted philosophers, lawyers and scripture. It was evidently influenced by (or was in accord with) the arguments of the National Campaign for the Abolition of the Death Penalty and the Howard League. It was chaired by a liberal churchman and abolitionist, a man described by an opponent on the Committee as motivated by a 'crusading fervour',[250] and one who saw Jesus Christ Himself as a victim of capital punishment.[251] Two of its members were Quakers. In the names of reason, progress and civilisation, it proposed abolition:

> … there will come, through the carrying into law of the proposals we are about to make, an ever-increasing security and an ever-increasing respect for human life. Humanity and security, indeed, will walk hand in hand.

And it is the more humane spirit in our people that makes a more humane penal code now possible; so, on the other hand, in humanising our punishments, we will yet further humanise our people. On the one side, and on the other, humanity will beget humanity, as nobleness enkindleth nobleness. (para. 456)

Yet, following the pattern of its predecessors, the Committee was discordant. Six of the fifteen members, all Conservatives, left at the drafting stage, declaring that the report would be 'so one-sided that it failed adequately to represent certain important aspects of the evidence,[252] and thereby tended to create an erroneous impression in the mind of the public and of Parliament'.[253] Sir Gervais Rentoul,[254] the dissidents' spokesman, informed the Committee on 2 December, a week before the report was to be submitted to Parliament, that 'in the event of the Committee deciding not to adjourn in order that those of the Committee who held views opposed to those embodied in the Draft Report proposed by the Chairman, might prepare and bring in an alternative Draft Report after the Christmas adjournment of the House, he and other members of the Committee would withdraw and take no further part in the proceedings'.[255] The Committee voted and it split down the middle. There was no adjournment and no minority draft report. The report that was submitted, endorsed by eight of the members (described as an 'absolute majority of the Committee'[256] by the chairman), concluded that:

Our prolonged examination of the situation in foreign countries has increasingly confirmed us in the assurance that Capital Punishment may be abolished in this country without endangering life or property, or impairing the security of Society. Further, we have the repeated assurances of the Home Office itself that Abolition of the death penalty will not bring with it any serious or insoluble problem of administration. (paras. 453–454).

Whilst the eight authors of the majority report professed that they were confident of their judgement, to be doubly certain, and to reassure the public, they suggested that there should be an experiment 'to precede the final judgment of the Nation': 'We therefore propose that Capital Punishment should be abolished by law for a period of 5 years' (paras. 460, 461). During the ensuing hiatus, 'it would be intolerable that Capital Punishment should ... be inflicted on any criminal' (para. 463). They therefore propounded three Definite Recommendations:

I.   That a Bill be introduced and passed into law during the present Session, providing for the Abolition of the Death Penalty for an experimental period of five years in cases tried by Civil Courts in time of peace.

II. That meantime and forthwith a Resolution be passed by the House of Commons declaring that the Secretary of State for Home Affairs and the

Secretary of State for Scotland, in tendering advice as to the exercise of the Royal Prerogative of Mercy, should recommend in each case that the Death Sentence should be commuted.

III. In regard to the penalty that should be substituted for the Sentence of Death in the cases referred, we recommend that it be the Penalty now attached to reprieved murderers, interpreted and administered in the same way as at present. (para. 475)

The Report was presented on 9 December 1930 and, again following precedent, the Government of Ramsey MacDonald and successor governments were not moved. Requests in the House of Commons for a debate on the Report were repeatedly staved off. Neither were executions reprieved (five were to be carried out in the seven months that followed the Report's publication[257]). In January 1931, the Home Secretary, John Clynes, said 'There has been no opportunity for seeing what is the opinion of Parliament on the recommendations contained in the report of the Select Committee set up as the result of discussion on a private Member's Motion. At present I cannot announce the intentions of the Government with regard to the report'.[258] By the end of the year, in October 1931, his government had fallen and he was no longer Home Secretary ('we were', he said afterwards, 'turned out of office before anything could be done to alter the law'[259]). But, despite his own antipathy to hanging, there had been little enough evidence of an appetite for change whilst he and his colleagues *were* in office.

The substance of Clyne's initial reply was to be repeated again and again over the next few years.[260] It was said that 'The Government do not propose at present to take any action concerning the report of the Select Committee';[261] and that 'In view of the state of Parliamentary business, I can hold out no hope of facilities being given for the discussion of this report at present'.[262] And, to be sure, there were crises and problems enough in the early 1930s: there was unrest in Egypt; agitation in India; the invasion of Abyssinia; unemployment (which was of 'paramount importance'[263]); proposals for a channel tunnel; strikes; the rise of fascism, communism and the Communist International; the Baghdad-Haifa Railway and Pipeline; the Gold Standard; colonial sugar policy; the Rhineland; rearmament and disarmament; the League of Nations; and much else.

But Vyvyan Adams was assiduous in keeping the matter of the report and abolition alive. In 1934, for instance, he asked the Home Secretary 'how many executions have occurred in England and Wales since the Select Committee in 1930 reported in favour of the abolition of the death penalty for an experimental period of five years; and how many of the offenders so executed were of the male sex?'[264] His last motion, 'That this House would welcome legislation by which the death penalty should be abolished in time of peace for an experimental period of five years,' was introduced in November 1938. It met with opposition from the Home Office, was subject to a free vote and, after lengthy debate, received a majority of 114 to 89 in favour. But abolition was not to be part of the Criminal Justice Bill, 1938,[265] an amendment having been resisted by the Home Secretary who said that the government should not experiment in the matter of murder,[266] and the Bill itself was suspended in November 1939 because of the onset of war.[267] Adams himself was not returned to Parliament after the war and died in 1951.

The Criminal Justice Act 1948

Even after the war, sixteen years after the Report's publication, the same sequence of events was to be re-enacted all over again,[268] and, unlike the *sequelae* of the First World War and their impact on courts martial, it was virtually unaltered by any response to the brutalities and mass killings of 1939–1945. Marie Gottschalk, the comparative historian of the politics of criminal justice, pointed out to me that 'In contrast to what happened on the Continent, the inheritance of World War II, notably concerns about excessive state power and the widespread use of state executions during the Holocaust, had little influence on debates about abolition in Britain'.[269] The new administration may have been the first majority Labour Government, having come to power in an election in 1945 that furnished 393 Labour MPs (who had captured 48% of the vote), 197 Conservative MPs with 36%, and 23 Liberal MPs with 9%. It may have been bent on a radical programme. Its election manifesto may have proclaimed: 'The nation needs a tremendous overhaul, a great programme of modernisation and re-equipment of its homes, its factories and machinery, its schools, its social services. All parties say so – the Labour Party means it. For the Labour Party is prepared to achieve it by drastic policies'. There may have been economic reform through the nationalisation of industry; the implementation of the 1944 Education Act; the introduction of the National Health Service; the beginnings of decolonisation and much else.[270] There may have been a preparedness to bring corporal punishment and penal servitude to an end, an abolitionist Home Secretary may have been in place, but on capital punishment, and despite the hopes of the Howard League and its allies,[271] the Cabinet was split, it had experienced no epiphany, the government was not to be swayed, and its great reforming Criminal Justice Bill contained no reference to abolition.[272] That there had been some consideration of a compromise proposal is clear. The would-be abolitionist Home Secretary, Chuter Ede, reminded Cabinet on 28 July 1947 that:

> At their meeting on 15th July ... the Cabinet invited me to ascertain whether it would be possible to draft the title of the Criminal Justice Bill in such a way as to exclude any amendment for the abolition of capital punishment and to circulate a memorandum on the suggestion that it might be possible to distinguish between certain types of murder for which capital punishment would be retained and other types for which it would be abolished. I do not see on what grounds it could be argued that an amendment on the subject of Capital Punishment is outside the scope of

a comprehensive Bill amending the law relating to the methods by which the courts are empowered to deal with offenders.

He went on to say that 'An amendment on the subject of Capital Punishment was proposed on the Criminal Justice Bill of 1939. No suggestion was then made that the amendment was out of order'. However, it proved to be all too demanding. He reviewed the arguments of past committees, including the 1930 Select Committee, to conclude presciently that 'There is no possible method of defining by law the cases in which the motive for taking human life is sufficiently excusable to warrant treating them as a distinct class. ...' There was an insuperable 'difficulty of defining by any statutory provision the types of murder which ought to be excluded from the death penalty ... any attempt to grade murders by statutory provisions would be fruitless'. Moreover, 'a proposal to limit the death penalty to certain types of murder would not be acceptable to those who are in favour of the abolition of capital punishment'.[273] Total abolition was then a step too far. The introduction of degrees of murder was impracticable.

That was the case argued *in camera* but, publicly, there was 'no [visible] indication that the Government [had] altered their views'.[274] What *had* changed was the composition of the House of Commons: there was a new cohort of younger and more reformist Members. An abolitionist amendment to the Bill was tabled by 147 Members, an amendment reciting that 'During the continuance in force of this Section, no person shall be sentenced by a court to death for murder; and every enactment requiring a court to pronounce or record a sentence of death in any case of murder shall be construed as requiring the court to sentence the offender to imprisonment for life'.[275] The amendment was moved by Sydney Silverman, an independent-minded, 53-year-old, radical Labour MP and solicitor, the last in the line of baton bearers,[276] who had embarked on his election to the House of Commons in 1935 on what his obituary was to call 'nearly thirty years of dogged endeavour'.[277]

Sydney Silverman died in 1968, a few years after he won success, and published sources are not forthcoming about why and how he should have so dedicated himself to abolition. Yet one of his sons, Roger, did shed light on his motivation. Sydney Silverman had been born in 1895, he said, 'the eldest son of a poor Jewish refugee from Rumania'. In 1916, he had been:

Conscripted into army. Due to his socialist as opposed to religious objections to military service, was denied recognition as a conscientious objector. Arrested for refusing to obey military orders, sentenced to two years' hard labour. Went on hunger strike, lived for a year on a daily pint of milk. Sentence commuted. On release, found a military escort waiting to conscript him at the prison gates. Once again defied orders, was court-martialled and jailed again. Spent a total of 2 years 3 months in jail. [He] ... did not talk much about his experiences in prison during the First World War, but I know that his hatred of capital punishment started there. When conscription was introduced, he was 21 and a student at Liverpool University. He was already a committed socialist and opposed the war on political grounds. When conscripted, he refused all military orders, and was arrested. He was refused recognition as a conscientious objector, and was jailed either for mutiny or desertion. War resisters were subject to special discrimination and brutal treatment, and at least one of his fellow prisoners died in his cell. Sydney himself staged a hunger strike, and eventually lived for one year on nothing more than a daily pint of milk. I believe that prisoners in his jail were executed during his term of imprisonment, and that that experience inspired his lifelong campaign against capital punishment.[278]

Sydney Silverman's amendment, his first salvo, based on the Select Committee's Report's principal recommendation, was passed on a free vote[279] by 245 to 222 on 14 April 1948. The Home Secretary, Chuter Ede,[280] an abolitionist in private, was obliged reluctantly to obey the principle of Cabinet unity,[281] and adhere to the conventional government line by affirming in conventional language and resorting to the conventional narrative that the time was not right; that the public was against abolition; that trials and appeals worked well[282] ('I am quite certain that if anyone listens to the summing up of the judge when he always warns the jury, in any kind of case, that any reasonable doubt must be resolved in favour of the prisoner, that applies even more to the consideration which is given at the final stage in these cases'[283]); and that the efficacy or inefficacy of deterrence was unproven:[284]

> ... the time is not ripe for undertaking this particular reform. I do not myself believe that public opinion in the country is in favour of this Clause at this time ... it is a very great thing for this country that the ordinary citizen believes that the law and those who administer it are sufficiently strong to prevent evil-doing and to punish evil-doing appropriately when it has occurred. I do not think that public opinion in this country shares the view ... that there is something intrinsically wrong in taking the life of a person who has deliberately and of malice aforethought taken the life of another person. There may come a time when that will be the general feeling in the country, but I am certain that it is not the feeling in the country at the moment. ... In 1938, 97 murders of persons over one year of age were committed in this country. In 1946 the figure was 138 and in 1947 it was 134. I know my hon. Friends who support the Motion say that that is in spite of the death penalty, but neither side can prove anything in regard to its deterrent effect. I am perfectly entitled to say that in my view but for the death penalty the figure would have been much higher. ...[285]

A small majority of the House of Commons had set itself against a government and cabinet that was itself internally riven. It was, said *The Times*, an 'embarrassment to the Government'.[286] The government conceded privately that the political situation was not entirely predictable,[287] they bowed and declared that the bill would be accepted if it passed all its stages. In the interim, there would be no outright abolition but a presumption of a reprieve of execution in all capital cases other than those where public opinion would not condone it.[288]

The bill did not pass all its stages. The clause was heavily defeated in the House of Lords two months later.[289] These were dangerous days, the peers said. Violence was rampant. The time was not ready for an experiment. The public did not support it.[290] Trial and appeal procedures worked well. The Archbishop of Canterbury, Geoffrey Fisher, described by Tuttle as a 'middle way advocate',[291] was unsure about the prudence of moving too far in advance of public opinion;[292] of flouting the views of judges and of past and present Home Secretaries; and of risking mob action:

> I would say that, as upon one or two other occasions, the Government have got themselves and all of us into great trouble by well intentioned but hasty and ill-considered action. I think that they, like the rest of us, must wish now that the matter had never been raised at this moment, or that if it had, they had firmly secured its rejection … it is quite vain to suggest that five years is necessarily an appropriate period for drawing conclusions. Secondly, the clause should certainly be amended so as to retain the death penalty for certain offences.[293]

The Leader of the Opposition in the House of Lords, the Marquess of Salisbury, said:

> I cannot but feel that what we are expected to do is to try an experiment – in plain words, to gamble with the lives of our fellow citizens – and this at a time when we know that the circumstances are most unfavourable to the success of that gamble. I suppose that there has never been a period – I will not go back into ancient history – within the last 150 years during which there has been a more catastrophic decline in the standard of public morals.

The Marquess of Reading[294] said:

> This Bill takes shape at a time when we are affected by a shortage of manpower, by a shortage of materials, and by an outbreak of lawlessness and lack of observance of even the smallest aspects of the law that has probably been unparalleled for many years. It is not good policy to put Utopia into a Statute unless at the same time you are in a position to put it into operation.

And the staunchly retentionist Lord Goddard,[295] the Lord Chief Justice and President of the Court of Appeal, remarked that he and his fellow judges were wholly against the amendment:[296]

Never in the last hundred years has there been such an outbreak of crimes of violence, accompanied, usually, by lethal weapons. ... I do say that if you are going to make the experiment, this is not the time to make it. Can any member of your Lordships' House pick up his newspaper any morning without seeing a report of some crime of violence – all too often the crime of murder? ... I hope that your Lordships will stand firm in accepting this Amendment and rejecting the clause, and, if you do, I am bound to say that I hope you will also stand firm in rejecting a compromise. I say that for this reason. I believe, with all my heart, that our present system, under which the Secretary of State reviews every case which comes before him, has worked well in the past and will work well in the future.[297]

The Lords were adamant, and the Criminal Justice Bill was returned to the House of Commons in early June with the clause deleted.[298] The abolitionist Attorney-General, Sir Hartley Shawcross,[299] then moved on 15 July 'That this House doth disagree with the Lords in the said Amendment';[300] but behind the motion there was a concession. There had been earlier talk of threatening to invoke Lloyd George's Parliament Act of 1911,[301] but instead, and partly because the majority of the cabinet were not unsympathetic to the stance adopted by the Lords; partly because the political environment was so difficult (not least because the Labour Government was contemplating reform of the House of Lords and had no wish to confer on that body the appearance of greater popular legitimacy than the House of Commons[302]); what was in fact proposed was a new, compromise clause, agreed between the Home Secretary and the abolitionists,[303] to retain the death penalty for certain, especially heinous classes of murder,[304] including the killing of police and prison officers.[305] It will be recalled that the Home Secretary had earlier warned about the impracticality of such a course, but it was nevertheless revived as a possible solution to a difficult dilemma.[306] (Tim Newburn commented that such a compromise was probably inevitable: the 'Government position was surely deeply influenced by the fact that the 1948 Bill was perceived to be of great importance – it was a major reformist move – and they were concerned that the capital punishment issue had the potential to derail the whole thing').

The Attorney-General proceeded to say that the House of Lords had actually done the duty of a second chamber.[307] It had expressed the will of the people. It was far more representative of the views of the nation than was the House of Commons:[308] 'We propose in the Clause ... fully to meet the anxiety which has been expressed by public opinion in regard to the matter. That involves a compromise. It involves asking my hon. Friends to accept less than most of them would have liked to see achieved, but I dare say those who believe, as I believe, that capital punishment is wrong in principle, also believe, and again as a matter of principle, that half a loaf is better than no bread'.[309] The House of Commons did pass that motion, no longer on a free vote, on 15 July, and it did so by a substantial majority that included two future Home Secretaries,

Frank Soskice and Roy Jenkins, the first of whom was to play a critical future role in the politics of abolition.

Five days later, the House of Lords again considered its position. The Lord Chancellor, again speaking for the government and conciliation, observed: 'We [cannot] simply go back to where we had been; we [have] to see whether it was not possible to work out some compromise. It has been, as it always is, an exceedingly difficult matter to think out the lines on which a compromise might be reached, because the issue of the marriage of pro and con is often apt to be a rather misshapen infant'.[310] He moved 'That this House do agree with the Commons in their Amendments made in lieu of the Lords Amendment to leave out Clause 1'. But the House of Lords did not agree. Lord Llewellin[311] said:

> What it really amounts to is this, that this clause which the Government have now, at the eleventh hour, produced, is akin to the Highway Code. If anyone who uses the roads observes the Highway Code, in every particular, he will not be prosecuted. This clause is the Murderer's Code; if the murderer reads, marks and observes, all these provisions he can so conduct his affairs that he can murder the person he wants to murder and have no chance of forfeiting his own life.

The Lord Chief Justice said:

> A few weeks ago your Lordships rejected by an emphatic vote the clause which had been sent up from another place abolishing capital punishment. It is agreed on all hands – it has been conceded in another place and certainly in the public Press – that the action of your Lordships was in accord with the opinion of the vast majority of people in the country. If that is so, I ask: What is there to compromise about? With whom are we compromising? Why should there be a compromise?

The motion was rejected by 99 votes to 19. There were no clerics amongst the abolitionists: the sole Lord Spiritual who voted, Cyril Garbett, the new Archbishop of York, and successor to Archbishop Temple, voted with the Not Contents.[312] The part that the Church of England played at that and other points should be heeded because it was to undergo a significant *volte face* later on.

The Law Lord, Lord Simonds,[313] who had professed himself an opponent of the House of Common's amendment – opposed because he was uncertain about its wisdom and impact – again followed precedent and, seeking to defuse an apparently irresoluble constitutional conflict, proposed the formation of yet another committee of inquiry:

> When I look at this clause, it seems to me impossible to regard it as anything but a face-saving device by which His Majesty's Government

control their recalcitrant supporters. For if it is not so, if the Government of the day seriously intend to amend the law in relation to murder, what is the course which they must inevitably take? Surely it is this: to institute a Committee or Commission of Inquiry in order to learn so much that is to be learned, and to place it before your Lordships and the public at large, so that they may be instructed upon this matter.[314]

And Viscount Templewood, a former Home Secretary and a convert to abolition,[315] one of a line of Quaker penal reformers[316] and the chairman of the council of the Howard League,[317] suggested that that committee of inquiry might take the form of a Royal Commission, 'to collect the facts ... to convince the public as a whole'. (He was later to publish an abolitionist book, *The Shadow of the Gallows*,[318] on the platform of the facts that he had himself collected for the Royal Commission).

The Criminal Justice Act c. 58 that was passed in July 1948 introduced detention and attendance centres; abolished penal servitude, hard labour, prison divisions[319] and the majority of powers to impose corporal punishment; and it prohibited the execution of offenders who had been 18 or younger at the time when the killing had taken place; but it made no other alteration to the law on capital punishment. It had been agreed that the clause on which the Houses disagreed, and which had been 'severely mauled', 'riddled' and 'shot to pieces' by the peers, must be deleted[320] so that the Bill could pass.[321] In its stead there was the placatory promise of a Royal Commission.

Two days after the second rebuff by the House of Lords, the Home Secretary told the House of Commons that he would explore 'practical means of limiting the death penalty', and, five months later still, on the day that a man was hanged at Norwich Prison, he announced that a Royal Commission would inquire into 'the questions whether liability under the criminal law in Great Britain to suffer capital punishment for murder should be limited or modified, what alternative punishment can be substituted and what are the changes in the law and the prison system involved by any alternative punishment'.[322]

The Royal Commission on Capital Punishment

A Royal Commission was thus established in January 1949 to ease government out of a difficult stalemate, but, somewhat disconcerting the abolitionist Members of Parliament,[323] its terms of reference did not talk of ending the death penalty or of the five-year moratorium that had been a staple recommendation of private members' bills after the 1930 Report. Perhaps it was thought yet again to be an unripe moment because the country was palpably marked by a degree of social instability and *anomie* in the wake of the Second World War, an instability that was accentuated by the return of thousands of service personnel who had become inured to violent death and did not always find easy the transition to civilian life.[324]

The Commissioners were confined instead to a rather narrow exploration of the *impasse* that had been reached and the compromise which could not be agreed upon, being invited 'To consider and report whether liability under the criminal law in Great Britain to suffer capital punishment for murder should be limited or modified, and if so, to what extent and by what means, for how long and under what conditions persons who would otherwise have been liable to suffer capital punishment should be detained, and what changes in the existing law and the prison system would be required; and to inquire into and take account of the position in those countries whose experience and practice may throw light on these questions'. That 'Retention of capital punishment posited in the Royal Warrant circumscribed the Commissioners' inquiry',[325] for the Prime Minister had said:

> It would be much more useful if the Royal Commission inquired into modifications or alternatives, because the straight issue of capital punishment is one on which Parliament in due course will have to take its decision. It is not very suitable to put it before a Royal Commission. ... I am quite sure that if we put up a Royal Commission with terms of reference to consider abolition, we should merely get majority and minority reports, and I think it is much more useful to set up a Commission with these terms of reference.[326]

The Commission's chairman was to be Sir Ernest Gowers,[327] then 69, a barrister and civil servant, who had in the past chaired numerous committees and commissions, and its members included Sir Alexander Maxwell, the recently retired Permanent Under-Secretary at the Home Office; Norman Fox-Andrews, a Recorder; George Montgomery, an advocate and Professor of Scots Law at Edinburgh University; Leon Radzinowicz; and Eliot Slater, a psychiatrist.

The Royal Commission deliberated for four years, reporting in September 1953.[328] It reflected with some disingenuousness that although its terms of reference had precluded it from considering whether it would be desirable to abolish capital punishment it had decided to hear evidence on the theme, and, in particular, on how far it might be possible to narrow the use of the death penalty 'without impairing the efficacy attributed to it. ... This led us to examine the evidence as to how far capital punishment has in fact that special efficacy it is commonly believed to have' (para. 15). The Chairman later recalled that 'We were not concerned on that Commission with the question whether capital punishment should be abolished or retained. ... But evidence directed to the question whether the scope of capital punishment could safely and properly be limited is often no less relevant to the question whether it could safely and properly be done away with altogether'.[329] Commissioners were also to consider how provocation, mental impairment, age and sex might impair an offender's liability for the death sentence.

The Commission was to produce another lengthy report of over 500 pages that followed the pattern that had been set by other committees on the same theme. It held 63 meetings and heard testimony from 118 witnesses, including Roy Calvert, Cicely Craven and Frank Dawtry of the Howard League; the Director of Public Prosecutions; lawyers and judges, including Lord Goddard; and representatives of the Home Office, the Prison Commission, the Prison Officers' Association, the Prison Governors; the Prison Medical Association, Chief Police Officers, the Police Federation and the Church. It proceeded, first, by perusing data about the effects of abolition from the Commonwealth, Europe and the United States. Next there were visits to prisons in Europe and the United States to ascertain what the alternatives to a sentence of death might be. It surveyed the recent history of murder[330] and executions in the United Kingdom (some 1,200 men and women had been sentenced to death, and 655 had actually been executed, between 1900 and 1949). It considered the alternatives to the penalty of death and the efficacy and character of different methods of execution.

Murder, it reflected, is a variegated offence, embracing very different circumstances, and, although it was commonly held that only the most heinous offences should culminate in execution, there was an inflexibility in the law: 'In Great Britain the law still reflects the concept of an earlier age that every murderer forfeits his life because he has taken another's life. This rigidity is the outstanding defect of our law of murder' (para. 22). It reviewed arguments about the abolitionist case and the more general role of punishment in criminal justice, listing its objects as retribution, reformation[331] and deterrence.[332]

Deterrence was held to be the most problematic of the three: 'Capital punishment has obviously failed as a deterrent when a murder is committed. We can number its failures. But we cannot number its successes' (para. 59). Yet there were those especially exposed to risk, the police and prison officers, who were insistent that it *did* deter, and that the removal of hanging would put their lives at hazard (para. 61).[333] The strength of that argument was difficult to determine, said the Commissioners, because all comparative analysis is fraught. The best conclusion they could form was that 'there is no clear evidence of any influence of the death penalty on the homicide rates of [the] States [that were examined] … and that as soon as a country has become accustomed to the new form of the extreme penalty, abolition will not in the long run lead to an increase in crime' (paras. 64, 65).

As to mitigating the death penalty, the report explored the emergence of the law of murder and the various ways in which homicide might be reclassified for purposes of assessing an offender's eligibility for execution, concentrating in particular on the concepts of 'constructive malice' and 'malice aforethought', and on the aggravation of the offence by contingent features such as murder performed during the commission of some other crime or in resisting apprehension. The doctrine of constructive malice was thought to be especially difficult to defend because people should not be punished for the consequences of acts which they did not foresee.

Possible mitigation was to serve as the core of the report. The Commissioners dwelt on the problem of applying a doctrine of degrees of murder, and they looked especially closely at the practice in the United States of America. There, murder in the first degree tended to be identified as wilful, deliberate and premeditated, marked by such criteria as the use of poison, 'by [the killer] lying in wait', or by its commission during acts of rape, arson, robbery or burglary; whilst murder in the second degree was a residual category of 'all other murders' (para. 517). The difficulty in applying those criteria, the report said – relying heavily on the testimony of American witnesses such as Thorsten Sellin of the University of Pennsylvania – was that the key terms had become obscure and ineffectual over time: premeditation no longer meant a calm, purposeful resolve before the act; the period of time preceding a murder was no longer clearly specified; the defendant's state of mind no longer had to be composed; the precise amount of time devoted to premeditation had become uncertain; and the simple intent to kill had itself become regarded in some jurisdictions as sufficient proof of premeditation. The result, said the Commissioners, was that 'the advantages [of degrees of murder] are far outweighed by ... theoretical and practical objections. ... We conclude with regret that the object of our quest is chimerical and that it must be abandoned' (para. 534).

The report's chief conclusions had to be correspondingly thin. They had not been permitted to touch on abolition (although Sir Ernest Gowers was later to say that the facts and arguments had led him 'to the conclusion that capital punishment ought to be abolished'.[334] Indeed, Sir Louis Blom-Cooper remarked in interview that Sir Ernest 'could absolutely say that at the end of it, all the commissioners would have said if they'd been asked, you must abolish the death penalty'). The search for the Prime Minister's quest for 'modifications or alternatives' had proved to be quixotic. What *was* determined was that the law of murder was marred by the application of a single punishment for a 'crime widely varying in culpability'; that degrees of murder could not satisfactorily be fixed; that the exercise of the Royal Prerogative of Mercy may have acted to soften that rigidity but was 'open to criticism';[335] and that it was impossible to demonstrate the deterrent impact of the death penalty.

The report's recommendations were themselves thin in proportion. The doctrine of constructive malice should be abolished, but accomplices to murder should still be liable to capital punishment. The existing law distinguishing between murder and manslaughter should remain intact. No one under the age of 21 should be hanged. Yet, for all its work, and in common with its predecessors in the 19th century, its proposals could advance but little from the vexed position which had confronted Parliament, the government and the Royal Commission at the outset. It did tentatively recommend ceding from judge to jury the power to decide on the facts of each case whether extenuating circumstances permitted the imposition of a sentence of imprisonment rather than of death,[336] but a more formal, legal differentiation of one case from another was not feasible: 'It is impracticable to frame a statutory definition of murder which would effectively limit the scope of capital punishment and which would not have overriding disadvantages in other respects; ... It is impracticable to find a satisfactory method of limiting the scope of capital punishment by dividing murder into degrees ...' (para. 790). It ended by returning intact and unresolved the problem which it had been asked to consider by the government and Parliament: 'We recognise that the disadvantages of a system of "jury discretion" may be thought to outweigh its merits. If this view were to prevail, the conclusion would seem to be inescapable that in this country a stage has been reached where little more can be done effectively to limit the liability to suffer the death penalty, and that the issue is now whether capital punishment should be retained or abolished' (para. 790). Looking back, Sir Louis Blom-Cooper was able to talk about the 'hopelessness of establishing categories of murder, ... and ... the absurdities and injustices of the concepts of capital and non-capital murder ...'[337] Sir Ernest Gowers himself later claimed that his experience as Chairman of the Royal Commission had converted him to abolition:

> Before serving on the Royal Commission I, like most other people, had given no great thought to the problem. If I had been asked for my opinion, I should probably have said that I was in favour of the death penalty, and disposed to regard abolitionists as people whose hearts were bigger than their heads. Four years of close study gradually dispelled that feeling. In the end I became convinced that abolitionists were right in their conclusions – though I could not agree with all their arguments – and that so far from the sentimental approach leading into their camp and the rational one into that of the supporters, it was the other way about.[338]

In July 1953, and before the report was even published, Sydney Silverman embarked on what was to be the resumption of a barrage that lasted another twelve years. He sought again to introduce a bill to implement the 1930 Select Committee's five-year moratorium under the 10-minute rule, a procedure for initiating supernumerary private member's bills. His broad defence was that it was proper to do so because, on the one hand, abolition, temporary or otherwise, had fallen outside the Royal Commission's terms of reference, and on the other, and more immediately, because of the apparent, recent collapse of one of the arguments against abolition marshalled by the man who had now become Home Secretary. Sir David Maxwell Fyfe had claimed in 1948[339] that the system of protections built into trial and appeal procedures in capital cases of the argument was practically infallible, but the case of Timothy Evans, hanged in 1950,[340] newly risen to prominence, pointed to the possibility of an unmistakable miscarriage of justice.[341] Sydney Silverman's motion failed by 195 votes to 256.

When the report *was* published, Sydney Silverman read it as abolitionist in tenor and he demanded a debate:

> The report makes it perfectly clear ... that the royal commission do not really believe that their proposed changes really make much difference, and they say expressly that the state of the law now is such that you cannot

really make many changes. The real question that emerges is whether to abolish the death penalty or not.[342]

He was not alone, being joined by Hector Hughes, the QC and Labour Member for Aberdeen North, and Jo Grimond, also a barrister and the Liberal Member for Orkney and Shetland, and together they put a succession of questions about when the Royal Commission's recommendations would be debated.[343] The matter was raised in the House of Lords by the retentionist Lord Simon, an erstwhile Attorney-General, Solicitor General and Home Secretary, who wished to deplore the report's recommendation about raising the age at which offenders might be hanged and, in particular, the recommendation that decisions about the death sentence might be devolved to juries:[344] and he was to be reassured by Viscount Jowitt,[345] the Lord Chancellor, that he, Lord Jowitt, was 'not in a position to make any pronouncement on behalf of Her Majesty's Government in regard to the issues raised'.[346]

The government did not find itself in such a position for some time. It was not to be until December 1954 that Jo Grimond was told by the Home Secretary that 'I hope that the House will have an opportunity of discussing these recommendations in the not too distant future'.[347] And that 'long-deferred'[348] debate that would lead to a free vote did at last take place in February 1955. It had not been agreed with any eagerness by Cabinet,[349] and it was opened rather cautiously by the Home Secretary, Major Lloyd-George.[350] The government had formed some 'provisional' views and, he said, 'I use the word "provisional" advisedly. The Government have not as yet come to any final conclusion about the major proposals of the Commission. They propose to examine them again in the light of the debate this afternoon'.[351] The government, he said, were not well-disposed to raising the minimum age at which an offender could be hanged (they 'share the natural desire to spare a young life wherever possible. But they are also disposed to agree with the minority that there are very strong objections to raising the age limit, and, in particular, that it would be dangerous and inopportune to do so at a time when crimes of violence on the part of persons between 17 and 21 are, unfortunately, so prevalent'). They were not well disposed to the recommendation that juries should decide whether a man should be hanged or sentenced to imprisonment ('it would impose on them a responsibility which they were not equipped to discharge, since they would never have such full information about every aspect of the offence and of the offender as is available to the Secretary of State ... it was not fair to ask 12 citizens selected at random, whose duty was already onerous and arduous enough, to bear this additional burden; and ... it would lead to inequalities and anomalies in a field where the interests of justice imperatively demand the maintenance of a uniform standard'). And, above all, the government were not well disposed to the abolition of capital punishment itself; and that was for three familiar reasons:

First, although there may be differences of opinion − and, of course, there are − about the deterrent value of the death penalty in general and in particular cases or types of cases, they are not disposed to reject the evidence of many experienced persons that it is a uniquely effective deterrent to professional criminals ... Secondly, although the Government have carefully studied the views of the Royal Commission on the question of imprisonment as an alternative to the death penalty, they are not convinced that the detention of some murderers for very long periods ... would not give rise to much more serious difficulty than the Commission expects. ... detention for more than 20 years in the conditions of a closed prison would be likely to lead to serious deterioration, as well as causing grave problems of security. Thirdly, irrespective of these considerations, the Government have no doubt that it would be entirely wrong to abolish capital punishment unless there were clearly overwhelming public sentiment in favour of this change. The Government have no reason to think that public opinion is in favour of abolition, or of suspension. Indeed, they believe that the contrary is true.

Sir Frank Soskice, the former Solicitor-General and Attorney-General, and the man who would be Home Secretary when abolition *was* finally enacted, chose to argue the reformers' case for civilisation and progress:

There is something utterly repellent in the infliction of the death sentence. According to our particular inclinations we use words like "immoral," or "uncivilised," or "shocking," but broadly speaking what we are all pointing to, whatever adjective we may choose, is the fact that we are deeply disturbed at the idea that a human being is deliberately and solemnly done to death by the will of society, in whatever circumstances. ... I put it to the Home Secretary and to the House – because we are all proceeding to exercise our judgement on a free vote and independently, as we should in a matter of this sort – that that leaves the matter in this position: ex concessis here is something which is inherently horrible. Investigation has shown that it is impossible to draw any safe conclusion to justify it. ... One has only to look back at the history of the last 50 years to realise what a delicate fabric civilisation is, and also to realise how utterly dangerous is anything which tends in the least to undermine the foundations on which that fabric rests.

Chuter Ede, the former Home Secretary who had been obliged by Cabinet decision to resist the recommendations of the 1930 Select Committee, spoke – and his was a public recantation.[352] He was still uncertain whether capital punishment was a deterrent, but he did note that the offences for which flogging had been prescribed had declined in number since the sentence had been abolished by the 1948 Act. He conceded that public opinion remained resistant to the abolition of the death penalty, but 'I doubt, also, whether, at any time during the last hundred years, a plebiscite would have carried any of the great penal reforms that have been made'. But what had prompted him to speak publicly above all was a personal matter which touched on decisions he had had to make whilst Home Secretary. He had had to say in the debate on the abolitionist amendment to the 1948 Criminal Justice Bill that sure procedures were installed to prevent innocent men and women being hanged, but the probable miscarriage of justice which had resulted in the execution of Timothy Evans in 1950[353] now obliged him very openly to reverse his declared position:[354]

> The evidence was overwhelming against Evans and then, years afterwards, the bodies of six women were found in that house and the other man admitted the murder of those six women. If those facts had been known to the jury at the time, they might perhaps have found Evans guilty of murder in conjunction with Christie; I doubt whether they could have found Evans guilty of murder in any other circumstances. I was the Home Secretary who wrote on Evans' papers, "The law must take its course." I never said, in 1948, that a mistake was impossible. I think Evans' case shows, in spite of all that has been done since, that a mistake was possible, and that, in the form in which the verdict was actually given on a particular case, a mistake was made. I hope that no future Home Secretary, while in office or after he has left office, will ever have to feel that although he did his best and no one would wish to accuse him of being either careless or inefficient, he sent a man to the gallows who was not "Guilty as charged."

The final words were those of the Attorney-General, Sir Reginald Manningham-Buller,[355] and he put the stock case of government and retentionists that spoke of the hazards of violence, the unripe time, and the danger of experimentation:

> … it is not proved that abolition will not result in someone being murdered who, if the death sentence stood, would remain alive. I ask hon. Members opposite in all seriousness to consider this point. I know, from listening to their speeches, how they feel. But have they considered at all what the results would be if the experiment which they are asking the House to make failed? I do not suppose that any one of us would suffer as a result of it, but if there are cases where the death sentence is now a deterrent, then I suggest that suspension of the death sentence is a most dangerous and risky step in the present state of our society. Knowing, as we do, the rising figures of crimes of violence, and that the figures for the first nine months of 1954 are much bigger than the figures for the first nine months of 1953, I suggest that we really should not run this risk with others at this time.[356]

With the support of 25 Labour Members and four Conservative Members of Parliament, Sydney Silverman then once more renewed his call for the implementation of the main recommendation of the 1930 Select Committee: the House, he proposed, 'taking note of the Report of the Royal Commission, is of opinion that for a period of five years persons convicted of murder in the United Kingdom should be sentenced, in place of the death penalty, to imprisonment for life; and calls upon Her Majesty's Government forthwith to introduce legislation to that end'. Parliament, he said, had made no progress since 1930 and would have to revert to the unsatisfactory state which the Royal Commission had condemned: 'if we do not abolish the penalty, if, nevertheless, we want to vary the penalty, if, nevertheless, we want to reject the recommendation of the Royal Commission that the jury or the court shall decide, then we are driven back upon the present method of using the Prerogative of mercy as though it were a judicial process'.

The political composition of the House of Commons (and, eventually, the House of Lords) was to count. There had been a general election since the issue was last fully debated in 1948 in an overwhelmingly Labour House of Commons; a Conservative administration now maintained power with a small majority of 17 seats; and the motion was lost by 245 votes to 214. 194 of those voting for the amendment were Labour (including Chuter Ede), 17 were Conservative and three were Liberal. Of those who voted against, 239 were Conservatives, five were Labour and one was a Liberal. 160 Members did not vote, including Clement Attlee and Herbert Morrison. And that was to remain the position for a while. When on the 14 July 1955 Arthur Lewis asked the Home Secretary, Major Lloyd-George, whether 'he will now introduce the necessary legislation for the abolition of the death penalty', the answer was a monosyllabic 'no'.[357] And 'no' it remained.[358] At the end of the year, Major Lloyd-George declared that the Government accepted none of the Royal Commission's recommendations on the death penalty[359] (Sydney Silverman's comment was that 'I do not know what dark, secret, noisesome influence it is in the Home Office that seduces every Home Secretary in turn'[360]).

The Homicide Act 1957

And still the backbenchers tried. Immediately after the Home Secretary's announcement, Geoffrey de Freitas[361] attempted to promote a motion for the suspension of the death penalty for the experimental period of five years.[362] Three days later, Sydney Silverman, supported by 11 Members, including Chuter Ede, introduced yet another bill, unopposed at first reading, 'to abolish or for a period suspend the passing and execution of the death sentence on conviction of murder and to substitute an alternative penalty therefor'.[363] Two days later still, 166 Members declared their support for a discussion of a Motion for the Second Reading of Silverman's Bill but they were refused leave for a debate.[364] A month later, and just before the Christmas recess,[365] Sydney Silverman pressed again for a Second Reading, and was told that there would be a debate on the penalty for murder 'very soon'.[366]

That debate did eventually materialise in February,[367] although the government had attempted unsuccessfully to stall it.[368] It followed custom and was conducted on a free vote. A Conservative Home Secretary and Lord

Chancellor shared none of the doubts about retention that had preoccupied their predecessors in the Labour administration,[369] but the political situation was quite unpredictable. They would 'put down [their own] motion which avoided the direct issue of abolition',[370] Cabinet would then take account of what transpired, scrutinising patterns of voting as an index of public opinion, and then formulate what might have to be a grudging response. In the short term:

> The House of Lords would ... almost certainly reject any proposal to abolish capital punishment. If the majority in the Commons was small, the Government could maintain that the balance of public opinion did not justify steps being taken to over-rule the House of Lords. On the other hand, if there were a large majority in the Commons, the Government might have to accept that as evidence that public opinion was overwhelmingly in favour of abolition.[371]

The Home Secretary further reflected that the government was in a great dilemma. It would be very difficult for the government to introduce a bill on the death penalty, because that would represent a greatly embarrassing *volte face*. The government's advice had been rejected and it now was up to the House of Commons to take responsibility and for the government 'to make way gracefully for those who believe in abolition'.[372] But the cabinet was still not without aspiration even if there should prove to be a large majority in the Commons. With the Marquess of Salisbury, as Lord President of the Council, in attendance, it agreed that it was reasonable to predict that the Lords would trump a vote in the House of Commons and thereby introduce a hiatus within which there might emerge a growing public resistance to change.[373]

The debate was opened by the Home Secretary and he was tentative, and more than somewhat restrained in what he could say and what he could promise and aware that any proposals were likely to culminate in anomalies and difficulties of drafting.[374] 'Poor Gwilym Lloyd-George', wrote Hugh Klare, 'found himself in the position of the Roman general who led his troops across a bridge: those behind cried forward and those in front cried back'.[375] He proposed the motion that 'this House is of opinion that, while the death penalty should be retained, the law relating to the crime of murder should be amended'.[376] The government still could not reconcile themselves to abolition, he said, and they recognised they had an obligation to give guidance.[377] And his arguments then followed an entirely familiar path. There might be a risk to the public:

> ... the House [is] to consider the straight issue of retention or abolition – that, I think, is the only issue – and [the Government] have themselves reached the conclusion, after long and anxious consideration, that capital punishment should be retained. ... The Government, at any rate, are bound to start from the assumption that in a matter of this kind the law

ought not to be changed unless it can be clearly shown that there is good reason for the changing and that that change would not prejudice the safety or well-being of the public. The Government's first and fundamental duty is to maintain law and order.

It could not, he continued, be demonstrated statistically that capital punishment was not a deterrent: 'The [Royal] Commission meant precisely what it said – that there is no evidence; statistics are incapable of providing evidence one way or another. ... I do not believe that what cannot be proved by statistics cannot be true'. There were in place abundant safeguards to prevent miscarriages of justice: 'Let us consider how many institutions, before an innocent man is hanged, must make not only a mistake but the same mistake. The police, the judge, the Court of Criminal Appeal, the Home Secretary – all, though anxiously searching for the truth, have to fall into error'. Capital punishment conveyed an important symbolic truth about the heinousness of murder: 'The first function of capital punishment is to give emphatic expression to society's peculiar abhorrence of murder. It is because murder is the crime of crimes and taking life is to be sharply distinguished from taking property that there is reserved for it the supreme and unique penalty of death'. These were dangerous times in which violence flourished and it would be foolish to put people at greater risk: 'I ask the House to take note of the continuing increase in the number of crimes of violence against the person. First, the number of murders. Excluding murders of children under one year of age, the number of murders is about one-third above the pre-war figure ...'

An hour into the debate, the former Home Secretary, Chuter Ede, the man who could now again publicly declare himself an abolitionist, then spoke, and he raised the problem of trials miscarrying:

I beg to move, to leave out from "House" to the end of the Question and to add instead thereof: believes that the death penalty for murder no longer accords with the needs or the true interests of a civilised society, and calls upon Her Majesty's Government to introduce forthwith legislation for its abolition or for its suspension for an experimental period. About a year ago I followed the Home Secretary in a similar debate. On that occasion I made certain personal statements which it seemed to me I owed to the House in the line that I proposed to take. The House was very generous to me on that occasion. I hope that the particular incident is not out of the minds of hon. Members; I do not propose to say very much about it today. ... As the Home Secretary who was responsible when the Evans case had to be decided, I say that I do not believe that if, between the time the Court of Criminal Appeal gave its decision and the time when the man was hanged, there had been found on those premises those other bodies from which life had been taken by exactly the same modus operandi as was used in the case of Mrs. Evans and her daughter – I do not believe that public opinion in this country would have allowed that execution to have taken place.

The amended bill received its second reading in the House of Commons by 292 votes to 246 and cabinet had begun to wonder if there was scope for some sort of latitude by, say, exempting the murder of police officers and prison officers from the abolition of the death penalty ('quite a few abolitionists on Govt side are now ready for compromise. ...'. Sydney Silverman himself might give ground and accept amendments, it was thought[378]). But the House of Commons did not seem ready to compromise. The third reading passed in late June 1956 by 152 votes to 133 and the bill moved to the House of Lords where the Lord Chancellor again urged the rejection of the bill and the retention of capital punishment.[379] Lord Goddard talked about the absence of any evidence of public demand for abolition; how violence was soaring; an ill-manned police force was vulnerable to attack ('do not', he pleaded, 'gamble with the lives of the police – because I believe it will be gambling with the lives of the police if this penalty is taken away'); a serious crime merited severe punishment ('The country should be willing to avenge crime; for, so far as I understand, that is the only way in which the community can show their detestation of crime and their resolve that, if possible, it should be stamped out'); and the defendant was adequately protected ('The present system works well because of the exercise of the Royal Prerogative in all cases where any mitigation is perceivable'[380]). The arguments were the same and the outcome was the same. The Lords emphatically rejected the Amended Bill by 238 votes to 95,[381] and the government was offered a new opportunity to legislate for less than total abolition.

The cabinet had been placed in a position riddled with contradictions. It could not accept abolition outright. Not only was it opposed to any such measure in principle but a reversal of its former position would entail a significant loss of political face.[382] Yet any compromise, including the retention of capital punishment for the most heinous murders, was known to be laden with pitfalls.[383] Indeed, the Home Secretary disliked the very word 'compromise'.[384] A memorandum submitted to cabinet at the end of March 1956 reflected: 'The Lord Privy Seal and the Home Secretary both said in the debate on 16th February, 1956, that the Government did not think that the problem could be solved by attempting to define murder or degrees of murder. Once a departure is made from total abolition or total retention anomalies are bound to arise because there are no logical or moral grounds for distinguishing between one category of murder and another'. And, to complicate matters yet further, they had, they claimed, a duty to support the agencies of the State: 'in view of our special responsibilities, we cannot oppose amendments specifically intended to protect policemen and prison officers'.[385] Cabinet was reported to have come to the unenviable and confusing conclusion that:

> ... the retention of capital punishment as a penalty for murders of speci-
> fied classes of persons would introduce into the law the conception of

degrees of murder, to which the Government had hitherto been opposed. Moreover, if in relation to these or other amendments the Government gave definite advice to the House, they would find themselves in an embarrassing position if on a free vote the decision went against the advice which they had given. Opinion on this question in the House of Commons was changing, and some of the Government supporters who had previously favoured abolition were now prepared to consider some compromise. Some of them, for example, had indicated their readiness to accept the amendment ... which would have the effect that capital punishment would be retained for murder committed by a lethal weapon in the course of burglary, house-breaking or robbery, or by a prisoner serving a life sentence. Acceptance of this amendment would, however, leave the law in an anomalous condition.[386]

There was widespread agitation in the party. Conservative associations and organisations across the country passed condemnatory resolutions.[387] One, from Yorkshire in 1956, informed Central Office that:

At the meeting of my General Purposes Committee it was the unanimous decision of all present that the great majority of women, not only in the organisation but in Yorkshire as a whole, were strongly opposed to the abolition of capital punishment. From my own experience of meetings in various constituencies during the past ten days, I can confirm that this is a true expression of general feeling ...[388]

It was 'Another straw in the wind, which is beginning to blow hard', Mrs Henry Brooke, the Joint Vice-Chairwoman of the Conservative Party Organisation, remarked to the Conservative Party Vice-Chairman — and it was a wind that could blow very hard indeed. It blew at a meeting of the Conservative Women's National Advisory Committee in June 1956.[389] The Chairman of the Conservative Party was told:

My wife — representing our Division — attended the above. Not surprisingly, she was completely astonished with the fantastic scenes that welcomed opposition to the current Bill to withdraw hanging. In view of the absolutely overwhelming — and vociferous — opposition to the withdrawal of hanging, I would like to know what action Central Office propose to take in acquainting Conservative M.P.s with this unrehearsed and unpremeditated (since it was an emergency Motion) demonstration of public feeling.[390]

There was anger at the Conservative Party conference in October 1956.[391] Government was lobbied and petitioned from without.[392] Government deliberated within, concluding that the House of Commons had flouted the general will[393] and that, despite manifest difficulties, it might yet secure support for the retention of capital punishment if it restricted the death penalty to only a few of the more egregious forms of murder.[394] In the event it determined to seize control[395] and, despite some remonstration,[396] pre-empt the fresh attempts that were beginning to loom to bring about abolition by private member's bill.[397] (One such possibility was a bill that would have been brought by Alice Bacon, and supported by Sir Frank Soskice, the future minister and Home Secretary at the time of abolition. But Alice Bacon drew eighth place in the private members' ballot at the beginning of the session.[398] She would have reintroduced Sydney Silverman's earlier bill at the beginning of February,[399] but there had not been time enough for her to do so[400]). Indeed, it was argued by the Marquess of Salisbury, that the vote in the House of Lords had given government the chance it had sought:

> … the Attorney-General had previously put forward the proposal that in the next session of Parliament the Government should themselves introduce legislation to alter the law of murder and should then be prepared, if necessary by the use of the Government Whip, to prevent the passage of any Private Members Bill providing for the total abolition of the death penalty. Before the debate in the House of Lords [the Marquess] had not been attracted by this proposal. During that debate, however, both the Archbishop of Canterbury and Lord Samuel had put forward, in moderate terms, the suggestion that the Government should themselves introduce legislation designed to narrow the scope of the death penalty and had argued that, if this were done, the retention of capital punishment would command a wider measure of support throughout the country. These speeches had made a substantial impression on the House of Lords; and there might now be an opportunity for the Government by this means to recapture the initiative in this matter. Discussion showed that there was a substantial body of opinion in the Cabinet in favour of taking this course. It would be consistent with the arguments advanced on the Government's behalf in the House of Commons, both in the discussion of the original motion, in which the Government had offered to take steps to amend the law of murder, and in the proceedings on the Death Penalty (Abolition) Bill. It would meet the view, which was widely held, that in a matter so closely affecting the preservation of law and order the Government should themselves assume responsibility.

A Cabinet committee was then straightaway formed at that meeting in July 1956, consisting of the Lord Chancellor, the Home Secretary, the Secretary of State for Scotland, the Attorney-General and the Lord Advocate, to frame legislation 'to restrict the scope of capital punishment'.[401] What the Lord Chancellor next proposed was, he said, a bill that 'does not seek to introduce degrees or categories of murder which distinguish some murders from others on the basis of moral heinousness, but to retain capital punishment for those forms of murder which most clearly strike at the maintenance of law and order and are most likely to be amenable to the deterrent effect of the death penalty.[402] It is aimed at the professional criminal, the person who carries a gun, the killer of the agents of law and order, and the rare but dangerous multiple killers of the type of Christie and Heath. ... The Bill expresses the present state of public opinion which, though not abolitionist, would like to see some amendment of the law to reduce the number of capital sentences ...'[403] On the very opening day of the new Session of Parliament, on 7 November 1956, the government proposed that compromise.[404] It recognised that its Homicide Bill[405] would meet with opposition:[406] indeed, so close was the vote expected to be that members of the government were required to vote for the bill unless doing so would deeply affront their consciences.[407]

Described as a bill to amend the law of homicide and to limit the scope of capital punishment, it was intended to reconcile those who did not support outright abolition but were discontent with the law as it stood: 'It appeared from the debate here, and from discussions elsewhere,' said the Home Secretary, 'that there was a considerable body of opinion which, while opposing abolition, would welcome some restriction of its scope, either by a more extensive use of the Royal Prerogative ... or by restricting sentences of death to certain types of cases'.[408] The bill accordingly introduced a distinction between what were to be known as 'capital murders' (that is, those subject to the death penalty) and other categories of murder for which the death penalty would be abolished. Capital murders were chiefly those committed in connection with theft or attempted theft or entry or attempted entry into enclosed premises with intent to steal; murders by shooting or by causing an explosion; murders committed in the course or for the purpose of resisting or avoiding or preventing a lawful arrest, or of effecting or assisting an escape or rescue from legal custody. They were particularly heinous and they were deemed amenable to deterrence. They were the maximum that could be retained in the face of parliamentary opposition.[409] This was the 'solution'[410] that had been debated and discussed many times over the previous ninety or so years and had been roundly rejected by the Royal Commission in the early 1950s as a 'chimera'.[411] It had an unopposed Second Reading on 15 November 1956, was considered in Committee for a further two months, and received its third reading at the beginning of February (despite an amendment by Sydney Silverman urging its rejection[412]). It then went to the House of Lords on 21 February 1957 (where it was presented as a compromise that should be agreeable to the peers[413]).

It is important to mark what the Lords Spiritual said on that occasion. It mattered. Potter observed that 'In a Christian country, such as England was, a death penalty devoid of religious sanction could not have survived. It was an issue over which the church could have exercised a moral hegemony and failed to do so. It shadowed public opinion rather than led it'.[414] The arguments of the Archbishop of Canterbury, Geoffrey Fisher,[415] might have turned at least some part of the House of Lords against capital punishment, but he made it plain that he believed that the death penalty was neither immoral nor contrary to Christian doctrine:

... the Lord Archbishop of York and I [have] made as clear as we could what the doctrine of the Church is in the matter of capital punishment. We said that the State has a right, in the name of God and of society, to impose the death penalty, whether as an act of justice or for the protection of its own citizens from violence. ... I feel bound to repeat what the most reverend Primate and I said last time, that there is no immorality in it at all. It may be wise or unwise, expedient or inexpedient; but it is not against the laws of God or the doctrine of the Christian Church.

But it is also significant that he then proceeded to trace a divergence between the two archbishops:

My fellow Archbishop believes, as I do, that the choice for or against abolition of the death penalty does not rest on any absolute principle, but is a matter of weighing the total moral effects upon the county if one line or the other is taken. My co-Primate, so weighing the matter, found himself in favour of total abolition. My own conclusion was different. I could not, as things are at present, support total abolition; but neither could I support the present system unchanged, believing that in several respects, and especially in the fact that 50 per cent of those condemned to death were in fact reprieved, the present system was very clumsy in its working, uncertain in its effect, and so clumsy as to rob the death penalty of the kind of solemnity and power in the public life of the community that it ought to have. So I sought for myself something which would limit the field in which the death penalty operated but would make it in that limited field almost certain to be imposed, thus creating, if there is such a thing as a deterrent in this world, a real deterrent. That seemed to be, in the present position of society and of public opinion, the right line to take.[416]

The Homicide Act was enacted on 21 March 1957, the Conservative Government's public view being that it was the best that could be accomplished in a difficult political situation. A minister reflected a few years later that:

[It] made a number of fundamental changes. It abolished the doctrine of constructive malice. It introduced the doctrine of diminished responsibility. It extended the scope of provocation as a defence to a charge of murder; and it provided that the survivors of suicide pacts should no longer be guilty of murder. But the main provision of the Bill ... was to abolish capital punishment for all murders except those coming within five specified categories. ...

The Royal Commission had reached the conclusion that it was not possible to divide murder into two degrees, capital and non-capital, so as to confine the death penalty to the more heinous. The Government accepted this view and the distinction embodied in the Act was based on a different principle. It was explained during the debate that these categories of murder were not necessarily those which were considered the most wicked but were those which struck especially at the maintenance of law and order and on the commission of which the deterrent effect of capital punishment was most likely to operate.[417]

But there were to be other views. The Lord Chancellor, Lord Kilmuir, later reflected that 'This compromise solution ... made the worst of the situation. Lloyd George was made to look foolish, as his advice was consistently ignored by the House; and the Government made to look weak and vacillating. ... The ... result was a discomfited Government, a divided party, and a measure – the Homicide Act of 1957 – which was something less than perfect'.[418]

Conclusion

For over a century, abolitionists and retentionists had repeatedly pitted the same arguments against one another in a debate that ended effectively in an unsatisfying stalemate. One rhetoric talked of barbarism and the lack of evidence for the value of the death penalty; the other of the defence of society and the lack of evidence for the absence of risk if there were to be abolition. It was a stalemate that came to be built into the very fabric of the Homicide Act of 1957, and the act was anything but a final answer to the difficulties which the government, and other governments, had faced. It housed what would in time come to be represented as a set of troubling dilemmas that demanded yet further political attention (Christoph observed that the 'enemies of capital punishment ... saw it as at best a palliative brimming with anomalies'[419] and another commentator, Judge Eric Stockdale, called it 'a ghastly compromise'[420]). What could only resolve the *impasse* was a change in the balance and composition of hitherto irreconcilable political forces.

Acknowledgements

I am grateful to Sir Louis Blom Cooper, Professor Marie Gottschalk and Tank Waddington for their comments on earlier drafts of these two chapters.

Notes

1 Christoph surmised that 'because of the reluctance of the normal motive force – the Government – to give a lead on many questions of penal policy, organized groups seeking change have had to rely upon back-benchers ... to press their case in Parliament'. J. Christoph (1962); *Capital Punishment and British Politics*, London: George Allen & Unwin, 180.
2 Lord Windlesham; *Responses to Crime, op. cit.*, 157.
3 Editorial, *The Times*, 10 February 1955.
4 See the letter from Lord Quickswood, the former Member for Greenwich, to *The Times*, 19 February 1955.

5　See the letter from Hugh Klare, Secretary of the Howard League, to *The Times*, 16 February 1955.

6　See M. Douglas and A. Wildavsky (1982); *Risk and Culture: An Essay on the Selection of Technical and Environmental Dangers*, Berkeley: University of California Press, 187.

7　J. Freeman (1961); Foreword to A. Koestler and C.H. Rolph; *Hanged by the Neck: An Exposure of Capital Punishment in England*, Baltimore, Maryland: Penguin Books, i.

8　Writing about the contemporary United States, David Garland said that 'There is very little in today's debates that would not be familiar to those who addressed the issue 200 years ago, as a glance at the writings of Cesare Beccaria, Jeremy Bentham, or Benjamin Rush will quickly reveal'. D. Garland (2010); *Peculiar Institution*, Cambridge, Massachusetts: Belknap Harvard, 10.

9　C. Cunningham; 'Some Practical Considerations', in L. Blom-Cooper (ed.) (1969); *The Hanging Question*, London: Gerald Duckworth, 109.

10　http://www.hup.harvard.edu/catalog.php?isbn=9780674057234

11　D. Garland (2009); '"Symbolic" and "Instrumental" Aspects of Capital Punishment', in C. Lanier, W. Bowers and J. Acker (eds.) *The Future of America's Death Penalty*, Durham, North Carolina: Carolina Academic Press, 421–452.

12　J. Gusfield (1963); *Symbolic Crusade*, Urbana: University of Illinois Press.

13　D. Garland; *Peculiar Institution, op. cit.*, 144.

14　Marie Gottschalk made much the same claim about the politics of abolition in the United States, except that the campaigning liberal elite in the USA failed to attain their object. See M. Gottschalk (2006); *The Prison and the Gallows*, Cambridge: Cambridge University Press, 206.

15　Mick Ryan claimed that the politics of the period were marked by the capacity of liberal groups to work despite populist clamour. That would, he said, change later. See M. Ryan (1983); *The Politics of Penal Reform*, London: Longman.

16　J. Horder (2012); *Homicide and the Politics of Law Reform*, Oxford: Oxford University Press, especially Ch. 1. And that is an argument that has been developed about the politics of capital punishment in other jurisdictions. For example, Garland says of the United States, that 'Abolition has been a top-down, countermajoritarian reform, imposed with limited popular support, and usually in direct contravention of majority public opinion'. *Peculiar Institution, op. cit.*, 130.

17　Ray Paternoster, for instance, opens his analysis of capital punishment in America with the statement: 'There are few topics as controversial as capital punishment. It seems to stir great passion and debate among those who support its infliction on serious criminal offenders and those who oppose it'. R. Paternoster (1991); *Capital Punishment in America*, New York: Lexington Books, i.

18　R. Jenkins (1959); *The Labour Case*, Mddx.: Penguin, 136.

19　For a broad overview of those trends, see S. Pinker (2012); *The Better Angels of Our Nature: A History of Violence and Humanity*, London: Penguin Books, esp. Ch. 3.

20　M. Eisner (2003); 'Long-Term Historical Trends in Violent Crime', *Crime and Justice*, Chicago: University of Chicago Press, Vol. 30, 99.

21　*Ibid.*, 85.

22　P. Spierenburg (2008); *A History of Murder*, Cambridge: Polity, 203.

23　See M. Eisner (2001); 'Modernization, Self-Control and Lethal Violence. The Long-term Dynamics of European Homicide Rates in Theoretical Perspective', *The British Journal of Criminology*, Vol. 41, No. 4, 639–655.

24　N. Elias (1978); *The Civilizing Process*, New York: Pantheon Books.

25　See E. Leyton (1995); *Men of Blood: Murder In Modern England*, London: Constable.

26　See J. Sharpe (2016); *A Fiery and Furious People: A History of Violence in England*, London: Random House.

27　See J. Sharpe (1990); *Judicial Punishment in England*, London: Faber and Faber.

28 *Report* (1931); Select Committee on Capital Punishment, Cmd. 15, London: HMSO, viii.
29 See Justice (1989); Evidence submitted to the House of Lords Select Committee on Murder, Manslaughter and Life Imprisonment, 1.
30 See A. Sarat (2001); *When the State Kills*, Princeton: Princeton University Press.
31 See H. Bleackley and J. Lofland (1977); *State Executions Viewed Historically and Sociologically: The Hangmen of England and the Dramaturgy of State Executions*, originally published 1929, reprinted by New Jersey: Patterson Smith; and J. Lofland (1975); 'Open and Concealed Dramaturgic Strategies: The Case of the State Execution', *Journal of Contemporary Ethnography*, Vol. 4, 272–295.
32 See J. Garner (2015); 'The Sheriff's Picture Frame:' Art and Execution in Eighteenth-Century Britain, Yale University, ProQuest Dissertations Publishing, 5.
33 'Execution of Gleeson Wilson', *The Times*, September 17, 1849.
34 See 'The Bermondsey Murder. Execution of the Mannings', *The Times*, November 13, 1849.
35 See 'Execution At The Old Bailey', *The Times*, October 21, 1862.
36 G. Wilkinson (no date); *The Newgate Calendar Improved*, London: Thomas Kelly, Vol. 3, 211–212.
37 G. Wilkinson; *The Newgate Calendar Improved*, op. cit., Vol. 5, 358.
38 A ritual that was echoed elsewhere. In Bedford, for instance, the bells of St. Paul's church would toll on execution days.
39 See D. Cooper (1974); *The Lesson of the Scaffold: The Public Execution Controversy in Victorian England*, Athens: Ohio State University Press, esp. 5.
40 See M. Merback (1999); *The Thief, the Cross and the Wheel: Pain and the Spectacle of Punishment in Medieval and Renaissance Europe*, London: Reaktion Books.
41 See P. Smith (2008); *Punishment and Culture*, Chicago: University of Chicago Press.
42 As a matter of course, *The Newgate Calendar* reported the comportment and last words of the dying man or woman as if to provide a moral epilogue to the offence and the offender. One such instance was the case of William Honeyman, 'the young swindler', executed on Pennenden Heath in 1806 who was reported to have said '... I confess, with the greatest contrition, the crime which has brought me to this horrid place, and admit the justice of my sentence, while I am sinking under its severity; and I earnestly exhort you all, my fellow prisoners, and young men at liberty, to acknowledge the offences you have been guilty of and to bequeath to your country that confidence in public justice without which there can be neither peace nor safety in this world ... we humbly trust, our sorrowful prayers and tears will be acceptable in [Christ's] sight. Thus shall we be qualified, through Christ, to exchange this dismal body and these uneasy fetters, for the glorious liberty of the sons of God ...' *The Newgate Calendar Improved*, op. cit., Vol. 3, 184–5. And see J. Sharpe (1984); 'Last dying speeches: religion, ideology and public execution in 17th-century England', *Past and Present*, 107, 144–67.
43 A. McKenzie (2007); *Tyburn's Martyrs: Execution in England 1675–1775*, London: Hambledon Continuum, 163.
44 Based on the entry on 'gallows' in the *Oxford Dictionary of Folklore*, http://www.oxfordreference.com/views/ENTRY.html?subview=Main&entry=t71.e396&category=
45 See R. Richardson (1987); *Death, Dissection and the Destitute*, London: Routledge and Kegan Paul.
46 Jack Ketch, for instance, was notorious for botching his job. See http://217.169.56.135/view/article/15479?docPos=1
47 Thus William Johnson and Jane Housden were said from the time of their conviction in 1712 for murder 'to that of their execution, and even at the place of their death, they behaved as if there wholly insensible of the enormity of the crime which they had

committed; and notwithstanding the publicity of their offence, to which there were so many witnesses, they had the confidence to deny it to the last moment of their lives: nor did they shew any signs of compunction for their former sins …' *The Newgate Calendar Improved, op. cit.*, Vol. 1, 124.

48 D. Garland (2006); 'Concepts of Culture in the Sociology of Punishment', *Theoretical Criminology*, Vol. 10, No. 4, 420–21.

49 Anon (1922); 'The Pros and Cons of Capital Punishment', *The Howard Journal*, Vol. 1, No. 2, 19.

50 For a complementary description of the manner in which ritual may have embedded capital punishment in North American sensibilities, see M. Davidson (2011); 'The Ritual of Capital Punishment', *Criminal Justice Studies*, Vol. 24(3), 227–240.

51 D. Hay (1975); 'Property, Authority and the Criminal Law', in D. Hay, P. Linebaugh and E. Thompson (eds.) *Albion's Fatal Tree*, London: Allen Lane, 17.

52 L. Radzinowicz (1948); *A History of English Criminal Law and its Administration from 1750*, London: Stevens and Sons, Vol. 1, 4. According to Beatty, the precise number of capital statutes was obscure, even to contemporaries: J. Beatty (1974); 'The Pattern of Crime in England 1660–1800', *Past and Present*, No. 72, 48.

53 *Report*, Select Committee on Capital Punishment, *op. cit.*, vii.

54 See L. Gabel (1929); *Benefit of Clergy in England in the Later Middle Ages, Smith College Studies in History*, Vol 14, Nos 1–4.

55 The third Baron Suffield, 1781–1835, sat in the House of Commons from 1806–1812, and from 1820–1821. He was a campaigner for liberal causes, pressing for an inquiry into the Peterloo massacre, the improvement of prison discipline, a relaxation of the game laws, and the abolition of the slave trade. He was chairman of quarter sessions in Norfolk. (Based on Anon.], *rev.* H. C. G. Matthew, T*he Oxford Dictionary of National Biography* on-line: http://www.oxforddnb.com/view/article/12232)

56 123 years later, Gerald Gardiner, the future Lord Chancellor, made precisely the same allegation about pious perjuries. G. Gardiner (1956); *Capital Punishment as a Deterrent: And the Alternative*, London: Victor Gollancz, 38.

57 D. Hay; 'Property, Authority and the Criminal Law', *op. cit.*, 46–49.

58 See P. Rock (1977); 'Law, Order & Power in Late Seventeenth and Early Eighteenth Century England', *Annales Internationales de Criminologie*, Vol. 16, Nos. 1 and 2, 191–221.

59 *Report*, Select Committee on Capital Punishment, *op. cit.*, ix.

60 Source http://www.capitalpunishmentuk.org/hanging1.html

61 See P. Spierenburg (1984); *The Spectacle of Suffering: Executions and the Evolution of Repression: From a Preindustrial Metropolis to the European Experience*, Cambridge: Cambridge University Press.

62 See P. Smith (1996); 'Executing Executions: Aesthetics, Identity, and the Problematic Narratives of Capital Punishment Ritual', *Theory and Society*, Vol. 25, No. 2, 235–261. Giddens talked about a growth of rationality in the administration of the State and Foucault claimed that the shift was from a public scourging of the body as a display of power under autocracy to a private disciplining of the soul in institutions such as penitentiaries, as part of a larger project of taming the masses in readiness for the demands of a nascent capitalist society. The two explanations are actually quite complementary. See M. Foucault (1979); *Discipline and Punish*, Harmondsworth: Penguin.

63 Romilly observed that 'There is probably no other country in the world in which so many and so great a variety of human actions are punishable with loss of life as in England. These sanguinary statutes, however, are not carried into execution. For some time past the sentence of death has not been executed on more than a sixth part of all the persons on whom it has been pronounced, even taking into the calculation crimes the most atrocious and the most dangerous to society, murders, rapes, burning

of houses, coining ...' S. Romilly (1810); *Observations on the Criminal Law of England, As It Relates to Capital Punishments*, London: T. Cadell and W. Davies, 3.

64 J. Sharpe, *Judicial Punishment in England, op. cit.*, 40.

65 Langbein talked about how 'As on the Continent, the decline in England's "penal death rate" came about because of the development of an alternative to the blood sanctions: transportation of convicts for terms of labor as indentured servants in the overseas colonies. Transportation of felons began as a trickle in the years 1615–1660, became substantial in the period 1660–1700, and expanded greatly after 1717'. J. Langbein (1976); 'The Historical Origins of the Sanction of Imprisonment for Serious Crime' *The Journal of Legal Studies*, Vol. V, No. 1, 54. See, for example, HC Deb 18 February 1819 Vol. 39 cc464–509.

66 Richards suggests that the campaign against capital punishment can be crudely divided into three phases: first, attempts to limit the number of offences punishable by death; second, the campaign to end public executions; and, finally, the campaign for total abolition. P. Richards (1970); *Parliament and Conscience*, London: George Allen and Unwin.

67 And treason included offences against the currency and, as petty treason, the wife's murder of her husband.

68 See J. Ridley (2001); *Bloody Mary's Martyrs*, London: Constable.

69 See http://www.exclassics.com/newgate/ng708.htm

70 1814 Chapter 146 Geo. 3. The preamble had run: 'Whereas in certain cases of high treason, as the law now stands, the sentence or judgement required by law to be pronounced or awarded against persons convicted or adjudged guilty of the said crime in such cases is that they should be drawn on a hurdle to the place of execution and there be hanged by the neck, but not until they are dead, but that they should be taken down again, and that when they are yet alive their bowels should be taken out and burnt before their faces, and that afterwards their heads should be severed from their bodies, and their bodies be divided into four quarters, and their heads and quarters to be at the King's disposal: And whereas it is expedient in the said cases of high treason to alter the sentence or judgement now required by law ... ' to death by hanging, followed by posthumous quartering, and later to hanging alone in 1870 under the Forfeiture Act (c. 23), s. 31. The current penalty is imprisonment for life.

71 http://lcjb.cjsonline.gov.uk/Cambridgeshire/3506.html

72 For an account of the last public procession see S. Devereaux (2009); 'Recasting the Theatre of Execution: The Abolition of the Tyburn Ritual', *Past and Present*, Vol. 202, No. 1, 127–174.

73 Cited in A. Griffiths (1896); *The Chronicles of Newgate*, London: Chapman and Hall, 72.

74 See V. Gatrell (1994); *The Hanging Tree: Execution and the English People, 1770–1868*, Oxford: Oxford University Press.

75 See R. McGowen (1994); 'Civilizing Punishment: The End of the Public Execution in England', *Journal of British Studies*, Vol. 33, No. 3, 257–282.

76 Charles Dickens to the Editor of *The Times*, Letters, November 13, 1849.

77 The Act's long title was the Capital Punishment Amendment Act 1868. Chapters 24, 31 and 32 Vict.: An Act to provide for carrying out of Capital Punishment within Prisons, and it laid down that 'Judgment of death to be executed on any prisoner sentenced on any indictment or inquisition for murder shall be carried into effect within the walls of the prison in which the offender is confined at the time of execution'.

78 And, indeed, as we shall see, those arguments were to be urged in the other two case histories of abortion and homosexual law that succeed this chapter.

79 See L. Farmer (2016); *Making the Modern Criminal Law: Criminalization and Civil Order*, Oxford: Oxford University Press, esp. ch. 3.

80 See A. Jorns (1931); *The Quakers as Pioneers in Social Work*, New York: Macmillan, 192.

81 There had, for example, been earlier Leveller voices demanding the restriction of the death penalty to only the gravest of crimes. See R. Zaller (1987); 'The Debate on Capital Punishment during the English Revolution', *The American Journal of Legal History*, Vol. 31, No. 2, 126–144.

82 And that was an argument that was made on both sides of the Atlantic. Benjamin Rush (1792) claimed that capital punishment might encourage others to kill and excited an unwarranted sympathy for the condemned. See *Considerations on the Injustice and Impolicy of Punishing Murder by Death*, Philadelphia: Matthew Carey.

83 See, for example, J.S. Mill (1869); *On Liberty*, Longman, London: Roberts and Green.

84 Romilly argued that 'it is universally agreed, that the certainty of punishment is much more efficacious than any severity of example for the prevention of crimes. Indeed this is so evident, that if it were possible that punishment, as the consequence of guilt, could be reduced to an absolute certainty, a very slight penalty would be sufficient to prevent almost every species of crime, except those which arise from sudden gusts of ungovernable passion'. *Observations on the Criminal Law of England, as It Relates to Capital Punishments, op. cit.*, 20.

85 See H. Bedau; 'Bentham's Theory of Punishment: Origin and Content', Paper given at the Bentham Seminar, University College, London, 10 March 2004, http://www.ucl.ac.uk/Bentham-Project/journal/Bedau.htm

86 J.S. Mill (1950); *Bentham and Coleridge*, originally published 1838, republished by London: Chatto and Windus, 75.

87 Speeches, 1838, in L. Radzinowicz; *A History of English Criminal Law, op. cit.*, 355.

88 J. Plamenatz (1949); *The English Utilitarians*, Oxford: Basil Blackwell, 59.

89 J.S. Mill (1910); *Utilitarianism, Liberty and Representative Government*, first published in 1861, republished by London: J.M. Dent, 55.

90 Cited in H. Bedau (1983); 'Bentham's Utilitarian Critique of the Death Penalty', *The Journal of Criminal Law and Criminology*, Vol. 74, No. 3, 1036.

91 He argued in a speech to the House of Commons on 21 April 1868: 'If, in our horror of inflicting death, we endeavour to devise some punishment for the living criminal which shall act on the human mind with a deterrent force at all comparable to that of death, we are driven to inflictions less severe indeed in appearance, and therefore less efficacious, but far more cruel in reality, Few, I think, would venture to propose, as a punishment for aggravated murder, less than imprisonment with hard labour for life; that is the fate to which a murderer would be consigned by the mercy which shrinks from putting him to death ... if it really is what it professes to be, and if it is realised in all its rigour by the popular imagination, as it very probably would not be, but as it must be if it is to be efficacious, it will be so shocking that when the memory of the crime is no longer fresh, there will be almost insuperable difficulty in executing it. What comparison can there really be, in point of severity, between consigning a man to the short pang of a rapid death, and immuring him in a living tomb, there to linger out what may be a long life in the hardest and most monotonous toil, without any of its alleviations, or rewards – debarred from all pleasant sights and sounds, and cut off from all earthly hope, except a slight mitigation of bodily restraint, or a small improvement of diet?'

92 The Howard League declared that 'Human justice is admittedly fallible. ... The infliction of capital punishment is ... to be avoided as removing the last chance of reversing a sentence proved later to be erroneous'. Anon; 'The Pros and Cons of Capital Punishment', *op. cit.*, 19.

93 Sir Samuel Romilly, 1757–1818, was called to the Bar in 1783. A friend of William Wilberforce, Jeremy Bentham and William Petty, he was a member of high Whig society. He became MP for Queenborough in Kent and served as Solicitor General

between 1806 and 1807. He campaigned against the liberal use of the death penalty, especially for petty offences, the pillory and flogging in the Army and Navy. He sought unsuccessfully to mitigate the punishments for treason. Source: R. A. Melikan's entry in *The Oxford Dictionary of National Biography* on-line: http://217.169.56.135/view/article/24050?docPos=2

94 See E. Tuttle (1961); *The Crusade against Capital Punishment in Great Britain*, London: Stevens and Sons, 3.

95 He recalled that he had been persuaded by Lord Abinger to 'attempt at once to repeal all the statutes which punish with death mere thefts, unaccompanied by any act of violence, or other circumstances of aggravation. This suggestion was very agreeable to me. … I determined to attempt the repeal of them one by one; and to begin with the Act of Queen Elizabeth, which makes it a capital offence to steal privately from the person of another'. (1840); *Memoirs of the Life of Sir Samuel Romilly Written by Himself*, London: John Murray, Vol. 2, 239. (Lord Abinger, 1769–1844, was a judge, at one time the most successful advocate of his day, who was elected a Member of Parliament for Peterborough in 1819, becoming Attorney General in 1827 and then lord chief baron of the exchequer in 1834 (G. F. R. Barker, *rev.* Elisabeth A. Cawthon in *The Oxford Dictionary of National Biography* on-line: http://217.169.56.135/view/article/24783).

96 It was to be his only successful abolitionist Bill despite having 'every year introduced Bills to abolish capital punishment for minor offences, and in particular for the offence of stealing goods to the value of 40s. or more in a private dwelling house, and the offence of stealing 5s. or more in a shop'. G. Gardiner; *Capital Punishment as a Deterrent: And the Alternative, op. cit.*, 24.

97 S. Romilly, *Memoirs of the Life of Sir Samuel Romilly Written by Himself, op. cit.*, 247–248.

98 *Ibid*, 244.

99 Quakers, for instance, had railed against capital punishment from the first. An early Friend, John Bellers (1654–1725), writing in 1699, was one of the very earliest English abolitionists (see his *Essays about the Poor, Manufactures, Trade, Plantations, & Immorality*, London: T. Sowle). Others followed, prominent amongst them being Elizabeth Fry, who was mocked for her 'extreme opinions against capital punishments' (review of a 'Memoir of the Life of Elizabeth Fry, Edited by two of her Daughters', *The Quarterly Review*, Vol. 82 (163), 1847, 115). The case they put was plain and unvariable. Hanging was inimical to Christianity. In 1956, when the homicide Bill was being discussed, it was decided at the London yearly meeting of the Society of Friends that 'We feel we should at this time declare once again our unwavering opposition to capital punishment. The sanctity of human life is one of the fundamentals of a Christian society and can in no circumstances be set aside'. In 1957, when the Bill had passed, the Quakers' own journal, *The Friend*, announced that 'Friends will have cause for thankfulness that the Government Homicide Bill has received the Royal Assent, and that this will result in a considerable reduction of hangings. … [However] Many Friends will regret that the Government agreed to [a] compromise and did not support the complete abolition of the death penalty …', *The Friend*, 29 March 1957, 262. The current position, conveyed by the Society of Friends' *vade mecum*, is that 'No man is ever utterly lost, and however deep he is sunk in evil, the only just approach to him is to work for his recovery'. *Quaker Faith and Practice* (2013); Fifth edition, Yearly Meeting of the Religious Society of Friends (Quakers) in Britain, London, 23.95.

100 See, for example, W. Eden (1771); *Principles of Penal Law*, London: B. White.

101 J. Langbein; 'The Historical Origins of the Sanction of Imprisonment for Serious Crime', *op. cit.*, 35.

102 E. Tuttle; *The Crusade against Capital Punishment in Great Britain, op. cit.*, 2.

103 C. Beccaria (1995); *On Crimes and Punishments*, originally published in 1764, republished by Cambridge: Cambridge University Press, 70.

104 J.S. Mill; *Bentham and Coleridge, op. cit.,* 75, 76.

105 House of Commons debates, 21 April 1868.

106 *The Times,* 22 December 1875.

107 See B. Wootton (1992); *Selected Writings: Volume 1: Crime and the Penal System,* Houndmills: Macmillan, 87.

108 The Howard League said that 'The deliberate putting to death of a fellow creature, though the State might benefit from its removal, is a task so abhorrent to a decent human being that it is wrong to demand it'. Anon; 'The Pros and Cons of Capital Punishment', *op. cit.,* 19.

109 See L. Sklair (1970); *The Sociology of Progress,* London: Routledge and Kegan Paul.

110 Ernest Thurtle, 1884–1954, served in a London regiment in the first World War and was severely wounded. He was the unsuccessful candidate for the National Federation of Discharged Sailors and Soldiers in 1918 but succeeded in winning the seat of Shoreditch in 1923. He became a junior whip in 1930. Stephen Brooke, his biographer for the Oxford Dictionary of National Biography, stated that 'Appalled by the cruelty of military punishment during his time in the trenches, he spearheaded a campaign to abolish the death penalty for offences such as desertion and cowardice, also publishing two books on the question, *Military Discipline and Democracy* (1920) and *Shootings at Dawn* (1929). In 1924 he introduced a bill to abolish the death penalty in such cases, and achieved his aim in 1930, a considerable personal triumph that did much to humanise military justice in Britain'. http://217.169.56.135/view/article/69843/39412

111 House of Commons Debates, 3 April 1930, Vol. 237 cc1564–627.

112 K. Younger; 'The Historical Perspective' in L. Blom-Cooper (ed.) *The Hanging Question, op. cit.,* 6–7.

113 Sir Robert Peel in the House of Commons, HC Deb 30 May 1832 Vol. 13 cc195–209.

114 *Report of the Select Committee on Capital Punishment, op. cit.,* para. 248.

115 *Ibid., op. cit.* para. 321.

116 Sir John Walsh, 1798–1881, the Member for Radnorshire, speaking in 1864. He added that, 'since the foundation of Christianity, capital punishments had been almost universally adopted by mankind'. HC Deb 3 May 1864 vol 174 cc2055–115. He could be described as conservative, having been a strenuous opponent of the 1832 Reform Act (he published a pamphlet titled 'The Practical Results of the Reform Act') and, in 1859, when proposing to stand for re-election, telling his constituents that 'A warm attachment to our mixed form of Government and constitutional monarchy have ever rendered me cautious in the path of innovation, lest I should disturb a balance it would be impossible to restore' (*The Times,* 9 April 1859).

117 The Common Serjeant answered a Parliamentary Question by reflecting: 'How comes it then that our laws are severe? It is because we love freedom and happiness; because we are jealous of previous restraint and controul of our actions; because we wish to avoid the teasing vigilance of the perpetual superintendence of the law; because we would not purchase exemption from crime, by the loss of virtue. If, from the want of this superintendence and controul, crimes are more difficult to detect; if, from the nature of our modes of trial, and from the scrupulous and jealous exactness with which testimony is scrutinised, criminals are with more difficulty convicted, and we have been thus obliged to counterbalance these inconveniences by the terror of severer sanctions, such sanctions are the price we pay for our liberties. And cheerfully ought we to pay this price, even though we were convinced that, by other courses of action, we might have fewer crimes. But have we failed in obtaining the objects we have sought? We have every way attained them. We have formed the character of people, which I will not trust myself to describe, but which I trust I shall never live to see

altered. Have severe laws made us cruel, or humbled or broken down our spirit? Are we a mean, creeping, overawed people? I never look at the people without feelings of respect, affection, and admiration, which overcome me'. HC Deb 29 March 1811 Vol. 19 cc644–61.

118 A. Koestler and C.H. Rolph (1961); *Hanged by the Neck, op. cit.*, 34.

119 William Frankland MP, 1761–1816, asked the House of Commons in a debate on the second reading of a bill for the more exemplary punishment of persons destroying or injuring any Stocking or Lace Frames, 'when the law was openly violated, it was the duty of the legislature to enact severer laws. If the parent were not obeyed, while mild and indulgent, who would maintain that he ought not to change his countenance, and express his indignation?' HC Deb 17 February 1812 Vol. 21 cc826–41.

120 The Earl of Liverpool, again talking about the Bill for the more exemplary punishment of persons destroying or injuring any Stocking or Lace Frames, reflected that 'The chief difficulty in the present case, he repeated, was the difficulty of detection under the existing applicable law; and he believed at the same time, that the operating dread of the severer punishment would, in the present case, be attended with beneficial effects'. HL Deb 27 February 1812 Vol. 21 cc964–79.

121 An MP, Richard Ryder, 1766–1832, confessed that he was was glad to hear the sentiments which he had so often expressed on the question before the House, confirmed by the Solicitor-General, who, it must be allowed by all, had more practical knowledge of the criminal law than any man in parliament. In his opinion the circumstances attendant on the case of the depredators on the river afforded the most ample proof of the advantage of allowing the [capital] law to remain on the statute book'. HC Deb 17 February 1813 Vol. 24 cc562–75.

122 Sir George Lewis, 1806–1863, a lawyers and barrister, occupied a number of ministerial posts, including that of parliamentary under-secretary at the Home Office in 1848. He pronounced in the debate on the New Trials in Criminal Cases Bill that 'The hon. and learned Member had not had the boldness to declare that innocent men were frequently found guilty in this country. ... All he (Sir George Lewis) could say was, that upon the strongest evidence of the Judges, of persons acquainted with prisoners and convicts, it was clear that such cases were of very rare occurrence'. HC Deb 15 May 1861 Vol. 162 cc2067–74. And see the evidence of Sir James Purves-Stewart cited by the *Report of the Select Committee on Capital Punishment, op. cit.*, para. 209.

123 A Home Secretary was quoted as saying in 1948, 'One of the great privileges and advantages we have in our present system of procedure is that the Home Secretary is unfettered as to the advice which should be tendered in the use of the Royal Prerogative. At every point in our system of criminal justice the benefit of the doubt is given to the accused. At every point in the subsequent consideration of a capital sentence, when it has been passed, the same bias is shown in favour of the convicted person. But when justice and the law have done their best within their limits, when precedents have been searched and weighed, mercy still roams around the prison seeking for some chink by which she can creep in'. HL Deb 16 December 1953 Vol. 185 cc137–88.

124 The Solicitor-General addressing the House of Commons, HC Deb 17 February 1813 vol 24 cc562–75.

125 See the argument by Moss Turner-Samuels, MP for Gloucester: 'I am in my submission ... entitled to argue that, as murder has gone down, there is some sort of deterrent somewhere, and I am entitled to believe on the facts that the deterrent is capital punishment. After all, death is the strongest deterrent, and there is no reason to suppose that it does not exert its dreadful influence in this lethal sphere. That appears to me to be an absolutely reasonable deduction to make'. HC Deb 10 February 1955 vol 536 cc2064–183.

126 The Home Secretary said 'I have always taken the view that, if a satisfactory alternative could be found, I should welcome the abolition of capital punishment – and, when I

say satisfactory, I mean satisfactory as a deterrent and also something that is satisfactory to the public conscience – but that, until it was clearly established that such an alternative existed, the death penalty must remain and must be carried out in appropriate cases'. HC Deb 10 February 1955 Vol. 536 cc2064–183.

127   The Prison Commissioner, Sir Alexander Paterson, was reported by the Home Secretary to have said that 'in his opinion and with all his experience, there was no alternative. He did not regard long imprisonment as a humane alternative to capital punishment'. HC Deb 10 February 1955 Vol. 536 cc2064–183.

128   See HL Deb 16 December 1953 Vol. 185 cc137–88.

129   See HC Deb 15 April 1935 Vol. 300 c1603.

130   'I do not wish to declare on the merits of [that] proposal to abolish capital punishment proposal; it may have been right or it may have been wrong; but one thing is certain: that it did not represent the majority views of the electorate', said the Marquess of Salisbury in the debate on the Queen's Speech. HL Deb 5 November 1953 Vol. 184 cc105–92.

131   See HC Deb 19 December 1935 Vol. 307 c1940; HC Deb 21 April 1936 vol 311 c19.

132   See HC Deb 3 December 1953 Vol. 521 c151W.

133   HC Deb 15 July 1948 Vol. 453 cc1411–545.

134   Frank Dawtry, 1902–1968, was a probation service organiser and employee of the National Association of Discharged Prisoners' Aid Societies, the precursor of NACRO. Between 1948 and 1967, he served as general secretary of the National Association of Probation Officers, and was on the executive committee of the Howard League for Penal Reform. (Based on Kenneth Thompson's entry in the *The Oxford Dictionary of National Biography*, http://217.169.56.135/view/article/32755.)

135   F. Dawtry (1966); 'The Abolition of the Death Penalty in Britain', *British Journal of Criminology*, Vol. 6, No 2, 187. And see D. Garland (2005); 'Capital Punishment and American Culture', *Punishment and Society*, Vol. 7, No. 4, and R. Hood (2002); *The Death Penalty*, Oxford: Oxford University Press.

136   See HC Deb 2 March 1819, Vol. 39 cc777–845.

137   Sir James Macintosh told the House of Commons: 'If a foreigner were to form his estimate of the people of England from a consideration of their penal code, he would undoubtedly conclude that they were a nation of barbarians. For what other opinion could a humane foreigner form of us, when he found, that in our criminal law there were two hundred offences against which the punishment of death was denounced, upon twenty of which only, that punishment was ever inflicted—that we were savage in our threats, and yet were feeble in our execution of punishments – that we cherished a system, which in theory was odious, but which was impotent in practice, from its excessive severity?' (HC Deb 21 May 1823 Vol 9 cc397–432)

138   The list was comprehensive:

1. That it is expedient to take away the punishment of death in the case of larceny from ships, from dwelling houses, and on navigable rivers.
2. That it is expedient to repeal so much of the statute 9 Geo. 1, commonly called the Black Act, as creates capital felonies, excepting the crimes of setting fire to a dwelling house, and of maliciously shooting at an individual.
3. That it is expedient to repeal so much of the statute 26 Geo. 2, c. 33, commonly called the Marriage Act, as creates capital felonies.
4. That it is expedient to repeal so much of the statute 21 Jac. 1. c. 26, relating to fines and recoveries; of 6 Geo. 2, c. 37, relating to cutting down banks of rivers; of 27 Geo. 2, c. 19, relating to threatening letters; of 27 Geo. 2, c, 19, relating to the Bedford Level; of 3 Geo. 3, c. 16, relating to Greenwich Pensioners; of 22 Geo. 3, c. 4, relating to cutting serges; and of 24 Geo. 3, c. 24, relating to convicts returned from transportation, as subjects persons convicted of the offences therein specified, to the punishment of death.

5. That it is expedient to take away the punishment of death in the cases of Horse Stealing, Sheep Stealing, and Cattle Stealing.

6. That it is expedient to take away the punishment of death in the cases of Forgery, and of uttering forged instruments.

7. That in the case of all the aforesaid offences, which are not otherwise sufficiently punishable by law, the punishments of transportation for life or years, or of imprisonment with or without hard labour, shall be substituted for death, in such proportions and with such latitudes of discretion in the judges as the nature and magnitude of the respective offences will require.

8. That it is expedient to make provision that the Judges shall not pronounce sentence of death in those cases where they have no expectation that such sentence will be executed.

9. That it is fit to take away the forfeiture of goods and chattels in the case of Suicide, and to put an end to those indignities which are practised on the remains of the dead, in the cases of Suicide and High Treason'. (HC Deb 21 May 1823 Vol. 9 cc397–432)

But the bill proposing it, and moved by Sir James Macintosh, was defeated by 76 votes to 86.

139 HL Deb 6 September 1831 Vol. 6 cc1172–83.

140 William Ewart, 1798–1869, was described in his biography as a 'Liberal with radical leanings'. He not only succeeded in initiating the Act of 2–3 Will. IV c. 62 but was responsible for other pieces of abolitionist legislation. (Based on an entry by S.M. Farrell in *The Oxford Dictionary of National Biography*, http://217.169.56.135/view/article/9011?docPos=1.)

141 An Act for abolishing the Punishment of Death in Certain Cases, and substituting a lesser Punishment in lieu thereof. 2–3 Will. IV c. 62:

142 G. Gardiner; *Capital Punishment as a Deterrent: And the Alternative, op. cit.*, 29.

143 See L. Farmer (2000); 'Reconstructing the English Codification Debate: The Criminal Law Commissioners, 1833–45', *Law and History Review*, Vol. 18, No. 2, 397–425, and esp. 402.

144 *Second Report from His Majesty's Commissioners on Criminal Law*, 1836, (343), XXXVI, 19.

145 HC Deb 19 May 1837 Vol. 38 cc907–26. The Attorney-General professed in that debate that he 'rejoiced that the public voice went with the Legislature in those ameliorations of the criminal code – by which the punishment of death was about to be taken away from three-fourths of those offences to which it had before been applied. He had no hesitation in giving those measures his support, for he had no apprehension that the abolition of the capital punishment would in any of the cases here mentioned lead to the increase of crime; but he was not at all prepared to do away with the punishment of death in every case. The public mind was not at all prepared for such a change, and he had little doubt that there would be a general exclamation through the country against it'.

146 The rules laid down that a finding of insanity could be made if, 'at the time of the committing of the act, the party accused was labouring under such a defect of reason, from a disease of the mind, as not to know the nature and quality of the act he was doing; or, if he did know it, that he did not know he was doing what was wrong'. (*Queen v. M'Naghten*, 8 Eng. Rep. 718 [1843]).

147 Under s. 9, they reported that 'Respecting the Expediency of Abolishing Capital Punishments the Committee found scarcely any Difference of Opinion. Almost all Witnesses, and all Authorities, agree in Opinion that for Offences of the gravest Kind the Punishment of Death ought to be Retained'. *Second Report brought from the House of Lords appointed to inquire into the execution of the criminal law especially respecting juvenile offenders and transportation*, 1847, 534.

148 See M. Foucault (1979); *Discipline and Punish: The Birth of the Prison*, Harmondsworth: Penguin Books.

149 I have borrowed some of these ideas from D. Garland; *Peculiar Institution, op. cit.*

150 In 1854, for instance, the Bishop of Oxford presented to the House of Lords a petition from inhabitants of Aylesbury and the neighbourhood, praying for some alteration in the mode of administering capital executions. This subject had been recently brought to the attention of the petitioners by the execution of Moses Hatto,* which took place in that borough, and had forced upon their consideration what were the moral effects of a public execution; and they said, that from the experience of what took place on that occasion, they were convinced that the effect of the present publicity of executions, was not to deter men from crime, but, on the contrary, to shock the feelings of the better disposed, and to harden hopelessly the feelings of the more vicious'. (HL Deb 15 May 1854 Vol. 133 cc305–12)* Hatto, a groom, had murdered Mary Spurgeon in November 1853 and had been executed by Calcraft in front of the new county gaol on 24 March 1854 in Aylesbury. *The Times* reported that there had been only a small crowd in attendance, and 'little excitement was occasioned by the wretched man's appearance on the scaffold' (*The Times*, 25 March 1854).

151 HC Deb 10 June 1856 Vol. 142 cc1231–61.

152 Report from the Select Committee of the House of Lords, appointed "'to take into consideration the present mode of carrying into effect capital punishments;" and to report thereon to the House; together with the minutes of evidence, and appendix'. 1856 (366)

153 HC Deb 1 April 1856 Vol. 141 c278.

154 Sir John Hibbert, 1824–1908, was Member for Oldham on three occasions. At the time he spoke in 1864, he had been elected in 1862 and was to remain in his seat until 1874. He was to be Parliamentary Secretary on a number of occasions, the first in 1872, under-secretary between 1883 and 1884, and Financial Secretary in 1892.

155 Sir James Mackintosh of Kyllachy (1765–1832), was called to the Bar in 1796 and became, *inter alia*, the Recorder of Bombay in 1804, where he attempted 'to reform the police, the administration of penal law, and, in particular, the prison system. In the spirit of Beccaria and Bentham he sought to use prison as the principal instrument of punishment, and offended the resident British community by resisting the use of the death penalty'. He was was elected MP for Nairn in 1813 and then elected MP for Knaresborough in 1819. He was successful in promoting a Commons vote in favour of ending capital punishment for aspects of forgery in 1832. (Based on Christopher Finlay's entry in *The Oxford Dictionary of National Biography*, http://217.169.56.135/view/article/17620?docPos=1)

156 HC Deb 23 February 1864 vol 173 cc941–5. He alluded to an execution in the City of London which had been attended by disorder and signs of degradation: 'He really could not understand why the City should be made the scene of such a demoralising spectacle. It was very objectionable that the capital punishment of men convicted of such crimes as piracy should be carried out under the eyes of a civil population'. And see the letter on the subject to *The Times* by CIVIS, February 26, 1864. There was support for Mr Hibbert. The MP for Sheffield, George Hadfield, (1787–1879), said 'He remembered, when a young man, and a stranger in the gallery, hearing in that House an excellent speech from Sir Samuel Romilly – whose honoured name would figure in the history of the country for ages to come – on the mitigation of capital punishment for the crime of forgery and some other offences. The Law Officers of that day said that any mitigation of the law would upset their glorious constitution. But what had been the result? Had the crime of forgery, which in those times was never pardoned, but which marked the circuits of the Judges with blood, and caused the Bank of England to be stigmatised as "The Bloody Bank" – had the crime of forgery increased since capital punishment was abolished for that crime? No one could deny it

had decreased'. And Thomas Sidney, both an Alderman and an MP, said 'the inhabitants of that portion of the City where the execution took place were seriously annoyed at the time, and felt deeply humiliated at the remembrance of the spectacle. It was an act of intolerable injustice to the City of London'. (Alderman Sidney, 1805–1889, was Member for Stafford.)

157 HC Deb 3 May 1864 Vol. 174 cc2055–115.
158 *Report of the Capital Punishment Commission* (1986); 3590, London: HMSO, iii–iv.
159 The Lord Chancellor noted that in a speech to the House of Lords on 1 May 1866 that 'another of the Commissioners, one of the Irish Judges, agreed with these four Commissioners to this extent, that he thought the time would come when the punishment of death should be done away with, but that society was not yet ripe for such a change'.
160 The Lord Chancellor between 7 July 1865 and 26 June 1866 was Robert Rolfe, 1st Baron Cranworth, 1790–1868.
161 Lord John Russell, 1792–1878, was prime minister between 29 October 1865 and 27 June 1866.
162 John Romilly, first Baron Romilly, 1802–1874, was called to the Bar in 1827, and became recorder of Ludlow in 1836. He was MP for Bridport between 1832 and 1835, and again in 1846, and then for Devonport in 1847. He became attorney-general in 1848 and solicitor-general in 1850. He was appointed master of the rolls in 1851. He became a peer in 1866. Based on the entry by J. A. Hamilton, *rev.* Patrick Polden in *The Oxford Dictionary of National Biography*, http://217.169.56.135/view/article/24048.
163 HL Deb 30 January 1860 Vol. 156 cc253–5.
164 For a review of that distinction, see the *Report* of the Royal Commission on Capital Punishment 1949–1953, (1953); Cmnd. 8932, HMSO, London, esp. paras. 124 *et seq.* The report quotes at para. 125 Stephen's *History of the Criminal Law:* 'The moral character of homicide must be judged of principally by the extent to which the circumstances of the case show, on the one hand, brutal ferocity, whether called into action suddenly or otherwise, or on the other, inability to control natural anger excited by a serious cause'.
165 The principal architect of those attempts was Sir Eardley Wilmott.
166 Based on *Report of the Select Committee on Capital Punishment, op. cit.*, paras. 166–168.
167 Charles Henry Gordon-Lennox, sixth Duke of Richmond, sixth Duke of Lennox, and first Duke of Gordon, 1818–1903, was Conservative MP for West Sussex between 1841 and 1860. He became Tory Leader in the House of Lords in 1867. Based on the entry by F. M. L. Thompson in *The Oxford Dictionary of National Biography*, http://217.169.56.135/view/article/33468?docPos=7
168 1874 (44) Homicide Law Amendment: A bill to consolidate and amend the law relating to homicide.
169 The category of manslaughter would, for example, have included homicide occasioned when a person loses self-control through provocation, fear of imminent death or grievous bodily harm, loss of control in the killing of a child by reason of disease or state of mind induced by bearing the child. The penalty for murder would have remained death, but for manslaughter it would been a sentence of imprisonment.
170 Report from Select Committee on Homicide Amendment Bill (1874); 315.
171 In 1881, for example, a private member's bill (the Capital Punishment (Abolition) Bill), moved by Sir Joseph Pease, was heavily defeated by 175 votes to 79 (HC Deb 22 June 1881 vol 262 cc1037–85). The next year, Sir Joseph admitted the difficulty of his task: 'He had, on previous occasions, brought forward Bills or Motions providing for the total abolition of capital punishment summarily and at once; but anyone who had listened to the debates that had taken place must feel, as he had felt, that the subject

had been fully and fairly discussed, and that right hon. and hon. Members on both sides of the House had debated it in a way that was satisfactory; he therefore felt it was no longer of much use, in the present state of feeling, both in and out of the House, to occupy the time of the House in trying to pass a Bill for the total and immediate repeal of capital punishment'. (HC Deb 10 May 1882 vol 269 cc382–400) Nevertheless, he was to try again five years later, attempting to introduce a Bill declaring 'That, in the opinion of this House, the time has arrived for the abolition of the death penalty for the crime of murder', and was again defeated by 117 votes to 63 (HC Deb 11 May 1886 vol 305 cc767–90). Sir Joseph, 1828–1903, was a Quaker and pacifist who was married to a Gurney. He entered Parliament in 1865 as Liberal Member for South Durham until that seat was abolished in 1885. He stood successfully for the new seat of Barnard Castle which he retained until his death.

172 See 'Ilford Murderers Executed', *The Times*, January 10, 1923.

173 See V. Bailey, 'The Shadow of the Gallows: The Death Penalty and the British Labour Government, 1945–51', http://www.historycooperative.org/journals/lhr/18.2/bailey. html

174 Under The Infanticide Act, 1922 'provided that a mother who killed her newly born child when "she had not fully recovered from the effect of giving birth to such a child, but by reason thereof the balance of her mind was disturbed" would be guilty of infanticide rather than murder'. (Law Commission (2006); Consultation Paper No 177: *A New Homicide Act for England and Wales?*, http://www.lawcom.gov.uk/docs/ cp177_web.pdf, 214).

175 Children who broke the law were now dealt with in specialist juvenile courts and prisons. Relevant sections recited that:

'103. Sentence of death shall not be pronounced on or recorded against a child or young person, but in lieu thereof the court shall sentence the child or young person to be detained during His Majesty's pleasure, and, if so sentenced, he shall, notwithstanding anything in the other provisions of this Act, be liable to be detained in such place and under such conditions as the Secretary of State may direct, and whilst so detained shall be deemed to be in legal custody.

104. Where a child or young person is convicted on indictment of an attempt to murder, or of manslaughter, or of wounding with intent to do grievous bodily harm, and the court is of opinion that no punishment which under the provisions of this Act it is authorised to inflict is sufficient, the court may sentence the offender to be detained for such period as may be specified in the sentence; and where such a sentence is passed the child or young person shall, during that period, notwithstanding anything in the other provisions of this Act, be liable to be detained in such place and on such conditions as the Secretary of State may direct, and whilst so detained shall be deemed to be in legal custody'.

The clauses seem not to have been contentious. Much more time was given in debate to the problems of juveniles smoking, infanticide and the murder of children.

176 Under Sec 53 of The Children and Young Persons Act 1933 (23 & 24 Geo.5 c.12).

177 The Home Secretary reflected to the Cabinet that little change was involved because 'This proposal gives legislative effect to the long established administrative practice'. (Memorandum by the Home Secretary. Child and Young Persons Bill. CP 326 (31) 15 December 1931).

178 Children Bill, Memorandum by the Home Secretary, C.P. 5 (28).

179 Roy Calvert in evidence to the Select Committee on Capital Punishment, *op. cit.*, minutes of the meeting of 2 April 1930.

180 Cabinet discussions that took place in 1947 and 1948 about the possible abolition of the death penalty in the civil courts certainly invoked the argument that any such reform might have a wide impact elsewhere. In 1947, for instance, a Memorandum to

Cabinet from the Home Secretary asked 'What repercussions will the abolition of the death penalty for crimes tried by the civil courts of Great Britain have on the imposition of death sentences in the British Zone of Germany, in the Colonial Territories, and by Courts-Martial?' (Criminal Justice Bill: Capital Punishment: Memorandum by the Home Secretary. CP. (47) 306 13 November, 1947). Again, a Cabinet meeting was reported to have considered the contention that 'There would also be a demand for a consequential curtailment of the powers of courts-martial to impose the death penalty on members of the Armed Forces. The Cabinet were informed that the Service Ministers would agree that, if the criminal courts in this country ceased to have power to impose the death penalty for murder and treason, courts-martial should no longer have power to pass sentence of death for those offences. They were satisfied, however, that the death penalty should be preserved for certain military offences'. (CONCLUSIONS of a Meeting of the Cabinet held at 10 Downing Street, S.W. 1, on Tuesday, 18 November, 1947, at 11 a.m. CM. (17)).

181 See J. McHugh (1999); 'The Labour Party and the Parliamentary Campaign to Abolish the Military Death Penalty, 1919–1930', *The Historical Journal*, Vol. 42, No. 1, 233–249.

182 Based on 'British Army: Courts Martial: First World War, 1914–1918', http://www.nationalarchives.gov.uk/catalogue/RdLeaflet.asp?sLeafletID=40 And see the reply to the Parliamentary Question given by Duff Cooper, the Financial Secretary to the War Office. HC Deb 23 February 1932 vol 262 cc206–7.

183 See Oram who argues that courts martial were treated as instruments of control rather than of justice. G. Oram (2004); *Military Executions During World War I*, New York: Palgrave, 2004.

184 That process would be recapitulated after the Second World War. Edward Heath recalled how, as an adjutant, he had been obliged in September 1945 to take command of a firing squad mustered to shoot a soldier. He remarked that he 'found it difficult to sleep that night … I was acutely conscious of the heavy responsibility of giving the command to fire. … Looking back on it, I believe this made a mark on my mind which later crystallised the view to which I have adhered for nearly four decades of my political life, as to the justification for abolishing the death penalty in peacetime'. E. Heath (1988); *The Course of My Life: My Autobiography*, London: Hodder and Stoughton, 103. He then reported on 300 how he had voted for the permanent abolition of capital punishment in 1969. Edward Heath, 1916–2005, served in the Royal Artillery between 1940 and 1946, becoming a lieutenant-colonel. He became Conservative MP for Bexley in 1950, becoming Minister of Labour in 1959, Lord Privy Seal in 1960, President of the Board of Trade in 1963, and leader of the Conservative Party in 1965.

185 Reported in *The Howard Journal* (1924); Vol. 1, No. 3, 114.

186 The Committee was appointed in 1919, was chaired by Mr Justice Darling, and had a membership that included General The Earl of Cavan; Major-General Childs, Deputy Adjutant-General; Felix Cassel, K.C., Judge Advocate-General; and Brigadier-General J. G. S. Mellor, Deputy Judge Advocate-General. Its terms of reference were 'To inquire into the law and rules of procedure regulating courts-martial both in peace and war, and to make recommendations'. It unanimously supported the retention of the death penalty. It reported to Parliament later in the year.

187 Charles Darling, first Baron Darling, 1849–1936, was called to the bar in 1874. He became an MP in 1888 for Deptford and remained so until he became a judge in 1897. His entry in the *Oxford National Dictionary of Biography* remarked that 'the courts martial commission recommended that the evidence presented to it should not be published (it never was), and that Darling's ruling as chairman meant that it was prevented from fully investigating alleged miscarriages of justice'. (Neville Laski, rev. G. R. Rubin; http://217.169.56.135/view/article/32714?docPos=2)

188 The King's Bench Division was that part of the High Court, established by the Supreme Court of Judicature Act 1873, that dealt with weightier matters of civil law and with appeals from lower criminal courts. In announcing the bill, Lord Selborne, the Lord Chancellor, said 'All these Courts I propose to have united in one Supreme Court; which is to be divided into two permanent branches or Divisions: the one consisting of a High Court of Justice to exercise original jurisdiction, and also to hear appeals from Inferior Courts: the other being a Court of Appellate Jurisdiction, to be called the Court of Appeal'. HL Deb 13 February 1873 vol 214 cc331–65.

189 *Report of the Committee Constituted by the Army Council to Enquire into the Law and Rules of Procedure Regulating Military Courts-Martial* (1919); Cmd 248, para. 1.

190 It was noted that 'These reports ... have been circulated to Commands, all of which have expressed general agreement with the recommendations of the majority of the Committee'. (Sir H. Creedy; Precis for the Army Council, No 1018, February 1920, WO32/5478)

191 Sir H. Creedy, Secretary, War Office wrote to the Army Council on 18 February 1920 that 'No detailed criticisms [have] been received from members of the Council on the report of the ... Committee which has been circulated ...'

192 One was to carry out recommendations contained in paragraphs 6 and 7 of the Chairman's Report, 26 February 1920; the other to work out in detail the recommendations in connection with the appointment of legal advisers and legal education contained in paragraphs 8 to 16.

193 That stance was generally approved by commanding officers. For example, the Commander in Chief of the British Army of the Rhine commented in a letter of 2 December 1919: 'The deterrent effect of the capital sentence has repeatedly been shown during the war, and I am entirely in agreement with the views expressed in paras. 103–110'. (WO32/5478 Military Courts Martial Committee Report)

194 The ensuing history of courts martial encompassed the reforms which the minority report had advocated. Implementation of the report of the Army and Air Force Courts-Martial Committee 1946 (the Lewis Committee, Cmd. 7608, submitted in 1949), a committee formed, like the Darling Committee, against the backdrop of a world war, brought about a complete separation of judicial and prosecutorial functions. The former came under the direction of the Lord Chancellor's Department and the latter under the Directorates of Legal Services which remained within the War Office and Air Ministry (see HC Deb 21 September 1948 Vol. 456 cc690–2). Later legislation affecting the Judge Advocate General's office included the Courts-Martial (Appeals) Act 1951, which established the right to appeal against a conviction by court martial on a point of law (based on http://www.ndad.nationalarchives.gov.uk/AH/8/detail.html) And see J. Griffith (1949); 'Report of the Army and Air Force Courts-Martial Committee, 1946 (Cmd. 7608)', *The Modern Law Review*, Vol. 12, No. 2, 223–227. The Committee's terms of reference were:

> 'To bring under review in the light of the experience gained in the late war and of the composition of the Army and the Royal Air Force, the recommendations of the Army and Air Force Courts-Martial Committee, 1938 (Cmd. 6200) with special reference to the question whether it is desirable to provide any, and if so what, form of appeal from the findings or sentences of courts-martial; to investigate the powers of courts-martial and of commanding officers to award punishment and the nature and scale of such punishment; and to make recommendations upon these and kindred matters'.

195 Major Christopher Lowther, 1887–1935, was the elder son of Viscount Ullswater, the Speaker of the House of Commons. He was Hon. Attaché in the Diplomatic Service, Morocco, 1907; and in Mexico, 1907–09. He went out with the Westmorland and

Cumberland Yeomanry to France and Belgium where he was very seriously wounded in 1915. He was appointed assistant provost marshal on the staff of the London District in 1917, of the Eastern Command in 1917–18, and of the Scottish Command in 1918. He was elected Unionist MP for Northern Cumberland in November 1918, and served on the committee a year later. Disagreeing with his party, he resigned his seat and unsuccessfully contested Wallsend as an independent. This was based on *The Times* archives and *Who Was Who* online. There is no other information publicly available about him that I could discover. Neither were there relevant family papers in private hands. He is not listed in the *The Oxford Dictionary of National Biography* and his other papers, deposited in the Ipswich Record Office, make no reference to his activities as a Member of Parliament.

196 A provost marshal is an officer in the armed forces who is in charge of the military police.

197 Horatio Bottomley, 1860–1933, first entered Parliament in 1906 as the Liberal MP then, in 1918, as the independent MP for Hackney South. He was made bankrupt in 1912, and then, in 1922, was found guilty of twenty three charges of fraudulent conversion, sentenced to seven years imprisonment and discharged from the House of Commons. (Based on A. J. A. Morris's entry in *The Oxford Dictionary of National Biography*, http://217.169.56.135/view/article/31981)

198 Stephen Walsh, 1859–1929, became Labour Member for Ince in Lancashire in 1906. He became Vice-Chairman of the Labour Party in 1922. His biographical entry in reports that 'During the First World War, [he] strongly supported recruiting campaigns and was an advocate of compulsory military service', and he became Secretary of State for War and President of the Army Council' in the first Labour Government of 1924. (Based on the entry by A. E. Watkin, *rev.* Marc Brodie, *The Oxford Dictionary of National Biography*, http://217.169.56.135/view/article/36713)

199 The Acts would recite that they 'provide, during Twelve Months, for the Discipline and Regulation of the Army and Air Force'. (Taken from 16 Geo. 5, c. 6, 1926)

200 Thus the Army and Air Force (Annual) Act, 1924, 14 Geo. 5, Ch. 5, recited that 'And whereas no man can be forejudged of life or limb, or subjected in time of peace to any kind of punishment within this realm, by martial law, or in any other manner than by the judgement of his peers and according to the known and established laws of this realm; yet, nevertheless, it being requisite, for the retaining all … the forces, and other persons subject to military law … in their duty, that exact discipline be observed and that persons belong to the said forces who mutiny or stir up sedition, or desert His Majesty's service, or are guilty of crimes and offences to the prejudice of good order and … discipline, be brought to a more exemplary and speedy punishment than the usual forms of the law will allow'.

201 Major John Hills, 1867–1938, was Conservative Member for Ripon between 5 December 1925–24 December and 1938. He was a solicitor until 1912, having entered Parliament in 1906. He volunteered to become a captain in the Durham Light Infantry in October 1914 and, in October 1915, was promoted to the rank of major. He was badly injured at the Battle of the Somme. (Based on the entry by E. H. H. Green, *The Oxford Dictionary of National Biography*, http://217.169.56.135/view/article/45568?docPos=2)

202 His proposed amendment read:
'For the purpose of abolishing death as a penalty for certain offences the following Amendments shall be made in the Army Act:

(1) In Section four paragraphs (1), (2), (6), and (7) shall be omitted;
(2) In Section five the following paragraphs shall be inserted after paragraph (6):
   (7) Shamefully abandons or delivers up any garrison, place, post, or guard, or uses any means to compel or induce any governor, commanding

officer, or other person shamefully to abandon or deliver up any garrison, place, post, or guard which it was the duty of such governor or person to defend;

(8) Shamefully casts away his arms, ammunition, or tools in the presence of the enemy;

(9) Knowingly does when on active service any act calculated to imperil the success of His Majesty's Forces or any part thereof;

(10) Misbehaves or induces others to misbehave before the enemy in such manner as to show cowardice;

(3) In Sub-section (1) of Section six the words "if he commits any such offence on active service be liable to suffer death or such less punishment as is in this Act mentioned, and if he commits any such offence not on active service," shall be omitted;

(4) In Section seven, for the word "death," there shall be substituted the words "penal servitude" (HC Deb 29 March 1927 Vol. 204 cc1084–126).

203 R. C. Morrison, Member for Tottenham North, 1923–1931, and 1935–1945, in HC Deb 17 April 1928 Vol. 216 cc31–83.

204 Under the Army and Air Force (Annual) Act 1925, 15 & 16 Geo. V, c. 25. Introducing the amended bill in the House of Lords in April 1925, the Under-Secretary of State for War stated that 'The death penalty is abolished altogether in certain cases – namely, for impeding the Provost-Marshal in the execution of his duty or refusing to assist him, for attacks on those in charge of supplies, for irregularly detaining such supplies, or for committing any offence against the property or person or an inhabitant of the country in which operations are taking place. These offences, which were never before punished with the penalty of death in peace time, have now ceased to be punishable with the death penalty in time of war. As regards peace, the death penalty is abolished altogether for all military offences excepting the one offence of mutiny' (HL Deb 6 April 1925 Vol. 60 cc1012–5) And Ernest Thurtle had tried to add cowardice, shamefully casting away arms or ammunition, imperilling the success of armed forces, and abandoning a post to the list. See HC Deb 1 April 1925 Vol. 182 cc1349–97.

205 Under Sec. 4 of the Army and Air Force (Annual) Act, 1928, 18 Geo. 5, Ch. 7, the following offences were no longer subject to the death penalty: 'being a soldier acting as sentinel leaves his post before he is regularly relieved'; 'leaves his commanding officer to go in search of plunder'; 'forces a safeguard'; 'forces or strikes a sentinel'; 'breaks into any house or other place in search of plunder'; and being a soldier acting as sentinel sleeps or is drunk on his post'. The sentence of penal servitude was provided instead.

206 See the answer of the Secretary of State for War to the House of Commons on 7 November 1939.

207 The Army and Air Force (Annual) Bill. Memorandum to Cabinet, C.P. 102 (30) March 1930.

208 See HC Deb 3 April 1930 Vol. 237 cc1564–627.

209 See HC Deb 7 November 1939 Vol. 353 c13.

210 Its terms of reference were 'To examine the existing system of trial by court-martial under the Army and Air Force Acts and matters incidental thereto, and in particular to consider whether it is desirable and practicable that a person convicted by court-martial should have a right of appeal to a civil judicial tribunal against his conviction, and to make recommendations'. See HC Deb 15 March 1938 Vol. 333 cc188–9. When it was re-established as the Lewis Committee in November 1946, the Admiralty 'was carefully excluded' (HL Deb 16 March 1949 Vol. 161 cc429–47) and its possible implementation was then impeded because of the initiation of a separate enquiry into naval discipline, the Pilcher Committee. Reporting two years later, in April 1948, and

released in January 1949, the Lewis Committee recommended a courts martial appeal court. It was only in the next decade that measures were adopted to introduce that court under the Courts-Martial (Appeals) Act 1951 c.46 14 and 15 Geo 6.

211 In particular, the modest recommendations that there should be 'the setting up of Appeal Court under the presidency of a Chief Judge Martial … [and] that general courts-martial and district courts-martial, when trying serious cases, should have as president a civilian lawyer whose functions would be similar to those of a Judge in a Court of Assize'. Service Courts-Marshall, Memorandum by the Lord Chancellor and the Minister of Defence, C.P. (50) 180, 24 July 1950.

212 I was told by Professor Brendan O'Leary of the University of Pennsylvania that the execution of Irish men and women after the Easter Rising had made a comparable impact, but there was no evidence of its effects in government. Certainly there was discussion in the House of Lords in May 1916 about the imposition of martial law in Ireland, and there was criticism of summary killings by troops (see HC Deb 1 August 1916 Vol. 85 cc123–256 and HC Deb 22 August 1916 Vol. 85 cc2558–604) but none of it was critical of capital punishment proper.

213 See E. Tuttle; *The Crusade Against Capital Punishment, op. cit.*, 29.

214 The government lasted from December 1923 until October 1924.

215 Arthur Henderson, 1863–1935, became Labour MP for Barnard Castle in 1903. He was appointed chief whip on four occasions, was Chairman of the Parliamentary Labour Party between 1908 and 1910, Party secretary between 1912 and 1934, and Home Secretary in the first Labour Government of 1924. His biographer, Chris Wrigley, claimed that 'The Home Office reinforced his tendencies towards moderation and caution'. *The Oxford Dictionary of National Biography*, http://217.169.56.135/view/article/33807

216 HO 45/12914/154425/57.

217 Asked 'if any decision has been taken by the Cabinet on the question of capital punishment; and, if not, whether the Government will grant facilities for the introduction of a Bill for the abolition of capital punishment?', the Under-Secretary of State for the Home Department replied that 'the Government has come to no decision'. House of Commons debates, 25 February 1924.

218 James Ramsay MacDonald, (1866–1937), was the first Prime Minister of the Labour Government of 1924, and again between 1929 and 1935, having been elected as Member for Leicester in 1906–1918, and again in 1922, becoming party chairman in 1911. Based on entry by David Marquand in *The Oxford Dictionary of National Biography*, http://217.169.56.135/view/article/34704

219 He had other matters to deal with: unemployment, labour relations, foreign relations, the national debt and the economy; and he was anxious to present the new government, including as it did the Labour Party, as dependable and moderate (see D. Marquand (1977); *Ramsay MacDonald*, London: Jonathan Cape, esp. 310–311. Marquand's index has no reference to capital punishment, crime or the death penalty). MacDonald's (1921); *Socialism: Critical and Constructive*, London: Cassell and Company, made no reference at all to crime, punishment or the death penalty.

220 D. Marquand; entry on James Ramsay MacDonald in *The Oxford Dictionary of National Biography*, *op. cit.*

221 A. Morgan (1987); *J. Ramsay MacDonald*, Manchester: Manchester University Press, 102. Morgan's biography, again, has no reference to capital punishment, crime or the death penalty.

222 J.R. Clynes obituary, *The Times*, 25 October 1949.

223 The historian of the earlier stages of abolition, James Christoph, remarked that 'moral questions such as capital punishment have an uncertain relationship to the central body of doctrines held by each of the parties and, in the eyes of the parties' chief strategists, are politically unrewarding. Emotional issues that plumb deep-seated moral codes – for

example, birth control, prostitution, homosexuality and hanging – are 'hot potatoes' that party leaders find uncomfortable to handle, not least because the leaders fear for their unpredictable and often diversionary character. In Britain as elsewhere it seems to be true that politicians are most attracted to and at home in bread-and-butter economic questions, cautious and vague about foreign policy and colonial issues, and highly fearful of conflicts stemming from efforts to change traditional social and moral attitudes'. (J. Christoph; *Capital Punishment and British Politics*, *op. cit.*, 173)

224 V. Bailey; 'The Shadow of the Gallows: The Death Penalty and the British Labour Government, 1945–51', http://www.historycooperative.org/journals/lhr/18.2/bai ley.html Part of this section borrows generally from that article.

225 E. Tuttle; *The Crusade Against Capital Punishment*, *op. cit.*, 31.

226 For example, he introduced a Bill on 24 November 1933 'to provide for the abolition of the death penalty for an experimental period of five years in cases covered by civil courts in time of peace'. There were also attempts to legislate against the hanging of women, made on 21 December 1934.

227 Vyvyan Adams (Samuel Vyvyan Trerice Adams), 1900–1951, a barrister and Conservative MP for Leeds West between 1931 and 1945, was energetically engaged in the promotion of a number of liberal causes, including campaigns for disarmament and against the arms trade; the promotion of an international court and an international police force; and protests against Fascist demonstrations. His attempts were also largely fruitless although in 1938 he did succeed, after three years' campaigning, in extending the Infanticide Act 1922 to include the provision that the sentence imposed on a woman might be mitigated if 'at the time of the act or omission the balance of her mind was disturbed by reason of her not having fully recovered from the effect of giving birth to the child or by reason of the effect of lactation consequent upon the birth of the child'. HC Deb 16 November 1938 Vol. 341 cc954–1011.

228 He continued: 'I imagine that in a civilised community the functions of a penal system are three. You seek to punish the offender; you try to reform him; and you aim at deterring others from renewing his offence. There seems to me to be no case for precise retaliation and for exact retribution. Our penal practice is not founded on any such theory. When a crime is committed, nobody is permitted to wreak private and personal vengeance upon the offender'.

229 See HC Deb 1 April 1925 Vol. 182 cc1349–97.

230 Lord Birkenhead, 1872–1930, a former Lord Chancellor, was then Secretary of State for India.

231 Mr Baldwin had that exchange reproduced and circulated to members of the Cabinet (Cabinet Ministers and the Press, C.P. 285 (25).

232 William Brown, 1894–1960, was the Labour Member for Wolverhampton West from May 30, 1929 until October 27, 1931. He was a strong trades unionist, and campaigned inside and outside parliament for the abolition of capital punishment.

233 He opened: 'I beg to move, that, in the opinion of this House, capital punishment for civil crimes should be abolished. At the outset, I should like to express my appreciation of the help which has been forthcoming from Members of all parties in this House since it became known that this Motion was to be moved to-night. I draw from that circumstance the hope that, whatever may be the fate of my Motion, at least the Division will not be drawn on the narrow lines of party when we go into the Lobby. It is my conviction that there is no case for the continuance of capital punishment. There is a case against its removal, but that is quite a different thing. I believe that there is no man or woman in England, who realises what is involved in capital punishment, who would not be glad to see this country free of it ...' (HC Deb 30 October 1929 Vol. 231 cc241–93).

234 Joseph Kennedy, 1886–1953, was the Member for Kingston upon Hull Central from 1926–1931.

235 His actual words were that Sir Herbert 'wants to have some form of inquiry or Select Committee. I do hope that I can show my right hon. Friend why we might, perhaps, take the opinion of this House on the clear-cut issue. If my right hon. Friend the Home Secretary wishes to have an inquiry, I am sure, if he asks for it, it will be agreed to …'

236 He was to say later that 'Capital punishment is a grim and terrible business. To put to death, in cold blood, a fellow human being is an ordeal upon everyone who has to do with it, and it throws a heavy responsibility upon the whole nation, all of whom have authorised these things to be done in their name. There is no doubt but that a wholly civilised country would not include capital punishment in its penal code, but the mistake is to assume that we are already a wholly civilised country'. HL Deb 20 July 1948 Vol. 157 cc1004–73.

237 Sir Herbert Samuel, 1870–1963, became Liberal MP for Cleveland in 1902. In 1909, he was appointed Chancellor of the Duchy of Lancaster and then Home Secretary in 1916. Leaving Parliament, he became first High Commissioner in Palestine in 1920. On his return, he was to be chairman of the Liberal Party in 1927 and then MP for the Lancashire seat of Darwen in 1929. (Based on B. Wasserstein's entry in *The Oxford Dictionary of National Biography*, http://217.169.56.135/view/article/35928)

238 J.R. Clynes, *Memoirs, op. cit.*, 134.

239 *Ibid*, 134.

240 Conclusions of a Meeting of the Cabinet held on 30 October 1929. Cabinet 42 (29).

241 John Clynes, 1869–1949, entered Parliament in 1906 as the Labour Member for the North-Eastern (later Platting) division of Manchester and retained his seat until 1931; becoming chairman of the parliamentary party in 1921, and leading the party in the general election of 1922. He was Home Secretary between 1929 and 1931. He returned to Parliament in 1935 as Member for Platting until 1945. (Based on the entry by J. S. Middleton, *rev*. Marc Brodie in *The Oxford Dictionary of National Biography*, http://217.169.56.135/view/article/32461)

242 At its meeting of 30 October 1929, it was reported to have agreed that: 'The Home Secretary, as a matter of urgency, raised the question of the abolition of capital punishment, which was to be discussed in the House of Commons the same afternoon. The Cabinet agreed with the view of the Home Secretary that he should adopt a sympathetic attitude towards a Debate on this question and intimate that the Government would be glad to learn the views of the House of Commons. The Home Secretary should be authorised to announce, if necessary, that if the view of the House was clearly in favour of a change an Inquiry should be initiated'. (Conclusions of a Meeting of the Cabinet held at 10, Downing Street, S.W.1., on Wednesday, 30 October, 1929. Cabinet 42 (29))

243 HC Deb 7 November 1930 Vol. 244 c1283.

244 James Barr (1862–1949), was a minister of the United Free Church of Scotland, a campaigning prohibitionist, a pacifist, campaigner against capital punishment, and Labour Member of Parliament for Motherwell from 1924 to 1931, and then for Coatbridge from 1931 to 1935. (Based on James Smyth's entry in *The Oxford Dictionary of National Biography*, http://www.oxforddnb.com/view/article/40286?docPos=1)

245 Sir John Power, 1870–1950, was Conservative Member of Parliament for Wimbledon between 1924 and 1945.

246 Introduction to the Reprint Edition of R. Calvert (1973); *Capital Punishment in the Twentieth Century*, Montclair, N.J.: Patterson Smith, v.

247 She claimed that capital punishment was based on a discredited and outmoded theory of the criminal mind (many criminals were impulsive rather than rational beings who considered the possible consequences of their actions); a discredited and outmoded theory of crime causation (most influential is social reform, not punishment, she argued); capital punishment is not more effective as a deterrent than other methods of

punishment; it makes no provision for redress should there be a miscarriage of justice; it has 'an unwholesome social influence'; it involves unnecessary suffering in others; and it encourages perverse verdicts at trial.

248   Capital punishment, he said, 'makes no pretence at reforming the culprit, but its infliction recognizes that his death expiates his crime and makes to society all the amends of which he is capable. One object of all forms of punishment of the criminal is to diminish crime by preventing the offender from again, or for a certain time, offending. A second is to deter others from committing crimes. Capital punishment always accomplishes the first object, and I believe it often attains the second ...' (para. 1269).

249   William Temple, 1881–1944, was in his early years an avowed socialist and sometime president of the Workers' Educational Association, but he became more conservative in later life and rarely spoke in the House of Lords. He was a prolific writer and author of what he called a 'Christocentric metaphysic'. Between 1920 and 1929, he was to be Bishop of Manchester, between 1929 and 1942, Archbishop of York and then, in 1942, Archbishop of Canterbury. (Based on the entry by Adrian Hastings in *The Oxford Dictionary of National Biography*, http://www.oxforddnb.com/view/article/36454?docPos=6) Carpenter described him as the proponent of a 'caring Church which believed that social justice mattered'. E. Carpenter (1997); *Cantuar: The Archbishops in their Office*, London: Mowbray, 467.

250   The remark was made by Sir Ronald Ross, 1888–1968, the Member for Londonderry between 1929 and 1951 (HC Deb 14 April 1948 Vol. 449 cc979–1098).

251   He was to say 'To me, the most fundamental teaching of Jesus Christ, enforced by His example, was that He despaired of no man, that to Him no man was beyond redemption. In His practice He did not deal much with self-righteous people such as we are. He dealt with those who were the despair of all others, and when He Himself – may I say it reverently – became the victim of the death penalty, He still exercised His calling, He still showed his unquenchable faith in man, He still sought to convert and raise the two thieves on either side of Him, and not without success. ... The scaffold has not taught men to venerate life; it has cheapened life. It has not repressed crime; it has perpetuated it'. (HC Deb 16 November 1938 Vol. 341 cc954–1011)

252   One member, Cyril Culverwell, was subsequently to recall that 'out of the 29 witnesses from this country 21 were in favour of the retention of capital punishment. But it is not only the numbers in favour of the retention of capital punishment which should impress the House, it is the experience which they have had. When I tell the House that these 21 included five governors of prisons, two chief officers, one senior medical officer, one chaplain to His Majesty's prisons, two Prison Commissioners, two ex-Home Secretaries, two judges, the representatives of the Council of the Law Society and of the Home Office, and that among the minority in favour of the abolition of capital punishment were the Secretary of the Society for the Abolition of Capital Punishment, the Secretary of the Society of Friends, which opposes capital punishment on principle, and an experienced prison doctor who considered that abolition should await a thorough reform of the whole penal system, I think the House will agree that, so far as the ability, experience and capacity of the witnesses to judge of this matter is concerned, the weight of evidence certainly lay with those who favour the retention of capital punishment'. (HC Deb 16 November 1938 Vol. 341 cc954–1011) Cyril Culverwell, 1895–1963, was the Unionist Member of Parliament for Bristol West between 1928 and 1945 (http://www.ukwhoswho.com.gate2.library.lse.ac.uk/view/article/oupww/whoswho/U56656/CULVERWELL_Cyril_Tom?index=1&results=QuicksearchResults&query=0)

253   *The Times*, 10 December 1930.

254   Sir Gervaise Rentoul, 1884–1946, was the Metropolitan Magistrate for West London. Interestingly, like so many retentionists, he came in time publicly to recant, saying

'Surely the time has come when we should be justified in making a notable experiment, and of proving, by the suspension of the death sentence, whether the jurists are right or whether, once again, the enlightened conscience of humanity is not a surer guide'. Sir G. Rentoul (1939); 'Second Thoughts on Capital Punishment', *The Penal Reformer*, Vol. 6, No. 1, 1–2.

255 Minutes of the meeting of 2 December 1930.

256 James Barr; letter to *The Times*, 20 December 1930.

257 See HC Deb 23 July 1931 Vol. 255 cc1657–62. Clynes reported in 1937 that 'I still remember with sorrow and uneasiness the names and faces of men hanged by the neck until they were dead, who might have been alive today had I been able to recommend that the King's clemency should be exercised in their cases. This is too dread a burden for any man to be made to bear'. J.R. Clynes, *Memoirs, op. cit.*, 145.

258 See HC Deb 20 January 1931 Vol. 247 c22; HC Deb 21 April 1936 Vol. 311 c19;

259 J.R. Clynes, *Memoirs, op. cit.*, 134.

260 See HC Deb 26 February 1931 Vol. 248 cc2262–3; Characteristic was the answer of John Clynes who said in July 1931: 'until Parliament has had an opportunity of considering and pronouncing upon the recommendations of the committee, I am afraid I could not see my way to propose legislation on this question'; and when asked when that might be, he replied 'I am unable to say'. (HC Deb 23 July 1931 Vol. 255 cc1657–62). Five years later, the same replies were being given (see HC Deb 21 April 1936 Vol. 311 c19).

261 HC Deb 29 January 1931 Vol. 247 c1143.

262 HC Deb 9 June 1931 Vol. 253 c804.

263 Conclusions of a Meeting of the Cabinet, 4 June 1930, Cabinet 31 (30).

264 HC Deb 31 January 1934 Vol. 285 c360.

265 There was, however, to be yet another minor step. A Private Bill introduced by Edith Picton-Turbervill to 'prohibit the passing of the sentence of death upon expectant mothers' was adopted by Government to become the Sentence of Death (Expectant Mothers) Act 1931 (c.24) and passed on first reading. The bill had arisen out of a capital charge of a woman about to become a mother ('A very poor woman, who was an expectant mother, made heroic efforts to provide food and shelter for her babe nine months old. She tried to secure this in every available quarter without success and finally killed her child by gas poisoning'. (HC Deb 4 February 1931 Vol. 247 cc1815–9)). Cabinet reasoned that the bill 'would effect a humane and necessary reform in procedure under the Criminal Law; that it was not controversial, since no one could object to the reform which the Bill proposed to effect; and that it was evident from the public interest in the case referred to, that legislation on the lines of the Bill would command general support'. (Meeting of the Cabinet, 11 March 1931. Cabinet 17 (31)). Edith Picton-Turbervill, 1872–1960, was Labour MP for the Wrekin between June 1929 and October 1931.

266 See *The Times*, 21 April, 1939.

267 See *The Times*, 10 and 15 November 1939.

268 See the Home Secretary's, Chuter Ede's, reply to a Parliamentary Question in November 1946: 'Legislation would be necessary to implement this recommendation and I can hold out no prospect of legislation on this subject in this Session'. (HC Deb 28 November 1946 vol 430 cc1751–2)

269 Email to Paul Rock of 3 March 2011.

270 Herbert Morrison who drafted the 1945 election manifesto recalled; 'We had not been afraid to be frank about our plans. There would be public ownership of fuel and power, transport, the Bank of England, civil aviation, and iron and steel. We proposed a housing programme dealt with in relation to good town planning. We promised to put the 1944 Education Act into practical operation. We said that wealth would no longer be the passport to the best health treatment. We promised that a Labour

Government would extend social insurance over the widest field'. (*An Autobiography* (1960); London: Odhams Press).

271 Just after the War, the League and its allies had arranged a meeting advertised by the statement that 'It is hoped that the Home Secretary will introduce a new Criminal Justice Bill before Christmas. ... The Bill will no doubt contain many of the propos-als of Sir Samuel Hoare's Criminal Justice Bill, 1938, which would have reached the Statute Book in 1939 but for the outbreak of war. But the new Bill must go further and provide for the abolition of the Death Penalty, as recommended by the Report of the Select Committee of the House of Commons in 1930. Otherwise it will be inconclusive and unsatisfactory in that it will leave untouched a barbaric survival of the old penal law which denies the basic principles of the Bill. If the Bill does not, in its original form, provide for abolition, every endeavour will be made to secure this amendment, or by a separate Bill'. (Notice: 'To Abolish the Death Penalty. Meeting and Conference arranged by the Howard League for Penal Reform[;] the Penal Reform Committee of the Society Of Friends[;] the National Campaign for the Abolition of the Death Penalty[.] September 1946'.)

272 There were other amendments proposed in addition to the implementation of the five-year moratorium on hanging. One was the introduction of degrees of murder (see *The Times*, 6 January 1948).

273 Capital Punishment: Memorandum by the Home Secretary, C.P. (47) 217 28 July 1947.

274 *The Times*, Monday, 12 April 1948.

275 HC Deb 14 April 1948 vol 449 cc979–1098.

276 Born in 1895, and dying in 1968, he was an inveterate campaigner. A solicitor, he became Labour Member of Parliament for Nelson and Colne in 1935 and retained his seat until his death. The criminologist, Sarah McCabe, remarked that after his failure to secure abolition in 1948, he became 'the acknowledged parliamentary protagonist of abolition, although outside the house and in the newly founded Campaign for the Abolition of the Death Penalty he had neither the reputation nor the force of the other determined reformers, Sir Victor Gollancz and Arthur Koestler' (*The Oxford Dictionary of National Biography*, http://www.oxforddnb.com/view/article/36093). Silverman said in debate on his amendment in 1948: " ... it was said that crimes of violence are increasing because the sense of the sanctity of human life is lower than it used to be, and that for that reason we should ourselves destroy life. I think that the argument is really all the other way ... it is the duty of all of us who value our civilisation not to depress still further those moral and spiritual values, but to seek to raise them, and to seek to raise them at precisely this moment when they are most in danger. ... ' That, said his biographer, 'was Silverman's case for the suspension of the Death Penalty ... the case for which he had repeatedly to argue for nearly twenty years'. E. Hughes (1969); *Sydney Silverman: Rebel in Parliament*, London and Edinburgh: Charles Skilton, 107.

277 *The Times*, 10 February 1968.

278 Email, 25 October 2010.

279 However, Labour ministers were allowed to abstain but not to vote in favour of the amendment. See *The Times*, 15 and 16 April 1948.

280 James Chuter Ede, 1882–1965, a nonconformist, was Labour MP for South Shields between 1929 and 1931, and again between 1935 and 1964, becoming Home Secretary between 1945 and 1951. Opposed to abolition in 1948, his biographer stated that 'The public issue which overshadowed Ede's later life was that of the death penalty. Growing evidence emerged in the mid-1950s that a serious miscarriage of justice had taken place in the case of Timothy John Evans, who had been sentenced to death for murder during Ede's term as home secretary. Ede maintained that he could not have granted a reprieve to Evans on the basis of the evidence available to him at

the time, and in this he was supported by official inquiries. But his anguish over the case encouraged him to revise his view of capital punishment. In old age Ede campaigned for the abolition of the death penalty and for a posthumous free pardon in the case of Evans, whose remains he argued should be transferred from prison to family relatives'. (Entry by K. Jefferys in *The Oxford Dictionary of National Biography*, http://www.oxforddnb.com/view/article/32414) Bailey claimed that 'Ede was a moderate, cautious, and practical politician, certainly no innovator, and, as such, likely to listen to his permanent officials. He tended to steer clear of controversy within the party, preferring the part of conciliator, and the capital punishment debate cannot have been to his liking. It is a telling point against him, moreover, that he was abolitionist both before and after his stint as home secretary, but retentionist when in office'. (http://www.historycooperative.org/journals/lhr/18.2/bailey.html)

281 There is a major difference between his public and private utterances, just as there was in Cabinet. Notes of a Cabinet meeting just before the 1948 Bill was about to be debated record him saying that 'Don't think a case has bn. made out tht. risks wd. be increased. ... I wd. say no suff. reason qua effects to vote v. abolition. If Private Member I wd. vote for abolition. ... No statistics to show tht. abolition in f. countries has led to increase. Traditional view of police & "experts" has always bn. wrong'. Caution trumped his doubts. The Lord President, Herbert Morrison, was reported to have said that 'Must watch public opinion – not convinced tht. it wants this change'. Stafford Cripps, the Chancellor of the Exchequer, said 'I cdn't vote in favour of prolonging it. Wd. want liberty to vote for abolition'. On a vote of 10–5, it was agreed that "Time not opportune," and that 'Give that advice. But allow free Vote of H/C. Ministers shd. not speak against Govt. view'. The Prime Minister was said to have asked 'Shd. they abstain from voting?' and was told by a number, including Herbert Morrison, that it was 'Constitutionally wrong to register divided views. Abstention shd. be enough,' and that 'we can't divide in diff. Lobbies'. The Home Secretary was then recorded as reflecting that 'I shall have to vote in acc. with my statement. That will be v. my conscience. Other Ministers who favour abolition will abstain & it will be noticed. Is that any better than allowg. them to vote v. Govt. line'. (CAB195/5 Cabinet Minutes C.M.(47)1st Meeting (Cont'd) – C.M.(47) 2 January 1947)

282 In the context of today's defence of capital punishment in the United States of America, Garland lists a number of 'narratives and metaphors' which are routinely put to work. One is 'The metaphor of rules [which] frames the death penalty as a constitutionally approved undertaking, a matter of legal determinations rather than personal decisions, an outcome of painstaking procedural safeguards that amount to "super due process"'. D. Garland; *Peculiar Institution, op. cit.*, 61.

283 HC Deb 14 April 1948 Vol. 449 cc979–1098.

284 He was to submit a rather different gloss on that ambiguous proposition in a Memorandum to Cabinet of November 1947. There, he said, 'in countries where the death penalty has been abolished, abolition has not been followed by any increase in the number of murders. So far as can be judged from the evidence collected by the Select Committee of 1930, there are no reliable figures showing that in any country which has abolished the death penalty there has been subsequently any significant increase in the number of murders. ...' He then proceeded to speculate about the repercussions of the abolition of the death penalty for the British administration of occupied Germany and for the colonies. (Memorandum by the Home Secretary, Criminal Justice Bill: Capital Punishment. CP. (47) 306 13 *November* 1947)

285 HC Deb 14 April 1948 Vol. 449 cc979–1098

286 *The Times*, 16 April 1948.

287 Cabinet determined that 'the debate on capital punishment should be taken during the Committee Stage. It seemed likely that the Lords would invite the Commons to reconsider the new Clause suspending capital punishment as a penalty for murder

but that, if the Commons insisted on it, they might acquiesce in its becoming law'. Conclusions of a Meeting of the Cabinet, 22 April 1948. Cabinet (29) 48.

288 See *The Times*, 10 June 1948. The Home Secretary was reported to have told the Cabinet that 'my situation now v. diff. Man awaiting execution now: v. serious case: Jury recommended to mercy: Judge doesn't endorse it. While Bill still before Parlt. murderer of P.C. Edgar likely to be convicted. Believe exp[n] of H/C. view can't be ignored. H/C. wdn't stand for executions while Bill pending. If disagreemt. with H/L. shd. kill the Bill this Session, law wd. revive in full force. Short of that, however, I must administer the law in acc. with exp[n] of H/C. opinion. Therefore intend to recommend reprieve in every case'. Herbert Morrison's reflection was said to be that 'Doubtful. Hope H/L. won't put us in diffy'. (CAB 195/6 C A B I N E T M I N U T E S C.M.(48)1st Meeting – C.M.(48) 15 April, 1948.) The Home Secretary was referring to the case of Donald Thomas who was about to be executed for the murder by shooting of Police Constable Nathaniel Edgar on 13 February 1948 (see *The Times*, 6 March 1948).

289 Amongst the 28 supporters was the Lord Chancellor, Lord Jowitt, who voted for the amendment as the will of the House of Commons, although he was opposed to it (*The Times*, 28 April 1948). Opposed were 181 members of the House.

290 Lord Simon said 'there is the question of the importance of public opinion in this matter. Your Lordships will have noted that in the course of the whole debate yesterday nobody, whatever his view on the clause, dared to suggest that the mass of public opinion was in its favour. Nobody did so'. HL Deb 1 June 1948 vol 156 cc19–75.

291 E. Tuttle; *The Crusade against Capital Punishment in Great Britain, op. cit.*, 136.

292 And, indeed, public opinion polls conducted at the time confirmed his view. Of three surveys, the largest proportion of respondents reported to favour an experimental moratorium on capital punishment was 26%, the smallest 13%. Those disapproving were between 66% and 77%. See L. England (1948); 'Capital Punishment and Open-End Questions', *Public Opinion Quarterly*, Vol. 12, No. 3, 412–416.

293 HL Deb 1 June 1948 Vol. 156 cc19–75.

294 Gerald Isaacs, the second Marquess of Reading, 1889–1960.

295 An editorial in the Howard Journal pronounced that 'The present Lord Chief Justice believes ... that it is necessary to prevent the crime of murder. He is so firmly convinced on *a priori* grounds that the fear of death is the most potent influence on the mind of man that he fears almost any relaxation of the present law'. 'Royal Commission on Capital Punishment', *Howard Journal*, Vol. VIII, 1 (1949–50) 2.

296 A statement he would later retract: *The Times*, 1 July 1948.

297 HL Deb 2 June 1948 Vol. 156 cc102–218.

298 The Bishop of Chichester had voted for abolition, the Bishop of Winchester against. No other Lords Spiritual voted. That was to change, and we shall see that the position of the bishops would later be pivotal to the enactment of the 1965 Bill.

299 Sir Hartley Shawcross, 1902–2003, was a barrister who became Labour MP for St Helens in 1945, becoming Attorney General in that year. He was to be the lead British prosecuting counsel in the Nuremberg trials.

300 HC Deb 15 July 1948 Vol. 453 cc1411–545

301 The Parliament Act 1911 c.13 (An Act to make provision with respect to the powers of the House of Lords in relation to those of the House of Commons, and to limit the duration of Parliament), curtailed to two years the power of the House of Lords to obstruct or delay the passage of legislation approved by the House of Commons. That period was to be further restricted to one year in 1949 under The Parliament Act 1949 c.103.

302 See J. Horder, *Homicide and the Politics of Law Reform, op. cit.*, 223.

303 Sydney Silverman recalled that 'I and my hon. Friends negotiated with my right hon. Friend the then Home Secretary and said, "Let us abandon our Clause and see whether we can devise a new Clause in which we will retain the death penalty for just those categories for which the House of Lords says we must retain it and abolish it for the others"'. HC Deb 10 February 1955 vol 536 cc2064–183.

304 The Attorney-General said 'The purpose of the new Clause, to put it in a phrase, is to include those cases in which public opinion feels that the suspension of the existing arrangements in regard to the death penalty might involve risks which ought not to be taken at this time'. HC Deb 15 July 1948 Vol. 453 cc1411–545.

305 *The Times*, 7 July 1948.

306 In what proved to be an anticipation of much of the 1957 Act, Cabinet had unanimously resolved on a draft clause on 3 June that 'the death penalty should be retained only for certain specified classes of murder. The effect of this clause was to retain the death penalty for murder committed either in the course of a felony involving violence or in resisting or avoiding arrest, or by the administration of any poison or other destructive thing. The death penalty would also be retained for the murder by a prisoner of a prison officer acting in the execution of his duty or for a murder committed by a person who had previously been convicted of murder'. CONCLUSIONS of a Meeting of the Cabinet held at 10 Downing Street, S.W. 1, on Monday, 7 June. 1948, C A B I N E T 36 (4 8).

307 James Christoph observed that 'the situation enhanced the power of the House of Lords, for it was clear that on this bill, unlike most of the measures that had been sent to them by the Labour-controlled House of Commons, the Lords were actually supporting the Government against a Commons' majority'. J. Christoph (1962); 'Capital Punishment and British Party Responsibility', *Political Science Quarterly*, Vol. 77, No. 1, 24.

308 *The Times*, 16 July 1948.

309 HC Deb 15 July 1948 Vol. 453 cc1411–545.

310 HL Deb 20 July 1948 Vol. 157 cc1004–73.

311 Lord Llewellin, 1893–1957, was a barrister, and the Conservative Member of Parliament for Uxbridge from 1929 to 1945 when he became a peer. He was President of the Board of Trade and Minister for Aircraft Production in 1942; and Minister of Food in 1943. (Based on Jonathan Lewis' entry in *The Oxford Dictionary of National Biography*, http://www.oxforddnb.com/view/article/34563).

312 Cyril Garbett, 1875–1955, became Bishop of Southwark in 1919, Bishop of Winchester in 1932, and Archbishop of York in June 1942. The webpage of the current Archbishop of York, John Sentamu, called him 'Known as a strong, often ruthless character who was respected rather than loved' (http://www.archbishopofyork.org/214). His was a far from monochromatic world view (see, for instance his portrait in *Time*, 17 April 1944), but it is possible that his muscular attitude to punishment was shaped by the Second World War, during which he lamented the frailty of civilisation and had been adamant about the need for retribution on the Germans who were massacring Jews: 'cold-blooded, cowardly brutes' (*The Times*, 12 December 1942). He later said, 'Let the German people know what was being done in their name. Let the German people also be told solemnly and repeatedly that sure retribution awaited not only the master criminals who had ordered these horrors but also their brutal underlings ...' (*The Times*, 15 March 1943 and see his observations reported in *The Times* of 8 January 1944 in which he talked of how 'there was only a thin crust between civilisation and utter chaos. ... Justice demanded that those responsible for ... abominations should be treated with the utmost severity'). He refused to condemn the mass bombing of Germany, saying that 'Often in life there is no clear choice between absolute right and wrong; frequently the choice has to be made of the lesser of two evils, and it is a lesser evil to bomb a war-loving Germany ...' (*The Times*, 25 June 1943). That theme

of the precariousness of civilisation was to endure after the war and into the period marked by the passage of the Criminal Justice Bill (see *The Times*, 23 June 1948). There was what he called a 'startling rise in the number of crimes' and 'a largely lost sense of moral obligations in the present generation' (*The Times*, 3 November 1948). 'The old homely virtues of honesty and truthfulness were vanishing. ... The first cause is the war' (HL Deb 23 November 1948 vol 159 cc511–38) (He was to deplore the Government's attempt to bring in the abolitionist amendment: 'the importance of the Bill had been ... largely overshadowed and obscured by the discussion of one clause. It was a great mistake to have introduced a clause dealing with capital punishment into this Bill'. (*The Times*, 21 July 1948).

313 Lord Simons, 1881–1971, was Lord of Appeal in Ordinary, 1944–51; later to become Lord High Chancellor of Great Britain, 1951–54.

314 HL Debate, 20 July 1948 Volume 157.

315 See B. Block and J. Hostettler (1997); *Hanging in the Balance*, Winchester: Waterside Press, 110.

316 See the Rt. Hon. Viscount Templewood (1948); 'The Criminal Justice Bill: International Aspects of Prevention and Treatment', *Journal of Criminal Law and Criminology*, Vol. 39, No. 2, 135.

317 Viscount Templewood, Samuel Hoare, 1880–1959, was elected to Parliament as the Conservative MP for Chelsea in 1910. He was to be Secretary for Air, Foreign Secretary, First Lord of the Admiralty, and then ambassador to Spain. He became the chairman of the council of the Howard League between 1947 and 1959, and was described as an energetic supporter of 'penal reform and particularly the 1947 Criminal Justice Bill and the movement to abolish capital punishment'. (Based on R. Adams' entry in *The Oxford Dictionary of National Biography*, http://www.oxforddnb.com/view/article/33898)

318 S. Hoare, Viscount Templewood (1951); *The Shadow of the Gallows*, Victor Gollancz, London. The short book consisted of the author's views on capital punishment with appendices on such matters as 'Murder Statement for the Years 1900–1948, prepared by the Home Office, 1949; Males Convicted of Murder Executed and Respited, 1900–48, analysis by age, statement prepared by the Home Office, 1949; and Summary of the Treatment in Prison and Release of Murderers in Abolitionist States.

319 The divisions were introduced under the 1898 Prisons Act, (61 & 62 Vict) C. 41, under which 'prisoners should be treated as offenders either of the first or the second division where there is evidence of good character over a considerable period of time ... 'S. Hobhouse and F. Brockway (eds.) (1922); *English Prisons To-Day*, London: Longmans, Green and Co., 214.

320 Herbert Morrison summarised the position by saying that 'The House of Lords rejected [the] proposition. It went back again under a compromise proposal, with whatever adjectives hon. Members may wish to apply to it. That was not acceptable; it came back again and, finally, the question of the abolition of capital punishment was removed from the bill altogether. All this was done within three or four weeks'. HC Deb 31 October 1949 Vol. 469 cc45–167.

321 See *The Times*, 21 and 22 July 1948.

322 HC Deb 18 November 1948 Vol. 458 cc564–5.

323 See *The Times*, 21 January 1949.

324 For a revealing social history of the period, see S. O'Connor (2013); *Handsome Brute: The Story of a Ladykiller*, London: Simon and Schuster.

325 M. Wingersky (1954); 'Report of the Royal Commission on Capital Punishment (1949–1953): A Review', *The Journal of Criminal Law, Criminology, and Police Science*, Vol. 44, No. 6, 695.

326 HC Deb 20 January 1949 Vol. 460 cc329–31.

327 Sir Ernest Gowers, 1880–1966, was called to the Bar in 1906. He had a long and varied career, including being private secretary to a number of parliamentary under-secretaries, principal private secretary to the Chancellor of the Exchequer, chief inspector of the National Health Insurance Commission, secretary to the Conciliation and Arbitration Board and chairman of the Coal Mines Reorganisation Commission. It is said that his chairmanship of the Royal Commission converted him to abolition. (Based on R. Burchfield's entry in *The Oxford Dictionary of National Biography*, http://www.oxforddnb.com/view/article/33497)

328 *Report of the Royal Commission on Capital Punishment* 1949–1953, *op. cit.*

329 E. Gowers (1956); *A Life for a Life? The Problem of Capital Punishment*, London: Chatto and Windus, 7.

330 The numbers of murders had shown no uniform trend between 1938 and 1951, there having been two peaks in 1942 and 1944, and a trough between 1949 and 1951 when the Commission was sitting (319).

331 Retribution seemed to be out of vogue, having been supplanted by reformation, and even murderers, it said, demonstrated a capacity for reformation in abolitionist countries (paras 52–55).

332 It was difficult to assess the deterrent impact of capital punishment, it said: 'Capital punishment has obviously failed as a deterrent when a murder is committed. We can number its failures. But we cannot number its successes' (para. 59).

333 It was recorded that the 'representatives of the Chief Constables' Association and the Police Federation were strongly opposed to any change in the existing law' (para. 103), but the Royal Commission dismissed their opposition as founded on an exaggeration of the consequences that might stem from abolition (para. 110).

334 E. Gowers, *A Life for a Life?*, *op. cit.*, 133.

335 That criticism was principally that a measure designed to exercise clemency in exceptional circumstances had become so routine that half of all capital sentences were reprieved; that the Secretary of State, the man responsible for advising on clemency, was obliged in effect to become an extra-judicial court of appeal 'sitting in private, judging on the record only, and giving no reasons for his decisions'. However capable the Home Secretary's advisers might be, and however much they might be able to rely on precedent, their role could not but be constitutionally anomalous (para. 47).

336 It said that 'The alternative of empowering the jury to decide in each case whether punishment by imprisonment for life can properly be substituted for the death penalty … is the only practicable way of enabling the courts, instead of the Executive, to take account of extenuating circumstances so as to correct the rigidity which is the outstanding defect of the existing law'. (para. 790)

337 L. Blom-Cooper (1973); 'The Penalty for Murder', *The British Journal of Criminology*, Vol. 13, No. 2, 188.

338 In J. Barry (1958); '… Hanged the Neck Until …' *The Sydney Law Review*, Vol. 2, No. 3, 403.

339 Sir David Maxwell Fyfe, 1900–1967, was a barrister and Conservative Member of Parliament for Liverpool West Derby Division between 1935 and 1954. He became Attorney General in 1945 and Home Secretary, 1951–1954 (http://www.ukwhoswho.com.gate2.library.lse.ac.uk/view/article/oupww/whowaswho/U47933/KILMUIR?index=1&results) His collected letters and speeches housed in the Churchill College Archives make no reference at all either to the debates about capital punishment or to the founding of the Wolfenden Committee, events in which he was pivotally engaged.

340 Timothy Evans, 1924–1950, had been accused of killing his wife and daughter in Notting Hill in 1949. At his trial, he accused John Christie, his neighbour, of the offence. Three years later, after Evans' execution, it became evident that Christie

was a serial killer who had murdered a number of women (see the reports in *The Times*, 25 March 1953: 'Three Women Found Dead In Flat: Bodies Concealed In Recess'; 26 March 1953: 'Fourth Strangled Woman Found'; 4 April 1953: 'Christie Further Remanded On Murder Charges'; and 15 May 1953: 'Body Of Mrs. Evans To Be Exhumed: Licence Granted To Defence'). By the end, six bodies were found. For an early synopsis of the case, see L. Kennedy (1961); *Ten Rillington Place*, London: Victor Gollancz. After prolonged campaigning by a number of prominent men, including Ludovic Kennedy and David Astor, Sir Frank Soskice, the then Home Secretary, ordered a new inquiry under Sir Daniel Brabin, a High Court judge, in 1965–66. Sir Daniel found it was "more probable than not" that Evans had murdered his wife but not his daughter. Sir Frank Soskice's successor, Roy Jenkins, announced that 'In all the circumstances, I do not think it would be right to allow Evans's conviction to stand. I have, therefore, decided that the proper course is to recommend to Her Majesty that she should grant a Free Pardon, and I am glad to be able to tell the House that The Queen has approved my recommendation and that the Free Pardon was signed this morning'. (HC Deb 18 October 1966 Vol. 734 cc38–40).

341 He said that 'The right hon. and learned Gentleman who is now Home Secretary [said]: "There is no practical possibility. The hon. and learned Member asks me to say that there is no possibility. Of course, a jury might go wrong, the Court of Criminal Appeal might go wrong, as might the House of Lords and the Home Secretary: they might all be stricken mad and go wrong. But that is not a possibility which anyone can consider likely. The hon. and learned Member is moving in a realm of fantasy when he makes that suggestion". I should like to know from the Home Secretary today whether he still believes that. Was my hon. and learned Friend moving in a realm of fantasy? This week we have had completely established that a case was made against a man on a charge of murder; that it succeeded; that the appeal failed; the application for reprieve failed; the man was hanged, and we know today that he was convicted and hanged on a false case'. HC Deb 1 July 1953 Vol. 517 cc407–19

342 *The Times*, 25 September 1953.

343 In November 1953, for example, Sydney Silverman was told by the Leader of the House that it would 'be premature to make any statement, because, as I think everybody knows, it took the Royal Commission about five years to study this question, and the Report was presented to Parliament only in September. This is a matter upon which not only hon. Members of this House but the whole country would desire to form an opinion'. HC Deb 26 November 1953 Vol. 521 cc526–9. He was told in December that 'I do not see any opportunity in the immediate future of a debate on this subject' (HC Deb 3 December 1953 Vol. 521 cc1314–9). And so it went on.

344 He said: 'I doubt very much whether we ought to tamper with the view that anyone who has been proved to have taken the life of another human being feloniously shall be liable to the capital sentence and will receive it. It seems to me that the fact that so awful a crime, whatever be the motive, is followed by this dreadful punishment, may well be a necessary mark which the community puts upon murder and one of the ways in which we seek to discourage people from committing it'. HL Deb 16 December 1953 Vol. 185 cc137–88.

345 Lord Jowitt, 1885–1957, was called to the bar in 1909, became a Liberal Member of Parliament for Hartlepool between 1922 and 1924, and again a Liberal Member, and then Labour Member for Preston in 1929, becoming Attorney-General in Ramsay MacDonald's Government. He was Solicitor-General between 1940 and 1942, and Lord Chancellor in 1945. His biographer claims that he was opposed to the suspension of the death penalty in the debates during and after the passage of the Criminal Justice Act. (Based on T. Legg's and M-L. Legg's entry in *The Oxford Dictionary of National Biography*, http://www.oxforddnb.com/view/article/34246)

346 HL Deb 16 December 1953 Vol. 185 cc137–88.

347 HC Deb 9 December 1954 Vol. 535 c58W.

348 *The Times*, 4 February 1955.

349 The record of Cabinet discussion suggests that it was rather grudging: 'The Cabinet were informed that facilities would have to be provided before long for the House of Commons to debate the Report of the Royal Commission on Capital Punishment. It must be assumed that, when this was debated, means would be found of forcing a division on the question whether capital punishment should be abolished in this country. On this issue the Government might find it necessary to allow a free vote'. Conclusions of a Meeting of Cabinet held on 27 January 1955. C.C. (55) 7.

350 Gwilym Lloyd George, 1894–1967, was the National Liberal and Conservative Member for Newcastle upon Tyne North, and he served as Home Secretary between 1954 and 1957. In the 1950s, he was said to have been 'firmly opposed to the abolition of capital punishment' (based on the entry by Kenneth Morgan in *The Oxford Dictionary of National Biography*, http://www.oxforddnb.com/view/article/34571). His obituary in *The Times* of 15 February 1967 stated that his 'liberal, but essentially right-wing views, perhaps made it difficult for him to be sympathetic to the parliamentary agitation that was then growing for the abolition of the death penalty. In this, it should be said, he reflected the general views of his colleagues in the Cabinet ...'

351 HC Deb 10 February 1955 vol 536 cc2064–183.

352 Although he had supported Vyvyan Adams' amendment on the five-year experimental abolition of the death penalty in the debate on the aborted 1938 Criminal Justice Bill. See HC Deb 16 November 1938 Vol. 341 cc954–1011.

353 And there were other cases that made their mark throughout the latter years of the campaigning – that of Ruth Ellis in particular.

354 R.A. Butler was to be less impressed. He read Ludovic Kennedy's book and his conclusion was that 'whether Evans was guilty or not, *it cannot now be established that he was innocent of the murder of the child*. If so, there could be no question of giving him a Free Pardon'. [Emphasis in the original] Capital Punishment; Memorandum [to Cabinet] by the Secretary of State for the Home Department, C. (61) 20, 8 February, 1961.

355 Sir Reginald Manningham-Buller, 1905–1980, was a barrister and the Conservative Member for Northamptonshire South. He had been Solicitor-General, 1951–1954, and Attorney-General, 1954–1962. He has been described as 'a tough and effective debater, though his abrasive style never really endeared him to the House of Commons, even on his own side of the chamber. ... He was out of sympathy with much of the changing mood of the 1960s, opposing the abolition of the death penalty and the legalisation of homosexuality'. (D. J. Dutton's entry in *The Oxford Dictionary of National Biography*, http://www.oxforddnb.com/view/article/31409).

356 HC Deb 10 February 1955 Vol. 536 cc2064–183.

357 HC Deb 14 July 1955 Vol. 543 c196W.

358 See, for example, HC Deb 21 July 1955 Vol. 544 cc541–3.

359 *The Times*, 11 November 1955.

360 HC Deb 15 November 1955 Vol. 546 cc207–10.

361 Geoffrey de Freitas, 1913–1982, was a barrister, Labour Member of Parliament for Central Nottingham, 1945–1950, for Lincoln 1950–1961, and for Kettering 1964–1979. He had been Parliamentary Private Sec. to Prime Minister, 1945–46; Under-Secretary of State for Air, 1946–50; and Under-Secretary of State, Home Office, 1950–51. (Based on his entry in *Who was Who*: http://www.ukwhoswho. com.gate2.library.lse.ac.uk/view/article/oupww/whoswho/U164347/de_ FREITAS_Rt._Hon._Sir_Geoffrey_Stanley?index=1&results=QuicksearchResults& query=0)

362 *The Times*, 12 November 1955.

363 HC Deb 15 November 1955 Vol. 546 cc207–10.

364 Tony Benn remonstrated that 'Mr. Speaker will correct me if I am wrong – when the records of the House show that the House gave a First Reading to a Bill for the abolition of the death penalty, it is in accordance with the dignity of the Government and the House that he should have allowed it to receive a First Reading without dissent and then suggest that it is no concern of his, as Leader of the House, to provide an opportunity for the Bill to proceed further?', but the Leader of the House, Harry Crookshank, said 'there is no question of the Government giving time for a debate on a Bill which, after all, is only at the stage of having received leave to be introduced, and which, moreover, is a Private Member's Bill'. HC Deb 17 November 1955 vol 546 cc780–90.

365 HC Deb 20 December 1955 Vol. 547 cc1863–75

366 HC Deb 24 November 1955 Vol. 546 cc1653–4

367 There had in the interim been published in January 1956 what was represented as a compromise solution between outright abolition and the law as it then stood. It was propounded in a report of a committee of the Inns of Court Conservative and Unionist Society, under the chairmanship of Lionel Heald, the Attorney General from 1951–54, published in 1956, and it proposed a restriction of the death penalty to those who had had a 'clear intention to kill'. *Murder: Some Suggestions for the Reform of the Law relating to Murder in England*, London: Society of Conservative Lawyers. For greater detail, see Lionel Heald's observations on that report in debate. It was to be his argument that 'We retain the rifle, but we strive to our utmost to reduce occasions for its use to the minimum. That is the principle we adopt. I would like to know how it can be suggested that one can logically depart from that principle as regards the death penalty. Can we, as Members of Parliament, deny to the State the ultimate sanction of life and death? That is what we are going to decide tonight. The penalty is a terrible one, but crimes also are terrible'. HC Deb 16 February 1956 Vol. 548 cc2536–655. The Home Secretary believed that that report might lend weight to the Government's position. It was, he said, 'likely to exercise a substantial influence over Government supporters in the House of Commons'. CONCLUSIONS of a Meeting of the Cabinet held at 10 Downing Street, S.W. 1, on Tuesday, 31 January, 1956, at 11 a.m. C M. (56).

368 The Home Secretary had also floated the possibility of 'persuading the Commons to agree to the retention of the death penalty if they offered to introduce legislation at the earliest practicable opportunity on three of the secondary recommendations of the Royal Commission ...' CONCLUSIONS of a Meeting of the Cabinet held at 10 Downing Street, S.W. 1, on Tuesday, 31 January, 1956, at 11 a.m. C M. (56).

369 At a Cabinet meeting on 3 January 1956, the Home Secretary, Major Lloyd-George, had said that 'he had set out fully the arguments for and against capital punishment as it was important that the Government should decide on the line to be taken in the debate which was due to take place when Parliament reassembled. He recommended that capital punishment should not be abolished, but that a more extensive use should be made of the Prerogative of Mercy. ... And the Lord Chancellor said 'that in his view the most important arguments in favour of the retention of capital punishment were those given in ... the Home Secretary's paper. Although there could be no statistical proof, the retention of the death penalty must have some deterrent influence. This deterrent was of most value in its effect on professional criminals who, if capital punishment were abolished, would be more likely to carry arms'. (CONCLUSIONS of a Meeting of the Cabinet held at 10 Downing Street, S.W. 1, on Tuesday, 3 January 1956, at 3 p.m. C M. (56))

370 *Ibid.*

371 *Ibid.*

372 Memorandum by the Secretary of State for the Home Department and Minister for Welsh Affairs: Legislation to Abolish Death Penalty for Murder, C.P. (56) 43 21 February 1956.

373 It was said that 'In the House of Lords there was a great body of authoritative legal opinion in favour of retaining the death penalty. Even if this Bill should pass the Commons, it was likely to be rejected by the Lords. Public opinion on this question was divided and this would, therefore, be a proper occasion for the exercise of the power of the House of Lords to delay the passage of legislation. There were already indications of a growing volume of public support for the retention of the death penalty; and it was to be expected that this movement would grow during the period between the first rejection of the Bill by the House of Lords and its subsequent presentation to the Upper House'. (CONCLUSIONS of a Meeting of the Cabinet held in the Prime Minister's Room, House of Commons, S.W. 1, on Wednesday, 22 February, 1956, at 4 p.m. CM. (56) 16th Conclusions)

374 Cabinet had agreed that 'the forthcoming debate on this subject should be held on a Government motion. On the form of this motion, and on the statements to be made by ministers speaking in support of it, the following points were raised:

> (a) Government supporters would be more likely to vote in favour of the motion if it emphasised the need for legislation to amend the law defining the crime of murder. The motion should not, however, be so phrased as to imply that the death penalty would be abandoned when that amending legislation had been passed.
>
> (b) The motion should relate to capital punishment as the penalty for murder. The House need not be invited to express any opinion on the retention of capital punishment as a penalty for treason, piracy or arson in dockyards.
>
> (c) The amendment of the law defining the crime of murder would present formidable legal difficulties. The Government spokesmen in the debate should therefore be guarded in their statements about the content of this legislation. It could be said that, in determining its content, the Government would take account of suggestions made in the debate. ...'

(CONCLUSIONS of a Meeting of the Cabinet held at 10 Downing Street, S.W.1, on Wednesday, 8 February, 1956, at 12 noon C M. (56)).

375 H. Klare (1963); review of J. Christoph; *Capital Punishment and British Politics, Annals of the American Academy of Political and Social Science*, Vol. 347, 168.

376 HC Deb 16 February 1956 Vol. 548 cc2536–655.

377 R.A. Butler wound up the debate by saying 'It may seem peculiar that we have a Government Motion and a free vote, but I think that on this issue that is the right decision. The Government should give a lead, the Government have a mind on the matter, as I shall indicate, and the Government have great responsibility to the public on this matter as the supreme authority. We are therefore right to put down a Government Motion, and the fact that we happen to have a free vote is the right way to handle the debate'. HC Deb 16 February 1956 Vol. 548 cc2536–655.

378 CAB 195/14 10 April 1956.

379 He argued that 'I believe that the death penalty is a uniquely effective deterrent, but I do not believe its effect is universal – obviously, it is not. No deterrent will deter the insane or those who kill in moments of blind rage or passion, without thought of the consequences. Some people do not count the cost to themselves of what they do. The ability not to count the cost may produce great acts of heroism in some fields or foolish recklessness in others. But the fact that human beings do sometimes act without thought of the consequences puts them at times – I repeat at times – beyond the reach of deterrents. But murder is not a thing that occurs to the human mind only in moments of passion or frenzy. The mind is capable of calculating the advantage to be gained by eliminating a particular person or by accepting the risk of killing in the course of a particular enterprise. It is here that the natural disinclination to take in cold

blood a substantial risk of death may tip the balance against murder'. (HL Deb 9 July 1956 Vol. 198 cc564–676). His wife wrote to him afterwards to say that: 'That was a marvellous speech darling. We met Priscilla who was quite breathless with enthusiasm. She said she had never heard you so good, that it was a historic speech & if they heard that in the Commons it might have changed the whole thing. ... It was a great triumph'. KLMR 4/20, Churchill College Archives.

380 HL Deb 10 July 1956 Vol. 198 cc679–843.

381 Significantly, the Church was more prominent in the voting, and more abolitionist. Nine bishops, including the Archbishops of Canterbury and York, voted for abolition, one only – the Bishop of Rochester – against.

382 The Home Secretary argued that 'I do not see how we could advocate a step which we have so recently urged the House, for reasons which still seem to me to be cogent, to reject. I think that people outside the House who are against abolition would be very critical if we executed a volte face of this kind; and we should put those of our supporters who voted with us in an impossible position if, having urged them to vote according to conscience on the motion, we put the Whips on to compel them to vote in support of the Bill ...' (Memorandum by the Secretary of State for the Home Department and Minister for Welsh Affairs. 21 February 1956. CP. (56) 43).

383 The Home Secretary reflected that the Heald Committee's recommendations might offer a way forward, but that they had their hazards: 'The Committee suggested that if these recommendations were adopted the effect would be that the death sentence would be passed only on those who have committed a heinous crime and the discussion on the desirability of retaining the death penalty would not be confused with extraneous disputes. I do not myself think that it is wholly true to say that if the recommendations of the Committee were adopted the sentence of death could be passed only in really heinous cases, but I have little doubt that the Committee's report and the suggestion that the area of disagreement can be narrowed will impress our supporters and particularly those who are with us on the main issue of the retention of the death sentence, but are disturbed about its present scope ... legislation on this subject may expose us to embarrassment ...' (Memorandum to Cabinet by the Home Secretary and Minister for Welsh Affairs, Amendment of the Law Relating to Murder. 20 January 1956. CP. (56) 27)

384 Four years after the event, Charles Cunningham noted to Francis Graham-Harrison, the Assistant Under-Secretary of State, Home Office, 1957–63, that 'You will recollect that the Secretary of State did not like the description of the Homicide Act as a compromise between the Government's point of view and that of the abolitionists. ...' CCC to Graham-Harrison, 20 March 1961 (CRI60 431/5/79).

385 D E A T H P E N A L T Y (A B O L I T I O N) B I L L: Memorandum to Cabinet by the Home Secretary and Minister for Welsh Affairs and the Secretary of State for Scotland, CP. (56) 92, 29 March, 1956. The Memorandum continued:

> '3. As Secretaries of State we are responsible for the maintenance of law and order and we have a special position in relation to the services by which law and order is maintained, the police and prison services. The members of both look to us to defend their interests, and it would be extremely undesirable, in view of the difficulty of recruiting for both these services, to give them the impression that we are indifferent to the increased danger to which the abolition of capital punishment will expose them. ...
>
> 4. We therefore propose that the Government should support amendments designed to preserve capital punishment as the penalty for:
> (i)   the murder of a police constable in the execution of his duty, and
> (ii) the murder of a prison officer by a prisoner.
> 5. We recognise that these amendments will create anomalies'.

386 CONCLUSIONS of a Meeting of the Cabinet held at 10 Downing Street, S.W. 1. on Tuesday 10 April 1956, at 11 a.m. CM. (5 6)

387 For example, by the Annual Conference of the Federation of University Conservative and Unionist Associations. 28–31 March 1955: "this conference upholds the principle of capital punishment"; and by the East Salford Conservative Association Executive Council. The latter read: "this meeting of the executive council of the East Salford Conservative Association expresses the view that the retention of capital punishment is essential in that it acts as a necessary deterrent to possible would be murderers". (Passed with two dissentients, 1.12.1955. 34 present)'. (CC04/6/45 1955 Conservative Party Archives at the Bodleian Library)

388 From the Hon. Secretary, National Union of Conservative and Unionist Associations (Yorkshire Provincial Area) Women's Advisory Committee, undated. CC04/8/27 Conservative Party Archives at the Bodleian Library.

389 See the report ('Death Penalty Opponent Booed by Women Conservatives') in *The Times*, 13 June 1956.

390 Letter from T.P. Child to O. Poole, Chairman of the Conservative Party, 14 June 1956. CC04/8/27 Conservative Party Archives at the Bodleian Library.

391 See *The Times*, 13 October 1956.

392 See *The Times*, 22 October 1956.

393 The Lord Chancellor said that 'The attitude which the House of Commons had adopted towards this question did not fairly reflect the state of public opinion in the country. There was good reason to believe that majority opinion in the country, while favouring some amendment of the law of murder, did not wish the death penalty to be wholly abolished. The Government therefore had a duty to bring forward a compromise measure …' The Home Secretary added that 'from informal soundings which had been taken, it seemed reasonable to assume that among those Conservative Members who had previously supported Mr. Silverman's Bill there would be a sufficient measure of support for a Government Bill on the lines of the draft … to ensure its passage through the House of Commons. It seemed likely that most of these Members would vote in favour'. And the decision was taken to move forward with legislation. CONCLUSIONS of a Meeting of the Cabinet held at 10 Downing Street, S.W. 1, on Wednesday 26 September 1956, at 10.30 a.m. C M. (56).

394 The Lord Chancellor put it to Cabinet that 'Those with whom he had discussed a [measure to amend the law of murder so as to restrict the scope of capital punishment] were disposed to think that [it] … would attract the support of a fair number of those Government supporters in the House of Commons who had originally favoured the abolition of the death penalty. He also had reason to believe, from informal discussions with the Lord Chief Justice and the Lord President of the Court of Session, that a Bill on these lines would be generally acceptable to judicial opinion. In discussion it was argued that it would accord with majority opinion throughout the country if capital punishment were retained only for those types of murder which directly threatened the preservation of law and order in a civilised society. There was, therefore, much to be said for the proposal that the Government should themselves introduce a measure based on that principle. It would, however, be important to secure the support of as many as possible of those Conservative Members of Parliament who had voted in favour of the total abolition of the death penalty; and it might be necessary on that account to define rather more narrowly … the categories of murder for which capital punishment would be retained. Thus, it was perhaps arguable that it was not essential for the preservation of law and order that the death penalty should be available for murders committed in connection with theft or house-breaking. … It was clear that a Bill on the lines envisaged would be carried, if at all, by a narrow majority; and it would not be possible to estimate whether a majority could be obtained without sounding informally all of the Government supporters who had previously favoured

abolition'. The Prime Minister said that 'in these circumstances it would be inexpedient for the Government to make a hasty announcement of their intentions. He recognised that moderate opinion throughout the country would welcome a decision by the Government to regain the initiative in this matter by introducing a measure on the lines proposed. But the Government must also take into account the tactical difficulties of handling the matter in Parliament and the political risks involved. It was clear that the Government could not take a final decision on this question until they had a clearer picture of the state of opinion among their supporters in the House of Commons'. CONCLUSIONS of a Meeting of the Cabinet held at 10 Downing Street, on Thursday 26 July 1956, at 11 a.m. C M. (56)

395 The Lord Chancellor told the Cabinet at the end of September that 'This would enable the Government to regain the initiative in his controversy and to resume their rightful responsibility for leading Parliament on a matter which directly affected the preservation of law and order. The Bill which had been prepared represented a middle course which, he believed, reflected majority opinion throughout the country'. CONCLUSIONS of a Meeting of the Cabinet held at 10 Downing Street, S.W.1, on Wednesday, 26 September 1956, at 10.30 a.m. C M. (56) The decision to include a Homicide Bill in the Legislative Programme for 1956–1957 was taken in October 1956 (Legislative Programme: 1956/57 Session Memorandum by the Lord Privy Seal [R.A. Butler]. 6 October 1956. C.F.(56) 233) Earlier, R.A. Butler had flagged that it was imperative to allow for contingencies. The Government's compromise Homicide Bill was in competition with Sydney Silverman's abolitionist Bill: 'We must', he said, 'provide also some extra margin for the unforeseeable contingencies, including the possibility that the Death Penalty (Abolition) Bill may have to be given a second run next Session'. (Legislative Programme: 1956–57 Session Memorandum by the Lord Privy Seal. 4 July 1956 CP. (56) 162)

396 Rather disingenuously, R.A. Butler told Sydney Silverman: 'our Bill should be published so that people can see what is in it [and] we should follow the usual procedure over Private Member's Bills'. HC Deb 6 November 1956 Vol. 560 cc20–84.

397 The Home Secretary was reported to have said 'It was to be expected that the Opposition would allege that the Government were under an obligation to accept the decision of the House of Commons and allow the Death Penalty (Abolition) Bill to be passed into law under the Parliament Act. In fact, the Government were not committed to that course, and they would not be guilty of any breach of faith if they brought forward a compromise measure on the lines now proposed. They could, however, blunt this Opposition criticism by undertaking that, if the Death Penalty (Abolition) Bill were again introduced by a Private Member, they would not block it or seek to secure its defeat by the use of the Government Whip. They could also undertake that, if this Bill were introduced under the ten-minute rule, time would be found for a Second Reading debate. In either event the Bill could not come forward before January 1957. By then, the Government measure should have made good progress, if indeed it had not been passed into law; and in that event it might be expected that the Death Penalty (Abolition) Bill would, even on a free vote, be defeated'. (CONCLUSIONS of a Meeting of the Cabinet held at 10 Downing Street, S.W.1, on Wednesday, 26 September 1956, at 10.30 a.m. C M. (56)) At the beginning of the new year, it could be reported that 'it was hoped to secure the Third Reading of the Homicide Bill on 6 February. Thereafter, if Miss Bacon's Bill had been successfully blocked in the meantime, the rules of procedure would prevent the introduction during that session of any further Bill providing for the abolition of capital punishment'. (CONCLUSIONS of a Meeting of the Cabinet held at 10 Downing Street, S.W. 1, on Thursday 31 January 1957, at 11 a.m. C.C. (57) 5th)

398 *The Times*, 16 November 1956.

399 *The Times*, 20 November 20 1956.

400 *The Times*, 2 February 1957.

401 Conclusions of a Meeting of the Cabinet held at 10 Downing Street, S.W.1, on Wednesday 11 July, 1956, at 11 a.m. C M. (56) 48th Conclusions.

402 And it was that dimension which Sir Louis Blom-Cooper believed to have been the more important. He said in interview in September 2011: 'When you go to … the classification of capital or non-capital, the selected ones were all on the basis that they were the kinds of offences which were more likely to deter people from engaging in it, didn't have any other justification other than to try and get out of the category of those liable to the death penalty, those for reasons that they were still subjected to a general deterrence argument, ought to remain death penalty. … They were all on the basis that these kinds of murders are the ones where the killers, potential killers, might be deterred'.

403 Memorandum by the Lord Chancellor: Capital Punishment, C.P. (56) 214 24 September 1956.

404 He then floated the idea in debate of 'making exclusions … in the case of armed criminals and the shooting of a policeman, the murder of a prison officer, and the like' (HL Deb 10 July 1956 Vol. 198 cc679–843).

405 A draft Bill had been circulated to Cabinet on 25 September 1956.

406 R.A. Butler reflected that the 'Abolitionists are determined to obstruct'. (CAB 195/16 C.M. (57) 2nd Meeting – C.C. (57) 81st Meeting, 8 January 1957)

407 Just before the opening of Parliament, a meeting of Cabinet was reported to have decided that 'it had been suggested that members of the Government, though they would be expected to vote in support of a Government measure on the lines of the draft … might be free to refrain from voting on an amendment designed to convert that Bill into a measure for the abolition of capital punishment. On further reflection it seemed doubtful whether this freedom could be allowed to members of the Government. This would be a Government Bill, introduced with the support of the Government Whip; and it would seem illogical that members of the Government should be free to abstain from voting against an amendment which was designed to defeat the whole purpose of the Bill. There was also the practical argument that, if it were known that members of the Government were to be free to refrain from voting against this amendment, it would be difficult to persuade those back-bench supporters of the Government who favoured the abolition of capital punishment to follow the Government Whip in voting against the amendment. The Chief Whip's calculation of the prospects of defeating the amendment had been based on the assumption that members of the Government would vote against it. In discussion the suggestion was made that freedom to abstain from voting on this amendment might be conceded only to those members of the Government who had very strong conscientious scruples about the retention of the death penalty'. (CONCLUSIONS of a meeting of the Cabinet on Monday 8 October 1956, held at 10 Downing Street, S.W. I. C M. (56) 69th Conclusions)

408 HC Deb 15 November 1956 Vol. 560 cc1144–259.

409 Sir Louis Blom-Cooper said in September 2011: 'It was utterly politically motivated by Kilmuir and his colleagues, all in the Tory Party, who were worried that … they were going to have to give up the death penalty which they passionately believed in'.

410 Jocelyn Simon, the Joint Parliamentary Under-Secretary of State at the Home Office and Conservative Member of Parliament for Middlesbrough West, recommended it to the House of Commons as 'an important Measure of penal reform, a solution which is in accord with public opinion in the country, a provision which preserves capital punishment only where it is particularly likely to act as a deterrent and a necessary deterrent, and, finally, a Measure which can properly bring this painful and protracted controversy to an end'. HC Deb 6 February 1957 Vol. 564 cc454–568.

411 Peggy Duff, secretary of the National Campaign for the Abolition of Capital

Punishment, said 'The effect of the Bill would be to institute degrees of murder which we have always opposed and which was opposed in 1948 by the Law Lords. We shall do everything we can to see Mr Silverman's Bill come up again'. *The Times*, 9 November 1956.

412 The amendment read 'this House, while welcoming the removal of certain anomalies in the law of murder and the abolition of the death penalty in respect of certain offences, cannot assent to a Bill which is an affront to constitutional propriety, fails to satisfy the public sense of justice and is in defiance of the principle which this House has already approved, namely, that the death penalty for murder no longer accords with the needs or the true interests of a civilised society'. It was rejected by 217 votes to 131. HC Deb 6 February 1957 Vol. 564 cc454–568.

413 The Lord Chancellor opened by saying that 'I do not propose to-day to repeat the arguments for and against capital punishment. The Government's opinion is already known: that its retention is necessary in some cases to safeguard law and order. That principle is preserved by this Bill, but we have thought it right to go a long way to meet the views of those who are opposed to the application of capital punishment under the present law. We have introduced this Bill because it is a matter of such grave importance and because, in such a matter, it is the duty of the Government to give a lead and to try to find a solution acceptable to a majority, both in Parliament and in the country. This Bill, I believe, contains such a solution'. Lord Goddard gave the Bill a grudging welcome: 'I cannot pretend that I look on the Bill with great enthusiasm, although I think there are some useful changes in the law of homicide, apart from questions of punishment, in the first Part of the Bill'. HL Deb 21 February 1957 Vol. 201 cc1165–84.

414 H. Potter (1993); *Hanging in Judgment: Religion and the Death Penalty in England*, *op. cit.*, 204.

415 Geoffrey Fisher, 1887–1972, was ordained as a priest in 1913 and became headmaster of Repton the following year. He became Bishop of Chester in 1932; Bishop of London in 1939; and Archbishop of Canterbury in 1945. His biographer, Alan Webster, describes him as having had a 'Victorian upbringing [which] perhaps led him to miss the massive changes in English ways of thinking and believing. He had come from a different age'. But he also adopted a utilitarian stance towards homosexual law reform, arguing that there is 'a realm which is not the law's business; a sacred area of privacy where people make their own choices and decisions into which the law must not intrude' (E. Carpenter (1991); *Archbishop Fisher: His Life and Times*, Canterbury Press, London, 393). (Based on an entry by Alan Webster in *The Oxford Dictionary of National Biography*, http://www.oxforddnb.com/view/article/31108)

416 HL Deb 21 February 1957 Vol. 201 cc1186–242.

417 D. Vosper; 'Capital punishment. Notes for a speech in reply to a resolution to be proposed at the meeting of the Central Council of the Conservative Party on 23 March 1961'. 431/5/79 CRI60. Tim Newburn commented that his was 'an argument that seems hard to sustain given it specifically included crimes involving firearms (which one can imagine being used without much forethought) but excluded poisoning (which it is hard to imagine being used without forethought)'.

418 The Earl of Kilmuir (1962); *Political Adventure: The Memoirs of the Earl of Kilmuir*, London: Weidenfeld and Nicolson, 264.

419 J. Christoph; *Capital Punishment and British Politics*, *op. cit.*, 169.

420 'Recent Reforms in English Criminal Law', *American Bar Association Journal*, Vol. 57 (May 1971) 484.

Bibliography

Anon (1922); 'The Pros and Cons of Capital Punishment', *The Howard Journal*, Vol. I, No. 2, 18–25

Anon editorial (1949–50); 'Royal Commission on Capital Punishment', *Howard Journal*, Vol. VIII, 1, 2

V. Bailey (nd); 'The Shadow of the Gallows: The Death Penalty and the British Labour Government, 1945–51', http://www.historycooperative.org/journals/lhr/18.2/bailey.html

J. Barry (1958); '... Hanged by the Neck Until ...' *The Sydney Law Review*, Vol. 2, No. 3, 401–413

C. Beccaria (1995); *On Crimes and Punishments*, originally published in 1764, republished by Cambridge: Cambridge University Press

H. Bedau (1983); 'Bentham's Utilitarian Critique of the Death Penalty', *The Journal of Criminal Law and Criminology*, Vol. 74, No. 3, 1033–1065

H. Bleackley and J. Lofland (1977); *State Executions Viewed Historically and Sociologically: The Hangmen of England and the Dramaturgy of State Executions*, originally published 1929, reprinted by New Jersey: Patterson Smith

B. Block and J. Hostettler (1997); *Hanging in the Balance*, Winchester: Waterside Press

L. Blom-Cooper (1973); 'The Penalty for Murder', *The British Journal of Criminology*, Vol. 13, No. 2, 188

R. Calvert (reprint edition 1973); *Capital Punishment in the Twentieth Century*, Montclair, N.J.: Patterson Smith

Report of the Capital Punishment Commission (1866); 3590, London: HMSO

E. Carpenter (1997); *Cantuar: The Archbishops in their Office*, London: Mowbray

J. Christoph (1962); *Capital Punishment and British Politics*, London: George Allen & Unwin

—(1962); 'Capital Punishment and British Party Responsibility', *Political Science Quarterly*, Vol. 77, No. 1, 19–35

His Majesty's Commissioners on Criminal Law, 1836, *Second Report*, (343), London: Printed by W. Clowes and Sons for HMSO

Report of the Committee Constituted by the Army Council to Enquire into the Law and Rules of Procedure Regulating Military Courts-Martial, (1919); Cmd 248, London: HMSO

D. Cooper (1974); *The Lesson of the Scaffold: The Public Execution Controversy in Victorian England*, Athens: Ohio State University Press

C. Cunningham (1969); 'Some Practical Considerations', in L. Blom-Cooper (ed.) *The Hanging Question*, London: Gerald Duckworth, 109–114

M. Davidson (2011); 'The Ritual of Capital Punishment', *Criminal Justice Studies*, Vol. 24(3), 227–240

F. Dawtry (1966); 'The Abolition of the Death Penalty in Britain', *British Journal of Criminology*, Vol. 6, No 2, 183

S. Devereaux (2009); 'Recasting the Theatre of Execution: The Abolition of the Tyburn Ritual', *Past and Present*, Vol. 202, No. 1, 127–174

M. Douglas and A. Wildavsky (1982); *Risk and Culture: An Essay on the Selection of Technical and Environmental Dangers*, Berkeley: University of California Press

M. Eisner (2001); 'Modernization, Self-Control and Lethal Violence. The Long-term Dynamics of European Homicide Rates in Theoretical Perspective', *The British Journal of Criminology*, Vol. 41, No. 4, 639–655

—(2003); 'Long-Term Historical Trends in Violent Crime', *Crime and Justice*, Chicago: University of Chicago Press, Vol. 30, 83–142

N. Elias (1978); *The Civilizing Process*, New York: Pantheon Books

L. England (1948); 'Capital Punishment and Open-End Questions', *Public Opinion Quarterly*, Vol. 12, No. 3, 412–416

L. Farmer (2016); *Making the Modern Criminal Law: Criminalization and Civil Order*, Oxford: Oxford University Press

M. Foucault (1979); *Discipline and Punish*, Harmondsworth: Penguin

J. Freeman (1961); Foreword to A. Koestler and C.H. Rolph; *Hanged by the Neck: An Exposure of Capital Punishment in England*, Baltimore, Maryland: Penguin Books, 9–10

L. Gabel (1929); *Benefit of Clergy in England in the Later Middle Ages, Smith College Studies in History*, Vol 14, Nos 1–4

G. Gardiner (1956); *Capital Punishment as a Deterrent: And the Alternative*, London: Victor Gollancz

D. Garland (2006); 'Concepts of Culture in the Sociology of Punishment', *Theoretical Criminology*, Vol. 10, No. 4, 419–447

—(2009); '"Symbolic" and "Instrumental" Aspects of Capital Punishment', in C. Lanier, W. Bowers and J. Acker (eds.) *The Future of America's Death Penalty*, Durham, North Carolina: Carolina Academic Press, 421–452

—(2010); *Peculiar Institution*, Cambridge, Massachusetts: Belknap Harvard

J. Garner (2015); *'The Sheriff's Picture Frame': Art and Execution in Eighteenth-Century Britain*, Yale University, ProQuest Dissertations Publishing

V. Gatrell (1994); *The Hanging Tree: Execution and the English People, 1770–1868*, Oxford: Oxford University Press

M. Gottschalk (2006); *The Prison and the Gallows*, Cambridge: Cambridge University Press

E. Gowers (1956); *A Life for a Life? The Problem of Capital Punishment*, London: Chatto and Windus

J. Griffith (1949); 'Report of the Army and Air Force Courts-Martial Committee, 1946 (Cmd. 7608)', *The Modern Law Review*, Vol. 12, No. 2, 223–227

A. Griffiths (1896); *The Chronicles of Newgate*, London: Chapman and Hall

J. Gusfield (1963); *Symbolic Crusade*, Urbana: University of Illinois Press

D. Hay (1975); 'Property, Authority and the Criminal Law', in D. Hay, P. Linebaugh and E. Thompson (eds.) *Albion's Fatal Tree*, London: Allen Lane, 17–63

E. Heath (1988); *The Course of my Life: My Autobiography*, London: Hodder and Stoughton

S. Hoare, Viscount Templewood, (1951); *The Shadow of the Gallows*, Victor Gollancz, London.

S. Hobhouse and F. Brockway (eds.) (1922); *English Prisons To-Day*, London: Longmans, Green and Co.

J. Horder (2012); *Homicide and the Politics of Law Reform*, Oxford: Oxford University Press

R. Jenkins (1959); *The Labour Case*, Mddx.: Penguin

A. Jorns (1931); *The Quakers as Pioneers in Social Work*, New York: Macmillan

L. Kennedy (1961); *Ten Rillington Place*, London: Victor Gollancz

J. Langbein (1976); 'The Historical Origins of the Sanction of Imprisonment for Serious Crime' *The Journal of Legal Studies*, Vol. V, No. 1, 35–60

H. Klare (1963); review of J. Christoph; *Capital Punishment and British Politics, Annals of the American Academy of Political and Social Science*, Vol. 347, 167–168

Law Commission (2006); Consultation Paper No 177: *A New Homicide Act for England and Wales?*, http://www.lawcom.gov.uk/docs/cp177_web.pdf

J. Lofland (1975); 'Open and Concealed Dramaturgic Strategies: The Case of the State Execution', *Journal of Contemporary Ethnography*, Vol. 4, 272–295

J. R. MacDonald (1921); *Socialism: Critical and Constructive*, London: Cassell and Company

R. McGowen (1994); 'Civilizing Punishment: The End of the Public Execution in England', *Journal of British Studies*, Vol. 33, No. 3, 257–282

J. McHugh (1999); 'The Labour Party and the Parliamentary Campaign to Abolish the Military Death Penalty, 1919–1930', *The Historical Journal*, Vol. 42, No. 1, 233–249

A. McKenzie (2007); *Tyburn's Martyrs: Execution in England 1675–1775*, London: Hambledon Continuum

'Memoir of the Life of Elizabeth Fry, Edited by two of her Daughters', *The Quarterly Review*, Vol. 82 (163), 1847, 115

M. Merback (1999); *The Thief, the Cross and the Wheel: Pain and the Spectacle of Punishment in Medieval and Renaissance Europe*, London: Reaktion Books

J.S. Mill (1869); *On Liberty*, Longman, London: Roberts and Green

—(1910); *Utilitarianism, Liberty and Representative Government*, first published in 1861, republished by London: J.M. Dent

—(1950); *Bentham and Coleridge*, originally published 1838, republished by London: Chatto and Windus

A. Morgan (1987); *J. Ramsay MacDonald*, Manchester: Manchester University Press

H. Morrison (1960); *An Autobiography*, London: Odhams Press

S. O'Connor (2013); *Handsome Brute: The Story of a Ladykiller*, London: Simon and Schuster

G. Oram (2004); *Military Executions During World War I*, New York: Palgrave, 2004

R. Paternoster (1991); *Capital Punishment in America*, New York: Lexington Books

S. Pinker (2012); *The Better Angels of Our Nature: A History of Violence and Humanity*, London: Penguin Books

J. Plamenatz (1949); *The English Utilitarians*, Oxford: Basil Blackwell

H. Potter (1993); *Hanging in Judgment: Religion and the Death Penalty in England*, London: SCM Press

Quaker Faith and Practice Fifth edition, (2013); Yearly Meeting of the Religious Society of Friends (Quakers) in Britain, London: Religious Society of Friends

L. Radzinowicz (1948); *A History of English Criminal Law and its Administration from 1750*, London: Stevens and Sons, Vol. 1

Sir G. Rentoul (1939); 'Second Thoughts on Capital Punishment', *The Penal Reformer*, Vol. 6, No. 1, 1–2

R. Richardson (1987); *Death, Dissection and the Destitute*, London: Routledge and Kegan Paul

P. Richards (1970); *Parliament and Conscience*, London: George Allen and Unwin

J. Ridley (2001); *Bloody Mary's Martyrs*, London: Constable

P. Rock (1977); 'Law, Order & Power in Late Seventeenth and Early Eighteenth Century England', *Annales Internationales de Criminologie*, Vol. 16, Nos. 1 and 2, 191–221

S. Romilly (1810); *Observations on the Criminal Law of England, as It Relates to Capital Punishments*, London: T. Cadell and W. Davies

—(1840); *Memoirs of the Life of Sir Samuel Romilly Written by Himself*, London: John Murray, Vol. 2

B. Rush (1792); *Considerations on the Injustice and Impolicy of Punishing Murder by Death*, Philadelphia: Matthew Carey

M. Ryan (1983); *The Politics of Penal Reform*, London: Longman

A. Sarat (2001); *When the State Kills*, Princeton: Princeton University Press

Select Committee on Capital Punishment (1931); *Report*, Cmd. 15, London: HMSO

J. Sharpe (1984); 'Last dying speeches: religion, ideology and public execution in 17th-century England', *Past and Present*, 107, 144–67

—(1990); *Judicial Punishment in England*, London: Faber and Faber

—(2016); *A Fiery and Furious People A History of Violence in England*, London: Random House

L. Sklair (1970); *The Sociology of Progress*, London: Routledge and Kegan Paul

P. Smith (1996); 'Executing Executions: Aesthetics, Identity, and the Problematic Narratives of Capital Punishment Ritual', *Theory and Society*, Vol. 25, No. 2, 235–261

—(2008); *Punishment and Culture*, Chicago: University of Chicago Press

P. Spierenburg (1984); *The Spectacle of Suffering: Executions and the Evolution of Repression: From a Preindustrial Metropolis to the European Experience*, Cambridge: Cambridge University Press

—(2008); *A History of Murder*, Cambridge: Polity

E. Tuttle (1961); *The Crusade against Capital Punishment in Great Britain*, London: Stevens and Sons

G. Wilkinson (no date); *The Newgate Calendar Improved*, London: Thomas Kelly, Vol. 3

Lord Windlesham (1993); *Responses to Crime*, Volume 2, Clarendon Press, Oxford

M. Wingersky (1954); 'Report of the Royal Commission on Capital Punishment (1949–1953): A Review', *The Journal of Criminal Law, Criminology, and Police Science*, Vol. 44, No. 6, 695–715

B. Wootton (1992); *Selected Writings: Volume 1: Crime and the Penal System*, Houndmills: Macmillan

K. Younger (1969); 'The Historical Perspective' in L. Blom-Cooper (ed.) *The Hanging Question*, London: Gerald Duckworth, 5–11

R. Zaller (1987); 'The Debate on Capital Punishment during the English Revolution', *The American Journal of Legal History*, Vol. 31, No. 2, 126–144

3 The Liberal Hour I

The Murder (Abolition of Death Penalty) Act 1965 c.71; Consummation

Introduction

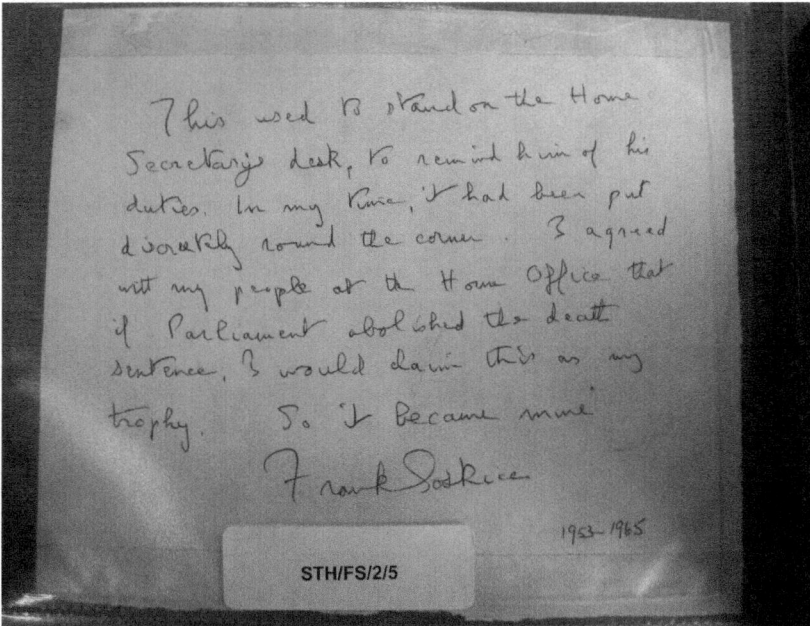

Figure 3.1 Note on a stand

My image of a note attached below a wooden stand retained in the Parliamentary Archives, STH/FS/2/5. I am grateful to Miss Claire Batley, Senior Archivist, for permission to reproduce it.

The compromise represented by the Homicide Act failed to appease protagonists on either side of the debate about the death penalty, and the statistical evidence about trends in homicide after the partial abolition of capital punishment in 1957 certainly did not help to elucidate matters clearly, at least to those who were *parti pris*. The numbers of murders and executions occurring were actually extraordinarily small,[1] they displayed no obvious pattern, and it would have been difficult to draw any strong inferences about them:

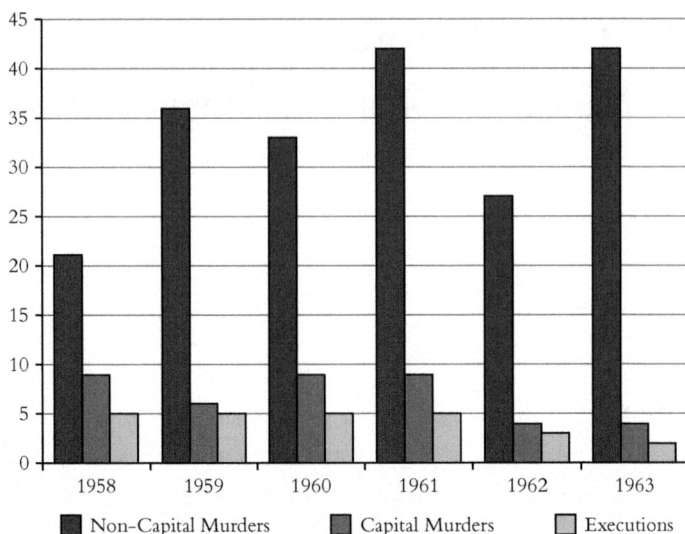

Figure 3.2[2] Capital murders, non-capital murders and executions 1958–1963

To make matters of argument yet more complicated, the exigencies of cabinet government brought it about that ministers, like John Clynes and James Chuter Ede, had had from time to time to use ambiguous materials to construct and defend positions in public from which they demurred in private.[3] After all, the issue was more momentous for government than for individual backbench Members of Parliament. There was a consciousness always of the political and practical risks that could follow in the wake of abolition: the possibility of increases in professional crime,[4] violence, homicide and assaults on police and prison officers that would inevitably be laid at the government's door;[5] and the popular discontent, reverses in parliament and electoral losses that could well follow,[6] and follow, politicians might argue, for no unavoidable reason. Governments were quite understandably nervous about committing themselves to legislation: abolition said Christoph, was 'too hot to handle and too unpredictable in its political effects ...'[7] Almost to the very end, and even during the so-called liberal hour, governments could not bring themselves to take an unambiguously decisive stand on a moral issue,[8] although what was defined as a moral issue seemed at times to be a little arbitrary (why should capital punishment have been regarded as a 'moral issue' when neither corporal punishment nor imprisonment was?). They preferred to temporise or to ease legislation from the sidelines rather than to lead (the former Conservative Home Office minister, Lord Windlesham, commented that 'Procrastination, compromise and delay had been the response of successive governments of both political parties'[9]). When the abolitionists did make headway, governments tended to trim. Yet, step by small step,[10] executions changed in number and character, although the arguments levelled on both sides changed but little and appeared to be of diminishing marginal utility over the decades. Sydney Silverman asserted at one point during a debate of 16 February 1956 that 'I have taken part in too many of these debates to feel it possible to advance anything very new'.[11] Eight years on, he reflected, there had still been no alteration: 'I think that this controversy has gone on long enough. The arguments both ways are clear, and I think that everybody knows what they are. I think that everybody has made up his mind about where the balance between the two arguments lies'.[12] An unchanging case for abolition was met ever by an unwavering case for retention.

I shall show in this chapter that, after a lull in which reform was becalmed under the Conservative Government of 1959–1964, abolition came about because it was the balance of political forces, rather than the balance of political arguments, which tilted, the only remaining escape route, further reform, having been closed by the 1957 Act. The Lord Chief Justice, Lord Goddard, was to retire at the age of 75 to be replaced by Lord Parker. Geoffrey Fisher was to be replaced as Archbishop of Canterbury by the abolitionist, former Archbishop of York, Michael Ramsey,[13] and it was as the senior bishop that Michael Ramsey would dragoon the Lords Spiritual in the votes that were to come.[14] (He would, said his biographer, play 'a key part. ... The change of archbishop ... made a difference'[15]). The Conservative architects of the compromise solution would no longer be in office, but Alice Bacon and Frank Soskice, the Members who had sought to introduce alternative abolitionist legislation by means of a Private Member's Bill, would by then be Home Office ministers. There would again be a Labour majority in the House of Commons.[16] The House of Lords would have undergone a sea change. And, appearing in the wings, there was a revived lobby, the National Campaign for the Abolition of the Death Penalty, whose chairman, Gerald Gardiner, was to become Lord Chancellor, the man critically responsible for legislation in the House of Lords. Sir Louis Blom-Cooper said 'If Gerald Gardiner had one wish in the whole of this life, it was to get rid of the death penalty'.

Dramatis personae

I shall concentrate on a short span of time and review in finer detail than before the chronology of events and the cast of people and organisations which resolved that *impasse* and brought about the effective abolition of capital punishment in 1965. The main action was again to take place not in the courts or the streets, but in Parliament and Whitehall, and it is not evident how decisively influential was the campaigning that occurred outside Westminster. But consequences there were, and they merit consideration. Information was continually fed by outsiders into the political arena[17] (although the most critical and timely information was probably that generated from within the Home Office itself by its new Research Unit[18]). Campaigners could move bodily into Parliament as Members. And the clamour that they made, like that of a Greek chorus, could create a sense of external constraint and external demand, an objectification of liberal commentary, that served partially to counter the other voices and representations of public opinion.

The Howard League for Penal Reform

Bob Morris, who had been an official in the Home Office during the pivotal period, reflected in interview that 'one has to remember that the confederation of organised pressure groups in social policy areas was very, very much less than it is now'. One of that small cluster of pressure groups, The Howard Association, founded in 1866 under the patronage of the utilitarian Lord Chancellor, Lord Brougham, and with the support of that energetic Member of Parliament, William Ewart,[19] had been abolitionist from its inception.[20] It had joined with the Prison Reform League in 1921 to form The Howard League for Penal Reform, and it played a modest part, secondary to that of the National Campaign for the Abolition of the Death Penalty,[21] in the early and middle history of the larger abolitionist campaign in the twentieth century,[22] organising a number of conferences, particularly before the 1948 Criminal Justice Bill was presented to Parliament,[23] and collating and disseminating information.[24] As a body with a broad interest in penal reform, attempting to appear balanced in its work,[25] it had resolved in 1960 that its contribution to a single-issue campaign should be rather modest[26] and it moved to the wings. In a small network of linked organisations with overlapping memberships and exchanges of observers,[27] it was agreed that the main labour of agitation would be undertaken by the National Campaign for the Abolition of the Death Penalty, although the Howard League did choose to return to the field from time to time.[28]

The National Campaign for the Abolition of the Death Penalty

The National Campaign for the Abolition of the Death Penalty (also calling itself on occasion the National Campaign for the Abolition of Capital Punishment) had been established in imminent expectation of success[29] in 1925 as a consortium of groups and individuals by Roy Calvert,[30] a devout Quaker, and a prison visitor, who died soon after, in 1933.[31] In the aftermath of the passage of the 1957 Homicide Act, the National Campaign had decided not to disband,[32] but for a while to suspend its activities.[33] Its Treasurer, Lord Altrincham, had written to Gerald Gardiner in January 1957: 'Even under the Government's grotesque Homicide Bill, few if any murderers would be hanged; and when a Labour Government comes in (you notice I say "when" rather than "if") Abolition will be formalised. I feel the National Campaign need not exert itself any more. The public is now preoccupied with other, and to be frank, greater issues; and to plug the cause of Abolition at the moment would, I am convinced do more harm than good'.[34] (Underlined in pencil in the original.)

There was thus to be a lull, but the National Campaign was then revived by the socialist publisher, Victor Gollancz,[35] who financed it in money and in kind[36] in 1960 to 'continue unremittingly' for total abolition under the joint chairmanship of the former Chairman of the Bar Council, Gerald Gardiner,[37] and himself. They reconvened an Executive Committee composed of John Collins,[38] Canon of St Paul's Cathedral; C.R. Hewitt (whose *nom de plume* was C.H. Rolph); Christopher Hollis;[39] Arthur Koestler[40] (whom Victor Gollancz credited with much of the renaissance of the Association); Reginald Paget;[41] and Sydney Silverman. In the recruitment of that committee and in all other aspects of its work, the Council was concerned always with the tactical politics and public appearances of persuasion. It was designed to be, and to be seen to be, a responsible, respectable and distinguished body whose public face was represented by politicians of the three parties[42] and by men and women high in the hierarchies of class, status, the arts, science and the professions. The endorsement of great people was sought and encouraged. On one occasion, for example, it noted with obvious pleasure a letter of support from the Marquess of Hertford.[43] It paid particular attention to the standing of its office-holders, appointing Lord Altrincham[44] as its treasurer; and Lord Harewood, 'of the blood royal',[45] a patron of the arts[46] and the husband of the Princess Royal, as the Chairman of a 'Committee of Honour' made up, *inter alia*, of Lord Russell, the artists Augustus John, Henry Moore and Graham Sutherland, the novelist Rebecca West, and the poet, Edith Sitwell. [47] Its Vice-Presidents included the actor, Sybil Thorndike, the politicians Vyvyan Adams and Nancy Astor, and the author, Osbert Sitwell.

There was early talk of programmes on the BBC and sympathetic articles being placed in *The Observer* newspaper[48] ('Both Mr Hollis and Mr Gollancz thought that Mr David Astor, the Editor ... would be agreeable to publishing such an article'[49]). The National Campaign organised the drafting of replies to hostile letters in the local press.[50] It distributed speakers' notes containing, amongst other items, digests of arguments from testimony delivered by Roy Calvert,[51] Margery Fry and others to the 1930 Select Committee and the 1949 Royal Commission.[52] It prepared petitions. Its chairman, Gerald Gardiner, wrote continually to the Home Secretary to argue the case for reprieves in specific cases. Despite some qualms about engaging in wider campaigning about individuals awaiting execution, its members and local groups did try to canvass support from time to time, the Bristol group being especially active.[53] They sometimes wrote letters *en masse* to *The Times*, one particular object of concern at the beginning of the new campaign being the impending execution in the autumn of 1960[54] of the 18-year-old, George Forsyth.[55] Alice Bacon and Sydney Silverman adopted the case of Forsyth as a *cause célèbre* in their quest to prevent the executions of those aged under 21, and they proposed an amendment to legislation on young offenders then before Parliament.[56] (The Home Secretary, R.A. Butler, was unmoved: he may possibly have been an abolitionist[57] but he had no wish to renew discussion of the death penalty,[58] and nothing came of their attempt. He told fellow-ministers that 'This amendment

I propose to resist, on the ground that it is undesirable to amend the law of murder in a particular respect, and that consideration of it as a whole is not relevant to the Criminal Justice Bill which is concerned only with offenders under the age of twenty-one'[59]).

There was also talk at the first meeting of relaunching the campaign with local meetings[60] and 'a big public meeting' in the Royal Festival Hall or the Royal Albert Hall[61] ('in spite of the size ... it could be respectably filled'[62]); and it was reported that Peter Kirk MP, Lady Violet Bonham Carter, Sydney Silverman MP, the Bishop of Colchester, Christopher Brasher and Gerald Gardiner would speak. But there was less certainty about others who might be invited: 'Two members of the Committee were strongly of the opinion that the speakers should include Adam Faith[63] or an equivalent representative of his generation. Others felt that his inclusion would detract from the apparent responsibility of the movement'.[64] And the idea of securing speakers from the masses did not quite die. At a meeting in March 1962, it was made known that 'The Chairman reported that the Archbishop of York and the Earl of Harewood had agreed to speak, and suggested that the following people should also be approached: Graham Sutherland, Rebecca West and a prominent Fellow of the Royal Society. An alternative suggestion was to have as one of the speakers a genuine man in the street'.[65] This was status politics indeed.

The campaign would again have to centre principally on the House of Commons.[66] 'Everything depended on the MPs', Gerald Gardiner argued, and there was to be a monthly briefing of possibly sympathetic Members of Parliament (and particularly of Conservative members in a Conservative Parliament whose voting would be pivotal).[67] Its first attempts to initiate legislation failed, having met with no success in securing a place for abolition in the lottery for Private Member's Bills,[68] but the re-formed and reinvigorated National Campaign was nevertheless ready to move into action just before the start of the new 1961–1962 Parliamentary session. 'The time had now come', said the ever-energetic Sydney Silverman, 'for a renewed and intense effort to be made in Parliament. There were a number of important points in the Campaign's favour: the proposed initial trial period[69] of the Homicide Act had almost expired, we were roughly midway between elections which left the Government comparatively free from electoral embarrassment, [and] the Home Office Research Unit Report "Murder"[70] upheld the abolitionist argument ...' He proposed that:

(a) an entirely informal all-Party group should see the Home Secretary [R.A. Butler] to sound him out on the probability of Government legislation to abolish the death penalty or alternatively on the Government's attitude to a free vote on a Private Member's Bill, (b) all known abolitionist Members of Parliament should be asked to take part in the ballot for Private Members' Bills and, if successful, to present a Bill, and Mr Silverman would undertake to draft the necessary letter which would be sent out by the Campaign office, (c) failing success in the ballot, an attempt to introduce a Bill would be made under the Ten Minute Rule.[71]

The Conservative Party

The Parliament upon which the Campaign intended to work at the beginning of the 1960s was once again divided. In 1959, for the third time in succession, and with a majority of 100 and 58% of the votes, a Conservative Government had been returned to power, and the Conservatives did not lean towards the idea of abolition. James Christoph, the historian of the earlier phase of abolition, observed:

> Throughout the dispute it was asserted that the fate of capital punishment was not a party political issue. In some respects this was quite true. ... Nevertheless, the behaviour of the politicians who were drawn into the controversy followed reasonably clear party lines. Labour M.P.s provided the big battalions upon which the abolitionists attempted to build their majorities ... [and] it can be shown that the retentionist centre of gravity remained always on the Conservative benches.[72]

When the new Executive Committee of the National Campaign sought to ascertain in late 1960 what the views of the new Parliament might be,[73] it did discover what might have been a preponderance of abolitionists, but it declared the result 'disappointing': '276 Abolitionists, 230 Retentionists (the remainder [of 124] uncertain)', reported Gerald Gardiner, but 'there was dissatisfaction in the House generally about the 1957 Homicide Act'.[74]

The government itself was yet again decidedly loath to act. The election had been fought with scarce reference to the politics of crime, criminal justice and law and order,[75] but the abolition of capital punishment had been almost always uniformly unpopular within the Conservative Party before the passing of the 1957 Act and it continued to remain so thereafter.[76] Lord Meston observed in 1961 that 'in the Conservative Party there is a solid and dominating bloc who are opposed to any abolition or reform, and when they cannot block it entirely they put up a rearguard action. That is exactly what happened in 1957'.[77] Opponents to, or sceptics about, reform were lodged deep in the Cabinet itself. Although Selwyn Lloyd, the Chancellor of the Exchequer, and Iain Macleod, the Secretary of State for the Colonies, may have been abolitionist, others were not. Above all, Harold Macmillan, the prime minister until 1963, was publicly cautious. A defender of the 1957 compromise,[78] he had written to a Conservative Association just before the bill was passed:

> ... I am, of course, well aware of the strongly held view of many supporters of our Party on the subject of capital punishment. It was because the Government believed that the country as a whole was not in favour of total abolition that the present Bill was introduced. Your members will be

aware of the principle on which this Bill is based – the retention of capital punishment for the type of murder which strike [*sic*] particularly at the maintenance of public order. ...[79]

Viscount Kilmuir, the Lord Chancellor until 1962, who, as David Maxwell Fyfe, had been Home Secretary between 1951 and 1954, was a stalwart retentionist (he had said of Sydney Silverman's 1956 bill that it was 'an unwise and dangerous measure, the presence of which on the statute book would be a disaster for the country and a menace to the people'[80]). His successor, Reginald Manningham Buller, Lord Dilhorne, was like-minded. The Lord President of the Council, chairman of the Conservative Party, and Minister of Science in the early 1960s, Lord Hailsham, a man who had played a pivotal part in the election, [81] was signally averse to abolition. He had told a party member on 12 November 1957, just after the passage of the Act:

> ... Unfortunately, the House of Commons by a majority passed a bill for the abolition of hanging altogether. I could not disapprove of this more than you do, and I voted against this Bill in the House of Lords when it came up.[82] The only way in which the Government could control the situation was to pass a compromise Bill. I was a member of the Government which did so. I entirely agree with you that it was not as good as the Law which existed before. But if people will elect as many Socialist Members of Parliament, they must expect to abide by the consequences. I am sorry to say that some of ours voted with them but that was not with my approval or with that of the Government.[83]

R.A. Butler was the Home Secretary until July 1962[84] and I have observed that he was nervous, having delivered a 'robust defence of hanging'[85] in the debate of January 1956.[86] Wedged uncomfortably between those who would abolish and those who would restore capital punishment, committed to an uneasy and hard-won compromise that he had constructed in its later stages but could not justify with much conviction, he and his fellow Home Office ministers were reluctant to resuscitate questions about a vexed policy so soon after the Act[87] and when there was little prospect of change. He preferred to adhere to the stance he had adopted after 1957[88] and lie low and wait and see. So it was that he told his colleagues in 1961:

> I should, on the whole, propose to leave the law unchanged for the time being. The settlement of 1957 was designed to keep the death penalty for those crimes – the murder of a police or prison officer, murder by shooting, and murder in the course or furtherance of theft – which were thought to be most prejudicial to law and order. It has been in operation for only four years. It has always been in view that it should have a five years' run before we attempted to reassess it. I think this is right. But there are two difficulties which we have to keep in mind. The more we imply

that we intend to review the law in the relatively near future, the more we are bound to give the impression that we shall then change it one way or the other. The second is that the longer we shelve the issue – especially if there were to be any sort of inquiry – the nearer we get to an election; and we do not want this to become an election issue. In spite of these dangers, however, *I am disposed to think the right course is to play the matter long.* At the moment, an abolition Bill certainly would not commend itself to the majority of our supporters, or, I think, to public opinion; and a Bill restoring the death penalty for murders which are not now capital would be opposed by a strong minority of our own people, as well as by the Opposition.[89] [Emphasis in original]

And that was to be the standard line, echoed, for example, by his Minister of State, Dennis Vosper, in an address to a party grouping at much the same time:

The Home Secretary and the Secretary of State for Scotland are keeping the working of the Homicide Act under close and constant review, but the Government consider that it is too soon to review the solution reached after much discussion less than four years ago, or to consider amending the Act in any way – either to make capital punishment once again the penalty for all murders or for additional categories of murder, or, as many people would wish, to abolish it entirely.[90]

Theirs was a seemingly intractable political dilemma which induced the Cabinet Secretary, Norman Brook, to record that:

There is a growing recognition that the Homicide Act, 1957 was a mistake. It was inherently unsound to distinguish between capital and non-capital murder – and experience is emphasising the anomalies to which this gives rise.

   On the other hand, if the law is to be changed, there are only two alternatives – to restore the death penalty for all murders or to abolish it altogether. And on this public opinion is pretty evenly divided. The pressures on the Home Secretary come from both sides – from people who want capital punishment extended and from those who want it abolished. And, as always on this subject, feelings on both sides run high.

   As there is unlikely to be a clear majority support for either course of action, the Home Secretary favours taking none: he suggests that he should play this long. ... The second point is the pressure under which the Home Secretary comes on his decisions on capital cases. The Cabinet will no doubt endorse his view that he should continue to resist demands for debates on these.

And that was not all. It was recognised that the so-called five-year experimental period introduced by Mr Brooke would end in March 1962, and that it would then become 'necessary to have some sort of enquiry in order to prevent this from becoming an issue at the next Election. A further enquiry might be something of an embarrassment'.[91]

It is evident that ministers were unwilling to commit or expose themselves. When Members of Parliament, representing the National Campaign for the Abolition of the Death Penalty, did see the Home Secretary on 8 March 1962 at the meeting initiated by Sydney Silverman, they were given no encouragement. According to the Permanent Under Secretary's note, Peter Kirk, Jeremy Thorpe, James Chuter Ede and Sydney Silverman told R.A. Butler on that occasion that there was still an abolitionist majority in the House of Commons, although it was more slender than before; that the figures of murder had changed very little and the deterrent effect of capital punishment still could not be demonstrated; the Act had undoubtedly worked unfairly and the only possible change was to abolish the death penalty altogether. The Home Secretary, in his turn, then proceeded to temporise by laying out his own difficulties, stuck uneasily, as he was, between Scylla and Charybdis: 'There were', he was reported to have said, 'some people who wanted to see the law strengthened, just as there were many who were in favour of abolition. The situation was a difficult one to hold. It was not an easy Act to defend – he himself had only become Home Secretary when the policy of the Act had been determined. It was difficult, short of abolition, to get a clear decision; he did not think that any extension of the penalty, short of complete restoration, was possible; and he did not propose complete restoration'.[92]

The magic number of five years, in currency since the 1930 Select Committee Report's recommendation of an experimental period of abolition, and raised by R.A. Butler in his memorandum and by Sydney Silverman in his request to see the Home Secretary,[93] may – as Norman Brooke had remarked – have introduced an expectation[94] that there would be an imminent review of the working of the Homicide Act,[95] but R.A. Butler would not promise a review.[96] He may have disliked capital punishment, but he chose not to act.[97] If, at some point, he said, there *were* to be a prospect of change, he would undoubtedly have to take account of the bishops. And he would also have to take account of the judges (there had been no collective expression of view by the judges, but he knew that the new Lord Chief Justice and others were tending to 'move away from the death penalty'). I shall return to the bishops and the Lord Chief Justice below.

Sydney Silverman's own report of that meeting also contained no promise of government action or support:

> The deputation was received in a most friendly manner and the interview lasted approximately fifty minutes. Mr Silverman put to the Home Secretary the reasons leading to the conclusion that this was an appropriate time to make a change: the situation created by the Homicide Act was indefensible, the five year trial period of the Act had almost expired, no harm had been done by reducing the number of executions, there had

been a significant change of opinion towards abolition, e.g. the Bishops, there was still a substantial period ahead, presumably, before the next General Election. The Home Secretary appreciated all these points and realised that the trend was clearly towards abolition, and that this would undoubtedly come. He asked Mr Silverman for his assessment of the number of abolitionists in the House and Mr Silverman stated that he felt that abolition could just be carried but with a decreased majority. It was felt that the Home Secretary was not satisfied that there was strong enough Conservative support to justify the introduction, at this stage, of Government legislation. Mr Silverman commented to the Committee that what was needed at the moment was a concentrated attack on Conservative Members. The Home Secretary had not yet made up his mind and would not do so just at present, but he was obviously disturbed about the situation. He invited the deputation to keep in touch with him and to inform him if it was felt at any time that a significant swing towards abolition in the House had occurred.[98]

In the previous year, the National Campaign for the Abolition of the Death Penalty had begun to prepare a new 'Memorial' ('as the Campaign could now claim the support of even greater numbers of distinguished people'[99]) which would eventually be signed by 6,825 people, including 39 bishops, 709 writers, artists, architects and musicians, 91 Fellows of the Royal Society, and 70 senior and principal probation officers (such people had been targeted and a very precise tally of their composition was kept and reported). Tendering it to the prime minister and Home Secretary in July 1962,[100] four months after the disappointing meeting with the Home Secretary, the delegation was again given no grounds for hope. Lord Harewood may have told *The Times* that ministers had been 'impressed',[101] but Gerald Gardiner seemed less sure:

> The Memorial ... was presented to the Prime Minister and each member of the deputation spoke in turn, the Bishop of Exeter as a Christian, Mr Gardiner as a lawyer, Mr Chuter-Ede as an ex-Home Secretary, outlining the recent history of the fight for abolition, whilst Lord Harewood gave his personal reasons for becoming an abolitionist, and Mr Gollancz spoke about the Memorial itself. The Home Secretary, referring to the [Home Office] pamphlet Murder, said that he was not convinced that the death penalty was not a deterrent. The Prime Minister said that abolition was a matter of timing, but would not commit himself to the view that abolition was, therefore, inevitable. It was considered that there was no likelihood whatsoever of the present Government introducing legislation to abolish capital punishment.[102]

The Executive Committee of the National Campaign were accordingly obliged to conclude that any future agitation would have to be largely defensive: 'The main effort of the Campaign in the next few months should be concentrated on influencing Members of Parliament as it seemed unlikely that this Government would abolish capital punishment but we should at least try to prevent any retrogressive legislation'.[103] There was to be no reason to alter that view throughout the remaining life of the Conservative government. The journalist, Anthony Howard, writing in February 1962, observed that 'Political forecasts remain gloomy': 'it would still need something like 50 Conservative votes for an abolitionist bill to be home and dry. ... What at least seems certain is that now the only thing standing in the way of its being put to the test is a Conservative administration that is manifestly far more interested in its own political tranquillity than in the anxieties caused even to members of its own party by the anomalous activities of the hangman'.[104]

Ministers' replies to hostile letters grew ever more perfunctory, no longer minded to explain, defend or enlarge upon what the government had done or would do in the future.[105] Capital punishment, it was thought within the Home Office, was a problem best left fallow.[106] Even if it was becoming difficult to justify,[107] the line could still be held for a while longer. The Permanent Undersecretary, Sir Charles Cunningham, a man sympathetic to abolition, reflected in March 1961 that:

> ... the position can be maintained for the present that it is too soon to contemplate a change in the law. It is likely however, that pressure for the reconsideration of the death penalty will grow. We contemplate laying a White Paper very soon, with an analysis of the capital offences committed since the law was altered in 1957; and, although no undertaking has been given, there has been an assumption that the Government will review the whole position five years after the passing of the 1957 Act. We may therefore expect strong pressure for a reconsideration of policy, and a clear indication of the Government's view during the next Session of Parliament. ... It is already clear that the statistics will prove nothing. It seems probable that the number of capital offences is not seriously influenced by the penalty with which those convicted of them may be visited. If this is the result of an impartial view of the position, the case of the abolitionists will not be easy to answer. The present law is illogical and not easily defended. The restoration of the death penalty for all murders would be difficult to justify; and the obvious way of removing the illogicality of the present position would be to abolish it. It may be doubted, however, whether public opinion generally would accept abolition in the present state of crime. It is one thing to refuse to reintroduce corporal punishment; it would be quite another to do away with capital punishment even to the extent to which Parliament retained it in 1957. In practice this may point to a continuation of the present position; but dialectically this may be difficult to maintain.[108]

The politics of abolition were thus in obvious suspense during the Conservative Government of the early 1960s. The National Campaign decided to cancel the rally at the Royal Albert Hall that had been booked first for 18 April[109] and then for 9 May 1962 ('It was felt that the Government was quite unlikely to introduce abolition at this stage in its life, and in view of its present difficulties. An Albert Hall Rally would, therefore, have little point'.[110]) It routinely canvassed candidates at by-elections.[111] But it otherwise bided its time until the political prospects of abolition had changed and another election effected a shift in the composition of the House of Commons. An undated press release was prepared in readiness for what might come: 'The National Campaign for the Abolition of Capital Punishment intends to get a Bill to achieve our object introduced into the House of Commons as early as possible in the life of the Parliament to be elected at the General Election. ... The next House of Commons will be younger than the present one and we are confident that, whichever party is in power, capital punishment will be abolished by the next Parliament'.[112]

Senior members of the Conservative government were also confident of that fact. They would not be able forever to continue playing long. Just over three weeks before the general election, on 22 September 1964, a note for the record reported that the Prime Minister had had a 'general talk' with the Home Secretary in which it was concluded that 'The Homicide Act is unworkable in its present form and the next Home Secretary, of whatever party, will have to end the death penalty'.[113]

The Labour Party

If 'For some reason the issue of hanging [had] always aroused strong emotions in the Conservative Party,'[114] the Labour Party had itself not vigorously espoused abolition in the 1950s and early 1960s. A Labour Government had resisted amendments to the 1948 Criminal Justice Act, requiring James Chuter Ede, the Home Secretary, reluctantly to make out a public case for retention. There was no reference to capital punishment in its annual reports for the period. There was no reference to criminal justice policy in *The New Britain*, its 1964 election manifesto. There was no reference to criminal justice policy in the debates that framed the campaign.[115] The Leader of the Labour Party, Harold Wilson, had evinced no obvious interest in criminal justice policy[116] (an economist, he was more preoccupied with education, the new technology, economic planning, 'modernisation' and overseas aid). And the National Campaign for the Abolition of the Death Penalty, deferring to the *Realpolitik* of the situation, itself resolved to be quiescent before and during the general election.[117] It announced in a letter to its members in April 1964 'the abolition of capital punishment will not be an issue in the election and we are satisfied that it would not be in the interest of the Campaign to try to make it one. We do not therefore propose to take any active part in the election'. Its executive committee held no meetings between February and September. It continued to bide its time.

Yet when the new Labour Government was returned to power in October 1964 with 317 seats, the Conservatives with 304 and the Liberals with nine, it came armed with what was not quite tantamount to a White Paper on criminal justice,[118] the new prime minister, Harold Wilson, had made a public promise to allow time for a debate on abolition,[119] and there were to be convinced abolitionists lodged in the most senior posts in the Home Office and the Lord Chancellor's Office. The Chairman of the Labour Party's Study Group on Crime Prevention and Penal Reform, Lord Longford, an abolitionist, was himself to become the new Leader of the House of Lords. 'They all were, all … abolitionists. I mean Gerald Gardiner, Barbara Wootton,[120] were so intent upon getting rid of the death penalty', recollected the barrister and criminal justice reformer, a man who had been a protagonist at the time, Louis Blom-Cooper,[121] in interview.

Gerald Gardiner, 'a dominant figure',[122] was the new Lord Chancellor, [123] and he was a dedicated abolitionist who, in his previous incarnation as Chairman of the National Campaign for the Abolition of the Death Penalty,[124] had petitioned ministers, written papers and engaged in copious correspondence with the Home Secretary[125] and newspapers about individual cases and general principle. It was he who had written in 1956:

> Capital punishment is a convenient phrase: but what it means is that once a month they take some man, woman or youth out of a cell and kill him or her on a gallows. … Who … is responsible for these killings? You and me. No one else. … My view is simply that one requires some justification before deliberately killing people and that, while I dare say that there are a good many things to be said against capital punishment, the real point is that there is nothing whatever to be said *for* it.[126]

Profoundly influenced by the arguments of the 1930 Select Committee and the Royal Commission,[127] Gerald Gardiner believed that capital punishment did not deter; that the state's executing a murderer was prompted by the same discreditable emotions as those that had stirred the murderer himself or herself to kill; that it was impossible to establish grades of murder; and that there were alternatives enough to the death penalty. It was a *bouleversement* indeed. The man who had much earlier chaired a Subcommittee on Capital Punishment of the Society of Labour Lawyers,[128] who had urged that 'members of the Committee [of the National Campaign] should take every opportunity to urge the introduction of abolition, particularly when in touch with likely members of the next Government',[129] who had suggested that Sydney Silverman prepare a new bill to present immediately the new government took office,[130] who had indeed drafted a bill himself on the very eve of the election,[131] who had minuted that 'Efforts [sh]ould be made … to discover what action the Labour Party might take should it be successful in the next General Election',[132] was now a senior member of that selfsame Labour Government himself and his view was that the Homicide Act was 'absolute rubbish'[133] – quite immoral, irrational and beyond repair.[134] He was to say 'What I had to discover when I became Lord Chancellor was how large and effective the role of Lord Chancellor in the field of law reform could be made to be'.[135] Louis Blom-Cooper and Terence Morris argued that 'His great enthusiasm lay in the field of penal reform and, above all, with the abolition of the death penalty. It had become his great project and he was determined that the window of legislative opportunity which presented itself should not be missed. ...'[136] Yet it should also be said that he acknowledged that there were constraints on how that opportunity could and should be seized: 'I've always fought against capital punishment being a party political question. I've always been in favour of it being dealt with on a free vote, and indeed the Labour Party always has'.[137] And there were other, constitutional constraints as well. Capital punishment was properly the preserve of the Home Secretary, not that of the Lord Chancellor. Sir Derek Oulton, his private secretary in 1964 and 1965, said in interview in January 2014: 'I think he recognised that it wasn't actually really very much Lord Chancellor's business. It was very much Gerald Gardiner business. I don't think we were briefing him at all on it'. What did allow him to become engaged with that business was not a departmental mandate but his almost unassailable moral and personal authority as a lawyer and man somehow above politics who had nevertheless come to occupy a central position in the Cabinet. He was, continued Sir Derek, 'a true goody among a number of baddies or a number of inerts'.

The man in whose domain the issue of capital punishment *did* lie, the new Home Secretary, Sir Frank Soskice, was both a close friend of Gerald Gardiner and himself a confirmed abolitionist. His son, David, said in interview 'He had very strong views indeed about capital punishment' and added that Harold Wilson had been told that he would not take the post unless it was understood that he would reprieve every prisoner sentenced to death ('he needed to say that to Wilson because he thought Wilson was wobbly on this').

Sir Frank had been born in Geneva in 1902, the son of David Soskice, a barrister, prominent Russian revolutionary, supporter of Kerensky, a Jew, the *Manchester Guardian* correspondent in Moscow, and 'an inveterate opponent of political terror',[138] who had witnessed first the oppressive power and anti-Semitic cruelties of the Tsarist state and then, as an activist and a journalist, the rise to power of the equally oppressive Bolsheviks, a man who became intensely anti-Communist, and it was that, his daughter-in-law, Professor Nicola Lacey, contended, which had underpinned his antipathy to the violent deployment of state power.[139] It must have been a powerful force in the home where Sir Frank was raised. But there were other, more immediate reasons as well. A conversation with Sir Frank's other son, Oliver, suggested that his father had come even more firmly to oppose capital punishment during his period as Solicitor General between 1945 and 1951 and in response to the furore about the execution of Timothy Evans who had been hanged on 9 March 1950.[140] On taking office – Oliver continued – Sir Frank had been further distressed when he 'had visited the Governor of Pentonville [Prison] and was taken through every step of the prisoner's calvary, including having a noose put around his neck'. He and Alice Bacon, the new Minister of State, had formally supported bills and voted for abolition in the past, and he would do so again. He had spoken in the debates on the 1957 Act, although, as a man who was far from radical and on the right of the Labour Party, as a careful lawyer and as a former Solicitor-General and Attorney-General, he had done so chiefly to raise technical points about flaws and contradictions in drafting.[141] If there was to be a law, he had said, it should be 'as good ... as it can be made', but, he was also unequivocally to add, 'I would like to see the capital penalty abolished completely'.[142] That was clear enough. More emphatic still were Victor Bailey's assertion that Sir Frank had 'fire in his belly'[143] on the issue and the recollection of the former official, Bob Morris, who had worked in his Private Office at the time: 'The continuing discussions about capital punishment [were] ended as far as Soskice was concerned. I mean he marched into the office and said, "I'm not going to hang anybody you know". Everybody was respited thereon. ... he found capital punishment abhorrent for a number of reasons. ...' including, Bob Morris believed, the execution of Ruth Ellis in 1955.[144] And Sir Frank Soskice kept his word. Everyone sentenced to death during his period of office was reprieved and there were to be no executions thereafter.[145] The note attached to the wooden stand portrayed at the top of this chapter is proof of the matter. To be sure, matters were somewhat complicated because, according to both his sons, Sir Frank Soskice, had, for personal reasons, an antipathy to Sydney Silverman, the chief torchbearer of abolition, who, in Oliver's words, 'was an intellectual and my father had a bit of a thing about intellectuals. He believed that they did not have their feet on the ground and was distrustful of ideology, and particularly of Marxist ideology...' There may also have been sensitivities about what was, in effect, their common background. David said:

> He always felt, he always saw himself, as this son of a Russian Jewish immigrant and always, always had to behave in a more English way than you can possibly imagine. So ... when he became a peer, what did he do? He changed his name from Soskice to Stow Hill... Quite what my father's views were about Sydney Silverman as a person, I don't know. But it wouldn't surprise me, you see, [if they were affected by] this business about Jewishness which I think ... was a more common thing than it is now. I think that he just didn't want to be Jewish.

And if there was no formal election commitment to abolition, there was a text to cite. As a moderniser, Harold Wilson had marshalled his experts, 'people with special knowledge and experience' in different fields in the shadow of a looming election, and the Study Group on Crime Prevention and Penal Reform, chaired by Lord Longford, had been convened in December 1963 to review criminal justice policy. One of its members, the abolitionist Alice Bacon, who was to become Minister of State at the Home Office from 1964 to 1967, had promised that its recommendations would be heeded if Labour came into office[146] (although George Brown, the Member for Belper, a recently defeated contender for the leadership of the Labour Party and about to be the First Secretary of State and Secretary of State for Economic Affairs, elected to disown that pledge in his preface to the report. It was not, he said, 'a policy statement by the Labour Party, but a report submitted to it'[147]).

The Longford Committee had had strong abolitionist markings. Amongst its members were the future Attorney-General, Elwyn Jones; Alice Bacon, a future Home Office Minister; and the ubiquitous C.H. Rolph (or C.R. Hewitt), a member, and Gerald Gardiner, the Chairman, of the National Campaign for the Abolition of the Death Penalty. '[F]or the first time in the history of the penal reform movement,' said the criminologist Terence Morris, himself a member of the Committee, an abolitionist and co-author of an analysis of trends in murder,[148] 'a political leader who was about to assume power had actually invited the reformers in to advise in advance of legislation ...'[149]

The Committee's agenda was tripartite: reform of the prison system; the treatment of juveniles; and the law of murder. Its prime stress was placed on the reform of the juvenile justice system and the proposal that there should be a new family service (18 of its 78 pages were devoted to the theme). But the theme of abolition was also there, occupying the equivalent of a page. In setting out the committee's agenda, members had been invited to list their priorities and C.H. Rolph had proposed that it should concentrate on ten points, the very first item in his list being 'Abolish capital punishment'.[150] Under the heading of 'capital punishment', the committee's working notes for a preliminary outline reported just as simply 'A New Driving Force Needed'.[151] And Gerald Gardiner had drafted a passage which recited that:

> A large majority of the western democracies have long since given up the use of death as a punishment for murder. The Homicide Act has neither a rational nor an ethical basis, and no one defends our present murder law. The House of Commons resolved in 1956: "The death penalty no longer accords with the needs or the true interests of a civilised society." We agree with that view and in our opinion it should forthwith be abolished.[152]

Crime A Challenge appropriated his text *verbatim* and expanded it to touch on the problem posed by some of the sentences passed where there was a finding of 'diminished responsibility'. It recommended on page 40 that 'in cases of diminished responsibility and in all those which now fall under the definition of murder, the sentence should be one of imprisonment for life subject to the Home Secretary's power of release ...'

Yet, when the Labour Party was returned to power, it was perhaps inevitable that tactical political decisions taken about the death penalty could not be entirely straightforward. Although there was undoubtedly a fair wind, the awkward *Realpolitik* of abolition had not wholly dissipated, and, despite its commitment, the government had still to determine how best to proceed in Parliament. Bob Morris recalled:

> You have to remember it had a very small majority to begin with and they weren't looking for controversial measures. And I don't know what the

rules, the Whips' calculations were, … but it wasn't clear that such a Bill would have necessarily passed the first Labour Government … And … Wilson wasn't an enthusiast, he wasn't hyperactive in those sort of areas … [it is difficult to say] whether it's a matter of conscience or a matter of political calculation … I mean mostly I'd say political calculation, that is that this was controversial business which, the success of which, was not necessarily guaranteed and could certainly take up a lot of Government time.

The Whips did calculate politically. It was, they said, impossible at the beginning of a new Parliament to fathom how a government bill on abolition might fare, the government's majority of four was slender, it could fall,[153] and any prospect of political embarrassment should be avoided. This would have to be a disciplined parliament with members in attendance at every possible opportunity and with pairing arrangements strictly followed[154] (pairing arrangements are based on agreements between members of opposing parties that, with the consent of the whips, one will not vote if the other is unable to do so). Risk-laden policy initiatives were thus far from welcome. The new Chief Whip, Edward Short, gave his advice on the proposed bill on 21 October 1964, immediately before the new session:

I promised to look at the prospects of a Death Penalty (Abolition) Bill. On the first point as to the strength of voting, I really cannot hazard a guess. We have, of course, so many new Members that without a Whips' exercise I cannot hope to assess what the outcome would be: you will understand that it would not be possible for me to put the Whips on to this until sometime after the State Opening, which I imagine will be too late for your purposes.

On the second question of whether it should be a Government Bill with the Whips on, or whether it should be even a Government Bill, I must be influenced by the fact that in a matter of such importance if we were to take it on and be defeated, then the consequences would obviously be serious. Moreover, on a matter of conscience, could we really attempt to Whip in – particularly in view of the Prime Minister's recent public statement that he would like to see far more free votes? The circumstances leave me at present to conclude that the latter might have to be decided by means of a Private Members' Bill with the Whips off.[155]

Entrusting the matter to a free vote was never a wholly instrumental matter. Brian Cubbon, the Home Office official who was later to be become Permanent Secretary, interviewed by David Dagan, an American graduate student, in 2002, said: 'I think there was always something in the genuine, personal conscience point of view. And I think that people really embraced the arguments of principle for the free vote, while realizing in their sober moments that the alternative could be worse politically'.[156] But it is evident that there were instrumental dimensions too, and Harold Wilson was anxious to steer away from that worse alternative. David Soskice recalled:

> It would surprise me if Wilson wasn't opposed to capital punishment but I think he was absolutely very nervous about doing something [with] this wafer-thin majority. I'm sure [my father] would have loved it to have been a government bill. And ... I've always assumed that ... Wilson's view was that the only way we can avoid having to take responsibility for this is to make it a free vote... [My father] thought Wilson was wobbly on this. And indeed having a Private Member's Bill, having a free vote and so on, was a reflection of wobbling on it. ...

If the form of an abolitionist bill was in doubt, so too was its timing. The new government had been in waiting for thirteen years and it had an appreciable legislative programme. In a cabinet meeting held to discuss the contents of the very first Queen's speech, the Lord President of the Council listed the items which had to be included in the first session (and they centred on such matters as iron and steel nationalisation, a Highlands development board, and monopolies and restrictive practices) and those which were inessential, including abolition (*they* centred on 'Bills on racial discrimination, capital punishment, Law Commissioners and the Parliamentary Commissioner for the investigation of grievances'[157]). So strong had the abolitionists become, however, that they now constituted a major bloc inside the government. They were not to be stalled. Sir Charles Cunningham, a man whose views were in accord with those of Sir Frank,[158] even said that they could ride roughshod over possible objections by police and prison officers.[159] Organisations representing the police, 'a powerful opponent of the abolition of the death penalty'[160], did protest[161] and they were indeed not heeded.

Cabinet decided on 27 October[162] to accept capital punishment as 'a firm commitment' although, it was noted, it 'might be by Private Member's Bill'. Sir Charles Cunningham's own view from within the Home Office was that that was *not* the best course to follow:

Abolition of the Death Penalty

...

2. I recognise that the Government may feel that they must allow a free vote. I would, however, submit that there is still a strong case for Government legislation, on the ground that:
   (a) A matter of such importance calls for Government legislation, particularly since:
   (b) While there are issues of conscience, there is also the major issue whether or not the Death Penalty, as it now exists, is needed for the preservation of law and order. This was the fundamental issue underlying the Homicide Act, 1957. It is one on which the Government would no doubt be expected to have a clear view

of its own, and it might also be expected to take the initiative in giving effect to it, rather than leaving the initiative to a Private Member.

(c) Abolition is likely to raise some important consequential issues. For instance, Lord Longford's Committee expresses the view (page 40 of their Report) that … in all cases of murder, the sentence should be one of imprisonment for life; and the Lord Chief Justice [Lord Parker] is, we have reason to think, critical of the whole concept of diminished responsibility. These are issues on which the Government would probably wish to reach its own conclusions …

(d) Even with a free vote on the major issue, it would be easier with Government legislation to keep control over proceedings and over the line to be taken on amendments (for example, to retain the Death Penalty for the murder of a policeman or prison officer, or for treason, or to provide for a minimum term of detention for murderers sentenced to life imprisonment).

3. If the matter were dealt with in Government legislation, the question arises whether it should be dealt with in a Criminal Justice Bill or in a separate measure. Its inclusion in a Criminal Justice Bill would give the Bill much greater importance; …

4. An alternative course would be to debate the matter in the first instance on a Motion. (In 1956, the Government of the day allowed a free vote on its own Motion, 'that this House is of opinion that, while the Death Penalty should be retained, the law relating to the crime of murder should be amended'.) The Government could then undertake that if the Motion were carried it would introduce early legislation to give effect to the decision of the House.

C.C.C. [163]

But the Chief Whip prevailed. Cabinet was not *that* resolute (and Lord Gardiner had long anticipated that abolition would not be by government legislation.[164]) The next day, it determined that 'Capital Punishment could best be tackled by means of a Private Member's Bill – on which there should be a free vote. The Lord President was invited together with the Home Secretary, to give further consideration to the proposal that facilities should be provided at an early date for the introduction of a Private Member's Bill …'[165] A commitment was thereby inserted into the draft text of the Speech from the Throne ('Facilities will be provided for a free decision by Parliament on the issue of capital punishment'[166]) and it was awarded priority. Emboldened by a decision of the first meeting[167] of the Home Affairs Committee[168] on 6 November,[169] a meeting that had stressed the importance of gauging the temper of the House before Christmas, the Lord President of the Council, Herbert Bowden, came to recommend that it should be included amongst those 'Bills to which the Government are committed, together with a very few other Bills of exceptional urgency and importance'.[170] What lay before the new Government would none the less be what G. Otton in the private office called 'a particularly difficult Session' with a great deal of business to despatch.

When the Home Secretary, the Lord Chancellor, the Secretary of State for Scotland, the attorney general, Sir Elwyn Jones, and the Minister of State next met to discuss capital punishment on 18 November, their aim was what the Home Secretary called 'the passage of a Bill whose main object is the speedy abolition of the death penalty'.[171]

The introduction of a bill should be rapid and its wording simple and uncluttered.[172] It would be debated, as the Home Secretary had wished, before Christmas[173] – and it was spurred on in some small part by the prospect of a number of imminent executions which would demand a decision and give unwelcome prominence to the politics of hanging. Sir George Coldstream, the Permanent Secretary at the Lord Chancellor's Department, was reported to have informed Robert Beloe,[174] the Archbishop of Canterbury's private secretary, in January 1965 that 'there is the position of the Home Secretary to consider. He should not be left in the present great difficulty that he was experiencing over the death sentence longer than was necessary'.[175] One case that loomed especially large was that of Ronald Cooper, who had been brought back from the Bahamas in October to be charged with murder by shooting and with attempted murder in the furtherance of burglary.[176] G. Otton warned that:

> If we take the worst possible assumption, Cooper might well be con-
> victed by, say, 20th November. He could then appeal to the C.C.A.
> [Court of Criminal Appeal] by, say, 2nd December. His appeal could be
> rejected by 9th or 10th December. An execution date could then be fixed
> for 31st December. The Cooper case will probably not move as fast as
> this, but we cannot take risks and must be prepared for it to do so. This
> means, therefore, that we must have Second Reading of a Bill before
> the Christmas recess. As I have indicated above, this will require special
> management …[177]

Sir Charles Cunningham accepted the need for haste, saying that he 'agree[d] that S. of S. should have this useful note. It seems best to introduce this Bill as soon as possible and take the Second Reading immediately afterwards'.[178] In the event, the movement of Cooper's case was protracted: he was convicted on 14 December 1964; he appealed, and then withdrew his appeal; was due to be hanged on 5 January 1965 and was reprieved seventeen days later (as was quite inevitable). Yet his progress through the courts had run in tandem with the movement of the bill, and it was thought that it might well have provided the foundation for a running commentary on hanging and the abolitionist case. (In fact, when the time came, no allusion at all was made to Ronald Cooper in Parliamentary debate.)

Sydney Silverman told his colleagues on the National Campaign a month after the election that, because the government had agreed to provide time for a Private Member's Bill, he needed to proceed neither by means of the lottery nor the 10-minute rule. 'He intended simply to present a Bill to the House. ... he hoped therefore to present his Bill on 4th December and it was understood that the business statement on 10th December would indicate a date for the second reading'.[179] He knew whereof he spoke. On 4 December the business of the House included a bill drafted by Lord Gardiner[180] and his 'law reform lot'[181] and introduced by Sydney Silverman. It was a:

> Bill to abolish capital punishment in the case of persons convicted in Great Britain of murder or convicted of murder or a corresponding offence by court-martial and, in connection therewith, to make further provision for the punishment of persons so convicted, presented by Mr. Sydney Silverman; supported by Mr. Humphry Berkeley, Mrs. Braddock, Mr. Christopher Chataway, Mr. Michael Foot, Sir Geoffrey de Freitas, Mr. Leslie Hale, Mr. Stan Newens, Mr. Paget, Mr. Shinwell, Mr. Jeremy Thorpe, and Mrs. Shirley Williams; read the First time; to be read a Second time upon Monday next and to be printed. [Bill 42.][182]

'The abolition of the death penalty is now regarded as certain', reported *The Times* the next day. 'No organised opposition is expected, though the Bill could run into trouble in the Lords, where in 1956 Mr. Silverman's earlier abolition Bill was refused a second reading'[183] (and that was a judgement shared by the Executive Committee of the National Campaign[184]). On 10 December, and again as Sydney Silverman had foretold, the date of the debate on the Second Reading of the bill was announced:[185] 21 December. The government itself was to be more than thorough in paving the way for abolition: with only a slim majority, cabinet determined that members could vote according to their conscience, but they would be allowed to do so only after a fashion:

> it was agreed in discussion that, although there would be a free vote, any Ministers who supported the retention of the death penalty should prefer-ably abstain from voting rather than vote against the Bill. Ministers should inform junior Ministers and Parliamentary Private Secretaries accordingly, on the understanding that they would not be pressed to act otherwise than in accordance with their conscience.[186]

Sydney Silverman opened the debate in the mid-afternoon of 21 December: 'My first word must be one of appreciation and gratitude to the Government for having provided the House and those of us who wish to see a final end of the last remnant of a grotesque barbarity with the opportunity of seeing the end of it at last'.[187] 'This is a Private Member's Bill,' he continued. 'The Government are officially neutral about it. The vote will be, as it has always been with the notable exception of that on the Homicide Act, 1957, a free vote of the House, but I hope that on this occasion we may count on the neutrality of the Government being a benevolent neutrality'. The decision before the House was no longer whether to abolish the death penalty for murder, because, he claimed, that had already been undertaken in the 1957 Act. The decision was whether to abolish it for the small rump of cases which that Act had retained.[188] Members should not heed public opinion but act according to their conscience and intellect: 'I should like hon. Members to imagine what their duty would be if they had the responsibility of deciding, if there were a man whom they knew it would be wrong to kill, if, in respect of that man, there were violent public pressure, nevertheless to kill him. Would it be right for a responsible legislator or member of the Government to kill that man, whom he thought he ought not to kill, because of some popular immediate pressure which might change its mind the next morning?' It was not possible rationally to distinguish and defend the cases of murder which were eligible for the death penalty and those which were not, he continued. The 1864 Royal Commission had failed to do so. The 1949 Royal Commission had failed to do so. The 1957 Act had failed to do so:

> No one could think that the exceptions in the 1957 Act were the worst murders. Those who accept the position of the 1957 Act accept that the murderers of children shall not be hanged. Those who accept the 1957 Act accept that cold, calculated, premeditated murders shall not be capital. Those who accept the 1957 Act accept that foul sexual crimes shall not be capital. Those who accept the 1957 Act accept that if a man waylays his enemy around a dark corner of a back street and stabs him in the back with a knife, that shall not be capital murder, whereas if he waits for him with a revolver and shoots him in the front, that is capital murder. Anyone who tried to justify the exceptions in the 1957 Act on the ground that it was a successful attempt to distinguish between the gravest kinds of murder and crimes which were not so grave would have an impossible task. Let the House remember that Ruth Ellis would still have committed a capital crime under the Homicide Act because she used a revolver instead of a knife.

There were those who opposed Sydney Silverman's case, and they said so frequently and at length, but perhaps the most significant intervention stemmed from Henry Brooke, the former Home Secretary,[189] who told the House of Commons that he had been a junior minister and a firm retentionist at the time of the debate on the 1957 Act, although he had not then chosen to speak. On becoming Home Secretary in 1962, however, he had:

> ... immediately asked for a report on the working of the Homicide Act, because one was aware of criticism; one was aware of anomalies in its working, and I was anxious to know whether it would be possible to improve the Act by any form of amendment that might be generally acceptable. The Act, as has been said, was designed to protect society by a special deterrent against carrying of lethal weapons or compounding

theft with murder, and to protect public servants such as police officers and prison officers in carrying out their dangerous duties. ... I realised very soon in my study of the matter that any amendment, while it might remove some anomalies, would be virtually certain to create others, and I must advise the House that we can find no escape from our problem this afternoon by that road. It has not been suggested in the debate that the right solution might be to alter the demarcation line between capital and non-capital murder, nevertheless there are some outside who think that that is the right solution. I must say with such authority as I can command that it is useless to study further the possibility of improving the law of murder by retaining the distinction between capital and non-capital murder but drawing a different demarcation line.

As Home Secretary, he had been obliged on some twelve occasions to consider whether to recommend the exercise of the Royal Prerogative of Mercy.[190] In six cases it had been difficult to do so as the law then stood. It had been, he said, a quite indefensible situation:

> I gave all of them very long thought, yet every now and again it used to come over me that while I was having to determine whether persons sentenced to death for capital murder should be hanged or not, other murderers whose crimes were indeed worse than the one which I had under consideration at that moment were not liable to the death penalty. It did not even come to the Home Secretary in those cases to consider whether or not a reprieve should be recommended. ... At the end of my time at the Home Office, I had become convinced that the case for retaining the death penalty was no longer strong enough to justify retention and that we were coming to the time when we ought to make trial of abolition. ... I shall press strongly in Committee for the Bill to be amended ... [so] that after a period of, say, five years, it should be incumbent on the Government, whatever Government may be in power, to have to bring forward an affirmative Resolution for a further continuance of the operation of the Act.

His successor, Sir Frank Soskice, then observed:

> As a former Home Secretary, [Henry Brooke] made a speech with which all of us listening to it had great sympathy and which we heard with deep admiration. He spoke from the experience he derived from holding the office which I now hold. I find myself so close in thought to him on this topic that I must say that I would be only repeating much of what he said if I deployed the thoughts with which I approached the debate. ... whether we support or oppose the Bill we regard the deliberate taking by a machine of another person's life as something so grave that we cannot avoid questioning its necessity. We cannot possibly accept it as something

which is just part of the ordinary order of things. It is something which we must keep constantly under review and with regard to which we must ask ourselves whether it can be shown – and I use the word deliberately – conclusively, or nearly conclusively, that it is essential that we should do that thing to protect society and prevent evil from falling upon innocent persons. … I therefore very much hope, speaking from the Government Bench, that the House will agree that the time has come when we should put an end altogether to the death penalty for the crime of murder.

Despite the fillip that Mr Brooke's recantation had given to abolition, he had reinstated the magical figure of the five-year trial period as an amendment (the sole amendment accepted[191]) 'against Government advice'[192] and in Sydney Silverman's absence abroad,[193] appearing as clause 3 of the Bill and section 4 of what would become the Act. After some seven hours of debate, the House of Commons divided, and the bill was passed on second reading with a large majority of 355 votes to 170. Henry Brooke, the Chief Labour Whip, the Prime Minister, the Home Secretary, Alice Bacon, Reginald Paget and Jeremy Thorpe voted for it. Eighty Conservative Members voted for it. Only one Labour backbencher voted against it. 44 Labour Members and 47 Conservatives abstained, including, it seems,[194] R.A. Butler. Quintin Hogg, the former Lord Hailsham who had resigned his peerage in 1963, voted against it.

When asked what he proposed to do next, Sir Frank Soskice declared that, until the bill had passed, he would continue to review individual cases as before.[195] 'The question now in everybody's mind', said Sydney Silverman's biographer, 'was whether the Lords had changed their minds since 1956 or would they turn the Bill down again and risk a constitutional clash with a Labour Government'.[196]

The legislative programme in that first Session was congested, and Sir Frank Soskice was necessarily much occupied with the bill in the new year. He had to attend 21 Standing Committee and other meetings on the death penalty in 1965. He had to fend off pleas from the Police Federation[197] to exempt the killing of officers from the Act.[198] He and his colleagues had to deal with a succession of attempts to stall or end the progress of the bill, and animosities mounted. The government's response at the beginning of March was to put the whips on in the vote to send the bill to the House of Lords, and, in retaliation,[199] it was agreed on 5 March at Committee Stage in the House of Commons that the bill be referred back to 'a committee of the whole House', a move that Cabinet understood would have undone all the work that had taken place so far.[200] The Lord President of the Council, Herbert Bowden, proposed in his turn, and exceptionally, that the House of Commons would have to meet on Wednesday mornings to expedite progress,[201] and, again exceptionally, the whips were put on.[202] Another plethora of retentionist amendments was tabled:[203] for example, to retain the death penalty for the murder of police officers, or for a second murder. Henry Brooke and a number of Conservative backbenchers again tabled their own amendment that the Act should be in force for an experimental five years and then be reviewed and voted upon in parliament.

What Sydney Silverman would not do was compromise the principle of complete abolition[204] (he wrote to members calling Henry Brooke's proposed amendment 'objectionable' and a 'constitutional absurdity'[205] which should be deleted) and, in that posture, he was supported by the National Campaign for the Abolition of the Death Penalty.[206] What the government was not prepared to do in the summer of 1965 was imperil a very full programme of legislation, including a Finance Bill, a Trades Disputes Bill and a Race Relations Bill. 'Conservative opponents of the Bill [would keep] up pressure to the end'[207] and cabinet's answer was to ease the passage of the bill by instructing Sydney Silverman that it would only afford time for a Third Reading debate if he were succinct in what he said and if he withdrew his opposition to the amendment:[208]

> On the Murder (Abolition of Death Penalty) Bill, half a day should be sufficient to dispose of the amendments relating to the penalty for murder and, if the Speaker were prepared to accept the closure, to secure Third Reading by a reasonable hour; but there would be a serious risk of losing the Bill if time were spent on an amendment put down by the sponsor, Mr. Sidney Silverman, to remove the clause (clause 3) limiting the operation of the Bill to five years. Mr. Silverman should accordingly be informed that, while the Government were willing to provide a half day for the remaining stages of the Bill, they were not prepared to jeopardise their own legislation in order to secure its passage, and that this time would be made available only on condition that he withdrew his amendment. It should be impressed on the sponsors of the Bill that they should confine their own speeches to the minimum ...[209]

So it was that for reasons somewhat tangential to the immediate logic of abolition, reflecting in part, perhaps, some of the antipathy in the cabinet to Sydney Silverman's personal style, Henry Brooke's amendment, proposing the five-year experiment, was perfunctorily built into the bill in May 1965.

The House of Lords, the Judiciary and the Churches

Although there was some confidence about how members of the House of Lords might vote, there was also said to be a possibility of substantial opposition and of 'backwoodsmen' again attending in numbers as they had done in 1956.[210] Two of the most important protagonists, legislators as well as authorities on the law and morals, Lords Goddard and Fisher, had impeded the passage of legislation in 1956. How their successors would act could be critical.

There appear, perhaps by design, to be almost no surviving records of the correspondence and deliberations of the Lord Chief Justice and the senior judges on the death penalty before the introduction of a new abolitionist bill in 1964.[211] But there is some evidence of a shift in thought.[212] That defender of the death penalty, Lord Goddard, had retired at the age of 75 to give way to Lord Parker as Lord Chief Justice in 1958 and, by 1962, the Home Office was aware that Lord Parker had let it be known privately that he considered the 1957 Act to be so riddled with anomalies that it was unworkable[213] (and that was the argument he would later put in debate). Sydney Silverman himself had certainly become more optimistic about the judges' stance in 1965 (he was reported to have told the Archbishop of Canterbury's Private Secretary that 'He believed that the Judges and the Lord Chief Justice in particular would support the Bill'[214]). Lord Parker had accepted an invitation from the chairmen of the National Campaign to attend a performance of 'Hang Down Your Head and Die',[215] a polemical musical play produced by the Oxford University Experimental Club,[216] in April 1964, an acceptance that was read as significant. And Sir Louis Blom-Cooper recalled that Lord Parker had told him that he 'loathed the thought of putting on the black cap'.[217] I also learned from the journalist, Antony Howard,[218] that whilst Lord Parker attended and spoke at the annual meeting of the Canadian Bar Association[219] and received an honorary degree from the University of British Columbia[220] in September 1959[221] he had 'attacked both the Homicide Act and the more recent Street Offences Act'.[222] Some say that the shift in the stance adopted by the judges, led by the Lord Chief Justice, may have played its part and that the lawyer-members of Parliament would have been influenced by what the judges said, although senior members of the former government, and a former prime minister above all, were unimpressed. Harold Macmillan was to ask Viscount Kilmuir 'Can you do anything about the Lord Chief Justice? How I wish I had appointed the Attorney-General [Sir Reginald Manningham-Buller] in his place. Is he at all ashamed of the follies he has committed … ? I suppose he would not be likely to move?'[223]

54 members of the Lords in the mid-1960s were solicitors (six of whom voted for abolition and none for retention in October 1965) or had been called to the Bar (23 of whom voted for abolition, eight against). There were 74 barristers and 33 solicitors in the House of Commons in 1965[224] and 60% of those who voted did so in favour of abolition on the crucial Third Reading in July 1965,[225] a little less than the proportion in the entire body of the House of Commons itself where 67% voted in favour. What *is* significant is that 12 of the 46 barristers, all Conservatives, who had taken what might be construed as an anti-abolitionist position in the Third Reading vote in 1957 had changed their minds and decided to support abolition by 1965.[226] The lawyer, Louis Blom-Cooper, reflected in interview:

> Lawyers were very powerful in Parliament. There were a very large number of them. People in those days used to practise and be members of Parliament. … There were 40–50 practising members of the Bar who were members of Parliament at that time. And the influence of the legal profession I think is comparable if not greater, than the Church.

[One] group which was important in influencing Parliamentarians was [therefore] the Judiciary. ... by 1961 with three-four years' experience of the Homicide Act, Parker had become totally convinced that it was a nonsense. He may have thought it was a political nonsense or not but he wasn't, as Lord Chief Justice, he was not going to live with it. ... In 1961, a half of the High Court (and in those days only the High Court judges could try murder cases, so it's only 20–30 High Court judges ...) he said, half of them would favour abolition. ... there was a major change among the Judiciary.

The Westminster diocesan files of the Roman Catholic Church have no record of Cardinal Archbishop Heenan's or the Hierarchy's position or actions on the politics of capital punishment at the time. Neither does the Archbishop's autobiography.[227] But the Church had by doctrine long been committed to the death penalty. Cardinal Godfrey, Archbishop Heenan's predecessor until his death in 1963, adhered to the traditional position of the Roman Church, a position that maintained that 'When it is a question of the execution of a condemned man, the State does not dispose of the individual's right to life. In this case it is reserved to the public power to deprive the condemned person of the enjoyment of life in expiation of his crime when, by his crime, he has already disposed himself of his right to live'.[228]

But the views of the other churches were moving fast away from retention,[229] and those of the Church of England in particular were to make a significant impact on the progress of the debate in the House of Lords. It was Harry Potter's judgement that:

[The churches'] central importance is explained by the fact that hanging was an institution which demanded, and even craved for, religious sanction. The Church by Law Established provided the intellectual and theological justification for hanging, and suggested the means by which those aspects of it which gave rise to most public outcry could be amended, and thus hanging be preserved. Judicial killing was sanctioned by bishops, and its execution presided over by chaplains. Had the church denounced it, it would have withered and died...[230]

The Church of England did come to denounce it and it did wither and die. The causal chain is not overwhelmingly solid, but the Church and its bishops certainly came to provide a number of the tactics, votes and arguments which weighed in the debate in the House of Lords. Canon John Collins of St Paul's Cathedral and Canon Edward Carpenter, the treasurer of Westminster Abbey, were on the Executive Committee of the National Campaign for the Abolition of the Death Penalty. There had been an upheaval in the ranks of the bishops: the abolitionist Michael Ramsey had replaced the retentionist Geoffrey Fisher as Archbishop of Canterbury in 1961, and twenty-one of the twenty-nine diocesan bishops in the Province of Canterbury at the time of the debate had been appointed between 1956 and 1962. Sixteen of the twenty-one were entirely new to the episcopacy.[231]

One, the new Bishop of Southwark, Mervyn Stockwood, appointed in 1959, was a campaigning abolitionist who had brought a successful compromise motion on the death penalty, built again on the magical five-year moratorium, that was unanimously supported by the Upper House of the Convocation of Canterbury, in January 1962.[232] It was a compromise intended to win over a divided body that had hitherto been hesitant about pronouncing on the subject, and whose head, the Archbishop of Canterbury, had had until then to be publicly circumspect. The Archbishop was reminded by the Church's Chief Information Officer in October 1961 that:

> Your Grace will recall that you recorded a short statement for B.B.C. television in connection with their documentary programme on Capital Punishment. In this your Grace said that "The Church of England has never pronounced officially on the subject of capital punishment, but amongst its members two views are sincerely held." Since then, however, there has been the resolution by the Lower House of the Convocation of Canterbury,[233] and I thought, therefore, to avoid possibility of misunderstanding the B.B.C. should cause the following to be said at the end of the programme. "Since the Archbishop ... made this recording, the Lower House of the Convocation of Canterbury has passed a resolution calling for the abolition of capital punishment or at least its complete suspension for five years".[234]

The votes in both Houses of Convocation had given Archbishop Ramsey an opportunity to declare himself on a position to which he already adhered,[235] and he was now able tell the Archbishop of York that 'the sponsors of the [Silverman] Bill will rightly expect some substantial support from the bishops, since the Bishops in the two Convocations have passed Resolutions on the matter'.[236] And there was an expectation in Lambeth Palace that 'a majority of the Peers Spiritual, possibly a considerable majority, will wish to support the Bill'.[237]

It is worth looking attentively at how the bench of bishops did come to give that support. The archive of Archbishop Ramsey's papers in the library of Lambeth Palace is so replete that it prepares the foundation of an unusually informed understanding not only of some parts of the process by which the politics of abolition were negotiated in the House of Lords but also of the special role played by the Church.

There was to be an interesting coalition of State and Church. Informally and in the wings, the government played a major strategic role in steering the legislation through Parliament. It organised logistics, personnel and devices. It afforded time for debate in the House of Commons. It prepared a path in the House of Lords, the domain of the Lord Chancellor. It liaised closely with the bishops. Louis Blom-Cooper was to observe in interview:

The time allotted or the time permitted by government to consideration of the Bill in committee in the Commons was huge. It was totally disproportionate to any other legislation. My recollection (this is all impressionistic) that from January right through, almost I think to June, the committee sat twice a week, debating amendments and … this was extraordinary because it, technically it was a Private Members' Bill. So government involvement in it was just as if they had produced the Bill … it was quite clear that the proponents of the Bill, that is to say, not just the sponsors but the Labour Party, were insistent on getting rid of the death penalty full stop.

The government's liaison with the Church was to be particularly intimate, extensive and intensively planned, and especially so as the movement of the bill to the Upper House began to become imminent. Formally, the government could not itself introduce what was not a government bill, and it sought a proxy.[238] In February 1965, and in anticipation of that move, Sydney Silverman requested the Archbishop of Canterbury formally to introduce his bill in the House of Lords [239] (and he, Robert Beloe and officials of the House of Lords met periodically thereafter to review tactics[240] although Beloe reported that he did not find him easy to work with[241]). But Silverman's move lagged behind that of the government: Robert Beloe, had already met Sir George Coldstream, the Permanent Secretary at the Lord Chancellor's Office, in January to discuss the part which Michael Ramsey might play. It was, said Sir George, 'an open secret' 'in certain quarters of the Lords' that this might happen, an open secret that had indeed already prompted Lord Longford, the Leader of the House, to feel emboldened enough to tell the Archbishop of Canterbury that 'it is wonderful news that you are ready to handle the Abolition Bill in the Lords'.[242] Yet it was also appreciated, said Robert Beloe, that a heavy burden would be placed on the archbishop who would be expected to 'pilot the Bill through all its stages … though he would, of course, have expert help from the peers who supported him'.[243] There was also the difficulty that the archbishop would be in Australia and New Zealand in Easter when the bill might be before Parliament (although it soon became clear that the bill was making slow progress and would not reach the House of Lords until after that time[244]).

Robert Beloe and Sir George Coldstream considered the disposition of the 26 senior bishops entitled to a seat in the House of Lords. There might, they thought, be 25 bishops who would vote for abolition, but the mere act of their voting would not be enough: 'it was desirable that some Bishops should take part. Coldstream thought that Exeter [who spoke for the bishops on social affairs] would be very helpful. I [Beloe] said that I wondered whether Leicester would be useful and I also said that in the absence of the Archbishop of Canterbury a lead might be taken by the Archbishop of York'.[245] In the interim, the Archbishop of Canterbury would brief himself on the matter of capital punishment with papers, consisting largely of memoranda prepared by the National Campaign for the Abolition of Capital Punishment, bearing on their masthead Gerald Gardiner's name in his earlier incarnation as Chairman.[246] The Archbishop of York too asked Robert Beloe for papers in readiness for his part in what was to come,[247] and he agreed, subject to the constraints of his own diary, to introduce the bill should the Archbishop of Canterbury be absent from the country.[248]

Timing continued to be a problem in what was to be a painstaking mustering of votes. The Archbishop of Canterbury might well be out of the country; the Archbishop of York might be busy with a diocesan campaign; but Robert Beloe reported to Sir George Coldstream that a 'majority of the Bishops would be prepared to come. The earlier we can get a certain date around which they can adjust their other engagements the more Bishops will be able to come'.[249] Robert Beloe was in fact becoming not only an intermediary and plenipotentiary but also the eyes and ears of the archbishop, reporting to him with great frequency about the state of play in the House of Lords, and particularly when the archbishop was absent in Australasia in March 1965.

As the archbishop's position became known, so the bill's proponents[250] and opponents gathered, and he became exposed to efforts internally[251] and externally to dissuade him from supporting the bill. For instance, Lord Dilhorne, the Lord Chancellor who had preceded Lord Gardiner, began what was to be a running correspondence[252] to say:

> I have heard a rumour which I hope is not true, that you have agreed to pilot Silverman's Abolition of the Death Penalty Bill in this House. … Frankly I do feel it would be most unwise and inappropriate for the Head of our Church to move the second reading of this Bill. It is a most controversial measure on which feelings run high. While of course it is right that the views of the Archbishops and the Bishops should be made known, it is a very different thing for an Archbishop to take charge of the conduct of the Bill.
>
> The Gallup polls show that the majority of the population are against the Bill, and I am sure that you will not mind my saying that a very great number of Church people will think it most inappropriate. … I have no doubt that if you do it, it will give rise to very strong criticism both in the House and outside which is bound to impair your position and that of our Church. …[253]

The archbishop was also to be warned that, although there was an expectation by officials of the House of the Lords that the bill would pass, he should suppose that his role in its passage would be time-consuming, bruising and arduous, and that he himself could become painfully embroiled in partisan politics. Peter Henderson, the Clerk at the Table who dealt with public bills, and David Stephens, the Clerk of the Parliaments at the House of Lords, cautioned Robert Beloe in March 1965 that anyone who introduced a bill would be obliged to 'give the final answer at the Committee Stage on any amendment,' and there would be:

a long tussle which would create more and more ill feeling and that in spite of the support by some Conservatives the opposition would more and more pin the Bill down as a Government measure, the more so as the Bill was becoming more unpopular in the country owing to the recent increase of violent crime. ... It was during the Committee Stage that the real difficulty would arise. The archbishop would not be treated differently from anybody else who introduced a controversial Bill. Among the opponents of the Bill would be the most adept Parliamentarians who would give no quarter in a matter of this kind. ... [Henderson and Stephens] spoke both as devoted admirers of the Archbishop and in their professional capacity. In the first capacity they did not like the idea of the Archbishop being subjected to the kind of attacks which would almost undoubtedly come upon him in the House at Committee Stage. In the latter capacity they doubted whether he would have the parliamentary expertise with which to cope with some of the cleverest attacks on the Bill in Committee. I [Beloe] said that they must assume that the Archbishop would not fear opposition from the opponents of the Bill however strong it was. I felt that he himself would probably think that his introduction of the Bill would tend towards taking the partisanship out of the atmosphere. Surely there was a good deal to be said for this.[254]

That warning did give the archbishop pause. On his return from Australasia, he reported to Sydney Silverman that he had been given to understand from 'not unfriendly sources' that 'there are likely to be some keen and expert attacks ... in all the ways open to Parliamentary procedure during [the Bill's] passage through the Lords. I feel I ought to ask you whether you are satisfied that in such circumstances I would be the best person to take charge. I am not expert in Parliamentary procedure nor can I be completely free to devote myself to the House. ... I write this merely in the hope that I might work out with you what is the best action to take so as to ensure that the Bill passes through the Lords. ...'[255] Sydney Silverman was not to be dissuaded,[256] but, in the event, Michael Ramsey did decide to step down,[257] although he and his secretary remained active behind the scenes, picking their way carefully through the hazards lying ahead. In this, as in other matters of social reform, he was what Baden Hickman of *The Guardian* newspaper called 'discreet but most active and committed'.[258] It was a perceptive comment. Discretion did rule. Michael Ramsey told Sydney Silverman, for example, that his making a public statement on hanging 'would antagonise some members in the Commons and ... would probably prejudice the position from which I could speak in the House of Lords'.[259]

But the archbishop nevertheless continued to act behind the scenes. He marshalled the bishops. On hearing the likely date of the debate, Robert Beloe wrote to him in June to say that 'it would be wise to warn all the Bishops immediately',[260] and the archbishop duly wrote to every bishop to declare that he was 'very grateful for all the help that Bishops were prepared to give' and promised that he would 'let them know as soon as possible what are likely to be the debates for the Second Reading in the House of Lords'.[261] He then proceeded to put all the bishops but two, both retentionist, on notice when the date had become certain. He was, in effect, acting as a whip for the Lords Spiritual.[262]

The archbishop and his private secretary compiled a tally of those likely to come: five bishops on 19 July when the speeches would be made; thirteen on the 20th when the vote would be taken. And there was to be much further correspondence and whipping at every turn when it was realised that the bill's progress would be slow and that dates for debate had to change and timetables reorganised. When it was known that the Third Reading would be on 26 October, for instance, bishops were advised by Robert Beloe that the archbishop 'very much hopes that there will be strong support ... from the Bench of Bishops and has bidden me write to express the hope that you will be able to go. It is not certain how matters will go, but I think it is very likely that there will be a Division in which an episcopal vote will mean more than just one vote. Could you possibly very kindly let me know if you propose to attend the debate?'

The bishops who might speak were briefed in detail on amendments and opposition arguments as they arose. For example, Robert Beloe produced an *aide memoire* on the apparent impact of abolition on attacks on police officers, based on *Hansard*, and citing work by Thorsten Sellin in the United States that showed that there were slightly more assaults in cities where the death penalty remained in place than in those cities where it had been abolished.[263] In October, again, he briefed the Archbishop of York, saying that:

> I think that the kind of speech that will prove most helpful from you will depend upon the atmosphere in the Third Reading debate ... I am told that the Bill's supporters think that they must be prepared for a strong attack. Therefore the eight or nine votes which the Bishops will contribute are considered to be very important. ... I am pretty sure that the House will need to be reminded of the kinds of thing which the Archbishop of Canterbury and the two other Bishops were interested in in the Second Reading debate, for other speakers do not make that kind of contribution with any sure touch. I would say that a fairly short speech of 15 to 20 minutes at most covering the moral principles and expressing the hope that the Bill would become law before the end of the Session would be the right intervention from you.[264]

After the Archbishop of Canterbury had resiled from opening the Second Reading debate, there had inevitably been some scurrying for an alternative. Sydney Silverman; the Lord Chancellor; Lord Longford; Lord Shepherd, the Government Chief Whip; and Robert Beloe conferred on 16 June to conclude that it might be best to turn to a member of the Opposition or the Liberal Party to placate the Conservatives. But Lord Byers was ruled out because the

Conservatives 'were inclined to be irritated by the Liberals' and R.A. Butler was 'not thought to ... be willing', and it 'was not certain that he [too] would not irritate Opposition Peers'. Lords Carrington or Jellicoe might be possibilities.[265]

In the event, it was to be 'that formidable debater',[266] the friend of Sir Ernest Gowers, a member of the Committee of Honour of the National Campaign, Barbara Wootton, and not Michael Ramsey, who would introduce the Second Reading on 19 July. Lady Wootton, said her biographer, Ann Oakley, 'was implacably opposed to [the death penalty], as she was to almost all forms of violence'.[267] She was a woman driven always by a regard for the evidence,[268] and she proposed to argue on the evidence that the public imagery of murder and murderers was misinformed and that the death penalty did not deter.[269] She began:

> This is an extremely simple Bill and it will require very little exposition. I think I may take it that the substance of it is already familiar to every Member of your Lordships' House. The main effect of this Bill is to provide that an automatic sentence of life imprisonment shall follow upon any conviction for murder. The later clauses of the Bill provide that murders committed by members of the Armed Forces shall be in like case with those committed by civilians ... [Thereby realising the ambition of Major Lowther some forty years before]. The final clause of the Bill provides [following Henry Brooke's amendment] that the Bill shall remain in operation for only five years unless an Affirmative Resolution of both Houses of Parliament shall otherwise determine. ... I would say first that I am very well aware that there are grave moral issues involved in the principle of this Bill, and if I say very little about the moral issues it is not because I underestimate their force but because I hope that in the subsequent debate there are those whose views on moral questions will command greater respect than I would venture to claim in this House for my own [and she had in mind what the Archbishops of Canterbury and York might say]. ... I should like to remind the House that notwithstanding the Title of this Bill, and notwithstanding the fact that during this debate we shall be concerned, I am sure, almost exclusively with the efficacy of the death penalty, this is not a Bill for the abolition of the death penalty. This is a Bill for the abolition of those exceptions to the rule that the sentence for murder is life imprisonment. It is a Bill for the abolition of those exceptions which were contained in the Homicide Act 1957 [and here she recapitulated the earlier argument of Sydney Silverman].[270]

She recited how the long history of abolition had advanced by small increments; how the worst fears of the retentionists had never been realised; how Professor Sellin's work in the United States showed that abolition did not appear to lead to an increase in homicide; and how the 1957 Act was 'a disastrous failure ... [that] has produced not justice but anomalies' and which led to the execution of those 'who could not possibly have been described as professional criminals'. Abolition would entail taking only a very small step because so few people were actually executed each year.

She was to be countered by a number of peers, including Lord Dilhorne, who dismissed the argument that cited the small number of executions as irrelevant to their deterrent potential and declared that he found the anomalous state of the present law unobjectionable ('Rather than do something which might lead to more loss of innocent lives, might it not be better that the anomaly in sentence in particular cases should be accepted? But, if the law should not be left as it is, it can be argued that the right change to make would be to make non-capital murders capital and to improve the machinery for granting reprieves'[271]).

The Archbishop of York followed Robert Beloe's prompting and pronounced that:

> to adopt that which we condemn, and to kill the killer, is not, in my view, the best way of exacting retribution. I suspect that to act thus is to take on ourselves a measure of vengeance which is best left to the Deity. There is about capital punishment a dreadful irrevocability which belongs to no other sphere of justice. ... All of us – every one of us – stand under the judgement of God. I do not think we should ask any of our fellow citizens – Home Secretary, judge or hangman – to participate in a function which rightly does not belong to mortal man.[272]

The Archbishop of Canterbury said:

> I support this Bill. My first speech in your Lordships' House was made in July 1956, in support of the abolition of the death penalty. ... there ought to be beyond the penalty the possibility of reclamation. I mean the possibility of the person being alive, repentant and different. If this can happen in this world, and not only for the world to come, we should strive for that to be so. Secondly, there ought to be recognition of the fact that the taking of life as a penalty does devalue human life. It means society saying, in effect: "This man has killed someone. Very well; we will kill him too." This does not enhance the sacredness of human life. I believe that it derates it further. ... in another place, two successive Home Secretaries, different in their politics and different in their initial approach to the abolition question, have told how they have found intolerable moral issues in the distinction of sentence between capital and non-capital murder. On the one hand, a murderer kills while stealing, perhaps on a sudden, delirious impulse – the death penalty. On the other hand, a murderer poisons after loathsome, vicious premeditation – not the death sentence. If, penalties other than the death penalty were involved, the moral arbitrariness of the distinction might be swallowed. But where the penalty is sometimes to kill the murderer, sometimes to

sentence the murderer to death, and sometimes not, it seems that law and morality have gone apart on the very point where it is imperative for them to go together.

And Lord Parker talked about the unworkability of the Act:

It is said that the death penalty is a unique deterrent, and I should be the last person to vote in favour of the abolition of something which I believed was a really unique deterrent. But your Lordships probably know the figures. Out of some 170 murderers every year, only a minute percentage are ever hanged. After all, it is the certainty of punishment which is the only real deterrent. Secondly, murder is in quite a different category from, say, many other offences. I suppose that 90 per cent., or more, of all murders arise in some domestic situation which will never arise again, or in the course of some sexual crime.[273] Nothing, I venture to think, in those cases will be a deterrent at all.

It is always said that judges are reactionary; that they never want any change in the law. But they sit there every day seeing where the shoe pinches and where injustice is being done. For seven years I have presided in the Court of Criminal Appeal, to whom almost every capital murderer appeals, and for the last four of those seven years I have been so disgusted (if I may put it that way) with the anomalies that arise, with the injustices that are done as between man and man – one man is hanged and another, equally blameworthy, imprisoned for life – that I determined four years ago that something ought to be done, and I was in favour of abolition.

When one gets to that stage, there are only three courses open. The first is to amend in some respect the Homicide Act. I venture to think that that is quite impossible. It is impossible to legislate for every type of crime which may occur at any time in the future. Whatever one does, there will be anomalies.

The leaders of the Church and the Bench, of morality and the law, had thus come prominently to the fore, and theirs must have been a consequential role. Gerald Gardiner, the Lord Chancellor, noted in the debate that:

I believe that there has been a great change in informed opinion. Generally, our great enemies have been the Bishops – if they do not mind my saying that: I mean historically, of course – but there was a change in 1956, when the then most reverend Primate, the Archbishop of Canterbury, said he did not approve of complete abolition but was going to vote for the Second Reading. As I understand it – and I shall be corrected if I am wrong – since 1956 all the Bishops of the Convocation of Canterbury have voted for abolition, as have all the Bishops of the Convocation of York,[274] except one; and yesterday for the first time in English history a Lord Chief Justice spoke in favour of the Second Reading of a Bill to abolish capital punishment, saying – and I submit he was right – that as the Judges ought not to be required to work an Act which causes so much injustice, and as the only two alternatives are either to go back to what the law was fifteen years ago or to abolish the death penalty, the latter was the only thing to do, provided that the alternative was satisfactory.

On 20 July, the bill passed on Second Reading in the House of Lords by 204 votes to 104. The Lord Chief Justice, the Archbishop of Canterbury and 10 bishops voted for abolition. No bishop voted against it. On 26 October, it passed on Third Reading by 169 votes to 75. The Lord Chief Justice, the Archbishop of York and seven bishops voted for abolition. No bishop voted against it. The Murder (Abolition of Death Penalty) Act 1965 c.71[275] came into effect on 8 November. Hanging having been brought to an end, the Secretary of State acquired the power to determine the minimum length of time to be served.[276]

Epilogue

The National Campaign for the Abolition of the Death Penalty resolved to retain its funds and return to a state of suspended animation, to be revived if necessary after the expiration of the five-year moratorium introduced by Section 4 of the 1965 Act.[277] It had indeed to be revived in reply to a succession of attempts to introduce private member's bills and ten-minute motions to restore hanging,[278] particularly by Duncan Sandys, the Conservative Member for Norwood.[279] Capital punishment became contentious again in 1966[280] and then in 1968, and the National Campaign[281] and the Howard League[282] were obliged once more to mobilise themselves. By late 1968 and early 1969, the politics of abolition were becoming especially fraught as the moratorium was coming to a close; by-elections loomed in October and a general election was in the offing; another, much-publicised private member's bill was mooted, again by Duncan Sandys; and there were reports of a rise in the numbers of murders[283] (although they were still very low by contemporary standards: there had been 96 murders in 1968 compared with 90 in 1967 and 88 in 1966 and, the Cabinet Secretary advised the prime minister, 'No conclusion can be fairly drawn from these figures'[284]).

Capital punishment remained a volatile, politically awkward problem in the late 1960s, and the Labour Government vacillated about what it should do, just as other governments had done in the past. It was not at all comfortable that 'The parliamentary controversy over hanging could ... flare up again at time when electioneering has taken over politics'.[285]

The prime minister was cautious.[287] The Home Secretary was indecisive. The chief whip noted that the subject was 'likely to cause a great deal of emotion and little understanding of the facts'.[288] Yet a judgement had to be made about what action, if any, the government should take.

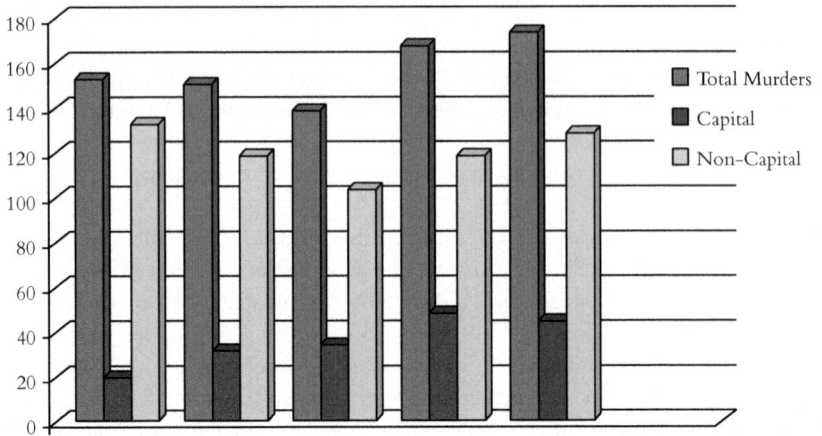

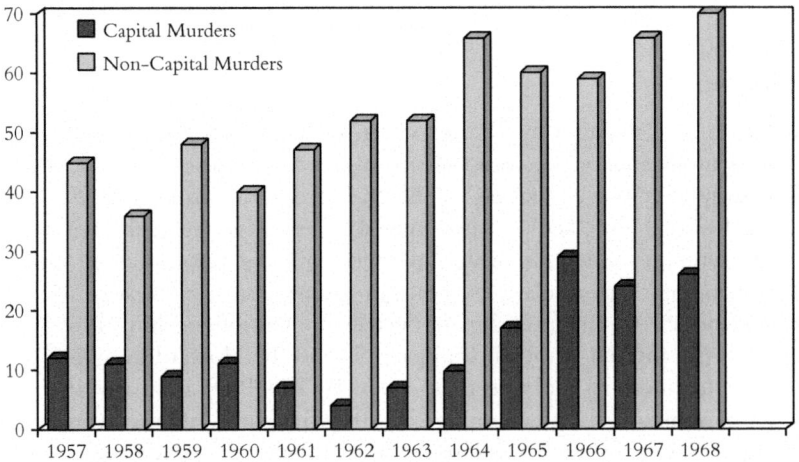

Figure 3.3 'Capital' and 'non-capital' murders 1957–1968[286]

The Home Secretary, James Callaghan, and the Secretary of State for Scotland urged 'the Government [to] take the initiative in bringing about the permanent abolition of capital punishment for murder':

> The essential case for abolition is in our view a moral one. Capital punishment is a barbarous penalty which the community has no right to exact, however heinous the crime. There are however other subsidiary arguments in favour of abolition. The death penalty is a denial of the principle underlying the rest of our penal thinking, that no criminal is beyond the hope of redemption. In the event of doubt arising about the verdict after the sentence has been carried out, there is no opportunity to right the wrong. We think that those who advocate capital punishment are under

Numbers per Million of Home Population

Murders in England and Wales

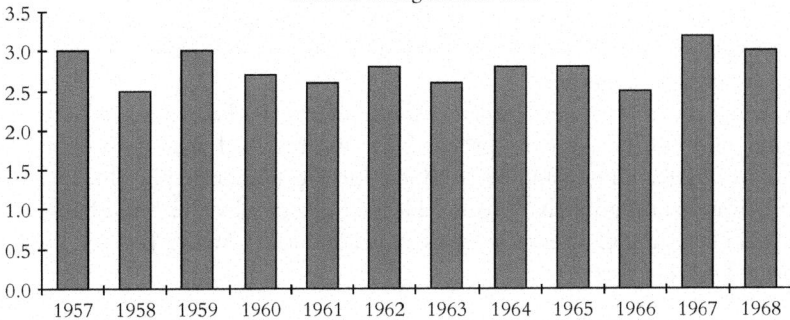

Figure 3.4 Murders in England and Wales

the onus of establishing that this barbarous penalty is a unique deterrent; but there is no conclusive evidence.[289]

But the cabinet remained uncertain about *when* precisely it would be best to act. Decisions were taken and reversed and reversed again. In May 1969 it was agreed to invite the Home Secretary 'to move the Resolutions required to continue the abolition of capital punishment permanently during the spill-over period towards the end of the present Session'.[290] James Callaghan duly noted that a second 'analysis from the Home Office Research Unit[291] ... was on the whole helpful from the government's point of view; and he had undertaken that he would publish this before capital punishment was next debated in Parliament'. The analysis should, he said, be published in October 1969 and the bill to make abolition permanent introduced in November before the general election: 'It would be better to introduce the resolutions during the spill-over period,[292] in order to get the issue which was unpopular in the country generally, out of the way as soon as possible'. That was a 'decision that should, however, remain confidential for the time being'.[293] It was a decision that Cabinet reassessed (in July it was decided that 'the precise timing of this would require further consideration in September'[294]) and then assessed again ('the resolutions on capital punishment should not be moved during the present Session'[295]). 'The Home Secretary', the prime minister was told in September, 'had already made representations to the Chief Whip urging that the Resolutions should not be made during the spill-over and suggesting that it might be politically advantageous to defer them until the beginning of 1970'[296] after the majority of the pending by-elections had taken place (five were to take place on 30 October alone[297]). Yet a government that deferred debate courted risk, and the cabinet secretary, Burke Trend, wondered 'if the matter waits for the new Session, must it then be mentioned in the Queen's Speech? And if so, is it then liable to attract more attention and to become a rather bigger issue than if it were disposed of relatively unobtrusively in the spill-over?'[298] Within a week, James Callaghan was reported again to have offered the provisional recommendation that the Order to make the 1965 Act permanent should be dealt with in the spill-over. And yet, at a further meeting, held in October, ten days after the new Session had begun, the decision to stall was again taken,[299] despite growing political pressure fuelled by statements made by Duncan Sandys.[300]

It was only in the penultimate month of the Parliamentary session that Cabinet did finally agree to proceed. It was resolved that debate in both Houses of Parliament would be conducted in December despite threats delivered privately and publicly[301] to the Home Secretary by the 'mild hanger',[302] Quintin Hogg, the Conservative spokesman on Home Affairs. James Callaghan informed cabinet that:

> Mr Quintin Hogg, had asked to see him on 24th November to discuss capital punishment. Mr Hogg had said that there would be great opposition within the Conservative Party to any proposal to make the Murder (Abolition of Death Penalty) Act 1965 ... permanent before the five-year period came to an end in July 1970. He thought they would vote against any resolutions to make the Act permanent before Christmas and urged that the Government should introduce a short Bill to extend the period by, say, a further 18 months, in order to bring the period to an end at a time well clear of the next General Election and so prevent capital punishment becoming an election issue.[303]

Capital punishment should not be made a party issue, Quintin Hogg was reported to have said. There could be no return to the 1957 Act, and the only choice was between making abolition permanent, new legislation retaining the death penalty in some form or, perhaps, extending the 1965 Act by a year and a half. Were he to become Home Secretary, he certainly would not operate a system of capital punishment without a Reprieve Board to advise him. But he did urge the Home Secretary 'not to introduce the resolutions before Christmas on the grounds that to do so would provoke the united hostility of the determined hangers, of those who thought that the experiment should run its full course, and of those who thought that the present Parliament was dead and had lost its authority'. But James Callaghan had by then become adamant:

> I challenged Quintin Hogg's statement that [such a step] would prevent capital punishment from becoming an election issue, and he gave no convincing answer to my suggestion that candidates would be faced with questions about their attitude, whatever action may or may not be taken between now and the date of the election. I told him that I did not think the groups he had mentioned would be assuaged any more easily by a debate in June rather than in December ... I suggested that it would also place him in an uncomfortable position since it would open his flank to Mr. Sandys and his followers, and said that I doubted whether he would

be able to carry the Conservative Party with him. I put it to him that he was attempting to walk in the middle of the road and was therefore liable to be knocked over. He replied that if we did not allow him to walk in the middle of the road he would walk on the right.[304]

James Callaghan pressed on. He reported to Cabinet on 4 December that:

> there were overwhelming arguments in favour of the early introduction of Resolution to make the Continuance of the Murder (Abolition of Death Penalty) Act 1965, permanent. There was no need to wait for further figures to become available; while too much reliance should not be placed on statistics when such small numbers were involved, the figures published in the Home Office research study "Murder: 1957 to 1968" would certainly not support the argument that the suspension of the death penalty had resulted in a substantial increase in the number of murders. To extend the five-year trial period by 18 months, as Mr. Quintin Hogg had suggested, would not in his view prevent capital punishment from becoming an election issue. He could see no merit in extending the period for another five years since at the end of this further period capital punishment was likely to be just as controversial an issue as it was now...[305]

The announcement of a debate was made simultaneously in both Houses of Parliament, on the very eve of that cabinet meeting. It might be a close-run thing. It certainly required political confidence. Lord Gardiner had written to Harold Wilson that there was a probability that, if the Conservatives did indeed vote as a party, 'we could be defeated in the Lords';[306] and there were indeed to be later rumours that the Opposition in the Lords was considering issuing an official whip against any government resolution on capital punishment.[307] *The Times* predicted a defeat.[308] But the Member of Parliament, Leo Abse, recollected that 'Jim Callaghan, the Home Secretary in 1969, was too shrewd a political operator to require any second reminder of the need at all costs to avoid capital punishment becoming an election issue: for taking away the death penalty for ever would be interpreted by many as a severe and intolerable deprivation. I knew in 1969 it was then or never'.[309]

The Home Secretary was determined. So was Gerald Gardiner. His private secretary, Michael Blair, recalled in interview that 'Gerald would have resigned from the Cabinet if they hadn't been willing to go ahead with this. He was able to hold them to ransom in effect. But he wasn't sure … after the relevant meetings that he would be able to come back with a result'.

On 16 December 1969, the Home Secretary moved that 'the Murder (Abolition of Death Penalty) Act 1965 shall not expire as otherwise provided by section 4 of that Act', and, by a 'thumping majority'[310] of 343 votes to 185, the House of Commons did at last so vote (50 Conservative Members were amongst those who voted in favour), and, although it was thought by some that the position was 'much more open'[311] in the House of Lords, their vote was mirrored two days later by 220 to 174 in the Upper House, Gerald Gardiner having spoken at length. He talked for 40 minutes, with conviction and as a lawyer, chronicling all the legislative steps which had culminated in the contradictions of the 1957 Act and their resolution in the 1965 Act. He talked about the ambiguity of the murder statistics and the uncertainty of the impact of the death penalty.[312] He ended:

> I have sought to deal with this matter by rational arguments. I have not involved myself in emotional arguments, those being the words used by people to describe other people's moral views with which they do not agree. But I should not like to conclude without making it plain that I do not think that the practice of putting men and women who are your prisoners to death, in cold blood, and telling them a fortnight beforehand that you are going to do so, is right. I believe it to be wrong; and I applaud the moral courage – which is not required in the same sense in this House – of those in another place (many of whom had their seats and their way of life to lose) ...[313]

'This', said Michael Blair, 'was his great moment on his way out ... he carried that debate. He listened to every debate, every speech for two days, on the Woolsack, in this ghastly uniform. And made an impassioned speech at the end and it was carried'. And Sir Derek Oulton, who had been Lord Gardiner's private secretary between 1961 and 1965, reflected in interview that 'I remember the night when the key vote was passed in the Lords, he was very, very emotional indeed'.

Conclusion

The long debates over capital punishment had continually foundered on the apparent dilemmas that deterrence could neither be proved to work nor not to work; that the experience of other states might or might not offer a useful precedent; that legislators had to choose whether to heed or steer public opinion; that the risk of even a minute increase in the number of killings might or might not be worth taking;[314] and that arguments based on the supposed sanctity of life made it equally possible to represent capital punishment as Christian or unchristian, appropriate or inappropriate, immoral or moral.[315] Even the protagonists were obliged sometimes to concede that the arguments and evidence were equivocal. For instance, the Executive Committee of the National Campaign for the Abolition of the Death Penalty concluded in the summer of 1960 that 'the murder rate figures, since the [1957] Act was brought in, could be made to prove or disprove any point of view. ...'[316] The Conservative Party advised its canvassers in the 1964 general election that 'In fact, as far as can be judged, the changes in the Homicide Act have made little difference to the incidence of murder...'[317] And Barbara Wootton, who had opened the debate on abolition in the House of Lords in 1965, herself remarked that: 'although much of the discussion turned on the efficacy of capital punishment as a deterrent, the ultimate issue is a matter of moral judgement. Arguments about deterrence are invariably inconclusive, inasmuch as nowhere in the world is there evidence of a stable correlation between the death penalty and the frequency of murder'.[318]

Something deeper was evidently at stake than disputes about statistics and the practical efficacy of the death penalty. How else could one account for their interminable and irreconcilable character? It was as if they stirred up sentiments of symbolic threat and danger quite disproportionate to the actual numbers of homicides and executions involved. The gallows was either a powerful bulwark of social order and stability or a barbaric relic unbefitting a civilised society, but it was never merely a technical means of implementing a sanction against a very small number of people.[319] It raised profoundly moral questions that roused men and women (David Garland talked about 'punishment's connection to the binary oppositions of sacred and profane, good and evil, orderly and disorderly'[320]). It raised troubling political questions that went straight to the role and responsibilities of the state. Having read drafts of these two chapters, Peter ('Tank') Waddington, Professor of Social Policy at the University of Wolverhampton, asked:

> why the fate of a handful of murderers aroused so much passion? At the time all this was being debated road fatalities were running at around 8,000 pa. It would be an interesting, albeit gruesome task, to calculate how many people were killed on British roads whilst parliament sat deliberating this issue. On the face of it, the whole thing – abolitionist and retentionist – seems supremely marginal. So, what explains it? It seems to me that murder and capital punishment lie right at the centre of the fundamental paradox of state legitimacy. The state claims to protect us as a Leviathan against wrongdoers, but it also claims to protect us – under the rule of law – against arbitrary state power. Loss of life is the ultimate wrong from which we seek protection and so the state goes to extraordinary lengths to find murderers and punish them, hopefully thereby to deter would-be murderers. Retentionists give primacy to this side of the equation. Yet, if an innocent person is convicted of murder and loses *their* life, then this too must be the ultimate affront to the rule of law, to which abolitionists draw attention. I think this is genuinely the horns of a dilemma: we can't have it both ways – complete protection without risk of arbitrary state power. Abolitionists (and I am one!) try to hide behind the 'evidence', but this is no protection because the rights of citizens are indivisible, hence if one person is murdered when they might have been spared, or one person is wrongly executed, then the wrong is done and legitimacy is damaged.[321]

These were questions so irresoluble and so fraught that governments chose not to venture out and hazard electoral defeat or defeat in Parliament. It was instead incumbent on a succession of dogged individuals – William Ewart, Vyvyan Adams, Sydney Silverman, Sir Frank Soskice and Lord Gardiner – to act as champions against or within governments cowed by *Realpolitik*. If the abolition of capital punishment was an instance of the liberal hour, it was a vicarious liberalism long protracted, a liberalism which was a century or more old, an act finally enabled and spurred on by government, but not performed by government itself. There clearly had to be *some* form of action – the 1957 Act had become quite untenable and its life was coming to an end. Defendants were still being sentenced to death (recall Figure 3.2) but the Home Secretary was refusing to hang anyone, and he was the first ever to have done so. The Lord Chancellor was threatening to resign. The archbishops and the Lord Chief Justice were very publicly opposed to capital punishment. But political action lacked popular support. It risked alienating the electorate. A private member's bill and a free vote were perhaps the only solution.

Although the campaigns to mitigate and ultimately eliminate the death penalty may in consequence have looked like the struggles of lone men against the state, much larger forces were actually deployed in their rear. Sydney Silverman had been briefed by the National Campaign at almost every turn. He had been aided by the Church. He had been assisted by the state. He may have been solitary at the beginning, but he was far from solitary at the end, and it was the support he secured, sometimes *malgré lui*, which accounted for his success. Indeed, many Home Secretaries and others (including Sir Ernest Gowers and Lord Gardiner) in the twentieth century were advocates of – or in office became converted to – abolition, although they had often to be guarded in what they said and did.

763 people were executed in England and Wales in the twentieth century. The very last to be hanged were Peter Allen and Gwynne Evans for the murder of John West, and they died on 13 August 1964,[322] in the fading days of a Conservative Government, and whilst Henry Brooke was Home Secretary. There was then a sea change. A new Labour Government and a new Secretary of State came into office two months later, and Sir Frank vowed never to allow another execution to take place. With Lord Gardiner, he effectively abolished the death penalty, at first unofficially in 1964, and then officially (albeit provisionally), in November 1965. England and Wales at that point joined the vanguard of an ever-growing number of abolitionist states (only 12 had abolished capital punishment for crimes in times of peace by 1965), and they were in their turn to be followed by a great retinue of 58 states between 1965 and 1995,[323] and another 37 after that. By 1969, another Home Secretary, James Callaghan, had become convinced that the matter of the so-called five-year trial period must finally and unequivocally be settled and in December he was brave enough to deliver the *coup de grâce*. Three months later still, he asked the Criminal Law Revision Committee, in a reference on offences against the person, to look at the crime and penalty for murder in the light of what was called the permanent abolition of the death penalty.[324] That, said Sir Louis Blom-Cooper, the prime insider, 41 years later, was 'the real cut-off', and it

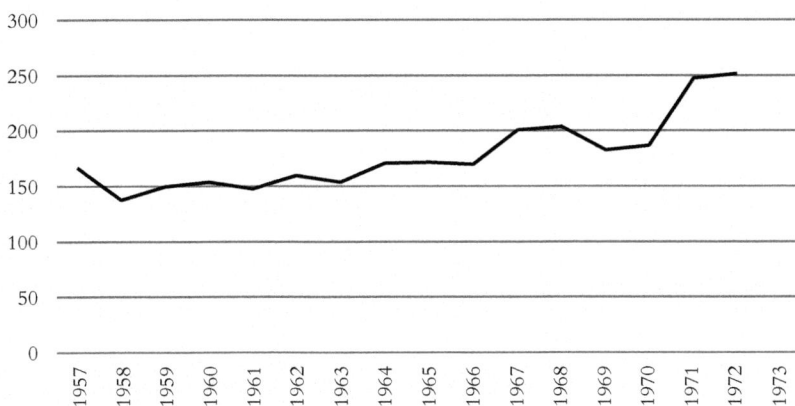

Figure 3.5 Murders known to the police 1957-1972

was a cut-off that was looked upon as the lifting of a pall by many officials in the Home Office. David Faulkner reflected in 1991:

> The work of the Office, and especially of the Criminal Departments and the Prison Service, is no longer darkened by the shadow of capital punishment. The notorious executions of the '50s and early '60s – Derek Bentley, Ruth Ellis, James Hanratty – affected the whole Department, and there was a universal sense of relief when capital punishment for murder was abolished in 1964 and its abolition was made permanent in 1969.[325]

What of the murder rate after the abolition of hanging? As ever, it was ambiguous. The numbers of murders known to the police certainly continued to climb erratically but steadily after 1965, although they were never absolutely large, and they climbed less steeply than other offences of violence. And then, after 1989, they declined again.[326] Murder is an offence with its own dynamic.[327] It would no doubt still be difficult to draw any unequivocal conclusions about what those numbers portended, and whether or not offending had been prevented, but, after all, the debate about abolition had never ever centred solely on the case for deterrence.

In the next two case studies in liberal legislation, lone figures again seemed to play their parts in the cockpit of Parliament, but they too were sustained, advised, briefed and indeed parried by organisations behind the scenes. In that sense they were the practical face of organisational conflict, an expression of what has been called inter-organisational negotiation,[328] mediating the play of significant institutions in and around the moral politics of the time. I shall turn first to abortion law reform and David Steel, its champion, and then to Lord Arran and the reform of the law on male homosexuality. Each came to represent much larger configurations of religious, professional and moral belief, and their resolution changed the landscape of regulation in England and Wales.

Notes

1 Barbara Wootton's speaking notes for the debate on abolition in the House of Lords in 1965 recited that 'Total abolition a small step inasmuch as it means end to hanging about two or three people annually; a big step inasmuch as it may save one or two lives. Present law cannot be regarded as effective deterrent: chance of a murderer being hung is now less than 2 per cent'. in Correspondence and papers of Lord Gardiner conc. the National Campaign for the Abolition of the Death Penalty 1927–1969, Add. 56455 The British Library.

2 Answer to Parliamentary Question: HC Deb 14 December 1964 Vol. 704 cc22–3W22W.

3 He was to speak in favour of abolition in debate in July 1965. See HL Deb 20 July 1965 Vol. 268 cc590–714.

4 So it was that Captain Duncan, Member of Parliament for South Angus, chose in the debate on the death penalty to quote Lord Cooper's observation to the Royal Commission: 'Twice over in my life I have experienced what looked like, and probably would have been, the development of a very ugly situation in connection with gangster warfare, which was nipped in the bud by sternly repressive measures and by the execution of the death sentence in several cases'. (HC Deb 16 May 1956 Vol. 552 cc2019–169)

5 The Lord Chief Justice, Lord Goddard, had said 'We must remember that the police of this country are armed with only a short baton – that is the only weapon they have against gunmen and other people who do not hesitate, if they think it necessary, to shoot and take the lives of policemen'. (HL Deb 10 July 1956 Vol. 198 cc679–843).

6 Thus the files of the Conservative Party held at the Bodleian Library contain an undated letter that opened 'Re the Murderers Protection Bill. Are you surprised at the bye-election results? Murderers lives are precious. Your tory government has passed a law making it illegal to hang a diabolical murderer. ...' And the Prime Minister, Sir Anthony Eden, received a letter dated 20 February 1956: 'I am a member of the Conservative Party and utterly deplore the recent decision by the Government to abolish hanging. It is, in my opinion, just another "give way" by the Conservative Government to the bleatings of the socialists. When all is said and done the country was behind the Government on this subject. Why then was a free vote given to a bunch of weak-kneed individuals?' And there were many more of the same ilk.

7 J. Christoph; 'Capital Punishment and British Party Responsibility', *Political Science Quarterly*, *op. cit.*, 32.

8 However, 1969 was not to be the complete end. There were between 1969 and 1988 fourteen unsuccessful attempts made in Parliament to reintroduce the death penalty.

9 Lord Windlesham (1993); *Responses to Crime*, Vol. 2, Oxford: Clarendon Press, 86.

10 Lord Silkin said in July 1956 that 'we have moved from stage to stage along a road towards constant amelioration of the brutalities of punishment'. HL Deb 10 July 1956 Vol. 198 cc679–843.

11 HC Deb 16 February 1956 Vol. 548 cc2536–655.

12 HC Deb 21 December 1964 Vol. 704 cc870–1010.

13 Although he was reluctant to take a prominent role or campaign in individual cases before the Church as a whole had declared its support for abolition. In July 1964, for example, he wrote to one who had asked him to support a petition for the reprieve of a convicted murderer: '... I am myself in favour of the abolition of capital punishment, and supported the Bill for abolition in Parliament a few years ago, and I think the Law is very unsatisfactory. At present the Home Secretary has the great responsibility of considering sentences and weighing all the claims to clemency. When the facts are before him together with all the considerations drawn from local knowledge, circumstances and feeling, I do not feel that it is helpful for widespread petitions to go before

him. I am sure you will understand my meaning'. (Lambeth Palace Archives. Ramsey 33: 250)

14 And he would dragoon them on other liberalising issues such as homosexual law reform (see O. Chadwick (1990); *Michael Ramsey A Life*, Oxford: Clarendon Press, 148).

15 *Ibid*, 157, 159.

16 Carpenter talked about how Ramsey's 'liberality ... burst forth ... to the great good of the nation. The Britain of Harold Wilson's Labour government somehow made this possible, and it is from 1965 that one finds Ramsey providing a strong lead on a number of important social matters – the passing of a new law protecting homosexuals from legal persecution following the recommendation of the Wolfenden Report; ... the abolition of capital punishment ...' E. Carpenter; *Cantuar, op. cit.*, 528.

17 For example, the archive of Archbishop Ramsey's papers in the library of Lambeth Palace is replete with briefings from the National Council. James Christoph said of the National Council for the Abolition of the Death Penalty, it 'saturated the country with its message' and he proceeded to claim that it affected public opinion. He cited polls conducted by Mass-Observation in April 1948 and February 1956 which showed that the percentage of support for capital punishment declined from 69% to 45% and approval of a trial suspension of capital punishment increased from 13% to 69%. J. Christoph; 'Capital Punishment and British Party Responsibility', *op. cit.*, 27. He may have been a little sanguine. In late 1964, just before attempts were renewed to introduce abolitionist legislation, it was reported to the National Council that a National Opinion Poll taken between 5 and 9 November showed that 65.6% of the public were in favour of retaining the death penalty, 21.4% in favour of abolition and 13% 'don't know'. Minutes of the Meeting of the National Campaign for the Abolition of Capital Punishment Executive Committee 24 November 1964 in the House of Commons.

18 And, in particular, E. Gibson and S. Klein (1961); *Murder*, London: Home Office. The Lord Chancellor, Lord Gardiner, drew comfort from what had been said. It is evident that he had studied the report closely. In his undated notes for a speech to be delivered in the debate on the 1965 Murder (Abolition of Death Penalty) Bill, he reflected that 'The Home Office Research Unit report "Murder" contains full figures analysing murders known to the police up to the end of 1960 and comparing the position before and after the Homicide Act ... It will be seen ... that there has been some increase since the Homicide Act in the total number of murders. Since over 80% of murders are non-capital this increase is more obvious in the non-capital category than in the capital category. To what extent the increase in the non-capital category is due to the removal of the death penalty for this category in 1957, rather than to other factors quite unrelated to the penalty, it is impossible to say. What is significant is that the proportion of capital to non-capital murders has altered very little [underlined in pencil] since the Homicide Act. Such increases in the murder rate as have taken place have been very much less than the increase in other crimes ... between 1931 and 1960 the annual number of murders per million of population fluctuated between 3.1 and 3.9 ... ; whereas the number of indictable offences as a whole, rose from an annual average of 6,047 per million of population in the period in 1931–1940 to 16,216 in 1960 ...' (In the Gardiner Papers, British Library).

19 See *The Howard Association Annual Report*, 1897, 3.

20 Its very first annual report of 1867 recorded that the Association's efforts had been focused on 'the promotion of reformatory and remunerative prison labour, and the abolition of capital punishment'.

21 See E. Tuttle (1961); *The Crusade Against Capital Punishment, op. cit.*, 46.

22 Under the spell of what was then current forensic psychiatry, the view of some its officers was that murder was the result of mental disturbance, not rational planning, and was not amenable to normal deterrence. Hugh Klare, its Secretary, claimed

in 1956 that 'There are three types of murderers. By far the largest proportion are psychotic, and no less than 70% of all suspected or proved murderers either commit suicide in circumstances providing clear evidence of a disordered mind, or are found insane before, during, or after trial'. Letter to *The British Medical Journal* (1956); Vol. 1, No 4962, 349.

23   One such meeting took place in October 1946 under the joint auspices of the Friends' Penal Reform Committee, The Howard League for Penal Reform and The National Council for the Abolition of the Death Penalty. The chairman was Lord Chorley, who would just have retired as the Sir Ernest Cassel Professor of Commercial and Industrial Law at the London School of Economics. He was to play a major role in the debates that took place in the House of Lords. The principal speakers included Esther Watson, the Honorary Secretary of the Friends' Penal Reform Committee; Cicely Craven, the Honorary Secretary of the Howard League for Penal Reform; and Frank Dawtry, the Secretary of The National Council for the Abolition of the Death Penalty.

24   Its *Annual Reports* for 1960–1961 stated on p. 3 that 'Since the revival of the National Campaign against Capital Punishment at the end of 1960, the League has been glad to co-operate closely by sending a representative to the Executive Committee of the Campaign, supplying background information from its records maintained over the years, and helping with arrangements for meetings. Since the League is concerned with the wider aspects of the penal system, and with its limited funds and staff must keep a balance between its various activities, it welcomes the work of an organisation which can devote all its efforts to the one end'. They also recorded that its files of press cuttings of murders had been put to 'particularly good use', serving as the main data basis for the analysis of murders since the Homicide Act conducted by Dr T.P. Morris and Mr L. Blom-Cooper, and published in *The Observer* in April 1961. Dr Glanville Williams, they reported, also used the cuttings as the foundation for his lecture to members of the League on "The Workings of the Homicide Act" which was published in the 1961 issue of the *Howard Journal.* 'Both studies have proved extremely helpful in illustrating the anomalies and injustice of the Homicide Act. …' Again, at the end of 1963, Hugh Klare prepared 'Notes on Capital Punishment' to spur on the campaign.

25   It is significant, for instance, that Hugh Klare would report more than once about how he had acted to correct any impression that the League was uncritically and wholly committed to the mitigation of severe sentences. In July 1961, the minutes of the 401st meeting of the Executive Committee: 'COMPENSATION FOR VICTIMS OF VIOLENCE Mrs Howard reminded the Committee that this idea has originated with Miss Margery Fry. The Working Party set up by the Home Office to examine the subject had just published its report. This, however, consisted mainly of an enumeration of the difficulties involved in different schemes examined. "Justice" had decided to enquire further into the matter and had set up their own committee, of which Mr Hewitt was a member. It seemed a subject which should be further pursued, especially as it helped to contradict the accusation often levelled against the League that it gave no consideration to the victims of attacks'. Again, it was recorded five months later in the minutes of the 405th meeting of the Executive Committee: 'Diminished responsibility Mr Klare felt that the section on diminished responsibility in the Homicide Act had resulted in a number of sentences of comparatively short fixed sentences which, seeing that the people who had committed these crimes were seriously disturbed, might constitute a real danger to the community. He thought that the League should suggest a change in the law to the effect that manslaughter due to diminished responsibility should be liable to an indeterminate sentence. This would also show that the League, which was concerned to abolish capital punishment, was equally concerned to protect the public. He thought that he might write a letter to the

Home Secretary at an opportune moment, and release the content to the press. The Committee approved of this proposal'.

26 It reported afterwards that '. ... The League's own part in the abolition of capital punishment is difficult to assess. It was different in the pioneering days of Roy Calvert. It was he who really posed the problem in rational terms for the first time. His analysis of the statistics then available was the great break-through and the beginning of the modern debate. And although fuller and more sophisticated information has since become available, the case has basically remained the same. The League's task has been to put that case in a reasonable and moderate way and make all the relevant information available to all who needed it. For this purpose a number of short pamphlets were printed. ... ' *Howard League Annual Report* 1969–70, 2.

27 It was agreed in 1961, for instance, to exchange representatives who would act as observers on the executive committees of the two bodies: Frank Dawtry attended meetings of the Howard League, and Hugh Klare the meetings of the National Council. Minutes of the Meeting of the Executive Committee of the National Council, 28 March 1961 at the House of Commons.

28 For example, the Executive Committee of the National Council noted 'that the Howard League was to be more active on this subject in the future'. Minutes of the Meeting of the Executive Committee 15 November 1960 at the House of Commons.

29 See E. Roy Calvert; 'Murder and the Death Penalty', *The Nation*, October 16 1929, 407.

30 'My purpose is not a sentimental one', Calvert had written in 1927, '[m]y objection to the death penalty is based upon the conviction that it is both futile and immoral'. E. R. Calvert (1927); *Capital Punishment in the Twentieth Century*, London: G. P. Putnam's Sons, preface to the first edition. He had prepared a small, unpublished compendium of speakers' notes for those who were about to campaign for abolition. It listed the law on capital punishment, mapped the spread of abolition (starting with Holland in 1870 and Italy in 1889), and marshalled the arguments and counter-arguments that might surface as the campaign advanced. On p. 5, for example, he observed that the deterrent effect of the death penalty decreased as its certainty decreased and claimed that hanging was the least certain of all punishments (between 1909 and 1913, there had been 783 murders known to the police, 510 persons tried for murder, 143 sentenced to death, and 79 actually executed): '*A murderer, therefore, has nine chances out of ten escaping the death penalty*' (italics in the original)). On p. 9, and wholly consonant with the teachings of the Society of Friends, was his suggestion that speakers might conclude that capital punishment, 'is immoral and unchristian. The whole social meaning of Christian is that our attitude to any man, no matter how evil or depraved he may be, must be one of uncompromising love i.e. it must be redemptive'. *Speakers' Notes*, National Council for the Abolition of the Death Penalty, London, 1925. Box 463/14 /1543, Archives of the Religious Society of Friends.

31 See his obituary in *The Times*, July 18, 1933. It had been his argument that capital punishment defeated its own object: it 'always militates against certainty of conviction. The death penalty is so horrible and the danger of inflicting an irrevocable punishment upon an innocent person so real, that ... juries hesitate to convict and often return verdicts contrary to the evidence ... the abolition of capital punishment and the substitution of a penalty which eliminated sentiment and commanded a greater measure of public support would do much to increase that certainty of conviction upon which the reduction of violent crime depends'. E. Roy Calvert; 'Murder and the Death Penalty', *op. cit.*, 406.

32 Its Chairman wrote to the Editor of *The New Statesman* on 22 July 1957 to say that 'I should be grateful if you would allow me to make it clear that we are continuing the Campaign until capital punishment has been abolished. ...'

33 Lord Altrincham had written to Lord Gardiner on 11 January 1957 '... As you say, the outcome of present discussions in Parliament about the death penalty is uncertain; but I stick to my view that the issue is, in effect, settled'. (Correspondence and papers of Lord Gardiner conc. the National Campaign for the Abolition of the Death Penalty 1927–1969, Add. 56455 The British Library.)

34 Letter of 11 January 1957, Gardiner Papers, British Library.

35 Victor Gollancz, 1893–1967, was a schoolmaster, teaching at Repton, where he was dismissed for his airing of political ideas by the Headmaster, Geoffrey Fisher, later the retentionist Archbishop of Canterbury. He joined the publishing firm of Benn Brothers in 1921, and then branched out to establish his own publishing house seven years later. As a socialist, he published a number of left-wing books and, eventually, a series, The Left Book Club, that was initiated in 1936. He founded or joined a number of organisations, including the National Committee for Rescue from Nazi Terror (1943), (with John Collins), Christian Action (1946), the Jewish Society for Human Service (1948), and the Association for World Peace (1951). He joined the National Council for the Abolition of the Death Penalty in 1955. (Based on the entry by Sheila Hodges in *The Oxford Dictionary of National Biography*, http://www.oxforddnb.com/view/article/33446) His case for abolition was simple and passionate and redolent of the argument put forward in 1930 by Barr, the Chairman of the Select Committee: 'It is doubtful whether as many irrelevancies are talked on any other topic as that on capital punishment. Almost everything that is said about it is irrelevant: absolutely everything, indeed, except one thing only. Nineteen and a half centuries ago a woman was taken in adultery and brought to Christ by a mob of her fellow-countrymen. ... he spoke a word that is still, perhaps, the greatest word ever spoken: he said "He that is without sin among you, let him first cast a stone at her." ... Murder will progressively cease (it may never cease altogether) as a habit of spiritual and physical gentleness becomes more and more instinctive in the human mind – as the very idea of violence, and above all of the ultimate, comes to seem, more and more, "something out of the question": or something, rather, that could simply never enter into anybody's heart or head. ... if the continued existence, anywhere in the world, of any sort of humane civilisation, of "civilisation" itself, were the matter at issue, and if the price for preserving it appeared ... to be the deliberate torture of a single child – the overwhelming majority ... would ... refuse, without the slightest hesitation, so much as to the consider the possibility. For you cannot preserve civilisation by an act that essentially negates it. ...' V. Gollancz (1955); *Capital Punishment: The heart of the matter*, London: Victor Gollancz, 1, 2 5 and 6. Gollancz was an assiduous campaigner, sending, for example, copies of Gerald Gardiner's *Capital Punishment as a Deterrent and the Alternative* (which he had published) to a number of peers, including Lord Beveridge, at a time of the debate on capital punishment.

36 He gave them free accommodation, for instance.

37 Gerald Gardiner, 1900–1990, was called to the Bar in 1925, and became a QC in 1948. He was a Member of the Lord Chancellor's Law Reform Committee, 1952–63. In 1960, he successfully defended the publishers of *Lady Chatterly's Lover* against a prosecution under the Obscene Publications Act, 1959; and Leon Uris in what was in effect the first trial centred on the Holocaust in 1964. He became Chairman of the Bar Council in 1958 and 1959. He joined the Haldane Society, and then became one of the founders of the Society of Labour Lawyers, of which he became chairman; and of Justice, the British branch of the International Commission of Jurists. He had stood unsuccessfully for Parliament in 1951, but was made a peer by Harold Wilson in 1963, becoming Lord Chancellor in 1964. (Based on the entry by Norman Marsh in *The Oxford Dictionary of National Biography*, http://www.oxforddnb.com/view/article/40090 and the entry in *Who was Who*, http://www.ukwhoswho.com.gate2.library.lse.ac.uk/view/article/oupww/whowaswho/U164420/GARDINER?index=1&results=QuicksearchResults

&query=0). In 1956, Gerald Gardiner published *Capital Punishment as a Deterrent: and the Alternative* (London: Victor Gollancz) in which he dilated on deterrence and the difficulty of establishing degrees of murder.

38 John Collins, 1905–1982, was ordained in 1928, became chaplain at Sidney Sussex College, Cambridge, and then Dean of Oriel College, Oxford, in 1938, the year he joined the Labour Party. His faith and politics were to be fused in Christian Action, an organisation he founded in 1946, and, attracted to his stance, two years later, Clement Attlee appointed him Canon of St. Paul's. Christian Action was a small but vigorous campaigning body which gave support, *inter alia*, to the abolition of capital punishment. (Based on the entry by Trevor Beeson in *The Oxford Dictionary of National Biography*, http://www.oxforddnb.com/view/article/30954?docPos=8)

39 Christopher Hollis, 1902–1977, was Conservative MP for the Devizes division of Wiltshire between 1945 and 1955.

40 Arthur Koestler, 1905–1983, a prominent public intellectual in the 1960s, had been the *News Chronicle* correspondent during the Spanish Civil War and had been captured and condemned to death by the Fascists in 1937. He reported that he had expected every day to be shot. See his *Darkness at Noon* (1940); London: Cape.

41 Reginald Paget, 1908–1990, was called to the Bar in 1934, becoming a QC in 1947. He was elected Labour MP for Northampton in 1945 and remained a Member until 1974 when he became a peer. He was co-author with Sydney Silverman of a book about the infamous murder by Christopher Craig and Derek Bentley in 1953. (Based on the entry by Anthony Howard in *The Oxford Dictionary of National Biography*, http://www.oxforddnb.com/view/article/39854)

42 At its rebirth, the Executive Committee 'agreed … that a well-known Conservative MP would be an asset to the Committee: Christopher Chataway, Geoffrey Johnson Smith and Julian Critchley were put forward as possible supporters'. Minutes of the Meeting of the Executive Committee 19 July 1960 at the House of Commons. In the event, the Executive Committee recruited Julian Critchley, Jeremy Thorpe and Wayland Young, thereby having as members one Liberal, two Conservative and two Labour Members of Parliament.

43 Minutes of the Meeting of the National Campaign for the Abolition of Capital Punishment Executive Committee 21 November 1961 at 90 Eaton Place. The chief interests of the Eighth Marquess of Hertford, 1930–1997, were listed in *Who's Who* as estate management and fox hunting.

44 John Grigg, second Baron Altrincham, 1924–2001, was a journalist and historian, writing for *The Guardian* and *The Times* newspapers and publishing a number of political biographies. He had aspired unsuccessfully to become a Conservative Member of Parliament but, on the death of his father in 1955, he succeeded to the peerage and became what his biographer called a radical Tory. (Based on Geoffrey Wheatcroft's entry in *The Oxford Dictionary of National Biography*, http://www.oxforddnb.com/view/article/76657?docPos=2)

45 See *The Times*, 12 January 1962.

46 He was, for example, the director of the Edinburgh Festival in 1961; a television presenter on arts programmes; and the first Chancellor of the new University of York.

47 *The Times*, 8 December 1960. Lord Hinchingbrooke and the Bishop of Birmingham had declined to join.

48 There had earlier been a lengthy analysis of murder printed in *The Observer* and reproduced in pamphlet form in April 1956. The eight-page article, 'Patterns of Murder: A Five-Year Survey of Men and Women Executed in England, Scotland and Wales (1949–53)', by 'Vigil', listed cases *seriatim* and then concluded that murder was not the crime of the criminal classes but *crimes passionelles* or the crimes of 'the disordered mind'. It was not premeditated, the result of malice aforethought, but more commonly

the outcome of mental instability (although it was not possible to classify them into distinct categories of murder): 'the execution of the mentally abnormal on the pretext that they do not fit into the traditional classification of insanity contradicts the practice of other civilised countries and is morally indefensible' (p. 9).

49 Minutes of the Meeting of the Executive Committee 19 July 1960 at the House of Commons.

50 'The need for answering all hostile letters in the local press was stressed. Mrs Howard reported that the Howard League would be unable to undertake this work in a general way. The Campaign office was instructed to open a subscription with Durrants for cuttings of all letters and leading articles on capital punishment from all papers, national and local, and Mr Hewitt, Mr Kirk and Canon Carpenter offered to answer'. Minutes of the Meeting of the Executive Committee, 2 May 1961 at the House of Commons.

51 Calvert's case, to be found in his *Capital Punishment in the Twentieth Century, op. cit.*, rested principally on the arguments that there was no statistical evidence of a deterrent effect, and that the death penalty was, as he said in the opening page of the preface to the first edition, both '*futile* and *immoral*' (emphasis added).

52 Those notes reminded speakers that 'abolition had not caused an increase in murder in a single European country: in most instances abolition has been followed by a decrease ... Those who support Capital Punishment claim that without it there would be an increase in murder. ... It is not denied that the fear of death is a deterrent. But this does not justify Capital Punishment even on grounds of expediency unless it can be proved to be the most effective deterrent... In spite of Capital Punishment we still have murders. There have been about 150 murders a year in England for fifty years. ... A strong argument against the Death penalty is that it is irrevocable and an innocent man may be hanged. ... Capital Punishment inflicts suffering upon prison officials who have to carry out the sentence. ... Most authorities agree that the carrying out of a Capital Sentence in a Prison, and the period of waiting between sentence and execution has a bad effect on other prisoners. ... Capital Punishment inflicts terrible suffering upon the innocent relatives of the condemned person. ... '. (Capital Punishment Speakers' Notes)

53 In July 1964, one of the many leaflets they issued read:

THE BRISTOL CAMPAIGN FOR THE ABOLITION OF CAPITAL
PUNISHMENT

HANGING'S NO ANSWER

GWYNNE OWEN EVANS (age 24)   due to be hanged
PETER ANTHONY ALLEN (age 21)   during August

These two young men were convicted of killing and robbing a 53 year old man in Lancashire. Had they killed without stealing they could not have been sentenced to death.

Two young men were hanged last December for a similar crime.

These and other hangings clearly did not deter these two young men.

Statistics show that hanging is not a unique deterrent.

Hanging is demoralising and degrading.

Hanging is an uncivilised form of punishment.

Hanging should be at once abolished.

54 See, for example, the report of the dismissal of appeals in *The Times*, 25 October 1960.

55 The 18-year-old Teddy Boy, George Forsyth, was tried with others in 1960 for the robbery and murder of Alan Jee. See '"No Word Of Remorse" By Young Men On Murder Charge "Victim Left Bleeding On Footpath"', *The Times*, 21 September 1960. A letter was published on 1 November 1960 by a number of imposing grandees

arguing that 'There could be no greater affront to the Christian or the humanist conscience than to kill, in cold blood, a youth of 18, whatever his crime'. It was signed by many members of the National Council: Kingsley Amis, Linton Andrews, A. J. Ayer, Gerald Barry, Leonard Birmingham, Edward Carpenter, Hugh Casson, L. John Collins, John Freeman, Victor Gollancz, Gilbert Harding, Harewood, Harmsworth, Jacquetta Hawkes, Christopher Hollis, Christmas Humphreys, Julian Huxley, Augustus John, Rosamond Lehmann, J. B. Priestley, Ravensdale Of Kedleston, Michael Redgrave, Russell, Donald O. Soper, Stephen Spender, Sybil Thorndike, Richard M. Titmuss, Edward R. Wickham, Bishop of Middleton, Leonard Woolf, and Wootton of Abinger.

56 An amendment, supported by 80 MPs, was tabled to the Criminal Justice Bill then moving through Parliament (see *The Times*, 12 December 1960) It read: 'That this House places on record its profound regret that the Secretary of State for the Home Department failed to advise Her Majesty the Queen to exercise Her Royal Prerogative of mercy in the cases of Francis Forsyth and Norman Harris, the first of whom was only a month or two over eighteen years of age and the other twenty-three years of age, both of whom were said by the learned counsel who prosecuted them to have had no intention to kill, and one of whom, namely, Norman Harris, was admitted to have struck no blow and was not present when any fatal act of violence was committed'. (HC Deb 20 December 1960 Vol. 632 cc1069–72) Forsyth was never the less executed. (Apparently, it was a convention that sentences under review could not be the subject of parliamentary questions (see *The Times*, Wednesday 15 February 1961)). The Bill was to become The Criminal Justice Act 1961, c. 39, on 19 July 1961. Its long title was 'An Act to amend the law with respect to the powers of courts in respect of young offenders; to make further provision as to the treatment of prisoners and other persons committed to custody, including provision for their supervision after discharge, and the management of prisons, approved schools and other institutions; to re-enact with modifications and additions certain statutory provisions relating to the removal, return and supervision of prisoners within the British Islands; and for purposes connected with the matters aforesaid'.

57 Antony Howard, one of his biographers, was evidently not sure about the matter: 'The suspicion, at least in liberal circles, was that Rab himself was a secret abolitionist. But there was scant sign of this in the various speeches he made on the floor of the House. ...' A. Howard (1987); *RAB: The Life of R.A. Butler*, London: Jonathan Cape, 253.

58 He informed the cabinet that 'pressure might develop for a debate to be held before the Christmas recess on the question of capital punishment. The Opposition had ... tabled an amendment to the Criminal Justice Bill to raise the age below; which sentence of death may not be passed and that amendment would afford an opportunity for a full discussion on the death penalty. It would be preferable to avoid having a separate debate on this subject'. CONCLUSIONS of a Meeting of the Cabinet held' at Admiralty' House S.W. 1, on Thursday 8 December 1960, at 10.30 a.m. C.C.(60) 62nd conclusions.

59 He went on 'Mr. Sydney Silverman, M.P., has had on the Order Paper for some time a Motion criticising my decision to let the law take its course in the recent cases of Harris and Forsyth – Forsyth being only eighteen years of age. I have avoided a debate on this Motion so far'. Capital Punishment; Memorandum [to Cabinet] by the Secretary of State for the Home Department, C. (61) 20, 8 February 1961.

60 They were to be called Questions and Answers Meetings. Lord Altrincham later suggested 'that a way to the big "middle" section of the community was through organisations – such as Rotary Clubs including in their activities a talk on capital punishment'. Minutes of the Meeting of the Executive Committee 6 June 1961 at the House of Commons.

61 Minutes of the Meeting of the Executive Committee 16 February 1961 at the House of Commons.

62 Indeed, so great were the committee's expectations that it was believed that 'we can not only pack the great hall itself but may even achieve an overflow at the Kensington Town Hall, which we have booked for the purpose'. Letter from Gerald Gardiner and Victor Gollancz to *The Spectator*, 17 March 1961, 361.

63 Adam Faith, 1940–2003, was a popular singer who had started as the lead vocalist in The Worried Men.

64 Minutes of the Meeting of the Executive Committee 16 February 1961 at the House of Commons.

65 Minutes of the Meeting of the National Campaign for the Abolition of Capital Punishment Executive Committee 13 March 1962 at the House of Commons.

66 '... in the last analysis, power of Abolition rested with Parliament, and it was ... felt on Parliament that the Committee should concentrate. The Committee generally felt that the House of Lords would not again frustrate any action taken towards Abolition initiated by the Commons'. Minutes of the Meeting of the Executive Committee 15 November 1960 at the House of Commons.

67 'Mr Gardiner ... wondered whether we ought not to send [the MPs] something every month. Mr Kirk offered to prepare a list of about 20 Conservative MPs who might vote for abolition if their constituencies could be converted, and suggested that Questions and Answers meetings might be organised in these constituencies. Mr Kirk also promised to ask Mr Chataway and Mr Geoffrey Johnson Smith to do what they could'. Minutes of the Meeting of the Executive Committee 2 May 1961 at the House of Commons. Six months later, 'The Chairman ... had drafted circulars to be sent weekly to all M.P.s from 30 October, and arrangements are being made for these circulars to be printed ...' Minutes of the Meeting of the Executive Committee 20 September 1961 at Caxton Hall.

68 Minutes of the Meeting of the National Campaign for the Abolition of Capital Punishment Executive Committee 21 November 1961 at 90 Eaton Place.

69 An expectation that was based on the recommendation of the 1930 Select Committee which had never, in fact, been incorporated in the 1957 Act.

70 That report, *Murder*, by E. Gibson and S. Klein, had concluded that, although there had been fluctuations in the number of murders over the years, averaging some 3.2 to 3.7 cases of murder and manslaughter per million population over a thirty-year period, it was impossible to argue that they had been affected by the 1957 Act. Lord Stonham was to tell the House of Lords just after its publication that 'It is clear that the Homicide Act has not produced a murder wave. The tragic increase in the general crime rate is not reflected in the murder rate. Murder is a crime apart... the fears in some minds that the partial dropping of the death penalty would lead to an increase in murder have proved groundless. The proportion of non-capital murders has in fact declined. In 1952 it was 87.9 per cent; last year it was 81.3 per cent'. HL Deb 9 November 1961 Vol. 235 cc435–502.

71 Minutes of the Meeting of the National Campaign for the Abolition of Capital Punishment Executive Committee 2 November 1961 at 90 Eaton Place.

72 J. Christoph, *Capital Punishment and British Politics, op. cit.*, 172–3.

73 'The views of the new Tory back-benchers would be of vital importance with regard to any new advance in the House, and it was therefore decided that Mr Gardiner would write to all members returned since 1957 to discover their attitude to Abolition'. Minutes of the Meeting of the Executive Committee 19 July 1960 at the House of Commons.

74 Minutes of the Meeting of the Executive Committee 15 November 1960 at the House of Commons.

75 The Conservative Party Manifesto, *The Next Five Years*, talked briefly and generally about protecting citizens, compensating victims and reforming criminals, but there was

no allusion at all to capital punishment. The Labour Party manifesto, *Britain Belongs to You*, had nothing to say about crime and criminal justice.

76 The papers of the Conservative Party are replete with hostile resolutions from local associations. Examples include that passed by the Committee Meeting of the Knaresborough and District Conservative Association held on 5 July, 1956: 'The Committee unanimously express their deep concern at the action of the House of Commons in passing the Silverman Bill for the Abolition of the Death Sentence. East [sic] member of this Committee is aware through personal contact of the mounting feeling of alarm of great numbers of voters, irrespective of parties, who fear the consequences to the country of the passage of this bill, and who also feel that they have not had the opportunity of expressing their views. ...' and that passed in November 1956 by the Honiton Division Political Education Conference: 'That this Conference is of the opinion (a) that capital punishment should be retained for certain classes of murder, especially those related to custodians of the Law in the execution of their duties; for all cases of treason; and for certain murders committed in connection with robbery; and (b) that the Law relating to murder should be revised'. (CC04/6/45 1955 Conservative Party Archives at the Bodleian Library). There were also a number of profoundly critical letters. One read:

> 'May I enquire why Edwards and Edwardson, the foul murderers of two small children were not condemned to death? The people of this country have not given the government a mandate for imprisonment instead of hanging. They believe in a life for a life. It is only common justice. Yet since 1945 we have had sloppy Home Secretaries reprieving every murderer. No wonder that there is practically a violent murder every day. ...
>
> It is obvious that if the government is not going to protect the public from criminals, then the public will have to take steps to protect itself, by arming. I have a revolver, and if anyone unauthorised enters my house I shall shoot and ask questions after.
>
> If after the war the birch had restored to the police courts for boys, instead of putting them on probation, there would not now be any Teddy Boy problem. Also if flogging had been brought in for robbery with violence it would have stopped in a week, instead of which it is daily on the increase.
>
> What is also wanted is castration for crimes of sex and hanging for all murderers from the age of 16...' (Letter from T.P. Child to O. Poole, Chairman of the Conservative Party, 14 June 1956. CC04/8/27 Conservative Party Archives at the Bodleian Library).

The reference was to Horace Edwards who was charged on 16 August 1957 with the murder of a seven-year-old boy in Loughton Essex (see *The Times*, Saturday 17 August 1957) and to the murder of Edwina Taylor by Derek Edwardson on 31 August 1957. The Taylor family's Member of Parliament, Frederic Harris, told the House of Commons that 'This murder has not only caused great sorrow to the child's parents and to all connected with her, but it has outraged the feelings of all decent people in the country and, particularly, of my constituents. A Streatham housewife, herself the mother of two children, has launched a petition calling on the Government to establish an institution where sexual offenders against young children can be detained and treated. The response to her petition has been overwhelming and has by no means been confined to the locality. It is estimated that in the first week some 4,000 signatures were obtained, although the petition was not what one would call a properly organised effort'. (HC Deb 18 November 1957 Vol. 578 cc165–74)

77 HL Deb 9 November 1961 Vol. 235 cc435–502 Lord Meston, 1894–1984, was a barrister and unsucessful Liberal candidate in two parliamentary elections.

78 Mr Macmillan had been Chancellor of the Exchequer at the time of the passage of the 1957 Act. I could find no record of his having made a public statement on the bill or the Act.

79 Letter of 27 February 1957. CC04/8/27 Conservative Party Archives at the Bodleian Library.

80 House of Lords Debates, Vol. 198, col. 586.

81 It was said of him that 'he played a key role in rallying the party faithful around the country demoralized by Suez, helping to deliver a surprise election win in 1959 ...' J. Doering (1 February 2002); 'Lord Hailsham: The Reluctant Peer', *Contemporary Review*, 94.

82 He had said in debate on the Homicide Bill: 'To my mind, the conclusive argument is the fact that, if this Bill becomes law, and your Lordships deliberately substitute life imprisonment for the penalty of death, we shall have a situation in which there will be a certain number of murders, possibly more numerous than the advocates of the Bill are prepared to admit, where there will be no deterrent for murder at all, or where the additional deterrent is only marginal. When I am faced with this proposition I am compelled to say that I regard the burden of proof as upon those who wish to bring about that situation. To my mind, that is a conclusive argument upon the merits of the debate. ... It is only a Bill for the attachment of a different penalty to murder. In so far as it can be amended, it can be amended only by taking out of that general exclusion an inner circle of non-exclusion, by citing particular kinds of murder which are not affected by the general ban on the death penalty while leaving the substantive law of murder unaltered. I do not believe that that is a dignified or, in the last resort, a possible method of promulgating to the country what the law of murder or the death penalty should he'. HL Deb 9 July 1956 Vol. 198 cc564–676.

83 CC04/8/27 Conservative Party Archives at the Bodleian Library, *op. cit.*

84 When he was succeeded by Henry Brooke who, as I shall observe, was himself initially a strong retentionist.

85 A. Howard, RAB: The Life of R.A. Butler, *op. cit.*, 225.

86 See the report in *The Times*, 9 March 1962. Appointed Home Secretary in January 1957, he had inherited the Homicide Bill in its last stages and had 'deftly put it on the statute-book'. As Lord Privy Seal, he had defended the bill, as he was obliged to, arguing that hanging was preferable to life imprisonment, and that the Timothy Evans case had been unique and unrepeatable. The nub of his argument was that which John Stuart Mill had put before him: 'I think that what some hon. Members fear is the sense of finality in the process of hanging. What is the alternative? The alternative is, not a quick death, but a slow death and a lingering execution. Instead of the fear of finality there is certainty of an excruciating uncertainty which and I quote from one of our most prominent experts on this subject – might "permanently impair something more precious than the life of the physical body"'. (HC Deb 16 February 1956 Vol. 548 cc2536–655.) He was to become an abolitionist whilst Home Secretary although he did not reprieve all those cases that came before him. (See his biography in *The Oxford Dictionary of National Biography*, http://www.oxforddnb.com/view/article/30886?docPos=2)

87 In January 1960, the Home Secretary wrote to Sir Eric Edwards, the deputy chairman of the party 'Changes in the law relating to capital punishment were made as recently as 1957 under the Homicide Act of that year. The Government would not, therefore, feel justified in making further changes in the law in connection with capital punishment at the present time. The operation of the 1957 Act will, of course, be kept under close review'. Letter dated 11 January 1960, CC04/8/27 Conservative Party Archives at the Bodleian Library.

88 See, for example, his written answer to a question from Jo Grimond in 1959: HC Deb 14 May 1959 Vol. 605 c167W.

89 Capital Punishment; Memorandum [to Cabinet] by the Secretary of State for the Home Department, C. (61) 20, 8 February 1961.

90 Notes for a speech [by D. Vosper] in reply to a resolution to be proposed at the meeting of the Central Council of the Conservative Party on 23 March 1961. CRI60 431/5/79. Dennis Vosper, 1916–1968, was Minister of State, Home Office, 1960–61.

91 Capital Punishment (C.(61) 20), 10 February 1961, PREM 11/4690. I am grateful to Tim Newburn for introducing me to this and another document in PREM 11/4690.

92 Note by C.C.C. [Charles Cunningham], 8 March 1962, CRI61 431/5/34.

93 A memorandum to the Home Secretary had reported that, in his letter, Mr Silverman says 'we should like to discuss generally the present position now that five years have almost elapsed since the Homicide Act and the prospects and desirability of Parliamentary action in the near future whether on an official or an unofficial basis'. Mr. Sydney Silverman, M.P., Asks to Bring an All-Party Deputation to Discuss the Future of the Act with the S. of S. CRI 61 431/5/34.

94 See the Parliament Question and Answer of April 1961: HL Deb 19 April 1961 Vol. 230 cc599–601

95 The report of the meeting stated that 'There had been no pledge of a review in five years' time; but the impression had undoubtedly got abroad that a review was due'. Note by C.C.C. [Charles Cunningham], 8 March 1962, CRI61 431/5/34.

96 But see the note of a conversation between Mr Butler and the prime minister reported below.

97 His autobiography is uninformative on the matter. His one brief and somewhat gnomic comment was to the effect that 'there can be no doubt that the possibilities raised by the Evans case provided a weighty argument for abolition. By the end of my time at the Home Office I began to see that the system could not go on, and present-day Secretaries of State are well relieved of the terrible power to decide between life and death'. R. Butler (1971); *The Art of the Possible: The Memoirs of Lord Butler K.G., C.H.*, London: Hamish Hamilton, 202.

98 Minutes of the Meeting of the National Campaign for the Abolition of Capital Punishment Executive Committee 13 March 1962 at the House of Commons.

99 In their planning, they sought the 'thousands of signatures, particularly from Probation Officers, Senior Nursing Staff, Sportsmen – including Olympic teams, cricketers, tennis, football (ask Jimmy Hill), General Councils of all Trade Unions, Magistrates and J.P.s, Important people in industry and commerce (chairmen and managing directors of big companies?) [and] Captains of big liners' Minutes of the Meeting of the Executive Committee 6 June 1961 at the House of Commons.

100 PREM 11/3686: Gerald Gardiner and Victor Gollancz; Memorial to the Prime Minister, 5 July 1962.

101 *The Times*, 6 July 1962.

102 Minutes of the Meeting of the National Campaign for the Abolition of Capital Punishment Executive Committee 13 September 1962 at Caxton Hall.

103 Minutes of the Meeting of the Executive Committee 20 September 1961 at Caxton Hall.

104 A. Howard, 'Parliament and the Gallows', *New Statesman*, 23 February 1962, 250. It is interesting that a copy of this article was lodged in the Cabinet files: CRI 61 431/5/34.

105 For instance, a letter was sent by his private Secretary on 6 February 1959: 'The Home Secretary has asked me to let you know that he has received your letter of 5th February forwarding a resolution about corporal punishment and hanging which was adopted by the Walton Conservative Association Finance and General Purposes Committee on 23rd October 1958'.

106 A Home Office note on a forthcoming meeting of the United Nations Congress on Prevention of Crime and Treatment of Offenders, to be held at Stockholm in 1965,

disclosed that the government believed that 'The [U.K.] delegation should oppose any suggestion that Capital Punishment should be one of the major items on the agenda … because full scale discussion might lead to embarrassment for H.M. Government …' CRI 61 431/5/28.

107 'The Home Secretary was advised by Sir Charles Cunningham that The justification for the present categories of capital murder was that such murders strike at the roots of law and order, and are those on which the uniquely deterrent effect of the death penalty is most likely to operate. The case against the law, as it now stands, is two-fold. First, it is widely felt that there are other types of murder – for example, sex murders – which are socially no less objectionable, and which in many cases are morally more reprehensible. Secondly, the claim that the death penalty has a uniquely deterrent effect is not supported by the facts quoted in the preceding paragraph. Murders in the non-capital categories have increased since 1957 by %,* murders in the capital categories by %.*' [*The blank spaces would be filled by 'Incorporat[ing] any summary of the analysis of murders now being made, here, H.O.R.U'.] 'Brief for S. Of S'. Meeting with Conservative Party Home Affairs Committee on 2.2.61, Draft. CRI 60 431/5/62 31 January 1961.

108 Note by Sir Charles Cunningham for Discussion on Crime: The Rising Incidence of Crime; 10 March 1961 CRI 60 431/5/92.

109 Kensington Town Hall had also been booked for a possible overflow meeting. Minutes of the Meeting of the Executive Committee 16 February 1961 at the House of Commons.

110 Minutes of the Meeting of the National Campaign for the Abolition of Capital Punishment Executive Committee 20 June 1962 Caxton Hall.

111 Its stock letter recited that 'I appreciate that as a Parliamentary candidate in a by-election you will have a great deal to do, and little time to spend considering questions which you may not already have had occasion to consider in any detail. The subject of capital punishment, however, is one on which large numbers of our fellow citizens feel strongly. If you have time just to turn the pages of the enclosed Memorial … you will see that a large number of men and women holding responsible positions in all aspects of our national life are firmly in favour of abolition. We believe that opinion on this subject primarily depends on a knowledge of the relevant facts, and, while realising how busy you must be, I feel it is not unreasonable to ask you at least not to form a view hostile to the abolition of capital punishment until you have had time to consider the facts we have put before you. …' G. Gardiner Papers Vol. V 5649C, British Library.

112 G. Gardiner papers Vol. V 5649C, British Library.

113 Note for the Record, PREM 11/4690.

114 H. Berkeley (1972); *Crossing the Floor*, London: George Allen and Unwin, 126.

115 In one of a series of articles on issues that would be neglected in the campaign, Nigel Walker wrote 'One of the issues on which the coming election will certainly not be fought is penal reform. As a national phenomenon serious crime is not yet prevalent enough to provoke a major reaction of the kind which led to the creation of police forces in the 19th century. Even the much publicised (and probably exaggerated) rise in the rates of crimes of violence, sex or … have [failed] to arouse the alarm which they used to. Property crimes are less rare, but cause less genuine suffering in an affluent, and heavily insured society …' 'Crime and Punishment', *New Society*, 12 March 1964, 15.

116 See, for example, G. Eyre Noel (1964); *Harold Wilson and the 'new Britain': The Making of a Modern Prime Minister*, London: Campion Press; B. Pimlott (1992); *Harold Wilson*, London: HarperCollins: and B. Donoghue (2005); *Downing Street Diary: With Harold Wilson in No. 10*, London: Jonathan Cape, none of which contains a reference to crime and justice.

117 'After a long discussion, it was decided that no action should be taken before, or during, the General Election, but immediately Parliament resumed every effort should be made to introduce a Private Member's Bill which Mr Silverman was asked to draft'. Minutes of the Meeting of the National Campaign for the Abolition of Capital Punishment Executive Committee 24 February 1964 at the House of Commons.

118 *Crime, a Challenge to Us All; Report of the Labour Party's Study Group* (1964) London: Home Policy Committee, Labour Party. *The Times* of 30 May 1964 remarked that 'It will be presented not as a statement of party policy but as a set of proposals intended to stimulate public interest'. The Longford Committee were, in effect, in competition with the Conservative Government's own draft White Paper on Penal Policy (which was to become *The War Against Crime in England and Wales* (H.M.S.O., London, April 1964, Cmnd. 2296)). The Cabinet Secretary, Burke Trend, had noted that 'The Home Secretary was asked to revise the draft in consultation with the Ministers principally concerned, with a view to its publication before Easter, in order to forestall the expected publication of the report of a committee set up by the Labour Party under Lord Longford to consider penal policy'. (CRI15/1/6 Penal Reform Generally White Paper on Penal Policy – Burke Trend to Prime Minister, 23 March 1964) The Home Secretary, Henry Brooke, had himself written to the Secretary of State for Scotland to say 'There is something to be said for publication before Easter. I am, as you know, concerned that we should take the initiative before the Labour Party's committee on Penal Policy under the chairmanship of Lord Longford are able to produce their Report. If we do not achieve publication before Easter, we shall have to wait until the Thursday after the Budget (16th April) ... To delay so long increases the risk that the Labour Party's Report may forestall us'. (PREM 11 4691 letter from Henry Brooke to Secretary of State for Scotland, 20 March 1964.)

119 When asked on the television programme, *This Week*, what he would do about the abolition of capital punishment, he replied that the matter would be left to a free vote in Parliament and, with a Labour Government in power, he knew what the outcome would be. See *The Times*, 17 January 1964. There was another allusion made by the new prime minister to a free vote: 'This brings me to the Homicide Act. I think that it is generally agreed now that the Homicide Act has neither a rational nor a moral basis and few can be found to defend the present law. We feel that, as this is an issue on which people have strong views and which is to some a matter of conscience, it should be left to a free vote of the House and we are prepared to find Government time for it. I think that on this sort of issue the House of Commons is at its best when each Member is expressing his own individual view'. ('Liberty and the Law'. Harold Wilson's speech to the Society of Labour Lawyers on 20 April 1964.)

120 As a peeress, she was to initiate the debate on the abolition of the death penalty in the House of Lords. She spoke as an atheist and a utilitarian with 'a profound sense of the value of human life and of human personality. This can hardly be surprising. Those who believe that this life is all that we can expect to have naturally hold it dear. To me at least, except in a few extreme cases of mercy killing, it is unthinkable to contemplate taking the life of another human being. On this ground alone, I am irrevocably opposed to capital punishment in any circumstances, even apart from the cogent arguments as to its ineffectiveness, and I am very proud that it fell to my lot to introduce into the House of Lords the Bill which has, I hope, finally abolished this barbarous practice in this country'. B. Wootton (1967); *In a World I Never Made: Autobiographical Reflections*, London: George Allen and Unwin, 173.

121 Sir Louis Blom-Cooper, was born in 1926, became a barrister in 1952 and a Q.C. in 1970. He was a member of the Howard League and the National Campaign for the Abolition of the Death Penalty; a member of the Home Secretary's Advisory Council on the Penal System, 1966–78; and Joint Director of the Legal Research Unit, Bedford College, University of London, 1967–82.

122 The term is Sir Louis Blom-Cooper's in interview, 2010.

123 See M. Box (1983); *Rebel Advocate: A Biography of Gerald Gardiner*, London: Victor Gollancz, 170.

124 He had resigned on taking office in government.

125 Quite typical of the very many letters he wrote was his appeal of 22 May 1964 to Henry Brooke, then Home Secretary, about an impending execution: 'This case seems a beautiful example of the futility of the Homicide Act. It seems clear that Masters was not a professional criminal of the type against whom the Act was aimed and that if he is hanged he will be hanged not for having committed a murder but for theft. … I feel sure that you must be as dissatisfied as we are at the difficult question to which the implementation of the Act has given rise but we are naturally hoping that you may in this case continue your apparent policy of advising a reprieve where the man convicted is not one of the class of men at whom this section was aimed'. G. Gardiner Papers Vol. V 5649C, British Library.

126 G. Gardiner; *Capital Punishment as a Deterrent: And the Alternative*, *op. cit.*, 7–8. Lord Beveridge commented on the eve of the debate in the House of Lords that he had read 'the book with great interest and admiration … I think it definitely brings me over to his side … ' Letter to Victor Gollancz (the publisher), 9 March 1956 (Beveridge/6/53 in the Archives of the British Library of Political and Economic Science).

127 He was to argue that the Royal Commission was right. The 1957 Act was "inherently impossible': it lacked a definition of the 'worst' murders which should still be subject to the penalty of hanging; it relied on a wholly impracticable notion of premeditation; and it simply could not contend with 'the infinitely varying circumstances' in which murder was committed. G. Gardiner, 'The Point About the Homicide Act', *New Statesman*, 10 February 1961, 208.

128 The Sub-Committee had decided unanimously 'that, subject only to the possible exception of murders of prison officers by prisoners, the death penalty is unnecessary and should be abolished and they accordingly unanimously recommend That the Society should submit a Memorandum to the Royal Commission advocating (1) That the death penalty should be limited to cases of the murder of prison officers by prisoners. (2) That other convicted murderers should be sentenced to imprisonment for life, to be served in the same circumstances and subject to the same conditions as to release as now apply to those convicted and reprieved'. Note by Gerald Gardiner, Chairman, 20.1.1950. (Papers of the Society of Labour Lawyers, SLL/6/14 in the archives of the British Library of Political and Economic Science.)

129 Minutes of the Meeting of the National Campaign for the Abolition of Capital Punishment Executive Committee 23 July 1963 at the House of Commons.

130 He had said in a letter to Sydney Silverman, 30 July 1964: 'You may remember that you were kind enough to say that you would draft for the Campaign a bill to abolish capital punishment for murder. My law reform lot have also drafted a bill, and I enclose a copy of it for your consideration. … As you will appreciate, a Labour Government would not sponsor such a bill itself but would merely afford time for a private member's bill. …' (Correspondence and papers of Lord Gardiner concerning the National Campaign for the Abolition of the Death Penalty 1927–1969, Add. 56455 The British Library.)

131 An early draft of his proposed bill was designed 'to abolish the death penalty for murder and amend the law relating to the punishment of murder and of homicide by persons suffering from diminished responsibility. After discussion, the Committee agreed that this draft Bill should be simplified to deal only with the abolition of the death penalty for murder and should include no reference to diminished responsibility or to the law relating to treason or cowardice'. Minutes of the Meeting of the National Campaign for the Abolition of Capital Punishment Executive Committee 16 September 1964 at Caxton Hall.

132 Minutes of the Meeting of the National Campaign for the Abolition of Capital Punishment Executive Committee 23 July 1963 at the House of Commons.

133 'Lord Gardiner Interviewed', *The Economist*, 28 March 1964, 1212.

134 He had written that 'When the Homicide Act was being passed many pointed out that it had neither a moral nor a rational basis. This is at last being generally recognised. For example:

   1)   If a man kills his wife by the nearest weapon to hand, which is a gun, this is capital murder; but if the nearest weapon to hand is a hatchet, this is non-capital murder.

   2)   If a man rapes a girl, strangles her and takes her handbag, this is in practice capital murder; if he does not take the handbag, it is not...

       Realising this at last, many people think (quite naturally) that if we took some classes of murder out of the Homicide Act and put others in, all would be well. This is a delusion and it is important to see exactly why it is a delusion. ... For over four years the Royal Commission considered every scheme or proposal for limiting capital punishment to the worst murders, or for grades or degrees of murder ... and they unanimously reported that any such scheme or proposal would result in so many anomalies that it could not be supported. All the Homicide Act has done is to show that the Royal Commission was right and no tinkering with the Homicide Act will make workable that which is inherently impossible...'

   1)   The first difficulty is that, while it is easy to talk about the 'worst' murders, few have considered what they mean. Some mean premeditated murders as against those which are not premeditated. Most people probably mean the murders which are committed with the greatest degree of brutality – but these are usually murder by the insane or aggressive psychopath.

   2)   The second difficulty is that of definition. If the premeditated murder were to be selected as one category ... men's lives would be left to depend on the particular jury's idea, unaided by any definition, of what "premeditated" meant. ...

   3)   The third difficulty is the greatest ... [there] is a chain of infinitely varying circumstances and the truth is that it is, and always will be, quite impossible to put one's finger down at any point in the chain and say "Everyone to the right deserves to die but not those to the left", for, wherever you put your finger down, the case to the immediate right and the case to the immediate left will be almost exactly the same case. ...'

(Undated speaking note: THE POINT ABOUT THE HOMICIDE ACT Correspondence and papers of Lord Gardiner conc. the National Campaign for the Abolition of the Death Penalty 1927–1969, Add. 56455 The British Library)

135 Letter to R. Heuston written in 1984, in R. Heuston, *Lives of the Lord Chancellors, op. cit.*, 231.

136 L. Blom-Cooper and T. Morris (2004); *With Malice Aforethought: A Study of the Crime and Punishment for Homicide*, Oxford: Hart Publishing, 5. A later Lord Chief Justice, Lord Phillips, reflected that 'capital punishment was effectively abolished by a Labour administration, largely as a result of the personal intervention of the Lord Chancellor, Lord Gerald Gardiner'. Lord Phillips, Lord Chief Justice of England and Wales; Crime and Punishment, High Sheriff's Law Lecture, Oxford, 10 October 2006.

137 'Lord Gardiner Interviewed', *op. cit.*, 1212.

138 B. Hollingsworth (1976); 'David Soskice in Russia in 1917', *European Studies Review*, Vol. 6, 78. I am grateful to Niki Lacey for sending me a copy of this article.

139 He said afterwards that 'Deliberately to break a man or woman's neck by a machine, whatever they had done, seemed an act of obsolete and obscene barbarism' Lord Stow Hill (1967); 'The Abolishment of Capital Punishment in England', *Women's Law Journal*, 53, 7.

140 See his obituary in *The Times* of 16 November 1979.

141 David Soskice remarked that 'He'd really wanted – [Hugh] Gaitskell had promised him – that he would be Lord Chancellor if [he] won the election. He didn't really want to be Home Secretary. … It was much more exposed and the only thing he knew how to do was to go by precedent'.

142 HC Deb 4 December 1956 Vol. 561 cc1073–198.

143 V. Bailey; 'The Shadow of the Gallows: The Death Penalty and the British Labour Government, 1945–51', http://www.historycooperative.org/journals/lhr/18.2/bailey.html

144 Ruth Ellis had murdered her lover in April 1955, was sentenced to death two months later (see *The Times*, 22 June 1955), and was hanged on 13 July of that year. She was the last woman to be executed in the United Kingdom, and attained great symbolic importance in the subsequent campaigns for abolition. Sir Louis Blom-Cooper said in interview in September 2011: 'the third element which I think goes both to Parliamentarians and to the public were miscarriages of justice. … I think you could just simply [point to] Ruth Ellis, Timothy Evans and Derek Bentley … The idea in the ordinary, in the mind of the ordinary citizen in this country, that somebody might have been executed who ought not to have been executed, either because they were innocent or because there were such mitigating factors, … was a powerful factor in leading some people, particularly Parliamentarians, to become abolitionists'.

145 The last two people hanged were Peter Allen and Gwynne Evans in August 1964 whilst Henry Brooke was Home Secretary.

146 See J. Mack (1965); review of *Crime A Challenge*, *The British Journal of Criminology*, Vol. 5, No. 1, 103–4.

147 Foreword, *Crime A Challenge*, v.

148 T. Morris and L. Blom-Cooper (1964); *A Calendar of Murder; Criminal Homicide in England since 1957*, London: M. Joseph, was based on press cuttings compiled by the Howard League and was intended, in part, to review the development of homicide since the passing of the 1957 Act (the book, Morris said, 'gave thumb-nail sketches of all people who had been indicted for murders committed between 21st March 1957 (the date the Homicide Act came into force) and 31st December 1962'. Minutes of the 414th meeting of the Executive Committee of the Howard League for Penal Reform, 18 January 1963). Morris and Blom-Cooper had previously published an article based on the same bank of materials in *The Observer* newspaper in April 1961.

149 T. Morris, *Crime and Criminal Justice since 1945, op. cit.*, 114.

150 Study Group on Crime Prevention and Penal Reform, RD732/March 1964, The Labour Party Archive in the People's History Museum, Manchester.

151 Study Group on Crime Prevention and Penal Reform: Preliminary Outline for Report, RD727/March 1964, The Labour Party Archive in the People's History Museum, Manchester.

152 Draft prepared by Gerald Gardiner; Study Group on Crime Prevention and Penal Reform, RD706/Feb 1964, The Labour Party Archive in the People's History Museum, Manchester.

153 And, indeed, Harold Wilson decided that his majority made government so unworkable that he had to call another election in March 1966 which he then won much more comfortably.

154 See *The Times*, 27 October 1964.

155 CRI 64 431/9/1.

156 In D. Dagan, 'Defiance and Death: Public Opinion, Politicians, and the Abolition of Capital Punishment in Great Britain and the United States', Master's Thesis, Brandeis University, undated, 88.

157 Cabinet: The Queen's Speech on the Opening of Parliament C. (64) 3 20 October 1964.

158 David Soskice said in interview that 'The truth of the matter was [my father] got on incredibly well with Cunningham. He and Charles Cunningham were really two of a kind ...'

159 Charles Cunningham wrote 'I see no point in consulting the police and the prison officers; their views cannot influence the decision, which is one of principle'. CRI 64 431/9/1 23 October 1964. Sir Frank Soskice did indeed not heed the police view that the abolition of capital punishment for the murder of police officers would have dire consequences. He was to say in debate on 4 February 1965 that 'The Police Federation have represented to me that capital punishment should be retained for the murder of a police officer acting in the execution of his duty or of any person coming to his assistance. With regard to extra protection, I am satisfied that other penalties which are available to the courts for attacks on police officers whilst on duty are adequate. ... If we start retaining the death penalty for individual types of murder, we are back to where we were in the Homicide Act, 1957'. HC Deb 4 February 1965 Vol. 705 cc1260–1

160 A. Koestler and C.H. Rolph; *Hanged by the Neck, op. cit.,* 57.

161 For example, the Police Federation circulated all Members of Parliament in December 1964 to argue that whilst it 'has no mandate to comment on the wider issues surrounding the proposal to abolish capital punishment, ... we firmly request the retention of capital punishment for the murder of a police officer acting in the course of his duty, or any person coming to his assistance. ... on the special protection afforded to police officers by the Homicide Act, the Police Federation must consider the position of its members, whose duty requires the highest degree of courage and tenacity in the pursuit and apprehension of criminals. ... We are aware of statistics which indicate the abolition of capital punishment in some other countries did not of itself result in more policemen being murdered than heretofore. However, this is not a safe comparison. The policeman in Great Britain is unique amongst most other overseas forces in carrying out his duties unarmed and, to a greater extent than abroad, alone. ... '. (In the Gardiner Papers, British Library) Protests from the Police Federation continued after the passing of the 1965 Act. See, for example, *The Times,* 13 August 1966.

162 C. (64) 6 27 October 1964.

163 CRI 64 431/9/1 28 October 1964.

164 He had said in a letter to Sydney Silverman of 30 July 1964 that 'As you will appreciate, a Labour Government would not sponsor such a bill itself but would merely afford time for a private member's bill. ...' Gardiner Papers, British Library.

165 Conclusions of a meeting of the Cabinet, held on 29 October 1964, C.C.(64) 4th Conclusions.

166 And that was how it would eventually appear in the Speech from the Throne. The Queen promised that 'Facilities will be provided for a free decision by Parliament on the issue of capital punishment'. HL Deb 3 November 1964 Vol. 261 cc9–13. It was, said Sydney Silverman's biographer, 'the first time in history that a Private Member's Bill had been mentioned in a Queen's Speech) and it was a bold and courageous decision for a Government with such a small majority to take'. (E. Hughes (1969); *Sydney Silverman: Rebel in Parliament,* London and Edinburgh: Charles Skilton, 172).

167 The meeting had been preceded two days before by a memorandum by the Home Secretary (H(64)3) which aired the issues to be discussed: should abolition cover only the categories retained under the 1957 Act? Sir Frank argued that if the Government were opposed to the use of the death penalty, it could be argued that, on the one hand, any legislation should embrace all the offences which were currently subject to capital punishment, but, on the other, to make it too complicated might simply invite delaying tactics from its opponents. Should life imprisonment become the penalty

for all cases of murder? Should the defence of diminished responsibility be retained? And he then turned to the matter of timing, citing the problem of the man who had 'just been committed for trial at the Central Criminal Court on a charge which is doubly capital [he was presumably alluding to the case of Ronald Cooper] ... It is quite likely that this case may present no mitigating features at all; and on the face of it, it is precisely one of those murders at which the Homicide Act was specially aimed. My colleagues will understand that I may find myself in a most painful position if by the time the House has risen in December it has not had an opportunity of reaching a view, at any rate in principle, on the question of capital punishment'. Accordingly he requested colleagues to agree to the drafting of a bill to be handed to a private member as soon as possible so that the House could express its view before the Christmas Recess.

168 The Committee was attended by Herbert Bowden, the Lord President of the Council; Sir Frank Soskice, the Home Secretary; Richard Crossman, the Minister of Housing and Local Government; Gerald Gardiner, the Lord Chancellor; James Griffiths, the Secretary of State for Wales; Fred Peart, the Minister of Agriculture, Fisheries and Food; and Niall MacDermot, the Financial Secretary to the Treasury. Six other ministers were 'also present'.

169 H64(1) In the interests of simplicity, and following his memorandum of 4 November, the Home Secretary was reported to have said that the bill should be confined to the abolition of capital punishment for murder, and not other 'relatively rare' civil offences such as treason and arson in H.M. dockyards. Neither should it cover military offences for which the penalty was death. Were that to be the case, the penalty for murder would become imprisonment for life. There was some discussion in committee about whether it would be right to retain the death penalty for military offences; the retention of defences of diminished responsibility; the provision of a minimum period of detention, and the need to award the Home Secretary discretion to release on licence a prisoner sentenced to life imprisonment 'at any time to take account of the wide variety of circumstances in which murder was committed'. In the event, the bill that was presented on 4 December did propose, under s. 3, the abolition of the death penalty for offences of murder tried in military courts. Hanging for treason and piracy when murder was attempted was abolished only under s. 36(4) and (5) of the Crime and Disorder Act 1998, c. 37.

170 Cabinet: Legislative Programme 1964–65 – Memorandum by the Lord President of the Council; C. (64) 16 17 November 1964.

171 Draft letter to Lord Gardiner of 5 November 1964. CRI 64 431/9/1.

172 Their sole outstanding focus was to be on the problem of whether to retain the defence of diminished responsibility which had been introduced in the 1957 Act and which had been the subject of some correspondence with the Lord Chief Justice and the Lord Chancellor. 'If the death penalty were done away with', they reasoned, 'this justification disappeared, and there was no logical reason why the doctrine should apply in cases of murder and not in the case of other criminal offences'. Note to Mr Gwynn from Sir Charles Cunningham, 18 November 1964, CRI 64 431/9/1.

173 Conclusions of a Meeting of the Cabinet held at 10 Downing Street, S.W.1, on Thursday, 19 November, 1964, at 10.30 a.m. CC. (64) 9th Conclusions.

174 Robert Beloe, 1905–1984, a former Chief Education Officer, was the first lay secretary successively to Archbishops Fisher and Ramsey between 1959 and 1968.

175 Note from Robert Beloe, 7 January 1965, Archbishop Ramsey's papers Ramsey 76:146. Library of Lambeth Palace.

176 See the reports in *The Times*, 28 October 1964, 15 and 19 December 1964, and 13 and 23 January 1965.

177 G.J. Otton to Sir Charles Cunningham, 30 October, 1964, CRI 64 431/9/1.

178 Note of 31 October 1964. CRI64 431/9/1.

179 Minutes of the Meeting of the National Campaign for the Abolition of Capital Punishment Executive Committee 24 November 1964 in the House of Commons.

180 Sydney Silverman had written to Lord Gardiner on 2 September 1964 to say that '... I have found your letter and enclosures of the 30th July. I had myself prepared a first draft of such a Bill, but I think the draft you send me is better and as far as I can see adequate for its purpose'. Gardiner Papers, British Library.

181 Letter from Lord Gardiner to Sydney Silverman, 30 July 1964. Gardiner Papers, British Library.

182 HC Deb 4 December 1964 Vol. 703 cc927–8.

183 *The Times*, 5 December 1964.

184 'Members of the Committee expressed their confidence about the outcome of the second reading debate in the Commons, but were informed by the Chairman of certain doubts expressed by Lord Gardiner ... about the outcome in the Lords, where he thought the campaign should now direct its efforts. Members were aware of the danger that any campaign with members of the House of Lords might have the undesirable effect of reminding the retentionists of the situation. It was agreed to postpone any decision about action in the Lords until after the second reading debate in the Commons. Personal approaches to selected members of the House of Lords might then be considered useful, but it was agreed that at the appropriate time there should be consultation with Lord Gardiner and with Lord Shepherd'. Minutes of the Meeting of the National Campaign for the Abolition of Capital Punishment Executive Committee 24 November 1964 in the House of Commons.

185 HC Deb 10 December 1964 Vol. 703 cc1819–29.

186 Conclusions of a meeting of the Cabinet held at 10 Downing Street on 15 December 1964.

187 HC Deb 21 December 1964 Vol. 704 cc870–1010.

188 Section 1 stated emphatically 'No person shall suffer death for murder, and a person convicted of murder shall be sentenced to imprisonment for life'. Murder (Abolition of Death Penalty) Act 1965, 1965 c.71.

189 *The Times* said that Mr Brooke was 'not a man who changes his mind easily. As Home Secretary, although his honesty was respected, his stubbornness was notorious. It must have taken courage to come to the Commons today and confess that although he had once been in favour of hanging all murderers, and had disliked the 1957 Homicide Act for that reason, his years at the Home Office had convinced him that the death penalty was no longer justified'. *The Times*, 22 December 1964.

190 An interesting insight into the process was provided by a senior civil servant who had worked closely with Sir Frank Newsam, the Permanent Undersecretary between 1948 and 1957. 'The Home Secretary never used to see anyone about a capital case. It was thought that it was not fair to him to be subject to the emotional pressure of seeing the relatives. And Newsam saw them. Newsam used to see them and they often were accompanied by Sydney Silverman. And Newsam seeing the relatives was a case study. He would give them a complete hearing, interrupting them only very occasionally and then he said, "is that what you want to say?" "Yes." And he'd turn to me and say, "get Miss Judd." Miss Judd was his shorthand writer. He'd then dictate, in front of the relatives, a brilliant summary of what they'd said, which dazzled them. He'd then say to them, "do you agree with that? It's a summary. Anything to add?" "No." "Miss Judd, new paragraph. I've dictated this note in the presence of the relatives of whoever it was, who've been good enough to say that it contained an accurate record of the representations they wish to bring to the notice of the Secretary of State. Now get that typed and in the Home Secretary's box tonight". Now a bit of showmanship, but very human and very careful'.

191 Sir Louis Blom-Cooper said in interview in September 2011 that 'the time taken was in a huge number of amendments, all of which were rejected and rejected

absolutely. There was never an amendment. The only amendment accepted ... was the procedural one by Henry Brooke about [the] five year probationary period'.

192 The Permanent Abolition of Capital Punishment for Murder, Memorandum by the Secretary of State for the Home Department and the Secretary of State for Scotland, 6 May 1969. (C (69) 48)

193 Gerald Gardiner would later observe that 'it was an unfortunate day. Mr. Sydney Silverman was fulfilling a longstanding speaking engagement on capital punishment in Canada. The Amendment was moved at half-past ten in the morning. The House had risen only at 6.39 that same morning, and, as was pointed out as soon as the noble Lord (as he now is) rose to move his Amendment, there appeared to be no abolitionists there. At all events, the Amendment was carried. Mr. Sydney Silverman told me afterwards that he was quite sure that the Amendment would be taken out on the Report stage'. HL Deb 17 December 1969 Vol. 306 cc1106–258.

194 His name does not appear in the lists prepared by the tellers.

195 *The Times*, 24 December 1964.

196 E. Hughes; *Sydney Silverman: Rebel in Parliament, op. cit.*, 179.

197 The Labour Member of Parliament for Rochester and Chatham, Anne Kerr, was reported by Roger Moody of *Peace News* to have said that 'Considerable pressure is being brought to bear on Sir Frank Soskice by such bodies as the Police Federation, to retain the Death Penalty. We cannot expect such pressure to decrease, in fact the greatest is yet to come. Sir Frank is in a most difficult position due to this. Being both a Lawyer and an Abolitionist, it is practically impossible for him to make any decision without feeling he may have fallen in error'. Minutes of the Meeting of the Bristol Campaign for the Abolition of Capital Punishment, 26 January 1965. Anne Kerr, 1925–1973, was said by her biographer Amanda Capern, to have been 'deeply involved in the campaign for the abolition of the death penalty and befriended the family of Derek Bentley, an intellectually disabled epileptic hanged in January 1953 for the murder of a policeman'. (*The Oxford Dictionary of National Biography*, http://www. oxforddnb.com/view/article/42089)

198 He was to tell the House of Commons: 'The Police Federation have represented to me that capital punishment should be retained for the murder of a police officer acting in the execution of his duty or of any person coming to his assistance. With regard to extra protection, I am satisfied that other penalties which are available to the courts for attacks on police officers whilst on duty are adequate. ... If we start retaining the death penalty for individual types of murder, we are back to where we were in the Homicide Act, 1957'. HC Deb 4 February 1965 Vol. 705 cc1260–1.

199 Robert Beloe told the Archbishop of Canterbury that 'The opponents of the Bill took great exception to the Government's decision to put the Whips on in the vote when after the Second Reading had been passed they decided to send the Bill upstairs rather than to keep it on the floor of the House at the Committee Stage. All this has added up to a determination on the part of the opponents of the Bill to impede it and they succeeded on Friday, 5th March in passing the motion to return the Bill to the floor of the House for the Committee Stage'. (Note of 12 March 1965) Ramsey 76:183, Lambeth Palace papers.

200 See B. Block and J. Hostettler; *Hanging in the Balance, op. cit.*, 239; and 'A Matter of Life or Death', *The Times*, 6 July 1965.

201 More precisely, Cabinet resolved 'To accept the decision of the House but to secure, by Resolution, that the House should sit on Wednesday mornings for consideration of the Committee stage of the Bill. If all amendments could be defeated, this would enable the Government to dispense with a Report stage. ...' CONCLUSIONS of a Meeting of the Cabinet held at 10 Downing Street, S.W.J, on Thursday, 11 March, 1965, at 10 a.m. CC (65) 15th Conclusions.

202 Reginald Paget and Geoffrey Howe had served as informal whips for the abolitionist cause in the House of Commons.

203 See *The Times* articles: 'Delays Threaten No Hanging Bill', 25 June 1965; 'Lords Get August Sitting Warning', 3 July 1965.

204 Robert Beloe, the Archbishop of Canterbury's Private Secretary, reported after a meeting that 'Silverman is, of course a man dedicated to the abolition of capital punishment and he showed clearly that he was not willing, nor I think would he be able, to compromise on the question of abolition. He said quite definitely that he was not prepared to accept any amendment of principle, and by principle he meant any amendment that would retain hanging for any kind of murder'. (Note of 11 March 1965). Later, Beloe observed that 'So far Silverman has taken the line in Committee that it is not for the Committee to alter the principle of complete abolition'. (Note of 12 March 1965) Ramsey 76:184; Lambeth Palace papers.

205 Letter to Members of Parliament, 22 June 1965, PREM 13 2552.

206 'The Committee endorsed Mr Silverman's view that no concessions to any proposal to retain the death penalty under certain circumstances, e.g. for the murder of a prison officer, should be made'. Minutes of the Meeting of the National Campaign for the Abolition of Capital Punishment Executive Committee 4 February 1965 in the House of Commons.

207 *The Times*, 14 July 1965.

208 It was further agreed in other meetings to tailor the parliamentary timetable to accommodate the bill if Sydney Silverman cooperated. Burke Trend's Cabinet Minutes for 10 March read 'HS ... Can't drop the Bill' and for 15 July 1965: 'Capital Punishment: L.P. Can still be completed if extension into August and fortnight's spill-over in autumn (?). But involves debate after 7 p.m. with suspension; and must accept risk Bill may be lost. P.M. Agree – provided promoter (Silverman) cooperates as regards amendments on report ("life sentence") and length of speeches on 3R. Must also press Speaker to accept closure if necessary'.

209 CONCLUSIONS of a Meeting of the Cabinet held at 10 Downing Street, S.W.1, on Thursday, 1 July 1965, at 10.30 a.m.

210 See *The Times*, 17 July 1965.

211 An official at the Royal Courts of Justice reported by email on 14 January 2010 that 'I asked a member of my staff to undertake some investigations on your behalf to see if we could find anything that might relate to the records that you are seeking, however regretfully he has not been able to located anything. It should of course be remembered in view of the age of the records that you are interested in, that if they had been selected for permanent preservation they would have been transferred to the National Archives'. Nothing is on record in the National Archives.

212 One tantalising snippet, undated and unsigned, is a note to Lord Gardiner from someone on R.M.S. Queen Elizabeth stating that 'The L.C.J. is on board, & I had a good talk with him about Cap. Pun. – I –?, but am not quite sure, that he told you what he told me: namely that (a) he is in favour of abolition, + the judge to sentence to a definite term of imprisonment & (b) – if I understood him aright – he is definitely coming out with the proposal about five years after the Homicide Act'. Gardiner Papers, British Library.

213 A note to file reported that: 'Lord Parker gave his views on capital punishment to a group of Lobby and Press Gallery correspondents. The talk was off the record but it was clear that correspondents could use the information given so long as the views were not attributed to Lord Parker. In essence he said that although he was once against abolition he had become over the last three years an abolitionist himself. Not for sentimental, social or religious reasons but because of the anomalies of the present law. He gave examples of this. He felt, however, that some kind of deterrent was necessary to take the place of hanging, which, in his opinion, is a deterrent at present.

Further, he felt that public opinion regarded it as a deterrent and would not be happy if it were abolished and not replaced with something else. He dismissed the possibility of going back to the position before the Homicide Act with the phrase 'we must go forward and not back'. ... The solution which he favours, and which he thinks would be acceptable to the police and to public opinion, is to abolish capital punishment but to allow judges to place restrictive conditions on the life sentences which they must by law impose. These restrictions would not interfere with the Home Secretary's functions but he would have regard to them when life sentences came up for review. I understand that in private conversation Lord Parker left the impression that this solution would be acceptable to 'more than half the judges in England'. 14 February 1962 CRI/ 61 431/5/36.

214 Note to Archbishop, 11 March 1965; The Ramsey Papers 76:178. Library of Lambeth Palace.

215 The title was taken from a popular song sung by the Kingston Trio. The play transferred to the Mayfair Theatre. A review appearing in *The New York Times* of 19 October 1964 reported that 'Mr. Wright and Mr. Murray [who had devised and staged it] are evidently young men with strong convictions, and 'Hang Down Your Head and Die' is almost furiously single-minded in its detestation of capital punishment. Executions by gas, the electric chair and the firing squad are as odious to this 'entertainment' as hanging. But the noose is England's lethal weapon and, like good Englishmen, Mr. Wright and Mr. Murray devote most of their attention to the English way'.

216 Others, including Lord Kilmuir, refused the invitation. The play, written by David Wright, encountered some difficulty with censorship imposed by the Lord Chamberlain. Intervention by Lord Gardiner and others led to the restoration of the episodes that had been cut, including a rehearsal of a hanging with sandbags. See *The Times*, 8 February 1964.

217 Conversation with Sir Louis, 22 May 2010.

218 I am grateful to Anthony Howard for pointing me to the relevant passage in his *RAB: The Life of R.A. Butler.*

219 I am very grateful to Karen Dickson of the University of British Columbia Law Library for finding and sending me a copy of that speech. The formal text, 'The Rule of Law in a Changing Society', actually focused solely on the civil law and the relation between formal law and administrative rules.

220 See *The U.B.C. Alumni Chronicle*, Autumn 1959, Vol. 13, No. 3, 27.

221 What Howard said was that 'Political forecasts – despite the sudden resurrection last week of views already expressed by Lord Parker at Vancouver in September 1959 – remain gloomy'. 'Parliament and the Gallows', *New Statesman, op. cit.*

222 A. Howard; *RAB, op. cit.*, 271–2.

223 Harold Macmillan to Lord Kilmuir, 1 November 1959. Kilmuir papers, Churchill College Archives.

224 There were seven solicitors and 47 barristers in the House of Lords of the mid-1960s. The House of Commons elected in 1959 contained 19 solicitors (11 Conservatives and eight members of the Labour Party); and 83 members of the Bar (50 Conservatives, 2 Liberals and 21 members of the Labour Party). The legal composition of the October 1964 Parliament was little changed: 33 solicitors (21 Conservatives and 11 members of the Labour Party); and 77 members of the Bar (54 Conservatives, three Liberals and 20 members of the Labour Party). Based on *Dod's Parliamentary Companion 1964* (1964) London: Business Directories Ltd., and *Dod's Parliamentary Companion 1965* (1965) London: Business Directories Ltd.

225 Five members of the Labour Party who were solicitors and 18 who were barristers, one member of the Conservative Party who was a solicitor and 12 who were barristers, and three members of the Liberal Party who were barristers, voted for abolition. 20 barristers and two solicitors, all Conservatives, voted in favour of retaining the death penalty.

226 46 Conservative and two Labour Members who had been called to the Bar voted in favour of the Government in 1957; one Conservative, 11 Labour and four Liberals voted against.

227 See J. Heenan (1974); *A Crown of Thorns: An Autobiography 1951–1963*, London: Hodder and Stoughton.

228 Pope Pius XII; 'The Moral Limits of Medical Research and Treatment', an address given on 14 September 1952 by His Holiness to the First International Congress on the Histopathology of the Nervous System. http://www.ewtn.com/library/ PAPALDOC/P12PSYCH.HTM

229 The Methodists, for instance, had assumed an abolitionist position at the time of the 1956 debate on the Homicide Bill, and they had advised Methodist Members of Parliament accordingly. It was reported that 'The whole matter came on to the Committee Agenda early in the Connexional Year on account of a request from the British Council of Churches that we should submit a memorandum on the subject to their Social Responsibility Department. We undertook a further study based upon a summary of facts and arguments prepared by the Chairman of the Standing Committee. In the subsequent discussion the Committee reached the unanimous judgment that capital punishment should be abolished or suspended. This judgment was submitted to the Executive Committee, who confirmed it, with two dissentient voices. It is interesting to report that, after a discussion based on the Memorandum submitted by the Department of Christian Citizenship, the Social Responsibility Department of the B.C.C. voted unanimously in favour of abolition or suspension ... the matter was debated in the House of Commons, when a majority voted in favour of abolition or suspension. A letter was sent to all Methodist Members of Parliament and to members of the Government prior to the debate indicating the judgment of the Executive Committee of the Department'. Report of the Methodist Conference Leeds, Representative Session, 2 July 1956: 7–8.

230 H. Potter, *Hanging in Judgment: Religion and the Death Penalty in England*, op. cit., vii.

231 Based on *ibid*, 192.

232 See 'Bishops want Death Penalty Ended or Suspended'. *The Times*, 18 January 1962. An earlier motion brought to the Lower House in October 1961 'was carried by a considerable majority'. Letter from the prolocutor, the Ven. G. Hilder, to Lord President of the Convocation of Canterbury, 6 October 1961. The Ramsey Papers 1961. Ramsey 76:4; Library of Lambeth Palace.

233 See 'Church call for Abolition of Capital Punishment', *The Times*, 6 October 1961.

234 Letter 19.10.61: From Ronald Hornby, Chief Information Officer, Church Assembly, to Cantuar; The Ramsey Papers 1961. Library of Lambeth Palace.

235 Robert Beloe told John Sainty in the government whips' office in the House of Lords that 'The Archbishop has been very anxious to take possibly a very prominent part in the Second Reading in the Lords ...' Letter of 8 February 1965; The Ramsey Papers 76:169. Library of Lambeth Palace.

236 Letter of 27 January 1965; The Ramsey Papers 76:166. Library of Lambeth Palace.

237 Robert Beloe to John Sainty, 8 February 1965; The Ramsey Papers 76:169. Library of Lambeth Palace.

238 The Archbishop of Canterbury informed the Archbishop of York that 'The Leader of the House [Lord Longford] and the Lord Chancellor had put to me the idea that I might introduce the Bill in the Lords as it cannot be treated as a Government Bill'. Letter of 27 January 1965; The Ramsey Papers 1965 76:166. Library of Lambeth Palace.

239 Letter of 17 February 1965. The Archbishop's reply was that 'I think you know that I am about to leave on a six week tour abroad, but on the assumption that the Bill will not be going to the House of Lords until after the Easter recess, I gladly accept your invitation, and will do my best. I am, of course, only an amateur Parliamentarian, but

I know I can count on considerable help from the Lord Chancellor and others ...'
Letter of 19 February. Ramsey 76, ff. 145–229; The Ramsey Papers 1965. Library of
Lambeth Palace.

240 Based on a letter from Sydney Silverman of 1 March 1965; The Ramsey Papers
76:175. Library of Lambeth Palace.

241 He observed in a note to the Archbishop, 'Silverman ... is completely dedicated to
abolition [and] has made things very difficult with the Conservatives who oppose this
Bill owing to his doctrinaire, unbending and waspish behaviour in the House and in
Committee'. (Note of 12 March 1965; Ramsey 76:182)

242 Undated letter. The Ramsey Papers. 76:177; Library of Lambeth Palace.

243 Note, 7 January 1965. Ramsey 76:146; The Ramsey Papers. Library of Lambeth
Palace.

244 Letter from John Sainty to Robert Beloe, 11 February 1965. Ramsey 76, ff. 145–229;
The Ramsey Papers. Library of Lambeth Palace.

245 Note from Robert Beloe. 10 January 1965; The Ramsey Papers 76:170. Library of
Lambeth Palace.

246 Letter from Sir George Coldstream to Robert Beloe, 13 January 1965; The Ramsey
Papers 76:147. Library of Lambeth Palace.

247 Letter from Archbishop of York to Robert Beloe, 27 January 1965; The Ramsey
Papers 76:166. Library of Lambeth Palace.

248 Letter, Robert Beloe to Sir George Coldstream, 1 February 1965; The Ramsey Papers
76:167. Library of Lambeth Palace.

249 Letter of 4 February 1965; The Ramsey Papers 76:168. Library of Lambeth Palace.

250 Mervyn Stockwood, for instance, sent the archbishop an account of the part played by
the Church in previous debates with the observation that he hoped the bishops would
'turn up in large numbers [to vote in the House of Lords] to undo the mischief of
their predecessors'. Letter of 12 March 1965. The Ramsey Papers 76:186. Library of
Lambeth Palace.

251 For example, Robert Beloe told the Archbishop that Robert Stopford, the Bishop of
London, was uneasy about the prospect of abolition impairing the safety of the police
force. Between 1925 and 1935, Stopford had been senior history master at Oundle,
one of his pupils having been Sir Joseph Simpson, later the Metropolitan Police
Commissioner. 'There is no doubt that opposition is building up among a lot of quite
ordinary people', said Bedoe. 'Robert London, mentioned your proposed part in it.
He did not, of course, question it, but said that he supposed that there were moments
when the Bishops should come down into the arena but that if they were to do so
they must ensure that the police has as full protection as it was possible to give them
without capital punishment. Simpson is one of his pupils from Oundle days and he has
no doubt been talking to him. Simpson is quite a sound man'. Note of 6 March 1965.
Ramsey 76:176; The Ramsey Papers 1965. Library of Lambeth Palace.

252 He said elsewhere that 'I am sure that no one could possibly object to your speaking
strongly in favour of the Bill, but if you took it over and made yourself responsible for
its conduct, I am equally sure that a very great many people both inside the House and
elsewhere would be – perhaps shocked is too strong a word – but at least very greatly
upset'. Letter of 24 March 1965; The Ramsey Papers 76:191. Library of Lambeth
Palace.

253 Letter of 26 February 1965; The Ramsey Papers 176:174. Library of Lambeth
Palace.

254 Robert Beloe, note of 12 March 1965; The Ramsey Papers 76:183. Library of
Lambeth Palace.

255 Letter of 27 May 1965; The Ramsey Papers 76:196. Library of Lambeth Palace.

256 Letter to the Archbishop of Canterbury, 18 June 1965. He said 'so far as the interests
of the Bill are concerned both in the House of Lords and in the country, it would be a

tremendous advantage to its supporters if, after all, you were able to take charge'; The Ramsey Papers 76:203. Library of Lambeth Palace.

257 He said in a letter to Sydney Silverman on 23 June 'my best way of helping the Death Penalty Bill … will not be by moving the Second Reading and having charge of the Bill. … I shall do my utmost to assist whoever is in charge of the Bill, and to help it at every stage that I can'. Ramsey 76:203; The Ramsey Papers. Library of Lambeth Palace.

258 'Inspired Leader', *The Guardian*, 12 March 1974.

259 Letter of 24 June 1965; The Ramsey Papers 76:206. Library of Lambeth Palace.

260 Letter of 10 June. The Ramsey Papers 76:200. Library of Lambeth Palace. There was a Church Assembly likely to meet at what was projected to be the time of the debate, and there was some effort to ensure that only a quorum would attend, freeing the other bishops for the debate.

261 Letter of 29 June 1965. The Ramsey Papers 76:209. Library of Lambeth Palace.

262 Robert Beloe wrote to one such Peer on 9 July to say that the archbishop 'would be so grateful if you could give him an idea of whether you can attend. … It seems more than likely that there will be enough speakers for one day and that the vote will, therefore, be taken on 20th July. There is likely, I am told, to be considerable opposition to the Bill'; The Ramsey Papers 76:211. Library of Lambeth Palace.

263 Note of 19 July 1965; The Ramsey Papers 76:212. Library of Lambeth Palace.

264 Letter of 18 October 1965; The Ramsey Papers 76:226. Library of Lambeth Palace.

265 Robert Beloe, Note of 17 June 1965; The Ramsey Papers 76:201. Library of Lambeth Palace.

266 *The Sunday Telegraph*, June 27 1965.

267 A. Oakley, unpublished typescript of biography of Barbara Wootton, Ch. 14, 345.

268 Ann Oakley reflected of her *Social Science and Social Pathology* that it 'was an enterprise much ahead of its time in insisting that social science work must respect canons widely accepted in the broader scientific community as to what counts as knowledge'. Unpublished typescript of biography of Barbara Wootton, Ch. 12, 5.

269 Her speaking notes recited that she would:

> 'Open with assumption that all sides in the controversy are at one in wishing to respect human life, and that only difference is how best to achieve this. …
>
> Homicide Act compromise indefensible. This alone the present issue. Examples of its working. Total abolition a small step inasmuch as it means end to hanging about two or three people annually; a big step inasmuch as it may save one or two lives. Present law cannot be regarded as effective deterrent: chance of a murderer being hung is now less than 2 per cent.
>
> Aim of present law is to frighten off the professional criminal; but 75% capital murderers have no previous history of violence; 25% have no previous convictions of any kind and less than 50% have convictions for property offences.
>
> Law does not result in professional criminals being hung. …
>
> Fear of increase in murders if no death penalty. Experience abroad. Most valuable evidence from neighbouring states with or without D.P. in USA and Australia. In these no perceptible difference in trend.
>
> Public opinion hostile to abortion. What public opinion does not know. Public visualise murders of defenceless old women or in course of bank robberies etc: in fact high proportion of family murders. Public does not appreciate high proportion of murderers who commit suicide or are mentally unbalanced. Public does not visualise the whole revolting procedure involved in an execution. … Public does not appreciate the very small proportion of murderers who are now hung.

The risks of abolition. Of course there are risks – as in everything. … No one can escape risks'. (Gardiner Papers, The British Library)

270 HL Deb 19 July 1965 Vol. 268 cc456–76.

271 Barbara Wootton recollected how: '… in the House of Lords debates in 1965 on the Bill to abolish the death penalty for murder[,] [o]n the crucial question of the risk that, without the deterrent of capital punishment, murders might become more frequent one or two speakers produced a wealth of evidence as to the experience of other countries in which the death penalty had already been abolished. This for the most part suggested that the risk was minimal. Yet no attempt whatever was made, by those who advocated the retention of hanging, either to criticise this evidence or to produce further facts that pointed in a contrary direction. One after another these speakers were content to say that in their opinion (based one can only suppose upon introspection into their own sanguinary impulses), more murders would follow if murderers were no longer hanged. Between the two groups there occurred absolutely no meeting of minds'. B. Wootton, *In a World I Never Made: Autobiographical Reflections, op. cit.*, 214.

272 HL Deb 26 October 1965 Vol. 269 cc529–48.

273 That was certainly the thrust of Terence Morris and Louis Blom-Cooper's *A Calendar of Murder*, London: Michael Joseph, which had been published the year before. On p. 280, they wrote 'In this country, murder is overwhelmingly a domestic crime in which men kill their wives, mistresses and children, and women kill their children'. It is not certain whether it was that study which Lord Parker had in mind, but there is a strong probability that it played its part.

274 See 'Conversion In The Death Cell', *The Times*, 16 May 1962.

275 Its long title was 'An Act to abolish capital punishment in the case of persons convicted in Great Britain of murder or convicted of murder or a corresponding offence by court-martial and, in connection therewith, to make further provision for the punishment of persons so convicted'.

276 The decision was the result of a lengthy tussle between the judges and politicians over who should control the decision to release those sentenced to life imprisonment. As early as 1961, Sir Charles Cunningham had briefed the Home Secretary to the effect that: 'Before a decision is taken, we ought to give closer consideration to the Lord Chief Justice's unofficial proposition that the death penalty should be abolished and that the courts should be given discretion to impose instead a sentence of imprisonment of whatever length they think is justified by the gravity of the crime. I think the Lord Chief Justice concedes that the Secretary of State would still have to review life sentences or other sentences of great length, from time to time; but he argues that the courts should be free to indicate by the severity of their sentence what was their view of the seriousness of the crime and that this would assist the Secretary of State in exercising his power of recommending remission. There are obvious difficulties in this scheme: but we should prepare ourselves to comment on it if the Lord Chief Justice puts it forward officially'. A year later, a Home Office note recorded that 'The solution which [the Lord Chief Justice] favours, and which he thinks would be acceptable to the police and to public opinion, is to abolish capital punishment but to allow judges to place restrictive conditions on the life sentences which they must by law impose. These restrictions would not interfere with the Home Secretary's functions but he would have regard to them when life sentences came up for review' (CRI/ 61 431/5/36). On 27 of July, Lord Parker did indeed move an amendment whose object, he stated 'is very simple, … to abolish once and for all a fixed penalty for murder; in other words, to prevent life imprisonment from being the only sentence which can be passed. The Amendment is in simple terms. If it is passed, subsection (1) will read: … a person convicted of murder shall … be liable at the discretion of the court to imprisonment for life… I dislike a fixed sentence, and now that it is proposed to abolish the fixed sentence of the death penalty I do not wish to

see another fixed sentence in its place. In a fixed sentence there is no room for any matters of mitigation. The sentence is passed; and the prisoner is removed from the dock, when almost the only things that have been said publicly are things which are against him. No one hears of his home circumstances or his background. I do not think that any Home Secretary would claim to have a monopoly of the quality of mercy' (HL Deb 27 July 1965 Vol. 268 cc1191–272) Sir Louis Blom-Cooper's recollection of what then transpired is quite graphic: 'Hubert Parker who was then Lord Chief Justice moved two amendments to the Bill. And the first was to get rid of the mandatory life sentence and make life imprisonment the maximum penalty. As an alternative he said, we'll have a minimum recommendation which ultimately became subsection one, subsection two. And on the abandonment to the mandatory penalty, he won the vote by, he won the vote by two votes. And so at the very end of July of '65, we had got rid of the mandatory penalty for life imprisonment which we've been saddled with for 40 years since. Then what happened was he got nobbled by Soskice who was then Home Secretary. The Home Office wanted to keep the question of discharge, remember this is all pre-parole which is '67 Act. And eventually he was prevailed upon to abandon his main amendment and second best, to move this second amendment which became part of the Bill. When it, when it came back to the Commons at the end of October in '65, they had to approve the second amendment which was the sub-section one, sub-section two, the minimum recommendation. And every speaker except the minister from the Home Office, were totally in favour of Parker's first amendments but they all said, look, we're nearly at the end of the Parliamentary session, if we go back on that, go back to the first amendment, it'll have to go back to the Commons, er, go back to the Lords again and we'll be in the peat bog situation. And Gerald Gardiner was doing his nut, was saying, we'll lose our death penalty and we can't have that. So they all said, well, for the sake, because of the timescale, and the sake of saving the abolition of the death penalty, we'll accept the second amendment'. Section 2 of the Act accordingly recited: 'On sentencing any person convicted of murder to imprisonment for life the Court may at the same time declare the period which it recommends to the Secretary of State as the minimum period which in its view should elapse before the Secretary of State orders the release of that person on licence under section'.

277 Minutes of the Meeting of the National Campaign for the Abolition of Capital Punishment Executive Committee 21 January 1966 in the House of Commons.

278 T.P. Morris and L. Blom-Cooper estimate that there were to be 14 attempts to reintroduce the death penalty just in the years when Mrs Thatcher was in office. T. Morris and L. Blom-Cooper (2011); *Fine Lines and Distinctions: Murder, Manslaughter and the Unlawful Taking of Human Life*, Hook: Waterside Press, ix.

279 Duncan Sandys, 1908–1987, had been Minister of Supply, Minister for Housing and Local Government and Secretary of State for Defence in the 1950s. He was heavily implicated in campaigns against immigration, Rhodesian sanctions and the Race Relations Act, and had become one of the more prominent advocates of restoration. He had helped to found the Campaign for the Reintroduction of the Death Penalty in 1966,and had pursued his case vigorously in the mass media and Parliament. He had, for instance, appeared on a *Man Alive* television programme on 30 January 1968 to argue the case for the death penalty, claiming that 'Since the suspension of capital punishment, criminals have shown greater readiness to carry guns'. *The Times*, 31 January 1968. He was to reiterate that theme over the months to come, saying, for instance, in July 1968 that 'Now that the deterrent of the death penalty has been removed, criminals no longer hesitate, as they did before, to carry a gun'. (*The Times*, 25 July 1968). He talked in the summer of 1969 about introducing a bill to bring back hanging (see *The Times*, 16 June 1969), but his attempt was unsuccessful. On 24 June, he was denied leave to initiate legislation by 256 votes to 126.

280 Each time, the government was obliged to consider its own response, declaring itself anxious not to make the death penalty a party issue and considering how to manage the politics of the debate. One possibility, mooted in 1966, was to try to arrange for a Conservative back-bencher to oppose Duncan Sandys. (Note to Prime Minister of 21 September 1966, PREM 13 1563).

281 It was agreed in October 1968 that 'The National Campaign must ... be ready to conduct an active campaign from the autumn of 1969, particularly if the Government did not indicate active endorsement of new abolitionist legislation. The Chairman and Honorary Treasurer would seek an interview with the Leader of the Opposition to discuss his position and in particular his attitude to the Duncan Sandys campaign. The Campaign must in good time produce a document with the up-to-date facts for use against the Sandys campaign and in readiness for the introduction of new legislation when the subject of abolition would again receive considerable publicity'. Minutes of the Meeting of the National Campaign for the Abolition of Capital Punishment Executive Committee 22 October 1968 at 2 Amen Court.

282 It reported in its 1968–9 Annual Report that 'the Trustees of the Calvert Memorial Fund have made over the money ... for the purpose of informing the public of the facts and figures. A short pamphlet, 'Murder and Capital Punishment', was produced in time to counter an initial attempt by Mr. Duncan Sandys to restore the death penalty. ... informal meetings have been held with a parliamentary group, with the Executive Committee of the Campaign for the Abolition of Capital Punishment whose Chairman is now Canon Collins; and with other interested voluntary bodies'.

283 It was a rise noted with some unease by a National Council for the Abolition of the Death Penalty: 'There were also unpublished indications that the numbers of murders in course of theft had increased – a point much stressed by Mr Duncan Sandys. The Honorary Treasurer was asked to put three questions to Mr Blom Cooper, who was at present carrying out a research project with Dr Terence Morris, and who had agreed to furnish the Campaign with information. These questions concerned diminished responsibility, the effect of abolition on the murder rate in other abolitionist countries and the relationship, if any, between the increase in the murder rate and the present instability of society'. Minutes of the Meeting of the National Campaign for the Abolition of Capital Punishment Executive Committee 22 October 1968 at 2 Amen Court.

284 Burke Trend to the Prime Minister, 10 December 1969. Emphasis in the original. PREM 13 2552.

285 *The Times*, 3 November 1969. The next general election was in fact to be on 18 June 1970.

286 Based on E. Gibson and S. Klein; *Murder: 1957 to 1968, op. cit.*

287 A note was made of a meeting between the National Council for the Abolition of the Death Penalty and the Lord Chancellor: 'The Chairman [Lord Altrincham] reported on a meeting with Lord Gardiner. A fresh Bill would be required when the present Act expired in July, 1970. This legislation could be expected to be mentioned in the Queen's Speech in October 1969, but doubts were expressed on this score in view of the political difficulties of the present Government'. Minutes of the Meeting of the National Campaign for the Abolition of Capital Punishment Executive Committee 22 October 1968 at 2 Amen Court.

288 Minute of 16 April 1969, PREM 13 2552. Duncan Sandys was inevitably less sure. He remarked that 'the Home Office report does nothing to weaken and much to strengthen the case for restoring capital punishment'. *The Times*, 7 November 1969.

289 The Permanent Abolition of Capital Punishment for Murder, Memorandum by the Secretary of State for the Home Department and the Secretary of State for Scotland, 6 May 1969.

290 Note to Prime Minister of 17 September 1969, PREM 13 2552.

291 The report argued that the risk of becoming a victim of murder had remained unchanged at three in a million between 1959 and 1966.

292 'The Commons usually reassembles for a short period, normally two to three weeks, in October (after the Party Conferences) to finish off any business not completed before the summer recess. This period is known as the spillover. Any remaining legislation that is not completed in this spillover period has to be re-introduced in the next session if the government wants to continue with it'. (http://news.bbc.co.uk/democracylive/hi/guides/newsid_82000/82033.stm)

293 Conclusions of a Meeting of the Cabinet held at 10 Downing Street … 22 May, 1969, CABINET CC (69) 24th Conclusions.

294 Note to Prime Minister of 17 September 1969, PREM 13 2552.

295 Conclusions of a Meeting of the Cabinet held at 10 Downing Street … 25 September, 1969 Cabinet CC (69) 45th Conclusions.

296 Note to Prime Minister of 17 September 1969, PREM 13 2552.

297 See *The Times*, 14 October 1969.

298 Note from Burke Trend to the Prime Minister, 24 September 1969, PREM 13 2552. The Cabinet Notebook recorded 25/9/69 3. <u>Capital Punishment</u> (oral) HS – Argues against dealing with issue of abolition lapsing if left till next session, after "Murder" available. Best fit it in now into "spillover". Danger of reversion to 1957 Act.

   L.Ch. Better to publish before Cons. Party Conf.?

   LPS – and to get it through the Lords. Against that, case for deferring wiser (?) – due to danger of influencing by-elections.

299 Conclusions of a Meeting of the Cabinet held at 10 Downing Street … 23 October, 1969 Cabinet CC (69) 51st Conclusions. The Cabinet Notebook records 3. <u>Cap. Pun.</u> (oral)

   HS – Warding off Tory Oppn. Proposal to set up an independent committee to review murder stats. Counter with statement that HO already have this material and "Murder" doc.

   P.M. Don't give them a chance to make pol. Capital out of this, least of all before by-elections. Best to publish first and draw their attention to it "as a matter of conscience, not statistics".

300 Duncan Sandys had publicly floated the idea that the government would move on the final abolition of capital punishment before the Christmas recess (see *The Times*, 7 November 1969). He had not been deterred by his defeat in the House of Commons. In October 1969 he resumed campaigning, claiming that he would present a petition to the House of Commons when it reassembled (*The Times*, 9 October 1969), and the petition was duly presented on 15 December.

301 See *The Times*, 16 December 1969.

302 The label was Quintin Hogg's own. Letter from Home Secretary to the Prime Minister, 26 November 1969. PREM 13 2552.

303 Conclusions of a Meeting of the Cabinet held at 10 Downing Street … 27 November, 1969 CABINET CC (69) 57th Conclusions.

304 Letter from Home Secretary to the Prime Minister, 26 November 1969. PREM 13 2552.

305 Conclusions of a Meeting of the Cabinet held at 10 Downing Street … 4 December, 1969 CABINET CC (69) 59th Conclusions.

306 Letter to the Prime Minister, 28 November 1969. PREM 13 2552.

307 Note to the Prime Minister, 5 December 1969. PREM 13 2552.

308 See 'Sandys petition opens hanging debate today', *The Times*, 15 December 1969.

309 L. Abse (1973); *Private Member*, London: MacDonald, 109.

310 *The Times*, 17 December 1969.

311 *The Times*, 15 December 1969.

312   The figures 'show what they usually show; they show that murder is, in the main, a family affair; they show that in one-third of all cases the murderer commits suicide either at the time or soon afterwards in cases suggestive of a disordered mind. As to numbers, in the first full year after abolition, 1966, they fell; in 1967, they rose; in 1968, they fell; and it looks as if in 1969 they are likely to have fallen again. There is one thing which I should like to make clear, because this is a subject on which, rightly or wrongly, I have always said what I think myself. I think it is absolutely useless to try to guess what would have happened in murder cases if the Homicide Act had been there when it was not there'. HL Deb 17 December 1969 Vol. 306 cc1106–258.

313   *Ibid.*

314   Barbara Wootton, addressing the House of Lords on the 1965 Bill, remarked that 'My Lords, of course we run risks. One cannot avoid risks in this world. We know that risks are inherent in the work of the police officer and the prison officer, and we are all profoundly grateful for the courage with which the members of those services face those risks a courage which on occasions seems almost to pass the bounds of credibility. We know that old ladies like myself living in isolated circumstances run risks, and they are risks which we are well prepared to take, knowing that as yet we still live in a community with a small minority of dangerously unbalanced and irresponsible people. In one sense, your Lordships are being asked to take a very large step, because anything that is concerned even with a single human life is a large step. In another sense, you are being asked to take a very small step: you are being asked to reduce the chance that a murderer will be hanged, from a rate of something of the order of 1½ per cent. to zero. There is reason to hope that in this very small step the additional risks that are to be taken will be minimal'. HL Deb 19 July 1965 Vol. 268 cc456–76.

315   Those arguments continue to rumble on outside England and Wales. They are still alive in the United States, for instance. See the article on the debate between candidates for the position of Attorney General of Massachusetts in September 2010 (*The Boston Globe*, 1 October 2010).

316   Minutes of the Meeting of the Executive Committee 19 July 1960 at the House of Commons.

317   General Election 1964 Questions of Policy. Society of Friends (Quakers) Questionnaire.

318   B. Wootton (1992); *Selected Writings: Volume 1: Crime and the Penal System*, Houndmills: Macmillan, 87.

319   David Garland remarked of capital punishment in the United States of America that it 'is largely an expressive measure today, held in place chiefly by emotionally charged political considerations rather than by more instrumental concerns such as deterrent crime control'. 'Capital Punishment and American Culture', *op. cit.*, 349.

320   D. Garland (2009); 'A Culturalist Theory of Punishment?', *Punishment and Society*, Vol. 11, No. 2, 260.

321   Email, 10 August 2014.

322   See *The Times*, 12 August 1964.

323   See R. Hood (1996); *The Death Penalty: A World-Wide Perspective*, Oxford: Clarendon Press, 7–8.

324   'I have asked', he said, 'the Criminal Law Revision Committee to review the law relating to, and the penalties for, offences against the person, including homicide, in the light of, and subject to, the recent decision of Parliament to make permanent the statutory provision abolishing the death penalty for murder'. HC Deb 05 March 1970 Vol. 797 c150W.

325   D. Faulkner (1991); *Continuity and Change in the Home Office*, Home Office Papers by Senior Officers, Occasional Papers in Administrative Studies, London: Home Office, 7.

326 See 'Violent Crime and Sexual Offences Homicide', Office for National Statistics, 2015 (http://www.ons.gov.uk/ons/dcp171776_394478.pdf).

327 Of patterns in the United States, Blumstein talks about what he calls 'trendless crimes' (Blumstein, A. (2006); 'Disaggregating the Violence Trends', in A. Blumstein and J. Wallman (eds.) *The Crime Drop in America*, Cambridge, Cambridge University Press, 19). Compared with the number of woundings known to the police in England and Wales (an admittedly broad and disparate category that included the infliction of relatively mild injuries), not only were there very few murders, but their rate of increase in what was considered to be a troubled time was very much less substantial (they grew from a small base by some 150% compared with a growth in woundings of over 500% during the period). It was those trends that had long encouraged academics and others to contend that the aetiology of the crime of murder must be treated as if it were *sui generis*:

Woundings Known to the Police: 1957–1972

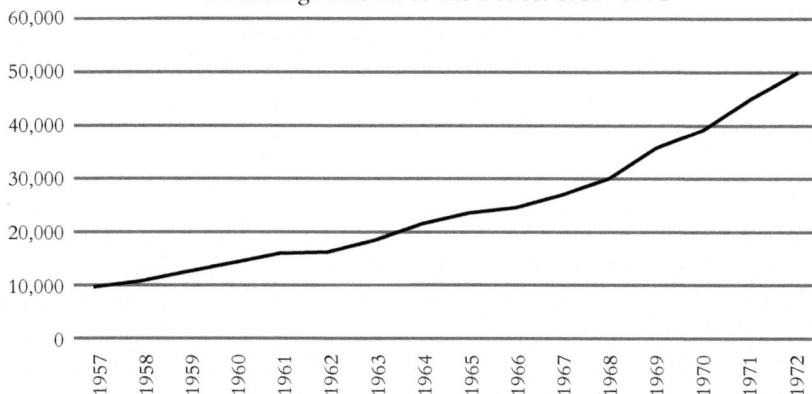

328 See A. Strauss (1982); 'Interorganizational negotiation', *Journal of Contemporary Ethnography*, Vol.11, No. 3, 350–367.

Bibliography

V. Bailey (nd); 'The Shadow of the Gallows: The Death Penalty and the British Labour Government, 1945–51, http://www.historycooperative.org/journals/lhr/18.2/bailey.html

H. Berkeley (1972); *Crossing the Floor*, London: George Allen and Unwin

B. Block and J. Hostettler (1997); *Hanging in the Balance*, Winchester: Waterside Press

L. Blom-Cooper and T. Morris (2004); *With Malice Aforethought: A Study of the Crime and Punishment for Homicide*, Oxford: Hart Publishing

A. Blumstein (2006); 'Disaggregating the Violence Trends', in A. Blumstein and J. Wallman (eds.) *The Crime Drop in America*, Cambridge: Cambridge University Press, 13–44

M. Box (1983); *Rebel Advocate: A Biography of Gerald Gardiner*, London: Victor Gollancz

R. Butler (1971); *The Art of the Possible: The Memoirs of Lord Butler K.G., C.H.*, London: Hamish Hamilton

E. Roy Calvert, (1927); *Capital Punishment in the Twentieth Century*, London: G. P. Putnam's Sons

—(1929); 'Murder and the Death Penalty', *The Nation*, October 16th, 406

E. Carpenter (1997); *Cantuar: The Archbishops in their Office*, London: Mowbray

O. Chadwick (1990); *Michael Ramsey A Life*, Oxford: Clarendon Press

J. Christoph (1962); 'Capital Punishment and British Party Responsibility', *Political Science Quarterly*, Vol. 77, No. 1, 19–35

—(1962); *Capital Punishment and British Politics*, London: George Allen & Unwin

D. Dagan (nd); *Defiance and Death: Public Opinion, Politicians, and the Abolition of Capital Punishment in Great Britain and the United States*, Master's Thesis, Brandeis University

Dod's Parliamentary Companion 1964 (1964); London: Business Directories Ltd.

Dod's Parliamentary Companion 1965 (1965); London: Business Directories Ltd.

J. Doering (2002); 'Lord Hailsham: The Reluctant Peer', *Contemporary Review*, 1 February, 92–97

B. Donoghue (2005); *Downing Street Diary: With Harold Wilson in No. 10*, London: Jonathan Cape

D. Faulkner (1991); *Continuity and Change in the Home Office*, Home Office Papers by Senior Officers, Occasional Papers in Administrative Studies, London: Home Office

G. Gardiner (1956); *Capital Punishment as a Deterrent: And the Alternative*, London: Victor Gollancz

—'Lord Gardiner Interviewed' (1964); *The Economist*, 28 March 1964, 1209–1212

D. Garland (2009); 'A Culturalist Theory of Punishment?', *Punishment and Society*, Vol. 11, No. 2, 259–268

E. Gibson and S Klein (1969); *Murder, 1957 to 1968: a Home Office Statistical Division report on murder in England and Wales*, London: HMSO

V. Gollancz (1955); *Capital Punishment: The heart of the matter*, London: Victor Gollancz

J. Heenan (1974); *A Crown of Thorns: An Autobiography 1951–1963*, London: Hodder and Stoughton.

B. Hollingsworth (1976); 'David Soskice in Russia in 1917', *European Studies Review*, Vol. 6, 73–97

Home Policy Committee, Labour Party (1964); *Crime, a Challenge to Us All; Report of the Labour Party's Study Group* London: Labour Party

A. Howard (1962); 'Parliament and the Gallows', *New Statesman*, 23 February, 250

—(1987); *RAB: The Life of R.A. Butler* London: Jonathan Cape

Howard League (1970); *Annual Report 1969–70*, London: Howard League

E. Hughes (1969); *Sydney Silverman: Rebel in Parliament*, London and Edinburgh: Skilton

A. Koestler (1940); *Darkness at Noon*, London: Cape

—and C.H. Rolph (1961); *Hanged by the Neck: An Exposure of Capital Punishment in England*, Baltimore, Maryland: Penguin Books

J. Mack (1965); review of *Crime A Challenge*, *The British Journal of Criminology*, Volume 5, No. 1, 103–4

T. Morris (1989); *Crime and Criminal Justice since 1945*, Oxford: Basil Blackwell

—and L. Blom-Cooper (1964); *A Calendar of Murder; Criminal Homicide in England since 1957*, London: M. Joseph

—and L. Blom-Cooper (2011); *Fine Lines and Distinctions: Murder, Manslaughter and the Unlawful Taking of Human Life*, Hook: Waterside Press

G. Eyre Noel (1964); *Harold Wilson and the 'new Britain': The Making of a Modern Prime Minister*, London: Campion Press

B. Pimlott (1992); *Harold Wilson*, London: HarperCollins

H. Potter (1993); *Hanging in Judgment: Religion and the Death Penalty in England*, London: SCM Press

Lord Stow Hill (1967); 'The Abolishment of Capital Punishment in England', *Women's Law Journal*, 7

A. Strauss (1982); 'Interorganizational negotiation', *Journal of Contemporary Ethnography*, Vol.11, No. 3, 350–367

E. Tuttle (1961); *The Crusade against Capital Punishment in Great Britain*, London: Stevens and Sons

The U.B.C. Alumni Chronicle (1959); Vol. 13, No. 3, 27

Lord Windlesham (1993); *Responses to Crime*, Vol. 2, Oxford: Clarendon Press

B. Wootton (1967); *In a World I Never Made: Autobiographical Reflections*, London: George Allen and Unwin

—(1992); *Selected Writings: Vol. 1: Crime and the Penal System*, Houndmills: Macmillan

4 The Liberal Hour II – The Abortion Act 1967 c. 87

Foundations[1]

The Abortion Act of 1967 is rightly viewed as one of the most important pieces of social legislation in the post-war period, and perhaps in the twentieth century.[2]

Introduction

There may have been in the 1960s what Roy Jenkins called the liberal hour, or Jeffrey Weeks the 'golden age of liberal-humanitarian reforms',[3] amounting to a new sensibility, a *Zeitgeist* of a sort, that framed a receptiveness to reform, but it had been decades in the making and there was a marked split between the way in which the situation was regarded by the individuals and organisations that peopled the world immediately around Parliament, on the one hand, and, on the other, by some observers during and after the time. Many individual Members of Parliament and senior civil servants did not seem to have conceived the various bills and measures they were promoting to be part of a collective enterprise. Embedded in the day-to-day, case-driven, practical work of policymaking, it was not immediately evident that there was any general tide of concerted liberal change in which they were playing a part. From within the Home Office, Bob Morris observed in interview about the arguments on liberalisation: 'these are retrospective glosses on events ... [which] presented as individual problems; and how to deal with capital punishment, how to deal with homosexual law reform, how to deal with abortion, weren't seen as part of some liberal process. They were seen as discrete problems which needed particular political solutions'. He was later reported to have said that it was 'difficult to arrive at a collective view on a subject in the Home Office because the issues under discussion were invariably difficult, complex questions to which there were no easy answers: abortion, racial disadvantage ...'[4] His colleague, David Faulkner, concurred when he said that 'quite a lot of time ... was taken up by discussing the best way in which it should be handled in Parliament – you know, Private Members' Bills would be the best way ... so ... a lot [of the focus] was on the logistics of it rather than the morality or whatever'[5] (although he did later say that decency was a common thread amongst his colleagues). And from within Parliament, the former Liberal Member of Parliament, David

Steel, now a member of the House of Lords, the prime mover in the reform of the law on abortion, said, also in interview, that he had had no liaison at all with the promoters of the abolition of capital punishment, the reform of the law on homosexuality or any other movements of the day: 'I think it was coincidence that you had at that period in the '60s ... a whole raft of legislation, capital punishment, homosexuality, abortion, but they were not coordinated. There was no part of a plan. They just all happened to come together at the same time. ... there was nothing as grand as a planned series of Bills ... they just all happened to coincide'. Indeed, he was later to say that he had not appreciated what a revolution he was effecting: 'I didn't realise at the time that people would, 40 years on, be looking back and saying that this was a fundamental change, but of course it was'.[6]

Yet the late 1950s and the 1960s were a remarkably fertile period politically in the criminal justice system, the culmination of decades of striving, and there was at the outset (David Steel nevertheless noted in his autobiography) something of a recognised menu of linked 'great social reforms', that might be attempted by one who, like himself, had succeeded in winning a place in a private members' ballot in the mid-1960s:

> I early on decided that third place in the ballot was too precious to be wasted either on any such minor cause which should be tabled by government or on any tilt at a gigantic windmill. ... it seemed right to take up one of the great social reforms. Capital punishment and divorce law reform had both been tackled. That left the more touchy topics of homosexuality and abortion, both of which bills had successfully passed through the House of Lords and were awaiting champions in the Commons.[7]

Although the principals did not always think of themselves, or chose not to *speak* of themselves,[8] as collaborating in a common enterprise, and there was no formal weaving together of strategies, there *was* a more or less tenuous web of relationships and connections being woven beneath the surface that joined the different reforms together in loose fashion. Because projects coincided in time,[9] various bills moved through Parliament in parallel, steered by like-minded people, and concessions and adjustments had continually to be made in the legislative timetable.[10] The successful passage of one liberal reform made it more likely that principals would believe that others could then follow as if in convoy. Alistair Service, the chairman both of the Family Planning Association and of the Abortion Law Reform Association (ALRA) in the 1960s said that 'the abolition of capital punishment had got through in 1964/65, and that broke the dam for social reform. Gradually we started to realise after the 1966 general election that everything had changed'.[11] Vera Houghton, sometime Chair of ALRA, said much the same: 'The Lords saw themselves as a great reforming chamber and had just reformed capital punishment when Lord Silkin, in conversation with Mrs Schofield Allen whose husband was an MP, said: 'What can we do next?' She replied: 'Abortion law reform' and he seized upon it'.[12] The character of the procession was recognised by the press. *The Times* talked in the beginning of December 1965 about how the House of Lords had achieved a 'hat-trick. After helping to abolish hanging and giving the Commons a lead on homosexual law reform, it voted [last night] ... in favour of a Private Member's Bill by Lord Silkin to change the law on abortion'.[13] And just as the proponents of reform sometimes saw what was in train as a series of linked measures, so did their opponents. In mounting their opposition, they gave unity and coherence to what was afoot.

There was also institutional and political convergence, the memberships of different organisations and campaigns sometimes overlapping. One man, C.H. Rolph, was ubiquitous, for instance, being on the committees of the Howard League and the National Council for the Abolition of the Death Penalty, working with the National Association for Mental Health and acting as the Chairman of both the Homosexual Law Reform Society and the Albany Trust, and those organisations would have in effect converged in and through his person. The Member of Parliament, Ernest Thurtle, active as a would-be abolitionist of capital punishment and a reformer of court martial procedure in the 1930s, was vice-chairman of ALRA, and he was married to Dorothy, ALRA's Vice-President. Victor Gollancz published many of the tracts advocating the abolition of capital punishment and abortion law reform. Christopher Chataway,[14] the Conservative Member of Parliament, and Lord Amulree were both active in support of abortion law reform and Sydney Silverman's bill on capital punishment. Humphrey Berkeley, another Conservative Member of Parliament, seconded Sydney Silverman's bill and introduced his own bill on homosexual law reform. And so it went on.

There was talk between the different reforming organisations about the possibility of working together on joint projects, such as public opinion surveys on problems of shared concern.[15] And there were a number of attempts, some successful, others less so, to forge alliances between bodies,[16] particularly by novice organisations seeking guidance, strength and authority from those better established. The members of those older organisations were obliged in their turn to confer and take stock of the political, social and moral standing of the newcomers who were so wooing them. In a revealing instance, the secretary of one central body, the Church of England Moral Welfare Council,[17] Ena Steel, reported in 1958 to its Chairman, Edward Jones, the Bishop of St. Albans:

> I want to bring you up to date with the campaign which Mr Dyson [of the newly-formed Homosexual Law Reform Society] is organising. I heard from the secretary of the Howard League that he had been to see him about a fortnight ago, taking with him a young clergyman called Hallidie Smith ... He also told me that these two young men had received so much support for what they were doing that it was going to be difficult to put the brake on. Mr Sainsbury[18] had seen them and although he was not impressed he was considering giving them a small sum of money to see

what progress they made, but without committing himself to giving any more unless he approved of what they were doing.[19]

Above all, perhaps, and as Ena Steel's letter suggests, it was the Churches that knitted together some parts of the networks in mid-century. The Church of England was solidly implanted in the House of Lords. Its bishops were by calling and duty professionally dedicated to shaping the public response to matters of moral importance. They equipped themselves with special committees for the purpose, the Church of England Moral Welfare Council being just such a body, and they continually viewed and reviewed what others were saying and doing. Although church membership may have been in decline, it was a still not insignificant activity in the lives of the population of England and Wales (some 19% of the population claimed membership in 1960[20]), and 'religion in the 1960s continued to be ... widely featured in public debate'.[21] The churches came together singly or collectively to prepare public and private pronouncements about social problems and, in so doing, they constructed, framed and synthesised many of the lengthier and more considered arguments which others would put to use in the explanation of their activities. It was in this vein that James Beckford wrote about the manner in which 'religious discourse about social problems [was] more salient and more influential than theories of secularisation have led us to expect'.[22] If only because others lacked the authority, time, training, courage or competence thoroughly to riddle out ethical and theological problems, the views of the churches were commonly invoked,[23] particularly at turning-points, by members of the professions, policy officials, politicians and activists. In November 1965, *The Times* noted, for example, that the fate of Lord Silkin's Abortion Bill in a debate in the House of Lords was 'likely to turn on the views expressed by the Church of England spokesman ... Several peers will be guided by the bishops when they come to vote on the second reading, which is being challenged by Catholic peers'.[24] And at a critical time in the deliberations on that bill, a month after it had received its first reading, the Church of England Assembly's Board for Social Responsibility did indeed publish a report on the ethical questions posed by abortion which came to provide guidance on what was then under way.[25]

The Churches were routinely invited by the campaigning organisations to peruse and comment on what was proposed.[26] They were invited to post their representatives on the committees of activist organisations, and any decision to do so would be fateful because, were it to be taken, they could, on the one hand, bestow significant approval and authority, and, on the other, not only themselves be praised or criticised for their own good or poor judgement but become implicated in whatever then transpired.

It was in this fashion that the Churches found themselves willing or unwilling central participants,[27] commentators, exemplars and coaches in the politics of morality.[28] They were not always in harmony (there was no agreement, for example, on abortion in the British Council of Churches), and they were more prominent in some arenas than in others, but they did hold sway in the politics of the day, perhaps if only because they assumed, and it was assumed by others, that they did and should hold sway – influence, in effect, being thrust upon them. One theme of the next chapter will be the roles played by the Church of England in effectively endorsing, and the Roman Catholic Church in ineffectually opposing, David Steel's bill. It will become apparent that the Hierarchy of the Roman Catholic Church in particular not only sought to intervene (albeit discreetly and covertly) but that it was under unremitting pressure to do so. The Churches could not have abstained from involvement in a matter touching on the sanctity of life even if their officials had wished them to do so.

Any proposed change in the law and the relations and duties it sketched out would also inevitably impinge on a mass of secular organisations, including the professions, and it was a part of the regular work of those bodies to keep a weather eye open for what would affect their members, and then to mobilise, advise, encourage and warn them about the steps, if any, they could and should take. The medical associations, above all, came vigorously to participate at first and second hand in the debates about homosexuality and abortion,[29] the social problems that were at once medical, moral and legal, and they marked out lines and structures of action as they did so. Another theme of this and the next chapter must therefore be the roles played by the British Medical Association, founded in 1832, and the Royal College of Obstetricians and Gynaecologists, founded in 1926.

Finally, and most obviously, links, fractures and formations had to be mediated administratively by the officials and politicians who worked in and around the government of the 1960s to superintend the passage of the bills that were being funnelled through Whitehall and Westminster. It was through the state always that major reforms were conducted in England and Wales, and the state's action or inaction was critical (Diane Munday of the Abortion Law Reform Association remarked that 'Everything we did was aimed at influencing MPs and the Government. The parliamentary and public campaigns meshed together'[30]). If governments did not always overtly promote or impede change, they did from time to time do so covertly by easing or blocking the passage of private member's bills, and I have shown how active the Wilson Government had been in supporting Sydney Silverman's Bill in 1965. Bob Morris reflected that 'that was the convenient way of dealing with it. It was a way the government could distance itself from doing good. You can say that was a very positive and sensible thing. And the other way, you could say it's a very cowardly way of doing things'.

In a centralised polity, where it was taken on trust that the state had diffuse responsibility for the moral, social and economic well-being of the populace, governments were in any event required to respond to events, crises and representations as they arose, and the same ministers, politicians and officials could be found fielding discussions across the entire range of reforms. Being involved in more than one issue, they effectively crafted and aligned the policies that passed before them. A small cast of people could as a result be seen at work on one reform after another, often in conjunction with one another.[31] In the opening days of the 1964 Labour Government, Brian Cubbon had decided, for example, that it would be sensible to brief Sir Frank Soskice on homosexual law reform and abortion law reform in a single memorandum. Three years later another Home Secretary, Roy Jenkins, recalled that 'In late June and July of 1967 there was a rather odd quirk. We were running the Homosexual Reform Bill and the Abortion Bill in double harness. I would say that I attached equal importance to both'.[32] And as Lord Chancellor, Lord Gardiner dealt, sometimes at the very same time, and sometimes most energetically, with members of the National Council for the Abolition of the Death Penalty (of which he had been the President), the Homosexual Law Reform Society and the Abortion Law Reform Association (to which he had been 'a longstanding adviser'[33]). He had, it was reported, delivered a Fabian Society lecture in 1960 in which he had 'outlined a list of legal issues to which he thought the next Labour Government should apply itself [and he] ... mentioned in passing that the abortion law needed to be reformed'.[34] It was his view, he said just before Labour returned to power and he became Lord Chancellor, that 'we are justi-fied in treating as axiomatic the proposition that much of our English law is out of date, and some of it shockingly so. ... Nothing else will do than the setting up within the Lord Chancellor's Office of a strong unit concerned exclusively with law reform ...'[35] (and what he had in mind was the Law Commission which he came to found in 1965).

Again, the Members of Parliament, Reginald Paget and Kenneth Robinson, were both involved in the campaigns about abortion law reform and the aboli-tion of capital punishment. Sir Frank Soskice was well disposed to the aboli-tion of capital punishment but he was queasy about abortion law reform, and he chose to divert discussion away to larger questions of moral decline. Leo Abse,[36] the champion of a host of liberal causes, was hostile to abortion law reform and fought it in the House of Commons – it was his contention that the campaign was sullied by its origins: 'It carried forward the fallacies of the earlier eugenicists, claiming that, without abortion, as the professional classes and more intelligent mastered the art of birth control, the feckless and unfit would breed the next generation of Britons. ...'[37] And, what is more pertinent to my argument, he came to claim further that his opposition to abortion had practical ramifications for his own pursuit of homosexual law reform:

> The Abortion Bill had been proceeding contemporaneously through the House and my onslaughts on this bungling Bill had estranged many of those who had given support to my homosexual Bill. I was nearly impaled upon my own attempts to reshape the Abortion Bill: yielding to the political blackmail, I let it be known that I would lapse into silence on the abortion issue...[38]

In all that jostling, in that work of selection, symbiosis, synthesis, co-operation, detachment and conflict, a complicated, moving political landscape was pieced together. Organisational manoeuvring was to be particularly stark in the history of the next liberal reform I shall consider, the 1967 Abortion Act, the outcome of a private member's bill, whose history 'reflect[ed] the clash of totally incompatible moral attitudes'[39] between those professing to champion the rights of the pregnant woman and those professing to champion the rights of the unborn child.

Scene-setting: The 1861 Offences Against the Person Act

Abortion had from an early stage been chiefly regarded as a criminal rather than a medical matter.[40] Under the common law, women could undergo induced abortions until the time of quickening but the act became a statutory offence under the Malicious Shooting or Stabbing Act – Lord Ellenborough's Act, (43 Geo. III, c. 58) of 1803 – there having been, as its preamble stated, 'no adequate means ... hitherto ... provided for the prevention and punishment of such offences'. Lord Ellenborough[41] was then the Lord Chief Justice, and it has been conjectured that he sought not only to revise the law on abortion in order to lend clarity to an ill-defined area, but also, John Keown believes, to protect the hitherto legally vulnerable pre-quickened foetus[42] and buttress that protection with the capital penalty as part of his vigorous enlargement of the so-called Bloody Code. The Act's first clause provided that 'if any person or persons ... shall wilfully, maliciously, and unlawfully administer to, or cause to be administered to or taken by any of His Majesty's subjects, any deadly poison, or other noxious and destructive substance or thing, with intent ... or thereby to cause and procure the miscarriage of any woman, then being quick with child ...' they would be guilty of felony, punishable by death without benefit of clergy.

The 1803 Act was riddled with uncertainties. It appeared to criminalise only the administration of poisons or 'other noxious substances' (an anomaly which was rectified 25 years later[43]); it left unclear whether a woman who aborted herself was liable to prosecution;[44] and it was confined to instances where the woman was 'quick with child'.[45] Above all, the vagueness of the word 'unlawfully' was to be critical. Its introduction and subsequent retention in the law on abortion were to become a running source of confusion and litigation until the end.

The Act and its successors were continually amended, in some measure as part of the emergence of the rational-legal utilitarianism of the bureaucratic state with its comprehensive legislative reforms, more carefully calibrated punishments and nurturing of the fledgling penitentiary system[46] as a substitute for the death penalty. In 1828, Section XIII of Lord Lansdowne's Act,[47] The Offences Against the Person Act (9 Geo.4 c.31), again talked about an intention 'unlawfully and maliciously' to commit abortion, but it added the phrase 'any Instrument or other Means whatever' to 'Poison or other noxious Thing', and it removed the death penalty, and substituted transportation or imprisonment with hard labour, for attempts to procure an abortion where the woman was not, or not proved to be, quick with child. In 1837, under the Benthamite

Offences Against the Person Amendment Act, 1 Vic., c. 85, introduced by the Prime Minister, Lord John Russell, as the product of a commission to 'consider, first the propriety of revising the whole of the unwritten criminal law on the one side, and of revising the whole of the written criminal law on the other; and, finally, ... to consider the expediency of consolidating the whole',[48] the death penalty was abolished for the core offence of committing abortion itself. And then that Act, and other pieces of legislation, were swept up into the omnibus 1861 Offences Against the Person Act, 24 & 25 Vict. c.100[49] ('An Act to consolidate and amend the Statute Law of England and Ireland relating to Offences against the Person'), the last of that great series of criminal reform acts, 'a statute which remains at the heart of the law today',[50] initially instigated by the utilitarian Lord Brougham, the Lord Chancellor and author of the Poor Law Amendment Act of 1834, the reformer of the civil courts, the pilot of the 1832 Reform Act, and much else.[51] It was an Act that had been 'the result of the labours of successive Governments, whether Liberal or Conservative, for nearly thirty years'.[52] Under sections 58 and 59, it touched on abortion, declaring that:

> Every woman, being with child, who, with intent to procure her own miscarriage, shall unlawfully administer to herself any poison or other noxious thing, or shall unlawfully use any instrument or other means whatsoever with the like intent, and whosoever, with intent to procure the miscarriage of any woman, whether she be or be not with child, shall unlawfully administer to her or cause to be taken by her any poison or other noxious thing, or shall unlawfully use any instrument or other means whatsoever with the like intent, shall be guilty of felony, and being convicted thereof shall be liable to be kept in penal servitude for life.

Self-administered abortions were now criminal. The word *unlawfully*, inherited from 1803, and recited in statutes thereafter, still remained undefined (indeed, a lawyer Member of Parliament, Sir George Bowyer,[53] complained about a general lack of precision of its key terms at the time of the Second Reading of the bill[54]). And other anomalies and difficulties survived. For over a century, subsequent history was to be punctuated with attempts, largely made through test cases, parliamentary questions and legal advice, to ascertain when, if at all, abortion was *not* unlawful.

In April 1896, for instance, the Committee on Criminal Abortion of the Royal College of Physicians, appointed in the previous year 'to define in a legal sense the proper conduct of a Practitioner when brought into relation with a case of acknowledged or suspected criminal abortion; with power to take legal advice', sought, on the recommendation of the Solicitor to the College, the guidance of two counsel, Sir Edward Clarke, a former Solicitor-General,[55] and Horace Avory.[56] That advice opened by making it plain that there were in effect two classes of abortion and abortionist, the morally deserving and the morally undeserving. In the former instance, 'the woman often suffers severely and her life may be at stake, so that the Practitioner naturally finds it necessary or desirable to obtain information as to what has actually taken place by any means in his power'. Communication made to a practitioner so placed, counsel went on, is not legally privileged: but 'If he divulges the information so obtained, he would certainly be regarded by the woman in question, and probably by her family, to have been guilty of a gross breach of professional confidence, whilst if he keeps the secret it may well be that he will render himself amenable to the criminal law'. On other occasions, the practitioner may himself or herself be asked to perform the abortion: 'There can, of course, be no doubt but that his duty is to refuse to have anything to do with the matter, but does his legal obligation end there?' Practitioners, counsel believed, had an obligation in law to report abortions lest they be 'guilty of misprision of felony and punishable accordingly'. However – and this was to be of the greatest significance – 'It not infrequently happens that a Medical Practitioner who is in attendance on a woman during her pregnancy, or at her confinement, becomes convinced that she will almost certainly die unless the child is in some way got rid of. He sees that unless something of the sort is done both mother and child may perish, but that the former can be saved at the expense of the destruction of the latter'. The conclusion drawn by counsel in that instance, and relying on the sometimes rather casuistical doctrine of double effect,[57] was that 'the law does not forbid the procurement of abortion during pregnancy, or the destruction of the child during labour, where such procurement or destruction is necessary to save the mother's life. If we are right in our views, no alteration of the law would probably be desired'. Given, no doubt, the sensitivity of the subject and the physician's vulnerability, that advice was to be treated as a matter of the utmost secrecy, and it was marked 'confidential', but it was of great professional importance and it was never the less leaked anonymously to *The Scalpel*[58] and then, later, to *The Medical Press*.[59]

Some years later, and as a result of a case in 1914 in which a woman had died and her two doctors had not reported the name of the abortionist (which they had been given in confidence) to the police, the Royal College again sought legal advice[60] and were told that a medical practitioner had a moral obligation to respect the confidence of his or her patient; that where there was the belief that an abortion had been performed, the woman should be urged to make a statement 'which may be taken as evidence against the person who has performed the operation … [but] That in the event of her refusal to make such a statement, he is under no legal obligation (so the College has been advised) to take further action, but he should continue to attend the patient to the best of his ability'.[61]

Elaboration of the 1861 Act was secured in a number of pieces of amending legislation,[62] including the Infant Life (Preservation) Act of 1929, Chapter 34 19 and 20 Geo 5,[63] moved by Lord Darling, which laid down that the destruction of children in the process of being born or 'capable of being born alive'[64] was a criminal offence (hitherto it had been illegal to abort a child *in utero*, and to kill a child who had been born, but there was no provision for killing one during the transitional process of labour itself). 'Its purpose', said Lord Darling, 'was to prevent children being destroyed at birth'.[65] The new Act decreed that, on the one hand, 'any person who, with intent to destroy the life of a child capable of being born alive, by any wilful act causes a child to die before it has an existence independent of its mother, shall be guilty of felony, to wit, of child destruction, and shall be liable on conviction thereof on indictment to penal servitude for life'; but, on the other, again tacitly invoking the doctrine of double effect, and reinforcing the Royal College of Physicians' counsel's opinion delivered in 1896, it declared 'that no person shall be found guilty of an offence under this section unless it is proved that the act which caused the death of the child was not done in good faith for the purpose only of preserving the life of the mother'. The bill was read for the first time in February 1929, the second time in March, and a third time in May 'with only two formal drafting Amendments',[66] leaving virtually no trace of debate or discussion, only passing references in the professional journals and newspapers, no remaining record in the Home Office archives, and no clear evidence at all why the last clause should have been introduced. It is possible that the major thrust of the bill was thought to be in conformity with established legal opinion. It is more possible still that there was a great rush to despatch legislation between the reassembly of Parliament on 15 April and its dissolution on 10 May (formally announced on 24 April) in anticipation of the general election at the end of the month. The bill certainly passed through Standing Committee with celerity on 25 April (it was discussed for only 15 minutes[67]). There was other major legislation in motion, and a local government bill touching on the organisation of hospitals, in particular, to preoccupy Members of Parliament and the medical associations. In the midst of much political, economic and social turmoil, on the eve of the Great Depression, when the unemployment rate in some parts of the country had reached over 15%,[68] and just before a general election, legislators' minds must have been turned elsewhere. The Act nevertheless came to have a 'profound influence on clinical practice'.[69]

There was thus a continuing and very practical question of legal interpretation that confronted lawyers and the physician and surgeon who worked in obstetrics in the latter half of the nineteenth century and the early half of the twentieth century (although governments for a number of years claimed there was no reason further to amend the law[70]). And there were clear divisions in the profession about the propriety of abortion itself.

Fears were prevalent amongst a number of doctors and others that, as abortion appeared to be becoming more common, they would be exposed to an ever-greater and increasingly undesirable demand to terminate pregnancies. Consider the judgements aired at a professional meeting in 1927: 'The effect of the spread of loose views was to produce a vicious circle, for as the public learned that abortion could be easily procured under the guise of medical indications, each individual failed to see why her medical attendant should hesitate in her case, and thus pressure was put upon doctors', said one doctor. The eugenicist, Lord Riddell, declared that abortion 'was not justified for the purpose of avoiding the minor risks of pregnancy. The practitioner must not be influenced by the appeals of the patient or her relatives to relieve her of these ordinary risks and discomforts, nor by economic considerations'. And the lawyer, Earl Russell,[71] said that, 'in view of the existing law, it struck him as curious that from some of the cases quoted on the medical side the practice of gynaecologists should have been extended to a degree which went far beyond the narrow consideration of risk to life or health, and amounted in many cases to relieving the patient from a very inconvenient and unpleasant time'.[72] They were arguments that were sometimes elaborated to highlight what was thought to be the problem that the availability of abortion might encourage promiscuity amongst working-class women[73] (and that argument, I shall later show, was to give Frank Soskice, the Home Secretary, pause when the issue of abortion came before him).

But there were contending opinions. At a meeting of the Kensington branch of the British Medical Association three years later, the opening speaker said that he 'considered that abortion should be legal for any woman who had had two children. The objection could hardly be made that this would encourage immorality. It would eliminate the almost constant fear of a failure in contraception, and do away with the irksome need to take extra precautions because of the absence of any second line of defence'. And Dr. C. Killick Millard,[74] the eugenicist Medical Officer of Health for Leicester, confessed that:

> they all must be impressed by the hardship entailed upon married women who had large families of children, more than they could probably bring up, and they all knew to what desperate straits these poor women were reduced. In spite of severe penalties, illicit or criminal abortion was still common, and brought about grave injury to health. It was this injury to health which made him, as a medical officer of health, wonder whether any modification of the law was desirable whereby abortion might be carried out under recognised conditions of reasonable safety.[75]

'Against a background of falling population,[76] economic uncertainty, high maternal mortality resulting from criminal abortion, and threatening war',[77] and uncertainty about the future of the race – a thoroughly confusing background it might be thought – that desire to modify the law was eventually to become embodied in a new campaigning organisation. Foreshadowed by what was in effect a public manifesto published in 1935,[78] a private declaration,[79] and 'an informal conference on abortion'[80] held in the lawyer, Clifford Chance's, office in February 1936, the Abortion Law Reform Association came into existence in March 1936. Its core members were Chance's wife, Janet, Eleanor Hawarden,[81] Alice Jenkins[82] E.T. Hitchcock, Bertha Lorsignol,[83] and Stella Browne,[84] 'a group of radically minded women, several of whom had been active in the early days of the birth control movement,[85] some of whom were women doctors, newly emergent on the professional scene,[86] and several of whom had links with the Labour Party'.[87]

Part of that background was clearly eugenicist, but the links were not unambiguous and there were other, powerful factors in play.[88] It is undoubtedly the case that eugenics, the science of genetics, racial purity and the nation's strength, was in vogue at the time of the new Association's inauguration[89] (Ann Oakley claimed that it 'dominated the public discourse about health in Britain and other countries'[90] in the first half of the century); a number of the Association's members had links with eugenics;[91] there was an overlapping membership of the early committees of the Abortion Law Reform Association and the Eugenics Society;[92] and those advocating abortion in the 1930s had to engage with eugenics as a matter of course. One of the Association's earliest manifestos certainly enlisted its arguments, if only because it was constrained to do so in the political landscape of the time. Janet Chance,[93] its author, stated that:

> ... this Association claims that the fear of under-population must not be met by the tacit conscription of the mother, but by a readiness to face all the factors in the problem of racial welfare and, if it be found that more children are in fact racially beneficial, by a provision of those conditions which will release the normal desire for parenthood. It also appears to us unlikely that the best racial interests are served by a system which leads large numbers of mothers to injure the very reproductive processes by which they are to fulfil their social function. In short, it is in the name of racial amelioration, and as one of the bases on which a eugenic and hygienic education of our race may be built that we ask a revision of the abortion laws.[94]

But it is also apparent that she was much more impressed by the simpler and more practical problems of the lot of poor women struggling to cope with too many children and excessively demanding partners:

> There are those who act as though ... women had no right to be heard on the disposal of their lives and bodies, and who claim that the Abortion Laws are required by racial and social ideals. This Association holds that such persons are bemused by vague ideas of the power of the State or the future of the race; and have not sufficiently considered the ends for which we desire a State to be powerful nor the quality of the physical and cultural legacy we are handing on to our children; nor the limitations of our present knowledge of the optimum population for this country.[95]

The Association's early members joined with her to assert that the law on abortion, such as it was, discriminated against the often desperate poor. Theirs was a left-leaning movement clearly grounded in a politics of class. Its founder, the gynaecologist, Dr Joan Malleson,[96] said that: 'Women of the upper and middle classes are generally disallowed to continue a pregnancy which endangers life or subsequent health. But the working-class mother – upon whose health the well-being of the whole family depends – is, in practical fact, often compelled to run … risks, since for her investigation and relief are seldom accessible'.[97] She was also to say that 'there may be certain situations in a woman's life when nothing will deter her from seeking abortion; to increase restrictive measures is absolutely futile, for she is prepared to face death itself rather than carry on with the pregnancy'.[98]

The Abortion Law Reform Association's initial aims were to 'advocate: – the repeal of the Abortion Laws; the passing of an Act to legalise abortion when performed by the medical profession, subject only to restrictions imposed by medical and humanitarian considerations; and to penalise abortions by unqualified persons'.[99] Its 1938 draft constitution, drawn up in its original version by the eminent physician, Lord Horder,[100] further stated that its members:

> are convinced that the widespread practice of secret abortion, whereby unqualified persons endanger the lives of pregnant women, will not be ended by the present abortion laws. Maintain that this problem cannot be adequately solved until the reasons for the refusal of motherhood are given the attention they deserve. Advocate that the contraceptive services be improved and the right to them be freely given. That abortion by qualified practitioners be legalised within such limitations as may be considered advisable.[101] [Emphases in the original]

Like the National Association for the Abolition of the Death Penalty, formed at very much the same time, the new organisation was designed to appear authoritative and respectable.[102] It had to be so if it was to gain any measure of success at all, especially in Parliament, the invariable target of campaigning. It was not, and could not be, a mass movement and it recruited its members and directed its attention elsewhere.[103] Stella Browne reported that the Association 'has already focussed eminent support amongst doctors and lawyers … and has secured leaders in literature and public affairs amongst its Vice-Presidents'.[104] At the end of its first year,[105] it had been established with eight Vice-Presidents, including Julian Huxley, H.G. Wells, and four Members of Parliament: Robert Boothby,[106] Mavis Tate, Ernest Thurtle and Sir Arnold Wilson.[107] Its 'Medico-Legal Council' consisted of James Abraham, Lord Horder, Joan Malleson, Denis Pritt,[108] Sydney Smith and Gerald Thesiger.[109] It began with 35 members in 1936. Four years later, it had grown to nearly 400. It assembled a library. It disseminated speakers' notes prepared by Janet Chance. It organised meetings.

The Association's repeated argument was that women, and especially poor women, should have the right not only to full information about birth control but also to be relieved of the misery of excessive child-bearing, unduly large families and hazardous, criminal and furtive procedures to deal with unwanted pregnancy. It was rooted in what it called the principle of 'voluntary parenthood', it being for the woman to decide how many children she should have: 'A large family is no longer the ambition of the average woman. Instead she demands a smaller family, and for herself a greater leisure and more comforts, even small luxuries, as some might term them, such as hairdressing, silk stockings, cigarettes'.[110] Medical practice at the time, Lord Horder observed, was 'an anomaly that allows the well-to-do to get rid of the unwanted child before it is born, without damage to life and reputation, yet denies such relief to the poor ... [it is] a stigma to which society is at last awakening'.[111] And Maud Ryan, one of the Association's Vice-Presidents, argued:

> We know only too well the many circumstances, too numerous and unnecessary to mention, that make a woman go through hell from fear of pregnancy. We know, too, the dreadful ends to which women will go in an attempt to end an unwanted pregnancy... We believe that a woman should be able to go to a doctor and to ask for pregnancy to be terminated; should have the right to have expert medical attention under hygienic conditions, and so end the need for going to "Quacks" and the various people who make money out of the misery of their fellow creatures.[112]

The situation which they wished to reform was legally fraught and socially and economically discriminatory. Abortion was practised illegally by so-called 'back-street abortionists'[113] and with uncertain legality by medical practitioners. It was known that doctors performed abortions and that some did so in bad faith. It was also known that patients sometimes had to lie in order to procure a termination with a semblance of legality.[114] But prosecutions were few ('[o]nly the worst cases get there'[115]); charging policy was confused; judges were sometimes inconsistent;[116] and governments (and others[117]) did not know,[118] and often claimed that they did not wish to know, how many abortions – criminal or therapeutic – were actually carried out, or how many maternal deaths ensued.[119] When, for example, Sir Edward Hilton Young,[120] the Unionist Minister of Health, was asked in 1932 if 'he [would] make a return of the number of [therapeutic abortions] carried out in hospitals under his authority in the past quarter', he replied simply, 'I am not aware of the existence of any organised arrangements in any part of this country for the performance of therapeutic abortion as distinct from other forms of obstetrical treatment. I do not think that any useful purpose would be served by obtaining such a return as is suggested in the question'.[121]

There was a deep ambivalence. Abortion was, and remains, a divisive, taboo and opaque subject that was not readily discussed in public.[122] It touched on shameful, controversial and secretive matters of crime, sexuality and death about which respectable people did not and should not know too much[123] ('... the illegal operation goes on in silence and darkness, ... it is unmentioned and unmentionable ...'[124] said Janet Chance). Particularly illuminating is an anecdote offered by Alice Jenkins, another founder member of ALRA, who recalled how as a young woman she had spoken to Gertrude Tuckwell,[125] a campaigner in the 'field of maternal welfare':

> ... in the course of our conversation I reminded her of deaths of mothers from what was described in newspaper columns as "the illegal operation", suggesting that the subject needed enquiry. My story being finished, there was a pause which could be felt. I waited expectantly for some sign that she understood and would give an opinion. Her face registered nothing, the pause lengthened, and when she spoke again it was on some other aspect of maternity.[126]

Abortion was a difficult matter to raise in public meetings (a resolution sent to the Maternal Mortality Committee in 1935 was ignored because it might 'disrupt the united front'[127]). It could excite strong passions (a reviewer of the early treatise, *Abortion: Three Views*, fulminated that 'Miss Stella Browne, burning with feminist zeal, preaches ... that if a woman does not want a baby why should she have one?'[128]) Members of Parliament sometimes appeared to be diffident in touching on the subject. Lady Astor[129] told Parliament in 1935 that 'I am going to say something upon a subject which is not so easy or so pleasant. We have talked about maternal mortality for a long time, but there are certain facts that we do not like to face. We have to face them, although we think we cannot face them because they are controversial. A high percentage of maternal mortality is due to attempted abortion'.[130] And a fellow Member of Parliament, Mavis Tate,[131] was said to have observed with 'courage'[132] in the same debate, 'To return to the maternal mortality rate, there are questions which none of us care altogether to face, but it is time that they were faced. One of the causes of the ill-health of mothers in the urban and industrial areas is the tremendous amount of abortion'.[133] Yet, rather paradoxically, there was also at the same time sustained medical and political interest in the problem of maternal mortality, a problem that was itself almost certainly closely allied – and known to be closely allied – to ineptly-performed abortions. Over 1200 articles and letters appeared on the theme in *The British Medical Journal* between January 1928 and December 1940, allowing a doctor writing to the journal on 12 January 1935 to talk about 'The unrestrained publicity given to the subject of maternal mortality in this country ...'

Talk about abortion and maternal mortality was set against a backcloth of fears about a plummeting birth rate, 'race suicide'[134] and national decline (Janet Chance was obliged to say in her 1936 manifesto for abortion that 'To many people the fall in the birth-rate is so alarming that they believe that any measure that might prevent births ... must be resisted in the interests of race-preservation'[135]). They were fears complicated by the difficulty of making confident assumptions about population trends. The 1931 census was not to be published until 1950, the war having intervened, and data derived from it would not have been widely known during the era when the concern about maternal and infant mortality was at its height[136] (in fact, the population was actually increasing during the period, and census returns show a

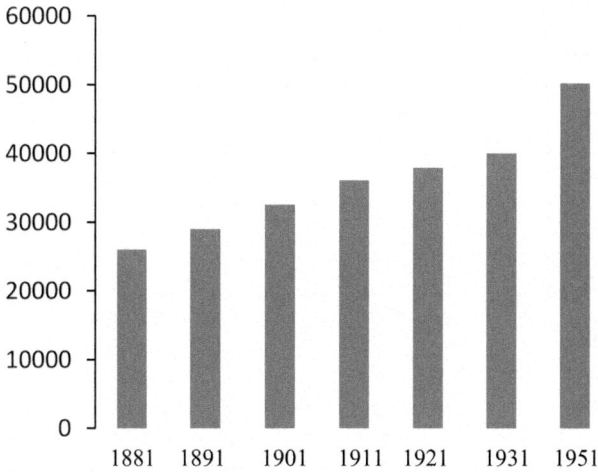

Figure 4.1 Population of England and Wales 1881–1951 (in 0000s)

Figure 4.2 % Incremental increases in the population of England and Wales 1881–1931

steady growth). But the *rate* of increase was certainly declining (the Royal Commission on Population commented in 1948 that 'In recent decades – broadly speaking, since about 1910 – the growth of population has slackened considerably in Great Britain …'[137]).

And the diminishing rate of increase was due chiefly to the reduction in fertility which the eugenicists and others feared. 'By the 1930s, fertility had dropped to historically low levels. …' said Sigle-Rushton, and, she continued, 'Assumptions that the sharp downward trends in fertility would continue unabated led to implausible projections …'[138] On the one hand, the rate at

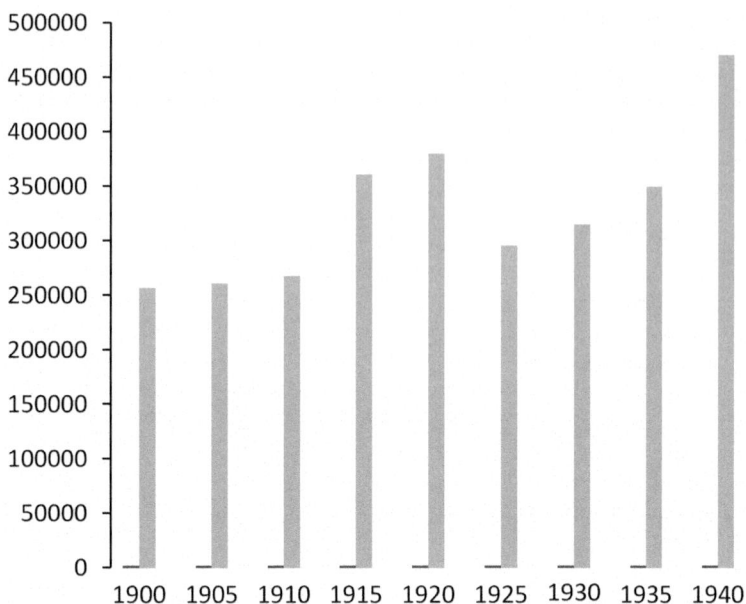

Figure 4.3 Numbers of marriages in England and Wales 1900–1940[139]

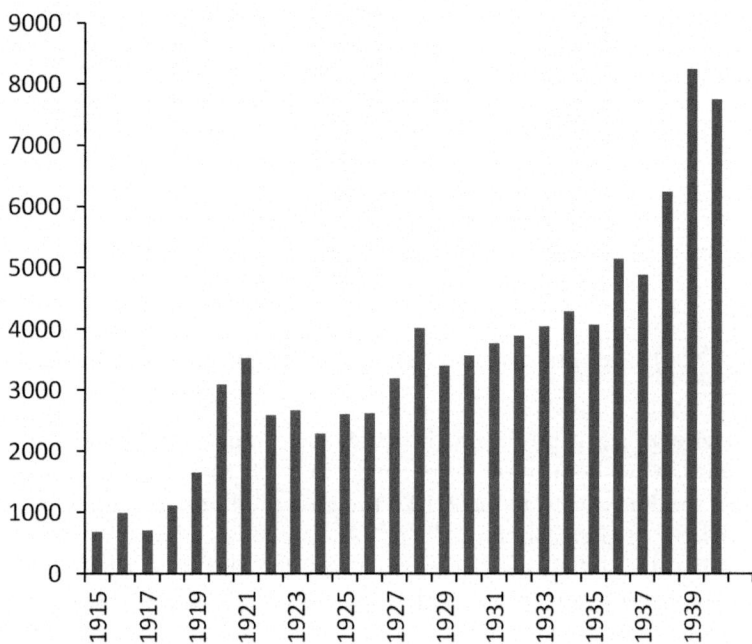

Figure 4.4 Numbers of divorces in England and Wales 1915–1940[140]

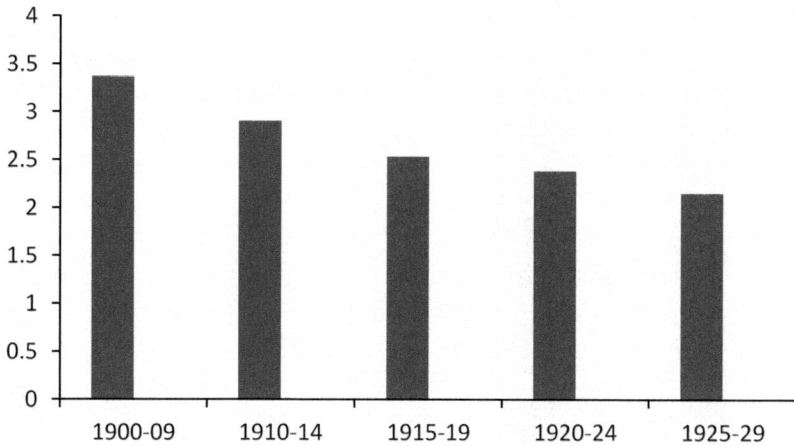

Figure 4.5 Estimated average size of completed family of women married 1900–1929[141]

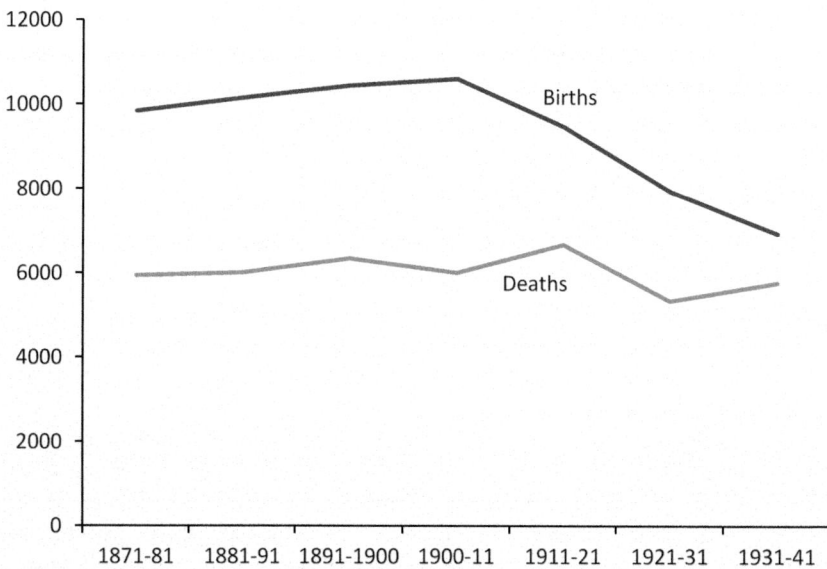

Figure 4.6 Births and deaths in Great Britain[142]

which people were marrying was volatile, but largely growing, and there were very few divorces in England and Wales (although the numbers were certainly growing). But, on the other hand, average family size was decreasing.

The net result looked ominous. The report of the Royal Commission on Population reported on page 17 that 'In the decade 1931–41, the excess

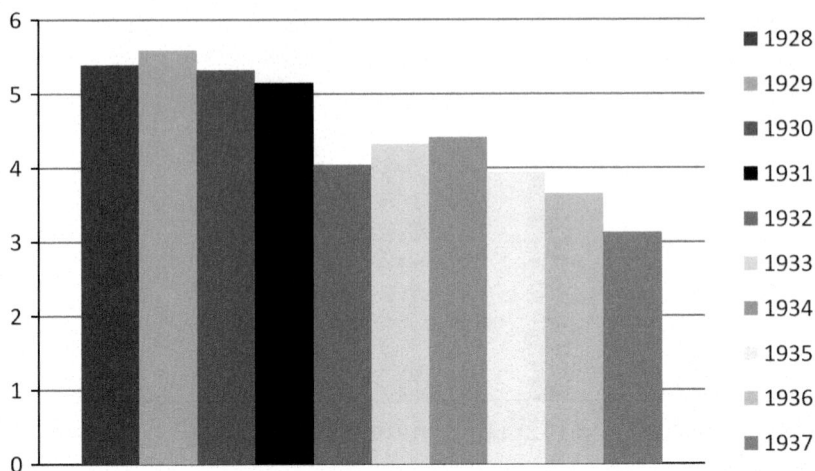

Figure 4.7 Maternal mortality rate per 1000 live births[143]

of births over deaths showed a considerable … decline compared with the previous decade … [if other things had remained equal] the rate of growth of population would have come down to a very low figure indeed'.

The loss of population and the loss of actual and potential mothers through abortion and other misadventures appeared to be linked.[144] One woman in every 250 lost her life giving birth in 1935. Whether and to what extent abortions, induced or spontaneous, legal or illegal, actually contributed markedly to the decline in live births and the slowing of population growth was then moot, but the question did feed into the political and medical narratives of a demographic crisis.

Research on the matter was thin and inconclusive. Boyle observed that 'For obvious reasons, reliable figures on the number of illegal abortions carried out each year are difficult to come by. … The number of prosecutions for breaches of abortion legislation was tiny in comparison with the number of abortions carried out'.[145] Efforts at rigorous inquiry did certainly begin in the late 1920s. The Ministry of Health's Maternal Mortality Committee had been set up in 1928 under the Chairmanship of its Chief Medical Officer, Sir George Newman,[146] in response to reports of a very high incidence of deaths.[147] It produced an interim report on 2000 deaths and then a final *Report of an Investigation into Maternal Mortality*, based on 770 deaths, and in that second statement it was obliged to say that the information 'on which conclusions could be based was found to be very limited. The gravity of the problem was admitted, but even its extent was found to be unknown'.[148] Its estimate was that 14 per cent of all puerperal deaths could be attributed to abortion[149] (and that figure stuck for a while: it was, for example, the number that would be given by Lady Astor in a debate in the House of Commons[150]).

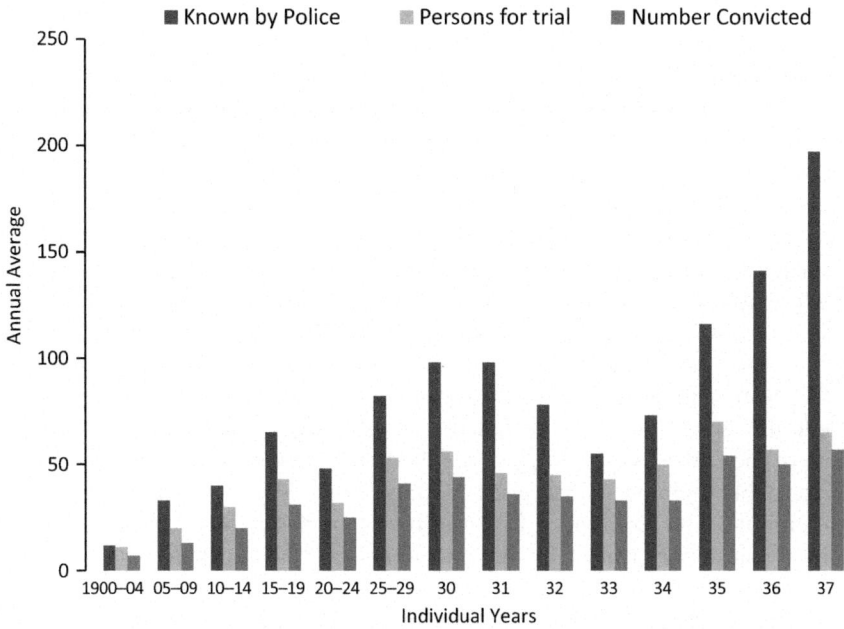

Figure 4.8 Numbers of offences known to the police, committed for trial and convicted under sections 58 and 59 of the Offences Against the Persons Act 1861[151]

The Report of the Committee on Medical Aspects of Abortion

Representatives of the British Medical Association had taken it in 1933 that it should also respond to the troubling uncertainties of law and practice, and its response was to be a motion proposing the convening of a special Committee on Medical Aspects of Abortion. It is evident that that proposal was hedged around with some diffidence: abortion was a moral and political thicket in which the Council of the BMA did not wish to become entangled. The Council had actually argued against the formation of such a committee, having declared in its report to the Annual Representative Meeting the following year that it been unsure about how problematic the law actually was (it questioned 'the alleged uncertainty of the medical practitioner as to his freedom to perform therapeutic abortion'); and it was reluctant to engage with the larger social, political and ethical questions clustered around abortion, questions which lay outside the specific professional competence of the medical practitioner.[152] The Council's own recommendation to the Association was that it should adopt the position that 'while [it] would be willing to contribute expert medical assistance and/or evidence to any committee set up by the Government to examine the various relations of the practice of abortion, [it] is of opinion that the subject has predominating interests other than medical, and that the initiation of the proposed inquiry does not properly fall within the responsibilities of the medical profession'. But, reluctantly, it conceded that 'if any real uncertainty existed on this point it might be well to get it resolved'.[153]

The 1934 Annual Representative Meeting did pass a resolution based on the first part of the Council's recommendation (declaring that it would 'be willing to contribute expert medical assistance and/or evidence to any committee set up by the Government to examine the various relations of the practice of abortion'). However it also went against the latter part, resolving that Council should be requested to 'set up a special committee "to consider and report upon the medical aspects of abortion"'. A Committee on Medical Aspects of Abortion was accordingly established on 25 July 1934 and reappointed on 23 July 1935, and a report was written. Doctors, said the report's *Preliminary*, published in 1936, 'were unwilling to perform therapeutic abortion – that is, abortion for medical reasons – owing to their sense of legal risk arising from the uncertain state of the law; and, secondly, ... the medical profession should endeavour to guide public opinion, which was becoming more and more interested in this question'.[154] The Committee followed the Council by electing from the start not to venture into realms in which it had no special competence:

> It has ... regarded abstract and specific questions of economics, equity, morality, and religion as being outside the scope of its inquiry. While it could not entirely exclude from its purview all questions which have legal, economic, ethical, or religious bearings, it has confined its attention to matters with which the medical practitioner is concerned in the course of his professional work.[155]

And that was a position which the BMA would steadfastly maintain in the decades to come. The report continued by rehearsing the familiar argument about the difficulties posed by the word 'unlawful' that was lodged in the existing statutes:

> Within recent years there has been considerable agitation in favour of a revision of the law of abortion. With many aspects of this movement the committee is not concerned. It has, however, been represented on many sides, both by the profession and by the public, that there is need for an investigation of the whole question with an object of clarifying the position of the doctor in regard to the law. With this the committee is in agreement. While it is manifestly impossible to provide exact indications for the induction of abortion, the committee considers it most desirable that the law should at least contain an explicit statement of the principles which should govern the lawful artificial termination of pregnancy. ...[156]

The law, it was noted, gave no indication of when an abortion was lawful, and there was an urgent need to elucidate the situation. It was the Committee's conclusion that there must be new legislation and new and proper checks on medical procedure: 'The committee therefore strongly recommends not only the clarification of the legal position, but also the institution of some system of authorisation of abortion in the individual case. It suggests that the doctor contemplating therapeutic abortion should be obliged to obtain the sanction of a professional colleague of recognised status. ...'[157]

The Bourne Case

A convenient and very probably orchestrated opportunity to resolve some of that long-lingering legal muddle arose when a rape was reported to the police[158] and a gynaecologist freely admitted to having carried out an abortion in June 1938 on a young girl,[159] a virgin, who had been raped by soldiers 'with great violence in circumstances which would have been terrifying to any woman, let alone a child of fourteen ...'[160] Aleck Bourne,[161] a consultant at St Mary's and Queen Charlotte's Hospitals,[162] a member of ALRA's Medico-Legal Committee, described by *The British Medical Journal* as 'a man of great compassion and understanding',[163] had terminated the pregnancy, said *The Lancet*, as 'an example of disinterested conduct in consonance with the highest traditions of the profession'.[164] After another obstetrician had refused to conduct the abortion,[165] he had been invited to operate by Joan Malleson, the founder of ALRA (although Bourne himself, in his memoirs, talked neither of his nor of her affiliation[166]), to whom the girl had been referred by the organiser of the schools care committee, but to operate secretly at the request of the victim's father, in the full knowledge that, were he to do so, he would be probing the legal limits of therapeutic abortion.[167] Mr Bourne, it was reported, 'had not courted publicity but had been willing, when the proper case came along, to have the matter dealt with. That this had happened in the particular case had been none of his doing'.[168] He himself was said to have testified that:

> The views of his professional brethren varied enormously. In October, 1935, he had been about to terminate pregnancy in a child of 15, and his house-surgeon had declined to assist him and, on Mr. Bourne's invitation, had walked out of the operation theatre. That doctor had only recently been qualified and had objected on religious grounds. This refusal had led Mr. Bourne to think very hard, and he had determined to obtain the ruling of the Court on the next occasion. That was why they were there.[169]

What followed proved to be a test case that lent a little clarity to a law, 'the statutory exception of which Mr Bourne rightly and humanely took advantage'. The case was deemed to be of sufficient moment to be prosecuted in person by Sir Donald Somervell, the Attorney-General. The trial judge, Sir Malcolm Macnaghten,[170] himself held the view that:

> It is, I think, a case of first instance, first impression. The matter has never, so far as I know, arisen before for a jury to determine in circumstances

such as these, and there was, even amongst learned counsel, some doubt as to the proper direction to the jury in such a case as this. ... It is said ... that this is a case of great importance to the public, and more especially, to the medical profession. ...[171]

The trial itself took place in the Central Criminal Court on 18 and 19 July 1938, the defence case being argued, not on the grounds of public, health or medical policy in general, but specifically on the lawfulness of Mr Bourne's action under the 1861 and 1928 Acts. The word 'unlawful' had not appeared in the original indictment but was inserted at the express insistence of Roland Oliver K.C., his counsel, 'who maintained that nearly the whole of his case rested on the interpretation of the word'.[172] The defence was to be simple: 'What I have done', Aleck Bourne would say, 'is lawful, right, and honest, and I have committed no offence at all'.[173] And, maintained Roland Oliver, 'Russell on Crimes said that the word "unlawfully" excluded from the section acts done in the course of proper treatment in the interest of the life or health of the mother'.[174] Despite Russell's apparent authority[175] and the firmer authority of the 1929 Act,[176] evidence was tendered at trial that doctors were more than doubtful about the state of the law. Joan Malleson, was reported to have said in cross-examination:

> ... there was very great variation of opinion among obstetricians and medical people generally about what was lawful in regard to the procuring of abortion. Some went so far as to say that it was not permissible in any case even to save life, and others took the view that it was lawful in the interests of the health of the mother. She shared that view, and held that it was better to perform an abortion than that a woman should be physically, mentally, or nervously broken down by having a child, particularly conceived in such circumstances.[177]

The attorney general talked of the sanctity of life and of the critical difference between preserving life and preserving health, but the judge was not impressed. In his summing up, he seized on the word 'unlawfully'[178] and reviewed step by step the precautions that Aleck Bourne had taken: the girl was pregnant as a result of the rape; she was not infected with venereal disease; she was neither 'feeble-minded' nor of a 'prostitute mind'; and she was a 'normal girl in every respect' for whom the continuance of the pregnancy would 'probably cause serious injury ... injury so serious as to justify the removal of the pregnancy at a time when the operation could be performed without any risk to the girl'. An expert witness in medical psychology had testified that 'if the girl gave birth to a child, the consequence was likely to be that she would become a mental wreck'.[179] Sir Malcolm Macnaghten compared the case with another which had come before him, that of a 'woman without any medical skill or medical qualifications ... [who had] unlawfully used an instrument for the purpose of procuring the miscarriage of a pregnant girl; she did it for money ... She used her instrument, and, within an interval of time measured not by minutes, by seconds, the victim of her malpractice was dead on the floor'. She afforded a bleak contrast to Aleck Bourne who was a professional man in high social standing on whom it was difficult to bestow disrepute.[180] His case, said the judge:

> is very different. A man of the highest skill, openly, in one of our great hospitals, performs the operation. Whether it was legal or illegal you will have to determine, but he performs the operation as an act of charity, without fee or reward, and unquestionably believing that he was doing the right thing, and that he ought, in the performance of his duty as a member of a profession devoted to the alleviation of human suffering, to do it.

In a critical passage, Sir Malcolm directed that the jury would have to determine:

> beyond reasonable doubt that the defendant did not procure the miscarriage of the girl in good faith for the purpose only of preserving her life. ... the words "preserving the life of the mother" must be construed in a reasonable sense. They are not limited to the case of saving the mother from violent death: they include the case where continuance of the pregnancy would make her a physical or mental wreck. ... If the doctor is of opinion, on reasonable grounds and with adequate knowledge, that the probable consequences of the pregnancy will be to make the woman a physical or mental wreck, the jury are quite entitled to take the view that the doctor who, under these circumstances and in that honest belief, operates, is operating for the purpose of preserving the life of the mother.

And the jury did acquit Mr Bourne. *The British Medical Journal* put it that doctors had asked:

> the meaning of "unlawfully" and were told that it had never been defined, either by Parliament or by a judge, but that the law almost certainly allowed the termination of pregnancy for the purpose of saving the mother's life. ... The lawyers [have been] content, in other words, to assume that an abortion was carried out lawfully when a doctor performed it in good conscience, after careful thought and observation and under proper conditions, for the substantial benefit of the patient. They felt that, so long as the law refrained from saying what a doctor could do, the question of what he could not do need not arise so long as he acted bona fide ... This attitude, however, did not allay the anxiety of medical men, and the situation was resolved last week in an English court of law. Mr. Aleck Bourne has for some time been among the chief of those who have desired to know clearly where they stood under the law.[181]

It was a decision and a judgement that some could claim had come to 'represent the law of England and Wales';[182] it could be read as having 'extended [the law] to cover the mother's health as well as her life';[183] it emphasised, in Aleck Bourne's words, 'the impossibility, in certain circumstances, of making a sharp distinction between life and health';[184] but it did not actually succeed in dispelling all doubt. Two articles by the Recorder of Cambridge, Roland Burrows, K.C.,[185] issued immediately in the wake of the judgement and published in the *Law Journal* of September 1938, were not encouraging. They argued, *per contra*, that the Bourne judgement 'is not of absolutely binding authority';[186] that it still remained evident that social reasons were irrelevant to lawful abortion; considerations of the care and cure of the patient were inconclusive; the border between maladies dangerous to health and maladies dangerous to life stayed unclear, and the doctor was ill-equipped to judge the facts; surgeons were obliged to obey the law, and, if a surgeon were to abort a woman whilst tending only to her proper care and treatment, 'but not for the purpose of saving her life',[187] he or she would still be guilty of a criminal offence. [188] 'It is impossible', Burrows said:

> to withhold sympathy from medical men if they complain that the law, while seeming to admit that there are cases where abortion can be performed without committing a crime, omits to give any definite guidance to those who have to obey the law when dealing with problems involving a determination whether or no abortion is to be performed. ... The [1861] Act is not altogether so clear as might be desired.[189]

And an editorial in *The Lancet* agreed: 'Acquittal has left the legal position – except for two passages in the judge's summing-up – only a little less obscure than before... The verdict of the jury does not amend the law. The all-important word "unlawfully" remains a forensic football... Do we wait patiently while the medical profession gradually extends the field of therapeutic abortion by the process of appearance in the dock?'[190] Beyond the law, moreover, there still lay unresolved moral and religious matters to trouble the profession. The judge, Sir Malcolm Macnaghten, had reflected in his summing-up that:

> Apparently there is a great difference of opinion even in the medical profession itself. Some there may be, for all I know, who hold the view that the fact that a woman desires the operation to be performed is a sufficient justification for it. Well, that is not the law: the desire of a woman to be relieved of her pregnancy is no justification at all for performing the operation. On the other hand there are people who, from what are said to be religious reasons, object to the operation being performed under any circumstances. That is not the law either. On the contrary, a person who holds such an opinion ought not to be an obstetrical surgeon, for if a case arose where the life of the woman could be saved by performing the operation and the doctor refused to perform it because of his religious opinions and the woman died, he would be in grave peril of being brought before this Court on a charge of manslaughter by negligence. He would

have no better defence than a person who, again for some religious reason, refused to call in a doctor to attend his sick child, where a doctor could have been called in and the life of the child could have been saved.

To ensure that members of the medical profession acted lawfully in the future, Sir Malcolm suggested, they 'no doubt ... would act only in consultation with some other member of the profession of high standing, so as to form the view that the circumstances were such that an operation had to be performed and was legal'.

The Inter-Departmental Committee on Abortion[191]

It was the judgement of *The British Medical Journal* that 'the medicolegal aspects of the case must be reserved for future discussion',[192] and the next step, immediately after the Bourne case, taken not only as a direct response to the case and to the report of the Ministry of Health's committee on maternal mortality,[193] but also as an indirect response to agitation from those who would become members of the future investigation,[194] was the convening of an Inter-Departmental Committee under the auspices of the Ministry of Health and the Home Office, and chaired by Norman Birkett,[195] to 'inquire into the prevalence of abortion, and the present law relating thereto, and to consider what steps can be taken by more effective enforcement of the law or otherwise to secure the reduction of maternal mortality and morbidity arising from this cause'. Abortion had become a matter of acute professional, social and political interest, and the government had surmised (it was observed much later[196]) that, 'If this were not done, doctors would be left in a state of uncertainty; some women would have to go to unqualified people; and ... doctors are more likely to take a sympathetic view of the legality of an abortion in the case of a fee-paying patient'.[197]

The report of the Inter-Departmental Committee, published in 1939, recited on pages 29 *et seq.* the legal circumstances flowing from the Bourne case under which it had been appointed: 'The learned Judge had ruled that the word ['unlawfully'] was not meaningless and that its use in the statute implied that there might be such a thing as the lawful procurement of abortion. ... if a pregnancy was likely to make the woman a physical or mental wreck, the jury were quite entitled to take the view that a doctor who in those circumstances and in that honest belief operated, was operating for the purpose of preserving the life of the woman'. It was that ruling, it said, which had acted as a catalyst for the Committee's deliberations.

The report itself opened with a discussion of the prevalence of abortion, and it again pointed to the difficulties entailed in estimating the scale and nature of the problem ('the nature of abortion is such that its occurrence will not readily be disclosed even when it is spontaneous' (para. 16), and 'a very large number of criminal abortions are never brought to light' para. 128). Offences known to the police and prosecuted in the criminal courts were no guide at all to the 'actual' incidence and prevalence of abortion.[198] Estimates varied widely,[199] and the available statistics were 'very imperfect' (para. 117). The Abortion Law Reform Association, in its own submission to the Committee, had been obliged to report that 'we have no statistics to offer on the subject-matter of this Memorandum'. But the Committee did venture its own figure. Acting on the basis of a British Medical Association contention that 16–20% of all pregnancies ended in an abortion,[200] the numbers of abortions occurring annually in England and Wales were held to fall between 110,000 and 150,000 (paras. 20–23). Calculated conservatively, the Report said, 66,000 abortions were probably spontaneous and 44,000 procured; and abortion itself was likely to have been responsible for the deaths of some 400–500 women a year between 1926 and 1935[201] (that number of around 100,000 then became what was tantamount to the received figure,[202] in circulation for the next thirty years[203]). Glanville Williams' comment, made at a much later date, was that, 'Assuming the lower of these two figures, it means that there are over 120 illegal abortions taking place every day in this country, in circumstances of misery and wretchedness, or one every twelve minutes round the clock … It is difficult to imagine the blight of life involved in these statistics'.[204]

Abortions might be procured, the Report stated, because the woman was poor, or a sole wage earner, because she was in ill health, fearful of transmitting hereditary diseases or defects, or the victim of incest or rape. But it was also true that 'selfishness' might well be a cause in a number of instances, where a woman 'who is in a position to give a child an excellent upbringing may prefer to avoid the inconvenience entailed and continue to lead the life to which she and her husband have become accustomed' (p. 39).

The majority Report held that the ruling in the Bourne judgement 'is not binding upon Judges of the High Court' (para 200), and it recommended that it should be so elucidated in law as to make it clear that the induction of abortion would be legal when it was carried out to save the life,[205] or to prevent the impairment of health, of a pregnant woman.[206] It did allude to the proposal made by the Abortion Law Reform Association, based on Janet Chance's principle of 'voluntary parenthood', that 'abortion should be made available to any woman who so wishes' (para 227),[207] but it declared that it was 'strongly opposed' to that and other like suggestions: 'We regard such proposals as contrary to religious and ethical teaching and to fundamental principles on which society is based, and we believe that, if given effect, they would have serious consequences' (para 230), including, it was thought, an unwelcome decline in the size of the population.[208] The Committee *was* cautiously favourable to the extension of abortion to pregnancies induced by rape[209] (although it professed there would be grave practical difficulties of drafting and implementation where rape might be no more than a matter of unproven allegation[210]), but it was adamant that there should be no other liberalisation of the law: 'The induction of abortion is on ethical, social, and medical grounds an undesirable operation, justifiable only in exceptional circumstances, and the Committee is strongly opposed to any broad relaxation of the law designed to make social, economic and personal reasons a justification for the operation' (p. 123).

Two members demurred about one section of the report and advocated a greater dissemination of advice about birth control. There were others who disagreed with the finding that 'No practicable scheme of compulsory notification of pregnancy is likely to contribute much to the problem of abortion' (p. 124). Dorothy Thurtle, born to the Labour purple,[211] produced a minority report which recommended the legalisation of abortion in cases of rape, incest, unlawful carnal knowledge and high fertility. But then matters stalled. Like much else in the area of criminal justice reform, the Second World War brought about a cessation of criminal justice policymaking and campaigning. It was Alice Jenkins' judgement that 'had it not been for the onset of war, it is likely that the high mortality rate [of abortions] recorded at that time would have caused the recommendations of the Government Report to be implemented'.[212]

A steady trickle of prosecutions resumed at the war's end.[213] One centred on two doctors, Eleanore Bergmann, an obstetrician, and Mary Ferguson, a referring psychologist based at the Tavistock Clinic, who were tried in May 1948[214] on a charge of unlawfully conspiring to procure a miscarriage in four women between December 1947 and January 1948. Alice Jenkins attended the trial, and she talked of her pain 'to see such women standing in the prisoner's dock'.[215] Dr Ferguson was examined at length on the reasons she had advanced in letters of referral to support abortions, including exhaustion and digestive troubles. She talked, for example, about 'a psychoneurotic girl who had in addition chest trouble', and termination had been recommended 'on both physical and mental grounds'. The case for her defence was that, 'whilst it was vitally important that the unborn should not be unlawfully destroyed, it was equally important that women whose pregnancy, if it was allowed to continue, might disastrously affect their health and endanger their life should be free and able to have their pregnancy terminated under safe conditions. It would be utterly wrong if the result of this case was to deter doctors from doing their duty'.[216]

In his summing-up to the jury, the judge, Mr Justice Morris, argued, as Sir Malcolm Macnaghten had argued before, that the defendants were not, as was common in most abortion cases, 'unqualified people', and he recited at length Sir Malcolm's reading of the word 'unlawfully' in *Rex v. Bourne*: 'I fully adopt those words and invite you to bear them very much in mind'. It was not, he said, part of the jury's duty to determine whether a referral letter had arrived at the right conclusion about the desirability of an abortion, 'A difference of opinion might obtain between members of the medical profession, and it might be difficult to find out which opinion should be preferred'. Whether 'Dr Ferguson was correct or incorrect in the view that she had formed was not for the jury'. Once again, the defendants were found not guilty, the doctor's good faith rather than the correctness of her diagnosis having been ruled the point at issue.

A later, rather more ambiguous case, that of Dr Louis Newton and Dr Ellis Stungo, stemmed from an inquest verdict, passed in March 1958,[217] of manslaughter against a specialist who had conducted an abortion on a woman whom he believed might otherwise have committed suicide and who had died shortly thereafter as a result of damage to her kidneys following an injection Dr Newton had administered. Dr Stungo, the referring psychiatrist, had told the Coroner, Sir Bentley Purchase, that 'I would say she was a good type of woman fundamentally, and I felt very sorry for her. I thought she was in a desperate state. I thought there was a severe risk of suicide'. The doctors were committed for trial at the beginning of May, the defence mounted by Christmas Humphreys that there was no case to answer having been rejected (Christmas Humphreys asked later 'How in future will any doctor have the courage to form an opinion, or express it, that an abortion is right in particular circumstances – if it turns out that the authorities take the view that it should not have been done, and prosecute?'[218]). The prosecution itself would again hinge on whether the jury believed that the doctors had acted in good faith when they had brought about the abortion ('The basis for the charge of the Crown ... was that this was not a *bona fide* operation'[219]). The trial judge, Mr Justice Ashworth, then chose to discharge Dr Stungo at the close of the prosecution, asserting that there was no case to answer – the defence had claimed that the prosecution had had to establish bad faith, but had failed to do so.

In a separate trial, Dr Newton testified that he had believed that the woman was suicidal: 'I thought that left alone she might quite easily have done something desperate to herself'.[220] He was nevertheless found guilty and imprisoned for five years for manslaughter on a charge that related to medical negligence in the administration of the injection rather than to the unlawfulness of the abortion itself (and it is evident that some regarded that verdict as perverse[221]). In his summing-up, the judge had again flagged the construction of the word 'unlawful': abortion was 'unlawful unless [it] was in good faith for the purpose of preserving the life or health of the woman. ... There was no immunity for doctors in the operation of the criminal law ... and if a doctor decided to terminate a pregnancy merely in order to oblige the woman, or to relieve her of embarrassment, or for a substantial reward, if it were merely for that then he was just as guilty of the criminal offence of abortion as would be the woman in the back street'.[222] ALRA concluded that, overall, the doctors' trials had 'led to a re-emphasis of psychiatric health as grounds for abortion'.

Early Attempts at Legislation

The Abortion Law Reform Association had been launched in the 1930s with enthusiasm, confidence and optimism: 'in the early stages we were so convinced of the rightness, necessity and justice of our cause that we were far from realising the opposition we should encounter, the difficulty of getting the subject across to the Press, and the amazing apathy of the general public'.[223]

But abortion, like homosexual law reform and the abolition of capital punishment, was deemed by successive governments to be a hazardous area for the politician, likely to inflame opposition, divisive of political party and unpopular with the electorate. The Member of Parliament, Robert Boothby, had warned members of the Association at a meeting held as early as 1936 that 'Governments would not move because they were afraid of losing the votes of people who otherwise would support them'.

Campaigning had ceased during the Second World War although ALRA remained in place as night watchman, its members giving occasional talks on topics such as 'Women and Post-War Problems', when asked to do so. The Association did put out occasional feelers to sympathetic advisers like Lord Listowel[224] and Lord Huntingdon,[225] but they were repeatedly cautioned that abortion reform would be difficult and that they could expect to make no progress in time of war.[226]

The Committee was reconvened in 1945 after what Lord Listowel called its 'wartime hibernation', but it was reconvened without confidence, it having been acknowledged that abortion remained a 'highly controversial'[227] area that could be approached only with the greatest trepidation and discretion. Alice Jenkins wrote that 'Both Mrs Chance and I were convinced that on such a controversial issue much reserve and circumspection was needed ... Many family friends knew nothing of my connection with the cause ...'[228] The Association resolved to proceed slowly and gingerly, issuing leaflets, speaking to meetings, writing letters to the press, and it made little impact. There was some discussion about whether a memorandum should be submitted to the 1944–1949 Royal Commission on Population and a new draft law prepared, but it was decided after all not to proceed but to send a simple letter instead in which it was suggested that illegal abortions might cause sterility 'which could be avoided by a proper amendment of the Abortion Law'. 'We are not in a position to provide evidence that it does have this effect', the letter continued, 'but the allegation is a serious one and we think should be taken up by your Committee'.[229]

In what was then to be a flurry of failed attempts to reform the law, sympathetic Members of Parliament made it evident that they believed that they could not proceed too fast or too radically. They were obliged to declare, at least in public, that their intent was simply to aid and support members of the medical profession by clarifying the meaning of the 1861 Act. A private member's bill 'to amend the law relating to abortion', drafted by Glanville Williams, introduced cautiously in November 1952 by Joseph Reeves,[230] the Labour Member of Parliament for Greenwich; supported, *inter alia*, by Douglas Houghton and Ernest Thurtle; and designed to 'remove doubt about certain cases where abortion might be necessary to save life or preserve health';[231] was 'talked out' three months later, having been given a mere ninety seconds of Parliamentary time. Parliamentary draftsmen had declined to include the word 'therapeutic' in the bill on the curious grounds, Alice Jenkins claims, that Members of Parliament would not know what it meant.[232] And the bill had consequently been attacked, particularly by the Hierarchy of the Roman Catholic Church, because it was claimed that it would allow non-therapeutic abortions to be performed in liberal numbers. The bill, said Cardinal Griffin, the Archbishop of Westminster,[233] would 'legalise practices in direct contravention to the natural law. ... The Christian principle is: Thou shalt not kill'. In the wake of the Second World War, the precept could well be established that it was permissible to sanction 'killing the innocent unborn, the aged, incurables, and even political undesirables ... should the State consider them inconvenient and harmful to the life of the nation. The Bill must be opposed ...'[234] A defensive Joseph Reeves protested that his purpose had not been:

> to extend the practice of abortion. On the contrary, it is to confine it to cases where, in the view of competent medical practitioners, it is in the interest of the mother's health and for the prevention of injury to her body. In such cases unmistakable authority should be given to the medical profession to act in the interests of the patient. Under the law at present, a great deal of uncertainty prevails, although certain judgements have seemed to provide protection for qualified practitioners performing operations in the interests of the mother. Many doctors are inhibited in their duty to their patients on account of the existing statutes on this subject.[235]

But it came to nothing. Two years later, in January 1954, a physician, Lord Amulree,[236] brought in another bill to amend the 1861 law by seeking to exempt from prosecution an abortion carried out by a registered practitioner, acting to preserve the life of a mother, or acting with the concurring opinion of a second registered practitioner, to prevent injury to the mother in body or health. But it was withdrawn before second reading.

The Magistrates Association passed by a small majority a resolution in favour of the liberalisation of law, proposed by Mrs Child, and seconded by Dorothy Thurtle, at its 1955 annual Conference.[237] And Members of Parliament asked a succession of questions in the House, one being the future Minister of Health, Kenneth Robinson, who was told in 1956 by the then Home Secretary, Major Lloyd George, that 'I can hold out no hope of legislation on this controversial subject'.[238] The Labour Member of Parliament, Lena Jeger,[239] was told by the ever-cautious R.A. Butler in like manner that he had no intention of implementing the recommendations of the Birkett Committee: 'Legislation for this purpose would be highly controversial and I have no reason to think that there is any practical need for it. I do not propose to introduce legislation to implement certain minor recommendations designed to facilitate prosecutions for criminal abortion'.[240]

By 1960, ALRA was twenty-four years old, emaciated and failing. Its original committee members were dead or elderly: Janet Chance had died in 1953, Stella Browne in 1955 and Joan Malleson in 1956. Its remaining 200 members were said to believe 'that they were the guardians of a lost cause'.[241]

Rather poignantly, and at the age of 72, one of the survivors, Alice Jenkins, embarked once more on making the case for reform, saying that she had done so 'at the request of friends who believe that no one else now has the knowledge to write [it]. Other founders ... particularly Mrs. Janet Chance or Miss Stella Browne, could have done the work much better, had they been here to do it'.[242]

In her *Law for the Rich*, published in that year of 1960, Alice Jenkins reiterated the arguments which had underpinned the Association from the first. Abortion was a crime without victims. There was, she said, quite unnecessary misery inflicted on women, their families and perpetrators by the gross social inequities and hazards attending the unwanted pregnancies and unwanted children of those in the greatest poverty. She countered the stock objections to abortion by affirming that it was a safe procedure when professionally performed under sterile conditions; that the law was draconian in the letter but ineffectual in its implementation; that it was highly misleading to represent the aborted foetus as a baby who could hear, see or feel; that abortion was an unpleasant procedure which women would seek only *in extremis*; that there was no reason to suppose that its liberalisation would lead to greater promiscuity ('the principal beneficiary under new law would be the decent mother of a family who has as many children as she can cope with' − 90% of illegal abortions 'are suffered by married women'); and there was 'no valid reason for insisting on the birth' of the unwanted children of promiscuous liaisons. The chief opponent to reform was the Roman Catholic Church which upheld the sanctity of life, but, she contended:

> "Sanctity of life" can mean little when referring to a tiny piece of undifferentiated human tissue measuring one hundredth of an inch across ... It seems to me that a doctrinal leadership takes upon itself an omniscient attitude when it presumes to know the entire unalterable law of God. ... It is time that more cognisance is taken of the fact that Roman Catholics number only about ten per cent of our community and receive their instruction from a celibate priesthood who can have only theoretical knowledge of what marriage and parenthood entail.[243]

The families of the poor (including Roman Catholic families) were large, and the size of their family exacerbated their poverty. Abortion, in short:

> presses most cruelly on the unenlightened poor, who cannot command the medical advice and surgical relief which have become increasingly available to the woman with knowledge, influence and financial resources. Illegal abortions now fall into two completely different categories: in the first, exceedingly dangerous operations are performed in an atmosphere charged with apprehension and, unless the patient's condition becomes immediately dangerous, are unaccompanied by post-operative treatment of any kind; in the second, secret but safe surgery is performed

by qualified operators under aseptic conditions in hospital or nursing home.[244]

It was, said a later Secretary of ALRA, to be an argument that became 'A staple ALRA text in the 1960s ... it made the case eloquently that if you had money you could buy a safe abortion privately, but if you were poor you risked your life and health at the hands of a backstreet abortionist'.[245] And it was to be an argument that was recited by the future Minister of Health, Kenneth Robinson, in his attempt to introduce a Medical Termination of Pregnancy Bill, 'a modest and a moderate Measure', in February 1961.

Kenneth Robinson was obliged to step warily in raising 'a very emotive' matter: 'I appreciate that it is ... a subject that is distasteful to many people, which makes it all the more necessary that we should think about it clearly and dispassionately. I hope that the House will keep an open mind on the matter, because from some quarters there have been certain reactions to the publication of this Bill that I can only describe as hysterical'.[246] His was not a bill to legalise abortion, because abortion was already legal, having been legitimated in the unsuccessful prosecution of the 'sordid case' that had led to the Bourne judgement. Abortion, he said, following the standard template that contrasted the morally deserving with the morally undeserving woman, and the morally deserving with the morally undeserving abortionist, was performed by two groups, one represented by the unskilled, back-street abortionists who practised on the poor and the other by 'the skilled, fully qualified professional abortionist who is known, I believe, as the Harley Street abortionist'. And here he turned to the work of Alice Jenkins. 'This leads in the simplest possible terms to a situation in which there is one law for the rich and one law for the poor. If there were no other arguments for amending the law, I submit that that is a very powerful one'. His Medical Termination of Pregnancy Bill was 'based on a draft Bill which is included in a book called A Law for the Rich'. It proposed that 'it should be lawful for a registered practitioner, acting in good faith, to terminate in the belief that there would be grave risk of serious injury to the patient's physical or mental health if she were left to give birth to and care for the child' (and one supporting illustration was the abortion of a pregnant woman who had contracted German measles); or if the pregnancy results from rape or incest, or if a girl of 13 years or under is pregnant, provided that rape or incest can be established. It laid down that abortion could not take place after the thirteenth week, and that the decision to terminate should always require a second, concurring opinion of another registered medical practitioner.

The bill attracted criticism.[247] The government claimed to have received the legal advice that 'the question of legalising abortion in certain circumstances cannot be dealt with in such simple terms as are proposed by Mr Robinson'[248] (and it had particularly in mind the problem of establishing rape). It attracted the criticism of the Churches and their clerical and lay members. The Moral Welfare Council of the Church Assembly Board for Social Responsibility convened a small expert committee, including the Bishop of Exeter,[249] both a member of the House of Lords and a prince of the Church, to review the bill, and its conclusions were condemnatory: what was proposed was based on hazardous speculation about the risk of foetal abnormality and largely unsustainable allegations of rape or some other criminal offence.[250] Canon Geoffrey Bentley, the Bishop of Exeter's examining Chaplain and an author of essays on sexual morality,[251] wrote to *The Times* to say that the bill would legalise actions that were not only morally wrong but would also further 'muddle and mislead the public conscience' by making the law 'explicitly sanction killing an unborn child for fear that, if it were permitted to live, it would become a burden to its mother or to the state'.[252] Peter Rawlinson,[253] a Catholic and Conservative Member of Parliament, later a Solicitor General, argued in the House of Commons that the law as it stood was perfectly satisfactory and that Kenneth Robinson's bill would both 'widen and loosen the safeguards which a state or community is entitled to demand in the care which must be devoted to living but unborn children'; and promote 'a more irresponsible attitude towards sex, and a looseness in behaviour ...' And David Renton,[254] a Home Office Minister, speaking for the government, stated that there was no need for change: 'By far the greater number of illegal abortions are performed not because the woman fears danger to her life or health, but simply because, for one reason or another, she does not want a child'. The law was in no need of amendment: 'To the extent that the Bill would make statutory the present case law and practice which has grown up round it, we do not consider it necessary to have a Bill for that limited purpose for it would make no substantial change in the law. To the extent that it would make a change, it would be restrictive ... [in that it would lay down] that the operation shall not be performed after the end of the thirteenth week of pregnancy'. He added that the bill would extend:

> the opportunities for legal termination of pregnancy, and in doing so it gives rise to some serious practical and legal difficulties ... it is still not possible to predict with any confidence in any particular case whether a child will exhibit some form of abnormality or how severe that abnormality will be. Where the transmission of abnormality is most probable and the degree of severity greatest it is the general experience that the state of mind of the expectant mother is such as justifies the termination of her pregnancy on the grounds of her health, and we do not believe, with the discretion which the present law allows that responsible doctors feel there is an unreasonable restriction by the absence of any provision relating specifically to the circumstances provided for in this Clause.

As for the clause permitting abortion in cases of rape and incest: 'we have the complication that there would be many cases in which a woman who had behaved indiscreetly, and found she was pregnant, would try to get out of her difficulty by saying that this was the result of one of those two criminal offences'. Generally:

> The existing law already allows termination of pregnancy where it is necessary to avoid serious damage to the health of the mother and regardless of the circumstances in which the pregnancy came about. Therefore, the enactment of these provisions ... would represent proposals which many people would support in principle, but which many others would oppose very strongly and they would in practice, as the Bill stands, not provide a satisfactory solution to the problems which, according to the declared intention of the hon. Member, the Bill is designed to meet.

And that Bill was also defeated, talked out by Anthony Fell,[255] another Catholic Member of Parliament, by 4 pm.

Thalidomide

The Abortion Law Reform Association had attempted on a number of occasions to introduce bills and it had failed. Its original membership were elderly or dead; its numbers were in decline; and it seemed to have lost momentum. Yet it was to revive, and what led to its rebirth was a concatenation of three catalysts: a crisis in 1961–2, a report in 1965 and the emergence of a new generation.

The crisis was generated by thalidomide.[256] Madeline Simms was to say that 'The drug thalidomide was the motor that reinvigorated the Abortion Law Reform Association and which paved the way for reform. ...'[257] Thalidomide, or Distaval, was a drug that had been prescribed in Europe and Canada since 1958 to allay the morning sickness that could accompany pregnancy. Doubts were first raised about its direct impact on patients,[258] and then about its impact on the babies to whom women gave birth. A warning[259] was first fired publicly in December 1961when an Australian doctor, William McBride, notified *The Lancet* that there had been an unexpected increase in the numbers of babies with 'severe abnormalities' delivered of women 'who had been given the drug thalidomide'. Had any readers, he wondered, 'seen similar abnormalities in babies delivered of women who have taken this drug during pregnancy?'[260]

Thalidomide was withdrawn in the United Kingdom in that very same month after its local producer, the Distillers Company, received what it called 'reports from two overseas sources possibly associating thalidomide ('Distaval') with harmful effects on the foetus in early pregnancy'.[261] Two papers in *The Lancet* then turned to the issue. The first, in February 1962, talked about 'disturbing reports from abroad of an increased incidence of certain malformations in newborn babies'.[262] A second, four months later, discussed a study in Liverpool which 'confirms the association previously reported between thalidomide and ectromelia [a congenital condition where long bones are

missing or underdeveloped] and between thalidomide and microtia [a congenital deformity where the outer ear is very small and underdeveloped]'. The
paper's author claimed that there must already in England and Wales have
been some 500 malformed babies born in 1960 and 1961 and that another
300 would be born in 1962.[263] At first the Ministry of Health resisted making
a count of thalidomide-related abnormalities,[264] but it succumbed under continual Parliamentary pressure, and the numbers it reported were progressively
whittled down. It at first fixed the numbers at 805 malformed babies born in
1960 and 1961 and in the first eight months of 1962.[265] In December 1962, it
put the total figure at 390;[266] and three months later at 349, of whom 267 were
then still surviving.[267] About 40 per cent of babies with thalidomide-induced
defects were said to have died before their first birthday.[268] Globally, it was
thought, the use of thalidomide had led to some 10,000 babies being born with
missing or severely deformed limbs.

The social problem of abortion had become abruptly dramatised. The historian, Barbara Brookes, talked about the 'public outrage at the thalidomide
disaster and at the lengths women had to go to get an abortion …'[269] But
there was no discernible immediate impact on the Conservative Government
then in power and very little on the Labour Government which succeeded
it. When, in July 1962, the doctor-peer, Lady Summerskill,[270] asked in the
House of Lords 'whether it can become permissible for a doctor to terminate
the pregnancy of a woman when it has been definitely established that thalidomide has been administered to her,' Lord Dilhorne, the Lord Chancellor,
maintained that the position was unchanged:

> … the circumstances in which a pregnancy may lawfully be terminated
> were indicated in the direction given to the jury in 1938 in the leading
> case of Rex v. Bourne; that is, that the act must be done in good faith to
> preserve the mother's life. The fact that the pregnancy, if allowed to take
> its course, would be likely to make the woman a physical or mental wreck
> would entitle the jury to take the view that the operation was for the
> preservation of the mother's life. The possibility that a child may be born
> deformed because, for example, the mother had taken thalidomide is not
> in itself a lawful ground for terminating a pregnancy.[271]

Yet evidence of a crisis continued to mount.[272] Observing the situation from
the United States, where thalidomide had not been approved for use, *Time
Magazine* recorded how 'Appalling reports continued to roll in. So far as is
known, close to 8,000 babies have been born deformed because their mothers
used a sleeping-pill-tranquilizer called thalidomide … All this added up to the
greatest prescription disaster in medical history'.[273] An oft-cited[274] article in *The
British Medical Journal* of July 1962 by two lecturers in the Department of Social
Medicine, University of Birmingham, one of them the Medical Officer of
Health for the city, graphically flagged quite how rapidly thalidomide-related
malformations seemed to be growing in Birmingham:

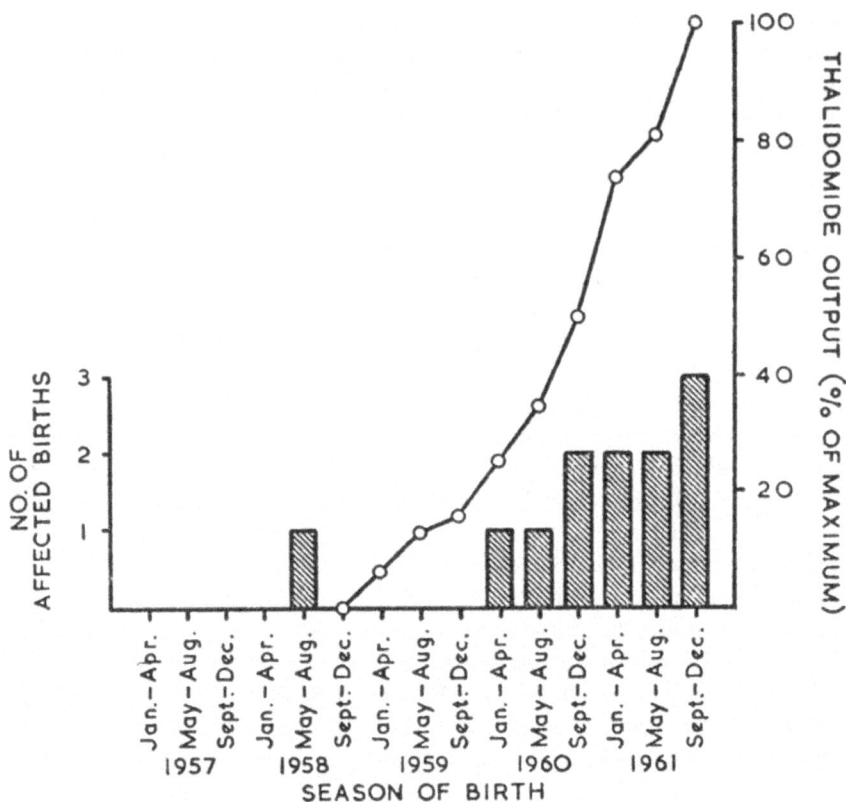

Figure 4.9 Thalidomide-related deformities in Birmingham 1957–1961[275]

I am very grateful to the *British Medical Journal* for giving me permission to reproduce this image.

There was talk of widespread public anxiety[276] and popular sympathy for a liberalisation of the law. A National Opinion Poll reported in the *Daily Mail* disclosed that almost 80 per cent of the public was in favour of legislation to enable a woman to have an abortion should she wish to do so, rather than be forced to give birth to a seriously deformed child.[277] There were reports about doctors in Arizona seeking leave to abort a woman who had taken thalidomide during the early stage of her pregnancy; the American courts denying her relief; and her pregnancy eventually being terminated in Sweden in August 1962,[278] despite the condemnation of the Vatican which claimed that the foetus was a human.[279] A family in Liège in Belgium was brought to trial in September 1962 for killing their malformed child with the assistance of their doctors:[280] the mother having protested that 'I just thought you could not let a baby like that live. I thought it could never be happy in its whole life'.[281] The family were to be acquitted by the jury,[282] and the case and the verdict led to a flurry of interest and numerous letters to the press, including those from Norman St John Stevas, a Catholic MP and a staunch opponent of abortion;

Barbara Wootton who raised doubts about the Roman Catholic Church's general stance on the sanctity of life;[283] and Glanville Williams who fused the issues together in a composite discussion of abortion, mercy killing and the law on homicide.[284] At a time when ALRA was regrouping, thalidomide offered a *casus belli* indeed. It was difficult in Parliament and Whitehall not to allude to it in discussion of the possible medical grounds for termination. A *New Society* article, dated August 1964 and tellingly deposited in the Home Office papers on abortion, stated that:

> For the first time, the problem of abortion has become a matter of wide-spread public concern and discussion. The Thalidomide tragedy, in par-ticular, brought home to many people the startling fact that in Britain, almost alone of the non-Catholic countries, there are no clearly defined grounds for the legal termination of pregnancy.[285]

Madeline Simms, one of the core members of the newly regrouped Association, recalled that 'Thalidomide was my original motivation [to join ALRA]. ... I became really active when the Thalidomide tragedy occurred. I have always been particularly concerned about the prevention of handicap, and it struck me as so appalling that there were people around who were actually prepared to compel women to have handicapped babies when this could be avoided'. She continued:

> We were the second wave of ALRA activists. Alice Jenkins and her friends Janet Chance and Stella Browne had founded ALRA in 1936. They did a lot of educational work and held meetings and conferences, but when the war came, the whole thing went into hibernation. When I joined 25 years later, there were a lot of elderly and rather respectable people running it, with an Indian army Colonel as the chair, which was not quite what I had expected. They were restrained and discreet. They felt you could hardly mention abortion in public, you could not write letters to the press about it, nor even to MPs unless you knew them personally. But in the 1960s we younger members started writing letters all over the place and found they were often printed. ... The group of people who came together in the 1960s was formidable. Getting to know them well was one of the marvel-lous side effects of being so closely involved in this cause. I suppose it was in the spirit of the age to some extent. Reform was in the air.[286]

It was thus precisely at the moment that thalidomide dawned as a social, ethical and medical problem that the Association came to reinvent itself. It acquired a new president, the eminent legal scholar, Glanville Williams,[287] in 1962, and a new constitution in November 1964, with the object of securing 'a change in British law such as will allow medical termination of pregnancy on wider grounds':[288] 'We were getting rid of the last bits of Victorian baggage that were surplus to requirements – the 1861 Offences Against the Person Act in our case,'[289] said Simms. A year later, in 1965, the Association had grown to 1,000 members.[290] It founded local branch associations – Birmingham ALRA Group in 1962, the North-West London and Bristol Groups in 1963, the Manchester Group in 1964, and the South East London Group in 1965. It commissioned polls. It sought to influence other organisations working in neighbouring regions of public policy (although abortion continued to be identified as a taboo area in some quarters[291]). And it worked hard in lobbying Members of Parliament: 'We started with about 30 known supporters in the House of Commons and we built this up until at one time an overall majority of members of the Commons were known supporters ... There were well over 100 new Labour MPs from professional backgrounds who, we thought, probably felt the same as us on this issue'.[292] It had especial success with the new generation of Members who entered Parliament after the 1964 general election, the generation that were supporting Sydney Silverman and his bills on capital punishment. By September 1965, it estimated that there were 300 Members sympathetic to change;[293] and Glanville Williams asked them to consider introducing legislation to amend the 1861Offences Against the Person Act.

Messages began to circulate within government itself about the growing interest in abortion law reform. A note to the Private Office in November 1964, at the very beginning of the new Labour Government's first session, reported that 'we are asked to make an early submission to S. of S. [Secretary of State] on the desirability of offering to a Private Member successful in the Ballot, a Bill on "Abortion Law Reform". Mr McMurray[294] does not know the source of the suggestion to the Whips' Office but it might, he thinks, have been the Labour Party Headquarters or the Whips might have discovered that some Private Members were interested'.[295] A briefing for the new Home Secretary reflected on liberalisation and the possible impact of thalidomide:

> Previous governments have not objected to such proposals but doubtful whether doctors would welcome it. Ministry of Health, after enquiries in 1960, were satisfied that the present state of the law imposed no real difficulty on responsible gynaecologists and that a strong body of opinion in the medical profession was in favour of leaving the law as it is. Might make it more difficult for them 'to convince a patient not requiring abortion on medical grounds that an abortion would be against the law. Ministry have no reason to suppose that they have changed their minds since 1960.
>
> Interdepartmental Cttee recommended against legalising abortion in cases of abnormality because medical science was not sufficiently advanced to forecast with reasonable certainty that a particular pregnancy would result in an abnormal child. This remains the case. Much would have to be left in the doctor's judgement with a real risk of unnecessary abortions and considerable abuse.
>
> Recent suggestion that there is an especially strong case for legalising abortion where the expectant mother has taken thalidomide which is known to result in abnormalities. But even here prediction is inexact.

Just as great a risk with German measles. Venereal disease not germane – doctors consider they should treat the mother in cases of syphilis rather than terminate her pregnancy.[296]

So framed, it is not perhaps remarkable that interest in law reform was so muted at first and that Home Office officials, the Home Secretary and Prime Minister were nervous about becoming involved. The Prime Minister, Harold Wilson, had no appetite for reform. [297] The Home Secretary was reticent. Officials were less than enthusiastic. Brian Cubbon's note to Sir Frank Soskice at the opening of the new session of the new government recited that it would be possible to:

[i] put the case law on a statutory basis; [ii] legalise abortion where some abnormality is expected in the child; [iii] permit abortion after a sexual assault. Questionable whether legislation would be desirable on ii or practicable on iii. No objection in principle to i but no reason to suppose that the views of doctors have changed since 1960 when M of Health found that there was strong medical opinion in favour of leaving the law as it is.[298] Law would be difficult to draft and Parliamentary Counsel are busy. Recommend that Cabinet Office should be told that it would not be possible to have a bill ready for a private member this session.[299]

Since 1961, the note continued, there had been the problem of thalidomide, but, repeating the arguments of the earlier submission, it was not of crucial significance:

Recent suggestion that there is an especially strong case for legalising abortion where the expectant mother has taken thalidomide which is known to result in abnormalities. But even here prediction is inexact. Just as great a risk with German measles. Venereal disease not germane – doctors consider they should treat the mother in cases of syphilis rather than terminate her pregnancy.

And there was the problem of pregnancy induced by rape or other sexual offence:

[The] Interdepartmental Cttee rejected this as a possible ground for medical abortion – welcomed on humanitarian grounds but overwhelming practical difficulties in deciding whether the pregnancy was in fact the result of an offence. May be delays in bringing offender to trial. Offender may not be caught. Not a question to be determined by a doctor.

Brian Cubbon concluded: 'There is of course a sizeable body of opinion which will vigorously oppose on religious and ethical grounds any legislation to legalise abortion, especially if it goes further than the present case law'.

The new Home Secretary, Sir Frank Soskice, hesitated. His answering note had initially opened with the phrase 'I agree. But'. However the phrase was struck out and he had begun again:

> I should like to think more about abortion. Whilst I agree we can't get a bill ready for this session, I do not feel convinced about the arguments in [the attached note]. To take a case of a child who has been raped, or a mother who has taken thalidomide or some other dangerous drug and who wants an abortion because she is anxious lest her child may be deformed, my own view would be that it is uncivilised to refuse her abortion, and that the rule in Bourne leaves the matter much too uncertain. I feel there may be great tragedies in situations of this kind, such as in the case in Belgium when a jury let a mother off a murder charge. I of course realise that there will be strong religious and moral objections, but my provisional feeling is that we should in due course consider legislation in spite of this.[300]

Four days later, however, he decided not to give any support to abortion law reform in the coming session. He was minded, he said, to 'explore the possibility in the first place of making clear in legislation what the common law is in upon the principle of the Bourne case. Secondly, I suggest that conceivably it might be possible [following that case] to make abortion legal in the case of a child under, say, 14 who had been made pregnant or the victim of a rape or a woman who had taken some drug such as thalidomide which was highly likely to cause a deformed birth'. What, however, had given rise to his hesitation and subsequent decision not to endorse legislation for the time being was the problem of moral hazard. In the dawn of what was coming to be called the permissive society,[301] there was, he feared, the possibility that liberalisation would promote promiscuity:[302]

> ... my own feeling is that we should contemplate measures for tightening up the law to lessen the sense of utter irresponsibility which seems to be prevailing about illegitimate conceptions. ... Moreover I have been considerably shocked by the apparent callousness with which some girls and young women who are unmarried and pregnant seem to think that they can load on to the community the child who is born and wholly discard any responsibility for it. ... [303] The general objective ... would be to bring home to young people that they really must be more self-controlled in their sex relationships. The extent of illegitimacy is, I understand, attaining alarming proportions and I feel that it is time to react against it if possible.[304]

From without, the Association sought to approach the new government, and Vera Houghton arranged, 'Through the good offices of my husband [Douglas], [a meeting with] the Home Secretary ...'[305] A record of that meeting, held on 2 February 1965, reported Sir Frank's ambivalence:

The Home Secretary opened by saying that he was in favour of allowing abortion on grounds relating to the health of the mother, in cases of rape and unlawful sexual intercourse with young girls, and in cases like the Thalidomide tragedy. He was not in favour of complete legalisation. ... [Glanville] Williams asked whether the Whips Office might not be supplied with a Bill like Mr Robinson's, which they might recommend to any private member who had been successful in the ballot and who came for advice. The Home Secretary thought that the measure would be too controversial to be dealt with in this way. In his opinion the task of the Abortion Law reform Association was to crystallise public opinion in support of legislation.[306]

Vera Houghton's own note stated that 'Our hope was that the Home Secretary might indicate to us that the Government would be willing to consider providing time for a private member's bill or giving some encouragement to a private member lucky in the next ballot. ... I am very sorry to report that this turned out to be a false hope and that the situation with this Government is little different from that of the previous one ...'[307] Diane Munday of ALRA recalled with some asperity, that 'she came away with the message, reinforced later from Harold Wilson, that abortion law reform was a highly sensitive issue; there was no public demand for it and therefore no government would touch it with a barge pole'.[308] And, the Association noted, Sir Frank needed more evidence of public demand for the measure before contemplating lending it his support.[309]

That was the seeming end of public discussion, although internally, within the Home Office, abortion law reform did continue to be deliberated. It was concluded there that it would almost certainly remain a public issue which required a response. There was a case to extend the provision of legal abortion to pregnancies incurred after rape, where the mother was very young and where she had taken thalidomide. But those deliberations were intimately coupled to, and complicated by, the rather special lens introduced by the supposed problem of sexual promiscuity. The Home Secretary, Permanent Secretary and Lord Stonham, the Home Office Minister in the House of Lords, sought to tie any reform of the law to forthcoming proposals on affiliation orders whereby young men who had fathered illegitimate children might be induced financially to support them, and, in the process, curtail the number of births outside wedlock. Sir Frank was reminded that he had 'suggested that, to combat the increase in illegitimate births and to encourage self-control in young people, changes should be considered in the law of affiliation designed to bring home a continuing sense of responsibility to the putative father and mother. ...'[310] It might be timely, it was thought, to temper the undesirable effects of liberalising abortion law by tightening provisions for the support of unwed mothers and their children. An undated note of an undated meeting records that:

S. of S. took the opportunity of a discussion with Mr Cubbon on another matter yesterday to raise again the question of Abortion Law Reform.

Lord Stonham was present and expressed support for the Home Secretary's view that we ought to consider once again whether the Government should make any move on this subject at the present time. Both S. of S. and Lord Stonham are certain that the subject will not be allowed to rest and that there will be continuing pressure on the Government. They would like the possibility explored of our putting proposals to Home Affairs Committee either for Government legislation or for the preparation of a Bill to be handed to a Private Member. S. of S. outlined his ideas on the content of legislation. He would like to see it deal with the issue on two fronts. First there should be statutory provision to permit abortion in certain defined circumstances. These should include pregnancies after rape; pregnancies where the mother had taken thalidomide (there should be power to prescribe by statutory instrument other drugs which might later be thought dangerous); cases where it was desirable to terminate pregnancy in the interests of the mother's health or of the child. Statutory effect should be given to the judgement in the Bourne case. The second approach should be to make more stringent provision for maintenance and affiliation payments. S. of S. has in mind the establishment of a fund into which the fathers of illegitimate children should be required to make payments for as long as the child needs support.[311]

What the ministers had in mind was the National Assistance Bill then moving through Parliament intended 'to deal with maintenance of the deserted or divorced wife under a maintenance order, or the support of the illegitimate child under an affiliation order;'[312] and it illustrates how events linked together in time may become linked causally and thematically.[313] That yoking together of two rather different issues then tended to impede the progress of any further decision-making. Some sort of new, 'general policy' might have been in distant sight, but, a note from the private office to Sir Charles Cunningham reported, 'S of S has accepted that an Abortion Bill is out of the question for this Session & I have informed Cabinet Office'.[314] But it was also acknowledged that that could not be the end of the matter: 'The subject will come up again in the New Year on the 65/66 legislative programme, if not before'. What was deemed unacceptable was 'the whole principle of permissive abortion', to which the Home Secretary maintained a 'strong opposition'.

It was an opposition that led the government to look with some distaste at a bill introduced in the summer of 1965 under a new procedure, the ten-minute rule,[315] by Renée Short,[316] the new Labour Member for Wolverhampton North-East. She would have made it possible 'lawfully [to] terminate a pregnancy in good faith in the belief that there would be a grave risk of the child being born grossly deformed or with a physical or mental abnormality which would be of a degree to require constant hospital treatment or special care throughout life'.[317] The impact of thalidomide had, she said, underscored the importance of the matter: 'Since my right hon. Friend the Minister of Health [Kenneth Robinson] attempted to introduce his own Private Member's Bill in

1961, the thalidomide tragedy has occurred. This adds urgency to the need for reform. It caused a great shift in public opinion'.[318]

Sir Charles Cunningham hoped to see the bill rejected ('the only question is whether the Government should take any steps to block the Second Reading in the likely event of no other objection being made. A case could be made out for blocking the Bill on the ground that, whatever the merits, a Bill of this kind ought not to be given approval in principle without a debate, but on the whole I suggest that it should be left to the personal convictions of Members to decide whether to object. ...'[319]) However, in the event, and following convention, Cabinet resolved that, if the motion were opposed, government supporters should be free to vote according to their conscience.[320]

The bill received an unopposed first reading on 29 June 1965 but failed to secure a second reading on 2 July, having been opposed by the Roman Catholic MP,[321] William Wells, Q.C.,[322] crying 'Object' (he was later to write expressly as a Catholic to *The Times* 'Without wishing to oversimplify a difficult problem, the foundation of the case against abortion is the commandment not to kill'[323]). There had been some attempt to counter him ('letters were addressed to Alra members in Walsall. ... asking them to write to Mr Wells and encourage other constituents to do so, pointing out that he was taking unfair advantage of Parliamentary procedure to express his religious views'[324]), but it was to no avail. 'It was near the end of the parliamentary session and [William Wells] knew that there would be no further opportunity for private members' business...'[325] In any event, an informal poll of Members of Parliament conducted by ALRA members had been more than a little discouraging: 228 Members had said they would not attend the second reading, 41 said they would.[326]

One of the prime reservations voiced within the Home Office to the bill had been that 'Where this defence of [a grave risk to the child] was raised, it would be up to the Crown to prove that the pregnancy was not terminated in that belief – a very difficult burden. Unreasonable to expect the Crown to have this burden'.[327] Others took notice as well. On 9 July 1964 the British Medical Association's annual representative meeting passed a resolution from the Birmingham Division, a division whose members were particularly averse to reform, 'That, in view of the present agitation for reform in the law concerning abortion, (1) the Council of the BMA should set up a special committee to evaluate the therapeutic indications; (2) the Government should be asked not to introduce any new legislation until this committee has reported'. It was clear that some medical practitioners considered that others, including ALRA, were beginning to encroach on territory that was their own.[328]

At precisely the time that Renée Short's Bill was being defeated, the Home Secretary was still engaged in his somewhat tangled exchange of notes with Sir Charles Cunningham about the prospects of some other venture that could at once liberalise abortion and rein in promiscuity. Any Bill would probably be best entrusted to a Private Member, it was thought, and Sir Charles foresaw abundant difficulties ahead: 'Although sympathy for abortion law reform has probably grown, there remains strong opposition to the whole principle of permissive abortion, and this was reflected in the discussion in the Legislation Committee on Mrs Short's recent Motion for a Ten Minute Bill'. A bill that would satisfy the reformers must fulfil three conditions that had been abstracted from ALRA publications and from Kenneth Robinson's failed 1961 bill:[329] abortions would become legal '(a) where they are permitted under the present case-law; (b) where an abnormal child is expected; and (b) where the pregnancy is the result of a criminal offence'.[330] The medical profession had not been consulted and might raise objections. There were moral hazards attendant on ceding the right to an abortion to all girls under 16:[331] 'It would ... be necessary to decide whether the Bill should cover all girls under 16. In their case the pregnancy must have resulted from a criminal offence, but to give <u>carte blanche</u> for abortions in these cases would in practice condone promiscuity and might even encourage it. ... '.

Yet the Home Secretary did not cease being exercised by the problem. Two months later he asked Sir Charles 'Are we giving thought to this? It is not practicable to introduce legislation at the moment. But I am sure pressure will continue and grow. I am myself in favour of it, on lines which I have previously indicated to the dept'.[332] A little later, towards the end of the Session, he would again say:

> I think pressure will grow, and my feeling is that while there would obviously be bitter opposition in some quarters, there is a broad and growing measure of public support for some reform in the existing law. We should leave the matter at the moment. But I should be grateful if the dept. would bring the matter forward for re-consideration at the end of the year, so that we can consider whether it would be right to try to test public and medical opinion in some way.[333]

So it came about that Alice Bacon, Minister of State between 1964 and 1967, signalled publicly in July 1965 that the government would not discourage a private member's bill in the next Session ('The Government', she said, 'are of the opinion that as there are divergent views of both sides of the House, this might be a good subject for a Private Member's Bill in the new Session, when the opinion of this House could be tested'[334]). An anonymous note to the Home Secretary recorded '<u>Abortion</u> ... Sir Charles Cunningham's submission of 28/6 and ... the last PQ exchange on the subject. It seems we can now only await the result of the ballot and whether any member takes up the very broad hint given by Miss Bacon'.[335]

Failing to take that hint, Renée Short was to complain that there was no provision for government support for an Abortion Bill by private Member or government in the Queen's Speech in November 1965 at the opening of the new session of Parliament:[336] 'I am ... rather sorry' she said, 'about the absence of another item from the Gracious Speech. I refer to proposals I looked for from my right hon. and learned Friend the Home Secretary for the reform of the law relating to abortion. Such a Bill would have been welcomed with acclaim on both sides of the House and by the general public'.[337]

The absence of a reference to reform must be explained by the difficulty the ailing Sir Frank had encountered in steering between the Scylla of promoting promiscuity and the Charybdis of excessive restraint on abortion. But just before Christmas he was to be replaced by a new Secretary of State, Roy Jenkins, who would adopt a less hesitant stance. Roy Jenkins, reported *The Times*, had made it clear that he was 'a campaigner for specific social reforms':

> He has backed the Wolfenden recommendations for reform of the law on homosexuality … has described the law on abortion as archaic. … Taking over the department when the Queen's Speech is already unfolding in legislation, he can at least be sure that he has not been committed to Bills over whose drafting he has had no influence. But, more important, there are three private members' Bills imminent that are well suited for him to show his reformist impact: on homosexuality …, abortion … and Sunday observance …[338]

'I supported abortion law reform for all the classical reasons of choice', he was to say later, 'a woman's right to have one if she wished – not as a backstreet, illegal operation. I considered it to be one of a number of health and social problems that needed to be addressed at the time. When I became Home Secretary in 1965 I very much wanted to see a proper measure of reform brought forward'.[339] He was powerfully supported by Vera Houghton's husband, Douglas Houghton, who was the Chairman of the Parliamentary Labour Party, and in Cabinet by John Silkin, Lord Silkin's son and the Chief Whip; Antony Crosland, Secretary of State for Education and Science; Richard Crossman, Minister of Housing and Local Government; the Lord Chancellor, Gerald Gardiner; and Kenneth Robinson.[340] 'I was lucky because there were a lot of friends at court', said Lord Steel about the ground that was being prepared for his own entrance. Reform appeared imminent.

Notes

1 I am most grateful to David Steel for having read and commented on this and the next chapter.
2 Stephen Brooke, Professor of History at York University, Canada, speaking at the ICBH Witness Seminar Programme, 10 July 2001, http://www.kcl.ac.uk/sspp/departments/icbh/witness/PDFfiles/AbortionAct1967.pdf, 22. He is the author of *Sexual Politics: Sexuality, Family Planning and the British Left from the 1880s to the Present Day*, Oxford: Oxford University Press, 2011.
3 J. Weeks (1990); *Coming Out: Homosexual Politics in Britain from the Nineteenth Century to the Present*, London: Quartet, 173. He went on to list as evidence the single-issue campaigns on 'the abolition of capital punishment and abortion-law reform and divorce-law reform as well as homosexual law reform. …'
4 Note for the record of a meeting between Mr. Callaghan, Lord Allen, Bob Morris and Nigel Bowles at the House of Commons on 9 March 1982. Callaghan Papers, BWA4, Special Collections, Bodleian Library.

5   He was later to write in a grand overview of the work of the Home Office and of the part he played in it 'The early and mid-1960s are often thought of as a period of liberal reform, and so they were in many ways, but we did not think of ourselves as driving that process in any visionary way so much as doing what we could do to make things better – more efficient, more fair, more suited to what was expected'. (D. Faulkner (2014); *Servant of the Crown*, Hook: Waterside Press, 21).

6   BBC interview: DP_KEEP_CHANGEMAKER_1200_3_12_millbank_219759.wmv

7   D. Steel (1989); *Against Goliath: David Steel's Story*, London: Weidenfeld & Nicolson, 10–11.

8   A retired Home Office official, a member of the small group of those who were central to the events of the time, told me me that they might not have said that they were engaged on a liberal, reforming project, but what they believed in private could well have been otherwise.

9   For instance, just as the new Labour Cabinet was readying itself to deal with the abolition of capital punishment in November 1964, there was a note in a Home Office file from 'HBW': 'In response to an earlier request by the S. of S. Mr Cubbon had prepared a draft note on the abortion law, with which I agreed, but deferred submitting it until a note on Wolfenden, for which S. of S. had asked at the same time, was ready (it will be shortly)'. Home Office File 219/1139: Abortion: Miscellaneous and General – Proposed Private Member's Bill to amend the Law on Abortion. And there was inevitable cross-influence: for example, the latitude allowed Sydney Silverman in passing his abolition bill was to be cited as a precedent in a request for extra Parliamentary time to be afforded the Abortion Bill (see Parliamentary Debates: Oral Answers: 8 July 1965).

10 The *Daily Mail* commented at one point that 28 October 1965 'was a curious parliamentary day. Only the vast central lobby separated two silver-haired St. Georges battling against their own private dragons of prejudice and hostility. In the Commons, Mr Sydney Silverman … was crowning his political ambitions by shepherding through the last stages of his "No Hanging" Bill. Across the hall, Lord Arran … was earning a 5–2 third reading for his measure to erase the stigma of criminality from acts between consenting adults'. (29 October 1965).

11 In *Pioneers of Change: Interviews with people who made the 1967 Abortion Act possible*, http://www.bpas.org/js/filemanager/files/abortion_pioneers.pdf, 24.

12 In *Pioneers of Change: Interviews with people who made the 1967 Abortion Act possible*, http://www.bpas.org/js/filemanager/files/abortion_pioneers.pdf, 30.

13 *The Times*, 1 December 1965.

14 He was also a member of the Executive Committee of the Homosexual Law Reform Society.

15 For instance, it was hoped that a consortium of campaigning organisations would share the cost of a survey: 'The Secretary [of the Homosexual Law Reform Society] reported that the British Market Research Bureau was now starting the attitude survey which had been agreed upon at the previous meeting, and it was proposed that an approach should be made to other bodies such as the Abortion Law Reform Society, Divorce Law Reform Society, Marriage Law Reform Society, Progressive League and the Married Women's Association, in the hope that they would bear a portion of the cost of the survey, since they would benefit from the results of this research'. Minutes of a Meeting of the Executive Committee, Homosexual Law Reform Society, 18 July 1963.

16 So it was that A. Dyson, one of the founders of the Homosexual Law Reform Society and the Albany Trust, wrote at an early stage to Ena Steel of the Church of England Moral Welfare Council, 'Our aim, as you know, will be to avoid such controversial issues as might divide supporters, and to work in full co-operation with all those who wish to see the law reformed. I am hoping that it will soon be possible to establish a

permanent liaison with yourselves, the Howard League and all other interested parties … ' Lambeth Palace papers: letter of 18 May 1958; BSR/AB.

17 The Church of England Moral Welfare Council was established in 1939 to supervise the work of the White Cross League, and the Advisory Board for Moral Welfare Work. It described itself as 'the central council of the Church for the co-ordination of thought and action in relation to sex, marriage and the family in the Christian life'. It was placed under the Board of Social Responsibility in 1958, and appears to have been active until the following year. http://www.dango.bham.ac.uk/record_details. asp?recordType=ngo&id=3157

18 This must have been Simon Sainsbury, 1930–2006, who had been a director of the family firm since 1959, becoming deputy chairman in 1969. He was the substantial, if unobtrusive, financial patron of a number of organisations, including the Monument Trust which he established in July 1965, and which gave money to a variety of causes, including HIV and AIDS sufferers and to Stonewall, the Gay Rights campaigning organisation. He and his male partner of 40 years' standing entered into a civil partnership in January 2006. (Based on http://www.oxforddnb.com/view/article/97474?docPos=7). The Monument Trust describes itself as making 'grants in the following areas:

   • Health and Community Care – substantial HIV/AIDS projects in the UK and Africa, social exclusion, the sexual health of young people, and hospices
   • Arts and Heritage – arts, architectural and environmental projects of national or regional importance, including galleries, museums, and historic houses and gardens. Proposals are particularly welcome for cultural projects which will make a major contribution to improving economically depressed areas.
   • Criminal justice – including prisoners resettlement, advice and mentoring, and alternatives to custody. (http://www.sfct.org.uk/monument.html)

19 Lambeth Palace papers: Letter of 27 May 1958; BSR/AB.

20 See P. Brierley (1999); *Religious Trends 1999–2000*, No. 2, London: Christian Research Association.

21 S. Newcombe (2009); review of H. McLeod (2007) *The Religious Crisis of the 1960s*, Oxford: Oxford University Press, in *The Historical Journal*, Vol. 52, No. 3, 849.

22 J. Beckford (1990); 'The Sociology of Religion and Social Problems', *Sociological Analysis*, Vol. 51, No. 1, 9.

23 For example, the medical associations sometimes turned to the Church for guidance or support on the morals of abortion and homosexuality. In one communication about the Abortion Bill, it was reported that 'The following document was approved by the Council of the B.M.A. at its meeting of 21 December': 'we would like to see included in the Bill a subclause to the effect that in deciding whether or not to terminate the pregnancy in the interests of the health of the mother, "account may be taken of the patient's total environment, actual or reasonably foreseeable". The words in quotation marks are taken from the draft bill recommended by the Report of the Church Assembly Board for Social Responsibility …' Medical Termination of Pregnancy Bill Views of the British Medical Association and the Royal College of Obstetricians and Gynaecologists', *British Medical Journal*, 31 December 1966, 1649.

24 'Bishops Will Sway Vote on Abortion Bill', *The Times*, 27 November 1965.

25 See the editorial in *The Times*, 1 February 1966.

26 Some part of the interplay between the National Campaign for the Abolition of the Death Penalty and the Church of England was traced in the last chapter. Similar interaction will be mapped in my description of the campaigns for abortion and homosexual law reform.

27 See H. McLeod (2007); *The Religious Crisis of the 1960s*, Oxford: Oxford University Press, esp. 233.

28 Thus Ena Steel, of the Church of England Moral Welfare Council, wrote to Tony Dyson of the embryonic Homosexual Law Reform Society: 'You know, I think, that our feeling is that there is work to be done, but this will be effective only if it is carried out by a very small and carefully chosen group of people who have special knowledge of this problem. Do you think that those who have said that they would be willing to serve on an Executive body would be willing to appoint such a group and then leave it to that body to carry out the work there is to do? The members of your Committee of Honour could be kept informed from time to time, but we should hope that there would be no public advertisement of this organisation or their names'. Lambeth Palace papers: 8 May 1958: letter from Miss Steel to A. Dyson; BSR/AB.

29 For example, the British Medical Association proclaimed in November 1965 that it would oppose any changes in the law on abortion, then pending in a bill before the House of Lords, until it had itself deliberated on the matter and made its views known. See 'B.M.A. Concern Over Abortion Bill', *The Times*, 30 November 1965. It then began to negotiate with Lord Silkin about the terms of his bill immediately after it had passed its first reading (*The Times*, 2 December 1965).

30 In *Pioneers of Change: Interviews with people who made the 1967 Abortion Act possible*, http://www.bpas.org/js/filemanager/files/abortion_pioneers.pdf, 10.

31 Letter of 16 November1964.

32 In *Pioneers of Change: Interviews with people who made the 1967 Abortion Act possible*, http://www.bpas.org/js/filemanager/files/abortion_pioneers.pdf, 54.

33 L. Hall, 'Historical Summary', List of Papers in the Contemporary Medical Archives Centre at the Wellcome Institute for the History of Medicine. (But there are no references to Abortion Law Reform in the Gardiner Papers held at the British Library (http://www.bl.uk/catalogues/manuscripts/DESC0010.ASP?source=DESC0000. ASP)

34 M. Simms in *Pioneers of Change: Interviews with people who made the 1967 Abortion Act possible*, *op. cit.*, 15.

35 G. Gardiner and A. Martin (1964); 'The Machinery of Law Reform', in G. Gardiner and A. Martin (eds.) *Law Reform Now*, London: Victor Gollancz (the book had been sponsored by the Society of Labour Lawyers). The mechanism in question was to be the Law Commission which he founded. He did not proceed to specify the laws that needed reform, but C.H. Rolph in his separate chapter on 'Criminal Law', did list capital punishment, homosexual law reform and abortion law reform (227–269). On the law on abortion, C.H. Rolph recited much of the argument and the evidence presented to the Inter-Departmental Committee and argued, summarising Dorothy Turtle's minority report, that 'being illegal, [abortion] is, unless the woman is wealthy, liable to take place under the dreadfully insanitary conditions which are well known. ... This law, like so many others, is out of harmony with the opinion of a large section of the public in this country' (240–1). Gerald Gardiner would, of course, have known and presumably approved what C.H. Rolph wrote.

36 Leo Abse, 1917–2008, was Labour Member of Parliament for Pontypool between 1958 and 1983. He introduced Infanticide Bills in 1964 and 1969 to amend the law relating to child murder; led the final parliamentary campaign for the abolition of capital punishment in 1969; and was the sponsor or co-sponsor of Private Members' Acts relating to divorce, homosexuality and family planning. (*Who's Who and Who was Who*, http://www.ukwhoswho.com.gate2.library.lse.ac.uk/view/arti cle/oupww/whowaswho/U4950/ABSE_Leo?index=1&results=QuicksearchResult s&query=0)

37 L. Abse (1973); *Private Member*, London: MacDonald, 217.

38 *Ibid*, 157.

39 B. Wootton (1992); *Selected Writings: Volume 1: Crime and the Penal System*, Houndmills: Macmillan, 85, 86.

40 A letter from Mrs. Street, of C4, dated 4 February 1985, reports that 'The Home Secretary has a general responsibility for abortion legislation, because it is bound up with the general criminal law on offences against the person (including child destruction)'. HO CRI/84 770/2/2.

41 Edward Law, Lord Ellenborough, 1750–1818, was called to the Bar in 1769, became a K.C. in 1787, and became Attorney General in 1801. A year later he became Lord Chief Justice, and he remained so until his death.

42 J. Keown (1988); *Abortion, Doctors and the Law*, Cambridge: Cambridge University Press, esp. 20.

43 In The Offences against the Person Act, 1828 (9 Geo.4 c.31).

44 It was later held necessary for a woman to be with child if she was to be punished for procuring her own abortion, but an attempt by others remained criminal even if she were not pregnant [R. v Whitchurch, 1890 (24 QBD 420)].

45 See A. Grubb (1990); 'Abortion Law in England: The Medicalization of a Crime', *Law, Medicine and Health Care*, Vol. 18, Nos 1–2, 146–161.

46 The new penitentiaries, designed to induce repentance in carefully controlled conditions of isolation, began to be built in the 1840s after the Penitentiary Act of 1799. The first national penitentiary was completed at Millbank in London, in 1816. It was followed, amongst others, by the new model penitentiary at Pentonville in 1842 and the New City Prison at Holloway in 1852.

47 Lord Lansdowne, 1780–1863, was the son of William Petty, Lord Shelburne, whose friend was Jeremy Bentham, and who acted as something of a mentor. He became minister without portfolio in 1827 and then Home Secretary.

48 HC Deb 23 March 1837 Vol. 37 cc709–33.

49 That section of the 1861 Act was itself a re-enactment of earlier statutes, the first of which was 43 Geo. 3, c. 58, s. 1, the Malicious Shooting or Stabbing Act 1803, also known as Lord Ellenborough's Act, which made any attempt to induce the abortion of a quickened foetus with poisons a capital felony, and any attempt to induce an abortion before quickening (or without proof of quickening) subject to fine, imprisonment, pillory, whipping, or transportation to the penal colonies for up to 14 years.

50 L. Farmer, *Making the Modern Criminal Law, op. cit.*, 234.

51 Henry Brougham, 1778–1868, was called to the Scottish Bar in 1800 and to the English Bar in 1803, appearing before Lord Ellenborough in 1811 when he successfully defended two defendants despite an adverse judicial summing-up in favour of conviction. He became involved with the Clapham set and the campaign against slavery in the early 1800s and entered Parliament in 1810 as a Whig which he held for two years. He returned to Parliament in 1815 as the member for Winchelsea. He was an educational reformer, a reformer of the law on charities, bringing in the introduction of Charities Commissioners, and helped to found the University of London. He was appointed Lord Chancellor in 1830, in which post he embarked on a wholesale reform of the legal system, instituting a Royal Commission on the criminal law in 1833. (Based on the entry by M. Lobban in the *Oxford Dictionary of National Biography*, http://www.oxforddnb.com/view/article/3581?docPos=2)

52 HL Deb 14 May 1860 Vol. 158 cc1200–3.

53 Sir George Bowyer, 1811–1883, had been called to the Bar on 7 June 1839, 'a fervent whig and an enthusiastic supporter of Lord Henry Brougham', he was elected as the Member for Dundalk in 1852. (Based on the entry by Michael Lobban in the *Oxford Dictionary of National Biography*, http://www.oxforddnb.com/view/article/3090?docPos=2)

54 'There was a great want of scientific arrangement in these Bills, and a great deal of repetition and unnecessary matter might have been spared had there been proper scientific definitions of what constituted certain offences, such as murder and assaults.

The whole Bill did not contain a definition of any offence'. HC Deb 11 June 1860 Vol. 159 cc270–80.

55 Sir Edward Clarke, 1841–1931, had been called to the Bar in 1864, became a Member of Parliament in 1880 and again in 1906, was Solicitor-General between 1886 and 1892. (http://www.ukwhoswho.com/view/article/oupww/whowaswho/U207546/ CLARKE_Rt_Hon._Sir_Edward_George?index=8&results=QuicksearchResults&q uery=0).

56 Horace Avory, 1851–1935, was called to the Bar in 1875 and became Junior Counsel to the Treasury at the Central Criminal Court in 1889 (http://www.ukwhoswho.com/ view/article/oupww/whowaswho/U205485/AVORY_Rt._Hon._Sir_Horace_Edm und?index=1&results=QuicksearchResults&query=0).

57 'The doctrine (or principle) of double effect is often invoked to explain the permissibility of an action that causes a serious harm, such as the death of a human being, as a side effect of promoting some good end. It is claimed that sometimes it is permissible to cause such a harm as a side effect (or "double effect") of bringing about a good result even though it would not be permissible to cause such a harm as a means to bringing about the same good end'. *Stanford Encylopedia of Philosophy*, http://plato.stanford.edu/ entries/double-effect/ It was a doctrine that was attacked by Pope Pius XII in his statement that '… to save the life of the mother is a most noble end, but the direct killing of the child as a means to this end is not licit'. In a speech by Kenneth Robinson in the House of Commons: HC Deb 10 February 1961 Vol. 634 cc853–92.

58 *The Scalpel*, 1896, 1, 160.

59 *The Medical Press*, 1 (1896); 591. The President of the Royal College of Physicians was obliged to report that the College had: 'learned with extreme disapproval that a Report, marked '*Confidential*,' concerning the legal position of Practitioners in relation to abortion, which was circulated to the Fellows, and to them only, … which was … laid before the Comitia and ordered to be classed among the '*Secreta Collegii*,' has been communicated to certain journals and by them published. The College declines to assume the possibility that any Fellow could, in violation of his undertaking on admission, be guilty of thus communicating what he was required by the College to keep secret, or that he could commit so grave an impropriety as to give for publication a document which he has received from the Registrar as '*Confidential*'. The College cannot but suppose that the Document in question was obtained by some surreptitious means, but desires to call the attention of the Fellows to the circumstance, with the view of obviating any such accident in the future'. Resolution adopted at the General Meeting of the Fellows, 30 July 1896, Royal College of Physicians. According to the archivist of the Heritage Centre, Royal College of Physicians, such admonitions were most uncommon and reflected disapproval both of the fact of the breach itself and of the disclosure of material on such a difficult area as abortion.

60 See A. Cooke (1972); *A History of the Royal College of Physicians*, Oxford: The Clarendon Press, Volume Three, 982.

61 Resolutions Concerning the Duties of Medical Practitioners in Relation to Cases of Criminal Abortion, Royal College of Physicians, 27 January 1916.

62 Including ss. 42 and 43 in 1925 (which increased the level of fines which could be imposed for common assault and battery (see Memorandum by the Home Secretary, Criminal Justice Bill 1925, C.P. 83 (25)).

63 Its long title was 'An Act to amend the law with regard to the destruction of children at or before birth'.

64 It was explained in Section 2 as 'For the purposes of this Act, evidence that a woman had at any material time been pregnant for a period of twenty-eight weeks or more shall be prima facie proof that she was at that time pregnant of a child capable of being born alive'. That twenty eight week period would, as I shall show in the next chapter, prove to be an object of later contention.

65 'Medical Notes in Parliament', *The British Medical Journal*, 1 December 1928, 1014. It was, said Mr. Justice Talbot: 'a felony to procure abortion and it is murder to take the life of a child when it is born, but to take the life of a child while it is being born and before it is fully born is no offence whatever'. Medical Notes in Parliament, *The British Medical Journal*, 30 June 1928, 1130.

66 HL Deb 8 May 1929 Vol. 74 c456.

67 *The Times*, Friday, Apr 26, 1929.

68 See W. Garside (1990); *British Unemployment 1919–1939*, Cambridge: Cambridge University Press, 9–10.

69 The phrase is to be found in 'Fetal Viability and Clinical Practice', the report of a 'representative Committee' of practitioners, including representatives of the Royal College of Obstetricians and Gynaecologists, the Royal College of Midwives and others, which met on 16 January 1985.

70 See, for example, the reply given by the attorney general to a Parliamentary Question. HC Deb 21 March 1932 Vol. 263 cc717–8W.

71 Frank, Second Earl Russell, 1865–1931, was an electrical engineer; Barrister-at-law; and, in 1929, Parliamentary Secretary to Ministry of Transport.

72 'Report of a joint meeting of the Medico-Legal Society and the Section of Obstetrics and Gynaecology of the Royal Society of Medicine', *The British Medical Journal*, 29 January 1927, 188.

73 See S. Brooke (2001); '"A New World for Women"? Abortion Law Reform in Britain during the 1930s', *The American Historical Review*, 106(2), 431–459, esp. 436–7.

74 Dr Killick Millard, 1870–1952, was appointed assistant Medical Officer of Health for Shropshire in 1894, and then Medical Officer of Health for Leicester in 1901, a post he retained until his retirement in 1935. Whilst at Leicester, he established a birth control clinic and was influential in persuading the Eugenics Society to advocate birth control between the wars. He promoted the sterilisation of the 'mentally incompetent'. He campaigned too for the legalisation of voluntary euthanasia. (Based on the entry by N. Kemp in the *Oxford Dictionary of National Biography*, http://www.oxforddnb.com/view/article/74648).

75 Notes of a meeting of the Kensington Division of the British Medical Association, *The British Medical Journal*, 26 November 1932, 968.

76 There was a marked fear of population decline at the time. See, for example, M. Teitelbaum and J. Winter (1985); *The Fear of Population Decline*, Orlando: Academic Press.

77 K. Hindell and M. Simms (1968); 'How the Abortion Lobby Worked', *The Political Quarterly*, Vol. 39, No. 3, 270.

78 S. Browne, A. Ludovici and H. Roberts (1935); *Abortion: Three Views*, London: George Allen and Unwin. Stella Browne, who was to be a founder member of ALRA, had in the introductory essay ('Ton Corps est à Toi') effectively made out a case for the woman's right to choose. Roberts, a doctor, argued that there was scope for modification of what was then the present state of the law on abortion, ('when the operation … is performed by competent surgeons … the dangers are reduced to a fraction'), but that the operation must be carried out with due safeguards and under 'proper conditions'.

79 A meeting of a number of women, including Stella Browne, Frida Laski, Dora Russell, Alice Jenkins and Janet Chance, resolved on 24 January 1936 to invite Joan Malleson and Dr Newfield to proceed to organise a new Association 'To repeal the present law and substitute one freeing the medical profession from all legal restrictions except those required by medical or humanitarian restrictions. That the only restriction on which we are all clear is that forbidding all unqualified persons to perform abortions'. Papers of the ALRA, Wellcome Institution Library.

80 A. Jenkins (1960); *Law for the Rich: A Plea for the Reform of the Abortion Law*, London: Victor Gollancz, 47.

81 Eleanor Hawarden was a South African broadcaster and teacher and the author of *Prejudice in the Classroom* (1966); Johannesburg: South African Institute of Race Relations.

82 Alice Jenkins, 1886–1967, became involved in the 1920s with the National Birth Control Association, later the Family Planning Association, the Workers' Birth Control Group and worked in the Islington family clinic where she was to become a campaigner for the legalisation of abortion.

83 Bertha Lorsignol, said Alice Jenkins, was an Englishwoman married to a French banker who 'addressed many meetings of the Women's Co-operative Guilds on abortion and allied matters'. *Law for the Rich, op. cit.*, 46.

84 Stella Browne, 1880–1955, was a Canadian, living in England, who supported herself by journalism, reviewing and translating (she had, for instance, translated T. van de Velde's (1930); *Ideal Marriage; Its Physiology and Technique*, New York: Random House). (Despite going through 35 printings between 1941 and 1958, *Ideal Marriage*, like abortion, touched on the taboo area of sexuality. Its author was compelled to state in a 'Personal Introductory Statement', that 'This book will state many things which would otherwise remain unsaid. Therefore it will have many unpleasant results for me. I know this, for I have gradually attained to some knowledge of my fellow human beings and of their habit of condemning what is unusual and unconventional'). Stella Browne was an advocate of birth control, and was a member of the British Society for the Study of Sex Psychology and of the Women's Social and Political Union.

85 And the socialist Workers Birth Control Group, in particular, that had been established in 1924 by H.G Wells, Dora Russell, Susan Lawrence and others to advocate the spread of contraception.

86 See E. Moberly Bell (1953); *Storming the Citadel: The Rise of the Woman Doctor*, London: Constable. Bell documents the rise of medical schools catering for women, the founding of the Medical Women's Federation and the emergence of women doctors, particularly during and after the First World War, but makes no mention either of any of the principals in this history or of the Abortion Law Reform Association. The 1930s do seem to have been a pivotal decade for women doctors. The first woman fellow of the Royal College of Physicians was appointed in 1934 (http://www.rcplon don.ac.uk/about/history/women-rcp) and the numbers of women practitioners grew appreciably from 477 to 2,810 during the first three decades of the twentieth century:

Male and Female Physicians

Census Years 1911–1931

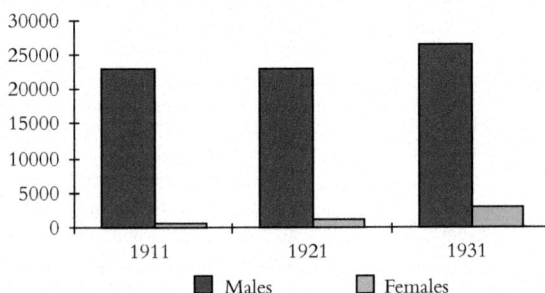

(source: http://www.visionofbritain.org.uk/census/table_page.jsp?tab_id=EW1931OC C_M16 and http://www.visionofbritain.org.uk/text/chap_page.jsp?t_id=SRC_P&c_id =8&cpub_id=EW1921GEN)

87 M. Simms (1974); 'Abortion Law and Medical Freedom', *The British Journal of Criminology*, Vol. 14, No. 2, 121.

88 See S. Brooke; '"A New World for Women"?' *op. cit.*

89 Argument about the eugenicist roots of the abortion movement may be found in B. Brookes (1988); *Abortion in England, 1900–1967*, London: Croom Helm, 61. That there were eugenicist arguments being put at the time when the movement started is indisputable. In 1932, for instance, Lord Riddell was reported to have said that 'The exponents of birth control … characterised the sentimental objection as absurd. It was easy, … in conclusion, to appreciate the arguments against abortion and birth control among the normal; but from a logical, ethical, and economic point of view it seemed to him that the arguments of those who demanded sterilisation of the mental defective were unanswerable'. 'Ethics of Abortion, Sterilisation, and Birth Control Address', *British Medical Journal*, 16 January 1932, 106. Lord Riddell, 1865–1934, a newspaper proprietor and publisher, was said by A. Morris to have 'a particular concern for medical charities, and provided handsome endowments for the Royal Free Hospital, London, and the Eastman Dental Clinic'. (*Oxford Dictionary of National Biography*, http://www.oxforddnb.com/view/article/35749).

90 A. Oakley (1991); 'Eugenics, social medicine and the career of Richard Titmuss in Britain 1935–5', *The British Journal of Sociology*, Vol. 42, No. 2, 165.

91 One was Professor Glanville Williams, the author of *The Sanctity of Life and the Criminal Law* (1958); London: Faber and Faber, who wrote an approving introduction to Alice Jenkins' *Law for the Rich*, in which he remarked as late as 1960 that 'Neither Government nor Parliament has attempted even a start upon the most important task of all – the improvement of our eugenic heritage… the Eugenics Society, for all its splendid work in encouraging ideas and research, has little to show in the way of official response'. Introduction to *Law for the Rich: A Plea for the Reform of the Abortion Law*, *op. cit.*, 11. Another was the socialist author, journalist and visionary, H.G. Wells, 1866–1946, who was intrigued by the possible futures of mankind, envisaged, in bleak form in his *The Time Machine*. In an early essay, he wrote: 'we are under the dominion of a logic that obliges us to take over the actual population of the world with only such moral and mental and physical improvements as lie within their inherent possibilities, and it is our business to ask what Utopia will do with its congenital invalids, its idiots and madmen, its drunkards and men of vicious mind, its cruel and furtive souls, its stupid people, too stupid to be of use to the community, its lumpish, unteachable and unimaginative people? And what will it do with the man who is "poor" all round, the rather spiritless, rather incompetent low-grade man who on earth sits in the den of the sweater, tramps the streets under the banner of the unemployed, or trembles – in another man's cast-off clothing, and with an infinity of hat-touching – on the verge of rural employment? These people will have to be in the descendant phase, the species must be engaged in eliminating them; there is no escape from that, and conversely the people of exceptional quality must be ascendant. The better sort of people, so far as they can be distinguished, must have the fullest freedom of public service, and the fullest opportunity of parentage. And it must be open to every man to approve himself worthy of ascendency. The way of Nature in this process is to kill the weaker and the sillier, to crush them, to starve them, to overwhelm them, using the stronger and more cunning as her weapon. But man is the unnatural animal, the rebel child of Nature, and more and more does he turn himself against the harsh and fitful hand that reared him. He sees with a growing resentment the multitude of suffering ineffectual lives over which his species tramples in its ascent. In the Modern Utopia he will have set himself to change the ancient law. No longer will it be that failures must suffer and perish lest their breed increase, but the breed of failure must not increase, lest they suffer and perish, and the race with them'. 'A Modern Utopia' (np) (http://ebooks.adelaide.edu.au/w/wells/hg/w45mu/index.html) Elsewhere, Wells was more circumspect about the possibilities of a science of eugenics. In 'The Problem of the Birth Supply, Chapter II of *Mankind in the Making*, he argued that too little was known

about the workings of heredity to permit intelligent intervention in the transmission of characteristics (New York: Charles Scribner's Sons, 1904).

92 In 1937, for instance, Lord Horder was President of the Eugenics Society and a member of the Association's Medico-Legal Council, and Julian Huxley was a Vice-President both of the Eugenics Society and of the Association. The Eugenics Society's Honorary Treasurer was Janet Chance's husband.

93 Janet Chance, 1886–1953, was a member of the Malthusian League and the Workers' Birth Control Group (WBCG), an organisation founded in 1924 by Stella Browne and Dora Russell, and a co-founder of the Abortion Law Reform Association. (Based on the entry by S. Brooke in the *Oxford Dictionary of National Biography*, http://www.oxforddnb.com/view/article/57857).

94 J. Chance (1936); *The Case for the Reform of the Abortion Laws*, London: Abortion Law Reform Association, 13–14.

95 *Ibid*, 12–13.

96 Joan Malleson, 1899–1956, was the daughter of the socialist owner of a coal mine and a brickworks. She studied medicine at University College and then at Charing Cross Hospital, and was a member of a liberal social circle that included Bertrand and Dora Russell, Cyril Joad and A. S. Neill. She became a MRCS LRCP in 1925 and acquired the degree of MB BS (Lond.) in 1926. She was to specialise in the area of fertility, reproduction, and sexuality, becoming both a general practitioner and a consultant. She was a member of the Eugenics Society. (Based on the entry by D. Martin in the *Oxford Dictionary of National Biography*, http://www.oxforddnb.com/view/article/54690). She submitted a Memorandum to the Inter-Departmental Committee on Abortion in which she alleged that there was substantial class bias in the existing practice of abortion. There should, she said, be a new institution, 'Mothers' Welfare Centres', which could give general advice and support for pregnant women, 'where cases which might require therapeutic abortion could be referred'. A doctor could then 'decide upon the validity of the patient's claim and then refer her for expert opinion. … the practitioner's role [would be to protect] the health, in its truest sense, of the pregnant woman under his care; and disinclined as he may be to consider her social status in relation to her pregnancy, he cannot with honesty fulfil his role if he ignores those environmental factors which determine her choices of subsequent life and health'. Memorandum by Dr. Joan Malleson to The Inter-Departmental Committee on Abortion, London: HMSO, 1939.

97 Memorandum by Dr. Joan Malleson to The Inter-Departmental Committee on Abortion, *op. cit.*

98 Foreword to A. Jenkins (1938); *Conscript Parenthood?, The Problem of Secret Abortion*, London: George Standring.

99 Inaugural Meeting of the Proposed Abortion Law Reform Association, 17 February 1936, Papers of the ALRA, Wellcome Institution Library.

100 Thomas Horder, 1871–1955, was appointed assistant physician at St Bartholomew's; became a senior physician in 1921 and retired in 1936. He was chairman of the Ministry of Health advisory committee, 1935–9. (Based on entry by L. Witts in the *Oxford Dictionary of National Biography*, http://www.oxforddnb.com/view/article/33985)

101 Abortion Law Reform Association Draft Constitution, Adopted by the Executive Committee, 27 January 1938. Amended and Adopted at the Annual General Meeting, 25 March 1938 and amended 17 October 1947. Papers of the ALRA, Wellcome Institution Library.

102 And that continued for a long while. Diane Munday, a prominent member of ALRA in the 1960s, 'doing the main public appearances', recollected that she had elected to wear a pink twin set, a 'horrible pink hat' and a pearl necklace when she addressed audiences of women: 'so that immediately they felt comfortable with me' ('The Abortion Act 50 years on', *BBC Woman's Hour*, 24 January 2017).

103 See S. Brooke (2009); 'The Sphere of Sexual Politics: The Abortion Law Reform Association, 1930s to 1960s' in N. Crowson, M. Hilton and J. McKay (eds.) *NGOs in Contemporary Britain: Non-State Actors in Society and Politics Since 1945.* London: Palgrave, 81–2.

104 S. Browne (January 1937); 'The A.L.R.A'., *The New Generation*, 5.

105 Abortion Law Reform Association (1937); *First Annual Report, 1936–7*, London.

106 Robert Boothby, 1900–1986, was the Conservative Member of Parliament for East Aberdeenshire, from 1924 to 1958, when he became a peer.

107 Sir Arnold Wilson, 1884–1940, became a National Conservative Member of Parliament for Hitchin at a by-election in 1933, being re-elected in 1935. 'As well as favouring birth control and easier divorce, he called for a comprehensive state system of social insurance, including family allowances'. (Based on entry by R. Pearce in the *Oxford Dictionary of National Biography*, http://www.oxforddnb.com/view/article/36944)

108 Denis Pritt, 1887–1972, was a lawyer and political activist. He became K.C. in 1927 and was Member of Parliament for North Hammersmith, first as a left-wing Labour member in 1935, and then as an independent in 1945.

109 Gerald Thesiger, 1902–1981, was called to the Bar in 1926, and was a member of the General Council of the Bar, 1936–41.

110 M. Edgecombe (1947); 'Marital Difficulties and Abortion Law Reform', in *Back-Street Surgery: A Study of the Illegal Operation which is Performed Probably about 100,000 Times a Year in England and Wales*, Fordingbridge: The Abortion Law Reform Association, 6.

111 Quoted on the frontispiece of A. Jenkins; *Law for the Rich, op. cit.*, no page number.

112 Introductory Letter, *Back-Street Surgery: A Study of the Illegal Operation which is Performed Probably about 100,000 Times a Year in England and Wales, op. cit.*, 3.

113 The future Minister of Health, attempting to introduce a private member's bill in 1961, described them as 'unskilled so-called back-street abortionists. These are people, mostly women, who perform the operation often in totally unhygienic surroundings and with unsterilised instruments'. HC Deb 10 February 1961 Vol. 634 cc853–92.

114 See the letter from Letitia Fairfield to *The Lancet*, 1 October 1938, 804–5, which claimed that a girl, made pregnant by her fiancé, had been obliged to allege that she had been raped by 'a degenerate' in order to obtain an abortion.

115 J. Chance, 'Back-Street Surgery', *op. cit.*, 10.

116 Mr Justice McCardie, born in 1869, was a judge on the King's Bench from 1916 until his death in 1933. His biographer, A. Lentin, claims in the *Oxford Dictionary of National Biography* that 'His reserved judgements were as comprehensive and as carefully crafted as though written for a legal monograph' and that 'he showed himself on the bench to be a rebel and a crusader, a critic and opponent of much in the system he was appointed to administer. … he supported his judgements with observations on the realities of modern life, especially the position of women, and with arguments in favour of birth control, lowering the age of consent, and the legalisation of abortion'. (http://www.oxforddnb.com/view/article/34677) 'Mr Justice McCardie … seemed to use every effort to discountenance and discourage such prosecutions, whereas his colleagues showed no such inclination' reported *The Lancet* in Rex v. Bourne, *The Lancet*, 23 July 1938, 201. In a 1931 case, he stated that an abortionist had had no wish to cause the death of a mother and described the charge against her as 'brutal': 'The law of abortion as it exists ought to be substantially modified. It is out of keeping with conditions that prevail in the world around us. … It is plain to me that many of those who seek to uhold this law of abortion are wholly ignorant of the social problems which menace the nation'. (*The Times*, 1 December 1931) he was to talk in favour of abortion in a lecture on 'My Attitude on Eugenics', delivered to the Eugenics Society (see A. Jenkins, *Law for the Rich, op. cit.*, 28.)

117 Alice Jenkins of ALRA said in 1960 '[N]o one knows'. In *Law for the Rich, op. cit.*, 33.

118 There was, for instance, no requirement on 'members of the medical and nursing professions to certify and notify to the medical officers of health all operations for abortion'. HC Deb 25 July 1938 Vol. 338 cc2710–1.

119 See HC Deb 24 November 1936 Vol. 318 cc232–3. 29 years later, Renée Short would claim in the House of Commons that 'Abortion is the second most common cause of maternal death; 61 per cent. are procured by the patient herself, 22 per cent. of deaths from this cause occur among women with four or more children'. HC Deb 15 June 1965 Vol. 714 cc254–8.

120 Sir Edward Hilton-Young, 1879–1960, studied for the Bar but did not pursue a career in the law. He first entered Parliament as a Liberal in 1918, lost his seat in 1923 and regained it a year later. Opposed to the General Strike, he joined the Conservative Party and was to become the Unionist Member for Sevenoaks between 1929 and 1935. In 1931, he was appointed Minister of Health under Ramsay MacDonald's coalition Government. On Ramsay MacDonald's resignation in 1935, he quit the House of Commons to become Lord Kennet. (Based on the entry by W. Kennet in the *Oxford Dictionary of National Biography*, http://www.oxforddnb.com/view/article/37071?docPos=3)

121 See HC Deb 9 May 1932 Vol. 265 c1555W.

122 It is interesting that even the Quakers found discussion of the matter difficult, complicating their ability to arrive at a collective stance. As late as 1994, Ann Hosking wrote in the Quaker *vade mecum*, 'There are many reasons why a person may consider an abortion. Friends in this yearly meeting have no united view on abortion in general, nor is there agreement on principles. Understandably there has been little open sharing of experience, and, therefore, sadly, almost no public discussion among Friends'. *Quaker Faith and Practice* (2013); Fifth edition, Yearly Meeting of the Religious Society of Friends (Quakers) in Britain, London, 22.54.

123 Diane Munday, who became involved in the second wave of campaigning in the 1960s, recalled that 'I suppose I was very naïve but [in the 1950s] it was something that was never discussed; it was a word that was never said' (ICBH Witness Seminar Programme, 10 July 2001, http://www.kcl.ac.uk/sspp/departments/icbh/witness/PDFfiles/AbortionAct1967.pdf, 27).

124 J. Chance, 'Back-Street Surgery', *Back-Street Surgery: A Study of the Illegal Operation which is Performed Probably about 100,000 Times a Year in England and Wales, op. cit.*, 9.

125 Gertrude Tuckwell, 1861–1951, was a school teacher, trade unionist and social reformer, the honorary secretary of the Women's Trade Union League, one of the first women magistrates, and the co-founder of the Ministry of Health's Maternal Mortality Committee. (Based on A. John's entry in *Oxford Dictionary of National Biography*, http://www.oxforddnb.com/view/article/36572)

126 A. Jenkins, *Law for the Rich, op. cit.*, 23.

127 *Ibid*, 47.

128 Anonymous review, *The British Medical Journal*, 25 January 1936, 161.

129 Nancy, Lady Astor, 1879–1964, was the first woman Member of Parliament, a Conservative, elected in 1919. She came to be treated as the woman's representative in the House of Commons, and she spoke on 'women's issues including the provision of nursery schools, widows' pensions, equal employment, women police, and measures to reduce the maternal mortality rates'. (M. Pugh's entry in the *Oxford Dictionary of National Biography*, http://www.oxforddnb.com/view/article/30489)

130 HC Deb 17 July 1935 Vol. 304 cc1059–180.

131 Mavis Tate, 1893–1947, was the National Conservative Member of Parliament for Frome between 1935 and 1945. 'By the mid- and late 1930s she found herself taking an increasingly feminist stance on such issues as maternal mortality rates, birth control clinics, women's nationality, and equal pay'. (M. Pugh's entry in the *Oxford Dictionary of National Biography*, http://www.oxforddnb.com/view/article/39185)

132 The word is that of her fellow Member, Sir Arnold Wilson, speaking at an Abortion Law Reform Association Conference, 15 May 1936.

133 HC Deb 17 July 1935 Vol. 304 cc1059–180. As late as 1966, the Conservative Member of Parliament, Simon Wingfield Digby, could say 'For a long time people have tended to evade this subject'. HC Deb 25 February 1966 Vol. 725 cc837–56.

134 See 'Race Suicide Peril: Western Civilisation Threatened', *The Times*, 11 October 1919; and V. Cornish (1922), *A Geography of Imperial Defence*, London: Sifton Praed & Co.

135 *The Case for the Reform of the Abortion Laws*, *op. cit.*, 13.

136 See: http://www.histpop.org/ohpr/servlet/View2?ResourceType=Census&Resourc eType=Legislation&ResourceType=Essays&ResourceType=Registrar%20General& ResourceType=TNA&SearchTerms=population%20england%20and%20wales%2019

137 Royal Commission on Population (1949); *Report*, Cmd. 7695, London: HMSO, 8.

138 W. Sigle-Rushton (2008); 'England and Wales: Stable Fertility and Pronounced Social Status Differences', *Demographic Research*, Vol. 19, 455.

139 Based on tables available on http://www.statistics.gov.uk/statbase/Product.asp?vlnk= 14275

140 Based on tables available on http://www.statistics.gov.uk/StatBase/Product.asp?vln k=581

141 Based on Table XVI of *Report*, Royal Commission on Population, *op. cit.*, 25.

142 Based on Table V of *Report*, Royal Commission on Population, *op. cit.*, 10.

143 Based on figures given in 'National Maternity Service Memorandum', *The British Medical Journal* (7 December 1935); 246, and 'Maternal Mortality Rates', *The British Medical Journal* (5 November 1938); 950. Some part of the decline may be attributed to the changes in the clinical management of childbirth that culminated in the passing of the The Midwives Act, 1936.

144 See J. Hobcraft (November 1996); 'Fertility in England and Wales: A Fifty-Year Perspective', *Population Studies*, Vol. 50, No. 3, 485–524.

145 M. Boyle (1997); *Re-Thinking Abortion: Psychology, Gender, Power and the Law*, London: Routledge, 13, 14. See I. Dawson; 'The Confidential Enquiry into Maternal Deaths: Its Role and Importance for Pathologists', *op. cit.*, 820. The statement made in the House of Commons at the time was that the Minister of Health was 'proposing to appoint a special Committee on maternal mortality, one of whose functions will be to consider the need for further research into the question ...' HC Deb 25 April 1928 Vol. 216 cc899–900.

146 Sir George Newman, 1870–1948, was a physician sympathetic to Beatrice Webb's idea of a national health service aired in the Royal Commission on the Poor Laws. In 1907, he became chief medical officer to the Board of Education, chief medical officer to the Local Government Board in 1919, and later in that year chief medical officer to the Ministry of Health, a post he held until 1935. (Based on the entry by S. Sturdy in the Oxford Dictionary of National Biography, http://www.oxforddnb.com/view/ article/35215

147 See The *British Medical Journal* (3 August 1957); 280.

148 Nursing Notes, (September 1937); 151.

149 See S. Brooke; '"A New World for Women"? Abortion Law Reform in Britain during the 1930s', *op. cit.*, 435; and the report in *The British Medical Journal* (8 May 1937); where it was said on p. 972, that 'Attempted abortions appear to be frequent and to be increasing, and to be responsible for a number of deaths from puerperal sepsis'.

150 HC Deb 27 October 1937 Vol. 328 cc87–214.

151 Based on table in report of The Inter-Departmental Committee on Abortion, *op. cit.*, 45.

152 It said that: 'While medical practitioners as citizens are entitled to hold individual opinions and cultivate activities on these several issues the medical profession as such

has no special right and no special competence to deal with them, and the Council therefore considers that any proposal that the profession ought to lead public opinion in such questions is one to be resisted. The medical profession in its corporate activities will best preserve its influence by keeping within the boundaries fixed by the particular technical knowledge of its members'. *Report of Committee on Medical Aspects of Abortion* (July 1936); B.M.A., 3.

153 *Ibid*, 3.

154 *Ibid*, 3.

155 *Ibid*, 6.

156 *Ibid*, 20.

157 *Ibid*, 24.

158 *The British Medical Journal* remarked that 'It was courageous and public spirited of him to invite prosecution in order to get the law declared on a matter of great importance to the public and more especially to the medical profession'. 'The Trial of Mr. Bourne', *The British Medical Journal* (23 July 1938); 185. His own account was somewhat different. He claims that police officers were independently investigating the rape, one of whom had instructed him, after the abortion had been carried out, that 'in no circumstances could he countenance the operation. I made it plain to the Inspector that I could not recognise his right to dictate to me what I, as a surgeon, should or should not decide to do in the best interests of my patient … and that in any event I had already operated on the girl and, if he wished, he could arrest me'. A little earlier, however, he stated that it had been his intention when next asked to undertake an abortion 'I would report what I had done to the police'. A. Bourne (1962); *A Doctor's Creed: The Memoirs of a Gynaecologist*, London: Victor Gollancz, 99.

159 His actual words to the police were said to be 'I emptied the uterus this morning; I want you to arrest me'. In 'Charge Of Procuring Abortion: Rex v. Bourne', *British Medical Journal* (23 July 1938); 200.

160 The King v. Bourne, (1938 1 KB, 687).

161 Aleck Bourne MA, MB, FRCS, FRCOG, 1886–1974, was a consulting obstetrician based in London.

162 He was to be described much later as 'an elegant, well-mannered man of academic brilliance with left wing political views and a very strong social conscience'. A. Fraser (2007); 'George Douglas Pinker: Obituary', *British Medical Journal*, Vol. 334, 1378.

163 Obituary, *British Medical Journal* (January 1975); 99.

164 Rex v. Bourne, *The Lancet* (23 July 1938); Volume 232, Issue 5995, 202.

165 The victim's doctor reported to Aleck Bourne that 'Unfortunately the matter is made a little more difficult by the fact that the girl was admitted to St. Thomas's Hospital under Mr., who I think from the report of his attitude must be Catholic. He took the conventional standpoint that 'he would not interfere with life because the child may be the future Prime Minister of England,' and 'that anyhow, girls always lead men on'. Charge Of Procuring Abortion: Rex v. Bourne', *op. cit.*, 199.

166 *A Doctor's Creed: The Memoirs of a Gynaecologist, op. cit.*

167 The actual referral letter read: 'I have been consulted by the organiser of the Schools Care Committee about a girl of 14 called –. It is possible that you saw in the paper some three weeks ago that this girl was assaulted in Whitehall by some soldiers. The actual facts were that she was with two girl friends, who ran off and left her, and she was held down by five men and twice assaulted. It appears that she is free of venereal infection, but the Z.A. test has just come back positive. I gather from the lady who brought her that everybody connected with the case, i.e., the police surgeon, the doctor at her work, the school doctor, etc., all feel that curettage should be allowed her; and I understand that Dr. –' and possibly some other psychiatrists of good standing, would be prepared to sponsor 'therapeutic abortion'. I presume they must mean on grounds of prophylaxis, because there does not appear to be any nervous disorder

present. All this, of course, gets us nowhere unless someone of your standing were prepared to risk a cause celebre and undertake the operation in hospital. Many people hold the view that the best way of correcting the present abortion laws is to let the medical profession gradually extend the grounds for therapeutic abortion in suitable cases, until the laws become obsolete, so far as practice goes. I should imagine that public opinion would be immensely in favour of termination of pregnancy in a case of this sort. If there is any chance that, given adequate professional backing, you feel prepared to consider this, I would take a lot of trouble to get people of high standing to see this girl, and should of course feel that it was most valuable if the case was conducted publicly in hospital. I am told that a rather grim twist is added to this case by the fact that the girl's parents 'are so respectable that they do not know the address of any abortionist'; and are, I gather, having to set about to find one, for they 'could not possibly let her go through with this'. She seems a normal, healthy girl, and on medical terms there is obviously nothing to be said'. (In 'Charge Of Procuring Abortion: Rex v. Bourne', *British Medical Journal* (23 July 1938); 199)

168 The words are those of Aleck Bourne's defence counsel, reported in 'Charge Of Procuring Abortion: Rex v. Bourne', *op. cit.*, 201.

169 In 'Charge Of Procuring Abortion: Rex v. Bourne', *op. cit.*, 201.

170 Sir Malcolm Macnaghten, 1869–1955, was Recorder of Colchester from 1924–1928, and a Judge of the High Court of Justice, King's Bench Division, from 1928–1947. He married the daughter of the social reformer Charles Booth, and had three daughters, all of whom became socialists and married Communists. His obituary, in *The Times* of 25 January 1955, was headed 'a humane judge'. The obituary went on to say that the acquittal in the Bourne case 'was generally approved'.

171 The King v. Bourne, (1938 1 KB, 687).

172 'Charge Of Procuring Abortion: Rex v. Bourne', *op. cit.*, 199.

173 In 'The Trial of Mr. Bourne', *op. cit.*, 185. There were members of the Abortion Law Reform Association who believed that he should have used the trial as a forum to promote the idea that abortion should be conducted on health grounds (see A Jenkins, *Law for the Rich*, *op. cit.*, 59).

174 In 'Charge Of Procuring Abortion: Rex v. Bourne', *op. cit.*, 200.

175 See R. Ross (1936); *Russell On Crime: A Treatise on Felonies And Misdemeanors By Sir William Oldnall Russell*, 9th edition, London, Sweet & Maxwell. The 1923 edition of *Russell On Crime* states on p. 787 that 'the word 'unlawfully' excludes from the section acts done in the course of proper treatment in the interest of the life or health of the mother'. The position is a little confused. *Russell on Crime* refers to A. Taylor; *The Principles And Practice Of Medical Jurisprudence*. The fourth edition, edited by Thomas Stevenson (1894); London: J. Churchill, discusses the meaning of the word 'unlawful' at some length in Vol. 2, 200–209 but gives no instances of *lawful* abortion. A later, seventh edition of the work, published in 1920, affirms that 'Strictly speaking … there is no such thing as justifiable abortion; the law recognises no such possibility; a medical man must always recognise this when he contemplates emptying a pregnant uterus'. *Taylor's Principles and Practice of Medical Jurisprudence*, London: J. Churchill, 147. The most recent edition held by the British Library was that of 1891. A survey of the Bodleian Library and the University of Cambridge Newton library catalogues produced nothing more recent.

176 The 1939 report of The Inter-Departmental Committee on Abortion, London: HMSO, was later to say on p. 29 that 'The wording of this section [of the 1929 Act] has been held to have an important bearing upon the question in what circumstances it may be lawful to induce abortion. The absence until very recently of any case law which might have helped to decide this question has given rise to much uncertainty'.

177 In 'Charge Of Procuring Abortion: Rex v. Bourne', *op. cit.*, 199.

178 Kenneth Robinson, introducing his Medical Termination of Pregnancy Bill in the House of Commons, HC Deb 10 February 1961 Vol. 634 cc853–92.

179 Editorial, *The Times*, 20 July 1938.

180 For a wider discussion of the links between deviant ascriptions and social standing, see J. Douglas (ed.) (1970); *Deviance and Respectability: The Social Construction of Moral Meanings*, New York: Basic Books.

181 'Therapeutic Abortion and the Law', The British Medical Journal (30 July 1938); 225–6.

182 The Church Assembly Board for Social Responsibility (1965); *Abortion: An Ethical Discussion*, London: Church Information Service, 11.

183 Kenneth Robinson in HC Deb 10 February 1961 Vol. 634 cc853–92.

184 A. Bourne, *A Doctor's Creed: The Memoirs of a Gynaecologist*, *op. cit.*, 103.

185 Sir Roland Burrows, 1882–1952, was called to the Bar in 1904, became Private Secretary to Sir Frederick Smith, the Solicitor-General and Attorney-General, 1915–19; and Assistant Private Secretary to the Lord Chancellor, 1919–22. He was Recorder of Chichester between 1926 and 1928 when he became Recorder of Cambridge. (http://www.ukwhoswho.com.gate2.library.lse.ac.uk/view/article/oupww/whow aswho/U235312/BURROWS_Sir_Roland?index=1&results=QuicksearchResults& query=0)

186 R. Burrows (1938); 'The Law of Abortion', *The Law Journal*, Vol. LXXXVI, 170.

187 *Ibid.*

188 Summarised in 'Rex v. Bourne Again', *The Lancet* (24 September 1938); 731–2.

189 R. Burrows (3 September 1938); 'The Law of Abortion', *The Law Journal*, Vol. LXXXVI, 154, 155.

190 Rex v. Bourne, *The Lancet* (23 July 1938); 201. Glanville Williams could say twenty two years later that 'the practice of the courts is now to treat a termination of pregnancy performed on medical grounds as legal ... [but] doctors are still understandably shy of the law'. Glanville Williams, introduction to A. Jenkins; *Law for the Rich*, *op. cit.*, 14.

191 It appears that the Home Office had no records on this committee, or on Home Office involvement in this area.

192 'The Trial of Mr. Bourne', *op. cit.*, 185.

193 The Minister of Health, Sir Kingsley Wood, stated: 'I have already taken action on the principal recommendations in this report. ... I am in communication with the Medical Research Council on the questions recommended in the report for further research, and, as I informed the House last Monday, I have, in conjunction with my right hon. Friend the Home Secretary, already appointed a committee to inquire into the prevalence of abortion and to consider what steps can be taken, by more effective enforcement of the law or otherwise, to secure the reduction of maternal mortality and morbidity arising from this cause'. HC Deb 27 May 1937 Vol. 324 cc417–8. He was to say later: 'There is no doubt that in connection with maternal mortality a good many people think the practice of abortion plays an important part, and I thought in view of the statements that were made by responsible people the best thing would be to have an inquiry made, and a committee is now sitting ...' HC Deb 27 October 1937 Vol. 328 cc87–214. Sir Kingsley Wood, 1881–1943, was the Conservative Member of Parliament for Woolwich West between 1918 and 1943, and Minister of Health, 1935–1938. As Minister, he presided over a substantial reduction in infant mortality as a consequence of his Midwives Act of 1936, an Act which provided for the better training, regulation and employment of midwives. See J. Buchan (June 1936); 'The Midwives Act, 1936, and Its Operation', *The Journal of the Royal Society for the Promotion of Health*, Vol. 57, 420–436. Within two years, 7,500 full-time midwives were employed by local authorities in England and Wales under the Act (see HC Deb 14 November 1938 Vol. 341 cc525–648).

194 In February 1936, a deputation from the National Council of Women, led by Lady Astor, and including a number of future members of the Birkett Committee, informed the Minister of Health that the 'council had considered recent figures relating to maternal mortality in England and Wales and to the deaths attributable to abortion included in these figures; and urged, first, that the Government should appoint a representative committee to inquire into the incidence of abortion and as to the law and its administration dealing with criminal abortion and attempted abortion, and to consider what measures, if any, are advisable to improve the existing position ...' *The British Medical Journal* (22 February 1936); 378.

195 William Norman Birkett, 1883–1962, was a British barrister, judge, politician and preacher. He was elected Liberal Member of Parliament for Nottingham East in 1923 and again in 1929. He was Judge of the King's Bench Division, High Court of Justice, 1941–50; and Lord Justice of Appeal, 1950–57. He became a peer in 1958.

196 That is the sole surviving reference. There were no records on the decision to establish the Committee in the Home Office archives.

197 Home Office File 219/1139: Abortion: Miscellaneous and General – Proposed Private Member's Bill to amend the Law on Abortion. 17 November 1964 – Brief on law on abortion.

198 The report stated that 'Only a fraction of the number of abortions procured come to the knowledge of the police, and even when a offence is strongly suspected, it may be impracticable to institute proceedings' (119).

199 Between, for example, 7% and 17% of all pregnancies in different studies (para. 20).

200 Committee on Medical Aspects of Abortion (1936); *Report*, London: British Medical Association.

201 Higher figures were offered for some local areas. For instance, in Sheffield in 1934, it was thought that abortions had led to 39 per cent of total maternal deaths. See T. McIntosh (2000); '"An Abortionist City": Maternal Mortality, Abortion, and Birth Control in Sheffield, 1920–1940', *Medical History*, Vol. 44, 75–96.

202 See, for example, M. Ryan, M. Edgecombe and J. Chance (1947); *Back-Street Surgery: A Study of the Illegal Operation, which is Performed Probably about 100,000 Times a Year in England and Wales*, Fordingbridge, Hants: ALRA, 12. None the less the study goes on to say that 'neither the Birkett Report nor any other report really has any solid facts about the frequency of illegal abortions. At best the figures are only reasonable guesses'.

203 See, for example, the account given of a meeting of ALRA attended in 1963 by Alastair Service, in *Pioneers of Change: Interviews with people who made the 1967 Abortion Act possible*, http://www.bpas.org/js/filemanager/files/abortion_pioneers.pdf, 24.

204 Introduction to A. Jenkins, *Law for the Rich, op. cit.*, 13.

205 The Secretary to the Committee, A. Moshinsky, had written to the Registrar of the Royal College of Physicians to peruse the report of its Committee on Criminal Abortion and the Resolutions which it had passed: 'It was no doubt of these that the witness who stated that he was under the impression that the Royal College of Physicians had been advised that a therapeutic abortion performed after a bona fide consultation between medical men in the interests of the mother's life was legal, was thinking'. Letter of 29 January 1938. Heritage Centre archives, the Royal College of Physicians.

206 The exact phrasing was 'We recommend ... that the law should be amended to make it unmistakably clear that a medical practitioner is acting legally, when in good faith he procures the abortion of a pregnant woman in circumstances which satisfy him that continuance of the pregnancy is likely to endanger her life or seriously to impair her health' (para 201).

207 In her own submission to the Committee, tactfully presented as 'suggestions', Joan Malleson had proposed that 'Therapeutic" abortion should be legalised. The less rigid

the instructions laid down to the medical profession the greater latitude would be given to the doctor for admitting the "desperate" woman to medical care. ... [there should be provision for women to] 'make application to have their cases considered in certain instances of special distress, which were based on other than purely health grounds'.

208   Lord Silkin, the mover of a reform bill in the 1960s, would say later that 'Their views were to some extent coloured at that time by the fact that it appeared that the population of this country was declining'. HL Deb 3 February 1966 Vol. 272 cc491–557.

209   It stated that 'There can be no doubt that on humanitarian grounds there would be widespread support for a proposal that a woman or girl who has become pregnant as a result of rape should be permitted by law to have her pregnancy terminated. ... Considerable practical difficulties are revealed, however, in any attempt to formulate a working scheme'. (paras. 241, 242). The report continued, for instance, to point to the need to secure a conviction for rape before an abortion could safely proceed.

210   And, in their hesitation, they were at one with other commentators at the time. Roland Burrows remarked after the Bourne trial that 'Many pregnant women seek to cover their folly by asseverations of force or fraud. Many of their relatives are prone either to believe or to affect to believe such asseverations, being anxious to avoid what may be an unpleasant scandal or disgrace. ... to suggest that [a doctor] should come to an irrevocable decision on a serious issue on the strength of *ex parte* and possibly biased or hearsay statements, is to put upon a medical man an unfair burden'. R. Burrows (10 September 1938); 'The Law of Abortion', *The Law Journal*, Vol. LXXXVI, 170.

211   Dorothy Thurtle, 1890–1973, was the daughter of George Lansbury, becoming a member of the Women's Freedom League and the Women's Labour League. She was General Secretary of Shoreditch Trades Council and Labour Party, and was to be elected to Shoreditch Borough Council in 1925 and mayor of Shoreditch in 1936. She and her husband were founding members of the Workers' Birth Control Group in 1924, and she was to become in 1936 one of the first members of ALRA, its Vice-President until 1962. (Based on S. Brooke's entry in the *Oxford Dictionary of National Biography*, http://www.oxforddnb.com/view/article/69843).

212   A. Jenkins, *Law for the Rich, op. cit.*, 60.

213   For instance, in England and Wales 51 persons were committed for trial in 1956 for offences under Sections 58 and 59 of the Offences against the Person Act, 1861:

	Males	Females
Acquitted	3	2
Conditional Discharge	1	3
Recognizances	4	5
Probation	—	3
Fine	1	1

Imprisonment:

	Males	Females
For 6 months and under	—	1
For over 6 months and up to 1 year	1	7
For over 1 year and up to 2 years	1	8
For over 2 years and up to 3 years	2	6
For over 3 years and up to 4 years	1	1
Total imprisonment	5	23
TOTAL	14	37

(Taken from HC Deb 21 November 1957 Vol. 578 cc552–3)

214   See *The Times*, 15 May 1948.

215   A. Jenkins, *Law for the Rich, op. cit.*, 67.

216 *The British Medical Journal* (22 May 1948); 1008.

217 This account of the inquest is based on a report in *The Times* of 18 March 1958.

218 *The Times*, 3 May 1958.

219 *The Times*, 15 May 1958.

220 'Criminal Abortion and Manslaughter', *The British Medical Journal* (24 May 1958); 1245.

221 Lord Denning was much later to say in the House of Lords 'Justice Ashworth gave a direction on the law which, so far as I know, has always been accepted. He told the jury: The law about the use of instruments to procure a miscarriage is this: 'Such use of an instrument is unlawful unless the use is made in good faith for the purpose of preserving the life or health of the woman'. When I say health, I mean not only her physical health but also her mental health. But also I have said 'it is unlawful unless'. I must emphasise and add that the burden of proving that it was not used in good faith is on the Crown. *In spite of that direction to the jury*, Dr. Newton was found guilty'. (Emphasis added) (HL Deb 30 November 1965 Vol. 270 cc1139–241)

222 *The Times*, 20 May 1958.

223 A. Jenkins, *Law for the Rich*, *op. cit.*, 50.

224 Lord Listowel, 1906–1997, was a socialist hereditary peer, who sat on the Labour front bench in the House of Lords from 1936, and became opposition chief whip in 1941. In October 1944, he became under-secretary of state at the India Office, becoming Secretary of State in 1947. (Based on the entry by G. Ireland in the *Oxford Dictionary of National Biography*, http://www.oxforddnb.com/view/article/65196)

225 The 16th Earl of Huntington, 1901–1990, was a left-wing artist who became Diego Rivera's assistant and who later painted a mural at the Marx Memorial Library, London, entitled *Worker of the Future Upsetting the Economic Chaos of the Present*. (Based on the entry by W. Wyatt in the *Oxford Dictionary of National Biography*, http://www. oxforddnb.com/view/article/40204?docPos=6) He was later to say in the Second Reading debate on Lord Silkin's Bill: 'the first object of this Bill, as has been so well said before, is to relieve the distress of thousands of women who, for one reason or another – whether they cannot cope with more children; whether it is the young girl who has a job which she could not keep if she had an unwanted child, or whether it is someone frightened of bearing a deformed, mad or abnormal child – cannot face having this child. Certainly this Bill will help to relieve this distress. But what is, I think, far more important is the question of the unwanted child. The unwanted child is in a most difficult and unpleasant position, psychologically and in every way; and although it is perfectly true that in some cases adoption works very well, in other cases it does not'. HL Deb 30 November 1965 Vol. 270 cc1139–241.

226 For example, Janet Chance wrote to Lord Listowel and Lord Huntingdon in April 1943 to ask whether 'there is any likelihood of the abortion question being raised in the Lords in the midst of post-war plans'; and Lord Listowel replied to say that he was 'delighted that your Committee is coming to life again after its wartime hibernation', but, he was to say in a later letter of 17 October 1944, 'I am sure you were right in deciding that the time is not yet ripe for a Bill, and that the best we can do at the moment is to try to wake up the public and to put personal pressure on the right people. I regard a debate in the Lords as mainly educative, and I hope it won't be delayed too long'. Lord Huntingdon gave a similar reply on 24 September 1943: 'I do think that this is not a very opportune time for pressing the matter. Possibly the position will change nearer the end of the end of the war, or when it is over'. The next year, when the war had indeed ended, Lord Listowel wrote again to say that 'I very much hope that now the war is over you may be able to do more in Parliament about your proposals for Law Reform, and if I can help you at any time with advice I shall be honoured to receive a request'. Abortion Law Reform Association papers at the Wellcome Institute for the History of Medicine.

227 B. Wootton, *Selected Writings: Volume 1: Crime and the Penal System*, *op. cit.*, 85.

228 *Ibid*, 68.

229 Letter from Janet Chance, Chairman, ALRA, to the Secretary, Royal Commission on Population, 1 January 1946.

230 Joseph Reeves, 1888–1969, was a Member of Parliament between 1949 and 1959.

231 *The Times*, 20 December 1952.

232 A. Jenkins, *Law for the Rich*, *op. cit.*, 71.

233 Bernard, Cardinal Griffin, 1899–1956, was ordained a priest in 1924, became secretary to Archbishop McIntyre, became a parish priest in 1937, and then an Assistant Bishop in 1938. He became Cardinal Archbishop of Westminster in 1943. (Based on the entry by M. Walsh in the *Oxford Dictionary of National Biography*, http://www.oxforddnb. com/view/article/33575?docPos=7)

234 *The Times*, 17 February 1953.

235 HC Deb 27 February 1953 Vol. 511 c2506.

236 Basil Mackenzie, Lord Amulree, MRCS, LRCP, MRCP, MD, 1900–1983, inherited his title as the second Baron. He was a pathologist who joined the Ministry of Health as a cancer specialist and then a specialist in the care of the chronic sick before returning to consultant practice as a physician in geriatric medicine. He was a member of the Society for the Study of Medical Ethics. (Based on the entry by T. Arie in the *Oxford Dictionary of National Biography*, http://www.oxforddnb.com/view/article/55504?docPos=1)

237 For fuller detail see the discussion in the next chapter.

238 HC Deb 26 January 1956 Vol. 548 c47W.

239 Lena Jeger, 1915–2007, was Labour Member of Parliament for Holborn and St. Pancras South between 1953 and 1959 and 1964–74, and for Camden, Holborn and St. Pancras South, 1974–79.

240 HC Deb 20 December 1957 Vol. 580 cc121–2W. She was to be told too in another Parliamentary written answer that 'During the period 7th June, 1954, to 4th June, 1955, some 190,000 days of incapacity for work, among about 6,000 insured women, were certified for National Insurance purposes as due to "abortion" which is the term used to cover all types of miscarriage'. HC Deb 29 January 1958 Vol. 581 c84W.

241 Alastair Service, in *Pioneers of Change: Interviews with people who made the 1967 Abortion Act possible*, http://www.bpas.org/js/filemanager/files/abortion_pioneers.pdf, 24.

242 A. Jenkins, *Law for the Rich*, *op. cit.*, no page number.

243 *Ibid*, 43.

244 *Ibid*, 35–36.

245 D. Cossey in *Pioneers of Change: Interviews with people who made the 1967 Abortion Act possible*, http://www.bpas.org/js/filemanager/files/abortion_pioneers.pdf, 23.

246 HC Deb 10 February 1961 Vol. 634 cc853–92.

247 Although the principle of clarifying the law was generally welcomed by the BMA which put out a press statement in January 1961 saying: 'There is … considerable uncertainty regarding the present legal position. If, as is sometimes believed, termination of pregnancy for therapeutic reasons is in fact permissible under existing law, it is highly desirable that the legal position should be made clear'. It also insisted that 'The question whether or not to terminate pregnancy for therapeutic reasons in any particular case, within the limitations imposed by the law, must be left to the decision of the doctor concerned'.

248 *The Times*, 3 February 1961.

249 Robert Mortimer, 1902–1976, studied moral theology at the University of Oxford and then proceeded to Wells Theological College in 1925. He was first a deacon in Bristol and then a lecturer in theology at Christ Church, Oxford, in 1929, where he studied canon law. In 1944 he was appointed Regius Professor of Moral and Pastoral Theology and, in 1949, Bishop of Exeter. He was, his biographer states, 'recognised

as a leader of the Anglo-Catholic wing of the church'. In 1955, he received a peerage and 'was soon recognised as one of the church's leading spokesmen on moral and social questions'. (Based on the entry by J. Porter in the *Oxford Dictionary of National Biography*, http://www.oxforddnb.com/view/article/31472?docPos=2)

250 The precise wording was 'The Bill is to be judged primarily by whether it will help or hinder [the medical practitioner] in making … judgements responsibly and effectively for the good of his patients. … Clause 1(c) and (d) would make extremely bad law, and ought to be resisted. Gross deformity or physical or mental abnormality can seldom be predicted of a foetus under thirteen weeks old; the likelihood of such a condition, as consequent upon certain known or suspected conditions in the mother, can never amount to certainty. Nor would it be safe to just to terminate a pregnancy on the ground of an unproven allegation of rape or incest, and proof by conviction in a court of law could seldom be obtained within thirteen weeks'. The Medical Termination of Pregnancy Bill, Report of a small expert Committee, appointed by the Moral Welfare Council of the Church Assembly Board for Social Responsibility, Chairman the Lord Bishop of Exeter, 8 February 1961.

251 Canon Bentley, 1909–1996, was a contributor to R. Acland, G. Bentley and C. Gough (1965); *Sexual Morality: Three Views*, London: Arlington Books; and R. Channer (ed.) (1985); *Abortion and the Sanctity of Human Life*, Exeter: Paternoster.

252 *The Times*, 6 February 1961.

253 Peter Rawlinson, 1919–2006, was a Catholic barrister and a politician, the Conservative Member of Parliament for Epsom between 1955 and 1979, when he became a peer. He opposed reform of the divorce, abortion, and homosexual laws. He was solicitor general from 1962 and 1964, when the Labour Party came to power. (Based on the entry by G. Howe in the *Oxford Dictionary of National Biography*, http://www. oxforddnb.com/view/article/97248).

254 David Renton, 1908–2007, was a barrister and Member of Pariament for Huntingdonshire, first as a National Liberal and then as a Conservative between 1945 and 1968. He was Minister of State, Home Office, between 1961 and 1962.

255 Anthony Fell, 1914–1998, was the Conservative Member of Parliament for Yarmouth, Norfolk, 1951–66 and 1970–83.

256 According to the American medical charity, the March of Dimes: 'In 1961, doctors in Germany, Australia and Great Britain noted a significant increase in the number of babies born with severely malformed or missing arms and legs. These birth defects were traced to the use of thalidomide during early pregnancy, when a baby's arms and legs begin to form. The most well-known defect, a severe shortening of the arms or legs with flipper-like hands or feet, is called phocomelia. Affected babies almost always have defects on both sides and often have both the arms and legs malformed. In especially severe cases, the babies have complete absence of limbs. The drug also causes malformations of the eyes and ears, heart, genitals, kidneys and digestive tract (including the lips and mouth)'. http://www.marchofdimes.com/alcohol_thalidomide.html

257 K. Hindell and M. Simms; *Abortion Law Reformed, op. cit.*, 108.

258 See the letter to *The British Medical Journal* from Denis Burley, 'Is Thalidomide to Blame?' (14 January 1961); 130. Initially the response had been merely guarded ('While the proportion of patients taking thalidomide who develop a polyneuropathy is small, and while the incidence of this complication of treatment is not sufficient, in view of its other advantages, to suggest that the drug should never be prescribed, greater caution in its use is needed and it should not be prescribed for long periods' 'Thalidomide Neuropathy', *The British Medical Journal* (30 September 1961); 876) but it became clear that thalidomide did have toxic properties.

259 Dr McBride had first made the connection between thalidomide and birth defects in June 1961, but his initial letter reporting the finding to *The Lancet* was rejected as 'interesting but not important'.

260 'Thalidomide and Congenital Abnormalities', Letters to the editor, *The Lancet* (16 December 1961); 1358.

261 *Ibid.*

262 A. Speiers (10 February 1962); 'Thalidomide and Congenital Abnormalities', *The Lancet*, 303.

263 R. Smithells (16 June 1962); 'Thalidomide and Malformations in Liverpool', *The Lancet*, 1272.

264 See HC Deb 26 June 1962 Vol. 661 c132W where Edith Pitt replied to a question: 'The deformities due to this drug cannot always be distinguished from those due to other causes. The number of deformed, births could not be ascertained without a detailed examination of hospital and other records, which I do not consider would be justified'. Edith Pitt, 1906–1966, was Conservative Member of Parliament for the Edgbaston Division of Birmingham, and Parliamentary Secretary, Ministry of Health, 1959–1962.

265 *The Times*, 30 October 1962.

266 HC Deb 10 December 1962 Vol. 669 cc21–2.

267 See *The Times*, 19 February 1963.

268 http://www.nytimes.com/2010/03/16/science/16limb.html

269 B. Brookes, *Abortion in England 1900–1967, op. cit.*, 151.

270 Edith Summerskill, 1901–1980, had qualified as a doctor in 1924 and entered Parliament as the Labour Member for West Fulham, 1938–55, and then as Member for Warrington, 1955–61. She became a peer in 1961.

271 HL Deb 19 July 1962 Vol. 242 cc767–70.

272 An article in *The British Medical Journal* at the end of 1962 talked about how 'Much evidence has now accumulated, strongly suggesting that gross abnormalities of the limbs of the newborn … may be due to the exhibition of the drug thalidomide during early pregnancy'. M. A. Lécutier (1 December 1962); 'Phocomelia and Internal Defects due to Thalidomide', *The British Medical Journal*, 1448. There was an abundance of other articles in the medical journals. See, for example, S. Ward (8 September 1962); 'Thalidomide and Congenital Abnormalities', *The British Medical Journal*, 646–7; and L. Gillis (8 September 1962); 'Thalidomide Babies: Management of Limb Defects', *The British Medical Journal*, 647–8.

273 'Medicine: The Thalidomide Disaster', *Time*, 23 August 1962.

274 See, for instance, the report, 'More Deformities in Limbs', in *The Times*, 9 July 1962.

275 I. Leck and E. Millar (7 July 1962); 'Incidence of Malformations since the Introduction of Thalidomide', *The British Medical Journal*, 16.

276 See *The Times*, 24 July 1962.

277 The survey was of 1997 electors (1,049 women 948 men). In answer to the question, 'do you think that abortion should be legal in all cases, in some cases, or illegal in all cases, the replies were:

Legal in all cases	6.4%
Legal in some cases	66.1%
Illegal in all cases	24.1%
Don't know	3.5%

278 *The Times*, 24, 26 and 27 July 1962. The mother's application to court was rejected and she turned to clinicians abroad for a termination – see *The Times*, 1 and 6 August 1962, eventually finding relief in Sweden.

279 *The Times*, 20 August 1962.

280 *The Times*, 13 September 1962.

281 *The Times*, 6 November 1962.

282 *The Times*, 12 November 1962.

283 *The Times*, 15 November 1962.

284 *The Times*, 19 November 1962.

285 P. Darby (13 August 1964); 'Legal abortion', *New Society*.

286 In *Pioneers of Change: Interviews with people who made the 1967 Abortion Act possible*, http://www.bpas.org/js/filemanager/files/abortion_pioneers.pdf, 15.

287 Glanville Williams, 1911–1997, was called to the Bar in 1935, became reader in English law, professor of public law, and then Quain Professor of Jurisprudence in the University of London; and then, in 1955, he became a fellow of Jesus College Cambridge, until his death. In his celebrated *The Sanctity of Life and the Criminal Law* (Faber and Faber: London, 1958) he reviewed the philosophical arguments underpinning the law on contraception, sterilisation, artificial insemination, abortion, suicide, and euthanasia. (Based on the entry by J. Spencer in the *Oxford Dictionary of National Biography*, http://www.oxforddnb.com/view/article/66017)

288 Constitution adopted at the Annual General Meeting held on 21 November 1964, Abortion Law Reform Association papers at the Wellcome Institute for the History of Medicine.

289 Madeline Simms in *Pioneers of Change: Interviews with people who made the 1967 Abortion Act possible*, http://www.bpas.org/js/filemanager/files/abortion_pioneers.pdf, 17.

290 Abortion Law Reform Association Annual Report 1964–65, 1.

291 Minutes of the Meeting of the Executive Committee of the Abortion Law Reform Association, 7 September 1965. ALRA Papers in the Wellcome Institute for the History of Medicine.

292 Note from HBW 16th November 1964; Home Office File 219/1139: Abortion: Miscellaneous and General – Proposed Private Member's Bill to amend the Law on Abortion.

293 Minutes of the Meeting of the Executive Committee of the Abortion Law Reform Association, 7 September 1965. ALRA Papers in the Wellcome Institute for the History of Medicine.

294 I could not establish who Mr McMurray was.

295 Note from HBW 16 November 1964; Home Office File 219/1139: Abortion: Miscellaneous and General – Proposed Private Member's Bill to amend the Law on Abortion.

296 Brief on law on abortion, 17 November 1964. Home Office File 219/1139: Abortion: Miscellaneous and General – Proposed Private Member's Bill to amend the Law on Abortion.

297 Vera Houghton recalled that 'I once tackled Harold Wilson during one of the Queen's flights. I said: 'I didn't see you having anything to say about abortion' and he replied: 'And you won't''. In *Pioneers of Change: Interviews with people who made the 1967 Abortion Act possible*, http://www.bpas.org/js/filemanager/files/abortion_pioneers.pdf, 31.

298 The note said later: 'Ministry of Health, after enquiries in 1960, were satisfied that the present state of the law imposed no real difficulty on responsible gynaecologists and that a strong body of opinion in the medical profession was in favour of leaving the law as it is. Might make it more difficult for them 'to convince a patient not requiring abortion on medical grounds that an abortion would be against the law'. Ministry have no reason to suppose that they have changed their minds since 1960'.

299 Note to S. of S. on the Law on Abortion – 17.11.1964. Home Office File 219/1139: Abortion: Miscellaneous and General – Proposed Private Member's Bill to amend the Law on Abortion.

300 Note of 19 November 1964. Home Office File 219/1139: Abortion: Miscellaneous and General – Proposed Private Member's Bill to amend the Law on Abortion.

301 See J. Ayto (2006); *Movers and Shakers: A Chronology of Words that Shaped Our Age*, Oxford: Oxford University Press, 172.

302 It is not evident what his larger views on sexual morality may have been. Sir Frank was a religious man, but not, it seems, in a conventional sense. His son, Oliver, recalled in

conversation that 'He did believe in the immortality of the soul although I never knew what his religious beliefs were. ...' There are hints of a more orthodox religiosity in a speech he gave at prize-giving day to St. Anselm's College, a Merseyside grammar school, in 1950: 'What is lacking in the world today is not knowledge but the simple kindnesses which enable us to use everything for the common benefit of mankind. The aim of life should be to live it in the true Christian sense and I know that at this school the stress is on the need to live in the Christian manner'. *St Anselm's College Magazine*, Vol. 1, No 2 (Spring 1950) 6.

303 According to Pat Thane, using the Registrar-General's figures, there were 5.5 illegitimate births for every thousand unmarried women aged 15–44 in the 1920s and 1930s; the number then rose steadily through the 1950s to reach 19 in 1961–5. "Happy Families?' history and policy', http://www.historyandpolicy.org/papers/policy-paper-107.html The reasons are multiple, not least being the growing availability of contraceptives. In the latter half of the 20th century, the proportion of illegitimate births in the United Kingdom was higher than anywhere else in Europe. See A. Sprangers and J. Garssen; 'Non-marital fertility in the European Economic Area', Division of Social and Spatial Statistics, Department of Statistical Analysis, Statistics Netherlands, http://www.cbs.nl/NR/rdonlyres/441AC4F4-0ED5-4E32-B12D-A100BC83552E/0/nonmarital.pdf. On p. 10, they claim that 'The level of non-marital fertility in the United Kingdom is some 40% above the EEA-average. In 1998 more than one out of three newborn babies had an unmarried mother'.

304 Note to Sir Charles Cunningham, 4 December 1964. Home Office File 219/1139: Abortion: Miscellaneous and General – Proposed Private Member's Bill to amend the Law on Abortion.

305 Letter to Members of the Executive Committee, 6 January 1965, ALRA Papers in the Wellcome Institute for the History of Medicine.

306 Confidential Note of a Interview with the Home Secretary, Sir Frank Soskice, 2 February 1965, ALRA Papers in the Wellcome Institute for the History of Medicine.

307 To Vice-Presidents, members of the Medico-Legal Council and (for information) to members of the Executive Committee, Deputation to the Home Secretary, 6 February. ALRA Papers in the Wellcome Institute for the History of Medicine. Keith Hindell and Madeline Simm said later: 'Towards abortion reform Soskice was really no more helpful than his three Conservative predecessors who had made bland assurances that nothing needed to be done'. *Abortion Law Reformed, op. cit.*, 129.

308 In Pioneers of Change: Interviews with people who made the 1967 Abortion Act possible, http://www.bpas.org/js/filemanager/files/abortion_pioneers.pdf, 10.

309 Minutes of the Meeting of the Executive Committee of the Abortion Law Reform Association, 7 September 1965. ALRA Papers in the Wellcome Institute for the History of Medicine.

310 Draft submission for S. of S. on his suggested reform of the law relating to affiliation 13.5.1965, Home Office File 219/1139: Abortion: Miscellaneous and General – Proposed Private Member's Bill to amend the Law on Abortion.

311 Undated, minute anonymous minute to H.B. Wilson. Home Office File 219/1139: Abortion: Miscellaneous and General – Proposed Private Member's Bill to amend the Law on Abortion.

312 See HL Deb 11 March 1965 Vol. 264 cc273–8.

313 See E. Husserl (1990); *On the Phenomenology of the Consciousness of Internal Time*, Dord recht: Kluwer Academic Publishers.

314 Note to Charles Cunningham 23.11.64, Home Office File 219/1139: Abortion: Miscellaneous and General – Proposed Private Member's Bill to amend the Law on Abortion.

315 Vera Houghton, the Chairman of ALRA, explained to members in a circular letter that 'Under this procedure the mover speaks for ten minutes and only one speech in reply is allowed. If the House divides, as it almost certainly will, there is a free vote. ... Whereas the two previous Bills, introduced ... in 1953 and by Mr Kenneth Robinson in 1961, were talked out, the present procedure will at least allow the opportunity of testing for the first time the strength of support in the House of Commons for Alra's aims, and the result will have an important bearing on future actions'. Undated letter. ALRA Papers in the Wellcome Institute for the History of Medicine.

316 Renée Short, 1916–2003, was elected to Parliament in 1964 and was described as 'one of the most dedicated advocates of abortion reform in the 1964 and 1966 parliaments'. (Based on the entry by D. Howell in the *Oxford Dictionary of National Biography*, http:// www.oxforddnb.com/view/article/88761)

317 The Bill read in full: ' ... it shall be lawful for a registered medical practitioner to terminate pregnancy in good faith:-

    (a) for the purpose of preserving the life of the patient, or

    (b) in the belief that there would be a grave risk of serious injury to the patient's physical or mental health if she were left to give birth to and care for the child, or

    (c) in the belief that the patient became pregnant as the result of intercourse which was an offence under sections 1 to 11 inclusive of the Sexual Offences Act 1956'.

The long title of the Sexual Offences Act 1956, CHAPTER 69, was 'An Act to consolidate (with corrections and improvements made under the Consolidation of Enactments (Procedure) Act, 1949) the statute law of England and Wales relating to sexual crimes, to the abduction, procuration and prostitution of women and to kindred offences, and to make such adaptations of statutes extending beyond England and Wales as are needed in consequence of that consolidation'. Those sections proscribed sexual intercourse under a variety of conditions, under Section 5, 'unlawful sexual intercourse with a girl not under the age of thirteen but under the age of sixteen'.

318 HC Deb 15 June 1965 Vol. 714 cc254–8.

319 Note from Charles Cunningham to S. of S. on the law on abortion 28 June 1965. Home Office File 219/1139: Abortion: Miscellaneous and General – Proposed Private Member's Bill to amend the Law on Abortion.

320 Conclusions of a meeting of the Cabinet held at 10 Downing Street on 3 June 1965.

321 See *The Times*, 23 July 1966.

322 William Wells was Labour MP for Walsall North, 1955–1974.

323 Letter to *The Times*, 21 April 1976. He did go on to remark that 'and we all know how difficult it is to say when, and whether, a foetus is alive'.

324 Appendix 5 to agenda for E.C. Meeting of 3 August 1965, ALRA Papers in the Wellcome Institute for the History of Medicine.

325 K. Hindell and M. Simms; *Abortion Law Reformed, op. cit.*, 88.

326 Replies received from members to Memorandum on Renée Short's Bill. Abortion Law Reform Association papers at the Wellcome Institute for the History of Medicine.

327 17.11.64 – Secretary of State's brief on law on abortion; 17.11.1964. Home Office File 219/1139: Abortion: Miscellaneous and General – Proposed Private Member's Bill to amend the Law on Abortion.

328 Introducing the motion, Dr Heath of the Birmingham branch said that: 'the pressure for the reform of the law on abortion continued from all directions. Recently there had been slanted television and radio programmes, press articles, resolutions from women's organisations, and a Private Member's Bill in Parliament. This was a medical matter. It was doctors who advised their patients, undertook the necessary treatment,

and bore the ultimate responsibility. It should therefore be their duty, right, and indeed privilege to advise the Government on any reform of the law. His Division felt that it was time for the profession to set up a subcommittee to evaluate and report on the therapeutic indications. The Government should be asked not to introduce any new legislation until that committee had reported'. Supplement to *The British Medical Journal* (17 July 1965); 54. Later, there was to be some professional dispute between the BMA and the Royal College of Obstetricians and Gynaecologists about which practitioners could and should be involved in the decision to terminate a pregnancy. The BMA declared that it was reluctant to cede the role to the Royal College. (See *The Times*, 26 January 1967)

329 Sir Charles noted that 'These proposals were in the Bill introduced by the present Minister of Health in 1961 and are advocated by the Abortion Law Reform Association'.

330 Note from Charles Cunningham to S. of S. on the law on abortion 28 June 1965. Home Office File 219/1139: Abortion: Miscellaneous and General – Proposed Private Member's Bill to amend the Law on Abortion.

331 The age of consent had been fixed at 16 in 1885 under the Criminal Law Amendment Act (which also extended the sodomy laws that will be the focus of other chapters). Its long title was The Criminal Law Amendment Act 1885 (48 & 49 Vict. c.69: An Act to make further provision for the Protection of Women and Girls, the suppression of brothels, and other purposes.

332 21 August 1965: Note from S. of S. Home Office File 219/1139: Abortion: Miscellaneous and General – Proposed Private Member's Bill to amend the Law on Abortion.

333 Note by S. of S. 6 September 1965, Home Office File 219/1139: Abortion: Miscellaneous and General – Proposed Private Member's Bill to amend the Law on Abortion.

334 Indeed, she went on to say in reply to a question by William Hamilton, 'if any of my hon. Friends, or any Member of this House, were to be lucky in the Ballot, then the Government would have to see what their attitude would be about doing the same as they did in the case of the Bill of my hon. Friend the Member for Nelson and Colne' [Sydney Silverman]. HC Deb 8 July 1965 Vol. 715 cc1789–91.

335 Note to Secretary of State of 3 September. Home Office File 219/1139: Abortion: Miscellaneous and General – Proposed Private Member's Bill to amend the Law on Abortion.

336 There had been references to measures 'to improve the administration of justice and to reform and modernise the law' and to 'the development of new means of dealing with young persons who now come before the courts and the advancement of penal reform', but that was all. HL Deb 9 November 1965 Vol. 270 cc1–5

337 HC Deb 10 November 1965 Vol. 720 cc166–310.

338 'The Home Office under New Management', *The Times*, 24 January 1966.

339 In *Pioneers of Change: Interviews with people who made the 1967 Abortion Act possible*, http://www.bpas.org/js/filemanager/files/abortion_pioneers.pdf., 54.

340 See Alastair Service, in *Pioneers of Change: Interviews with people who made the 1967 Abortion Act possible*, http://www.bpas.org/js/filemanager/files/abortion_pioneers.pdf., 26.

Bibliography

L. Abse (1973); *Private Member*, London: MacDonald

Anon (1927); 'Report of a joint meeting of the Medico-Legal Society and the Section of Obstetrics and Gynaecology of the Royal Society of Medicine', *The British Medical Journal*, 188–193

Anon (1928); 'Medical Notes in Parliament', *The British Medical Journal*, 1011–1014

Anon (1928); 'Medical Notes in Parliament' *The British Medical Journal*, 1116–1118

Anon (1936); 'Maternal Mortality and Abortion. Deputation from the National Council of Women', *The British Medical Journal*, 378

Anon (1938); 'The Trial of Mr. Bourne', *The British Medical Journal*, 185

Anon (1938); 'Charge Of Procuring Abortion: Rex v. Bourne', *British Medical Journal*, 199–205

Anon (1938); 'Rex v. Bourne', *The Lancet*, Volume 232, Issue 5995, 201–202

Anon (1966); 'Medical Termination of Pregnancy Bill Views of the British Medical Association and the Royal College of Obstetricians and Gynaecologists', *British Medical Journal*, 1649–1650

J. Beckford (1990); 'The Sociology of Religion and Social Problems', *Sociological Analysis*, Vol. 51, No. 1, 1–14

M. Boyle (1997); *Re-Thinking Abortion: Psychology, Gender, Power and the Law*, London: Routledge

P. Brierley (1999); *Religious Trends 1999–2000*, No. 2, London: Christian Research Association

British Medical Association (1936); *Report of Committee on Medical Aspects of Abortion*, London: B.M.A.

S. Brooke (2001); '"A New World for Women"? Abortion Law Reform in Britain during the 1930s', *The American Historical Review*, 106(2), 431–459

—(2009); 'The Sphere of Sexual Politics: The Abortion Law Reform Association, 1930s to 1960s' in N. Crowson, M. Hilton and J. McKay (eds.) *NGOs in Contemporary Britain: Non-State Actors in Society and Politics Since 1945*, London: Palgrave, 77–94

—(2011); *Sexual Politics: Sexuality, Family Planning and the British Left from the 1880s to the Present Day*, Oxford: Oxford University Press

B. Brookes (1988); *Abortion in England, 1900–1967*, London: Croom Helm

S. Browne (1937); 'The A.L.R.A'., *The New Generation*, 5

—and A. Ludovici and H. Roberts (1935); *Abortion: Three Views*, London: George Allen and Unwin

J. Buchan (1936); 'The Midwives Act, 1936, and Its Operation', *The Journal of the Royal Society for the Promotion of Health*, Vol. 57, 420–436

R. Burrows (10 September 1938); 'The Law of Abortion', *The Law Journal*, Vol. LXXXVI, 170

J. Campbell (1932); 'Notes of a meeting of the Kensington Division of the British Medical Association', *The British Medical Journal*, 960–963

J. Chance (1936); *The Case for the Reform of the Abortion Laws*, London: Abortion Law Reform Association

The Church Assembly Board for Social Responsibility (1965); *Abortion: An Ethical Discussion*, London: Church Information Service

A. Cooke (1972); *A History of the Royal College of Physicians*, Oxford: The Clarendon Press

V. Cornish (1922); *A Geography of Imperial Defence*, London: Sifton Praed & Co.

I. Dawson (1988); 'The Confidential Enquiry into Maternal Deaths: Its Role and Importance for Pathologists', *Journal of Clinical Pathology*, Vol. 41, 820–825

J. Douglas (ed.) (1970); *Deviance and Respectability: The Social Construction of Moral Meanings*, New York: Basic Books

M. Edgecombe (1947); 'Marital Difficulties and Abortion Law Reform', in *Back-Street Surgery: A Study of the Illegal Operation which is Performed Probably about 100,000 Times a Year in England and Wales*, Fordingbridge: The Abortion Law Reform Association

L. Farmer (2016); *Making the Modern Criminal Law: Criminalization and Civil Order*, Oxford: Oxford University Press

A. Fraser (2007); 'George Douglas Pinker: Obituary', *British Medical Journal*, Vol. 334, 1378

G. Gardiner and A. Martin (1964); 'The Machinery of Law Reform', in G. Gardiner and A. Martin (eds.) *Law Reform Now*, London: Victor Gollancz, 1–14

W. Garside (1990); *British Unemployment 1919–1939*, Cambridge: Cambridge University Press

A. Grubb (1990); 'Abortion Law in England: The Medicalization of a Crime', *Law, Medicine and Health Care*, Vol. 18, Nos 1–2, 146–161

E. Hawarden (1966); *Prejudice in the Classroom*, Johannesburg: South African Institute of Race Relations

K. Hindell and M. Simms (1968); 'How the Abortion Lobby Worked', *The Political Quarterly*, Vol. 39, No. 3, 269–282

J. Hobcraft (1996); 'Fertility in England and Wales: A Fifty-Year Perspective', *Population Studies*, Vol. 50, No. 3, 485–524

E. Husserl (1990); *On the Phenomenology of the Consciousness of Internal Time*, Dordrecht: Kluwer Academic Publishers

The Inter-Departmental Committee on Abortion (1939); *Report*, London: HMSO

A. Jenkins (1938); *Conscript Parenthood?, The Problem of Secret Abortion*, London: George Standring

—(1960); *Law for the Rich: A Plea for the Reform of the Abortion Law*, London: Victor Gollancz

J. Keown (1988); *Abortion, Doctors and the Law*, Cambridge: Cambridge University Press

T. McIntosh (2000); '"An Abortionist City": Maternal Mortality, Abortion, and Birth Control in Sheffield, 1920–1940', *Medical History*, Vol. 44, 75–96

H. McLeod (2007); *The Religious Crisis of the 1960s*, Oxford: Oxford University Press

E. Moberly Bell (1953); *Storming the Citadel: The Rise of the Woman Doctor*, London: Constable

S. Newcombe, review of H. McLeod (2007); *The Religious Crisis of the 1960s*, Oxford: Oxford University Press, in *The Historical Journal*, Vol. 52, No. 3 (September 2009), 848–849

A. Oakley (1991); 'Eugenics, social medicine and the career of Richard Titmuss in Britain 1935–5', *The British Journal of Sociology*, Vol. 42, No. 2, 165–194

Lord Riddell (1932); 'Ethics of Abortion, Sterilization, and Birth Control Address', *British Medical Journal*, Vol. 1, No. 3706, 106

R. Ross (1936); *Russell On Crime: A Treatise on Felonies and Misdemeanors By Sir William Oldnall Russell*, 9th edition, London, Sweet & Maxwell

Royal Commission on Population (1949); *Report*, Cmd. 7695, London: HMSO

M. Ryan, M. Edgecombe and J. Chance (1947); *Back-Street Surgery: A Study of the Illegal Operation, which is Performed Probably about 100,000 Times a Year in England and Wales*, Fordingbridge, Hants: ALRA

W. Sigle-Rushton (2008); 'England and Wales: Stable Fertility and Pronounced Social Status Differences', *Demographic Research*, Vol. 19, 455–502

M. Simms (1974); 'Abortion Law and Medical Freedom', *The British Journal of Criminology*, Vol. 14, No. 2, 118–131

D. Steel (1989); *Against Goliath: David Steel's Story*, London: Weidenfeld & Nicolson

A. Taylor (1894); *The Principles And Practice Of Medical Jurisprudence*, fourth edition, edited by Thomas Stevenson, London: J. Churchill

M. Teitelbaum and J. Winter (1985); *The Fear of Population Decline*, Orlando: Academic Press

T. van de Velde (1930); *Ideal Marriage; Its Physiology and Technique*, New York: Random House

J. Weeks (1990); *Coming Out: Homosexual Politics in Britain from the Nineteenth Century to the Present*, London: Quartet

H.G. Wells (1904); *Mankind in the Making*, New York: Charles Scribner's Sons

G. Williams (1958); *The Sanctity of Life and the Criminal Law*, London: Faber and Faber

B. Wootton (1992); *Selected Writings: Volume 1: Crime and the Penal System*, Houndmills: Macmillan

5 The Liberal Hour II – The Abortion Act 1967 c. 87

Culmination

The new generation of ALRA members busied themselves preparing materials for the private member's bill which Alice Bacon had solicited. They constructed the evidence of public sentiment which the Home Secretary had required in their meeting in February, evidence which might persuade a cautious government that support would not be electorally hazardous. One source was the *Daily Mail* and National Opinion Polls which had conducted a national survey of electors in March 1965 to ascertain their stance towards the existing law: 72.5% were said to be in favour of reform,[1] supplying an argument that enabled Glanville Williams to claim that all that ALRA sought to accomplish was to 'remove a criminal prohibition from the medical profession to the extent that this accords with general opinion'.[2] The survey also enabled Simon Wingfield Digby, a Conservative Member seeking to introduce a new private member's bill in February 1966, to talk about the revelation of women's 'great uncertainty … as to their rights'.[3] Another influential step had been the North-West London ALRA group's submission of a questionnaire to some 2,000 doctors in the London area at the end of 1964. Over 750, or 37.5%, of the doctors had replied, and, in answer to the question 'Do you feel that the present laws make it sufficiently easy for you to know when abortion is legal?', 50.5% of those questioned had said 'No' and only 36.5% had said 'Yes'; 69.5% had stated, in answer to another question, that they approved of ALRA's aims; only 10.5% had said that they did not approve; 84% had considered that abortion undertaken in hospital conditions in the first 12 weeks of pregnancy was a safe operation for a woman in good health; and 75.5% thought that the operation ought to be available on the National Health Service.[4] It was evidence that could be deployed to dispel some of the prevailing assumptions about medical resistance to reform, and it was certainly put to use, for example by Lord Stonham, the Joint Parliamentary Undersecretary of State, Home Office, in a debate in the House of Lords in November 1965.[5]

I spoke of the intense lobbying conducted by the revived ALRA after the election of the first Wilson Government of 1964. ALRA meticulously prepared and continually revised lists recording the sympathies of Members of Parliament:[6] 390 Members of the new House of Commons had indicated their willingness to support reform, and there were others in both Houses of

Parliament who declared that they were prepared to introduce legislation.[7] One was Lord Silkin,[8] father of the Government Chief Whip, who had replied on 17 August 1965 that he was 'definitely in favour of ALRA's proposals' and was 'prepared to consider introducing a Bill in the House of Lords'. He told the Association that he hoped to get a date for a second reading after the Queen's Speech had been 'dealt with and before Bills from the Commons started crowding the Lords'. He had in mind, he said, a 'slightly more liberal Bill'[9] than those previously introduced, retaining the freedom afforded a doctor under the Bourne judgement to terminate a pregnancy on health grounds; but fixing a period beyond which an abortion on sexual grounds could not take place except in an emergency; and making provision for a new clause, in accord with established ALRA thinking, stipulating what were called social conditions, including difficult living conditions and family size, as lawful indications for termination. He asked Glanville Williams to prepare a draft bill which, in addition to the new clauses (including what Glanville Williams called 'the eugenics grounds' of abortion for foetal abnormality or deformity), would contain presentational changes which might ward off some of the attacks that had been levelled at Kenneth Robinson's Bill in 1961.[10] There was now, for example, no reference to what was thought to be the emotionally laden word 'child' except for the neutral allusion to a child coming into existence only if the pregnancy were allowed to continue. Were the bill to receive a second reading, remarked Lord Silkin, it would be able to proceed to the House of Commons where, if the government ceded time, it could be despatched before the end of the session.[11]

Lord Silkin introduced his bill on 11 November 1965 and, he said, its prime goal was familiar enough, the reform of a century-old law: 'Abortion is a criminal offence under Section 58 of the Offences Against the Person Act 1861. It is stated to be punishable by life imprisonment. Any woman who with intent to procure a miscarriage administers to herself any poison or drug or who uses any instrument for the like purpose commits an offence. So does any other person who administers drugs or uses any instrument on a woman for the same purpose'. Some mitigation of the impact of the law had been introduced in the judgements passed in and after the Bourne case that appeared to make abortion lawful 'where the mother's life or health is seriously endangered – but it is still a fact that this decision depended upon directions to the jury by three specific judges. There has been no decision of any higher Court; therefore there is still a considerable element of doubt and uncertainty as to what the law is'. He talked about the harm that illegal abortion procedures inflicted on the women who underwent them: 'in 1964 there were 50 deaths from abortion not carried out by doctors. There were also between 30,000 and 40,000 cases of abortion, or attempted abortion, admitted into hospital at public expense; and the number is steadily increasing. ... Many women to-day are so desperate that they resort to means which are gravely damaging to their health, or even to their life, to create an abortion. They take drugs and pills, such as quinine pills, which are calculated to end pregnancy; they insert things into the womb by means of a syringe; they use disinfectants, running a grave risk of serious injury to tissues and organs; they use methods of violence, such as moving heavy furniture and jumping down stairs'. What he proposed was, he maintained, modest enough:

> The Bill before the House is designed, first, to make the law on abortion clear and certain, so that no medical practitioner need fear prosecution if in good faith he carries out an abortion on a patient whose circumstances fall within the provisions of this Bill. I want to make it clear at this stage that the conditions in the Bill are carefully circumscribed, and it is not a general licence to a medical practitioner to carry out abortions on anybody who desires an abortion. ... Clause 1(c) relates to the health of a patient or the social conditions which make her unsuitable to assume the legal or moral responsibility of parenthood. I have in mind cases of women between 40 and 50 years of age who have conceived a child, some of them grandmothers, some with five or six children, who are so desperate that in a number of cases they have attempted suicide, and in some cases have carried out the attempt successfully. ... Clause 1(d) provides for cases where the patient becomes pregnant as the result of intercourse which is an offence under Sections 1 to 11 of the Sexual Offences Act 1956. These are cases which involve rape, sexual intercourse with a child under 13, sexual intercourse with a child over 13 (where the conditions and the penalty are rather different), sexual intercourse with a woman who is insane or mentally defective, or sexual intercourse as the result of administering drugs to a woman so as to make her unconscious. There are various cases of a kind which will be familiar to most lawyers, but these are all cases where there is involuntary intercourse on the part of the woman, with one possible exception – incest.[12]

The government, under a Harold Wilson with scarce taste for the politics of abortion, and in the last weeks of Sir Frank Soskice's tenure of the Home Office, was not much moved and it announced its neutrality (as was customary with private member's bills).[13] Cabinet had noted with disapproval five days before the Second Reading debate, on 25 November, that the Bill:

> went further in a number of respects than the earlier proposals for reform which had been put forward by the Abortion Law Reform Association. In particular, it sought to legalise abortion on grounds connected with the social conditions in which the mother was living; and the effect of such a provision could be regarded as removing, in effect, any restraint on abortions. Moreover, the General Council of the British Medical Association had recently set up a committee to consider the reform of the law [which I shall discuss below] ... and had called upon the Government to refrain from any action in this regard pending the committee's report.[14] There was general agreement that in these circumstances the Government's

spokesman should maintain an attitude of strict neutrality towards Lord Silkin's Bill.[15]

At Second Reading, that government spokesman, Lord Stonham, did indeed announce to the House of Lords that 'it is easier to deplore and recognise the evil, than to find an effective and acceptable remedy. This is a most difficult and controversial subject on which there are widely divergent, and sincerely held, views. These divergencies have little connection with social class and none with Party politics. It is for this reason that Her Majesty's Government's attitude to the Bill is one of strict neutrality'.[16] Nevertheless, he said, the bill was not satisfactory, and it was not satisfactory for a litany of reasons, some of which had been rehearsed for decades. There should be a second opinion where the decision to terminate was being considered. The burden of proof would prove excessive: the 'Bill preserves the present position under the Bourne and Newton and Stungo judgements, which place on the Crown the onus of show-ing lack of good faith. But we have to ask ourselves whether, with this very considerable extension of the grounds for legal abortion, the burden on the prosecution might not become so onerous that enforcement of the law would be virtually impossible'. The clause referring to social conditions was overly vague and required doctors to exceed their competence: 'It is not primarily a medical ground, and it is arguable that it should not be left to doctors to decide. "Social conditions", would presumably cover the case of a woman with five or six children living in two rooms. It may be undesirable to bring another child into the world in such conditions; but it is surely arguable that rehousing, not abortion, is the answer'. The clause referring to rape was not satisfactory: 'The problem is who is to decide, and how, that the pregnancy has resulted from a criminal offence. The matter is not wholly a medical one; and there are obvious opportunities for alleging an assault simply to get rid of an unwanted pregnancy. Any limitation to cases where there has been a conviction would exclude very deserving cases – for example, where the offender cannot be found or, for some reason, cannot be proceeded against. This would probably delay action until it was too late'. Should a pregnant girl under the age of 16 be aborted where she had consented to intercourse?: 'it is a fact that consent is often freely given. We have to ask: is it right in these circumstances that a girl who has willingly entered into sexual intercourse, in the full knowledge of what it means, should be entitled by law to have an abortion procured?' Above all, he believed that the bill was premature because 'the House should bear in mind that the medical profession, whose members would have to operate the new law, have not yet committed themselves to support any change'.

Viscount Dilhorne, the former attorney general, Reginald Manningham-Buller, a man who tended generally to be antipathetic to liberal reform, claimed that he supported the aims, but not the phrasing of the bill. It was, he said, 'a badly drawn, wholly inadequate, and to me, I say quite frankly, a most disappointing Bill'. So important a decision as the termination of a pregnancy, a decision that could result in 'trauma, physical or mental, which may be serious and prolonged, and possibly irreversible', should depend on the judgement of not one but two practitioners; and the need for a termination should be notified, with an accompanying justification, to a health authority within 48 hours of the decision being made. It was disturbing that doctors could be empowered to take a life if they merely suspected that the birth of a child would cause hardship for the mother: 'I do not see how the destruction of a potential human being can be justified on the ground that the woman, who can without risk to herself bear the child, may be thought likely to suffer in health "from the strain of caring for it"'. Doctors were in no position to judge the veracity of claims of rape or incest: 'how is a doctor going to satisfy himself that a criminal offence has been committed? What evidence will he have before him? The only evidence is likely to be that of the girl or woman concerned'. And, 'whether a criminal offence of having unlawful intercourse with a girl between 13 and 16 has been committed may in some cases depend on the accused's belief as to the girl's age. If [a defendant] is under 24 and has not previously been charged with a like offence, he is not guilty of having unlawful intercourse with a girl between 15 and 16 if he believes her to be 16 or over and has reasonable cause for that belief'. As to foetal abnormality: 'Is it to be said and I am looking at this now not from the point of view of the mother but from that of the child – that there is a grave risk of abnormality where the mother has German measles, when 30 per cent. of the children have been born deformed? Is the potential life of the remaining 70 per cent. to be destroyed on that account? I must say that I find this a very difficult question upon which to express an opinion'. He was troubled by the clause which alluded to the inadequacy of the mother to be:

> To destroy a potential human life because in the opinion of a doctor the mother is unable to assume the legal and moral responsibility of caring for it is, I think, quite unjustifiable. If, after the child has been born, it appears that the mother is not suitable to look after it, then, surely, provision can and should be made for its proper care and custody. But to say that, because of an opinion before the birth of the child, the mother is unsuitable to assume legal or moral responsibility for it, seems to me a wholly inadequate ground for making sure that the child shall never be born.

He was troubled by the way in which a burden of proof was placed on the prosecution:

> It requires the prosecution to prove beyond reasonable doubt that the operation was not performed in good faith in the belief specified in this Bill. But how on earth the prosecution are going to be able to prove conclusively that the man does not believe what he says he believes, I do not know. The prosecution might adduce a mass of evidence to show that his belief was wholly unfounded, that it was totally unreasonable, and that there were no adequate grounds for it. None the less, unless they could

prove that he did not hold the belief he said he held, any prosecution would be bound to fail.

Mervyn Stockwood,[17] the socialist Bishop of Southwark, similarly declared himself well disposed to the ends but not to the substance of what was proposed: 'I agree with the basic aims of this Bill, but the wording is unsatisfactory. In fact, that is an understatement, for it is so unsatisfactory that I hope the noble Lord, Lord Silkin, will withdraw the Bill and bring us something better... Abortion happens every day: if a woman has the money, then in a nursing home; if she has not, then in a back street. ... our choice is between recognising abortion or conniving at it; between taking steps to regularise it and allowing it to happen in secret and, perhaps, in sordid and dangerous conditions'. There should, he said, be a right to consult the prospective father. The decision to abort was a heavy one, and it would be better to enlist the aid of another doctor or a special tribunal. The allusion to the mother's 'strain' was disturbing: 'the nurturing of a child usually involves strain. How can a medical practitioner decide, before birth, the degree of strain that will be placed upon the mother after birth? And even if it could be proved that the strain of nurturing would be excessive, does it necessarily follow that the child should not be born?' The allusion to 'social conditions' was disturbing: 'What is meant by "social conditions"? And how does one become qualified to pass a judgement upon them? Are we to assume that a degree in medicine gives to the holder of it such insights into sociological problems that he is competent to determine by himself?'

The stance of the Church of England, so important at the time in framing moral questions, was more formally conveyed by the Bishop of Exeter,[18] the Church's social affairs spokesman and the erstwhile chairman of the small expert committee on Kenneth Robinson's 1961 bill, and he did give some ground. He was no longer quite so unequivocal in his condemnation of proposals to reform the law, but he was no enthusiast:

> We are here, as I see it, confronted with a choice between, on the one hand, the obvious humanity which inspires this Bill, the desire to reduce the sum of human misery by relieving a certain class of individuals of a heavy and great load of unhappiness which they carry by reason of fear or anxiety occasioned by their pregnancy. But, on the other hand, we know that it is our duty as legislators to do nothing which would have the effect, or be likely to have the effect, of cheapening the value set in our society upon human life. What we have really been discussing the whole of this afternoon and evening is the value which we are to place upon human life, because whatever an unborn baby is or is not, at least it is certain that it is not a mere inconvenience to its mother.

It could be argued, he said, anticipating a more official statement of the Church of England's position, that was then in preparation, that 'the fœtus becomes a member of the human race at the moment of its conception ... This, as I understand it, is the doctrine of the Roman Catholic Church and is not at all irrational. At one time, when I was younger, I held it myself, and if one holds it follows, as an unavoidable conclusion, that all abortion must be treated as a form of murder or homicide'. But it could also be argued (and this was the view of Michael Ramsey, the Archbishop of Canterbury[19]) that, although the foetus is sacred, it has only a *potentiality* for life, and abortion is not infanticide. Where its interests conflicted with those of the mother, the mother's life should take precedence:

> From this it will be clear to your Lordships that our attitude is that we support the principle which underlies ... this Bill, which would legitima- tise abortion where the interests of the mother vitally require it. Where there is a grave threat to her life, to her physical health or to her mental health, we maintain that abortion may be legitimate. For my own part, I would go even further. The phrase in the clause about the strain of their upbringing is certainly obscure, but I take that to mean that in considering the vital interests of the mother one should not exclude either the duties of the mother towards the living members of her family. I understand that what lies behind that phrase is that the total environment of the mother, including the rights of the already born children to the care and protection of the mother, should be taken into account as one factor in reaching a decision as to whether the threat to the mother and her environment is so severe as to override the rights of the potential human being present in the baby... What to do about the Second Reading of this Bill, I am not quite so sure. It seems to me that it would be almost impossible, and incredibly tedious, to get this Bill into an acceptable shape in the Committee stage on the Floor of this House. I should much prefer, if it were possible, that it were referred to some body which could consult with doctors, with lawyers, and with social workers, as well as, perhaps, with the clergy. That body could then produce a new Bill, so drafted as to be acceptable to the majority opinion in this country; a Bill which would be proof against any abuse in the direction of making an abortion available on demand.[20]

The neurologist, Lord Brain,[21] spoke, as it were, for the medical profession, and he said:

> the present state of the law relating to abortion is unsatisfactory. It is unsat- isfactory that doctors should be put into the position of having to make up their minds whether what they may do will fall within the interpretation of the law as decided by judges many years ago. I am told that, as a result, it is often difficult to get a gynæcologist to terminate pregnancy in a case where all the doctors are agreed that on medical grounds it is desirable. The law, therefore, I am sure, needs to be defined; but I am bound to say that in many respects I think the present Bill falls far short of a satisfactory definition.

He accepted that the law must stipulate that two medical opinions should be sought in the decision to terminate a pregnancy; but he held that some of the other doubts expressed by speakers were overly cautious. The criterion of excessive strain being placed on the mother was not unreasonable: it was the current practice to take it into account to some extent, and in suitable cases. 'For example, if a woman has severe heart disease or a disabling disease of the nervous system, it is relevant to consider not only what the immediate effects on her physical health of the pregnancy going to term will be, but also what will be the effects on her physical and mental health of having to care for the child after it is born. I am told that is a current consideration in many cases'. In the assessment of the possibility of foetal abnormality, there 'are a wide variety of risks here, some of which are easy to estimate and some of which are very difficult to estimate. I think I should say something particularly about rubella (German measles) where the risk varies a great deal according to the precise stage of pregnancy at which the disease occurs. If it is at the most vulnerable phase – I think that is about the sixth to ninth week – then the risks are extremely high, and very responsible gynæcologists have told me they would regard that established fact as in itself indication for the termination of pregnancy'. But the House of Lords was not the proper forum to judge these and other, often quite technical matters. The best course, he thought, echoing the Bishop of Exeter, was for the government to establish a new inter-departmental committee.

Another physician, and the previous sponsor of a similar bill, Lord Amulree, also declared himself a supporter:

> The Bourne judgement, one might think, would be sufficient to give the medical profession complete trust and faith, but there is always the fear that it might be reversed in the Appeal Court, and it does not satisfy a great many doctors. ... The effect of a back-street abortion, of course, can be terrible. It can lead to chronic ill-health in the mother; and, also – a tragic thing, supposing she should wish to become pregnant subsequently – the chances of her being sterile are enormously increased. The other thing which I think one finds is that if they have been to a back-street abortionist they get a much greater feeling of guilt when the operation has been carried out and they come away, than they do if it is done in a legal manner.

Nevertheless, he said, 'I entirely agree with what was said by ... Lord Dilhorne. [The Bill] seems to me to be badly drawn, and that it would be quite impossible to enforce it in a correct way'. Above all, abortion should be the work of a specialist, not any practitioner; and there should always be a second opinion.

And a few Catholic peers spoke. The Earl of Iddlesleigh did so. So did Lord Clifford: 'Here we are having legalised abortion. What will it be next? – euthanasia, then sterilisation will be added en passant, and man, in all his arrogance, will have allotted to himself that function which those of simpler beliefs have considered to be until now the prerogative of the Almighty. Surely it can never be anything but morally wrong, and therefore, one hopes, legally wrong, for man to solve his problems by death, whether it is death at the beginning, in the middle or at the termination of his life span. It seems to me that Hitler tried to solve some of his problems that way'.[22] The Catholic Lord Craigmyle spoke:

> There are objections based on the natural order. The sanctity of human life is there, whether you happen to be a Mohammedan or a Roman Catholic or a member of the Church of England. ... The Abortion Law Reform Association is avowedly humanist and non-Christian. Those of us who are Christian may think they are in fact anti-Christian, although they would not say that themselves. This Bill is a humanist Bill. It springs from the line of thinking which supposes for some reason or other that a woman has the power of life and death over her own offspring. The same line of thought in ancient times led Greek mothers to expose their unwanted babies on the cold hillside, or the Canaanite mothers to offer their babies in fire to the idol Moloch.

Despite that small welter of criticism, the bill did receive its Second Reading on 30 November by 70 votes to eight. It was amended after discussion with members of the British Medical Association and with Lord Dilhorne; and was considered in Committee in February 1966,[23] the Home Office, now under Roy Jenkins, still professing its neutrality, but offering, as was customary for a bill that had advanced thus far, assistance with further drafting.[24]

Lord Silkin raised at Committee Stage the talks he had had with the BMA, Lord Dilhorne and the Churches, and he disclosed the amendments he proposed, including the removal of the 'social conditions' clause. He sounded uncomfortable, conceding that 'I have not been entirely successful. No Private Member who tries to draft a Bill can be assured that he will get exactly the right words to meet what he wants to do'.[25] His Bill was nonetheless approved on 3 February with the clause on inadequacy 'intact' and the clause permitting abortion for girls under the age of 16 retained. But the forensic problems of establishing rape brought it about that, at the instigation of Lord Dilhorne, it was withdrawn as grounds for a lawful abortion (Lord Stonham supported him, saying that 'it had not been possible to solve the problem of how a doctor was to decide whether it was a genuine case of rape. To await the prosecution or conviction of an offender would delays things too much to perform an abortion. In any case, there would be no help for the woman unless the offender was caught'[26]). The bill received a further reading on 7 February in its now more restricted version which talked neither about rape nor about the mother's and existing children's social conditions but still listed the mother's inadequacy[27] (a clause to which Lord Dilhorne[28] and the Archbishop of Canterbury, following the Bishop of Exeter, objected[29]). The government, in the meanwhile, resolved yet again to remain neutral, although, again as was customary when a private bill had made headway, it publicly confirmed its willingness to help with drafting in future.[30]

Lord Silkin had admitted at the outset that 'This Bill will obviously need amendment', and some commentators began to argue that the progress of the legislation had become so increasingly and worryingly irresolute that it was time to put it aside, seek the counsel of the medical profession, and clarify a number of ethical dilemmas, particularly those which appeared to introduce eugenicist arguments. It was, *The Times* said, 'a botched job':

> Fundamental questions of conscience or social policy have been raised, half-examined, and lost to sight ... One object ... is to reduce the number of "unwanted children" who are born into the world ... and by so doing to alleviate besetting social problems ... If Parliament is prepared to con-template the use of abortion for the purposes of voluntary social eugenics, it should do so with its eyes open.[31]

Yet the bill nonetheless successfully completed Committee Stage on 23 May,[32] making it possible for Glanville Williams to talk confidently about the House of Lords being favourable to reform,[33] and for ALRA to say that 'After thirty years of public debate the argument had virtually been concluded in favour of reform by all but a tiny minority who, for religious or other moral reasons, oppose any change'.[34] In the interim, Lord Silkin, Glanville Williams and Vera Houghton had met on 18 May to hear Lord Silkin declare that he would be prepared to withdraw his bill should one of the Members of the House of Commons successful in the private member's ballot announced on 12 May wish to proceed with his or her own measure, bills introduced in the Commons taking precedence over those in the Lords,[35] and his own bill having run out of time and been effectively lost.[36] ALRA itself concluded that 'In view of the bill now to be taken in the House of Commons ... it is very unlikely that Lord Silkin will proceed with his bill to a third reading as it would have to take its turn at the end of the queue in the Commons, long before which we hope that the new bill to be introduced in the Commons will have reached the Lords'.[37] And its more general verdict was that:

> Whatever were considered to be the drawbacks of Lord Silkin's bill, there is no doubt about the tremendously significant part it has played in the campaign for reform and in preparing the ground for a much more liberal bill. The publicity which resulted from the long debates in the House of Lords, occupying nine sitting days over a period of six months, the con-troversies which raged in the correspondence columns of the press, the feature articles, the editorials, for and against, the documentaries on televi-sion and sound radio programmes, and the urgency which the prospect of legislation gave to the deliberations of bodies like the Church Assembly, the British Medical Association and the Royal College of Obstetricians and Gynaecologists, did more to awaken the country to the pressing need for reform than anything else had done.[38]

Intermission I: The doctors and abortion

Let me turn round to review those deliberations. The medical profession had again been stirring. Abortion was a matter that touched it immediately, Lord Silkin's bill looked for a while as if it might come to fruition, a number of medical practitioners had spoken at the debate in the House of Lords, and the profession was obliged to consider its position. A Special Committee, composed of representatives of constituent committees and divisions of the British Medical Association,[39] had been established in response to a resolution of the October 1965 Annual Representative Meeting that had talked about 'the present agitation for reform in the law concerning abortion'. The government, the resolution had continued, 'should be asked not to introduce any new legislation until this committee has reported'.[40] That committee, it was decided on the very day that Lord Silkin's bill received its Second Reading, 'proposes to carry out its task by bringing up to date the 1936 report of the BMA entitled "Medical Aspects of Abortion"'.[41] It would re-examine the therapeutic conditions for abortion;[42] consider a second draft of the bill, 'together with a copy of his adviser's [Glanville Williams'] notes';[43] and produce comments, at Lord Silkin's invitation, before the Committee stage that had been scheduled for 1 February (at his meeting with Lord Silkin on 14 December, the Undersecretary of the BMA, Dr. Gullick, had ascertained that 'Lord Silkin had made it clear that he would welcome the advice and comments of the medical profession on the re-drafting of his Bill').

There were voices in that Special Committee opposing any reform. The Birmingham Division[44] looked upon Lord Silkin's bill (and David Steel's subsequent bill[45]) with some distaste: and its representative, the consultant psychiatrist, Myre Sim,[46] urged on this occasion, as he had done at other times, a categorical rejection of liberalisation:

> It has been a medical ethic since the days of Hippocrates that a doctor should preserve life and this has been generally practised to date. The free advocacy of abortion offends this ethic and it would very difficult for doctors to retain their image as the preservers of life when they condemn unborn, healthy and innocent babies to death for what is mainly a social convenience. Society may insist on abortion on demand, but the psychiatrist should be very cautious in lending his support to such a policy. He will certainly not be acting on medical evidence and will be involving his profession in conduct which is the antithesis of ethical medical practice.[47]

There was also a marked show of reticence about some of the possible therapeutic signs. Josephine Barnes, a gynaecologist, and another member of the committee, wrote:

> I think the gynaecological indications are very rare indeed, and as I have remarked, I have never terminated pregnancy for a gynaecological

condition that I can remember. Again I would be nervous that a woman with a small fibroid causing perhaps a small amount of pain might get her pregnancy terminated. This would not only be quite wrong in my opinion but might even be dangerous...[48]

There was opposition conveyed to the Special Committee by the BMA membership. One doctor said, for instance, that:

at present ... a practitioner in his consulting room is able to state to a patient, or parent with a patient, that it is unlawful to procure an abortion when confronted with a direct request. The reversed position will place the onus of supporting a negative reply on the General Practitioner. It is the frequent task of a General Practitioner to comfort, sustain, and encourage a patient and parents against censure and what is seen as utter disgrace and ruin. Far more frequently than not, one year, eighteen months, at most two years sees a happy ending with a family supporting an "erring" member, often bringing out hidden stores of courage and goodwill. The proposals in the Bill even as amended introduce, almost a 'carte blanche'. The Welfare State mentality is a demanding one, immediately insisting on rights. The present state of the law is in my opinion a protection to the doctor against unreasonable demands and a protection for the individual against precipitate panic measures. ... If the new Bill redrafted became law a sizable [sic] proportion of the general-practitioner body would encounter great difficulties of conscience in complying with it. To the majority of these the reply to a direct request can only be a negative one. Similarly in the hospital field a large proportion of medical and nursing personnel will find conscientious difficulty in carrying out the work which will result from the Bill becoming law.[49]

But the bulk of the committee resolved that 'revision of the law was most desirable, and it also agreed on the importance of accepting the invitation to comment upon the Bill'.[50] It next proceeded to scrutinise the bill clause by clause and unearthed what it believed were the chief problems for the profession. It was, for example, difficult to forecast foetal abnormality. À propos the position 'of the girl under 16 years of age; it was agreed to recommend that these words be deleted, since there were no medical indications for termination on grounds of age alone'.

So protracted had proceedings become that the bill lapsed at the end of the 1964–5 session of Parliament, but it was reintroduced later in the new year, and Lord Brain openly urged the Special Committee to remain *in situ* to respond to whatever might be attempted, and, when they did so, to make their conclusions forcefully and publicly: 'What disturbs me ... is how little impression on the whole any medical views so far expressed have had on the Peers, and I doubt whether it is worth while to go over all this again, unless the views of doctors can somehow be given much more publicity'.[51] The Special

Committee did remain in place, and it was urged by its Chairman to publish its revised version of the 1936 report before the bill was debated at Committee Stage towards the end of May.[52] Working closely with other professional bodies such as the Royal College of Obstetricians and Gynaecologists,[53] and carefully skirting the wider politics and morality of abortion, an area in which it claimed no special competence, it had agreed on a number of points which centred squarely on practical, medical questions of professional powers and protections. It wished, in particular, to retain sovereign control over the decision to abort on therapeutic grounds: the Special Committee, said John Havard, its Secretary, 'should make it clear that, subject to the necessary safe-guards, termination of pregnancy in the interests of the health of the mother should be permissible; the law should not be formulated too strictly and it should be left to medical discretion in the light of all the circumstances to take the decision as to whether therapeutic abortion should be undertaken. This would safeguard the doctors' right to decide what was best for his patient'. They further agreed:

(i) That there was need for reform of the law on termination of pregnancy.
(ii) That new legislation should include "safeguards" to determine the person carrying out the operation and the place of operation. [Previous discussion had flagged the fact that any medical practitioner could call himself or herself a gynaecologist or obstetrician.]
(iii) That the normal system of medical consultation be used to give an opinion regarding termination of pregnancy in individual cases, rather than that a tribunal or panel should be appointed.
(iv) That there should be confidential notification of the operation, purely for scientific and statistical purposes.
(v) That failure to comply with rules for notification should be treated simi-larly to failure to comply with other forms of notification, and should not be considered a criminal offence.[54]

At their concluding meeting of 9 June 1966, they discussed a final draft of the report that recited all the problems arising from the 1861 Act, the Bourne judgement, and subsequent 'judicial decisions, reported and unreported, which interpret the Act in the light of conditions after more than a century of medical progress...' Whilst it appeared lawful to terminate a pregnancy to protect the life and health of the mother, it was simply not feasible to lay down with any exactitude the criteria that should inform that decision in a particular instance: 'the possibility of damage to the health of the mother and environmental factors may need to be considered in reaching a medical opinion on the desirability of termination. Accordingly it is important that the law should not attempt to define too precisely the circumstances in which pregnancy may be terminated in such cases'. Citing the stance taken by a recently published report of the Church Assembly Board for Social Responsibility,[55] a report to which I shall turn, they maintained that it was for the physician alone to determine when an abortion should take place. The BMA's overriding interest lay not only in preventing the law from encroaching too generously on the professional autonomy of the practitioner but also in protecting doctors from litigation:[56]

> From the point of view of the medical profession the decision to advise termination must be taken in the light of the circumstances of the particular case. It is not possible, except in certain exceptional conditions, to specify the maternal disorders which must be present before pregnancy may properly be terminated. Furthermore, in the present dynamic state of medical knowledge, what may be regarded as medically justifiable now, will not necessarily be so regarded in the future... Accordingly, the Committee recommends that the legal indications for terminating pregnancy in the interests of the health of the mother should not be too closely defined. ...

The physician, it was argued, should protect the mother's life: that much was evident not only from medical ethics but from the Bourne judgement. Medical science had advanced appreciably since 1936, and, because the practitioner could now predict severe foetal abnormality with some confidence, such a diagnosis could properly become a therapeutic indication (the report reflected that: 'the rhesus factor was not [then] appreciated[57] and it was not known that certain diseases in the mother, including rubella, could damage the foetus. Although it was known that certain drugs which were taken for the specific purpose of inducing illegal abortion might damage the foetus there were no drugs in current therapeutic use, such as thalidomide, which were known to have this effect'). But the committee did not wish to recommend terminations in circumstances where the grounds were *not* strictly medical: where, for example, the expectant mother was under 16; even although they did concede, somewhat reluctantly, that other, possibly valid principles were in play in cases of rape and incest:

> it will very often happen that continuation of pregnancy would not be in the interests of the health of the mother and this situation would be covered by the changes in the law already recommended in this report. In other cases we appreciate that the social and moral conscience of the community would be affronted by the prospect of a mother being forced to continue her pregnancy to term ... In some cases of pregnancy following incest it may happen that the relationship is such that there is a risk of serious foetal abnormality. In other cases the social and moral conscience of the community would again be affronted by the prospect of a child being born as a result of such a relationship ... Similar considerations apply in the case of pregnancy as a consequence of unlawful intercourse with a mentally subnormal woman...

But here, where the decision impinged awkwardly on evidential and moral matters lying outside medical science and the competency of the practitioner, it is not remarkable that the committee should have stood back and havered: 'From the medical point of view the fact that pregnancy has resulted from a sexual encounter which was unlawful is not, in itself, an indication for terminating pregnancy. ... We do not consider any extension to the changes in the law already recommended in this report would be necessary to cover such cases'. Its overall, somewhat defensive, conservative[58] and narrow conclusion, a conclusion[59] endorsed by the Royal College of Gynaecologists and Obstetricians in March 1966,[60] was, in effect, that the case law from the Bourne case and its successors should be ratified in legislation with the sole addition of a new provision for severe foetal abnormality:

> The law should be amended to provide that therapeutic abortion is lawful only if carried out by a registered medical practitioner of the required skill and experience, in an approved hospital or nursing home after consultation and with the approval of a professional colleague who has examined the patient. Subject to the above conditions the law should be further amended to provide that it is lawful for a registered medical practitioner to terminate pregnancy in good faith in the interests of the health of the mother and/or the serious risk of gross abnormality of the foetus. Termination of pregnancy in the absence of the above indications is not justifiable on the grounds that the girl was under the age of 16 years at the time of conception. In other cases of pregnancy resulting from an unlawful act further amendment of the law would give rise to serious problems of law enforcement and of medical ethics.

Intermission II: The churches and abortion

The Churches had also been stirring. Abortion was a troubling, shifting,[61] divisive[62] area (in the words of the Reverend Greet, a Methodist minister, 'the Roman Catholic Church [was] at one end and the Free Churches at the other, with the C. of E. in the middle'[63]), but they could not help but comment on an issue of such current controversy, an issue that centred on what was conventionally described as the sanctity of life, and what they said would make an impact.

The Roman Catholic Hierarchy's position was and remained simple and categorical. God's law was immutable. Abortion was the sinful taking of life,[64] and it could never be condoned (except, significantly perhaps, where the principle of double effect applied[65]). In 1930, a papal encyclical had asked:

> Can any reason ever avail to excuse the direct killing of the innocent? For this is what is at stake. The infliction of death whether upon mother or upon child is against the commandment of God and the voice of nature: "Thou shalt not kill!" The lives of both are equally sacred and no one ... can ever have the right to destroy them.[66]

Thirty-six years later, the Hierarchy of England and Wales repeated and reinforced that doctrine by issuing a statement after a meeting of Roman Catholic Bishops on 22 October 1966 and at the time when another abortion bill was proceeding through Parliament: 'All direct destruction of life in the womb is immoral,' it said. 'No civil law can change the moral law which we are bound to obey'.[67] Cardinal Heenan,[68] the head of the Church in England and Wales, pronounced that 'The Church has never varied in her teaching on Abortion. It is immoral to destroy by direct action life in the womb'.[69] But the Roman Catholic Church was alone, and knew itself to be alone. The Cardinal wrote sadly in a letter of 16 June 1966 that 'I am afraid that we shall fight a losing battle on the Abortion Bill because even the Anglican bishops were in favour. We cannot impress Parliament that it is a Christian issue if the established Church is not on our side'. David Steel, the man who was to sponsor a private member's bill, reflected that 'The religious objection came fundamentally from the Roman Catholic Church because they've taken a consistent line throughout that they don't sanction abortion at all. But the other churches were calling for support'.[70]

ALRA's response to the Catholic position was hostile in private but largely (but not invariably[71]) muted in public. Vera Houghton noted that 'The Sun [newspaper] phoned me yesterday and asked for my views on the Catholic campaign. ... Hope I wasn't too virulent!'[72]

Moral theology in the Protestant Churches had long been less than absolute on the matter. As early as 1937, the Church of England Modern Churchmen's Union[73] had submitted a memorandum to the Inter-Departmental Committee on Abortion to argue that 'We know of no specific Christian principle which would condemn abortion on all and every ground. ... The present law, forbidding it altogether, is cruel, inhuman, ineffective and un-Christian'.[74] Later, in 1955, Geoffrey Fisher, the then Archbishop of Canterbury, had declared his support for the somewhat restricted position flowing from the judgement in the Bourne case. In a letter to a Roman Catholic lay woman who had invited him[75] to join with other Churches in condemning a resolution that was to be put to the Magistrates Association,[76] he said that he believed that the Church of England would support the resolution's first clause, a clause that talked about physicians acting in good faith to save the life of a mother, but not the other clauses which would have enlarged the existing provisions to cover matters of maternal health and infant deformity:

> ... It would indeed be a grave thing if the resolution as it stands were passed since parts of it are open to serious objection. So far as I am able to judge general opinion in the Church of England, the first clause (a) would be supported as giving a very much desired relief to the consciences of doctors. Unlike the Church of Rome general opinion in the Church of England thinks that the preservation of the life of the mother takes precedence. There would be much divided opinion about (b) (i) and I should be in total opposition to (b) (ii).[77]

That was the established stance: a guarded endorsement of what seemed to be the accepted position in law, not a complete proscription on abortion, but also an acknowledgement of the opposition and controversy that legal reform could excite and a reluctance to extend the law further (ALRA itself recognised that in the 1950s 'The Church of England was deeply divided on the issue of abortion …'[78]) It was a position that remained intact for some while. It will be recalled, for instance, that a later review conducted by the Bishop of Exeter's small expert committee had been largely unsympathetic to provisions of Kenneth Robinson's 1961 bill that would have made abortion lawful where there had been an allegation of rape or a possibility of foetal abnormality. The impact of those divisions of opinion to which the archbishop referred was real enough, and members of ALRA had had a long acquaintance with them. Encounters between the proponents of reform and some members of the Church had in the past been more than a little abrasive. In 1958, for instance, Shirley Emerson of the Chichester Diocesan Moral Welfare Association had written to Ena Steel of the Moral Welfare Council of the Church Assembly Board for Social Responsibility about her encounter with members of ALRA:

> The meeting was quite terrifying, and the Doctor who came from the Abortion Law Reform Association was quite fanatical. They say they only want the law changed to protect doctors in certain cases, but in actual fact I think they would like to see it possible for any woman, married or unmarried, to get an abortion if she wants to. They make a certain appeal to people's emotions, because they talk of overcrowded homes and drunken husbands – in fact at one time we were beginning to wonder if all England was like that! The other two doctors who spoke were both opposed to it and were both excellent. I think in the end we carried the day, but I think this body of rather fanatical people might need watching.[79]

But the events of the mid-1960s, including the crisis of thalidomide and the Belgian trial; the emergence of a more vigorous ALRA, and the legislation then in train had given the problem of abortion a renewed salience. The Churches had to clarify their position and the Church of England's Church Assembly Board for Social Responsibility, a board which again included as a consultant member the Bishop of Exeter, the bishop charged with speaking on social affairs in the House of Lords, elected to return to the problem. In 1965, it produced *Abortion: An Ethical Discussion*, as part of its occasional series of 'serious studies of difficult social questions'.[80] It was a report that furnished the rather elastic estimate that there were between 10,000 and 100,000 illegal abortions a year in England and Wales; and then posed an opening trio of key questions:

> For some mothers there is a genuine risk that their health, physical or mental, may be impaired if the pregnancy goes to term; for some few, a

risk to life. ... the crux of the matter is ... in the decision that the life of the foetus has to be sacrificed to the interest of the mother in her own continued life, health, and, it may be, her continued service to her husband and family. For other mothers there is a risk that their child may be born deformed. If the mother has already contracted rubella ... and the virus is still active at the time of her conception, there is a high risk that her child will be defective in eyes, ears, heart and brain. ... the question then arises, ought the life of the foetus to be sacrificed to ... family interests? Thirdly, there is the interest of the unborn child itself: [and here, significantly, the matter of thalidomide and the Liège homicide was raised] is it better to allow it to be born, with a calculable statistical probability of deformity of some sort, or for it not to be born at all?[81]

There was, the argument continued in familiar vein, the inequity of the wealthy obtaining safe abortions and the poor being at risk from dangerous procedures. There were the 'girls or women against whom a sexual offence has been committed, the victims of rape or of incest, or young girls below the age of consent. ... it is to be noted that the existing case law, which has secured to medical practitioners a tenuous right lawfully to terminate a pregnancy which threatens the mental health of the mother, arose from the [judgement in the Bourne case about the] termination of the pregnancy of a girl who, while three months under the age of fifteen, had conceived as a result of a criminal assault upon her'.[82] Those were questions that raised, in their turn, other, larger problems: the right to life which was protected in English law unless, in the last remaining days of capital punishment, it was not rendered forfeit by one's own unlawful act; (with a whiff of eugenics) the right of a society to protect its survival and the future of its population; the declaratory obligation to bear 'witness that some acts are morally reprobate within that society';[83] and the professional right of medical practitioners to protect themselves: 'it lies with the prosecution to prove that a doctor who terminated a pregnancy was not acting in good faith and in the reasonable belief that the operation was necessary to preserve the life or health of the mother. The medical practitioner has a clear interest to defend in this matter. He has to defend the autonomy of his professional judgement ...'[84] None of these problems was susceptible of a simple answer. And what followed was a most consequential deduction:

the primary and general intention of the law has been to preserve as inviolable the right of the unborn child to live; yet the number and extent of the exceptions and accommodations are such that this right to live cannot be described as absolute and *in all circumstances* inviolable. The Christian moral and legal tradition recognises implicitly that there are circumstances in which the killing of the unborn child does not come under the general condemnation attaching to murder.[85] [Emphasis in original]

Even if the foetus were thought to be human and to possess a soul, '… circumstances can be envisaged in which it may be a duty to extinguish the rights of the very young foetus in order to do justice to those of an adult person, say of the mother, and, indeed, of her other children whose 'rights' might be infringed if the foetus were left undisturbed. It would then become a moral question of some intricacy to decide on the balance of those rights …'[86] Following the formula set out by Clarke and Avory in 1896, substantially developed and amended by Glanville Williams and ALRA and then qualified in the discussion of Lord Silkin's bill, the report then declared that abortion could be permissible where it was recommended by two qualified medical practitioners and where the pregnancy constituted a grave threat to the mother's life or health (p. 33); there was a calculable risk of the birth of a deformed or defective child (p. 36); and the child has been conceived as a result of rape or some other criminal offence (p. 45). Its overall judgement was that '[a]fter surveying the matter afresh … our broad conclusion is that in certain circumstances abortion can be justified. This would be when, at the request of the mother and after the kind of consultation which we have envisaged in the report, it could be reasonably established that there was a threat to the mother's life or well-being, and hence inescapably to her health, if she were obliged to carry the child to term and give it birth'.[87]

The report, reflected David Steel in interview, was 'very important indeed, partly because [it] was well circulated and publicised and partly because it influenced lesser reports from the Methodists and the Church of Scotland'. He was to say elsewhere that it had affected him personally, calling it 'a very substantial document from the Church of England [that] influenced me greatly as the Bill was going through …';[88] 'I have yet to see anything which so powerfully states a positive Christian attitude to this most complex subject'.[89]

Others deliberated in the report's wake, and it also affected their position. I have shown that the BMA had alluded to it in the report of its Special Committee on Therapeutic Abortion. Cardinal Heenan, the head of the Roman Catholic Church in England, praised it although he himself did not accept its reasoning or conclusions.[90] And the Methodist Church was to absorb some of its argument. The Methodists had earlier taken the stand that abortion was an unmitigated and unambiguous wrong:

> The Christian conscience condemns abortion as a means of family limitation. The practice, when successful, involves the destruction of human life, and when unsuccessful the risk of grave injury in body and mind to the child born in spite of it. The life of the mother may also be placed in jeopardy. …[91]

But a later report, submitted to the 1966 Methodist Conference, asserted:

> The problem of abortion has presented us with a great difficulty. It concerns an area in which medical, social, moral, and theological considerations

overlap. For this reason we have been unable to accept the suggestion made by some that the whole subject falls outside the concern of the Churches. ... The debates in the House of Lords on Lord Silkin's Bill to amend the law on abortion revealed a wide measure of support for reform, but considerable diversity of opinion on the complex moral questions involved. Careful consideration of the issue in the B.C.C. [British Council of Churches] Advisory Group on Sex, Marriage and the Family failed to produce any agreed judgement. Accordingly the Moral Welfare Committee set up a small group to study the matter. The statement which follows owes much to the guidance given by that group. ...[92]

In its preamble, that new statement by the Methodists talked about how much turned on a definition of the status of the foetus and its claim to the 'full rights of legal protection of life which are given to human beings'.[93] Everything hinged on what was meant by *human*: 'Many people who have wrestled with this question must have wished that they were able to accept the comparatively simple Roman Catholic position ... We do not accept this view...':

> Granted that it is a basic function of the law to seek to safeguard life, in the case of a pregnant woman, we have to consider her life and that of the foetus. *Where the two may be in conflict the former must be regarded as more important than the latter... One practical conclusion which follows ... is that in cases where the continuance of pregnancy would involve serious risk to the life or grave injury to the health of the pregnant woman, abortion should be permitted.* We believe there is widespread support for this position. The Anglican Report, with which we are thus far in agreement, would not carry the definition of legal abortion beyond that point ...[94] [Emphasis added]

A recommendation flowing from this argument might possibly have been the wholesale decriminalisation of abortion, but 'We do not think that such a step would be acceptable to the British public and we believe the consequences of such action are too much in doubt to make it right or desirable. ...'[95] What was recommended instead to the Methodist Conference in July 1966, put in the form of a resolution, and then passed, was a motion broadly similar to the terms of the ALRA draft legislation, Lord Silkin's Bill, the report of the Church of England's Church Assembly Board for Social Responsibility and, in part, the judgement in the Bourne case. Abortion, it was agreed, should be legal if, in the view of a medical practitioner, termination was necessary because 'The continuance of the pregnancy would involve serious risk to the life or grave injury to the health whether physical or mental of the pregnant woman whether before, at or after the birth of the child'; 'There is a substantial risk that if the child were born it would suffer from such physical or mental abnormalities as to deprive it of any prospect of reasonable enjoyment of life'; and 'The pregnant woman became pregnant while under the age of sixteen, or as the result of intercourse which was a criminal offence'.[96]

The Steel Bill

Just as Lord Silkin had anticipated, there were parallel stirrings in the House of Commons as private member's bills were drafted in the new Session of Parliament. One such bill, initiated by the Conservative Member for Dorset West, Simon Wingfield Digby, and with support from the Labour Member, Renée Short, and the Conservative Member, Joan Vickers, had been introduced on 12 February. It was a bill more restricted in wording than Renée Short's and Lord Silkin's own earlier draft legislation, having attempted to avoid some of the difficulties encountered by Lord Silkin's bill,[97] but it was couched in what were tantamount to proto-feminist terms[98] and it was buttressed by the provision of milder penalties for illegal abortions. Its object, said its sponsor, was again to 'alter the Victorian law', the Offences Against the Person Act, 1861, and 'make it permissible positively to carry out an abortion in certain clearly defined circumstances'.[99] It suffered a like fate to Kenneth Robinson's and Renée Short's bills, being 'talked out' by two brothers, both Catholic Labour MPs, Simon and Peter Mahon.[100] Simon Mahon's argument was simple and it came straight from doctrine:[101]

> I am not presuming to speak for the Catholics. I am a layman. I am not a doctor, I am not a lawyer, I am not a priest. Are these the only people qualified to speak on a matter like this? I was 14 when I left school, and I have done my best ever since to try to use whatever enlightenment I was given to put forward the case of my own people. It comes down in the end to whether men can believe that, once conception has taken place, it can be lawful to kill. That is the whole crunch of the argument. All over the world, people are trying to find ways of reducing population and feeding people properly. We are not arguing about contraception, but about conception, and, once it has taken place, is it right and proper to kill that life? ... I wonder whether I dare say to the House and to the country that at one time there were people who did not say, "We will destroy you because you are imperfect, or because you are in the way, but we will destroy you because you are a Jew. We will destroy you because you are a Catholic. We will destroy you because you do not believe what we believe." I have lived through those days, and it is the memory of them which comes to mind when I think of this Bill. ... I am a Catholic, but I am not a Catholic theologian. I do not want anyone to be in any difficulty in understanding the Catholic position in this matter. The responsible voice of Catholicism in this country, the Cardinal Archbishop of Westminster, says that Catholics would not oppose efforts to tidy up the existing law on abortion, just as they did not object to legislation on divorce, but that they cannot, in conscience, support either abortion or divorce.[102]

Another Member whom ALRA had lobbied had been the new Liberal MP for Roxburgh, Selkirk and Peebles, David Steel:[103]

In the beginning I knew very little about abortion. As parliamentary candidates in the 1964 general election, we were lobbied by the Abortion Law Reform Association (ALRA) as to what our attitude would be. I looked at the literature and I ticked the box saying that I would be a supporter of abortion law reform if elected to Parliament. And that was really about the sum total of my thinking on the subject. I did not get elected at the 1964 election but I came in at a by-election six months later. When I drew number three in the Ballot of course I was lobbied by everybody under the sun, including ALRA, so the question then was, would I actually introduce a Bill myself? I did a bit of reading including Alice Jenkins' book A Law for the Rich, and obviously met with ALRA and with Home Office Ministers ... [I] decided this was definitely a worthwhile reform, long overdue, and I was lucky enough to have the place in the Ballot to do it.[104]

It was, he repeated, Alice Jenkins' 'movingly impressive'[105] *Law for the Rich* that had particularly weighed with him. He said in interview:

Alice Jenkins' book, *Law for the Rich*, was one of the things that influenced me to do the Bill 'cause I read that book.... that was indeed the point, it was a law for the rich and in fact, the only time I saw an abortion carried out before the passage of my Bill, was by the General Secretary of the Royal College of Obstetricians and Gynaecologists, ... and when I looked at the case notes that he was dealing with, "I said to him that you know, this is obviously a very articulate, it was a school teacher, a very articulate woman who's been able to persuade you that this is within the law. But it looks to me to be skating on very thin ice." And he said, "yes, but that's why I support your Bill." So in other words, somebody, not necessarily rich with money, but somebody who was well endowed either with money or with ... the gift of argument, could secure an abortion by some means, whereas ordinary women with no money and no persuasive powers, really couldn't.

Abortion law reform as he conceived it was thus focused on redeeming the lot of poor, inarticulate, burdened women who could not get access to safe medical procedures. It was not a matter of eugenics.[106] Neither was it a feminist matter of a woman's right to control her own body. That came later.[107] It was not the case made by ALRA,[108] and it was not the case he made:

... it wasn't even on the radar at that time. It is interesting how things have evolved that the woman's right to choose has become a sort of slogan, not just in this country but in the United States and you could argue internationally. But I don't think that featured at all in the 60s. It was simply a question of trying to undo the damage which was being done by the supposed prohibition on abortion. In other words, the number of deaths, the number of admissions for septic and incomplete abortions as it was called then, in all the hospital wards. ... I don't think, if you look in the *Hansard*, I'm sure you won't, I don't think you'll even find the phrase, a woman's right to choose.

David Steel consulted his constituents and his family about what bill he should seek to introduce. His Abortion Bill, supported, amongst others, by his unsuccessful predecessors, Simon Wingfield Digby and Renée Short, was then presented on 15 June, and was granted a Second Reading on 22 July, just before the summer recess. Although the government again remained neutral on what was deemed to be 'a controversial subject on which wildly differing views are held both in [the] House [of Commons] and in the country',[109] it announced[110] that it would be awarded some extra time by Roy Jenkins,[111] a professed partisan, who had persuaded the cabinet to afford it time and assistance with drafting.[112]

ALRA's drafting committee, including Glanville Williams, observed with satisfaction that the bill was very similar to Lord Silkin's,[113] although it now once again included the provision for termination in cases of rape.[114] They also approved its championing by a Liberal Member who was less markedly aligned with the two major parties ('we could go through the middle',[115] one member recalled). ALRA unanimously endorsed it at its Annual General Meeting in October 1966,[116] and there then began what it believed would be a big, perhaps final, push:

> Should David Steel fail to get the second reading on 22 July (this ... could happen if there were not at least 100 supporting M.P.s voting for the closure at 4 o'clock) the whole campaign would be wrecked and it might be several years before we could again persuade a [*sic*] M.P. with an equally favourable place in the ballot to take a.l.r. [abortion law reform] ... it is generally agreed that this is the moment at which to throw everything we've got (cash included) into making sure that as many M.P.s as possible are persuaded of the vital importance of being present on 22 July.[117]

So it was that ALRA circulated the 382 Members of Parliament it understood to be sympathetic, urged its 1,100 members to write to their Members (although it was noted that they were concentrated in only a few constituencies); commissioned letters to be written by different combinations of committee members to newspapers; arranged a press conference for 14 July; and a mass lobby of the House of Commons on 19 July.[118]

David Steel opened the Second Reading by confessing that he would have preferred the bill to have been a government measure:

> ... this has been a difficult choice for me. It remains my view that it is unfortunate that the practice in the House is for controversial social issues of this kind – issues such as the abolition of capital punishment – to be left

entirely to private Members to bring forward. In my opinion, it would be better if the Government, as part of their social reform, were prepared to bring forward these Measures, although leaving them to be decided entirely on a free vote of Members of the House and of the Government. But this is not so, and I therefore had to consider my choice in the light of the present practice of the House.[119]

He proceeded to recite the judgement in the Bourne case, and observed that 'The judge, in directing the jury, stated that where a medical practitioner was convinced that the effects of a pregnancy on his patient would be to make the woman a physical or mental wreck, he was justified in carrying out the operation. There has been a series of cases since then which have developed this aspect of the law. But there is total uncertainty about the exact legal position. It is left far too much to the judgement of individual practitioners whether they are or are not within the law'. Successive judges had advocated a change in the law. The BMA some thirty years before had come out in favour of change. The Inter-Departmental Committee had argued for change. 'In recent years, the Churches have added their weight to the demands for reform – the Church of England Assembly, the Methodist Conference and, this year, the General Assembly of the Church of Scotland'.[120] There were between 40,000 and 200,000 illegal abortions a year. His bill, partially revised in the aftermath of the House of Lords debate, proposed that an abortion could be performed only if, in the judgement of two qualified medical practitioners, 'the continuance of the pregnancy: …would involve serious risk to the life or of grave injury to health, whether physical or mental, of the pregnant mother, whether before, or after the birth of the child'; if 'there [was] a substantial risk that if the child were born it would suffer from such physical or mental abnormalities as to be seriously handicapped' (and here David Steel pointed to the shift in professional opinion between the 1936 and 1966 BMA reports); if 'a pregnant woman [was] a defective or [had become] pregnant while under the age of 16 or … as a result of rape'; or if there were, more controversially, what were called 'social' circumstances 'other than risk to physical or mental health'. 'If we in Parliament', he continued, 'decide that we want cases of severe social hardship to be considered, we ought to say so. We ought not to demand of the medical profession that they should slip these in under a general Clause relating to physical and mental health'. He then touched on the impact of the bill on the major grouping averse to abortion, the Roman Catholic Church (he had had meetings with the members of a Catholic seminary in his own constituency and was conscious of their position,[121] and he had also received numerous protests from Catholic groups[122]). There would, he said, be a conscience clause that would exempt doctors and nurses opposed to abortion from participating in the procedure:[123]

I entirely respect the doctrine and beliefs of that Church in this matter, but I would point out that the doctrine of the Church is not necessarily permanent. We are seeing now the possibility of a great change in the attitude of the Catholic Church to the whole question of contraception which would have been unthinkable twenty or thirty years ago. My respect for the Catholic position on this question is occasionally dented by references to euthanasia and other matters which are in no way connected with the Bill. There is also nothing in the Bill which compels a Catholic patient or a Catholic doctor to be in any way involved in the termination of a pregnancy, and there is also a clear statement in the Bill that nothing in the Bill affects the protection afforded by the law to the viable foetus.

Roy Jenkins, the Home Secretary, declared his personal support, saying that:

I am myself convinced that the existing law on abortion is uncertain and is also, and perhaps more importantly, harsh and archaic and that it is in urgent need of reform. I take this view because I believe that we have here a major social problem. How can anyone believe otherwise when perhaps as many as 100,000 illegal operations a year take place, that the present law has shown itself quite unable to deal with the problem? I believe this, too, because of the danger which exists at present to those who are forced to resort to back-street abortionists and to the misery which is caused to some of those who fail to get an abortion. I certainly shall have no hesitation in voting for the Second Reading of the Bill. ... I believe it also because it causes many otherwise thoroughly law-abiding citizens to act on the fringe, or perhaps on the wrong side, of the law. As the Minister responsible for law enforcement, I believe that to be a thoroughly bad thing. In addition, there is mounting evidence that public opinion outside is now strongly in favour of a change.[124]

Doctor-MPs, including David Owen[125] and Michael Winstanley,[126] spoke in favour of the bill. But there was also vociferous opposition. Jill Knight,[127] one of the bill's most determined critics, a woman who would fight with great tenacity at the Committee stage, cited the views of gynaecologists working in the city of Birmingham in which her constituency was set,[128] and argued that:

There is something very wrong indeed about this. Babies are not like bad teeth to be jerked out just because they cause suffering. An unborn baby is a baby nevertheless. Would the sponsors of the Bill think it right to kill a baby they can see? Of course they would not. Why then do they think it right to kill one they cannot see? It seems to me that this is a most important point. I have come to believe that those who support abortion on demand do so because in all sincerity they cannot accept that an unborn baby is a human being. Yet surely it is. Its heart beats, it moves, it sleeps, it eats. Uninterfered with, it has a potential life ahead of it of 70 years or more. ... I wish ... to speak about the girl under 16. ... Of course, it is a tragedy that little girls should have babies when they are only 12, 13, or 14 or even 11. But is it morally right to destroy one child to help another, and is having an abortion all that much better than having a baby which, after all, if the mother wants, will quite easily be adopted by parents who want it deeply and will give it a good life?

And the Catholics spoke. One was Kevin McNamara:[129]

> In the Declaration of Human Rights, passed in Plenary Session of the United Nations in 1959, there appeared the following resolution: "The child by reason of its physical and mental immaturity needs special safeguards and care, including appropriate legal protection before as well as after birth". This quotation contains not only the essence of Christian belief, not only the common law of our land, but, from the nature of the Assembly which passed it, the common law of humanity. This is what the Bill seeks to change, for if it does nothing else it legalises the taking of human life... The phrases which are used "substantial risk", "seriously handicapped" – are difficult to interpret and are incapable of precise definition. What exactly does "substantial risk" mean? When Lord Brain wrote his commentary on the first bill of Lord Silkin in the British Medical Journal he pointed out the difficulties which their Lordships have had medically and legally in trying to find a meaning. It is almost impossible to give a definition. How are we to measure this? Where do we draw the line? Rubella was mentioned earlier and the 30 per cent chance of a child being born deformed, but what of the other 70 children in that statistical 100?

The prominent Catholic, Norman St John-Stevas[130] also spoke, although he professed to accept the *Realpolitik* of the debate:

> My personal religious commitments are probably known to hon. Members. I do not seek to build my case against the Bill on those today. In our contemporary pluralist society, which is secular in substance although not in form, religion cannot play a determining role. For better or for worse, theology is no longer queen of the sciences – not absolute ruler, not even a constitutional sovereign; but the voice of theology can be raised, although I should be the first to agree that it should not be imposed. I accept that position fully. There is one point nevertheless which I must stress – and that is the position of those in the medical profession who have a conscientious objection to abortion. I should, therefore, like to see a conscience Clause included in the Bill which would specifically safeguard the interests of those doctors and nurses so that under no circumstances would they be compelled to take part in abortions which were against their conscientious convictions. That would be a fair balance for the extension provided by the Bill.

And Leo Abse raised his fears of eugenics:

> Hon. Members on this side of the House, and many on the other side, too, must believe that, ideally, a society should be such that every child, whether born fatherless, whether born handicapped, whether born in a palace or in a manger, should be received with warmth and be endowed with care. This is our starting point. Let no one suppose that a Bill of this kind can be a triumph for the community. There are societies which are impatient of doctrines which place the same ultimate worth on each personality. These societies are ready to rid themselves of all the weak, whom they regard as encumbrances. The Nazi society, the great life deniers, killed off the aged and the mentally backward. The primitive African tribes, which some of us may have known from our military experience during the war, still commit infanticide against a child lacking a limb, and not long ago the Chinese were leaving the new-born female child to die of exposure and succouring only the male child. Respect for life is the cornerstone of our society today.

(David Steel's much later retort in interview was: 'Nonsense. I remember him saying that and we puzzled over why, why did he take such a strong line? Some unkind people said simply because he'd been involved in all the other three bits of social legislation [homosexual law reform, divorce reform and the abolition of capital punishment], wasn't involved in this and was, therefore, rather jealous'.)

Yet the bill passed on second reading by a substantial and 'unexpectedly large'[131] majority of 223 votes to 29, and next moved on 18 January[132] into a 'long and unhappy'[133] committee stage dominated by supporters, but with four members identified by ALRA as opponents,[134] a stage which was portrayed by ALRA as 'protracted and at times bad-tempered, with extremist views expressed from both sides'.[135] Leo Abse, a hostile member of that committee, offered his own rather dyspeptic recollection of what transpired:

> Any hopes that I had that in the committee stages the Bill could be improved were to be dashed. For two-and-a-half months over twelve bitter sittings, the thirty of us selected to serve were embroiled in the most disagreeable of committee proceedings in my experience. A holy war was waged between the proselytising abortionists and their outright opponents, mostly Catholics; their taunts and jibes, increasingly emotive as time went on, inflamed each other to an unyielding dogmatism ...[136]

David Steel himself 'sat at the ministerial bench, with three ministers from the Home Office, the Ministry of Health and the Scottish Office alongside to give 'expert' guidance. ...'[137] It was in committee that the bill's survival would be resolved, and the committee was awash with stalling amendments.[138] It was there, too, that, in the words of the Secretary of the British Medical

Association, 'its final form will be substantially determined',[139] and members of the Committee were continually lobbied by those who had a stake in what was afoot, including ALRA,[140] the churches and the BMA. The Council of the BMA, for instance, briefed at every step by Sharpe Pritchard, its parliamentary agents, sympathetic lay MPs[141] and its own members in Parliament, talking frequently to David Steel,[142] 'had been very actively engaged in trying to ensure that any legislation which may be enacted shall be acceptable to the majority of the medical profession'.[143] The BMA also carried out a flurry of consultations with members of other organisations in its own hinterland, with, for example, the Medical Defence Union,[144] and the Royal College of Obstetricians and Gynaecologists, as problems arose.[145] It was particularly exercised over proposals for the compulsory notification of abortions and what was called the 'social clause' in the grounds for termination, but it was not to be entirely successful in its representations.[146] It had tried to insist that two medical practitioners should agree on the need for a termination, one of whom should be 'a practitioner having special experience', and it was to be satisfied in the first but not the second particular; it had sought to insist that abortions should be carried out in approved premises, and here, too it had been satisfied; but it had also been averse to the 'inclusion in the grounds for termination of the risk of injury to the physical or mental health of the family, [whereby] Parliament has introduced a non-medical reason for termination of pregnancy which we and the R.C.O.G. profoundly deplore. The effect of this "social clause"', it was to conclude, 'is to introduce into a medical decision non-medical grounds and, in fact, to provide for lawful abortion for reasons which, strictly speaking, are non-therapeutic so far as the patient herself is concerned'. It was to be discontented with the phrasing of the conscience clause, claiming that physicians might not always be able to defend themselves when they chose not to terminate a pregnancy.[147]

It is difficult and probably unnecessary to trace every turn in the bill's serpentine route through the final phases of its progress through Parliament (the discussion centred mainly on the qualifications of the practitioners concerned and the grounds to be specified for the lawful termination of pregnancy[148]) but it should be remarked that it was fought unremittingly. There were opponents within, led principally by the Members of Parliament, Norman St. John-Stevas, Jill Knight and Sir Bernard Braine. There were opponents without, their voices arising from a great ferment of meetings, petitions and lobbies across the land – opponents who were to gather and consolidate themselves, most markedly and formally as S.P.U.C., the Society for the Protection of the Unborn Child,[149] a new organisation specifically launched in January 1967 to defeat the bill and stop the 'wanton killing of many healthy babies'.[150] Its visible leadership was composed of a group of public men and women, in large part practitioners, amongst whom, it is to be noted with some surprise, was Aleck Bourne, who announced that he was distressed that the case to which his name had been attached was being cited in the campaign for enlarging the scope of lawful abortion.[151] Bourne's memoirs had been published in 1962, five years before the founding of S.P.U.C., but he did say there that:

> I have always been very strict in the interpretation of the law. Many times I have been asked if, in my opinion, the law should not be radically liber-alised, as in Sweden, to permit abortion for almost any woman who wants the operation, even on the flimsiest grounds. ... . Those who plead for an extensive relaxation of the law ... have no idea of the very many cases where a woman who, during the first three months, makes a most impas-sioned appeal for her pregnancy to be 'finished,' later, when the baby is born, is thankful indeed that it was not killed while still an embryo. During my long years in practice I have had many a letter of the deepest gratitude for refusing to accede to an early appeal.[152]

The sole pretext for change he would have admitted in 1962 would be that which had emerged very narrowly from the judgement in his own case 24 years before:

> I would like to state what I think about the reform of the law of abortion. With no reservations I would include as an unquestioned justification the termination of pregnancy which has followed the rape of a girl below the age of consent ... provided that she is not a mental defective who is quite indifferent to her pregnancy or even does not realise it, and excluding also the prostitute.[153]

In May 1967, chaired by the eleventh Viscount Barrington, a barrister and dip-lomat, S.P.U.C.'s Executive Committee was composed of a Deputy Chairman, Professor J.S. Scott, M.D., F.R.C.S., F.R.C.O.G.; Edward Henderson, the Bishop of Bath and Wells; Owen Barfield, a writer, poet, solicitor and former Inkling; Professor Sir Andrew Claye, M.D., F.R.C.S., F.R.C.O.G. emeritus professor of obstetrics and gynaecology, Leeds University, and a former presi-dent of the Royal College of Obstetricians and Gynaecologists; Professor Ian Donald M.D., F.R.C.S., F.R.C.O.G., Regius Professor of Midwifery at the University of Glasgow; Frances Foxton SRN, SCM, MTD; Lady Glyn; C.B. Goodhart; the Conservative Member of Parliament for Pudsey, Joseph Hiley; Professor Peter Huntingford M.D., F.R.C.S., F.R.C.O.G. an obstetrician and gynaecologist; Alasdair Mackenzie, Liberal Member of Parliament for Ross and Cromarty; Professor J.C. McClure Browne F.R.C.S., F.R.C.O.G.; Professor H.C. McLaren M.D., F.R.C.S., F.R.C.O.G., Professor of Obstetrics and Gynaecology at the University of Birmingham; the Bishop of Exeter; Dr R.A. Newton, M.D., F.R.C.O.G.; Gordon Oakes, Labour M.P. for Bolton West; Dame Hilda Rose D.B.E., F.R.C.S., F.R.C.O.G.; and Dr Myre Sim, M.D., D.P.M.

It is worth reproducing that list in full because it offers a number of points of interest. There was a great preponderance of eminent doctors and especially of gynaecologists (enabling Cardinal Heenan to observe that 'The pressure is mounting against the Bill. ... Some powerful medical voices have been added to our own ...'[154]) There were two bishops, one of whom, the Bishop of Exeter, the Church of England spokesman on social issues in the House of Lords, had chaired the small sub-committee on abortion at the time of Kenneth Robinson's 1961 bill, and he had spoken prominently, although in measured fashion, in the debate on Lord Silkin's Bill. Dr Myre Sim, it will be remembered, had been a member of the 1966 Committee on Therapeutic Abortion.

Although S.P.U.C. had ties with the churches, and had adopted the *icthos* or ⊂⊗ (representing the first letters of the Greek words for 'Jesus Christ, Son of God') as its symbol,[155] none of the members of that Executive Committee, including the Members of Parliament, was publicly identifiable as a Roman Catholic. Indeed, Catholics were by design to play no part at all in S.P.U.C. The Deputy Chairman, Professor James Scott, told Cardinal Heenan on 31 January 1967: 'I am sure you will appreciate that it is for reasons far removed from religious prejudice that we have deliberately avoided having a Catholic on the Committee...' The Cardinal's reply, two days later, said:

> I am very grateful to you and all concerned for not having a Catholic on the committee. As we agreed in our earlier correspondence it is most important that this should be recognised as an issue not concerning one denomination but all men who regard the moral law as sacred. ... I know that our people will support your society both by attending the meetings and by contributing to the funds. I shall not make a personal subscription for obvious reasons but I shall see that support is forthcoming.[156]

The Society and others who acted in parallel with it inside and outside Parliament had of political necessity to receive only discreet support from a Roman Catholic church which supposed that too close and public a connection with the Hierarchy would blight all prospects of success.[157] It was believed from the outset that it would be unfortunate if there were a suggestion that any group was acting as a Catholic lobby.[158] Cardinal Heenan's Secretary, Monsignor David Norris, wrote to a lay Catholic on 16 May 1967:

> I think that the Cardinal has been working on the lines you suggest, namely, that this is a question of morals and not just a matter of a Catholic pressure group. He feels, therefore, that the Church should try to work with all those people who are attempting to prevent the present Bill from becoming law. We have some hope that the House of Commons will reject the Bill. Mr Norman St John-Stevas who has been fighting the Bill in the House of Commons has some hopes of getting a majority against this present Bill. I think it is most important that the opposition to the Bill should be seen as coming from all Christian bodies and also from those who have no Christian beliefs but some morality.[159]

But his confidence was to evaporate. The Hierarchy took itself more and more to be the voice of an embattled and vilified[160] Christian minority[161] struggling on its own in a largely secular and indifferent world, fearful about the calamity which abortion law reform would bring about.[162] The Cardinal wrote to another Catholic lay person on 26 September 1966: 'It is only by action of people like yourself and your friends – both Catholic and Protestant – that the moral issue on abortion can be presented. If we were to make an appeal for all Catholics to write to their Members of Parliament the cry of "pressure group" would soon be made and resistance would be made more stiff. I suggest therefore that you ask people to write to their M.P. in their own way not making this a Catholic issue but simply one of good ethics'. And that was to be an argument repeatedly made. Catholics inside and outside Parliament[163] could not and should not speak *as* Catholics, because that would only discredit their cause: 'We have organised opposition among well-disposed Members of Parliament but we must be careful not to make this into a Catholic issue. If abstaining from abortion were thought to be a Catholic foible like abstaining from meat on Friday the Bill would have a triumphant progress'.[164] Wherever possible, Catholics should join with those of other faiths or none to obviate the idea that it was they alone who were campaigning against reform.[165] Neither should there be any threat of the withdrawal of Catholic votes at elections: 'there is a clique of M.P.s who are using precisely this argument to show that Catholics are attempting to force Members to vote against their conscience. They are well aware of the numbers of Catholic constituents upon whose votes they rely, and to remind them of this would only tend to exacerbate the argument and lend force to these Members' suggestion that Catholics are using unfair means. ...'[166]

On 21 October 1966, the Hierarchy issued a public statement in an attempt to 'to get the more distasteful parts of the Bill defeated'.[167] A segment of what was said, categorically denouncing the immorality of abortion, has already been cited. It continued:

> Many citizens do not accept the Catholic view. We do not doubt their sincerity and fully understand their desire to amend existing legislation to protect women from the so-called 'back street abortionists'. Catholics do not demand that their own convictions should be imposed by law upon all citizens. They do however claim that doctors, nurses and others who may be affected by the proposed legislation shall not be asked to act against their own conscience. It is our duty to point out that certain clauses of the proposed Bill are contrary to the ethical code hitherto accepted not only by Catholics but by all who hold life sacred. These clauses have already been contested in Parliament. We are confident that Members of Parliament of all creeds will support appropriate amendments.

More privately, a resigned Monsignor Norris observed twelve days later that:

> It has been clear for some time that this Bill will be passed. The opposition to it is so very small that, as a result of established Parliamentary procedure,

the Bill will almost certainly become law next year. There are, however, certain clauses (for example, those concerning "abortion on request") which it may be quite possible to have amended. You will see from the phrasing of the Hierarchy's statement that the bishops are anxious not to give the impression that opposition to these clauses is based exclusively on Catholic doctrine or discipline, but rather on the much broader basis of the universal sanctity of life. The reason for the bishops' anxiety in this regard is their fear that our opposition will be less effective if it is thought to come only from "the Catholic Church". The impression could be given that opposition to abortion is one of those things peculiar to Catholics, like abstaining from meat on Fridays.[168]

The Cardinal and the Hierarchy were thus obliged to act quietly behind the scenes as a source of guidance[169] and exhortation for opposition and doubters, including doubters who, like the Labour Member of Parliament, Tam Dalyell,[170] were not themselves Catholic (Tam Dalyell had voted for David Steel's Bill on Second Reading but did not so again, after his conversation with the Cardinal, on Third Reading). Their aim could no longer be to defeat 'this rather unpleasant Bill'[171] but to curtail the damage it might cause: 'The extent of our opposition is such that we cannot hope to prevent the passing of the … Bill; all our efforts therefore must be directed towards the introducing of amendments which will reduce the number of situations when foetal life can be taken'.[172] What campaigning there was thus tended to be *sub rosa*, conducted by a vanguard composed of the laity[173] rather than of the Church and Catholics,[174] intended to mitigate or delay[175] harm, and inspired by little animosity to ALRA[176] or David Steel personally[177] but by objections flowing from theology and the teachings of the Church. The Church would do what it could, it would make its case, it would work discreetly,[178] but it anticipated no victory:

> Catholic M.P.'s have had a number of meetings about the Abortion Bill. The Catholics in the House of Lords made some good speeches in opposition. Doctors and M.P.'s are having regular meetings and planned strategy for when the Bill comes to the Commons. There is not the slightest chance of stopping its passage but you may be quite sure that Catholic voices will be raised against it.[179]

By March 1967, the passage of David Steel's bill, like that of Sydney Silverman's other bill which was before Parliament at much the same time, hinged critically on the ceding of enough time to allow the third reading, and attempts were made to prevent that happening.[180] ALRA wrote to its members:

> The opposition will undoubtedly stake everything on being able either substantially to amend the Bill, even at that late stage, or to frustrate the Third reading on the same day. If the opposition tactics succeed, the Bill

will not get its Third reading and will then fall UNLESS the Government is willing to provide time for its completion in the House of Commons. This is by no means likely. In any case, if the Bill is to become law it still then has to go through the House of Lords, and if all this is not completed by August 3rd the Bill will lapse altogether.[181]

Norman St. John-Stevas[182] exhorted the cardinal to emerge publicly to appeal to the Prime Minister, Harold Wilson, to deny the bill the time it needed to pass ('I think', he said, 'it would also be of considerable help if you could write a personal letter to him saying that Catholics would be greatly distressed if the Government facilitates the passage of the Bill by granting it time'[183]). But the Cardinal remained reluctant, replying on 23 March: 'What I am anxious to avoid is handing ammunition to the proposers of the Bill – who repeatedly say that the only opposition is from R.C.'s – by writing to Wilson. That I had done so would soon be known throughout Parliament. If all else fails then I shall call to see Wilson at 10 Downing Street. That would be better than writing a letter'. Six weeks later, on 9 May, Norman St. John-Stevas wrote again in what was to be his last fling:

> The position now is that the Bill is down for Report and Third Reading on June 2nd. We have tabled various amendments to the Bill, and it is not quite clear that the Report Stage cannot be concluded at the Report Stage, let alone the Third Reading. The only other Private Members' Day left is June 16th and there are already five bills down for consideration on that day. This means that the Abortion Bill can only pass if the Government gives it time. I therefore think it of vital importance that you should see the Prime Minister privately and express the view that the Catholic population would be outraged if the Government facilitates the passage of this bill. I think the best time to see him would be early June. Certainly as soon after June 2nd as possible.

The cabinet was still displaying some signs of nervousness in its deliberations. It was evident that, despite the support of individual ministers, it continued to treat the issue of abortion with trepidation. The Prime Minister was advised by the cabinet secretary, Burke Trend, that 'to give time would be in accordance with the view that the Government ought to facilitate Parliamentary consideration of social issues on which they do not feel able to promote legislation themselves, particularly where there is a fair measure of Parliamentary support for reform; and there is much to be said for enabling Bills to get through if a little Government help now will avoid pressure for more Government help to be given next session in the event of their failing this session'. Yet there were also difficulties, Burke Trend continued: the Bill had met with significant opposition; it would require a significant amount of Parliamentary time – more perhaps than the government could cede; the Government itself was not well disposed to the clause allowing abortion to preserve the well-being of the woman, although removing that clause would not meet with the support of the reformers: 'But if in order to get the Bill put in proper form the Government have to say that they will accept the Bill so amended but not otherwise must they not expect Ministers to vote in support of this stand?'[184] And might not the attempt to secure the passage of a bill so amended signal that the government had departed from its policy of neutrality?

Roy Jenkins, the Home Secretary reported how, at its meeting of 11 May, Cabinet had resolved uneasily to ask the Legislation Committee to consider whether to award the Bill extra time: 'The Committee met on 30th May and there was general agreement, the Lord Privy Seal [the Catholic Lord Longford] dissenting, that Government time should if necessary be found for the remaining stages of the Bill'.[185] And, he was to tell Cabinet:

> The Bill was down for consideration of Report and Third Reading on 2nd June but was unlikely to be completed in the House of Commons unless the Government provided time. This might be found after 7 p.m. on 3rd July, when the 10 o'clock Rule could be suspended to enable the debate to continue until completed.

Cabinet was reported to have been in a dither:

> It was pointed out however that to provide Government time for the Bill would imply that the Government were in favour of its principle, on which they had so far taken no view; and, while this would be welcome to some sections of public opinion, it would undoubtedly alarm others. On the other hand it was arguable that on an issue of such social importance the Government ought to give time (unless the Bill as it emerged from Committee was bad in form) notwithstanding that this might be thought to imply Government support for the principle. The provision of time might indeed afford an opportunity for the opponents of the Bill to deploy their arguments in favour of its rejection and the appointment of a Royal Commission to consider the whole problem.[186]

Cardinal Heenan did eventually take Norman St. John-Stevas' advice and approached the Prime Minister, and supporting him inside the Cabinet itself, Lord Longford, the devoutly religious Lord Privy Seal, described by Cardinal Heenan as an 'excellent Catholic',[187] sought to put the case that abortion was not properly a Catholic issue at all but one for the public as a whole:

> Recent articles in the Press suggesting that the Government proposed to "come to the rescue" of the Bill and to "defeat a filibuster" had created an impression of Government support which would be confirmed in the public mind if Government facilities were now given. This might do harm to the Government's reputation with considerable sections of

public opinion which were by no means wholly Roman Catholic, as was illustrated by the collection of 500,000 signatures to a petition against the Bill which had been organised by [S.P.U.C.] a non-Roman Catholic Committee.[188]

But the Cardinal and Lord Longford were rebuffed. A cabinet stocked with members sympathetic to the bill[189] resolved at last on 1 June that: 'if the Bill failed to complete its remaining stages in Private Members' time Government time should be given on one evening after 7 p.m. The Lord President in announcing this decision later in the day should make it clear that the Government were providing time in order to enable the House to reach a decision on the Bill and that the Government's attitude of neutrality was maintained. Ministers should be free to vote as they considered right ...' So it was that Harold Wilson came to tell the cardinal six days later:

> I was interested to read what you said about the Abortion Bill. I am afraid you will not agree, but I am sure it is right that the Government should provide time for the remaining stages of this Bill. It received a Second Reading by a decisive majority, and although I am certainly receiving a large number of letters opposing the Bill, I am also receiving many supporting it. The opinion polls suggest that in the country as a whole there is a strong majority in favour of abortion law reform. The Steel Bill, as it came out of Committee, contained a number of objectionable features, but the sponsors have themselves put down amendments to overcome those. In these circumstances the Government felt that, while maintaining a position of neutrality towards the Bill itself, it would be quite wrong to allow it simply to be talked out, as would undoubtedly happen if more time were not provided. If the Bill is enacted, its provisions will not of course force anyone who has conscientious scruples to undergo or carry out an abortion, and while I deeply respect your own feelings on this subject, and agree that it raises ethical rather than primarily religious issues, I cannot believe it would be right to prevent Parliament from reaching a decision on the Bill now, or that a further inquiry would add any very useful information.

When the bill did come before the House of Commons again for the Report Stage on 2 June, it was to confront a mass of 57 amendments, some supported signally by the Church of England.[190] There was, for example, the amendment arguing for the need to establish a 'panel of medical practitioners ... including physicians, surgeons and psychiatrists to undertake compliance' with the requirements of the Bill'. Quintin Hogg, then in opposition, protested that 'There are no adequate safeguards against a racket'. But David Steel objected that protections were already built into the proposed legislation, that the intervention of such a panel would only delay an operation which 'should be carried out at the earliest possible opportunity', and that the proposal had not received universal support from members of the medical profession. And the amendment was defeated by 184 votes to 116.[191] There were other attempts to amend the bill some three weeks later. One sought to restrict the indications for abortion, say, to 'cases where there was "a probability of death or severe permanent" damage to health' instead of the presence of a mere 'risk'. And here, as in other debates, the Minister of Health, Kenneth Robinson, entered to support the existing wording of the bill: 'I draw the attention of the House to a letter in *The Times* of 29 May last, signed by the President of the Royal College of Obstetricians and Gynaecologists, the Chairman of the British Medical Association's Council and other distinguished doctors, setting out the terms of the bill which they would support and, relative to this series of amendments, they have no qualifications about the matter'. The amendment was defeated by 179 votes to 97.[192] Another attempt, chiefly undertaken by Jill Knight, to remove the 'social conditions' clause of the bill, was defeated by 166 votes to 66.[193] And so it went on, in a 12-hour debate lasting until 10 o'clock the following morning, a debate in which allegations of filibustering were angrily made and angrily rejected. In yet another protracted debate on 13 July, lasting from 10.45 p.m. to 3 a.m. the next day, there was further discussion of those 57 amendments, including an amendment to the clause on rape, which again rehearsed the arguments about the evidential and forensic difficulties of establishing whether an offence had taken place (one Member observed 'One does not have to be a lawyer to know the difficulty of proving an allegation of rape. One is not proved guilty by two doctors and an allegation'.[194]); although, on this occasion, Jill Knight favoured the retention of the clause if the woman alleging rape reported it to the police within 48 hours. *The Times* observed the next day that 'Barring total collapse by Mr St. John–Stevas and his fellow opponents of the Medical Termination of Pregnancy Bill it was clear by 3 a.m. today that the report stage would not be concluded by the time the debate would have to give way to today's Government business'.[195] The Leader of the House would not commit himself towards the very end, at 10.15 in the morning, on the question of whether the government would yet again afford extra time ('We shall think over it' he said. 'As for our intentions about the Bill, we must await the next business statement'). The bill was evidently in 'serious trouble', and the cabinet was obliged to consider 'whether further all-night sittings should be arranged to allow the forces for and against the Bill to battle it out to the bitter end. But Ministers are under pressure from M.P.s who object to such special treatment being given to one particular private member's measure'.[196]

David Steel did get his third reading on 14 July, Roy Jenkins telling the House of Commons that a decision should be reached whatever it might be. David Steel recalled:

> The Second Reading was carried overwhelmingly … and that was a good start. But in Committee, the opponents were very vocal and were determined … Because, as you know, one of the weapons in opposition

to any legislation is delay. Put down lots of amendments, beaver away at it. And actually at Report Stage we ran out of time because we didn't finish on the day we were allocated. And I had to go to the Government and ask for another day. Now that's unusual. You don't get other days given to private Members. And I had to go to see Richard Crossman, who was the Leader of the House, and I remember it well. ... I was in awe of this great man. You know, I'm a new, very young MP and he was the Leader of the House, a senior political figure. And I had to see him in his room and ask if the Government would allocate another day to get this Bill finished and ... his colleagues in the Cabinet were ... saying "come on, you've got to give it another day because otherwise this issue is going to keep coming back, this is the 7th bill we've had so far. Let's get this thing finished one way or another." So the Government did give a second day to the report stage and without that it would never have got through.[197]

Peter Jackson, the Labour Member for High Peak, reflected long afterwards that 'there had not ... been an occasion when a Private Member's Bill had been so accommodated by a government'.[198]

It was to be another long debate. Norman St. John-Stevas himself put it that it was not a filibuster but a determination to make use of normal Parliamentary procedures as a legitimate means of delaying the passage of a bill to which there were strong objections of principle, but others demurred. It was to be an acrimonious debate in which Peter Mahon asserted, for example, that the choice was between life sanctified by God and legalised infanticide. It was won by the reformers by 167 votes to 83 and moved to the House of Lords on 19 July, where Lord Longford, the Leader of the House, removed himself from the government front bench and sat amongst the bishops to attack it.

A 'conscience clause', promised by David Steel, was inserted (and later accepted on third reading in the House of Commons). The 'social clause' was again assailed by the Archbishop of Canterbury and successfully removed by a single vote (and then restored in an amendment introduced by Lord Silkin in October). The bill was finally approved on Third Reading in the Commons on 25 October by 188 votes to 94. 'We dealt', remembered Roy Jenkins, with a 'fourteen-hour filibuster only by making it clear that we were prepared if necessary to keep the House sitting throughout Friday night and Saturday to get the bill. The 120 people (against 40 on the other side) who had already stayed voluntarily throughout two nights ... were resolved to complete the job. It was indeed the liberal hour'.[199]

The Act received Royal Assent at the end of October 1967 but, just as had been the case with the abolition of capital punishment, there was to be no cessation to the altercation about the law on and surrounding abortion. A succession of private member's bills attempted to undo all or part of the 1929 and 1967 Acts. Bills were presented by a number of Members of

Parliament – David Alton, John Campbell, Sir Bernard Braine, John Benyon and Norman St. John-Stevas – some of whom were prominent Catholics. One bill, moved by John Corrie, the newly elected Conservative Member for Cunninghame North, cited the recommendation of a 1970 report by the Department of Health and Social Security, and proposed an upper limit of 20 weeks pregnancy for lawful terminations.[200] It fell, despite significant support, in March 1980, but it is instructive briefly to consider the course of discussions about its consequences because it underscores a number of the themes that I have sought to advance.

Ministers of the Department of Health and Social Security had approached the Royal College of Obstetricians and Gynaecologists for their advice on foetal viability after the debate on the Corrie Bill. The ensuing report of the Royal College's Working Party, sent to the Department's Chief Medical Officer, recommended that the clinical judgement exercised in the 1920s was no longer appropriate and that there should be a reduction in the presumptive age of capacity to be born alive in section 1(2) of the Infant Life (Preservation Act) 1929 from 28 weeks to 24 weeks, the chance of survival in the 1980s for babies of 27 weeks' gestation having, it was claimed, become greater than 50%. Yet it was recognised that abortion remained highly controversial, the 1929 and 1967 Acts were fused together in the political mind, and any suggested amendment to the one could revive debate about the other. It was an area, some thought, best left alone.[201] When a DHSS official broached a proposal to his counterpart in the Home Office that 'we need seriously to consider … the possibility of legislation to reduce the 28 weeks in ILPA to around 24',[202] another Home Office official notably observed that 'it seems to me extraordinary that DHSS should seem to think that the 1929 Act could easily be amended without opening up the general question of abortion legislation in Parliament. … The fact remains that the two Acts are publicly seen to be connected. I suspect that the last thing our Ministers would want is would be [sic] to involve themselves in this area of controversy'.[203]

Some Ministers in the Conservative administration under Margaret Thatcher continued to be minded to act, and the Secretaries of State for the Home Office and Department of State for Social Services resolved in late 1984 that there should be discussion about amending legislation to bring practice into greater conformity with current medical judgement.[204] One catalyst was the failed Corrie Bill; a second was yet another, impending private member's bill; a third the report of the Royal College's working party; and the last a consciousness of the way in which the 1929 Act appeared vulnerable to abuse:

> there are a small number of doctors who continue to carry out late terminations (which can be lucrative), relying on the letter of the law to justify non-compliance with recommended clinical practice. In many such cases the effect must be to destroy a child capable of being born alive, and thus to render the doctor liable in principle to prosecution, since strictly

speaking the Act already protects all babies capable of being born alive, and thus to render the doctor liable in principle to prosecution, since strictly speaking the Act already protects all babies capable of being born alive ... But in practice it is impossible to find evidence sufficient to negative the presumption; it is only those who carry out the operation who could supply the evidence.[205]

Ministers thought there should be no government bill (abortion had always been a matter for private Members and governments had always professed their neutrality), but a private member's bill with government support: 'The proposal is that the Bill should be drawn very narrowly indeed: quite simply, that it should substitute '24' for '28' in the 1929 Act'. They recognised that 'Any Bill inevitably presents some risk of fuelling controversy about the abortion law in general ... and it will therefore be important to resist any pressure to widen the scope of the Bill and to maintain neutrality on abortion itself'.[206]

In the event, although a proposal was indeed made that a suitable bill should be included on the list of those suitable for offering to private members successful in the ballot, it soon evaporated. The Home Office might have remained steadfast, but the Department for Health and Social Services, the department that had first mooted legislation, began to falter. Whilst the Home Secretary, Leon Brittan, was noted by his officials to be eager to promote legislation,[207] Kenneth Clarke, the Minister for Health, had begun to entertain doubts, saying to him:

> I understand you are inclined to seek colleagues' agreement to offer-
> ing a private member a short bill to amend the ... Act, in the autumn.
> I am writing to express my strong reservations about Government
> initiation of legislative action. ... there is ... diehard opinion on both
> sides of the abortion argument which would, in my opinion, make
> compromise on even [a] single measure impossible. Nor would there
> be any prospect of all-party agreement as opinions are cross-party and
> fundamental.[208]

Leon Brittan's reply was: 'I entirely agree that there can be no question of adding a Government Bill ... to the next Session's legislative programme. I also accept that it must be doubtful whether such a Bill, if entrusted to a Private Member, would have an easy passage. I do, however, wonder whether that is a sufficient reason for not making the attempt'.[209]

After a change of ministers, Leon Brittan having been succeeded by Douglas Hurd, and Kenneth Clarke by Barney Hayhoe in September 1985, the Home Office continued to push matters forward, albeit in gingerly fashion, and it gave instructions to Parliamentary Counsel in October 1985.[210] But the nervousness of the Department for Health and Social Services had increased (the new Home Secretary was advised that 'despite a very encouraging letter from Mr Hayhoe on 20 September, DHSS Ministers now seem to be considerably less enthusiastic about a Bill than Home Office Ministers'.[211]) The proposal did go forward to a delayed meeting of H Committee of Cabinet on 23 October 1985, and it was endorsed, but any possible legislation was then stalled until what was thought to be another contentious and loosely coupled matter, the report of the Warnock Committee on human fertilisation and embryology, came before Parliament. The one controversy, it was thought, might profitably be used to distract attention from the other. [212]

John Biffen, the Lord Privy Seal and Leader of the House of Commons, wrote to Douglas Hurd on 12 November 1985:

> I have concluded that it would not be right to include the Bill on the Private Members' handout list for this Session. I am sure that the measure would be entirely suitable for any Session in which we were taking action on the Warnock Report, or after we had done so, but I would not wish to risk upsetting the delicate balance we are trying to construct to delay action on the Warnock Report this Session by stimulating other measures affecting the unborn child.[213]

Douglas Hurd's observation on 13 November was:

> I would like to sign off by repeating my belief that it is wrong to leave a matter of this importance to voluntary arrangements, and that early legislation is therefore desirable. But I must reluctantly accept his and DHSS' judgement on the relationship with Warnock.

And matters remained stalled. Douglas Hurd was informed by John Biffen six months later:

> … I do not think we should offer the Infant Life Preservation Bill for next Session. As you know, Cabinet has decided not to include a Warnock Bill in next Session's programme and I am concerned that the absence of a Government Bill might provoke a Private Member's Bill. I have been discussing the problems this might cause with Norman Fowler [the Secretary of State for Health and Social Security] and our current intention is that we should publish a consultation paper on the Warnock proposals at the beginning of the Session. While your Bill does not deal with issues directly relevant to those covered in the Warnock Report, I think that the timing of its possible passage through the House would be extremely awkward in the light of these plans.[214]

Delay continued. It was not to be until 1987 that an announcement about legislation on the Warnock Report was announced;[215] 1988 when a White Paper was announced;[216] 1989 when legislation was proposed;[217] and 1990 when an Act, the Human Fertilisation and Embryology Act (c. 37), was passed, establishing a regulatory authority to license the 'use in treatment, storage and research of human embryos outside the body'.[218] Folded into that Act, almost secreted as it were, was Section 37 which amended the 1967 Abortion Act to provide for a shorter period of 24 weeks before the termination of pregnancy became unlawful.[219] Moving it on second reading, the Lord Chancellor, Lord Mackay, talked exclusively about the Warnock Report, the treatment of infertility and research on embryos, and made no reference at all to abortion.[220] During the eight-hour debate that followed, there was scarce mention of abortion and the 1929 and 1967 Acts. What *was* said consisted of exhortations not to allow the debate to stray into what was represented as an unrelated area. Lord Ennals,[221] for example, observed:

> In the Long Title of the Bill the Government have incorporated the words: "To make provision in connection with human embryos and any subsequent development of such embryos". That was clearly a decision paving the way for this Bill on embryo research and in vitro fertilisation to be used as a vehicle for a wide ranging discussion of decisions and amendments raising again the whole issue of the 1967 Abortion Act. I cannot say that I am other than saddened by the possible effect on the quality of our debate on the Bill. It is a decision I greatly regret. The issues tackled by the noble Baroness and her team and by the Bill are quite different from the issue of the medical termination of pregnancy.

And that was to be a plea that was echoed by a number of peers who wished to sever discussion of what they considered to be the overwhelmingly important implications of the Warnock Report from a consideration of abortion law reform. The former President of the British Medical Association and of the General Medical Council, Lord Walton,[222] remarked that 'attempts to amend the 1967 Abortion Act are irrelevant in relation to the Human Fertilisation and Embryology Bill and should be addressed quite separately and on another occasion. Otherwise, there is a serious danger that attention might well be diverted from the vital matters which we are considering today'. Lord Henderson[223] said: 'There is no doubt that, from all quarters of the House, the plea has been made, as it was made most seriously and effectively by Sir George Porter, the president of the Royal Society, that the two subjects of the Warnock legislation, as one might loosely call it, and abortion should be kept severely apart'. No amendments on abortion were tabled, the period in which terminations could take place was abridged, and the law passed.

It is clear that after 1967 many politicians felt loath to become mired again in the controversies which abortion stirred up. The rate of terminations was to climb steadily and then reached something of a plateau just below 200,000 a year, 91% of which were funded by the National Health Service:[224] Abortion had become firmly institutionalised as a lawful procedure in England and Wales:

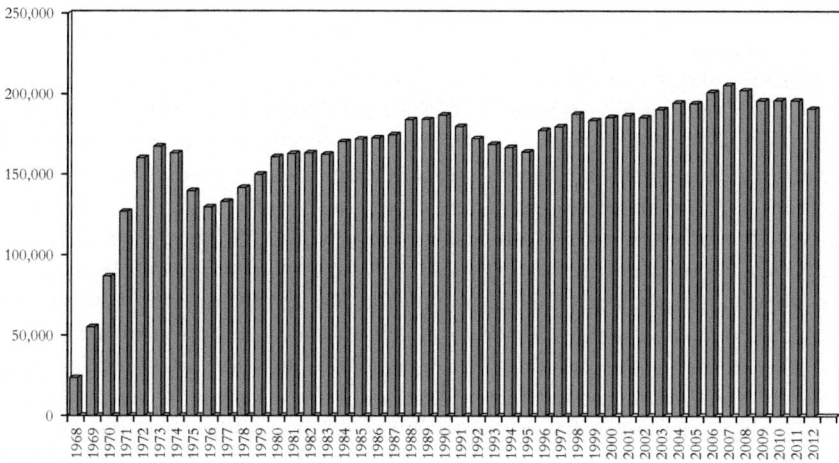

Figure 5.1 Abortions in England and Wales 1968–2012

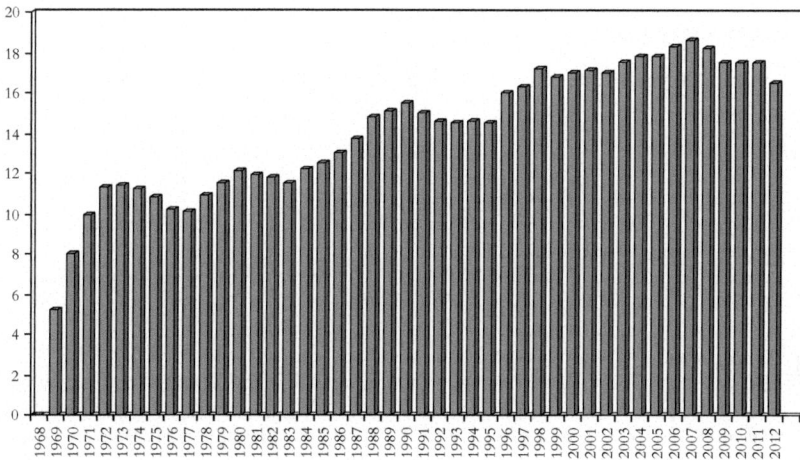

Figure 5.2 Rate of abortions per 1,000 women residents aged 15–44 in England and Wales 1968–2012

(Based on *Statistical data on abortion statistics in England and Wales for 2012*, Department of Health, July 2013: https://www.gov.uk/government/statistical-data-sets/statistics-on-abortions-carried-out-in-england-and-wales-in-2012)

Conclusion

The matter of abortion had been from the first a difficult and sensitive area of law, morals, practice and politics, central to religion and conceptions of what was called the sanctity of life, and it impinged heavily on the churches and the professions. It demonstrates how the criminal justice system is not neatly bounded or contained but merged almost seamlessly with other institutional and professional domains. There could be no final, agreed resolution of the interminable debates about its reform. Like capital punishment, it was contested in Westminster, the core institution of a centralised state, but it was considered terrain best avoided by government, entrusted, if at all, to private members who faced a prolonged struggle. Like capital punishment, it was infused, on the one hand, with a distinctively British utilitarianism that stemmed from the great reforming era of the 1830s, a utilitarianism[225] that lent itself to synthesis with a moderate theology emanating from the Moral Welfare Committee; and, on the other, with an absolutist morality which stemmed from Roman Catholicism and the fundamentalism of a Christianity of the Book. In the end it was utilitarianism that trumped absolutism, the reasoning contrived by the Committee making it possible for an unconditional proscription on killing to give way to the felicific calculus and a weighing of the value of one life against another. And each successive piece of legislation in the history of its reform was indissolubly linked to its fellows, so that the legal and political ramifications of the 1861, 1929 and 1967 Acts so continually played on one another that it was difficult to amend the one without raising the spectre of the others.

Acknowledgements

I am grateful to Lord Steel for commenting on an earlier draft of this chapter.

Notes

1   Minutes of the Meeting of the Executive Committee of the Abortion Law Reform Association, 7 September 1965, Appendix 1. ALRA Papers in the Wellcome Institute for the History of Medicine.
2   Letter to *The Times*, 31 January 1966.
3   HC Deb 25 February 1966 Vol. 725 cc837–56.
4   Abortion Law Reform Association (1964–65); *Annual Report*, 1.
5   Almost as if seeking for corroboration, Lord Stonham said in debate that 'Your Lordships will know that I have consistently held that Parliament should do what it considers right and refuse to be governed by Gallup Poll, but we can be in no doubt that attitudes toward abortion have changed and are changing. There is an increasing public awareness of the serious social problem of illegal abortions and a greater understanding of the distressing circumstances which can lead women to it. There is a substantial body of opinion which believes that the present law is unrealistic and inhumane. ... We must also attach special weight to the views of the medical profession', he said. 'The proposed changes would impose considerable responsibilities upon doctors, and we have to be sure that they are willing and able to carry them. Last year, as I understand, 70 per cent. of the 750 London doctors who took part in a survey organised by the Abortion Law Reform Association pronounced in favour of reform of the law, and the Socialist Medical Association are also in favour'. HL Deb 30 November 1965 Vol. 270 cc1139–241.
6   And it was able to brief members about whom to approach. To one woman in Glasgow, for instance, Dilys Cossey, the Secretary could write on 11 July 1966: 'Why don't you write to all the Glasgow MPs whose constituencies you cover using the address of the person who actually lives in the constituency and all signing the letter... Of the Glasgow MPs the following are for some reform of the abortion law [and six names were listed]. We know nothing of the opinions of [six named MPs]. Edward

Taylor, Cathcart, could do with shaking up; we talked to him at some length at the time of Mrs. Renee Short's Bill in June, 1965, and he felt that his constituents did not think that this was necessary. The two remaining MPs, Mrs. Alice Cullen, Gorbals, and Richard Buchanan, Springburn, are both Roman Catholics'.

7 Minutes of the Meeting of the Executive Committee of the Abortion Law Reform Association, 19 May 1966. ALRA Papers in the Wellcome Institute for the History of Medicine.

8 Lewis Silkin, 1889–1972, became Labour Member of Parliament for Peckham in 1936 until his seat was abolished and he accepted a peerage in 1950, becoming deputy leader of the opposition in the House of Lords in 1955. (Based on the entry by R. Weight in the *Oxford Dictionary of National Biography*, http://www.oxforddnb.com/view/article/31684?docPos=1). His son, John Silkin, 1923–1987, became Labour Member of Parliament for Deptford in 1963 and Chief Whip between 1966 and 1969.

9 Minutes of the Executive Committee of the Abortion Law Reform Association, 7 October 1965.

10 Clause C of his draft bill contained, for example, the provision that abortion would be lawful if it were conducted 'in the belief that the health of the patient or the social conditions in which she is living (including the social conditions of her existing children) make her unsuitable to assume the legal and moral responsibility for caring for a child or another child as the case may be …' Minutes of the Meeting of the Executive Committee of the Abortion Law Reform Association, 7 October 1965. Appendix 3. ALRA Papers in the Wellcome Institute for the History of Medicine. That clause was later to be amended to contain the phrase 'the pregnant woman's capacity as a mother would be (severely) overstrained by the care of a child or another child as the case may be'. Minutes of the Meeting of the Executive Committee of the Abortion Law Reform Association, 19 May 1966.

11 Minutes of the Meeting of the Executive Committee of the Abortion Law Reform Association, 7 September 1965. ALRA Papers in the Wellcome Institute for the History of Medicine.

12 HL Deb 30 November 1965 Vol. 270 cc1139–24.

13 Lord Gardiner, the future Lord Chancellor, said just before the general election that he was in favour of abortion law reform but 'This again is another question which I think a Labour government, if it thought it had time for it at all, would probably leave to a free vote of the House'. 'Lord Gardiner Interviewed', *The Economist*, 28 March 1964, 1212.

14 The early view of that Committee was that: '<u>Maternal Health</u> We prefer the wording contained in Clause 1 of the Church Assembly Board for Social Responsibility. <u>Other Indications</u> We consider that the physical or mental inadequacy of the woman to be a mother … or the fact that she is under age of 16, are not, in themselves, sufficient grounds for terminating pregnancy. <u>Safeguards</u> We attach the greatest importance to the inclusion of a provision to regulate the places in which such operations may properly be carried out and to ensure that the management of the case is in experienced hands. <u>Notification</u> We do not approve of the police being given access to the register of operations'. (David Stevenson, Secretary of the BMA, to Lord Cohen, 31 January 1966). Later comments, made in November 1966, said flatly that 'Clauses 1(c) and (d) are objectionable in specifying indications which are not medical. They will, in our opinion, give rise to serious difficulties in practice. They might well lead to an excessive demand for termination on social grounds and this would be unacceptable to the medical profession. …' ALRA's observation was that all these recommendations were excessively restrictive, arguing, for example, that 'The insistence that the operation "has to be carried out in a National Health hospital or other place approved for the purpose by the Minister", and the consequent deletion of a registered nursing home from the Bill is another piece of restrictionism. … ALRA cannot believe

that the insistence upon the use of a consultant is motivated by a desire to protect the patient from unskilled operators – rather it is the result of a particular moral or religious bias which we should not seek to enforce by law. ... There is already severe pressure on beds in hospitals and maternity units. If places are excluded where terminations are now being performed and no alternative accommodation is provided, the result will be the opposite of the intention of the Bill, namely to liberalise the law and practice and so bring about a decrease in the number of unqualified operators. ... Indications ... For the BMA and RCOG to say ... that clauses 1(c) and (d) "are objectionable in specifying indications which are not medical" indicates a serious confusion of thought. The fact that the operation is being carried out by a medical practitioner need not carry the automatic implication that it is carried out on medical grounds'. (Letter from Vera Houghton, ALRA, to David Stevenson, Secretary BMA, 16 January 1967) Elsewhere, Madeleine Simm was to argue that there were only 500 suitable consultants in the field, 'many of [whom] had religious or conscientious objections to the operation. If every woman requiring legal abortion had to pass through this narrow filter, then the "reform" might well, as Mr. Richard Sharpies, M.P. observed in Committee (March 1, col. 353), "restrict abortions beyond the existing law established by case law"'. (M. Simms (April 1974); 'Abortion Law and Medical Freedom', *The British Journal of Criminology*, Vol. 14, No. 2, 121.)

15 Conclusions of a Meeting of the Cabinet held at 10 Downing Street ... on 25 November, 1965. CC (65) 64th Conclusions.

16 HL Deb 30 November 1965 Vol. 270 cc1139–241.

17 Mervyn Stockwood, 1913–1995, 'an outspoken socialist', read theology at Cambridge University, becoming a deacon and then a priest in Bristol. He was to become Bishop of Southwark in 1958. (Based on the entry by M. De la Noy in the *Oxford Dictionary of National Biography*, http://www.oxforddnb.com/view/article/57972)

18 According to the Parliamentary adviser to the Bishop of London, with whom I had a conversation, it was understood conventionally and after discussion amongst the Peers Spiritual that there should be a division of labour in which different bishops addressed different areas of policy.

19 See his address on abortion to the Convocation of Canterbury on 17 January 1967, in *Canterbury Pilgrim* (1974); London: SPCK, 165.

20 HL Deb 30 November 1965 Vol. 270 cc1139–241.

21 Lord Brain, 1895–1966, was consultant neurologist at the London Hospital; president of the Royal College of Physicians, 1950–57; president of the Association of Physicians, 1956; president of the Association of British Neurologists in 1960; president of the International Society of Internal Medicine (1958); and president of the British Association for the Advancement of Science, 1963–4. He was made Baron Brain of Eynsham in 1962. (Based on the entry by G. Pickering in the *Oxford Dictionary of National Biography*, http://www.oxforddnb.com/view/article/32035).

22 Lord Clifford sent a copy of his speech to Cardinal Heenan, who replied: 'It seems so sad that it is left mainly to Catholics to object to the Abortion Bill. I am so afraid that the general public will think that this has nothing to with ethics but is just another example of the funny ideas Catholics have. ...' Papers of Cardinal Heenan in the Westminster Diocesan Archives. AAW HE/A1(a)

23 Where, for example, the Bishop of Exeter raised doubts about terminating pregnancies where there was a risk of abnormality: was it right, he asked, to say that it would be better if a child with abnormalities should not be born? *The Times*, 2 February 1966.

24 See *The Times*, 19 February 1966.

25 HL Deb 3 February 1966 Vol. 272 cc491–557.

26 *The Times*, 4 February 1966.

27 The new clauses read that an abortion would be lawful if '(a) the continuance of the pregnancy would involve serious risk to the life or grave injury to the health whether

physical or mental of the pregnant woman whether before at or after the birth of the child; or (*b*) the child if born would be likely to suffer from such physical or mental abnormalities as to deprive it of any prospect of reasonable enjoyment of life; or (*c*) the pregnant woman is or will be physically or mentally inadequate to be the mother of a child or of another child as the case may be; or (*d*) the pregnant woman is a defective or became pregnant when under the age of sixteen or as the result of rape or of intercourse which was an offence under section 128 of the Mental Health Act 1959 or section 97 of the Mental Health (Scotland) Act 1960 (relating to sexual intercourse with patients)". HL Deb 3 February 1966 Vol. 272 cc491–557.

28 He asked 'What exactly is meant by "inadequate to be the mother"? If it is intended to mean and the phrase is capable of this meaning – that she is not, or will not be, a good mother, are two doctors, no matter how high in the positions they hold, the right persons to judge of this? No question of health is involved, only adequacy. But even if it were right to prescribe that two doctors should judge of this, surely it cannot be right to destroy a potential life on the ground that it is thought the mother is not, or will not be, a good mother. Surely the right course is not to terminate the pregnancy but to seek to remedy the inadequacy'. He was echoed by the Bishop of Exeter: 'I cannot think what reason could have persuaded the noble Lord, Lord Silkin, to put it down. It seems to me to be an extraordinary assumption of arrogance that I, or any one of your Lordships, or any two medical practitioners, should determine whether a woman is or is not "adequate" to be the mother of a child'. HL Deb 3 February 1966 Vol. 272 cc491–557.

29 He said that 'I regret a clause has got into the present Bill which allows abortion when it is held that the woman would be inadequate as a mother. That seems to open the door to almost anything and to allow abortion just when it is convenient to have it'. *The Times*, 10 February 1966. 'Inadequacy' was a term then much in vogue, particularly to describe deviant women. It conjures up what David Garland (2001) would call 'penal welfarism', the doctrine that criminals and deviants are impaired people requiring often coercive measures of treatment and correction (*The Culture of Control: Crime and Social Order in Contemporary Society*, Chicago: University of Chicago Press). And see P. Rock (1996); *Reconstructing a Women's Prison*, Oxford: Clarendon Press.

30 At a Cabinet meeting of 3 February, 'They endorsed the recommendation of the Home Affairs Committee that the Government as a whole should adopt an attitude of neutrality …, on the understanding that this need not preclude individual Ministers from expressing, if they so wished, personal sympathy with the objectives of the proposed legislation and that, in the case of the Abortion Bill, it might be appropriate to offer to make available the services of the official draftsman to assist in the preparation of any measure which might appear to be acceptable in principle to the House'. (Conclusions of a Meeting of the Cabinet held at 10 Downing Street, S.W.1, on Thursday, 3 February, 1966. CC(66) 5th Conclusions).

31 See the editorial in *The Times*, 22 February 1966.

32 See *The Times*, 24 May 1966.

33 See his letter to *The Times*, 15 July 1966.

34 Circular letter, January 1966, ALRA Papers in the Wellcome Institute for the History of Medicine.

35 Minutes of the Meeting of the Executive Committee of the Abortion Law Reform Association, 19 May 1966. ALRA Papers in the Wellcome Institute for the History of Medicine.

36 See *The Times*, 2 June 1967.

37 Abortion Bills, 14 June 1966, ALRA Papers in the Wellcome Institute for the History of Medicine.

38 Abortion Law Reform Association; *Annual Report 1965–66*, 16.

39 Including the Central Consultants and Specialists Committee; the General Medical Services Committee; the Central Ethical Committee; the Public Health Committee; the Committee on Medical Science, Education and Research; the Committee on Psychological Medicine; the Medical Women's Federation; and representatives of divisions which had submitted motions on abortion at the Annual Representative Meeting: Birmingham (which was adamantly hostile to legal reform); Chesterfield and East Herts Division.

40 Committee on Therapeutic Abortion, Session 1965–66, Meeting of 30 November 1965, Papers held in the archives of the British Medical Association. I am grateful to the help I received from the archivist.

41 Minutes of the Meeting of Committee of 30 November 1965, British Medical Association archives.

42 It was noted that 'One of the most important parts of this task is to prepare an up-to-date review of the medical conditions which may provide grounds for termination of pregnancy'. Letter to Miss Holloway, secretary, RCOG, from joint secretaries, 10 March 1966.

43 Glanville Williams' notes sent to the Committee on 22 December 1965, *inter alia*, alluded to the repeated employment of the word *belief* in the draft bill:

'It shall be lawful for a registered medical practitioner to terminate pregnancy in good faith –
(a) in the belief that if the pregnancy were allowed to continue there would be grave risk of the patient's death or of serious injury to her physical or mental health resulting either from giving birth to the child or from the strain of caring for it, or
(b) in the belief that if the pregnancy were allowed to continue there would be grave risk of the child being born grossly deformed or with other serious physical or mental abnormality, or
(c) in the belief that the health of the patient or the social conditions in which she is living (including the social conditions of her existing children) make her unsuitable to assume the legal and moral responsibility for caring for a child or another child as the case may be, or
(d) in the belief that the patient became pregnant as the result of intercourse which was an offence under sections one to eleven inclusive of the Sexual Offences Act 1956 or that the patient is a person of unsound mind'.

The notes reported 'This word must … be read in the light of Clause 3, which requires the doctor if charged to adduce evidence of his belief. If he fails to show any reasonable grounds for holding the belief that he professed to hold, this will entitle the jury to find that he did not in fact hold the belief. …' Committee on Therapeutic Abortion, Papers held in the archives of the British Medical Association.

44 Birmingham seemed to have been an unusually strong site of opposition to abortion law reform. Members of its BMA division were strenuous in making a critical case to the press (six, for example, wrote letters to *The Church Times, Methodist Recorder* and *Baptist Times* in September 1966). A Birmingham Member of Parliament, Jill Knight, citing the representations of doctors in her constituency, was prominent in mounting the campaign to defeat David Steel's bill.

45 It attempted, for example, to move a stalling resolution in the Annual General Meeting of the BMA in July 1967 declaring that ' … the British Medical Association, in support of its resolution passed unanimously at the Annual General Meeting in Swansea 1965, requests all Members of both Houses of Parliament not to approve legislation on Medical Termination of Pregnancy until all relevant facts have been collected, scrutinised and reported on by an independent tribunal such as a Royal Commission'.

46 Dr Sim, 1914–2010, M.B., Ch.B., MD, was registered in 1938, became a Consultant Psychiatrist at the United Birmingham Hospitals, and was later to be a member of the

Society for the Protection of the Unborn Child (he spoke at an annual meeting of the Society in 1973, calling the law on abortion 'a sorry mess' (*The Times*, 17 December 1973)). He was one of the opponents of the bill in a public debate on abortion conducted at Aberdeen University on 26 February 1966 and at the Hastings Centenary Clinical Meeting on Therapeutic Abortion later that year. It was there that he argued that 'A doctor ... should preserve life. Society might insist on abortion on demand, but the psychiatrist should be very cautious in supporting such a policy' (*The British Medical Journal* (30 April 1966); 1105). He was to protest frequently and vehemently about the bill and the Act over the years – in letters to *The Times* (where, for instance, on 31 January 1966 he attacked the Committee for rushing to premature support of the bill: 'The prospect of hasty legislation based mainly upon propaganda and argument must appal doctors and is surely undeserved by the country'), and to *The British Medical Journal* of 14 September 1963, 26 October 1963, 19 June 1965, 26 January 1966, 20 May 1967, 4 November 1967 and 5 April 1969. His obituary in *BCMJ*, the *British Columbia Medical Journal* (2009), Vol. 51(9), 386, recorded that 'Dr Sim had strong opinions regarding the major ethical problems facing psychiatry today and, as can be expected, such opinions tend to foster both vocal advocates and adversaries. As is typical of the medical profession, the old adage nil nisi bonum de mortuis will hopefully be honored at this time'.

47 Minutes of the Meeting of the Committee on Therapeutic Abortion of 22 December 1965.

48 Letter of 28 March 1967. Committee on Therapeutic Abortion, Papers held in the archives of the British Medical Association.

49 Papers of the Meeting of the Committee on Therapeutic Abortion of 11 January 1966. Papers held in the archives of the British Medical Association.

50 Minutes of the Meeting of the Committee on Therapeutic Abortion of 11 January 1966.

51 Letter in *The British Medical Journal*, 19 March 1966.

52 Minutes of the Meeting of the Committee on Therapeutic Abortion of 9 May 1966.

53 The Secretary of the BMA in a general letter of 2 January 1967 had stated that 'throughout 1966 the Council of the Association has been very actively engaged in trying to ensure that any legislation which may be enacted shall be acceptable to the majority of the medical profession. In this campaign the Council has recently been collaborating with the Council of the RCOG'. BMA Loose Papers 1967, BMA.

54 Minutes of the Meeting of the Committee on Therapeutic Abortion of 9 May 1966, BMA Archives.

55 The Report argued that 'the assessment is essentially a medical one; no one other than the medical practitioners involved – not even the mother herself – can make the assessment which has to be made as to the ground of a decision, whether the pregnancy should be terminated or not'. Church Assembly Board for Social Responsibility, (1965); *Abortion – An Ethical Discussion*, Church House, Westminster, 38.

56 A member of the Committee told John Havard on 12 April 1967: 'I still hold the view that while we seem to be committed to presenting a list of indications there should be emphasis on the fact that the lists are purely for guidance and generally for medical guidance. You will remember at an early stage I hoped they would not just provide a battlefield for contesting barristers (- on interpretation) – or even for search by unscrupulous doctors for a plausible excuse within a wide catalogue'.

57 The 'rhesus factor' referred to a possible problem caused by the incompatibility of blood types in the mother and foetus. The American Pregnancy Association reports that 'If a small amount of the baby's blood mixes with your blood, which often happens, your body may respond as if it were allergic to the baby. Your body may make antibodies to the Rh antigens in the baby's blood. This means you have become sensitised and your antibodies can cross the placenta and attack your baby's blood.

They break down the fetus's red blood cells and produce anemia (the blood has a low number of red blood cells). This condition is called hemolytic disease or hemolytic anemia. It can become severe enough to cause serious illness, brain damage, or even death in the fetus or newborn'. http://americanpregnancy.org/pregnancycomplica tions/rhfactor.html

58 It was a conclusion that was not unanimously approved by the profession. A letter from John Howells of the Institute of Family Psychiatry in Suffolk to *The British Medical Journal* reported, for example, that: 'Last March, at an introductory course in family psychiatry at this institute, a group of 21 general practitioners and colleagues in public health expressed their views on the grounds for the termination of pregnancy. Thirteen doctors (62% of the sample) expressed themselves in favour of the first alter-native of granting termination to the woman at her request in the first three months, thus extending birth control into the first trimester. A further six supported the second alternative that social grounds should be taken into account when termination is considered by the doctor; they thus supported [reform]. No doctor favoured the third alternative of merely making present case law into legislation – the B.M.A. viewpoint. Two dissented from any of the above three views. Thus 90% of this sample of doctors were in favour of progressive legislation. The sample is small, but no smaller than the B.M.A. committee representing the views of the profession. The sample may not have represented doctors as a whole; neither may have the B.M.A. committee. It would be sad if a committee supposedly acting for the profession succeeded in limiting the ill now before Parliament and produced an Act to which the majority of doctors were not attuned'. *The British Medical Journal* (29 April 1967); 314.

59 The Secretary of the BMA had written a letter to cognate professional organisations on 2 January 1967 soliciting their approval for the stance which the Association was taking.

60 The Royal College stated that 'The Council of the College accepts that there is a case for amending the law to make it positively rather than negatively clear that there are circumstances where abortion is justified, namely, when it is in the interests of the physical and mental health of the woman. ... If a new law were enacted it would be wise to include as an indication a considerably increased risk that the baby if born would be seriously handicapped either physically or mentally'. Cited in HC Deb 22 July 1966 Vol. 732 cc1067–165.

61 Methodist Conference Wolverhampton Representative Session (1 July 1966); *Report*, 5. Archives, Methodist Church House, London.

62 The head of the Roman Catholic Church in England and Wales, Cardinal Archbishop Heenan, wrote to Norman St. Stevas, the Catholic Member of Parliament, at a time when the abortion campaign was coming to a head: 'I do not think that there is any chance of a joint statement on Abortion. I am sure that the Archbishop of Canterbury would be willing but there are many Anglicans – Mervyn Stockwood, for example, who would repudiate his views. The Free Churches would give us very little support'. Letter of 10 May 1967. Papers of Cardinal Heenan in the Westminster Diocesan Archives.

63 In Appendix 3 for agenda for the meeting of the Executive Committee of the Abortion Law Reform Committee, 19 May 1965. ALRA Papers in the Wellcome Institute for the History of Medicine.

64 Thus the Roman Catholic Bishop of Northampton, Monsignor Parker, talked at a public meeting on 31 October of 'the legalisation of murder of innocent persons who are allowed no self defence'. (*The Northampton Chronicle and Echo*, 1 November 1966).

65 Cardinal Heenan did write to tell a lay woman in a letter of 17 June 1966 that '... The Church has never varied in her teaching on Abortion. It is immoral to destroy by direct action life in the womb. The matter is quite different when, for example, an

operation had to be performed and as an indirect result the foetus is lost. ...' Papers of Cardinal Heenan in the Westminster Diocesan Archives. AAW HE/A1(b)

66 Encyclical Letter of Pope Pius XI, *Christian Marriage*, 1930, Catholic Truth Society, Unwin Brothers, Woking, 1962, 31.

67 Statement from the Hierarchy of England and Wales, 21 October 1966, Papers of Cardinal Heenan in the Westminster Diocesan Archives. AAW HE/A1(a)

68 Significantly perhaps, the cardinal made no reference at all to abortion or to criminal justice matters in his autobiography (1974); *A Crown of Thorns: An Autobiography 1951–1963*, London: Hodder and Stoughton.

69 Letter of 17 June 1966. Papers of Cardinal Heenan in the Westminster Diocesan Archives. AAW HE/A1(a)

70 BBC Change Makers: November 2010 -zztest_cutback_1541_3_12_millbank_219822. wmv (268.93 MB) <http://rapidshare.com/files/434728346/zztest_cutback_1541_ 3_12_millbank_219822.wmv?bin=1>

71 One member wrote to *The Manchester Guardian* on 19 October 1966: 'I write in great anger ... The Guild of Catholic Doctors have no need to be interested in our Protestant <u>Reform</u> of our Laws. Surely they can exercise their Catholic prejudices in their consulting rooms as much as they like. ...'

72 Undated note to file. ALRA Papers in the Wellcome Institute for the History of Medicine.

73 The Modern Churchmen's Union had been formed on 27 July 1898, by a group who, in the face of modern science, were persuaded that there was a need for a forum to air 'progressive religious thought': 'The thinking layman no less than the thinking clergyman required that religious truths should be elucidated in such a way as to afford intellectual conviction; that, in any case, the laity declined to be fettered by the dead past, and required recognition of the living truths of to-day'. The Union was 'primarily intended to be a union of Churchmen, who desire to promote the clearer statement of Christian truth in accordance with the advance in knowledge that has been made in modern times'. (Revd. T. Brocklehurst (April 1911); 'The Birth of the Churchman's Union', *The Modern Churchman*, Vol. 1, No. 1 (https://modernchurch. org.uk/our-history/journal/the-birth-of-the-churchmen-s-union).

74 The submission was approved by a number of clerical and lay members of the Church of England, including the Bishop of Birmingham.

75 Her letter of 10 October 1955 said in part; 'I endeavoured to have this withdrawn before the meeting but I am told that this is not possible. In view of the pernicious character of this resolution and its possible effect upon the nation it would seem to call for action by Christians acting in defence of our traditional belief in the dignity and sanctity of human life. ...'

76 The resolution read in full: That the law regarding abortion be amended. ...
   (a) no registered medical practitioner shall be found guilty of an offence ... unless it is proved that the act charged was not done in good faith for the purpose of preserving the life of the mother
   (b) no registered medical practitioner who acts with the concurring opinion of a second registered medical practitioner shall be found guilty of an offence ... unless it is proved that the act charged was not done in good faith:
      (i) for the purpose of preventing serious injury to the mother in body or health, or
      (ii) in the belief that there was grave risk of the child being born grossly deformed or lacking normal physical or mental faculties or incapable of normal mental physical or mental development'.
   The resolution was passed by a small majority.

77 Letter of 14 October 1955 in the Lambeth Palace archives; BSR/AB.

78 K. Hindell and M. Sims (1971); *Abortion Law Reformed*, London: Owen, 90.

79 Letter of 24 February 1958 in the Lambeth Palace archives; BSR/AB. There was no information about where and when the meeting took place, nor about who Shirley Emerson might have been. The diocese of Chichester did not reply to my query about her identity or about the occasion to which she referred.

80 The Church Assembly Board for Social Responsibility (1965); *Abortion: An Ethical Discussion, op. cit.*, 3.

81 *Ibid*, 8.

82 *Ibid*, 11.

83 *Ibid*, 19.

84 *Ibid*, 22.

85 *Ibid*, 24.

86 *Ibid*, 29.

87 *Ibid*, 61. In that production of a measured argument permitting abortion in certain circumstances, the Board for Social Responsibility defied some of the conventional analyses which commentators have advanced about the relations between religion and abortion (see, for example, J. Kelley, M. Evans and B. Headey (1993); 'Moral Reasoning and Political Conflict: The Abortion Controversy', *The British Journal of Sociology*, Vol. 44, No. 4, 589–612).

88 BBC Change Makers: November 2010 -zztest_cutback_1541_3_12_millbank_219822. wmv (268.93 MB) <http://rapidshare.com/files/434728346/zztest_cutback_1541_3_12_millbank_219822.wmv?bin=1>

89 D. Steel; *Against Goliath: David Steel's Story, op. cit.*, 49.

90 He was to say that 'Anglicans do not feel bound to take a similar stand [to that of the Roman Catholic Church]. In a recent publication the Church Assembly Board for Social Responsibility makes this clear. It deliberately rejects what it recognises to be the traditional Christian view that the killing of the foetus is a form of homicide. The principle is too simple, the Board says, to fit the complexities of the case and abortion, like divorce, cannot be unconditionally condemned. While disagreeing with its conclusions we must pay tribute to the learning and compassion of the authors of this little book. It is described as 'an ethical discussion' and it is informative and fair in every way. It is refreshingly free from the fault of modern controversialists who often cite only those examples and statistics which support their own side'. 'The Cardinal's Message: Life is God's Gift', *Westminster Cathedral Chronicle*, February 1966.

91 Cited in *Report* to the Methodist Conference Wolverhampton Representative Session, 1 July 1966, 5. Archives, Methodist Church House, London.

92 *Ibid*, 5.

93 *Ibid*, 7.

94 *Ibid*, 8.

95 *Ibid*, 9.

96 Resolution before the Methodist Conference Wolverhampton Representative Session, 1 July 1966.

97 He informed the House of Commons: 'It remains for me to say why certain other rather more controversial features have not been incorporated in the Bill – what has been known as the social Clause, what has been called the rape Clause and what has been called the under-16 Clause. I have much sympathy with all the cases which people have in mind who have put forward these Clauses, but there are three reasons why I have not attempted to include them in the Bill. The first is the difficulty of adequate definition, and I again remind the House that we are dealing with the criminal law. The second is my wish to keep the authority to the doctors as simple and unelaborate as possible. The third is my desire to get maximum support to re-write the law, which I believe to be so important. I realise that I am open to criticism from both sides – from those who think that I have not gone far enough and from some who may think that

I have gone too far, although I am scarcely going beyond the law as it is at present practised'. HC Deb 25 February 1966 Vol. 725 cc837–56.

98 He said: 'in many ways this is really a woman's problem. I read in the Evening Standard a very cryptic letter about the way in which assemblies, predominantly male, have been discussing this subject. I regard this as one of the last steps in the emancipation of women'. HC Deb 25 February 1966 Vol. 725 cc837–56.

99 HC Deb 25 February 1966 Vol. 725 cc837–56.

100 See K. Hindell and M. Simms; *Abortion Law Reformed, op. cit.*, 88. The brothers were born into an Irish Catholic family in Liverpool, Peter in 1909 and Simon in 1914. They were educated at Irish Christian Brothers school and became Labour Members of Parliament for Preston South, 1964–70, and for Bootle, 1955–79, respectively. When Peter Mahon lost his seat and was not selected for a vacant Liverpool seat in 1971, he stood unsuccessfully as an Independent Labour and Anti-Abortion candidate (see S. Bruce (1995); *Religion in Modern Britain*, Oxford: Oxford University Press, 123).

101 The Church's position was quite unequivocal. It had been voiced in 1930 and in 1966. Twenty-four years later, the position remained the same: "Nothing and no one can in any way permit the killing of an innocent human being, whether a foetus or an embryo, an infant or an adult, an old person, or one suffering from an incurable disease, or a person who is dying. Furthermore, no one is permitted to ask for this act of killing, either for himself or herself or for another person entrusted to his or her care, nor can he or she consent to it, either explicitly or implicitly. Nor can any authority legitimately recommend or permit such an action". (Congregation for the Doctrine of the Faith, 'Declaration on Euthanasia *Iura et Bona*' (5 May 1980), II: *AAS* 72 (1980), 546. And see 'Pope says respect embryos', *The Philadelphia Inquirer*, 28 November 2010.

102 HC Deb 25 February 1966 Vol. 725 cc837–56.

103 David Steel, born in 1938, was elected at a by-election in 1965 as Liberal Member of Parliament for Roxburgh, Selkirk and Peebles.

104 In *Pioneers of Change: Interviews with people who made the 1967 Abortion Act possible*, http://www.bpas.org/js/filemanager/files/abortion_pioneers.pdf, 50.

105 D. Steel; *Against Goliath: David Steel's Story, op. cit.*, 49.

106 Although eugenicist echoes were still to be heard. It will have been noted that Glanville Williams had talked about one of the clauses he had drafted as being on 'eugenicist grounds'. And in a letter about a draft constitution to the Secretary of the revived ALRA, a committee member, J. Brander remarked that one of the strengths of an increased provision for abortion would be that 'Unwanted children are not only a burden on the families, but create many of the criminals now afflicting this country'. Letter of 28 October 1964 in the ALRA Papers in the Wellcome Institute for the History of Medicine. (The argument about the role played by abortion in preventing crime and criminals was aired by Glanville Williams in 1958, *The Sanctity of Life and the Criminal Law*, London: Faber and Faber, 99–100, and in S. Levitt and S. Dubner (2005); *Freakonomics:* A Rogue Economist Explores the Hidden Side of Everything, London; Allen Lane. It was scotched in F. Zimring (2007); *The Great American Crime Decline*, Oxford: Oxford University Press).

107 The first women's liberation conference was held in Oxford in 1970, after the Act was passed (see S. Brooke; 'The Sphere of Sexual Politics: The Abortion Law Reform Association, 1930s to 1960s', *op. cit.*, 77.

108 Madeline Simms said 'I have often heard people say at meetings that the Abortion Act was the result of the women's movement, but this isn't so. The women's movement did not really start until the 1970s'. In *Pioneers of Change: Interviews with people who made the 1967 Abortion Act possible*, http://www.bpas.org/js/filemanager/files/abortion_pioneers.pdf, 18.

109 Roy Jenkins, speaking at the Second Reading of the Bill, HC Deb 22 July 1966 Vol. 732 cc1067–165.
110 *Ibid.*
111 See HC Deb 1 June 1967 Vol. 747 cc259–66.
112 P. Allen (2004); 'A Young Home Secretary' in A. Adonis and K. Thomas (eds.) *Roy Jenkins: A Retrospective*, Oxford: Oxford University Press, 64.
113 And David Steel claimed that his bill 'was the same as Lord Silkin's successful measure from the Lords'. D. Steel; *Against Goliath, op. cit.*, 50.
114 Minutes of the meeting of the Executive Committee of the Abortion Law Reform Committee, 14 July 1966. ALRA Papers in the Wellcome Institute for the History of Medicine.
115 In 'The Abortion Act 50 years on', *BBC Woman's Hour*, 24 January 2017.
116 Memorandum from Vera Houghton, 27 October 1966. ALRA Papers in the Wellcome Institute for the History of Medicine.
117 Appendix 1 to agenda of the meeting of the Abortion Law Reform Committee, 21 June 1966. ALRA Papers in the Wellcome Institute for the History of Medicine.
118 Minutes of the meeting of the Executive Committee of the Abortion Law Reform Committee, 21 June 1966. ALRA Papers in the Wellcome Institute for the History of Medicine.
119 HC Deb 22 July 1966 Vol. 732 cc1067–165.
120 The position taken by the Church of Scotland in 1966 was '"The foetus is, from the beginning, an independent human being" and therefore it can be threatened "only in the case of threat to maternal life, and that after the exhaustion of all alternatives"'. http://www.googlesyndicatedsearch.com/u/churchofscotland?q=abortion+1966&sa=Google+Search
121 He recalled in interview that 'I had a very big Catholic seminary in my constituency which has since closed down but it was called Drygrange and ... I had more than one meeting with them 'cause they were resolutely opposed to it. ... you know, there was just no meeting of minds ... but by going courteously to see them 'cause they were constituents of mine, and just arguing the case and saying, "well I'm sorry, if you start from the proposition that full human life exists from the moment of conception, then there can be no meeting ground. You cannot have an abortion. I understand that, but most people do not accept that and what's more, most Catholics do not accept it." ... the conscience clause which was added during the committee stage was very much as a result of that discussion that I had with the seminary in my constituency. And I thought there was a reasonable point that if you have Catholic or others who were doctors and nurses and they don't want anything to do with this, then their job should be protected. And so the conscience clause was written in. And to some extent, that was a sop to the Catholic faith but they accepted that'. (The Archdiocesan Seminary, St. Andrew's College, at Drygrange, near Melrose, was opened in 1953. It later moved to Gillis in Edinburgh. See http://www.archdiocese-edinburgh.com/documents/CELEBRATIONOFTHEFEASTOFSTANDREW30Nov2010.pdf)
122 An appendix to the agenda of the Executive Committee of the Abortion Law Reform Committee for 15 September 1966 recorded, for instance, that he had received a 'protest telegram' from 30,000 members of the Union of Catholic Mothers.
123 That was a reassurance he was also to make to a Catholic guild of doctors: 'I can confirm that it is my intention to introduce a "conscience clause" to my Bill at Committee Stage. ...' Letter from David Steel to Dr Dignan, Guild of St. Luke, SS. Cosmos and Damian, 8 November 1966. The Guild had issued an undated statement (ABORTION BILL – Catholic Doctors' View) in which it had claimed that '... the <u>amendments</u> to the existing case law ... would in our opinion be

deplorable for the mothers, their doctors and the public at large, for the following reasons:

Clause 1 (i) b gives doctors authority to terminate if there is a "substantial risk" that the child would be "seriously handicapped in mind or body". Doctors [must] ask what is meant by "substantial risk"? How is such a risk to be assessed by a doctor? ...
Clause (i) c we find peculiarly alarming. It allows abortion if the doctor thinks that the pregnant woman's "capacity as a mother will be severely overstrained ..." For the first time in British history doctors are to ... destroy life for undefined personal or social reasons, which they have no special competence to assess ...
Clause 1 (i) d extends the right to abort to three medico-social situations, although the intention to do this is denied by many supporters of the bill. In each case, something very like "right to abortion" is created. Firstly, where the woman is a severely subnormal defective...
... Thirdly – in case of rape. This clause was dropped in the House of Lords, in spite of the deep sympathy it aroused, because it would be impossible to administer. It would put a premium on false stories of assault, and would encourage false accusations against individuals.
... In conclusion, we desire to reaffirm our view that the human embryo is from the moment of fertilisation a distinctively human organism entitled to the protection of the law at every stage of its development. ...' (Archive of the Archbishop of Westminster).

124 HC Deb 22 July 1966 Vol. 732 cc1067–165.
125 David Owen had been a Neurological and Psychiatric Registrar, 1964–66; and Labour Member for Plymouth Sutton, 1966–74.
126 Michael Winstanley was a surgeon, the Liberal Member of Parliament for Cheadle, 1966–70, and the Liberal Spokesman on Health.
127 Jill Knight was the Conservative Member for Birmingham, Edgbaston. She was to liken abortion to euthanasia (see *The Sunday Telegraph*, 7 August 1966).
128 See http://www.historyofparliamentonline.org/volume/oral-history/member/knight-jill-1923
129 Kevin McNamara was the Labour Member of Parliament for Kingston-upon-Hull between 1966 and 1974.
130 Later Lord St. John of Fawsley, Norman St. John-Stevas, born in 1929, was a barrister and Conservative Member of Parliament for Chemsford, 1964–1987. He was a prominent Catholic, having been educated at St. Joseph's Salesian School, and, briefly, for the Roman Catholic priesthood at the English College in Rome. He was the author of a number of essays and books on abortion and allied issues, including (1963); *The Right to Life*, London: Hodder and Stoughton, and (1961); *Life, Death and the Law: A Study of the Relationship between Law and Christian Morals in the English and American Legal Systems*, London: Eyre and Spottiswoode. His obituary in *The Times* of 6 March 2012 said that 'In a period when many politicians and Whips preferred to eschew controversial "moral" issues such as abortion, euthanasia ... he was one of those who took a very determined view ...'
131 Abortion Law Reform Association; *Annual Report 1965–1966*, 18.
132 It was just before that date, on 17 January, that Michael Ramsey gave an address to the Convocation of Canterbury in which he maintained the sanctity of the foetus but did not conflate abortion with infanticide. See O. Chadwick, *Michael Ramsey: A Life*, *op. cit.*, 154.
133 The phrase was used in a report in *The Times*, 10 May 1967.
134 Minutes of the meeting of the Executive Committee of the Abortion Law Reform Committee, 14 July 1966. ALRA Papers in the Wellcome Institute for the History of Medicine. Standing Committee F met on twelve occasions between 18 January and 5 April 1967. At its first meeting, one of those opponents, Norman St. John Stevas,

declared roundly that 'strong views are entertained in the country about the Bill and they should be strongly expressed in this Committee. Strong words are needed about the Bill. A heavy responsibility lies on hon. Members in seeking to improve what I consider to be a dangerous, unnecessary, cruel and heartless Bill – one of the most reckless Bills that has ever come before the House of Commons. Far from clarifying the law, as it claims in its Long Title, it confuses it. It strikes a blow at one of the fundamental moral principles on which our society is based, namely, respect for the sanctity of life'. *Official Report*, London: HMSO, 1967, col. 15. And at its fifth meeting, on 15 February, Jill Knight said 'Sponsors of this Bill really must try to understand that millions of people in this country feel that getting rid of the child is an extreme step to take. I am sorry if they do not accept this, but I really must point out that this is a view which it is sincere to hold and perfectly proper to hold, and this is the view which I put forward'. *Official Report, op. cit.*, col. 211.

135 D. Steel, *Against Goliath: David Steel's Story, op. cit.*, 50.

136 L. Abse; *Private Member, op. cit.*, 227.

137 *Ibid.*, 50.

138 For example, Jill Knight and Bernard Braine moved separately that the text should be amended on 'Page 1, line 7 [Clause 1] [to] leave out 'a registered medical practitioner' and insert 'or under the supervision of, a registered medical practitioner holding an appointment as a consultant in the National Health Service or a registered medical practitioner of equivalent experience approved for the purposes of this section by the Minister or Secretary of State'. Norman St. John-Stevas later wrote on 29 December 1967 to Cardinal Heenan, 'Mrs Knight was indefatigable in her opposition to the Bill and without her we could not have obtained such success as we had. ... I feel, myself, that it would be appropriate if [her] efforts received some recognition from the Vatican in the form or an award or decoration ...'

139 Letter of 2 January 1967 from Secretary of BMA to the Chairman of the Committee on Therapeutic Abortion. And it was an engagement that continued after Committee Stage. For example, David Steel wrote to the Secretary of the BMA on 25 April 1967: 'Now that the Medical Termination of Pregnancy Bill has emerged from Committee and is to be reported to the House on June 2nd, I think it would be useful if one or two of its supporters were able to meet representatives of the British Medical Association in order to discuss the Bill as it now stands. ...' Papers of the Committee on Therapeutic Abortion, Archives of the British Medical Association.

140 ALRA, for instance, sent all those members of the Committee who were thought to be supportive copies of a Newsletter, a lecture by the Bishop of Woolwich, the ALRA annual report, ALRA's reply to the BMA report and other materials, including ALRA's commentary on proposed amendments. And there was more diffuse lobbying. The report of ALRA's 1967 annual general meeting recorded that Peter Jackson MP had urged 'the importance of continued pressure on MPs. He advised members whose MPs had not been present at the Second Reading to write regretting that it had not been possible for the MP to attend and hoping that he would be able to support the bill in its later stages. Mr Jackson said that Catholic opposition must not in any way be underestimated. Many MPs had already received letters from RC constituents and these might cause them to waver especially in marginal constituencies'.

141 One was Bernard Braine. A typical example of such a briefing was his communication to David Gullick of the BMA on 17 July 1967: 'Herewith the Official Report of the all-night sitting. You will see that a concession was made in respect of an amendment in regard to emergency operations. I made a slip of the tongue at the foot of column 1324 but realised I had done so halfway down column 1325. This is part of the price one pays for talking through the night in a state of near exhaustion!!! I am most unhappy about the whole affair as you will judge from my remarks'. On another occasion, he wrote to David Stevenson: 'As promised I enclose a copy of the letter I have written to

the Parliamentary Secretary. I hope that the meeting with the Minister will now take place very soon. Presumably you will renew your request for this, but in any event it would be helpful, as I suggested to Sir John Peel last night, if the BMA and the Royal College would not only make their wishes known to the Minister but would issue a joint statement. Bearing in mind the way in which the sponsors of the Bill (helped by some doctors) were able to throw doubt on the views of the leaders of their profession it is imperative in my view that this time there is no doubt and I can quote a firm statement when I address the House, My impression is that if you are firm the Minister will agree; if you are not, he will stand aloof until after the Bill has got a third reading in the Commons. Unless we resolve this matter by giving a firm lead the Bill may not get a third reading. There is a lot of misgivings about it at the moment'. His letter to the Parliamentary Secretary recited that 'I enclose a copy of the amendment to which I referred. This has the full support of the B.M.A. and the R.C.O.G. It does not spell out how the additional doctors would be approved, nor is this thought necessary. If such a duty is accepted by the Minister, he would undoubtedly wish to consult the profession as to how best to carry it out. The Amendment has the merit, I think, of covering all the contingencies envisaged when we discussed the matter in Standing Committee, (such as the need to make provision for those parts of the country where a consultant gynaecologist is not available but a consultant surgeon is ...) ... I understand that the B.M.A. together with the Royal College, asked to meet the Minister some weeks ago, but so far no meeting has been arranged. As time is getting short I have now tabled the amendment. If you are happy about it then, of course, no difficulty arises, but perhaps we could have a further word when you have had the opportunity of meeting the profession's representatives'. British Medical Association archives. His amendment, unsuccessful in the event, read: 'delete "a registered medical practitioner" and Insert "or under the supervision of a registered medical practitioner holding an appointment as a consultant in the National Health Service or a registered medical practitioner approved for the purposes of this section by the Minister or Secretary of State'. Bernard Braine, 1914–2000, was Conservative Member for South-East Essex between 1955 and 1983.

142 In a typical instance, the Secretary of the BMA wrote to David Steel on 10 April 1967 to say 'I was most interested to see that this Bill has now emerged from committee after very prolonged discussion. I believe during the final twelfth sitting you did in passing express a wish to have an opportunity between now and the Report stage to discuss the present position with the professional organisations concerned. I am merely writing to say that we should be very happy indeed to meet with you and I shall look forward to hearing from you ... '

143 *Ibid.*

144 The Medical Defence Union had been founded in 1885 to indemnify doctors for incidents arising from their clinical care of patients (http://www.themdu.com/about-mdu).

145 In October 1967, for instance, there was correspondence about the implications of the impending legislation for professional disciplinary procedures. A letter was sent to the Medical Defence Union: 'I am writing both to yourself and Dr Constable because an interesting point has been brought to my attention by one of our members arising out of the decision yesterday by the House of Lords to reintroduce into the legislation the possibility of abortion being carried out because of the prospect of injury to a woman's other child or children. Our member telephoned to say that if, as seems more than likely, the Bill should reach the Statute Book in this form it is likely to raise a considerable problem because of the present terms of the statement by the General Medical Council contained in its booklet "Functions, Procedure, and Disciplinary Jurisdiction". You will not need reminding I am sure that the relevant sentence reads "The Disciplinary Committee has always regarded induced non-therapeutic abortion

as so grave an offence as to lead almost invariably to erasure of the doctor's name from the Register". British Medical Association archives.

146 Its position was to change over time. Initially it reported that 'the text of the Bill now corresponds fairly closely with the recommendations of the Special Committee which were published in the B.M.J. in July of last year and we believe that this is not entirely coincidental. The joint action which has been taken in the past twelve months by the Association and [the RCOG] and the advocacy of members of both Houses of Parliament with whom they have been in touch have been effective'. (Letter of 23 August 1967 from John Havard and Derek Gulluck to members of the committee on therapeutic abortion). Two months later, on 24 October 1967, it voiced its discontents in a press statement. What Madeline Simm called the withdrawal of two 'wrecking amendments' in the House of Lords was greeted by the BMA as a major setback: 'The decision of the House of Lords on 23 October to reintroduce lawful abortion so as (1) to include risk to the health of the other children and (2) to require no particular experience of either of the doctors involved is in the view of the R.C.O.G. and the B.M.A. weakening the safeguards which it is believed the women concerned must be entitled to. The R.C.O.G. and the B.M.A. hope that no further amendments weakening the position will be made during the concluding stages of the Bill'. Simm's own account is that '... The passage of this Bill became possible when the House of Lords had second thoughts about the wisdom of pursuing the two 'wrecking' amendments it had inserted into the Bill earlier in the summer. In the event, the social clause was left intact, and the operation was not made dependent upon the consent of a consultation or doctor on a special list to be drawn up by the Minister of Health (who had anyway already stated that he was not prepared to draw up such an 'invidious' list). So all was well, and the Bill was, at long last, transformed into an Act. ... The Act ... says quite plainly that in determining whether the continuance of the pregnancy would involve risk to health 'account may be taken of the pregnant woman's actual or foreseeable environment'... The British Medical Association ... tried hard to ensure that the two 'wrecking' amendments were retained in the Bill' (M. Simms (January 1968); 'The Abortion Act, 1967', *Family Planning*, Vol. 16, No. 4, 117).

147 The Under Secretary of the BMA observed that 'Clearly, the Roman Catholic physician and others with similar religious scruples will have no difficulty in proving their conscientious objection and, in any event, are extremely unlikely because of their convictions ever to be involved in the termination of pregnancy. However, we are strongly of the opinion that a much larger section of the profession may be placed in real difficulty. We would recognise that there are bound to be many middle-of-the-road gynaecologists who, in some cases, feel justified in terminating a pregnancy and in others slightly different in circumstances would have an ethical objection to so doing. In this kind of case if the surgeon is challenged as to why he failed to advise termination for one woman having terminated others, he may be in a very real difficulty to demonstrate the proof of his conscientious objection. ...' Under Secretary of the BMA to Dr A. Peart, General Secretary, Canadian Medical Association of Toronto, 26 October 1967. British Medical Association archives. In the event, and after protracted consultations, a meeting took place on 8 February 1968 between a Joint BMA/RCOG deputation and Lord Cohen of Birkenhead, MD, FRCP, Hon. Master of the Bench, Inner Temple and a former Professor of Medicine at the University of Liverpool, concerning the ethical implications of the Abortion Act in which the following points were established:

1. Whether or not termination of pregnancy in certain circumstances could be regarded as "unethical" is a question which could be determined by the [BMA], but that it certainly does not follow that a particular course of conduct amounts to "infamous conduct in a professional respect" merely because it is unethical.

2. Lord Cohen accepted the possibility that there may come a time when legislation of such a nature, e.g. euthanasia, is introduced that the GMC would have to take a positive action in support of medical ethics, nothwithstanding the wishes of parliament.

3. Lord Cohen explained that the present paragraph in the Disciplinary Notice relating to non therapeutic abortion would carry an asterisk, the footnote to which would state that the paragraph was under review pending the introduction of the Abortion Act, 1967.

148 The argument put was that, except in an emergency, an abortion could be performed lawfully only by a consultant qualified in gynaecology, and that was defeated by 13 votes to 11. Three sittings were devoted to the grounds for abortion, and the clause eventually agreed was 'that the continuance of the pregnancy would involve risk to the life or of injury to the physical or mental health of the pregnant woman or the future well-being of herself or the child or her other children'.

149 Although there were other organisations. An appendix to the agenda of the meeting of the Executive Committee of the Abortion Law Reform Association of 15 September 1966 alluded, for example, to a new body, the Committee in Defence of Innocent Life, that had been formed in London, Liverpool and Manchester (and see *The Catholic Herald*, 9 September 1966). ALRA meticulously scoured newspapers for information about groups opposed to its campaign.

150 *The Times*, 25 January 1967. David Steel observed that amongst those campaigning for reform, the SPUC was known as the Society for the Promotion of Unwanted Children (http://www.kcl.ac.uk/sspp/departments/icbh/witness/PDFfiles/AbortionAct1967. pdf, 42).

151 It was said that Aleck Bourne 'had become increasingly appalled that his case was being used to justify the new legislation' (http://www.S.P.U.C..org.uk/) And see C. de Costa (August 2009); 'The King versus Aleck Bourn', *Medical Journal of Australia*, Vol. 191, No. 4, 230–1.

152 A Bourne, *A Doctor's Creed, op. cit.*, 103, 105.

153 *Ibid*, 108.

154 Letter of 20 December 1966, Westminster Diocesan Archives. AAW HE/A1(a)

155 Thus a leaflet distributed by the Medway Towns Society for the Protection of Unborn Children to promote a march and petition to the Prime Minister on 20–21 May 1967 recited that: '… THE NEW BILL will allow abortion on the grounds of a mother's 'environment'. This is so vague that it will result in **ABORTION ON DEMAND**. AT THE MOMENT OF CONCEPTION THERE IS A NEW LIFE. There is a tiny perfectly formed baby by the time a woman knows for certain that she is pregnant. **THIS LIFE IS SACRED**. The new bill will allow it to be destroyed for purely selfish reasons. … In our SYMBOL the Fish represents a united Christian endeavour, the Triangle is composed of the Three main Christian Faiths acting in unison'.

156 William Wells, a Labour, Catholic Member of Parliament, prominent in the campaign against abortion, wrote to Monsignor Norris on 28 January 1967: 'since the supporters of the Bill are trying to misrepresent the opposition as being exclusively, or almost exclusively, Roman Catholic (vide Friday's Times), the more that can be done to dispel this illusion and the sooner the better. … I think the fairly considerable activity of certain doctors against the Bill, notably Professor McCarthy, and the formation of the new Society for the Protection of Unborn Children, with I think I am right in saying no Catholics prominent in its membership, will do this part of our work for us gradually but pretty effectually. …' The report to which he alluded was in *The Times*, Friday, 27 January 1967. Headed 'Postbag Pressure on M.P.s', it talked about how 'The voice of the people has been coming through to Westminster very stridently for six months, with all the signs of energetic organisation by Roman Catholic guilds and groups and by the Society for the Protection of the Unborn Child … David

Steel ... reckons that 150 letters come from doctors in support of the Bill. Most of the rest are hostile and, he is sure, have been organised by Roman Catholic priests and opinion-makers. Many of them are virtually identical and make use of what nearly all non-Roman Catholic M.P.s have come to recognise as a tell-tale phrase – "legalised murder."' Westminster Diocesan Archives AAW HE/A1(b)

157 Cardinal Heenan wrote to a lay member on 7 February 1967: 'I have deliberately not identified myself with the anti-abortion campaign. To have done so would have given me much personal satisfaction but would have practically guaranteed the passage of the Bill unchanged. Once the public have the idea that only Catholics are against abortion the cause is lost. I am in close contact with the B.M.A. and, especially, with the founders of the Society for the Protection of the Unborn Child. This society refuses to have any Catholics on its committee in order to demonstrate that this is a question of moral decency and not of denominational bias. ...' Westminster Diocesan Archives AAW HE/A1(b).

158 That was also the judgement formed by some members of ALRA. Some time after the event, Keith Hindell and Madeline Simms observed that 'There was ... evidence ... that the Catholics were no longer able to reply on Government timidity in face of outrageous demands... From the early 1960s Catholic opposition to birth-control and abortion was greeted with increasing resistance'. K. Hindell and M. Simms; *Abortion Law Reformed*, *op. cit.*, 87.

159 In the papers of Cardinal Heenan in the Westminster Diocesan Archives. AAW HE/A1(b)

160 The Member of Parliament, Simon Mahon, the man who had previously succeeded in 'talking out' a private member's bill, wrote to Cardinal Heenan on 8 March 1967, 'I am writing to inform you of my opinion with relation to the Abortion Bill, now in Committee Stage here. Firstly, (and not most important), I point out that I believe that certain Catholic people and organisations, have quite deliberately left out, so far as they are able, people like myself from deliberations inside of this House and outside. I have borne my Irish name for so long that I am well used to this form of activity, and it is only when important 'causes' may be harmed that I complain. Fortunately experience lessens the intended effect, and I will leave the matter there ... 'Westminster Diocesan Archives AAW HE/A1(a). It was the view of the archivist of the Westminster Diocesan Archives that Cardinal Heenan himself may have been equally sensitive about his Irish origins.

161 There were, the Church believed, some 5,000,000 Catholics amongst the 54,350,000 population of the United Kingdom. A memorandum prepared for The Inter-Diocesan Council of Parents and Electors Regarding Prospective Legislation on Abortion in July 1966 stated that 'Catholics in this country are in a minority – a recently quoted figure being five millions, i.e. about 10 per cent of the population. In a democratic society we have every right to express our view but in a democratic society we should not seek to impose our view'. Westminster Diocesan Archives. AAW HE/A1(a)

162 Cardinal Heenan said in a letter of 14 June 1966: 'Unless good sense prevails we shall see an even greater holocaust than Vietnam'. Westminster Diocesan Archives AAW HE/A1(a).

163 According to *The Catholic Directory for the Year of Our Lord 1966*, London: Burns and Oates, there were in Parliament 32 MPs and 49 peers declaring themselves Roman Catholic.

164 Letter from Cardinal Heenan, 11 October 1966. Elsewhere he wrote 'I have taken the line – with which the other bishops agreed at our last meeting – that if we are to succeed in blocking the most objectionable clauses from the Bill it is important that we do not present this as a Catholic issue. That is why our protests have been so mild' (letter of 4 November 1966, Westminster Diocesan Archives AAW HE/A1(a)). That analogy was a routine component of argument. In another letter of 5 July

1966, the Cardinal said, 'Once the Catholic attitude to abortion is classified with the fish-on-Friday outlook the dechristianisation of this country takes a further step'. Westminster Diocesan Archives AAW HE/A1(a).

165 So it was that, James Dunn, a Catholic Labour Member of Parliament, wrote to the Guild of St Luke, SS. Cosmos and Damian on 2 December 1966: 'One suggestion I make to you is that a number of non-Catholic Doctors should be encouraged to co-operate in joint representations made to all members of Parliament on this very important matter. There is a tendency at the moment to say that opposition to the Bill is canalising itself into objections made by Roman Catholics only. I have projected that we act only as a catalyst and that objections are made in their widest sense and then conveyed to us and we, in turn, express it publicly. ...' Westminster Diocesan Archives AAW HE/A1(a).

166 Letter from Father Burke, Cardinal Heenan's Private Secretary, 29 November 1966. Westminster Diocesan Archives AAW HE/A1(a). It is interesting that Harold Wilson appears to have been quite mindful about the possible impact of proposals for reform on Catholic voters in marginal constituencies, and that impact made him cautious about proceeding (see http://www.kcl.ac.uk/sspp/departments/icbh/witness/PDFfiles/Ab ortionAct1967.pdf, 37).

167 Letter from Monsignor Norris, 26 October 1966, Westminster Diocesan Archives AAW HE/A1(a).

168 Letter from Monsignor Norris, 2 November 1966, Westminster Diocesan Archives AAW HE/A1(a).

169 On 5 July 1966, for instance, the Catholic Conservative MP for Hornsey, Hugh Rossi wrote to the Cardinal: I am greatly troubled by the proposed private members bill for the amendment of the law relating to Abortion on which I have received a number of supporting letters from Catholics. ... I would be grateful for guidance ... If it is not too much of an imposition an early reply from yourself or the Moral Theologian charged with the problem would be gratefully appreciated'. The Chancellor's observation on that letter was simple: 'As the whole issue of abortion is repugnant to the moral law I am puzzled when Rossi asks for guidance ... As the proposed Bill deals entirely with making legal actions which are now illegal and which are also contrary to the moral law none of its provisions are acceptable as such. ...'

170 Tam Dalyell, born in 1920, was the Labour Member for Linlithgow between 1962 and 1983, acting as Secretary of State for the Social Services, 1964–70.

171 In a letter from Monsignor Norris, 12 August 1967. Westminster Diocesan Archives AAW HE/A1(b).

172 Letter from Monsignor Norris, 19 November 1966. Westminster Diocesan Archives. AAW HE/A1(b).

173 The Bishop of St. Andrews and Edinburgh wrote to Cardinal Heenan to say 'I think the line you are taking regarding the Abortion Bill ... is wise. I had the feeling myself that any kind of opposition to this proposed legislation should come rather from the laity than from the Bishops'. Letter of 6 July 1966. Westminster Diocesan Archives AAW HE/A1(a).

174 The Cardinal wrote on 20 July 1966: 'I have insisted all the time that we must not make this a Catholic "thing" like fish on Friday. Much of the opposition in the House of Lords came from Catholic Peers and we want, if possible, to make other Christians stand up and speak this time'. Westminster Diocesan Archives AAW HE/A1(a).

175 For instance, a Parliamentary motion, designed to be a *coup de grace* to the bill, organised *inter alia* by Norman St. John-Stevas, and supported by some 100 Members of Parliament, called for the setting up of a Royal Commission on abortion. See *The Times*, 10 May 1967.

176 Cardinal Heenan wrote rather poignantly: 'The supporters of the Bill are decent people who are horrified by what are called back street abortions but do not realise

what we mean by the sanctity of human life. They regard life in the womb as having no more sanctity than an abscess or a tumour. ...' Letter of 28 June 1966. Westminster Diocesan Archives AAW HE/A1(a).

177 James Dunn, the Catholic Labour Member of Parliament for Liverpool Kirkdale since 1964, wrote to a group of Catholic doctors on 2 December 1966: 'David Steel ... is now finding that opinion on Abortion Law Reform is not as he was lead [*sic*] to believe, so strong in favour of the Bill that he has sponsored in the "House". It may well be that he now finds himself a prisoner of circumstances and indeed of other personalities who are co-sponsors of the Private Members Bill. In all justice to him, it is my opinion that he has acted in good faith and from deep sincerity in the cause that he attempting to champion. Emotionally he has reacted against back street abortionists in such a way as to lead him into proposing action which gives all appearances of removing this cancerous disease from our community. One can only sympathise with his revulsion against back street abortionists and express our concern and contempt for this practice also'. Westminster Diocesan Archives, AAW HE/A1(a).

178 The Cardinal's phrase was 'we are more likely to serve the cause of God by going to work quietly. ...' Letter of 16 February 1967. Westminster Diocesan Archives AAW HE/A1(b)

179 Letter from Cardinal Heenan, 27 June 1967. Westminster Diocesan Archives AAW HE/A1(b).

180 Norman St. John-Stevas, for example, asked the Speaker of the 16 March to give 'an assurance that it is not the intention of the Government before or after Easter to give time to facilitate the passage of the Medical Termination of Pregnancy Bill', only to be reminded that 'We cannot have negative questions on business'. (HC Deb 16 March 1967 Vol. 743 cc715–32.) He tried again a week later by asking the Prime Minister 'whether he will recommend the appointment of a Royal Commission to investigate the facts and law in relation to abortion;' and he was again rebuffed: 'the whole House knows – none more than the hon. Gentleman – this is a very important and highly controversial matter, a matter on which the House should be left to come to its own judgement. If, at the end of proceedings which it would clearly be out of order for me to refer to [because the Bill was in Committee], the House made its views clear in the sense indicated in the hon. Gentleman's Question, the Government would obviously have to give very close consideration to any such expression. But the House must be free to make its own decision on the matter'. (HC Deb 23 March 1967 Vol. 743 cc1908–9)

181 *alra newsletter* Spring 1967, – No 18.

182 He had earlier unsuccessfully asked the Speaker, Horace King, 'May we have an assurance that it is not the intention of the Government before or after Easter to give time to facilitate the passage of the Medical Termination of Pregnancy Bill'. HC Deb 16 March 1967 Vol. 743 cc715–32.

183 Letter of 22 March 1967.

184 Note to Prime Minister, 'Parliamentary Business: Private Members' Bills', 10 May 1967, PREM 13 1563.

185 Medical Termination of Pregnancy Bill: Memorandum by the Secretary of State for the Home Department, 31 May 1967, C(67) 90.

186 Conclusions of a Meeting of the Cabinet held at 10 Downing Street, S.W.1, on Thursday, 11 May, 1967, CC (67).

187 Letter to the Bishop of St Andrews and Edinburgh, 2 July 1966, Westminster Diocesan Archives AAW HE/A1(a).

188 Conclusions of a Meeting of the Cabinet held at 10 Downing Street, S.W.1, on Thursday, 1 June, 1967. CC (67) 35th Conclusions. For details of the petition, including its sponsorship by four Members of Parliament, including the Catholic, Norman St. John Stevas, see *The Times*, 8 March 1967.

189 David Steel recalled in interview that 'John [Silkin, the son of Lord Silkin] was in a pivotal position as a government chief whip in the decision about time. Roy was Home Secretary, was pushing for it. ... Kenneth Robinson was the Minister of Health and he had himself promoted a Private Member's Bill which ran out of time earlier on, so he was sympathetic. So you had within the Cabinet, a group of people who were very keen to get this thing through. And therefore, the request for time, although technically in the hands of Richard Crossman, I don't know whether it was ever discussed in the Cabinet or not, but certainly had colleagues around who were very pro, not forgetting Douglas Houghton who was then Chairman of the Parliamentary Labour Party'.

190 The Archbishops of Canterbury and York, and the Bishops of London and Durham, the great princes of the Church of England, had written to *The Times* on 23 May, 'at a crucial stage in the discussion of the Medical Termination of Pregnancy Bill, to say, citing *Abortion: An Ethical Discussion*, that they supported a termination conducted to save the life of the mother and that 'the lawful grounds for abortion should be contained in this single principle'. They supported neither the abortion of potentially deformed foetuses nor the clause offering as grounds the impact on other children.

191 HC Deb 2 June 1967 Vol. 747 cc450–93.

192 HC Deb 29 June 1967 Vol. 749 cc895–1102.

193 HC Deb 29 June 1967 Vol. 749 cc895–1102.

194 HC Deb 13 July 1967 Vol. 750 cc1161–239.

195 'MPs in Marathon Fight', *The Times*, 30 June 1967.

196 'Doubt for Abortion Bill', *The Times*, 1 July 1967.

197 I am grateful to the BBC for allowing me to see this interview: zztest_cutback_154_13_12_Millbank_219822

198 ICBH Witness Seminar Programme, 10 July 2001, http://www.kcl.ac.uk/sspp/departments/icbh/witness/PDFfiles/AbortionAct1967.pdf, 36.

199 R. Jenkins, *A Life at the Centre, op. cit.*, 210.

200 'A Bill to amend The Abortion Act 1967; to make further provisions with respect to the termination of pregnancy by registered medical practitioners; and for connected purposes'. It was presented by John Corrie and supported by Sir Bernard Braine, Leo Abse, Jill Knight, Elaine Kellett-Bowman, Gordon Wilson, W. Benyon, James Hamilton, Michael Ancram, James White, Ian Campbell and Janet Fookes. HC Deb 27 June 1979 Vol. 969 c45. John Corrie opened by saying that 'I found it a complicated matter to try to amend the Abortion Act 1967, which in turn must be read in conjunction with the Infant Life (Preservation) Act 1929'.

201 It is significant that the Home Office file on the proposed change to the 1929 Act contained a newspaper cutting from *The Times* of 22 July 1985, reporting the possibility of legislation, whose headline was 'BMA fears abortion controversy'.

202 Letter from Mrs J. Firth to W. Bohan, 7 February 1984. HO CRI/84 770/2/2.

203 Letter from M. Head to S. Street, 9 April 1984. HO CRI/84 770/2/2.

204 And there was the prospect in early 1985 of yet another private member's bill in the offing, to be moved by Edward Leigh, the Conservative MP for Gainsborough and Horncastle, that would amend the 1929 Act to prevent late abortions. Mr Leigh was averse to all abortion, arguing that 'everyone had the right to life, the mentally retarded as much as the normal, the old, sick, weak and stupid as much as the young, strong and clever'. *The Times*, 12 February 1985.

205 Infant Life (Preservation) Act 1929: Memorandum to the Home and Social Affairs Committee by the Secretary of State for the Home Department and the Secretary of State for Social Services. No date, *ca* September 1984, para. 6.

206 *Ibid.*

207 An amended version of the joint memorandum was accompanied by a note stating that 'The case for change is made more positively, according to the Home Secretary's wishes'. Mrs. S. Street to Mr. Fittall, 1 October 1985, HO CRI/84 770/2/2.

208 Letter of 23 July 1985. HO CRI/84 770/2/2.

209 Letter of 31 July 1985, HO CRI/84 770/2/2.

210 Those instructions noted that 'The need for the Bill arises from increased concern about the number of late abortions: the Abortion Act 1967 (c. 87) ceases to bite where the 1929 Act becomes effective …, and experience has shown that it is virtually impossible for a conviction to be secured under the 1929 Act …' HO CRI/84 770/2/2.

211 Brief for the Home Secretary: Infant Life (Preservation) Act 1929, Home and Social Affairs Committee, Cabinet, H(85) 43. October 1985.

212 The Committee had been established in July 1982 "To consider recent and potential developments in medicine and science related to human fertilisation and embryology; to consider what policies and safeguards should be applied, including consideration of the social, ethical, and legal implications of these developments; and to make recommendations". It reported on 18 July 1984. The Home Office's reading of the stance taken by the DHSS was that 'the Bill will be offered only if it is necessary to do so in order to buy off the threat of action on the Warnock Report or an abortion issue. The attraction of this course to DHSS is that they would be substituting a lesser controversy for a greater by persuading a Member to switch to the 1929 Act amendment, and this may indeed prove attractive to a member who is interested in abortion issues generally'. (Letter of 15 October 1985. HO CRI/84 770/2/2.) The relevant Cabinet minutes and Sir Robert Armstrong's Cabinet Minute Book could not be found.

213 Letter of 12 November 1985. HO CRI/84 770/2/2.

214 HO CRI/84 770/2/2.

215 HL Deb 30 June 1987 Vol. 488 cc239–40WA

216 HL Deb 15 January 1988 Vol. 491 cc1450–508

217 HL Deb 7 December 1989 Vol. 513 cc1002–114.

218 http://www.hfea.gov.uk/2068.html

219 The section read: (1) For paragraphs (a) and (b) of section 1(1) of the Abortion Act 1967 (grounds for medical termination of pregnancy) there is substituted –

'(a) that the pregnancy has not exceeded its twenty-fourth week and that the continuance of the pregnancy would involve risk, greater than if the pregnancy were terminated, of injury to the physical or mental health of the pregnant woman or any existing children of her family; or

(b) that the termination is necessary to prevent grave permanent injury to the physical or mental health of the pregnant woman; or

(c) that the continuance of the pregnancy would involve risk to the life of the pregnant woman, greater than if the pregnancy were terminated; or

(d) that there is a substantial risk that if the child were born it would suffer from such physical or mental abnormalities as to be seriously handicapped'.

220 HL Deb 7 December 1989 Vol. 513 cc1002–114. There was, in parallel, a separate Abortion (Amendment) Bill passing through the House of Lords that sought to implement the report of a Select Committee of the House of Lords and its recommendation that 28 weeks be reduced to twenty-four. Its mover, Lord Houghton, said 'the content of the Bill can be briefly summarised by saying that we recommended that up to the end of the 24th week the existing conditions and criteria in the 1967 Act should continue to apply, while after the 24th week stiffer conditions and sterner tests should be applied. Whatever limits are fixed there have to be exceptions'. HL Deb 14 December 1989 Vol. 513 cc1461–502.

221 David Ennals, 1922–1995, had been the Labour Member for Dover between 1964 and 1970 and for Norwich North between 1974 and 1983. He was to become Parliamentary Undersecretary at the Home Office between 1967 and 1968; Minister of State at the Department of Health and Social Security between 1968 and 1970; and Secretary of State for Social Services between 1976 and 1979. He became a Life

Peer in 1983. http://www.ukwhoswho.com/view/article/oupww/whowaswho/
U172317/ENNALS?index=1&results=QuicksearchResults&query=0.

222 Born in 1922, he had been President of the British Medical Association between 1980
and 1982, President of the General Medical Council between 1982 and 1989 and
President of the Royal Society of Medicine between 1984 and 1986.

223 Lord Henderson, 1922–2000, had been Clerk, House of Lords, 1954–60; he was
seconded to HM Treasury as Secretary to the Leader and Chief Whip, House of
Lords, 1960–63; Reading Clerk and Clerk of Public Bills, 1964–74; Member of the
Committee on Preparation of Legislation, 1973–74.; and was made a life peer in
1984. Based on entry in *Who was Who*, http://www.ukwhoswho.com/view/article/
oupww/whowaswho/U179134/HENDERSON_OF_BROMPTON?index=1&res
ults=QuicksearchResults&query=0.

224 Department of Health, (2009); *Abortion Statistics, England and Wales: 2008*, Statistical
Bulletin, http://www.dh.gov.uk/prod_consum_dh/groups/dh_digitalassets/docu
ments/digitalasset/dh_099714 Figure 5.1 is also taken from that bulletin.

225 It is interesting that Glanville Williams, the lawyer-philosopher president of ALRA
in its second and victorious incarnation, could criticise Lord Devlin for 'his apparent
inability to conceive the possibility of a utilitarian morality. He recognises that moral
rules may (by accident, it seems) have a utilitarian justification, but their moral status
does not depend on it in his eyes: they go historically back to Christian teaching, and
are supposed now to exist as customary morality independently either of utilitarian
justification or of religious belief. He thinks of the rules being in fact God-given …'
(March 1966); 'Authoritarian Morals and Criminal Law', *Criminal Law Review*, 138.

Bibliography

P. Allen (2004); 'A Young Home Secretary', Ch. 6 in A. Adonis and K. Thomas (eds.) *Roy
Jenkins: A Retrospective*, Oxford: Oxford University Press, 61–84

Revd. T. Brocklehurst (April 1911); 'The Birth of the Churchman's Union', *The Modern
Churchman*, Vol. 1, No. 1 (https://modernchurch.org.uk/our-history/journal/the-birth-
of-the-churchmen-s-union)

S. Bruce (1995); *Religion in Modern Britain*, Oxford: Oxford University Press

The Church Assembly Board for Social Responsibility (1965); *Abortion: An Ethical Discussion*,
London: Church Information Service

Congregation for the Doctrine of the Faith (1980); 'Declaration on Euthanasia *Iura et Bona*',
II: *AAS* 72

Encyclical Letter of Pope Pius XI (1930); *Christian Marriage*, Catholic Truth Society, Unwin
Brothers, Woking, 1962, 31

'Lord Gardiner Interviewed' (28 March 1964); *The Economist*, 1209–1212

D. Garland (2001); *The Culture of Control: Crime and Social Order in Contemporary Society*,
Chicago: University of Chicago Press

H. Heenan (1974); *A Crown of Thorns: An Autobiography 1951–1963*, London: Hodder and
Stoughton

K. Hindell and M. Sims (1971); *Abortion Law Reformed*, London: Owen

J. Kelley, M. Evans and B. Headey (1993); 'Moral Reasoning and Political Conflict: The
Abortion Controversy', *The British Journal of Sociology*, Vol. 44, No. 4. 589–612

S. Levitt and S. Dubner (2005); *Freakonomics: A Rogue Economist Explores the Hidden
Side of Everything*, London: Allen Lane

M. Ramsey (1974); Convocation of Canterbury on 17 January 1967, in *Canterbury Pilgrim*,
London: SPCK, 163–167

'Obituary: Dr. Sim' (2009); *British Columbia Medical Journal*, Vol. 51(9), 386

P. Rock (1996); *Reconstructing a Women's Prison*, Oxford: Clarendon Press.

M. Simms (1974); 'Abortion Law and Medical Freedom', *The British Journal of Criminology*, Vol. 14, No. 2, 118–131

N. St. John-Stevas (1961); *Life, Death and the Law: A Study of the Relationship between Law and Christian Morals in the English and American Legal Systems*, London: Eyre and Spottiswoode

G. Williams (1958); *The Sanctity of Life and the Criminal Law*, London: Faber and Faber

—(1963); *The Right to Life*, London: Hodder and Stoughton

—(1966); 'Authoritarian Morals and Criminal Law', *Criminal Law Review*, 132–147

F. Zimring (2007); *The Great American Crime Decline*, Oxford: Oxford University Press

6 The Liberal Hour III – The Sexual Offences Act 1967 c. 60

Prologue

Introduction

What was variously and uncertainly[1] called 'indecency', an 'unnatural' act, an 'infamous crime', 'buggery' or 'sodomy'[2] (but not homosexuality or sexual inversion until the new science of sexology emerged under Krafft-Ebbing[3] and Havelock Ellis[4] in the late 1880s[5]) had been an offence in law since 1533, when, under the Buggery Act of 25 H. VIII C6, conceiving sodomy to be an idolatrous and heretical sin inimical to the proper purpose of sexual congress,[6] a sin linked to the monkish practices then under the censure of the new Protestant reformers[7], transgressive because it straddled what were thought to be natural boundaries,[8] 'the detestable and abominable Vice of Buggery committed with mankind or beast' was made punishable by death.[9] It was a penalty that was first imposed in 1540, lapsed briefly in 1553 when Queen Mary ascended the throne to repeal a mass of Henrician legislation, reinstated ten years later under an Act for the Punishment of the Vice of Sodomy, 5 Eliz. C. 17, and then continued to be imposed for some three centuries thereafter.[10]

Changes in the sodomy laws were to move through many of the same stages and substantially in step with the other legislative developments I have charted so far. They were, as importantly, to be framed within much the same general debate between an absolutist ethics that talked about damage to the moral and spiritual fabric of the community, condemned by God, and a utilitarianism[11] that talked, in this instance, about the autonomy of the responsible individual.[12] Sodomy remained a hanging offence, the wording intact from the sixteenth century, in Lord Lansdowne's Act of 1828[13] (according to Harvey, some 50 to 60 men were hanged for sodomy between 1800 and 1835, there having been more executions for sodomy than for murder in 1806[14]), but it effectively lapsed as a capital crime in the mid-1830s. There was an abortive attempt to abolish the imposition of the death penalty in law in 1841 with the unsuccessful Punishment of Death Bill.[15] And then the offence was swept up in the great wave of consolidating and liberalising legislation which marked the utilitarian-inspired state-building project of the mid-nineteenth century, becoming exempt from hanging under the omnibus 1861 Offences Against the Person Act[16] which, under Sec. 61, still retained the older wording from the sixteenth century but substituted a new sentence of penal servitude for between ten years and life.[17]

A critical transformation was next introduced somewhat abruptly and, to some, seemingly inexplicably in August 1885 by the so-called Labouchère Amendment[18] 'which stole into the Criminal Justice (Amendment) Act[19] [*sic*] in the middle of the Report stage of the Bill',[20] almost, many commentators would believe, in a fit of absence of mind.[21] That 'infamous'[22] Act was inspired by a collective endeavour to confront moral corruption[23] in sexual and domestic relations, having been in part instigated by the campaigns of the Social Purity movement, and, especially, of the Society for the Suppression of Vice founded at the beginning, and by the Society for the Prevention of Cruelty to Children founded at the end of the nineteenth century. After a number of unsuccessful attempts at legislation, it was quite deliberately[24] spurred on by William Stead's[25] revelations of child prostitution in 'The Maiden Tribute of Modern Babylon' published in *The Pall Mall Gazette* in July 1885[26] – revelations which likened London to a Minotaur that devoured its young through 'The sale and purchase and violation of children; II The procuration of virgins; III The entrapping and ruin of women; IV The international slave trade in girls; [and] V Atrocities, brutalities, and unnatural crimes'.[27]

Stead had made no reference to young male prostitutes,[28] and the 1885 bill touched at first only on offences against females. It would have raised the age of female sexual consent to 16 and devised new penalties for sexual offences against women and minors (its long title was 'An Act to make further provision for the protection of Women and Girls, the suppression of brothels, and other purposes', and its principal sections touched on 'Procuring woman to be a common prostitute or to enter a brothel'; 'Procuring defilement of woman by threats or fraud'; 'Defilement of girl under thirteen years of age'; 'Defilement of girl between thirteen years and sixteen years of age'; 'Abduction of girl under eighteen with intent to have carnal knowledge'; and 'Power, on indictment for rape, to convict for indecent assault').

Henry Labouchère's[29] late and unexpected intercession posed two problems. It seemed to go quite against the grain of the bill (Charles Warton, the member for Bridport, protested that it 'dealt with a totally different class of offence to that against which the Bill was directed'[30]). It also introduced a new, 'unspecified'[31] and umbrella crime of 'gross indecency' between *males* (but not females) of all ages, extending the existing law well beyond the simple act of sodomy[32] to encompass 'all forms of sexual intimacy between men'.[33] The Earl of Dundee asserted eighty years later that 'it was not until very near the end of the Report stage that Mr. Labouchere suddenly got up and moved his new clause. Until then, sodomy had been the only kind of homosexual act which came within the range of the criminal law. This new Labouchere clause brought every other kind of homosexual act within the range of the criminal law'.[34] That clause, section 11, recited that:

'Any male person who, in public or private, commits, or is a party to the commission of, or procures or attempts to procure the commission by any male person of, any act of gross indecency with another male person, shall be guilty of a misdemeanour, and, being convicted thereof, shall be liable, at the discretion of the Court, to be imprisoned for any term not exceeding one year with or without hard labour'.

Sodomy and homosexuality were difficult, taboo subjects, too awkward to form a proper subject of parliamentary debate, and it is not remarkable that Labouchère himself should have been diffident about expatiating on them in public. Indeed, he was reluctant even to name them. His actual purpose in moving the amendment has in consequence remained somewhat obscure. None of his obituaries[35] or biographies makes any mention of the Act or the Amendment,[36] his personal papers were largely destroyed,[37] and he was to offer different and contradictory reasons for his action over the years. All he had to say at the time was that 'The meaning of it was that at present any person on whom an assault of the kind here dealt with was committed must be under the age of 13, and the object with which he had brought forward this clause was to make the law applicable to any person, whether under the age of 13 or over that age'.[38] His amendment was thereby to become something of a Rorschach blot which has baffled the occasional commentator[39] and excited quite different interpretations.

In common with many others, he certainly appeared to have a marked antipathy to homosexuals and the alleged cabals that sustained them[40] (an allegation that continued to be made by others for decades,[41] not surprisingly, perhaps, when many homosexual activities were obliged to be collaborative and clandestine (as David Matza once said, deviation must often become devious[42])). So it was that, five years after the passing of the Act, in 1890, some light was thrown on his action when he was 'named' and suspended from the House of Commons for making charges against the Home Secretary and the attorney general for their conduct of the prosecution of a group of men, including an aristocrat, Lord Arthur Somerset, who had been arrested at a male brothel in Cleveland Street,[43] notorious for its *poses plastiques*, but was allowed to fly to France.[44] 'Practically my charge', he said, 'is that certain official persons confederated together to defeat the course of justice by interfering to prevent their friends being put on trial for a crime in regard to which two persons were tried and convicted'.[45] More particularly, he asserted – still shying away from the actual use of unspeakable words – that in 'consequence of collusion between the counsel for the prisoners and the Treasury counsel, an inadequate sentence was passed upon [two defendants] and that [another] was allowed to escape from justice':[46]

> There is no doubt that of late years a certain offence – I will not give it a name – has become more rife than it ever was before. Before 1885 the law was insufficient to deal with it, because the offence had to be proved by an accessory, and many other offences very much of the same nature were not regarded as crimes at all. In 1885, when the Criminal Law Amendment

Bill was before a Committee of the House, Mr. Stead – who, it will be remembered, took a very active part in urging that Bill on the attention of the House – sent me a report with reference to this offence,[47] giving particulars and evidence which went to show the extent of its prevalence. I was requested to read this report to the House, but I did not think it desirable to do so, although I thought the case was pretty well proved. I proposed the addition to the Bill of a special clause which I took from the French Code, and this clause was submitted to the Attorney-General and Lord Cross,[48] and, with some verbal alterations, accepted and incorporated in the Bill, and is now the law of the land. Therefore, in 1885, Parliament armed the guardians of public morality with full powers to deal with this offence.[49]

The Australian historian, Barry Smith, contended that this was an implausible argument – there was, for example, no such clause in the French legal code[50] – and the Amendment was little more than a piece of obstructive mischief-making by a man who had not hitherto busied himself in the area of sexual regulation,[51] was unsympathetic to the wider intentions of the Bill and sought to embarrass its sponsors.[52] Sanna supposed that it was a characteristically repressive piece of Victorian legislation[53] (although it would be hard to cast Labouchère himself as oppressively moralistic[54]). Some have portrayed the Amendment as a rather marginal addition to a misogynistic Act that was motivated by hostility to the exploitation of working class youths by aristocratic men.[55] Others have looked upon it as a reasonably commonplace and intelligible coupling[56] that had its origins in an effort to defend the integrity of the family[57] by policing men's sexuality and controlling private morality,[58] a coupling that persisted up to the convening in 1954 of the committee on homosexual offences and female prostitution, chaired by Sir John Wolfenden, whose work will be the culmination of this chapter. Labouchère himself talked about how he had been prompted by Stead's seemingly undisclosed report. But much more direct, and much more compelling, is Louise Jackson's argument[59] that it simply extended a provision regulating the abuse of young females to the abuse of young males.[60]

There was, she writes, a growing public apprehension in the 1880s that young males were also being sexually exploited, and that their exploitation represented a repugnant problem which demanded redress. The courts were beginning to accept that males under the age of 12 could not give consent to indecent assault, but there was a difficulty with those who were older. It was to be a subject of comment by Howard Vincent,[61] the occupant of the newly created post of Director of Criminal Investigations with the Metropolitan Police, when he testified before the 1881 Select Committee on the Protection of Young Girls.[62] The committee had been established in the belief that 'prostitution was increasing with fearful rapidity in London, and that, under the present law, it was perfectly easy and safe for persons in this country to carry on a traffic in English girls for purposes of prostitution'.[63] It was not supposed to occupy itself with the protection of young boys, and Vincent's brief and anomalous intervention – amounting to what was almost an aside – was the only reference in the minutes of evidence to indecency and the need to guard vulnerable male youth against the temptations of homosexual London. Indeed, what he said was in answer to a question about female prostitution:

> I should like to make one observation first of all, and that is, that I do not think the evil of juvenile prostitution is entirely confined to females; I think it is applicable to a very large extent indeed to males. I mean that everything centreing [*sic*] in London, as it does in this country; all examinations are held in London; everybody sends their sons up to London necessarily for examination; and a boy must be a paragon of virtue, who, at 16 or 17, can walk from 11 o'clock at night till half-past 12 in the morning, from the top of the Haymarket to the top of Grosvenor-place without being solicited to such an enormous extent, that he is almost certain to fall.[64]

That *obiter dicta* did not make its way into the Committee's report. It was not recorded in the newspapers.[65] It was not the subject of the many petitions presented to Parliament in the years following the report on the protection of young girls. It was not quoted in the debate on the 1885 Act. It was not mentioned in Howard Vincent's biography,[66] although his evidence to the committee about the 'immoral traffic in young girls' *was* cited, and other matters, such as his role in combatting Fenians and anarchists, and in drafting an unsuccessful Stolen Goods Bill received lengthy attention. It was not even mentioned by Labouchère as he proposed his amendment. But Labouchère certainly knew Vincent quite well[67] and what he had said might quite conceivably have swayed him. After all, it had entered the published record of a committee that was the linear antecedent of the Act. It is possible to argue, Jackson writes:

> that the outlawing of gross indecency in 1885 must have been an attempt to deal with the perceived problem of boys aged 14–18 who were picked up by adult men, whether these boys were 'innocent' parties or openly pursuing business as male prostitutes. The 'gross indecency' clause, read purely as an attempt to stop consensual sex between men, is often seen as incongruous in a bill which otherwise aimed to 'protect young girls'. If, however, its central aim was the protection of young boys (whatever purposes it was actually put to), the clause fits neatly into place.[68]

It was a measure that was thought to be so self-evidently commendable that it needed no defence: Henry Labouchère himself said that he did not 'think it necessary to discuss the proposal at any length, as he understood Her Majesty's Government were willing to accept it. He, therefore, left it for the House and the Government to deal with as might be thought best'.[69] And the Amendment was subject to only the most meagre debate, possibly, some argue, because MPs were eager to return home to campaign for an impending general election or, as others would say, because it was not a subject that could be discussed without embarrassment.[70]

There have been scholarly doubts aired about the amendment's meaning[71] and practical impact,[72] but Jeffrey Weeks, the prime authority in the area, has made the claim that it led to a new and unequivocal:

> Focus specifically on male-male sexual activities short of sodomy. Gross indecency was the indication of this. As far as I am aware it did not appear in statute before 1885, and was I believe exclusively used for male-male activity. Prior to this all acts short of penetration were dealt with as acts likely to lead to sodomy. [And the amendment became] a symbolic focus of a more refined and shifting approach to the regulation of homosexuality. It is striking how it was seen by an emergent homosexual theorisation as the focus of a new hostility, not least as the 'Blackmailer's charter'.[73] It may also be read as part of a running project to instil moral purity and to defend the respectability of the family by policing the sexual conduct of women *and* men.[74]

Male Homosexuality in the 1950s

Reinforced by clauses regulating importuning in the Vagrancy Acts 1898[75] and 1912, the 1885 Act cast a wide net over men who became ever more nervous about their vulnerability to exposure – the standard epithet repeatedly applied was, in Weeks' words, the 'blackmailer's charter'.[76] Peter Wildeblood, the author and journalist who was himself convicted under the amendment, wrote to the Wolfenden Committee that: 'A large number of men ... continue to live ... in fear of prosecution. Blackmail ... continue[s] to flourish. Lord Jowitt has said that during his term of office as Lord Chancellor 95 per cent of all blackmail cases had homosexuality as their root cause[77]. ...'[78] And another letter written to Sir John Wolfenden reported that:

> With the newspaper strike "on", you have, possibly, not noticed a very unpleasant Blackmail case, as a result of which two Metropolitan Police Constables have been sentenced to 2 years imprisonment, each, for attempted blackmail of a Commercial Traveller, in Piccadilly Circus.[79] One of these blackguards accosted the man, and, then, said he was going to arrest him for importuning. Then the other fellow appeared on the scene, and suggested it might be possible to "square" things. They arranged to meet the victim the next night. In the meantime the victim, with great courage, had gone to the police and acted under their instruction. The result as I have, already, stated [is that]. ... every Tom, Dick, and Harry (male AND female) seem to spend their time "snooping" and

"pimping" for, possible, homosexual actions among their friends, and neighbours... [80]

Sir John Wolfenden himself would later reflect that there was 'ample opportunity for blackmail, compounded by the danger that if a man who was being blackmailed revealed the fact to the police he might be charged and sentenced for homosexual offences'.[81] It was under Section 11 of the Criminal Law Amendment Act that Oscar Wilde was convicted in 1895[82] and Alan Turing was convicted in 1952.[83] Trends in the numbers of prosecutions for 'unnatural offences' and 'gross indecency' reflect the intersecting vagaries of reporting, recording, policing and charging practices,[84] supplying a rough index of the interest which the state and its agencies took in the problem, and it may be seen from Figure 6.1 that, although they were never massive in scale, those trends did rise steadily, steeply and continuously across England and Wales over the first half of the twentieth century, causing apprehensions that they marked a very real and disturbing change in behaviour,[85] and engendering and being engendered by what Tim Newburn called a 'moral panic'.[86] It was a panic that some have supposed reflected and exacerbated anxieties about the new 'delinquent generations' and the proper development of masculine identity after the upheavals of war[87] (a matter which I discussed in Chapter 1); a number of well-publicised scandals;[88] and apprehensions lurking at the very heart of the Home Office and Scotland Yard.

Yet, if a moral panic or a moral crusade *was* in train, it is a little difficult after sixty years to decipher quite what it entailed. It was certainly a repressive era (Weeks remarks that 'In the 1950s Britain was widely regarded as having one of the most conservative sexual cultures in the world, with one of the most draconian penal codes'[90]). There were certainly the signs of a campaigning rhetoric in the air. The Commissioner of Metropolitan Police, Sir John

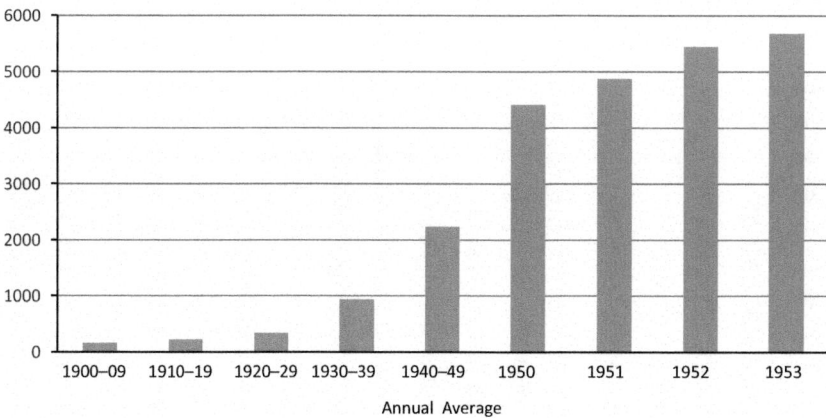

Figure 6.1 Number of persons tried on indictment and summarily for 'Unnatural Offences and Attempts' 1900–1953[89]

Nott-Bower,[91] appointed in 1953 on the strong recommendation of his pre-decessor, Sir Harold Scott, and of the Home Secretary, was widely reported to have promised to 'rip the cover off all London's filth spots ... [and to have] enlisted the support of local police throughout England to step up the number of arrests for homosexual offences',[92] but it seems that he otherwise made scant public reference to 'filth spots' or 'unnatural offences' in his speeches or annual reports[93] (it was his predecessor who flagged their increase in *his* reports[94]). He left no personal papers,[95] autobiography or biography. I was told that there are no documents in the possession of the Metropolitan Police touching on Sir John's policies, actions and views on the 1861 and 1885 Acts.[96] There are no references at all to his sentiments on the theme in *The Times*, *Manchester Guardian* and *Observer* archives. In all the correspondence about his appointment, there was only one minor allusion, made by the Prime Minister, Winston Churchill, to what might be deemed 'filth spots',[97] and there is no evidence that it was conveyed to Sir John himself. In all probability, Sir John was not questioned at his job interview about anything to do with 'filth spots' or 'gross indecency' (the questions focused principally on police recruitment and traffic enforcement[98]). But there is a clue to trends in the volume of 'unnatural offences' recorded in the Metropolitan police area in the late 1940s and early 1950s, just before and during the time of his appointment. Sir John told the Wolfenden Committee that there had been a modest increase in the complement of officers from three to seven specifically dedicated to investigat-ing male importuning, and that their surveillance was heavily concentrated in a number of public lavatories in central London.[99] It would be difficult to accept that the impact of that heightened vigilance by a few policemen had led to a dramatic increase (see Figure 6.2).

Neither, should it be observed, was there much evidence of an especially vigorous campaign being mounted in that part of Hampshire where arrests were made in late 1953 in what was to become known as the Montagu affair, an affair with critical consequences, to which I shall return (see Figure 6.3).

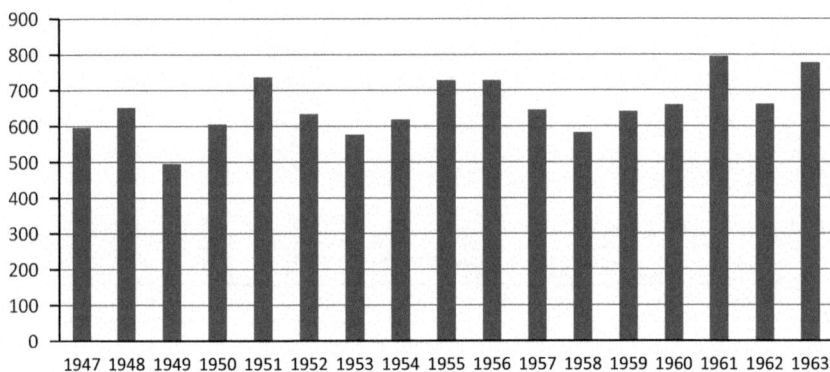

Figure 6.2 'Unnatural Offences' known to the Metropolitan Police[100]

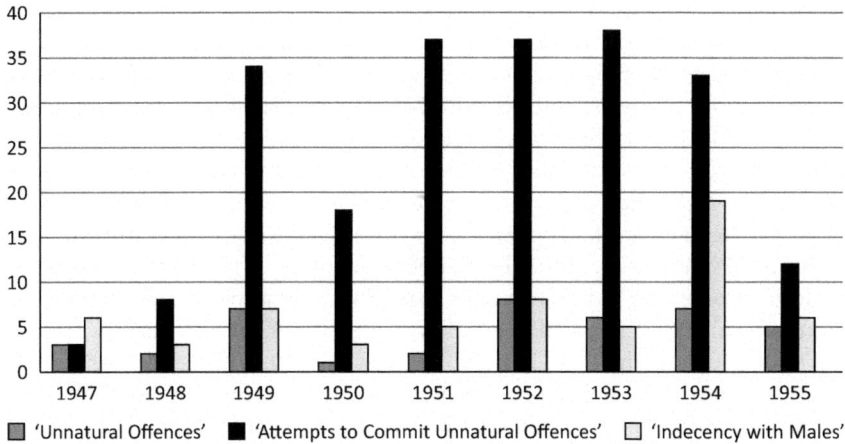

Figure 6.3 Recorded offences in the County Borough of Southampton 1947–1955*

* Taken from *Annual Report of the Chief Constable for 1947*, County Borough of Southampton, Chief Constable's Office, Southampton, 16 February 1948 and successive reports thereafter. I am grateful to the Archives department of the Hampshire Record Office in recommending this and other materials on local events in the county in the 1950s.

The Home Secretary, Sir David Maxwell Fyfe,[101] appointed in 1951, is also said to have egged prosecutions along,[102] and he had undoubtedly promised 'a new drive against male vice' that would 'rid England of this plague'.[103] He told the House of Commons in 1953 that 'homosexuals in general are exhibitionists and proselytisers and are a danger to others, especially the young, and so long as I hold the office of Home Secretary I shall give no countenance to the view that they should not be prevented from being such a danger'.[104] Perhaps because he too found the subject literally almost unspeakable, his memoirs make no mention of homosexuality or policing policy,[105] and he said little else in public, but he was a man avowedly driven by strong convictions[106] and had 'a well-served reputation for being exceptionally unsympathetic to homosexuals'.[107] It was to be an ironic and unintended consequence of that hostility that the law was reformed.

Formally and informally, the social problem of homosexuality was for the most part subterranean in the first half of the twentieth century, apprehended through half-truths and generally little discussed.[108] In a fragment of autobiography, Anatole James observes that 'in the Britain of pre-1914 [when James was 22] [a]mong the so-called "normal" & respectable people, the subject of homosexuality was absolutely unmentionable – in fact the whole subject was absolutely unmentionable. The whole subject was, among very large sections of the public, unknown. They just didn't realise it went on'.[109] Homosexuality may indeed have been susceptible to the workings of what John Dollard once called 'pluralistic ignorance', a divergence between what people may privately have believed, known and thought themselves, and what they believed, knew and thought others believed, knew and thought.[110] Those who might have known something or someone in private would profess their innocence in public because any hint of familiarity with the phenomenon could itself confer a taint. Bob Morris, the former civil servant who had been in the Home Office at the time of the work on the 1967 Sexual Offences Bill recalled in interview in 2010: 'Well, there was this enormous prejudice against them [in the Home Office] ... it struck atavistic chords you know, that they were going to interfere with children and so on, ... on the one hand. On the other, I mean there was toleration often where it occurred face-to-face. ... And this was understood, you know, at that level, but at the policy level it was a "no-no"'. Sir John Wolfenden,[111] the man who chaired the Departmental Committee on Homosexual Offences and Prostitution in the 1950s, wrote, perhaps in *faux naïf* fashion that, at the time, homosexuality was 'not mentioned in polite society. Most ordinary people had never heard of homosexuality; and of those who had the great majority regarded it with something nearer to disgust than understanding'.[112] Indeed, it will become apparent that members of the Wolfenden Committee were themselves to be troubled by the prospect of getting too close to homosexuality and to their homosexual witnesses[113] (just as those witnesses were to be fearful of exposure[114]). And those who *did* discuss homosexuality – even those who professed to do so for scientific reasons – often seemed obliged as a matter of etiquette or prudence to distance themselves from the phenomenon. In 1897, for example, the man who opened up what purported to be the scientific investigation of sexuality, Havelock Ellis, began his *Sexual Inversion* with the statement that:

> I had not at first proposed to devote a whole volume to sexual inversion. It may even be that I was inclined to slur it over as an unpleasant subject, and one that it was not wise to enlarge on. But I found in time that several persons for whom I felt respect and admiration were the congenital subjects of this abnormality. At the same time I realised that in England, more than in any other country, the law and public opinion combine to place a heavy penal burden and a severe social stigma on the manifestations of an instinct which to those persons who possess it frequently appears natural and normal. It was clear, therefore, that the matter was in special need of elucidation and discussion.[115]

It was a squeamishness that prevailed from first to last.[116] Some sixty years later, at the time of the first meetings of the Wolfenden Committee, the child psychiatrist, Kenneth Soddy,[117] chose to open a paper in *The Lancet* with the observation that 'The word "homosexuality" brings with it, to some people, a sensation of abhorrence that is deeper than reason'.[118] Significantly, too, perhaps, and as I have hinted, Sir John Wolfenden was constrained publicly to pretend to an ignorance of the subject that was belied in private.[119] There was certainly no doubt that homosexuality could not be openly celebrated by men and women as a desirable way of life freely chosen (and the conditions under which many had to labour could indeed make it far from pleasant[120]).

They tended not to speak thus in public and perhaps not necessarily to think thus in private.[121] Rather, homosexuality tended chiefly to be seen as a *problem*, defined through the lenses supplied by different vocations and life-worlds; regarded at best as an affliction, biological predisposition or illness to be pitied and treated,[122] or at worst as an abomination to be deplored, deterred and punished[123] (although the one stance could leach into the other, so that, as I shall argue, the supposedly clinical looked at times as if it were remarkably moralising[124]). Not atypical was the observation offered by the journalist, Percy Cudlipp,[125] when he talked about the 'unfortunate and tragic mental quirk which makes [men] homosexuals'.[126] Even the members of the organisation that was set up to champion homosexual law reform took it upon themselves, in good or bad faith,[127] publicly to declare that:

> When the Homosexual Law Reform Society was founded in 1958 some of those who gave it their support may have been under the impression that homosexuals were a tiny, freakish minority and that the law ... affected the lives of perhaps only a few hundred people. ... [T]here are probably at least one million men in this country, and quite possibly a far higher number, who are wholly or predominantly homosexual in temperament if not in overt behaviour. ... We believe that the law as it stands ... gives rise to much objectionable behaviour of a homosexual nature (public indecency and importuning) which would almost certainly diminish considerably if legal sanctions against private consenting homosexual behaviour were removed. ... The present law also undoubtedly deters a great many men – especially young men and adolescents – from seeking psychological or medical treatment at the earliest possible moment. Because of the widespread fear of exposure which exists, a great deal of neurotic illness, and also of venereal disease, goes untreated. Reaction to the law tends to turn many homosexuals into either moody, neurotic depressives or else into frivolous, irresponsible, badly-integrated personalities. ...[128]

Many homosexual men and women led shadowy lives, hidden from common view, liable on occasion to accept adverse judgements about themselves,[129] and apparently themselves prone to pluralistic ignorance.[130] 'I thought I was, like a lot of people do, I was the only one in the world and there was something terribly strange and dreadful about it. It wasn't until I went to university and was a bit older, that I actually met people who identified as gay'[131] said Antony Grey, the secretary of the Homosexual Law Reform Society. They frequently resorted to a common stock of metaphors to describe their condition. Peter Wildeblood, for example, reflected that 'I have been on both sides of the fence which separates Society from its misfits, the world from the underworld, and the no-man's land which surround it is a territory which I have crossed and recrossed many times. It is a bare and comfortless place ... [and] most of the men and women in it are prisoners. They are not enclosed by bricks and mortar, but by their circumstances and desires; some are the prisoners of their upbringing, some of their poverty, others of their wealth; there are prisoners of the flesh and of the spirit ...'[132] And Anthony Grey, a man impelled to adopt a *nom de guerre*[133] (his original name was Edgar Wright), recalled in the early 1990s that as a teenager:

> I ... became aware that there is a hideous aura of criminality, degeneracy and abnormality surrounding the matter. ... growing up during the war, I increasingly felt where sex was concerned like a member of the Resistance in enemy-occupied territory. ... Homosexual men were smothered by [a] blanket of silence and lived in an atmosphere of secrecy, of insecurity and frequently of considerable ignorance. ... It is hard for anyone now aged under fifty to imagine what living in this oppressive atmosphere was like.[134]

He did not exaggerate. He lived a secretive life, marked by caution,[135] and he was constrained sometimes to engage in subterfuge when he spoke publicly as a homosexual man. A letter he received at the Homosexual Law Reform Society from the Head of News at Independent Television for South Wales and the West of England in March 1961 said, for instance:

> We are very glad to hear that you are arranging for a spokesman for your Society to take part anonymously in our programme "In the News" on Friday evening. For the sake of convenience in these rather special circumstances, there are one or two arrangements which we must make. The contract for your spokesman ... . plus first class return rail fare from London, must be made payable to an individual, and will therefore be made out to you. ... For convenience only – and because we must have a name for our various Studio documents, we shall be calling your spokes-man, for the period of his visit to Cardiff, "Mr. William Johnson" [altered to Antony Grey after this was written]. We are booking a room for him for Friday night ... in this name, and he will be described by this name on his Studio pass ...[136]

Homosexual men, in short, kept their heads down. The distinguished crimi-nologist and 'sexologist', Donald West, remarked in his frank sexual auto-biography, that 'To be taken seriously in the Fifties, one had to keep a low profile and avoid public admission of a homosexual orientation (fortunately something it was unlikely people would dare to ask outright)'.[137]

What did eventually dramatise the social problem of homosexuality, push-ing it publicly and politically into the open, was a number of scandals, two of which were prolonged, centred on prominent people and arising in close juxtaposition.[138] One was the arrest for 'persistent soliciting' and for importun-ing a police officer in October 1953 of Sir John Gielgud, the actor. He was fined £10 at West London magistrates court on 21 October and was told by the magistrate, who had not recognised him, that 'this conduct is dangerous to other men, particularly young men, and is a scourge in this neighbourhood'.[139] His court appearance had however been noted by a reporter from the London *Evening Standard*, was prominently publicised in the newspaper, and 'was soon front-page news'.[140] In the event, little enough was said: Gielgud was described in the *Evening Standard* as having 'thinning hair' and wearing 'horn-rimmed spectacles', and that, and the rest of the text, was reproduced wholesale and without much amendment in other newspapers the next morning. The report-ing was uniformly bald and its tenor was muted, no new investigation having been undertaken by journalists. Sir John Gielgud's public standing seemingly neutralised the obloquy he might have suffered, and there was little specific detail offered of the offences themselves. All that was problematic was the issue of how the conviction might affect his stage career. The *Daily Express* of 22 October, for example, talked about how his 'Agent and friends [had] urge[d] 'act on' ...') The *Daily Mail's* sub-headline on that day's front page was 'Will he appear in new play?' And the *Daily Telegraph* reported that the manager of the Royal Court Theatre, Liverpool, needed to know Sir John's plans about the play he was to direct ("'I must know tomorrow," said Mr Mason, "so that I can alter my advertising if necessary'''). Although the scandal affected Sir John himself deeply, colleagues and theatre audiences were forbearing,[141] press reporting was neither searching nor prurient, and media interest died down quite quickly.

A second scandal was the unfolding exposure of Guy Burgess[142] and Donald Maclean,[143] the so-called Cambridge spies, who had been part of a larger circle of Soviet sympathisers and homosexuals, centred on the Apostles (the 'best known and at the same time most secretive of all undergraduate societies'[144]), recruited at Cambridge University in the 1930s, and then established in the Secret Service and the Foreign Office. It was a circle which was said to have inflicted significant damage on defence and security,[145] and it contributed to a loss of American faith in British intelligence.[146]

The homosexual[147] Guy Burgess had joined the News Department of the Foreign Office in 1944, became assistant private secretary to the Secretary of State for Scotland, and then Second Secretary at the British Embassy in Washington in 1950. The bisexual Donald Maclean was head of the American Department of the Foreign Office. Together they fled to France in May 1951 and from thence to a destination that remained undisclosed for several years, but which was later identified as Moscow; and the circumstances of their appointment, activities, surveillance and disappearance were to be the subject of repeated questioning inside and outside Parliament.[148] Some public clarification of what had happened was eventually provided when Vladimir Petrov,[149] a Soviet agent who had defected in Australia, made allegations about Burgess and Maclean in a front page article in the *People* newspaper of 18 September 1955.[150] 'Today', the newspaper claimed, ''The People' lays before the world the complete solution to the mystery of the missing British diplomats ...' It proceeded both to summarise the substance of an Australian Royal Commission report on Soviet espionage[151] that had been prompted by

Vladimir Petrov's defection and to publish an account by Petrov himself.[152] Petrov did talk there about how Burgess and Maclean 'became close friends after their Cambridge days' but he said nothing at all explicitly about their sexuality. 'At last', thundered *The Times*, 'a newspaper has rung the bell. There have been countless (costly) stories of Mr. MACLEAN and Mr. BURGESS, of the Foreign Office, since they vanished four years ago. Now the tale told … the *People* as from Mr. PETROV … is admitted by the Foreign Office to be in certain essentials true'.[153] A few days after the publication of that story, and following on the heels of the report of the Australian Royal Commission, the British government released its own eight-page White Paper[154] on the affair in which again nothing was said about sexuality. In paragraph 9, for example, it stated that:

> The question has been asked whether the association of these two officers with each other did not give rise to suspicion. The fact is that although we have since learned that Maclean and Burgess were acquainted during their undergraduate days at Cambridge, they gave no evidence during the course of their career in the Foreign Office of any association other than would be normal between two colleagues.

There seemed in fact to have been a thoroughgoing and not uncharacteristic reticence to allude to the near-taboo matter of Burgess' and Maclean's sexuality, and it may not have been centrally at issue in the beginning. None of the telegrams, reports and correspondence which first brought the problem before the Prime Minister in 1951 made any direct reference to the matter.[155] In the House of Commons debate on the White Paper on 7 November 1955, there was much circumlocutory talk about Burgess and Maclean being 'undesirable types'[156] who had 'chips on their shoulders'[157] and a record of 'misbehaviour' demonstrated by Maclean's 'disgraceful conduct in Cairo' and what was called Burgess's 'indiscretion' and his 'troubles … in Washington'.[158] It is consequently not evident when, to what extent and by whom, their sexuality was explicitly taken to be problematic, partly because the language in use at the time was almost invariably so elliptical.[159] Quite typical was the encrypted comment made by the Member of Parliament, Sir Godfrey Nicolson, that:

> So far as vulnerability is concerned, there have been references to the unfortunate habits of Burgess and various people. Without delivering moral judgement, we must face the fact that people who are perverted in their tastes are extremely vulnerable to blackmail. I did not know Burgess well. I met him once or twice. [But] [o]ne had only to look at his eyes to see that he was an unreliable and shifty type, brilliant though he was. I believe that if in those days there had been the same careful scrutiny of people's character, habits and background as there is today he would not have been in the Foreign Office for one week.[160]

Only one bald reference to homosexuality was made in that debate, and that was offered by Alfred Robens, the 'forthright' Labour Member for Blyth,[161] who asked 'how can it be that a couple of drunks, a couple of homosexuals well-known in the City, could for so long occupy important posts in the Foreign Office?' 'Whitehall floundered in this unpleasant scandal of espionage, sex, and conspiracy',[162] and the supposed links, if any, between Burgess' and Maclean's homosexuality, treason, recruitment and conspiracy were left largely tacit.[163] But connections were certainly being mapped by officials *sub rosa*,[164] and new vetting procedures were introduced to include questions about sexual propensity.[165] Moreover, according to a report in *The Sydney Morning Telegraph* of 25 October 1953:

> Special Branch began compiling a "Black Book" of known perverts in influential Government jobs after the disappearance of the diplomats Donald Maclean and Guy Burgess, who were known to have pervert associates. Now comes the difficult task of side-tracking these men into less important jobs – or of putting them behind bars.

A third, contemporaneous episode was similarly protracted and much publicised, and it centred on a scandal in the very heart of the English aristocracy. There had long been a history of promiscuity amongst the upper classes, but it tended to be concealed by the taboos attached to the explicit naming of homosexual acts and actors, discreet cover-up and, *in extremis*, a resort to calling on men to fall on their sword or quit the country.[166] The so-called Montagu affair was different. Driven by what has been described as feverish press interest,[167] it began first with the issuing of a warrant against Lord Montagu of Beaulieu[168] and another in October 1953;[169] a preliminary hearing by the Lymington Magistrates in Hampshire in November 1953 and their subsequent trial in December at Winchester Assizes for committing 'a serious offence against a young person',[170] a boy scout, one of a number then camping on his estate. Lord Montagu's defence counsel, William Fearnley-Whittingstall,[171] observed as he opened his case that 'the trial was taking place at a time when public attention had been focused on this type of vice. The Press, prominent men, and divines of all sects had written about it; it was in that atmosphere that the trial took place'.[172] It was, said the local newspaper, a *cause célèbre*;[173] 'played out', remarked the arresting officer, 'amid an unprecedented blaze of publicity'.[174] It was not the only case of offences against young boys prosecuted at the same Autumn Assizes – an Alderman[175] and a schoolmaster[176] were also being tried in separate cases. It was in that setting that the Dean of Winchester was moved to preach in his Remembrance Day Service in the local cathedral about 'the present concern being expressed in this country ... on every side to-day voices are raised warning us how disastrously in our own country moral standards are being allowed to lapse'.[177]

The case turned on the credibility of the alleged victim, and Lord Montagu was to be acquitted on 16 December of the first charge of committing an unnatural offence under the 1861 Offences against the Person Act, but the jury were unable to decide on the second charge of indecent assault,[178] and a retrial was ordered for the next Assize (in the event, that retrial was abandoned, the indictment being 'allowed to lie on the file',[179] the prosecuting counsel, Jeremy Hutchinson, having declared much later that he had told the Director of Public Prosecutions that he thought that the new trial was ill-advised, although it was, he said, advice that was not well-received[180]).

Lord Montagu was then rearrested in January 1954[181] and, with his second cousin, Michael Pitt-Rivers,[182] and Peter Wildeblood, tried over eight days at Winchester Assizes in March 1954 on eighteen fresh counts of conspiracy to commit acts of gross indecency under the 1885 Act. The principal Crown witnesses, two R.A.F. men, John Reynolds and Edward McNally, had been offered immunity from prosecution, and there was some scepticism about the reliability of their testimony (one of the prosecution counsel, G.D. Roberts, himself admitted that they were 'perverts, men of the lowest possible moral character, men who were corrupted ... [and who] were willing parties to these unnatural offences'[183]). Never the less, Michael Pitt-Rivers was found guilty on one count and Peter Wildeblood was found guilty on a number of counts, and they were sentenced to 18 months' imprisonment. Charges of 'unnatural offences' against Lord Montagu were dismissed on the judge's instructions, but he was found guilty of two counts of gross indecency and of one offence under Section 11 of the 1885 Act, and was sentenced to 12 months' imprisonment. In sentencing them, the judge declared that 'the accused men were being dealt with in the most lenient way ...'[184]

The defendants were all prominent, newsworthy and vulnerable to the risk of a great social fall (the head of the local C.I.D., Walter Jones, said that they were 'three of the most celebrated prisoners of the last quarter of a century'[185]). Lord Montagu himself had protested to the Chief Constable about the first charge in 1953 that 'I realise only too well the extreme danger to someone in my position of such a charge being publicly made ...';[186] and Peter Rawlinson,[187] defending Peter Wildeblood at the second trial, said that 'But for the personalities in this case ... what interest would any normal person have in it? One wondered why people should queue up to see what they did see when Wildeblood was giving evidence ...'[188] He went on say in his auto-biography that:

> I and my colleague and friend, Bill Fearnley-Whittingstall, were both angered and resentful over the circumstances surrounding the prosecution of three men of otherwise undoubted quality accused of sex in private with other adult men, two airmen in the RAF who looked browbeaten when they gave evidence and who were neither seduced nor seductive. The case also involved illegal police searches of premises and a denial of access to lawyers while a statement was obtained in such circumstances that the judge at the trial eventually forbade its use in evidence. The whole prosecution had to me the savour of a witch-hunt. ... The trial was sad

and sordid; the witnesses for the prosecution in contrast to the bearing of the accused, sullen and unappealing. The police irregularities, searches without warrant, were revealed. ... The prosecution seemed to me at the time, as it seems to me today, thirty years later, to have been an act of public cruelty. It contributed to a change in the climate of opinion which, a decade later, led to a change in the law.[189]

It is tempting to conjecture that it was the moral and social standing of Michael Pitt-Rivers, Peter Wildeblood and Lord Montagu and their breaching of class lines to consort with disreputable members of the lower orders that prompted press interest.[190] It was the many incongruities between their erstwhile respectability; the inferior status and disreputability of their partners and accusers, the witnesses for the prosecution;[191] and the methods by which they had been apprehended;[192] that encouraged a belief that something momentous had occurred, and that the proper order of things was out of joint and in need of correction.[193] Lawyers, including Mr Justice Ormerod, the judge in the case,[194] inclined to the view that the conduct of the defence deserved some approbation.[195] But it was not an unambiguous affair, and very different inferences could be drawn about its nature and implications. Lord Montagu was said to have believed that he had been deliberately targeted by a homophobic Home Secretary and that the police had been 'out to get him' because of their failure to secure a conviction in the first trial.[196] Walter Jones, the arresting officer, formulated his own, rather personal set of conclusions when he stated that:

> had the case been lost, my career in the police would have been badly damaged. In the eyes of some, I was the villain of the piece. ... my reputation ... was also on trial that day. ... I suppose the overwhelming majority of people felt sympathy for Montagu, Wildeblood and Pitt-Rivers. ... The Montagu Case did me no good at all. Certain people in high places were strongly critical of such a prosecution because they thought it did more harm to the police image and the Force's public relations.[197]

The trial received a critical response from Roy Jenkins which would later affect the course of legislation.[198] It received a response from the Moral Welfare Council of the Church of England, whose secretary, Sherwin Bailey,[199] had earlier published 'The Problem of Sexual Inversion' in the form of a long letter in *Theology* in February 1952 (and later, in 1955, a book, *Homosexuality and the Western Christian Tradition*[200]). Under the impact of the new sciences of psychology and sexology,[201] and fusing rationalism with theology, Bailey had argued that the Church should re-examine the problem of the legal position of homosexuals:[202] 'It is clear', he said in that piece in 1952:

> that the innate invert ought not be penalised on account of his condition ... it is not the invert's condition, but the specific sexual expression

which his condition demands, that renders him liable to the penalty of the law. ... society must demand of the invert the same restraint and responsibility in sexual matters as it demands of the heterosexual. From neither, very properly, will the law tolerate sexual offences with or against those under the age of consent; from neither will it allow anything coming within the category of personal assault; in both, it will punish nuisance and public indecency. There is no discrimination against the homosexual here. But the British law goes further, and in its intrusion into the privacy of the invert's sexual life is not only grossly unfair, but itself conduces to crime. It is, without doubt, a Christian duty to press for the removal of this anomalous and shameful injustice, which has done untold harm, and has achieved no good whatever, and it is to be hoped that those who looked to the Church for a lead will not be disappointed.[203]

Grimley argues that 'Having received a large postbag about this article, he persuaded the Moral Welfare Council to convene [in 1953] a panel of doctors, lawyers and clergy',[204] a panel that was to be known as the Inversion Group, as part of a continuing Church project to undertake what might be called the secularisation of sin by breaking the link between private immorality and the public law. The group's interim report, *The Problem of Homosexuality*,[205] issued at a propitious moment in 1954, ostensibly private but widely circulated to politicians and others,[206] thereafter helped to shape the way in which the problem of homosexuality was to be framed.[207]

The Problem of Homosexuality enlarged on the argument of 'The Problem of Sexual Inversion'. Homosexuality was taken to be a deplorable but normal enough condition which was largely beyond the individual's control. It was nonetheless a sin, and, it was argued on page 13, 'we may expect him by the grace of God to resist the temptations to which his condition gives rise, and to come to terms with his "condition"'. But it was also the case that the criminalisation of a man's homosexuality exacerbated whatever problems he may have had. The prevailing law promoted blackmail and the formation of criminal subcultures. It could lead to the ruination of careers and to suicide. There was manifest inequality in the differential treatment of female homosexuals, who were exempt from prosecution, and male homosexuals who could be charged under the 1861 and 1885 Acts. There was manifest inequality in the differential treatment of male homosexuals and of no less harmful adulterous and philandering male heterosexuals. What applied to the one should apply to the other.[208] It was an argument that impelled the Moral Welfare Council to recommend in December 1953 and again in February 1954 that the Home Secretary should investigate 'the whole matter of homosexuality'.[209] It was an argument that was to be reiterated in the Council's submission to the Wolfenden Committee in 1955.

There were editorials about the Montagu trial in the press. One, quite blunt, in *The Sunday Times*, talked of the prosecution revealing 'not a momentary scandal but a deep-rooted malady', and it went on to declare that:

the so-called Montagu case has exposed with peculiar sharpness some of [the problem's] more disturbing aspects. The chief witnesses for the prosecution were the accomplices – equally guilty with the accused of whatever acts were proved between them. We may well ponder, first, the fact that one set of parties goes free while the other takes the punishment. ... Notorious inverts occupy eminent places, and few people of wide acquaintance would be prepared to say that they know no one whom they could suspect of conduct which – if found out – would bring legal punishment and social disgrace. In all this matter, our society is riddled with hypocrisy. ... The case for a reform of the law as to acts committed in private between adults is very strong. The case for authoritative inquiry into it is overwhelming. '[210]

Then too there were the reactions to Peter Wildeblood's own account of his trial in *Against the Law*, published the next year, in 1955, and sent to every Member of Parliament, which encouraged one commentator later to contend that it had 'prompted debates in both houses of Parliament[211] and led to the establishment ... of the Wolfenden Committee ... ';[212] and the political journalist, Daniel Finkelstein, to declare much later still that the book 'produced an outcry. As occasionally happens in politics, this prosecution suddenly revealed a great injustice that had been there all the time, unnoticed. And the Home Secretary responded to the fuss by setting up a commission under Lord Wolfenden ...'[213]

There was indeed to be a sustained series of Parliamentary questions put by Desmond Donnelly[214] the Labour Member for Pembrokeshire, Sir Robert Boothby,[215] the Conservative Member for East Aberdeen, and others, who, beginning in late 1953,[216] had sought to initiate an inquiry into the 'nature and treatment of homosexuals'.[217] Without expressly alluding to the Montagu case, Sir Robert later recalled a speech he had made in February 1954 to the Hardwicke Society in which he had asserted that the homosexual suffered from 'a biological and pathological condition for which the victim is only to a small degree responsible', a condition 'which may sometimes be cured'[218] but which should not be punished as a crime:

> [The law] regarding homosexuality was iniquitous, and ... the clause in the Act which made indecency between consenting male adults in private a crime should be removed from the statute book. ... The press reported my speech widely, and this led me to put down some questions in the House of Commons, and to write to the Home Secretary ...[219]

But there is actually very little hint of how much, if at all, those events weighed with Home Office officials and politicians as a number of important formative decisions were being made within government. The Home Secretary, David Maxwell Fyfe, was once again silent in his memoirs and archived private papers about how and why he had sought the appointment of John Wolfenden[220] and his committee (although there is a remote possibility that an article, appearing in *The Sunday Times* a little time prior to the decision may have been the trigger – an article in which John Wolfenden, as the former headmaster of an independent school, discussed with a fictional mother the sexual problems faced by boys at boarding school[221]). What may be telling is that, quite contrary to the utilitarian arguments that were later to be deployed by the Church and the Wolfenden Committee,[222] the Home Secretary, himself a deeply religious man much preoccupied with the growing gulf between scientific and moral progress, a man who had addressed the General Assembly of the Church of Scotland in 1955 on the 'Faith of a Politician',[223] a man who had held private, unreported meetings with magistrates about London's morals,[224] took it that the business of politics was actively to shape moral conduct and promote the cohesion of the family. He had long held that a goal of the Conservative Party must be to 'ensure that the spiritual stature of man in Britain makes comparable advances and improvements with scientific progress',[225] and he said that:

> When I was young, it used to be a remark frequently made in discussions of crime and morals that you cannot make people good by Act of Parliament. There are a number of partial truths latent in this sentiment, but at its face value it is liable to be accepted as meaning that you should not try to make people good by Act of Parliament; and further that it is not the business of those who administer Acts of Parliament to try to make people good. ... These are unexceptionable maxims, as far as they go: but when more and more people begin to commit offences against the criminal law, is it not the duty of Government to seek means to induce them not to do so?[226]

No clarification is to be secured from the Permanent Under-Secretary of the time, Sir Frank Newsam. He left no relevant correspondence, speeches, biography or autobiography.[227] His account of the work of the Home Office is silent on the matter.[228] And it is disappointing that the pertinent Home Office records have been destroyed as part of the general cull I described in Chapter 1. The Home Office departmental records officer informed me that 'the only files of this age that we continue to hold are casework files that we have to retain for legal reasons'.[229] We are thus left with no way of knowing just how and why the political problem of homosexuality came to assume its very particular genesis in government circles in the mid-1950s.

David Maxwell Fyfe certainly invoked none of the many frequently cited pretexts for his action in instituting the Committee in the documents which are now in the public domain. Neither did he refer to the extraordinarily prescient questions put to him in February and March 1954 by George Craddock, the Labour MP for Bradford South,[230] who wished to 'safeguard public morals by preventing the publication in the Press of gross and unnecessary details in cases of homosexuality', and to ensure public protection against knowledge of the 'innermost secrets of persons mentioned in the question'[231] (the

Home Secretary replied merely that he had 'under consideration the general question of the law relating to sexual offences and of the treatment of sexual offenders … but I do not think that the appointment of a committee… would be justified'[232]). Why it was that George Craddock chose to raise those questions, and why he did so at just that moment, is another of the unexplained gaps which I have been unable to fill. Almost nothing is to be learned about him as a man, moralist and politician.[233]

Yet something can be established. What ensued within government itself looks as if it were actually quite tangential to all that external clamour. The first surviving record of the Home Secretary raising the possibility of an inquiry is a memorandum submitted to Cabinet in February 1954, and that talked largely of prostitution.[234] He announced that 'The prevalence of sexual crime and the activities of prostitutes soliciting in the streets of London have attracted much attention and there have been demands in Parliament, in the press and from leaders of the Churches for more effectives measures to check these evils and, more, recently, for the appointment of a Royal Commission to enquire into certain aspects of this problem and to review the existing Law'. 'I have thought it right', he continued, 'to raise … the question whether such a commission should be appointed'.[235]

Figure 6.4 shows that, although they were again low by contemporary standards, the figures of reported 'offences by prostitutes' were rising appreciably in England and Wales during this period – from 3,192 in 1938 to 102,291 in 1952; predominantly in London where they rose from 2,966 to 9,756; largely, it has been conjectured, as a result of increases in the numbers of police and the establishment of dedicated vice squads;[236] and there was a continual, companion flow of allegations of police corruption, particularly in the West End's Vice Squad,[237] where, 'Between them the police and the prostitutes', it was said, had 'come to what might almost be termed a happy compromise to make the law into a working, though pointless compromise'.[238] It was that growth in recorded offending and its concomitant neutralisation – indeed subversion – of policing at a time when tourists were about to come to London for the 1953 coronation which may have been chiefly responsible for the inception of the Wolfenden Committee.

In his first memorandum to cabinet, David Maxwell Fyfe did also raise the problem of homosexuality, but it was consigned to a place of much less importance, and he was anything but eager to investigate or reform the law bearing upon it. On the one hand, he conceded, just as was the case with prostitution:

> There has been a serious increase in offences of this kind. The number of unnatural offences of the gravest kind (sodomy and bestiality) known to the police in England and Wales rose from 134 in 1938 to 670 in 1952; the number of attempts to commit unnatural offences (a category which includes not only attempts to commit sodomy and bestiality, but also indecent assaults on male persons and a small number of cases of importuning dealt with on indictment) rose from 822 to 3,087; and the number of

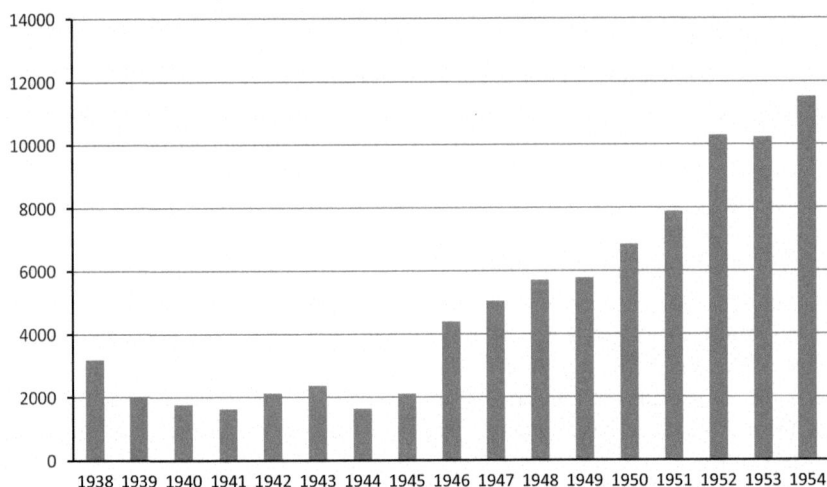

Figure 6.4 'Offences by Prostitutes' recorded for England and Wales 1938–1954[239]

offences of gross indecency rose from 320 to 1,686. Corresponding figures for offences of importuning by male persons are not available, but in 1952, proceedings were taken in the Metropolitan police district in 373 cases. ... Experience shows that only a minority of homosexual offenders are likely to benefit by psychiatric treatment. So far as such treatment is useful, it can be, as it is now, provided in prisons, although there may be some scope for development here, particularly when it is possible to open the institution for mentally abnormal offenders [later called Grendon Underwood Prison which opened in 1962]. There is a considerable body of opinion which regards the existing law as antiquated and out of harmony with modern knowledge and ideas, and, in particular, represents that unnatural relations between consenting adults, which are not criminal except in Great Britain and the United States, should no longer be criminal in this country, and that the criminal law, in dealing with unnatural, and with normal, sexual relations, should confine itself to the protection of the young and the preservation of public order and decency.

But, he concluded on the other hand, that:

I do not myself believe that there is any case for altering the law relating to homosexuality and I think that the most profitable line of development is to improve, so far as finances permit, the facilities for the treatment of homosexuals sentenced by the courts; but there is a sufficient body of opinion in the country in favour of setting in train some inquiry into homosexual offences to warrant my bringing the question before my colleagues. The setting up of a Royal Commission or other form of inquiry *might lead to a belief that the Government thought that the law ought to be changed, and would later expose us to the danger of receiving embarrassing recommendations for altering the law.* [Emphasis added]

He was then to declare at the next meeting of Cabinet that the law had to be strengthened if the substantial increase in the number of convictions for prostitution was to be curbed, 'particularly by increasing the penalty and by modifying the requirement to prove "annoyance"'. But he also acknowledged that any proposals were likely to be contested, especially by women's organisations, and it was vital to support them by 'the findings of an authoritative enquiry'. There had, he once more added, been an even greater proportionate increase in the number of homosexual offences, and, although he was averse to changing the law in this area, there were many 'responsible people [who] believed that homosexual practices between consenting adults should not be a criminal offence. In the present state of public opinion, there would certainly be criticism if an enquiry were held into prostitution and no similar investigation were made into homosexuality'. Quite why it was thought that such criticism might emerge is far from clear, but it was a linkage customarily forged, evident, for instance, in the 1885 Act, and the discussion that followed in Cabinet touched first on offences of prostitution and then moved on to homosexuality, where the emphasis was quite distinct:

> The suggestion was made that newspapers might be prohibited from publishing details of criminal prosecutions for homosexual offences. If a Private Member could be persuaded to introduce a Bill for this purpose under the ten-minute rule, the arguments for and against a restriction on the reporting of these cases could be publicly stated. If there then appeared to be a substantial amount of public support for such a measure, the Government might facilitate the further stages of the Bill. ...[240]

And it was agreed that the cabinet would resume at a later meeting the discussion of a formal enquiry into the law relating to prostitution and homosexual offences. It is plain that, quite contrary to the later received accounts,[241] there was no enthusiasm for measures to mitigate the law and treatment of homosexuality.[242] That was not the object of interest. The interim report of the Moral Welfare Council, the stir created by the perceived injustice of the Winchester trial, representations made by bodies such as the Howard League[243] and parliamentary questions may indeed have supplied a context for reform (and they would have a discernible impact at a later date, becoming the received story about what happened[244]), but what was actually seizing the mind of the Home Secretary, Prime Minister and cabinet at the time was something quite separate and different. It was anxiety about the supposed moral contamination and public alarm that could flow from the publicity attached to the much-blazoned, disreputable actions of eminent men that appeared to be the prime motive for the decision eventually made to hold an inquiry. Sir John Wolfenden himself recollected that 'In the three or four years before our appointment there had been a number of rather sensational cases of prosecutions for homosexual offences. ... there was a widely-voiced fear that what was called "this kind of behaviour" was becoming increasingly widespread, especially in certain intellectual and artistic circles, and was damaging the nation's moral fibre'.[245] He said further that:

> The Home Secretary's problems had lately been brought to a head by two cases which had attracted considerable public notice. So there was a very odd atmosphere. The vast majority of the population were probably unaware that there was such a thing as a homosexual offence; of the aware minority a majority regarded the whole business as distasteful and shocking, while a few were tolerant and sympathetic.[246]

George Craddock's questions about the reporting of trials may thus have resonated, anticipated and even crystallised, Sir David Maxwell Fyfe's own views. The two men *were* in remarkably close accord: they both believed that the unwholesome publicity and *brouhaha* flowing from criminal proceedings was one of the chief problems and catalysts of the rise in the volume of homosexual acts and that, if there were to be legislation, it should take the form only of action to control the distressingly prurient details of what the public learned. But external influences of any kind were only very vaguely mentioned in what the Home Secretary said in cabinet or Parliament, and it is impossible to know now whether and to what degree they weighed with him. What evidently *did* count was the seemingly inexplicable and unwelcome growth in the volume of offending, a problem which required elucidation before it could be solved, and it was the supposed need for that elucidation which may have inclined him to weaken. Where so little was known, he was to argue, political action had to wait on an inquiry. At the next meeting of Cabinet, held in March 1954, the Home Secretary restated his cautious case for an investigative committee:

> The prevalence of prostitution, particularly in London, and the unexplained increase in homosexual offences, constituted a serious problem which the Government could not ignore; [and] that, without support from the findings of an independent and authoritative enquiry the Government would not be in a position to promote legislation, or to take other measures, to deal with this problem; and that in these circumstances the only course open to them was to appoint a Royal Commission or other appropriate form of enquiry to examine the problem and to suggest appropriate remedies.[247]

The ensuing discussion continued to fuse homosexuality and prostitution together as a pair of troublesome sexual offences that were symptomatic of a wider moral decline (although, to be sure, it was conceded some years later that the link was tenuous[248]); it disclosed that Ministers remained reluctant to legislate; and it showed that their gaze, in the lesser matter of homosexuality, was turned almost wholly on the problem of curbing the growth of offending and the undesirable consequences of the publicity that attended it.

The Home Secretary confronted a dilemma. As a former solicitor general and attorney general, an experienced and conventionally minded trial lawyer, who had served 'with distinction'[249] as the deputy to Sir Hartley Shawcross, the chief British prosecutor at the Nuremberg trials, and who had edited the series of volumes covering the war crimes trials in the interests of promoting public awareness of atrocity,[250] he was neither able nor likely to be disposed to ban trial publicity.[251] Criminal justice 'should be done in public' and publicity might always attract fresh evidence, but some restriction of objectionable reporting was never the less necessary, and that would be a difficult reform indeed to pass through Parliament. The Lord Privy Seal and Leader of the House of Commons, Harry Crookshank, said, in the Cabinet Secretary's notes taken of the meeting, that 'it wdn't get a run in H/C unless Govt. adopted it. We mightn't wish to do so'. Lord Salisbury, the Leader of the House of Lords, in the sole reference made to the Winchester case, was reported to have interjected 'Wd. also look bad to introduce in H/L. soon after Montagu case! ... [But] Somethg. should be done. Nothg. can be done w'out R. Comm^n. This is surely a strong case for enquiry on this occasion'.[252] The upshot, said the Prime Minister, was that:

> the prudent course would be to take no action save to encourage a Private Member to introduce in the House of Commons, under the ten-minute rule, a Bill designed to prohibit the publication of detailed information of criminal prosecutions for homosexual offences. The Home Secretary said that he would be ready to submit to the Cabinet a memorandum examining the arguments for and against such restrictive legislation. But he pointed out that such legislation, even if it had the effect of allaying public anxiety about homosexuality, would make no contribution whatever towards a solution of the problem of prostitution. This, in his view, was the more urgent and obvious problem ...[253]

It was agreed to invite the Home Secretary to prepare yet another memorandum and to 'resume, when it was available, their discussion of the proposal to hold a formal enquiry into the law relating to prostitution and to homosexual offences', conceived, it would seem, very narrowly indeed.

That new memorandum, submitted in April 1954, reported that the publication of indecent material was already prohibited under Section 1 of the Judicial Proceedings (Regulation of Reports) Act of 1926; that it was the Home Secretary's conviction that trials for homosexual offences could not and should not be held *in camera*; and that there remained only an issue of whether there should be publication confined solely, in the words of the Section I(b) of the Act, to such materials as 'a concise statement of charges, defences and counter-charges in support of which evidence has been given; [and] submissions of law and the decision of the court thereon'. In the most useful and transparent account of his understanding of the problem, the Home Secretary said it might be:

> (i) that the publication of full and detailed reports of these unsavoury cases panders to the salacious reader, may corrupt the innocent, and is in general injurious to public morals; (ii) that sensational accounts of criminal offences may lead to their imitation by others; and (iii) that the amount of space devoted by the Press to some notorious cases of this kind may give rise to exaggerated ideas of the prevalence of homosexual vice and that restriction of Press reports would tend to allay public anxiety.

However:

> (i) Any restriction on the liberty of the Press can be justified only by a clear and compelling need in the public interest; but the sensational treatment of an occasional notorious case is exceptional, and the majority of such cases are reported briefly, if at all. ... (iv) The publicity given to the preliminary proceedings before examining Justices sometimes leads to witnesses coming forward who can give evidence of value to the prosecution or the defence. Curtailment of reports at this stage might therefore be prejudicial to the administration of justice. (v) It is in the public interest that cases of this kind, however unpleasant, should be reported, so that everyone may know that conduct of this kind is an offence against criminal law and may realise what is punishment for committing that crime. ... (vi) If ... legislation were now introduced by a Private Member and accepted by the Government, and at the same time the Government announced that they did not propose to undertake any inquiry into the law relating to homosexual offences, it would be said that the Government had not merely declined to hold an inquiry, in spite of the great and unexplained increase in such offences and of the fact that the existing law was regarded as unsatisfactory by many respectable people, but were endeavouring to suppress the publication of evidence which showed the need for an inquiry.[254]

In short, he concluded, the objections to any legislation to restrict publication of the details of criminal prosecutions 'outweighed any advantage it might have. ... There was ... force in the argument that, if the Government supported this legislation and at the same time declined to hold an enquiry, they would be open to the criticism that they were trying to suppress the publication of evidence showing the need for an enquiry'. There was a surfeit of Royal Commissions at the time but 'he was ready to agree that this enquiry should be made by a Departmental Committee ... '.[255] Moreover it may have been germane that, although this aspect of the decision was not mentioned in the cabinet papers, unlike Royal Commissions, Departmental Committees were under no obligation to publish what could, in this instance, be highly sensitive material.[256] Cabinet accordingly agreed on 15 April 1954 that a Departmental Committee should be appointed to enquire into the law 'relating to prostitution and homosexual offences;' and that the Home Secretary would consult with the Prime Minister about its membership.

Several quite independent and parallel conversations and histories were thus in train. Conversations outside cabinet, many highlighting the case at Winchester Assizes, talked about the oppressiveness, antiquatedness, irrationality and inequity of the laws of 1861 and 1885. Another conversation, taking place *within* the cabinet, making no appreciable reference to the views of Members of Parliament, the Churches or any other body, was on the surface solely preoccupied with ways of safely regulating the ill effects of publicity stemming from the prosecution of distasteful offences, offences which were thought without demur or discussion to demand robust enforcement.[257] Demands made in the name of the one conversation were thus being met with replies made in the name of the other; although, over the course of time, those who, like Sir Robert Boothby,[258] had posed those demands would later claim an influence and causal impact which cannot now be substantiated.

A few days after cabinet had made its decision to commission an inquiry, but before its decision was disclosed, Desmond Donnelly,[259] again professed himself to be disquieted by the inappropriateness of the methods employed to deal with homosexuality, a medical rather than a criminal matter, and he declared to the House of Commons that there must be better ways of managing the problem:

if a Royal Commission is appointed it should look into this matter with a view to seeing what medical treatment can be provided. I am advised that this is not mainly a glandular problem; it is a psychiatric problem and the answer can very often be found in psychiatric treatment in cases where this is possible, or, more particularly, in studying the problem of the treatment of young people in their nursery years, because this is the crux of the whole matter. A Royal Commission should go into this aspect and see that there is a widespread public knowledge of how this sort of thing can be avoided. ... if we are to treat people for this sort of offence, prison is the very worst way in which to treat them. I believe it only makes the situation much worse. Sensitive people are taken there and placed with criminals guilty of a completely different crime against society – if one is to call this a crime against society; and this action by itself creates an additional social problem, because people who would not otherwise come into contact with homosexuality are thus indoctrinated.[260]

Sir Robert Boothby again followed suit, no doubt motivated by a measure of hidden self-interest,[261] acting as one of a number of homosexual and bisexual campaigners who could not and would not fight under their own colours. His final question to the Home Secretary at the end of April 1954 put it that:

In most of our great cities, there is a homosexual underground which is a constant menace to youth; and we ought to bear that always in mind. The sporadic campaigns of the police against homosexuality ...

are often accompanied ... by methods of great dubiety; and do nothing, in my opinion, towards its eradication. On the contrary, they intensify the squalor by which it is surrounded, and widen the areas in which the underground flourishes. For these methods I do not blame the police, but the existing law. In cases involving alleged acts of indecency committed in private, where there is no injured party, witnesses are almost invariably tainted; which means that they are accomplices actuated by motives of avarice, jealousy or fear. That is what makes the field of homosexuality a happy hunting ground for the blackmailer.[262]

He and others were, in short, arguing for an inquiry into ways of ending or reducing the harmful impact of the criminalisation of homosexuality whilst the Home Office and cabinet were seeking something quite different (indeed, Sir Robert Boothby himself remembered that David Maxwell Fyfe had told him that 'I am not going down to history as the man who made sodomy legal'[263]). In April 1954, Sir Hugh Lucas-Tooth, the Undersecretary, finally replied to Desmond Donnelly and Sir Robert Boothby to say that the Home Secretary:

> ... has authorised me to inform the House that he and the Secretary of State for Scotland have decided to appoint a committee to examine both these questions [of prostitution and homosexual offences]. He feels that a committee would be more appropriate in this connection than a Royal Commission. But he is anxious to secure the services of able and experienced men and women to serve upon this committee and, therefore, it may be some little time before he is in a position to announce its membership and terms of reference.[264]

The Wolfenden Committee

So it came about that, on 8 July 1954, David Maxwell Fyfe officially announced the formation of a committee under the chairmanship of the vice chancellor of the University of Reading, Sir John Wolfenden, and, given its genesis, its terms of reference might seem to have been somewhat tangential. They were 'To consider –

1. (*a*) the law and practice relating to homosexual offences and the treatment of persons convicted of such offences by the courts; and
2. (*b*) the law and practice relating to offences against the criminal law in connection with prostitution and solicitation for immoral purposes.[265]

In tracing what happened next I shall occupy myself solely with the committee's deliberations on homosexuality because it was they which were to lead to the 1967 Act. It is not evident that it had ever been made clear to members of the committee that their task in this area was supposed to be the investigation of the effects of noxious publicity (that was not apparent in the terms of reference or the official papers and the idea's author, David Maxwell Fyfe, was shortly to move on to become Lord Chancellor, replaced as Home Secretary in October 1954 by Gwilym Lloyd-George). Indeed, the members professed that they had no clear conception of what they should do or what ideas they could and should bring to bear. Sir John recollected that 'They [were] not supposed to be experts'.[266] They were instead obliged to claim naively or not so naively, following the vein of pluralistic ignorance and their supposed remoteness from a taboo subject, to know little of the field. Sir John Wolfenden certainly pretended to an unfamiliarity. His biographer, Jeffrey Weeks, wrote that 'He confessed in his autobiography that when approached to chair the committee, he had little personal knowledge of homosexuality. This was, however, somewhat disingenuous. He already knew that his eldest son, Jeremy ... was ostentatiously homosexual'.[267] Indeed, Jeremy Wolfenden had 'come out' whilst a young pupil at Eton, and had finally informed his parents about his sexuality after one of the masters had written a letter of complaint to them in 1952. On his appointment to the committee, Sir John was reported by Jeremy to have said simply that it would be best if 'we stay out of each other's way for the time being', and that 'you should wear rather less make-up'.[268] A *cordon sanitaire* was in place.

Before the committee lay what they chose to represent as *terra incognita*. Sir John Wolfenden wrote at the outset that 'we are going to find it a pretty arduous job, and I have no sort of idea yet what recommendations, if any, we are likely to make. But I expect that in the course of the next two years we shall gradually move towards some conclusions of some kind. ...'[269]

But the committee's very composition did map a preliminary conception of the character of the problems they faced: they consisted of those concerned with the welfare of the young; with education; with problems of morality and religion; and with politics, law and medicine.[270] One, Goronwy Rees, was later to be exposed as having had links (although no sexual liaison) with Burgess and was obliged to resign, his lack of candour being deemed a handicap.[271]

Confronting allegedly unexplored terrain, they acted, in effect, as the Lewis and Clarke of sexual inversion. Frank Mort has described how 'Wolfenden and his team embarked on a massive information gathering exercise, listening to witnesses and exchanging sexual knowledge that went far beyond their original brief ...'[272] The committee began by drafting lists of organisations to consult. Homosexuality was a medical problem, questions of treatment were involved,[273] and one of its members, the consultant psychiatrist, Desmond Curran,[274] recommended making approaches to the Royal Medico-Psychological Association; the British Medical Association; Prison Medical Officers; and The National Institute for the Scientific Treatment of Delinquency ('Clearly they should have a lot of experience, but my personal view is that the personnel there is of variable quality'). Homosexuality was a problem of morality and law enforcement that touched especially on the corruption of youth, and Sir Hugh Linstead,[275] the Member of Parliament, recommended approaching the police ('Home Office can advise'); prisons;

lawyers; judges;[276] churches ('Do we go to the Archbishop, the Cardinal and the Moderator?'); youth organisations ('Nat. Assn. of Boys Clubs'); schools ('Headmasters' Conference,? Assn. of Headmasters of Secondary Schools'); Social Workers; and 'Society representing Probation Officers'. Homosexuality touched on problems of human rights, and the Secretary of the Committee consulted the European Convention on Human Rights.[277]

From the first, therefore, the Committee determined that they would explore, listen and learn on a very broad front rather than proceed on the foundation of the government's one, lone, morally condemnatory definition of homosexuality as a condition whose prosecution generated unwelcome and unpleasant publicity, but they did not do so without quite express qualms. Their task was said to be distasteful[278] and they routinely hedged it about with a strange, half-aversive, half-jocular,[279] public school 'othering' argot that talked about 'Huntleys' and 'Palmers', the name of a biscuit-manufacturing company[280] located in Wolfenden's home town of Reading, rather than about homosexuals and prostitutes.[281] It would be laid out in three stages: 'an appraisal of the present situation'; 'consideration of proposals for amendment of the existing law and practice'; and 'treatment of (homosexual) offenders'.[282] As they proceeded, they would acquire a sizeable and quite diverse portfolio of submissions from different bodies, some invited, others uninvited (the Secretary called them 'a motley collection of professional organisations, government departments and officials, and individuals of one sort or another. ...'[283]). Just as the politics of capital punishment and abortion had galvanised medical, religious and campaigning groups into forming committees and drafting reports, so the Wolfenden Committee stirred the professions and churches into formulating their stance (although some campaigning and educational groups, such as the Homosexual Law Reform Society and the Albany Trust, were to emerge only at a later point, when the Committee had actually reported).

Like most enquiries of its kind, the Committee was to become inundated with paper and argument. Indeed, there was to be a rapidly developing sense that it was becoming overwhelmed by the flow of what was frequently opinionated evidence. By June 1955, only nine months after it had begun work, the Chairman declared 'We could go on almost indefinitely listening to more and more experts and more and more people who think they know the answers, but we shall have to try to draw a line somewhere, and I think we shall have to close down by the end of this year. Then there will be the very difficult business of drafting the report and agreeing on its terms. ...'[284]

The submissions they elicited were diverse indeed. They received an unusually libertarian memorandum from the Institute for the Study and Treatment of Delinquency and the Portman Clinic which simply advocated *laissez-faire, laissez-aller*. Its editor, Edward Glover, a psychoanalyst and one of the first editors of *The British Journal of Delinquency*, said:

> ... psychological treatment should not, under existing conditions, be looked on as the answer to the problem. This is strictly in keeping with the

view that in a so-far unascertained but certainly large proportion of cases, *there is no answer to homosexuality save tolerance on the part of the anti-homo-sexual groups in the community* ... [in the majority of instances] there is no answer to homosexuality and, in the sense of criminal conduct, no need for an answer.[285] (Emphasis in the original)

They received a submission from the Church of England's Moral Welfare Council, a submission that was, in effect, a succinct summary and revision of the council's earlier interim report, and there are a number of matters to note: the submission refrained from overt moralisation, grounding itself instead in a version of pragmatic liberalism that appeared to have fed on the arguments of John Stuart Mill[286] and to have anticipated those of Isaiah Berlin;[287] and, like its report on abortion that I discussed before, it was to be massively influential in organising the moral responses of others. It confirmed the strategic part the Church would come to play in framing the dimensions of the problem of homosexuality; developed the idea of a division of regulatory responsibilities between Church and state; and offered an authoritative moral licence and a narrative path to others who might wish to accede to the idea of reform.

The law, the council's submission repeated, was 'not ... equal in its injustice. Whilst the male homosexual is heavily penalised for his offences, the female homosexual is ignored ...' It then went on to declare in a key passage that:

> ... we have purposely refrained from touching upon the moral and religious aspects of the question, since these lie outside the Government Committee's terms of reference. We are, nevertheless, acutely aware of the need for careful study of the whole subject from the pastoral and theological standpoints. Moreover, while advocating reform of the law, and concerned that the public shall be enlightened, we would not have it thought that we are unmindful of the widely-held conviction that homosexual acts are unnatural and immoral ... We would submit, however, that it is not the function of the state and the law to constitute themselves the guardians of <u>private</u> morality, and that to deal with <u>sin as such</u> belongs to the province of the Church. On the other hand, it is the duty of the state to punish crime, and it may properly take cognisance of offences against <u>public</u> morality, and (in certain circumstances) those sins which incite thereto.[288] [Emphases in the original]

The Roman Catholic Cardinal Archbishop Griffin had established his own advisory committee to prepare a submission to the Wolfenden Committee, and its conclusions[289] ran remarkably in parallel to those developed by the Moral Welfare Council. Together, the two Churches[290] (and the Methodists[291]) argued in virtually identical words the utilitarian case that the business of the Church was with sin and the business of the state was with crime, and that the state had no business interfering in sinful private behaviour that did no palpable public harm – and that was a stance that Sir John and the members of his committee, many of them committed Christians, would themselves come to embrace.[292]

The Catholic position did weaken over time, but it was never to be as unequivocally condemnatory of this sin as it had been in the earlier agitation over abortion law reform. When the Wolfenden Committee reported a year later, Archbishop Griffin's successor, Cardinal Godfrey, decided to issue a public statement that entrusted moral judgement to the individual consciences of members of the Church.[293] And a decade later, at a time when legislation was in prospect, and Cardinal Godfrey's own successor, Cardinal Heenan, received a number of anguished letters,[294] he nevertheless refused to intervene, saying, in one instance, 'I think that Catholic opinion is by no means unanimous on the question you mention and for this reason it might be very difficult for a member of the hierarchy to make any public statement'.[295] The Church of England[296] and the Catholic Church may have been internally divided, but important voices did thereby well up from prominent clergyman to deplore the sinfulness of homosexual acts, on the one hand, whilst refusing to endorse their continuing criminalisation, on the other.[297] Theirs was an interesting and considered merger of what has been called 'public reason and comprehensive doctrines'[298] that led to the principle of a division of moral labour in which state and Church should play their separate and distinctive roles.

Again and by invitation, the British Medical Association convened its own committee on homosexuality and prostitution, 'a special Committee consisting chiefly of experts',[299] in December 1954 to prepare evidence for submission to the Departmental committee. It was initially composed of psychiatrists interested in the psychopathology of homosexuality; endocrinologists seeking to ascertain the physiological roots of homosexuality; and forensic specialists and specialists in venereal medicine, but its scope was to grow as, at Desmond Curran's instigation, affiliated professional bodies were invited to submit their own evidence to be collated, synthesised and forwarded to the Wolfenden Committee: The Institute of Psycho-Analysis; the Royal Medico-Psychological Association; The Royal College of Physicians; The Medical Women's Federation; The Tavistock Clinic and others. The B.M.A. Committee was itself to be allied to a much larger confederation of fifteen organisations, brought together by the Magistrates Association, that would 'present the factual evidence on the law and practice relating to homosexuality in other countries to the Departmental Committee'.[300] It already had before it the report of a committee of physicians and psychiatrists, produced just five years before, which had examined homosexuality through the very particular lens of the medical professions to conclude that:

> those charged with sexual offences should be dealt with by the courts by a procedure that in some respects differs from that which is used for the generality of accused persons. The principal reason for this is medical. ... punishment without treatment is not likely to have a beneficial effect;

indeed, it can make these offenders worse, and thus more likely to repeat their offences. In a high proportion of cases imprisonment without treatment may have consequences to the community even more dangerous than to the offenders themselves. ...[301]

The task which the new B.M.A. committee set itself at its first meeting of 6 December 1954 was a comprehensive mapping of the problem of homosexuality medically conceived: there would be separate reports 'on environment as a factor in homosexuality in the male' and the female; 'genetic studies of homosexuality'; and modes of treatment. The committee's manner of reasoning merits some comment because it diverged so markedly in method, mode and content from that of the Churches.

Consider first that paper on treatment, prepared by Trevor Gibbens[302] of the Institute of Psychiatry in February 1955, which proffered a typology of male homosexuals:

(1) 'Well compensated homosexuals of good character. These are either unaware of their tendency or have successfully struggled against it, and may be successfully married. ...
(2) Well preserved personalities who have accepted their homosexuality and intend to practise it: somewhat egocentric but otherwise law-abiding ...
(3) Young adults and adolescents. The youngest require protection from effects which might delay their transition through a temporary phase. ...
(4) Seriously damaged personalities. The commonest of these in outpatient practice is a group of intensely lonely, shy, inadequate persons, whose only affectionate or social contact may be in fleeting lavatory offences or minor play with children... Secondly, a very effeminate and essentially narcissistic group who like to be admired and feather their nest but have little real interest in sex and are usually harmless. Thirdly, a group of anti-social and often aggressive characters. The mixture of other perversions – especially fetichism [sic] and sado-masochism – with homosexuality ... is most apparent here and makes the outlook worse. ...
(5) Homosexuality with serious mental abnormality – psychosis, mental deficiency, psychopathic personality'.

The paper then proceeded to lay out a companion list of the types of treatment on offer:

(1) 'Analytical psychotherapy ...
(2) Group treatment
(3) Psychiatric treatment
(4) Physical treatment. ECT, abreaction etc. are indicated for any accompanying mental illness rather than for homosexuality. The main treatment here is the use of oestrogens ... to produce temporary cessation of sexual desire. ...

(5) Social measures as used by the psychiatric social workers and probation officer.

(6) Punishment must be included. The part played by the psychiatrist is to allow the good effects to operate while minimising undesirable side-effects by means of rehabilitation and after-care. ...[303]

Consider too the memorandum by S. Leonard Simpson, the endocrinologist, which the Committee examined at its next meeting in March 1955:

> Those who have been in contact with the problem over a number of years appear to find that an appreciable proportion of homosexuals have physical characteristics indicating the lack of normal virile features or the positive presence of feminine features. ... it would appear that [there is a call] for some change in the attitude of the general public and of many doctors to the problem of homosexuality. It seems that only a proportion of homosexuals can be regarded as unworthy evil persons to be morally condemned and criminally punished. On the other hand, it might well be correct for a community ... to form the opinion that the existence and/or spread of homosexuality is not in the best interests of the community and must be discouraged by all justifiable methods. ...
>
> Addendum
> The claim that homosexuals are especially artistic or show special aptitudes in the artistic sphere is one which intrigues many and which I think is substantially well founded. ...[304]

Consider finally the submission by John Glaister, Regius Professor of Forensic Medicine at the University of Glasgow, which came before the Committee in June 1955:

> ... the main object of all courts must always be the protection of the public, but in [a number of] instances ... the public are not primarily involved. The question must arise, whether, as in heterosexual relationships, what happens in private between two consenting adults, is, within limits, their own affair? The further question is whether the law should only step in when certain limits have been exceeded, e.g. assault, the involvement of a minor, blackmail, etc.? ... I hold the view that the law should assume a very stern aspect towards certain manifestations of homosexuality. I refer to sodomy. I refer to homosexual practices between an adult and a minor. I refer to importuning for homosexual purposes. ...[305]

It may be noted that, whilst there were strands in these arguments that leaned towards what purported, albeit not always successfully, to be a disinterested emphasis on scientific taxonomy and therapeutic intervention, there was also a persistent, judgemental and condemnatory stress on the deviant, and, indeed, on the moral dimensions of homosexuality.[306] It was moreover a stress coaxed continually into being by the Committee's Secretary, Ernest Claxton MRCS LRCP, the Assistant Secretary of the B.M.A.

Ernest Claxton had been born in India, the son of missionaries and brother to the Bishop of Blackburn. He was a member of the Churches' Council on Health and Healing, a body revived after the Second World War that was concerned with unifying the Churches and the medical profession.[307] His outlook, his obituary came to say, 'was global, based on a sense of morality and a dependence on God's guidance to put his beliefs into practice'.[308] He endeavoured always to set the problem of sexuality in moral and religious context.[309] 'The right use of sex', he was to declare at the Committee's meeting of 19 July 1955, was 'related to responsibility. Stable marriage, the nurture and education of children and their development as responsible citizens were basic to the nation's wellbeing. If children were allowed to think that sex could be separated from responsibility, the door was opened to both homosexual and heterosexual indulgence...'

Claxton's solution to the problem of homosexuality was not to be sought in tolerance, punishment or treatment but in religious conversion: 'The Assistant Secretary ... said that ... he had personal knowledge of four more cases of conversion ... the Committee's report should make it clear that homosexuality in its accepted sense was part of a moral decline throughout the country and the answer to the problem lay in the general promotion of higher moral standards ...'[310]

The Committee's report passed through successive drafts in September and thence to Council on 4 November 1955. In its final version it was some forty pages long, and it adopted a moral, indeed a eugenicist, tone. It opened by saying on page 7:

> Homosexuality and prostitution are essentially social rather than medical problems, but, since health depends largely on environmental and sociological conditions, the Council welcomes the opportunity of advising on their nature and causes and of making suggestions for their control and cure. The individual doctor, and the medical profession as a whole, regard as their function the prevention of illness, the treatment of the sick, and the promotion of health in its widest sense. Everything which helps to encourage physical and mental health, social responsibility and stable family life is the concern of the medical profession, for on these factors the virility and soundness of the national life are founded. ...

It went on to say:

> The proper use of sex, the primary purpose of which is creative, is related to the individual's responsibility to himself and the nation, and the Committee believes that any weakening of personal responsibility with regard to social and national welfare in a significant proportion of the population is one of the causes of the apparent increase in homosexual practices and in prostitution.

It declared that it endorsed the submission of the Church of England's Moral Welfare Council, but then introduced its own *caveat*:

> The attempt to suppress homosexual activity by law can only be one factor in diminishing this problem. A public opinion against homosexual practices is a greater safeguard, and this can be achieved by promoting in the minds, motives and wills of the people a desire for clean and unselfish living.

It reproduced its typology of homosexual men,[311] commenting that:

> Not all homosexual persons can be identified as such by their appearance and manner, for many have no special characteristics. Homosexuals themselves are usually able to recognise each other in various ways, including gestures, smiles and manners, and peculiarities of appearance and habits. In some there is a tendency to self-display in dress and hair styles and in the use of scent and make-up. In this effeminate type of male there is often a certain softness which is difficult to describe but easy to sense. The voice may be high-pitched and facial hair scanty.

And of homosexual practices themselves it said:

> Not only are the actual practices repulsive, but the behaviour and appearance of homosexuals congregating blatantly in public houses, streets, and restaurants, are an outrage to public decency. Effeminate men wearing make-up and using scent are objectionable to everyone.

Unlike the B.M.A.'s earlier treatment of abortion (where there had been an unsullied emphasis solely on professional matters) and, curiously, unlike the Churches, it could not abstain from moralising:

> With reference to homosexual offences the Association's Committee has found it impossible to isolate from each other the varying causes, degrees and effects of homosexuality, and if it were to confine itself to purely medical considerations, its evidence would be so restricted as to be almost valueless. ... It is for this reason that the memorandum discusses aspects of homosexuality and prostitution which at first sight seem to extend beyond the medical sphere. It would urge that the Departmental Committee should examine the subject of sexual licence in all its extensive ramifications ... [and should make an] ... emphatic statement that, even though the Committee's conclusions might lead to a recommendation for the relaxation of the law, it must not be thought to condone in the slightest degree homosexual practices. Young people must not be allowed to acquire the view that homosexual practices were unobjectionable.[312]

It moved on to list both the adverse consequences of the existing law on homosexual practices (and here it echoed the arguments of the Church of England Moral Welfare Council in condemning the potential for blackmail and for the 'excessive penalisation of conduct which would not be punished if it were heterosexual; discrimination between the sexes ...'), and the positive consequences, applauding the manner in which criminalisation protected the young, and reinforced public opinion and moral boundaries by 'instil[ling] in the public mind the idea that homosexual practices are reprehensible and harmful'.

It considered the available treatments: analytical psychotherapy; non-analytic psychotherapy ('is applicable to a wide range of cases'); group treatment ('said to be effective but raises problems of secrecy'); physical and drug treatment; (may not help with homosexuality but could help accompanying conditions); castration (effective in a small number of cases – a radical treatment that could be recommended only it were almost invariably effective) and penal treatment. And finally and significantly, it showed the hand of the committee's secretary in its observation that:

> Individuals cannot of course be "dragooned" into a religious experience and pressure in this direction would defeat its own object. There should, however, be a recognition of the fact that homosexuals can acquire a new direction in their lives through religious conversion, and opportunities should be available to them to discover for themselves a basis of life that proves a reality to many people.

In all this, there is to be detected an interesting test and qualification of the entrenched sociological argument that medicine had replaced religion as the 'social guardian of morality'[313] and that this was part of a secularising process that entailed (in Bryan Wilson's words) a 'transfer of property, power, activities, and both manifest and latent functions, from institutions with a supernaturalist frame of reference to (often new) institutions operating according to empirical, rational, pragmatic criteria',[314] or, in David Martin's simpler phrase, the 'notion that religion and modernity are necessarily incompatible'.[315] Doctors may indeed have become moral guardians, but, in this instance, they were far from modernist, secular, empirical, rational or pragmatic as they sermonised through a loose compound of religiosity, clinical judgement and casual stereotypy. It was the *clergy* who deliberately eschewed the supernatural to look at homosexuality calmly, rationally, directly and professionally.

The Committee on Homosexual Offences and Prostitution heard from lawyers, including Lord Goddard, the Lord Chief Justice,[316] whose view that homosexual acts 'contain none of the elements of a crime'[317] was not always shared by his colleagues. Lawyers, like doctors, could also lapse into moralising. The Council of the Law Society, for example, declared that it had found it difficult to exclude moral criteria from their deliberations (it is, the council said, 'impossible entirely to divorce the legal from the social and moral aspects and it has accordingly been found necessary here and there in this memorandum to express views which are perhaps outside the strict province of the law as such ...') Those views led it to profess that it had followed Jeremy Bentham's 'six principles'[318] to conclude that the law should *not* be changed:

> Judged by these tests, the Council thinks that both buggery and gross indecency should remain criminal offences even when committed in private between consenting male persons of full age. The offences are productive of great evils (1) inasmuch as they (i) tend to reduce the inclination to marry; (ii) militate against the procreation of children; (iii) are calculated to result in damage to the State if they get too strong a hold; (iv) are likely (if legalised in private between genuine homosexuals) to contaminate others (and particularly the young); (v) may well, if allowed to go unchecked, result in male brothels; and (vi) probably tend to spread venereal disease.[319]

The Wolfenden Committee was to receive oral testimony. Quite bravely, a number of homosexual men wished to come forward to put their view of the world as a counter to the conventional medico-legal discourse of the time.[320] Quite bravely, too, in the prevailing moral climate, the Secretary, W. Roberts, also recommended talking to them, and it is evident that he believed they had something worth contributing,[321] but he did so employing the peculiar argot that had emerged even at a very early stage in the life of the committee, and there are strong hints that homosexual men (and prostitutes) would be regarded more as interesting specimens[322] than as straightforward, competent witnesses whose judgement and evidential authority counted like that of any other.[323] 'What about our Huntley and Palmers?' he asked.

> What are they thinking and saying? What are their complaints about the police? What are their grudges against society? They are not likely to come as official witnesses and if they did they would hardly be at their best when cross-examined by a committee. But I hope that some of us as individuals or in small groups can find ways of meeting some of those who are in daily touch with the realities of our enquiry and get them to talk off the record about what really happens under the surface of the law and its administration.

Throughout the committee's work, it should be noted, there was to be a continual process of vetting to establish a hierarchy of credibility[324] which would rank witnesses in terms of the weight which should be attached to their testimony:[325]

> Clearly, it will be for the convenience of the Committee and for the witnesses themselves that those who are to give oral evidence should be heard in some sort of order. ... Although it may be some time before we can hear a particular organisation or individual, it would be useful to have

what they are going to say at the back of our minds when considering the evidence of other witnesses whom we are seeing in the meantime. If you agree, therefore, I would propose to proceed as follows:

(1) Where the memorandum is from a responsible organisation or individual whom we must inevitably see, or whose evidence we must inevitably consider, I will circulate the memorandum as soon as may be after receipt.

(2) Where the memorandum is of doubtful value of where there might be some doubt about the bona fides of the author, I will seek your directions.

For the latter purpose, I have devised a form which will save you the trouble of writing letters. ...'[326]

It is evident that submissions from homosexual men tended in the main to be regarded as 'of doubtful value'. Even Peter Wildeblood, the defendant in the Montagu case, a hitherto respectable man, a successful journalist and author, who had submitted a lengthy written statement and was prepared to be questioned in person, was to be treated gingerly. Perhaps deferring to common stereotype, Sir John Wolfenden told the Secretary that 'I confess I am not looking forward very much to our interview with Mr Wildeblood; but I guess that once he gets going he will do most of the talking...'[327]

One other indication of the cautious manner in which the proceedings about prostitution and homosexuality were approached was that, despite copious and prolonged protests, it was decided to hold meetings *in camera*.[328] All efforts to reverse the decision were rebuffed by a committee that believed themselves at times to be under siege, particularly in their discussion of prostitution and particularly from women's organisations, who were typically dismissed as 'the ladies'. In one instance, demands from the federal Association for Moral and Social Hygiene[329] were dismissed as 'either an impertinence or a threat'.[330] Later, the chairman said of the Association's further request, 'These people really are the limit. Why should we be subjected to a mass meeting? The answer really is, of course, that the various Societies do not trust each other and each wants to have its watch-dog (if that is the right sex) to keep an eye on the others'.[331]

Throughout, the chairman and secretary of the Committee on Homosexual Offences and Prostitution maintained a critical distance from much of what they were told, even by those who were supposed to be professional experts. Thus, on one occasion, they were disinclined on libertarian grounds to accept the Prison Commissioners' recommendation that homosexual men should be administered hormones.[332] They were particularly wary of the enthusiasms of lobbies. In April 1955, the secretary wrote to the chairman: 'I am writing merely to let you know the "menu" for next week ... On Thursday we have the Labour Lawyers. ... On Friday we start with the Progressive League ... In the afternoon we are to have the Howard League. This will dispose, I think, of the more zealous reformers on the homosexuality side, though we shall no doubt hear from time to time from others who would favour reform'.[333] There was also a distinct uneasiness about much of the correspondence which the secretary received. He referred to it as 'fan mail', and often passed it on to the chairman with the observation that it might be found amusing.

By September 1955, Sir John Wolfenden had moved to the position that would later be taken by the majority of the Committee and embedded in its report: homosexual acts between consenting adults[334] in private were offensive and sinful but there were no good reasons why they should remain criminal, and it is clear that he, as a 'good Anglican layman',[335] had been much influenced by the arguments developed by the Moral Welfare Council. He had, he told the secretary:

> ... the feeling that genuinely private sexual behaviour between consenting adults, although some of its forms may be distasteful to ordinary people and although they may appear to many to be sinful, ought not to be the subject of legislation; ... . the feeling that homosexuals (as defined) ought not to be the only people for whom the only alternative to compulsory lifelong chastity is the risk of severe legal penalties. ... I agree with the Church of England pamphlet. I think it could be argued that other forms of sexual misbehaviour (adultery, rape and many forms of heterosexual perversion) are more harmful, both to the individual and to society, than are private homosexual acts between consenting adult males. ... There are many forms of behaviour which are legal but which are not therefore regarded as respectable; and there are many forms of behaviour which are tolerated although they are illegal... I am not sure how best to put into statutory language the change in the law which I think should be advocated. ... it looks as if the deletion of 'in private' from the Labouchere amendment is what I really mean.[336]

In short, and put simply, he was to say that private behaviour that did no harm to others was not the law's business: it 'goes beyond the proper sphere of the law's concern. We do not think that it is proper for the law to concern itself with what a man does behind closed doors unless it can be shown to be contrary to the public good to such an extent that the law ought to intervene in its function as the guardian of that public good'.[337] Almost all the other members of the Committee concurred (the sole dissenter was James Adair, the former Procurator-Fiscal for Glasgow, chairman of the Scottish Council of the Young Men's Christian Association and an Elder of the Church of Scotland, who asserted that liberalisation would have an injurious impact on public morals[338]). The Catholic barrister and Member of Parliament, William Wells, even took it that that position should be strengthened further to set the law in England and Wales firmly in contrast to the moral and political absolutism of totalitarian states.[339] And the Churchman and Regius Professor of Moral and Pastoral Theology at the University of Oxford, Canon Vigo Demant,[340] said that 'Homosexual acts between adult consenting males should not be an offence in the criminal law, and no distinction should be made in this respect between different kinds of such acts'. It is significant to note that it was he, a churchman and theologian, who was entrusted by Sir John Wolfenden to produce the next draft of the report's chapters which touched on the moral compass of the law. Submitting that draft, he reported to Sir John:

> It is practically a repetition of your excellent draft, which I find more concise than Roberts! [The secretary] I have changed a word or phrase here and there, and made some additions to the earlier part, in order to ... state a little more fully and firmly what we consider the functioning of the law to be, before stating what it should not cover, and to relate the law to the moral issues. ...[341]

The report was finally presented to Parliament in September 1957, its first print of 5,000 copies selling out within hours of publication. Its approach was stated simply: 'We clearly recognise that the laws of any society must be acceptable to the general moral sense of the community if they are to be respected and enforced. But we are not charged to enter into matters of private moral conduct except in so far as they directly affect the public good'.[342] It followed that 'Certain forms of sexual behaviour [may be] regarded by many as sinful, morally wrong, or objectionable for reasons of conscience, or of religious or cultural tradition; and such actions may be reprobated on these grounds. But the criminal law does not cover all such actions at the present time; for instance, adultery and fornication are not offences for which a person can be punished by the criminal law. ...'[343] There were to be some conceptual problems with the precise meanings of each key term that followed, but it concluded that 'We accordingly recommend that homosexual behaviour between consenting adults in private should no longer be a criminal offence. ...'[344]

Conclusion

The Wolfenden Committee had been established in 1954 by Sir David Maxwell Fyfe and the Conservative Government in part to stem what was deemed to be the unwelcome impact of unwholesome publicity about trials for indecent and unnatural offences under the 1861 and 1885 Acts. It took advice from experts in medicine, psychology, psychiatry[345] and law,[346] some of whom took a liberal, utilitarian view, others of whom moralised and supported the retention of control through law enforcement or therapeutic intervention,[347] and some of whom did both simultaneously. But it is notable that much of that advice was disregarded (and it is also notable that the older, vague offences of indecency and male importuning did give way under the influence of the new medical sciences to a new conception of homosexuality, the very first time that the word was about to be used in criminal law[348]). Instead, following the liberal reasoning of the Moral Welfare Council of the Church of England, the Committee came to adopt a position that might have been advocated by John Stuart Mill, 'the standard libertarian':[349] sinful acts committed in private that

432 *The Sexual Offences Act 1967: Prologue*

were innocuous to the public good should not be exposed to the criminal law. The Church had provided a simple, clear moral philosophy to order its conclusions, and the Committee's debt to its theologians was made quite explicit. Sir John Wolfenden was later reported to have said:

> A clergyman had told him that the answer was perfectly plain: the root of all law was to be found in the Ten Commandments. But if you looked at the Ten Commandments dispassionately, how many were embodied in the law of this country? Either three and a half or four and a half according to how you defined "to bear false witness." It was simply not the case that there was identity between the adjectives of morality and adjectives of criminality. It was desirable to be clear about this …[350]

The Moral Welfare Council itself recognised the importance of the role it had played in its own commentary on the report: it was, it said, content to 'endorse[] the proposals made by the Committee for a reform of the law which follow almost exactly in substance those advocated by the Council'.[351]

The future of the committee's pivotal recommendation would subsequently turn on an acceptance of the idea of a publicly innocuous private immorality (most famously to be contested in the debate between Herbert Hart and Lord Devlin,[352] itself a reprise of an earlier debate between John Stuart Mill and James Fitzjames Stephen[353]), and a political readiness in cabinet and Parliament to implement what would be yet another contentious liberalising measure in law.

Notes

1 Weeks states that 'as late as 1871, concepts of homosexuality were extremely undeveloped both in the Metropolitan Police and in high medical and legal circles, suggesting the absence of any clear notion of a homosexual category or of any social awareness of what a homosexual identity might consist of'. J. Weeks (1989); *Coming Out: Homosexual Politics in Britain from the Nineteenth Century to the Present*, London: Quartet Books, 101.

2 Sodomy appears to have been understood rather loosely as disorderly sexuality rather than as simple anal penetration.

3 See R. v. Krafft-Ebing (1887); *Psychopathia Sexualis*, Stuttgart: Verlag von Ferdinand Enke.

4 See H. Ellis (1897); *Studies in the Psychology of Sex: Vol. 1. Sexual Inversion*, London: University Press.

5 See *The Oxford English Dictionary*.

6 See R. Warnicke (1987); 'Sexual Heresy at the Court of Henry VIII', *The Historical Journal*, Vol. 30, No. 2, esp. 250.

7 Robert Burton (1883) spoke, for instance, in *The Anatomy of Melancholy*, of the 'mastuprations, sodomies, buggeries of monks and friars', Chatto and Windus, London, 343; and see P. Ackroyd (2017); *Queer City: Gay London from the Romans to the Present Day*, London: Chatto and Windus, 43.

8 See R. Scott (1972); 'A Proposed Framework for Analysing Deviance as a Property of Social Order', in R. Scott and J. Douglas (eds.); *Theoretical Perspectives on Deviance*, New York: Basic Books, 9–36.

9 The Act was repealed in 1553 and then restored ten years later under Queen Elizabeth 1.

10 A typical report, published in the *Daily Universal Register* in August 1787 talks of how:
    'At the assizes at Exeter, which ended on the Crown side on Thursday evening, six
    prisoners were capitally convicted, and received sentence of death, viz. Thomas Ayre,
    for stealing a mare saddle, &c. John Piper, for house-breaking; Thomas Crispin, aged
    45, for committing an unnatural crime on the body of Hugh Gribble, aged 20; and
    said Hugh Gribble, for permitting him so to do ...' in Rictor Norton (ed.) 'Newspaper
    Reports, 1787', *Homosexuality in Eighteenth-Century England: A Sourcebook*, 14 May
    2010; http://rictornorton.co.uk/eighteen/1787news.htm. That website is an invalu-
    able source of information about reports on and surrounding the history of prosecu-
    tions for sodomy.

11 Barbara Wootton was to say that 'this [1967 Sexual Offences] Act is of special interest
    inasmuch as opposition to it could only be based on moral grounds. The performance
    of homosexual acts by consenting adults in private is one of the rare examples of
    behaviour which can be said to have practically no effect upon anyone other than
    those who engage in it. Not surprisingly, therefore, it has become *par excellence* the
    battle-ground between the moralists who regard certain actions as inherently wicked,
    irrespective of their effect on the community at large, and the secular utilitarians in
    whose view no action is immoral which does not cause damage to someone other than
    the person who performs it. ...' B. Wootton, *Selected Writings: Volume 1: Crime and the
    Penal System, op. cit.*, 85.

12 See L. Mulcahy (2011); *Legal Architecture: Justice, due process and the place of law*, London:
    Routledge, 63.

13 An Act for Consolidating and Amending the Statutes in England Relative to Offences
    Against the Person, 9 Geo IV, where it was confirmed that 'every person convicted
    of the abominable crime of Buggery, committed either with mankind or with any
    animal, or aiding or abetting such crime, shall suffer Death as a Felon'.

14 A. Harvey (December 1978); 'Prosecutions for Sodomy in England at the Beginning
    of the Nineteenth Century', *The Historical Journal*, Vol. 21, No. 4, 939–948. I have
    constructed the following chart on the basis of the table he presents on 947:

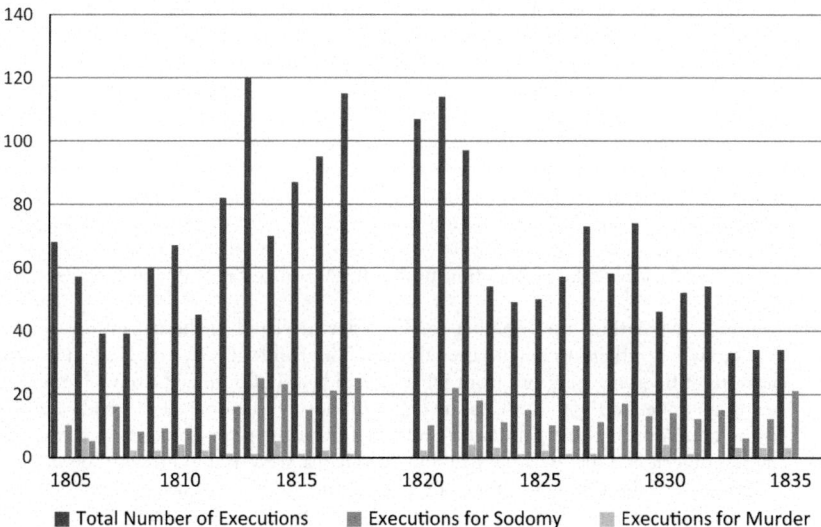

Executions in England and Wales – 1805–1835

Legend: Total Number of Executions Executions for Sodomy Executions for Murder

15 See HL Deb 17 June 1841 Vol. 58 cc1552–60.

16 23 Vict. Under Sec. LXIII ('Unnatural Offences') it was stipulated that 'Whosoever shall be convicted of the abominable Crime of Buggery, committed either with Mankind or with any Animal, shall be liable to be kept in Penal Servitude for Life'.

17 The actual phrasing was 'Whosoever shall be convicted of the abominable Crime of Buggery, committed either with Mankind or with any Animal, shall be liable, at the Discretion of the Court, to be kept in Penal Servitude for Life or for any Term not less than Ten Years'.

18 It was not the only amendment he proposed to the bill. He also proposed that young girls should no longer be subject to the control of parents who connived in their immorality and that guardians should be appointed to protect those who were under 16 years old (*The Times*, 6 August 1885).

19 It was actually the Criminal Law Amendment Act 48 & 49 Vict. c.69, and its long title was 'An Act to Make Further Provision for the Protection of Women, Girls, the Suppression of Brothels and Other Purposes'.

20 Sydney Allen, Member of Parliament for Crewe, speaking in a debate on the Wolfenden Report in the House of Commons, HC Deb 29 June 1960 Vol. 625 cc1453–514.

21 See Roy Jenkins' depiction of the introduction of the amendment in the House of Commons debate of June 1960 (HC Deb 29 June 1960 Vol. 625 cc1453–514).

22 http://yourarchives.nationalarchives.gov.uk/index.php?title=Gay_and_Lesbian_ History_at_the_National_Archives:_An_Introduction

23 See L. Farmer; *Making the Modern Criminal Law*, op. cit., 277.

24 Stead claimed that he had published the report precisely to rescue the Criminal Law (Amendment) Bill which was then in the doldrums (see his 'Notice to our Readers: A Frank Warning', published in *The Pall Mall Gazette* on 4 July 1885). Indeed, it appears that the Act was known at the time as 'Stead's Act'. See D. Gorham (1978); 'The "Maiden Tribute of Modern Babylon" Re-Examined: Child Prostitution and the Idea of Childhood in Late-Victorian England', *Victorian Studies*, Vol. 21(3), 354.

25 William Stead, 1849–1912, was first to become assistant editor of *The Pall Mall Gazette* in 1880 and then its editorial director in 1883, in which post he sought to make it a 'tribune for the poor'. (Based on the entry by J. Baylen in *The Oxford Dictionary of National Biography*, http://www.oxforddnb.com/view/article/36258) The only recent biography published of Stead talks about his relation with Labouchère, and talks about the 1885 Criminal Law Amendment Act, but it makes only a perfunctory mention of the Labouchère amendment itself, saying, without naming Labouchère that a Member had 'speculatively motioned that 'gross indecency with another male person, shall be guilty of misdemeanour" (W. Robinson (2012); *Muckraker: The Scandalous Life and Times of W.T. Stead*, London: The Robson Press, 101.) Stead notoriously changed his opinions on a number of moral issues, but it is interesting that he would condemn in his *Pall Mall Gazette* the prosecution under the Act of Oscar Wilde in 1895 (see *ibid*, 225).

26 Alexander McArthur, the Member for Leicester, declared in the debate on the Act that he 'was not there to defend the editor of The Pall Mall Gazette. He had not the pleasure of knowing him; but from what he had heard of him, and from what he had heard in connection with this case, he believed, notwithstanding all that had been said to the contrary, that that gentleman had acted from the purest motives and with the highest object, and that what he had done had had a great deal to do with the success-ful progress of the Bill. It was perfectly true, as the Home Secretary had pointed out, that this Bill had been prepared two or three years; but he was convinced that if it had not been for The Pall Mall Gazette, another year, at least, would have been allowed to elapse without its being passed. He had no doubt that considerable injury had been done by The Pall Mall Gazette by the publication of these articles; but he believed that

the arousing of the people of the country to these abominations and terrible crimes would more than counterbalance any amount of evil that had been done'. HC Deb 6 August 1885 Vol. 300 cc1386–428.

27 http://www.attackingthedevil.co.uk/pmg/tribute/mt1.php

28 See B. Lewis (2011); Review Essay: The Maiden Tribute of Modern Babylon: The Report of the Secret Commission. By W. T. STEAD', *Journal of the History of Sexuality*, vol. 20 (1), 200.

29 Henry Labouchère, 1831–1912, a journalist and politician, was a radical Liberal Member of Parliament for Windsor between 1865 and 1866; for Middlesex between 1867 and 1868, and for Northampton between 1880 and 1906. His biographer observed that 'Though in general libertarian, Labouchere was a strong opponent of homosexuality; it was his clause added to the Criminal Law Amendment Act 1885 by which Oscar Wilde was tried; Labouchere regretted that Wilde got only two years' hard labour; his original proposal would have permitted seven' (http://www.oxforddnb.com/view/article/34367?docPos=2)

30 HC Deb 6 August 1885, vol 300 cc1386–428.

31 The adjective is that employed by Kenneth Robinson in the debate on the Wolfenden Report in the House of Commons HC Deb 29 June 1960 vol 625 cc1453–514.

32 There had been no prior legislation proscribing homosexual practices other than anal penetration (see A. Harvey, 'Prosecutions for Sodomy in England at the Beginning of the Nineteenth Century', *op. cit.*, 941) although Jeffrey Weeks reminded me that 'before 1885 homosexual acts short of buggery were not ignored but were prosecuted as acts likely to lead to the major offence' (email, 29 April 2012).

33 See M. Foldy (1997); *The Trials of Oscar Wilde: Deviance, Morality, and Late-Victorian Society*, New Haven: Yale University Press, 31.

34 HL Deb 12 May 1965 vol 266 cc71–172

35 For example in *The New York Times* of 17 January 1912; *The Saturday Review*, 20 January 1912.

36 There is no reference to any of the matters that would arise in connection with the events traced in this chapter (prostitution, Howard Vincent, *Select Committee of the House of Lords on the Law Relating to the Protection of Young Girls*, the Criminal Law Amendment Act, homosexuality and the like) in A. Thorold (1913); *The Life of Henry Labouchere*, London: Constable; H. Pearson (1945); *Labby (The Life and Character of Henry Labouchere)*, London: Hamilton; and R. Hind (1972); *Henry Labouchere and the Empire 1880–1905*, London: The Athlone Press. The only reference to his engagement with matters of criminal justice was to the Crimes Bill of 1882 which was deeply embedded in the Irish politics about which he entertained passionate sentiments (A. Thorold, *The Life of Henry Labouchere*, 169–170).

37 See F.B. Smith (October 1976); 'Labouchère's amendment to the Criminal Law Amendment Bill', *Australian Historical Studies*, Vol. 17, No. 67, 167.

38 HC Deb 6 August 1885 Vol. 300 cc1386–428.

39 'Labouchère had never before shown any particular interest in matters of sexuality, and it is a puzzle why he proposed his amendment,' stated Caryn Neumann; (http://www.glbtq.com/social-sciences/labouchere_amendment.html) J. Coleman (2014) simply said that the amendment was passed 'mindlessly'. *Rent: Same-Sex Prostitution in Modern Britain, 1885–1957*, PhD dissertation, the University of Kentucky, 31.

40 He was not alone. The criminal justice politics of the homosexual underworld was quite febrile at the time. See N. McKenna (2013) *Fanny & Stella: The Young Men who Shocked Victorian England*, London: Faber and Faber. Labouchère was not even particularly preoccupied with those politics. One of his biographers, H. Pearson, stated that 'The subject that brought forth all Labby's powers of invective, mockery and scorn, was war. It was the only subject on which he spoke with strong feeling and bitterness'. *Labby (The Life and Character of Henry Labouchere)*, op. cit., 171.

41 The Conservative Member of Parliament for Cheadle, William Shepherd, wrote to a newspaper to complain that 'The homosexual belongs to a "freemasonry," and this means that – unlike offenders in the other classes – he will on discovery be most reluctant to give any information about fellow homosexuals involved in the net. …' (Cutting from an unnamed, undated newspaper filed in the papers of the Committee on Prostitution and Homosexual Offences, CRI 477/8/67). He was to question the Prime Minister about the number of cases of 'male perversion' coming before the courts (see *The Times*, 4 December 1953) and was to be a staunch opponent of homosexual law reform (see *The Times*, 29 June 1960; and 7 February 1966). No doubt the fear of apprehension drove many gay men into defensive groups.

42 D. Matza (1969); *Becoming Deviant*, Englewood Cliffs: Prentice-Hall, 38–39.

43 See *The Times*, 24 December 1889.

44 See L. Chester, D. Leitch and C. Simpson (1976); *The Cleveland Street Affair*, London: Weidenfeld and Nicholson, and K. Hindmarch-Watson (2016); 'Sex, Services, and Surveillance: The Cleveland Street Scandal Revisited', *History Compass*, June 2016, Vol.14(6), 283–291.

45 HC Deb 28 February 1890 Vol. 341 cc1523–611.

46 *The Times*, 1 March 1890.

47 *The Maiden Tribute* touched only on the exploitation of young girls. Robinson's biography of Stead, *Muckraker*, makes no mention of a report about the exploitation of young boys, and I have been unable to trace it elsewhere.

48 Sir Richard Cross, later Lord Cross, 1823–1914, had been Member of Parliament for SW Lancashire, 1868–85 and Lancashire (Newton), 1885–86; and Home Secretary, 1874–80 and 1885–1886.

49 HC Deb 28 February 1890 Vol. 341 cc1523–611.

50 Nancy Erber said simply 'the French legal code, unlike those of its neighbors, "tolerated" homosexual acts because it was silent on them'. (N. Erber (1996); 'The French Trials of Oscar Wilde', *Journal of the History of Sexuality*, Vol. 6, No. 4, 550). Some confusion may have arisen because Labouchère claimed at the time to have based other amendments, relating to the treatment of girls under 13, on the French penal code (see HC Deb 3 August 1885 Vol. 300 cc850–922). His early biographer and nephew, Algar Labouchère Thorold, 1866–1936, also employed by *Truth*, did say that he had an 'embroidering memory' See the anonymous review of his *The Life of Henry Labouchère*, in *The Nation*, 11 December 1913, Vol. 97, No. 2528, 564; and *The Times*, 8 March 1912. And note the phrase '*mutatis mutandis*' which he employed when, in 1895, commenting on the conviction of Oscar Wilde – without entering into any detail about what he considered to be the facts of the case – he stated that 'Wilde and Taylor were tried on a clause in the Criminal Law Amendment Act which I had inserted, in order to render it possible for the law to take cognisance of proceedings like theirs. I took this clause *mutatis mutandis* from the French code. The then Home Secretary and Attorney-General, both most experienced men, however, suggested to me that, in such cases, convictions are always difficult, and that it would be better were the maximum to be two years'. Of Wilde himself, he reflected that 'the curious thing in the man is that he seems to have been proud of the avowal of doctrines which the most abandoned would, even if they held to them, carefully conceal. … There are those who think that a case like this does more harm than good. That is not my view. I regard it rather as a storm that will clear the moral atmosphere'. 'A Righteous Verdict', *Truth*, Vol. XXXVII, No. 961 (30 May 1895), 1331–2.

51 That is a contention which seems to run counter to the fact that Labouchère had played an active and wide-ranging part in many of the debates on the bill and had attempted at committee stage and after to introduce other amendments touching more nearly on the central theme of the legislation. He spoke more often and with

greater emphasis, for example, on the problem of the continuing parental control of young girls who had been seduced. He also tried to add a clause stating that 'In all cases where it can be proved that the carnal connection of an unmarried girl under the age of twenty-one with a man has been encouraged, favoured, or facilitated by the father, mother, or guardian, such father, mother, or guardian shall cease to have any authority over her'. And, he said, 'he had given Notice of another clause on the same subject, but he did not see it on the Paper. ... It was – And in such cases where the girl is under the age of sixteen any magistrate shall have authority on proof of the offence to send her to a reformatory or industrial school, or to commit her to the custody of any person or persons whom he may think fit until the age of seventeen' (HC Deb 3 August 1885 Vol. 300 cc850–922)

52 F. B. Smith; 'Labouchère's amendment to the Criminal Law Amendment Bill', *op. cit.*, 169–170.

53 A. Sanna (2012); 'Silent Homosexuality in Oscar Wilde's Teleny and The Picture of Dorian Gray and Robert Louis Stevenson's Dr Jekyll and Mr Hyde', *Law & Literature*, 24:1, 21–39. On p. 23 he asserts that 'late-Victorian law described homosexuality as an unhealthy form of malady; it stated that homosexuality was unacceptable by contemporary society and threatened to punish its practitioners, commanding them not to indulge in any form of physical contact. We could then consider the Labouchère amendment as a humanly made creation of a society, which was driven by the antipermissiveness and puritanism of the period'.

54 Pearson, for example, described him in Chapter VIII of *Labby (The Life and Character of Henry Labouchere)*, as an agnostic, a pacifist, anti-imperialist and a republican; and W.S. Blunt's diary claimed that he was to be found 'entirely in the society of whores and croupiers' in *Henry Labouchere and the Empire 1880–1905, op. cit.*, 1.

55 See J. Walkowitz (1980); 'The Politics of Prostitution', *Signs*, Vol. 6 (1), 128, and J. Walkowitz (1982); 'Male Vice and Feminist Virtue: Feminism and the Politics of Prostitution in Nineteenth Century Britain', *History Workshop*, No. 13, 79–93. She says on p. 85 that 'An anti-aristocratic bias may have prompted the inclusion of this clause ... as homosexuality was associated with the corruption of working-class youth by the same upper-class profligates, who, on other occasions, were thought to buy the services of young girls'.

56 In 1951, for example, discussion in the House of Commons of a proposal by the Paddington Moral Reform Council to establish a committee to investigate prostitution in London was to include the suggestion that such a committee should also consider homosexuality (HC Deb 5 April 1951 Vol. 486 cc367–8). Again, in a contemporary review of laws proscribing homosexuality, Hélie talks of 'a strong connection between homophobic assaults by fundamentalists and those directed against women who do not "behave."' A. Hélie (2004); 'Holy Hatred', *Reproductive Health Matters*, Vol. 12, No. 23, 120.

57 See J. Weeks; *Sex, Politics and Society, op. cit.*, 106.

58 See S. Rowbotham (2008); *Edward Carpenter: A Life of Liberty and Love*, London: Verso, 103.

59 I am grateful to Louise Jackson for pointing me to her work.

60 L. Jackson (2000); *Child Sexual Abuse in Victorian England*, London: Routledge, esp. 100–106.

61 Sir Howard Vincent, 1849–1908, served in the army, worked as a journalist, was called to the Bar in 1876 and then, two years later, was recruited to become the first director of criminal investigation at Scotland Yard, in which role he was called upon to reorganise the detective department. In 1885, he was elected as the Conservative Member of Parliament for Central Sheffield (http://www.oxforddnb.com.gate2.library.lse. ac.uk/view/10.1093/ref:odnb/9780198614128.001.0001/odnb-9780198614128-e-36660?rskey=C7bByu&result=1). At first, his chief responsibilities as Director seem

to have been in surveilling the activities of anarchists, socialists, Fenians and Social Democrats, and supervising murder investigations.

62 See the *Report from the Select Committee of the House of Lords on the Law Relating to the Protection of Young Girls*; House of Lords (August 1881). Cm. 448. The committee had been convened, announced the Earl of Dalhousie, in response to reports about the decoying and ill treatment of young English girls to houses of ill repute in Belgium and, it was believed, Austria and France (HL Deb 30 May 1881 Vol. 261 cc1603–13). No mention was made on that occasion about young boys, and the committee submitted only the briefest of reports without any reference to male homosexual relations.

63 Statement by the Earl of Dalhousie, reported in The Times, 1 March 1882. And see S. Petrow (1994); *Policing Morals: The Metropolitan Police and the Home Office 1870–1914*, Oxford: Clarendon Press, Ch. 5.

64 Report from the Select Committee of the House of Lords on the Law Relating to the Protection of Young Girls, *op. cit.*, paragraph 646). It seems that he saw his role to be as much focused on crime prevention as arrest and punishment, believing that his first duty was to 'save the [offender] from the natural consequences of his actions when he is caught' ('Mr Howard Vincent and the Criminal Classes', *The Saturday Review*, 23 December 1882, Vol. 54 (1417), 815). He was involved, for example, in establishing children's courts (see the review of his biography in *The Manchester Guardian* of 4 November 1912 and T. Bridgwater (1906); 'Children's Courts', *Journal of the Society of Comparative Legislation*, Vol. 7, No. 2, 375–383).

65 The press focused solely on the white slave trade in young girls. See, for example, the lengthy editorial in *The Times* of 25 August 1881.

66 Neither was there any reference to the Criminal Law (Amendment Act) although Vincent was an M.P. when it passed through Parliament.

67 There appear to have been a number of meetings before and during his time as an M.P. For instance, he and Labouchère dined together as guests of the then Prince of Wales, and the two of them were to sponsor a bill prohibiting the importation of brushes manufactured in foreign prisons (see S. Jeyes (1912); *The Life of Sir Howard Vincent*, London: George Allen and Company, 233).

68 *Child Sexual Abuse in Victorian England, op. cit.*, 105–6.

69 HC Deb 6 August 1885 Vol. 300 cc1386–428.

70 See A. Travis, 'Repercussions of scandals still linger', *The Guardian*, 20 November 2002.

71 The sometime attorney general, Viscount Dilhorne, was to say that 'I found some difficulty in knowing what was the intention which lay behind that Amendment, because it was never debated in Parliament. There is no report of any discussion at all' (HL Deb 28 October 1965 Vol. 269 cc677–730)

72 See H. Cocks (2003); *Nameless Offences: Homosexual Desire in the Nineteenth Century*, London: I.B. Tauris. And see Bristow, who observed in a review of C. Upchurch's *Before Wilde: Sex between Men in Britain's Age of Reform*, that 'legal developments such as the Labouchère Amendment ... which banned sexual relations between men even in private, did not accomplish a decisive shift when it specified a maximum sentence of two years with hard labour for men who were found guilty of committing acts of "gross indecency"' ((April 2010); review of C. Upchurch (2009) *Before Wilde: Sex between Men in Britain's Age of Reform*, Berkeley: University of California Press, in *The Journal of British Studies*, Vol. 49, No. 2, 480). And see A. Adut (July 2005); 'A Theory of Scandal: Victorians, Homosexuality, and the Fall of Oscar Wilde', *American Journal of Sociology*, Vol. 111, No. 1, 213–248. Adut states on p. 213 that 'the Victorian authorities rarely and only reluctantly enforced homosexuality laws'.

73 Email to Paul Rock, 3 February 2011.

74 Weeks referred to 'a wider change in social roles and sexual attitudes which was to see in the next generation the reconceptualisation of social attitudes to the family, the

role of women and in society, and the position of children and adolescents ... It is significant ... that legislation on homosexuality should have been intimately tied in with changes in the law regarding prostitution ...' J. Weeks, *Sex, Politics and Society: op. cit.*, 15–16.

75 The Vagrancy Act c. 39, s.1(b) amended earlier legislation to penalise any person who 'in any public place persistently importunes or solicits for immoral purposes' and deemed him to be 'a rogue and a vagabond ... and may be dealt with accordingly'. The Criminal Law Amendment Act 1912, & 3 Geo. 5, c. 20, s. 1 stipulated that 'A constable may take into custody without a warrant any person whom he shall have good cause to suspect of having committed, or of attempting to commit, any offence against section two of the Criminal Law Amendment Act, 1885 (which relates to procuration and attempted procuration); and under s. 3. 'Any male person who is convicted under section two of the Criminal Law Amendment Act, 1885, may, at the discretion of the court, and in addition to any term of imprisonment awarded in respect of the said offence be sentenced to be once privately whipped, and the number of strokes and the instrument with which they shall be inflicted shall be specified by the court in the sentence'.

76 The phrase seemed first to have appeared in G. Westwood (1952); *Society and the Homosexual*, London: Victor Gollancz. It was then frequently repeated thereafter, in, for example, 'The Homosexual, The Law, and Society: Evidence submitted by the Church of England Moral Welfare Council to the Government Committee on Homosexual Offences and Prostitution'; the report of the Methodist Conference, Newcastle Upon Tyne, Representative Session, 7 July 1958, 6 Moral Welfare; and 'Homosexuality and the Law', *The Lancet*, 12 December 1959, 1071. Leo Abse was eventually to say that 'No argument had swayed the House in passing the relieving Act more than that the old punitive law was a charter for blackmailers. ...' 'The law that failed to liberate the gays', *The Times*, 28 July 1982. The allegation has been contested by Peter Alldridge (Autumn 1993) who claimed that the blackmail of homosexual men had been practised long before the 1885 Act and that there is no clear evidence of any increase in its incidence after its enactment: 'Attempted Murder of the Soul': Blackmail, Privacy and Secrets', *Oxford Journal of Legal Studies*, Vol. 13, No. 3, 368–387.

77 His reference was to a statement made in the House of Lords by Lord Jowitt who said that: 'When I became Attorney-General, I became oppressed by the discovery that there was a much larger quantity of blackmail than I had ever realised. I have no figures – I do not suppose one can get figures in a case of this sort – but I can certainly charge my recollection to this extent. It is the fact – I do not know why it is the fact, but it is the fact – that at least 95 per cent. of the cases of blackmail which came to my knowledge arose out of homosexuality, either between adult males or between adult males and boys'. HL Deb 19 May 1954 Vol. 187 cc737–67.

78 Departmental Committee on Homosexual Offences and Prostitution: Statement Submitted by Mr. Peter Wildeblood (Age 32 – Sentenced to 18 months imprisonment, March, 1954. Served sentence at H.M. Prison Winchester and Wormwood Scrubs. Released March, 1955). Document no. CHP/51.

79 See the report, 'Policemen's Conviction Upheld', in *The Times* of 27 May 1955.

80 Letter from Anatole James to John Wolfenden 30 March 1955 (HO345/2). An associate of Havelock Ellis (see P. Grosskurth (1980); *Havelock Ellis: A Biography*, New York: Alfred A. Knopf, 218), James died in 1979. He was the author of an unpublished autobiography which was described in the archive where it is housed as 'Gays-- England--20th century' (Division of Rare and Manuscript Collections, Cornell University Library: http://rmc.library.cornell.edu/ead/htmldocs/RMM07660.html) The archivist of the Collections did not respond to a request to supply further information about James. However, I did manage to learn something about James through a friend of a friend, Eisha Prather, Special Collections Assistant and Exhibition

Coordinator at the University, who wrote to say that James 'was born April 7, 1892. He and his family lived in and around Hull. His father was a solicitor, and he had three sisters. He was never sent to school, but was educated at home by governesses and tutors. In 1909 he joined his father's solicitor's office, where he worked until his first arrest for gross indecency and sodomy in August 1917. … He mentions once that at the time of his arrest he was called "Geoffrey," so Anatole James is probably not his real name. He mentions having been in 10 different prisons, and refers to having been arrested several times since 1917 on similar charges'. I am most grateful to Eisha Prather for his help.

81 J. Wolfenden (1976); *Turning Points: The Memoirs of Lord Wolfenden*, London: The Bodley Head, 131.

82 See *The Times*, 8 April 1895.

83 See http://www.turing.org.uk/bio/part8.html

84 Nigel Walker wrote very near the time that franker discussion of sexual matters and the more graphic newspaper reporting of homosexual incidents might have brought it about that 'Not only may the ordinary member of the public be persuaded into sufficient alarm or moral indignation, but the police themselves may be stimulated into more active enquiries. This is probably the explanation of the trend of reported homosexual offences in the nineteen-fifties'. N. Walker; *Crime and Punishment in Britain, op. cit.*, 26.

85 Sir Hugh Linstead, a politician and member of the Wolfenden Committee appointed to report on homosexuality and prostitution, would later say in debate to another Member of Parliament that 'If the hon. and learned Gentleman will look at the table of offences known to the police he will see a spectacular increase in the number of those offences, which can be explained only on the basis of a considerable increase in the condition of homosexuality in the community. I do not think any competent observer would deny that'. HC Deb 26 November 1958 Vol. 596 cc365–508.

86 T. Newburn, *Permission and Regulation, op. cit.*, 49.

87 That certainly is the contention of Houlbrook who argued that 'rising rates of juvenile crime, dramatised by repeated panics surrounding metropolitan youth cultures, focused attention upon young men's socialisation into normative masculinities. That youths were growing up in female-dominated households, without suitable male role models, made their future cause for massive concern'. M. Houlbrook (July 2003); 'Soldier Heroes and Rent Boys: Homosexuality, Masculinities, and Britishness in the Brigade of Guards, circa 1900–1960', *The Journal of British Studies*, Vol. 42, No. 3, 384.

88 See F. Mort; 'Scandalous Events: Metropolitan Culture and Moral Change in Post-Second World War London', *Representations*, (2006), Vol. 93(1), 106–137.

89 Based on Table E, *Criminal Statistics England and Wales* 1936, Cmd. 5690, HMSO, London, 1938; and Table E, *Criminal Statistics England and Wales* 1953, Cmd. 9199, HMSO, London, 1954.

90 J. Weeks, 'Wolfenden and Beyond: The Remaking of Homosexual History', http://www.historyandpolicy.org/papers/policy-paper-51.html

91 Sir John Nott-Bower, 1892–1972, was made Assistant Commissioner of the Metropolitan Police in 1940, Deputy Commissioner in 1946, and Commissioner in 1953. There is no entry for him in the *Oxford Dictionary of National Biography*, neither does he appear to have been the subject of a biography or autobiography.

92 *The Sydney Morning Telegraph*, 25 October 1953.

93 He did refer without amplification to the fact that he had been invited by the Departmental Committee on Homosexual Offences and Prostitution [otherwise known as the Wolfenden Committee] on p. 14 of his report for 1954: *Report of the Commissioner of Police of the Metropolis for the Year 1954*, Cmd. 9471, London: HMSO, 1955.

94 See, for instance, *Report of the Commissioner of Police of the Metropolis for the Year 1950*, Cmd. 8359, London: HMSO, 1951, 11; and *Report of the Commissioner of Police of the Metropolis for the Year 1951*, Cmd. 8634, London: HMSO, 1952, 9.

95 An extensive search on, for example, http://archiveshub.ac.uk/search/search.html, proved to be barren.

96 Letter from Ruth Allen, Information Manager, Metropolitan Police, 16 February 2011.

97 Winston Churchill said in a letter to David Maxwell Fyfe: 'I do not consider this is the moment to appoint a policeman [in contrast to a retired military officer] to this particular job. There are many new problems which lie before the police on which a fresh eye would be advantageous. Have you heard no rumours about corruption in the difficult and doubtful area around the Eros monument?' (Letter of 9 July 1953, POL 726/1/38). He would no doubt have had in mind the kind of incident to which Anatole James later referred. But there were other events recently reported: for example, in *The Times* of 8 and 17 January 1953, which touched on the arrest and trial of a bio-chemist for importuning for immoral purposes which turned on the defendant's denial of police allegations; and, more immediate to the Prime Minister, in *The Times* of 26 January and 21 February 1953 which centred on the arrest and trial of William Field, the Labour Member for North Paddington, for persistent importuning.

98 'Some suggested questions might be put to candidates from within the police service'. (POL 726/1/38) That preoccupation with recruitment and novel problems of traffic control was to dominate during the decade. See, for instance, *The Times*, 1 October 1953; 1 September 1954; and 20 January 1955. He would talk elsewhere about allegations of police corruption and the increase in crimes of violence and against property. See, for instance, the report of the 14 August 1958 in *The Manchester Guardian*, titled 'Crime in London area nearly up to post-war peak: Robbery still on the increase'. But he did not discuss offences of sodomy or indecency.

99 Reported in L. Moran (1996); *The Homosexual[ity] of Law*, London: Routledge, 130–1. I am grateful to Tim Newburn for bringing the reference to my attention.

100 Based on successive annual reports of the Commissioner of Police for the Metropolis.

101 David Maxwell Fyfe, later the Earl of Kilmuir, 1900–1967, was called to the Bar in 1922, became the Conservative Member of Parliament for the West Derby division of Liverpool in a by-election in July 1935, and was to be appointed Home Secretary in 1951. His biographer, D. Dutton, states that 'On most issues he was on the progressive wing of his party, and he opposed the re-introduction of corporal punishment ...' He was, however, averse to the abolition of capital punishment. (Based on the entry in *The Oxford Dictionary of National Biography*, http://www.oxforddnb.com/view/article/33301)

102 See P. Wildeblood (1955); *Against the Law*, London: Weidenfeld and Nicolson, 45–46.

103 See http://www.dailymail.co.uk/news/article-468385/Lord-Montagu-court-case-ended-legal-persecution-homosexuals.html#ixzz1CzFAodxO

104 HC Deb 3 December 1953 Vol. 521 cc1295–9.

105 What his memoirs of the period do touch upon are the great national political questions of the day, including the abolition of registration cards, the Suez crisis, disarmament and housing and, more particularly, the east coast floods of February 1953, and the 1953 coronation. He was also to devote considerable space to a discussion of the design of his armorial bearings when he was raised to the peerage. Above all, he seemed to have treated his period of office as Home Secretary as a series of diverting social occasions. A not untypical passage recited that 1953 'opened with my first official visit to Pembrokeshire, taking in Cardiff *en route*, where I enjoyed a fascinating all-Welsh lunch, was presented with a Caerphilly cheese, and addressed the Welsh Travel Association. I then spent three hectic but delightful days in Pembrokeshire; on one

day I inspected a land reclamation scheme, a model stock farm, opened a new housing estate (where, with characteristic Welsh kindness, there was a 'Maxwell Fyfe House'), opened a new part of the cattle market in Pembroke with an earnest speech on bovine tuberculosis ... '. and on and on. The Earl of Kilmuir (1964); *Political Adventure: The Memoirs of the Earl of Kilmuir*, London: Weidenfeld and Nicolson, 204–5.

106 He said that 'lack of conviction can so often be attributed to laziness of mind. Nowhere is there less scope for such an attitude than in politics. A politician must have the courage of his convictions, he must have some convictions to hold fast to, and he must have the courage to face the firmly held convictions of others'. The Findlay Memorial Lecture, Cardiff High School for Boys, 7 May 1954. KLMR 4/9. Churchill College Archives.

107 R. James (1991); *Bob Boothby: A Portrait*, London: John Curtis, 370.

108 Antony Grey said 'I always used to find when I went around giving talks about this, I was much more fortunate in a way because people didn't know anything about it. It was a totally secret subject'. The Generation Gap, BBC Radio 4, 2 March 2010.

109 Ms. in Cornell University Division of Rare and Manuscript Collections.

110 See J. Dollard (1937); *Caste and Class in a Southern Town*, New Haven: Institute of Human Relations.

111 John Wolfenden, 1906–1985, becoming successively head of Uppingham and and Shrewsbury schools; Vice-Chancellor of Reading University in 1950; and the full-time chairman of the University Grants Committee between 1963 and 1968. (Based on J. Weeks' entry in the *Oxford Dictionary of National Biography*, http://www.oxforddnb.com/view/article/31852)

112 J. Wolfenden; *Turning Points: The Memoirs of Lord Wolfenden, op. cit.*, 132.

113 Much of the Committee's internal correspondence was couched in a jocular vein which hinted at a profound disease at engaging too closely with its subjects and subject matter. On 28 June 1955, for example, the Committee's secretary wrote to John Wolfenden: ' ... If the idea is merely to let the Committee see what a few Huntleys look and behave like, then the proceedings could be informally conducted over a cup of tea. If, however, you think what they have to say will be worth preserving for the record we shall have to cease clattering the cups before we see them ...' HO345/2. See S. Freud (2002); *The Joke and Its Relation to the Unconscious*, London: Penguin.

114 A draft memorandum prepared by the Secretary of the Committee stated that 'The Chairman reported that he had been approached by a number of homosexuals anxious to discuss their problems with him. He had consented to see a number of them, if only as part of his personal education, and he had no doubt that other members had been approached by, and had seen, other individuals on a similar basis. He felt, however, that among these were some who could add something useful to the Committee's knowledge of the problem, and invited the Committee to consider the possibility of setting up some machinery to deal with these cases. Some of the men concerned were in responsible positions; they had successfully concealed their inversion and were naturally anxious to continue to do so, and whilst they were ready to help the Committee so far as they could do so without jeopardising their positions they would be reluctant to reveal their identity to a body as large as the Committee'. W. Roberts to Sir John Wolfenden, 19 January 1955. HO345/2.

115 H. Ellis; *Studies in the Psychology of Sex*, Vol. 2, *op. cit.*, i.

116 Lindsay Farmer pointed out to me that Jeremy Bentham declined to publish his essay on pederasty. It was only to be printed online in 2008, long after his death, by Louis Crompton in the *Journal of Homosexuality* (http://www.tandfonline.com/doi/abs/10.1300/J082v03n04_06#.U1ZPfVVdVMA).

117 Dr Soddy, 1911–1986, was Lecturer in Child Psychiatry, University College Hospital, London, 1948–76.

118 K. Soddy (11 September 1954); 'Homosexuality', *The Lancet*, 541.
119 Geraldine Bedell of *The Observer* wrote that 'Wolfenden had a gay son, Jeremy. Antony Grey [the Chairman of the Homosexual Law Reform Society] told me that when Wolfenden accepted the job, he wrote to Jeremy saying it would be better if he weren't seen around him too often in lipstick and make-up'. 'Coming out of the Dark Ages', *The Observer*, 24 June 2007.
120 Anthony Grey wrote to the *Wolverhampton Express and Star* in May 1963 that it was not surprising 'that a lot of homosexuals are highly strung, neurotic and troubled people. The laws which make their private lives a private crime are responsible for far more psychological disturbance and general ill-health among them than is their homosexuality itself. ...' And the Albany Trust stated that all homosexuals ... have to face difficulties of adjustment to life which impose upon them a strain greater than most of us have to bear. ...' *Some Questions and Answers about Homosexuality*, London: Albany Trust, undated, 16. (The Albany Trust was founded in the United Kingdom as a charity in May 1958 to complement the Homosexual Law Reform Society).
121 So it was that Anthony Grey wrote: 'One recognises, of course, that no homosexual relationships can ever be 'moral' in the sense that marriage is the only truly moral sexual relationship; but by frowning less heavily upon the invert's attempt to obtain a permanent connection based upon affection than upon promiscuous behaviour akin to prostitution, society would be pointing a way to the solution of the invert's personal problems, and thus helping to lessen his incidence as a social problem'. A. Grey (1997); *Speaking Out: Writings on Sex, Law, Politics and Society 1954–95*, London: Cassell, 5.
122 A report of a 1949 BMA Committee had concluded that 'The main object of all courts must always be the protection of the public. The Committee is convinced that, in regard to sexual offenders, punishment without treatment is not likely to have a beneficial effect; indeed, it can make these offenders worse, and thus more likely to repeat their offences. In a high proportion of cases imprisonment without treatment may have consequences to the community even more dangerous than to the offenders themselves. ... In all charges arising out of homosexual conduct it is in our opinion essential that no sentence should be passed on an offender without examination and report by a duly qualified doctor after a verdict of guilty. ...' *The Criminal Law and Sexual Offenders*, A Report of the Joint Committee on Psychiatry and the Law appointed by the British Medical Association and The Magistrates' Association, BMA, London, 1949, 5, 11.
123 A later committee of the British Medical Association, the Committee on Homosexuality and Prostitution, established on 6 December 1954 following a Council decision to appoint a body to prepare evidence for submission to the Departmental Committee on Homosexual Offences and Prostitution, resolved that it 'should study the scientific aspects of the subject with a view to establishing whether or not there was agreement as to the nature of homosexuality; whether it was innate, genetic or produced by environmental conditions and experience in early life, and whether endocrines played any part in it. The conclusions of such a study would enable the Committee to indicate methods of prophylaxis and treatment, including correction, and to comment on the law and practice relating to homosexual offences'. BMA Archive.
124 For example, the report of the British Medical Association Committee on Homosexuality and Prostitution opened with the statement on p. 7 that 'Homosexuality and prostitution are essentially social rather than medical problems, but, since health depends largely on environmental and sociological conditions, the Council welcomes the opportunity of advising on their nature and causes and of making suggestions for their control and cure. The individual doctor, and the medical profession as a whole, regard as their function the prevention of illness, the treatment of the sick, and the

promotion of health in its widest sense. Everything which helps to encourage physical and mental health, social responsibility and stable family life is the concern of the medical profession, for on these factors the virility and soundness of the national life are founded. ... Homosexuality and prostitution are problems of ancient origin ... The proper use of sex, the primary purpose of which is creative, is related to the individual's responsibility to himself and the nation, and the Committee believes that any weakening of personal responsibility with regard to social and national welfare in a significant proportion of the population is one of the causes of the apparent increase in homosexual practices and in prostitution'. BMA Archive.

125 Percy Cudlipp, 1905–1962, worked on a variety of newspapers, including the *Evening Standard* and the *News Chronicle*. His last post was as editor of *New Scientist*.

126 In *Any Questions*, BBC Home Service, 15 November 1957 http://www.bbc.co.uk/archive/gay_rights/12002.shtml

127 A revealing interview conducted by Jeffrey Weeks and Ken Plummer with Mary McIntosh, published in 1981, disclosed how members of the society were obliged publicly to present the society and themselves: 'I remember writing a letter to the Homosexual Law Reform Society at one stage, supporting the cause in general, but saying that I had a lot of reservations about the nature of the argument they were putting forward because I could not really accept the view that homosexuality was a sickness. And they wrote back and said that they had a lot of sympathy with my position but that at the time they had to use the arguments that were suited to the moment'. 'Postcript: 'the homosexual role' revisited', in K. Plummer (ed.) *The Making of the Modern Homosexual*, Hutchinson, London, 1981, 44. I am indebted to Jeffrey Weeks for bringing this to my attention.

128 Departmental Committee on Homosexual Offences and Prostitution Action on the Report: Memorandum from the Homosexual Law Reform Society, May 1965 (CRI 477/8/50).

129 See, for instance, G. Smith, A. Bartlett and M. King (21 February 2004); 'Treatments of Homosexuality in Britain since the 1950s – An Oral History: The Experience of Patients', *British Medical Journal*, Vol. 328, 427–29.

130 B. Charles, one of the Mass Observation diarists who recorded his everyday doings in the years immediately after the Second World War, reflected that 'a few years ago, if you *mentioned* the subject, in the most guarded way possible, you were criticised ... It is very difficult to know what the average person thinks about it. I feel, of course, that there are a very great many people who do not realise that there is such a thing as congenital homosexuality at all'. In S. Garfield (ed.) (2004); *Our Hidden Lives: The Everyday Diaries of a Forgotten Britain 1945–1948*, London: Ebury Press, 219.

131 In a BBC Radio 4 programme, *The Generation Gap*, broadcast on 2 March 2010, just before his death in June.

132 P. Wildeblood (1956); *A Way of Life*, London: Weidenfeld and Nicolson, 10, 11.

133 His obituary, published in *The Times* on 4 May 2010, said that the name had been adopted in 1962 'when there were real dangers of police attention for any campaigner for gay rights'. He was not alone. Michael Schofield believed that he was constrained on occasion to publish under the name of Gordon Westwood, for instance. Schofield was a fairly prolific writer on sexual behaviour: works published under his own name included (1965); *Sociological Aspects of Homosexuality: A Comparative Study of Three Types of Homosexuals*, London: Longmans (1976); *Promiscuity*, London: Gollancz and (1965); *The Sexual Behaviour of Young People*, London: Longmans. But, at an earlier time, it is evident that he was reticent about publishing works on homosexuality in his own name. As Gordon Westwood, he wrote (1952); *Society and the Homosexual*, London: Gollancz and (1960); *A Minority: A Report on the Life of the Male Homosexual in Great Britain*, London: Longmans.

134 A. Grey (1992); *Quest for Justice: Towards Homosexual Emancipation*, London: Sinclair-Stevenson, 2, 20. But even he then treated homosexuality as in some manner pathological: 'I think it's true to say that it's not inborn, but it's a thing which is developed in the very earliest years of one's life through the general relationships within the family: either a boy gets too closely fixated upon his mother, or there's some trouble with his relationship with his father and he doesn't develop normally'. (Transcript: BEHIND THE HEADLINES; A television interview on HOMOSEXUALITY and the LAW between Godfrey Lagden, M.P., Antony Grey and John Meade, 10 March 1961, in the Homosexual Law Reform Society and the Albany Trust Papers at the British Library of Political and Economic Science).

135 He recollected in the *The Generation Gap* how 'the first thing that any gay person knew in those days was that you should never, never give your name, address and telephone number to anybody else and let them put it in their diary. Because if the police got wind of somebody and thought they might be gay, they would go and do a search of their home and go through all their personal papers and they'd take their diaries and address books away. And then they would have these prison sentences. I mean people committed suicide'.

136 In the Homosexual Law Reform Society and the Albany Trust Papers at the British Library of Political and Economic Science.

137 D. West (2012); *Gay Life Straight Work*, London: Paradise Press, 63.

138 See http://www.glbtq.com/social-sciences/wolfenden_report.html For a discussion of a not dissimilar episode in the United States of America that occurred at much the same time, see E. Sutherland (September 1950); 'The Diffusion of Sexual Psychopath Laws', *The American Journal of Sociology*, Vol. 56, No. 2, 142–148. Sutherland's abstract at the head of the article on p. 142 states that 'The diffusion of sexual psychopath laws has followed this course: a community is thrown into panic by a few serious sex crimes, which are given nation-wide publicity; the community acts in an agitated manner, and all sorts of proposals are made; a committee is then appointed to study the facts and to make recommendations. ...'

139 *The Times*, 22 October 1953.

140 http://www.oxforddnb.com/view/article/74146

141 See G. Brandreth (2000); *John Gielgud: An Actor's Life*, Stroud: Sutton Publishing, 96 *et seq.*

142 Guy Burgess, 1911–1963, attended Trinity College, Cambridge, 'already known for his drinking and homosexuality', was recruited by the KGB in 1934 and by the British secret service in 1938. He defected with Donald Maclean in 1951. (Based on the contribution by S. Kerr in *The Oxford Dictionary of National Biography*, http://www.oxforddnb.com/view/article/37244)

143 Donald Maclean, 1913–1983, went up to Cambridge University in 1931 where he joined a socialist society whose other members included Guy Burgess, Anthony Blunt and Kim Philby. He was recruited by the KGB in 1934. He entered the diplomatic service in 1935, becoming third secretary at the Paris embassy. In 1951 he and Guy Burgess defected to the USSR. (Based on the contribution by R. Cecil in *The Oxford Dictionary of National Biography*, http://www.oxforddnb.com/view/article/31394?docPos=3)

144 W. McCann (Winter 1984–1985); "Apostles' in Belfast: H.O. Meredith & E.M. Forster', *The Linen Hall Review*, Vol. 1, No. 4, 11. And see W. Lubenow (1998); *The Cambridge Apostles, 1820–1914: Liberalism, Imagination, and Friendship in British Intellectual and Professional Life*, Cambridge: Cambridge University Press.

145 See N. West and O. Tsarev (1999); *The Crown Jewels: The British Secrets at the Heart of the KGB Archives*, New Haven: Yale University Press.

146 See S. Paul (2000); *Nuclear Rivals: Anglo-American Atomic Relations, 1941–1952*, Columbus: Ohio State University Press and A. Lownie (2015); *Stalin's Englishman: The Lives of Guy Burgess*, London: Hodder.

147 I am mindful that such terms as 'homosexual' and 'bisexual' are clumsy but they are employed here merely as a shorthand to expedite description.

148 See, for example, the questions to David Maxwell Fyfe and other ministers in the House of Commons, HC Deb 18 June 1951 Vol. 489 cc30–3; HC Deb 26 June 1951 Vol. 489 cc137–8W; HC Deb 30 January 1952 Vol. 495 c171; HC Deb 15 May 1952 Vol. 500 c144W; HC Deb 2 July 1952 Vol. 503 cc416–8; HC Deb 17 February 1953 Vol. 511 c126W.

149 An MVD agent, he had been Third Secretary and Consul at the Australian Embassy since February 1951. An earlier defector, Konstantin Volkov, had also made allegations in 1945 but they were ignored by the British Vice-Consul and the Consul General in Istanbul to whom they had been made (see K. Jeffery (2011); *MI6: The History of the Secret Intelligence Service 1909–1949*, London: Bloomsbury).

150 See *The Times*, 19 September 1955.

151 The Royal Commission on Espionage. An interim report was submitted to the Governor-General on 21 October 1954 and the final report was submitted to the Governor-General on 22 August 1955 and to Parliament on 14 September 1955. See http://www.naa.gov.au/about-us/publications/fact-sheets/fs130.aspx#section2

152 'I can now disclose', he said, 'that beyond all doubt these two men regularly supplied the Kremlin with all the information they could lay their hands on as trusted servants of the Foreign Office'.

153 *The Times*, 19 September 1955.

154 *Report concerning the disappearance of two former Foreign Office officials* (1955); Cmd. 9577, London: HMSO.

155 For example, a number of cabinet documents of discussion and correspondence on Burgess and Maclean do not touch directly on the matter but their catalyst, an American news report, is a little less obscure. The sequence began when the British Embassy in Washington sent a telegram to the Foreign Office on 8 June 1951 reproducing a United Press item which said that 'The Central Intelligence Agency and the State Department are highly disturbed over the disappearance of Donald Maclean and Guy Burgess British Foreign Office officials. They said there is not the slightest doubt that both the agencies will make strong representations that the Foreign Office should clean house regardless of whom may be hurt. They said that in view of their records, the two men should not have continued to occupy posts in the British Foreign Office. They pointed out that in the State Department repeated drunkenness, recurrent nervous breakdowns, sexual deviations and other human frailties are considered security hazards ...' An accompanying memorandum from the Embassy stated that 'both Burgess and Maclean are well known in Washington press and other circles and it is impossible to attempt to conceal any of the facts about them, most of which were in any case more or less in public property here'. The Prime Minister, Clement Attlee, then requested a report from the Foreign Office on the two men on 10 June 1951, observing that 'It appears to be known that their characters were unsatisfactory'. The reply took the form of a letter of 13 June 1951 from the Foreign Secretary, Herbert Morrison, which stated, again a little obliquely, that, 'as a result of intensive investigation by the Security Service and of statements volunteered by acquaintances and friends of the two men, we have learned a good deal about their character and personal behaviour which we did not know before. The problem of how to keep an adequate check on the personal behaviour of members of the Foreign Service without at the same time instituting a system of spying which would be both repugnant to our traditions and destructive of morale is one to which the Foreign Office are giving anxious thought'. (PM/51/39). An undated report in the Prime Minister's papers (PREM/8/1524) talked about how Donald Maclean had exhibited uniformly good conduct until 1950 when he was 'suffering from a form of collapse induced at least in part by excessive drinking. ... Shortly afterwards it was learned that he, with another

man, had in a drunken state broken into the flat occupied by the Private Secretary of the U.S. Ambassador in Cairo and had done considerable damage'. There were other references in the report to how Maclean might have another breakdown were he to be subject to more strain, but none directly to homosexuality. An accompanying report on Guy Burgess referred to his 'irresponsible and indiscreet behaviour while on leave in Tangier … in 1949'; 'reckless driving' in 1951; and doubts entertained by the Head of Security at the Foreign Office since 1948 (PREM/8/152) but, once more, sexuality was not mentioned.

156 The phrase was that of the Member of Parliament, Sir Arthur Irvine, in the House of Commons, HC Deb 7 November 1955 Vol. 545 cc1483–611.

157 See the remarks of Peter Rawlinson in the House of Commons, HC Deb 7 November 1955 Vol. 545 cc1483–611.

158 See the statement by the Foreign Secretary, Harold Macmillan, in the House of Commons, HC Deb 7 November 1955 Vol. 545 cc1483–611.

159 As far as I can establish, it was not until 1959 that Burgess' homosexuality was explicitly mentioned in Cabinet papers. There was some concern that he might apply to return to visit his sick mother, and the notes of the Cabinet meeting of 17 February, 1959 record that R.A. Butler, the Home Secretary, said that 'Deteriorating – drink, homosexuality, megalomania. May well present himself (sick mother). Cdn't then refuse admission: or prosecute'. The judgement of the Attorney General was that 'S.2 offence wd. be v. technical: he left behind some official pp., but they were of no importance. We shd. be ridiculed if we prosecuted' and of the Prime Minister: 'F.O. and H.O. to concert means of keeping him away'. (C.C. 10(59)).

160 HC Deb 7 November 1955 Vol. 545 cc1483–611.

161 Alfred Robens, 1910–1999, was Labour Member for Wansbeck (later named Blyth) from 1945 until 1960. His biographer remarks on his 'forthright, common-sense views'. (G. Tweedale in *The Oxford Dictionary of National Biography*, http://www. oxforddnb.com/view/article/72445). His obituary in *The Independent* declared that he was a 'big, jolly man, a supreme extrovert [with] boundless self-confidence, vigour and strength of feeling …' (*The Independent*, 29 June 1999)

162 S. Kerr in *The Oxford Dictionary of National Biography*, http://www.oxforddnb.com/ view/article/37244

163 Interestingly, Sir John Wolfenden's son Jeremy, also a homosexual, was also said to have worked 'in Moscow for the *Daily Telegraph* [where h]e was set up in a gay honey-trap by the KGB, caught and blackmailed by them'. (http://www.sebastianfaulks. com/index.php?page_id=32) See S. Faulks (1996); *The Fatal Englishman: Three Short Lives*, London: Hutchinson.

164 See C. Andrew (2009); *The Defence of the Realm: The Authorized History of MI5*, London: Allen Lane.

165 See P. Hennessy (2010); *The Secret State*, London: Penguin, 103; and Statement on the Findings of the Conference of Privy Councillors on Security 1956, CAB 129 80.

166 See the lengthy treatment of the matter in J. Mulvagh (2008); *Madresfield: The Real Brideshead*, London: Black Swan, esp. ch. 14. I am grateful to Larry Sherman for bringing the book to my attention.

167 See J. Bengry (2014); 'Profit (f)or the Public Good? Sensationalism, homosexuality, and the postwar popular press', *Media History*, Vol. 20(2), 146–166.

168 Lord Montagu, born in 1926, was the third Baron. He has been prominent in the world of private museums focused on transport and historic houses. He is the author of many books on Beaulieu and on motoring and motorists, but appears not to have written his autobiography nor to have been the subject of a biography.

169 See *The Times*, 17 October 1953.

170 See *The Times*, 9 November 1953.

171 William Fearnley-Whittingstall, 1903–1959, was called to the Bar in 1925, was Recorder of Grantham, 1946–1954 and of Lincoln between 1954–1957 (http://www. ukwhoswho.com/view/article/oupww/whowaswho/U237157/FEARNLEY-WHITTINGSTALL_William_Arthur?index)

172 *The Times*, 16 December 1953.

173 *Hampshire Chronicle and General Advertiser*, 19 December 1953.

174 W. Jones (1966); *My Own Case*, Maidstone, Kent: Angley Books, 111. He also said on p. 110 that 'What is true I do not care for homosexuals. Some people do. I don't. And … they broke the law …' There were other local manifestations of distaste and disquiet at the time, but, again, it is difficult to find evidence of a moral panic in Hampshire where Beaulieu is set. The Hampshire Constabulary was formed in 1967 when the Isle of Wight Constabulary amalgamated with the forces of Portsmouth and Southampton. The only surviving police reports appear to be those of the Chief Constable for the County Borough of Southampton, an area of just over 9,000 acres with a population of 181,000 in the early 1950s (or some 30% of the total population of the county (http://www3.hants.gov.uk/hampshire_county_historical_profile-3.pdf)), and, taken as a rough proxy index of policing in the county as a whole, they suggest that the numbers of reports of, and arrests for, offences under the 1861 and 1885 Acts fluctuated, but were always so minute in scale as to be virtually insignificant. What is most important is that it was in that police area that the arrests were made (see the Bradford *Telegraph and Argus*, 1 February 1954). Any regulation of covert offences without victims and with few witnesses must typically rely on entrapment, coercion or surveillance, and it seemed to have been no preoccupation of the chief officers of the time. They appear to have been more exercised by problems of traffic and bicycle theft, making only one solitary allusion to unnatural offences and offences of indecency, when, in the report for 1953, it was said merely that 'There has been no rise in unnatural offences and attempts to commit this class of crime during the year, but a large proportion, nearly 90%, have been detected'.

175 *Hampshire Chronicle and General Advertiser*, 19 December 1953.

176 *Hampshire Chronicle and General Advertiser*, 5 December 1953.

177 *Hampshire Chronicle and General Advertiser*, 14 November 1953.

178 *The Times*, 17 December 1953.

179 *The Times*, 26 March 1954.

180 See his letter to *The Times* of 29 July 2017.

181 See *The Times*, 11 January 1954.

182 Michael Pitt-Rivers, 1917–1999, was a landowner.

183 *The Times*, 16 March 1954.

184 *The Times*, 25 March 1954.

185 W. Jones, *My Own Case*, *op. cit.*, 108.

186 *The Times*, 16 November 1953.

187 Peter Rawlinson, 1919–2006, was a barrister and then a Conservative Member of Parliament for Epsom, inheriting the seat from David Maxwell Fyfe when the Home Secretary was appointed Lord Chancellor. He was a member of Gerald Gardiner's chambers. His biographer, Geoffrey Howe, states that 'Initially he spoke in defence of capital punishment and against reform of divorce, abortion, and homosexual law. But by the time he took silk in 1959 he spoke, for example, on the Wolfenden report (on homosexual law reform) with compassion and common sense, and was serving on the council of Justice and as a trustee of Amnesty International'. *The Oxford Dictionary of National Biography* (http://www.oxforddnb.com/view/article/97248)

188 *The Times*, 23 March 1954.

189 P. Rawlinson (1989); *A Price Too High: An Autobiography*, London: Weidenfeld and Nicolson, 58, 59.

190 See H. Hughes (1940); *News and the Human Interest Story*, Chicago: University of Chicago Press. In particular, there was an article in *The Sunday Times*, entitled the 'Law and hypocrisy', which was published in March 1954.

191 Prosecuting counsel opened by saying that his two principal witnesses were worthless men of 'the lowest possible moral character' who had 'cheerfully accepted corruption, long before they met these three men'. In W. Jones; *My Own Case, op. cit.*, 119. He had gone on to talk about the 'unusual association of these persons of such social disparity'. *The Times*, 16 March 1954.

192 Thus a film, photographs and diaries which the police seized from Lord Montagu's flat in London were deemed at trial to be inadmissible as evidence. See the Bradford *Telegraph and Argus*, 30 January 1954.

193 See K. Erikson (1966); *Wayward Puritans*, New York: John Wiley; and J. Douglas (ed.) (1970); *Deviance and Respectability*, New York: Basic Books.

194 He wrote to Peter Rawlinson on 25 March 1954: 'I hope you will not mind my saying how good I thought your work was in the defence of Wildeblood. You had an extremely difficult case to handle. I hope you were not disappointed by the result. It was certainly not due to any shortcomings on your part'. Rawlinson papers, RWSN 3/6, Churchill Archives, Cambridge.

195 William Fearnley-Whittingstall, who defended Lord Montagu, wrote to Peter Rawlinson, who defended Peter Wildeblood, to say 'Believe me, no-one could have defended Wildeblood with greater courage or eloquence than you exhibited and people on [both] sides said so. We will have a drink one day when it is all a less bitter memory'. Letter of 29 March 1954. Rawlinson papers, RWSN 3/6, Churchill Archives, Cambridge.

196 See his obituary in *The Times*, 1 September 2015.

197 W. Jones, *My Own Case, op. cit.*, 109, 110, 123.

198 He was to write that there should be legal reform so that 'private relations between adult men are not an affair which concerns the state'. *The Current*, 21 April 1954.

199 Sherwin Bailey, 1910–1974, was Chaplain to Anglican students at the University of Edinburgh, 1944–1951; and Central Lecturer at the Church of England Moral Welfare Council between 1951 and 1955.

200 (1955); *Homosexuality and the Western Christian Tradition*, London: Longmans, Green and Co., His principal argument was that there should be a repeal of relevant clauses in the 1861 and 1885 Acts. A reviewer observed that he had 'produced not only a scholarly but an entirely fair-minded book, urging a more liberal attitude to inverts and the repeal of certain clauses in the Acts of 1861 and 1885. His book advocates also that the public should be educated to "a sense of understanding and responsibility for the men and women who labour under this peculiar handicap"'. Review by Kenneth Walker (8 October 1955); in *The British Medical Journal*, 892.

201 See G. Willett (December 2009); 'The Church of England and the Origins of Homosexual Law Reform', *Journal of Religious History*, Vol. 33, No. 4, 418–434.

202 This was not the first attempt made within the Church of England to reformulate its stance on homosexuality and the law. See T. Jones (January 2011); 'The Stained Glass Closet: Celibacy and Homosexuality in the Church of England to 1955', *Journal of the History of Sexuality*, Vol. 20, No. 1, 132–152.

203 S. Bailey (February 1952); 'The Problem of Sexual Inversion', *Theology*, Vol. 55, No. 380, 49.

204 M. Grimley (2009); 'Law, Morality and Secularisation: The Church of England and the Wolfenden Report, 1954–1967', *The Journal of Ecclesiastical History*, Vol. 60, No. 4, 725.

205 Church of England Moral Welfare Council (1954); *The Problem of Homosexuality*, London: Church Information Board.

206 And subsequently submitted to the Wolfenden Committee.

207 See J. Carey (1988); 'D.S. Bailey and "the Name Forbidden among Christians"', *Anglican Theological Review*, Vol. 70, No. 2, 152.

208 It was an argument that would later be extended and elaborated to effect in the Moral Welfare Council's submission to the Wolfenden Committee: 'The Homosexual, The Law, and Society: Evidence submitted by the Church of England Moral Welfare Council to the Government Committee on Homosexual Offences and Prostitution', The submission began 'comments and criticisms evoked by the interim Report have been carefully studied and collated, and the general conclusions to be drawn therefrom have been placed at the disposal of the Moral Welfare Council for use in preparing its evidence for the Committee of Enquiry. ...'

209 See *The Times*, 5 December 1953 and HC Deb 10 December 1953 Vol. 521 cc2160–1.

210 'Law and Hypocrisy', *The Sunday Times*, 28 March 1954.

211 Antony Greenwood, the Labour Member of Parliament, would refer to it in debate as 'a most sensitive work'. HC Deb 26 November 1958 Vol. 596 cc365–508.

212 W. Honan; 'Peter Wildeblood', *New York Times*, 21 November 1999. And see the obituary in *The Independent* which asserted that 'it was Wildeblood who received the publicity and ... made a personal stand. When Against the Law appeared in 1955, its account of his experiences, not only at the hands of the law and the British establishment, but the appalling conditions in Wormwood Scrubs, encouraged a campaign for ... homosexual, reform'. (P. Hoare, 'Peter Wildeblood', *The Independent*, 25 November 1999).

213 *The Times*, 16 February 2011.

214 Desmond Donnelly was the Labour Member for Pembrokeshire (defeating the erstwhile Home Secretary, Gwilym Lloyd-George) from 1950 to 1968.

215 Robert Boothby, 1900–1986, won the seat of East Aberdeenshire as a Conservative Member of Parliament in 1924 which he held until he entered the House of Lords in 1958.

216 See HC Deb 26 October 1953 Vol. 518 cc328–9W.

217 See P. Wildeblood, *Against the Law, op. cit.*, 70.

218 In R. James, *Bob Boothby, op. cit.*, 369.

219 R. Boothby (1978); *Boothby: Recollections of a Rebel*, London: Hutchinson, 211–212. The Home Secretary's replies were more than a little guarded. In December 1953, for example, he replied to a renewed request put by Desmond Donnelly and Sir Robert Boothby:

'The general question of the law relating to sexual offences and of the treatment of sexual offenders is engaging my attention ... [but] I must make clear to the House that one element in dealing with this matter is the protective element in punishment, because homosexuals in general are exhibitionists and proselytisers and are a danger to others, especially the young, and so long as I hold the office of Home Secretary I shall give no countenance to the view that they should not be prevented from being such a danger'. (HC Deb 3 December 1953 Vol. 521 cc1295–9)

220 Roy Jenkins, his successor some 13 years later, conjectured that the case had weighed with him. He said that 'Their trial in 1954 probably played into the decision of the Home Secretary, David Maxwell-Fyfe, to establish the Wolfenden Committee to consider whether a change in the law was necessary'. R. Jenkins; *A Life at the Centre, op. cit.*, 180.

221 J. Wolfenden, 'Sons, Mothers & Schools', *The Sunday Times*, 3 January 1954. In that article, John Wolfenden answered the opening question about the frequency of 'cases of immorality in the schools' by saying that 'I don't claim to know the whole truth about this subject: he would be a rash man who thought he did'. He went on to remark that there were two types of 'sexual misbehaviour between boys': 'coarse physical violence' which is 'very rare', and 'a quite different kind, and this is where it gets difficult. Some of what you may well think of as 'immorality' has in it a strong element of affection

between the boys concerned. ... I am not saying that if two boys are close friends they are to be excused if their friendship results in sexual misbehaviour. What I am saying is that there are quite a lot of 'romantic friendships', if that is the right way to describe them, and that some of them do end in sexual behaviour that you would not like your own boy to take part in. I am not excusing it, or saying that it ought to be tolerated, still less encouraged; I am only saying that it happens. ... It is now pretty widely recognised that there is a stage in the adolescence of practically every body which can be called, absolutely innocently homosexual ... I am quite sure that there is very little connection between any of this and the 'adult male homosexuality' which from time to time causes so much public concern. ...' It may be supposed that it is possible that that piece established John Wolfenden as a suitable person to chair an inquiry.

222 Although interestingly enough, he was to engage them in other contexts. For instance, in a lecture on the relations between the state and private individuals, he reflected that '(a) increasing interference by the State in every aspect of his life means that the citizen is repeatedly faced with a real conflict between his own interest and that of the public; (b) our task is to find some way of resolving those conflicts without detriment to the public interest and with the minimum injustice to the citizen'. (April 1957); 'The State, The Citizen and the Law', *The Law Quarterly Review*, 175.

223 He claimed on that occasion that 'in no other sphere of activity are there greater opportunities for doing good or evil, for causing misery or happiness ...' KLMR 4/11, Churchill College Archives.

224 See 'LONDON'S MORALS: Home Secretary Confers with Magistrates', *The Manchester Guardian*, 27 October 1953.

225 He went on to say that 'I am convinced that a great deal of the increase in crime is due to a lowering of our moral standards, unsatisfactory homes and the fact that religion is no longer a practical sanction in daily life', Notes for a Speech by the Home Secretary and Minister for Welsh Affairs at a Young Conservative Rally, 10 June 1953. KLMR 4/9, Churchill College Archives.

226 'Virtue, the State and the Family', William Ainslie Memorial Lecture, 8 July 1954, KLMR 4/9, Churchill College Archives.

227 Sir Frank Newsam, was Permanent Under Secretary between 1948 and 1957. He left some papers which were deposited at the Open University's International Centre for Comparative Criminological Research, but they appear to contain nothing that could explain why homosexuality was construed as a problem or why it took the form it assumed in the deliberations of the Home Office. *The Times* newspaper archive is also unhelpful.

228 F. Newsam (1954); *The Home Office*, London: George Allen and Unwin.

229 And even then the record-keeping was imperfect. A senior civil servant, who had entered the Home Office in the early 1950s to reach high rank, said in interview in 2015 that 'the Home Office is based on cases very largely. And the influence of cases is so powerful – capital cases is a striking example – and just as an aside, I find to my horror that weeders have been destroying old free pardon files on the grounds that they didn't illustrate a development of policy'.

230 Described by the *Daily Telegraph* as a constituency which was 'Liberal-held in the 1920s and 1930s, but has returned a Labour MP most time since 1945, usually with a comfortable majority. It has been described as a tough inner-city constituency with a few middle-class pockets'. http://ukpolitics.telegraph.co.uk/Bradford+South

231 See *The Times*, 5 March 1954.

232 *The Times*, 19 February 1954.

233 George Craddock, 1897–1974, was MP for South Bradford, between 1949 and 1970. Those two questions were the only interventions on homosexuality he was to make in the House of Commons. There appears to be very little documentation about George Craddock: he was principally interested in foreign affairs and matters of

nuclear disarmament, but he was also a member of the Committee on Administrative Tribunals and Enquiries (the Franks Committee) between 1956 and 1957. What else George Craddock believed or why he said what he did at that time is not recorded. I received no assistance at all from the national Labour Party, and no replies to my enquiries from the local constituency organisation or the incumbent Member for Bradford South in my attempt to learn more about him. The Bradford local newspaper, the *Telegraph and Argus*, did carry quite extensive coverage of the Montagu case – it was certainly more extensive than in *The Times* or the *Hampshire Chronicle and General Advertiser*. On the 25 and 30 January, for example, there was generous *verbatim* reporting of the trial proceedings; and the reporting continued on succeeding days well into March and the trial's conclusion. It was to feature on the front page on a number of occasions – for example on 16, 18, 19, 23 and 24 March. But there was but one reference to George Craddock and his questions about the 'danger to public morale' in the newspaper, on 3 February 1954, it was brief and it contained nothing that could not have been read in *Hansard*. His question of 19 February was not reported. Neither was there any other report of trials under the 1861 and 1885 Acts in the paper at the time. In short, no light at all was thrown on why he chose to intervene about the publicisation of trials for homosexual offences. Neither was there any other report of trials under the 1861 and 1885 Acts in the newspaper at the time.

234 In a major book on the theme, Frank Mort talks about how 'London's sexual notoriety was obsessively dissected throughout the 1950s when anxieties about public and private vice pressed hard on national politics'. F. Mort (2010); *Capital Affairs: London and the Making of the Permissive Society*, New Haven and London: Yale University Press, 3.

235 Sexual Offences, Memorandum by the Secretary of State for the Home Department and Minister for Welsh Affairs, C. (54) 6, 17 February, 1954.

236 See Slater, who argues that 'All the evidence points to an increase in manpower being responsible for the increased number of arrests of prostitutes. From 1948, specific patrols were utilised in the Paddington division to deal with prostitutes, and by the mid-1950s, "C" Division's rowdyism patrol had increased to fourteen men'. S. Slater (April 2010); 'Containment: Managing Street Prostitution in London, 1918–1959', *The Journal of British Studies*, Vol. 49, No. 2, 354.

237 See, for example, *The Times* for 18 November 1955; 14 February 1956 and 29 June 1956.

238 C. Rolph (1955); *Women of the Streets*, London: Secker and Warburg, 26.

239 Based on successive reports of Home Office Criminal Statistics, beginning with *Criminal Statistics England and Wales 1939–1945*, Cmd. 7227, London: HMSO, 1947.

240 Conclusions of a Meeting of the Cabinet held at 10 Downing Street, S.W.1, on Wednesday, 24 February 1954, at 11 00 a.m., C. C. (54) 11th Conclusions.

241 For example, that offered by Brian Lewis, Professor of History at McGill University, in an article marking the 50th anniversary of the Sexual Offences Act (August 2017); 'Homosexuality and the Law: A Gay Revolution?', *History*, 63.

242 The Secretary of State for Scotland, James Stuart, believed, for instance, there was no case for a complementary inquiry into matters in Scotland. There have, he said, 'been no recent indications of public concern about this social evil [prostitution] in Scotland; and I have received no representations about it. …' The number of reported cases of homosexuality was very small. 'It will be apparent', he concluded, 'that the Scottish problem would not in itself justify an inquiry. If, however, it should be decided to appoint a Royal Commission I think it would clearly need to have terms of reference for the whole of Great Britain'. Sexual Offences: Memorandum by the Secretary of State for Scotland. C. (54) 61 17 February 1954.

243 See *The Times*, 13 January 1954.

244 See, for example, 'Lord Montagu on the court case which ended the legal persecution of homosexuals', *Evening Standard*, 14 July 2007 and the report, 'The stately saviour risen from a gay sex scandal', in *The Sunday Times* of 17 April 2016 that claimed baldly that the 'Montagu case led directly to the publication of the Wolfenden report three years later, which recommended homosexuality be decriminalised'.

245 J. Wolfenden (December 1968); 'Evolution of British Attitudes Toward Homosexuality', *American Journal of Psychiatry*, Vol. 125, No. 6, 792.

246 J. Wolfenden; *Turning Points: The Memoirs of Lord Wolfenden*; *op. cit.*, 131.

247 Conclusions of a Meeting of the Cabinet held at 10 Downing Street, S.W.1, on Wednesday, 17 March, 1954, at 11.30 a.m., C. C. (54) 20th Conclusions.

248 The Home Secretary, R.A. Butler, introducing the House of Commons debate on the report would say that 'I think it can now be said that the two parts of the Report have not very much to do with one another'. (HC Deb 26 November 1958 Vol. 596 cc365–508)

249 Q. Wright (September–October 1951); review of *Trial of Sumida Haruzo and Twenty Others*, in *The Journal of Criminal Law, Criminology, and Police Science*, Vol. 42, No. 3, 375.

250 He had written in the foreword to the first book in the series: 'It is of the highest importance that there should be some selected record of selected trials for as many types of war crimes as possible … (for then) the would-be apologist will be faced by an impregnable fortification of truth'. Foreword to J. Cameron (ed.) (1948); *The 'Peleus' Trial*, War Crimes Trials Series, Vol. 1, London: Hodge and Co., xv.

251 There were, of course, quite strict controls already in place under the *sub judice* rules. See Glanville Williams (January 1952); 'Pre-Trial Publicity', *Modern Law Review*, Vol. 15, No. 1, 98–99. For a reasonably contemporary comparison between provisions in England and Wales and the USA, see T. Taylor (January 1966); 'Crime Reporting and Publicity of Criminal Proceedings', *Columbia Law Review*, Vol. 66, No. 1, 34–61.

252 C. 20(54) 17 March 1954.

253 Conclusions of a Meeting of the Cabinet held at 10 Downing Street, S.W.1, on Wednesday, 17 March, 1954, at 11.30 a.m., C. C. (54) 20th Conclusions.

254 Restrictions on Reporting of Proceedings for Homosexual Offences, Memorandum by the Secretary of State for the Home Department and Minister for Welsh Affairs, C. (54) 121, 1 April 1954.

255 Conclusions of a Meeting of the Cabinet held on Wednesday, 15 April, 1954, at 11.30 a.m., C. C. (54) 29th Conclusions.

256 See (9 July 1960); 'Crime and Sin: Sir John Wolfenden at Winchester', *British Medical Journal*, 140.

257 It was Roy Jenkins' conjecture that the Home Secretary might have wished, 'by handing over to a committee, to shelve the issue. Perhaps he assumed Wolfenden would find against, in which case, he chose a curious chairman, because Wolfenden had a gay son, Jeremy'. R. Jenkins, *A Life at the Centre*, *op. cit.*, 180.

258 Sir Robert said 'eventually [the Home Secretary] asked me to write him a memorandum on the subject. This I did and, after considering it for some time, he wrote and told me that he had decided 'with reluctance', to refer the matter to a committee presided over by Sir John Wolfenden'. (R. Boothby; *Boothby*, *op. cit.*, 212) There is no reference to Sir Robert Boothby or his memorandum in any of the surviving cabinet papers and one may only conclude that this is probably another instance of *post hoc ergo propter hoc* reasoning.

259 The reasons for Desmond Donnelly's interest in the subject are obscure. There is no biography or autobiography to supply an answer, and his writings are principally on matters such as the Cold War and trade with communist countries.

260   HC Deb 28 April 1954 Vol. 526 cc1745–56.

261   The language in which he spoke should be noted because it once more displays that curious flagging of an ignorance about behaviour that the speaker, a bisexual politician and the lover of the gangster, Ronnie Kray, and of youths in Kray's social circle, did not maintain in private (Thorpe said of him that 'His private life, especially by the standards of the day, could be described as unorthodox. A passionate man, he was promiscuous and bisexual ...' (Extract from D. Thorpe (2010); *Superman: The Life of Harold Macmillan*, London: Chatto and Windus, in *The Times*, 28 August 2010.)) It is indicative of that bravado that he said of himself 'Since the war my life has been lived in the full glare of publicity – as a Member of Parliament, as a working journalist, and under the arc lamps of television. In a sense I have had no private life at all'. (Lord Boothby (1962); *My Yesterday, Your Tomorrow*, London: Hutchinson, xi) It was an instance, perhaps, of what Laud Humphreys once dubbed the donning of 'a breastplate of righteousness', where those with the greatest personal familiarity with homosexuality are constrained to pretend to the greatest aversion to it (see L. Humphreys (1970); *Tearoom Trade: A Study of Homosexual Encounters in Public Places*, London: Duckworth). No man or woman in policy or political circles in the 1950s could easily admit to an intimate acquaintance, or to having a wish to have an intimate acquaintance, with the nameless, 'unpleasant subject' (Lord Jowitt HL Deb 19 May 1954 Vol. 187 cc737–67) of homosexuals or homosexuality without jeopardising his or her reputation. A staunch opponent of reform, Sir Cyril Osborne, once told the House of Commons that 'I know nothing, or very little, about what is called buggery, but from what I do know about it I hate it and I dislike it'. HC Deb 11 February 1966 Vol. 724 cc782–874. Cyril Osborne, 1898–1969, was Conservative Member of Parliament for the Louth division of Lincolnshire from 1945 to 1969.

262   HC Deb 28 April 1954 Vol. 526 cc1745–56.

263   R. Boothby, *Boothby*, *op. cit.*, 212.

264   HC Deb 28 April 1954 Vol. 526 cc1745–56.

265   HC Deb 8 July 1954 Vol. 529 cc2313–4.

266   'Crime and Sin: Sir John Wolfenden at Winchester', *op. cit.*, 140.

267   J. Weeks in *The Oxford Dictionary of National Biography*, *op. cit.* Jeremy Wolfenden, 1934–1965, was educated at Eton and Oxford, becoming the Moscow correspondent of the *Daily Telegraph* (when rumours circulated about his possible involvement in espionage and the circle centred on Guy Burgess (see F. Mort (1 October 2016); 'Victorian Afterlives: Sexuality and Identity in the 1960s and 1970s', *History Workshop Journal*, Volume 82, Issue 1, 199–212). He then removed to America where his death, it was said, was 'early and mysterious' (*The Times*, 15 February 1997).

268   Quoted in S. Faulks (1997); *The Fatal Englishman: Three Short Lives*, London: Vintage, 242.

269   Letter to Dame Rachel Crowdy, 21 September 1954. HO345/2. Rachel Crowdy, 1884–1964, was a nurse and social reformer.

270   Its other members were James Adair, O.B.E. former Procurator-Fiscal for Glasgow; Mrs. A.M. Cohen, vice-president of the City of Glasgow Girl Guides, Chairwoman of the Scottish Association of Girls' Clubs; Dr Desmond Curran; Rev. Canon V.A. Demant (Canon of Christ Church, Oxford and Regius Professor of Moral and Pastoral Theology at the University of Oxford); Sir Hugh Linstead, Conservative MP for Putney, and pharmaceutical chemist.; The Marquess of Lothian a Foreign Office minister; Mr Victor Mischcon, solicitor and Labour member of the London County Council; Mr Goronwy Rees, Principal of the University College of Wales, Aberystwyth; Lady Lily Stopford, Doctor, Magistrate and wife of the Vice-Chancellor of the University of Manchester; Rev. R.F.V. Scott, Presbyterian Minister of St. Columba's Church, London (Church of Scotland); Mr. W.T. Wells, Labour MP for Walsall North and

Barrister; and Dr Joseph Whitby, general practitioner with psychiatric experience. Its secretary was W.C. Roberts of the Home Office.

271 'On five consecutive Sundays between 11 March and 8 April 1956 articles on Burgess were published in The People, written anonymously by 'his most intimate friend – a man in high academic position''. (http://www.archiveswales.org.uk/anw/get_col lection.php?inst_id=1&coll_id=20438&expand) Their author, Goronwy Rees, was later exposed in the 'Peterborough' column in *The Daily Telegraph* on 21 March 1956. Sir John Wolfenden wrote to Sir Frank Newsam on that day: 'If Peterborough is right in identifying him with the anonymous writer of articles about Burgess in the Sunday People, and if Rees is advertising himself as Burgess' "closest friend", I think this makes considerable awkwardness for the Committee. It is pretty tricky, in any case, that one of the members of the Committee should now be revealed as having this particular connection with such a notorious homosexual. If it turns out – as it well may – that the Committee recommends some 'liberalisation' of the law about adult male homosexuals in private we really shall be in a mess. Such a recommendation will be a good deal discredited if it is signed by "Burgess' closest friend." It would be regrettably easy for the 'Telegraph' – or anybody else – to say 'What could you expect, with this man as a member of the Committee? Clearly we can pay no attention to anything they say on this subject'. Sir Frank was to reply on 18 April 1956: 'Rees has replied that he realises the embarrassment which might be caused and he assumes that the Home Secretary would wish him to retire from the Committee; he has asked that no public announcement of his resigna- tion should be made or at least postponed as long as possible. He makes this plea on account of the difficulties which will be caused to his College rather than to him if an announcement were made at present'. HO345/2 And see *The Times*, 26 February 1957; and http://www.walesonline.co.uk/news/uk-news/2010/04/02/ mystery-of-the-soviet-spy-radio-found-in-a-welsh-field-91466-26160416/

272 F. Mort, *Capital Affairs, op. cit.*, 145.

273 Desmond Curran wrote to the Secretary on 16 September 1954: 'my own view is that the medical evidence, dealing as it will with highly controversial questions of possibili- ties in treatment, should only be taken towards the end of our deliberations when the members of the Committee will have a wider background of knowledge of the subject than perhaps some of them may possess at the moment'. HO345/2.

274 He was later to write (6 April 1957); 'Homosexuality: An Analysis Of 100 Male Cases Seen In Private Practice', *The British Medical Journal*, Vol. 1, No. 5022, 797–801.

275 Hugh Linstead to Chairman, 28 September 1954, HO345/2.

276 W. Roberts was to report that 'I have today received the Lord Chief Justice's [Lord Goddard's] contribution [not in the files]. This is surprisingly moderate in tone. He suggests whipping in certain cases, but on the whole he is for ignoring gross indecency in private. …' W. Roberts to Sir John Wolfenden 24 November 1954. HO345/2.

277 He concluded that 'The relevant articles of the European Convention are 8 and 14. You will observe that Article 8 allows public authorities to interfere with the exercise of the right concerned where this necessary not only "… for the prevention of … crime" but also … "for the protection of … morals". It seems to me that there is nothing in Article 14 or elsewhere to prevent any State from deciding that an act of gross indecency between male persons should be a crime even though an act of indecency between females may not be … … Even if the law were changed in such a way that homosexual acts between consenting adult males were no longer criminal, "the protection of morals" would cover quite a lot!' (W. Roberts to Chairman, 5 November 1955, HO345/2.) Article 8, on the right to respect for private and family life[1], recited that 'Everyone has the right to respect for his private and family life, his home and his correspondence. There shall be no interference by a public authority with the exercise of this right except such as is in accordance with the law and is

necessary in a democratic society in the interests of national security, public safety or the economic well-being of the country, for the prevention of disorder or crime, for the protection of health or morals, or for the protection of the rights and freedoms of others'. Article 14, on the prohibition of discrimination, recited that 'The enjoyment of the rights and freedoms set forth in this Convention shall be secured without discrimination on any ground such as sex, race, colour, language, religion, political or other opinion, national or social origin, association with a national minority, property, birth or other status'.

278 Sir John Wolfenden wrote on 20 June 1955: 'It is an extremely interesting enquiry, though in many respects a distasteful one. Whether we shall in the end have anything of value to say I would not like to prophesy. But one thing I think is fairly certain, that when our report does appear it will create a certain amount of stir ...' (HO345/2)

279 He said in that selfsame letter: 'Mrs Cohen has also suggested that we should see individual Palmers, but this will perhaps be difficult if we don't get any volunteers. Mrs Cohen's idea seems to be that we should pick one or two from a list of regular clients at Bow Street and ask them to come along. I can foresee some amusing possibilities if this procedure is followed, but there may be some way of getting one or two ladies to come along'. *Ibid.*

280 See http://www.huntleyandpalmers.com/index.php/about-us

281 So it was that W. Roberts wrote to the Chairman on 24 November 1954, 'You will by now have received the Huntley memorandum from the Commissioner of Police (and a dull bit of reading it is, too. I gather he has been a little reticent for fear of shocking the ladies, but I have told Baker that when we see them we shall want dirt and all!)' (HO345/2)

282 Draft undated letter Sir John Wolfenden to Sir Frank Newsam, early February 1955. HO345/2.

283 W. Roberts to Chairman, 30 September 1954, HO345/2.

284 Letter of 20 June 1955, HO345/2.

285 E. Glover (ed.) *The Problem of Homosexuality: A memorandum presented to the Departmental Committee on Homosexual Offences and Prostitution by a Joint Committee representing the Institute for the Study and Treatment of Delinquency and the Portman Clinic (I.S.T.D.),* Published by the Institute for the Study and Treatment of Delinquency, no provenance, no date, 20–21.

286 John Stuart Mill argued: 'The acts of an individual may be hurtful to others, or wanting in due consideration for their welfare, without going the length of violating any of their constituted rights. The offender may then be justly punished by opinion, though not by law. As soon as any part of a person's conduct affects prejudicially the interests of others, society has jurisdiction over it, and the question whether the general welfare will or will not be promoted by interfering with it, becomes open to discussion. But there is no room for entertaining any such question when a person's conduct affects the interests of no persons besides himself, or needs not affect them unless they like (all the persons concerned being of full age, and the ordinary amount of understanding). In all such cases there should be perfect freedom, legal and social, to do the action and stand the consequences. ... neither one person, nor any number of persons, is warranted in saying to another human creature of ripe years, that he shall not do with his life for his own benefit what he chooses to do with it'. (J. Mill; *On Liberty*, Chapter IV: 'Of the Limits to the Authority of Society over the Individual', (originally published in 1869), republished as (1960); *Utilitarianism, Liberty, Representative Government*, London: J.M. Dent, 132).

287 Isaiah Berlin opened his essay on 'Two Concepts of Liberty' with the observation that: 'The first of [the] political senses of freedom or liberty (I shall use both words to mean the same), which (following much precedent) I shall call the 'negative' sense, is involved in the answer to the question 'What is the area within which the

subject – a person or group of persons – is or should be left to do or be what he is able to do or be, without interference by other persons?' The second, which I shall call the 'positive' sense, is involved in the answer to the question 'What, or who, is the source of control or interference that can determine someone to do, or be, this rather than that?' The two questions are clearly different, even though the answers to them may overlap'. (I. Berlin (1958); "Two Concepts of Liberty," in I. Berlin (1969) *Four Essays on Liberty*, Oxford: Oxford University Press, 2.) That is, there are acts which may be condemned but are never the less to be tolerated because they do not harm others.

288 'The Homosexual, The Law, and Society: Evidence submitted by the Church of England Moral Welfare Council to the Government Committee on Homosexual Offences and Prostitution', undated.

289 The report, published in *The Dublin Review* in 1956, said that 'Crime is a social concept not a moral one and therefore is a problem to be tackled by the State with the assistance of its specialists in jurisprudence and psychiatry. Sin is not the concern of the State but affects the relations between the soul and God'.

290 The 'sexologist' Eustace Chesser was to publish a long essay on the Wolfenden Report in which he made the observation that 'The point of the Report was that a distinction must be drawn between crime and sin, and this was very clearly realised by those who approved in the main of its recommendations. No doubt the path had been smoothed by the guidance given by representatives of the leading Churches. Both the Church of England Moral Welfare Council and the Roman Catholic Advisory Committee appointed by the late Cardinal Griffin agreed that 'it is not the business of the State to intervene in the purely private sphere, but to act solely as the defender of the common good'. E. Chesser (1958); *Live and Let Live: The Moral of the Wolfenden Report*, London: Heinemann, 14.

291 'We are generally agreed that the function of the law, at any rate in relation to sexual behaviour, is… the preservation of public order and decency and the protection of the citizen, particularly the young and vulnerable citizen. It is not the function of the law to interfere with private behaviour unless it can be shown that such behaviour is detrimental to the public good in an extraordinary degree. Thus, adultery, fornication and prostitution, though they are grievous sins, are not offences for which a person can be punished by the criminal law. Sin and crime are not synonymous terms'. (Methodist Conference Newcastle Upon Tyne, Representative Session, 7 July 1958)

292 Sir John Wolfenden recalled on a BBC *Any Questions* programme almost immediately after the publication of his Committee's report: 'As I ventured to say to the Archbishop of Canterbury on one occasion, "we on the committee have modestly confined ourselves to *crime*. It is for you, your Grace and your colleagues, to turn your attention to *sin*," and that *moral* leadership is precisely what I think is properly the function of the Church. And we for our part on this Committee dealt with the crime part of it'. *Any Questions*, BBC Home Service, 15 November 1957, http://www.bbc.co.uk/archive/gay_rights/12002.shtml

293 THE FOLLOWING STATEMENT APPEARS IN THE DECEMBER ISSUE OF THE WESTMINSTER CATHEDRAL CHRONICLE PUBLISHED 2 DECEMBER 1957.

WOLFENDEN REPORT
IN VIEW OF THE ENQUIRIES WHICH HAVE REACHED ARCHBISHOP'S HOUSE FOLLOWING THE PUBLICATION OF THE REPORT OF THE HOME OFFICE DEPARTMENTAL COMMITTEE ON PROSTITUTION AND HOMOSEXUALITY, HIS GRACE THE ARCHBISHOP OF WESTMINSTER HAS THOUGHT IT USEFUL TO SET FORTH THE FOLLOWING PRINCIPLES WHICH SHOULD BE BORNE IN MIND

WHEN CONSIDERATION IS GIVEN TO THE PROPOSALS REGARDING
HOMOSEXUAL ACTS BETWEEN CONSENTING ADULTS:-

The civil law takes cognisance primarily of public acts. Private acts <u>as such</u> are outside its scope.

However, there are certain private acts which have public consequences in so far as they affect the public good. These acts may rightly be subject to civil law.

It may be, however, that the civil law cannot effectively control such acts without doing more harm to the common good than the acts themselves would do. In that case it may be necessary in the interests of the common good to tolerate without approving such acts.

It has, for example, invariably been found that adultery or fornication (which, however private, have clear public consequences) cannot effectively be controlled without provoking greater evils.

Applying those principles to the question of homosexual acts between consenting males:

1. As regards the moral <u>law</u>, Catholic moral teaching is:
   (i)   Homosexual acts are grievously sinful.
   (ii) That in view of the public consequences of those acts, e.g. the harm which would result to the common good if homosexual conduct became widespread or an accepted mode of conduct in the public mind, the civil law does not exceed its legitimate scope if it attempts to control them by making them crimes.

The teaching authority of the Bishops is primarily concerned with laying down those two principles of <u>law</u> which cannot be denied by any Catholic.

2. However, two questions of <u>fact</u> arise:-
   (i)   If the law takes cognisance of private acts of homosexuality and makes them crimes, do worse evils follow for the common good?
   (ii) Since homosexual acts between consenting males are now crimes in law, would a change in the law harm the common good by seeming to condone homosexual conduct?

Ecclesiastical authority could rightly give a decision on this question of fact as well as on the question of the moral law, if the answers to the questions of fact were overwhelmingly clear. As, however, various answers are possible in the opinion of prudent men, Catholics are free to make up their own minds on these two questions of fact.

294 One said, for instance: 'I love England but I am so deeply concerned for the future of my baby son that I would emigrate rather than remain in a country where depravity could become commonplace. It is not just that the morality of the nation should be endangered for the sake of a perverted minority. How can the morality of our own youth be safeguarded if such a law is passed. It would be the beginning of the end of all that is decent in English life. I beg you your Eminence to speak out against such a law for the sake of all who have families to bring up in what is already a difficult world. ...' Letter of 27 May 1965, Westminster Diocesan Archives. AAW HE1/W10.

295 Letter of 1 July 1965, Westminster Diocesan Archives, AAW, HE1/W10.

296 For example, the Bishop of Rochester would write to Sir John Wolfenden that 'I am writing about a book "Sexual Offenders and Social Punishment" issued by the Church of England Moral Welfare Council. It recommends that homosexually can be legally practised between male persons in private, if they are above the age of seventeen years. I am quite certain that this is not the view of the Church of England as a whole, and only represents the Moral Welfare Council. Some of us have had experience of homosexual

clubs. The Police know about them. And we should not be happy that such should be allowed to operate with lawful sanction'. Letter of 1 August 1956. (HO345/2) Christopher Chavasse, 1884–1962, was an evangelical Christian and supporter of Billy Graham who was nominated Bishop of Rochester on 19 March 1940, consecrated on 25 April the same year, and served in that position until his resignation on 30 September 1960. More importantly, the Archbishop of Canterbury, Geoffrey Fisher, wrote in the November 1953 issue of the *Canterbury Diocesan Notes* that he was appalled that homosexuals "have been encouraged to think, and are often very ready to think, that these inclinations are a misfortune that they cannot control or even a fortune that with a clear conscience they can indulge ... homosexual indulgence is a shameful vice and a grievous sin from which deliverance is to be sought by every means". (Taken from G. Willett, 'The Church of England and the Origins of Homosexual Law Reform', *op. cit.*, 427.)

297 The Bishop of Exeter, for instance said quite boldly that 'the function of the criminal law in this field was to preserve public order and decency, to protect the citizen from what is offensive or injurious, and to provide sufficient safeguards against exploitation and corruption of others. Where no right either of the community or the individual was threatened, then the criminal law had no place'. (Notes on a Church Assembly Debate relating to Homosexual acts in private: Autumn 1957. Lambeth Palace Library: MWC/HOM/7.)

298 The phrase is that employed by Peter Sedgwick (2009); in 'The Public Presence of Religion in England', in N. Biggar and L. Hogan (eds.) *Religious Voices in Public Places*, Oxford: Oxford University Press, 248.

299 Introduction to Draft Report, 30 June 1955, BMA Archive: Committee on Homosexuality and Prostitution.

300 BMA Archive: Committee on Homosexuality and Prostitution (SA/MWF/A.4/13).

301 *The Criminal Law and Sexual Offenders*, A Report of the Joint Committee on Psychiatry and the Law appointed by the British Medical Association and The Magistrates' Association, BMA, London, 1949, 5.

302 Trevor Gibbens, 1912–1983, had been a consultant at the Bethlem Royal and Maudsley Hospitals since 1951. He was later to become Professor of Forensic Psychiatry, Institute of Psychiatry, London University, 1967–78.

303 Memorandum by T.C.N. Gibbens on the Treatment of Homosexuality for the Meeting of the Committee on Homosexuality and Prostitution to be held on 3 February 1954. BMA Archive (SA/MWF/A.4/13).

304 S. Simpson; 'Meeting to be held on 31 March 1955: Some thoughts on Homosexuality and the Trend of our Deliberations', BMA Archive (SA/MWF/A.4/13).

305 Memorandum by Professor J. Glaister for the meeting to be held on 30 June 1955, BMA Archive (SA/MWF/A.4/13).

306 Michael King and Annie Bartlett reported how, 'In order to report to the Wolfenden Committee on homosexuality and prostitution, the British Medical Association (BMA) assembled doctors drawn mainly from psychiatry, forensic medicine, venereology and general practice ... Despite reluctantly conceding that the age of consent for men should be 21 years, the BMA report was replete with moral disdain for homosexuals, who were considered in the same light as prostitutes'. (1999); 'British Psychiatry and Homosexuality', *The British Journal of Psychiatry*, 175, 107.

307 The Churches' Council for Health and Healing "overarches" Christian agencies and provides a link between them and the Royal Colleges of Medicine. See C. Hamel-Cooke and D. Cope (24–31 December 1983); 'Not an alternative medicine at St Marylebone Parish Church', *British Medical Journal*, Vol. 287, 1934.

308 *British Medical Journal*, (30 April 1988); Vol. 296, 1268.

309 He was also to rail against the new oral contraceptives (see *The Times*, 3 December 1963).

310 Minutes of meeting of 30 June 1955. BMA Archive (SA/MWF/A.4/13). That conversation about the competing merits of conversion and psychiatry continues. See D. Sanderson; 'Christians and psychiatrists clash over 'gay cure'', *The Times*, 15 April 2015.

311 This was based in part on S. Simpson's own analysis of a small sample of men which talked about how homosexuals were characterised by the presence of a:

1. 'Voice high in excitement is so frequent as to be a positive characteristic.
2. Appearance younger than age is almost equally a positive characteristic.
3. Artistic temperament and sensitivity etc. again sufficiently frequent to be a definite characteristic.
4. At least half of the patients were poor at games and at running at School.
5. Delayed puberty and youthful appearance in adult life occurs in at least 33%.
6. Although only two patients grew in height after the age of 20, the span is greater than the height in 7 patients ...'

(Memorandum from S.L. Simpson, BMA Committee for the meeting to be held on 19 July 1955, BMA Archive (SA/MWF/A.4/13))

312 Minutes of meeting held on 19 July 1955, BMA Archive (SA/MWF/A.4/13).

313 I draw here on an article by Malcolm Bull, (June 1990); 'Secularization and Medicalization', *The British Journal of Sociology*, Vol. 41, No. 2, 245–261.

314 B. Wilson (1985); 'Secularization: The Inherited Model', in P. Hammond (ed.) *The Sacred in a Secular Age*, Berkeley: University of California Press, 11.

315 D. Martin (September 1991); 'The Secularization Issue: Prospect and Retrospect', *The British Journal of Sociology*, Vol. 42, No. 3, 465; and see B. Hayes (September 1995); 'Religious Identification and Moral Attitudes: The British Case', *The British Journal of Sociology*, Vol. 46, No. 3, 457–474.

316 The Secretary, W. Roberts, reported to Sir John Wolfenden in November 1954: 'I have today received the Lord Chief Justice's [Lord Goddard's] contribution. This is surprisingly moderate in tone. He suggests whipping in certain cases, but on the whole he is for ignoring gross indecency in private. ...' W. Roberts to Sir John Wolfenden 24 November 1954. HO345/2.

317 Note by the Chairman: Comments on the Secretary's Note of September 1955, HO345/4.

318 '(1) The objectionable practice should be productive not merely of evils, but of evils so great as to counter-balance the suffering, direct and indirect, which the infliction of criminal punishment necessarily involves; (2) It should admit of being defined with legal precision; (3) It should admit of being proved by cogent evidence; (4) The evidence should be such as can usually be obtained without impairing the privacy and confidence of domestic life; (5) It must be reprobated by the current feelings of the community; and (6) It must be a practice against which adequate protection cannot be secured to the community by the milder sanctions which Civil Courts can wield'.

319 Memorandum of the Council of the Law Society, June 1955, Document No. CHP/61.

320 One man wrote to Sir John on 1 July 1955, 'This letter is to entreat that, apart from having any use for me at any time, your Committee will really try to get the point of view of the kind of problem I [would like to] outline to you. I know how easily you will get other points of view, including psychotherapists and doctors quoting cases. My great hope is that you will hear <u>at first hand</u> some of those cases; for there are many, so many, who go through vexation and deep frustration at the hands of psychotherapists and hosts of others who just do not get at or understand such problems – and they could give your Committee false, one-sided picture'. HO345/2.

321 He wrote to Sir John Wolfenden in December 1954 to say: '... I very much agree with you that there is much to be said for setting up the panel to interview individuals and getting on with this part of the job fairly soon, and for two reasons. In the first place, the individuals will be able to tell us things that will help in framing questions

to those that come before the Committee later. In the second, there is a danger that if they are kept waiting too long the enthusiasm of the volunteers might wane. ...' Letter of 29 December 1954. HO345/2.

322 Consider the tenor of the note sent by the Secretary to the Chairman on 28 June 1955: 'If the idea is merely to let the Committee see what a few Huntleys look and behave like, then the proceedings could be informally conducted over a cup of tea. If, however, you think what they have to say will be worth preserving for the record we shall have to cease clattering the cups before we see them ...' (HO345/2) Such notes would receive replies in the same vein, suggesting that this was an entirely appropriate and consensual way of treating the subject of the inquiry.

323 'The individual Huntley and Palmers I know you already have very much in mind. I have had letters from two or three Huntleys who want to say something and there are indications that there may be others later. I asked one of my correspondents (who is an old friend of the Home Office) to put in a written statement first, but he seems to be boggling at that, and has suggested the possibility that one or two members of the Committee (one perhaps a psychiatrist) might consent to see him'. *Ibid.*

324 See H. Becker (1967); 'Whose Side Are We On?', *Social Problems*, Vol. 14, No. 3, 234–47.

325 For example, on one occasion, W. Roberts wrote to Sir John Wolfenden to say: '(i) The writer of the enclosed letter [not retained] evidently wants to pour out his heart to you personally. If you would like to shunt him on to me, please do so by all means. This brings me to (ii) You will remember that I told you that I was proposing to see an invert in a responsible University post to see whether, knowing now the composition of the Committee, he was still anxious to help. He called to see me last Friday, and he would be quite willing to come and talk to a small sub-committee such as you have in mind. Moreover, he has no objection to the revelation of his identity to such a sub-committee – in fact, he feels that you ought to know who he is so that you may judge the better how much weight to attach to his evidence. I think he will be a useful witness; unlike so many with his particular disability he has no axe to grind – he merely feels that he has a duty to come forward and place his special knowledge at the Committee's disposal. I don't think he will be able to tell us anything of the seamier side of things because he has been careful to steer clear of homosexual coteries (most of his friends – few of whom know of his inversion – are normals of his own standing), but nevertheless I think what he has to say will be well worth hearing. He struck me as being a very decent sort of chap (the personification, in fact, of the D.P.P.'s "genuine" homosexual!)'. Note the persistence of the jokey, distancing tone. Letter of 15 December 1954. Elsewhere Sir John said to Roberts: 'why not mobilise the Recorder of Portsmouth and the Boy Scouts man? Little Morgan of the Boy Scouts' Association I have met many times before; he is a pleasant person who will give us all the orthodox stuff in a prim way. ...' Letter of 14 January 1955. In Roberts' reply there was the compliment: 'Morgan, Boy Scouts. (I enjoyed your description, by the way!)' Letter of 20 January 1955. HO345/2.

326 W. Roberts to Chairman, 4 October 1954, HO345/2.

327 Note of 23 May 1955, HO345/2.

328 The Committee were also reluctant to be exposed to the kind of pressure they imagined would be exercised in public meetings. Of a coalition of women's organisations, the Status of Women Committee, W. Roberts wrote to Sir John Wolfenden: 'I have not the slightest doubt that within the next week or so you will be receiving representations from most of the women's organisations about closed sittings. ... This would enable them to organise pressure groups in an endeavour to counteract the possible effect of evidence with which they do not agree. This is quite legitimate politics, but would not tend to help the Committee in its difficult task. ... 'Letter of 26 October 1954. HO345/2 A memorandum by the Secretary of 1 November 1954 reflected that

'Both problems under consideration by the Committee are extremely controversial, and the organisations interested in these problems hold widely different views as to the ways in which they should be dealt with. There is every probability that if the meetings were open to the public the various organisations would send observers to each meeting and subsequently organise campaigns to counteract the views expressed by organisations or individuals with whom they disagreed...' HO345/2

329   The Association for Moral and Social Hygiene was founded in 1915 following the merger of the Ladies' National Association and the British Continental and General Federation for Abolition of Government Regulation of Prostitution (later to become the International Abolitionist Federation).

330   W. Roberts to Sir John Wolfenden 10 May 1955, HO345/2.

331   Sir John Wolfenden to W. Roberts, 11 May 1955 HO345/2.

332   Thus Sir John Wolfenden wrote to W. Roberts on 12 February 1955: 'I have been making one or two enquiries about this form of treatment, and what I wrote to Newsam is exactly what I myself, as an ordinary individual, think about it at the present state of my knowledge. If the experts can provide us with something like reliable opinion, well and good. But it seems to be one thing for a private patient to undergo treatment of this sort of his own free will and accord, but quite another thing for the Prison Commissioners to bounce in with it for prisoners. I can see that the Home Secretary may be afraid of criticism if a form of treatment accepted in the medical world is not available for prisoners. On the other hand, I should have thought there was much more political risk in laying himself open to a charge of using prisoners as guinea pigs for the doctors. I should have thought that there would have to be much stronger medical backing for it before it could be used in prisons without the danger of this sort of accusation. ...' (HO345/2). The decision was subsequently taken in 1958 that such treatment should be administered with the prisoner's consent (CRI 477/8/50).

333   Letter of 19 April 1955, HO345/2.

334   That emphasis on adults was to assume great importance because it countered the persistent apprehension that greater liberalisation would lead to a greater corruption of the young. Sir John was to reflect that 'It seems from practically all the evidence we've had that ... there are two kinds of men, two broad categories of men of this kind: those who prefer contemporaries as their partners, and those who prefer boys or young men, and that very seldom do the two overlap. That is the medical evidence. ... There are men who commit homosexual acts with boys and they will still be liable to the law. ...' In *Press Conference*, BBC Television, 6 September 1957. http://www.bbc. co.uk/archive/gay_rights/12001.shtml

335   O. Chadwick; *Michael Ramsey: A Life, op. cit.*, 145.

336   Note by the Chairman: Comments on the Secretary's Note of September 1955, HO345/4.

337   Draft summary of recommendations, undated, HO345/4. The draft went on: 'We regard it as the function of the law to protect society from morally and socially destructive forces in so far as it is able to do so. It is not in our view its function to intervene in the private lives of citizens, or to seek to enforce any particular pattern of personal behaviour, further than is necessary to carry out the purposes we have outlined'.

338   He said: 'The influence of example in forming the views and developing the characters of young people can scarcely be over-estimated. The presence in a district of, for example, adult male lovers living openly and notoriously under the approval of the law is bound to have a regrettable and pernicious effect on the young people of the community. No one interested in the moral, physical or spiritual welfare of public life wishes to see homosexuality extending its scope, but rather reduced in extent, or at least kept effectively in check. ... Existing homosexual trends and tendencies are currently the cause of much public concern and disgust, and the case for relaxing legal restrictions does not appear to me to be a compelling one. ...' Reservation by

Mr Adair, Home Office and Scottish Home Office (September 1957); *Report of the Committee on Homosexual Offences and Prostitution*, Presented to Parliament, Cmnd. 247. For a discussion of the Scottish context and the ramifications of his minority report, see R. Davidson and G. Davis (2004); 'A Field for Private Members': The Wolfenden Committee and Scottish Homosexual Law Reform, 1950–67', *Twentieth Century British History*, Vol. 15, No. 2, 174–201. Davidson and Davis contend that the overwhelming majority of the Scottish evidence tendered to the Committee was antagonistic to liberalisation of the law, and they talk of 'homophobic prejudices within the Scottish legal establishment' (187), but they do not explore the particular reasons for Adair's adamant opposition.

339 He commented on a draft of the report on 29 February 1956: 'Rather interestingly, I went last week to a party at the Soviet Embassy to meet a Russian lawyer … He told me that the law as to homosexuality in Russia was substantially the same as the law here, and I am beginning to think that in order to make our distinction between the public good and the sphere of private morals at all intelligible to the ordinary half-educated reader, we have got to paint the picture with a broad brush and point out that in a free society there are certain things you cannot do without imperilling freedom: and it will help us to build this case if we can show that the only European countries where the law is the same as it is here are Russia, which has never known a free society, and Germany, which destroyed it in the 1930s'. HO345/2.

340 Canon Vigo Demant, 1893–1983, had been the Director of Research to the Christian Social Council, 1929–33 and Canon of Christ Church and Regius Professor of Moral and Pastoral Theology in Oxford University, 1949–71. (http://www.ukwhoswho. com.gate2.library.lse.ac.uk/view/article/oupww/whowaswho/U163518/ DEMANT_Rev._Vigo_Auguste?index=1&results=QuicksearchResults&query=0).

341 Letter of 15 February 1956, HO345/2.

342 *Report of the Committee on Homosexual Offences and Prostitution, op. cit.*, para 12.

343 *Ibid*, para 14.

344 *Ibid*, para 62.

345 The Institute of Psychiatry of the University of London did take the view in its own memorandum to the Departmental Committee that 'the law should not concern itself with homosexuality in private between consenting adults, nor should it differentiate between the form of gratification adopted (manual, interoral, anal, oral etc) by consenting adults'. And The Royal Medico-Psychological Association said 'Where a society punishes its members for some act committed in private, which is harmful, if at all, only to the offender himself, the situation is usually one of a majority imposing a law on a minority. Many homosexuals feel they are members of a persecuted minority. …' (No CHP/58).

346 The Magistrates Association argued to the Committee that 'the law should be amended and that homosexual conduct between consenting adults in private should no longer, within certain limits, be a criminal offence. … In putting [this recommendation] forward the Council wishes to make it clear that it in no way departs from the general view that homosexual practices are undesirable and dangerous, both for individuals and the community. The Council was influenced by the fact that there are many evils, such as adultery and lying, which have to remain outside the criminal law unless there are additional circumstances which make the intervention of the criminal law'. (CHP/64)

347 The staff of the psychoanalytically inclined Tavistock Clinic asserted that they were 'unanimously of the opinion that homosexuality is a disorder of personality and as such to be regarded as an illness affecting both sexes and resulting from many and complex factors. … homosexuality is an illness whose impact falls chiefly on the mind and emotions… [As a result] Homosexual acts between consenting adults committed in private should not be classed as criminal offences'. (DOCUMENT CHP/76)

348 See L. Moran (1995); 'The Homosexualization of English Criminal Law', in
     D. Herman and C. Stychin (eds.) *Legal Inversions: Lesbians, Gay Men, and the Politics of
     Law*, Philadelphia: Temple University Press, 3–28.
349 A. Lough (January 1968); 'Sins and Crimes', *Philosophy*, Vol. 43, No. 163, 38.
350 'Crime and Sin: Sir John Wolfenden at Winchester', *op. cit.*, 142.
351 *Comment on the Wolfenden Report, 1957 by the Church of England Moral Welfare Council*,
     no date, no provenance, 2.
352 See H. Hart (1963); *Law, Liberty and Morality*, Stanford: Stanford University Press, and
     P. Devlin (1965); *The Enforcement of Morals*, Oxford: Oxford University Press. *Law,
     Liberty and Morality* was an extension of an earlier article ('Immorality and Treason',
     Listener, 30 July 1959, 162) which served as a reply to Devlin's attack on John Stuart
     Mill and the Wolfenden Report (P. Devlin (1959); 'The Enforcement of Morals',
     Proceedings of the British Academy, XIV). The argument was to become quite heated.
     Herbert Hart later said: 'I think Devlin's arguments are really bad and mislead-
     ing and enable reactionary people to claim a philosophical mantle, which is quite
     wrong' (in D. Sugarman and H. Hart (June 2005); 'Hart Interviewed: H.L.A. Hart
     in Conversation with David Sugarman', *Journal of Law and Society*, Vol. 32, No. 2,
     285). Lord Devlin was nevertheless later to make a recommendation in April 1965
     that that the consent of the Attorney General should be required for a prosecution for
     certain homosexual offences; 'Lord Devlin has written suggesting that as a first reform
     it might be best to provide that no prosecution for a homosexual offence between
     consenting adults should be instituted without the consent of the Attorney General
     (Departmental Committee on Homosexual Offences and Prostitution Action on the
     Report: Note of a meeting held in Lord Stonham's room at the HO on 22 April to
     discuss Lord's Arran's Motion on Homosexuality. CRI 477/8/50).
353 See J. Stephen (1883); *A History of the Criminal Law of England*, London: Macmillan,
     Vol. II, Ch. 17. For a rather partisan reading of the context of the quarrel between
     Mill and Stephen, see R. Kirk (December1952); 'The Foreboding Conservatism of
     Stephen', *The Western Political Quarterly*, Vol. 5, No. 4, 563–577.

Bibliography

P. Ackroyd (2017); *Queer City: Gay London from the Romans to the Present Day*, London:
     Chatto and Windus

A. Adut (July 2005); 'A Theory of Scandal: Victorians, Homosexuality, and the Fall of
     Oscar Wilde', *American Journal of Sociology*, Vol. 111, No. 1, 213–248

Albany Trust (nd) *Some Questions and Answers about Homosexuality*, London: Albany Trust

P. Alldridge (1993); 'Attempted Murder of the Soul : Blackmail, Privacy and Secrets',
     Oxford Journal of Legal Studies, Vol. 13, No. 3, 368–387

C. Andrew (2009); *The Defence of the Realm: The Authorized History of MI5*, London: Allen Lane

Anon (1882); 'Mr Howard Vincent and the Criminal Classes', *The Saturday Review*, Vol. 54
     (1417), 814–815

S. Bailey (1952); 'The Problem of Sexual Inversion', *Theology*, Vol. 55, No. 380, 47–52

—(1955); *Homosexuality and the Western Christian Tradition*, London: Longmans, Green
     and Co.

H. Becker (1967); 'Whose Side Are We On?', *Social Problems*, Vol.14, No. 3, 234–47

J. Bengry (2014); 'Profit (f)or the Public Good? Sensationalism, homosexuality, and the
     postwar popular press', *Media History*, Vol. 20(2), 146–166

I. Berlin (1958); 'Two concepts of liberty : an inaugural lecture delivered before the
     University of Oxford on 31 October 1958', Oxford: Clarendon Press

R. Boothby (1978); *Boothby: Recollections of a Rebel*, London: Hutchinson

M. Bull (1990); 'Secularization and Medicalization', *The British Journal of Sociology*, Vol. 41, No. 2, 245–261

G. Brandreth (2000); *John Gielgud: An Actor's Life*, Stroud: Sutton Publishing

T. Bridgwater (1906); 'Children's Courts', *Journal of the Society of Comparative Legislation*, Vol. 7, No. 2, 375–383

J. Bristow (2010); review of C. Upchurch (2009); *Before Wilde: Sex between Men in Britain's Age of Reform*, Berkeley: University of California Press, in *The Journal of British Studies*, Vol. 49, No. 2, 480–482

R. Burton (1652, rep. 1883); *The Anatomy of Melancholy*, Chatto and Windus, London

J. Carey (1988); 'D.S. Bailey and "the Name Forbidden among Christians"', *Anglican Theological Review*, Vol. 70, No. 2, 152–173

E. Chesser (1958); *Live and Let Live: The Moral of the Wolfenden Report*, London: Heinemann

L. Chester, D. Leitch and C. Simpson (1976); *The Cleveland Street Affair*, London: Weidenfeld and Nicholson

Church of England Moral Welfare Council (1954); *The Problem of Homosexuality*, London: Church Information Board

H. Cocks (2003); *Nameless Offences: Homosexual Desire in the Nineteenth Century*, London: I.B. Tauris

J. Coleman (2014); *Rent Same-Sex Prostitution in Modern Britain, 1885–1957*, PhD dissertation, the University of Kentucky

Commissioner of Police of the Metropolis (1951); *Report of the Commissioner for the Year 1950*, Cmd. 8359, London: HMSO (1952); *Report of the for the Year 1951*, Cmd. 8634, London: HMSO

D. Curran (1957); 'Homosexuality: An Analysis Of 100 Male Cases Seen In Private Practice', *The British Medical Journal*, Vol. 1, No. 5022, 797–801

R. Davidson and G. Davis (2004); 'A Field for Private Members': The Wolfenden Committee and Scottish Homosexual Law Reform, 1950–67', *Twentieth Century British History*, Vol. 15, No. 2, 174–201

P. Devlin (1959); 'The Enforcement of Morals', *Proceedings of the British Academy*, XIV, London: British Academy

—(1965); *The Enforcement of Morals*, Oxford: Oxford University Press

J. Dollard (1937); *Caste and Class in a Southern Town*, New Haven: Institute of Human Relations

J. Douglas (ed.) (1970); *Deviance and Respectability*, New York: Basic Books

H. Ellis (1897); *Studies in the Psychology of Sex: Vol. 1. Sexual Inversion*, London: University Press

N. Erber (1996); 'The French Trials of Oscar Wilde', *Journal of the History of Sexuality*, Vol. 6, No. 4, 549–588

K. Erikson (1966); *Wayward Puritans*, New York: John Wiley

L. Farmer (2016); *Making the Modern Criminal Law: Criminalization and Civil Order*, Oxford: Oxford University Press

S. Faulks (1997); *The Fatal Englishman: Three Short Lives*, London: Vintage

M. Foldy (1997); *The Trials of Oscar Wilde: Deviance, Morality, and Late-Victorian Society*, New Haven: Yale University Press

S. Freud (2002); *The Joke and Its Relation to the Unconscious*, London: Penguin

S. Garfield (ed.) (2004); *Our Hidden Lives: The Everyday Diaries of a Forgotten Britain 1945–1948*, London: Ebury Press

D. Gorham (1978); 'The "Maiden Tribute of Modern Babylon" Re-Examined: Child Prostitution and the Idea of Childhood in Late-Victorian England', *Victorian Studies*, Vol. 21(3), 353–379

A. Grey (1992); *Quest for Justice: Towards Homosexual Emancipation*, London: Sinclair-Stevenson
—(1997); *Speaking Out: Writings on Sex, Law, Politics and Society 1954–95*, London: Cassell

M. Grimley (2009); 'Law, Morality and Secularisation: The Church of England and the Wolfenden Report, 1954–1967', *The Journal of Ecclesiastical History*, Vol. 60, No. 4, 725–741

P. Grosskurth (1980); *Havelock Ellis: A Biography*, New York: Alfred A. Knopf

C. Hamel-Cooke and D. Cope (1983); 'Not an alternative medicine at St Marylebone Parish Church', *British Medical Journal*, Vol. 287 (6409), 1934–1936

H. Hart (1963); *Law, Liberty and Morality*, Stanford: Stanford University Press

A. Harvey (December 1978); 'Prosecutions for Sodomy in England at the Beginning of the Nineteenth Century', *The Historical Journal*, Vol. 21, No. 4, 939–948

B. Hayes (1995); 'Religious Identification and Moral Attitudes: The British Case', *The British Journal of Sociology*, Vol. 46, No. 3, 457–474

A. Hélie (2004); 'Holy Hatred', *Reproductive Health Matters*, Vol. 12, No. 23, 120–124

P. Hennessy (2010); *The Secret State*, London: Penguin

R. Hind (1972); *Henry Labouchere and the Empire 1880–1905*, London: The Athlone Press

K. Hindmarch-Watson (2016); 'Sex, Services, and Surveillance: The Cleveland Street Scandal Revisited', *History Compass*, June 2016, Vol.14(6), 283–291

M. Houlbrook (2003); 'Soldier Heroes and Rent Boys: Homosexuality, Masculinities, and Britishness in the Brigade of Guards, circa 1900–1960', *The Journal of British Studies*, Vol. 42, No. 3, 351–388

House of Lords Select Committee (1881); *Report on the Law Relating to the Protection of Young Girls*, Cm. 448, London: House of Commons

H. Hughes (1940); *News and the Human Interest Story*, Chicago: University of Chicago Press

R. James (1991); *Bob Boothby*, London: Hodder & Stoughton

K. Jeffery (2011); *MI6: The History of the Secret Intelligence Service 1909–1949*, London: Bloomsbury

R. Jenkins (1991); *A Life at the Centre*, London: Macmillan

S. Jeyes (1912); *The Life of Sir Howard Vincent*, London: George Allen and Company

L. Jackson (2000); *Child Sexual Abuse in Victorian England*, London: Routledge

Joint Committee on Psychiatry and the Law appointed by the British Medical Association and The Magistrates' Association (1949); *The Criminal Law and Sexual Offenders*, BMA, London

T. Jones (2011); 'The Stained Glass Closet: Celibacy and Homosexuality in the Church of England to 1955', *Journal of the History of Sexuality*, Vol. 20, No. 1, 132–152

W. Jones; *My Own Case* (1966); Maidstone, Kent: Angley Books

The Earl of Kilmuir (1954); The Findlay Memorial Lecture, Cardiff High School for Boys, KLMR 4/9. Churchill College Archives
—(1957); 'The State, The Citizen and the Law', *The Law Quarterly Review*, 172–180
—(1964); *Political Adventure: The Memoirs of the Earl of Kilmuir*, London: Weidenfeld and Nicolson

M. King and A. Bartlett (1999); 'British Psychiatry and Homosexuality', *The British Journal of Psychiatry*, 175, 106–113

R. Kirk (1952); 'The Foreboding Conservatism of Stephen', *The Western Political Quarterly*, Vol. 5, No. 4, 563–577

R. v. Krafft-Ebing (1887); *Psychopathia Sexualis*, Stuttgart: Verlag von Ferdinand Enke

B. Lewis (2011); Review Essay: The Maiden Tribute of Modern Babylon: The Report of the Secret Commission. By W. T. STEAD', *Journal of the History of Sexuality*, Vol. 20 (1), 198–205

A. Lough (1968); 'Sins and Crimes', *Philosophy*, Vol.43 (163), 38–50

A. Lownie (2015); *Stalin's Englishman: The Lives of Guy Burgess*, London: Hodder

W. Lubenow (1998); *The Cambridge Apostles, 1820–1914: Liberalism, Imagination, and Friendship in British Intellectual and Professional Life*, Cambridge: Cambridge University Press

D. Martin (1991); 'The Secularization Issue: Prospect and Retrospect', *The British Journal of Sociology*, Vol. 42, No. 3, 465–474

D. Matza (1969); *Becoming Deviant*, Englewood Cliffs: Prentice-Hall

David Maxwell Fyfe (1948); Foreword to J. Cameron (ed.) *The 'Peleus' Trial*, War Crimes Trials Series, Vol. 1, London: Hodge and Co, i–li

W. McCann (1984–1985); 'Apostles' in Belfast: H.O. Meredith & E.M. Forster', *The Linen Hall Review*, Vol. 1, No. 4, 11–13

N. McKenna (2013); *Fanny & Stella: The Young Men who Shocked Victorian England*, London: Faber and Faber

J.S. Mill (1960 originally published in 1869); *On Liberty*, Chapter IV: 'Of the Limits to the Authority of Society over the Individual', republished as *Utilitarianism, Liberty, Representative Government*, London: J.M. Dent, 65–174

L. Moran (1995); 'The Homosexualization of English Criminal Law', in D. Herman and C. Stychin (eds.) *Legal Inversions: Lesbians, Gay Men, and the Politics of Law*, Philadelphia: Temple University Press, 3–28

—(1996); *The Homosexual[ity] of Law*, London: Routledge

F. Mort (2010); *Capital Affairs: London and the Making of the Permissive Society*, New Haven and London: Yale University Press

L. Mulcahy (2011); *Legal Architecture: Justice, due process and the place of law*, London: Routledge

J. Mulvagh (2008); *Madresfield: The Real Brideshead*, London: Black Swan

T. Newburn (1992); *Permission and Regulation* London: Routledge

F. Newsam (1954); *The Home Office*, London: George Allen and Unwin

R. Norton (ed.) (14 May 2010); 'Newspaper Reports, 1787', *Homosexuality in Eighteenth-Century England: A Sourcebook*, http://rictornorton.co.uk/eighteen/1787news.htm

S. Paul (2000); *Nuclear Rivals: Anglo-American Atomic Relations, 1941–1952*, Columbus: Ohio State University Press

S. Petrow (1994); *Policing Morals: The Metropolitan Police and the Home Office 1870–1914*, Oxford: Clarendon Press

K. Plummer (ed.) (1981); *The Making of the Modern Homosexual*, Hutchinson, London

P. Rawlinson (1989); *A Price Too High: An Autobiography*, London: Weidenfeld and Nicolson

Report concerning the disappearance of two former Foreign Office officials (1955); Cmd. 9577, London: HMSO

W. Robinson (2012); *Muckraker: The Scandalous Life and Times of W.T. Stead*, London: The Robson Press

C. Rolph (1955); *Women of the Streets*, London: Secker and Warburg

S. Rowbotham (2008); *Edward Carpenter: A Life of Liberty and Love*, London: Verso

A. Sanna (2012); 'Silent Homosexuality in Oscar Wilde's Teleny and The Picture of Dorian Gray and Robert Louis Stevenson's Dr Jekyll and Mr Hyde', *Law & Literature*, 24:1, 21–39

M. Schofield (writing as Gordon Westwood) (1952); *Society and the Homosexual*, London: Gollancz

—(1960); *A Minority: A Report on the Life of the Male Homosexual in Great Britain*, London: Longmans

—(writing as M. Schofield) (1965); *The Sexual Behaviour of Young People*, London: Longmans

—(1965); *Sociological Aspects of Homosexuality: A Comparative Study of Three Types of Homosexuals*, London: Longmans

—(1976); *Promiscuity*, London: Gollancz

R. Scott (1972); 'A Proposed Framework for Analyzing Deviance as a Property of Social Order', in R. Scott and J. Douglas (eds.) *Theoretical Perspectives on Deviance*, New York: Basic Books, 9–32

P. Sedgwick (2009); in 'The Public Presence of Religion in England', in N. Biggar and L. Hogan (eds.) *Religious Voices in Public Places*, Oxford: Oxford University Press, 235–259

F.B. Smith (1976); 'Labouchère's amendment to the Criminal Law Amendment Bill', *Australian Historical Studies*, Vol. 17, No. 67, 165–175

G. Smith, A. Bartlett and M. King (2004); 'Treatments of Homosexuality in Britain since the 1950s – An Oral History: The Experience of Patients', *British Medical Journal*, Vol. 328, 427–29

K. Soddy (1954); 'Homosexuality', *The Lancet*, 267(6837), 54

J. Stephen (1883); *A History of the Criminal Law of England*, London: Macmillan, Vol. II

D. Sugarman and H. Hart (2005); 'Hart Interviewed: H.L.A. Hart in Conversation with David Sugarman', *Journal of Law and Society*, Vol. 32, No. 2, 267–293

E. Sutherland (1950); 'The Diffusion of Sexual Psychopath Laws', *The American Journal of Sociology*, Vol. 56, No. 2, 142–148

A. Thorold (1895); 'A Righteous Verdict', *Truth*, Vol. XXXVII, No. 961, 1331–2

—(1913); *The Life of Henry Labouchere*, London: Constable

D. Thorpe (2010); *Superman: The Life of Harold Macmillan*, London: Chatto and Windus

N. Walker (1965); *Crime and Punishment in Britain*, Edinburgh: Edinburgh University Press

J. Walkowitz (1980); 'The Politics of Prostitution', *Signs*, Vol.6 (1), 123–135

—(1982); 'Male Vice and Feminist Virtue: Feminism and the Politics of Prostitution in Nineteenth Century Britain', *History Workshop*, No. 13, 79–93

R. Warnicke (1987); 'Sexual Heresy at the Court of Henry VIII', *The Historical Journal*, Vol. 30, No. 2, 247–268

J. Weeks (1989); *Coming Out: Homosexual Politics in Britain from the Nineteenth Century to the Present*, London: Quartet Books

—(nd); 'Wolfenden and Beyond: The Remaking of Homosexual History', http://www.historyandpolicy.org/papers/policy-paper-51.html

D. West (2012); *Gay Life Straight Work*, London: Paradise Press

N. West and O. Tsarev (1999); *The Crown Jewels: The British Secrets at the Heart of the KGB Archives*, New Haven: Yale University Press

G. Westwood (1952); *Society and the Homosexual*, London: Victor Gollancz

P. Wildeblood (1955); *Against the Law*, London: Weidenfeld and Nicolson

—(1956); *A Way of Life*, London: Weidenfeld and Nicolson

G. Willett (2009); 'The Church of England and the Origins of Homosexual Law Reform', *Journal of Religious History*, Vol. 33, No. 4, 418–434

G. Williams (1952); 'Pre-Trial Publicity', *Modern Law Review*, Vol. 15, No. 1, 98–99

—(1960); 'Crime and Sin: Sir John Wolfenden at Winchester', *British Medical Journal*, Vol.2 (5192), 140–142

—(1968); 'Evolution of British Attitudes Toward Homosexuality', *American Journal of Psychiatry*, Vol. 125, No. 6, 792–796

J. Wolfenden (1976); *Turning Points: The Memoirs of Lord Wolfenden*, London: The Bodley Head

B. Wootton (1992); *Selected Writings: Volume 1: Crime and the Penal System*, Houndmills: Macmillan

Q. Wright (1951); review of *Trial of Sumida Haruzo and Twenty Others*, in *The Journal of Criminal Law, Criminology, and Police Science*, Vol. 42, No. 3, 373–375

7   The Liberal Hour III – The Sexual Offences Act 1967 c. 60

Consummation

Introduction

The Wolfenden report created a stir,[1] and it did so partly by design. It centred on a contentious theme and a bold proposal. Having laboured for three years, Sir John stated that he believed with some reluctance that he could not simply abandon it.[2] One hostile Member of Parliament reported in November 1958 that she had 'never known a Report which was so well boosted. There has hardly been a week since its publication when the author has not been appearing either in the Press or at public functions or on the B.B.C'.[3] A significant portion of the initial public response was quite favourably disposed to the report's principal recommendation on homosexual law reform.[4] The leading editorial in *The Times* newspaper that appeared the day after its publication opened with the pronouncement that 'Adult sexual behaviour not involving minors, force, fraud, or public indecency belongs to the realm of private conduct, not of criminal law. Nearly all civilised countries recognise the futility of making into crimes what are regarded as sins against morality'.[5] Much of the press concurred with that judgement.[6] The British Medical Association, the Howard League for Penal Reform and the National Association of Probation Officers supported it. The Committee's moral mentors supported it, including a number of committees of the Church of England,[7] and, most conspicuously, the two senior prelates, the Archbishops of Canterbury and of York (although the latter, Michael Ramsey, professed that he had not thought about the matter of homosexuality until he read the report, but was prepared instantly to accept its argument and actively supported change[8]). The Archbishop of Canterbury, Geoffrey Fisher, argued personally in its favour in the 24 September 1957 issue of *Canterbury Diocesan Notes*[9] and again in the House of Lords in December of that year.[10] The Church's Moral Welfare Council approved it,[11] as did, with a slight majority of 17, and after some labour by the Council's Central Lecturer, Sherwin Bailey, in what was described as a 'virtual revolution',[12] the 194 members of a meeting of the Church Assembly in the autumn of 1957[13] (Sir John Wolfenden, an Anglican layman, observed that the 'Church Assembly ... has shown very great courage, first of all in even discussing this matter, and, secondly, in the decision that it reached ...'[14]). The Lord Spiritual charged with speaking on social affairs for the Church in the House of Lords, the Bishop of Exeter, moving two motions on the Report at that meeting of the Church Assembly, said in strict utilitarian vein that 'Where no right either of the community or the individual was threatened, then the criminal law had no place. The scope and function of the criminal law was not to enforce the observance of a particular moral code'.[15] The Methodist Conference approved the recommendation in like manner: 'It is not the function of the law to interfere with private behaviour unless it can be shown that such behaviour is detrimental to the public good in an extraordinary degree'.[16] The Roman Catholic Archbishop of Westminster's Special Advisory Committee[17] approved it (although the archbishop himself, William Godfrey, adhering to the agreed position, abstained from making a formal pronouncement, allowing individual Catholics to weigh what was a divisive question for themselves[18]). Monsignor G.A. Tomlinson,[19] Chancellor of Westminster Cathedral, would in time accept an invitation to join the Honorary Committee of the society established to campaign for homosexual law reform,[20] and it is most unlikely that he would have done so without the approval of the cardinal archbishop of his day, Cardinal Heenan.[21] In short, there was a preparedness amongst many inside and outside the Churches to follow the Committee and apply John Stuart Mills' and Isaiah Berlin's doctrines of moral pluralism, personal liberty, the prevention of harm[22] and the limits of state power to the legal regulation of private sexual conduct (although curiously, as Jeffrey Weeks pointed out to me, the other target of the report, street offences committed by prostitutes, was not to be so treated).

Yet those who had written and those who later endorsed the report were not necessarily ready or able to proceed to what might be thought to have been the next step and abstain from condemning homosexual conduct itself. The two matters were treated as if they were independent of one another and it would seem that it remained politically and publicly difficult not to continue to denounce homosexuality, and to do so almost as a matter of course, as if to clear people of any unwelcome stain of approval or indeed personal complicity. Sir John Wolfenden himself certainly denounced it, saying on the B.B.C. radio programme, *Woman's Hour*, in the week after the report was issued, that 'I want to make it absolutely plain that we do not think that men who behave like this are doing something that is right. But it does not follow that they should be sent to prison'.[23] And that was a sentiment that he would continue to voice in his many pronouncements after the report was issued.[24] Even the homosexual campaigner, Antony Grey, believed that he was obliged to distance himself from 'the sort of conduct which [has been] described – the people who go around in dark corners and public lavatories, and the people who corrupt young children. I think this is thoroughly bad'.[25] Perhaps the very harshest supporter of all was the Bishop of Exeter, the mover of the reformist motions in the meeting of the Church Assembly, and a member of the Homosexual Law Reform Society's Honorary Committee (a body whose emergence I shall describe below). He told the 1,000 people who attended the society's inaugural meeting in Caxton Hall:

> I can say this in the name of the Church, and in absolute certainty I speak her mind, when I say that the Church still stands by the judgement pronounced on homosexuality by S. Paul in the Epistle to the Romans.[26] The Church sees no reason for revising or reconsidering that judgement – namely that homosexual practices between men and women are gravely sinful, and that they are indeed unnatural in a sense and in a degree in which heterosexual misbehaviour is not. ... The mere fact that many people do have these [homosexual] tendencies makes them neither natural nor normal. Cancer is quite clearly unnatural in that it is destructive to the human body. It has to be fought. It has to be brought under control. Homosexual tendencies in a similar way, according to the teaching of the Church, are foreign to human nature; they are abnormal to it ... And as cancer kills the body, so homosexual tendencies, if not controlled or eradicated, are destructive of human personality and of human society. The Church also holds that the only answer for man in dealing with his sexual impulses is the practice of chastity; and that chastity is not more impossible or indeed harder for persons with homosexual tendencies than it is for heterosexuals ...[27]

Archbishop Ramsey was to say after one of the great Parliamentary debates about the Wolfenden Report that his mistake had been to reveal that the report had induced him to study the subject of homosexuality – to know too much was evidently a fault.[28] If the Wolfenden Committee's supporters' arguments were circumspect and qualified, sometimes severely so, its critics tended not to be so guarded in what they said – theirs was a much less delicate and complicated task. The report scandalised many who read it, and there were many who were ready to *be* scandalised (the *News Chronicle* newspaper talked of how, 'To countless thousands of men and women, homosexuality is regarded with horror and disgust as something to be stamped out at all costs'[29]). Sir John Wolfenden recalled:

> It is difficult for me, and it must be nearly impossible for anybody else, to realise the to-do that followed. It entirely filled the front pages of Wednesday's evening papers, with VICE in inch-high capitals as the main headline. ... It went on for weeks. Gradually the almost hysterical uproar died down, and people began to ask what, if anything, the Government was going to do about it. They were not, understandably enough, in a tearing hurry to do anything.[30]

His recollection was accurate enough. Newspaper headline writers on 5 September 1957, the day after the report's publication, did choose almost identical wording to convey what had happened. Even the liberal *News Chronicle* talked of a 'SEX CLASH AHEAD' and anticipated that the Cabinet would 'shelve' the problem of 'homosexual reform:' 'One of the greatest moral controversies Britain has ever known will follow publication yesterday of an official report proposing a major relaxation in the law on homosexuality'.[31] The *Daily Mail* blazoned the headline 'VICE STORM BREAKING[:] Law for men unlikely to change', and it predicted that 'MPs will press for go-slow on the Wolfenden Report calling for relaxed sex law'. The headline in the *Daily Express* read 'VICE: THE STORM BREAKS[:] WOMEN 'Law should be stricter' – Government may agree[;] MEN 'Law should be easier' – Tory MPs disagree'. Derek Marks,[32] the newspaper's political correspondent, continued by predicting that 'The Government will not seek to implement the highly controversial recommendations of the Wolfenden Committee advising relaxation of the law against homosexuals'.

As the press had foretold, parliamentary opinion appeared to be against the Committee. There were indications that many Conservative electors appeared to be against it.[33] The Labour Party in opposition was hesitant to comment on it[34] and its silence was noted in parts of the press.[35] And successive Conservative Governments under Sir Anthony Eden, Harold Macmillan and Sir Alec Douglas Home[36] were nervous about taking any legislative action or, indeed, about discussing it at all. *Their* thoughts were not turned towards repealing the 1861 and 1885 Acts. Sir David Maxwell Fyfe, now Lord Kilmuir, the Lord Chancellor, remained a staunch opponent and a baleful presence.[37] The Home Secretary at the time, R.A. Butler, may have been reported to say that he had made it 'clear' to Simon Sainsbury in May 1958 that 'he would not mind being pressed' about reform,[38] and to the future founder of the Homosexual Law Reform Society, in fairly careful words, that he 'still has an open mind on this important subject and will welcome the fullest public discussion',[39] but he was actually timorous in his more public responses, as he had ever been, a moderate man surrounded by men less moderate, whenever controversial matters were aired. Throughout the year that followed publication there was, as a result, a chorus in sections of the press bewailing his and the government's 'shameful'[40] timidity.[41] Sir John Wolfenden alleged that the government 'feared to implement the recommendations of [his] committee for political reasons'.[42] Rather than willingly succumbing to pressure, it was Mr. Butler's declared position that 'it is always hard to find Parliamentary time for ... a discussion'[43] of the Committee's recommendation on homosexual relations; and that, despite the force of some of the Committee's arguments, it would not be prudent to flout strongly held public opinion[44] (and that was a line of argument sustained by his successors for a number of years to come[45]). The Conservative cabinet accordingly decided in November 1957 that it was not:

> practicable for the Government to promote legislation at the present time to change the law relating to homosexual offences. On that subject public opinion was divided and strong views were held; and there was not sufficient measure of public support for the Committee's recommendations

to justify the Government in introducing legislation to give effect to them. On the other hand it would be premature for the Government to announce a final decision on this point in the forthcoming debate in the House of Lords because Ministers had previously indicated that they would wish to take account of the general state of opinion in the House of Commons[46] before reaching their final conclusion.

Lord Kilmuir, the former David Maxwell Fyfe, now Lord Chancellor, a man deeply hostile to reform, was accordingly authorised to pronounce 'that there was no early prospect of Government legislation to amend the law relating to homosexual offences'[47] and it was to that phrase that he returned in his speech to the House of Lords on 4 December:

> I think that few people would disagree with the Committee's proposition that it is not the function of the law to attempt to cover all the fields of sexual behaviour. But when we seek to define the proper scope of the law, and to say what is the sphere of conduct which is best left to the individual conscience and what is the sphere in which the State, acting through the criminal law, has a duty to impose general standards, there are wide and deep differences of opinion. ... It is my considered view that it would obviously be a serious step to reverse the provisions of the criminal law which have stood for a long time, and any Government would be bound to think long and carefully before deciding to do so. There are cases, which I should be prepared to argue, with great enjoyment to myself, when it may well be the duty of a Government to lead rather than to follow public opinion, but in a matter of this kind the general sense of the community, particularly as expressed in Statutes which have been left undisturbed for long periods, is an important feature; and the community is entitled to its view as to what affects society as a whole. Her Majesty's Government do not think that the general sense of the community is with the Committee in this recommendation, and therefore they think that the problem requires further study and consideration. Certainly there can be no prospect of early legislation on this subject.[48]

Despite repeated calls for a debate in the House of Commons from a number of Members of Parliament[49] – including those who intended to attack the report[50] – it was said in characteristic fashion that the time was not yet ripe; the recommendation was highly controversial; public opinion had yet to declare itself;[51] and there was an urgent pressure of competing business.[52] Backbenchers said that there were weightier matters to discuss than the Report – the Navy estimates[53] or an economic conference to be held in Montreal, for example.[54] To be sure, the Home Secretary did have a meeting on 18 February 1958 to consider possible bills for the next session of Parliament, and the Committee's report was discussed, but no decision was taken (and it was only the proposals on prostitution that engaged his attention[55]).

Matters dragged on. Consideration was being given to the report, said Mr Butler in mid-June 1958, 'I often think about it, but I have not yet found time for a debate'.[56] The report came before a meeting of the Home Affairs Committee, a month later, on 25 July, but again it was only the recommendations on prostitution that were discussed.[57] It then went before yet another meeting of the Committee in October[58] where the Home Secretary said that:

> there could be no question of legislation in the next Session of Parliament on homosexual offences; but he proposed that arrangements should be made early in the new Session for a Debate on both aspects of the report, after which he would consult his colleagues further. There was no doubt that public opinion was becoming increasingly critical of Government inactivity on the report and in his view it had now become desirable to introduce a Street Offences Bill which would make it an offence for a common prostitute to loiter or solicit in a public place for the purpose of prostitution.[59]

Perhaps the subject was regarded as simply too disagreeable to be aired willingly (the MP, Leo Abse,[60] reported that Lord Kilmuir, the former Home Secretary, now Lord Chancellor, refused to attend any cabinet meetings where 'what he called this 'filthy subject' would be discussed,'[61] although his observation is mistaken – Lord Kilmuir *did* attend such meetings).

What the *Guardian* newspaper called a pattern of 'discreet avoid[ance]'[62] continued. When the Unionist Member, H. Montgomery Hyde,[63] the author of works on homosexuality and the trials of Oscar Wilde,[64] put down a notice of motion in the House of Commons for 13 June 1958, he was left with but a minute to move it. There was to be no reference to the report in the Speech from the Throne at the beginning of the 1958–1959 Session of Parliament,[65] but it *was* conceded that there might be a debate in the House of Commons before Christmas, even if it was unlikely that more than a single day could be allotted to it.[66] To the excitement of the press[67] and a newly formed Homosexual Law Reform Society,[68] a debate *was* then finally fixed for the afternoon of 26 November 1958, 14 months after the report had been submitted.

Opening the proceedings, the Home Secretary apologised for the delay and moved straight to the Committee's core proposal on homosexual law reform and the utilitarian framework within which it was lodged. They were not arguments the government could accept:

> I think we all agree that there is a sphere of conduct in which the behaviour of individuals must be controlled by the sanctions of the law, in their own interests, in the interests of others, and in the interests of society at large. I think it would be agreed that there is a sphere which it is proper to leave to the dictates of the individual conscience; I mean the individual and the individual conscience as fortified by the teachings of religion and the generally accepted standards of the society in which we live. ... What

kinds of conduct, the Committee asked, are so contrary to the public good that the law ought to intervene in its function as the guardian of that public good? It is really on the answer to that question, which I took from the Committee's Report, that the discussion on the Committee's recommendations on homosexual conduct has turned. Is such conduct between consenting adults in private injurious to society, or is it a matter entirely for the private consciences of the parties concerned? ... leaving homosexual conduct to the private conscience [can be accepted] only if one is convinced that society will not be harmed by so doing. That is a proposition which many people, after giving full weight to the Committee's arguments and to the views of the Churches, still find great difficulty in accepting.[69]

Mr Butler speculated whether the greater freedom envisaged for consenting homosexual adults might not corrupt those on the margins – the weak and vulnerable bisexual men, for instance, whom he supposed would not otherwise be seduced into sinful conduct. Might not an extension of freedom be read as signifying a formal condoning of homosexual practices? Given the decline in the moral influence of religion, was not the criminal law the only effective check on wrong conduct? Would not a liberalisation of the law offend a great many people? Was not ignorance about the causes and extent of homosexuality an impediment to making an intelligent judgement about the consequences of any action that might be taken? He recognised the ills wrought by the 1885 Act – the potential for blackmail and the manner in which imprisonment could exacerbate rather than mitigate problems – but he also concluded that the government were not satisfied that 'they would ... be justified at present, on the basis of opinions expressed so far, in proposing legislation to carry out the recommendations of the Committee'.

A few Members opposed what he said. Prominent amongst them was Anthony Greenwood,[70] 'a major political figure',[71] a member of the Labour Party National Executive Committee and a future Minister, who recited the libertarian argument underpinning the Committee's recommendation and made much of the way in which it had been endorsed by the Churches:

I am fortified in my view by the fact that it is shared by many of the great religious leaders of the country. The right hon. Gentleman referred to the variety of testimony given in the past, but there is a remarkable measure of agreement at the present time. So far as I can tell, none of our religious leaders believes that homosexual indulgence is anything but a sin; but many of them take the view that it should not be a crime. In the admirable words of the right hon. Gentleman, it is a matter which should be left to the dictates of the individual conscience. Like the right hon. Gentleman, I was impressed by the arguments advanced in another place by the Archbishop of Canterbury. The Archbishop of York has taken the same view and both of them have pronounced in favour of the Wolfenden Report. The Archbishop of York wrote a most courageous letter to The Times earlier this week.[72] The Church of England Moral Welfare Council, as well as the Church Assembly, have supported the Report. The views of the Methodist Conference were made unmistakably clear when, on the advice of its Department of Christian Citizenship, it passed a resolution endorsing the Wolfenden recommendation on homosexuality. ... With this weight of theological opinion behind me, I cannot feel that my acceptance of the Wolfenden Report is wrong.

A member of the Wolfenden Committee, the Conservative Member for Putney, Sir Hugh Linstead, recapitulated the major steps in the argument that had impelled him and his colleagues to recommend liberalisation, and, in particular, the contentions that the existing criminal law had no place in the regulation of private morality, and that it was ineffective, arbitrary and indefensibly discriminatory. Peter Rawlinson, the barrister, now the Conservative Member for Epsom, the man who had acted for the defence in the Montagu trial at Winchester Assizes, a trial where hitherto respectable defendants had been brought low by morally undeserving and marginal men, pronounced that he could not approve outright decriminalisation,[73] but, somewhat contradictorily, one may suppose, drawing on his experience at law, confessed that he found much amiss with the present system:[74]

> I can only say from my personal experience that I have left the court at the conclusion of some trials sickened by injustice, not so much of the verdict, but sickened by the injustice which does surround so many of this kind of crimes. To sit there and see a man, perhaps of talent and distinction, in the box, and to see the worthless wretched creatures being paraded there as witnesses for the Crown, pampered by the police as persons upon whom apparently there has been cast the mantle of perfection, to see it is to feel that it is a mockery by society, the mockery of the administration of the law, and it leaves an impression well nigh inerasable.

But they were unrepresentative of wider sentiment in the House of Commons, being quite outnumbered by opponents from both the major parties who entertained strong feelings and who spoke of them at length. The Labour Member, Emanuel Shinwell,[75] for example, interrupted Sir Hugh to ask him whether he was saying 'to homosexual activists ... "You must not do it in public because you may be penalised for so doing, but go and do it in private and you escape"'.? Frederick Bellenger, the Labour Member for Bassetlaw,[76] claimed in concert with other Members of Parliament that the Committee had been captured by a coterie of lawyers and psychiatrists, and was entirely unresponsive to the mass of lay opinion: 'in the eyes of most of our constituents, homosexuality ... is wrong. ... a malignant canker in the community and if this were allowed to grow, it would eventually kill off what is known as normal life. ... humanity would eventually revert to an animal existence if this cult were so allowed to spread that, as in ancient Greece, it overwhelmed the community at large'. Indeed, Jean Mann, the Labour Member for Coatbridge and Airdrie and a Christian Socialist, the woman who had deplored the volume of attention devoted to the Report, approvingly quoted her fellow Scot, James Adair, the sole dissenting member of the Wolfenden Committee, and proceeded to portray the clergymen, psychiatrists and intellectuals who condoned homosexuality as part of a powerful international homosexual conspiracy.[77] William Shepherd, the Conservative Member for Cheadle, a man who would maintain his opposition to the last,[78] 'was rather surprised, in fact rather annoyed, at the Wolfenden Committee refusing to accept that these [homosexual] practices are unnatural. I was very surprised that the members of the Committee should jib at that phrase. ... It is perfectly true that if one adopts a lax attitude towards homosexuality one promotes its growth. It is no credit to this community that homosexuality is known on the Continent as vice Anglais, but it is a discreditable reflection on our society and I believe it our duty to try to deal with it'. James Dance, another adamantine opponent, the Conservative Member for Bromsgrove,[79] at the height of the Cold War and the fear of a nuclear attack, likened the threat posed by homosexuals to that of the fall-out from strontium 90: 'too many people are looking into the mind of the homosexual rather than considering the repugnance which is caused to millions of decent people all over the country. There can be no question that this practice is a social evil and that it undermines the morals of the country'. Emulating Jean Mann, he again reminded the House of the words of James Adair who had talked about the potentially pernicious impact of homosexual couples 'living openly and notoriously under the approval of the law'. Dr. Broughton, the Labour Member for Batley and Morley,[80] approvingly read out a letter from a constituent:

> Men and women joined in true marriage are complementary the one to the other; the man with his strength, ruggedness, thoughtfulness and protective love and respect for his wife; and the woman with her sweetness, intuitive wisdom, love of beauty and reverence for her husband. I suggest that that is the type of love that we want to encourage. There is no getting away from it. We must say that homosexuality is biologically wrong.

And so it went on. Although no vote was taken, it was clear that very few from both the major parties supported the Wolfenden Committee. Most condemned it. They did not wish to encourage a wicked sin[81] and evil men.[82] They did not wish to flout the views of the public and their constituents.[83] They did not wish to risk the danger of homosexuality increasing. There could be no distinction between private immorality and public crime. Winding up the debate after some seven hours, David Renton, the Joint Undersecretary of State for the Home Department, a man who was himself profoundly opposed to change, said that 'the Government have to take note, both of the risk of homosexuality spreading, and of possible corruption and degradation in society if it does, if the law is changed... it is the instinct of most members of the public and of most Members of both Houses of Parliament to decline the Wolfenden proposal'.

It was, pronounced an editorial in C.H. Rolph's *New Statesman*, 'an example of the House of Commons at its worst'.[84] The much later verdict of the historian and sociologist, Jeffery Weeks, was that there was 'a crushing unwillingness on the part of the government to act. The Tories had a substantial parliamentary majority, but much of it consisted of backwoodsmen, interested in nothing more than the moral status quo'[85] (and, it might be added, and he later agreed, there were many Labour backwoodsmen as well). It was an inauspicious political birth.

The Homosexual Law Reform Society

Yet, and again as the press had anticipated, the government did not consider contentious the Committee's recommendations about prostitution, and they were dealt with expeditiously: the Home Secretary broached a Bill in Cabinet later in December 1958;[86] and, under the slogan of 'cleaning up the streets',[87] the Street Offences Act became law in 1959.[88] Section 1 of the Act made it criminal 'for a common prostitute to loiter or solicit in a street or public place for the purpose of prostitution'; and Section 4 increased the maximum penalty for living on the earnings of prostitution to seven years imprisonment. It was, R.A. Butler said in his autobiography, one of the three most important Acts he put through Parliament: 'I was moved to take such action by the condition of the streets around Mayfair and Piccadilly which were literally crowded out with girls touting for clients. This gave a very unhealthy look to the centre of our capital city'.[89]

But he made no mention at all of the other major recommendation in the Report. Homosexual law reform would take much longer. Indeed, under a consolidating Act introduced by Lord Kilmuir, and passed in 1956, the Sexual Offences Act, C 69 4 and 5 Eliz 2, the law on indecency and buggery had once again been confirmed on the very eve of the Wolfenden Report's publication.[90] It was reported too that David Renton, his new Parliamentary Undersecretary, had refused as a matter of conscience to assist any reform of the law,[91] and that was not an uncommon posture. Something of the loathing which was expressed around the time was conveyed by Gerald Sparrow, the former Labour Party and sometime Democratic Anti-Common Market Parliamentary candidate, a man of strong views,[92] and one of R.A. Butler's biographers:

> Although the Home Office drove the prostitutes from the streets no effort was made to ban the homosexual other than very rare prosecutions for soliciting. The growth of homosexuality and the enticement of young men into this filthy brotherhood has not been stopped or even discouraged.[93]

Offences against the 1861 and 1885 Acts continued to be reported to the police and prosecuted in the courts, although their numbers were in slow, albeit ragged, decline:

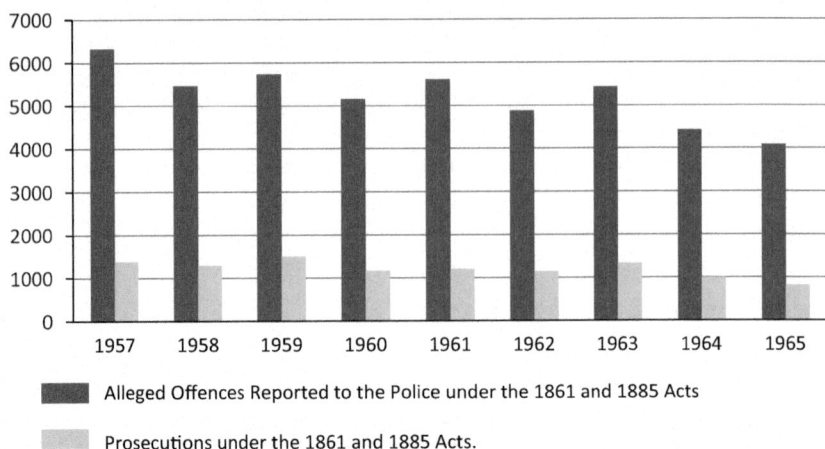

Alleged Offences Reported to the Police under the 1861 and 1885 Acts

Prosecutions under the 1861 and 1885 Acts.

Figure 7.1 Crimes of buggery and indecency reported and prosecuted in England and Wales under the 1861 and 1885 Acts 1957–1965★

★Based on *Criminal Statistics England and Wales 1959–60*, Cmnd. 1100, Home Office, London, 1961 and successive reports thereafter.

The men and women who had been encouraged by the publication of the report to coalesce politically around the prospect of law reform chose to liken what was happening in and around the criminal courts, especially outside the large urban areas, to 'provincial pogroms'.[94] One spate of arrests, alleged to have taken place in Wells, Somerset, in late 1957 or early 1958, at the very time the report was beginning to make an impact, was held to be particularly significant, a *casus belli*, although it is difficult now after some sixty years to establish precisely what may have happened, how much was exaggerated for political purposes and whether it could properly be described as a pogrom. The local police records appear no longer to be available;[95] the Somerset County Archivist informed me that the local magistrates' court records merely note 'at least one conviction' in the latter half of the 1950s;[96] and the local newspapers, the *Wells Journal* and the *Central Somerset Gazette*, both of which exhaustively reported the smallest events at length and in minute detail – including proceedings taken after a failure to stop at a halt sign; legal action pursued after a 'Lorry had inefficient brake and no speedometer'; and a man fined £2 for exceeding the speed limit – mention a total of but two prosecutions, one successful and the other unsuccessful, for offences of indecency in and around the city of Wells (but nothing really resembling a pogrom) between July 1957 and February 1958,[97] thereby tending to confirm the Archivist's report. Even the extensive records of LAGNA, the Lesbian and Gay Newspaper Archive, records that begin in August 1953, make no mention of anything resembling a Somerset pogrom.[98] Nevertheless, the writer of a letter to *The Spectator* on 3 January 1958, a man of local standing, was resolute that something *was* afoot in Wells, and his statement was to have consequences, being repeatedly cited to become a substantial social and political fact in its own right.[99] Dr Robert Reid[100] reported that:

> Even though the Government, for reasons which they are not prepared to give, are to throw over the recommendations of the Wolfenden Committee, one would still have expected the police authorities to pay *some* attention to them. ... The pogroms, however, continue ... The pattern is much the same in all these cases. The police go round from house to house, bringing ruin in their train, always attacking the younger men first, extracting information with lengthy questioning and specious promises of light sentences as they proceed from clue to clue i.e. from home to home ... This time the age range is seventeen to forty, which is about average. Last time a man of thirty-seven dropped dead in the dock at Assizes.[101]

It was his, and other, allied public statements, that prompted the publication of a spate of letters in newspapers, including an important joint letter that was organised by a 29-year-old academic, A.E. Dyson,[102] which appeared in *The Times* on 7 March 1958.[103] Many of those who signed it were 'the H-bomb names and the Treason Trial[104] names'[105] who had played a part in other liberalising movements, including the two campaigns I have described in preceding chapters,[106] and they formed, and must have known that they formed, the nucleus of yet another social movement. One, most importantly, was Isaiah Berlin, the author of *Two Concepts of Liberty*, a man who was personally discomfited by the presence of homosexuality[107] but whose philosophy embodied a version of the utilitarian politics of *laissez-faire*. *The Times* letter advertised its debt to the new theological utilitarianism by opening:

> ... homosexual acts committed in private between consenting adults should no longer be a criminal offence. The present law is clearly no long representative of either Christian or liberal opinion in this country, and now that there are widespread doubts about both its justice and its efficacy, we believe that its continued enforcement will do more harm than good to the health of the community as a whole. The case for reform has already been accepted by most of the responsible papers and journals, by the two Archbishops, the Church Assembly, a Roman Catholic committee, a number of nonconformist spokesmen, and many other organs of informed public opinion. ...

More letters followed[108] and it was that concatenation of events and that appearance of activity, partly fortuitous, partly enacted for dramatic ends,[109] an 'outcry ... busily being organised, in an efficient way',[110] that enabled A.E. Dyson,[111] to float the idea of a new campaigning organisation that would 'work for legal reform along the lines suggested by the Wolfenden Report, and ... promote a wider understanding of the problem of homosexuality as a whole'.[112] Such an organisation did indeed soon emerge, being inaugurated on 12 May 1958, and it began public recruiting a month later,[113] tracing its genesis to the outraged response to the alleged Wells pogrom: 'At the beginning of this year there were large-scale arrests in Wells. These resulted in correspondence which brought the Homosexual Law Reform Society into existence'.[114]

Like the National Campaign for the Abolition of Capital Punishment[115] and the Abortion Law Reform Association, the Society was quite deliberately and almost certainly necessarily configured to present an irreproachably respectable face to the world[116] – members of the elite calling upon their fellows for support. It was intended to cause as little preventable stir as possible (A.E. Dyson said that 'Our aim ... will be to avoid such controversial issues as might divide supporters, and to work in full co-operation with all those who wish to see the law reformed'[117]); it would not be overly or diffusely ambitious;[118] and it would draw on the close little world of publicly prominent and reputable intellectuals, artists, lawyers, medical men and women, politicians and churchmen, amongst them the signatories of the letter to *The Times*, who were so engaged at the time in and around the politics of criminal justice reform.[119]

The first chairman of its Executive Committee was a surgeon, psychiatrist and 'sexologist', Kenneth Walker,[120] and its founding members were A.E. Dyson (Vice-Chairman), Ambrose Appelbe,[121] Canon John Collins, Victor Gollancz, Jacquetta Hawkes, Dr W. Lindesay Neustatter,[122] the inevitable C.H. Rolph, Stephen Spender, Dr E.B. Strauss[123] and the Shadow Home Secretary between 1955 and 1957, Kenneth Younger, MP. Its Honorary Committee (mirroring the form and composition of similar campaigning organisations of the period) included the Archbishop of York and the Bishops of Birmingham, Exeter, Ripon and Reading.

The Society[124] and the Committee grew. Others, including Barbara Wootton, came in time to declare their sympathy, and others still, such as the priapic philosopher,[125] Professor A.J. Ayer, would formally join,[126] Ayer becoming the Society's president in 1963. Antony Grey (the public *persona* or 'gay name' adopted by Edgar Wright[127]), who, after a delay occasioned revealingly by the Society's anxieties about appointing a homosexual to the post,[128] was to be the Society's first salaried secretary in 1964, claimed that its members 'were mostly not homosexual themselves; they were very conscious of the delicate, and in some respects potentially dangerous, nature of the task which they had taken on, and they were understandably nervous of being 'railroaded' by a group who ... were all personally vulnerable in the existing state of the law and might do irreparable damage to the Society's cause if they put a foot wrong ...'[129]

Theirs was a well-founded nervousness. Although A.E. Dyson hoped that the new society would secure patronage, legitimacy and advice from other, better-entrenched institutions by 'establish[ing] contact with the most important Christian and secular bodies concerned with the problem',[130] and although he approached those bodies with what can only be described as diffidence,[131] their members were sometimes less than eager fully to respond to his overtures for reasons that may, no doubt, have been quite ambivalent. Chief amongst those bodies was the Church of England's Moral Welfare Council, the body whose reports had critically defined and, to a major extent, given legitimacy to the central posture of the Wolfenden Committee. Edward Jones, the Bishop of St Albans, the Chairman of the Moral Welfare Council since 1951, was invited to be the first Chairman of the new Honorary Committee but his 'first reaction, as usual, is to be reluctant to join ... – though that may be necessary – or to go on a deputation; the former because it is already sufficiently representative ... the latter because I know nothing of the rest of the party'.[132] Before the Society was launched, and seeking guidance, A.E. Dyson met Gordon Dunstan[133] and Ena Steel, the ever-cautious Secretary of the Moral Welfare Council,[134] and *her* inclination was to dismiss him as impetuous and politically naive, a man bent on making a commotion that would jeopardise the prospects of reform. She would be wary about what she deemed to be the fanaticism of the Abortion Law Reform Association and she was cautious about what she deemed to be the political inexperience of the new Homosexual Law Reform Society. Dyson was, she said:

> Well-intentioned, but very vague as to practical steps to be taken in the immediate or more distant future. ... It would appear that his objective is to press for legislation, but it was obvious that he had not given sufficient weight to the strength of resistance to a change in the law, and that he had not understood the underlying reasons for this resistance either in the Government, amongst the Bishops or in the community generally. ... I explained to him that ... if he wanted the support of the Council his Executive Committee must set out its aims and objects clearly, and these would be studied by our Council very sympathetically.[135]

The Reverend Professor Dunstan was even more apprehensive:[136]

> I was alarmed more by his lack of imagination than by his being an unlikely organiser or secretary. He had not thought out the certain impact upon the public mind of most of his propositions ... He had no idea of the emotional resistance which high pressure propaganda on this subject is bound to create, or of the antipathy automatically attaching to the names of some of his star supporters and already chosen committee members. He had not perceived the differences between education and a campaign to bring political pressure to bear ... With these defects I regard his efforts as being not simply harmless, but possibly dangerous in that he is bringing high powered people, hardened and impetuous campaigners, together for a work which he does not really understand and to become a force which he will find it impossible to control.[137]

Ena Steel would report to Gordon Dunstan that she had spoken to Hugh Klare of the Howard League (and it is interesting how, as a matter of course, members of the little world of established reformers worked together *sub rosa*, organisation talking to organisation, to negotiate a position on what was being bruited):

> I telephoned Mr Klare. He will be seeing Mr Dyson on Monday morning. As you know, he shares our dismay at the array of names collected by Mr Dyson,[138] and is appalled at the idea of high-powered public action. ... I told Mr Klare that one hope of salvaging Mr Dyson from the dead hand of his Executive Committee[139] would be to get them to agree to the setting up of a small working party on the lines suggested by Mr Klare, and to forswear a big public campaign. ...[140]

She suggested to A.E. Dyson that:

> ... the next step will be very important. You know, I think, that our feeling is that there is work to be done, but this will be effective only if it is carried out by a very small and carefully chosen group of people who have special knowledge of this problem. Do you think that those who have said that they would be willing to serve on an Executive body would be willing to appoint such a group and then leave it to that body to carry out the work there is to do? The members of your Committee of Honour could be kept informed from time to time, but we should hope that there would be no public advertisement of this organisation or their names.[141]

An anonymous note to file in the Lambeth Palace Archives, addressed to Gordon Dunstan in October 1958, makes it clear that there then followed a reluctance to embark on further meetings with representatives of the embryonic Society — in this instance with Andrew Hallidie Smith,[142] a married clergyman and the new secretary of the Homosexual Law Reform Society,[143] whose apparent heterosexuality was frequently advertised by A.E. Dyson in his correspondence with Ena Steel and others.[144] Homosexuals, those who gave them political succour, and organisations campaigning on their behalf, were still evidently thought to be dangerously discredited and discrediting (Andrew Hallidie Smith was reported to have admitted that 'A strong prejudice ... will always remain against this minority group'[145]). It is as if the existence of the Society was acknowledged, and that there was a modest willingness or sense of obligation to work with it, but that making its presence publicly known or entering into any visible dealings with it were viewed with more than a little queasiness, even by homosexual men and women themselves.

So it was that the homosexual philanthropist, Simon Sainsbury,[146] reluctantly agreed to donate a small sum[147] to establish 'a very small *anonymous* committee, working for (1) the drafting of a bill to implement the Wolfenden recommendation; (2) the asking of questions in Parliament; (3) the provision of material for the Press' (my emphasis added). He also arranged two dinners just before the launch, one attended by the then Home Secretary, Henry Brooke, and the other by Aneurin Bevan, but the results were not reassuring (Aneurin Bevan, then Labour Party treasurer and a figure of considerable political weight, was reported to have said that he thought that 'neither the Government nor the Opposition would provide time for a debate in the House'[148]).

Not only were the external responses to the new society frequently luke-warm or antagonistic, even from its allies or would-be allies, but, as I have already suggested, some of its own members appeared to be a little nervous about what was in train. They chose to adhere closely and publicly to the emerging, and for the time, no doubt, progressive view that homosexuality was an unfortunate condition which merited some form of medical or psycho-logical treatment,[149] and the society's Executive Committee, possibly reflecting the professional leanings of a number of its key members, spent time deliber-ating, in concert with a psychotherapist, Mrs. H. Malik,[150] and the National Association for Mental Health, how best to establish a 'clinic'[151] whose 'prin-cipal aim [would] be to assist homosexual men and women and others with psycho-sexual problems'[152] revealed, in part, by psychological research into pathologies in the early family relationships of homosexuals undertaken by a Dr Eva Bene.[153] (The archaeologist and patron of the Albany Trust, Jacquette Hawkes,[154] noted the likely import of what was being aired and would later recommend that the name of the clinic be given further consideration, 'so as not to imply that homosexuals were necessarily mentally disordered or in need of medical treatment'.[155])

A decade before what the Americans Haug and Sussman, came to call the 'revolt of the client'[156] when members of social movements challenged the power of others to define their condition, psychiatry and medicine offered one of the few public languages available to those who wished to talk about homosexuality, and it was in the main a language of clinical pathology. Plans for the society's public meetings took it that a number of the 'Speakers ... would be psychiatrists and others with specialised knowledge of the subject',[157] and psychiatrists and doctors were to be co-opted to work with the Executive Committee. The new organisation was certainly not, and, quite probably, politically could never have been in the 1950s and early 1960s, bent on openly championing homosexuality as a desirable, valid or pleasurable way of life freely chosen.[158] Neither was it permissible to embrace the idea that homosexuals could claim legitimacy, authority and expertise on the basis of their own experi-ence *as* homosexuals.[159] The Society could never be so forward (Antony Grey recalled that its 'activities ... have been flatteringly described in some quarters as 'sophisticated'. I would prefer to characterise them as 'discreet''[160]). There could be no resort to the 'speaking-out' or 'coming out' or 'reclaiming the night' or 'me-toos' that later, bolder groups would advocate.[161] It was obliged to dis-tance itself from any hint of such practices. Consider its response to a report in *The Times* of 7 November 1960 that had quoted the ambivalently supportive Professor Dunstan as saying that 'propaganda was coming into Britain from "powerful homosexual organisations" in the United States [and that] Apparent in it was a morally indifferent or "even approving" attitude, and if people in

Britain who supported homosexual law reform were seeking to propagate this attitude, they should be told that the Church is not on their side'. In his unpublished letter to the editor, the Society's Chairman replied:

> The Homosexual Law Reform Society, of which we are Executive Committee members, fully endorses this attitude, and does not subscribe to the type of propaganda mentioned by the Revd. Dunstan. ... Our Society stands among the firmest advocates of reforms, but far from seeking to condone homosexual behaviour, we share the view put forward by the Archbishop of Canterbury, that only with a change in the law will "the fresh air of normal morality begin to circulate far more easily" among homosexuals.[162]

The warnings which the Moral Welfare Council and others had meted out to A.E. Dyson and his committee were to be continually reiterated. A campaign for homosexual law reform was known to be an area fraught with political hazards. There were, for example, the findings of a survey commissioned by the society's twin organisation, the Albany Trust,[163] and carried out by the British Market Research Bureau in July and August 1963, that revealed substantial and growing public antagonism to legal reform:[164] only 16% of a national sample of 2,500 men and women interviewed were said to have supported the change in the law proposed by the Wolfenden Committee; 67% opposed it, and 17% declared that they were unsure.[165] The inference to be drawn, the Society's Executive Committee believed, was that 'Public opinion is so hostile to reform that it is useless to try and influence it, and efforts should be concentrated upon influencing Parliament ... [and that] the Society should spend virtually no money on advertising and publicity and concentrate all its efforts upon lobbying tactics in Parliament'.[166]

There were the doubts voiced by the MP and committee member, Kenneth Robinson, who wondered whether it would be prudent or politic to hold any public meetings.[167] There was the scepticism of a potential donor, Alfred Hecht,[168] who informed the executive committee that 'He questioned whether any attempts which the Society could make to influence public opinion would have any effect whatever'.[169] Provincial newspapers sometimes declined to accept the Society's advertisements.[170] Funding applications to support research into public attitudes to homosexual law reform did not bear fruit.[171] A meeting at the Home Office in 1963 concluded that 'no useful purpose would be served at present by embarking upon fresh research projects'[172] (although it will be recalled that the government *had* funded such studies in the preceding few years).

Parliamentary action

Change would again have to be effected through legislation in Westminster, but action in Parliament would be fraught. The response to the Report was taken to 'show[] that the most ignorant prejudice still flourishes in high places'.[173] The 'hysterical outbursts'[174] marking the initial Parliamentary response in 1958 had been so discouraging that the new Society had been temporarily paralysed. It refrained from lobbying and it deferred its inaugural public meeting for its first eighteen months[175] (although it did organise in the interim a spate of 'small meetings, representing various layers of responsible public opinion'[176]). It acknowledged that it would face 'a long hard slog'.[177] Antony Grey called it 'the long haul'.[178] By the mid-1960s, and in the face of sustained antipathy from a succession of Conservative governments, Alfred Hecht was reported to have said that 'the Committee had existed for six years and achieved nothing'.[179]

Despite the Society's apparent lack of early momentum, members of its Executive Committee were politically experienced and well-connected men and women. That was one of the reasons why they had been selected. They were adept at 'doing new things in old ways'.[180] Many had worked, or were working simultaneously in the late 1950s and early 1960s, in central roles on quite similar reform projects, including the two other liberalising criminal justice movements of the time, abortion law reform and the abolition of capital punishment; they gave succour to one another;[181] and they had accumulated stocks of recipe knowledge that could be applied to campaigning. They recruited or turned to the same experts whom they or others had consulted in other campaigns, and to the Society of Labour Lawyers, in particular,[182] for intelligence on parliamentary opinion, and guidance on the strategy, timing and drafting of possible legislation. It was as a result taken for granted that homosexual law reform would almost certainly have to follow a set pattern, being introduced by a Private Member, draft bills having to be prepared, possible sponsors being scouted out in both Houses of Parliament, and government and backbench support being mustered.

The bills that they drew up[183] tended generally (but not invariably[184]) to adhere strongly to the wording of the Wolfenden Report – that was the most prudent tactic – despite some private reservations about, for example, the age of consent being fixed at 21[185] (a matter which would become an object of successful future campaigning[186]). Again, following the model of other campaigns, they recognised that homosexual law reform was likely to be a protracted process – there might have to be not one but many attempts to introduce legislation. And the very first attempt was that undertaken by Kenneth Robinson, a member of the Society and a champion of abortion law reform, in June 1960 and it took the form of the motion 'That this House calls upon Her Majesty's Government to take early action upon the recommendations contained in Part Two of the Report of the Wolfenden Committee'.

Kenneth Robinson sought in his opening to undo some of the stereotypes that had been applied with such damaging effect in debates two years before (although it was perhaps inevitable that, in doing so, he was obliged to turn to the rival typification of the pitiable and hapless man then being fostered in reforming circles): 'in the light of things which were said on the last occasion when this subject was debated', he remarked, 'it is necessary to try to clear the air. It is widely held ... that all homosexuals are effeminate, depraved and exhibitionist. This may be true of a very small minority, those of a homopsychopathic character, but, after all, much the same could be said *mutatis mutandis* of a small minority of heterosexual people. The majority of homosexuals are useful citizens who go about quite unrecognised and unsuspected by most of us. ... these unfortunate people deserve our compassion rather than our contempt'. Just as inevitably, he cited the moral authority of the Churches and the political authority of the press: 'there is the opinion of the Churches, which is to some of us perhaps the most surprising and welcome feature of the debate. The Archbishops of Canterbury and York, the Church Assembly, the Methodist Conference and the Committee set up by the Roman Catholic Church to study the same problems as those studied by the Wolfenden Committee all support the same recommendation. Editorial opinion is heavily in favour of the recommendation. *The Times*, the *Guardian*, the *Observer*, the *Sunday Times*, the *Daily Mirror*, the *Star*, the *New Statesman*, the *Spectator*, and the *Economist* are all in favour of the Wolfenden recommendations'.[187] Despite that effort at remedial descriptive work, despite the invocation of religious legitimacy, despite the Homosexual Law Reform Society having mobilised itself, 'put itself into high gear, and arranged to hold its first public meeting at Caxton Hall on 12 May 1960,[188] shortly after sending a deputation to see the Home Secretary',[189] he was unsuccessful.

There was, to be sure, palpably more parliamentary support for reform on this occasion than there had been in 1958. Those who had urged the case did so again, and they were joined by new voices, but homosexuality remained an unwholesome and unwelcome subject and the bill's opponents were still solidly in place. The Labour Member, Dr. Broughton, who had spoken in 1958, wondered why Kenneth Robinson had sought to reintroduce such an unsavoury problem at all: 'I cannot congratulate him on his choice of subject', he said. Perhaps, he thought, Mr Robinson was the tool of a homosexual lobby: 'he might be well advised to inquire into the source of the present demand. If he does that, he may then find that behind the present small wave of pressure which has swept him to the fore there are homosexuals whose indignation at the attitude of the community towards them and whose fear of harsh laws urge them to try this means towards escape from the wrath of the law'. The Conservative, Godfrey Lagden, asked 'Have we reached the stage of misguided thinking that we say that, providing two evil people consent, then their actions should be considered legitimate? ... since time began those who have been put in authority have always been given a duty to see that good is upheld and evil is punished'. Brigadier Terence Clarke[190] asked 'If we are to allow this sort of thing to occur, would my hon. Friend be happy to go into a public house and find a couple of hairy old males sitting on each other's knees and liking it? Is that what we are going to allow?' R.A. Butler, the perennially hesitant Home Secretary, added a reference to the doctrine of unripe time: the issue was still too divisive to permit resolution and 'although we have made some considerable progress, no one who has to legislate or decide on this subject can deny that there is still a very great difference of opinion, and, in my opinion, a very great deal of work still to be done'.

A few Members conceded with Eirene White that, although they considered the subject 'difficult, embarrassing and distasteful ...', they were never the less prepared to apply the liberal argument that severed sin from crime and, 'faced with a practical and a moral choice in this matter ... [recognised that] the weight of evidence is emphatically on the side of changing the law'.[191] The future Home Secretary, Roy Jenkins, a man who had already come out publicly in favour of reform, remarked that 'no body of opinion in this House suggests that we should legislate against ... other sexual sins and that we should make them not merely sins but crimes as well. ... I do not believe that any body of opinion in the House, if the Labouchere amendment had not been slipped in on the Report stage of the 1885 Act, would now come forward with a proposal for the Labouchere amendment'. Yet even he believed that he was obliged to remain timid and cautious: 'we wish that the Labouchere amendment was not there. Of course, it creates an illogical position between homosexuality and Lesbianism. We wish that it was not there, but it is there and there is a difficulty about removing it lest it be thought that in doing so this House was proclaiming that homosexuality is a good thing. I do not believe that many people would take that view'.

Those few supporters spoke at greater length and more frequently than the bill's opponents, but they were guarded and they were again heavily outgunned. The majority of Members would have no truck with reform. And after a debate lasting for three hours, the bill was defeated by 213 votes to 99. The Homosexual Law Reform Society concluded that 'legal reform will not be just round the corner. Mr Butler has recently made it clear that the Government does not want early action. The position now is that reform can certainly be achieved within a few years, but only by further hard work and publicity'.[192] [Emphasis in the original.]

There was to be a second attempt when, having secured a place in the private member's ballot, Leo Abse[193] introduced a bill 'to amend the law relating to homo-sexual offences', supported *inter alia*, by Christopher Chataway, Jeremy Thorpe and now, it should be noted, by Peter Rawlinson, that passed at First Reading on 22 November 1961;[194] moved to second reading but was 'talked out' without a vote in a brief, hour-long debate in March 1962. Prepared in the aftermath of the first debate on the report and of Kenneth Robinson's earlier bill, the new bill had been diluted and bowdlerised. Instead of seeking the outright decriminalisation of private homosexual acts between consenting adults – that, it was thought, would still not have met with the approval of the House of Commons in 1961 – it proposed, first, that all criminal proceedings would have to be taken with the consent of the Director of Public Prosecutions, thereby lessening their frequency and the homosexual man's exposure to the risk of blackmail; and that, secondly, where a man was found guilty of a homosexual offence for the first time, medical evidence must be adduced before sentencing. It was, said Leo Abse, 'to allay some of the anxieties which were expressed by hon. Members who could not accept the major recommendation that I have been prompted to bring this Bill before the House'. As a man who sometimes resorted to a somewhat vulgar form of psychoanalysis,[195] announcing in a later interview that 'I was and am an ideologue … I am a Freudian',[196] he sought to build on and advance the medicalised model of homosexuality, observing that 'in many cases, fortunately, the condition can be treated'.[197] His bill was thus grounded in the newly alternative, therapeutic stereotypy running through much of the public thinking in and around the Homosexual Law Reform Society in the late 1950s and early 1960s, thinking that juxtaposed a positivistic model of crime and deviance as sickness requiring treatment with a utilitarianism talking about harm reduction. Homosexual men were to be regarded as the unfortunate and wretched members of a vulnerable minority, and it was the moral duty of the statesman to protect vulnerable minorities, 'whether those minorities be criminal or homosexual, gypsies, or sick or ill':

> Since the initiative taken by my hon. Friend the Member for St. Pancras, North, [Kenneth Robinson] the question has remained dormant. All action has been shirked. Meantime, every four hours it is calculated that an unfortunate baby is born in Britain who is fated to be a homosexual. It is said that at least one man in 25 is a homosexual. I know that homosexuals tend sometimes to exaggerate the extent of homosexuality because they wish, as it were, to minimise their sense of guilt. Whether that is true or not, it is said that there are half a million practising homosexuals in this country. Whether that is so or not, it obviously amounts to a substantial and unfortunate minority. Although they have not chosen their fate, most people recognise that there could be few individuals who would opt for homosexuality. For nearly all, if not all, their disposition arises from birth or a faulty family upbringing. They are doomed to be denied what to most of us who possess it is the greatest blessing God can give – a happy married life and the gift of children.

But the new typification still carried little political weight in 1961. Perhaps it was too new to have acquired authority. John Wells, the Conservative MP for Maidstone, would have none of it. Homosexuals were *not* corrigible: 'In spite of what the hon. Member for Pontypool has said, I have always been given to understand that a great majority of confirmed homosexual offenders are not amenable to treatment. If a man is not amenable to treatment, it seems absurd to set out at the public expense to seek to treat him. It will be throwing money away to no advantage to the nation and to no advantage to the man in question'. Homosexuals were wicked, not sick. To 'leonine growls of approval from some Conservatives',[198] Charles Doughty, the Conservative MP for Surrey East, objected to any mitigation of the response to a heinous act, and he objected to the very title of the bill: 'It abuses the words it uses and would mean a sort of glorification of these offences, which are rightly called "abominable" …' It was reported that Leo Abse came to conclude that there were 'no votes in trying to amend the law on homosexuality'.[199]

There were to be a few more sporadic efforts made in the months immediately thereafter. For example, the Secretary of the Church of England Board for Social Responsibility, the successor to the Moral Welfare Council since 1958, submitted the first of its own draft Bills,[200] drawn up by Gordon Dunstan and Quentin Edwards,[201] to Sir Charles Cunningham in November 1962 ('It occurred to us that it might be of value to you in advising the Home Secretary … '[202] Dunstan added). But there was no reported response.

Another draft bill was discussed by Lord Arran in an approach to Sir Alec Douglas-Home, the Prime Minister, some two years later. He himself left no record of why he chose at that stage to pursue legal reform, but a reason frequently offered is his bereavement after the death of his homosexual brother, the seventh earl, who had committed suicide in December 1958.[203] Unlike Members of the House of Commons he had no constituents to fear. And, more generally, something may be inferred from his maxim that 'It seems to be quite wrong to condemn people for sins which one is not oneself tempted to commit. … Of course, this is not to say that there is no such thing as right and wrong. Only that one shouldn't be too jolly smug about the bad things which others do and which one hasn't done oneself simply because one hasn't wanted to'.[204] It is a maxim that casts some light on what he said in his letter to the Prime Minister: 'I have long felt that action toward this end would not only be humane, but the sensible thing to do. … Many people tend to regard the Labour and Liberal Parties as the parties of compassion, and it would be useful, I feel, if the Tories were to give their blessing to this major piece of social legislation'.[205] Whatever his motivation may have been – and motives are often obscure even to those who possess them – Antony Grey came to conclude that at first 'he seemed a somewhat unlikely champion of social reform. … He struck me as too politically marginal and personally eccentric to be an effective champion,' but 'In fact he turned out to be a shining specimen of *noblesse oblige*'.[206]

Lord Arran's first overture was to no avail. The Prime Minister was reported to have told him that it would not be a good time to introduce a bill or a motion on homosexual law reform in the House of Lords and 'that he could not give any undertaking about the Government's attitude towards such a move before the election, as both [he] and the Home Secretary, who was keeping the matter under review, had seen no evidence of any alteration in Parliamentary or public opinion since the Debate in 1960'.[207]

The prospect of legal reform under a hostile Conservative Government and in an indifferent Parliament thereby continued to seem more than a little bleak. Somewhat forlornly, the Executive Committee of the Homosexual Law Reform Society resolved at its meeting on 14 January 1964, that 'it was unanimously decided that "the Society should intensify its efforts for law reform for a further three years, after which time the question of its future should be reviewed"'.[208] To be sure, there had in the interim been some small changes, and, in particular, a number of compromise measures intended to reduce the impact of the 1861 and 1885 Acts. Leo Abse's recommendation about prosecution policy had, for example, already been presaged in an agreement undertaken by chief constables to confer with the attorney general or the Director of Public Prosecutions before taking action against men arrested for committing offences in private,[209] and there had been a consequent decline from 781 in 1954 to 372 in 1963 in the number of persons received into prison under sentence for offences under the Sexual Offences Act, 1956, or for attempted buggery.[210] But it is evident that the law officers were uncomfortable about the procedure[211] and that they did not wish it to be incorporated more formally in law.[212]

If nothing major could be accomplished under a Conservative administration, hopes in the early 1960s were again perforce becoming attached to the change that a new and possibly more liberal Labour government might bring. The society began to discuss sounding out the leader of the opposition, Harold Wilson, about the prospects for reform should his party come to power, and there was a spate of reconnaissance expeditions and discussions with individual Members of both Houses of Parliament.[213] There had been conversations with Lord Arran and Baroness Wootton in the summer of 1963 about possible action in the House of Lords; but C.H. Rolph had ascertained that although she would support a bill, she was not prepared to introduce it herself. The Executive Committee of the Society thought that Lord Boothby or Lord Arran[214] might serve instead, but the presentational politics of sexual law reform were then in play and 'on consideration it was felt that a woman peeress, such as Lady Elliot of Harwood[215] or Lady Summerskill,[216] would be preferable. Mr Thorpe[217] said he would explore these ladies' views on the matter'.[218]

Harold Wilson's slim victory in October 1964, a victory secured with a majority of only four, was, said Antony Grey, an encouragement to 'our parliamentary supporters to plan an early debate on homosexual law reform'.[219] It was from thenceforth that those supporters, and Leo Abse, in the House of Commons, and Lord Arran, in the House of Lords, especially, assumed command over much of the pace and direction of what was done, leading some members of the Homosexual Law Reform Society later to believe that they had been rather roughly displaced.[220]

In the first session of the new Labour administration, in May 1965, it was Lord Arran who duly sought to introduce a Motion 'To call attention to the recommendations of the Wolfenden Committee on homosexual offences; and to move for Papers'. There were new men and women in power who might give legislation their blessing, and he told the Executive Committee of the Homosexual Law Reform Society that the Archbishops of Canterbury and York, and the Bishops of Ripon and Southwark, would support him and 'the Lord Chancellor and Lord Longford might ... speak. Lord Stonham (Joint Under-Secretary, Home Office) would wind up for the Government, it was hoped in an encouraging sense'. (Lord Longford, the Leader of the House of Lords, had been associated with Peter Wildeblood and Lord Montagu in establishing the New Bridge, an organisation for released prisoners, in 1956, despite his pronounced aversion to homosexuality that had been strengthened by his Catholicism. He was wont to argue, in the company of so many others, including St. Augustine, that one can hate the sin but love the sinner. He had led in the House of Lords debate on the Wolfenden Report in 1957,[221] acting, in Lord Boothby's phrase, as the 'non-playing captain of the homosexual team'[222] although he appeared to have taken no part in the 1967 debate). R.A. Butler, now Lord Butler, and Lord Devlin (who had mellowed on reform[223]) had also been approached, 'but the former would be abroad'. There would in the meanwhile be a continual supporting barrage of parliamentary questions.[224]

Newspapers shared some of his high expectation. The *Daily Mail* of 20 April 1965, for instance, reported that 'New pressure on the Government to reform the laws on homosexuality will begin in the House of Lords soon. Peers are to debate the controversial question of legalising private acts between consenting adults in view of these developments. *ONE*: Most of the Home Office Ministers, from the Lord Chancellor down, are sympathetic to a relaxation of present laws. *TWO*: Church opposition has receded. Anglican bishops are now believed to be overwhelmingly in favour of a more understanding approach'.

The familiar pattern of the progress of a private member's bill was thus about to unfold. Simultaneous action would be planned for the House of Lords, where Lord Arran would first introduce the motion and then, possibly, a bill, and for the House of Commons where the Labour MP, Leo Abse, and the Conservative MP, Christopher Chataway, now both members of the society's Executive Committee, talked of securing places in the private members' ballot to steer an identically worded bill through the House of Commons. At Christopher Chataway's suggestion, a deputation from the Homosexual Law Reform Society saw Sir Frank Soskice on 4 May before Lord Arran's motion was presented.[225] The new Home Secretary, thought Jeremy Thorpe and Norman St. John Stevas, might be asked to introduce legislation himself or, at the least, state his intentions about legislation.

But the reformers and the press had been overly optimistic. Harold Wilson was, as ever, not much interested in criminal justice reform.[226] Little palpably would change in the Home Office under Sir Frank and Lord Stonham, the Joint Parliamentary Undersecretary of State in the House of Lords, and, indeed, at first, under Sir Frank's successor, Roy Jenkins, although all three would declare themselves personally in favour of reform[227] and would vote for it when the time came. Indeed, in one Home Office file, an anonymous official had inserted an incredulous exclamation mark beside the key passages in the *Daily Mail*'s report about the support that would be forthcoming from ministers and peers.

Communications within the Home Office were cautious. It was the view of ministers that it would be best if Lord Arran withdrew his motion to avoid division and government discomfiture,[228] and, under their pressure, he did agree to do so at the very conclusion of the debate on 12 May. It was also their view that it would be best if Gerald Gardiner, the new Lord Chancellor, did not speak at all[229] (although, in the event, he was to do so). Lord Stonham's view was reported to be that 'The Lord Chancellor has very strong personal views on this subject[230] and it might be embarrassing for him to have to take part in a debate of this kind on behalf of the Government'.[231]

It is especially significant that, although Lord Stonham's own reply to the imminent speech from Lord Arran at the beginning of the session went through successive drafts, it steadfastly conveyed the position, conventional enough where reform was mooted by private members, that homosexual law reform was a matter for personal judgement[232] and that the government was neutral. But theirs was not a benevolent neutrality. Ministers wished to distance themselves from what was still quite evidently regarded as a difficult and distasteful subject; and, as a result, notes and draft speeches simply held the line and cannibalised statements made by R.A. Butler seven years before. It was suggested that Lord Stonham might open by saying:

> My Lords, whatever your views on the painful subject under discussion, it is impossible for you not to have been impressed, as I have, by the sincerity, conviction, and authority, of the speeches we have been privileged to hear [*sic*]. The great majority of us are born sound in body and mind and, because these priceless gifts are as natural as breathing, we are prone to undervalue them. Nevertheless, we are concerned for those who are broken in body or mind, and ready to give what help we can. In like manner, the great majority of us are happily heterosexual, but, in this vitally important part of life, we are not ready to help those who do not enjoy the priceless gift of normality. I think it is true of most of us, as Lord Arran said, that "we don't want to know about them." Certainly it was true of myself. I must have been remarkably lucky or exceptionally blind but, during a fairly active life among men, including 25 years participation in team games, I did not personally encounter homosexuality.

And it was further suggested that he would then repeat almost word for word some of the doubts that R.A. Butler had aired before him. Whilst he recognised that:

> not to legislate would condemn homosexuals to a life of furtiveness and ultimately neurosis and even suicide with … . a considerable risk of blackmail. … there are those who firmly believe that the present law acts as a very real deterrent to dissuade those − including many bi-sexuals − who might be tempted to experiment in homosexual behaviour from doing so, and that it provides a very real incentive to those who may have been lured into homosexual practices, to seek advice and help, to try to cure themselves of these tendencies.[233]

It was said, as was so often the case where such private member's bills were in the offing, that government support for a contentious matter could not be contemplated in the midst of a busy legislative programme and in the face of what the politicians steadfastly took to be a hostile public and a hostile and divided Parliament. Rather, in the correspondence passing within the Home Office before the 1965 debate in the House of Lords, the focus was not on applying the Wolfenden Committee's principal recommendation at all, but on concessions that might both partially mitigate the severity of the existing law and appease the campaigners. There was a question of enlarging and improving the provision of medical and psychiatric treatment to incarcerated homosexuals. There was also the possibility of continuing the *de facto* policy not only of diluting the severity but also reducing the number of prosecutions for indecency. Sir Charles Cunningham further talked of 'A compromise proposal which has received some support [and that] is that Parliament should repeal the "Labouchere Amendment" of 1885, [underlining in text by the Home Secretary] which first made indecency in private between males an offence. Such an amendment might not be so strongly opposed as the Wolfenden Committee's main recommendation, and it would considerably reduce the scope for prosecutions of homosexual conduct in private. On the other hand,' he reflected, 'it would make a distinction between one form of indecent conduct and others which would no apparent basis in logic or in morals. ... '[234] Other minor compromises, he thought, might be contemplated in due course.[235]

As was also conventional, Ministers declared that they would listen to what was said in debate and would not then stand in the way of parliamentary opinion should it be clearly expressed. They were uncommitted ('the Government would not think it right either to advise against implementation of the Wolfenden recommendation or to come out in support of it'[236]); and it was not taken at that stage to be the government's task to lead or even to ease the passage of legislation by promising extra Parliamentary time should it be called for.[237] Neither could it be assumed that there were many MPs who were willing to speak out. There was certainly not yet a strong enough case to follow the precedent established by Sydney Silverman's Murder (Abolition of Death Penalty) Bill.[238]

That was the line taken by a cautious Sir Frank Soskice when he met Lord Stonham on 26 April; at a meeting of the Cabinet Home Affairs Committee held on 30 April; and yet again in a memorandum presented to Cabinet. His own declared private preference was for reform, but there were forms, precedents and political constraints to heed (not least the much cited risk of flouting public opinion and incurring electoral disapproval[239]) and it would be better to follow the safe, formally disinterested approach set, say, by his recent response to a report on another contentious matter, that of Sunday Observance.[240] He proceeded gingerly in his search for a path between imposing what looked like an absolute veto and appearing to promote a politically barbed policy in a hostile environment: Government should, 'without giving any encouragement at all, try not to produce the impression that this is a taboo subject on which the Government mind is closed for good and all. ...'[241] That was the position he would put when he and Alice Bacon met members of the Homosexual Law Reform Society on 4 May.[242] And that was the position he put in a memorandum to cabinet submitted on the same day:

> I consider that the basic Government attitude should be that this is a matter for personal judgement; that debates of this kind serve the useful purpose of focusing public attention on the essential considerations; that the strongest opinions are at present widely held on both sides; and that the Government would not think it right either to advise against implementation of the Wolfenden recommendations or to come out in support of it. I am reluctant however to adopt a wholly neutral attitude, without offering some guidance to the growing body of opinion in favour of a change in the law on how in the Government's view a change might be brought about. For the foreseeable future Government legislation must I think be ruled out, and the question arises how far we should go in encouraging a Private Member's Bill. I think that the least that could be said would be that the appropriate course for those in Parliament who support a change in the law would be to introduce at a suitable opportunity so that Parliamentary opinion may express itself … and that while the Government could not undertake to provide time for the Bill, they would not wish to obstruct it and would be content with the decision Parliament reached on a free vote.[243]

So it came about that cabinet resolved to retain its distance from involvement at its meeting of 6 May.[244] Summed up in the shorthand notes of Sir Burke Trend, the Cabinet Secretary, the Prime Minister was reported to have said 'Treat in every way as Private Member's Bill which must take its chance in normal way…though imply that, if opinion develops, issue can always be reopened. Ministers should be free to vote in Lords'.[245] The new government's initial position was thus simply to stand back and wait and see.

It is worth reciting the form and substance of the ensuing debate on Lord Arran's motion at some length because it should make it evident that arguments were by then in the process of becoming routinised. The opponents of reform would argue, in a manner that can only be described as pre-Enlightenment, that homosexual acts were sinful, committed by predatory men, condemned by the Bible, revolting to the mass of the population and held in check chiefly by the criminal law. Proponents would, on the one hand, and also as a matter of course, profess their feelings of revulsion for homosexual conduct; but, on the other, cite the moral authority of Churches wielding arguments shaped by the Enlightenment; defend the preservation of personal liberty; and deplore the criminalisation of homosexual acts committed in private by consenting adults.

Opening his motion, Lord Arran was simple and direct and he spoke in what had become the stock rhetoric of reform. He was a Christian, he said, who was supported by the great Christian bodies,[246] and, as a Christian, he believed that 'we are persecuting a minority and we are being unjust. And these things,

I think, are unbecoming to our country'.[247] He did not condone homosexuality, but he did not think it right that the state should interfere in the publicly innocuous private lives of adults: 'If we can agree that men over 21 may do what they like together in private so long as no one else is the worse off because of it, then we have accepted the spirit of Wolfenden; and the rest, I believe, will follow. Can we accept that recommendation? Is it right or is it wrong that grown-up men with abnormal sexual desires who indulge their tastes together should be regarded as criminals and sent to prison?' The criminal law was ineffective but the social and psychological cost of its enforcement was high: homosexuals were, he said from close knowledge, obliged to live fearful lives, exposed to the risk of blackmail, and unable to seek the protection of the state.

He was followed by the Archbishop of Canterbury who deployed the same language to support Lord Arran: 'I want to start by making clear what is the moral standpoint from which I approach this question. I believe that homosexual acts are always wrong in the sense that they use in a wrong way human organs for which the right use is intercourse between men and women within marriage'. But then, equally predictably, he proceeded to the argument about personal liberty and social utility which his Church had positioned at the very centre of the debate:

> The case for altering the law in respect of homosexual acts between consenting adults in private rests, I believe, on reason and justice, and on considerations of the good of the community. As to the first, I think that there is real cogency in the plea of the Wolfenden Report that not all sins are properly given the status of crimes, not even such sins as the adulterous conduct of a man or woman, which can smash up the life of a family and bring misery to a whole family of children. If the line can reasonably be drawn anywhere, homosexual acts in private between consenting adults fall properly on the same side of the line as fornication. To say this is not to condone the wrongness of the acts, but to put them in the realm of private moral responsibility.

The Archbishop of York supported him, and citing Sydney Silverman's bill as a precedent, called on the government to allow time for debate. So too did the Bishops of Southwark[248] and Worcester. Lord Stonham replied, and he delivered the substance of his carefully prepared draft speech, beginning by talking about this, 'as I regard it, most distressing subject', and ending with a restatement of the government's neutrality:

> I must now make it crystal clear that the Government regard this as a moral issue which is essentially a matter for the personal judgement of each one of us. This Administration will not attempt to drive your consciences into one lobby or another on this issue. If a change in the law is to be made, I say frankly to your Lordships that it must be by a Private Member's Bill, with the decision left to a free vote of Parliament. The noble Earl, Lord

Arran, has not yet made his intentions known with regard to a Division: he may be deciding later in the debate. But if he does choose to divide the House on this Motion, then noble Lords on this side of the House, including Ministers, will be entirely free to vote according to their consciences.

The Liberal Leader, Lord Rea,[249] voiced his support for reform. So did Lord James of Rusholme[250] invoking John Stuart Mill. So did Baroness Gaitskell. So did the Marquess of Hertford. So did the former LSE Professor of Law, Lord Chorley, the co-signatory to the Archbishop of York's letter, who called the Wolfenden Report 'one of the most remarkable, courageous and farseeing social documents that has ever been produced by a Committee of this kind'. So did the Earl of Huntingdon, a member of the Homosexual Law Reform Society. So did a member of the Wolfenden Committee, the Marquess of Lothian. So, repeating the stock case, did Lord Francis-Williams:[251]

> I bring to this subject, as many of your Lordships also I am sure do, a natural repugnance which it is difficult to overcome. ... In so far as our knowledge of homosexuality goes – and as the most reverend Primate has already said, it does not go very far – we do not know, medical science does not know, the causes, nor has it been able to find a cure, but what does seem clear is ... it is the result of what can be called an illness. ... What we are now doing is to turn homosexuality into a secret society, with all the attractions that a secret society offers to the unbalanced young ... It is because I believe that it is immensely important that we should bring this matter out into the open that I support the noble Earl, Lord Arran, in this Motion.

What should happen next, it was said, was moot and there was to be some protracted discussion about whether Lord Arran could and should proceed to a division. The Earl's own view, contrary to the Government's wishes, was that a division would merely gauge sentiment and make a symbolic statement: 'I should be deeply sorry to have to withdraw [it]. It is couched in the most innocuous terms, and to withdraw it would seem to me rather to indicate that there was a feeling of disapproval in the House, which I do not think would correspond with the views of your Lordships. This Motion does not commit anyone to anything. It says simply that these matters are worthy of earnest consideration'. None the less he did defer to the government and agreed that there should be no vote:

> It had been my intention to ask the House to vote on my Motion – Heaven knows! it is couched in most innocuous terms – but I have been told by noble Lords who support the Motion that should be ill-advised to do so and that the terms of the Motion are such that to vote one way or the other would mean nothing. I am sorry about this. I think that a favourable vote would have been a clear message from this House, if only a

symbolic one. But I bow before the views of those wiser than myself who gave me their best advice. But, overwhelmed by the support for a change in the law as evinced by your Lordships' House this afternoon, I can say definitely that I will introduce a Private Member's Bill on this subject, and I hope that the Government will afford us the time and facilities. I would say squarely that the Government's reputation for genuine belief in social reform is at stake; and I hope that they will carry out their very clear obligations'.

The Lords present had favoured reform. No judges had spoken. Lords Kilmuir and Dilhorne, both hostile to change, had been silent. Of the 22 speakers in the five-hour long debate, 17, including two bishops and the two archbishops, had spoken in favour of the motion, and they had dominated the floor. No bishop had opposed the motion. The Bishops of Birmingham, Bristol, Exeter, London and St. Albans, unable to attend the debate, had published a letter in *The Times* on the previous day to signal their support for Lord Arran.[252] On a very rough count, just over half the time taken up in the debate was given over to speeches in favour of the motion; a third to speeches which were neutral or chiefly centred on procedural matters; and only an eighth to speeches which opposed the motion. The Deputy Speaker, Lord Jessel,[253] observed that 'In 1957, I recollect, there were several strong speeches against the Wolfenden recommendation, while to-day, certainly up to now, the majority of the speeches have been in favour of it'. Change seemed to be stirring. Lord Jessel continued:

I say quite frankly that in urging for this change in the law we are much more likely to get a sympathetic hearing from the present Government than we did from the previous Administration. The noble Earl the Leader of the House [Lord Longford] is well known for his interest in social misfits and down-and-outs. The noble and learned Lord Chancellor [Lord Gardiner] has campaigned for years for many kinds of law reform, and I hope that he will add this to his list. I feel sure that the change in the law is bound to come one day: but unless some Government are prepared to take positive action, or, as has been suggested, to give their blessing to a Private Bill, we may be having the same debate in another eight years' time.

The Lord Chancellor, Lord Gardiner, concluded in the neutral tone in which Lord Stonham had begun:

Any Member of Parliament is at liberty to introduce a Bill. I understand that in another place a Bill is about to be introduced. There is nothing whatever to stop any Member of your Lordships' House from introducing a Bill tomorrow. If that is done the Government are not prepared to give Government time for it, but they will not impede it in any way, and it will be a really free vote in which everybody, including Ministers, can vote as their consciences may dictate'.

Quite why the debate had taken that new tack is not self-evident, but a number of matters are suggestive. Opponents were absent or were quiet, keeping their powder dry. The Church was once again a Church Militant, as it was in the parallel campaigns of the time. Indeed, it had itself engendered the arguments that were so busily being put to work in the promotion of reform. It continually lent strength to Lord Arran – for example, in encouraging him by its actions to move on to the next stage of presenting a bill, and I have argued that the moral authority and the organisational competence of the Church could be quite crucial to the affairs of the House of Lords when it discussed difficult moral matters at the time.

Whilst there had been no organisation actively campaigning for reform in 1957, the Homosexual Law Reform Society had appeared in the intervening few years to attain some authority in fashioning and promoting a new public face for homosexuality. Lord Arran was able to call it 'that most learned and respectable body';[254] and both archbishops referred to the arguments it adduced (although the Archbishop of Canterbury was not wholly persuaded by every point that it made[255]).

And the result was that the framing of the problem of homosexuality jointly constructed by the Wolfenden Committee, the Homosexual Law Reform Society and significant portions of the Church and the medical profession had been honed, simplified and consolidated in the adversarial dialectics of Parliamentary debate. It worked well enough and was for the most part taken for granted by many, if only for a while.[256] It had become the standard, tried, approved and almost mechanical way of talking about the problem in many quarters. It did not demand fresh reflection each time it was applied. It was deployed by men and women of every sexuality. At a time when, some criminologists and sociologists would say, deviance was becoming medicalised,[257] the new and perhaps occasionally artful[258] typification of the unfortunate and unenviable man who was to varying degrees ill;[259] who needed compassion, protection and, possibly, treatment rather than punishment;[260] an emotionally disordered[261] man who practised abominable acts but who could not be blamed for them because he did not choose his sexuality;[262] someone who was quite different from the rest of us but nevertheless a potentially useful member of the community; enabled difficult, contradictory and indeed dangerous representations to be reconciled, consolidated and defended in a pragmatic synthesis without incurring outrage or the speaker's public shame or embarrassment. It brought about a severance of the sinner from the sin. And, most important perhaps, it protected the reformer and the reform from moral and political reproach.[263]

In effect, what had happened was part of a definitional transformation that amounted to what Joseph Gusfield, in his analysis of a similar process touching on drinking and the drinker, called a 'moral passage' from arguments centred on the 'enemy deviant' to others focused on the 'sick deviant'. And what distinguishes the sick deviant, Gusfield observed, is that 'Defining a behavior pattern as one caused by illness makes a hostile response toward the actor illegitimate and inappropriate'.[264] One might not care for homosexual men but it became rather more difficult to vilify them. Forty years later, and using slightly different language, criminologists would talk about the drift to what Garland called 'penal welfarism'[265] and Dario Melossi the shift from evil deviant to victim deviant (although one might question his addition of the idea of 'vicinity'):

> In the situation characterized by a tendency to exclusion, we may observe ... that criminologists (*as well as* public opinion *and* "aesthetic" productions, not to mention politics) assume an attitude of distance or antipathy toward the criminal: the deviant is the producer of evil ..., social order is represented as a given order that is to be established or re-established ... In the situation characterized instead by a drive to include, criminologists (as well as public opinion and fictional accounts) tend to assume an attitude of vicinity or sympathy toward the criminal: the deviant is seen as in some sense a victim of society ...[266]

The Lords' response to Lord Arran's motion could register no more than formal recognition of the chief recommendation of the Wolfenden Report. There had been no vote. There had been little criticism and no discussion about how the report could or should be implemented. That would demand a bill, and a bill was indeed introduced for first reading the very next day,[267] and for second reading twelve days later. It was all quite remarkably rapid. The churchman and peer, the Right Reverend Lord Sanford, wrote on 17 May 1965, five days after the debate, 'I did not realise ... that Lord Arran would move so quickly to introduce his bill ... I expect he was encouraged by the strong support he had from the bishops' bench!'[268]

The new bill was plain enough, an embodiment of the central Wolfenden proposal.[269] It would 'amend the law of England and Wales relating to homosexual acts. Para 1(1): Notwithstanding any statutory or common law provision, a homosexual act in private shall not be an offence provided that the parties consent thereto and have attained the age of 21 years. (2) The commission of any such act when more than two persons are present shall not be deemed to be in private'. It was, said Lord Arran, 'a Bill in its earliest and most unvarnished form; a Bill which, to judge by the number of speakers, has stimulated interest, some of it far from favourable'.[270]

It was certainly thought too unvarnished by some. The proposed legislation, the government was to say, was poorly drafted. In the speech prepared for him – but never actually delivered – Lord Stonham was invited to pronounce, certainly ironically (although his intention is not made pellucidly clear): 'Today we are debating a Bill and let me at once say it is a shockingly drafted Bill. Because my Lords IT IS SIMPLE; IT IS CLEAR; AND IT IS SHORT. No reputable Parliamentary draughtsman would have allowed a measure to emerge in a form which a child could understand. It must be full of legal loopholes. I do not intend to examine these because they will be matters for your consideration'[271] [capitalisation in the original]. That ironic tone disappeared somewhat when Ministers did decide to give assistance with drafting after the committee stage in July 1965.[272] The First Parliamentary Counsel was at that point instructed that 'The Wolfenden recommendations ... have never received detailed critical examination in the Home Office with a view to their implementation in legislation, and as so often happens in the case of such recommendations they simply fall to pieces in the hand in ... instances when one attempts to recast them in the form of definite instructions'.[273]

Those who had opposed legal change as members of the previous Conservative Government were led to believe that the bill's wording gave them ample scope to do so again, and they raised a scatter of objections (some of which were dismissed as 'nonsense' by Home Office officials[274]). Lord Dilhorne would have exempted sodomy and attempted sodomy from the new bill (Parliamentary counsel's judgement was that that exemption would have no basis in morals or logic[275]). Peers issued repeated warnings about hazards to the morale, proper relations[276] and good order of the armed forces (and, Lord Kilmuir pointed out, of the police and prison service as well[277]) that would arise should the law be changed; and they were warnings that demanded intense consultations with the Ministry of Defence (all the armed forces were consulted[278] but, in the event, Parliamentary Counsel made it clear that they would be exempted from the bill[279]). Similar problems, it was said, might arise in the merchant navy,[280] and the 'seafarers' unions and shipowners ... [were reported to have] expressed deep concern about [its] likely effects ... if it becomes law ...'[281] What of English ships sailing out of Scottish ports where homosexual acts remained criminal – would the new law apply to their crews? What of homosexual relations between passengers and crew? There were uncertainties about how many people needed to be present to transform a private occasion into a public one (Lord Dilhorne, it was reported, 'is worried about the homosexual orgy and takes the view that a homosexual act can be committed between more than two persons at the same time'[282]). There were anxieties voiced by the preceding Lord Chief Justice, Lord Goddard, and the preceding Lord Chancellor, Lord Kilmuir, about what they called 'buggers' clubs' and 'sodomitic societies' although the Director of Public Prosecutions claimed that the Metropolitan Police had found no evidence at all of their existence after the war.[283] There were uncertainties about the issue of consent where a 'defective' or a mentally disordered person was involved.[284] There were questions raised about whether the age of consent in homosexual relations should be 25 instead of 21.

The motion had been discussed without much rancour, but the later debate on the bill itself was fierce (at the very outset, Lord Byers,[285] the former Chairman of the Liberal Party, commented presciently '17 out of the 22 speakers in that debate were in favour of reform. Looking at the names of to-day's speakers I do not suppose that we shall have quite such a favourable ratio'). Lord Arran was in consequence obliged to try to forestall some of what was to come. One area of weakness foreseen would be the corruption of members of the armed forces, but 'the [Wolfenden] Committee pointed to Section 66 of

the Army Act, 1955, which provides for the punishment of disgraceful conduct, or conduct of an unnatural kind'. Another area would be the corruption
of the young:

> What are the things that are likely, in particular, to irk and disturb your
> Lordships? There is, first of all, the question of youth, of young people.
> It may be suggested, that the Bill disregards young people, inasmuch as
> it makes no mention of them. My Lords, it makes no mention of them
> because it in no way weakens or alters the present law in regard to their
> protection. For an older man sexually to interfere with a youth under
> the age of 21 would remain a criminal offence. The Bill does not say this
> because it does not need to be said ...

There then followed a straightforward confrontation between irreconcilable
representations, between the newly established image of the homosexual as
vulnerable, ill, wretched and unfortunate, the compound image sired jointly
by medicine, the liberal theology of the Church of England and the apologetics
of the Homosexual Law Reform Society; and the older image of the enemy
seducer, the predator, who exercised moral choice for the bad; and it was the
former typification, relayed repeatedly and intact, which held sway with the
greater number of peers. Lord Byers supported the bill: 'I do not believe ...
that it can be right to subject a substantial number of our fellow citizens to the
misery and degradation they suffer to-day because, in the eyes of the majority of us, they are not just different but abnormal'. The former Labour Prime
Minister, Clement Attlee, talked of his experience at the Bar and the persua-
siveness of the Wolfenden Committee: 'I believe it is false to imagine that
doing away with this matter as a criminal offence will in any way extend the
evil. I profoundly believe that the evil is mainly a matter of physical condition;
it is a matter of misfortune rather than crime'. Lord Francis-Williams said: 'All
the evidence suggests that those who are affected by homosexual tendencies
are so affected for physical and psychological reasons, of which we do not
know the cause and for which we do not know the cure; and that, on the
whole, when they have reached the age 21 and beyond they are, poor, unfortunate, creatures, set in their habits and cannot change them: and they cannot
change them because we do not know whether there is any cure or any way in
which this condition can be altered. We have to legislate in the world as it is;
in a world in which the vast majority of people follow ordinary normal sexual
lives, and only a comparatively small unfortunate minority is homosexual'. The
Marquess of Queensberry, the descendant of the man who had engineered the
fall of Oscar Wilde, said:

> I do not think that [homosexual men] are in any way more depraved or
> immoral than either myself, or any other normal man of my acquaint-
> ance. They came slowly to realise in early manhood what they were, not
> through any particular influence of which they were aware. They are

unable to explain why it should have been their lot to develop in this way, and I suggest to your Lordships that neither psychologists nor doctors are able to explain this, either. It would seem that it is much more to do with genetic predisposition and environment in early childhood, than it is to do with corruption at an impressionable age. ... I would suggest that the best possible solution, for society and for [the homosexual man], is that he has the opportunity to lead a quiet ordered life, finding, if he must, sexual satisfaction with another adult man. Yet at the moment this is exactly what our law denies to him.

The Bishop of Chichester said:

> We must, of course, continue to assert, as one of the most reverend Primates did, that homosexual acts are always in principle wrong. There is no intention on our part ... that we should appear to be condoning such conduct. ... But we must also assert that the law relating to private homosexual conduct between consenting adults does grave injustice to a large number of individuals. It is productive of much misery. It produces a squalid underworld of suspicion and fear. It leads to blackmail. It leads often enough to the tragedy of suicide.

Advancing the theme of medicalisation, the bishop also sought to introduce the stipulation about reports which Leo Abse had demanded in his failed bill: 'when a person under the age of 21 is found guilty of a homosexual offence, the court should be required to obtain a psychiatric report before sentence is passed. It is, in fact, for the inclusion within this bill of safeguards in respect of those under 21 for which we most strongly press'. The homosexual Bishop of Southwark, donning the breastplate of righteousness,[286] defensively condemning in public what he practised in private, said:

> I am not appealing to sentiment: I am appealing to reason. Here are people who are born like this, who become like this. We must try to help them. Time and time again, as one has heard their story, one has been, to put it frankly, revolted. ... [but] my reaction has been, I have said, "I am a pastor, and it is my job to help, so that they may win back their self-respect and play their part usefully in society".

The Home Office Minister, Lord Stonham, again emphasised that the issue was a divisive, cross-party matter of conscience on which strong feelings prevailed.[287] The government was formally neutral but he himself could no longer be neutral ('to avoid inflicting any more pain on your Lordships or myself, I shall conceal my personal views no longer. If it comes to a Division, I intend to vote for the noble Earl's Bill'). He supported Lord Arran's case that the corruption of minors would not be affected by the bill; that the Services would not be affected ('Service law creates offences and it could, if necessary, be used to deal with this matter irrespective of your Lordships' decision on this particular Bill'); and he flagged the fact that the existing law was manifestly ineffective ('Last year, the total of prosecutions for all homosexual offences, whether in public or private and whether committed against an adult or minor, was 1,300, out of we know not how many scores of thousands. The conviction rate is only a fraction of one per cent. I hope your Lordships, whether you support or oppose the main Wolfenden recommendation, will agree with me that this situation, is manifestly unsatisfactory').

But the image of the homosexual as enemy deviant had not been wholly exorcised. Lord Montgomery of Alamein, the former Field Marshal, did not heed Lord Arran's (or the Defence Minister, Lord Shackleton's[288]) reassurance about the corruption of youth and the armed services. Neither did he accept that homosexuality was not immoral:

> To condone unnatural offences in male persons over 21, or, indeed, in male persons of any age, seems to me utterly wrong. One may just as well condone the Devil and all his works. I am entirely opposed to this Bill ... My main reason is that a weakening of the law will strike a blow at all those devoted people who are working to improve the moral fibre of the youth of this country. ... The fighting men of Britain have been my comrades-in-arms for over half a century. What is the greatest single factor making for success in battle, or for efficient and well-trained Armed Forces in peace? It is morale. And what is the very foundation of morale? It is discipline. If these unnatural practices are made legal, a blow is struck at the discipline of British Armed Forces at a time when we need the very highest standard of morale and discipline, with those forces serving throughout the world.

Lord Kilmuir, the man who had deplored the unwholesome publicity attached to the prosecution of homosexual men, the man who, as David Maxwell Fyfe, the Home Secretary, had appointed the Wolfenden Committee in the hope that it would discover ways of dealing with that iniquity, insisted that the criminal law was vital to the enforcement of sexual morality, and that a decriminalised homosexuality would 'have a respectability that it never had before ... toleration of actions of lying and cruelty and indecency can never be right'. Homosexuals in the main were weak men 'who were simply not standing up to wickedness'. Lord Goddard, the former Lord Chief Justice, would not dismiss the enemy deviant either: 'I think I have to approach this subject with the view ... that homosexuality is not the result of a disease or of any illness or anything of that sort. You have to take those who practise it as being as responsible as any others who come before the courts'. Lord Rowallan, the former Chief Scout of the British Commonwealth and Empire, again not heeding what Lord Annan had said, quoted the Memorandum to the Wolfenden Committee produced by the Standing Conference of National Voluntary Youth Organisations: 'We are bound to uphold the position that our young members must be protected against sin and perversion and must also he fortified to overcome them if they meet them'. And Lord Dilhorne, the former attorney general and Lord Chancellor, said: 'if we give a Second Reading to this Bill to-night I cannot help but think that there will be many young people who will think that homosexuality is not as bad a sin as they were led to suppose'.

After some three hours' debate, Lord Arran's bill passed on second reading by 94 votes to 49 and was next expected to proceed to Third Reading in the House of Lords on 28 October. A number of the bishops who had spoken did not vote. Neither did the two archbishops. But four bishops did vote 'content' and none voted 'not content'.

Ministers had anticipated popular and Parliamentary opposition to the bill. But the peers had proved unexpectedly sympathetic, and the bishops had been exceptionally so (it was noted in one newspaper that the bill had 'won a majority in the House of Lords, with episcopal blessings'[289]). New polls showed that the public were becoming more inclined to reform.[290] Following convention, the government began formally to be drawn in, agreeing after second reading to aid peers, in particular the Archbishop of Canterbury and Lord Chorley, with the drafting of amendments ('It seems difficult to refuse these requests', said Brian Cubbon in a submission to Home Office Ministers, 'If the amendments were privately revised, it is almost certain that Lord Stonham would have to point out drafting objections on Report, and it is hardly dignified for the House to be frustrated in this way when its wishes were made known at the Committee stage'[291]). Brian Cubbon further noted that 'There is no possibility of its being passed during the current session as it has not yet been to the Commons, but it is expected that a similar Bill will be re-introduced next Session'.[292]

Ministers had evidently been taken somewhat aback. Still a little wary, a nevertheless sympathetic Lord Stonham noted that:

> I am certain that the support for Lord Arran on Third Reading will be just as strong and quite possibly stronger than it was at the earlier stages and that the Government will be pressed very heavily by ... peers on the lines that refusal to provide facilities has the same result as the positive obstructions of the previous Government. In the light of previous decisions I shall not be able to respond positively but I hope that I may say that the Government has been impressed by the arguments which have been presented, that it shares the view that if at all possible it is desirable for these important matters to be considered by both Houses of Parliament and that I will report the views expressed to you. I would of course add that the order of business in the House of Commons is a matter entirely for that House ... If the debate runs the way I expect and the public opinion polls show that there is more public sympathy for reform than had previously been believed I think we should go back to the Cabinet for authority to provide facilities for discussing this Bill when it is re-introduced in the

next session. The time is not now appropriate for such an approach and it may well be that we could not provide time until the session after next but I do not think we can maintain neutrality indefinitely. The surprisingly strong support Lord Arran has received in the Lords and the unexpected result of the public opinion poll create a new situation which justifies reconsidering the Government's attitude.[293]

Lord Arran's Bill moved to Committee Stage, the first of a series of debates on amendments being held on 21 June and the last on 16 July, where once again the government declared itself neutral. At that first debate, which had by now become utterly standardised and repetitive, Lord Dilhorne would have changed the bill to exempt sodomy, thereby restricting the bill to a repeal of the 1885 Act. He asked 'Are there not some forms of conduct so abominable in themselves and such an affront to decency that the State, whose function it is, as the Wolfenden Report recognises, to preserve public order and decency, should regard and treat them as criminals?'[294] Lord Arran's reply again combined a routine profession of his aversion for the sin with the utilitarian's wish for a Benthamite consistency, rationality and enforceability in a civilised legal system: 'We are being asked to say that homosexual practices shall remain a crime if they affect a certain part of the human body. To sexually normal people, as has been pointed out, the whole thing is unattractive enough; but to discriminate in this way, to say that one area is permissible and another is not, seems to me to be carrying one's instinctive physical distaste to an absurdity which is unbecoming in a civilised age'. The Archbishop of Canterbury again echoed the form of that argument precisely: 'I do not subtract one whit from the sense of the abominableness of it; yet it is impossible to distinguish between the abominableness of various kinds of homosexual actions, and I do not really think it makes for morality when there is embodied in the criminal law a distinction that is not really a rational moral distinction'. And Lord Kilmuir, a member of the Church of Scotland, retorted just as routinely with an argument couched in an older Biblical teaching: 'I know that my own country [of Scotland] has always been accused of attaching too great an importance to the Old Testament. I hope that I do not, but I would say that in my view it would be a great pity if the impression were to be created that the teaching and moral standards of the Old Testament are wrong simply because they occur in the Old Testament'.

Paradoxically, then, and just as had been the case in the bill's second reading, where the Church had invoked science, personal liberty and the sovereignty of reason, where it declared that it was not the business of the state to trample on what grown men did in private,[295] and where the archbishop lauded rationality in the criminal law,[296] the criminal lawyer turned to the Old Testament to condemn wrongdoing.

Lord Dilhorne's amendment was defeated by 86 votes to 52. Four bishops, including the Archbishop of Canterbury, voted against it. None voted for it. They had, in effect, been whipped just as they had been in the debates about capital punishment.[297]

The bill trundled on to a third reading that had been fatally postponed to 28 October because of the pressure of other government business, including the extended time afforded the passage of the debates on 'a long and complex'[298] criminal justice bill, penal reform, abortion and capital punishment. It was then fought 'without quarter' by a minority of peers, led by the 'patently fuming'[299] Lord Dilhorne, who engaged in what was equivalent to a renewed personal duel with the Archbishop of Canterbury about what he called 'this unsavoury subject'. Little new was said. Just as had been the case with the debates about the abolition of the death penalty, argument had become monotonous and stylised (Lord Dilhorne himself remarked that 'We have heard to-day a repetition of arguments which have been advanced before, seldom anything fresh …'). The third reading was passed by 96 votes to 31 votes, but it was a Pyrrhic result because the bill 'was doomed to extinction'[300] when the session ended the following week. It may have passed all its stages but it had to die with the session (Lord Arran reflected that 'one is tempted to wonder whether we should not give up and whether this Bill, even if it is approved, by your Lordships to-day … will not completely disappear'[301]). Supported by the Earl of Swinton, Lord Annan and the Bishop of St. Albans,[302] he then made a plea to the government that it should:

> most earnestly … face the position, which is this: here we have a Bill for homosexual law reform based on the Wolfenden Report. It was approved by the House of Lords, the Upper House of Parliament, on Second Reading by a majority of nearly two to one. It was considered at great length in Committee and on Report, and amended in detail but in no way weakened. It had the approval of the senior ecclesiastics of the Established Church of England, and of other great and good men in your Lordships' House. Doctors, school masters and sociologists among your Lordships have spoken in favour of it. It has been regarded indulgently even by those news papers which in the past were most violently against reform. Last and newest, and most important of all perhaps, it has, seemingly, the support of the people. … Will the Government not, if only as a courtesy, grant us the simple thing for which we ask – namely, time and facilities in the other place? They gave them, after all, to that other measure of social reform, the abolition of hanging, even though the opinion polls were two to one against abolition and the number of people actually hanged annually since the 1957 Act was passed have been under a dozen, whereas to-day we are talking in terms of hundreds of thousands. Will they not give us these same facilities, too?

Lord Stonham had originally been armed with a defensive reply in which he would have explained why the government had 'not sponsored this Bill and assured its passage'. He was primed to say that 'There is, I suppose, no issue which more deeply divides those who are concerned with the Criminal Law than the relationship which ought to exist between the Criminal Law and the accepted morality of the community... The reform in the law which we are now considering epitomises that moral challenge. ... [the issue was] essentially one which must be decided in a way which requires no one to act against his own moral feelings and conscience'. He was supposed too to justify the government's decision not to cede extra Parliamentary time: 'you will also appreciate the overwhelming difficulties which face those responsible for organising business in another place ... '[303] Yet, when the moment actually came, he again departed from that draft and from that noncommittal stance. His own sympathies were for reform, and it seems that he had listened to what had been said and noted how sentiment had changed. He became a little more encouraging:

> This subject is the very essence of a Bill for a Private Member and not for a Government. It would to me be quite remarkable if a Member of another place, fortunate in the Ballot, could not be found to sponsor it. Meanwhile, I will report the views of your Lordships' House to my right honourable friend the Home Secretary. I will also draw his attention to the other developments which have been illustrated in this debate. Since we last considered this issue there appears to have been a change, and I hope personally that, if it is possible to introduce the Bill, its progress will not be unduly delayed.

In the event, it was not to be Leo Abse or Christopher Chataway or any other politician connected with the Homosexual Law Reform Society, but the Conservative Member for Lancaster, Humphrey Berkeley, who won a second place in the ballot in the new session in November 1965 and proposed to sponsor the private member's bill that Lord Stonham had presaged. 'I was', he said, 'determined to use the occasion, which guaranteed a certain and early debate, for an important social measure'[304] and it was the implementation of the Wolfenden recommendation that, with the encouragement of the Archbishop of Canterbury, he chose. Although he offers no record of the precise reason why he did so, it is not difficult to suppose what he was thinking. He was homosexual himself [305] (the new Home Secretary, Roy Jenkins, reflected that 'He was gay and in many ways, the lobby, certainly Grey, would have preferred him' to Leo Abse[306]). Lord Arran's bill had only just failed for want of time; and it was Lord Arran's bill that he 'picked up'[307] and adopted word for word for steering through the House of Commons[308] (Lord Stonham would later comment that 'he did so without altering a single comma. ... they did not even correct the misprint'[309]).

Humphrey Berkeley wrote to the Home Secretary on 30 December 1965 seeking to enlist his help whilst, he said, understanding the restraints under which he laboured ('although I recognise that your Department's attitude must be at best one of benevolent neutrality I nevertheless believe that the guidance given by a senior member of the Government on this issue, could prove to be decisive'[310]). Roy Jenkins' reply five days later was conventional enough: 'it is not possible for me at this stage to give any undertaking as to what the Government's attitude is likely to be. However, you … can … take it that I shall give very careful consideration to the Bill's objectives when it appears…'[311] All the same, when the time did come, and in contrast to his predecessor, Sir Frank Soskice, the 'timid abstentionist',[312] he *did* intervene, and he did so decisively. He had, quite remarkably for the times, made an unambiguous case for homosexual law reform in *The Labour Case*,[313] published in 1959, and he argued it again when he entered office. Much later, he would look back at *The Labour Case* and quote himself on the dual standards and pusillanimity of the times:

> "The law relating to homosexuality remains in the brutal and unfair state in which the House of Commons almost accidentally placed it in 1885," was my next complaint. This was made worse by the fact that the clear recommendation of the Wolfenden Committee on the point had been ignored, while its much more vague proposals about prostitutes had been implemented in a way that considerably increased police power. Furthermore there was the hypocrisy that the leading members of previous governments applied no social disapproval to homosexual conduct which, for public consumption, they insist[ed] on keeping subject to the full rigours of the criminal law. …[314]

He was to become what he called a 'definitely benevolent neutral',[315] amending in his own hand a key phrase in the wording of a draft memorandum of 12 January 1966 to the Home Affairs Committee from 'it would be right, in view of the votes in the Lords and the apparent acceptance by a substantial proportion of public opinion that the law needs amendment, that our neutrality should be *reasonably benevolent*' to '*definitely benevolent*'[316] [my italics]. And he put that phrase to work in his own new wording of the draft: 'the Government's attitude to the principle of Mr Berkeley's Bill should be one of definitely benevolent neutrality and … drafting assistance should be provided at this stage for this purpose and for possible technical amendments; and later on for any amendments which would seem to be generally welcome and unobjectionable on policy grounds'.[317] The final version was submitted to the Home Affairs Committee on 18 January: the bill, Roy Jenkins repeated, had passed all its stages in the Lords, public opinion polls suggested that a majority in the country was now in favour of a change in the law, and the government should help with its drafting.[318] The Home Affairs Committee were not disposed wholeheartedly to support him (they 'thought that the Home Secretary should avoid giving the impression that the Government as such were in favour of the amendment of the law'[319]), but he persevered nonetheless.

Humphrey Berkeley's bill had already had its first reading in the House of Lords,[320] the Home Office had honoured its promise to assist with drafting, and the parliamentarians in the Homosexual Law Reform Society stirred themselves yet again into mustering those Members who might be sympathetic on Second Reading on 11 February 1966,[321] just as its opponents were stirring themselves with 'fury' and 'righteous indignation'[322] to resist what was identified, in a letter signed by the Members of Parliament, James Dance[323] and Sir Charles Taylor,[324] as a bill in 'favour of homosexuality'.[325]

Little would be new in what came next, the two opposing arguments having become frozen. The enemy deviant was once again set against the sick deviant. The reformers invoked the Church, medicine and reason. Their antagonists, not being able to cite the Church, turned to the bible of the Old Testament, the general will and popular morality. Towards the end, Christopher Chataway would reflect that 'It would have been surprising if during the course of this afternoon's debate many new arguments had been deployed. After all, it is eight years since the Wolfenden Committee reported'.

In his opening speech, Humphrey Berkeley, a homosexual and a practising Roman Catholic, was constrained, willingly or unwillingly, artfully or disingenuously, to resort to the stock iconography of the reform movement:[326]

> On the evidence available … the vast number of homosexuals … passionately wanted to be heterosexual and disliked intensely their own physical condition. As far as one can see from the evidence, it seems likely that their condition was in-born rather than the result of corruption, and the degree of proselytisation about which we have heard so much appears to have been greatly over-estimated. Those of us in the House who are practising members of the Christian faith – and I regard myself as one – are faced with something of a problem. All of us who are Christians, and probably many who are not, regard homosexual acts as morally wrong. On the other hand, all of us who are Christians, and many others, equally must have a feeling of compassion and justice for a minority of the population who find themselves in a condition for which they have no responsibility.

The bill, he said, 'implements in almost precise detail various recommendations of the Wolfenden Committee'. Homosexual acts in private between consenting adults should no longer be crimes. Those under 21 would still need the defence of the law ('If, as would appear to be the case, the homosexual condition is a form of emotional retardedness – and this is the most accurate description one can put on it – people who are vulnerable to pressures during adolescence must be protected'). The Churches remained adamant that such acts were sinful ('One of the objects of the Bill is to cease to make these offences a crime, while recognising, as all Christians must, that they are grave sins'). But the Churches wanted reform ('I understand that every major Christian body takes that view. Certainly every bishop who spoke and voted on this matter voted in favour of reform …'). The law was unenforced and unenforceable, arbitrary and discriminatory, although it still exposed homosexual men to the risk of blackmail. Reform was a matter of compassion and tolerance for the unfortunate: 'To those people who are, as it were, irreconcilable in their opposition to this Measure, I would say that I hope that they will thank God each day of their lives that they do not belong to this 5 per cent. of people who are exclusively attracted to their own sex, and who have, as far as we know, a normal sex urge'. The mood of the country was now more forbearing. Where once the criminalisation of homosexuality had been universally defended, there had been a change in political and public opinion – both Gallup and National Opinion[327] polls showing some 60% of the electorate now favouring reform.[328]

The ensuing arguments had been frequently rehearsed. George Strauss, the Labour Member for Vauxhall, argued that 'Nobody denies that a homosexual is a homosexual through no fault of his own. He is either born that way through some accident of genes or has become a homosexual through environment in his early life. If anybody denies that, he has the whole weight of the authority of psychiatrists against him. Homosexuals do not voluntarily give up the warmth and happiness of marriage, the conjugal home and the joy of children. It is not through choice that they are homosexuals'. Leo Abse asked:

> Have those blessed with the emotional security of a full, heterosexual life the right to demand total and permanent abstinence from those whose terrible fate it is to be homosexuals? ... I do not find it surprising as a result that in such a climate of opinion so many homosexuals lapse into near-paranoia. I do not find it surprising that they behave, as so many do, when they are put outside the community. I do not find it so surprising that they react, as many of them do, in such an anti-social manner. With all their original feelings of guilt, reinforced, as they must be, by our brutal laws, is it surprising that they sometimes protect their self-esteem by absurdly proclaiming their intellectual and artistic superiority to those who are mere heterosexuals?

Also electing to don the breastplate of righteousness, a homosexual Norman St. John Stevas[329] said:

> We know that a sizeable proportion of the population, through no fault of their own, are attracted sexually only to members of their own sex. This is not a question of diabolical lust. It is a question of misplaced affections and misplaced sexual drives. Some are capable of a degree of self-control, some are capable of a degree of self-sacrifice and sublimation, but most people in this situation are not. This is a fact which we have to face, and in this situation the law must be practical. It is not the function of the law to enforce every virtue or to forbid every vice. ... by making a change in the law one does not give moral approval to the homosexual. We are simply saying that criminal sanctions are inappropriate to deal with this subject. We are saying that it must be treated as adultery, fornication, and other sexual sins are treated. ... While we are right to condemn homosexuality as being morally wrong in the objective sense, we must realise, first of all,

that subjectively the moral guilt in the homosexual is much reduced, and we should take that into account.

The arguments against reform had also become rehearsed. There were those who claimed that the supporters of the bill did not speak for the mass of the population: Frank Tomney,[330] the Labour Member for Hammersmith North, said 'the Bill is signed by those who, in my opinion, have never had to lead the life of the ordinary people. The people who matter most are the ordinary people outside, the mums and dads carrying the responsibilities of society and of rearing this country's citizens. ... if we take off the checks and the balances of society at this moment we shall ask for trouble; and we shall certainly get it'. There were those who claimed that the criminal law was an important bulwark against moral decline: an adamantine William Shepherd asserted that 'Let us remember that the veneer of civilisation is incredibly thin. Certainly animal sexual behaviour which is physically directed, as ours is not, is less susceptible of variation'. Sir Cyril Osborne,[331] rejecting the image of the hapless homosexual, talked about the exercise of moral choice: 'I cannot accept the argument that homosexuals cannot help themselves; that they are born that way. I just do not accept it. I was brought up a Victorian by a very stern, puritan, Victorian father who taught me that we can do anything if we are sufficiently determined. I believe that organised society is not possible unless we can exercise self-control, and the Government have a duty on behalf of the majority to see that the minority who will not exercise self-control are controlled and, if necessary, are punished for not so doing'. Sir Cyril Black[332] talked about sin. He deprecated this 'debatable and unpleasant subject' and his 'duty [to discuss it] from which many of us would quite naturally shrink'. But to support the bill was to support evil:

> The Bible declares uncompromisingly that the wages of sin is death. In the case of the offences with which the Bill deals it is particularly true, involving, as these practices do, death to that which is most valuable in the body, the mind and the soul... I know nothing, or very little, about what is called buggery, but from what I do know about it I hate it and I dislike it. It is time that someone spoke from my point of view as a straightforward, simple square. I am rather tired of democracy being made safe for the pimps, the prostitutes, the spivs, the pansies and now, the queers. It is high time that we ordinary squares had some public attention and our point of view listened to.

And he prophesied:

> I do not believe that the Government will find Parliamentary time to see this Bill on to the Statute Book, even if we pass it today. The Parliamentary time-table is already overcrowded, so much so that the Government have rightly said, after great consideration, "We are sorry. We cannot carry on with the Steel Bill. We do not have the time"'.

The bill was given its second reading by 164 votes to 107.[333] For the very first time, the House of Commons had voted in favour of homosexual law reform. Humphrey Berkeley was triumphant, declaring that 'I am more proud of introducing the Sexual Offences Bill than of anything else that I did or said in six and a half years as a Member of the House of Commons'.[334] But Sir Cyril Black had been prescient. Parliamentary time would expire. With a majority of four, the government was weak; there was early talk of it falling;[335] an anxious monitoring of the auguries in a by-election in late January in Hull North;[336] and a general election that was proclaimed on 28 February, a mere seventeen days after the bill's second reading, to take place on 31 March. Even before the government decided that it would go to the nation, the Home Affairs Committee had persuaded Roy Jenkins[337] that the bill could be ceded no extra time.[338] Parliament was accordingly dissolved on 10 March; Members of Parliament ceased constitutionally to exist;[339] and 'all Private Members' Bills of this year, 1965–66, [were] lost',[340] including, to the delight of some,[341] Humphrey Berkeley's bill, a 'casualty of the General Election'.[342]

Yet a headwind had been created. The Labour Party was returned with a much larger majority of 98; there was an intake of new and possibly even more liberal Members of Parliament; and the campaign for reform did not die. There would be yet another attempt made that year, amounting to yet another last big push. On 10 May, Lord Annan reintroduced his bill in the House of Lords,[343] and Leo Abse, working in tandem, asked for enough time to ensure its proper consideration should it come before the House of Commons. Because the election had been called in March, there could be no private members' ballot until November, and, when it was eventually held, no eligible Member of the House of Commons wished to promote homosexual law reform.[344] The conditions for any likely progression of the reform therefore remained difficult and the government at first remained discouraging,[345] but then Roy Jenkins stepped in. He was said to have proposed that 'the Government should take a neutral line, tempered by an undertaking that, if there appears to be a general wish that a Private Member's Bill on the subject should be discussed and this could not be done unless the Government made time available, the Government would consider providing such time ...'[346] He summoned Leo Abse to assure him 'that if I could gain a decisive vote when, under the ten-minute-rule procedure, I was to ask leave to introduce the Bill, he would insist at Cabinet level for government time to be given to me. He was to prove as good as his word ...'[347]

In the meanwhile, the bill had gone back to a House of Lords whose arguments had grown stale (the Bishop of St. Albans complained that 'your Lordships' House [has had to] return to debating a Bill in regard to which the great majority of your Lordships have already, I suspect, made up your minds'[348]). Decisions reached before had to be reached again. There was nothing new to say. No one was likely to be converted (Lord Byers said 'there is a clear-cut division in the House, and I doubt whether any of us will convince others to a different way of thinking'). Yet Lord Arran, the Sisyphus of homosexual law reform, was constrained again to open what was to be a three and a half hours debate. For a second time he moved the second reading of his bill.[349] He again presaged the opposition it would almost certainly arouse, from Lord Rowallan of the Scouts and from the two former Lords Chancellor, Lords Dilhorne and Kilmuir. But he did announce that he was comforted by the fact that Lord Gardiner supported the bill and that 'the Lord Chief Justice, the noble and learned Lord, Lord Parker of Waddington, has authorised me to say that, though he is far from certain what the age of consent should be, he broadly approves of homosexual law reform so long as there is no question of corruption'. And he offered what had become the standard defensive argument for reform:

> It is estimated that there are between 500,000 and one million homosexuals in this country – a substantial minority. To some, they are sad men; to some, they are ridiculous; to many, they are morally evil; and to the law, they are criminal. The arguments for law reform are that these men do not choose to be homosexual; that no man would deliberately and obstinately forgo the choice of loving women – that no man, let along 500,000 or one million, would be so stupid. The argument is that nature makes her mistakes with human beings, as with animals: she makes some of us physically deformed; she makes some of us mentally deformed; and others she makes emotionally deformed. ... The Wolfenden Committee ... felt that there comes a time in a man's life when he must be allowed to decide for himself and to act according to what to him are his natural inclinations. This is what this Bill is about. We are saying that a grown-up man should not be a criminal because he is what he is, and because he may find someone else of like tastes and indulge in them privately. We are saying that such a man is evil, if you wish, but that he should not be sent to prison.

That too was the argument of the Chairman of the Moral Welfare Council, the Bishop of St. Albans: 'The supporters of this Bill desire to keep moral condemnation for homosexual acts. Frequently though this statement has been made, it needs to be said again and again. I hold this conviction strongly, and I am certain that Christians who think in these terms must be alive to the problems of homosexuals, and do their part to see they are reasonably and justly treated. I continue to support the Wolfenden proposals'. It was also the argument of Lord Byers, the leader of the Liberal peers: 'If I understand homosexual practices, then I find them abhorrent. But I find the law full of injustice; I find it full of stupidity as it stands at the present time, and my sympathy goes out to any such minority who are oppressed in this fashion'.

Then, as Lord Arran had foretold, Lord Kilmuir, a second Sisyphus, opened the attack. He began by lamenting that 'We have discussed this subject so often, and at such length ...' And he adduced a set of arguments that had been heard before. The bill would lead to a belittling and encouragement of sin: 'the lifting of the prohibition applies to the whole act of sodomy, and not only to the gross indecency covered by Mr. Labouchère's Amendment. I believe we are bound to consider the dangers of proselytising in this field, but it is my view that if we are lifting a statutory bar which has existed for over 400 years in regard to the full offence, we cannot do so without lightening the moral opprobrium with which the act is regarded'. Society would be debauched and weakened.[350] There would be a lessening of morale and a corrupting of men in the Armed Services ('How long will [a homosexual act] be considered "indecent and unnatural conduct" if your Lordships have changed the law and legalised sodomy, as is proposed?') There would be a corrupting of seamen. Male prostitution would increase.

Lord Dilhorne sounded as if he too had grown tired, saying 'I do not intend to repeat the arguments I advanced in the earlier discussions on this Bill', but he did return to Lord Kilmuir's conundrum of the English ship and the Scottish port; and he declared his anxiety about the ill-effects of a relaxation of moral standards (whatever the reformers might profess their intentions to be). The former Chief Scout, Lord Rowallan, again invoked the image of the evil corrupter that he had summoned up in a previous debate: 'We have heard a great deal about the persecution of the homosexual, but we have heard very little about the homosexual's persecution of those who do not fall in with his plans and his wishes... there are certain types of homosexuals whose delight it is to seduce young heterosexuals and lead them down the garden path which, as we have been told, leads to nothing but frustration, sorrow and degeneration'. Lord Ferrier[351] could not support the removal of the criminal sanction from a wicked act: 'I cannot see how a sin – and this act we are discussing is a hideous sin; I nearly said bestial, but beasts do not do it – is any more excusable morally because it is committed in private'. And Lord Stonham concluded by pronouncing that 'this debate has been less satisfactory than those which preceded it' and once more repeated the government's professed neutrality.

Lord Arran's verdict was more kindly: 'I did not think it was such a bad debate. Perhaps there was nothing particularly new to say'. Peers had spoken in equal measure for and against the bill (seven in favour and eight against); and the outcome had been much the same: 70 voted for a second reading of the bill, 29 against. Five bishops had voted for it. None was against. The bill had finally passed all its stages, but it had yet to be ratified in the other House.

The new bill introduced on 5 July by Leo Abse with Roy Jenkins' blessing was again largely identical for prudential reasons[352] to the one that had just passed in the Lords and had so nearly passed in the Commons, although it was now supposedly immunised against the attacks which had been made in earlier debates. Offences against young boys would remain criminal and heavily penalised (the 'penalty for a homosexual offence against any boy under the age of 16 ... could be up to life imprisonment'), as would offences against 'military discipline in the Army, the Navy and the Air Force, so that Section 66 of the Army Act would remain undisturbed – that Section providing punishment for disgraceful and immoral conduct'.[353] Politicians' anxieties about what had become known colloquially as 'buggers' clubs' would be allayed by the provision 'that any premises found to be used for homosexual practices would constitute a brothel, attracting the same penalties as would be the case for premises now used for heterosexual practices'.

The present law, said Leo Abse once more, was absurd and arbitrary. It could not be enforced except against a small fraction of those committing offences. It did not deter. It encouraged intimidation and blackmail. It 'brand[ed] [homosexual men] as criminals and outlaws, their isolation is intensified, they become increasingly estranged and many retreat into a ghetto, cut off from involvement in the community, feeling hostility from the community. Too often they react by succumbing to anti-social attitudes'. The penalties it imposed were only likely to exacerbate offending: 'to send homosexuals to overcrowded, hermetically-sealed male prisons is as therapeutically useless as incarcerating a sex maniac in a harem'. The Churches supported change because they had been moved by compassion, and compassion should move the politician too.

The only Member to speak against Leo Abse was Sir Cyril Osborne, and he refused to the last to be convinced or mollified. There was, he claimed, no mandate for change in any of the election manifestos issued by the parties; he was not persuaded that the armed services and young people would not be debauched; and there was no reassurance that these 'bestial habits' would not proliferate. No time for a second reading should be given to the bill.

Argument had patently become ritualised. Leo Abse had been brief; Sir Cyril Osborne had been brief; the entire debate had been brief – it was concluded in less than half an hour – and, Members having once again been rallied,[354] the vote for a First Reading was won by 244 to 100. Yet the structural constraints of the Parliamentary system remained formidable – other bills were also in train – and Sir Cyril Osborne's wish about the bill's mortality could yet be granted. Leo Abse was apprehensive that the second reading of the bill might not be reached in late November, and he sought leave from the Home Secretary to secure the promised extra time.

The combination of Roy Jenkins, as Home Secretary, and Lord Gardiner[355] as Lord Chancellor, both avowed advocates of reform, was again to be critical[356] (and Lord Gardiner had certainly hoped from the first that they would act *as* a combination. He had written to Roy Jenkins within days of his appointment to congratulate him 'on assuming what, from my point of view is the most important Ministry in the country. We have a lot to do together in the legal field and if at any time I can help in any way I would be most anxious to help in any way I can'[357]). Richard Crossman, the Lord President of the Council, reminded the Prime Minister that 'Roy Jenkins would like this to be done and done soon enough to enable the Bill to clear the Standing Committee sufficiently early to avoid, if possible, any further Government time being required ...'[358] And there were other supporters now in the Cabinet, including Anthony Greenwood, Lord Longford and Kenneth Robinson. The Executive Committee of the Homosexual Law Reform Society reported that 'The new Leader of the House (Mr Crossman) was known to be sympathetic', but 'the Government's heavy legislative timetable might render the provision of Government time difficult'.[359] Government neutrality may still have been maintained formally, but it was becoming ever more definitely benevolent. Roy Jenkins reminded the Cabinet at its meeting of 27 October 1966 that the House of Lords had twice passed Lord Arran's bill, and that the House of Commons had given a second reading to Humphrey Berkeley's bill and had had then given leave to Leo Abse to introduce a bill which was again effectively identical with Lord Arran's bill. He then said:

> While the Government should still adhere to its neutral attitude on principles, it would be under strong criticism, in view of the recent votes in both Houses, if some time were not provided to enable Mr. Abse's Bill to make progress. ... The arguments for providing Government time to the Bill were similar to those which had obtained in the case of Mr. Silverman's Bill to abolish capital punishment. In these circumstances the balance of advantage lay in making available half a day of Government time for the Second Reading debate on Mr. Abse's Bill.

The Prime Minister was himself less than eager to act[360] and there was a lingering reticence elsewhere in Cabinet to act on what had not ceased to be a controversial measure.[361] The customary objections were raised: 'there were still feelings on the issues involved'; giving government time would be 'widely interpreted as indicating Government support'; it might lead to further demands for time for the bill; and it would set an unfortunate precedent before the sponsors of other private members' bills.[362] But, *per contra*, it was also argued that allotting government time could be justified by the way in which both Houses of Parliament had expressed their will; and the risk 'that further Government time would have to be given might be avoided if it were made clear at the outset that thereafter the Bill would have to follow the usual course without Government assistance'.[363]

Roy Jenkins prevailed and an extra half day was made available, against Sir Cyril Osborne's remonstrations,[364] to be announced at the end of November[365] and confirmed in December for later in the month. The debate itself then began at 7 p.m. on 19 December[366] with a familiar recitation by Leo Abse: 'we are dealing with the largest number of those to be declared criminals in the land. To these men, what does the law say? It does not give them the choice of saying that they may live out their lives in discretion. It does not give them the choice that they may live out their lives away from public view provided that they do not flaunt their conduct. The law as it stands does not give them the choice to live out their lives provided that they never corrupt a young person. In fact, the law gives them a brutal choice. It offers them either celibacy or criminality, and nothing in between'. The law was unenforceable, yet men lived in fear. They were vulnerable to blackmail. When they were sent to prison they only found themselves beset by temptation. No therapy was offered to them. It was not remarkable that there 'are not a few homosexuals who almost lapse into near paranoia. It is not surprising, when the law puts them outside the community, that they behave as many do, that they should react as some of them do in an anti-social manner, with all their original feelings of guilt reinforced by repressive laws'.

He again attempted to forestall possible attack. The bill posed no threat to good order in the armed forces. Nor was it a threat to discipline on merchant ships, but, should anxiety persist, he 'would in no way resist an Amendment founded upon the principle that a merchant seaman should be in no worse or no better a position than a naval rating'. The innocence of the young would be protected by enhanced penalties. The law relating to the earnings of male prostitutes would attract the same punishment as that applied to female prostitutes. If all that were accepted, then the bill could be passed, and, said the Freudian, work could begin to intervene therapeutically to prevent the onset and development of homosexuality in the young:

> The paramount reason for the introduction of this Bill is that it may at last move our community away from being riveted to the question of punishment of homosexuals which has hitherto prompted us to avoid the real challenge of preventing little boys from growing up to be adult homosexuals. Surely, what we should be preoccupied with is the question of how we can, if it is possible, reduce the number of faulty males in the community. How can we diminish the number of those who grow up to have men's bodies but feminine souls? It is clear from the number of homosexuals who are about that, unfortunately, little boys do not automatically grow up to be men. Manhood and fatherhood have to be taught. Manhood has to be learnt.

He did not satisfy everyone. Captain Elliot,[367] the Conservative Member for Carshalton, wondered about the anomaly of the naval officer who went ashore to engage legally in homosexual acts, only to return to his ship where 'he may be called on to serve on a court martial and send a man to prison for indulging in them'. Were the bill to pass, 'We should, I presume, get a succession of plays on television and on the stage on the subject. We should get more books on it. We should get more clubs. I believe that the vice would be looked upon as a normal and natural part of our daily life, and all checks would be gone'.[368]

The debate nearly ran out of time – that presumably had been the bill's opponents' intention – until it was rescued by Roy Jenkins at 10 p.m. who awarded it two hours more. There followed something of a filibuster attacking the very fact that the bill had been given time.[369] And then, after only an hour, the extended debate expired early and unexpectedly. The Bill's opponents were 'caught napping',[370] and failed to return to support Simon Mahon's amendment demanding the bill's rejection. The bill moved to committee without a vote.

The bill's progress had always been hard fought, protracted and serpentine, subject to opportunistic attack and defence, and that is how it continued until the end. At report and third reading on 23 June 1967, there was to be another filibuster. Sir Cyril Osborne tabled some twenty-two amendments, including raising the age of consent to 25, but it was to be the discussion of his rather curious amendment on the publication of lists supposedly advertising the names of homosexual men that at first exhausted the time available.[371] What was claimed by numerous Members to be the rapid spread of those lists invited prolonged talk about 'people who indulge in this filthy business [and who] do not confine it to themselves but are great proselytisers, and are always trying to attract other people, especially other younger men, into this filthy business'.[372] Parliamentary time again lapsed. The bill, observed *The Times*, fell victim to a 'determined attempt to wreck [it] by a group of Conservative backbenchers. ... The repetitive oratory of Sir Cyril Osborne, ... Sir Cyril Black ... and their friends was too much to overcome'.[373]

Leo Abse had once more to solicit government help, and he was reported to be confident that it would be forthcoming.[374] His was one of several private member's bills, said the Lord President of the Privy Council, that 'had a good prospect of being enacted in the current Session if they were given some Government time, but not otherwise'[375] (Burke Trend had advised the Prime Minister on the day before the Cabinet meeting that 'You may think that the Bill's prospects are bright enough to be worth giving it a day'.[376])

And another day *was* given. Three weeks later, in the early morning of 4 July, the Sexual Offences (no. 2) Bill completed 'its stormy progress through the Commons', receiving its third reading by 99 votes to 14. Lord Arran's parallel bill simultaneously received its first reading in the House of Lords, was expected to 'have a quiet passage',[377] and moved on to gain its second reading on 13 July by 111 votes to 48. Homosexual acts conducted in private between consenting adults would no longer be criminal offences (although curiously enough, as Jeffrey Weeks reminded me in his comments on an earlier draft of this chapter, the Act was the first to place homosexuality explicitly into law[378]), and the Executive Committee of the Homosexual Law Reform Society proceeded to hold a celebratory dinner financed by a gift of £100 from a supporter.[379]

And what were the immediate consequences of the 1967 Act? Whilst neither the report nor the Act seemed to have made much of an impact on the number of offences recorded by the police, there *was* a palpable effect on the number of people arraigned for trial. Prosecutions for offences of buggery and attempted buggery slowly declined and then levelled off, whilst prosecutions for offences of indecency plummeted, recovering briefly, after the publication of the report in 1957 and then, more decisively and dramatically, virtually collapsed during and after the passage of 1967 Act.

There was a parallel decline in parliamentary and media interest in offences of indecency and buggery, save for the brief reporting of a flurry of acquittals of men who had been charged – without the consent of the Director of Public Prosecutions – with offences of indecency with males under that age under Section 8 of the Act.[380] The world, it seems, had moved on – at least for a while.[381]

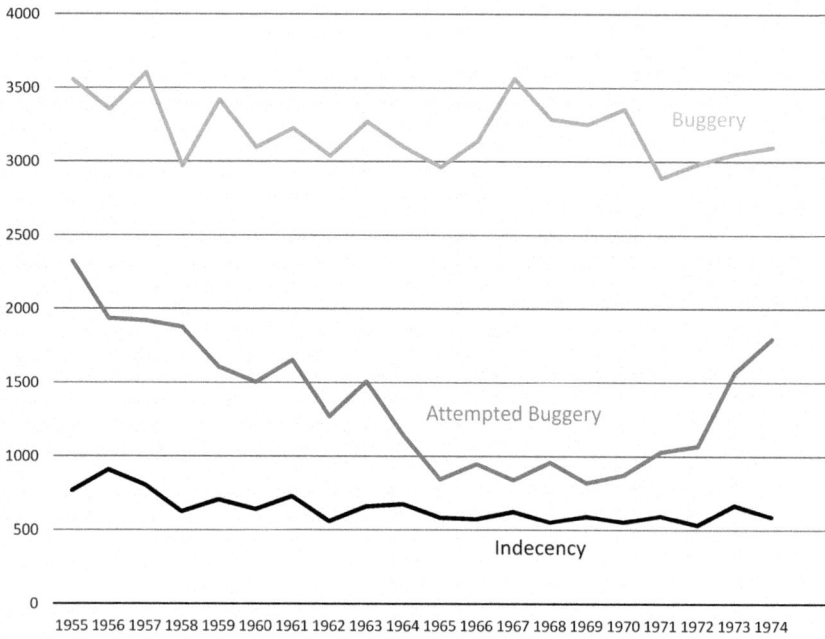

Figure 7.2 Offences known to the police 1955–1974

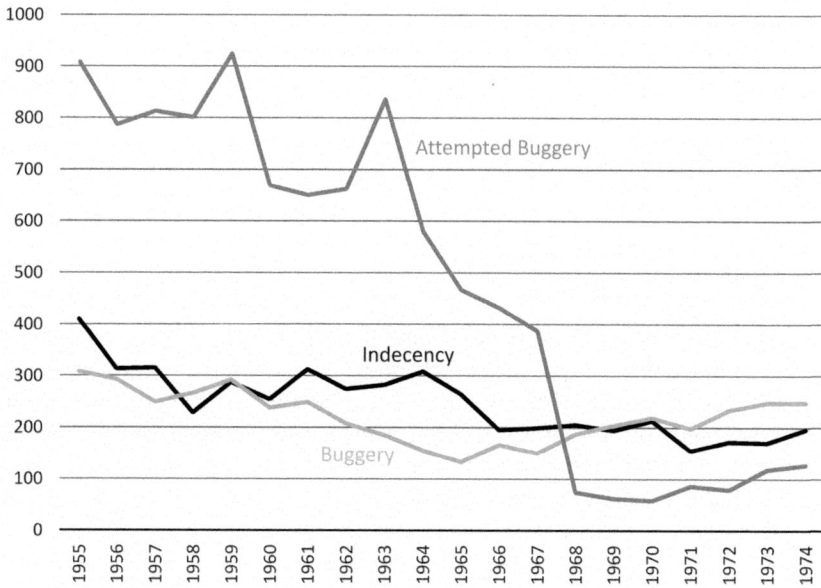

Figure 7.3 Assizes and Quarter Sessions and Crown Court: persons for trial
1955–1974

Conclusion†

A fairly consistent picture emerges from my description of the three great liberalising reforms of the criminal justice system introduced by private members in the 1950s and 1960s (and it is one that will apply in its turn to the histories of the founding of the Crown Court and the Crown Prosecution Service that are to come). First, they may all be represented as episodes in a continuing work of administrative improvement that had begun with Howard, Bentham and Romilly in the late eighteenth century and attained momentum next in the 1830s with Henry Brougham and then with James Fitzjames Stephen.[382] It was refined by John Stuart Mill to incorporate a new emphasis on personal liberty.[383] It was dedicated to transforming and modernising the state by imparting consistency, coherence and reason to what was depicted as a disorderly mass of arbitrary, ineffective and often oppressive and unnecessarily invasive laws, and it was said at the time that there had 'begun, with good auspices, a career of legal reformation ... [a] good work of simplifying the laws, purifying their administration, and bringing justice cheaply and expeditiously home to the people'.[384]

The project was grounded in liberal, utilitarian ideas loosely conceived and their core propositions that all lawmaking should be informed, on the one hand, by a careful and rational calculation of the effects it might confer on the sum of human happiness; and, on the other, by the precept that there should be equally careful limits set on the power of the state to encroach on individual liberty, even in the cases of sodomy and pederasty.[385] (That was a precept that led, *inter alia*, to a shift in the regulation of sexual mores from a conception of the victim as society writ large to the victim as an identifiable individual[386]). It was in this fashion that utilitarianism formed the core of a relatively unchanging set of foundational principles that supported much of the theory and practice of criminal law for over 150 years.[387] Sir Henry Maine observed it in 1875, saying 'I do not know of a single law reform effected since Bentham's time which cannot be traced to his influence'.[388] Lindsay Farmer, the legal historian and Professor of Law at the University of Glasgow observed it 135 years later. It is a tradition, he said, which is:

> typically concerned with the limits of state power and the maximizing of individual freedom ... [and it] sought to specify the conditions under which certain sorts of behaviour might properly be regarded as permitting state intervention. To a surprising degree, later writings more explicitly directed at the theme of criminalization have not advanced substantially beyond these early insights: most are conducted within the framework of liberal political theory laid out by Mill ...[389]

The framework is perhaps least evident in the commonplace discourse of politicians,[390] civil servants and practitioners in mid-twentieth-century England and Wales. Officials may have been called Platonic guardians, but there was actually very little of the ethos of *The Republic* about them. They formed no part of a state in which 'philosophers are kings, or the kings and princes of this world have the spirit and power of philosophy. ...'[391] There is no evidence in any interview conducted or paper consulted for this history that they were given to such grandiosity.[392] They did not philosophise. They and their predecessors never looked to the great criminological schools of thought.[393] They declined to accept identification with any overarching historical movement. A somewhat jaded Herbert Hart remarked at the time that 'No one expects judges or states-men occupied in the business of sending people to the gallows or prison, or in making (or unmaking) laws which enable this to be done have much time for philosophical discussion of principles which make it morally tolerable to do these things'.[394] That was not their style – they professed always to focus on the more immediate problems of lawmaking and practical administration. A civil servant who rose to high office at this time, Sir Brian Cubbon, said:

> A civil servant likes legislation 'cause it's exciting and it's important. And when you go home at night and your children ask you what you've done, if you've ever been in Parliament, you've got an answer. And so civil servants have an instinctive liking – or they don't mind – legislation. More than that, legislation's nice. At the same time, they're very conscious of the difficulty of a particular legislative subject and whether it's resources or principle or the interference of other departments and there are many factors that will, which will stop any rush to legislation. *Utilitarianism*, it's not a concept that comes naturally. ... Global questions [of philosophy] would come in only when the bill was drafted and you were writing the second reading speech and you wanted to have some nice high fallutin' words to get it through.

So it was elsewhere that signs of the framework had to be detected,[395] and where they were to be found was in what Husserl might have called the *Stiftung* or foundation of a number of demonstrably influential commentaries about criminal justice policy. That is certainly Lindsay Farmer's position. He argued that well into the twentieth century it diffusely permeated what was in effect the reformers' taken for granted conceptual environment, becoming what he called a part of their 'toolkit':

> The English (British) liberal tradition ... has been dominated by a utilitari-anism – it is hard to think of prominent liberal thinkers who have not been associated with it in some way. That said, the utilitarianism gets expressed in different ways, and might articulate differently around different issues. There is the strain of modernising justice and the state: clear, consistent, rational laws. And there is the strain of political utilitarianism (liberalism) articulated by Mill and later Berlin around the boundaries between public and private life. These two were not always consistent with one another (modernisers often supported moral repression of vice in the 19thC), but

they came together in Wolfenden and subsequent debates. And in the same way penal welfarists, such as Wootton, were utilitarian modernisers, though it was inflected through a medicalised discourse of treatment. All of which is by way of saying that... utilitarianism was part of the 'toolkit' of reformers, but was not determinative, in the sense that it underlay a range of different kinds of arguments.[396]

It was a toolkit that was influential in part because it was so practical. From time to time it answered remarkably well to the working needs of those who advocated or developed policy. It was not over-ambitious or intellectually extravagant. It supplied a want when direction or legitimation was sought or the ornamentation of 'high fallutin' words' was required. And it was the product of a distinct division of labour in which scholarly men and women quite deliberately set about constructing formal arguments for the potential use of others more practically engaged. After all, it is one of the chief roles of public intellectuals purposefully to cultivate and expound important ideas for a wider lay audience.

It was Herbert Hart, the man once described as the 'outstanding English philosopher of law in the twentieth century',[397] who embarked on a long and questioning conversation with the ghost of Bentham[398] and was inspired by John Stuart Mill's analysis of liberty,[399] to engage with Lord Devlin in a celebrated and much publicised debate about the Wolfenden Report.[400] Devlin, he said, was 'perverse in trying to make a case against John Stuart Mill'.[401] 'First, we must ask whether a practice which offends moral feeling is harmful, independently of its repercussion on the general moral code. Secondly, what about repercussion on the moral code? Is it really true that failure to translate this item of general morality into criminal law will jeopardise the whole fabric of morality and so of society?' The assertion that conduct generally deemed intolerable must be suppressed 'is no adequate substitute for a reasoned estimate of the damage to the fabric of society likely to ensue if it is not suppressed'.[402] His fellow philosopher, Isaiah Berlin, perhaps more liberal than utilitarian, nevertheless described himself as 'a last feeble echo of J.S. Mill ...'[403] and he did deploy a Millian argument when he offered his somewhat reticent support to the Wolfenden reforms and added his signature to the critical letter in *The Times* of March 1958. He once said that liberal societies 'proceed on the assumption that there is a frontier between public and private life, and that, however small the private sphere may be, within it I can do as I please'.[404] The criminologist, Barbara Wootton, supported the campaign for homosexual law reform (quoting Herbert Hart[405]) and led in the House of Lords on capital punishment. Her obituarist, Philip Bean, called her 'the perfect exponent of a Utilitarian creed and philosophy, and of the pure Benthamite version of Utilitarianism'.[406] And there were others. Amongst them was the academic lawyer, Glanville Williams, the author of *The Sanctity of Life and the Criminal Law*,[407] a man who played a prominent role in the abolition of capital punishment and the campaigns to reform the laws on abortion, suicide and euthanasia,[408] and was once described by Leon Radzinowicz as 'The Illegitimate Child of Jeremy Bentham'.[409]

If those public intellectuals were bent on elaborating utilitarianism, it was the Church of England in the 1950s and 1960s that lent it added practical, moral and indeed political force. The Church was quintessentially political, embedded physically in Parliament, part of the constitutional fabric of the nation.[410] It played a notable part as a moral tutor and mentor. It was a self-conscious source of ideas,[411] an ally of the reform movements and a reforming institution in its own right. It offered clear, straightforward and useful interpretations of current social problems. It gave headmasterly moral guidance and authority to those who sought change;[412] it petitioned politicians, often to effect;[413] and, as a hierarchical institution whose members deferred to the archbishops, it dragooned the Peers Spiritual in the House of Lords.[414] It was, in short, a significant political and didactic power and, unlike the political parties in the House of Commons, it had no constituents to fear. It was the Church that mediated, and took it that it was its role to mediate, a major portion of the ethical arguments that underpinned the reforming work of the lawyers and the politicians, and I have shown how its authority was repeatedly invoked. Peter Sedgwick, a Canon of Llandaff Cathedral, the Principal of an Anglican theological institution, St Michael's College, and the author of a number of works on theology, ethics and criminal justice,[415] said:

> They were seen as the moral guardians of the nation. ... Both William Temple, and Geoffrey Fisher who followed him as Archbishop of Canterbury, had been public school headmasters[416] and that was seen as a stepping stone from having been an Oxford don. You might do some time in parishes as well. You might not. You would then proceed either to a Deanery or to a Bishopric and so you would eventually get into a senior Bishopric and so into the House of Lords. And those people who had been public school headmasters up to I suppose the 1950s, very much as I don't need to tell you, would have seen their role as forming the moral character of the elite British Empire. ... Those that became headmasters and then Bishops in the Lords had a slightly paternal, particularly in the case of Geoffrey Fisher, view when he talked in that House of Lords. There were presumably, I don't know, some MPs who might have been at school, at Repton or whatever. There would certainly have been Peers that he would have either taught or would certainly have known. ... So you get the Establishment absolutely at work at this point. ...

At a number of junctures during the period there was something of a critical confluence or consonance between the world views of senior Anglicans and the lay reformers which stressed a civilised tolerance of diversity;[417] the close application of rationality; an acceptance of the evolution of morals;[418] and the sovereignty of reason in defying not only the will of the multitude (John Stuart Mill was a Theist[419] who once railed against 'mobocracy'[420]), but also the authority of an overbearing and absolutist secular ruler in trying to determine what was an appropriate moral rule. Most important of all, underpinning much of the liberalism of the time was the long-established recognition of two quite discrete spheres – the claims of conscience, which were the Church's business – and the claims of public order, which were the state's.[421]

It was a stance that was manifest not only in what was said about homosexuality but also in the concurrent and closely linked debate about the decriminalisation of attempted suicide.[422] Geoffrey Fisher, the then Archbishop of Canterbury, had said of the Wolfenden Report that there was a need to 'think about and compare the sphere of crime and the sphere of sin'.[423] And of suicide and attempted suicide, he likewise observed, 'Looking at it casually, now that we are getting the distinction between crime and sin on to a reasonable basis, I can myself see no grounds on which it is possible to go on treating attempted suicide as a crime. It hardly seems justifiable for the protection of the community, and seems to be very definitely more a piece of private morality than, for example, adultery, which is not a crime'.[424] He was to approve the commissioning of another committee of the Church's Board for Social Responsibility[425] which reported that suicide should be viewed as a personal tragedy and not as a crime,[426] and what it said convinced the Home Secretary[427] and speeded the passing of the 1961 Suicide Act.[428] In the debate on the matter, Lord Silkin made clear what had been done:

> We are taking the view that it is no longer the business of the community to preserve the life of a person who wants to end his life. Whether or not suicide is a sin is a matter which is not for this House, but in the future it will certainly not be an offence. … this change in outlook has been influenced by the very fine pamphlet which has been issued by the Churches and which I have had the pleasure of reading.[429]

It must be said that the part played by Geoffrey Fisher's successor, Michael Ramsey, the 'chief moralist of England',[430] is not always easy to fathom. Beyond his very particular interventions in and around the debates in the House of Lords, and his major, albeit sometimes ambivalent role in the reforms,[431] he said little about what he called his generation's 'old-fashioned liberalism'.[432] He said nothing on the matter of homosexual law reform in a collection of lectures on the pivotal issue of 'otherworldly and this-worldly aspects of Christianity' delivered at a critical time in 1964.[433] He abjured new priests neither to be overly involved in the wholly secular nor in the wholly spiritual,[434] although he did encourage them rather blandly to 'Help your congregation to be a caring congregation, active in its service of some human need or distress'.[435] His views on race relations and poverty were pronounced, but on sexuality they seem to have been conventional enough, arguing, as he did, that 'the essence of the Christian view is that sex is to be understood only in the context of the whole relation of man and woman'[436] and that 'the family is part of God's scheme of things'.[437] Homosexuals, he thought, should be offered pastoral care rather than punishment.[438] But at one point and at an important time, his larger intellectual position became quite transparent. He invoked the name of John Stuart Mill in the 1962 Robert Waley Cohen Memorial Lecture and then proceeded to recite the utilitarian doctrine that it was necessary to defend 'the freedom of an individual to think, believe and teach and do what he pleases so long as he does not injure his fellows in ways which the state must prevent or punish'.[439] And that, after all, was the crux of the argument that undergirded many of the liberalising criminal justice reforms of the 1960s.

Richard Chartres, the former Bishop of London and himself a member of the House of Lords, said to me that the Church of England had long been relatively pragmatic, 'immersed in the world', and led by the laity instead of being schooled somewhat at a remove in the seminary. It was well positioned to mediate between the divine, the philosophical and the practical. More, added a diocesan bishop, moral decisions at the time of the great liberal reforms of the 1960s were far simpler: the Church had then to contend with less of a cacophony of information and arguments in a simpler and smaller world which did not, for example, have to confront the strongly held and opposing views of the African and American churches.[440]

So it was that reformers, nonconformists and Churchmen alike argued that men and women must be allowed to make their own choices, even if they were choices for ill, choices of which one disapproved and for which they should be condemned, so long as no indefensible harm was done to others – that they should, in short, be judged only by the public impact of their actions.[441] To do otherwise would be a step too far (Peter Sedgwick reflected that the Church's view was that 'imprisonment was there for persistent burglars or acts of violence, rape and murder, not for sexuality, not for abortion, not for a whole range of things. I mean this is just off limits'). They deployed what appeared to be a calmly impersonal rationality and a variant of moral philosophy, express or implied, described by Christie Davies as 'causalism' or 'negative utilitarianism', akin in certain cases to the ideas of Bentham and Mill, and in others to the more involuted ideas of Henry Sidgwick,[442] to champion the difficult cause of discredited and unfortunate people with whom they professed to feel no great kinship, and, indeed, from whom they often sought visibly to distance themselves. Christie Davies asserted that 'They were not primarily concerned with (or at least did not openly press) the rights, freedoms and pleasures of women … or homosexuals but rather stressed the harm suffered by them as a result of the existing laws – bodged back-street abortions … [and] blackmailed sodomites'.[443] Theirs was an authority to which they could lay a special professional claim. After all, moralising was their trade, and it was a moralising grounded in a distinctively Protestant conception of conscience and its rights to freedom.[444] That authority on the sociology of work, Everett Hughes, once said that the professions:

> rest upon some branch of knowledge to which the professionals are privy by virtue of long study and by initiation and apprenticeship under masters

already members of the profession. ... They profess to know better than others the nature of certain matters, and to know better than their clients what ails them or their affairs. ... The professional is expected to think objectively and inquiringly about matters which may be, for laymen, subject to orthodoxy and sentiment which limit intellectual exploration'.[445]

Apply that definition to the thinkers of the Church of England and its Board for Social Responsibility and Moral Welfare Council. The impression created was that they were occupationally well-equipped to apply a reasoned, universalistic mode of argument to causes with which they may not always have had personal sympathy. They were obliged by their vocation to deal with mundane moral problems every day, and it is tempting to imagine that they were professionally trained to look on them with eyes that were frequently calmer, less confused, more experienced and better focused than, say, those of men and women whose expertise lay chiefly elsewhere, people whose moral judgments were effectively lay although they may have been formally presented in professional garb (one recalls, for instance, the occasional, rather clumsy ethical pronouncements of the special committees on abortion and homosexuality established by the British Medical Association and the Law Society). Doctors and lawyers were not always deft when they moralised. Ethics was acknowledged not to be their field and they were not at ease when they ventured into it.

To be sure, utilitarianism was never a lone voice, especially in the campaign to reform the 1885 Act. There were elements of what David Garland called 'penal welfarism' in a number of the arguments that deviants should be treated and assimilated rather than punished,[446] but they were always of minor importance, and they lent themselves perfectly well to an accommodation with utilitarianism.[447] Some, no doubt, were opportunistic, some a matter of conviction in the new therapies that were then in vogue, and some a simple corollary of the depiction of the homosexual man as pitiable and ill. But it was not those elements that held much sway. Neither were they inscribed in the 1967 Act. That was a liberalising rather than a therapeutic, measure.

It is impossible now to know how much of what was said was actually interested or disinterested, argued for reasons of state, rhetorical effect, self-protection or personal conviction (although it is evident that a number of the campaigners for the Wolfenden reforms were actually occasional or life-long 'closet' bisexuals or homosexuals – including, it seems, Mervyn Stockwood, Herbert Hart,[448] Roy Jenkins himself[449] and possibly Leo Abse[450] – and many, like John Wolfenden, were less distant from the problem than their protestations suggested). But it is plain that, whatever may have been believed or said by some lay men and women in private, no campaigner at the time could proclaim that a woman should have a simple right to choose to have an abortion, that she could, as would be said later, have a right to 'control her own body'. Neither could one proclaim that homosexuality was a proper or enviable way of life.[451] Lord Arran was obliged to reflect that 'it is true to say that, in all the discussions we have had, and in all the speeches, no single noble Lord or noble

Lady has ever said that homosexuality is a right or a good thing. It has been universally condemned from start to finish, and by every single Member of this House'.[452] But the reformers nevertheless did press a case for liberalisation, and they pressed it vigorously.

That work of rationalisation was sustained by men and women in the face of what were profound and opposing convictions about what was conceived to be the sanctity of life and the natural order of gender and sexuality, convictions that drew on an older religious authority, and most often the authority of the Old Testament. The two systems of belief are venerable[453] and largely incommensurable, and their chief theatre of war was Parliament, where, in a highly centralised polity, questions of criminal justice policy must be resolved. They transcended party divisions, they excited the deep and frequently hostile feelings of electors, and their presentation made governments timid. If there was to be legislative change, it had invariably to be entrusted to backbenchers who, usually with little official encouragement at first, worked with the vehicle of the private member's bill, and its fate rested on the resilience of a Member or Members prepared to struggle on in the manner of a Mother Courage. Indeed, in the instance of the repeal of the laws on abortion and capital punishment, it was to be a succession of Mothers Courage who trudged on, one after another, decade after decade, in a Parliamentary equivalent of the Thirty Years War. At least, that was certainly how it looked to those close to the principals. Roger Silverman, the son of Sydney, wrote of his father that he had 'staged a hunger strike in prison against brutal treatment as an opponent of the First World War. His 25-year parliamentary campaign against capital punishment met with bitter and unanimous opposition from successive governments, the Home Office, the police, the judges, the Press barons… that is, from every single part of the "establishment". … his ultimate victory in bringing to an end the barbarity of capital punishment in Britain – through a private members' bill, without government backing – represented a stunning historic defeat for the establishment'.[454]

As they were pitched against one another in Parliamentary debates that became ever more routinised, so, over time, contending arguments themselves became increasingly stylised in what resembled a form of political trench warfare. To be sure, the dialectics of an adversarial politics ensured that compromises and adjustments had continually to be made in small particulars, and proposals were modified to enhance their prospect of survival, but there could be no reconciling the core arguments about the right to take life or how one could behave sexually. The outcomes of parliamentary battles came then to centre less on reasoned argument about morality and policy, more on tactical manoeuvring, the outwitting of opponents, the securing of alliances, the winning of time allotted debates, shifting numbers in the Houses of Parliament, and, above all, the benevolence of the powerful.

Thomas Carlyle was right and Plekhanov was wrong. In a relatively small forum such as Parliament, and on a free vote, individual Members and individual ministers did matter. Without a Sydney Silverman, David Steel, Leo Abse or Lord Arran the course of events would probably have been different. But it was also inevitable that those individuals were constrained to act in conditions that were not of their own making. What they accomplished was structured by the manner in which they dealt with the play of institutional and procedural contingencies, by the composition of the House of Commons and the House of Lords, the rise and fall of administrations, the limitations imposed by the life of Parliaments, and competition from other legislative business. However able the reform-minded may have been, they managed to achieve little under the Conservative administrations of the 1950s and 1960s. They had to wait for the appearance of a more liberal judiciary, a more liberal body of peers and Members of Parliament and a cluster of extraordinary ministers, first Frank Soskice and Gerald Gardiner, and then Roy Jenkins, who had been appointed by Harold Wilson in the mid-1960s.

It must however be noted that whilst Gerald Gardiner stepped outside the constitutional boundaries of his office to effect change, and whilst Frank Soskice was determinedly opposed to hanging, a manifestly liberal Roy Jenkins, the author of articles in the 1950s urging reform in *Tribune, The Current*[455] and *The Labour Case*, the man who talked about the liberal hour, one of whom so much was expected,[456] and one who did intervene quite decisively at a number of points in this history, seemed actually to have been rather little interested in what might be called the more mundane workings of the criminal justice system before, during and after his twin periods of office as Home Secretary between 23 December 1965 and 30 November 1967, and 5 March 1974 and 10 September 1976. Although he had for years expressed an ambition to become Home Secretary,[457] and although his disengagement was not marked at first but grew with time, the 288 boxes of his papers deposited in the special collections of the Bodleian Library in Oxford, boxes containing copious speeches, letters, pocket diaries and a lengthy and extremely candid narrative journal, prepared, the Bodleian Archivist speculated, for a memoir – papers purporting to record the entire span of his public career as a politician – make *not a single reference* to the abolition of capital punishment,[458] homosexual law reform, abortion law reform, or the role of the police in prosecutions, the Maxwell Confait case and the Fisher Inquiry which are to be the themes of chapters to come. The 818 pages of *A Well-Rounded Life*, John Campbell's much lauded biography of Roy Jenkins, contain scant allusion to capital punishment and homosexual law reform, and *none at all* to Maxwell Confait, the Fisher Inquiry, the problems of police prosecutions, the Royal Commission on Assizes and Quarter Sessions or the Royal Commission on Criminal Procedure.[459] He was at times, said another biographer, Anthony Howard, something of 'a peripheral politician', 'a predominantly metropolitan figure',[460] who was more at home in the literary world than in the campaigning world of penal politics. There is, to be sure, evidence of his strong interest in criminal justice reform to be found in other places, particularly in the debates of the House of Commons and in cabinet and departmental papers, and I have turned to it where I could. He did intervene at critical points,[461] enjoying palpable success in introducing 'altogether more civilised standards into British life'.[462] And his stance may have been little more than an accentuation, as it were, of the conventionally cautious role-style associated with the post of Home Secretary (David Faulkner observed that 'intellectual and moral leadership in matters of penal and social policy has usually come from outside the [Home] Department ... The Home Office role is to recognise and seize opportunities for reform when they present themselves; but at the same time to keep a practical eye on cost and affordability; ... to avoid the dangers of political overreaction or short-term opportunism'[463]). Nevertheless, his archived papers suggest that his eyes were usually fixed elsewhere whilst he was in office. He told Robin Day, the broadcaster, that 'you should concentrate on relatively few issues on which you can really do something decisive ... not dissipate your energies over too wide a field'.[464] And it may have been for that reason that, in his capacity as Secretary of State, he was publicly preoccupied not with the routine (and even the not so routine) administration of the criminal justice system but with a more dramatic terrain that covered terrorist outrages, sex and race relations, reorganising the police, the 'Shrewsbury Two',[465] freedom of information, the laws of gambling and censorship and the future of broadcasting. He was to be periodically jolted into action by what Harold Macmillan would have called 'events' – by the prison escape of George Blake and the murders of police officers committed by Harry Roberts. But in his capacity as national politician and European politician in waiting, he talked more, and more often, about the case of his colleague, Reg Prentice;[466] economic performance; inflation; election campaigning; his own candidacy for the leadership of the Labour Party; and, above all else, the place of Britain in Europe, the referendum on membership of the Community that was announced at the beginning of 1975,[467] the Campaign for Europe which he founded,[468] and, towards the end, his own aspiration, realised in January 1977, to become President of the European Commission. By contrast, commonplace criminal justice affairs appeared from his own record to have been regarded as tedious, something of a side engagement, indeed a distraction.[469] It is, for instance, revealing that, at the very time when, as we shall see in the next volume of this history, the Member of Parliament, Christopher Price was busily agitating in and around the Home Office for an appeal against the conviction of three young constituents for the death of Maxwell Confait – an appeal that was to have momentous consequences – Roy Jenkins recorded nothing but social engagements, luncheons, dinner parties[470] and the politics of Europe in his narrative diary for the first half of 1975. He said in the late spring of that year:

> ... the Referendum activities and the Britain in Europe campaign ... absorb an increasing amount of my time. I think probably that from this post-Easter period onwards it was taking nearly 50% and as we got into May the figure became closer to 75% and probably at the very end even up to 90%. Fortunately Home Office affairs remained pretty quiet during this period and Arthur Peterson [the Permanent Under-Secretary of State] was undoubtedly helpful in ensuring that they didn't obtrude too much on my attention ...

All this is illuminating, if a little humbling, for the historian of criminal justice. His biographer, John Campbell, said of him and of his archive that he was 'very self-conscious about his own career',[471] but Roy Jenkins evidently chose chiefly to remember, and be remembered by,[472] events falling outside the ambit of this history, and that fact should be borne in mind whenever he appears. Given how controversial the reforms were at the time, it may explain why, although his sentiments were largely progressive, he tended characteristically to hold back, serving, as it were, as a benign extra (definitely benevolent neutrality being a phrase he was wont to employ in such matters – as did the government as a whole), rather than electing to drive vigorously from the front in the manner of Lord Gardiner.

The backbenchers who pressed for reform were not lone figures. Although the abolition of capital punishment is indelibly associated with the person of Sydney Silverman, abortion law reform with David Steel, and homosexual law reform with Leo Abse and Lord Arran, there were marshalled behind them interlocking associations of seasoned, competent and closely tied men and women who supplied them with advice and intelligence; crafted plans; lobbied and dragooned Members of Parliament; and secured the patronage of ministers. David Steel said, for instance, that 'I had a very close relationship with ALRA. They provided a great deal of the backing including … the organisation of the voting in the major parties'.[473]

It was acknowledged that the projected reforms were difficult, politically divisive and electorally unpopular. Abortion and homosexuality were literally almost unspeakable. They made governments timid. They had to be delegated to backbenchers. And where governments were timid, change seemed most likely to be achieved by those who operated in ways that would not frighten them further – the 'insider'[474] and 'acceptable'[475] groups who constructed a respectable public front and worked quietly from within rather than noisily from without; who applied tested formulae, skills and knowledge that were transferred from campaign to campaign, from decade to decade, and from group to group, beginning, in the case of the death penalty, in the eighteenth century; of abortion, in the 1930s; and of homosexual law reform, in the 1950s, allowing new things continually to be done in old ways.

Acknowledgements

I am grateful to Lindsay Farmer, Niki Lacey and Jeffrey Weeks for their comments on an earlier draft of this chapter.

Notes

1 David Astor's *Observer*, a staunch supporter of reform, reported in an editorial on 30 November 1958 that 'For more than a year the public in Britain has been discussing in pubs, clubs, newspapers and drawing-rooms (indeed wherever there is a radio or television set) the problem of homosexuality'.

2 He said 'I'm very much tempted to say that I've had enough of this particular topic over the last three years, but I think it's a sort of thing one can't escape. It sounds a most frightfully smug thing to say, I suppose, but we have put a fair amount of work into this, we have, some of us learned a great deal – the whole Committee lived through the whole of this learning, and it's very hard, having got as far as this in a subject, just to drop it and say it's no more concern of mine'. Replying to John Freeman in *Press Conference*, BBC Television, 6th September 1957, http://www.bbc.co.uk/archive/gay_rights/12001.shtml

3 Jean Mann, 1889–1964, Labour Member for Coatbridge and Airdrie, speaking at the debate on the report, HC Deb 26 November 1958 Vol. 596 cc365–508. Others concurred, arguing that the report was being zealously promoted by its advocates. Sir Cyril Black supported what she had said, remarking in the same debate on: 'the very high pressure campaign which has been undertaken in recent months in support of the recommendation of the Committee on which she has been speaking. Those who are in favour of the recommendation arid who seek to effect an alteration in the law are perfectly entitled to organise themselves for the purpose and to undertake any publicity and propaganda that they may wish in that direction. But I think the House should have its attention drawn to the fact that such a campaign has obviously been in progress'.

4 There were, to be sure, abundant critical voices. Lord Denning's was one. He maintained Lord Devlin's argument that there could be no private immorality nor could the law free itself from upholding moral standards. See *The Times*, 27 September 1957.

5 *The Times*, Thursday 5 September 1957.

6 An editorial in the *Observer* of 30 November 1958 remarked that 'The Press almost unanimously – from the *Daily Mirror* to *The Times* – advised the government to accept the Report's recommendation that homosexuality in private between male adults should be as legal as it is between females'.

7 However, the Church of Scotland, the Church of Ireland, the Salvation Army and the Baptists opposed it. It will be recalled that it was that stance of the Church of Scotland that encouraged David Steel not to pursue homosexual law reform when he won the private members' ballot.

8 He wrote to John Newall of the Homosexual Law Reform Society on 6 November 1961 that 'I am still as anxious as before to see reform along the lines of the Wolfenden Report on the matter of homosexuality'. Grey Papers, 1/6/49, Archives of the London School of Economics.

9 He said that 'In a civilised society all crimes are likely to be sins also, but most sins are not and ought not to be treated as crimes. Sin is an offence against God. Its measurements do not vary from age to age, as man's laws do'.

10 He again said there that 'The State and the Law are not concerned directly, as the Church is, with saving the souls of men from their own destruction. The right to decide one's own moral code and obey it, even to a man's own hurt, is a fundamental right of man, given him by God and to be strictly respected by society and the criminal code. ... I believe that the Report is right in recommending that, while all existing laws shall remain in force to protect and control those under 21, and to protect the unwilling over that age, homosexual acts between consenting adults in private should not come within the ambit of the law'. HL Deb 4 December 1957 Vol. 206 cc753–832. Indeed, his successor, Archbishop Ramsey, would later urge Lord Arran, the man who introduced a bill to implement the Wolfenden proposals, to persevere at a time when he was wavering under the advice not to proceed tendered by Lord Shepherd, then Labour Leader in the House of Lords (CRI477/8/55 Departmental Committee on Homosexual Offences and Prostitution Action on the Report – Sexual Offences Bill (House of Lords) Second Reading and Committee Stage 8: letter from Cubbon to DPP, 3 June 1965).

11 The Chairman of the Council, the Bishop of St. Albans, again said: 'It is good to be able to report that the Wolfenden Committee, in its proposals, followed almost exactly in substance the recommendations made by our Council'. HL Deb 4 December 1957 Vol. 206 cc753–832.

12 Gordon Dunstan, writing to *The Times*, about the work of Ena Steel, Eva Kennedy and Sherwin Bailey, the principal members of the Moral Welfare Council, remarked how 'Sherwin Bailey was leading the British Churches in a virtual revolution in their thinking about human sexuality, including prostitution and homosexuality. Under his guidance the council gave leading evidence to the Wolfenden Committee, and carried the Church Assembly in support of Wolfenden's proposed reform of the law on homosexual conduct. This ... required courage and calm in the face of determined opposition'. (Letter of 13th March 1982)

13 The Bishops of Plymouth, Carlisle and Chester spoke against it: the Bishop of Carlisle arguing, with Lord Devlin, that 'It was questionable whether immoral acts had to be done in public before they affected the public good. Private morality of any kind must affect the public life of the community. For the majority of people what the law permitted was right and what it forbad was wrong...' Their judgement was important because, it will be recalled, the senior bishops were also members of the House of Lords. Notes on a Church Assembly Debate relating to Homosexual acts in private, Archbishop Ramsey's Papers, Lambeth Palace Library (MWC/HOM/7). The Bishop of Chester was to reiterate his opposition to the report in his address to a diocesan conference in October 1957 (see *The Times*, 9 October 1957). The vote was assigned importance and later magnified for rhetorical purposes. In a debate at Committee Stage on Lord Arran's Bill, the Bishop of Lincoln talked about how 'the Wolfenden Report was given a long and careful debate in the Church Assembly and ... was over-whelmingly approved by the Church Assembly ...' HL Deb 21 June 1965 Vol. 267 cc287–317

14 Speaking in the BBC radio programme, *Any Questions*, 15 November 1957, http://www.bbc.co.uk/archive/gay_rights/12002.shtml, *op. cit.*

15 The first part "That this Assembly generally approves the principles on which the criminal law concerned with sexual behaviour should be based, as stated by the Wolfenden Committee" was carried by a clear majority. The second part, "and also its recommendations relating to homosexuality" was carried by 155 votes to 138 votes. ...' Notes on a Church Assembly Debate relating to Homosexual acts in private. Lambeth Palace archives (MWC/HOM/7).

16 Methodist Conference Newcastle Upon Tyne, Representative Session, 7 July 1958. The Conference further agreed that 'the Wolfenden Report is a sane and responsible approach to the difficult questions with which it deals'.

17 They argued that 'It should accordingly be clearly stated that penal sanctions are not justified for the purpose of attempting to restrain sins against sexual morality commit-ted in private by responsible adults'. Cited in the debate in a House of Commons, HC Deb 26 November 1958 Vol. 596 cc365–508.

18 One problem for the Hierarchy was posed by internal divisions within the Church. The Earl of Longford, for example, favoured reform. Cardinal Heenan would later write to the Archbishop of St. Andrews and Edinburgh: 'Regarding the Bill on Homosexuality we are in some difficulty. A number of Catholics, both clerical and lay people, think the law needs to be changed. We have excellent Catholics like Lord Longford and St John Stevas who would defend the Bill in their respective Houses. I think it would be wise, therefore, not to take any action'. Letter of 2 July 1966. The Heenan Papers in the Westminster Diocesan Archives (AAW HE/W10). When Leo Abse's bill was voted on at third reading in the House of Commons in July 1967, three of the 99 Members voting 'Aye', and one of the14 voting 'No' were recognised as Catholic (HC Deb 3 July 1967 Vol. 749 cc1491–525). Ten days later, in the House of

Lords, on the second reading of Lord Arran's bill, four of 111 Peers voting 'Content', and one of the 48 'Not Content' were so recognised (HL Deb 13 July 1967 Vol. 284 cc1283–323). Recognition was made by consulting *The Catholic Directory for the Year of Our Lord*, Burns and Oates, London, 1966, which listed a total of 32 MPs and 49 peers in 1966.

19 G.A. Tomlinson, 1906–1985, was ordained in the Church of England in 1930; received into the Catholic Church in 1932; became the Senior Catholic Chaplain to the University of London, 1953–64; and served as the Administrator of Westminster Cathedral, 1964–67. (Based on http://www.ukwhoswho.com/view/article/oupww/whowaswho/U169834/TOMLINSON_Rt._Rev._Mgr_George_Arthur?index=)

20 Minutes of Meetings of the Executive Committee of the Homosexual Law Reform Society, 13 April and 14 April 1965. (Papers of the Society are housed in the Archives of the British Library of Political and Economics Science at the London School of Economics under GB 97 HCA)

21 An inquiry to the diocese about the significance of his acceptance did not lead to a clear answer, but there appeared to have been agreement that, even although a Chancellor enjoyed an unusual measure of independence, his decision could not have been taken lightly.

22 John Stuart Mill wrote that 'the only purpose for which power can be rightfully exercised against any member of a civilised community, against his will, is to prevent harm to others'. *John Stuart Mill on Liberty and other Essays*, 1991 edition, Oxford: Oxford World Classics, 14.

23 *The Times*, Thursday 12 September 1957.

24 Six days earlier, immediately after the publication of the report, he emphasised that 'We're not to be taken, *I* don't want to be taken, as approving or encouraging, *morally* approving, of this sort of behaviour. The Churches don't. They say it's sin. … What we're saying is that we don't approve of it morally, just as we don't approve of all sorts of behaviour, but we don't see why this particular form of behaviour, which we regard, most of us, as morally repugnant, why that … form of behaviour, should be regarded as a criminal offence'. In *Press Conference*, BBC Television, 6 September 1957. http://www.bbc.co.uk/archive/gay_rights/12001.shtml

25 Transcript: BEHIND   THE   HEADLINES A   television   interview   on HOMOSEXUALITY and the LAW between Godfrey Lagden, M.P., Antony Grey and John Meade. Independent Television for South Wales and the West of England, 10 March 1961. Much later, Antony Grey recalled that 'I was in my early 20s then but I volunteered to go down and do a sort of back to the camera and shadows thing with one of the very hostile MPs. And it was really quite comical because he behaved as if I was a sort of dreadful wild beast or something and sort of crouched at the other end of the studio glaring at me'. *The Generation Gap*, BBC Radio 4, 2 March 2010. Godfrey Lagden, 1906–1989, was the Conservative Member for Hornchurch between 1955 and 1966.

26 What he was almost certainly referring to was Romans, Ch. 1, v. 27, in which there is an imprecation against 'the men [who], leaving the natural use of the woman, burned in their lust one toward another, men with men working unseemliness …'

27 Homosexual Law Reform Society – Part of a Report of Meeting held at Caxton Hall, Westminster, 12 May 1960. Lambeth Palace papers (BSR/MWC/HOM/1).

28 See O. Chadwick; *Michael Ramsey: A Life, op. cit.*, 159, 148.

29 *News Chronicle*, 5 September 1957.

30 J. Wolfenden; *Turning Points: The Memoirs of Lord Wolfenden; op. cit.*, 140–141.

31 *News Chronicle*, 5 September 1957. But there was also an article in the same newspaper on the following day by C.H. Rolph, titled 'Sin and Crime[:] Don't confuse the two – however much the Report may have set you arguing'. He said further that 'There is much in the Report to praise'; claimed that very little was known

about homosexuality; and put a case for research by the new Home Office Research Unit.

32 Derek Marks, 1921–1975, was a political journalist who had entered politics as a prospective Liberal candidate for the Cleveland division of Yorkshire in the 1940s. He was, said Edward Pickering, a man who 'bestrode the worlds of Fleet Street and Westminster … the outstanding lobby correspondent of his day, and could frequently record the private proceedings of parliamentary committees for his newspaper within minutes of the close of a meeting'. (http://www.oxforddnb.com/view/article/48464)

33 A letter dated 17 February 1957 and preserved in the Conservative Party Archives at the Bodleian Library stated that 'I enclose a cutting from the Daily Express. Will you tell me if this is what I have been voting for as a Conservative for the last thirty five years? I would not have done so if I had thought that the Party was in favour of unnatural practices, but now we know that their predilection is for unnatural, not natural however unsavoury, they are. This filthy urge of the Conservative Party must make one think the majority of the Party has these tendencies or sympathies, and I would be repulsed by their unnatural, filthy ideas … If this is what the Conservative Party produce they must have filthy minds, and one can expect their next programme will be advocating buggery! Of two alternatives the less evil is the best. I will therefore (against my will) work … to get the Labour Party returned to Parliament. … Will all perverts know that male Conservatives are fair game to be approached by these unspeakable males? …' The cutting from The Daily Express of 17 February 1957 reported that 'Highly controversial proposals for changes in the vice laws are about to be put before the Cabinet – and it can be regarded as almost certain that they will be accepted. An investigating committee will, it is understood, urge:- 1. Severer sentences for persistent prostitution … 2. Relaxation of the law covering homosexuality. It is suggested that the act between consenting adults should NOT be treated as criminal. This proposal will provoke sharp opposition in Parliament and from the Churches. …' A Gallup Poll taken in December 1958 showed that 48% of all voters interviewed, and 60% of Conservatives, supported the Government's rejection of the Committee's recommendation about the decriminalisation of homosexual acts between consenting adults in private (*News Chronicle*, 17 December 1958).

34 See Lord Pakenham's speech in HL Deb 4 December 1957 Vol. 206 cc733–50. There were no papers on the Wolfenden Report in the Labour Party Archive in the People's History Museum, Manchester.

35 An editorial in the *Daily Mirror* of 26 November 1958, headlined 'WHY ARE THEY SCARED?', complained that 'the Government has rejected the report's recommendation that homosexual acts between consenting adults should no longer be regarded as a criminal offence. Nor has the Labour Opposition declared its official attitude on this controversial issue. Both sides are frightened by public opinion. THE MIRROR DEPLORES THIS TIMOROUS BEHAVIOUR'.

36 Sir Alec would be reported as saying in early 1964 that 'he could not give any undertaking about the Government's attitude towards … a move before the election, as both the Prime Minister and the Home Secretary, who was keeping the matter under review, had seen no evidence of any alteration in Parliamentary or public opinion'. Meeting of the Executive Committee of the Homosexual Law Reform Society, 23 March 1964.

37 Leo Abse recalled that 'my private negotiations with the government, through Fletcher-Cooke, who was then Under Secretary of State at the Home Office, to accept [my] Bill, were of no avail. Fletcher-Cooke was wholly sympathetic but the figure of Lord Kilmuir, then Lord Chancellor, loomed in the background'. L. Abse, *Private Member*, *op. cit.*, 147.

38 Noted in a letter from Miss Steel to Gordon Dunstan, 7 May 1958, Lambeth Palace papers (BCC/SRD/7/4/1/12).

39 Letter from A.E. Dyson to the Bishop of St. Albans, 31 March 1958, Lambeth Palace papers (BCC/SRD/7/4/1/12).

40 The adjective was employed in an editorial in David Astor's *Observer* of 8 June 1958. David Astor, 1912–2001, was to be an important intermediary between the emerging Homosexual Law Reform Society and men and women of influence such as the philanthropist, Simon Sainsbury. It was at lunches which he arranged in 1963 that contacts were made between the Society and Henry Brooke, the Home Secretary, and Aneurin Bevan. He gave Andrew Hallidie Smith half a page in his broadsheet to write about 'Homosexuals: a Breeze of Change' on 19 June 1960.

41 Particularly prominent was the *Daily Mirror*. Take one editorial, that was published on 9 June 1958, and headlined 'GET A MOVE ON, MR. BUTLER'.

42 *The Times*, 3 September 1958.

43 HC Deb 26 November 1958 Vol. 596 cc365–508.

44 He said in debate: 'There is no doubt from the inquiries and researches I have made that many hon. Members and many people outside would at present misunderstand the removal of the prohibition as implying, if not approval, at least condonation by the legislature of homosexual conduct. We have to reflect that many people who are outside the influence of religion find no other basis for their notions of right and wrong but in the criminal law. Can we be sure that if we removed the support of the criminal law from these people they would find any other support? At any rate, what is clear, after taking this time to think it over and to receive all the impressions and consider the perplexities of this problem, is that there is at present a very large section of the population who strongly repudiate homosexual conduct and whose moral sense would be offended by an alteration of the law which would seem to imply approval or tolerance of what they regard as a great social evil. Therefore, the considerations I have indicated satisfy the Government that they would not be justified at present, on the basis of opinions expressed so far, in proposing legislation to carry out the recommendations of the Committee'. (HC Deb 26 November 1958 Vol. 596 cc365–508)

45 In May 1963, for example, members of the Homosexual Law Reform Society met the then Home Secretary, Henry Brooke, at the luncheon given by David Astor. They reported that he was 'personally sympathetic regarding the subject of homosexual law reform, though he had said that Government action was not politically possible at the present time'. Minutes of a Meeting of the Executive Committee of the Homosexual Law Reform Society, 18 July 1963.

46 Mr Butler had previously told the House of Commons that 'In view of the nature of the problem involved it is important to take account of public opinion and particularly of any views that may be expressed by hon. Members of this House, before coming to any final conclusions on the Committee's recommendations'. HC Deb 31 October 1957 Vol. 575 c87W.

47 Conclusions of a Meeting of the Cabinet held at 10 Downing Street, S.W. 1, on Thursday, 28 November, 1957, 82nd Conclusions, CC. (57).

48 4 December 1957 Vol. 206 cc733–50.

49 Following the usual pattern, there were to be questions in the House of Commons and letters to the press. One example was that of a pair of letters written by the MP, Kenneth Younger, and the Bishop of Exeter and published together in the *Observer* on 26 October 1958. Both lamented the government's concentration on the report's recommendations about prostitution and its neglect of homosexuality. The bishop said simply that 'If, as I hope, the Wolfenden Report is to be debated soon, it is in my opinion most important that adequate time should be devoted to the recommendations on homosexuality'. Another example, published at much the same time and appearing over the signatures of four people, including the Archbishop of York, asking 'whether it is in the best interests of British justice that there should remain on the Statute Book a law which is widely discredited'. (The *Times*, 24 October 1958)

50 One was George Rogers, 1906–1983, the Labour Member for Kensington North, who said that 'I think there are numerous aspects of our social life which have deteriorated during the past few years and that that has something to do with it. ... the deterioration in moral standards is due to the lack of belief by the great majority of people in any after-life'. HC Deb 31 October 1958 Vol. 594 cc476–577.

51 See, for example, R.A. Butler's statements in HC Deb 22 May 1958 Vol. 588 cc1475–6; HC Deb 12 June 1958 Vol. 589 cc411–6.

52 The Lord Chancellor said in the House of Lords on 30 October 1958: 'owing to the pressure of business there has not been a debate on that subject'. HL Deb 30 October 1958 Vol. 212 cc83–137.

53 See HL Deb 11 June 1958 Vol. 209 cc714–88.

54 See HC Deb 20 November 1958 Vol. 595 cc1324–9 and see the report in *The Times*, 17 July 1958.

55 Penal Reform General Suggestions for Inclusion in Legislation: HOME OFFICE LEGISLATION IN THE 1958/9 SESSION; HO291/504. It may be presumed that any Home Office bills that were contemplated at that meeting of 18 February would have touched, not on reforming the law on homosexual acts, but on prostitution.

56 HC Deb 19 June 1958 Vol. 589 cc1312–5.

57 Item 5: Report of the Committee on Homosexuality and Prostitution; H.A. (58) 16th meeting of the Home Affairs Committee, 25 July 1958.

58 It had as usual been preceded by a memorandum in which Mr Butler said merely 'I do not think that there can be any question at present of legislation on the Wolfenden Committee's recommendations on homosexual offences, though I propose that we should find time early in the new Session for a debate on both aspects of the Committee's report', before moving on to a lengthier discussion of matters that were to lead to the Street Offences Bill. (Report of the Committee on Homosexual Offences and Prostitution: Memorandum by the Secretary of State for the Home Office and Lord Privy Seal, Home Affairs Committee, 23 October 1958 (H.A.(58)123)).

59 H.A. (58) 20th meeting of the Home Affairs Committee, 24 October 1958.

60 Leo Abse, 1917–2008, was Labour Member of Parliament for Pontypool (later renamed Torfaen) for almost 30 years from 1958. It was said of him that 'No backbench MP could exceed his success in getting Private Member's Bills on to the statute book. His campaign for the normalisation of homosexual acts between consenting adults was of a piece with his tenacity and eloquence'. (www.timesonline.co.uk/tol/comment/obituaries/article4573641eceOBITUARIES)

61 L. Abse, *Private Member, op. cit.*, 147.

62 'The blind eye', *Manchester Guardian*, 14 June 1958.

63 H. Montgomery Hyde, 1907–1989, was the barrister, prolific author and Unionist Member of Parliament for North Belfast. He published a number of books on crime and homosexuality, and gave criminology as his recreation in *Who's Who*. (http://www.ukwhoswho.com/view/article/oupww/whowaswho/U165640/HYDE_Harford_Montgomery?index=1&results=QuicksearchResults&query=0)

64 The first edition of *Famous Trials: Oscar Wilde*, published by William Hodge and Co., London, appeared in 1948. The work covered the trials at length, but was not marked for its condemnation either of Wilde or of his prosecution. The *Preface* to the second edition, published by Penguin, London, in 1962, contained the following observation: 'there can be very little if any doubt that Wilde was justly convicted – indeed he admitted as much himself to friends with whom he was in touch both during and after his imprisonment. The best that can be said for him is that, so far as is known, he never debauched any innocent young men'. (p. 19) The imagery of the evil corrupter of the young was to play a large role in constructions of the enemy homosexual deviant.

65 See the remark made by Marcus Lipton in the debate on the address, HC Deb 28 October 1958 Vol. 594 cc8–142.

66 HC Deb 13 November 1958 Vol. 595 cc572–9.

67 An editorial in the *Star* of 10 October 1958 was headed 'Action at Last', and it continued 'We rejoice. At last the Committee's important findings … are to be discussed in the Commons. But what a reflection on MPs of all parties this delay has been. … Why on earth did MPs fight shy of it?'

68 The Society's secretary, Andrew Hallidie Smith, wrote to its members to say: ' … a situation of some urgency has been brought about by the Home Secretary's statement on October 9th, that there may be an early debate on the Wolfenden Report. We feel that now is the time when letters to Members of Parliament can be most effective. We suggest, therefore, that you write a letter or postcard to your own M.P. urging him to work for the implementation of the Wolfenden proposals on homosexuality'. Letter of 23 October 1958, Lambeth Palace papers (BCC/SRD/7/4/1/12).

69 HC Deb 26 November 1958 Vol. 596 cc365–508.

70 Anthony Greenwood, 1911–1982, was the Labour Member for Rossendale.

71 Kenneth Morgan in his entry in *The Oxford Dictionary of National Biography*, http://www.oxforddnb.com/view/article/31169

72 In that letter of 22 November, co-signed by John Baillie, Cynthia Colville and the lawyer and academic, Lord Chorley, the Archbishop of York, Michael Ramsey, had said simply that 'We understand that the Wolfenden Report is to be debated in the House of Commons. We hope that, in considering the proposals on homosexuality, members will bear in mind the question as to whether it is in the best interests of British justice that there should remain on the Statute Book a law which is widely discredited'. It may be presumed that John Baillie was the distinguished clergyman and academic, 1886–1960, who had been an Extra Chaplain to the Queen in Scotland since 1956; Chaplain to the Queen in Scotland, 1952–56 (and to King George VI, 1947–52); Principal of New College, Edinburgh and Dean of the Faculty of Divinity, 1950–56; and Professor of Divinity in the University of Edinburgh, 1934–56 (http://www.ukwhoswho.com/view/article/oupww/whowaswho/U234309/BAILLIE_Very_Rev._John?index=2&results=QuicksearchResults&query=0). Lady (Helen) Cynthia Colville, 1884–1968, was the twin sister of the Marquess of Crewe and the wife of Viscount Colville of Culross, a former Woman of the Bedchamber to Queen Mary, 1923–53; a social worker and a J.P. (http://www.ukwhoswho.com/view/article/oupww/whowaswho/U49104/COLVILLE_Lady_Helen_Cynthia?index=1&results=QuicksearchResults&query=0). She published her autobiography, *A Crowded Life* (Evans Brothers, London) in 1963, after the Wolfenden Report had been issued but some time before the appearance of that letter to *The Times*. *A Crowded Life* says nothing about Sir John Wolfenden or any of the other principals or developments in the politics of homosexual law reform, and her appearance as a co-signatory cannot be explained.

73 He pronounced that 'I cannot personally accept the main recommendation of the Wolfenden Committee in regard to homosexuals. I do believe as an individual – I may be right or I may he wrong – that there do exist private realms in which the State should intrude. I believe that the removal of this offence from the Statute Book would be at this time against the public interest'. Of the central tenet of the Wolfenden recommendation about the decriminalisation of sin, he would enquire in debate two years later should not 'the criminal law interfere with euthanasia, abortion and incest?' (HC Deb 29 June 1960 Vol. 625 cc1453–514)

74 He was later to be one of those who changed their mind.

75 Emanuel Shinwell, 1884–1986, was the Labour Member for the Easington Division of Durham between 1950–70. He was to occupy a number of ministerial posts.

76 Capt. Rt Hon. Frederick Bellenger 1894–1968, was Labour Member for the Bassetlaw Division of Nottinghamshire between 1935 and his death in 1968 (http://www.oxforddnb.com/view/article/92720).

77 Jean Mann, a Christian socialist, also quoted James Adair at length, and said that 'Neither psychiatrists nor the Churches condemn criminals. Ask the clergy what kind of sentence they would give to anyone. They would not want to give a sentence at all, regarding these people as poor, beloved sinners. … A very limited but very powerful and influential body is behind the Report, and behind the expense of the sending out of the Report. It has very wide ramifications. The evil thread runs through the theatre, through the music hall, through the Press, and through the B.B.C. It has international ramifications'. (For details of her biography see http://www.oxforddnb.com/view/article/50056))

78 See *The Times*, 12 February 1966.

79 James Dance, 1907–1971, became Conservative Member for Bromsgrove in 1955.

80 Dr. A.D.D. Broughton, 1902–1979, was a medical practitioner who was elected Member of Parliament in 1949.

81 Norman Cole, 1909–1979, the Liberal and Conservative Member for Bedfordshire, South, said, for instance: 'I do not want to provide any more opportunities for or in any way seem to condone what I and most other people believe to be a sin, whether it is called an unnatural practice, a deviation or anything else. … I believe in the moral sense of the majority of the public. I believe that when the House of Commons or any other legislature is in some doubt as to how far it should move, it is a pretty safe plan to rest on the majority feeling from the point of view of morals. I certainly am quite prepared to do that'.

82 Sir John Wolfenden commented that 'All the obvious points were made, with demands for ruthless suppression of 'evil men' … '*Turning Points: The Memoirs of Lord Wolfenden, op. cit.*, 142.

83 Kenneth Younger said of the Home Secretary's opening statement: 'I do not think the right hon. Gentleman argued much of the case on merits against the Committee's recommendations. He really based his decision not to accept the recommendations almost wholly upon his appreciation of the unreadiness of the public mind for a change of this kind, which he felt would be generally regarded as implying approval by the Government and by Parliament of homosexual acts. It is not unnatural that the public mind should be in this condition because, after all, this subject was almost undiscussed in public until the Wolfenden Report was published'.

84 'The Wolfenden Debate', *New Statesman*, 6 December 1958.

85 J. Weeks, *Coming Out: Homosexual Politics in Britain from the Nineteenth Century to the Present, op. cit.*, 168.

86 Memorandum by the Secretary of State for the Home Department [R.A. Butler] and Lord Privy Seal; 12th December, 1958, C. (58) 249.

87 See *The Times*, November 27, 1958.

88 Street Offences Act 1959 (7 & 8 Eliz. 2 c. 57).

89 R. Butler; *The Art of the Possible: The Memoirs of Lord Butler K.G., C.H., op. cit.*, 204.

90 It was an Act to consolidate 'the statute law of England and Wales relating to sexual crimes, to the abduction, procuration and prostitution of women and to kindred offences, and to make such adaptations of Statutes extending beyond England and Wales as are needed in consequence of that consolidation' (Lord Kilmuir speaking in the House of Lords, HL Deb 24 January 1956 Vol. 195 c489). Section 12 provided that 'It is felony for a person to commit buggery with another person'; and Section 13 that 'It is an offence for a man to commit an act of gross indecency with another man, whether in public or private, or to be a party to the commission by a man of an act of gross indecency with another man, or to procure the commission by a man of an act of gross indecency with another man'. The Act was represented by the attorney general as no more than a housekeeping measure not warranting much debate: it 'merely consolidates the existing statute law, with such corrections and minor improvements as may be authorised under that Act. Consequently, it would not be in order for me

to discuss the contents of the Bill'. (HC Deb 6 July 1956 Vol. 555 cc1750–1) And, indeed, it was passed at second reading in a few minutes, but it is interesting that it should have been introduced at a time when the Wolfenden Committee was in the latter stages of its deliberations.

91 See A. Howard, *RAB: The Life of R.A. Butler*, *op. cit.*, 264–5.

92 He had talked about how the Exeter Labour Party, for which he had been prospective Parliamentary candidate, had been 'infiltrated by people who, though they deny that they are Communists, advocate doctrines indistinguishable from Communist doctrine' (*The Times*, 28 August 1958).

93 G. Sparrow (1965); *"R.A.B."*: *Study of a Statesman*, London: Odhams Books, 173.

94 Letter from Dr R.D. Reid, *The Spectator*, January 1958.

95 The records of many small local police forces disappeared with the amalgamations of the 1960s and 1970s, and, in this instance, when the Avon and Somerset Police were formed in 1974. The Avon and Somerset Police did not answer my query about the location, if any, of records of policing in Wells in the 1950s and the archives in the Somerset Heritage Centre contained police records for the period relating only to the City of Bath.

96 Email from Graeme Edwards, 24 May 2011.

97 Extensive search found no evidence of a pogrom (although that cannot be the same as saying that no pogrom took place). A perfunctory report of preliminary proceedings on charges of gross indecency in the Wells magistrates court appeared in the *Central Somerset Gazette* on 14 February 1958. It simply recorded two cases, one of which was abandoned because 'a prima facie case had not been made out', without supplying detail apart from the name and occupation of the alleged offenders. The broadsheet *Wells Journal*, which could devote 20 column inches in its edition of 24 January 1958 to the prosecution of two youths who failed to show their bus tickets; nine column inches to the imposition of a £2 fine for speeding on 25 April 1958; and a third of its front page to a report of the Conservative club's new lounge bar on 4 April 1958; gave six column inches in an inside page to an identical report of the charges brought against the two men on 14 February 1958. The surviving case was tried at the Wells Assizes and reported in the *Wells Journal* of 23 May 1958: the 40-year old man was given a conditional discharge.

98 LAGNA, the Lesbian and Gay Newspaper Archive which is housed in the Bishopsgate Institute, the major news archive in the area, containing some 200,000 cuttings, has no direct reports at all of the allegedly heightened police activity in Wells (and I am grateful for the help we received from the LAGNA archivists).

99 For example, E.M. Forster wrote to the *Spectator* to talk about Dr Reid's 'disquieting account of the prosecutions at Wells' and how it 'should receive all possible publicity. Evidently the scientific conclusions and humane recommendations of the Wolfenden Report cut no ice in that city. Nor is Wells unique. ...' (letter published on 17 January 1958).

100 Robert Reid, 1898–1983, was the Headmaster of King's College, Taunton, 1933–37, and later became the High Constable and Deputy Mayor of the City of Wells (http://www.ukwhoswho.com/view/article/oupww/whowaswho/U168462/REID_Dr_Robert_Douglas?index=1&results=QuicksearchResults&query=0)

101 *The Spectator*, 3 January 1958, Vol. 200, No. 6758, 18.

102 See his letter to the *Observer*, 16 March 1958.

103 See A. Grey (1992); *Quest for Justice: Towards Homosexual Emancipation*, London: Sinclair-Stevenson, 26.

104 The Treason Trial involved 156 people, including Nelson Mandela, who had been arrested in a raid and accused of treason in South Africa in 1956.

105 D. Astor, 'Cry Wolfenden', the *Observer*, 8 June 1958.

106 They included (most notably) Isaiah Berlin; the Bishops of Birmingham and Exeter; Robert Boothby; Canon John Collins; Jacquetta Hawkes; J.B. Priestley; Kenneth Walker and Barbara Wootton.

107 See M. Ignatieff; *Isaiah Berlin: A Life*, *op. cit.*, 46. Ignatieff talks about Berlin 'recoiling at the homo-erotic affectation' of the Oxford of the 1920s.

108 See A. Grey; *Quest for Justice: Towards Homosexual Emancipation*, *op. cit.*, 27.

109 By 'enacted' I intend to convey the argument that those involved created the apparently external conditions to which they could then respond. See K. Weick (1979); *The Social Psychology of Organizing*, Reading, Mass.: Addison-Wesley.

110 The phrase is David Astor's in 'Cry Wolfenden', the *Observer*, 8 June 1958.

111 A.E. Dyson himself immediately contributed to that reflexively self-generating chain of letters by writing to the *Spectator* of 10 January 1958 to endorse what Dr Reid had said. He opened: 'I agree very much with Dr. Reid's letter, and would gladly belong to any society which existed to help the victims and their families of our homosexuality laws. But even more to the point would be the formation of a society concerned to work for a change in the laws themselves'.

112 Letter to the Bishop of St. Albans, 31 March 1958, Lambeth Palace papers (BSR/MWC/HOM).

113 As part of his enactment of events, A.E. Dyson wrote to the *Observer* of 16 June 1958 in reply to its editorial titled 'Cry Wolfenden' to say that 'the Homosexual Law Reform Society now exists ... and we shall welcome help from all those who wish to see this important and already overdue reform effected'. He published a virtually identical letter in the *Church of England Newspaper* of 20 June 1958. Advertisements appeared in periodicals such as the *New Statesman*, proclaiming that 'The Society is working for the implementation of the major Wolfenden proposal and welcomes support from all who agree with its aim' (issue of 20 September 1958).

114 *Progress Report of the Homosexual Law Reform Society*, London, April 1959 1st issue, Lambeth Palace Library (BSR/MWC/HOM/1).

115 The history of the National Campaign commented that 'All too often reformist groups put themselves beyond the pale of the political process by becoming identified with harmless or questionable fringe elements in society. Respectability is sometime attached to numbers, but also ... to association with powerful and respected sectors of the community. In their search for the power of respectability abolitionist groups employed several techniques. They emphasised the empirical nature of their case and went out of their way to dissociate themselves from highly emotional and sensational appeals ... They took special pains to include in their membership persons of avowed conservative views, such as a number of Tory humanitarians, peers and social leaders. ...' J. Christoph; *Capital Punishment and British Politics*, *op. cit.*, 189.

116 Jeffrey Weeks (1990); said that 'throughout the next eight years it maintained an air of well-drilled respectability. ...' *Coming Out: Homosexual Politics in Britain from the Nineteenth Century to the Present*, London: Quartet, 168. The illustrious composition of the Society's committee would be flourished continually to effect. In a letter to the *Daily Telegraph* on 5 November 1958, for instance, Andrew Hallidie Smith talked about how 'It cannot be without significance that our own committee list of over 100 distinguished people includes names of such eminence as those of the Archbishop of York and Lady Rothschild, and until recently those of the late Dr. Ralph Vaughan Williams and Dame Rose Macaulay'.

117 A.E. Dyson to Ena Steel, 18 May 1958. Lambeth Palace papers (BSR/MWC/HOM).

118 The society noted that 'It is clearly not within the competence of a law reform society to campaign for a radical and controversial change in social attitudes. We must work within the existing moral framework, and our purpose must be to encourage a change in laws which we not only regard as unjust and ill-advised but which bring within

the criminal sphere matters of purely private morality'. HOMOSEXUAL LAW REFORM SOCIETY, undated, Lambeth Palace papers (BSR/MWC/HOM/1).

119 It was those names which could usefully be paraded whenever it was necessary to underscore the legitimacy of the new society and its cause. For example, Antony Grey wrote to the *Bolton Evening News* of 13 August 1963 in reply to an earlier correspondent that she 'must be unaware that the Archbishops of Canterbury and York, together with many other prominent clergy from all the main denominations, members of both Houses of Parliament belonging to all three political parties, and eminent members of the legal, medical and other professions, form the honorary committee of this society, and are united in the view that the present law … is unworthy of a civilised, Christian country'.

120 Kenneth Walker, 1882–1966, was an author and urologist who was appointed officer in charge of the venereal diseases department at St. Bartholomew's Hospital, where he concentrated on the social and psychological consequences of sexual disorders. (See the entry by David Innes Williams in *The Oxford Dictionary of National Biography*, http://www.oxforddnb.com/view/article/56873). He resigned as Chairman in 1963, to be replaced by C.H. Rolph.

121 Ambrose Appelbe was a solicitor whose firm's website describes him thus: 'Ambrose Appelbe founded our firm in Lincoln's Inn in 1935 and gave discreet, personal advice to clients as varied as Ingrid Bergman, Mandy Rice-Davies and the murderer John Christie. He helped found the National Marriage Guidance Council (now Relate), Help the Aged and was a founding trustee of the Albany Trust which was the first national counselling service for gay men, lesbians and other sexual minorities'. http://www.ambrose.appelbe.co.uk/history The Past. He was a prolific letter correspondent in *The Times* on a wide range of matters, including the sighting of birds on Hampstead Heath, the conservation of Highgate Village and forms of marriage.

122 Dr W.L. Neustatter, 1904–1979, occupied a number of posts, his final position being that of consulting psychiatrist to the Royal Northern Hospital, London. His obituary on p. 278 of *The British Medical Journal* of 28 July 1979 called him 'the doyen of British forensic psychiatrists'.

123 E.B. Strauss, 1894–1961, was Consulting Physician for Psychological Medicine at St. Bartholomew's Hospital.

124 By the middle of March 1963, for example, it could claim 1,142 subscribing supporters.

125 See G. Wells (2011); *A House in France: A Memoir*, Bloomsbury, London.

126 Other recruits, joining in early 1965, were the Bishop of Woolwich; the Earl of Huntingdon; Norman St. John Stevas; W.T. Williams, Q.C.; and Christopher Chataway M.P.

127 See http://gayhistory.wordpress.com/2011/08/22/homosexual-law-reform-society/

128 See his obituary in *The Times*, 4 May 2010. In *The Generation Gap* of 2 March 2010, he recalled that 'It was quite a relief to me that you were able to get into the campaigning work because I could be more open around that. But even there, a lot of people would have preferred it I think if I hadn't been gay. Our committee, which was a committee of the Great and the Good and most of them were not gay, I think they felt very nervous at having a gay man doing most of the work in case I was busted by the police'.

129 A. Grey; Quest for *Justice: Towards Homosexual Emancipation, op. cit.*, 29.

130 Letter to the Bishop of St Albans, 31 March 1958, Lambeth Palace papers (BSR/MWC/HOM). Despite those difficulties, Antony Grey would later conclude that the results of those overtures had been critically important: 'Throughout the law reform campaign, we were in constant touch with leading members of various churches, and the support of the then Archbishop of Canterbury, Michael Ramsey, and several of his colleagues was crucial in the House of Lords'. 'Christian Society and the Homosexual', in *Speaking Out: Writings on Sex, Law, Politics and Society 1954–95*, Cassell, London, 1997, 135.

131 One of his early overtures to the Moral Welfare Council said that: 'I am afraid that I could give only the outlines of my plan, and until the Executive Committee has met ... it will be hard to put anything definite into writing. ... I realise, of course, that your own Council has been considering the problem, and working for reform, for a long time now, with far more expert knowledge than I could hope to assemble!' Letter to Ena Steel, 13 April 1958. Lambeth Palace papers (BSR/MWC/HOM)...

132 Letter from the Bishop of St. Albans to Ena Steel, 27 May 1958. Lambeth Palace papers (BSR/MWC/HOM). There were other refusals, some more emphatic than others. Some time later, the Bishop of Chester would tell Antony Grey, the society's secretary that: 'I accept that there are many cases which need pastoral and medical care rather than punishment by imprisonment. There are, nevertheless, in my opinion, grave possibilities of vicious and corrupting influences through the activity of consenting adults in private, and I cannot accept that it would be right for the law to be powerless to deal with such cases of behaviour which must have a deleterious effect upon the welfare of society'. Minutes of the Meeting of the Executive Committee of the Homosexual Law Reform Society, 23 March 1964. The bishop was formally to decline the invitation in a letter of 5 July 1958. Sherwin Bailey was regarded as the Moral Welfare Council's representative to the Society.

133 Professor the Reverend Canon G R Dunstan CBE, MA, HonDD, HonLLD, FSA, HonFRCP, FRCOG, HonFRCGP, HonFRCPCH, 1917–2004, was described as 'the leading English moral theologian of his time, committed to the multidisciplinary discussion of issues raised by the practice of medicine' (Obituary (2004); *Journal of Medical Ethics* 30, 233–234).

134 She had been the General Secretary of the Moral Welfare Council from 1944 and was to remain so until the Council was reinvented as the Church Council for Social Work in 1961 (see *The Times*, 1 September 1961).

135 Lambeth Palace papers: memorandum from Miss Steel to St. Albans, 9 April 1958 – MR DYSON (BSR/MWC/HOM).

136 That view was to linger. Dunstan was to write to D.S. Bailey, Study Secretary of the Church of England Moral Welfare Council, on 13 June 1958: 'Have you seen the statement put out by Mr Dyson and sent, I understand, to all M.P.s on behalf of the Homosexual Law Reform Society? It contains a quotation from para. 62 of the Wolfenden Report and eight reasons why the recommendation should be accepted. It is too naïve for words. Are you, as a signatory, consulted about what is put out in your name? If so, are you able to keep him from adding yet more confusion to public opinion in this way?' The statement to which he referred read:

> 'HOMOSEXUAL LAW REFORM SOCIETY Some reasons in favour of an early acceptance of this recommendation [Para 62 of the Wolfenden Report]
>
> 1. Homosexuality, as the Wolfenden Committee emphasised, is not a disease, and there is no reason to suppose it would become more widespread if the law were reformed. It is, rather, the sexual orientation of a small, though not unimportant minority of otherwise normal human beings; and in countries where the law has been amended no increase of any kind has taken place. [marginal comment inserted by the Bishop of St. Albans: 'too simple']
>
> 2. Homosexuality is not connected in any way with offences against children. Such crimes are just as likely to be perpetrated by heterosexuals ...' ['?' was inserted in the margin]

Dunstan's own utilitarian view attempted to balance competing imperatives: 'while the law should clearly protect the young and immature from corruption, and also the general public from being scandalised by immoral behaviour, it is not the task of the law to regulate the private behaviour of private persons. ... It is ... in principle wrong and unjust that homosexual relations between consenting male adults should be a crime, and that such persons should be open to the rigours of the law ...' (GRD February 1961: REFORM OF THE LAW ON HOMOSEXUAL OFFENCES Draft Report, Lambeth Palace papers.)

137 G.R.D.'s Postscript to memorandum from Miss Steel to St. Albans, 9 April 1958 – MR DYSON (BSR/MWC/HOM).

138 She did not make it evident what she found so distressing about the membership of the society's committees.

139 It is not clear which and why certain members of the committee were regarded as beyond the pale.

140 Letter from Ena Steel to Gordon Dunstan, 7 May 1958. Lambeth Palace papers (BSR/MWC/HOM).

141 Letter of 8 May 1958 (BSR/MWC/HOM).

142 Andrew Hallidie Smith graduated from Cambridge in 1955, attended Ely Theological College, and became the vicar attached to the Church of St. Mary, Pype Hayes in the Diocese of Birmingham in 1956 (based on *Crockford's Clerical Directory, 1957–58* (1958); London: Oxford University Press).

143 The note read: 'I rang up Mr Hallidie Smith of the Homosexual Law Reform Society. I told him you were very sorry you could not undertake to see him for some considerable time, as your programme was at present so very heavy, and that you were so committed to other duties that in any case you felt you could probably not be of very much help to him. Mr. Smith ... asked how soon you were likely to be able to see him. I said that I knew you were hopelessly committed throughout November, and that December also was very full, and he himself suggested that perhaps he had better wait until after Christmas, with which proposal I agreed. He then asked whether there would be any point in trying to get into touch with Miss Steel. I did not encourage him in this idea. I think he will probably not ask for an interview again for two or three months'. Anon to Mr Dunstan, 9 October 1958: NOTE FOR FILE (BSR/MWC/HOM).

A slightly more sympathetic response, evinced by Sherwin Bailey, was still reticent about Hallidie Smith and the Homosexual Law Reform Society. Sherwin Bailey told Ena Steel on 15 May 1958 that 'Yesterday evening I had a visit from Mr Halliday Smith, the clergyman associated with Mr Dyson in promoting the new society for reform of the homosexual offences law ... He gave me a very full account of the origin and plans of the society, from which I gained the impression that it is a serious venture, and that they are anxious to act wisely and responsibly. I expressed my own view (and yours) that action was perhaps precipitate at this stage, and that much more needed to be done educationally, but they believe that some action at least is necessary to prevent the authorities from shelving the matter and thus making it more difficult to revive interest. ...'

144 Thus A.E. Dyson referred to him in a general letter as a 'young married clergyman'. Lambeth Palace papers: letter dated 15 July 1958 (BSR/MWC/HOM).

145 Quoted in 'Heretics Discuss Perversion', *Varsity*, 22 November 1958.

146 Simon Sainsbury, 1930–2006, was a member of the Sainsbury family and the founder of the Monument Trust. He registered a civil partnership with his partner, Stewart Grimshaw, in January 2006 (see http://www.oxforddnb.com/view/article/97474)

147 Ena Steel reported to the Bishop of St. Albans on 27 May 1958 that 'Mr Sainsbury had seen them and although he was not impressed he was considering giving them a small sum of money to see what progress they made, but without committing himself to giving any more unless he approved of what they were doing. ... All we can do at the moment I think is to help [when] we are asked to do things that we feel should be done, otherwise to refuse. ...' Lambeth Palace papers (BSR/MWC/HOM).

148 Letter from Ena Steel to Gordon Dunstan, 7 May 1958. Lambeth Palace papers (BSR/MWC/HOM).

149 Although it was also accepted that many of the problems faced by homosexual men were, in effect, iatrogenic, the result of an oppressive criminal justice system. Antony Grey commented, for instance, at a meeting of the Executive Committee of the Homosexual Law Reform Society that 'it was evident that many doctors were not sufficiently conscious of how the social and personal problems of homosexuality were being aggravated by the present law'. Minutes of a Meeting of the Executive Committee of the Homosexual Law Reform Society, 16 April 1964. It is interesting that the position now appears to have been reversed, and that suggestions that homosexuals are treatable have been taken up by the religious right in America and are now regarded as reactionary by liberal law reformers (see the report by C. Lamb, 'From Tea Party kook to contender', *Sunday Times*, 19 June 2011). Public designations of homosexuality have evolved from the unnatural heretic, to evil man, to sick deviant, to the relative normalisation of the freely chosen way of life, and the presumption that the freely chosen is a remediable pathology is a target of resentment.

150 Under the auspices of the society, she carried out a survey in the early1960s to ascertain the clinical facilities then available for the treatment of homosexuals in the London area (reported, for instance, in the Minutes of a Meeting of the Executive Committee of the Homosexual Law Reform Society, 23 October 1963).

151 Minutes of a Meeting of the Executive Committee of the Homosexual Law Reform Society, 23 October 1963.

152 Minutes of the Meeting of the Executive Committee of the Homosexual Law Reform Society, 24 February 1965.

153 The outcome was published as (1965); 'On the Genesis of Male Homosexuality: An Attempt at Clarifying the Role of the Parents' in *The British Journal of Psychiatry*, 111 803–813. The article's abstract read 'The results confirm those of previous studies according to which homosexual men more frequently than heterosexual men had bad relations with their fathers, and had fathers who were ineffectual as parents and did not serve as models for their sons. … Since the present findings support those of previous investigations which suggest that homosexuality is furthered by the lack of good relations between the child and his father, it has been concluded that more attention needs to be given than is usual at present to the role of the father in the upbringing of the child'.

154 Jacquetta Hawkes, 1910–1996, was an archaeologist and civil servant, married to J.B. Priestley. It was their apartment in The Albany that lent its name to the Trust.

155 Minutes of a Meeting of the Executive Committee of the Homosexual Law Reform Society, 23 October 1963.

156 See M. Haug and M. Sussman (1969); 'Professional Autonomy and the Revolt of the Client', *Social Problems*, Vol. 17, No. 2, 153–161. They argue on p. 153 that, by the late 1960s, and a decade after the formation of the Homosexual Law Reform Society, 'The thrust of the client revolt is against the delivery system for knowledge application [*sic*], as controlled by the professionals …' A decade later still, and harking back to Haug and Sussman's work, Helena Lopata was to say in her presidential address to the Midwest Sociological Society that 'American society is witnessing a dramatic explosion and dissemination of knowledge, accompanied by the increasing refusal of patients, customers, students, and other types of clients to passively receive the services of the expert in any body of knowledge or skill'. (September 1976); 'Expertization of Everyone and the Revolt of the Client', *The Sociological Quarterly*, Volume 17, Issue 4, 435.

157 Lambeth Palace papers: memorandum from Miss Steel to St Albans, 9 April 1958 – MR DYSON (BSR/MWC/HOM).

158 It is interesting that even the 1961 film *Victim*, described by the British Film Institute as taking an 'unprecedentedly direct approach to homosexuality' (http://www.bfi.org.uk/whatson/bfi_southbank/film_programme/august_seasons/he_who_dared_dirk_

bogarde/victim), and starring Dirk Bogarde, who was himself a covert homosexual, was nevertheless constrained to depict 'all its gay characters [as] seem[ing] to regard their orientation as a burden' (E. Porter, 'Film Choice', *Sunday Times*, 27 July 2011).

159 Jeffrey Weeks pointed out to me in an email of 29 April 2012 that 'there were young gay men working as volunteers around HLRS from [the] mid 60s who were more radical, and in Manchester formed the embryo of what was to become the Campaign for Homosexual Equality. The real criticism of the earlier leaders, including Grey to some extent, was their slowness in recognising things were changing after 1967, and especially with the arrival of gay liberation after 1970'.

160 A. Grey; 'Homosexual Law Reform: From the Tactics of Pressure', in *Sex, Law, Politics Speaking Out: Writings on and Society 1954–95, op. cit.*, 33–34.

161 See his (1995); *Telling Sexual Stories*, London: Routledge. The book opens with the statement that 'Sex … has become the Big Story. From Donahue and Oprah getting folk to tell of their child sexual abuse … from … the collected writings of lesbians and gay men 'coming out' … a grand message keeps being shouted: tell about your sex. … in this late modern world … [sexual stories] seem to have gained an unusual power and prominence. It is curious, perhaps, that they should have become so celebrated. When I grew up as a child in the late 1940s and 1950s such stories resonated a deafening silence'. (4, 6)

162 Letter from the Chairman of the Homosexual Law Reform Society to the editor of *The Times*, 8 November 1960.

163 The Albany Trust was founded as a registered charity in May 1958 as a complementary body to the Homosexual Law Reform Society. Its objects were to 'promote psychological health in men through research, cultural and public education initiatives and to take suitable steps to improve the social and general conditions necessary for such healthy psychological development' (http://www.albanytrust.org/history.html) The Trust's founding Trustees were Anthony Edward Dyson, Jacquetta Hawkes, Kenneth Walker, Andrew Hallidie Smith and Ambrose Appelbe were drawn almost wholly from the Executive Committee of the Homosexual Law Reform Society.

164 A Draft Public Relations Policy prepared by the Homosexual Law Reform Society and dated 13 March 1964, reported that earlier surveys, carried out in the immediate wake of the publication of the Wolfenden report, suggested that just under 50% in favour of those interviewed in two National Opinion Polls supported legal reform.

165 Draft Public Relations Policy, *op. cit.*

166 *Ibid.* Somewhat gingerly, nevertheless, the society did decide to proceed with a public campaign on the supposition that 'The vague and confused state of public opinion indicated by the … survey is fertile ground for publicity designed to spread knowledge of the facts concerning homosexuality among the public at large and to secure support for reform of the law'.

167 Minutes of a Meeting of the Executive Committee of the Homosexual Law Reform Society, 23 October 1963.

168 Alfred Hecht, 1907–1991, was a picture framer and art dealer well established in the art world of London. He offered to hold a sale of art to raise funds for the society. See http://www.npg.org.uk/research/conservation/directory-of-british-framemakers/h.php.

169 Minutes of the Meeting of the Executive Committee of the Homosexual Law Reform Society, 23 March 1964.

170 Minutes of a Meeting of the Executive Committee of the Homosexual Law Reform Society, 18 July 1963.

171 Minutes of a Meeting of the Executive Committee of the Homosexual Law Reform Society, 23 October 1963.

172 Minutes of a Meeting of the Executive Committee of the Homosexual Law Reform Society, 18 July 1963.

173 *Progress Report of the Homosexual Law Reform Society*, London, April 1959, 2nd issue: The Commons Debate.
174 A. Grey; *Quest for Justice: Towards Homosexual Emancipation, op. cit.*, 41.
175 *Ibid*, 41.
176 A. Hallidie Smith, 'Homosexuals: a Breeze of Change', *The Observer*, 19 June 1960. He did add that 'Two years ago at these meetings, there was always a substantial minority who voiced robust disapproval of any change in the law'.
177 *Ibid*, 36.
178 A. Grey; 'Homosexual Law Reform: From the Tactics of Pressure', *op. cit.*, 32.
179 Meeting of the Executive Committee of the Homosexual Law Reform Society, 23 March 1964.
180 See   http://oai.dtic.mil/oai/oai?verb=getRecord&metadataPrefix=html&identifier= ADA130450
181 For example, the Minutes of a Meeting of the Executive Committee of the Howard League for Penal Reform held in January 1962, read: '<u>NEW BILL ON HOMOSEXUALITY</u> Mr Klare reported that the League had been approached for assistance with a new bill on homosexuality coming before Parliament in the next session. Mr. Leo Abse, M.P., who had drafted it, had drawn seventh place in the ballot for Private Members Bills, and had the support of several M.Ps, among them Mr Kenneth Robinson and Mr. Kirk. The Home Office had been consulted and Mr Klare thought that the bill, which was carefully limited to certain modifications in the present law, had a good chance of success, at least in the Commons. The League would give every possible help'.
182 Jean Graham Hall, the Honorary Secretary of the Society of Labour Lawyers, was to be especially important. On 12 June 1964, for example, she wrote to C.H. Rolph that 'We have at last among our members a member who is capable of drafting Bills for us in true Parliamentary fashion. He is in the Parliamentary department of one of the National Corporations, and he does not decide matters of substance for us, but drafts our memoranda in a fashion which Parliament would not fault. He takes the view that the Albany Trust Bill, although in the true spirit and what we want to do, is unfortunately not of sufficiently watertight standard to stand up to Parliamentary criticism. I enclose herewith an explanatory memorandum of the Bill which he suggests together with a draft Bill. If you have any comments or criticisms which you care to make, would you please do so by June 30th when he will be back from holiday…' Jean Graham Hall, 1917–2005, trained as a probation officer, worked at the Home Office with Barbara Wootton, was called to the Bar in 1951, and was the Honorary Secretary of the Society of Labour Lawyers between 1954 and 1964. Of a later stage, Antony Grey reported that the Society had 'consulted an eminent Queen's Counsel with parliamentary drafting experience' (A. Grey; *Quest for Justice: Towards Homosexual Emancipation, op. cit.*, 105). It is not clear whether or not that eminent Queen's Counsel was the same as the lawyer who had offered advice before.
183 The first, in October 1958, was drafted by the layman, C.H. Rolph (Andrew Hallidie Smith to Secretary, Church of England Moral Welfare Council, 25 October 1958, Lambeth Palace papers (BSR/MWC/HOM). Later, the drafting would become more professional under the guidance of the Society of Labour Lawyers. An undated, pencilled Home Office note on amendments forwarded by the Homosexual Law Reform Society to Lord Arran commented that they consisted of 'technical, legal wording much in line with the advice of Parliamentary counsel'. (CRI477/8/55 Departmental Committee on Homosexual Offences and Prostitution Action on the Report – Sexual Offences Bill (House of Lords) Second Reading and Committee Stage 9: Homosexual Law Reform Society Memorandum on Drafting of Sexual Offences Bill).

184 I shall show that Leo Abse's 1961 bill was a relatively modest affair which did not seek to implement the main Wolfenden recommendation, and that was because it was considered unlikely that a more ambitious bill would then pass.

185 Minutes of a Meeting of the Executive Committee of the Homosexual Law Reform Society, 24 February 1965.

186 After Leo Abse's bill had passed in July 1967, and in the light of the report of the Latey Committee, the Executive Committee resolved to campaign for the age of homosexual consent to be lowered to 18. Minutes of Meeting of the Executive Committee Homosexual Law Reform Society, 11 October 1967. The Latey Committee on the Age of Majority, Cmnd. 3342, was presented to Parliament in July 1967 and led to legislation the following year which 'reduce[d] from 21 to 18 the age at which a person has full powers to enter into a binding contract, to give a valid receipt and to hold and dispose of property' (the Lord Chancellor speaking in HL Deb 10 April 1968 Vol. 291 cc348–52). In 1979, the Home Office Policy Advisory Committee's Working Party report, *Age of Consent in relation to Sexual Offences*, recommended that the age of consent for homosexual offences should also be lowered to 18. The report of the full Advisory Committee, published in April 1981, pointed out in para 49 that: 'if the Wolfenden reform had been delayed until after 1969, 18 might well have been selected as the minimum age'. (This section is based on A. Thorpe; Research Paper 98/68, 'Age of Consent' for Male Homosexual Acts, Home Affairs Section, House Of Commons Library,19 June 1998.)

187 HC Deb 29 June 1960 Vol. 625 cc1453–514.

188 I have already suggested that the manner in which that inaugural meeting unfolded underlined both the conflicted character of support for the Society and the reasons why it was so very hard to mount political action. Some 1,000 people attended but what they heard was sometimes less than fulsome. Antony Grey said of the opening speech delivered, significantly, by the Bishop of Exeter, that it talked of this 'monstrously unjust law' – 'though [the Bishop] also angered some of the audience by likening homosexual tendencies to a cancer which, if not controlled or eradicated, would be destructive of human personality and society'. A. Grey; *Quest for Justice: Towards Homosexual Emancipation, op. cit.*, 41.

189 A. Grey; *Quest for Justice: Towards Homosexual Emancipation, op. cit.*, 41.

190 Terence Clarke, 1904–1992, was the Conservative Member for Portsmouth West between 1950–66.

191 The words are those of Eirene White, 1909–1999, the Labour Member for Flintshire. She was later to be Parliamentary Secretary, Colonial Office, 1964–66 and Minister of State for Foreign Affairs, 1966–67.

192 Homosexual Law Reform Society leaflet, 21 June 1960.

193 I could find no evidence to suggest why Leo Abse had elected to adopt this particular reform, unless it stemmed from his general interest as a Freudian in the control and therapeutics of sexuality.

194 HC Deb 22 November 1961 Vol. 649 c1353.

195 His political autobiography, *Private Member*, was infused with psychoanalytic observations (even its title playfully alludes to an interest in the phallic).

196 In G. Bedell, 'Coming out of the dark ages', *The Observer*, 24 June 2007.

197 HC Deb 9 March 1962 vol. 655 cc843–60.

198 *The Times*, 10 March 1962.

199 *Ibid.*

200 There would be a later attempt, at the time when Lord Arran's bill was being debated in the House of Lords. The Church's intention was to devise a way of decriminalising homosexual conduct between consenting adults in private without conveying approbation of what they did. It would be 'a means of releasing a considerable body of unfortunate men from the fear of criminal prosecution and at the same time maintaining the

law's witness that homosexual acts of fornication are no more approved of in our society than are such heterosexual acts. ...' Note from anonymous writer to the Archbishop of York, 28 April 1965. Lambeth Palace papers (BSR/MWC/HOM).

201 Quentin Edwards, 1925–2010, was the draftsman of a group convened by the Moral Welfare Council to consider the implications of the Church Assembly decision. He had been called to the Bar in 1948, and later became a QC and Circuit Judge. In a pamphlet, *What is Unlawful?*, published for the Church of England Moral Welfare Council by the Church Information Office. London, 1959, he was to argue 'there are certain acts which are now regarded as unlawful but are not punishable by the courts. Obvious examples are adultery, fornication and slander. ...'

202 Board for Social Responsibility: letter from Edwin Barker, Secretary, to Sir Charles Cunningham, 22 February 1962. Lambeth Palace papers (BSR/MWC/HOM1).

203 Lord Arran, 1911–1983, the eighth Earl of Arran, was a public servant and journalist. Antony Grey recalled in interview that 'He had inherited the title because his older brother, who was gay, had committed suicide. He wasn't the sort of person you'd think would do it. But he was invaluable. He was related to everyone and was always saying things like, "I'll have a word with Cousin Salisbury about that"'. In G. Bedell, 'Coming out of the dark ages', *The Observer*, 24 June 2007.

204 Lord Arran (1964); 'Danger, Arran at Work', in *Lord Arran Writes*, London: Hodder and Stoughton, 71. The book was a collection of weekly articles that originally appeared in the London *Evening News*. No date is given for 'Danger, Arran at Work'.

205 In A. Grey; *Quest for Justice: Towards Homosexual Emancipation*, op. cit., 87.

206 *Ibid*, *op. cit.*, 86.

207 Minutes of a Meeting of the Executive Committee of the Homosexual Law Reform Society, 23 October 1963.

208 The Homosexual Law Reform Society Public Relations Policy, Draft, 13 March 1964.

209 CRI 477/8/50: Departmental Committee on Homosexual Offences and Prostitution Action on the Report: Note from Graham Angel to Brian Cubbon.

210 HC Deb 28 June 1965 Vol. 715 cc28–9W.

211 It may be significant that the Secretary of the Executive Committee of the Homosexual Law Reform Society 'informed the Committee that the Attorney General had declined to receive a deputation from the Society to discuss the prosecution of homosexual offences, on the ground that this was not a field in which it would be appropriate for him to give directions to the Director of Public Prosecutions, who necessarily had to have regard to all the facts of every particular case referred to him. ...' (Meeting of the Executive Committee Homosexual Law Reform Society, 24 February 1965)

212 In 1965, at the time that the Homosexual Law Reform Society was mustering support, and private member's bills were being presented, the Legal Secretary to the Law Officers Department of the Home Office reported to Brian Cubbon that: 'Proposals have been made from time to time that the substantive law might be left unchanged but that the consent of the Attorney General or of the Director of Public Prosecutions should be required before any prosecution is brought for offences committed by consenting adults in private ... the Attorney General thinks it wrong that he or the Director of Public Prosecutions should have imposed on him the difficult and controversial duty of deciding whether it is in the public interest to prosecute in any particular case in respect of a homosexual act committed by consenting adults in private. Nevertheless, the Attorney General appreciates the fact that there may be considerable pressure on the Government to accept some proposal to restrict the right to prosecute... If it were thought right to give serious consideration to such a proposal, it must be recognised that the restriction could not be imposed except by legislation, the promotion of which by the Government would lay them open to almost as much criticism as if they were to seek to legislate the full proposals of the Wolfenden Committee. ... Departmental Committee on Homosexual Offences

and Prostitution Action on the Report: Letter from the Legal Secretary to the Law Officers' Department to Brian Cubbon, 11 May 1965. CRI 477/8/50. Brian Cubbon, born in 1928, entered the Home Office in 1951, and was an Assistant Secretary in the Criminal Department in 1965.

213 Minutes of a Meeting of the Executive Committee of the Homosexual Law Reform Society, 23 October 1963.

214 Lord Arran was semi-detached from the Homosexual Law Reform Society. He was not, for instance, a member of its Honorary Committee.

215 Lady Elliot of Harwood, 1903–1994, was a public servant and politician who in 1934 married Walter Elliot, the Conservative MP for Glasgow Kelvingrove. She became a life peeress in 1958 (http://www.oxforddnb.com/view/article/54942)

216 Edith Summerskill, 1901–1980, was a doctor and Labour politician, becoming the Member of Parliament for West Fulham in April 1938 and a life peeress in 1961 (http://www.oxforddnb.com/view/article/31734?docPos=1).

217 Jeremy Thorpe, born in 1929, was called to the Bar in 1954 and was to become Liberal Member of Parliament for North Devon between 1959 and 1979, when he was embroiled in a scandal that had been simmering for some years in the late 1970s and in which allegations of homosexuality and murder were rife (see http://www. liberalhistory.org.uk/item_single.php?item_id=19&item=biography)

218 Minutes of a Meeting of the Executive Committee of the Homosexual Law Reform Society, 18 July 1963.

219 A. Grey; *Quest for Justice: Towards Homosexual Emancipation, op. cit.*, 84.

220 See J. Weeks; *Coming Out: Homosexual Politics in Britain from the Nineteenth Century to the Present, op. cit*, 173, 176.

221 He talked then about hating the sin and loving the sinner, and chose closely to follow the line of argument propounded by the hierarchy: 'Evidence was given to the Committee by the Roman Catholic Advisory Committee on prostitution and homosexual offences, in which evidence a strong line was taken against the continuance of penal sanctions for homosexual offences in private between consenting adults. That was the evidence given by that Committee. Issues on this and other points they left open, as will be seen by a recent statement by the Archbishop of Westminster, for each Catholic to settle for himself. Clear guidance has been given to the Roman Catholic community regarding principles, but care has been taken not to prejudge questions of fact. ... the point of view of the Committee comes to this: that if a man ... is doing wrong the law must not intervene to stop him unless he is harming someone else; and if two or more men are doing wrong together, neither coercing the other nor taking advantage of his weakness, they must not be interfered with by the law unless their behaviour is harmful to a third party or parties. I think that is the simplest possible exposition of the juristic philosophy behind the Report. Again, I ask: can we accept this doctrine? By and large, though it is for each Member of the House to decide for himself, I believe that we can'. HL Deb 4 December 1957 Vol. 206 cc733–50.

222 See P. Stanford (2003); *The Outcasts' Outcast: A Biography of Lord Longford*, Stroud, Gloucestershire: Sutton Publishing, 242–3, 366.

223 With a group of bishops, he was to sign a letter supporting Lord Arran in *The Times* of 11 May.

224 The Secretary reported in February 1965 that 'Lord Arran hoped to introduce a Motion on the subject of homosexual law reform in the House of Lords on ... 12th May, when he believed he would receive support from the Archbishop of Canterbury, Lord Gardiner, Lord Longford and Lord Stonham'. Minutes of the Meeting of the Executive Committee Homosexual Law Reform Society, 24 February 1965.

225 It was reported that the Churches had again prepared the way: Antony Grey told the Committee that the 'Secretary of the British Council of Churches, the Rev. Kenneth Greet, had informed him that when a deputation from the Council had met the Home

Secretary recently they had found him both interested and sympathetic about homosexual law reform. The deputation had taken the opportunity to emphasise to the Home Secretary that they did not believe public opinion was now on balance against the Wolfenden recommendations'. Minutes of Meetings of the Executive Committee of the Homosexual Law Reform Society, 13 April and 14 April 1965.

226 See J. Weeks, *Coming Out: Homosexual Politics in Britain from the Nineteenth Century to the Present, op. cit.*, 175.

227 Lord Stonham would say that 'I shall conceal my personal views no longer. If it comes to a division, I intend to vote for Lord Arran's Bill. I have reached this decision as a result of the close study which I had to give to this subject in order to speak to your Lordships about it. I certainly approached it with no pre-disposition in favour of legalising homosexual conduct in any circumstances. But I am satisfied that the injustice and the evils of continuing the present law are greater, very much greater, than the risks involved in making the proposed change'. CRI477/8/52 3: Departmental Committee on Homosexual Offences and Prostitution Action on the Report – 2nd reading of the Sexual Offences Bill. 24 May 1965. Lord Stonham's speech.

228 A note from an indecipherable hand to Brian Cubbon in April 1965 said that 'it is most desirable that Lord Arran should be persuaded to withdraw his motion …' CRI 477/8/50: Departmental Committee on Homosexual Offences and Prostitution Action on the Report. Indeed, Lord Stonham bristled at the possibility of a vote. At his meeting with Lord Arran, held on 22 April 1965, in the month before the Motion would be presented, he:

> 'explained that if the Motion were strengthened to call upon the Government to implement the Wolfenden Report, he would have no alternative but to oppose it and that in the long run this would probably not be helpful to the aim which Lord Arran had in mind. He also advised against pressing the Motion to a division. The Government would certainly be able to accept the spirit of the Motion as it stood and he proposed, if he replied, to welcome the debate as an opportunity to ascertain the opinion of the House and, provided the debate manifested support for the Wolfenden proposals, to say that he had been impressed by the amount of support which the proposals had obtained and that he would report accordingly to the Home Secretary. …' (CRI 477/8/50: Departmental Committee on Homosexual Offences and Prostitution Action on the Report: Note of a meeting held in Lord Stonham's room at the HO on 22 April to discuss Lord's Arran's Motion on Homosexuality.)

> That position was then urged by the Home Secretary at a meeting of the Cabinet Home Affairs Committee held on 30 April: 'In order to avoid the embarrassment of a division, the Government spokesman might accept the Motion on the basis that the matter was one which merited discussion'. H (65) 9th Meeting.

229 A note about Lord Stonham's meeting with the Home Secretary in late April 1965 reflected 'Lord Stonham wishes to consult the H.S. on … discouraging the Lord Chancellor from speaking (Lord Arran is still hoping that he will take part in the debate and Lord Longford has suggested that he should be the second speaker for the Govt)'. (CRI 477/8/50: Departmental Committee on Homosexual Offences and Prostitution Action on the Report: indecipherable to Brian Cubbon).

230 See 'Lawyers: Labor's Lord High Chancellor', *Time*, 13 November 1964, where there was an explicit reference to Gerald Gardiner's personal desire to liberalise the law on homosexual conduct.

231 CRI 477/8/50: Departmental Committee on Homosexual Offences and Prostitution Action on the Report: written note from Graham Angel to Mr Otton [Sir Frank's Private Secretary], 14 April 1965. It is possible that Lord Stonham was mistaken, that Lord Gardiner had changed his mind, or that Lord Gardiner did not want to show his hand on a difficult subject, but it is interesting that he had declared just before

the general election that he had 'no strong views about it ... on the whole I think the advantages of implementing it are greater than the disadvantages'. 'Lord Gardiner Interviewed', *The Economist*, 28 March 1964, 1212.

232 A memorandum by Roy Jenkins in January 1966 recorded that 'The Government adopted a strictly neutral attitude to the principle of Lord Arran's Bill, on the ground that it raised moral issues which were essentially a matter for personal judgement rather than Government policy'. CRI 477/8/67 Homosexual Offences and Prostitution Sexual Offences Bill 7. Cabinet Home Affairs Committee Legislation on Homosexual Offences Memorandum by the Secretary of State for the Home Department, 12 January 1966.

233 CRI 477/8/50: Departmental Committee on Homosexual Offences and Prostitution Action on the Report: Note from Graham Angel to Brian Cubbon with revised draft of Lord Stonham's speech incorporating newly-drafted passages. May 11 1965.

234 CRI 477/8/50: Departmental Committee on Homosexual Offences and Prostitution Action on the Report: Charles Cunningham to S. of S., 9 December 1964. Lord Stonham would disagree. If there were to be significant change, it should not be by administrative stealth: 'If the law is to be changed, it must be changed by Parliament. Neither the Home Secretary, nor the Attorney General, nor the Director of Public Prosecutions, nor chief constables, nor anyone else, can properly implement the Wolfenden recommendations by administrative action or inaction'. HL Deb 12 May 1965 Vol. 266 cc71–172.

235 Brian Cubbon wrote after an important debate on 12 May 1965: 'all but 3 of the back-bench speakers were in favour of implementing the main Wolfenden recommenda-tion ... This Bill simply implements that recommendation. It is suggested that the Government spokesman should indicate on Second Reading that, if the Bill receives a Second Reading, it might be desirable in Committee to consider implementing some of the minor Wolfenden recommendations. ...' CRI477/8/52 1: Departmental Committee on Homosexual Offences and Prostitution Action on the Report – Note from Brian Cubbon, 17 May 1965.

236 The Law Relating to Homosexual Offences, Memorandum by the Secretary of State for the Home Department, Cabinet Home Affairs Committee, 28 April 1965, H. (65) 32.

237 The Cabinet Minutes for 6 May 1965 recite that: 'Item 5 The Cabinet considered a memorandum by the Home Secretary (C (65) 68) on the law relating to homosexual offences. The HS then described Lord Arran's HoL motion. Because of divided opin-ion ...the Govt. spokesman in the debate [Lord Stonham] should abstain from advising either for or against the implication of the Wolfenden Report's major recommenda-tions but should indicate that the proper course for those who wished to promote the amendment of the law was to introduce a Private Member's Bill. The Govt. would then accept the result of the free vote. Govt. time could be made available, but not in this Session. Strict neutrality should be observed, but the matter of a Friday slot this session could be reconsidered if favourable opinion prevailed'.

238 The Law Relating to Homosexual Offences, Memorandum by the Secretary of State for the Home Department, Cabinet Home Affairs Committee, 28 April 1965, H. (65) 32.

239 He wrote in December 1964 that 'It is, I think, best to have the debate. I very much dislike, in effect, sweeping social questions of this sort under the carpet; (and person-ally would like to give effect to Wolfenden) but I think there is little alternative at the moment. In my view, the best line in debate is to say that this question is very much one for personal judgement, on which the strongest individual opinions are held. Public opinion has changed about it in some measure, but it is not the intention (avoid using the word 'present' intention, which invites the question whether in the future the Government are saying there <u>will</u> be legislation) to bring proposals before

Parliament to amend the existing law'. CRI 477/8/50: Departmental Committee on Homosexual Offences and Prostitution Action on the Report: Copy of Note by the S. of S. 19 December 1964. He had written earlier: 'Personally I would like to see the Wolfenden report implemented; but I do not think we can force this on an unwilling public opinion, which is not yet ready for it. There is nothing we can do for the present'. CRI 477/8/50: Departmental Committee on Homosexual Offences and Prostitution Action on the Report: Note from S. of S., 12 December 1964.

240   The model set by the response to the reform of the law on Sunday Observance, recently debated, was particularly in officials' and politicians' minds. Sir Frank Soskice had opened discussion of the *Report of the Departmental Committee on the Law on Sunday Observance*, Cmnd 2528, presented on 9 December, 1964, with words that would be put to work again in virtually identical form in discussion of the Wolfenden Report: 'The subject matter of the Report is obviously one on which hon. and right hon. Members on both sides of the House hold the strongest feelings. One of the objects of this debate is to elicit and invite the fullest expression of opinion from both sides on a matter which cuts right across party lines and deeply affects people's feelings on subjects of this type. ... The object of this debate, as I said at the outset, is to afford an opportunity to hon. Members to express their views on the issues involved'. (HC Deb 15 February 1965 Vol. 706 cc858–964) Graham Angel had written to Mr Otton on 14 April 1965 to say that: "You will recall that the Home Secretary had instructed Lord Stonham to reply to the debate on 12th May on the lines of the speech about Sunday Observance making it clear that the Government could give no commitment on this subject but that he would report the views expressed in the House to the Home Secretary'. In what was an almost verbatim reprise of Sir Frank's earlier statement in February, it was reported that 'Lord Stonham agrees 'with the course of action proposed subject to the proviso that he would like, if the debate shows an impressive degree of support for the Wolfenden proposals, to indicate that he has been impressed by the weight of evidence in favour of them and will report accordingly to the Home Secretary'. (CRI 477/8/50: Departmental Committee on Homosexual Offences and Prostitution Action on the Report.)

241   CRI 477/8/50: Departmental Committee on Homosexual Offences and Prostitution Action on the Report: Copy of Note by the S. of S. 19 December 1964.

242   It was reported that 'the Home Secretary indicated to the deputation that he was personally in favour of implementing the recommendations of the Wolfenden Committee. The deputation would recognise, however, that this would be a difficult issue in Parliament and in view of their narrow majority the Government would see difficulty in presenting legislation. When public opinion were ready for the change, his view was that the Government might allow facilities for a measure to be discussed in Parliament on a free vote. It was, however, difficult to know whether public opinion was yet ready for such a development; he suspected it was not. The admitted shift of informed opinion on this subject did not necessarily reflect opinion in the country at large'. Note of a Meeting 4 May 1965. CRI477/8/59 Departmental Committee on Homosexual Offences and Prostitution – Action on the Report.

243   'The Law Relating to Homosexual Offences: Memorandum by the Secretary of State for the Home Department', 4 May 1965, C. (65) 63.

244   A record of its discussion recited that '[Lord Arran] was expected to address himself in particular to the recommendation that homosexual behaviour between consenting adults in private should cease to be a criminal offence; and he was likely to receive considerable support. But strong opinions were also held in the opposite sense; and the subject was not one on which the Government could contemplate introducing legislation in the foreseeable future. ... it was not clear, as it was in the case of the problem of capital punishment, that a majority of either the members of the House of Commons as a whole or the Government's own supporters were in favour of amending the

law on homosexual offences. ... In the present political situation, ... no undertaking should be given to provide time for a Private Member's Bill, although this need not preclude reconsideration of the matter in the light of any later developments in public opinion ...' Conclusions of a meeting of the Cabinet held at 10 Downing Street held on 6 May 1965. CC (65) 28.

245 Taken from Sir Burke Trend's Cabinet Notebook (CAB 195/25) (6 May 1965).

246 He said that 'it cannot be mere accident that the Wolfenden Committee's recommendations on homosexuality have been supported by the Church Assembly, The Church of England Moral Welfare Council, The Roman Catholic Advisory Committee set up by the late Cardinal Griffin, the Methodist Conference and an influential group of Quakers'.

247 HL Deb 12 May 1965 Vol. 266 cc71–172.

248 The bishop called on the government to act: 'I think noble Lords on this side just cannot wash their hands in this matter like Pilate. You have got to face facts. You have got to give a lead. If I may say so with respect to a Party which frequently talks about justice and the fullness of life, I think that to say the things that you did this afternoon is sheer humbug. From the last Government we had a lead so far as part of the Wolfenden Report was concerned'. (Arthur) Mervyn Stockwood, 1913–1995, was Bishop of Southwark from 1958–1979. He was a homosexual and a committed socialist. (see http://www.oxforddnb.com/view/article/57972)

249 Lord Rea of Eskdale, 1900–1981, was the Liberal Leader in the House of Lords, 1955–67.

250 Lord James of Rusholme, 1909–1992, was high master of Manchester Grammar School and then the founding Vice-Chancellor of the new University of York.

251 Lord Francis-Williams, 1903–1970, was a journalist and broadcaster who became editor of the *Daily Herald* in 1936. After the war, he was to be press relations adviser to the Labour Prime Minister, Clement Attlee, and, eventually, a Labour peer in 1962 (see http://www.oxforddnb.com/view/article/36919?docPos=1)

252 They concluded 'We hope that in response to the Motion, calling attention to the Wolfenden Committee's recommendations which Lord Arran is to move in the House of Lords on May 12 Her Majesty's Government will now recognise the necessity for this reform and will introduce legislation'.

253 Lord Jessel, 1917–1990, was Deputy Speaker between 1963 and 1977.

254 HL Deb 12 May 1965 Vol. 266 cc71–172.

255 He was to refer in the debate, for instance, to 'an over-simplification in a pamphlet issued by the Homosexual Law Reform Society, which states homosexuality is an involuntary emotional condition which in the present state of medical knowledge can only be cured in a tiny minority of cases'.

256 Lord Byers said that 'The [Wolfenden] Committee of eminent people studied this problem for three years, and they reported with a 12 to 1 majority. That, surely, must be an important factor in any consideration of this sort. But one must also notice the significant change in the opinions, of for instance, many Church leaders, of teachers, of dons at university and of others who are in continual and constant contact with young people. And this to me is a very significant change of opinion'. HL Deb 24 May 1965 Vol. 266 cc631–52.

257 See, for example, P. Conrad (1975); 'The Discovery of Hyperkinesis: Notes on the Medicalization of Deviant Behavior', *Social Problems*, Vol. 23, No. 1, 12–21; P. Conrad and J. Schneider (1980); *Deviance and Medicalization: From Badness to Sickness*, St. Louis: Mosby; T. Szasz (1970); *The Manufacture of Madness: A Comparative Study of the Inquisition and the Mental Health Movement*, New York: Harper and Row; and especially M. Foucault (1979); *The History of Sexuality*, London: Allen Lane.

258 An interview with Leo Abse disclosed that he believed that 'much of this was tactical. 'The thrust of all the arguments we put to get it was, "Look, these people, these gays,

poor gays, they can't have a wife, they can't have children, it's a terrible life. You are happy family men. You've got everything. Have some charity." Nobody knew better than I what bloody nonsense that was' in G. Bedell, 'Coming out of the dark ages', *The Observer*, 24 June 2007.

259   Donald West, a psychiatric criminologist and sexologist, wrote of the time that 'In the 1950s there was a tendency among homophile writers to emphasise the early onset and immutability of homosexual orientation, its probable biological origins, and its resistance to both treatments and social pressure to change. In short, a homosexual orientation was a fact of nature that the law had no business to denounce'. *Gay Life Straight Work, op. cit.*, 61. He was the author of a number of works on sexuality, including (1955); *Homosexuality*, London : G. Duckworth (1977); *Homosexuality Re-examined*, London : Duckworth; and (2000); 'Paedophilia: plague or panic?', *The Journal of Forensic Psychiatry*, Vol.11(3), 511–531.

260   Of course, the two alternatives are not wholly incompatible. See N. Lacey and H. Pickard (Spring 2013); 'From the Consulting Room to the Court Room? Taking the Clinical Model of Responsibility without Blame into the Legal Realm', *Oxford Journal of Legal Studies*, Vol. 33, No. 1, 1–29.

261   One eminent physician and medical administrator, Lord Brain, said 'Why should homosexuality concern the doctor? ... it is not a disease but a disorder of emotional development. Nevertheless, it impinges on medicine at many points. Doctors, and especially psychiatrists, are necessarily concerned with emotional problems, and it is easy to imagine the emotional stresses to which homosexuals are exposed in our present society'. HL Deb 24 May 1965 Vol. 266 cc631–52.

262   The Archbishop of Canterbury was to argue that: 'It is no use saying to a man of homosexual tendencies, "Stop having homosexual tendencies." It is no use saying to a man who is tempted to homosexual acts, "Do not be tempted to homosexual acts, and then you will not be blackmailed." What matters is that such people should be more accessible to the means available to help them; and the evidence is, I believe, overwhelmingly strong that the present law makes it difficult or impossible for many to make themselves accessible to those forces of grace which would help them'. HL Deb 28 October 1965 Vol. 269 cc677–730.

263   Although not absolutely. It is said that the sponsor of a private bill, Humphrey Berkeley, lost his seat in the 1966 general election because of his championing of homosexual law reform. His own concluding sentence in the debate of February 1966 constituted, he observed, 'the last words which I uttered as a Conservative Member of Parliament. ... I have no doubt that my promotion of this Bill cost me my seat'. H. Berkeley, *Crossing the Floor, op. cit.*, 139, 129. Lord Arran was not convinced: 'it is also true that Mr. William Shepherd, perhaps the strongest opponent of the Bill, also lost his seat, to a Liberal. But the percentage against them [Humphrey Berkeley and William Shepherd] was not very different. Further, it is a statistical fact that, of those who voted in favour of the Bill in another place, 7 lost their seats, whereas of those who voted against, 20 lost their seats' (HL Deb 10 May 1966 Vol. 274 cc605–52).

264   J. Gusfield (Autumn 1967); 'Moral Passage: The Symbolic Process in Public Designations of Deviance', *Social Problems*, Vol. 15, No. 2, 180. That was certainly the line adopted by the avowedly homosexual criminologist, Donald West, who argued much later in 1988 that 'sympathy for the situation of the homosexual minority might be increased by the thought that many of them have no power to change'. 'Homosexuality and Social Policy: The Case for a More Informed Approach', *Law and Contemporary Problems*, Vol. 51(1), 182.

265   See D. Garland (2001); *The Culture of Control: Crime and Social Order in Contemporary Society, op. cit.*

266   D. Melossi (2008); *Controlling Crime, Controlling Society*, Cambridge: Polity Press, 6–7.

267   HL Deb 13 May 1965 Vol. 266 c268.

268 Lambeth Palace papers (BSR/MWC/HOM1). Lord Sandford, 1920–2009, had been a Hertfordshire curate before becoming a Conservative whip between 1966–1970 and ultimately a junior minister in the House of Lords.

269 Sir John had written to Lord Arran 'It must be clear to everyone that the Bill lays down the basic principle which is recommended in our Report'. HL Deb 24 May 1965 Vol. 266 cc631–52.

270 HL Deb 24 May 1965 Vol. 266 cc631–52.

271 CRI477/8/52 3: Departmental Committee on Homosexual Offences and Prostitution Action on the Report – 2nd reading of the Sexual Offences Bill. 24 May 1965. Lord Stonham's speech.

272 Lord Stonham wrote to Barbara Wootton: 'I have, as promised, considered the whole position of Lord Arran's Bill now that the Committee stage has been completed and I am glad to be able to tell you that the Government are prepared to offer the assistance of Parliamentary Counsel in drafting those amendments which in debate were greeted with general agreement in principle'. CRI477/8/56: Departmental Committee on Homosexual Offences and Prostitution Action on the Report, 3 July 1965. He had earlier requested permission to instruct Parliamentary Counsel on the grounds that, in the words of the Home Secretary, 'Lord Chorley asked the Government for assistance in redrafting, and I have since had a similar request from the Archbishop of Canterbury in respect of three of his amendments. Lord Stonham thinks that it would be very difficult not to give this assistance, and I agree with him. It is reasonably certain that if it is not given, the amendments will be imperfectly revised and on Report stage Lord Stonham will have to point this out. Even though the Bill cannot pass into law this Session, it is hardly dignified for the House to be frustrated in this way when there is general agreement on what should be done'. Letter from HS to Herbert Bowden, Privy Council Office, 28 June 1965. CRI477/8/56: Departmental Committee on Homosexual Offences and Prostitution Action on the Report.

273 CRI477/8/56: Departmental Committee on Homosexual Offences and Prostitution Action on the Report – to Sir Noel Hutton QC, 2 July 1965. Noel Hutton, 1907–1984, was First Parliamentary y Counsel between 1956–68.

274 In the instance of the supposed impact of the proposed legislation on the armed forces, for example, Brian Cubbon wrote 'I have sorted this nonsense out with the Ministry of Defence …' – Handwritten note of 13 July 1965 by Brian Cubbon which was appended to a letter from the Private Secretary to the Ministry of Defence (Air Force) to Graham Angel on 12 July. That letter had reported that 'Lord Dilhorne felt that if the Sexual Offences Bill became law and it had been amended as proposed with regard to the Armed Forces, this would lead to a situation where courts martial would refuse to find that sodomy was disgraceful or indecent conduct. He felt that if sodomy were to be a military offence, it should be an offence against military law and that the Services Acts should be amended accordingly'. CRI477/8/56: Departmental Committee on Homosexual Offences and Prostitution Action on the Report.

275 CRI477/8/55 Departmental Committee on Homosexual Offences and Prostitution Action on the Report – Sexual Offences Bill (House of Lords) Second Reading and Committee Stage 2.

276 'It is inimical to Service discipline because it could have a deleterious effect on the proper relationships which must exist within a relatively close-knit community … It may also lead to improper pressure being exerted by senior on junior ranks' CRI477/8/56: Departmental Committee on Homosexual Offences and Prostitution Action on the Report – Brief for Minister (RAF) on the report stage of the Sexual Offences Bill (HL) 13 July 1965.

277 CRI477/8/56: Departmental Committee on Homosexual Offences and Prostitution Action on the Report – letter to Brian Cubbon from an official in F4: 15 October 1965.

278 CRI477/8/54 Departmental Committee on Homosexual Offences and Prostitution Action on the Report – Consultation with the service departments about service implications of a change in the law. Note of 20 May 1965.

279 Letter from the office of the Parliamentary Counsel, 4 August 1965. A brief prepared for Minister (RAF) put the argument that whilst members of the armed forces were subject to the civilian law, 'Nevertheless, the Serviceman is not just a civilian, he is also a member of a disciplined fighting Service in which personal relationships, exercise of authority, even his welfare and the nature of his communal life as a member of a disciplined body, impose upon him further obligations than those of the ordinary citizen. In these circumstances, certain behaviour, of which no notice need be taken in the case of a civilian must be repressed and, if necessary, punished ...' (BRIEF for Minister (RAF) on the report stage of the Sexual Offences Bill (HL) (Prepared by DS10 in consultation with Naval Law, G2 (AD), S10 (Air) and Treasury Solicitor)). (Lord Dilhorne declared that he was not persuaded by the brief. He was reported to have told Lord Shackleton, the Minister of Defence for the RAF, that 'if the Sexual Offences Bill became law and if it had been amended as proposed ... this would lead to a situation where courts martial would refuse to find that sodomy was disgraceful or indecent conduct ...' J. Carruthers, Private Secretary, Ministry of Defence, to G. Angel, Home Office, 12 July 1965). CRI477/8/56: Departmental Committee on Homosexual Offences and Prostitution Action on the Report.

280 It was suggested in a note by Brian Cubbon to Lord Stonham of 5 May 1966 that 'If homosexual acts on British merchant ships were no longer to be criminal offences, the master of a British ship would have no sanction to employ against members of his crew who engaged in homosexual practices'. (CRI477/8/59 Departmental Committee on Homosexual Offences and Prostitution – Action on the Report) The view eventually taken in an undated, anonymous note was that, akin to the disciplinary regulation of the armed services, 'The common law power of the master is understood to be to arrest and confine in a reasonable manner for a reasonable time any seaman or other person on his ship if he has reasonable cause for believing, and does in fact believe, that the arrest and confinement are necessary for the preservation of order and discipline, or for the safety of the vessel or persons or property on board'. (CRI477/8/71)

281 Letter from Douglas Jay, President of the Board of Trade, to Roy Jenkins, 26 October 1966 (CRI477/8/79) The General Secretary of the National Union of Seamen would write separately to the Prime Minister on 16 November to say that 'seamen spend most of their lives in a very confined space, and nothing could happen aboard ship which could be considered private to the rest of the ship's company'. The draft reply simply disowned responsibility for the projected measure: 'I can well understand the anxieties you feel in this matter. But this is a Private Member's Bill ... [and] we have declined to treat the Bill as a party matter ...' (CRI477/8/81).

282 Undated, anonymous note to Lord Arran, Lord Dilhorne was Reginald Edward Manningham-Buller, the Conservative Attorney General between 1954 and 1962, and Lord Chancellor between 1962 and 1964. Lord Dilhorne wrote to Lord Stonham on 29 July 1965: 'I hope it is recognised that there may be more than two parties to an act of gross indecency. I think it should cease to be in private if there are more than two parties'. CRI477/8/56: Departmental Committee on Homosexual Offences and Prostitution Action on the Report.

283 CRI477/8/55 Departmental Committee on Homosexual Offences and Prostitution Action on the Report – Sexual Offences Bill (House of Lords) Second Reading and Committee Stage 7: Letter from DPP to Brian Cubbon, 2 June 1965.

284 Parliamentary counsel advised that 'if a defective's consent is to be treated as void, he himself would be liable to prosecution for buggery. There is authority to show that his fears are unjustified. ... Whichever view you adopt, it will result in a severely subnormal person escaping punishment (to put it at its lowest) when the other party

to a homosexual act is convicted. ...' CRI477/8/56: Departmental Committee on Homosexual Offences and Prostitution Action on the Report – Parliamentary Counsel to James Nursaw, 13 July 1965. James Nursaw joined the Legal Adviser's Branch, Home Office, in 1959.

285 Lord Byers, 1915–1984, had been Liberal Member for North Dorset, 1945–1950; Chairman of the Liberal Party, 1950–1952; and was to become Liberal Chief Whip 1946–1950. He became a peer in 1964. (http://www.ukwhoswho.com/view/article/oupww/whoswho/U162583/BYERS?index=1&results=QuicksearchResults&query=0)

286 See L. Humphreys (1970); *Tearoom Trade: A Study of Homosexual Encounters in Public Places*, London: Duckworth.

287 He was empowered to make some small concessions should they seem necessary: 'the Government spokesman should indicate on Second Reading that, if the Bill receives a Second Reading, it might be desirable in Committee to consider implementing some of the minor Wolfenden proposals; in particular the recommendation (iv) ... that no proceedings be taken in respect of any homosexual act (other than indecent assault) committed in private by a person under 21, except by the Director of Public Prosecutions or with the sanction of the Attorney-General'. Extract from a Meeting of the Cabinet Legislation Committee held on 18 May 1965, LG(65) 16th Meeting.

288 Lord Shackleton had replied that 'The noble Viscount will know that the Government are taking an impartial view, but Section 66 of the Army Act will still apply. If it does not apply, as the noble and gallant Viscount knows, it is open to the Services to get rid of any undesirable person who practises disgraceful conduct – and I think there can be no argument on the subject that these practices are disgraceful conduct'. But Viscount Montgomery was not convinced.

289 *The Glasgow Herald*, 7ᵗ February 1966.

290 A copy of the *Daily Sketch* of 2 November 1965, filed in Home Office papers, reported that nearly 2/3 of the electorate believed in the decriminalisation of homosexual acts between consenting adults in private whilst a majority supported the retention of capital punishment. An anonymous comment by an official observed that 'Can it be that what you and I and the man next door think does not matter a tinker's cuss once some of our legislators get the bit between their teeth?' That and other polls were raised by Lord Arran in his discussions with Lord Stonham after his Motion was passed in the House of Lords (CRI477/8/56: Departmental Committee on Homosexual Offences and Prostitution Action on the Report.)

291 Note to Lord Stonham and S. of S., 27 June 1965. In the Home Secretary's formal request for drafting assistance from Parliamentary Counsel, the argument was put that 'When a redrafted amendment was moved on Report, Lord Stonham would remain neutral on the principle involved but could say that the drafting appeared correct'. Letter to Sir Herbert Bowden, 28 June 1965. CRI477/8/56.

292 CRI477/8/56: Departmental Committee on Homosexual Offences and Prostitution Action on the Report – Brian Cubbon to James F4 and Weiler Establishment Division 3, 7 October 1965.

293 CRI477/8/56: Departmental Committee on Homosexual Offences and Prostitution Action on the Report: Note from Lord Stonham to HS, 20 October 1965.

294 HL Deb 21 June 1965 Vol. 267 cc287–317.

295 The Bishop of Chichester said: 'we have supported the main proposal, not because we want to withhold our own condemnation of all these practices, each one of which is as disgusting as the other, but because we believe that they ought to be put on a level of personal, moral responsibility and not on the level of criminal offences'. HL Deb 21 June 1965 Vol. 267 cc287–317.

296 And he was followed by the Methodist minister, Lord Soper, who said homosexual practices: 'are unnatural; to me they are abhorrent – and I would use the word

"abominable". But having said that, I am sure that to discriminate between certain areas of human behaviour, and to say that certain of these practices are abominable to the extent that they should entail a criminal prosecution, while others may be committed in private, seems to me quite unrealistic and quite illogical ...'

297 See O. Chadwick; *Michael Ramsey A Life, op. cit.*, 148.

298 Roy Jenkins called it 'the first major piece of general legislation on criminal justice for nearly 20 years' (HC Deb 12 December 1966 Vol. 738 cc52–208)

299 *The Times*, 29 October 1965.

300 *Ibid.*

301 HL Deb 28 October 1965 Vol. 269 cc677–730.

302 'I believe that homosexual acts are wrong, for they misuse human organs for which the right use is intercourse within marriage between men and women. I am convinced that as fornication is always sinful, so homosexual acts are sins. But when circumstances are carefully weighed, it will be seen that there are degrees of culpability attached to these sins. ... [But the] decisive argument in the Wolfenden Report is found in paragraph 61, and this immediately precedes the recommendation which is the substance of the Bill before your Lordships' House. In that paragraph it is stated that both society and the law ought to attach importance to individual freedom, and there must, therefore, be a realm of private morality and immorality which is not the law's concern'.

303 Sexual Offences Bill, Third Reading, Notes for Speech. CRI 477/8/71.

304 H. Berkeley; *Crossing the Floor, op. cit.*, 128.

305 Humphrey Berkeley, 1926–1994, became Conservative Member for Lancaster in 1959. Antony Grey said that 'He knew more about the personal and social aspects of the homosexual issue than either Lord Arran or Leo Abse' (*Quest for Justice: Towards Homosexual Emancipation, op. cit.*, 111).

306 R. Jenkins, *A Life at the Centre, op. cit.*, 180.

307 The phrase is Lord Arran's. HL Deb 10 May 1966 Vol. 274 cc605–52.

308 Roy Jenkins explained in a Memorandum to the Home Affairs Committee that 'The Bill has not yet been published, but basically it will be the Bill, sponsored by Lord Arran, which passed all its stages in the Lords last session by comfortable majorities ... . Lord Arran has re-introduced his own Bill this session ... but he does not intend to proceed with it until the fate of Mr. Berkeley's Bill is known. ...' (CRI 477/8/67 Homosexual Offences and Prostitution Sexual Offences Bill. Cabinet Home Affairs Committee Legislation on Homosexual Offences Memorandum by the Secretary of State for the Home Department, 12 January 1966).

309 HL Deb 10 May 1966 Vol. 274 cc605–52.

310 In CRI477/8/59 Departmental Committee on Homosexual Offences and Prostitution – Action on the Report – Sexual Offences Bill (introduced by Humphrey Berkeley M.P.).

311 CRI477/8/59 Minister's Case – Departmental Committee on Homosexual Offences and Prostitution – Action on the Report – Mr. H. Berkeley MP requests any proposed H.O. amendments to Earl of Arran's Homosexuality Bill.

312 The epithet is Nora Beloff's in *The Observer*, 6 February 1966.

313 R. Jenkins (1959); *The Labour Case*, A Penguin Special, Mddx., 136.

314 R. Jenkins; *A Life at the Centre, op. cit.*, 180.

315 One may suppose that the phrase had come into currency with Frank Delano Roosevelt's declaration of a position towards the United Kingdom before the United States entered the Second World War. See TNA CAB/66/12/28.

316 CRI 477/8/67 Homosexual Offences and Prostitution Sexual Offences Bill 7. Cabinet Home Affairs Committee Legislation on Homosexual Offences Memorandum by the Secretary of State for the Home Department, 12 January 1966.

317 *Ibid.* The sea change is made even more clear in an undated note made by Roy Jenkins that was attached to a submission by Brian Cubbon. Brian Cubbon had written in the

cover minutes that 'It could be explained that we had not yet ascertained the views of the present S. of S.', to which Roy Jenkins had added: 'As amended. I think we can now be pretty definitely benevolent'. CRI 477/8/67.

318 Legislation on Homosexual Offences: Memorandum by the Secretary of State for the Home Department, H(66) 6 18 January 1966.

319 Note from Burke Trend to the Prime Minister; Parliamentary Business, 2 February 1966. PREM 13 1563.

320 See the address by Humphrey Berkeley in HC Deb 11 February 1966 Vol. 724 cc782–874.

321 It was reported that 'Mr Chataway and Mr Thorpe agreed to arrange a House of Commons meeting of at least 20 sympathetic MPs who would each be asked to persuade five other Members who had previously abstained on the issue of homosexual law reform to support Mr Berkeley's Bill'. Minutes of Meeting of the Executive Committee of the Homosexual Law Reform Society, 19 January 1966.

322 *The Times*, 12 February 1966.

323 James Dance, 1907–1971, was the Conservative Member for Bromsgrove.

324 Sir Charles Taylor, 1910–1989, was the Conservative Member for Eastbourne between 1935 and 1974.

325 *The Times*, 7 February 1966.

326 He gave no account at all of why he chose his particular form of words, although he does reproduce the speech in full in his autobiography, *Crossing the Line*, *op. cit.*

327 Home Office File CRI 477/8/67 contained the findings of the National Opinion Poll, appearing in the *Daily Mail*, October 1965, which reported the following results:

Which of the following statements do you agree with?
(a) Homosexuals are in need of medical or psychiatric treatment.
   93% agree
   6% disagree
   1% didn't know
(b) Homosexual acts between consenting adults (21+) in private should be criminal.
   36% agree
   63% disagree
   1% didn't know
(c) Homosexual acts involving people under 21 should be criminal.
   66% agree
   32% disagree
   2% didn't know

328 See *The Times*, 12 February 1966.

329 See http://www.dailymail.co.uk/news/article-2294622/Partners-50-years--Lord-St-John-tied-knot-save-money-Tory-dandy-married-gay-lover-secret-avoid-1-2million-inheritance-tax-bill.html. In the meeting of Standing Committee F on 19 April 1967, Mr St. John Stevas took care to distance himself from what he called 'the most distasteful thing about this distasteful subject [which] is that public lavatories are very often haunted by homosexuals driven on by the compulsions and the misery of their situation … '. *Official Report* at col. 21.

330 Frank Tomney, 1908–1984, had been Branch Secretary, General and Municipal Workers Union between 1940 and 1950 and was the Labour Member for Hammersmith North between 1950 and 1979. (http://www.ukwhoswho.com/view/article/oupww/whowaswho/U169835/TOMNEY_Frank?index=1&results=Quicks earchResults&query=0)

331 Sir Cyril Osborne, 1898–1969, was the son of a coalminer who was brought up in what he called 'a very stern puritan home'. He was the Conservative MP for the Louth division of Lincolnshire from 1945 until his death. A biographer, Robert

Pearce, claimed that he was 'noted for his opposition to generally progressive causes' (http://www.oxforddnb.com/view/article/40643) His obituary in *The Times* of 1 September 1969 remarked that 'Many of his views were controversial in the extreme'. He had opposed the abolition of the death penalty (see *The Times*, 27 January 1961); Commonwealth immigration to the United Kingdom (see *The Times*, 14 July 1960, and 24 March 1961) and much else.

332   Sir Cyril Black, 1902–1991, was Conservative Member for Wimbledon from 1950 until 1970. Devout, a member of the temperance movement, he was described as 'completely immoveable on his chosen subjects', campaigning against the liberalisation of the divorce laws, licensing laws and immigration controls. (Based on http://www. oxforddnb.com/view/article/49581)

333   48 Conservatives had voted for the bill. The previous Home Secretary, Sir Frank Soskice, and all the then current Home Office ministers did so too. (The Times, 14 February 1966).

334   H. Berkeley; *Crossing the Floor, op. cit.*, 129.

335   See *The Times*, 10 January 1966.

336   See *The Times*, 27 January 1966. In the event, the Labour Party 'romped home' (*The Times*, 28 January 1966).

337   A note to Roy Jenkins said that, 'As you will recall, the Home Affairs Committee took the view ... that pressure on the Government to provide time should be resisted. I understand that Mr. Berkeley thinks that the opponents of the Bill may try to spin out the proceedings on the two preceding Private Members Bills ... I have had a word with the Lord President's Private Secretary, who suggests that you should "play it long"'. (CRI 477/8/66 Homosexual Offences and Prostitution Sexual Offences Bill Committee Stage (Commons)) A note of the meeting between the Home Secretary and Humphrey Berkeley reported that 'S.of S. said he understood that the Lord President's view was that the Bill was likely to make as quick progress in Standing Committee C as in any other Standing Committee, though he (the Lord President) was prepared to discuss the matter with Mr. Berkeley. S. of S. indicated that his personal view was that it might be better for Mr. Berkeley not to be indebted to the Government for facilities at this stage, but to get his Bill through Standing Committee C in the normal way, and then, if necessary, seek help at Report Stage. ...' (CRI 477/8/66 Homosexual Offences and Prostitution Sexual Offences Bill Committee Stage (Commons): note of 18th February 1966).

338   'In discussion it was urged that any suggestion that the Government were sympathetic towards the Bill would be a departure from the line which the Cabinet had agreed should be taken on Lord Arran's Bill (CC(65) 28th Conclusion Minute 5) and would be liable to expose the Government to political embarrassment. The strictly neutral line adopted in the House of Lords had, however, left an impression that the Government were hostile to this Bill. This effect was also to be avoided. The Home Secretary should accordingly say that the matter was one for a free vote of the House on the principle of which the Government would not give advice one way or the other. The proposals could, however, be discussed in a sympathetic manner without appearing to be hostile to, or in favour of, the Bill. The Bill should have a good prospect of being passed in the House of Commons unless there were deliberate obstruction in Committee or at Report stage. In that event there might be some pressure on the Government to provide time, but this would be impossible without displacing the Government's own business; and, while it might be argued that where the House had shown a clear wish to discuss a problem the Government should enable it to do so, it would be impracticable either to concede that all Private Members' Bills which reached a specified stage were entitled to Government time for their remaining stages, or to make a selection among Private Members' Bills, many of which were of considerable value. ...' CRI 477/8/67 Homosexual Offences and

Prostitution Sexual Offences Bill. Meeting of Home Affairs Committee, 26 January 1966.

339 See http://www.parliament.uk/business/news/2010/04/dissolution-of-parliament-12-april-2010/

340 Graham Page speaking in HC Deb 27 April 1966 Vol. 727 cc846–907.

341 Sir Cyril Osborne had strenuously resisted the provision of extra Parliamentary time for Humphrey Berkeley's Bill and he sought assurances from the Government in May 1966 that they would neither offer it nor leave legislation to a private member. The Government's view remained that this was not a matter for them (CRI477/8/72).

342 Homosexual Law Reform Memorandum by the Secretary of State for the Home Department, 24 October 1966, C(66) 144.

343 HL Deb 10 May 1966 Vol. 274 cc605–52.

344 The matter was noted by David Steel in another instance of the interplay between campaigners. He made a strong case to resume the progress of what had been, in effect, Humphrey Berkeley's lost Bill: 'There was … one Bill which was in process in the last Parliament which shows no sign of reappearing in this Parliament, and that was the Private Member's Bill introduced by Mr. Humphrey Berkeley, the former Member for Lancaster, the Sexual Offences Bill. We have had the Ballot for Private Members' Bills. It would appear that none of the Private Members who have been successful in the Ballot and who are near the top of the list are likely to take up that Bill. Regardless of whether we as individual Members are in favour of or opposed to the Bill, the position is that the House of Commons has already decided by a vote in the previous Parliament to change the criminal law, that the House of Lords yesterday completed the Committee stage of the same Bill and has decided that there should be a change in the criminal law but that, none the less, the criminal law is remaining unchanged'. Herbert Bowden was unmoved: David Steel 'mentioned the fact that on the dissolution of the last Parliament the Sexual Offences Bill fell. So did all the other legislation that had not been completed at the time. Whatever may have happened in another place yesterday with regard to the Bill to which he referred, if it should so happen that it is picked up here it will have to take its chance with other Bills. I cannot promise to give it priority over every other Private Member's Bill. It must take its chance'. HC Deb 24 May 1966 Vol. 729 cc302–34.

345 The Lord President of the Council, Herbert Bowden, said he could not 'promise additional time beyond the normal private Members' time'. HC Deb 12 May 1966 Vol. 728 cc596–604.

346 Burke Trend to the Prime Minister, The Law Relating to Homosexual Offences, 5 May 1966. PREM 13 1563.

347 L. Abse; *Private Member, op. cit.*, 152.

348 HL Deb 10 May 1966 Vol. 274 cc605–52.

349 And it was on that selfsame day that the Second Reading of Lord Silkin's Abortion Bill was also heard in the House of Lords (see HL Deb 10 May 1966 Vol. 274 cc577–605).

350 Lord Arran retorted that 'Is it not true that the reason why the Athenian Empire fell was because the Athenians were beaten in battle by the Spartans, who were ten times as wildly homosexual as the Athenians themselves?'

351 Lord Ferrier, 1900–1992, was formerly the Chairman or President of a number of companies and organisations in India, including the Bombay Chamber of Commerce (http://www.ukwhoswho.com/view/article/oupww/whowaswho/U172413/FERRIER?index=3&results=QuicksearchResults&query=0)

352 Dick Taverne would later write to Edgar Wright (Antony Grey's *alter ego*) in May 1967 that 'I see from the note of your meeting that your members are anxious to avoid anything that might jeopardise the Bill's chances, and the sponsors would no doubt have to consider the possible effect on the progress of the Bill of any move to

make such amendments'. Dick Taverne was elected Labour Member of Parliament for Lincoln at a by-election in March 1962, became a QC in 1965, and served as a Home Office Minister from 1966 to 1968.

353 HC Deb 5 July 1966 Vol. 731 cc259–67.

354 Antony Grey wrote to all members at the end of June 1966 to say that 'On Tuesday 5 July, Mr Leo Abse, M.P., will ask leave of the House of Commons under the "Ten Minute Rule Bill" to introduce a Bill to enact the Wolfenden proposals on homosexuality. He will be opposed by Sir Cyril Osborne, which means that there is certain to be a vote. … It is therefore of the most crucial importance for homosexual law reform that as many Members of Parliament as possible should support Mr Abse next Tuesday afternoon. … A list is enclosed from which you can see whether your M.P. has voted on this issue in previous Parliaments, and, if so, how. Unless he is a known opponent of reform, please write to him AT ONCE urging him to support Mr Abse …'

355 See M. Box (1983); *Rebel Advocate: A Biography of Gerald Gardiner*, London: Victor Gollancz, 179.

356 The Permanent Secretary of the time, Sir Phillip Allen, believed that 'these … two measures, dealing with abortion and homosexual behaviour, are those most associated with Roy's first term of office as Home Secretary. They would never have become law without him'. Phillip Allen (2004); 'A Young Home Secretary' in A. Adonis and K. Thomas (eds.) *Roy Jenkins: A Retrospective*, Oxford: Oxford University Press, 65.

357 Letter of 3 January 1966, Roy Jenkins papers, Bodleian Library, University of Oxford.

358 Note to the Prime Minister, 21 September 1966. PREM 13 1563.

359 Minutes of a Meeting of the Executive Committee of the Homosexual Law Reform Society, 17 October 1966.

360 In considering whether extra time should be allotted to the Bills on the death penalty and sexual offences, he instructed that the office of the Chief Whip should be informed that 'he is more doubtful about the Sexual Offences Bill, and considers that the handling of this should be raised in Cabinet'. Note to the Office of the Chief Whip, 23 September 1966. PREM 13 1563.

361 The Cabinet Notebook records: 27/10/66 Item 3 Legislative Programme: Homosexual Law Reform C(66)144. HS argues strongly for an extra half-day, due to "continuing embarrassment" in the admin. Of criminal law. Fears of setting a precedent for other Private Member's Bills by LPS and Ch.Exch. L.P – "Because public opinion has shifted: and because law is in confusion".

362 Burke Trend reminded the Prime Minister that 'to give Government time to one Private Member may make it embarrassing to refuse it to another. Are the Lord President and the Chief Whip satisfied that a concession to Mr. Abse will not cause embarrassment in relation to e.g. the Sunday Entertainments Bill or the Abortion Bill … if these should run into difficulties?' 'Parliamentary Business: Private Members' Bills', Note to Prime Minister, 10 May 1967. PREM 13 1563.

363 Conclusions of a Meeting of the Cabinet … 27 October 1966. CC (66) 52nd Conclusions.

364 He said that 'The Bill will give great offence throughout the country. It is understood that there will be a free vote on it. Why are the Government taking up a Private Member's Bill like this, escaping the responsibility themselves in the most cowardly way, finding Government time for it and shutting out much more important business for which hon. Members on both sides of the House have pressed? This is a most cowardly thing to do'. HC Deb 8 December 1966 Vol. 737 cc1573–81.

365 Richard Crossman, the Leader of the House, said 'As the Bill has now been passed twice in another place, and a strong expression of opinion on it has been shown in this House, we have decided to give half a day's time shortly before Christmas for the Bill'. HC Deb 10 November 1966 Vol. 735 cc1551–62.

366 There was announced at the outset a proposed amendment from Simon Mahon, the Labour Member for Bootle, on the old theme of the corruption of seamen on merchant ships and of men in the armed services. 'That this House declines to give a Second Reading to a Bill which fails to afford the exemption and protection to the Merchant Navy, now provided in the Bill to Her Majesty's Royal Navy, Army, and Royal Air Force, and fails also to take into account that this omission will create circumstances which can lead to corruption of young seamen, and to conditions which will be prejudicial to the best interests of the Merchant Navy, and to the discipline and good order at sea which are vital to the best interests of our nation's Merchant Service'. (HC Deb 19 December 1966 Vol. 738 cc1068–129)

367 Walter Elliot, 1910–1988, served in the Royal Navy between 1929 and 1945, and was Member of Parliament for Carshalton and Banstead, 1960–1974. (http://www.ukwhoswho.com/view/article/oupww/whowaswho/U163887/ELLIOT_Captain_Walter?index=1&results=QuicksearchResults&query=0)

368 And that preoccupation with the dangers of corrupting seamen and military personnel would be mirrored incessantly in discussions in other forums – for example, in the deliberations on 19 April 1967 of Standing Committee F where, at col. 7 of the *Official Report*, Eric Ogden voiced the qualms of 'the National Maritime Board, which represents shipowners and all seafarers, giving reasons why they believe that the Merchant Service should be excluded from the provisions of the Bill' and was supported by other members of the committee, including Nicholas Ridley.

369 Launched principally by the Conservative Member for Southend East, Sir Stephen McAdden, 1907–1979, who opened with a lengthy complaint that the Bill had been awarded extraordinary favour by the Government: 'This Bill, which is alleged to be a Private Member's Bill, nevertheless has the support of Her Majesty's Government to such an extent that they are able to provide extraordinary privileges for it which they do not normally extend to a Private Member's Bill'. Roy Jenkins' reply was that 'the fact that we have provided this time does not mean that the attitude collectively of the Government towards the Bill is other than one of neutrality. But we felt that, in a situation where this House had twice expressed, by decisive majorities, its approval of the principles embodied in the Bill, and where a similar Bill had twice been passed through all its stages by substantial majorities in another place, it was only right to give the House the opportunity to accept or reject the change in the law proposed'. (HC Deb 19 December 1966 Vol. 738 cc1129–48)

370 *The Times*, 20 December 1966.

371 The amendment read 'Anyone who indulges in activities tending to promote acts of homosexuality between consenting adults through the publication of lists of names and addresses of known homosexuals, or otherwise, shall be guilty of a criminal offence and shall be liable on conviction to imprisonment for a term of five years or to a fine of £5,000'.

372 By Ray Mawby, Conservative Member for Totnes. HC Deb 23 June 1967 Vol. 748 cc2115–55.

373 *The Times*, 24 June 1967.

374 *Ibid.*

375 Cabinet: Extract from the Minutes of a Meeting held on 11 May 1967. CRI477/8/69.

376 'Parliamentary Business: Private Members' Bills', Note to Prime Minister, 10 May 1967. PREM 13 1563.

377 *The Times*, 5 July 1967.

378 See L. Moran; 'The Homosexualization of English Law', *op. cit.* Lindsay Farmer would add that the Act was also the first to refer explicitly by name to sexual offences.

379 Minutes of Meeting of the Executive Committee of the Homosexual Law Reform Society, 11 October 1967.

380 See 'Indecency Court Martial A Nullity', *The Times*, 21 November 1967; 'Sex Charges Man Freed', *The Times*, 16 March 1968; 'Proceedings Are A Nullity Without Dpp's Consent', *The Times*, 3 May 1968. Section 8 read 'No proceedings shall be instituted except by or with the consent of the Director of Public Prosecutions against any man for the offence of buggery with, or gross indecency with, another man, for attempting to commit either offence, or for aiding, abetting, counselling, procuring or command-ing its commission where either of those men was at the time of its commission under the age of twenty-one ...'

381 Those agitating for decriminalisation in the 1950s and 1960s had agreed for tactical reasons to defer resisting the Wolfenden Report's recommendation that the age of consent should be fixed at 21. They waited eight years before they regrouped (see 'Homosexuals to seek further reforms', *The Times*, 3 July 1975) and another nineteen years before they were successful (see 'MPs vote for homosexual consent at 18', *The Times*, 22 February 1994). It was then that the House of Commons voted for the simple amendment that 'In section 1 of the Sexual Offences Act 1967 ..., for 'twenty-one' in both places where it occurs there is substituted 'eighteen''. There had actually only been a modest number of prosecutions for consensual sex between males over and under the age of 21. In the late 1980s and early 1990s, for example, David Maclean provided the House of Commons with the following figures:

Number of persons prosecuted and convicted for consensual sexual offences[1], 1988–92

England and Wales	Number of persons	
Year	Prosecutions	Convictions
1988	19	24
1989	8	17
1990	10	9
1991	19	10
1992	14	12

1 Buggery or attempted buggery of a male of, or over 21 with another male under the age of 21 with consent. (HC Deb 17 January 1994 Vol. 235 cc372–3W)

382 Sir James Fitzjames Stephen, 1829–1894, was a High Court judge, legal reformer, an 'ardent student of Benthan and Austin' ('Death Of Sir James Stephen', *The Times*, 13 March 1894), and a legal historian (he wrote *The History of Criminal Law* (1883)) (see http://www.oxforddnb.com/view/article/26375?docPos=3). He was a liberal, albeit of a conservative bent, who eventually parted company with Bentham and Mill (see J. Stapleton (Winter 1998); 'James Fitzjames Stephen: Liberalism, Patriotism, and English Liberty', *Victorian Studies*, Vol. 41, No. 2, 243–263; and the review of Leslie Stephens' *The Life of Sir James Fitzjames Stephen* by J. G. Rosengarten (January 1896); in *The American Historical Review*, Vol. 1, No. 2, 351–355).

383 Niki Lacey put it to me that 'Mill introduce[ed] the principle of liberty as in some senses a constraint on pure utilitarianism. So it does very much seem to be, if one can put it this way, Millian Benthamism which finds its way into Wolfenden'. Email, 20 March 2015.

384 J. Douglas (1830); *Letter to Henry Brougham, Esq., on Law Reform in Scotland*, London: Longman, Rees, Orme, Brown and Green, 3–4.

385 See M. Sokol (April 2009); 'Jeremy Bentham on Love and Marriage: A Utilitarian Proposal for Short-Term Marriage' *Journal of Legal History*, Vol. 30, No. 1, 1–21. Bentham declared in his essay on pederasty, 'As to any primary mischief, it is evident that it produces no pain in anyone. On the contrary it produces pleasure, and that a pleasure which, by their perverted taste, is by this supposition preferred to that

pleasure which is in general reputed the greatest. The partners are both willing. If either of them be unwilling, the act is not that which we have here in view: it is an offence totally different in its nature of effects: it is a personal injury; it is a kind of rape.

As a secondary mischief whether they produce any alarm in the community
As to any secondary mischief, it produces not any pain of apprehension. For what is there in it for any body to be afraid of? By the supposition, those only are the objects of it who choose to be so, who find a pleasure, for so it seems they do, in being so.

Whether any danger
As to any danger exclusive of pain, the danger, if any, must consist in the tendency of the example. But what is the tendency of this example? To dispose others to engage in the same practises: but this practise for anything that has yet appeared produces not pain of any kind to any one'. ('Paederasty', written *ca.* 1785, http://www.columbia. edu/cu/lweb/eresources/exhibitions/sw25/bentham/)

386 Lindsay Farmer pointed me to a global survey of trends in sexual crimes between 1945 and 2005 which makes the argument that sodomy and adultery were increasingly decriminalised, whilst rape and child sexual abuse were increasingly criminalised during that period, raising 'the priority of individual consent and lower[ing] the priority of collective order across the policy field': D. Frank, B. Camp and S. Boutcher (December 2010); 'Worldwide Trends in the Criminal Regulation of Sex', *American Sociological Review*, Vol. 75, No. 6, 887.
387 The legal philosopher, Peter Ramsey, put it to me that 'utilitarianism is the dominant mode of thing, the only mode of thinking'.
388 H. Maine (1875); *Lectures on the Early History of Institutions*, New York: Henry Holt, 397.
389 L. Farmer (2010); 'Criminal Wrongs in Historical Perspective', in R. Duff *et al.* (eds.) *The Boundaries of the Criminal Law*, Oxford: Oxford University Press, 214. I am grateful to Arlie Loughlan for the reference.
390 Jeremy Bentham, John Stuart Mill and Isaiah Berlin *were* cited, but almost never in the context of the events laid out in these chapters. Ironically, the sole exception is that of R.A. Butler who claimed the support of John Stuart Mill in defence of capital punishment (HC Deb 16 February 1956 Vol. 548 cc2536–655).
391 *The Republic*, Book V, l. 473.
392 A revealing comment was made by Sir John Chilcot, who, at the beginning of his career, served as Assistant Private Secretary to Roy Jenkins in the mid-1960s. Talking about another area of policy formation altogether, the negotiation of a settlement in Northern Ireland, he alluded to what he called 'moral boundaries' in the giving of political advice. Those boundaries, he said, 'are felt and known. They do not need to be explicit' ('Negotiations and positions: an interview', in G. Spencer ed. (2015), *The British and Peace in Northern Ireland*, Cambridge: Cambridge University Press, 83). A version of utilitarianism, one may suppose, was also felt and known but did not need to be explicit.
393 See M. Wiener (1987); 'The March of Penal Progress?', *Journal of British Studies*, 2, 85.
394 H. Hart (1959–1960); 'Presidential Address: Prolegomenon to the Principles of Punishment', *Proceedings of the Aristotelian Society*, Vol. 60, 2.
395 Herbert Hart declared that the principles supporting the Wolfenden Report's recommendations were 'strikingly similar to those expounded by Mill in his essay *On Liberty*', and then proceeded to quote section 13 of the Report in support, remarking that 'Mill's principles are still very much alive in the criticism of law …' H. Hart (1963); *Law, Liberty and Morality, op. cit.*, 14, 15.
396 Email, 22 April 2014.

397 N. MacCormick (December 1993); 'Herbert L.A. Hart: In Memoriam', *Ratio Juris*, Vol. 6, No. 3, 337.

398 See, for example, H. Hart (1982); *Essays on Bentham: Jurisprudence and Political Philosophy*, Oxford: Oxford University Press; and H. Hart (1983); *Essays in Jurisprudence and Philosophy*, Oxford: Oxford University Press, where, on p. 183, he observed that Bentham's doctrines 'came to dominate English social thought for a long time. For much of the nineteenth century 'utilitarianism' became in England almost synonymous with progressive political and social thought'. Tony Honoré said that Hart was 'fascinated' by Bentham and devoted twelve years to his study (see http://www.oxforddnb.com/view/article/51089?docPos=1).

399 H. Hart (1963); *Law, Liberty and Morality, op. cit.*, See N. Lacey (2004); *A Life of H. L. A. Hart: The Nightmare and the Noble Dream*, Oxford: Oxford University Press, 221.

400 See A. Ryan (2008); 'Hart and the Liberalism of Fear' in M. Kramer *et al.* eds., *The Legacy of H.L.A. Hart: Legal, Political and Moral Philosophy*, New York: Oxford University Press; and P. Cane (January 2006); 'Taking Law Seriously: Starting Points of the Hart/Devlin Debate', *The Journal of Ethics*, Vol. 10, No. 1/2, 21–51.

401 In D. Sugarman and H. Hart (June 2005); 'Hart Interviewed: H.L.A. Hart in Conversation with David Sugarman', *Journal of Law and Society*, Vol. 32, No. 2, 284.

402 H. Hart, 'Immorality and Treason', *The Listener*, 30 July 1959, 162.

403 In M. Ignatieff (2000); *Isaiah Berlin: A Life*, London: Vintage, 255.

404 Quoted by P. Collins in *The Times*, 27 May 2011.

405 See HL Deb 23 May 1966 Vol. 274 cc1190–208.

406 P. Bean (1989); 'Barbara Wootton: Testament for a Social Scientist', *The British Journal of Criminology*, Vol. 29, No. 1, 74.

407 G. Williams (1958); *The Sanctity of Life and the Criminal Law*, London: Faber and Faber. Bertrand Russell's (March 1958); review in *Stanford Law Review*, Vol. 10, No. 2, 382 talks about how Glanville Williams pits a utilitarian against what he calls a 'taboo morality'.

408 John Spencer's obituary in *The Independent* of 17 April 1997 said that he was 'a convinced utilitarian, who held that punishment was an evil to be avoided unless there was a good reason for imposing it'.

409 In L. Farmer; 'The Modest Ambition of Farmer Williams', unpublished paper, 1.

410 See J. Beckford (Summer 1991); 'Politics and Religion in England and Wales', *Daedalus*, Vol. 120, No. 3, esp. 181, where he argues that 'the overwhelmingly higher profile of the Church of England in Parliament and in other parts of the public sphere means that this church is more involved in politics ...'

411 That was certainly David Steel's judgement: 'If you look at the debates that rage nowadays [in 2007] I object to people who say [of the opponents of abortion], 'Oh, this is a Christian viewpoint', meaning this is the viewpoint of the Roman Catholic church and some of the evangelicals in the Protestant churches. That is what they mean, but they attach themselves to the adjective 'Christian'. But what helped me was the report that the Church of England had produced in 1966 called *Abortion, An Ethical Discussion* which I still maintain to this day is the best argued document from a Christian standpoint in favour of having a positive law on abortion. And it counteracted better than I could the arguments of the Roman Catholic Church, and indeed was the foundation of the support that the bishops gave in the House of Lords'. (http://www.abortionreview.org/images/uploads/Abortion_Pioneers_%281%29.pdf)

412 I am indebted to the Reverend Canon Dr Peter Sedgwick, Principal of St. Michael's College, Llandaff, for his advice about the political role of the Church during this period.

413 *The Economist* observed on 20 January 1962 that 'The effect of the opinion of the Anglican Church on the views of Conservative backbenchers, although it is a force

that moves slowly and sometimes mysteriously, can be surprisingly decisive'. (Quoted in O. Chadwick, *Michael Ramsey: A Life, op. cit.*, 159.)

414 Owen Chadwick said that 'Ramsey took a lot of trouble to get other bishops to support him in the House of Lords. Five or six did so'. O. Chadwick; *Michael Ramsey: A Life, op. cit.*, 148. Peter Sedgwick said in interview that 'The Church of England remained an extraordinary hierarchical conservative institution until the 1990s. I remember talking to a Bishop in the 1990s about George Carey raising some questions and he said, 'well, Peter, you have to remember that for all that Bob Runcie appeared very left wing, if you were made a Bishop and you went into the House of Bishops and they met four times a year for four days, you actually spoke in terms of seniority and there were the first five Bishops that had authority anyway, Canterbury, York, London, Durham, Winchester, and then in order of seniority, you had to wait in a debate 'he said', until anybody more senior came on'.

415 Including, for instance, with Peter Jones, the co-edited work (2002); *The Future of Criminal Justice: Resettlement, Chaplaincy and Community*, London: SPCK.

416 Geoffrey Fisher had been Michael Ramsey's headmaster at Repton. It is interesting that the Anglican Sir John Wolfenden, had himself been a headmaster at Uppingham and at Shrewsbury.

417 See L. Hartz (1969); 'A Comparative Study of Fragment Cultures', in H. Graham and T. Gurr (eds.) *The History of Violence in America*, New York: Bantam Books.

418 Peter Sedgwick said in interview 'built in, which is part of the issue about sexuality today, built into the Church of England was and accepted in the non-technical way, [was the doctrine] of [moral] evolution. The debate had moved on. The moral education becomes more illuminated. The John Stuart Mill argument that debate in *On Liberty* actually moves the debate on. ... there was a feeling that the position that you held 50 years ago might not be the position you held today'.

419 See J.S. Mill (1885); *Nature: the Utility of Religion, and Theism*, London: Longmans Green; and J. Lipkes (1999); *Politics, Religion and Classical Political Economy in Britain: John Stuart Mill and his Followers*, Basingstoke: Macmillan, esp. 36.

420 He argued in 'On Liberty' that 'the strongest of all arguments against the interference of the public with purely personal conduct is that, when it does interfere, the odds are that it interferes wrongly, and in the wrong place'. J.S. Mill (1910); *Utilitarianism, Liberty and Representative Government*, London: J.M. Dent and Sons, 140.

421 See L. Siedentop (2014); *Inventing the Individual: The Origins of Western Liberalism*, London: Allen Lane.

422 I am grateful to Tony Bottoms for pointing me to the parallels between the two reforms.

423 HL Debate, 4 December 1957, c.735.

424 In S. Moore (http://etheses.lse.ac.uk/1573/1/U136493.pdf) 139–140. For a full treatment of the matter see her Ph.D. thesis, *The Decriminalisation of Suicide*, London School of Economics and Political Science January 2000.

425 Which included many of those who had drafted the Church's submission on homosexuality.

426 See *Ought Suicide to be a Crime?: A Discussion of Suicide, Attempted Suicide and the Law*, London: Church of England, Board for Social Responsibility, 1959. Its first recommendation was that 'Attempted suicide should cease to be a crime and that consideration be given to placing the law with regard to the liability of secondary parties to suicide on a more realistic basis by abolishing the felony of suicide and creating a new offence of aiding, abetting or instigating suicide of another'.

427 See http://bjc.oxfordjournals.org/content/1/3/275.2.full.pdf

428 Chapter 60 9 and 10 Eliz 2: An Act to amend the law of England and Wales relating to suicide, and for purposes connected therewith.

429 HL Deb 2 March 1961 Vol. 229 cc246–76.

430 O. Chadwick; *Michael Ramsey: A Life, op. cit.*, 147.

431 He argued as a liberal man uncertain about the Establishment that the role of the Lords Spiritual was valued and consequential, but that it was exacting of their time and energy, and he was unsure whether 'membership of the House of Lords is the most suitable and effective forum for the bishops' influence in moral and social questions today'. 'Church and State in England', in *Canterbury Pilgrim, op. cit.*, 181.

432 in (1972); *The Christian Priest Today*, London: SPCK, 41.

433 *Sacred and Secular, The Holland Lectures for 1964*, London: Longmans, 1965.

434 'Priest and Politics', *op. cit.*, 35–36.

435 *Ibid*, 41.

436 (1964); 'Sex and Civilization', *Canterbury Essays and Addresses*, London: SPCK, 88.

437 M. Ramsey; 'The Family', in *Canterbury Pilgrim, op. cit.*, 168.

438 See O. Chadwick; *Michael Ramsey: A Life, op. cit.*, 145.

439 'The Crisis of Human Freedom', Robert Waley Cohen Memorial Lecture, London: Council of Christians and Jews, 1962, 13.

440 That changed moral and political environment was to become quite visible on 4 April 2014 when the Archbishop of Canterbury expressed his trepidation about the links being forged between the Church and gay marriage. It was reported that he 'has said the Church of England accepting gay marriage could be "catastrophic" for Christians in other parts of the world. The Most Rev Justin Welby told LBC that hundreds of Christians in Africa had been killed by people who associated Christianity with homosexuality. He warned the same could happen if the Church of England backed gay unions. Same-sex marriage became legal in England and Wales last week, but is not supported by the Church'. (http://www.bbc.co.uk/news/uk-26894133)

441 John Stuart Mill put it that conduct which does not harm other people is never a fit subject for legal interference. See M. Nussbaum (May 2002); 'Millean Liberty and Sexual Orientation', *Law and Philosophy*, Vol. 21, No. 3, 322.

442 Henry Sidgwick, 1838–1900, a clergyman's son but an agnostic, lecturing in philosophy at the University of Cambridge, who was to be the author of *The Methods of Ethics*, published in 1874 as a defence and exploration of a consequentialist version of utilitarianism (see http://www.oxforddnb.com/view/article/25517?docPos=4) See H. Rashdall (April 1885); 'Professor Sidgwick's Utilitarianism', *Mind*, Vol. 10, No. 38, 200–226; and Leslie Stephen (January 1901); 'Henry Sidgwick', *Mind*, Vol. 10, No. 37, 1–17.

443 C. Davies (1989); 'Religion, Politics and the 'Permissive' Legislation', in P. Badham (ed.) *Religion, State, and Society in Modern Britain*, Lewiston: Edwin Mellen Press, 320.

444 See E. Andrew (2001); *Conscience and its critics : Protestant conscience, enlightenment reason, and modern subjectivity*, Toronto: University of Toronto Press.

445 E. Hughes; 'Professions' (1994); in L. Coser (ed.) *Everett C. Hughes on Work, Race, and the Sociological Imagination*, Chicago: University of Chicago Press, 38.

446 See *The Culture of Control: Crime and Social Order in Contemporary Society, op. cit.*

447 It was a juxtaposition in vogue at the time not only in England and Wales but also in the United States (and elsewhere). See T. Green (2014); *Freedom and Criminal Responsibility in American Legal Thought*, New York: Cambridge University Press, esp. Ch. 4.

448 Hart called himself a 'suppressed homosexual'. See N. Lacey, *A Life of H. L. A. Hart: The Nightmare and the Noble Dream, op. cit.*, 61, 74.

449 That is certainly the thesis of a biography of *Jenkins: A Well-Rounded Life*, by John Campbell, which alleges that he had had an affair with Antony Crosland (previewed in *The Daily Mail*, 11 March 2014).

450 Allegations were made after Leo Abse's death that he had been a paedophile rapist (see *The Sunday Times*, 22 March 2015).

451 Peter Sedgwick's supposition was that Churchmen at the time entertained a sense of 'genuine puzzlement [about homosexuality]. ... I think it wasn't something that Christian theology had given any attention to. ... it was just a no-go area really'.

452 HL Deb 16 June 1966 Vol. 275 cc146–77.

453 See N. Lacey (2009); 'Historicising Criminalisation: Conceptual and Empirical Issues', *The Modern Law Review*, Vol. 72, No. 6, 936–960.

454 Excerpt from a letter to the B.B.C. attached to an email from Roger Silverman, 9 April 2011.

455 *The Current* was an Indian journal in which Roy Jenkins aired arguments about homosexuality and capital punishment. See J. Campbell; *A Well-Rounded Life, op. cit.*, 152–3.

456 The Conservative Member for Chelmsford, Norman St. John Stevas, had written to him on his appointment to say that 'you will be a great Home Secretary'. Letter of 29 December 1965. George Thomas, Undersecretary of State for the Home Department, promised in a letter of 22 December a 'sincere welcome from your Ministerial colleagues ... I am delighted that you are coming to us for there is an enormous task ahead ... It will be a joy to work with you'. Roy Jenkins papers in the Bodleian Library, University of Oxford.

457 A letter from a friend with an indecipherable signature recalled at the time of his appointment that 'I remember you telling me, shortly before election day in 1959, that your dearest ambition at that time was to go to the Home Office and we reluctantly agreed that this was rather too lofty an aim'. Letter of 2 January 1965, Roy Jenkins papers in the Bodleian Library, University of Oxford. In an email of 11 March 2014, Darren Treadwell, the archive assistant of the Labour History Archive and Study Centre at the People's History Museum in Manchester, 'the main specialist repository for research into the political wing of the labour movement [which] holds the archives of working class organisations from the Chartists to New Labour, including the Labour Party and the Communist Party of Great Britain' (http://www.phm.org.uk/archive-study-centre/planning-a-visit/) surmised that the friend was probably the leader of the constituency Labour Party or his election agent.

458 To be sure, his narrative diary did contain a brief report of unsuccessful attempts in the House of Commons to restore the death penalty during the Irish bombing campaign of 1975.

459 J. Campbell; *A Well-Rounded Life, op. cit.*

460 http://www.oxforddnb.com/view/article/88739?docPos=1. His biographer adds that he 'hardly enjoyed the reputation of being a notably conscientious MP'.

461 John Halliday, who joined the Home Office as a junior civil servant in 1966, reflected in interview that 'the crucial thing was that Jenkins got the government to give the private members government time, otherwise it'd never got through and I think in some if not all of the cases, the government provided drafting assistance which meant that they weren't left to their own devices to produce a bill which the government would have to say was inadequate or wouldn't work and it would therefore fail. So with drafting, he was able to use government time to help David Steel in particular, with abortion, Leo Abse with homosexual law reform'.

462 http://www.oxforddnb.com/view/article/88739?docPos=1.

463 D. Faulkner; *Continuity and Change in the Home Office, op. cit*, 10.

464 In J. Campbell; *A Well-Rounded Life, op. cit.*, 267.

465 The two were pickets who appealed against conviction on charges of criminal conspiracy during the 1972 national building strike. See '50 MPs urge Mr Jenkins to free pickets', *The Times*, 31 October 1974. As Home Secretary, he was subject to considerable political pressure to exercise the prerogative of mercy. Roy Jenkins' case was that 'The central point is that it is a fundamental principle of our system of justice that the decision in individual cases is a matter for the courts. The rule of law

and the independence of the courts would be seriously undermined if Governments were to presume to re-judge the merits of cases decided by the courts'. Statement on Shrewsbury Pickets, January 1975. Roy Jenkins papers in the Bodleian Library, University of Oxford.

466   Reg Prentice, 1923–2001, had been Labour Member for Newham North-East, and, although he differed with Roy Jenkins about the matter of Europe, he has been described as Roy Jenkins' closest political ally. Geoff Horn (2013) remarks how the two 'often spoke in tandem, each supporting the stance of the other in Cabinet' (*Crossing the floor: Reg Prentice and the crisis of British social democracy*, Manchester: Manchester University Press, 77). Prentice was to become a casualty of the civil strife in the Labour Party of the 1970s, becoming the target of a left-wing campaign to oust him from his seat. In July 1975 a 29 to 19 majority of the general management committee of his constituency passed a resolution calling on Prentice to retire. There followed a protracted battle between different Labour Party factions, a battle in which Roy Jenkins played a vigorous part. Prentice resigned from the Cabinet at the end of 1976 and from the Labour Party itself a year later.

467   See D. Wood, 'Cabinet decides on EEC referendum before end of June', *The Times*, 24 January 1975. The referendum was to be the main focus of a lengthy interview he gave to Llew Gardner in the *People & Politics* programme at the end of January 1975. Roy Jenkins' papers in the archives of the Bodleian Library, University of Oxford.

468   See G. Clark, 'Mr Jenkins sees vote to leave Europe as catastrophe for Britain', *The Times*, 27 March 1975.

469   For instance, he interrupted an otherwise continuous account of enthusiastic campaigning about the European referendum in his narrative diary to report 'On Friday May 9th [1975], I flew up to Newcastle, back again in the afternoon, again by HS 125 but this time purely on Home Office business, in order to address the Probation Officers' Conference, an engagement which I would probably not have accepted had I realised that it was going to be at this stage of the Referendum Campaign'. Three days later, he recorded that he had seen 'Michael Swann the Chairman of the BBC – whom I had specifically not wanted to ask to come and see me in the Home Office because I was not seeing him as the minister responsible for broadcasting but as President of the Britain in Europe Campaign …'

470   John Campbell observes in an excerpt from his biography that 'He belonged to the most exclusive clubs and dining clubs in London and lunched with some member of 'the great and the good' almost every day of his adult life'. *The Daily Mail*, 11 March 2014.

471   http://www.bodleian.ox.ac.uk/__data/assets/pdf_file/0015/106224/Roys-diaries.pdf

472   And that is certainly reflected in *A Well-Rounded Life*.

473   http://www.abortionreview.org/images/uploads/Abortion_Pioneers_%281%29.pdf

474   See W. Grant (1989); *Pressure Groups, Politics and Democracy in Britain*, London: Philip Allan.

475   See M. Ryan; *The Acceptable Pressure Group: A Case Study of the Howard League for Penal Reform and Radical Alternatives to Prison, op. cit.*

Bibliography

L. Abse (1973); *Private Member*, London: MacDonald

P. Allen (2004); 'A Young Home Secretary', Ch. 6 in A. Adonis and K. Thomas (eds.) *Roy Jenkins: A Retrospective*, Oxford: Oxford University Press, 61–84

Lord Arran (1964); 'Danger, Arran at Work', in *Lord Arran Writes*, London: Hodder and Stoughton, 65–80

E. Andrew (2001); *Conscience and its Critics : Protestant Conscience, Enlightenment Reason, and Modern Subjectivity*, Toronto: University of Toronto Press

P. Bean (1989); 'Barbara Wootton: Testament for a Social Scientist', *The British Journal of Criminology*, Vol. 29, No. 1, 71–5

J. Beckford (1991); 'Politics and Religion in England and Wales', *Daedalus*, Vol. 120, No. 3, 179–201

E. Bene (1965); 'On the Genesis of Male Homosexuality: An Attempt at Clarifying the Role of the Parents', *The British Journal of Psychiatry*, 111, 803–813

H. Berkeley (1972); *Crossing the Floor*, London: George Allen and Unwin

M. Box (1983); *Rebel Advocate: A Biography of Gerald Gardiner*, London: Victor Gollancz

R. Butler (1971); *The Art of the Possible: The Memoirs of Lord Butler K.G., C.H.*, London: Hamish Hamilton

J. Campbell (2014); *A Well-Rounded Life*, Jonathan Cape, London

P. Cane (2006); 'Taking Law Seriously: Starting Points of the Hart/Devlin Debate', *The Journal of Ethics*, Vol. 10, No. 1/2, 21–51

O. Chadwick (1990); *Michael Ramsey A Life*, Oxford: Clarendon Press

J. Chilcot (2015); 'Negotiations and positions: an interview', in G. Spencer (ed.) *The British and Peace in Northern Ireland*, Cambridge: Cambridge University Press, 79–100

J. Christoph (1962); *Capital Punishment and British Politics*, London: George Allen & Unwin

Lady C. Colville (1963); *A Crowded Life*, London: Evans Brothers

P. Conrad (1975); 'The Discovery of Hyperkinesis: Notes on the Medicalization of Deviant Behavior', *Social Problems*, Vol. 23, No. 1, 12–21

—and J. Schneider (1980); *Deviance and Medicalization: From Badness to Sickness*, St. Louis: Mosby

C. Davies (1989); 'Religion, Politics and the 'Permissive' Legislation', in P. Badham (ed.) *Religion, State, and Society in Modern Britain*, Lewiston: Edwin Mellen, 321–342

J. Douglas (1830); *Letter to Henry Brougham, Esq., on Law Reform in Scotland*, London: Longman, Rees, Orme, Brown and Green

L. Farmer (2010); 'Criminal Wrongs in Historical Perspective', in R. Duff *et al.* (eds.) *The Boundaries of the Criminal Law*, Oxford: Oxford University Press, 214–237

D. Faulkner (1991); *Continuity and Change in the Home Office*, Home Office Papers by Senior Officers, Occasional Papers in Administrative Studies, London: Home Office

M. Foucault (1979); *The History of Sexuality*, London: Allen Lane

D. Frank, B. Camp and S. Boutcher (2010); 'Worldwide Trends in the Criminal Regulation of Sex', *American Sociological Review*, Vol. 75, No. 6, 867–893

'Lord Gardiner Interviewed' (1964); *The Economist*, 28 March 1964, 1209–1212

D. Garland (2002); *The Culture of Control: Crime and Social Order in Contemporary Society*, Oxford: Oxford University Press

W. Grant (1989); *Pressure Groups, Politics and Democracy in Britain*, London: Philip Allan

T. Green (2014); *Freedom and Criminal Responsibility in American Legal Thought*, New York: Cambridge University Press

A. Grey (1992); *Quest for Justice: Towards Homosexual Emancipation*, London: Sinclair-Stevenson

—(1997); 'Christian Society and the Homosexual' in *Speaking Out: Writings on Sex, Law, Politics and Society 1954–95*, Cassell, London, 135–137

J. Gusfield (1967); 'Moral Passage: The Symbolic Process in Public Designations of Deviance', *Social Problems*, Vol. 15, No. 2, 175–188

H. Hart (1959–1960); 'Presidential Address: Prolegomenon to the Principles of Punishment', *Proceedings of the Aristotelian Society*, Vol. 60, 1–26

—(1959); 'Immorality and Treason', *The Listener*, 162–163

—(1963); *Law, Liberty, and Morality*, New York: Vintage Books

—(1982); *Essays on Bentham: Jurisprudence and Political Philosophy*, Oxford: Oxford University Press

—(1983); *Essays in Jurisprudence and Philosophy*, Oxford: Oxford University Press

L. Hartz (1969); 'A Comparative Study of Fragment Cultures', in H. Graham and T. Gurr (eds.) *The History of Violence in America*, New York: Bantam Books, 107–126

M. Haug and M. Sussman (1969); 'Professional Autonomy and the Revolt of the Client', *Social Problems*, Vol. 17, No. 2, 153–161

G. Horn (2013); *Crossing the floor: Reg Prentice and the crisis of British social democracy*, Manchester: Manchester University Press

A. Howard (1987); *RAB: The Life of R.A. Butler*, London: Jonathan Cape

E. Hughes (1994); 'Professions' in L. Coser (ed.) *Everett C. Hughes on Work, Race, and the Sociological Imagination*, Chicago: University of Chicago Press, 37–49

L. Humphreys (1970); *Tearoom Trade: A Study of Homosexual Encounters in Public Places*, London: Duckworth

H. Montgomery Hyde (1948); *Famous Trials: Oscar Wilde*, London: William Hodge and Co.

M. Ignatieff (2000); *Isaiah Berlin: A Life*, London: Vintage

R. Jenkins (1959); *The Labour Case*, Mddx.: A Penguin Special

—(1991); *A Life at the Centre*, London: Macmillan

P. Jones and P. Sedgwick (2002); *The Future of Criminal Justice: Resettlement, Chaplaincy and Community*, London: SPCK

N. Lacey (2004); *A Life of H. L. A. Hart: The Nightmare and the Noble Dream*, Oxford: Oxford University Press

—(2009); 'Historicising Criminalisation: Conceptual and Empirical Issues', *The Modern Law Review*, Vol. 72, No. 6, 936–960

—and H. Pickard (Spring 2013); 'From the Consulting Room to the Court Room? Taking the Clinical Model of Responsibility without Blame into the Legal Realm', *Oxford Journal of Legal Studies*, Vol. 33, No. 1, 1–29

J. Lipkes (1999); *Politics, Religion and Classical Political Economy in Britain: John Stuart Mill and his Followers*, Basingstoke: Macmillan

H. Lopota (1976); 'Expertization of Everyone and the Revolt of the Client', *The Sociological Quarterly*, Volume 17(4), 435–447

N. MacCormick (1993); 'Herbert L.A. Hart: In Memoriam', *Ratio Juris*, Vol. 6, No. 3, 337–338

H. Maine (1875); *Lectures on the Early History of Institutions*, New York: Henry Holt,

D. Melossi (2008); *Controlling Crime, Controlling Society*, Cambridge: Polity Press

J.S. Mill (1885); *Nature: the Utility of Religion, and Theism*, London: Longmans Green

—*John Stuart Mill on Liberty and other Essays*, 1991 edition, Oxford: Oxford World Classics

S. Moore (2000); *The Decriminalisation of Suicide*, PhD dissertation, London School of Economics and Political Science

L. Moran (1995); 'The Homosexualization of English Criminal Law', in D. Herman and C. Stychin (eds.) *Legal Inversions: Lesbians, Gay Men, and the Politics of Law*, Philadelphia: Temple University Press, 3–28

M. Nussbaum (2002); 'Millean Liberty and Sexual Orientation', *Law and Philosophy*, Vol. 21, No. 3, 317–334

K. Plummer (1995); *Telling Sexual Stories*, London: Routledge

M. Ramsey (1962); 'The Crisis of Human Freedom', Robert Waley Cohen Memorial Lecture, London: Council of Christians and Jews

—(1964); *Canterbury Essays and Addresses*, London: SPCK

—(1965); *Sacred and Secular, The Holland Lectures for 1964*, London: Longmans

—(1972); *The Christian Priest Today*, London: SPCK

—(1974); *Canterbury Pilgrim*, London: SPCK

H. Rashdall (1885); 'Professor Sidgwick's Utilitarianism', *Mind*, Vol. 10, No. 38, 200–226

B. Russell (1958); review of *The Sanctity of Life and the Criminal Law* in *Stanford Law Review*, Vol. 10, No. 2, 382–385

A. Ryan (2008); 'Hart and the Liberalism of Fear' in M. Kramer *et al.* (eds.) *The Legacy of H.L.A. Hart: Legal, Political and Moral Philosophy*, New York: Oxford University Press, 315–330

M. Ryan (1978); *The Acceptable Pressure Group: A Case Study of the Howard League for Penal Reform and Radical Alternatives to Prison*, Farnborough: Saxon House

L. Siedentop (2014); *Inventing the Individual: The Origins of Western Liberalism*, London: Allen Lane

J. Rosengarten (1896); review of Leslie Stephens' *The Life of Sir James Fitzjames Stephen* in *The American Historical Review*, Vol. 1, No. 2, 351–355

M. Sokol (2009); 'Jeremy Bentham on Love and Marriage: A Utilitarian Proposal for Short-Term Marriage' *Journal of Legal History*, Vol. 30, No. 1, 1–21

G. Sparrow (1965); *"R.A.B.": Study of a Statesman*, London: Odhams Books

P. Stanford (2003); *The Outcasts' Outcast: A Biography of Lord Longford*, Stroud, Gloucestershire: Sutton Publishing

L. Stephen (1901); 'Henry Sidgwick', *Mind*, Vol. 10, No. 37, 1–17

T. Szasz (1970); *The Manufacture of Madness: A Comparative Study of the Inquisition and the Mental Health Movement*, New York: Harper and Row

A. Thorpe (1998); Research Paper 98/68, 'Age of Consent' for Male Homosexual Acts, Home Affairs Section, House Of Commons Library

J. Weeks (1989); *Coming Out: Homosexual Politics in Britain from the Nineteenth Century to the Present*, London: Quartet Books

G. Wells (2011); *A House in France: A Memoir*, London: Bloomsbury

D. West (1955); *Homosexuality*, London : G. Duckworth

—(1977); *Homosexuality Re-examined*, London : Duckworth

—(1988); 'Homosexuality and Social Policy: The Case for a More Informed Approach', *Law and Contemporary Problems*, Vol. 51(1), 181–199

—(2000); 'Paedophilia: plague or panic?', *The Journal of Forensic Psychiatry*, Vol.11(3), 511–531.

—(2012); *Gay Life Straight Work*, London: Paradise Press

J. Wolfenden (1976); *Turning Points: The Memoirs of Lord Wolfenden*, London: The Bodley Head

Index